THE BEAT GENERATION

A Gale Critical Companion

THE **BEAT** GENERATION

A Gale Critical Companion

Volume 1: Topics

Foreword by **Anne Waldman**
Distinguished Professor of Poetics
The Jack Kerouac School of Disembodied Poetics, Naropa University

Lynn M. Zott, *Project Editor*

GALE®

THOMSON
GALE™

Detroit • New York • San Diego • San Francisco • Cleveland • New Haven, Conn. • Waterville, Maine • London • Munich

THOMSON

GALE

The Beat Generation, Vol. 1

Project Editor
Lynn M. Zott

Editorial
Jessica Bomarito, Tom Burns, Jenny Cromie, Elisabeth Gellert, Edna M. Hedblad, Jeffrey W. Hunter, Justin Karr, Michelle Kazensky, Jelena Krstović, Michelle Lee, Allison McClintic Marion, Ellen McGeagh, Linda Pavlovski, Thomas J. Schoenberg, Russel Whitaker

Research
Nicodemus Ford, Sarah Genik, Barbara McNeil, Tamara C. Nott, Gary Oudersluys, Tracie A. Richardson

Editorial Support Services
Mark Hefner

Permissions
Edna Hedblad, Lori Hines

Imaging and Multimedia
Lezlie Light, Kelly A. Quin, Luke Rademacher

Product Design
Pamela Galbreath, Michael Logusz

Composition and Electronic Capture
Carolyn Roney

Manufacturing
Stacy L. Melson

LIBRARY OF CONGRESS CATALOGING-IN-PUBLICATION DATA

Zott, Lynn M. (Lynn Marie), 1969-
The beat generation : a Gale critical companion / Lynn M. Zott.
    p. cm. -- (Gale critical companion collection)
Includes bibliographical references and index.
ISBN 0-7876-7569-5 (hardcover set) -- ISBN 0-7876-7570-9 (v. 1) --
ISBN 0-7876-7571-7 (v. 2) -- ISBN 0-7876-7572-5 (v. 3)
1. American literature--20th century--History and criticism. 2. Beat generation. I. Title. II. Series.
PS228.B6Z68 2003
810.9'0054--dc21

2002155786

Printed in the United States of America
10 9 8 7 6 5 4 3 2 1

CONTENTS

v

VOLUME 2

VOLUME 3

In a recent class I taught at the Jack Kerouac School of Disembodied Poetics entitled "Liberation Now!," students fretted over the cultural imperialism and condescension of various "moderns"—Ezra Pound, William Carlos Williams, and the mad Antonin Artaud as well as the privileged lifestyle of independently "wealthy" Gertrude Stein and H. D. who could afford a "room of one's own" in Virginia Woolf's apt phrase. There was the sense of the white male gaze toward the Balinese and Tarahumara cultures, in the case of Artaud, and of Pound's dabbling with the Noh theatre of Japan and the troubadour tradition, not to mention his problematic anti-semitism. Was "orientalism" the problem here, exoticizing the problematic "other?" I tried to give some historical context and expressed my own gratitude as a writer to the investigative nature, in particular, of Pound's passionate magpie scholarship and how he had championed James Joyce (another sexist?) and T. S. Eliot and opened the floodgates for contemporary poets back into the beauties and exquisite lineaments of the past. Reinventing Chinese poetry, just one example, for our time. William Carlos Williams's "Beautiful Thing" had also been called into question in its objectification of women.

Was there an "internalized repression" going on in Stein's own anti-semitism? Or H. D.'s aristocratic classicism? Was there a reach for the heights of Olympus? A rejection of American democratic values? My advice was: Read the work, use your heads, don't respond with knee-jerk superficial assumptions or clichéd political correctness. It's a complicated world, it's a complicated time. Be investigative, go deeper, see the subtlety of the work, understand "influence," lineage, and also the radical departure from Victorian "official"—and mostly stultifying— "verse."

But I shuddered to think of the discourse we would have around certain so-called Beat writers, known superficially for macho views presented in particular writings: the sexism of Jack Kerouac in *On The Road*; the misogyny of William S. Burroughs in *The Wild Boys*. Was it up to me to contextualize, apologize, get defensive? I had personally seen "beyond" these mindsets in the work and in my own personal experience of these writers. And I had benefited from the liberating quality of the thinking, the imagination, the radical moves of their language and grammar. Just as Marcel Proust and James Joyce and Gertrude Stein had provoked a serious probe and delight in consciousness, pursued a grammar of thinking, as it were, Burroughs and Kerouac and others were raising the ante on what was possible in language. Their writing strove to capture the passing moment, the nuances of speech, the eidolons of history and philosophy and emotion. And I was also aware of the un-mined—in some cases un-voiced—richness of the work of the women writers associated with

ix

that community and working in the 1950s—that was immensely conditioning. In those times, the struggle for female individuality, for roles not defined by the Patriarchy, was immense. To fight against the tide of post-war materialism, conformity, the anathemas of "difference" (if one was lesbian, for example, or if one was in a bi-racial relationship, or if one got pregnant out of wedlock) was a constant struggle.

I myself, although a generation younger in most cases, was also being included in the Beat canon, and I felt the resonance of these same issues in my own work which is, in some cases, staunchly feminist. But I had benefited by the previous struggle of my comrades. And there were major differences in the backgrounds and lives and aesthetics and imagination of so many of these Beat writers, compared to the Moderns and compared with one another. Comparisons are odious! It is hard to generalize a generation, a literary movement. And then there was the enormity of influence and all the art, music, and performance that was spawned out of the maelstrom. Go to the work! That is my rallying cry. There is so much there to mine, to probe, to enjoy, that will enlighten you in a spiritual sense. I think I was able, as my class's discussion took shape, to manifest the huge debt I felt to these writers who blazed the way, who turned the establishment on its head!

The Beat literary movement conjures the rhizome as a metaphor or paradigm for its incredibly rich and enduring presence in the worlds of poetry, literature, performance, politics, culture. As such, it is a social phenomenon, a movement that extended and continues to extend beyond the usual parameters of literature and art. Rhizome refers to a living tuber system, literally "an elongate stem or branch of a plant that is often thickened or tuber shaped as a result of deposits of reserves (food) and is usually horizontal and underground, producing shoots above and roots below in which persistent growth and nourishment occurs, moving horizontally rather than vertically." This rhizome pattern might also be compared to Indra's Net or the Buddhist sense of "pratitya samutpada" which translates as interconnectedness. In their book *Rhizome: Introduction* (Minuit, 1976), the critical theorists Gilles Deleuze and Félix Guattari invoke the rhizome as creative paradigm: "Form rhizomes and not roots, never plant! Don't sow, forage! Be neither a One nor a Many, but multiplicities! A rhizome doesn't begin

and doesn't end, but is always in the middle, between things, interbeing, intermezzo."

It is a useful perspective in examining the multi-layered writings and the lives of a very exceptional community of writers which, in mid-20th-Century America, began to change all of our lives. It was propitious that such a conjunction of minds (and hearts) should occur and stimulate each other. That such a conjunction should root and flower in such remarkable and unique ways, having a ripple effect that moved into other realms of pop culture—fashion, film, music, theatre—and now, also, has staying power in the "academy" of officialdom; the Beat influence has been felt all over the world. It has spawned communities of writers and artists the world over. From the Jack Kerouac School of Disembodied Poetics at Naropa University in Boulder, Colorado, to the Schule für Dichtung in Vienna to the City Lights bookstore and publishing house in Florence, Italy. When Allen Ginsberg died, there were memorials in Britain, France, Italy, India, the Czech Republic, and across the United States. The writings of Beat authors are some of the most translated works in the annals of contemporary literature. The Beat movement holds and inculcates promise, fuels new generations of writers and scholarship. Beat writings demand readership, exploration, and scrutiny; their subtexts of gender, sexuality, queerness, race, and addiction beg to be deciphered. Also, importantly, the influence of jazz and negritude on Beat culture. For these writers were not operating in a vacuum: One could look at the political implications and the concern for the desecration of planet earth and notions of ecology in the work of Gary Snyder and Michael McClure. One could examine notions of spirituality (particularly the philosophy and psychology of Buddhism) and vision and the use of entheogens (Yage, mushrooms, peyote, marijuana).

Beats also felt themselves in a lineage with the antinomian William Blake, who referred to imagination as "Big Vision." Ginsberg had an audio-hallucination, imagining he heard Blake speak. This sensory experience fueled Allen's own identity as a mystic and prophet. Ginsberg taught classes in William Blake at Naropa University for years. Gregory Corso invoked the radical Percy Byshe Shelley on many occasions in his "socratic poetry raps." Eliot's "The Wasteland" was one of William Burroughs's favorite poems. Joanne Kyger has led workshops that stake out "location" and sites of activity and their literary histories, herself being the guardian of the coastal town of Bolinas for many years. Diane di Prima taught classes on light in John Keats. Keats' "negative capability" is the epigrammatic slogan of the Kerouac School and also serves as a description of the quality of mind of the Beat Generation. "Subterranean," "radical," "liberating," "subversive"; these are the adjectives that arise frequently in the discourse. One could add: "learned," "visionary," "empathetic."

This three-volume set, *The Beat Generation: A Gale Critical Companion,* covers a vibrant span of the literary movement. It gives ample space to key figures as well as others who were simpatico and shared the belletristic moments "in Eternity" and in community, and who also lived an alternative (and bohemian) lifestyle. Paul Blackburn—one example—fine poet and translator of the troubadours, affiliated with the praxis of Black Mountain, was a progenitor of the Poetry Project in New York, hosting the open and taping readings with his old Wollensack recorder. Chandler Brossard, a subterranean, almost noirish prose master. Neal Cassady, flamboyant muse and hero of Kerouac's novels, fabulous talker, although less prolific on the page. Robert Duncan and Jack Spicer, more associated with their own San Francisco Renaissance—and at times a more mystical poetics (Spicer speaks of receiving dictation from Mars)—shared a mutual "composition by field" approach with the Beats. Bill Everson, printer and former priest, as well as poet, shared an oppositional pacifism and confessionalism. Barbara Guest, historically placed as key among the New York School innovators (with Frank O'Hara, John Ashbery, Kenneth Koch, and James Schuyler), is possibly the most opaque and experimentally obtuse of the writers here and has always been considered a maverick. Other writers covered in this set's biographical entries are official progenitors of the scene and need less justification for inclusion. The topic entries (volume 1) in this collection are apt, up-to-date, expansive, and extremely useful for scholarship into the future. Entries pertaining to performing and visual arts make this collection particularly salient and useful as a full-bodied rhizomic chart of the ever-layered and expanded notion of a Beat Renaissance.

And this compendium also foregrounds the sites, the presses, and further disseminations of influence. It is a living, palpable transmission that continues because in many ways the Beat movement was a radically spiritual one and, as such,

continues a utopian transforming cultural intervention that is so desperately needed now, as it was in 1950s "art." The writing of poetry and fiction for many of these writers was viewed as a "sacred practice, with sacramental approach to each other as characters," as Ginsberg wrote. There's more power in a sacred approach than in a careerist one, which is why the work and activity of these writers resonates for a new audience—vital to these times, as society needs to re-examine its materialistic, conformist, and, in the case of the U.S., its Pax Americana New World Order modus operandi.

We had an ad for the creative writing program at Naropa: "Come to a school where your teachers have been jailed for their work and beliefs!" One feels that these writers and innovators had no choice in their paths. It was a calling that exacted a life commitment, demanding full attention to art and life and its concommitant camaraderie and vow of friendship. The combination of time and place with the intersection of so many prodigious "best minds" was indeed an auspicious and powerful one that is rare in literary annals. Ginsberg spoke of the establishment response to the threat of power in this movement in his introduction to *The Beat Book* (Shambhala), which I edited in 1999:

> This "beat generation" or "sixties" tolerant worldview provoked an intoxicated right wing to go into "Denial" (as in AA terminology) of reality, and reinforced its codependency with repressive laws, incipient police state, death-penalty demagoguery, sex demagoguery, art censorship, fundamentalist monotheistic televangelist quasi-fascist wrath, racism and homophobia. This counter-reaction seems a by-product of the further gulf between the rich and poor classes, growth of a massive abused underclass, increased power and luxury for the rich who control politics and their minions in the media.

These words seem ever more relevant as I write this in the shadow of war, in the aftermath of a highly publicized fracas over a planned (ultimately scuttled) literary event at the White House. First Lady Bush wanted, ironically—perhaps this is a call for help on Laura Bush's part!—to honor radical poets Emily Dickinson, Walt Whitman, and Langston Hughes (who themselves thought and wrote subtly about the horrors and implications of war). The First Lady made the mistake (at least from the perspective of the administration) of inviting Buddhist poet and editor Sam Hamill of

Copper Canyon Press. He responded by inviting poets all over the country to send protest poems opposing a war with Iraq to the White House. The situation prompted the White House to "delay" the First Lady's event. Despite this, over 5,000 poets have responded to Hamill's invitation. These writings can be seen on the poetsforpeace website, www.poets4peace.com. Lawrence Ferlinghetti, poet laureate of San Francisco, weighed in with the timely "Speak Out," first published in the San Francisco *Chronicle* (14 February 2003). In the poem he speaks to the dangers of war, the threats that confront civil liberties. He concludes with the warning lines:

All you lovers of Liberty . . .
Now is the time for you to speak
O silent majority
Before they come for you

As I sit here pondering the future of the planet, which has suffered so much war and

degradation already in the last century, and I contemplate how to best teach new "best minds" in the face of a war that threatens the stability the whole world over, I realize it behooves one to speak with passion and conviction in the spirit of the Beat Generation that tried to save America from itself. Read this historic canon as one might a sacred text, as unfettered imagination that inspires, guides, and reactivates human thought and emotion towards candor, delight, and compassion.

—Anne Waldman
Distinguished Professor of Poetics
Chair, Summer Writing Program
The Jack Kerouac School of Disembodied Poetics
Naropa University, Boulder, Colorado
and
Co-founder
Poetry is News Coalition, New York City

The Gale Critical Companion Collection

In response to a growing demand for relevant criticism and interpretation of perennial topics and important literary movements throughout history, the Gale Critical Companion Collection (GCCC) was designed to meet the research needs of upper high school and undergraduate students. Each edition of GCCC focuses on a different literary movement or topic of broad interest to students of literature, history, multicultural studies, humanities, foreign language studies, and other subject areas. Topics covered are based on feedback from a standing advisory board consisting of reference librarians and subject specialists from public, academic, and school library systems.

The GCCC is designed to complement Gale's existing Literary Criticism Series (LCS) , which includes such award-winning and distinguished titles as *Nineteenth-Century Literature Criticism* (*NCLC*), *Twentieth-Century Literary Criticism* (*TCLC*), and *Contemporary Literary Criticism* (*CLC*). Like the LCS titles, the GCCC editions provide selected reprinted essays that offer an inclusive range of critical and scholarly response to authors and topics widely studied in high school and undergraduate classes; however, the GCCC also includes primary source documents, chronologies, sidebars, supplemental photographs, and other material not included in the LCS products. The graphic and supplemental material is designed to extend the usefulness of the critical essays and provide students with historical and cultural context on a topic or author's work. GCCC titles will benefit larger institutions with ongoing subscriptions to Gale's LCS products as well as smaller libraries and school systems with less extensive reference collections. Each edition of the GCCC is created as a stand-alone set providing a wealth of information on the topic or movement. Importantly, 15% or less of the critical essays included in GCCC titles have appeared in LCS, ensuring that LCS subscribers who purchase GCCC titles will not duplicate resources in their collection.

Editions within the GCCC are either single-volume or multi-volume sets, depending on the nature and scope of the topic being covered. Topic entries and author entries are treated separately, with entries on related topics appearing first, followed by author entries in an A-Z arrangement. Each volume is approximately 500 pages in length and includes approximately 50 images and sidebar graphics. These sidebars include summaries of important historical events, newspaper clippings, brief biographies of important non-literary figures, complete poems or passages of fiction written by the author, descriptions of events in the related arts (music, visual arts, and dance), and so on.

The reprinted essays in each GCCC edition explicate the major themes and literary techniques of the authors and literary works. It is important to note that approximately 85% of the essays reprinted in GCCC editions are full-text, meaning that they are reprinted in their entirety, including footnotes and lists of abbreviations. Essays are selected based on their coverage of the seminal works and themes of an author, and based on the importance of those essays to an appreciation of the author's contribution to the movement and to literature in general. Gale's editors select those essays of most value to upper high school and undergraduate students, avoiding narrow and highly pedantic interpretations of individual works or of an author's canon.

Scope of The Beat Generation

The Beat Generation, the second set in the Gale Critical Companion Collection, consists of three volumes. Each volume includes a detailed table of contents, a foreword on the Beat Generation written by noted Beat scholar Anne Waldman, and a descriptive chronology of key events of the movement. The main body of volume 1 consists of entries on five topics relevant to the Beat Generation, including 1) The Beat Generation: An Overview; 2) The Beat "Scene": East and West; 3) Beat Generation Publishing: Periodicals, Small Presses, and Censorship; 4) Performing Arts and the Beat Generation; and 5) Visual Arts and the Beat Generation. Volumes 2 and 3 include entries on twenty-nine authors and literary figures associated with the movement, including such notables as William S. Burroughs, Gregory Corso, Lawrence Ferlinghetti, Allen Ginsberg, Jack Kerouac, and Kenneth Rexroth, as well as entries on individuals who have garnered less attention, but whose contributions to the Beat Generation are noteworthy, such as Diane di Prima, William Everson, Bob Kaufman, Ed Sanders, Gary Snyder, Lew Welch, and Philip Whalen.

Organization of The Beat Generation

A *Beat Generation* topic entry consists of the following elements:

- The **Introduction** defines the subject of the entry and provides social and historical information important to understanding the criticism.

- The list of **Representative Works** identifies writings and works by authors and figures associated with the subject. The list is divided into alphabetical sections by name; works listed under each name appear in chronological order. The genre and publication date of each work is given. Unless otherwise indicated, dramas are dated by first performance, not first publication.

- Entries generally begin with a section of **Primary Sources**, which includes essays, speeches, social history, newspaper accounts and other materials that were produced during the time of the Beat Generation.

- Reprinted **Criticism** in topic entries is arranged thematically. Topic entries commonly begin with primary sources, followed by general surveys of the subject or essays providing historical or background information, followed by essays that develop particular aspects of the topic. For example, the Publishing topic entry in volume 1 of *Beat Generation* begins with a section providing primary source material on publishing during the Beat Generation. This is followed by a section providing an overview essay on the topic, and three other sections: Beat Periodicals: "Little Magazines"; Beat Publishing: Small Presses; and Beat Battles with Censorship. Each section has a separate title heading and is identified with a page number in the table of contents. The critic's name and the date of composition or publication of the critical work are given at the beginning of each piece of criticism. Unsigned criticism is preceded by the title of the source in which it appeared. Footnotes are reprinted at the end of each essay or excerpt. In the case of excerpted criticism, only those footnotes that pertain to the excerpted texts are included.

- A complete **Bibliographical Citation** of the original essay or book precedes each piece of criticism.

- Critical essays are prefaced by brief **Annotations** explicating each piece. Unless the descriptor "excerpt" is used in the annotation, the essay is being reprinted in its entirety.

- An annotated bibliography of **Further Reading** appears at the end of each entry and suggests resources for additional study. In some cases, significant essays for which the editors could not obtain reprint rights are included here.

A *Beat Generation* author entry consists of the following elements:

- The **Author Heading** cites the name under which the author most commonly wrote, followed by birth and death dates. Also located here are any name variations under which an author wrote. If the author wrote consistently under a pseudonym, the pseudonym will be listed in the author heading and the author's actual name given in parentheses on the first line of the biographical and critical information. Uncertain birth or death dates are indicated by question marks.

- A **Portrait of the Author** is included when available.

- The **Introduction** contains background information that introduces the reader to the author that is the subject of the entry.

- The list of **Principal Works** is ordered chronologically by date of first publication and lists the most important works by the author. The genre and publication date of each work is given. Unless otherwise indicated, dramas are dated by first performance, not first publication.

- Author entries are arranged into three sections: **Primary Sources, General Commentary,** and **Title Commentary.** The Primary Sources section generally includes letters, poems, short stories, journal entries, novel excerpts, and essays written by the featured author, and sometimes commentary written about the author by the author's contemporaries. General Commentary includes overviews of the author's career and general studies; Title Commentary includes in-depth analyses of seminal works by the author. Within the Title Commentary section, the reprinted criticism is further organized by title, then by date of publication. The critic's name and the date of composition or publication of the critical work are given at the beginning of each piece of criticism. Unsigned criticism is preceded by the title of the source in which it appeared All titles by the author featured in the text are printed in boldface type. However, not all boldfaced titles are included in the author and subject indexes; only substantial discussions of works are indexed. Footnotes are reprinted at the end of each essay or excerpt. In the case of excerpted criticism, only those footnotes that pertain to the excerpted texts are included.

- A complete **Bibliographical Citation** of the original essay or book precedes each piece of criticism.

- Critical essays are prefaced by brief **Annotations** explicating each piece. Unless the descriptor "excerpt" is used in the annotation, the essay is being reprinted in its entirety.

- An annotated bibliography of **Further Reading** appears at the end of each entry and suggests resources for additional study. In some cases, significant essays for which the editors could not obtain reprint rights are included

here. A list of **Other Sources from Gale** follows the further reading section and provides references to other biographical and critical sources on the author in series published by Gale.

Indexes

The **Author Index** lists all of the authors featured in the *Beat Generation* set, with references to the main author entries in volumes 2 and 3 as well as commentary on the featured author in other author entries and in the topic volume. Page references to substantial discussions of the authors appear in boldface. The Author Index also includes birth and death dates and cross references between pseudonyms and actual names, and cross references to other Gale series in which the authors have appeared. A complete list of these sources is found facing the first page of the Author Index.

The **Title Index** alphabetically lists the titles of works written by the authors featured in volumes 2 and 3 and provides page numbers or page ranges where commentary on these titles can be found. Page references to substantial discussions of the titles appear in boldface. English translations of foreign titles and variations of titles are cross-referenced to the title under which a work was originally published. Titles of novels, dramas, nonfiction books, and poetry, short story, or essay collections are printed in italics, while individual poems, short stories, and essays are printed in roman type within quotation marks.

The **Subject Index** includes the authors and titles that appear in the Author Index and the Title Index as well as the names of other authors and figures that are discussed in the set. The Subject Index also lists titles and authors of the critical essays that appear in the set, as well as hundreds of literary terms and topics covered in the criticism. The index provides page numbers or page ranges where subjects are discussed and is fully cross-referenced.

Citing The Beat Generation

When writing papers, students who quote directly from the *BG* set may use the following general format to footnote reprinted criticism. The first example pertains to material drawn from periodicals, the second to material reprinted from books.

Podhoretz, Norman, "The Know-Nothing Bohemians," *Partisan Review* 25, no. 2 (spring 1958): 305-11, 313-16, 318; reprinted in *The Beat Generation: A Gale Critical Companion,* vol. 1, ed. Lynn M. Zott (Farmington Hills, Mich.: The Gale Group, 2003), 13-19.

Rexroth, Kenneth, "Disengagement: The Art of the Beat Generation." in *A Casebook on the Beat,* edited by Thomas Parkinson (New York: Thomas Y. Crowell Company, 1961), 179-93; reprinted in *The Beat Generation: A Gale Critical Companion,* vol. 1, ed. Lynn M. Zott (Farmington Hills, Mich.: The Gale Group, 2003), 6-13.

The Beat Generation *Advisory Board*

The members of the *Beat Generation* Advisory Board—reference librarians and subject specialists from public, academic, and school library systems—offered a variety of informed perspectives on both the presentation and content of the *Beat Generation* set. Advisory board members assessed and defined such quality issues as the relevance, currency, and usefulness of the author coverage, critical content, and topics included in our product; evaluated the layout, presentation, and general quality of our product; provided feedback on the criteria used for selecting authors and topics covered in our product; identified any gaps in our coverage of authors or topics, recommending authors or topics for inclusion; and analyzed the appropriateness of our content and presentation for various user audiences, such as high school students, undergraduates, graduate students, librarians, and educators. We wish to thank the advisors for their advice during the development of the *Beat Generation.*

Suggestions are Welcome

Readers who wish to suggest new features, topics, or authors to appear in future volumes of the Gale Critical Companion Collection, or who have other suggestions or comments are cordially invited to call, write, or fax the Project Editor:

Project Editor, Gale Critical Companion
  Collection
The Gale Group
27500 Drake Road
Farmington Hills, MI 48331-3535
1-800-347-4253 (GALE)
Fax: 248-699-8054

The editors wish to thank the copyright holders of the excerpted criticism included in this volume and the permissions managers of many book and magazine publishing companies for assisting us in securing reproduction rights. We are also grateful to the staffs of the Detroit Public Library, the Library of Congress, the University of Detroit Mercy Library, Wayne State University Purdy/ Kresge Library Complex, Oakland University Library, and the University of Michigan Libraries for making their resources available to us. Following is a list of the copyright holders who have granted us permission to reproduce material in this edition of *The Beat Generation*. Every effort has been made to trace copyright, but if omissions have been made, please let us know.

Copyrighted material in The Beat Generation *was reproduced from the following periodicals:*

American Book Review, v. 3, May-June 1981. Reproduced by permission.—*American Literature*, v. 65, No. 1, pp. 117-130, March 1993. Copyright, 1993, Duke University Press. All rights reserved. Used by permission of the publisher. —*American Poetry Review*, v. 23, November-December 1994. Reproduced by permission of the author—*American Studies*, v. 32, 1987; v. 29: 1, Spring 1988. Copyright © Mid America American Studies Association, 2002. Reproduced by permission from American Studies.—*American Studies*, v. 43, 1998. Reproduced by permission of the author.—*The Antioch Review*, v. 31, Fall 1971. Reproduced by permission.—*The Ark*, v. 14, 1980. Reproduced by permission.—*Arshile*, v. 5, 1996. Reproduced by permission of the author. —*Atlantic Monthly*, v. 221, March 1968. Reproduced by permission of Sterling Lord Literistic, Inc.—*Beat Scene*, Autumn, 1993. Reproduced by permission.—*The Cambridge Quarterly*, v. 22, 1993. Copyright © 1993 by the Editors. Reproduced by permission of Oxford University Press. —*Chicago Review*, v. 26, 1974. Reproduced by permission.—*College Literature*, v. 27, Winter 2000. Reproduced by permission.—*Commentary*, v. 49, January 1970. All rights reserved. Reproduced by permission.—*Concerning Poetry*, v. 2, Spring 1969; v. 20, 1987. Reproduced by permission.—*Contemporary Literature*, v. 31, n. 3, Fall 1990; v. 38, n. 2, Summer 1997; v. 42, n. 3, Fall 2001. Copyright © 1990, 1997, 2001 The Board of Regents of the University of Wisconsin System. All rights reserved. Reproduced by permission. —*The Critical Quarterly*, v. 8, Autumn 1966. Reproduced by permission of Blackwell Publishing Ltd.—*ENclitic*, v. 11, Spring 1989. Reproduced by permission of the author.—*Exquisite Corpse: A Journal of Letters and Life*, 2002. Reproduced by permission.—*Extrapolation*, v. 20, Winter 1979. Reproduced by permission.—*Film Quarterly*, v. 45, Spring 1992. Copyright © 1992 by The Regents of the University of California, www.ucpress.edu. Reproduced by permission.—*The Gazette*, September 9, 2000. Reproduced by permission of the

ACKNOWLEDGMENTS

author.—*Geographical Review*, v. 86, January 1996. Reproduced by permission of the American Geographical Society.—*Harvard Theological*, v. 84, April 1991. Reproduced by permission. —*Ironwood*, 1983. Reproduced by permission of the author.—*Journal of Modern Literature*, v. 2, 1971-72, for "Theory and Practice of Gary Snyder, by Thomas Parkinson. Reproduced by permission of Indiana University Press.—*Kenyon Review*, v. 14, Winter 1992. Reproduced by permission of the author.—*Literary Review*, v. 33, Spring 1990. Reproduced by permission of the author.—*MELUS*, v. 14, Fall-Winter 1987; v. 19, Fall 1994. Reproduced by permission.—*Midwest Quarterly*, v. 14, July 1973. Copyright © 1973 by The Midwest Quarterly, Pittsburgh State University. Reproduced by permission.—*Modern Drama*, v. 22, March 1979. Copyright © 1979 University of Toronto, Graduate Centre for Study of Drama. Reproduced by permission.—*Moody Street Irregulars*, Summer 1986. Reproduced by permission.—*The Nation,* v. 185, November 9, 1957; v. 186, March, 1958; v. 187, October 11, 1958. © 1957, 1958 The Nation magazine/The Nation Company, Inc. Reproduced by permission.—*New Orleans Review*, v. 19, Spring 1992. Copyright © 1992 by Loyola University. Reproduced by permission.—*New York Times*, August 9, 1996. Copyright © 1996 by The New York Times Company. Reproduced by permission.—*New York Times Book Review*, November 25, 1984. Copyright © 1984 by The New York Times Company. Reproduced by permission.—*New York Times Magazine*, November 16, 1952. Copyright © by Estate of John Clellon Holmes. Reproduced by permission of Sterling Lord Literistic, Inc.—*Newsweek*, November 22, 1971, Newsweek, Inc. All rights reserved. Reproduced by permission.—*North Dakota Quarterly*, Fall 1987. Copyright 1987 by The University of North Dakota. Reproduced by permission.—*Parnassus*, v. 1, 1973; v. 3, Fall-Winter 1974. Copyright © 1973, 1974 Poetry in Review Foundation, NY. Reproduced by permission of authors.—*Partisan Review*, v. 25, Summer 1958, for "The Know-Nothing Bohemians," by Norman Podhoretz. Copyright © 1958 by Norman Podhoretz; v. 25, Summer 1958, for a letter to the editor, by LeRoi Jones; v. 26, Spring 1959, for "The Other Night at Columbia: A Report from the Academy," by Diana Trilling. Copyright © 1959 by Partisan Review, renewed 1987 by Diana Trilling. Reproduced by permission of the author, publisher, and Wylie Agency respectively.—*Playboy Magazine*, v. 6, June 1959, "The Origins of the Beat Generation," by Jack Kerouac. Reproduced by permission of the publisher and Sterling Lord Literistic, Inc.—*Poetry*, v. 90, April 1957, for "Two New Books by Kenneth Rexroth," by William Carlos Williams. Copyright © 1957 by Paul H. Williams and the Estate of William Eric Williams. Reproduced by permission of New Directions Publishing Corp., agents.—*Publishers Weekly*, v. 248, May 7, 2001. Copyright 2001 by Reed Publishing USA. Reproduced from Publishers Weekly, published by the Bowker Magazine Group of Cahners Publishing Co., a division of Reed Publishing USA. Reproduced by permission.—*Religion and the Arts*, v. 2, 1998. Reproduced by permission.—*Review of Contemporary Fiction*, v. 3, Summer 1983; v. 7, Spring 1987; v. 19, Spring 1999. Copyright 1983, 1987, 1999 by John O'Brien. Reproduced by permission.—*Sagetrieb*, v. 2, Spring 1983. Copyright © 1983 by the author. Reproduced by permission of the author.—*The San Francisco Chronicle—Sunday Review Section*, April 22, 2001. Republished with permission of The San Francisco Chronicle, conveyed through Copyright Clearance Center, Inc.—*Sixties*, Spring 1962. Reproduced by permission of the Eighties Press.—*Small Press: The Magazine and Book Review of Independent Publishing*, August 1990. Reproduced by permission.—*Social Research*, v. 68, Fall 2001. Copyright 2001 by New School for Social Research. Reproduced by permission.—*Southern Humanities Review*, v. VI, Fall 1972. Reproduced by permission.—*Southern Review*, v. 21, January 1985. Reproduced by permission.—*Texas Studies in Literature and Language*, v. 44, n. 2, Summer 2002, pp. 211-28. "'The Brake of Time' Corso's Bomb as Postmodern God(dess)," by Christine Hoff Kraemer. Copyright © 2002 by the University of Texas Press. All rights reserved. Reproduced by permission.—*Third Rail*, v. 8, 1987. Reproduced by permission of Mr. Uri Hertz, Editor of Third Rail and the author.—*Times Literary Supplement*, June 3, 1983, pp. 586-7, for "Camp Follower," by James Campbell. © The Times Supplements Limited 1983; March 22, 1991, p. 21, for "The Steinberg Case," by Brian Masters. Reproduced by permission.—*TriQuarterly*, v. 43, Fall 1978. Reproduced by permission of author.—*Western American Literature*, v. 3, Fall 1968. Copyright 1968, by the Western American Literature Association. Reproduced by permission.—*Whole Earth*, v. 98, Fall 1999. Reproduced by permission. —*Women's Studies*, v. 30, 2001. © Gordon and Breach Science Publishers. Reproduced by permission.—*Woodstock Journal*, v. 7, February 2- 16, 2001; v. 7, May 11-25, 2001. Reproduced by permission.—*The Wordsworth Circle*, v. 22, Summer 1991. © 1991 Marilyn Gaull. Reproduced by permission of the editor.

Copyrighted material in The Beat Generation was reproduced from the following books:

Amram, David. From "This Song's For You, Jack: Collaborating With Kerouac," in *Beat Culture: The 1950s and Beyond*. Edited by Cornelis A. Minnen, Jaap van der Bent, and Mel van Elteren. VU University Press, 1999. Copyright © 1999 by Amerika Instituut, Amsterdam. All rights reserved. Reproduced by permission.—Berger, Maurice. From "Libraries Full of Tears: The Beats and the Law," in *Beat Culture and the New America: 1950-1965*, by Lisa Phillips et al. Whitney Museum of American Art, 1995. Copyright © 1995 by Whitney Museum of American Art. All rights reserved. Reproduced by permission.—Blaser, Robin. From "The Practice of Outside," in *The Collected Books of Jack Spicer*, by Jack Spicer. Edited by Robin Blaser. Black Sparrow Press, 1975. Copyright © 1975 by the Estate of Jack Spicer. All rights reserved. Reproduced by permission.—Burroughs, William S. From Introductory Essay to *Mindfield*. Thunder's Mouth Press, 1989. Copyright © 1989 by William Burroughs. Reproduced by permission of The Wylie Agency, Inc.—Burroughs, William S. From *Naked Lunch*. Grove Press Inc., 1959. Copyright © 1959 by William S. Burroughs. All rights reserved. Reproduced by permission.—Burroughs, William S. From *The Yage Letters*. City Lights Books 1963. Copyright © 1963, 1975 by William S. Burroughs and Allen Ginsberg. All rights reserved. Reproduced by permission.—Bush, Clive. From "'Why Do We Always Say Angel?': Herbert Huncke and Neal Cassady," in *The Beat Generation Writers*. Edited by A. Robert Lee. Pluto Press, 1996. Copyright © 1996 by Lumiere (Cooperative) Press Ltd. and Pluto Press. All rights reserved. Reproduced by permission.—Campbell, James. From "Behind the Beat: Neurotica," and "The Muses: Huncke-Junkie and Neo-Cassady," in *This Is the Beat Generation: New York—San Francisco—Paris*. Secker and Warburg, 1999 and the University of California Press. Copyright © 1999 by James Campbell. All rights reserved. Reproduced by permission of The Random House Group Limited and by the Regents of the University of California and the University of California Press.—Carpenter, David. From "Introduction: She That Looketh Forth as the Morning," in *The Integral Years: Poems 1966-1994*, by William Everson. Black Sparrow Press, 2000. Copyright © 2000 by David A. Carpenter. All rights reserved. Reproduced by permission.—Carroll, Paul. From "I Lift My Voice Aloud/Make Mantra of American Language Now.../I Here Declare the End of the War!" in *The Poem in Its Skin*. Follett Publishing Company, 1968. Copyright © 1968 by Paul Carroll. All rights reserved. Reproduced by

permission.—Cassady, Carolyn. From "Afterword," in *The First Third and Other Writings*. Edited by Lawrence Ferlinghetti and Nancy J. Peters. City Lights Books, 1981. Copyright © 1981 by City Lights Books. All rights reserved. Reproduced by permission.—Cassady, Neal. From Letter to Jack Kerouac (Kansas City, MO, March 7, 1947), in *The First Third & Other Writings*. City Lights Books, 1971. Copyright © 1971 by City Lights Books. All rights reserved. Reproduced by permission.—Cherkovski, Neeli. From "Bob Kaufman," and "The Memory of Love: John Wieners," in *Whitman's Wild Children: Portraits of Twelve Poets*. Steerforth Press 1999. Copyright © 1999 by Neeli Cherkovski (a.k.a. Neeli Cherry). All rights reserved. Reproduced by permission.—Christensen, Paul. From Introduction to *Two Novels: You Didn't Even Try: Imaginary Speeches for a Brazen Head*. Zephyr Press, 1989. Copyright © 1989 by Paul Christensen. All rights reserved. Reproduced by permission.—Christian, Barbara. From "Whatever Happened to Bob Kaufman," in *The Beats: Essays in Criticism*. Edited by Lee Bartlett. McFarland, 1981. Copyright © 1981 by Lee Bartlett. All rights reserved. Reproduced by permission.—Clark, Walter Houston. From "Historical Notes: The Harvard Incident," in *Chemical Ecstasy: Psychedelic Drugs and Religion*. Sheed and Ward, 1969. Copyright © by Sheed and Ward, Inc. All rights reserved. Reproduced by permission.—Clay, Steven, and Rodney Phillips. From "A Little History of the Mimeograph Revolution," in *A Secret Location on the Lower East Side: Adventures in Writing 1960-1980*. The New York Public Library and Granary Book, 1998. Copyright © 1998 by The New York Public Library, Astor, Lenox and Tilden Foundations and Granary Books. All rights reserved. Reproduced by permission.—Cohen, Ronald D. From "Singing Subversion: Folk Music and the Counterculture in the 1950s," in *Beat Culture: The 1950s and Beyond*. Edited by Cornelis A. Minnen, Jaap van der Bent, and Mel van Elteren. VU University Press, 1999. Copyright © 1999 by Amerika Instituut, Amsterdam. All rights reserved. Reproduced by permission.—Corso, Gregory. From "Marriage," in *The Happy Birthday of Death*. Copyright © 1960 by New Directions Publishing Corp. Reprinted by permission of New Directions Publishing Corp.—Creeley, Robert. From Introduction to *Black Mountain Review: Volume 1, 1954*. AMS Press, 1969. Copyright © 1969 by AMS Press Inc. All rights reserved. Reproduced by permission.—Creeley, Robert. From Preface to *Cultural Affairs in Boston: Poetry and Prose, 1956-1985*, by John Wieners. Edited by Raymond Foye. Black Sparrow Press, 1988. Copyright © 1988 by Robert Creeley. All rights reserved. Reproduced by permission.

—Davidson, Michael. From "'Spotting That Design': Incarnation and Interpretation in Gary Snyder and Philip Whalen," and From "'The City Redefined': Community and Dialogue in Jack Spicer," in *The San Francisco Renaissance: Poetics and Community at Mid-Century*. Cambridge University Press, 1989. Copyright © 1989 by Cambridge University Press. All rights reserved. Reproduced by permission of Cambridge University Press and the author.—Dickey, James. From "Kenneth Patchen," in *Babel to Byzantium Poets and Poetry Now*, by James Dickey. Copyright © 1968 by James Dickey. Reproduced by permission of Farrar, Straus, and Giroux, LLC.—Douglas, Ann. From "'Punching a Hole in the Big Lie': The Achievement of William S. Burroughs," in *Word Virus: The William S. Burroughs Reader*. Edited by James Grauerholz and Ira Silverberg. Grove Press, 1998. Copyright © 1998 by Grove Press. All rights reserved. Reproduced by permission.—Duncan, Robert. From "Often I am Permitted to Return to a Meadow," in *The Opening of the Field*. Copyright © 1960 by Robert Duncan. Reprinted by permission of New Directions Publishing Corp. —Dylan, Bob. From "Blowin in the Wind," in *The Free Wheeling Bob Dylan*. Copyright © 1962 by Warner Bros. Inc. Copyright renewed 1990 Special Rider Music. All rights reserved. International copyright secured. Reproduced by permission. —Dylan, Bob. From "The Times They are a Changin'," in *The Times They are A-Changin'*. Copyright © 1963 by Warner Bros. Inc. Copyright renewed 1991 Special Rider Music. All rights reserved. International copyright secured. Reproduced by permission.—Edmiston, Susan, and Linda D. Cirino. From "The East Village," in *Literary New York*. Houghton Mifflin Company, 1976. Copyright © 1976 by Susan Edmiston and Linda D. Cirino. All rights reserved. Reproduced by permission of the authors.—Ferlinghetti, Lawrence, and Nancy J. Peters. In *Literary San Francisco: A Pictorial from Its Beginning to the Present Day*. City Lights Books and Harper & Row, 1980. Copyright © 1980 by Lawrence Ferlinghetti and Nancy J. Peters. All rights reserved. Reproduced by permission of HarperCollins Publishers Inc., and the author.—Ferlinghetti, Lawrence, and Robert Dana. From "Lawrence Ferlinghetti," in *Against the Grain: Interview with Maverick American Publishers*. Edited by Robert Dana. University of Iowa Press, 1986. All rights reserved. Reproduced by permission of the author.—Ferlinghetti, Lawrence. From "Horn on Howl," in *On the Poetry of Allen Ginsberg*. Edited by Lewis Hyde. University of Michigan Press, 1984. Copyright © 1984 by University of Michigan Press. All rights reserved. Reproduced by permission of the author.—Ferlinghetti, Lawrence. From "I am Wait-

ing," in *A Coney Island of the Mind*. Copyright © 1958 by Lawrence Ferlinghetti. Reprinted by permission of New Directions Publishing Corp. —Ferlinghetti, Lawrence. From "Number 13: It Was a Face Which Darkness Could Kill," in *Pictures of the Gone World*. City Lights, 1955. Copyright © 1955 by Lawrence Ferlinghetti. All rights reserved. Reproduced by permission of the author.—Foster, Edward Halsey. From "Corso," and "Hipsters, Beats, and the True Frontier," in *Understanding the Beats*. University of South Carolina Press, 1992. Copyright © 1992 by University of South Carolina Press. All rights reserved. Reproduced by permission.—Foye, Raymond. From Introduction to *The Herbert Huncke Reader*. Edited by Benjamin G. Schafer. William Morrow, 1997. Copyright © 1997 by the Estate of Herbert E. Hencke, Jerome Poynton, Executor. All rights reserved. Reproduced by permission.—Foye, Raymond, and John Wieners. From Introduction to *Cultural Affairs in Boston: Poetry and Prose, 1956-1985*, by John Wieners. Black Sparrow Press, 1988. Copyright © 1988 by Raymond Foye and John Wieners. All rights reserved. Reproduced by permission.—French, Warren. From "On the Road: Work in Progress," in *Jack Kerouac*. Twayne Publishers, 1986. Copyright © 1986 by G.K. Hall & Co. All rights reserved. Reproduced by permission.—Fuller, Robert C. From "Psychedelics and Metaphysical Illumination," in *Stairways to Heaven: Drugs in American Religious History*. Copyright © 2000 by Westview Press. Reproduced by permission of Westview Press, a member of the Perseus Books, L.L.C.—Gelpi, Albert. From "Introduction: Everson/Antonius: Contending with the Shadow," in *The Veritable Years: Poems 1949-1966*, by William Everson. Black Sparrow Press, 1998. Copyright © 1998 by Albert Gelpi. All rights reserved. Reproduced by permission.—George, Paul S., and Jerold M. Starr. From "Beat Politics: New Left and Hippie Beginnings in the Postwar Counterculture," in *Cultural Politics: Radical Movements in Modern History*. Edited by Jerold M. Starr. Praeger, 1985. Copyright © 1985 by Praeger Publishers. All rights reserved. Reproduced by permission.—Ginsberg, Allen, "Early Journal Entries," found at *http://www.allenginsberg.org*. Copyright © 2000 by the Allen Ginsberg Trust. Reprinted with permission of The Wylie Agency, Inc.—Ginsberg, Allen. From An interview in *Jack's Book*, by Barry Gifford and Lawrence Lee. St. Martin's Press, 1978. Copyright © 1994 by Barry Gifford and Lawrence Lee. Reproduced by permission of St. Martin's Press, LLC.—Ginsberg, Allen. From Foreword to "Out of the World," *Deliberate Prose: Selected Essays 1952-1995*. Edited by Anne Waldman. Crown Publishers, 1991. Copyright © 1999 by Allen Ginsberg Trust. All rights reserved.

ling Lord Literistic, Inc.—Kerouac, Jack. From "Scripture of the Golden Eternity," in *Scripture of the Golden Eternity*. Totem Press, 1960. Copyright © 1960.by Jack Kerouac. All rights reserved. Reproduced by permission of Sterling Lord Literistic, Inc.—Kerouac, Jack. In *The Dharma Bums*. Copyright © 1958 by Jack Kerouac, © renewed 1986 by Stella Kerouac and Jan Kerouac. Used by permission of Viking Penguin, a division of Penguin Putnam, Inc. and Sterling Lord Literistic, Inc.—Kesey, Ken. From "Flowers for Tim," foreword to *On the Bus*, by Paul Perry. Thunder's Mouth Press, 1996. Copyright © 1964 by The Estate of Ken Kesey. All rights reserved. Reproduced by permission of Sterling Lord Literistic, Inc.—Kesey, Ken. From "The Day after Superman Died," in *Demon Box*. Copyright © 1979 by Ken Kesey. Used by permission of Viking Penguin, a division of Penguin Putnam Inc. and Sterling Lord Literistic, Inc.—Knabb, Kenneth, "The Relevance of Rexroth: Magnanimity and Mysticism," at *http://www.bopsecrets.org/PS/rexroth2.htm*. Published by Public Secrets, Bureau of Public Secrets, (1997). Reprinted with permission. —Knight, Brenda. Excepted from "Joan Vollmer Adams Burroughs: Calypso Stranded (1924- 1951)," "Anne Waldman: Fast Speaking Woman," "Eileen Kaufman: Keeper of the Flame (1922-)," "Joanne Kyger, Dharma Sister," "Joyce Johnson: A True Good Heart," and "ruth weiss: The Survivor (1928-)," in *Women of the Beat Generation: The Writers, Artists and Muses at the Heart of a Revolution*. Conari Press, 1996. Copyright © 1996 by Brenda Knight. All rights reserved. Reproduced by permission of Conari Press, an imprint of Red Wheel/Weiser. Ordering information: Red Wheel/Weiser 1-800-423-7087 Website: Conari.com. —Kowalewski, Michael. From "Jack Kerouac and the Beats in San Francisco," in *San Francisco in Fiction: Essays in a Regional Literature*. Edited by David Fine and Paul Skenazy. University of New Mexico Press, 1995. Copyright © 1995 by University of New Mexico Press. All rights reserved. Reproduced by permission.—Kupferberg, Tuli, and Theresa Stern, An interview with Tuli Kupferberg, *www.furious.com/perfect/tuli.html*. Published by Furious, (1997). Reprinted with permission.—Lauridsen, Inger Thorup, and Per Dalgard. From An Interview with Gary Snyder, in *The Beat Generation and the Russian New Wave*. Ardis, 1990. Copyright © 1990 by Ardis Publishers. All rights reserved. Reproduced by permission of Overlook Press, Inc.—Leavitt, Craig. From "On the Road: Cassady, Kerouac, and Images of Late Western Masculinity," in *Across the Great Divide: Cultures of Manhood in the American West*. Edited by Matthew Basso, Laura McCall, and Dee Garceau. Routledge, 2001. Copyright © 2001 by Routledge.

All rights reserved. Reproduced by permission of Routledge, Inc., part of the Taylor & Francis Group.—Levy, Peter B. From "Beating the Censor: The 'Howl' Trial Revisited," in *Beat Culture: The 1950s and Beyond*. Edited by Cornelis A. Minnen, Jaap van der Bent, and Mel van Elteren. VU University Press, 1999. Copyright © 1999 by Amerika Instituut, Amsterdam. All rights reserved. Reproduced by permission.—Maynard, John Arthur. From Introduction to *Venice West: The Beat Generation in Southern California*. Copyright © 1991 by John Arthur Maynard. Reproduced by permission of Rutgers University Press. —McCarthy, Mary. From "Burroughs' Naked Lunch," in *William S. Burroughs at the Front: Critical Reception, 1959- 1989*. Edited by Jennie Skerl and Robin Lydenberg. Southern Illinois University Press, 1991. Copyright © 1991 by Southern Illinois University Press, reprinted by permission of Harcourt, Inc.—McClure, Michael, and Eduardo Lipschutz-Villa. From "Wallace Berman and Semina," in *Lighting the Corners: On Art, Nature, and the Visionary, Essays and Interviews*. University of New Mexico College of Arts and Sciences, 1993. Copyright © 1993 by Michael McClure. All rights reserved. Reproduced by permission.—McClure, Michael. From "A Mammal Gallery," in *Scratching the Beat Surface*. North Point Press, 1982. Copyright © 1982 by Michael McClure. All rights reserved. Reproduced by permission of the author.—McClure, Michael. From "Bob Dylan: The Poet's Poet," and "Sixty-six Things About the California Assemblage Movement," in *Lighting the Corners: On Art, Nature, and the Visionary, Essays and Interviews*. University of New Mexico College of Arts and Sciences, 1993. Copyright © 1993 by Michael McClure. All rights reserved. Reproduced by permission.—McClure, Michael. From "Point Lobos: Animism," in *Hymns to St. Geryon and Other Poems*. Auerhahn Press, 1959. Copyright © 1959. by Michael McClure. All rights reserved. Reproduced by permission of the author.—Meltzer, David. From "Diane di Prima (1999)," and "Lew Welch (1969)," in *San Francisco Beat: Talking with the Poets*. City Lights Books, 2001. Copyright © 2001 by David Meltzer. All rights reserved. Reproduced by permission.—Meltzer, David, and Jack Shoemaker. From "Lawrence Ferlinghetti I (1969)," in *San Francisco Beat: Talking with the Poets*. Edited by David Meltzer. City Lights Books, 2001. Copyright © 2001 by David Meltzer. All rights reserved. Reproduced by permission.—Meltzer, David, and Jack Shoemaker with Michael McClure. From "Michael McClure I (1969)," in *San Francisco Beat: Talking with the Poets*. Edited by David Meltzer. City Lights Books, 2001. Copyright © 2001 by David Meltzer. All rights reserved. Reproduced by permission.—Meltzer, David. From "Poetry and Jazz," in *Beat Down to Your Soul: What Was the Beat Generation*. Edited by Ann Charters. Penguin, 2001. Copyright © 2001 Ann Charters. All rights reserved. Reproduced by permission.—Merrill, Thomas S. From "Ginsberg and the Beat Attitude," in *Allen Ginsberg*. Twayne Publishers, 1988. Copyright © 1988 by G.K. Hall & Co. All rights reserved. Reproduced by permission.—Merrill, Thomas F. From "Allen Ginsberg's Reality Sandwiches," in *The Beats: Essays in Criticism*. Edited by Lee Bartlett. McFarland, 1981. Copyright © 1981 by Lee Bartlett. All rights reserved. Reproduced by permission.—Miles, Barry. From "The Beat Generation in the Village," in *Greenwich Village: Culture and Counterculture*. Edited by Rich Beard and Leslie Cohen Berlowitz. Copyright © 1993, by the Museum of the City of New York. Reproduced by permission of Rutgers University Press.—Miller, Henry. From "Patchen: Man of Anger and Light," in *Kenneth Patchen: A Collection of Essays*. Edited by Richard G. Morgan. AMS Press, Inc. 1977. Copyright © 1977 by Richard G. Morgan. All rights reserved. Reproduced by permission.—Nelson, Raymond. From "Patchen: A Mystical Writer's Career," in *Kenneth Patchen and American Mysticism*. University of North Carolina Press, 1984. Copyright © 1984 by University of North Carolina Press. All rights reserved. Reproduced by permission.—O'Grady, John P. From "Kenneth Rexroth," in *Updating the Literary West*. Edited by the Western Literature Association. Texas Christian University Press, 1997. Copyright © 1997 by Western Literature Association. All rights reserved. Reproduced by permission.—Olson, Kirby. From "Gregory Corso: Doubting Thomist," in *Comedy after Postmodernism: Rereading Comedy from Edward Lear to Charles Willeford*. Texas Tech University Press, 2001. Copyright © 2001 by Texas Tech University Press. All rights reserved. Reproduced by permission.—Ossman, David and Imamu Amiri Baraka (LeRoi Jones). From "LeRoi Jones: An Interview on Yugen," in *The Sullen Art: Interviews by David Ossman with Modern Poets*. Corinth Books, 1963. Reprinted by permission of the author.—Parkinson, Thomas. From "Poets, Poems, Movements," in *Casebook on the Beat*. Edited by Thomas Parkinson. Thomas Y. Crowell Co., 1961. UMI Research Press, University Microfilms, Inc., Ann Arbor, Michigan, 48106. Copyright © 1987 by T. Parkinson. Reproduced by permission.—Patchen, Kenneth. From "The Artist's Duty," in *The Journal of Albion Moonlight*. Copyright © 1941 by Kenneth Patchen. Reprinted by permission of New Directions Publishing Corp.—Perloff, Marjorie. From "On the Other Side of the Field: The Collection Poems of Paul Black-

burn," in *Poetic License: Essays on Modernist and Postmodernist Lyric*. Northwestern University Press, 1990. Copyright © 1990 by Marjorie Perloff. All rights reserved. Reproduced by permission.—Perry, Paul. From "Origins," in *On the Bus*. Edited by Michael Schwartz and Neil Ortenberg. Thunder's Mouth Press, 1990. Copyright © 1990 by Paul Perry. All rights reserved. Reproduced by permission of the author.—Phillips, Rod. From "'Let Us Throw Out the Word Man': Michael McClure's Mammalian Poetics," and "'The Journal of Urban Withdrawal': Nature and the Poetry of Lew Welch," in *"Forest Beatniks" and "Urban Thoreaus": Gary Snyder, Jack Kerouac, Lew Welch, and Michael McClure*. Peter Lang, 2000. Copyright © 2000 by Peter Lang Publishing, Inc. All rights reserved. Reproduced by permission. —Porter, M. Gilbert. From "Kesey: The Man and the Artist," in *The Art of Grit: Ken Kesey's Fiction*. University of Missouri Press, 1982. Copyright © 1982 by The Curators of the University of Missouri. All rights reserved. Reproduced by permission of the University of Missouri Press.—Ratner, Rochelle. From "Loba," in *Trying to Understand What It Means to be a Feminist: Essays on Women Writers*. Contact II Publications, 1984. Copyright © 1984 by Contact II Publications. All rights reserved. Reproduced by permission of the author.—Rexroth, Kenneth. From "Disengagement: The Art of the Beat Generation," in *A Casebook on the Beat*. Edited by Thomas Parkinson. Thomas Y. Crowell Company, 1961. Copyright © 1961 by Thomas Y. Crowell Company. All rights reserved. Reproduced by permission.—Rexroth, Kenneth. From Introduction to *The Residual Years: Poems 1934-1948*, by William Everson. Copyright © 1968 by New Directions Publishing Corp. Reprinted by permission of New Directions Publishing Corp.—Rexroth, Kenneth. From "On Jazz and Poetry," in *The San Francisco Poets*. Edited by David Meltzer. Ballantine, 1971. Copyright © 1971 Ballantine. All rights reserved. Reproduced by permission.—Rexroth, Kenneth. From Letter to *The Village Voice Reader*. Doubleday, 1962. Copyright © 1962 by Doubleday. All rights reserved. Reproduced by permission. —Rexroth, Kenneth. From "Thou Shalt Not Kill," in *Collected Shorter Poems*. Copyright © 1956 New Directions Publishing Corp. Reprinted by permission of New Directions Publishing Corp. —Ricci, Claudia, "Anne Waldman: A Profile," *http://www.albany.edu/writers-inst/olv1n2.html*. Published by New York State Writers Institute, (Fall 1996). Reprinted with permission.—Roszak, Theodore. From "Journey to the East ... and Points Beyond: Allen Ginsberg and Alan Watts," in *The Making of a Counter Culture: Reflections on the Technocratic Society and Its Youthful Opposition*.

The Cult of Information: The Folklore of Computers and the True Art of Thinking. University of California Press, 1995. Copyright © 1986 by Theodore Roszak, the University of California Press, publisher. Reproduced with permission.—Russo, Linda. From "To Deal with Parts and Particulars: Joanne Kyger's Early Epic Poetics," in *Girls Who Wore Black: Women Writing the Beat Generation*. Edited by Ronna C. Johnson and Nancy Grace. Copyright © 2002 by Linda Russo. Reproduced by permission of Rutgers University Press. —Saroyan, Aram. From "Interview with Aram Saroyan," in *Off the Wall: Interviews with Philip Whalen*. Edited by Donald Allen. Four Seasons Foundation, 1978. Copyright © 1978 by Four Seasons Foundation. All rights reserved. Reproduced by permission of Aram Saroyan.—Skau, Michael. From "'The Comedy Gone Mad': Corso's Surrealism and Humor," in *"A Clown in a Grave": Complexities and Tensions in the Works of Gregory Corso*. Southern Illinois University Press, 1999. Copyright © 1999 by the Board of Trustees, Southern Illinois University. All rights reserved. Reproduced by permission.—Smith, Larry R. From "A Vision of Light and Art," in *Kenneth Patchen*. Twayne Publishers, 1978. Copyright © 1978 by G.K. Hall & Co. All rights reserved. Reproduced by permission.—Smith, Richard Candida. From "Woman's Path to Maturation: Joan Brown, Joy DeFeo, and the Rat Bastards," in *Utopia and Dissent: Art, Poetry, and Politics in California*. University of California Press, 1995. Copyright © 1995 by The Regents of the University of California. All rights reserved. Reproduced by permission.—Snyder, Gary. From "Riprap," in *Riprap and Cold Mountain Poems*. Four Seasons Foundation, 1958, 1965. Copyright © 1958, 1965. All rights reserved. Reproduced by permission of the author.—Snyder, Gary. From "The Smokey the Bear Sutra," in *The Fudo Trilogy*. Shaman Drum, 1973. Copyright © 1973 by Shaman Drum. All rights reserved. Reproduced by permission of the author.—Solnit, Rebecca. From "Culture and Counterculture: San Francisco's Fifties," and "Heyday," in *Secret Exhibition: Six California Artists of the Cold War Era*. City Lights Books, 1990. Copyright © 1990 by Rebecca Solnit. All rights reserved. Reproduced by permission. —Spicer, Jack. From "A Postscript to the Berkeley Renaissance," in *One Night Stand and Other Poems*. Grey Fox Press, 1980. Copyright © 1980 by Grey Fox Press. All rights reserved. Reproduced by permission.—Spicer, Jack. From "Sporting Life," in *The Collected Books of Jack Spicer*. Black Sparrow Press, 1975. Copyright © 1975 by Black Sparrow Press. All rights reserved. Reproduced by permission.—Stafford, William E. From "Brother Antoninus—The World as a Metaphor," in *The Achievement of Brother Antoninus: A Comprehensive Selection of His Poems with Critical Introduction*. Scott, Foresman and Company, 1967. Reproduced by permission of Pearson Education, Inc. —Stephenson, Gregory. From "Friendly and Flowing Savage: The Literary Legend of Neal Cassady," in *The Daybreak Boys: Essays on the Literature of the Beat Generation*. Southern Illinois University Press, 1990. Copyright © 1990 by the Board of Trustees, Southern Illinois University. All rights reserved. Reproduced by permission.—Stephenson, Gregory. From "Gasoline," and "The Happy Birthday of Death," in *Exiled Angel: A Study of the Work of Gregory Corso*. Hearing Eye, 1989. Copyright © 1989 by Gregory Stephenson. All rights reserved. Reproduced by permission. —Stephenson, Gregory. From "Homeward from Nowhere: Notes on the Novels of John Clellon Holmes," "The 'Spiritual Optics' of Lawrence Ferlinghetti," and "Allen Ginsberg's Howl: A Reading," in *The Daybreak Boys: Essays on the Literature of the Beat Generation*. Southern Illinois University Press, 1990. Copyright © 1990 by the Board of Trustees, Southern Illinois University. All rights reserved. Reproduced by permission.—Sterritt, David. From Introduction to *Mad to Be Saved: The Beats, the '50s, and Film*. Southern Illinois University Press, 1998. Copyright © 1998 by David Sterritt. All rights reserved. Reproduced by permission.—Stitch, Sidra and Brigid Doherty. From "A Biographical History," in *Jay DeFeo: Works on Paper*. Edited by Sidra Stitch. University of California, Berkeley Art Museum, 1989, pp. 11-25. Copyright © 1989 by The Regents of the University of California. All rights reserved. Reproduced by permission.—Sukenick, Ronald. From "Bleecker Street," in *Down and Out: Life in the Underground*. Beech Tree Books, 1987. Copyright © 1987 by Ronald Sukenick. All rights reserved. Reproduced by permission of the author.—Swartz, Omar. From *The View from On the Road: The Rhetorical Vision of Jack Kerouac*. Southern Illinois University Press, 1999. Copyright © 1999 by the Board of Trustees, Southern Illinois University. Reproduced by permission.—Tanner, Stephen L. From "Influences and Achievement," in *Ken Kesey*. Edited by Warren French. Twayne Publishers, 1983. Copyright © 1983 by G.K. Hall & Company. All rights reserved. Reproduced by permission.—Theado, Matt. From "Tristessa (1960), Visions of Gerard (1963), and Buddhism," in *Understanding Jack Kerouac*. University of South Carolina Press, 2000. Copyright © 2000 by University of South Carolina Press. All rights reserved. Reproduced by permission.—Thurley, Geoffrey. From "The Development of the New Language: Michael McClure, Philip Whalen, and Gregory Corso," in *The Beats in Criticism*. Edited by Lee Bartlett. McFarland, 1981. Copyright © by 1981 Lee Bartlett. All rights reserved. Reproduced by permission.—Tytell, John. From "Allen Ginsberg and the Messianic Tradition," and "The Black Beauty of William Burroughs," in *Naked Angels: The Lives and Literature of the Beat Generation.* McGraw-Hill Book Company, 1976. Copyright © 1976 by John Tytell. All rights reserved. Reproduced by permission of the author.—Tytell, John. From "The Frozen Fifties," in *Paradise Outlaws: Remembering the Beats, with Photographs by Mellon.* William Morrow and Company, Inc., 1999. Copyright © 1999 by John Tytell and Mellon. All rights reserved. Reproduced by permission of the author.—Waldman, Anne, "Angel Hair Feature," *http://jacketmagazine.com/16/ah1-wald.html.* Published by Jacket 16, (March 2002). Reprinted with permission of the author.—Waldman, Anne. From Foreword to *Strange Big Moon, The Japan and Indian Journals: 1960-1964*, by Joanne Kyger, published by North Atlantic Books. Copyright © 2000 by Joanne Kyger. Reproduced by permission of the publisher.—Waldman, Anne. From "Our Past," in *Blue Mosque.* United Artists Books, 1988. Copyright © 1988 by United Artist Books. All rights reserved. Reproduced by permission of United Artists Books and author.—Waldman, Anne, "The Weight of the World is Love," *www.naropa.edu/ginstributes8.html.* Published by Naropa Institute, (2002). Reproduced with permission of the author and Coffee House Press, Minneapolis, Minnesota.—Weinreich, Regina. From "The Sound of Despair: A Perfected Nonlinearity," in *The Spontaneous Poetics of Jack Kerouac: A Study of the Fiction.* Southern Illinois University Press, 1987. Copyright © 1987 by The Board of Trustees, Southern Illinois University. All rights reserved. Reproduced by permission of the author.—Whitmer, Peter O. with Bruce Van Wyngarden. From "The Beat Begins," in *Aquarius Revisited: Seven Who Created the Sixties Counterculture that Changed America*, William Burroughs, Allen Ginsberg, Ken Kesey, Timothy Leary, Norman Mailer, Tom Robbins, Hunter S. Thompson. Copyright © 1987 by Peter O. Whitmer. Reproduced by permission of Scribner, an imprint of Simon & Schuster Adult Publishing Group. —Widmer, Kingsley. From "The Beat in the Rise of the Populist Culture," in *The Fifties: Fiction, Poetry, Drama.* Edited by Warren French. Everett/Edwards, Inc., 1970. Copyright © 1970 by Warren French, reassigned 1985 to Kingsley Widmer. All rights reserved. Reproduced by permission. —Wilentz, Elias. From Introduction to *The Beat Scene.* Edited by Elias Wilentz. Corinth Books, 1960. Copyright © 1960 by Fred McDarrah and Elias Wilentz. All rights reserved. Reproduced by permission of the author.—Williams, Mary Elizabeth with Chuck Workman, "The Beats Go On: Filmmaker Chuck Workman on The Source, His Fawning Tribute to the Beat Generation," at *http:www.salon.com.* Published by Salon, (June 1, 1999). Reprinted with permission.—Williams, William Carlos. From "A Counsel of Madness: A Review of The Journal of Albion Moonlight," in *Kenneth Patchen: A Collection of Essays.* Edited by Richard G. Morgan. AMS Press, Inc., 1977. Copyright © 1977 by Richard G. Morgan. All rights reserved. Reproduced by permission. —Wisker, Alistair. From "An Anarchist among the Floorwalkers: The Poetry of Lawrence Ferlinghetti," in *The Beat Generation Writers.* Edited by A Robert Lee. Pluto Press, 1996. Copyright © 1996 by Lumiere (Cooperative) Press Ltd. and Pluto Press. All rights reserved. Reproduced by permission.—Zurbrugg, Nicholas. From "Will Hollywood Never Learn? David Cronenberg's Naked Lunch," in *Adaptations: From Text to Screen, Screen to Text.* Edited by Deborah Cartmell and Imelda Whelehan. Routledge, 1999. Copyright © 1999 by Nicholas Zurbrugg. Selection and editorial matter © Deborah Cartmell and Imelda Whelehan. All rights reserved. Reproduced by permission. —Zweig, Paul. From "A Music of Angels," in *On the Poetry of Allen Ginsberg.* Edited by Lewis Hyde. University of Michigan Press, 1984. © *The Nation* magazine/The Nation Company, Inc. Reproduced by permission of *The Nation* Magazine.

Photographs and illustrations in The Beat Generation *were received from the following sources:*

Beatniks, San Francisco, California, photograph. © Bettmann/Corbis. Reproduced by permission. —Berman, Wallace. *Semina,* assemblage of various photographs. Wallace Berman Estate, Courtesy of LA Louver Gallery. Reproduced by permission. —Blackburn, Paul, photograph. © by Fred W. McDarrah. All rights reserved. Reproduced by permission.—Bremser, Ray, photograph. Original caption: "Ray Bremser, Jazz-ear sound-Poetry genius, syncopating wow-sound word walloper, original N.Y. late-1950s coffee shop bard with Kerouac & Leroi Jones, his long-ago jail songs were noted by Bob Dylan in 'The Times They are a Changin,' at kitchen table, March 15, 1987, he stayed over to read poetry and teach my 'Literary History of Beat Generation' class Brooklyn College, come down from A.A. halfway house in Utica, N.Y., rare trip to the Apple for survivor with big fine beard." Allen Ginsberg/Corbis. Reproduced by permission.—Brown, Joan. *Fur Rat,* sculpture consisting of wood, chicken wire, and raccoon fur, photograph. Berkeley Art Museum, University of California. Reproduced by permission.—Burroughs, William S. (left), and Jack Kerouac in an apartment in New York City, photograph. © Corbis. Reproduced by permission. —Burroughs, William S., sitting in front of a typewriter, at his home in Paris, France, photograph. © Bettmann/Corbis. Reproduced by permission.— Burroughs, William S. (left to right), Lucien Carr, and Allen Ginsberg, sitting together in an apartment in New York City, photograph. © Allen Ginsberg/Corbis. Reproduced by permission. —Campus of Black Mountain College in North Carolina. Courtesy of the North Carolina Offices of Archives and History, Raleigh, North Carolina. Reproduced by permission.—Cassady, Neal, San Francisco, California, 1966, photograph by Ted Streshinsky. Corbis/Ted Streshinsky. Reproduced by permission.—Chase, Hale (left to right), Jack Kerouac, Allen Ginsberg, and William Burroughs, in Morningside Heights near Columbia University campus, New York, c. 1944-1945, photograph. © Allen Ginsberg/Corbis. Reproduced by permission.—City Lights Bookstore, San Francisco, photograph. City Lights Books, Inc. Reproduced by permission.—Corso, Gregory, photograph. © Christopher Felver/Corbis. Reproduced by permission.—Cover of the Black Mountain College publicity booklet, 1936-1938, photograph. Courtesy of the North Carolina Offices of Archives and History, Raleigh, North Carolina. Reproduced by permission.—Cover of "The Black Mountain Review," photograph. Courtesy of the North Carolina Offices of Archives and History, Raleigh, North Carolina. Reproduced by permission.—Defeo, Jay. *After Image,* artwork consisting of graphite, gouache, and transparent acrylic on paper with cut and torn tracing paper, photograph. The Henil Collection, Houston. Reproduced by permission. —di Prima, Diane, photograph. © Chris Felver. Reproduced by permission.—di Prima, Diane, sitting on top of piano, reading selections from her first published book of poetry "This Kind of Bird Flies Backward," to an assembled crowd at the Gas Light Cafe in New York City, photograph. © by Fred W. McDarrah. All rights reserved. Reproduced by permission.—Donlin, Bob, Neal Cassady, Allen Ginsberg, Robert LaVinge, and Lawrence Ferlinghetti (left to right) standing outside Ferlinghetti's City Lights Bookstore, photograph. © Allen Ginsberg/Corbis. Reproduced by permission.— Duncan, Robert, photograph by Nata Piaskowski. Courtesy of New Directions. Reproduced by permission. —Dylan, Bob, photograph. AP/Wide World Photos. Reproduced by permission.—Everson, William, photograph. © Chris Felver. Reproduced by permission.—Ferlinghetti, Lawrence, photograph. AP/Wide World Photos. Reproduced by permission. —Ginsberg, Allen, reading his poem "Howl," outside the U.S. Court of Appeals

in Washington, D.C., photograph. AP/Wide World Photos. Reproduced by permission.—Ginsberg, Allen, with fellow poets, original caption: "Philip Whalen, Jerry Heiserman (Hassan later as Sufi) & poet Thomas Jackerell who drove us Vancouver to San Francisco returning from poetry assemblage, we stopped to sightsee Portland where Philip had gone to Reed College with Gary Snyder & Lew Welch. End of July 1963. Vancouver," photograph. © Allen Ginsberg/Corbis. Reproduced by permission. —Ginsberg, Allen, speaking into microphone, 1969, photograph. AP/Wide World Photos. Reproduced by permission.—Guest, Barbara, photograph by Chris Felver. Reproduced by permission.—Guest, Barbara, standing and holding paper in hands while reading poetry at the Living Theatre, photograph. © by Fred W. McDarrah. All rights reserved. Reproduced by permission. —Gysin, Brion, portrait by Carl Van Vechten. The Library of Congress. Reproduced by permission. —Gysin, Brion, portrait by Carl Van Vechten. The Library of Congress. Reproduced by permission. —Holmes, John Clellon, photograph by Chris Felver. Reproduced by permission.—Huncke, Herbert, photograph by Chris Felver. Archive Photos. Reproduced by permission.—Johnson, Joyce, photograph. © Jerry Bauer. Reproduced by permission.—Kandel, Lenore, photograph. The Library of Congress.—Kaufman, Bob, reading his poems at Living Theatre, photograph. © by Fred W. McDarrah. All rights reserved. Reproduced by permission.—Kerouac, Jack, photograph. © Jerry Bauer. Reproduced by permission.—Kerouac, Jack (clockwise from top left), Allen Ginsberg, Gregory Corso, Peter Orlovsky and his brother Lafcadio on vacation in Mexico City, 1956, photograph. © Allen Ginsberg/Corbis. Reproduced by permission. —Kerouac, Jan, photograph. AP/Wide World Photos. Reproduced by permission.—Kesey, Ken, 1990, photograph. AP/Wide World Photos. Reproduced by permission.—Kyger Bolinas, JoAnne, photograph. © Chris Felver. Reproduced by permission.—Landesman, Fran, in a still from the documentary film "Gaslight Square—The Forgotten Landmark" by Bruce Marren. © 2002 Bruce Marren. Reproduced by permission.—Landesman, Jay Irving, in a still from the documentary film "Gaslight Square—The Forgotten Landmark" by Bruce Marren. © 2002 Bruce Marren. Reproduced by permission.—The Merry Pranksters' Bus, preparing it for its drive to the Acid Test Graduation, San Francisco, California, October, 1966, photograph. © Ted Streshinsky/Corbis. Reproduced by permission.—McClure, Michael, photograph. © Roger Ressmeyer/Corbis. Reproduced by permission.—Mingus, Charles (center), playing bass with other musicians during a live performance at the Five Spot Cafe in San Francisco, California, photograph. © by Fred W. McDarrah. All rights reserved. Reproduced by permission.—Mingus, Charles (center), playing bass with his ensemble, while Kenneth Patchen (right) reads poetry during a live performance at the Living Theatre, photograph. © by Fred W. McDarrah. All rights reserved. Reproduced by permission.—Monk, Thelonius, photograph by Jack Vartoogian. Reproduced by permission.—Nicholson, Jack (seated at table), and Vincent Schiavelli standing at left, in the 1975 movie version of "One Flew Over the Cuckoo's Nest," written by Ken Kesey, directed by Milos Forman, movie still. The Kobal Collection/United Artists/Fantasy Films. Reproduced by permission.—Orlovsky, Peter, photograph. AP/Wide World Photos. Reproduced by permission. —Patchen, Kenneth, photograph. Archive Photos, Inc. Reproduced by permission.—Rick Allmen's Cafe Bizarre on West Third Street in Greenwich Village, photograph. © Bettmann/Corbis. Reproduced by permission.—Rexroth, Kenneth, 1952, photograph. AP/Wide World Photos. Reproduced by permission.—St. Mark's-in-the-Bowery, an Episcopal Church built in 1799, photograph. © Lee Snider; Lee Snider/Corbis. Reproduced by permission.—Sanders, Ed, photograph by Chris Felver. Reproduced by permission of Chris Felver.—Snyder, Gary, photograph. AP/Wide World Photos. Reproduced by permission.—Solomon, Carl, photograph. © Allen Ginsberg/ Corbis. Reproduced by permission.—Students sitting under a tree at Columbia University, original caption: "Outdoor Class, Outdoor Class on Columbia University Campus is shown, as class was taken outside on this warm summer day," New York, May 7, 1959, photograph. © Bettmann/ Corbis. Reproduced by permission.—Village Vanguard nightclub, Greenwich Village, New York, January 1, 1967, photograph. © Bettmann/Corbis. Reproduced by permission.—Waldman, Anne, photograph. © Allen Ginsberg/Corbis. Reproduced by permission.—Waldman, Anne, reading a poem in tribute to the late Allen Ginsberg at the Wadsworth Theater in Los Angeles, California, photograph. AP/Wide World Photos. Reproduced by permission.—Washington Square in Greenwich Village and an arch, photograph. © Bettmann/ Corbis. Reproduced by permission.—weiss, ruth, photograph by Daniel Nicoletta. © 2002 Daniel Nicoletta. Reproduced by permission.—Welch, Lew, photograph. © by Fred W. McDarrah. All rights reserved. Reproduced by permission. —Weller, Peter, as Bill Lee in the 1992 film "Naked Lunch," based on the book written by William Burroughs, directed by David Cronenberg, movie still. The Kobal Collection/Recorded Picture Co/ First Independent. Reproduced by permission. —Whalen, Philip, 1984, photograph. © Allen Ginsberg/Corbis. Reproduced by permission. —Wieners, John, photograph. © Allen Ginsberg/ Corbis. Reproduced by permission.

● = historical event

■ = literary event

1914

● William Seward Burroughs is born on 5 February in St. Louis, Missouri. He is the heir to the Burroughs Adding Machine Corporation.

1915

● Herbert Edwin Huncke is born on 9 January in Greenfield, Massachusetts.

1919

● Lawrence Ferlinghetti is born 24 March in Yonkers, New York.

1922

● Jean-Louis (Jack) Kerouac is born on 12 March in Lowell, Massachusetts.

1926

● Neal Cassady is born 18 February in Salt Lake City, Utah, as his parents travel from Iowa to California.

● Irwin Allen Ginsberg is born on 3 June in Paterson, New Jersey.

1930

● Gregory Nunzio Corso is born on 26 March in Greenwich Village, New York.

1932

● Burroughs enters Harvard University as an English major.

1939

● Huncke arrives in New York City.

● Kerouac attends preparatory school before entering Columbia University on a football scholarship.

1941

● The U.S. Naval base at Pearl Harbor, Hawaii, is attacked by Japanese forces; the event spurs America's entry into World War II.

1942

● Kerouac enlists in the merchant marines, serving on the *S.S. Dorchester*.

● Burroughs finds work in Chicago as a pest exterminator.

1943

● Burroughs arrives in New York City.

Kerouac works on the novel "The Sea Is My Brother," which remains unfinished and unpublished.

Ginsberg meets Lucien Carr while attending Columbia. Carr introduces Ginsberg to Kerouac and Burroughs.

1944

Ginsberg, Kerouac, and Carr formulate and discuss "The New Vision" or "New Consciousness," a literary manifesto inspired by the work of such authors as Franz Kafka, Albert Camus, and W. H. Auden. "The New Vision" provides a framework for the Beat aesthetic.

Carr is arrested for the murder of David Kammerer; Kerouac is detained as a material witness. Kerouac marries Edie Parker as a means of raising money for Carr's defense. Carr is convicted and serves two years in prison.

Burroughs meets Huncke.

Kenneth Rexroth, Philip Lamantia, William Everson, and Robert Creeley orchestrate the Berkeley Renaissance.

1945

Ginsberg is suspended from Columbia. He moves to a communal apartment occupied by, among others, Kerouac and Joan Vollmer, who will become Burroughs's common-law wife.

World War II ends.

1946

Kerouac begins writing his first published novel, *The Town and the City.*

Huncke introduces Burroughs to heroin.

Cassady arrives in New York and begins a friendship with Ginsberg and Kerouac.

Corso begins a three-year prison sentence for grand theft; he begins writing poetry while incarcerated.

1947

Burroughs and Vollmer move to Texas, where their son, William Seward, Jr., is born.

Cassady meets Carolyn Robinson, who will become his second wife.

Kerouac travels to Denver, a trip that will inform *On the Road.*

The House Un-American Activities Committee (HUAAC) begins congressional hearings on suspected American communists.

1948

Burroughs moves his family to Louisiana.

Kerouac completes *The Town and the City.* He coins the phrase "Beat Generation." In the winter, he and Cassady travel the U.S., excursions which will be recounted in *On the Road.*

John Clellon Holmes meets Kerouac and Ginsberg in New York City.

Ginsberg has a series of visions involving William Blake.

1949

Ginsberg is arrested for allowing Huncke to keep stolen goods in his apartment.

Kerouac receives a $1000 advance from Harcourt, Brace for *The Town and the City.*

Burroughs's legal troubles force him to move his family to Mexico.

Trumpeter Miles Davis's album *The Birth of the Cool* marks the onset of the "Cool Jazz" movement and marks a period of renewed popularity for jazz music; the medium will have a great influence on Beat writers in the next decade.

1950

Kerouac's *The Town and the City* is published.

Burroughs starts work on *Junkie.*

Kerouac marries Joan Haverty.

Ginsberg meets Corso in Greenwich Village.

Ferlinghetti moves from New York to San Francisco.

1951

John Clellon Holmes completes *Go,* the novel is generally credited as the first to chronicle the Beat Generation.

Burroughs begins writing *Queer.*

Fueled by stimulants, Kerouac composes the scroll version of *On the Road* in one long writing session; the event is an early example of the nascent technique he has dubbed "spontaneous prose."

- In Mexico, Burroughs accidentally shoots and kills Vollmer; he credits her death as his motivation to seriously pursue a writing career.

- American forces join in the Korean War.

1952

- Kerouac visits the Cassadys in San Francisco, where he composes part of *Visions of Cody*. He has an affair with Carolyn Cassady. Later in the year, Kerouac will visit Burroughs in Mexico, where he writes *Doctor Sax*.

- Holmes's *Go* is published by Scribners; he writes the seminal article "This is the Beat Generation" for the *New York Times Magazine*.

1953

- Burroughs's *Junkie: Confessions of an Unredeemed Drug Addict* is published under the pseudonym William Lee by Ace Books.

- Ferlinghetti and Peter Martin open City Lights, the first paperback bookstore in the U.S.

- Burroughs and Ginsberg have a brief affair. At its end, Burroughs moves to Tangiers, where he will live for the next five years. While in Tangiers, he begins work on *Naked Lunch*.

- Kerouac writes *Maggie Cassidy* and *The Subterraneans*.

1954

- Attracted to the tenets of the religion, Kerouac begins studying Buddhism. He begins writing *San Francisco Blues* and *Some of the Dharma*, his unpublished musings on Buddhism.

- Ginsberg moves to San Francisco to work in market research and meets Peter Orlovsky; the two will become lifelong partners.

- In California, the North Beach bohemian scene, comprised of writers such as Jack Spicer, Richard Brautigan, Bob Kaufman, and John Weiners, finds expression in cafés, bars, and jazz clubs.

1955

- Corso publishes his first poetry collection, *The Vestal Lady on Brattle and Other Poems*.

- While in San Francisco, Ginsberg completes the majority of "Howl."

- Ferlinghetti founds City Lights Press; the first book on the imprint is his own *Pictures of the Gone World*; publication of works by Kenneth Patchen, Ginsberg, Corso, and Kerouac soon follow.

- Kerouac writes *Mexico City Blues* and starts work on *Tristessa*. Excerpts from *On the Road* are published in *New World Writing* and *Paris Review*.

- Kenneth Rexroth hosts the landmark poetry reading (organized by Ginsberg) at Six Gallery in San Francisco on 7 October; performers include Ginsberg, who performs a breakthrough reading of "Howl," as well as Philip Lamantia, Gary Snyder, Michael McClure, and Philip Whalen.

1956

- Kerouac completes *Tristessa* and begins work on *Visions of Gerard* and *Desolation Angels*.

- Ginsberg reads the complete "Howl" in Berkeley, California. City Lights publishes the poem in the collection *Howl and Other Poems* with an introduction by William Carlos Williams.

- Ginsberg's mother, Naomi dies; the event has a profound effect on the poet and will influence his later work, notably the poem "Kaddish."

1957

- Kerouac meets up with Ginsberg and Orlovsky in Tangiers where they assist Burroughs in the assembly of *Naked Lunch*.

- In March, copies of *Howl and Other Poems* are confiscated and later released by U. S. Customs officials. Ferlinghetti is subsequently arrested for selling the book, which is alleged to be a work of obscenity. In October, following the famous obscenity trial, Ginsberg's work is found to be "not obscene."

- Rexroth and Ferlinghetti perform their poetry accompanied by a jazz band in a San Francisco bar.

- Kerouac's *On the Road* is published by Viking. Reviews are favorable and the book and its author gain widespread popularity.

- Ginsberg begins writing "Kaddish" in memory of his mother.

The *Evergreen Review* publishes "San Francisco Poets" by Barney Rossett and Donald Allen; the piece is a special focus on the West Coast Beats.

1958

- Ginsberg, Orlovsky, Corso, and Burroughs move into the "Beat Hotel" in Paris.

- Corso's poem "Bomb" is published as a broadside; his collection *Gasoline* is published by City Lights.

- Grove Press publishes Kerouac's *The Subterraneans*; Viking publishes *The Dharma Bums*.

- Kerouac makes an appearance on *The Steve Allen Show*.

- An excerpt from Burroughs's *Naked Lunch* is published in the fall issue of the *Chicago Review*; the work's appearance results in controversy over censorship.

- Cassady begins a two-year prison sentence for possession of marijuana.

- Ferlinghetti's *A Coney Island of the Mind* is published by New Directions.

- Random House publishes Holmes's *The Horn*.

- LeRoi and Hettie Jones found Totem Press as well as the journal *Yugen*.

1959

- Burroughs's *The Naked Lunch* is published in Paris by Olympia Press; Grove will publish the book in the U.S. as *Naked Lunch* in 1962.

- Kerouac publishes several works this year, including *Doctor Sax, Maggie Cassidy, Mexico City Blues,* and *Excerpts from Visions of Cody.*

- Gary Snyder's *Rip Rap* is published in Japan by Origin Press.

- *Pull My Daisy* is produced; the Beat-themed film features appearances by Ginsberg, Corso, and Peter Orlovsky, and Kerouac serves as the narrator.

- Ginsberg records a version of "Howl" to be released on Fantasy Records, a major jazz label.

- Beat literature and lifestyle receives significant attention in publications such as *Time* and *Life,* as well as in the highly critical publication by Lawrence Lipton, *The Holy Barbarians.*

- 29 September debut of television series *The Many Loves of Dobie Gillis*, which features a Beatnik character, Maynard G. Krebs.

1960

- Kerouac publishes *Tristessa, The Scripture of the Golden Eternity,* and *Lonesome Traveler.*

- Corso's *The Happy Birthday of Death* is published by New Directions.

- Totem Press publishes Snyder's *Myths and Texts.*

- *The New American Poetry* is published by Grove Press; the volume is edited by Donald Allen and presents the work of several Beat poets.

- The film adaptation of Kerouac's *The Subterraneans* is produced by Metro-Goldwyn-Mayer.

- Inspired by interaction with Brion Gysin, Burroughs begins to experiment with the "Cut-up" literary technique for *Minutes to Go* and *Exterminator.*

- Seymour Krim's landmark chronicle, *The Beats,* is published by Gold Medal.

- The 7 October debut of the television series *Route 66,* which chronicles the cross-country travels of two young men; the show grew out of plans to create a television series based upon *On the Road;* the concept was rejected by Kerouac and re-tooled as *Route 66.*

1961

- Burroughs's *The Soft Machine* is published by Olympia.

- Corso publishes his only novel, *The American Express.*

- Kerouac begins writing *Big Sur* and completes *Desolations Angels;* he publishes *Book of Dreams* and *Pull My Daisy.*

- City Lights publishes Ginsberg's *Kaddish and Other Poems: 1958-1960;* Ginsberg travels to the Near and Far East.

1962

- Burroughs's *The Ticket That Exploded* is published in Japan; *Naked Lunch* is published in the U.S.

- Kerouac's *Big Sur* is published by Grove.

- Burroughs receives international notice when Norman Mailer and others hail his work at the International Writer's Conference in Edinburgh.

1963

- Kerouac's *Visions of Gerard* is published by Farrar, Strauss.

- Correspondence between Ginsberg and Burroughs is published as *The Yage Letters* by City Lights.
- City Lights publishes Ginsberg's *Reality Sandwiches*.
- Ginsberg is awarded a Guggenheim Fellowship.

1964

- Diane di Prima founds Poets Press.
- Kerouac moves to Tampa, Florida, where he resides with his mother; he and Cassady see each other for the last time.

1965

- Following his travels in France, Kerouac begins writing *Satori in Paris*; *Desolation Angels* is published by Coward-McCann.
- Poets Press publishes *Huncke's Journal*.

1966

- Burroughs moves to London and his novel *The Soft Machine* is published by Grove.
- Kerouac and his mother move to Hyannis on Cape Cod, Massachusetts, where she suffers a stroke. Kerouac marries Stella Sampas, his third wife, and the three move back to his hometown of Lowell.
- A decision is reached in the *Naked Lunch* obscenity trial, with the Massachusetts Supreme Court ruling that while the work is "grossly offensive," it is not obscene.

1967

- Kerouac begins work on *The Valley of Duluoz*.
- *The Ticket That Exploded* is published in America by Grove.
- *Nothing More to Declare* by John Clellon Holmes is published.

1968

- Kerouac's *The Valley of Duluoz* is published by Coward-McCann.
- After a night of heavy drinking, Neal Cassady wanders into the Mexican desert and dies of exposure.

- Ginsberg organizes a protest of the Vietnam War to coincide with the Democratic National Convention in Chicago, Illinois; rioting ensues and the National Guard is called out.

1969

- Kerouac completes his final work, *Pic*; his alcoholism is chronic by this point; on 21 October, a vein in his stomach bursts, and Kerouac dies in St. Petersburg, Florida; he is later buried in Lowell.
- Ginsberg is awarded a poetry grant from the National Institute of Arts and Letters.

1970

- Burroughs's *The Last Words of Dutch Schultz* is published in London; U.S. publication in an enlarged and revised format in 1975 by Viking.

1971

- Burroughs's *The Wild Boys: A Book of the Dead* is published by Grove.

1973

- Viking publishes Burroughs's *Exterminator!*.

1974

- Burroughs returns to America and takes a teaching post at the City College of New York.
- Ginsberg's *Fall of America* wins the National Book Award, and he is inducted into the American Academy of Arts and Letters.
- The Jack Kerouac School of Disembodied Poetics, Naropa Institute, is founded by Ginsberg and Anne Waldman in Boulder, Colorado.

1978

- Ginsberg's *Mindbreaths: Poems 1972-1977* is published by City Lights.
- *As Ever: The Collected Correspondence of Allen Ginsberg & Neal Cassady* is published by Creative Arts.

1981

- Burroughs moves to Lawrence, Kansas.

1982

- The Naropa Institute holds a twenty-fifth anniversary celebration of Kerouac's *On the Road.* In attendance are, among others, Ginsberg, Burroughs, Corso, Ferlinghetti, Michael McClure, Ken Kesey, Abbie Hoffman, Anne Waldman, Timothy Leary, and Herbert Huncke.

1985

- Viking publishes *Queer* by Burroughs.

1989

- Burroughs appears as the Tom, the Junky Priest, in director Gus Van Sant's film *Drugstore Cowboy.*

1990

- Burroughs releases the album *Dead City Radio,* which features readings of unpublished material.
- Director David Cronenberg's loose film adaptation of Burroughs's *Naked Lunch* is released; Peter Weller plays Bill Lee and Judy Davis plays Joan Vollmer.
- Burroughs has triple bypass heart surgery.

1992

- Burroughs and Kurt Cobain of the rock group Nirvana collaborate on the album *The Priest They Called Him.*

1993

- Burroughs collaborates with musician Tom Waits and director Robert Wilson on the musical play and album (released under Waits's name) *The Black Rider.*

1994

- Burroughs appears in Nike television advertisements.
- "The Beat Legacy and Celebration" is held on 18-21 May; sponsored by New York University, the event is chaired by Ginsberg and Ann Charters; speakers include Carolyn Cassady, Corso, Ferlinghetti, Hettie Jones, Ed Sanders, Hunter S. Thompson, and Anne Waldman, among others.

1995

- New York University sponsors "The Writing of Jack Kerouac Conference" on 4-6 June.

1996

- Huncke dies on 8 August from congestive heart failure in NewYork City.

1997

- Ginsberg dies on 5 April from complications of liver cancer in New York City.
- Burroughs dies on 2 August following a heart attack in Lawrence, Kansas.

2001

- Corso dies on 17 January from prostate cancer in Minnesota.

THE BEAT GENERATION: AN OVERVIEW

Originating in the 1950s and primarily centered in select communities of California, such as North Beach and Venice West, and New York City's Greenwich Village, the Beat Generation essentially constituted a countercultural movement in opposition to the traditional, established culture of mid-twentieth-century America. Extending in scope beyond the world of art, literature, painting, and music, the Beat movement included a wide variety of social expression. Adherents of the Beat Generation originally coined the term "beat" to signify their weariness with society in general, but also used the word in a spiritual sense, the beatific inspiration that many of them found in music and religion, including Buddhism, Zen, and other Eastern philosophies. Often using their lifestyle as a means through which to convey their alienation from contemporary society, the Beats expressed their defiance of convention through experiments with drugs, alternative modes of dress, and their writing, art, film, and drama.

Some of the best-known Beat writers include Allen Ginsberg, Gary Snyder, Jack Kerouac, William Burroughs, and Lawrence Ferlinghetti, all of whom used their writing, with its unstructured style and unconventional language, to convey their opposition to the cultural and aesthetic standards of previous generations. Technological advances had made mass media a significant presence in American life, and the Beats had a close relationship with the media. This attention helped these writers and artists to promote their work more easily, but it also publicized their lifestyle in a way that allowed "traditional" society to observe them in a way not possible for any previous countercultural movement. The exposure to stories about Beat colonies, drug use, and sexual escapades caused panic among authorities, leading to many confrontations between the Beats and the establishment. Confrontations with authorities spilled over into censorship of Beat writing and poetry, leading to several legal battles, including the famous trial of Lawrence Ferlinghetti on charges of obscenity in Allen Ginsberg's poem *Howl* (1956).

Beat writers and artists expressed disillusionment with scientific progress and what they perceived as the prevalence of Western technocracy. In opposition to these forces, the Beats searched for an alternative set of values and ethics. Ironically, however, their lifestyle and ideas gained a strong foothold in American popular culture, and in a little over a decade the movement itself became absorbed in mainstream life, with its original proponents scattered all over the world. At the core of the movement, in its heyday, efforts were centered on redefining or creating a new view of American life, an alternative to the conformity and uniformity of traditional culture. This effort, originating in the writings of Ginsberg, Kerouac, Burroughs, and others, soon expanded to include a vision of American society that celebrated alternatives to conventional modes of existence, including experimentation with drugs.

Although the use and study of the effects of psychedelic drugs began in the 1930s, interest in drugs and hallucinogenic substances surged among the Beats during the 1950s. One of the most famous personalities associated with drugs and related research was Dr. Timothy Leary, a lecturer at Harvard University, whose dismissal from his position on charges of drug usage and abuse led to a large amount of media attention. Leary originally began his research based on his belief that drugs could be used for effective psychotherapy. He continued his experiments while at Harvard, even involving some students as subjects. His eventual dismissal from his post, and several subsequent brushes with the law concerning drug usage, kept Leary in the public eye for many years, an active promoter of the use of drugs and psychedelic substances as a means of achieving spiritual nirvana. Although Leary lost his prominence by the 1970s, his influence was considerable, and he is credited as one of the leading inspirations for the hippie movement in the 1960s, as well as several churches that made drugs the center of their theological beliefs and practices.

The Beats themselves shunned the reality of everyday, traditional life in America, but they did believe that the artist had a central place in the evolution of a better society, and many were involved in radical political movements aimed at changing public opinion about the establishment. Conversely, their lifestyle and writing provoked the establishment, leading to an openly adversarial relationship with the authorities. Beat gatherings and establishments were often the targets of police raids, leading many of the Beats to get involved in protests against state attempts to regulate their lifestyle and ideology. Beat involvement in politics reached its highest intensity in the early 1960s. One of the most publicized incidents during this time was a protest led by many political radicals and Beats outside San Francisco city hall, against the committee that was investigating "subversive" elements in the area. The protestors were arrested or physically dragged away from the building, inciting a massive picketing effort the following day by thousands of activists. This event, which received extensive media coverage, is considered a significant milestone in the founding of the New Left in American politics. Ironically, however, the Beat involvement with politics was originally envisioned more as an op-

position to the state, a rebellion against control and establishment, viewing power as being inherently corrupt.

In their quest for an alternative to the norms of traditional society and religion, several of the Beats became followers of such Eastern religions as Buddhism and Zen. Both Ginsberg and Kerouac were active Buddhists, as were many others of the Beat Generation. They eagerly educated themselves about the religion, learning Chinese and Japanese, and reading Eastern religious texts. Kerouac's interest in Buddhism and religion can be traced in many of his novels written during the mid-1950s, including *The Dharma Bums* (1958), *Mexico City Blues* (1959), and *Desolation Angels* (1965). Although Kerouac returned to his Catholic roots after several years, Ginsberg continued his involvement with Buddhism, eventually expanding his interest in and study of other Eastern religions and even visiting India and other Asian countries in his spiritual endeavors. Similarly, Gary Snyder made several visits to Japan for Zen studies. Of all the spiritual scholars writing at that time, however, it was Alan Watts, who has become most identified as the man responsible for introducing the West to Zen. Beginning with his first book, *The Spirit of Zen* (1936), which he published at the age of twenty, Watts became famous for his series of lectures, books, and private classes on Zen. He regarded what he termed as "beat Zen" disparagingly, instead focusing on disseminating formal principles of Zen through his writings and lectures. Although spiritual concerns were fundamental to the Beats, critical appraisals of Beat literature have tended to treat the spiritual concerns in their writing as "tangential rather than constitutive," notes Stephen Prothero. Other scholars perceive the Beat spiritual concerns as yet another way in which these writers and artists lodged their protest against orthodox America.

REPRESENTATIVE WORKS

William Burroughs
Junkie: The Confessions of an Unredeemed Drug Addict [as William Lee] (novel) 1953; republished as *Junky* 1977

The Naked Lunch (novel) 1959; also published as *Naked Lunch,* 1962; restored text edition 2001

Lawrence Ferlinghetti
Pictures of the Gone World (poetry) 1955; enlarged edition 1995

A Coney Island of the Mind (poetry) 1958

Her (novel) 1960

Allen Ginsberg
Sunflower Sutra (poetry) 1955

Howl and Other Poems (poetry) 1956

Kaddish and Other Poems, 1958-1960 (poetry) 1961

The Fall of America (poetry) 1972

John Clellon Holmes
Go (novel) 1952

"This Is the Beat Generation" [published in *New York Times Magazine*] (newspaper article) 1952

The Horn (novel) 1958

Joyce Johnson
Minor Characters: A Young Woman's Coming-of-Age in the Beat Orbit of Jack Kerouac (autobiography) 1983

Door Wide Open: A Beat Love Affair in Letters, 1957-58 (letters) 2000

Bob Kaufman
Abomunist Manifesto (poetry) 1959

Does the Secret Mind Whisper (poetry) 1959

Second April (poetry) 1959

Jack Kerouac
On the Road (novel) 1957

The Dharma Bums (novel) 1958

Mexico City Blues (poetry) 1959

The Scripture of the Golden Eternity (poetry) 1960

Big Sur (novel) 1962

Desolation Angels (novel) 1965

Joan Haverty Kerouac
Nobody's Wife: The Smart Aleck and The King of the Beats (memoir) 2000

Timothy Leary
L.S.D. (sound recording) 1960

The Psychedelic Experience: A Manual Based on the Tibetan Book of the Dead (nonfiction) 1964

Turn on, Tune in, Drop out: Timothy Leary, Ph.D., Speaks on L.S.D. (sound recording) 1966

Norman Mailer
The Naked and the Dead (novel) 1948

The Deer Park (novel) 1955

The White Negro: Superficial Reflections on the Hipster (essays) 1957

Gary Snyder
Riprap (poetry) 1959

The Back Country (poetry) 1968

Earth House Hold (essays, reviews, journal entries) 1969

Alan Watts
The Spirit of Zen (nonfiction) 1936

The Supreme Identity (nonfiction) 1950

The Way of Zen (nonfiction) 1957

Psychotherapy East and West (nonfiction) 1961

Beat Zen, Square Zen, and Zen (essay) 1967

This Is It, and Other Essays on Zen and Spiritual Experience (essays) 1967

Ruth Weiss
Steps (poetry) 1958

Gallery of Women (poetry) 1959

South Pacific (poetry) 1959

Blue in Green (poetry) 1960

PRIMARY SOURCES

JOHN CLELLON HOLMES (ESSAY DATE 16 NOVEMBER 1952)

SOURCE: Holmes, John Clellon. "This Is the Beat Generation." *New York Times Magazine* (16 November 1952): 10-22.

In the following essay, written by Holmes in an effort to explain his generation, Holmes credits a then-unknown Jack Kerouac and defines the Beat Generation as having "no single philosophy, no single party, no single attitude."

Several months ago, a national magazine ran a story under the heading "Youth" and the subhead "Mother Is Bugged At Me." It concerned an eighteen-year-old California girl who had been picked up for smoking marijuana and wanted to talk about it. While a reporter took down her ideas in the uptempo language of "tea," someone snapped a picture. In view of her contention that she was part of a whole new culture where one out of every five people you meet is a user, it was an arresting photograph. In the pale, attentive face, with its soft eyes and intelligent mouth, there was no hint of corruption. It was a face which could only be deemed criminal through an enormous effort of righteousness. Its only complaint seemed to be: "Why don't people leave us alone?" It was the face of a beat generation.

That clean young face has been making the newspapers steadily since the war. Standing before a judge in a Bronx courthouse, being arraigned for stealing a car, it looked up into the camera with curious laughter and no guilt. The same face, with a more serious bent, stared from the pages of *Life* magazine, representing a graduating class of ex-GI's, and said that as it believed small business to be dead, it intended to become a comfortable cog in the largest corporation it could find. A little younger, a little more bewildered, it was this same face that the photographers caught in Illinois when the first non-virgin club was uncovered. The young copywriter, leaning down the bar on Third Avenue, quietly drinking himself into relaxation, and the energetic hotrod driver of Los Angeles, who plays Russian Roulette with a jalopy, are separated only by a continent and a few years. They are the extremes. In between them fall the secretaries wondering whether to sleep with their boyfriends now or wait; the mechanic berring up with the guys and driving off to Detroit on a whim; the models studiously name-dropping at a cocktail party. But the face is the same. Bright, level, realistic, challenging.

Any attempt to label an entire generation is unrewarding, and yet the generation which went through the last war, or at least could get a drink easily once it was over, seems to possess a uniform, general quality which demands an adjective . . . The origins of the word "beat" are obscure, but the meaning is only too clear to most Americans. More than mere weariness, it implies the feeling of having been used, of being raw. It involves a sort of nakedness of mind, and, ultimately, of soul; a feeling of being reduced to the bedrock of consciousness. In short, it means being undramatically pushed up against the wall of oneself. A man is beat whenever he goes for broke and wagers the sum of his resources on a single number; and the young generation has done that continually from early youth.

Its members have an instinctive individuality, needing no bohemianism or imposed eccentricity to express it. Brought up during the collective bad circumstances of a dreary depression, weaned during the collective uprooting of a global war, they distrust collectivity. But they have never been able to keep the world out of their dreams. The fancies of their childhood inhabited the half-light of Munich, the Nazi-Soviet pact, and the eventual blackout. Their adolescence was spent in a topsy-turvy world of war bonds, swing shifts, and troop movements. They grew to independent mind on beachheads, in gin mills and USO's, in past-

midnight arrivals and pre-dawn departures. Their brothers, husbands, fathers or boy friends turned up dead one day at the other end of a telegram. At the four trembling corners of the world, or in the home town invaded by factories or lonely servicemen, they had intimate experience with the nadir and the zenith of human conduct, and little time for much that came between. The peace they inherited was only as secure as the next headline. It was a cold peace. Their own lust for freedom, and the ability to live at a pace that kills (to which the war had adjusted them), led to black markets, bebop, narcotics, sexual promiscuity, hucksterism, and Jean-Paul Sartre. The beatness set in later.

It is a postwar generation, and, in a world which seems to mark its cycles by its wars, it is already being compared to that other postwar generation, which dubbed itself "lost". The Roaring Twenties, and the generation that made them roar, are going through a sentimental revival, and the comparison is valuable. The Lost Generation was discovered in a roadster, laughing hysterically because nothing meant anything anymore. It migrated to Europe, unsure whether it was looking for the "orgiastic future" or escaping from the "puritanical past." Its symbols were the flapper, the flask of bootleg whiskey, and an attitude of desperate frivolity best expressed by the line: "Tennis, anyone?" It was caught up in the romance of disillusionment, until even that became an illusion. Every act in its drama of lostness was a tragic or ironic third act, and T. S. Eliot's *The Waste Land* was more than the dead-end statement of a perceptive poet. The pervading atmosphere of that poem was an almost objectless sense of loss, through which the reader felt immediately that the cohesion of things had disappeared. It was, for an entire generation, an image which expressed, with dreadful accuracy, its own spiritual condition.

But the wild boys of today are not lost. Their flushed, often scoffing, always intent faces elude the word, and it would sound phony to them. For this generation lacks that eloquent air of bereavement which made so many of the exploits of the Lost Generation symbolic actions. Furthermore, the repeated inventory of shattered ideals, and the laments about the mud in moral currents, which so obsessed the Lost Generation, do not concern young people today. They take these things frighteningly for granted. They were brought up in these ruins and no longer notice them. They drink to "come down" or to "get high," not to illustrate anything. Their excursions into drugs or promiscuity come out of curiosity, not disillusionment.

Only the most bitter among them would call their reality a nightmare and protest that they have indeed lost something, the future. For ever since they were old enough to imagine one, that has been in jeopardy anyway. The absence of personal and social values is to them, not a revelation shaking the ground beneath them, but a problem demanding a day-to-day solution. *How* to live seems to them much more crucial than *why*. And it is precisely at this point that the copywriter and the hotrod driver meet and their identical beatness becomes significant, for, unlike the Lost Generation, which was occupied with the loss of faith, the Beat Generation is becoming more and more occupied with the need for it. As such, it is a disturbing illustration of Voltaire's reliable old joke: "If there were no God, it would be necessary to invent him." Not content to bemoan his absence, they are busily and haphazardly inventing totems for him on all sides. For the giggling nihilist, eating up the highway at ninety miles an hour and steering with his feet, is no Harry Crosby, the poet of the Lost Generation who planned to fly his plane into the sun one day because he could no longer accept the modern world. On the contrary, the hotrod driver invites death only to outwit it. He is affirming the life within him in the only way he knows how, at the extreme. The eager-faced girl, picked up on a dope charge, is not one of those "women and girls carried screaming with drink or drugs from public places," of whom Fitzgerald wrote. Instead, with persuasive seriousness, she describes the sense of community she has found in marijuana, which society never gave her. The copywriter, just as drunk by midnight as his Lost Generation counterpart, probably reads *God and Man at Yale* during his Sunday afternoon hangover. The difference is this almost exaggerated will to believe in something, if only in themselves. It is a *will* to believe, even in the face of an inability to do so in conventional terms. And that is bound to lead to excesses in one direction or another.

The shock that older people feel at the sight of this Beat Generation is, at its deepest level, not so much repugnance at the facts, as it is distress at the attitudes which move it. Though worried by this distress, they most often argue or legislate in terms of the facts rather than the attitudes. The newspaper reader, studying the eyes of young dope addicts, can only find an outlet for his horror and bewilderment in demands that passers be given the electric chair. Sociologists, with a more academic concern, are just as troubled by the legions of young men whose topmost ambition seems to be to find a secure berth in a monolithic corporation. Contemporary historians express mild surprise at the lack of organized movements, political, religious, or otherwise, among the young. The articles they write remind us that being one's own boss and being a natural joiner are two of our most cherished national traits. Everywhere people with tidy moralities shake their heads and wonder what is happening to the younger generation.

Perhaps they have not noticed that, behind the excess on the one hand, and the conformity on the other, lies that wait-and-see detachment that results from having to fall back for support more on one's capacity for human endurance than on one's philosophy of life. Not that the Beat Generation is immune to ideas; they fascinate it. Its wars, both past and future, were and will be wars of ideas. It knows, however, that in the final, private moment of conflict a man is really fighting another man, and not an idea. And that the same goes for love. So it is a generation with a greater facility for entertaining ideas than for believing in them. But it is also the first generation in several centuries for which the act of faith has been an obsessive problem, quite aside from the reasons for having a particular faith or not having it. It exhibits on every side, and in a bewildering number of facets, a perfect craving to believe.

Though it is certainly a generation of extremes, including both the hipster and the radical young Republican in its ranks, it renders unto Caesar (i.e., society) what is Caesar's and unto God what is God's. For the wildest hipster, making a mystique of bop, drugs and the night life, there is no desire to shatter the "square" society in which he lives, only to elude it. To get on a soapbox or write a manifesto would seem to him absurd. Looking at the normal world, where most everything is a "drag" for him, he nevertheless says: "Well, that's the Forest of Arden after all. And even *it* jumps if you look at it right." Equally, the young Republican, though often seeming to hold up Babbitt as his culture hero, is neither vulgar nor materialistic, as Babbitt was. He conforms because he believes it is socially practical, not necessarily virtuous. Both positions, however, are the result of more or less the same conviction—namely that the valueless abyss of modern life is unbearable.

For beneath the excess and the conformity, there is something other than detachment. There are the stirrings of a quest. What the hipster is looking for in his "coolness" (withdrawal) or "flipness" (ecstasy) is, after all, a feeling on somewhereness, not just another diversion. The young Republican feels that there is a point beyond which change becomes chaos, and what he wants is not simply privilege or wealth, but a stable position from which to operate. Both have had enough of homelessness, valuelessness, faithlessness.

The variety and the extremity of their solutions are only a final indication that for today's young people there is not as yet a single external pivot around which they can, as a generation, group their observations and their aspirations. There is no single philosophy, no single party, no single attitude. The failure of most orthodox moral and social concepts to reflect fully the life they have known is probably the reason for this, but because of it each person becomes a walking, self-contained unit, compelled to meet, or at least endure, the problem of being young in a seemingly helpless world in his own way.

More than anything else, this is what is responsible for this generation's reluctance to name itself, its reluctance to discuss itself as a group, sometimes its reluctance to be itself. For invented gods invariably disappoint those who worship them. Only the need for them goes on, and it is this need, exhausting one object after another, which projects the Beat Generation forward into the future and will one day deprive it of its beatness.

Dostoyevski wrote in the early 1880's that "Young Russia is talking of nothing but the eternal questions now." With appropriate changes, something very like this is beginning to happen in America, in an American way; a re-evaluation of which the exploits and attitudes of this generation are only symptoms. No single comparison of one generation against another can accurately measure effects, but it seems obvious that a lost generation, occupied with disillusionment and trying to keep busy among the broken stones, is poetically moving, but not very dangerous. But a beat generation, driven by a desperate craving for belief and as yet unable to accept the moderations which are offered it, is quite another matter. Thirty years later, after all, the generation of which Dostoyevski wrote was meeting in cellars and making bombs. This generation may make no bombs; it will probably be asked to drop some, and have some dropped on it, however, and this fact is never far from its mind. It is one of the pressures which created it and will play a large part in what

will happen to it. There are those who believe that in generations such as this there is always the constant possibility of a great new moral idea, conceived in desperation, coming to life. Others note the self-indulgence, the waste, the apparent social irresponsibility, and disagree.

But its ability to keep its eyes open, and yet avoid cynicism; its ever-increasing conviction that the problem of modern life is essentially a spiritual problem; and that capacity for sudden wisdom which people who live hard and go far possess, are assets and bear watching. And, anyway, the clear, challenging faces are worth it.

KENNETH REXROTH (ESSAY DATE 1957)

SOURCE: Rexroth, Kenneth. "Disengagement: The Art of the Beat Generation." In *A Casebook on the Beat*, edited by Thomas Parkinson, pp. 179-93. New York: Thomas Y. Crowell Company, 1961.

In this essay, originally published in New World Writing *in 1957, Rexroth surveys the development of a new youth culture, reflected in artistic movements in music, painting, and literature that are not merely reactions to the past but efforts to begin anew with fresh techniques and materials. Rexroth, whom Kerouac described as the father of young San Francisco poets, speaks from the perspective of an adult overlooking the progress of an up-and-coming generation, observing both the excitement of a growing avant-garde movement in the arts and the possibility that nihilism will overtake and eventually destroy young artists.*

Literature generally, but literary criticism in particular, has always been an area in which social forces assume symbolic guise, and work out—or at least exemplify—conflicts taking place in the contemporary, or rather, usually the just-past wider arena of society. Recognition of this does not imply the acceptance of any general theory of social or economic determinism. It is a simple, empirical fact. Because of the pervasiveness of consent in American society generally, that democratic leveling up or down so often bewailed since de Tocqueville, American literature, especially literary criticism, has usually been ruled by a "line." The fact that it was spontaneously evolved and enforced only by widespread consent has never detracted from its rigor—but rather the opposite. It is only human to kick against the prodding of an Erich Auerbach or an Andrey Zhdanov. An invisible, all-enveloping compulsion is not likely to be recognized, let alone protested against.

After World War I there was an official line for general consumption: "Back to Normalcy." Day by day in every way, we are getting better and better. This produced a literature which tirelessly pointed out that there was nothing whatsoever normal about us. The measure of decay in thirty years is the degree of acceptance of the official myth today—from the most obscure hack on a provincial newspaper to the loftiest metaphysicians of the literary quarterlies. The line goes: "The generation of experimentation and revolt is over." This is an etherealized corollary of the general line: "The bull market will never end."

I do not wish to argue about the bull market, but in the arts nothing could be less true. The youngest generation is in a state of revolt so absolute that its elders cannot even recognize it. The disaffiliation, alienation, and rejection of the young has, as far as their elders are concerned, moved out of the visible spectrum altogether. Critically invisible, modern revolt, like X-rays and radioactivity, is perceived only by its effects at more materialistic social levels, where it is called delinquency.

"Disaffiliation," by the way, is the term used by the critic and poet, Lawrence Lipton, who has written several articles on this subject, the first of which, in the *Nation,* quoted as epigraph, "We disaffiliate . . ."—John L. Lewis.

Like the pillars of Hercules, like two ruined Titans guarding the entrance to one of Dante's circles, stand two great dead juvenile delinquents—the heroes of the post-war generation: the great saxophonist, Charlie Parker, and Dylan Thomas. If the word deliberate means anything, both of them certainly deliberately destroyed themselves.

Both of them were overcome by the horror of the world in which they found themselves, because at last they could no longer overcome that world with the weapon of a purely lyrical art. Both of them were my friends. Living in San Francisco I saw them seldom enough to see them with a perspective which was not distorted by exasperation or fatigue. So as the years passed, I saw them each time in the light of an accelerated personal conflagration.

The last time I saw Bird, at Jimbo's Bob City, he was so gone—so blind to the world—that he literally sat down on me before he realized I was there. "What happened, man?" I said, referring to the pretentious "Jazz Concert." "Evil, man, evil," he said, and that's all he said for the rest of the night. About dawn he got up to blow. The rowdy crowd chilled into stillness and the fluent melody spiraled through it.

The last time I saw Dylan, his self-destruction had not just passed the limits of rationality. It had

assumed the terrifying inertia of inanimate matter. Being with him was like being swept away by a torrent of falling stones.

Now Dylan Thomas and Charlie Parker have a great deal more in common than the same disastrous end. As artists, they were very similar. They were both very fluent. But this fluent, enchanting utterance had, compared with important artists of the past, relatively little content. Neither of them got very far beyond a sort of entranced rapture at his own creativity. The principal theme of Thomas's poetry was the ambivalence of birth and death—the pain of blood-stained creation. Music, of course, is not so explicit an art, but anybody who knew Charlie Parker knows that he felt much the same way about his own gift. Both of them did communicate one central theme: Against the ruin of the world, there is only one defense—the creative act. This, of course, is the theme of much art—perhaps most poetry. It is the theme of Horace, who certainly otherwise bears little resemblance to Parker or Thomas. The difference is that Horace accepted his theme with a kind of silken assurance. To Dylan and Bird it was an agony and terror. I do not believe that this is due to anything especially frightful about their relationship to their own creativity. I believe rather that it is due to the catastrophic world in which that creativity seemed to be the sole value. Horace's column of imperishable verse shines quietly enough in the lucid air of Augustan Rome. Art may have been for him the most enduring, orderly, and noble activity of man. But the other activities of his life partook of these values. They did not actively negate them. Dylan Thomas's verse had to find endurance in a world of burning cities and burning Jews. He was able to find meaning in his art as long as it was the answer to air raids and gas ovens. As the world began to take on the guise of an immense air raid or gas oven, I believe his art became meaningless to him. I think all this could apply to Parker just as well, although, because of the nature of music, it is not demonstrable—at least not conclusively.

Thomas and Parker have more in common than theme, attitude, life pattern. In the practice of their art, there is an obvious technical resemblance. Contrary to popular belief, they were not great technical innovators. Their effects are only superficially startling. Thomas is a regression from the technical originality and ingenuity of writers like Pierre Reverdy or Apollinaire. Similarly, the innovations of bop, and of Parker particularly, have been vastly overrated by people unfamiliar with music, especially by that ignoramus, the intellectual jitterbug, the jazz aficionado. The tonal novelties consist in the introduction of a few chords used in classical music for centuries. And there is less rhythmic difference between progressive jazz, no matter how progressive, and Dixieland, than there is between two movements of many conventional symphonies.

What Parker and his contemporaries—Gillespie, Davis, Monk, Roach (Tristano is an anomaly), etc.—did was to absorb the musical ornamentation of the older jazz into the basic structure, of which it then became an integral part, and with which it then developed. This is true of the melodic line which could be put together from selected passages of almost any-body—Benny Carter, Johnny Hodges. It is true of the rhythmic pattern in which the beat shifts continuously, or at least is continuously sprung, so that it becomes ambiguous enough to allow the pattern to be dominated by the long pulsations of the phrase or strophe. This is exactly what happened in the transition from baroque to rococo music. It is the difference between Bach and Mozart.

It is not a farfetched analogy to say that this is what Thomas did to poetry. The special syntactical effects of a Rimbaud or an Edith Sitwell—actually ornaments—become the main concern. The metaphysical conceits, which fascinate the Reactionary Generation still dominant in backwater American colleges, were embroideries. Thomas's ellipses and ambiguities are ends in themselves. The immediate theme, if it exists, is incidental, and his main theme—the terror of birth—is simply reiterated.

This is one difference between Bird and Dylan which should be pointed out. Again, contrary to popular belief, there is nothing crazy or frantic about Parker either musically or emotionally. His sinuous melody is a sort of naïve transcendence of all experience. Emotionally it does not resemble Berlioz or Wagner; it resembles Mozart. This is true also of a painter like Jackson Pollock. He may have been eccentric in his behavior, but his paintings are as impassive as Persian tiles. Partly this difference is due to the nature of verbal communication. The insistent talk-aboutiveness of the general environment obtrudes into even the most idyllic poetry. It is much more a personal difference. Thomas certainly wanted to tell people about the ruin and disorder of the world. Parker and Pollock wanted to substitute a work of art for the world.

Technique pure and simple, rendition, is not of major importance, but it is interesting that Parker, following Lester Young, was one of the leaders of the so-called saxophone revolution. In modern jazz, the saxophone is treated as a wood-wind and played with conventional embouchure. Metrically, Thomas's verse was extremely conventional, as was, incidentally, the verse of that other tragic enragé, Hart Crane.

I want to make clear what I consider the one technical development in the first wave of significant post-war arts. Ornament is confabulation in the interstices of structure. A poem by Dylan Thomas, a saxophone solo by Charles Parker, a painting by Jackson Pollock—these are pure confabulations as ends in themselves. Confabulation has come to determine structure. Uninhibited lyricism should be distinguished from its exact opposite—the sterile, extraneous invention of the corn-belt metaphysicals, or present blight of poetic professors.

Just as Hart Crane had little influence on anyone except very reactionary writers—like Allen Tate, for instance, to whom Valéry was the last word in modern poetry and the felicities of an Apollinaire, let alone a Paul Éluard were nonsense—so Dylan Thomas's influence has been slight indeed. In fact, his only disciple—the only person to imitate his style—was W. S. Graham, who seems to have imitated him without much understanding, and who has since moved on to other methods. Thomas's principal influence lay in the communication of an attitude—that of the now extinct British romantic school of the New Apocalypse—Henry Treece, J. F. Hendry, and others—all of whom were quite conventional poets.

Parker certainly had much more of an influence. At one time it was the ambition of every saxophone player in every high school band in America to blow like Bird. Even before his death this influence had begun to ebb. In fact, the whole generation of the founding fathers of bop—Gillespie, Monk, Davis, Blakey, and the rest—are just now at a considerable discount. The main line of development today goes back to Lester Young and bypasses them.

The point is that many of the most impressive developments in the arts nowadays are aberrant, idiosyncratic. There is no longer any sense of continuing development of the sort that can be traced from Baudelaire to Éluard, or for that matter, from Hawthorne through Henry James to Gertrude Stein. The cubist generation before World War I, and, on a lower level, the surrealists of the period between the wars, both assumed an accepted universe of discourse, in which, to quote André Breton, it was possible to make definite advances, exactly as in the sciences. I doubt if anyone holds such ideas today. Continuity exits, but like the neo-swing music developed from Lester Young, it is a continuity sustained by popular demand.

In the plastic arts, a very similar situation exists. Surrealists like Hans Arp and Max Ernst might talk of creation by hazard—of composing pictures by walking on them with painted soles, or by tossing bits of paper up in the air. But it is obvious that they were self-deluded. Nothing looks anything like an Ernst or an Arp but another Ernst or Arp. Nothing looks less like their work than the happenings of random occasion. Many of the post-World War II abstract expressionists, apostles of the discipline of spontaneity and hazard, look alike, and do look like accidents. The aesthetic appeal of pure paint laid on at random may exist, but it is a very impoverished appeal. Once again what has happened is an all-consuming confabulation of the incidentals, the accidents of painting. It is curious that at its best, the work of this school of painting—Mark Rothko, Jackson Pollock, Clyfford Still, Robert Motherwell, Willem de-Kooning, and the rest—resembles nothing so much as the passage painting of quite unimpressive painters: the mother-of-pearl shimmer in the background of a Henry McFee, itself a formula derived from Renoir; the splashes of light and black which fake drapery in the fashionable imitators of Hals and Sargent. Often work of this sort is presented as calligraphy—the pure utterance of the brush stroke seeking only absolute painteresque values. You have only to compare such painting with the work of, say, Sesshu, to realize that someone is using words and brushes carelessly.

At its best the abstract expressionists achieve a simple rococo decorative surface. Its poverty shows up immediately when compared with Tiepolo, where the rococo rises to painting of extraordinary profundity and power. A Tiepolo painting, however confabulated, is a universe of tensions in vast depths. A Pollock is an object of art—bijouterie—disguised only by its great size. In fact, once the size is big enough to cover a whole wall, it turns into nothing more than extremely expensive wallpaper. Now there is nothing wrong with complicated wallpaper. There is just more to Tiepolo. The great Ashikaga brush painters painted wallpapers, too—at least portable ones, screens.

A process of elimination which leaves the artist with nothing but the play of his materials themselves cannot sustain interest in either artist or public for very long. So, in the last couple of years, abstract expressionism has tended toward romantic suggestion—indications of landscape or living figures. This approaches the work of the Northwest school—Clayton Price, Mark Tobey, Kenneth Callahan, Morris Graves—who have of all recent painters come nearest to conquering a territory which painting could occupy with some degree of security. The Northwest school, of course, admittedly is influenced by the ink painters of the Far East, and by Tintoretto and Tiepolo. The dominant school of post-World War II American painting has really been a long detour into plastic nihilism. I should add that painters like Ernie Briggs seem to be opening up new areas of considerable scope within the main traditional abstract expressionism—but with remarkable convergence to Tobey or Tintoretto, as you prefer.

Today American painting is just beginning to emerge with a transvaluation of values. From the mid-nineteenth century on, all ruling standards in the plastic arts were subject to continual attack. They were attacked because each on-coming generation had new standards of their own to put in their place. Unfortunately, after one hundred years of this, there grew up a generation ignorant of the reasons for the revolt of their elders, and without any standards whatever. It has been necessary to create standards anew out of chaos. This is what modern education purports to do with finger painting in nursery schools. This is why the Northwest school has enjoyed such an advantage over the abstract expressionists. Learning by doing, by trial and error, is learning by the hardest way. If you want to overthrow the cubist tradition of architectural painting, it is much easier to seek out its opposites in the history of culture and study them carefully. At least it saves a great deal of time.

One thing can be said of painting in recent years—its revolt, its rejection of the classic modernism of the first half of the century, has been more absolute than in any other art. The only ancestor of abstract expressionism is the early Kandinsky—a style rejected even by Kandinsky himself. The only painter in a hundred years who bears the slightest resemblance to Tobey or Graves is Odilon Redon (perhaps Gustave Moreau a little), whose stock was certainly not very high with painters raised in the cubist tradition.

The ready market for prose fiction—there is almost no market at all for modern painting, and very much less for poetry—has had a decisive influence on its development. Sidemen with Kenton or Herman may make a good if somewhat hectic living, but any novelist who can write home to mother, or even spell his own name, has a chance to become another Brubeck. The deliberately and painfully intellectual fiction which appears in the literary quarterlies is a by-product of certain classrooms. The only significant fiction in America is popular fiction. Nobody realizes this better than the French. To them our late-born imitators of Henry James and E. M. Forster are just *chiens qui fument,* and arithmetical horses and bicycling seals. And there is no more perishable commodity than the middle-brow novel. No one today reads Ethel L. Voynich or Joseph Hergesheimer, just as no one in the future will read the writers' workshop pupils and teachers who fill the literary quarterlies. Very few people, except themselves, read them now.

On the other hand, the connection between the genuine highbrow writer and the genuinely popular is very close. Hemingway had hardly started to write before his style had been reduced to a formula in *Black Mask,* the first hard-boiled detective magazine. In no time at all he had produced two first-class popular writers, Raymond Chandler and Dashiell Hammett. Van Vechten, their middle-brow contemporary, is forgotten. It is from Chandler and Hammett and Hemingway that the best modern fiction derives; although most of it comes out in hard covers, it is always thought of as written for a typical pocket book audience. Once it gets into pocketbooks it is sometimes difficult to draw the line between it and its most ephemeral imitators. Even the most *précieux* French critics, a few years ago, considered Horace McCoy America's greatest contemporary novelist. There is not only something to be said for their point of view; the only thing to be said against it is that they don't read English.

Much of the best popular fiction deals with the world of the utterly disaffiliated. Burlesque and carnival people, hipsters, handicappers and hop heads, wanted men on the lam, an expendable squad of soldiers being expended, anyone who by definition is divorced from society and cannot afford to believe even an iota of the social lie—these are the favorite characters of modern post-war fiction, from Norman Mailer to the latest ephemerid called *Caught,* or *Hung Up,* or *The Needle,* its bright cover winking invitingly in the drugstore. The first, and still the greatest, novelist of total disengagement is not a young man at all, but an elderly former I.W.W. of German ancestry, B. Traven, the author of *The Death Ship* and *The Treasure of Sierra Madre.*

It is impossible for an artist to remain true to himself as a man, let alone an artist, and work within the context of this society. Contemporary mimics of Jane Austen or Anthony Trollope are not only beneath contempt. They are literally unreadable. It is impossible to keep your eyes focused on the page. Writers as far apart as J. F. Powers and Nelson Algren agree in one thing—their diagnosis of an absolute corruption.

The refusal to accept the mythology of press and pulpit as a medium for artistic creation, or even enjoyable reading matter, is one explanation for the popularity of escapist literature. Westerns, detective stories and science fiction are all situated beyond the pale of normal living. The slick magazines are only too well aware of this, and in these three fields especially exert steady pressure on their authors to accentuate the up-beat. The most shocking example of this forced perversion is the homey science fiction story, usually written by a woman, in which a one-to-one correlation has been made for the commodity-ridden tale of domestic whimsey, the stand-by of magazines given away in the chain groceries. In writers like Judith Merril the space pilot and his bride bat the badinage back and forth while the robot maid makes breakfast in the jet-propelled lucite orange squeezer and the electronic bacon rotobroiler, dropping pearls of dry assembly plant wisdom (like plantation wisdom but drier), the whilst. Still, few yield to these pressures, for the obvious reason that fiction indistinguishable from the advertising columns on either side of the page defeats its own purpose, which is to get the reader to turn over the pages when he is told "continued on p. 47."

Simenon is still an incomparably better artist and psychologist than the psychological Jean Stafford. Ward Moore is a better artist than Eudora Welty, and Ernest Haycox than William Faulkner, just as, long ago, H. G. Wells was a better artist, as artist, than E. M. Forster, as well as being a lot more interesting. At its best, popular literature of this sort, coming up, meets highbrow literature coming down. It has been apparent novel by novel that Nelson Algren is rising qualitatively in this way. In his latest novel, thoroughly popular in its materials, *A Walk on the Wild Side,* he meets and absorbs influences coming down from the top, from the small handful of bona fide highbrow writers working today—Céline, Jean Genêt, Samuel Beckett, Henry Miller. In Algren's case this has been a slow growth, and he has carried his audience with him. Whatever the mertis of his subject matter or his thesis—"It is better to be out than in. It is better to be on the lam than on the cover of *Time* Magazine"—his style started out as a distressing mixture of James Farrell and Kenneth Fearing. Only recently has he achieved an idiom of his own.

There is only one thing wrong with this picture, and that is that the high-brow stimulus still has to be imported. Algren, who is coming to write more and more like Céline, has no difficulty selling his fiction. On the other hand, an author like Jack Kerouac, who is in his small way the peer of Céline, Destouches or Beckett, is the most famous "unpublished" author in America. Every publisher's reader and adviser of any moment has read him and is enthusiastic about him. In other words, anybody emerging from the popular field has every advantage. It is still extremely difficult to enter American fiction from the top down.

The important point about modern fiction is that it is salable, and therefore viable in our society, and therefore successful in the best sense of the word. When a novelist has something to say, he knows people will listen. Only the jazz musician, but to a much lesser degree, shares this confidence in his audience. It is of the greatest social significance that the novelists who say, "I am proud to be delinquent" are nevertheless sold in editions of hundreds of thousands.

Nobody much buys poetry. I know. I am one of the country's most successful poets. My books actually sell out—in editions of two thousand. Many a poet, the prestige ornament of a publisher's list, has more charges against his royalty account than credits for books sold. The problem of poetry is the problem of communication itself. All art is a symbolic criticism of values, but poetry is specifically and almost exclusively that. A painting decorates the wall. A novel is a story. Music . . . soothes a savage breast. But poetry you have to take straight. In addition, the entire educational system is in a conspiracy to make poetry as unpalatable as possible. From the seventh grade teacher who rolls her eyes and chants H. D. to the seven types of ambiguity factories, grinding out little Donnes and Hopkinses with hayseeds in their hair, everybody is out to de-poetize forever the youth of the land. Again, bad and spurious painting, music, and fiction are not really well-organized, except on obvious commercial levels, where they can be avoided. But in poetry Gresham's Law is supported by the full weight of the powers that be. From about 1930 on, a conspiracy of bad poetry has been as carefully organized as the Communist Party, and today controls most channels of publication except the littlest of the little magazines. In all other departments of American culture, English influence has been at a

steadily declining minimum since the middle of the nineteenth century. In 1929, this was still true of American poetry. Amy Lowell, Sandburg, H. D., Pound, Marianne Moore, William Carlos Williams, Wallace Stevens—all of the major poets of the first quarter of the century owed far more to Apollinaire or Francis Jammes than they did to the whole body of the English tradition. In fact, the new poetry was essentially an anti-English, pro-French movement—a provincial but clear echo of the French revolt against the symbolists. On the other hand, Jules Laforgue and his English disciples, Ernest Dowson and Arthur Symons, were the major influence on T. S. Eliot. Unfortunately Mr. Eliot's poetic practice and his thoroughly snobbish critical essays which owed their great cogency to their assumption, usually correct, that his readers had never heard of the authors he discussed—Webster, Crashaw, or Lancelot Andrewes—lent themselves all too easily to the construction of an academy and the production of an infinite number of provincial academicians—policemen entrusted with the enforcement of Gresham's Law.

Behind the façade of this literary Potemkin village, the main stream of American poetry, with its sources in Baudelaire, Lautréamont, Rimbaud, Apollinaire, Jammes, Reverdy, Salmon, and later Breton and Éluard, has flowed on unperturbed, though visible only at rare intervals between the interstices of the academic hoax. Today the class magazines and the quarterlies are filled with poets as alike as two bad pennies. It is my opinion that these people do not really exist. Most of them are androids designed by Ransom, Tate, and Co., and animated by Randall Jarrell. They are not just counterfeit; they are not even real counterfeits, but counterfeits of counterfeits. On these blurred and clumsy coins the lineaments of Mr. Eliot and I. A. Richards dimly can be discerned, like the barbarized Greek letters which nobody could read on Scythian money.

This is the world in which over every door is written the slogan: "The generation of experiment and revolt is over. Bohemia died in the twenties. There are no more little magazines." Actually there have never been so many little magazines. In spite of the fantastic costs of printing, more people than ever are bringing out little sheets of free verse and making up the losses out of their own pockets. This world has its own major writers, its own discoveries, its own old masters, its own tradition and continuity. Its sources are practically exclusively French, and they are all post-symbolist, even anti-symbolist. It is the Reactionary Generation who are influenced by Laforgue, the symbolists, and Valéry. Nothing is more impressive than the strength, or at least the cohesion, of this underground movement. Poets whom the quarterlies pretend never existed, like Louis Zukovsky and Jack Wheelwright, are still searched out in large libraries or obscure bookshops and copied into notebooks by young writers. I myself have a complete typewritten collection of the pre-reactionary verse of Yvor Winters. And I know several similar collections of "forgotten modernists" in the libraries of my younger friends. People are always turning up who say something like, "I just discovered a second-hand copy of Parker Tyler's *The Granite Butterfly* in a Village bookshop. It's great, man." On the other hand, I seriously doubt whether *The Hudson Review* would ever consider for a moment publishing a line of Parker Tyler's verse. And he is certainly not held up as an example in the Iowa Writers' Workshop. There are others who have disappeared entirely—Charles Snider, Sherry Mangan, R. E. F. Larsson, the early Winters, the last poems of Ford Madox Ford. They get back into circulation, as far as I know, only when I read them to somebody at home or on the air, and then I am always asked for a copy. Some of the old avant garde seem to have written themselves out, for instance, Mina Loy. There are a few established old masters, outstanding of whom are, of course, Ezra Pound and William Carlos Williams. I am not a passionate devotee of Pound myself. In fact, I think his influence is largely pernicious. But no one could deny its extent and power amongst young people today. As for Williams, more and more people, even some of the Reactionary Generation, have come to think of him as our greatest living poet. Even Randall Jarrell and R. P. Blackmur have good words to say for him.

Then there is a middle generation which includes Kenneth Patchen, Jean Garrigue, myself, and a few others—notably Richard Eberhart, who looks superficially as if he belonged with the Tates and Blackmurs but who is redeemed by his directness, simplicity, and honesty, and Robert Fitzgerald and Dudley Fitts. Curiously enough, in the taste of the young, Kenneth Fearing is not included in this group, possibly because his verse is too easy. It does include the major work, for example, *Ajanta,* of Muriel Rukeyser.

I should say that the most influential poets of the youngest established generation of the avant garde are Denise Levertov, Robert Creeley, Charles Olson, Robert Duncan, and Philip Lamantia. The most influential avant garde editor is perhaps Cid Corman, with his magazine *Origin.* Richard Emerson's *Golden Goose* and Robert Creeley's *Black Mountain Review* seem to have suspended publication temporarily. Jonathan Williams, himself a fine poet, publishes the Jargon Press.

All of this youngest group have a good deal in common. They are all more or less influenced by French poetry, and by Céline, Beckett, Artaud, Genêt, to varying degrees. They are also influenced by William Carlos Williams, D. H. Lawrence, Whitman, Pound. They are all interested in Far Eastern art and religion; some even call themselves Buddhists. Politically they are all strong disbelievers in the State, war, and the values of commercial civilization. Most of them would no longer call themselves anarchists, but just because adopting such a label would imply adherence to a "movement." Anything in the way of an explicit ideology is suspect. Contrary to gossip of a few years back, I have never met anybody in this circle who was a devotee of the dubious notions of the psychologist, Wilhelm Reich; in fact, few of them have ever read him, and those who have consider him a charlatan.

Although there is wide diversity—Olson is very like Pound; Creeley resembles Mallarmé; Denise Levertov in England was a leading New Romantic, in America she has come under the influence of William Carlos Williams; Robert Duncan has assimilated ancestors as unlike as Gertrude Stein and Éluard, and so on—although this diversity is very marked, there is a strong bond of aesthetic unity too. No avant garde American poet accepts the I. A. Richards—Valéry thesis that a poem is an end in itself, an anonymous machine for providing aesthetic experiences. All believe in poetry as communication, statement from one person to another. So they all avoid the studied ambiguities and metaphysical word play of the Reactionary Generation and seek clarity of image and simplicity of language.

In the years since the war, it would seem as though more and more of what is left of the avant garde has migrated to Northern California. John Berryman once referred to the Lawrence cult of "mindless California," and Henry Miller and I have received other unfavorable publicity which has served only to attract people to this area. Mr. Karl Shapiro, for instance, once referred to San Francisco as "the last refuge of the Bohemian remnant"—a description he thought of as invidious. Nevertheless it is true that San Francisco is today the seat of an intense literary activity not unlike Chicago of the first quarter of the century. A whole school of poets has grown up—almost all of them migrated here from somewhere else. Some of them have national reputations, at least in limited circles. For example, Philip Lamantia among the surrealists; William Everson (Br. Antoninus, O.P)—perhaps the best Catholic poet. Others have come up recently, like Lawrence Ferlinghetti, Allen Ginsberg, Gary Snyder, Philip Whalen, James Harmon, Michael McClure, and still have largely local reputations. But the strength of these reputations should not be underestimated. The Poetry Center of San Francisco State College, directed by Ruth Witt-Diamant, gives a reading to a large audience at least twice a month. And there are other readings equally well attended every week in various galleries and private homes.

This means that poetry has become an actual social force—something which has always sounded hitherto like a Utopian dream of the William Morris sort. It is a very thrilling experience to hear an audience of more than three hundred people stand and cheer and clap, as they invariably do at a reading by Allen Ginsberg, certainly a poet of revolt if there ever was one.

There is no question but that the San Francisco renaissance is radically different from what is going on elsewhere. There are hand presses, poetry readings, young writers elsewhere—but nowhere else is there a whole younger generation culture pattern characterized by total rejection of the official high-brow culture—where critics like John Crowe Ransom or Lionel Trilling, magazines like the *Kenyon, Hudson* and *Partisan* reviews, are looked on as "The Enemy"—the other side of the barricades.

There is only one trouble about the renaissance in San Francisco. It is too far away from the literary market place. That, of course, is the reason why the Bohemian remnant, the avant garde have migrated here. It is possible to hear the story about what so-and-so said to someone else at a cocktail party twenty years ago just one too many times. You grab a plane or get on your thumb and hitchhike to the other side of the continent for good and all. Each generation, the great Latin poets came from farther and farther from Rome. Eventually, they ceased to even go there except to see the sights.

Distance from New York City does, however, make it harder to get things, if not published, at least nationally circulated. I recently formed a collection for one of the foundations of avant garde poetry printed in San Francisco. There were a great many items. The poetry was all at least readable, and the hand printing and binding were in most

cases very fine indeed. None of these books were available in bookstores elsewhere in the country, and only a few of them had been reviewed in newspapers or magazines with national circulation.

Anyway, as an old war horse of the revolution of the word, things have never looked better from where I sit. That avant garde has not only not ceased to exist. It's jumping all over the place. Something's happening, man.

The disengagement of the creator, who, as creator, is necessarily judge, is one thing, but the utter nihilism of the emptied-out hipster is another. What is going to come of an attitude like this? It is impossible to go on indefinitely saying: "I am proud to be a delinquent," without destroying all civilized values. Between such persons no true enduring interpersonal relationships can be built, and of course, nothing resembling a true "culture"—an at-homeness of men with each other, their work, their loves, their environment. The end result must be the desperation of shipwreck—the despair, the orgies, ultimately the cannibalism of a lost lifeboat. I believe that most of an entire generation will go to ruin—the ruin of Céline, Artaud, Rimbaud, voluntarily, even enthusiastically. What will happen afterwards I don't know, but for the next ten years or so we are going to have to cope with the youth we, my generation, put through the atom smasher. Social disengagement, artistic integrity, voluntary poverty—these are powerful virtues and may pull them through, but they are not the virtues we tried to inculcate—rather they are the exact opposite.

NORMAN PODHORETZ (ESSAY DATE SPRING 1958)

SOURCE: Podhoretz, Norman. "The Know-Nothing Bohemians." *Partisan Review* 25, no. 2 (spring 1958): 305-11, 313-16, 318.

Podhoretz, a critic and classmate of Ginsberg's from Columbia, wrote the first in-depth criticism of the Beats, condemning their idiosyncratic style as a cloak for anti-intellectualism and excoriating the movement's libertine aesthetic as an endorsement for anti-socialism and violence.

Allen Ginsberg's little volume of poems, *Howl,* which got the San Francisco renaissance off to a screaming start a year or so ago, was dedicated to Jack Kerouac ("new Buddha of American prose, who spit forth intelligence into eleven books written in half the number of years . . . creating a spontaneous bop prosody and original classic literature"), William Seward Burroughs ("author of *Naked Lunch,* an endless novel which will drive everybody mad"), and Neal Cassady ("author of *The First Third,* an autobiography . . . which enlightened Buddha"). So far, everybody's sanity has been spared by the inability of *Naked Lunch* to find a publisher, and we may never get the chance to discover what Buddha learned from Neal Cassady's autobiography, but thanks to the Viking and Grove Presses, two of Kerouac's original classics, *On the Road* and *The Subterraneans,* have now been revealed to the world. When *On the Road* appeared last year, Gilbert Milstein commemorated the event in the New York *Times* by declaring it to be "a historic occasion" comparable to the publication of *The Sun Also Rises* in the 1920's. But even before the novel was actually published, the word got around that Kerouac was the spokesman of a new group of rebels and Bohemians who called themselves the Beat Generation, and soon his photogenic countenance (unshaven, of course, and topped by an unruly crop of rich black hair falling over his forehead) was showing up in various mass-circulation magazines, he was being interviewed earnestly on television, and he was being featured in a Greenwich Village nightclub where, in San Francisco fashion, he read specimens of his spontaneous bop prosody against a background of jazz music.

Though the nightclub act reportedly flopped, *On the Road* sold well enough to hit the best-seller lists for several weeks, and it isn't hard to understand why. Americans love nothing so much as representative documents, and what could be more interesting in this Age of Sociology than a novel that speaks for the "young generation"? (The fact that Kerouac is thirty-five or thereabouts was generously not held against him.) Beyond that, however, I think that the unveiling of the Beat Generation was greeted with a certain relief by many people who had been disturbed by the notorious respectability and "maturity" of postwar writing. This was more like it—restless, rebellious, confused youth living it up, instead of thin, balding, buttoned-down instructors of English composing ironic verses with one hand while changing the baby's diapers with the other. Bohemianism is not particularly fashionable nowadays, but the image of Bohemia still exerts a powerful fascination—nowhere more so than in the suburbs, which are filled to overflowing with men and women who uneasily think of themselves as conformists and of Bohemianism as the heroic road. The whole point of *Marjorie Morningstar* was to assure the young marrieds of Mamaroneck that they were better off than the apparently glamorous *luftmenschen* of Greenwich Village, and the

fact that Wouk had to work so hard at making this idea seem convincing is a good indication of the strength of prevailing doubt on the matter.

On the surface, at least, the Bohemianism of *On the Road* is very attractive. Here is a group of high-spirited young men running back and forth across the country (mostly hitch-hiking, sometimes in their own second-hand cars), going to "wild" parties in New York and Denver and San Francisco, living on a shoe-string (GI educational benefits, an occasional fifty bucks from a kindly aunt, an odd job as a typist, a fruit-picker, a parking-lot attendant), talking intensely about love and God and salvation, getting high on marijuana (but never heroin or cocaine), listening feverishly to jazz in crowded little joints, and sleeping freely with beautiful girls. Now and again there is a reference to gloom and melancholy, but the characteristic note struck by Kerouac is exuberance:

> We stopped along the road for a bite to eat. The cowboy went off to have a spare tire patched, and Eddie and I sat down in a kind of homemade diner. I heard a great laugh, the greatest laugh in the world, and here came this rawhide oldtimes Nebraska farmer with a bunch of other boys into the diner; you could hear his raspy cries clear across the plains, across the whole gray world of them that day. Everybody else laughed with him. He didn't have a care in the world and had the hugest regard for everybody. I said to myself, Wham, listen to that man laugh. That's the West, here I am in the West. He came booming into the diner, calling Maw's name, and she made the sweetest cherry pie in Nebraska, and I had some with a mountainous scoop of ice cream on top. "Maw, rustle me up some grub afore I have to start eatin myself or some damn silly idee like that." And he threw himself on a stool and went hyaw hyaw hyaw hyaw. "And throw some beans in it." It was the spirit of the West sitting right next to me. I wished I knew his whole raw life and what the hell he'd been doing all these years besides laughing and yelling like that. Whooee, I told my soul, and the cowboy came back and off we went to Grand Island.

Kerouac's enthusiasm for the Nebraska farmer is part of his general readiness to find the source of all vitality and virtue in simple rural types and in the dispossessed urban groups (Negroes, bums, whores). His idea of life in New York is "millions and millions hustling forever for a buck among themselves . . . grabbing, taking, giving, sighing, dying, just so they could be buried in those awful cemetery cities beyond Long Island City," whereas the rest of America is populated almost exclusively by the true of heart. There are intimations here of a kind of know-nothing populist sentiment, but in other ways this attitude resembles Nelson Algren's belief that bums and whores and junkies are more interesting than white-collar workers or civil servants. The difference is that Algren hates middle-class respectability for moral and political reasons—the middle class exploits and persecutes—while Kerouac, who is thoroughly unpolitical, seems to feel that respectability is a sign not of moral corruption but of spiritual death. "The only people for me," says Sal Paradise, the narrator of *On the Road,* "are the mad ones, the ones who are mad to live, mad to talk, mad to be saved, desirous of everything at the same time, the ones who never yawn or say a commonplace thing, but burn, burn, burn like fabulous yellow roman candles exploding like spiders across the stars. . . ." This tremendous emphasis on emotional intensity, this notion that to be hopped-up is the most desirable of all human conditions, lies at the heart of the Beat Generation ethos and distinguishes it radically from the Bohemianism of the past.

The Bohemianism of the 1920's represented a repudiation of the provinciality, philistinism, and moral hypocrisy of American life—a life, incidentally, which was still essentially small-town and rural in tone. Bohemia, in other words, was a movement created in the name of civilization: its ideals were intelligence, cultivation, spiritual refinement. The typical literary figure of the 1920's was a midwesterner (Hemingway, Fitzgerald, Sinclair Lewis, Eliot, Pound) who had fled from his home town to New York or Paris in search of a freer, more expansive, more enlightened way of life than was possible in Ohio or Minnesota or Michigan. The political radicalism that supplied the characteristic coloring of Bohemianism in the 1930's did nothing to alter the urban, cosmopolitan bias of the 1920's. At its best, the radicalism of the 1930's was marked by deep intellectual seriousness and aimed at a state of society in which the fruits of civilization would be more widely available—and ultimately available to all.

The Bohemianism of the 1950's is another kettle of fish altogether. It is hostile to civilization; it worships primitivism, instinct, energy, "blood." To the extent that it has intellectual interests at all, they run to mystical doctrines, irrationalist philosophies, and left-wing Reichianism. The only art the new Bohemians have any use for is jazz, mainly of the cool variety. Their predilection for bop language is a way of demonstrating solidarity with the primitive vitality and spontaneity they find in jazz and of expressing contempt for coherent, rational discourse which, being a product of the mind, is in their view a form of death. To be

articulate is to admit that you have no feelings (for how can real feelings be expressed in syntactical language?), that you can't respond to anything (Kerouac responds to everything by saying "Wow!"), and that you are probably impotent.

At the one end of the spectrum, this ethos shades off into violence and criminality, mainline drug addiction and madness. Allen Ginsberg's poetry, with its lurid apocalyptic celebration of "angel-headed hipsters," speaks for the darker side of the new Bohemianism. Kerouac is milder. He shows little taste for violence, and the criminality he admires is the harmless kind. The hero of *On the Road,* Dean Moriarty, has a record: "From the age of eleven to seventeen he was usually in reform school. His specialty was stealing cars, gunning for girls coming out of high school in the afternoon, driving them out to the mountains, making them, and coming back to sleep in any available hotel bathtub in town." But Dean's criminality, we are told, "was not something that sulked and sneered; it was a wild yea-saying overburst of American joy; it was Western, the west wind, an ode from the Plains, something new, long prophesied, long a-coming (he only stole cars for joy rides)." And, in fact, the species of Bohemian that Kerouac writes about is on the whole rather law-abiding. In *The Subterraneans,* a bunch of drunken boys steal a pushcart in the middle of the night, and when they leave it in front of a friend's apartment building, he denounces them angrily for "screwing up the security of my pad." When Sal Paradise (in *On the Road*) steals some groceries from the canteen of an itinerant workers' camp in which he has taken a temporary job as a barracks guard, he comments, "I suddenly began to realize that everybody in America is a natural-born thief"—which, of course, is a way of turning his own stealing into a bit of boyish prankishness. Nevertheless, Kerouac is attracted to criminality, and that in itself is more significant than the fact that he personally feels constrained to put the brakes on his own destructive impulses.

Sex has always played a very important role in Bohemianism: sleeping around was the Bohemian's most dramatic demonstration of his freedom from conventional moral standards, and a defiant denial of the idea that sex was permissible only in marriage and then only for the sake of a family. At the same time, to be "promiscuous" was to assert the validity of sexual experience in and for itself. The "meaning" of Bohemian sex, then, was at once social and personal, a crucial element in the Bohemian's ideal of civilization. Here again the contrast with Beat Generation Bohemianism is sharp. On the one hand, there is a fair amount of sexual activity in *On the Road* and *The Subterraneans*. Dean Moriarity is a "new kind of American saint" at least partly because of his amazing sexual power: he can keep three women satisfied simultaneously and he can make love any time, anywhere (once he mounts a girl in the back seat of a car while poor Sal Paradise is trying to sleep in front). Sal, too, is always on the make, and though he isn't as successful as the great Dean, he does pretty well: offhand I can remember a girl in Denver, one on a bus, and another in New York, but a little research would certainly unearth a few more. The heroine of *The Subterraneans*, a Negro girl named Mardou Fox, seems to have switched from one to another member of the same gang and back again ("This has been an incestuous group in its time"), and we are given to understand that there is nothing unusual about such an arrangement. But the point of all this hustle and bustle is not freedom from ordinary social restrictions or defiance of convention (except in relation to homosexuality, which is Ginsberg's preserve: among "the best minds" of Ginsberg's generation who were destroyed by America are those "who let themselves be —— in the —— by saintly motorcyclists, and screamed with joy, / who blew and were blown by those human seraphim, the sailors, caresses of Atlantic and Caribbean love"). The sex in Kerouac's books goes hand in hand with a great deal of talk about forming permanent relationships ("although I have a hot feeling sexually and all that for her," says the poet Adam Moorad in *The Subterraneans*, "I really don't want to get any further into her not only for these reasons but finally, the big one, if I'm going to get involved with a girl now I want to be permanent like permanent and serious and long termed and I can't do that with her"), and a habit of getting married and then duly divorced and re-married when another girl comes along. In fact, there are as many marriages and divorces in *On the Road* as in the Hollywood movie colony (must be that California climate): "All those years I was looking for the woman I wanted to marry," Sal Paradise tells us. "I couldn't meet a girl without saying to myself, What kind of wife would she make?" Even more revealing is Kerouac's refusal to admit that any of his characters ever make love wantonly or lecherously—no matter how casual the encounter it must always entail sweet feelings toward the girl. Sal, for example, is fixed up with Rita Bettencourt in Denver, whom he has never met before. "I got her in my bedroom after a long talk in the dark of the front room. She was a nice little girl,

simple and true [naturally], and tremendously frightened of sex. I told her it was beautiful. I wanted to prove this to her. She let me prove it, but I was too impatient and proved nothing. She sighed in the dark. 'What do you want out of life?' I asked, and I used to ask that all the time of girls." This is rather touching, but only because the narrator is really just as frightened of sex as that nice little girl was. He is frightened of failure and he worries about his performance. For *performance* is the point—performance and "good orgasms," which are the first duty of man and the only duty of woman. What seems to be involved here, in short, is sexual anxiety of enormous proportions—an anxiety that comes out very clearly in *The Subterraneans*, which is about a love affair between the young writer, Leo Percepied, and the Negro girl, Mardou Fox. Despite its protestations, the book is one long agony of fear and trembling over sex:

> I spend long nights and many hours making her, finally I have her, I pray for it to come, I can hear her breathing harder, I hope against hope it's time, a noise in the hall (or whoop of drunkards next door) takes her mind off and she can't make it and laughs—but when she does make it I hear her crying, whimpering, the shuddering electrical female orgasm makes her sound like a little girl crying, moaning in the night, it lasts a good twenty seconds and when it's over she moans, "O why can't it last longer," and "O when will I when you do?"—"Soon now I bet," I say, "you're getting closer and closer"—

Very primitive, very spontaneous, very elemental, very beat.

For the new Bohemians interracial friendships and love affairs apparently play the same role of social defiance that sex used to play in older Bohemian circles. Negroes and whites associate freely on a basis of complete equality and without a trace of racial hostility. But putting it that way understates the case, for not only is there no racial hostility, there is positive adulation for the "happy, true-hearted, ecstatic Negroes of America."

> At lilac evening I walked with every muscle aching among the lights of 27th and Welton in the Denver colored section, wishing I were a Negro, feeling that the best the white world had offered was not enough ecstasy for me, not enough life, joy, kicks, darkness, music, not enough night. . . . I wished I were a Denver Mexican, or even a poor overworked Jap, anything but what I was so drearily, a "white man" disillusioned. All my life I'd had white ambitions. . . . I passed the dark porches of Mexican and Negro homes; soft voices were there, occasionally the dusky knee of some mysterious sensuous gal; and dark faces of the men behind rose arbors. Little children sat like sages in ancient rocking chairs.

It will be news to the Negroes to learn that they are so happy and ecstatic; I doubt if a more idyllic picture of Negro life has been painted since certain Southern ideologues tried to convince the world that things were just as fine as fine could be for the slaves on the old plantation. Be that as it may, Kerouac's love for Negroes and other dark-skinned groups is tied up with his worship of primitivism, not with any radical social attitudes. Ironically enough, in fact, to see the Negro as more elemental than the white man, as Ned Polsky has acutely remarked, is "an inverted form of keeping the nigger in his place." But even if it were true that American Negroes, by virtue of their position in our culture, have been able to retain a degree of primitive spontaneity, the last place you would expect to find evidence of this is among Bohemian Negroes. Bohemianism, after all, is for the Negro a means of entry into the world of the whites, and no Negro Bohemian is going to cooperate in the attempt to identify him with Harlem or Dixieland. The only major Negro character in either of Kerouac's two novels is Mardou Fox, and she is about as primitive as Wilhelm Reich himself.

The plain truth is that the primitivism of the Beat Generation serves first of all as a cover for an anti-intellectualism so bitter that it makes the ordinary American's hatred of eggheads seem positively benign. Kerouac and his friends like to think of themselves as intellectuals ("they are intellectual as hell and know all about Pound without being pretentious or talking too much about it"), but this is only a form of newspeak. Here is an example of what Kerouac considers intelligent discourse—"formal and shining and complete, without the tedious intellectualness":

> We passed a little kid who was throwing stones at the cars in the road. "Think of it," said Dean. "One day he'll put a stone through a man's windshield and the man will crash and die—all on account of that little kid. You see what I mean? God exists without qualms. As we roll along this way I am positive beyond doubt that everything will be taken care of for us—that even you, as you drive, fearful of the wheel . . . the thing will go along of itself and you won't go off the road and I can sleep. Furthermore we know America, we're at home; I can go anywhere in America and get what I want because it's the same in every corner, I know the people, I know what they do. We give and take and go in the incredibly complicated sweetness zigzagging every side.

You see what he means? Formal and shining and complete. No tedious intellectualness. Completely unpretentious. "There was nothing clear about the things he said but what he meant to say was somehow made pure and clear." *Somehow.* Of course. If what he wanted to say had been carefully thought out and precisely articulated, that would have been tedious and pretentious and, no doubt, *somehow* unclear and clearly impure. But so long as he utters these banalities with his tongue tied and with no comprehension of their meaning, so long as he makes noises that come out of his soul (since they couldn't possibly have come out of his mind), he passes the test of true intellectuality.

Which brings us to Kerouac's spontaneous bop prosody. This "prosody" is not to be confused with bop language itself, which has such a limited vocabulary (Basic English is a verbal treasure-house by comparison) that you couldn't write a note to the milkman in it, much less a novel. Kerouac, however, manages to remain true to the spirit of hipster slang while making forays into enemy territory (i.e., the English language) by his simple inability to express anything in words. The only method he has of describing an object is to summon up the same half-dozen adjectives over and over again: "greatest," "tremendous," "crazy," "mad," "wild," and perhaps one or two others. When it's more than just mad or crazy or wild, it becomes "really mad" or "really crazy" or "really wild." (All quantities in excess of three, incidentally, are subsumed under the rubric "innumerable," a word used innumerable times in *On the Road* but not so innumerably in *The Subterraneans.*) The same poverty of resources is apparent in those passages where Kerouac tries to handle a situation involving even slightly complicated feelings. His usual tactic is to run for cover behind cliché and vague signals to the reader. For instance: "I looked at him; my eyes were watering with embarrassment and tears. Still he stared at me. Now his eyes were blank and looking through me. . . . Something clicked in both of us. In me it was suddenly concern for a man who was years younger than I, five years, and whose fate was wound with mine across the passage of the recent years; in him it was a matter that I can ascertain only from what he did afterward." If you can ascertain what this is all about, either beforehand, during, or afterward, you are surely no square.

In keeping with its populistic bias, the style of *On the Road* is folksy and lyrical. The prose of *The Subterraneans,* on the other hand, sounds like an inept parody of Faulkner at his worst, the main difference being that Faulkner usually produces bad writing out of an impulse to inflate the commonplace while Kerouac gets into trouble by pursuing "spontaneity." Strictly speaking, spontaneity is a quality of feeling, not of writing: when we call a piece of writing spontaneous, we are registering our impression that the author hit upon the right words without sweating, that no "art" and no calculation entered into the picture, that his feelings seem to have spoken themselves, seem to have sprouted a tongue at the moment of composition. Kerouac apparently thinks that spontaneity is a matter of saying whatever comes into your head, in any order you happen to feel like saying it. It isn't the *right* words he wants (even if he knows what they might be), but the first words, or at any rate the words that most obviously announce themselves as deriving from emotion rather than cerebration, as coming from "life" rather than "literature," from the guts rather than the brain. (The brain, remember, is the angel of death.) But writing that springs easily and "spontaneously" out of strong feelings is *never* vague; it always has a quality of sharpness and precision because it is in the nature of strong feelings to be aroused by specific objects. The notion that a diffuse, generalized, and unrelenting enthusiasm is the mark of great sensitivity and responsiveness is utterly fantastic, an idea that comes from taking drunkenness or drug-addiction as the state of perfect emotional vigor. The effect of such enthusiasm is actually to wipe out the world altogether, for if a filling station will serve as well as the Rocky Mountains to arouse a sense of awe and wonder, then both the filling station and the mountains are robbed of their reality. Kerouac's conception of feeling is one that only a solipsist could believe in—and a solipsist, be it noted, is a man who does not relate to anything outside himself.

Solipsism is precisely what characterizes Kerouac's fiction. *On the Road* and *The Subterraneans* are so patently autobiographical in content that they become almost impossible to discuss as novels; if spontaneity were indeed a matter of destroying the distinction between life and literature, these books would unquestionably be It. "As we were going out to the car Babe slipped and fell flat on her face. Poor girl was overwrought. Her brother Tim and I helped her up. We got in the car; Major and Betty joined us. The sad ride back to Denver began." Babe is a girl who is mentioned a few times in the course of *On the Road;* we don't know why she is overwrought on this occasion, and even if we did it wouldn't matter, since there is no reason for her presence in the book at all. But Kerouac tells us that she fell flat on her face while walking toward a car. It is impossible to believe that Kerouac made this detail up, that his

imagination was creating a world real enough to include wholly gratuitous elements; if that were the case, Babe would have come alive as a human being. But she is only a name; Kerouac never even describes her. She is in the book because the sister of one of Kerouac's friends was there when he took a trip to Central City, Colorado, and she slips in *On the Road* because she slipped that day on the way to the car. What is true of Babe who fell flat on her face is true of virtually every incident in *On the Road* and *The Subterraneans*. Nothing that happens has any dramatic reason for happening. Sal Paradise meets such-and-such people on the road whom he likes or (rarely) dislikes; they exchange a few words, they have a few beers together, they part. It is all very unremarkable and commonplace, but for Kerouac it is always the greatest, the wildest, the most. What you get in these two books is a man proclaiming that he is *alive* and offering every trivial experience he has ever had in evidence. Once I did this, once I did that (he is saying) and by God, it *meant* something! Because I *responded!* But if it meant something, and you responded so powerfully, why can't you explain what it meant, and why do you have to insist so?

I think it is legitimate to say, then, that the Beat Generation's worship of primitivism and spontaneity is more than a cover for hostility to intelligence; it arises from a pathetic poverty of feeling as well. The hipsters and hipster-lovers of the Beat Generation are rebels, all right, but not against anything so sociological and historical as the middle class or capitalism or even respectability. This is the revolt of the spiritually underprivileged and the crippled of soul—young men who can't think straight and so hate anyone who can; young men who can't get outside the morass of self and so construct definitions of feeling that exclude all human beings who manage to live, even miserably, in a world of objects; young men who are burdened unto death with the specially poignant sexual anxiety that America—in its eternal promise of erotic glory and its spiteful withholding of actual erotic possibility—seems bent on breeding, and who therefore dream of the unattainable perfect orgasm, which excuses all sexual failures in the real world. Not long ago, Norman Mailer suggested that the rise of the hipster may represent "the first wind of a second revolution in this century, moving not forward toward action and more rational equitable distribution, but backward toward being and the secrets of human energy." To tell the truth, whenever I hear anyone talking about instinct and being and the secrets of human energy, I get nervous; next thing you know he'll be saying that violence is just fine, and then I begin wondering whether he really thinks that kicking someone in the teeth or sticking a knife between his ribs are deeds to be admired. History, after all—and especially the history of modern times—teaches that there is a close connection between ideologies of primitivistic vitalism and a willingness to look upon cruelty and blood-letting with complacency, if not downright enthusiasm. The reason I bring this up is that the spirit of hipsterism and the Beat Generation strikes me as the same spirit which animates the young savages in leather jackets who have been running amuck in the last few years with their switch-blades and zip guns. What does Mailer think of those wretched kids, I wonder? What does he think of the gang that stoned a nine-year-old boy to death in Central Park in broad daylight a few months ago, or the one that set fire to an old man drowsing on a bench near the Brooklyn waterfront one summer's day, or the one that pounced on a crippled child and orgiastically stabbed him over and over and over again even after he was good and dead? Is that what he means by the liberation of instinct and the mysteries of being? Maybe so. At least he says somewhere in his article that two eighteen-year-old hoodlums who bash in the brains of a candy-store keeper are murdering an institution, committing an act that "violates private property"—which is one of the most morally gruesome ideas I have ever come across, and which indicates where the ideology of hipsterism can lead. I happen to believe that there is a direct connection between the flabbiness of American middle-class life and the spread of juvenile crime in the 1950's, but I also believe that juvenile crime can be explained partly in terms of the same resentment against normal feeling and the attempt to cope with the world through intelligence that lies behind Kerouac and Ginsberg. Even the relatively mild ethos of Kerouac's books can spill over easily into brutality, for there is a suppressed cry in those books: Kill the intellectuals who can talk coherently, kill the people who can sit still for five minutes at a time, kill those incomprehensible characters who are capable of getting seriously involved with a woman, a job, a cause. How can anyone in his right mind pretend that this has anything to do with private property or the middle class? No. Being for or against what the Beat Generation stands for has to do with denying that incoherence is superior to precision; that ignorance is superior to knowledge; that the exercise of mind and discrimination is a form of

death. It has to do with fighting the notion that sordid acts of violence are justifiable so long as they are committed in the name of "instinct." It even has to do with fighting the poisonous glorification of the adolescent in American popular culture. It has to do, in other words, with being for or against intelligence itself.

LEROI JONES (LETTER DATE SUMMER 1958)

SOURCE: Jones, LeRoi. Letter to the editor of *Partisan Review* 25, no. 3 (summer 1958): 472-3.

Jones, now known as Amiri Baraka, is a playwright and author. He was the host of frequent Beat author gatherings and is considered an important associate of the movement. In the following letter, he responds to the scathing indictment of the Beats written by Norman Podhoretz and published in the preceding edition of the Partisan Review.

Sirs:

It would seem that Norman Podhoretz, in his article "The Know-Nothing Bohemians," objected more violently to certain instances of socio-ethical non-conformity in the Beat Generation than to its paucity of erudition, as the title of his essay states. It would also seem that his essay was less an attempt at objective literary criticism than it was a kind of ill-concealed rant. . . . Can it be that the Beat Generation's biggest would-be detractors are so taken up by the "violence and madness" which they seem to point out so readily as the exclusive content of Beat literature, that they find no room for the normal functions of literary criticism? . . .

If any of the so-called criticism of the so-called "Beat Generation" needs a rebuttal (or at least an examination of motives) it is Mr. Podhoretz's claim that this whole movement made him nervous. . . . "Next thing you know," Mr. Podhoretz says, "he'll be saying that violence is just fine." Well, that's just it. Violence *is* just fine. I don't mean that someone ought to walk up to Mr. Podhoretz and smack him down, but that this generation of writers must resort to violence in literature, a kind of violence that has in such a short time begun to shake us out of the woeful literary sterility which characterized the '40's, to pull us out of what Dudley Fitts called (in his review of William Meredith's new book of verse) "an impoverished time, so far as poetry is concerned."

. . . I have read a great many of these scathing rants that are being palmed off as objective critical studies of the "New Bohemianism," and almost without exception they have come from

Hal Chase, Jack Kerouac, Allen Ginsberg, and William Burroughs (left to right) in Morningside Heights near the Columbia University campus, circa 1944.

the small coterie of quasi-novelists or *New Yorker* suburban intellectual types of the late '40's and early '50's which represents so much of what Beat is a reaction against. It seems to me that Beat is less a movement than a reaction. It is a reaction against, let us say to start, fifteen years of sterile, unreadable magazine poetry: poetry, as Mr. Fitts said so well, that is "neogeorgian, preserved from the almost obligatory dullness of the Georgians by a mild freshness of invention and an agreeably disturbing wit." To my mind, this is not what poetry ought to be. And Beat is also a reaction against what Randall Jarrell calls "The Age of Criticism."

. . . There was neither Bohemianism nor any great intellectual rebellion in the '40's, and there was no poetry to speak of. (Poor Dylan Thomas carried the ball all by himself in England, and we all know what happened when eventually he did get to America.) The only persons that caused even a semblance of a literary stir were a few addlebrained individuals mumbling under their breaths something about "creative criticism." There was nothing but one great big void.

I respect Randall Jarrell, Robert Lowell, Karl Shapiro, Delmore Schwartz, John Berryman, Peter Viereck, George Barker, Stephen Spender, Louis Macniece, and others who were so representative

of what poetry was in the '40's, as well as Eberhart, Wilbur, Meredith, Merwin, Bishop, the Pack-Simpson bunch, etc., who represent the academically condoned poetry of the '50's. But I wish to say emphatically that from this entire group of poets (which represents almost twenty years of poetry) we have about five poems of note. . . .

The Beat Generation, while not a movement as such, is a definite reaction to the void [of the '40's]. To deny the obvious immaturity and ingenuous quality of a good bit of the literature of this reaction would be absurd, just as it would be to say that all the art of such a parallel movement as Dada was purposeful and valid. . . . As with Dada, Beat represents a line of departure rather than a concrete doctrine. And even if this departure never produces another poem as influential or controversial as Allen Ginsberg's "Howl," there is no doubt in my mind that it will produce better ones. The same is true of Kerouac's *On the Road*. It breaks new ground, and plants new seeds . . .

[Podhoretz] shows an ignorance about the whole of the Beat reaction. . . . Statements like "Kerouac's 'bop prosody' is not to be confused with bop language itself, which has such a limited vocabulary you couldn't write a note to the milkman in it, much less a novel" show not only a basic ignorance . . . of the role of bop language in our society, but also a complete inability to see its possible function in literature per se. To write a novel in bop language is not the point, no more than it was Shakespeare's *point* to write his plays in Elizabethan English. A novel, play, etc. is about people, the ideas of people, not about language. . . . Of course *On The Road* is unthinkable without bop language, just as *Hamlet* is unthinkable without Elizabethan English. If one thinks the hipster's language meaningless, perhaps it is not entirely the hipster's fault. . . . The point is that the language can be extended and enlivened by just such prosody as Kerouac's if we are not too snobbish to accept it.

Another of Mr. Podhoretz's misconceptions is his rather early-'30's middle class assumption that "Bohemianism, after all, is for the Negro a means of entry into the world of the whites, and no Negro Bohemian is going to cooperate in an attempt to identify him with Harlem or Dixieland": Harlem is today the veritable capitol city of the Black Bourgeoisie. The Negro Bohemian's flight from Harlem is not a flight from the world of color but the flight of any would-be Bohemian from what Mr. Podhoretz himself calls "the provinciality, philistinism and moral hypocrisy of American life." Dixieland . . . is to traditional jazz what Rock and Roll is to Blues, or Rhythm and Blues—a cheap commercial imitation. The Negro intellectual certainly has no responsibility either for or to it.

Finally, a statement like "The only art the new Bohemians have any use for is jazz" . . . borders on back alley polemics, not at all in the tradition of the "coherent, rational discourse" Mr. Podhoretz says he cherishes.

JACK KEROUAC (ESSAY DATE JUNE 1959)

SOURCE: Kerouac, Jack. "The Origins of the Beat Generation." *Playboy* 6, no. 6 (June 1959): 31-2, 42, 79.

In the following article, Kerouac outlines the evolution of the Beat Generation, citing key figures, events, and the origin of the moniker "Beat."

This article necessarily'll have to be about myself. I'm going all out.

That nutty picture of me on the cover of *On the Road* results from the fact that I had just gotten down from a high mountain where I'd been for two months completely alone and usually I was in the habit of combing my hair of course because you have to get rides on the highway and

all that and you usually want girls to look at you as though you were a man and not a wild beast but my poet friend Gregory Corso opened his shirt and took out a silver crucifix that was hanging from a chain and said "Wear this and wear it outside your shirt and don't comb your hair!" so I spent several days around San Francisco going around with him and others like that, to parties, arties, parts, jam sessions, bars, poetry readings, churches, walking talking poetry in the streets, walking talking God in the streets (and at one point a strange gang of hoodlums got mad and said "What right does he got to wear that?" and my own gang of musicians and poets told them to cool it) and finally on the third day *Mademoiselle* magazine wanted to take pictures of us all so I posed just like that, wild hair, crucifix, and all, with Gregory Corso, Allen Ginsberg and Phil Whalen, and the only publication which later did not erase the crucifix from my breast (from that plaid sleeveless cotton shirt-front) was *The New York Times,* therefore *The New York Times* is as beat as I am, and I'm glad I've got a friend. I mean it sincerely, God bless *The New York Times* for not erasing the crucifix from my picture as though it was something distasteful. As a matter of fact, who's *really* beat around here, I mean if you wanta talk of Beat as "beat down" the people who erased the crucifix are really the "beat down" ones and not *The New York Times,* myself, and Gregory Corso the poet. I am not ashamed to wear the crucifix of my Lord. It is because I am Beat, that is, I believe in beatitude and that God so loved the world that he gave his only begotten son to it. I am sure no priest would've condemned me for wearing the crucifix outside my shirt everywhere and *no matter where* I went, even to have my picture taken by *Mademoiselle.* So you people don't believe in God. So you're all big smart know-it-all Marxists and Freudians, hey? Why don't you come back in a million years and tell me all about it, angels?

Recently Ben Hecht said to me on TV "Why are you afraid to speak out your mind, what's wrong with this country, what is everybody afraid of?" Was he talking to me? And all he wanted me to do was speak out my mind *against* people, he sneeringly brought up Dulles, Eisenhower, the Pope, all kinds of people like that habitually he would sneer at with Drew Pearson, *against* the world he wanted, this is his idea of freedom, he calls it freedom. Who knows, my God, but that the universe is not one vast sea of compassion actually, the veritable holy honey, beneath all this show of personality and cruelty. In fact who knows but that it isn't the solitude of the oneness of the essence of everything, the solitude of the actual oneness of the unbornness of the unborn essence of everything, nay the true pure forever-hood, that big blank potential that can ray forth anything it wants from its pure store, that blazing bliss, *Mattivajrakaruna* the Transcendental Diamond Compassion! No, I want to speak *for* things, for the crucifix I speak out, for the Star of Israel I speak out, for the divinest man who ever lived who was a German (Bach) I speak out, for sweet Mohammed I speak out, for Buddha I speak out, for Lao-tse and Chuang-tse I speak out, for D. T. Suzuki I speak out . . . why should I attack what I love out of life. This is Beat. Live your lives out? Naw, *love* your lives out. When they come and stone you at least you won't have a glass house, just your glassy flesh.

That wild eager picture of me on the cover of *On the Road* where I look so Beat goes back much further than 1948 when John Clellon Holmes (author of *Go* and *The Horn*) and I were sitting around trying to think up the meaning of the Lost Generation and the subsequent Existentialism and I said "You know, this is really a beat generation" and he leapt up and said "That's it, that's right!" It goes back to the 1880s when my grandfather

Jean-Baptiste Kerouac used to go out on the porch in big thunderstorms and swing his kerosene lamp at the lightning and yell "Go ahead, go, if you're more powerful than I am strike me and put the light out!" while the mother and the children cowered in the kitchen. And the light never went out. Maybe since I'm supposed to be the spokes-man of the Beat Generation (I *am* the originator of the term, and around it the term and the generation have taken shape) it should be pointed out that all this "Beat" guts therefore goes back to my ancestors who were Bretons who were the most independent group of nobles in all old Europe and kept fighting Latin France to the last wall (although a big blond bosun on a merchant ship snorted when I told him my ancestors were Bretons in Cornwall, Brittany, "Why, we Wikings used to swoop down and steal your nets!") Breton, Wiking, Irishman, Indian, madboy, it doesn't make any difference, there is no doubt about the Beat Generation, at least the core of it, being a swinging group of new American men intent on joy . . . Irresponsibility? Who wouldn't help a dy-ing man on an empty road? No and the Beat Generation goes back to the wild parties my father used to have at home in the 1920s and 1930s in New England that were so fantastically loud nobody could sleep for blocks around and when the cops came they always had a drink. It goes back to the wild and raving childhood of playing the Shadow under windswept trees of New England's gleeful autumn, and the howl of the Moon Man on the sandbank until we caught him in a tree (he was an "older" guy of 15), the maniacal laugh of certain neighborhood madboys, the furi-ous humor of whole gangs playing basketball till long after dark in the park, it goes back to those crazy days before World War II when teenagers drank beer on Friday nights at Lake ballrooms and worked off their hangovers playing baseball on Saturday afternoon followed by a dive in the brook—and our fathers wore straw hats like W. C. Fields. It goes back to the completely senseless babble of the Three Stooges, the ravings of the Marx Brothers (the tenderness of Angel Harpo at harp, too).

It goes back to the inky ditties of old cartoons (Krazy Kat with the irrational brick)—to Laurel and Hardy in the Foreign Legion—to Count Dracula and his *smile* to Count Dracula shivering and hissing back before the Cross—to the Golem horrifying the persecutors of the Ghetto—to the quiet sage in a movie about India, unconcerned about the plot—to the giggling old Tao Chinaman trotting down the sidewalk of old Clark Gable

Shanghai—to the holy old Arab warning the hot-bloods that Ramadan is near. To the Werewolf of London a distinguished doctor in his velour smoking jacket smoking his pipe over a lamplit tome on botany and suddenly hairs grown on his hands, his cat hisses, and he slips out into the night with a cape and a slanty cap like the caps of people in breadlines—to Lamont Cranston so cool and sure suddenly becoming the frantic Shadow going mwee hee hee ha ha in the alleys of New York imagination. To Popeye the sailor and the Sea Hag and the meaty gunwales of boats, to Cap'n Easy and Wash Tubbs screaming with ecstasy over canned peaches on a cannibal isle, to Wimpy looking X-eyed for a juicy hamburger such as they make no more. To Jiggs ducking before a household of furniture flying through the air, to Jiggs and the boys at the bar and the corned beef and cabbage of old wood-fence noons—to King Kong his eyes looking into the hotel window with tender huge love for Fay Wray—nay, to Bruce Cabot in mate's cap leaning over the rail of a fog-bound ship saying "Come aboard." It goes back to when grapefruits were thrown at crooners and harvestworkers at bar-rails slapped burlesque queens on the rump. To when fathers took their sons to the Twi League game. To the days of Babe Callahan on the waterfront, Dick Barthelmess camping under a London street-lamp. To dear old Basil Rathbone looking for the Hound of the Baskervilles (a dog big as the Gray Wolf who will destroy Odin)—to dear old bleary Doctor Watson with a brandy in his hand. To Joan Crawford her raw shanks in the fog, in striped blouse smoking a cigarette at sticky lips in the door of the waterfront dive. To train whistles of steam engines out above the moony pines. To Maw and Paw in the Model A clanking on to get a job in California selling used cars making a whole lotta money. To the glee of America, the honesty of America, the honesty of oldtime grafters in straw hats as well as the honesty of old-time waiters in line at the Brooklyn Bridge in *Winterset*, the funny spitelessness of old bigfisted America like Big Boy Williams saying "Hoo? Hee? Huh?" in a movie about Mack Trucks and slidingdoor lunchcarts. To Clark Gable, his certain smile, his confident leer. Like my grandfather this America was invested with wild selfbelieving individuality and this had begun to disappear around the end of World War II with so many great guys dead (I can think of half a dozen from my own boyhood groups) when suddenly it began to emerge again, the hipsters began to appear gliding around saying "Crazy, man."

When I first saw the hipsters creeping around Times Square in 1944 I didn't like them either. One of them, Huncke of Chicago, came up to me and said "Man, I'm beat." I knew right away what he meant somehow. At that time I still didn't like bop which was then being introduced by Bird Parker and Dizzy Gillespie and Bags Jackson (on vibes), the last of the great swing musicians was Don Byas who went to Spain right after, but then I began . . . but earlier I'd dug all my jazz in the old Minton Playhouse (Lester Young, Ben Webster, Joey Guy, Charlie Christian, others) and when I first heard Bird and Diz in the Three Deuces I knew they were serious musicians playing a goofy new sound and didn't care what I thought, or what my friend Seymour thought. In fact I was leaning against the bar with a beer when Dizzy came over for a glass of water from the bartender, put himself right against me and reached both arms around both sides of my head to get the glass and danced away, as though knowing I'd be singing about him someday, or that one of his arrangements would be named after me someday by some goofy circumstance. Charlie Parker was spoken of in Harlem as the greatest new musician since Chu Berry and Louis Armstrong.

Anyway, the hipsters, whose music was bop, they looked like criminals but they kept talking about the same things I liked, long outlines of personal experience and vision, nightlong confessions full of hope that had become illicit and repressed by War, stirrings, rumblings of a new soul (that same old human soul). And so Huncke appeared to us and said "I'm beat" with radiant light shining out of his despairing eyes . . . a word perhaps brought from some midwest carnival or junk cafeteria. It was a new language, actually spade (Negro) jargon but you soon learned it, like "hung up" couldn't be a more economical term to mean so many things. Some of these hipsters were raving mad and talked continually. It was jazzy. Symphony Sid's all-night modern jazz and bop show was always on. By 1948 it began to take shape. That was a wild vibrating year when a group of us would walk down the street and yell hello and even stop and talk to anybody that gave us a friendly look. The hipsters had eyes. That was the year I saw Montgomery Clift, unshaven, wearing a sloppy jacket, slouching down Madison Avenue with a companion. It was the year I saw Charley Bird Parker strolling down Eighth Avenue in a black turtleneck sweater with Babs Gonzales and a beautiful girl.

By 1948 the hipsters, or beatsters, were divided into cool and hot. Much of the misunderstanding about hipsters and the Beat Generation in general today derives from the fact that there are two distinct styles of hipsterism: the cool today is your bearded laconic sage, or schlerm, before a hardly touched beer in a beatnik dive, whose speech is low and unfriendly, whose girls say nothing and wear black: the "hot" today is the crazy talkative shining eyed (often innocent and openhearted) nut who runs from bar to bar, pad to pad looking for everybody, shouting, restless, lushy, trying to "make it" with the subterranean beatniks who ignore him. Most Beat Generation artists belong to the hot school, naturally since that hard gem-like flame needs a little heat. In many cases the mixture is 50-50. It was a hot hipster like myself who finally cooled it in Buddhist meditation, though when I go in a jazz joint I still feel like yelling "Blow baby blow!" to the musicians though nowadays I'd get 86d for this. In 1948 the "hot hipsters" were racing around in cars like in *On the Road* looking for wild bawling jazz like Willis Jackson or Lucky Thompson (the early) or Chubby Jackson's big band while the "cool hipsters" cooled it in dead silence before formal and excellent musical groups like Lennie Tristano or Miles Davis. It's still just about the same, except that it has begun to grow into a national generation and the name "Beat" has stuck (though all hipsters hate the word).

The word "beat" originally meant poor, down and out, deadbeat, on the bum, sad, sleeping in subways. Now that the word is belonging officially it is being made to stretch to include people who do not sleep in subways but have a certain new gesture, or attitude, which I can only describe as a new *more*. "Beat Generation" has simply become the slogan or label for a revolution in manners in America. Marlon Brando was not really first to portray it on the screen. Dane Clark with his pinched Dostoievskyan face and Brooklyn accent, and of course Garfield, were first. The private eyes were Beat, if you will recall. Bogart. Lorre was Beat. In *M*, Peter Lorre started a whole revival, I mean the slouchy street walk.

I wrote *On the Road* in three weeks in the beautiful month of May 1941 while living in the Chelsea district of lower West Side Manhattan, on a 100-foot roll and put the Beat Generation in words in there, saying at the point where I am taking part in a wild kind of collegiate party with a bunch of kids in an abandoned miner's shack "These kids are great but where are Dean Moriarty and Carlo Marx? Oh well I guess they wouldn't belong in this gang, they're too *dark*, too strange, too subterranean and I am slowly beginning to join a new kind of *beat* generation." The manuscript of *Road* was turned down on the grounds that it would displease the sales manager of my publisher at that time, though the editor, a very intelligent man, said "Jack this is just like Dostoievsky, but what can I do at this time?" It was too early. So for the next six years I was a bum, a brakeman, a seaman, a panhandler, a pseudo-Indian in Mexico, anything and everything, and went on writing because my hero was Goethe and I believed in art and hoped some day to write the third part of *Faust*, which I have done in *Doctor Sax*. Then in 1952 an article was published in *The New York Times* Sunday magazine saying, the headline, "'This is a Beat Generation'" (in quotes like that) and in the article it said that I had come up with the term first "when the face was harder to recognize," the face of the generation. After that there was some talk of the Beat Generation but in 1955 I published an excerpt from *Road* (melling it with parts of *Visions of Neal*) under the pseudonym "Jean-Louis," it was entitled *Jazz of the Beat Generation* and was copyrighted as being an excerpt from a novel-in-progress entitled *Beat Generation* (which I later changed to *On the Road* at the insistence of my new editor) and so then the term moved a little faster. The term and the cats. Everywhere began to appear strange hepcats and even college kids went around hep and cool and using the terms I'd heard on Times Square in the early Forties, it was growing somehow. But when the publishers finally took a dare and published *On the Road* in 1957 it burst open, it mushroomed, everybody began yelling about a Beat Generation. I was being interviewed everywhere I went for "what I meant" by such a thing. People began to call themselves beatniks, beats, jazzniks, bopniks, bugniks and finally I was called the "avatar" of all this.

Yet it was as a Catholic, it was not at the insistence of any of these "niks" and certainly not with their approval either, that I went one afternoon to the church of my childhood (one of them), Ste. Jeanne d'Arc in Lowell, Mass., and suddenly with tears in my eyes and had a vision of what I must have really meant with "Beat" anyhow when I heard the holy silence in the church (I was the only one in there, it was five P.M., dogs were barking outside, children yelling, the fall leaves, the candles were flickering alone just for me), the vision of the word Beat as being to mean beatific . . . There's the priest preaching on Sunday morning, all of a sudden through a side door of the church comes a group of Beat Generation characters in strapped raincoats like the I.R.A. coming in silently to "dig" the religion . . . I knew it then.

But this was 1954, so then what horror I felt in 1957 and later 1958 naturally to suddenly see "Beat" being taken up by everybody, press and TV and Hollywood borscht circuit to include the "juvenile delinquency" shot and the horrors of a mad teeming billyclub New York and L.A. and they began to call *that* Beat, *that* beatific . . . bunch of fools marching against the San Francisco Giants protesting baseball, as if (now) in my name and I, my childhood ambition to be a big league baseball star hitter like Ted Williams so that when Bobby Thomson hit that homerun in 1951 I trembled with joy and couldn't get over it for days and wrote poems about how it is possible for the human spirit to win after all! Or, when a murder, a routine murder took place in North Beach, they labeled it a Beat Generation slaying although in my childhood I'd been famous as an eccentric in my block for stopping the younger kids from throwing rocks at the squirrels, for stopping them from frying snakes in cans or trying to blow up frogs with straws. Because my brother had died at the age of nine, his name was Gerard Kerouac, and he'd told me "Ti Jean never hurt any living being, all living beings whether it's just a little cat or squirrel or whatever, all, are going to heaven straight into God's snowy arms so never hurt anything and if you see anybody hurt anything stop them as best you can" and when he died a file of gloomy nuns in black from St. Louis de France parish had filed (1926) to his deathbed to hear his last words about Heaven. And my father too, Leo, had never lifted a hand to punish me, or to punish the little pets in our house, and this teaching was delivered to me by the men in my house and I have never had anything to do with violence, hatred, cruelty, and all that horrible nonsense which, nevertheless, because God is gracious beyond all human imagining, he will forgive in the long end . . . that million years I'm asking about you, America.

And so now they have beatnik routines on TV, starting with satires about girls in black and fellows in jeans with snapknives and sweatshirts and swastikas tattooed under their armpits, it will come to respectable m.c.s of spectaculars coming out nattily attired in Brooks Brothers jean-type tailoring and sweater-type pull-ons, in other words, it's a simple change in fashion and manners, just a history crust—like from the Age of Reason, from old Voltaire in a chair to romantic Chatterton in the moonlight—from Teddy Roosevelt to Scott Fitzgerald . . . So there's nothing to get excited about. Beat comes out, actually, of old American whoopee and it will only change a few dresses and pants and make chairs useless in the livingroom and pretty soon we'll have Beat Secretaries of State and there will be instituted new tinsels, in fact new reasons for malice and new reasons for virtue and new reasons for forgiveness . . .

But yet, but yet, woe, woe unto those who think that the Beat Generation means crime, delinquency, immorality, amorality . . . woe unto those who attack it on the grounds that they simply don't understand history and the yearnings of human souls . . . woe unto those who don't realize that America must, will, is, changing now, for the better I say. Woe unto those who believe in the atom bomb, who believe in hating mothers and fathers, who deny the most important of the Ten Commandments, woe unto those (though) who don't believe in the unbelievable sweetness of sex love, woe unto those who are the standard bearers of death, woe unto those who believe in conflict and horror and violence and fill our books and screens and livingrooms with all that crap, woe in fact unto those who make evil movies about the Beat Generation where innocent housewives are raped by beatniks! Woe unto those who are the real dreary sinners that even God finds room to forgive . . . woe unto those who spit on the Beat Generation, the wind'll blow it back.

THOMAS PARKINSON (ESSAY DATE 1961)

SOURCE: Parkinson, Thomas. "Phenomenon or Generation." In *A Casebook on the Beat*, pp. 276-90. New York: Thomas Y. Crowell Company, 1961.

In the following essay, Parkinson comments on the social and cultural implications of the Beat Generation, characterizing it as a "social refusal rather than a revolt."

When the beat writers emerged in 1956 they struck so responsive a chord that they became the most widely discussed phenomenon of the late 1950's. If they represented a "generation," they replaced a remarkably short-lived and little-lamented "silent generation" which had dominated the first five years of the 1950's. Even in the accelerated pace of twentieth-century living, two generations per decade rather crowds things. Whether they represented an entire generation or a spasm of revulsion, the beat writers attained symbolic status, as did the until-then little-remarked Bohemian communities of New York's Greenwich Village and San Francisco's North Beach. When the San Francisco columnist Herb Caen dubbed the members of current Bohemia "beatniks," the derisive appellation stuck. Beatnik life became a subject of general interest, and that special nexus of jazz, Buddhism, homosexuality, drugs, and squalor was graphed and discussed in a wide range of media that reached a large audience.

It was easy to deride the nonconformist existentialist costumes, the sheer unpleasantness of texture in the dreary fakeries of beatnik art, and no one could defend the aimless self-destructiveness and occasional pointless criminality of conduct. But two basic problems were not so easily dismissed. The first was the genuine vigor and force of Allen Ginsberg and Jack Kerouac, the extraordinary wit and hilarity of Lawrence Ferlinghetti and Gregory Corso, the obvious intelligence, learning, and decency of Gary Snyder and Philip Whalen, the hard integrity of Michael Mc-Clure—in short, the simple literary expertise of several gifted writers who participated in many of the excitements and obsessions of current Bohemia. The second problem, essentially social, was how to estimate the importance of this extra-official mode of life. Was it spindrift or the point of an iceberg, this sudden revelation of resentment and bad feeling? Was it American Bohemia newly garbed, new beatnik being old bum writ bold? One commentator closed his very unfriendly article with somber tone: "A hundred million squares must ask themselves: 'What have we done to deserve this?'" A hundred million seems a modest estimate, but whatever the census, the refrain of puzzled commentators was a steady and repeated "What's wrong?" To many people the chief force of the beat movement was the suggestion that all was not well with our unrivaled happiness.

If not puzzled, commentators were pleased to see that the tradition of revolt was not dead, and many a patronizing phrase approved of youth having its fling. A surprising number of people seemed to assume that rebellion per se, whatever its means or ultimate goal, is a good thing. After ten years of literary dandies carefully machining their Fulbright poems in a social atmosphere of cold war and general stuffiness, the beats were welcomed. What troubled the most tolerantly disposed critics, however, was the refusal of beat and beatnik to play their proper social role. Their elders had a hazy rosy memory of their own daring youth in which they had been true radicals,

that is, left New Dealers relatively active in political affairs. To their sense of things, the true rebel might take his origins in blank resentment of the world, but he went on to formulate his motives in terms of some ideal mode of social organization. But the beat movement simply denied the role of social critic and took an indifferent and passive posture before the problems of the world. Fallout, population, medical care, legal justice, civil rights—the beats were concerned actively with these problems when they impinged on the printing of books with certain taboo words, or on the problems of dope addicts cut off from their source of supply, or on the rights of poets to say slanderous things about policemen. Otherwise their approach was sardonic, apocalyptic, or impudent.

With very few exceptions, the beat and beatnik compose a social refusal rather than a revolt: as Allen Ginsberg announced to his audience in Chile, he is a rebel, not a revolutionist. They take no particular pleasure in tearing down a social fabric that they see as already ruined, and their attitude toward society is suspicious and evasive rather than destructive. When their attitude becomes destructive, the result is pointless antisocial acts; they then cease to be beat and become unemployed delinquents. Many beatniks are college students who, after two or more years of college, are not certain that they intend to go on into the business and professional worlds that swallow up the graduates of American colleges and universities. So they take a year off and loaf and invite their souls on Grant Avenue or Bleecker Street or the Left Bank. Some find the atmosphere so congenial that they linger through several years, and a few of them become permanent Bohemians. In such an atmosphere the tone is naturally anti-academic and antiofficial.

In this sense the beatnik world is a continuation of the Bohemian world already familiar to observers of American life. The beats are differentiated from past Bohemians by their religiosity (Zen Buddhism, Christ-as-beatnik with sandals and beard), experimental interest in hallucinogenic drugs and occasional dabbling in addictive drugs, proximity to criminality (largely through association with drugs), and fascination with moral depravity for its own sake. The traditional antidomesticity of the Bohemian world is still prevalent, as well as the concomitant relaxation of sexual mores in this predominantly male society.

The differences between the intellectual and religious concerns of current Bohemia and those of the 1920s or 1930s are modes of differentiating the attitudes of those eras from our own. It seems to me fairly plain that American Bohemia in reacting against suburbia tends to produce a reverse image of the society that makes the hydrogen bomb, throws its money around an idiot frenzy, and refuses to vote for school bonds; the same moral flaccidity, the same social irresponsibility, the same intellectual fraudulence operate throughout the two worlds that are, finally, not opposed. Freud in the 1920s meant sexual liberation, whereas psychoanalysis in Bohemia and suburbia in the 1950s was primarily a mode of keeping going. The borderline between beatnik and psychiatric patient shifts constantly, claiming one and releasing another, and a surprising number of people in current Bohemia are under psychiatric care. This in turn reflects the rising commitment rate of American mental hospitals and the steady increase in the numbers of people seeking psychiatric aid so that they can continue their business and professional life. The indifference toward politics exhibited by Bohemia is matched by the neglect and cynicism of suburbia. The beatnik contempt for simple comfort and cleanliness is the counterpart of mindless possessiveness, status-seeking, and other elaborate forms of greed.

It would be easy to multiply points of comparison: the gray flannel suit and the existentialist costume, the smiling religious purveyor of togetherness and the egotism of Christ-as-beatnik, ranch house and pad, cocktails and marijuana. But it was not merely the direct parody that attracted so much attention; rather, the illusion of community promoted by the hip jargon, the agreed values, the common rites, and relaxed tone—this was the chief source of attraction and interest. What was sought by commentator and reader alike was a way of life that would answer their feeling of pointlessness and guilt in looking at their own unrewarding accumulation of commodities. The beatniks not only evaded a society that, even its friendliest critics are quick to admit, has lost all community of motive; they went further and created an impenetrable community that turned the well-adjusted member of suburbia into a frustrated outsider. They shaped a way of life at once public and arcane. No wonder that the spectacle of Grant Avenue has produced so many dances of uncomprehending rage.

And yet is it not pathetic that the alternatives of American society should be posed in terms of Beatville and Squareville? If the beat and beatnik are the only answer to the wasteful cupidity of suburbia, then the country is in a very nasty spot. In truth, there is a vast fund of good sense and social responsibility in this country, and the only

problem is to allow its voice to be heard more clearly and loudly. And if a rebellion is necessary, it will be fostered by people who have a sense of commitment to the insulted and injured of the world, who feel and act on an ideal of human conduct that sponsors change in individual experience, and who do not waste their substance on pointless conformity and aimless complaint. Some of those people live in suburbia, some in Bohemia, and many of them just anywhere; they respond to and shape their environment, and from such responsible shaping come the seeds of community and, finally, civilization.

In talking about the social phenomenon of the beat and beatnik, I deliberately distinguished between the two terms. The term "beat" I take to be descriptive, and its primary reference is to a group of writers, especially, who participate in certain common attitudes and pursue common literary aims. They may use the beatnik milieu as their subject and their ideas and attitudes may be widely shared by current Bohemia. The beatnik, on the other hand, is either not an artist or an incompetent and nonproductive one. The beatnik provides the atmosphere and audience of Grant Avenue and analogous areas, and he is frequently an engaging person. He may write an occasional "poem," but he has no literary ambitions.

The beat writer, on the other hand, is serious and ambitious. He is usually well educated and always a student of his craft. Sometimes, as is the case with Gary Snyder, he is a very learned man, and his knowledge of literature and its history is dense and extensive. Allen Ginsberg's public posture on literary matters is that of an innocent who writes from impulse, but he knows better. And one of my objections to Lawrence Ferlinghetti is that he is much too literary in tone and reference. He writes for the man in the street, but he chooses a street full of *Nation* subscribers and junior-college graduates, that is, Grant Avenue. In fact, the only untutored writer of the lot is Gregory Corso, and in his work this is neither a merit nor a handicap. His stock in trade is impertinence, and he learned that out of his own impish nature.

The reception of the beat writers, the extraordinary interest taken in the novels of Kerouac, Ginsberg's little pamphlet of poems, Ferlinghetti's *Coney Island of the Mind* (which has sold over 40,000 copies), the San Francisco issue of *Evergreen Review* (entering its seventh printing), and the publicity accorded the beat way of life by national magazines—all this has passed into not only social history but also literary history. When Meridian Books put out its anthology of *New Poets of*

England and America in 1957, it included none of the beat writers and none of the writers of the San Francisco school and the Black Mountain group. Any anthology of recent poetry now appearing would practically have to include Ginsberg and Snyder, to say nothing of the nonbeat writers who have by accident been associated with them: William Everson (Brother Antoninus), Robert Creeley, Robert Duncan, Denise Levertov, Charles Olson, Kenneth Rexroth, and Jack Spicer, to name only those I take to be most distinguished.

The beat writers are not, in short, the only writers in America who live outside the universities and are not interested primarily in perpetuating the iambic line. This fact needs underlining, for one unhappy result of the publicity attendant on the rise of the beat was, simply, the tarring of all writers with experimental motives with the single brush *beat* or the further implications that the only valid experimental writers *were* beat. The terms "San Francisco Renaissance" (awakening would be more fitting) and "San Francisco writers," for instance, were cheerily applied to any writer who knew Allen Ginsberg or was published by Lawrence Ferlinghetti. As a matter of fact, only one of the writers on the City Lights list was even born in California. The writer in question is Robert Duncan, who is one of the best poets now writing in English and as nonbeat as a person can get.

The association of the beat writers with San Francisco is not entirely fortuitous. From about 1944 on, the area has been distinguished by considerable artistic activity, and during that period it was one of the strongholds of experimental poetry. There was a great deal of other literary activity, and I do not intend to depreciate the products of Stanford's writing program or of the Activist group associated with Lawrence Hart or the numerous writers who simply lived in the San Francisco Bay area because life was pleasant there or because they had jobs in the various colleges. But what especially distinguished writing in the Bay area was a group of people—mainly poets—who were interested in creating and establishing a community of literary interest. They were like coral insects building a reef that might ultimately create the calm and pleasure of a lagoon. They were interested in forming a culture rather than in shaping unimpeachable structures out of the detritus of a museum civilization. The poetry they wrote and liked was deeply religious in tone, personalist in dramaturgy, imagist in iconographic habit, and experimentalist in prosody. With this poetics was associated a loose cluster of concerns and attitudes—anarcho-pacifism in politics, rela-

tively conservative (especially Roman Catholic) religious preoccupations, a generally receptive attitude toward Eastern art and thought that grew naturally out of the Pacific Basin orientation of the great port of San Francisco, intensive interest in the traditions of European experimentalism, and perhaps above all a very deep elegiac sense of the destruction of both the natural world and the possibilities of the American dream (its waste in the great wars and the frozen polity of the postwar period) dramatized in the brutal exploitation of California as its population swelled. Whatever was wrong with the poetry written out of these basic concerns, it was not a poetry that refused to meet squarely the challenges of great subjects.

This was accompanied by a widespread feeling of poetic community that took its center in activities organized by Robert Duncan, George Leite, and Kenneth Rexroth. George Leite's *Circle* magazine appeared first in 1944, and from then until 1950 he published ten issues of work local and international in origin. Its closest analogue in that period was the British magazine *Now,* which included many of the same contributors, and though Leite's editorial taste was far from infallible, the level of achievement was often very high. Some of his contributors—Henry Miller, Kenneth Rexroth, Josephine Miles, George P. Elliott, Robert Duncan, Brother Antoninus—have come to be well-known figures in current American letters, and a surprising number of his other contributors have been consistently productive. The attitudes that *Circle* espoused, both political and aesthetic, were hardly what could be called generally acceptable, and the magazine embodied the blithe indifference to the official culture that marked the early or postwar stages of the San Francisco Renaissance.

During the period of *Circle*'s publication, Berkeley and San Francisco woke from their literary sleep of years. The chief figure in this awakening was Kenneth Rexroth. He was a poet nationally known at the time, printed by Macmillan and New Directions, and one of James Laughlin's advisors at the latter publishing house. He was interesting, well informed, friendly to the young. He gave the impression of truly patriarchal longevity. I said to him once that I had lost all my illusions about the Soviet Union at the time of the Finnish war. He said, "That just shows how young you are. I lost *my* illusions with the Kronstadt Rebellion." It was only much later that I came to realize that at the time of the rebellion he was fifteen years old, for he gave the impression that he had turned his back on Lenin with sorrow and withdrawn his counsel from the baby Soviet republics, leaving them to stumble on into disaster. He had a trick of imaginative projection that allowed him to suggest he was a contemporary of Lenin, Whitman, Tu Fu, Thoreau, Catullus, Baudelaire, John Stuart Mill—they were all so real to him. The amount of labor and confusion that he saved younger people was immense; one could be painfully working his way out of Dublin Catholicism, and he would talk of Buber or Lao-Tzu. Or with difficulty one could be moving toward understanding of his locale, and he would make some casual statement about Pacific Basin culture, adducing Morris Graves as exemplar. It would be easy to multiply instances. His recent collection of essays—*Bird in the Bush*—gives some idea of the range of his interests and talk.

Beyond his work as poet and critic, Rexroth organized discussion groups at his home, chiefly on political subjects though he conducted some literary seminars. He was certainly one of the best close readers of texts that I have ever encountered, and his technical knowledge of verse was wide, detailed, exact. I stress this because he has insisted recently on the indifference of such analysis to the study and writing of verse ("I write poetry to seduce women and overthrow the capitalist system"), and the record should be clarified. Chiefly, however, the discussions were political and religious with literary figures (Lawrence, Blake, Yeats) seen in the perspective of Schweitzer, Buber, Berdyaev, Kropotkin, Emma Goldman, Toynbee, Gill, Boehme, Thoreau, Gandhi—the list could be extended indefinitely. When poetry was discussed directly, it tended to be French poetry since Apollinaire or the most recent British poetry; he was at that time engaged in his extensive translations from Léon-Paul Fargue, Cros, Carcot, Milosz, Desnos, Reverdy and in editing his anthology of British poetry since Auden. In addition to various poets and ordinary people, the discussions were attended by many of the conscientious objectors who after the war migrated in large numbers to the Bay area and had much to do with establishing the range of intellectual interest. For example, many of the founders of the famous listener-sponsored radio station KPFA-B (with branches now in Los Angeles and New York) were among the participants, and now that the station has become more staid and respectable, it is practically forgotten that the title of its governing board—Pacifica Foundation—was not a geographical but an intellectual designation.

In Berkeley too, partly because of the sudden upsurge of enrollment at the University of Califor-

nia after the war, there was a great deal of extra-academic literary activity. *Circle* was published there, and Bern Porter brought out some individual books of poetry. Robert Duncan, however, was most instrumental in organizing discussions and readings of poetry, and he was the first person in the Bay area who gave large-scale public poetry readings. These readings drew on the large and relatively mature postwar student body at the university for audience. As one sour witness put it, every clique must have its claque. Very true, but the extraordinary thing about the poets was their very great variety, their degree of disagreement. Through the poetry readings in Berkeley and San Francisco and—when it began operation in 1949—over KPFA, a fairly large audience was created that accepted and took interest in poetry readings.

From about 1950 to 1953, there was a period of dispersal when this embryonic literary community developed no further, and it was with the opening of the Poetry Center at San Francisco State College that poetry in the Bay area entered its most recent phase, in which the beat writers were involved. Through the Poetry Center, Mrs. Ruth Witt-Diamant brought to the area most of the important poets of the Anglo-American world, and it was largely because of the generosity of W. H. Auden that she was able to start this always precarious enterprise. Through her hard, thankless labor, a fixed center was established for poetry readings where widely recognized poets could be heard and young poets only emerging could get an immediate audience. As the writers associated earlier with the area began drifting back from their travels, things began to quicken again, and a newly emergent group of younger writers revived the earlier excitements. There were continuities between the by-now older poets and the younger, so that Michael McClure was in some ways a disciple of Robert Duncan, and Gary Snyder and Phil Whalen took much of their poetic method from Kenneth Rexroth. Duncan, through his association with Black Mountain College and his participation (by contributing) in *Origin*, helped to bring to the attention of the writers of the area the work of Charles Olson, Robert Creeley, and Denise Levertov; and Rexroth, who remained tirelessly interested in and receptive to experimental writing of all kinds, also kept people informed of the new and as yet generally unknown.

In other words, when Lawrence Ferlinghetti came to San Francisco in 1953 and Allen Ginsberg in 1954, they were not entering a cultural void, even restricting the sense of culture to experimental writing. It seems to me fruitless to argue whether writing in the San Francisco area has been notably original, just as it is fruitless to ask whether the San Francisco painters are really separable from the main currents of recent painting. In both instances it seems more useful to consider the quality of work produced and the extent to which the producers of the art learned from each other. In both painting and poetry, it seems to me perfectly clear that there *are* San Francisco schools, that is, significant groups of artists who have learned from each other profitably and have produced work capable of competing on equal terms with work produced in other cultural centers. In painting—David Park, Elmer Bischoff, Ernie Briggs, Sam Francis, Richard Diebenkorn, Clyfford Still; in poetry—Brother Antoninus, Robert Duncan, Michael McClure, Kenneth Rexroth, Jack Spicer, Gary Snyder, Phil Whalen. Naturally all these artists have affinities with painters or writers from other parts of the world, and it is for this reason that their names are often associated with those of artists with whom they have nothing in particular to do.

When the beat writers came to the San Francisco area, then, they found a sounding board, so that Allen Ginsberg wrote "Howl" and related poems only after moving out to the West Coast and read it first to Bay area audiences. The audience and structure of public address were there, and the literary atmosphere was receptive. Snyder, Whalen, and McClure, who were in effect a second wave of the Bay area awakening, joined forces with him, and when first Kerouac and later Corso made the trip, they also found an amiable reception. The presence of Lawrence Ferlinghetti as publisher also provided an outlet for at least Ginsberg and Corso, and so another phase in the literary life of the San Francisco area began.

In giving the historical background to the association of the beat writers with San Francisco, I am not trying to depreciate the personal role played by Allen Ginsberg in revivifying the poetic life of the Bay area. Too little stressed in all the public talk about Ginsberg are his personal sweetness and gentleness of disposition. He was a person more cohesive than disruptive in impact, and it was largely through his personal qualities, his extraordinary abilities as reader of his own verse, and his genuinely selfless dedication that the sense of literary community was again established. And he wrote well. In spite of all the miscellaneous demurs against "Howl," it still stands as a moving and important poem, and I suspect that it will hold up for a long time. And

Lawrence Ferlinghetti, with his quiet easiness of manner, his very great skill as public reader, and his persistent courage, was a force of equal importance and pertinacity. It takes nothing from either of them to say they were supported by an environment that, in turn, they changed. Their great contribution was in the expression of new motives and their creation—or recognition—of a new audience. The singular force of the beat writers is manifest in the fact that they did not merely reflect the audience of American Bohemia; they substantially altered that audience, and in so doing they liberated and clarified motives until then only imperfectly realized. The intensity of reaction to their work indicates that the motives embodied in Kerouac's *On the Road* and *The Subterraneans* strike some sensitive hidden nerve that is more important than, before the appearance of those works, many had cared to admit.

I have taken such historical pains because there are two confusions that I think should be unraveled. First, the best experimental poetry in the United States is not necessarily beat, any more than the beatnik pattern of conduct is the only valid response to the life of the organization man. Second, the beat writers, with the exception of McClure, Snyder, and Whalen, are all easterners whose relations with northern California are either fugitive or nonexistent. A person moving from the Left Bank to Greenwich Village to North Beach is not leaving home but is remaining in a basically constant society. The scene changes but the emotional milieu is fixed, existentialist costumes, jazz, and all. When Kerouac writes of the West Coast, he does so with a tourist's eye; it is all copy, raw material to be exploited, not substantial. No one objects to this seriously, but it is a little annoying to Californians to hear William Burroughs described as a San Francisco writer when he has not, so far as I know, ever set foot in the state. It is all the more annoying when the result is a distortion of historical fact that muddies waters.

More important than such minor pique, however, is the question of the association of all experimental writing with the beat movement. What happened in 1956 when the national news media became aware of the beat writers was a taking off of the lid. Laments had been issued because of the dullness and sameness of American poetry, and as the cold war thawed, there seemed room for a little more freewheeling treatment of experience. At the same time, there was no reason for taking such a matter too far, and the beats were suited for a surprisingly moderate role. They presented a spectacle of a romantically dark community that repelled and attracted, that satisfied and thrilled without inviting. It was possible to feel at once sympathetic, envious, and superior to the way of life they embodied. So too with the writing; if this was all that existed outside the finicky preciousness of the dandy and the plodding wholesomeness of the women's magazines, who could seek or be interested in a change of intellectual diet? In effect, it was possible to talk their work to death by considering only their odd habits, and since their contempt for the intellect preserved them from any rational critical self-defense, they could become figures of derisive fun. The fact that Gregory Corso publicly boasted that he has never combed his hair has led to the belief that he could not then have taken much care with his poetry. The quality of the work could then remain unexamined.

Of the writers represented in this casebook, several seem to me important figures, not merely as social phenomena but as literary artificers of some accomplishment. The best comments on "Howl" are probably those made by Kenneth Rexroth and Mark Schorer during the obscenity trial, and they suggest its remarkable qualities quite clearly. I have always felt that Ginsberg is the genuine article, and if he keeps on writing he will probably become a very important poet. Both he and Ferlinghetti are extremely gifted readers—entertainers—and they have been extraordinarily effective in bringing poetry to a widened audience.

A certain amount of ironic comment has been made on the importance of oral delivery and the writer's physical dramatic presence to the full impact of the poetry of Ginsberg and Ferlinghetti. Their poetry, and that of McClure and Whalen (and Snyder, to a lesser extent), attempts notation of the actual movement of mind and voice in full vernacular. It seems difficult to take this poetry off the page largely because the mode of poetic notation that fits the movement of American speech is still in the realm of the nonconventionalized. Accustomed to syllabic, stress and foot verse, the normal audience for poetry is not prepared to take into consideration intensity (loudness), pitch, and duration, and the concept of breath pause is far from being ritualized. The usual prosodic assumption is that the precise notation so readily accepted for music is not possible for poetry, that poetry will have to bumble along with concepts that more or less fit the products of another tone and tempo of speech. This seems to me predicated on a happy combination of ignorance and lazi-

ness, ignorance of the past and laziness in the face of actual problems of current experience. The primary problem of poetry is notation, through the appearance of poem on page to indicate the reality of articulation. A poem is a score.

Looked on in this way, much of the notation of this poetry ceases to seem odd or frivolous. The capital letters, the broken lines, the long long long lines, the shift from vernacular idiom to lofty rhetoric, these are attempts to shift from conventional idiom to actual, to increase the vocality of the verse. The experiments with jazz accompaniment are more dramatic instances of the stress on precision of notation.

Related to the concept of vocality that underlies much of this poetry and brings it over into the world of performance and entertainment is the concept of intimacy that affects both prose and poetry. The beat poet is best considered as a voice, the beat prose writer as an active revery. Into this revery come past and present, but the revery is chiefly preoccupied with keeping up with the process unfolding outside and inside the narrator. Hence the long sentences, endlessly attempting to include the endless, the carelessness—even negligence—with the ordinary rules of grammatical function, so that noun, adjective, and verb interchange roles; after all, if the process is endlessly unpredictable and unfixed, grammatical categories are not relevant. It is a syntax of aimlessly continuing pleasure in which all elements are "like." Release, liberation from fixed categories, hilarity—it is an ongoing prose that cannot be concerned with its origins. There are no origins and no end, and the solid page of type without discriminations is the image of life solidly continuous without discriminations in value, and yet incomplete because it is literally one damned thing after another with no salvation or cease. There are no last things in this prose whereas the very division of experience into lines compels the discrimination of element from element. Even a poetic catalogue, which is by definition one thing after another, moves in blocks which have weight, and even if each unit weighs the same, the total weight increases with each succeeding integer. Not so in prose, the only limits coming from the size of the page. The ideal book by a writer of beat prose would be written on a single string of paper, printed on a roll, and moving endlessly from right to left, like a typewriter ribbon.

Is there anything especially new about this sense of endlessness in prose or of vocal notation in poetry? *Finnegans Wake* and Molly Bloom's soliloquy at the close of *Ulysses* could also be printed on a ribbon without violating James Joyce's intention, and the classical experimental poetry of the twentieth century had as one chief aim the kind of precise notation that I have suggested as a major motive in beat poetry. There is nothing new under the sun, even the American sun, granted, but this would not disturb the beat writers. They are perfectly happy to place themselves in a tradition of experimental writing, and they are alert to the existence of writers they can claim as ancestors. They assume that this experimental tradition should be consolidated and extended, and they do not consider it as part of the conventional work of English writers. The experimental era could be looked on as an attempt to vivify the conventions of English verse and prose, that is, as extension of the normal performances of, say, Dickens and Tennyson, corrective to it, part of the loyal opposition. In this sense, it can be assimilated into the institution of literature as generally—that is, academically—understood, just as Blake can be memorialized in Westminster Abbey.

In another sense, the experimental writers destroyed convention in order to create a completely new way of looking at experience and cannot be assimilated into the existing institution. In this view, the aim of literary creation is not to enrich the tradition but to expose its poverty and irrelevance so that it can be swept aside in favor of a literature more responsive to the realities of experience. The question raised by this aim has wide implications, for education, for politics, for human understanding. I have heard William Carlos Williams say that the poet who invented a new measure, a new line, would change the world radically. The scientists at Alamagordo certainly did change the world, as did the biochemists who produced antibiotics, and the technicians working on increased automation. Whether a literature proportionate to technological change is in the process of being shaped is certainly a question worth asking. But by the same token, one might also ask whether this literature is not merely an expression of the hopelessness and consequent frivolity that affects a world shaken to its foundations as its population, power, and problems multiply.

These are fundamental questions that may be too large for the context of beat writing. In the history of American life and letters, the phenomenon of the beat may have been a spasm rather than a "generation," and the final importance of the movement will be seen only when a larger *œuvre* is available from its several writers. The test of literature is the knowledge it realizes, using knowledge in the fullest and least exclusive sense, and literature realizes knowledge by the labor of that intelligent love we think of as art. It may be an unfair comparison, but to read Theodore Dreiser after reading Jack Kerouac—Dreiser knew so much and had so intelligent a love of life and art that he could compose an image of an entire society. He established a norm for American writers, and it is against the measure of human force represented by Cowperwood, Witla, Carrie, Jennie Gerhardt, Lester Kane, and Clyde Griffiths that any claim to embodying an image for a generation has to be placed.

The image shaped by the beat writers is partial, but without it any sense of life in these post-atom bomb years is incomplete. The solution is not, as is often absurdly suggested, to add Bohemia to suburbia and divide by two, thus achieving a golden mean or a shabby compromise. The solution is to be, where you are, what you are, with such persistence and courage as can be called to life. The best of the beat writers exemplify precisely that state of secular grace. In this world of shifting conflicts the integrity of the person might not be enough, but without it, all else is lost.

OVERVIEWS AND GENERAL STUDIES

PETER O. WHITMER AND BRUCE VANWYNGARDEN (ESSAY DATE 1987)

SOURCE: Whitmer, Peter O., and Bruce VanWyngarden. "The Beat Begins." In *Aquarius Revisited: Seven Who Created the Sixties Counterculture that Changed America*, pp. 47-54. New York: Macmillan Publishing Company, 1987.

In the following essay, Whitmer and VanWyngarden provide character sketches of some of the personalities instrumental in developing the counterculture.

"L.A." I loved the way she said "L.A."; I love the way everybody says "L.A." on the Coast; it's their one and only golden town when all is said and done."

—Jack Kerouac, *On the Road*

Splitting the San Joaquin Valley north of Los Angeles is Route 5, running for 250 miles of eight-lane emptiness. The heat and haze obscure the mountains on either side. Few roads are more monotonous, more inviting to speed on, or more heavily patrolled by police. Your ego and superego debate loudly as the dashed lines in the asphalt become the pendulum swing of a hypnotist's watch.

Allen Ginsberg (top row, third from left) and fellow poets visit a poetry assemblage in Vancouver in 1963.

The only things to look at are oil wells, slowly pumping up and down. Many of the ugly devices have been covered by simple wooden cages, but a few are decorated with the festiveness of a Latin American bus. Some are painted emergency orange with black polka dots. Some are striped like zebras or have human figures painted at each end. And then there is *that* one painted black and red and white, with tail feathers attached to one end and wings painted on the middle. On top of the other, rocking end is a bright-red crest set above shiny black eyes and a long, sharp yellow beak. You can't miss it. It looks like a three-story-high woodpecker on Quaaludes.

Turning west at Lost Hills onto Route 46, away from the heat and toward the ocean, I find a wide, well-surfaced two-lane highway that traverses rolling cattle country as it heads toward the Tremblor Range. For nearly forty miles the road is almost perfectly straight; only two gradual turns break the monotony. In late September the days here are scorching, and the 105-degree temperature creates shimmering mirages.

The only place to stop before Paso Robles is Cholame, which consists of a Chevron station, a small restaurant, eight shade trees, and a myth that captured the world.

Stopping to put in twenty dollars worth of gas, I strike up a conversation with the attendant. He is a punker, with studded neck band and pumpkin-orange hair.

"What's the most common question you get asked by people stopping here," I ask above the endless ringing of the pump.

"Oh, I guess it'd be how hot it is," he replies.

"Other than that?"

"Well," he says, "then it'd have to be 'Why does the gas cost so much?'"

"What about what happened right down there, almost exactly thirty years ago," I say, pointing several hundred yards east of Aggie's Restaurant, to where James Dean was killed in a brutal head-on collision on September 30, 1955.

"Oh that . . . well, not that many ask about it." He shrugs. This latter information turned out to be completely contradicted by the waitress in Aggie's. The restaurant, with its hamburgers so thin they appear to have been sketched on the bun, serves as a virtual James Dean shrine. Perhaps those who know have no need to ask questions of gas station attendants.

* * *

A decade before James Dean began acting out the message and the rules of a new generation on the screen, Jack Kerouac, Allen Ginsberg, William Burroughs, and Norman Mailer had begun laying the foundation in their writing.

Jack Kerouac came to Columbia University in the fall of 1940, from the blue-collar mill town of Lowell, Massachusetts, on a football scholarship. By the time Allen Ginsberg entered Columbia in 1943, from Paterson, New Jersey, Kerouac had left formal education far behind. But the campus was a magnet, and after classes, the West End Bar was also. There, in June 1944, began a kind of social ripple effect. The first stone in the pond was Edie Parker, an art student at Columbia and Kerouac's live-in girlfriend. She was the daughter of a wealthy owner of a Grosse Pointe, Michigan, Buick dealership. Kerouac lived in her apartment when not at sea with the Merchant Marine or at home with his mother and terminally ill father.

The ripples quickly grew. Edie introduced Jack to Lucien Carr, who was taking art courses with her. In time, Edie's apartment became a focal point. Lucien brought over his dormmate, Allen Ginsberg, who was interested in Kerouac, having heard that he had already written "over a million words." After an initially rocky beginning, wherein Ginsberg's confused homosexuality sparred with Kerouac's confused heterosexuality, the two discovered they shared a vision of a new world.

Lucien Carr then brought into the circle a good friend of his from Saint Louis, who happened to be living in New York. William Burroughs wanted to find out from Kerouac how to go about getting papers for the Merchant Marine.

The ripples turned to splashes just before Christmas 1946. Justin Brierly, a Columbia grad as well as an attorney and high school counselor in Denver, Colorado, visited the campus in 1945 to see how his protégé, Hal Chase, was doing. He ended up like all the others, at Edie's, which in fact had become the archetype for the "crash pad." Brierly met the whole crowd, but he was most impressed by Kerouac, who was at that time typing the manuscript for his first book (great reviews, no sales), *The Town and the City*. What struck Brierly were the physical characteristics, manic energy level, and intellectual single-mindedness that Kerouac shared with Neal Cassady, a teenager he knew in Denver. Brierly was trying to counsel Cassady through a transition period between reform school (where he had been sent for stealing cars) and a possible formal education at Columbia.

When he returned to Denver, Brierly told Cassady about "the scene" at Columbia, and especially at Edie's apartment. Cassady decided he had to meet these "Ivy League poets, philosophers, and novelists." From Brierly's descriptions, it was Kerouac who intrigued him most; Cassady had a half brother whose part-Indian blood gave him the same coloring as Kerouac. His name was also Jack.

The wave of energy that Cassady injected into Edie's place when he first hit town was undeniable. Perhaps the fact that he was born in the backseat of his parents' car while they were driving through Salt Lake City may help to explain it. He was a high-powered, high-speed human dynamo who churned out schemes and thoughts and grandiose plans and who exuded a contagious sense of adventure, of life on the edge. Around him men's adrenaline pumped faster, young girls' nipples blushed, and married women worried over what ungodly form of trouble Cassady was going to drag their husbands into next. In the simplest of terms he was a benevolent sociopath, "benevolent" in that he was not a violent person, "sociopathic" in his lack of guilt over his compulsive car thefts (reportedly around five hundred—for joy riding) and insatiable sexual drive. He was a bigger-than-life, bicoastal, bisexual bigamist. He became a hero for two generations of counterculture: as Dean Moriarty in Kerouac's *On the Road* and, ten years later, as the manic, pill-popping driver of *Further*, Ken Kesey and the Merry Pranksters' magically painted bus.

Unlike Kerouac, Cassady never seemed to age. Kesey recalled him as "like a noisy, yappy little mutt dog—just always barking away, always underfoot. But lovable and entertaining as hell." Tim Leary's first contact with him was when Cassady made a surprise visit to Harvard after hearing from Allen Ginsberg of Leary's drug experiments. Leary recalls him as "the most horny, manic, chaotic fucker on earth. He would never slow down, let alone stop."

For young Jack Kerouac in the long days between his early vision and the fame that finally consumed him, Cassady served as student, muse, intellectual provocateur, literary stylist, and chauffeur nonpareil.

Cassady had read and loved the twenty-pound manuscript for *The Town and the City* that Kerouac carried around in an old leather bag for anyone to read—or publish. Back in Denver, Cassady would write letters to Kerouac (and later to Kesey), the style and content of which seemed to capture the essence of his manic, speedy view of the world; great, long kaleidoscope sentences that seemed to describe anything in mind or sight. One in particular was known as the "Joan Anderson Letter." It was written on Benzedrine and told a sordid tale of Cassady's life on skid row with a suicidal lover. Twenty-three thousand words of compressed volatility, it helped change Kerouac's writing from an imitative Thomas Wolfe style to the spontaneous, "sketching," jazzlike, write-as-you-see-and-feel prose that mirrored the driven emotionality of his generation. Kerouac felt that America in the 1950s was a vastly different, exponentially more complex place than it was before the war. Neal Cassady showed him that there was a different kind of life west of New York City—and how to record it.

Cassady's affect on Ginsberg was less definable. The two took to each other instantly, talking philosophy and poetry and becoming lovers almost overnight. Cassady's bisexuality made Ginsberg feel somewhat more comfortable with his own homosexuality, but as a creative inspiration, Cassady sometimes played a negative role: When he stood Allen up for a scheduled lovemaking session in Denver, Ginsberg's rejection was worked into the book of poems called *Denver Doldrums*.

To Burroughs, who slowly evolved into a writer, partly out of boredom, partly out of Kerouac's inspiration and Ginsberg's love, and partly as a way of explaining his drug addiction (his first book was *Junkie*), Cassady was a nagging, food-eating, beer-cadging, money-borrowing bother. Burroughs was never long on social facades, despite his blue-blooded heritage and Harvard education. He openly expressed his disdain for Cassady's mad automotive flailings across the country, which inevitably included a stop at wherever Burroughs happened to be. Cassady would descend with no warning, with a carful of people, and proceed to eat Burroughs's food, drink his liquor, smoke his dope, and pop his pills. Burroughs didn't appreciate being a pit stop.

Neal's trips possess a sheer compulsive pointlessness that compares favorably with the mass migra-

tions of the Trojans. To cross a continent for the purpose of transporting Jack to Frisco where he intends to remain for three days before starting back to New York . . . obviously the 'purpose' of this trip is carefully selected to symbolize the basic fact of purposelessness. Neal is, of course, the very soul of the voyage into pure, abstract, meaningless motion. He is the mover, compulsive, dedicated, ready to sacrifice family, friend, even the very car itself to the meaning of moving from one place to another.
—William Burroughs to Allen Ginsberg, 1949

The second big splash in the forming wave of counterculture came in the form of John Clellon Holmes, whose involvement with the Columbia crowd brought with it a singularly powerful force: media attention. The meeting of Holmes with Ginsberg, Burroughs, and Kerouac took place at a memorable three-day party, on the long July Fourth weekend of 1948.

Holmes and Kerouac had a mutual friend in Alan Harrington. He knew that both were involved with their first novels. Kerouac's manuscript was finished and actually in attendance at the Fourth of July party, nestled comfortably in its battered leather carrying case. Holmes was in the middle of his first novel, about which he now says, "It was never published. It was awful." The initial attraction between the two had little to do with their respective manuscripts: Both were New Englanders with some war involvement and a literary bent. It was later that the two got down to comparing literary notes.

Holmes grew close to the whole scene at Edie's place, finding Kerouac the most kindred soul. Ginsberg was fascinating but mystic and manic; blowing up flowerpots with firecrackers in the middle of parties, standing on couches reading his poetry to a heedless crowd. Burroughs was in his late thirties and "that seemed like an absolute greyed image" to Holmes.

Kerouac's novel was published first, and he was completing *On the Road* as Holmes was working on his second novel. But it was Holmes's second novel *Go,* an eloquent diary of his life amid the Columbia and New York City crowd between August 1949 and September 1951, that got the media ball rolling.

Holmes's book suffered a fate similar to Kerouac's, selling twenty-five hundred copies, then quickly disappearing until being reissued in the 1957 post-*On the Road*, Beat Generation mania that swept the nation. But a reviewer at the *New York Times,* Gilbert Millstein (who would later review *On the Road*), saw something significant in *Go* and asked Holmes to write an article for the

Sunday, November 16, 1952, *New York Times Magazine*. The article created a scene.

Go contains a good amount of sex, drugs, jazz, and a handful of wildly eccentric characters, but Holmes's point, as articulated in the article "This Is the Beat Generation," was that the manic excesses of the characters were simply symptomatic of a generation "moved by a desperate craving for affirmative belief."

> Their own lust for freedom and their ability to live at a pace that kills, to which war has adjusted them, led to the blackmarket, sexual promiscuity, narcotics and Jean Paul Sartre. The beatness set in later . . . the cohesion of things had disappeared. . . . Today's Wild Boys are not lost . . . drugs are a curiosity, not a disillusionment. They live with the future in jeopardy. . . . The hot rod driver steering with his feet is not fed up with life—he's affirming life the only way he knows how—at the extreme. They are the stirrings of a quest.

Holmes's article stirred more than four hundred letters. Teenagers wrote. Old people wrote. Taylor Caldwell (whose two sons were somewhat overage for Holmes's demographics, at twenty-eight and thirty-six) wrote, saying that Holmes must be from New York City, since the kids she saw were "healthy, courageous and ambitious."

The argument went on, week after week. A Harvard professor wrote saying that yes, the problem with life is essentially a spiritual one. Others wrote in, chalking off the whole problem to nuclear bombs. Regardless, the article galvanized the public, the media, and the people at the core of it all. The movement now had a single label—Beat—like it or not. Soon the media would provide it with a uniform (sandals, Kafka-black turtleneck sweaters, blue jeans) and other signs of membership, such as goatees, bongos, bare light bulbs, empty beer cans, cheap furniture, and an aversion to soap and water and social conformity. "Pad," which originally and literally meant a mattress on the floor, ended up implying a communal apartment where who-knows-what went on.

Television offered shows such as *Dobie Gillis* and *Route 66*; jazz, then rock and roll gained popularity; Smirnoff vodka advertised a drink called the Mule, which made "swingers go! go! go! and get their kicks." However, one point of confusion in the growth of the Beat Generation from a small handful of college students into a nationwide business was the meaning behind the word *Beat*. *Beat* was sort of like the Swiss Army knife of social terminology. It could mean: "tired," "raw," "beatific," "with-it," "out-of-it," "lost," "disoriented," "worn down," "cranked up," "cool," "hot," "used," "alive." Or maybe it had something to do with music, especially jazz, but very soon the *beat* of rock and roll. Some related to one of Kerouac's many definitions: "We were just a bunch of guys out trying to get laid." In the end the meaning of *beat* or *hip* (later turned into *hippie* as a derogatory term for imitators) was a multiple-choice test whose answer was probably "all of the above."

* * *

James Dean had the beat, and so did Norman Mailer. The two played influential roles in the maturing counterculture, if different in nature and in timing. Dean popularized it; Mailer legitimized it.

It took Norman Mailer only five years after graduating from Harvard (1943) to explode onto the literary scene with his war-and-manhood bestseller *The Naked and the Dead*. (The publisher Little, Brown offered a three hundred dollar advance, but only if he would clean up the language. Mailer went elsewhere.) He was lionized before he was twenty-six. He'd never had a job, yet he was a literary hero of the returning GIs with a book that sold over two hundred thousand copies.

His second book, *Barbary Shore*, was different in every respect. Political with clear overtones of Marxism, it met with poor reviews, and the timing couldn't have been worse; just a few months before its release, the Communist Chinese had entered into the Korean War. Things did not get better with his third book, *Deer Park*, published to consistently bad reviews. Mailer became involved with drugs—especially alcohol, sleeping pills, and marijuana. In 1955, he and three others started a little antiestablishment newspaper in Greenwich Village called the *Village Voice*. The *Voice*, of course, developed into a model for underground and countercultural newspapers. It carried the news (and strange want ads) for readers who wanted the news the *New York Times* felt was *unfit* to print, a sizable and growing population.

Mailer's second contribution to the burgeoning counterculture was his essay, "The White Negro," published by City Lights Books. The essay, which was later published in Mailer's fourth book, *Advertisements for Myself*, caused more controversy than Holmes's "Beat" article in the *New York Times*.

Mailer wrote that since the war the world had turned apocalyptic. Its future was so bleak and its culture so totalitarian that violence was the only remaining form of self-expression. The "hipster" (a term first seen in print in a 1948 *Partisan Review* article) was simply responding appropriately to his environment; his behavior was not unlike that of a psychopath or an angry black. He was simply turning his feelings of helplessness into violent actions. He was trying to beat the world at its own game. The new generation was heroic, not criminal.

By his own admission, Mailer's research was first person in nature.

> All I felt then was that I was an outlaw, a psychic outlaw, and I liked it. I liked it . . . better than trying to be a gentleman, and with a set of emotions accelerating one on the other. I mined down deep into the murderous message of marijuana, the smoke of the assassins, and for the first time in my life I knew what it was to make your kicks.
>
> —Norman Mailer *Advertisements for Myself*

Soon after Mailer's essay was published, Ginsberg—who already knew Mailer—and Kerouac made a number of visits to Mailer's Perry Street apartment. *On the Road* had been published the same year, and the two men were only months apart in age, but Mailer was much more naturally extroverted than the shy-when-sober Kerouac. Kerouac was appreciative of Mailer's early success, and he had also dated Mailer's wife, Adele Morales. Ginsberg recollects their meetings as congenial, gentlemanly, even scholarly. By 1958 Ginsberg was less impressed with Mailer's essay:

> I don't mean to be presumptuous, but I thought the essay was very square . . . the whole point of *On the Road* . . . as well as all of Burroughs's writings, all of mine, and everything else going on with the Beat thing had to do with American tenderheartedness. Norman's notion of the hipster as being cool and psychopathic and cutting his way through society with jujitsu was a kind of macho folly that we giggled at. We giggled because it's silly and misses the point. In '45 and '46 Burroughs was experimenting with what it was like to be a thief, rolling drunks.
>
> So Norman grasped the apocalyptic nature of mind literature in the late fifties and later in the sixties . . . our basic take was the same, and so "The White Negro" was something positive. It was the most intelligent statement I'd seen by any literary-critical person . . . there was such a poverty of intelligence at that point.

EDWARD HALSEY FOSTER (ESSAY DATE 1992)

SOURCE: Foster, Edward Halsey. "Hipsters, Beats, and the True Frontier." In *Understanding the Beats*, pp. 1-27. Columbia: University of South Carolina Press, 1992.

In the following essay, Foster examines Beat writing in the context of social concerns, noting the commonality of themes among the various writers of that generation.

> The fluency and ornaments of the finest poems . . . are not independent but dependent. All beauty comes from beautiful blood and a beautiful brain.
>
> —Walt Whitman, Preface to *Leaves of Grass*

The Beats, according to an article in *Life* magazine in 1959, were "the only rebellion around."[1] Whether their fiction and poetry altered the way people thought or merely reflected social and cultural change, the Beats were responsible for some of the most powerful writing in America at that time. As significant as the Beats may have been to American social history at mid-century, their books were their principal achievement.

There are four major beat writers: William S. Burroughs, Gregory Corso, Allen Ginsberg, and Jack Kerouac. Others with whom they were associated and who strongly affected their work—Neal Cassady, Herbert Huncke, and Carl Solomon, for example—were not as committed to writing as were the original four. Still others like Alan Ansen and John Clellon Holmes, although they dealt with similar materials and ideas, were stylistically more conservative and less adventurous.

In the late 1950s and early 1960s, journalists included several other writers among the Beats—Gary Snyder, Philip Whalen, Michael McClure, William Everson, and Lawrence Ferlinghetti, among others—but, as most of these writers themselves quickly pointed out, that was a mistake. Philip Whalen, for example, insisted that the word *beat* involved "a period in New York City that Allen and Jack and Clellon Holmes and Burroughs and Corso and many other people were involved in. I wasn't there. . . . I don't think of myself as a 'beat.'"[2]

The confusion arose initially from the fact that various beat writers were living in the Bay Area during the San Francisco Renaissance, that sudden flowering of poetry (and audiences for poetry) in San Francisco in the 1950s. Journalists, unable to distinguish between, say, Ginsberg's poems and Whalen's, decided that anyone who lived and wrote in North Beach must be part of the same revolution, and soon America thought so, too. Some academics also identified the Beats largely with writers associated in some way with San Francisco. Thomas Parkinson, for example, pointed out that San Francisco had developed its own characteristic poetry long before Ginsberg and Kerouac arrived there, yet he included Ferlinghetti, Snyder, Whalen, and McClure among the Beats in his influential 1961 anthology of poetry and criticism, *A Casebook on the Beat*.[3]

San Francisco poets, however, have continued to resist the label. Gary Snyder said that *beat* could be used in "[talking] about the overall social phenomenon," but that "as a poet I belong to the San Francisco renaissance; . . . I'm not a Beat poet." In fact, he has said, "I never did know exactly what was meant by the term 'The Beats.'" Ferlinghetti has insisted that he was not in any way influenced by the Beats and turned down the opportunity to publish *Naked Lunch* "because I didn't like that kind of writing."[4]

McClure's plays and poetry have little in common with Burroughs's fiction, and Snyder's aesthetics are very different from Ginsberg's. The word *beat* can too easily be appropriated to describe a range of experimental or innovative poets and novelists with little else in common except a general resistance to academic poetry and to conservative values and politics in America during the 1950s.

If one is talking, however, about the "Beat Generation" as a sociological rather than as a literary movement, then Snyder, McClure, Whalen, and so forth might be grouped with Burroughs, Corso, Ginsberg, and Kerouac. Over the years, McClure, for example, has adamantly insisted that, strictly speaking, he was never a Beat, although he could be included as one "in the broadest sense." In that case, however, Robert Creely and other Black Mountain poets should be included as well.[5] Ann Charters suggested the larger spectrum in *The Beats* (1983), which includes essays even on such writers as William Carlos Williams, Frank O'Hara, and Jack Spicer, who were in no sense Beats themselves but who influenced, or were at least aware of and criticized (quite negatively in Spicer's case), the work of those who were.

The word *beat* in the larger sense might also include writers from the 1960s such as Diane di Prima, LeRoi Jones (Amiri Baraka), Ed Sanders, Clark Coolidge, and Anne Waldman—writers, that is, whose poetry and fiction were influenced by the Beats or were at least similar to theirs. At that point, however, one is including a very large portion of contemporary innovative or avant-garde writers—so large in fact that the word again loses precision. It is better in this case to talk about a second generation.

Whalen was correct in locating the Beats geographically in New York, for it was there in the 1940s that their politics and literary ambitions were formed. Burroughs, Corso, Ginsberg, and Kerouac were friends long before they published anything of consequence. Kerouac and Ginsberg

knew each other as undergraduates at Columbia, and Burroughs met them both in 1944. Ginsberg met Corso six years later in 1950 and introduced him shortly afterward to Kerouac. The circle was complete in 1953 when Burroughs, who had been living in Mexico, returned to New York and met Corso. These four writers shared a set of experiences at a crucial moment in their lives (and, for that matter, in the course of American civilization) and developed political and social visions that often overlapped. They wrote about each other, solicited each other's criticism, and promoted each other's books. If in the end they seem very different writers (and even Burroughs himself has said, "You couldn't really find four writers more different, more distinctive"[6]), their careers did intersect at a crucial moment, giving them a shared perspective and sensibility.

These four writers are in many ways so distinctively individual that at times it may seem as if the entire beat phenomenon were nothing but a journalist's or a critic's fantasy. Nonetheless, when one puts the fiction and poetry of the Beats next to, for example, the work of John Updike, Saul Bellow, William Bronk, William Gaddis, John Barth, Robert Lowell, Anne Sexton, or even Gary Snyder and Michael McClure, among other writers who emerged as major figures between the end of World War II and the mid-1960s, it is clear that the Beats do comprise a separate group, not only because they strongly encouraged and influenced each other aesthetically but also because they shared a particular attitude, largely urban and Eastern in origin, about what they felt had gone wrong with America. As Corso said, "the beats that I really knew, Kerouac, Ginsberg, Burroughs, they were all very diverse in their writing styles, but," he adds, "there was a similarity . . . with their feeling of what was coming, of what was to be."[7]

Burroughs was much older than the other Beats,[8] and, unlike them, he was not at first interested in becoming a writer. It was Kerouac, he said, who encouraged him to write. Kerouac was obsessed with becoming a writer but had read much less than Burroughs. Columbia taught Ginsberg and Kerouac the classics, but Burroughs showed them what had been left out—Hart Crane, T. S. Eliot, Céline, Kafka, Cocteau, Spengler, and other modern writers.

Kerouac and Ginsberg met Burroughs through Lucien Carr, a fellow Columbia student with whom they discussed the possibility of a "New Vision"—a new way of understanding the world. This Rimbaud-like enterprise was certainly abetted by the kind of books Burroughs recommended and the people with whom he associated. Here was an equivocal realm of petty thieves and addicts, in some ways like the inhabitants of Céline's Paris, who constituted a largely self-sufficient world indifferent to conventional values and ideals. Here also were the beginnings of "hip" culture—the world of the hipster, which began to form in New York and other cities toward the end of the war.

The hipster, in Norman Mailer's classic definition, set out "to encourage the psychopath in oneself, to explore that domain of experience where security is boredom and therefore sickness, and one exists in the present, in that enormous present which is without past or future, memory or planned intention, the life where a man must go until he is beat, where he must gamble with his energies through all those small or large crises of courage and unforeseen situations which beset his day, where he must be with it or doomed not to swing."[9]

The hipster, said Mailer, knows that "new kinds of victories increase one's power for new kinds of perception; and defeats, the wrong kinds of defeats, attack the body and imprison one's energy until one is jailed in the prison air of other people's habits, other people's defeats, boredom, quiet desperation, and muted icy self-destroying rage."[10] Although hipsters were a national phenomenon, they were usually found in cities. Most of the other writers later associated with the Beats were at this time living abroad or in small cities and towns, and although they could not fail to encounter hipsters somewhere (for the cultural influence was seen from jazz to movies to the way people dressed), it would have been difficult to know the type as well or as intensely as Burroughs, Ginsberg, and Kerouac did. These writers were there, so to speak, at the creation, watching from Times Square as this new cultural force took shape, and all three, in their very different ways, adopted in their works an attitude and outlook that was unmistakably hip. Corso during these years was living on New York streets or in foster homes or in prison and absorbed the same sensibility more directly.

Burroughs introduced Kerouac and Ginsberg to the underside of Times Square, including the addicts Bill Garver, who supported his habit by stealing coats, and Herbert Huncke, who became, said Holmes, "a model of how to survive."[11] (Huncke's autobiography, published in 1990, was entitled *Guilty of Everything*.) Huncke was the first person Kerouac remembered using the word *beat*, a word which Kerouac thought might have come from "some mid-west carnival or junk cafeteria."[12]

Initially, according to Kerouac's *Desolation Angels,* beat simply meant "mind-your-own-business" as in "beat it" or get out of here.[13] It meant "poor, down and out, deadbeat, on the bum, sad, sleeping in subways" ("Origins," 363). In his first novel, Kerouac described, for example, a woman "wandering 'beat' around the city in search of some other job or benefactor or 'loot' or 'gold.'"[14] Holmes added in 1952 that "more than mere weariness, ["beat"] implies the feeling of having been used, of being raw. It involves a sort of nakedness of mind, and, ultimately, of soul; a feeling of being reduced to the bedrock of consciousness. In short, it means being undramatically pushed up against the wall of oneself."[15] Kerouac later decided that the word meant "beatific" as well ("Origins," 365).

Kerouac traced the Beat Generation back to that time when "America was invested with wild self-believing individuality" ("Origins," 361). By the 1940s, however, America seemed to have little use for "wild self-believing individuality." The frontier era was long past, and the labor movement, which had portrayed the worker as defiant and independent, had become respectable and middle-class. The laborer lived nearly as well as the professional, and no one needed a Eugene Debs or a Daniel Boone any longer. The self-reliant hero had survived in the Depression songs of Woodie Guthrie and the novels of John Steinbeck and had been transformed into the GI during World War II, but young men returning from Europe and the South Pacific were not told to brave frontiers but to get an education (at government expense under the GI bill), a family, and a home.

A generation later, John F. Kennedy's New Frontier—a frontier bureaucratized, sanitized, and domesticated—would exemplify the new male ideal: a man fundamentally impersonal and unemotional. But the type was already there in the years when the Beats began to write. Men were expected to be logical, efficient, and cool-headed, organizing their lives according to their employers' needs. There was no place for the excitable, intense, and independent personality exemplified by frontier America. That older hero survived in movies and popular fiction, but essentially he was identified now as an adolescent, a stage responsible men were supposed to outgrow. A nineteenth-century hero had become a problem for social workers in the 1950s: Cooper's Natty Bumppo was now a "juvenile delinquent."

William Burroughs, Lucien Carr, and Allen Ginsberg (left to right) sit together in a New York City apartment in 1953.

But juvenile delinquents, motorcycles, and leather jackets indicated a discontent that went much beyond adolescence. Convention and respectability had very nearly eradicated Kerouac's "America . . . invested with wild self-believing individuality," but he felt that the America he valued "suddenly began to emerge again" after World War II, when "the hipsters began to appear gliding around saying 'Crazy, man'" ("Origins," 361). The hipster adopted an ethic at odds with most Americans, and his values and view of the world soon became the Beats'. What was known in the 1950s as "beat" was essentially what had been called "hip" a decade earlier.

A few months after Burroughs, Ginsberg, and Kerouac became friends, they were brought even closer together by a murder case that led to Kerouac and Burroughs's first attempt at writing a novel. Lucien Carr had met an older man named Dave Kammerer, who fell in love with him and pursued him for several years. In the summer of 1944, Carr stabbed and killed Kammerer with a Boy Scout knife in a park near Columbia. Carr went to Kerouac and told him, and Kerouac helped him dispose of the murder weapon. They spoke to Burroughs who told Carr that he should turn himself in to the police. Two days later he did.

Burroughs and Kerouac made the Carr-Kammerer episode the subject of a jointly written novel, still unpublished, entitled "And The Hippos Were Boiled in Their Tank." (The title was taken from a radio news report of a fire at the zoo.) Aside from a few earlier sketches, this was Burroughs's first extended piece of writing, and he adopted for it the style of hard-boiled detective stories, a style which he would utilize in his first two novels, *Junky* (1953) and *Queer* (written immediately after *Junky* was completed but not published until 1985), as well as in much of his subsequent fiction. It was an ideal style with which to describe that world of moral ambiguity in which he and his friends found themselves. It was one way to deal with the hip world—a cold verbal surface beneath which, in a morass of moral ambiguities, there was always the threat of terrible violence. In *On the Road* (1957) Kerouac would develop a style which would more directly express that threat, a style which would seem intense, frantic, and driven, although two decades later when he returned to Kammerer's murder in *Vanity of Duluoz* (1968), he chose a style as cool and dispassionate as that of Burroughs.

Burroughs, who left New York in 1947, did not know Bill Cannastra, a Harvard graduate who took the cult of hip to an extreme, dancing (as reported in Ginsberg's "Howl" [1956]) "on broken wineglasses barefoot," teetering on the edge of his roof, defying violent death repeatedly, and who in 1950 was killed when he suddenly tried to climb out of the window on a subway train as it started to leave the station. He became Finistra in Kerouac's *Visions of Cody* (1972) and Agatson in Holmes's *Go* (1952). He was, in a sense, warning where the hipster's nihilism could lead (and that is how he is seen in Holmes's novel), but his life and death also exemplified the extremes to which conformist America drove the rebellious individual, and it was in that sense that he became one of the heroes, one of "the best minds," of Ginsberg's "Howl." "The first perceptions that we were separate from the official vision of history and reality, began around '45, '46, '47," Ginsberg said.[16] The official vision, the one to which the GIs returned, seemed a fantasy. The real one was a world of real horror—Kammerer's murder, Cannastra's death, and the addicts and petty thieves who passed before the windows of the Times Square cafeteria where the Beats would spend the time with Huncke or Garver. Huncke's addiction, according to Ginsberg, pointed out the difference between humanitarian matters—what the junkie need was "maintenance therapy—and official oppression" (*Composed,* 71).

Holmes thought his generation was "black, lost, wild and headed toward the deepest corner of the night," and yet, he insisted, "Our search is, I firmly believe, a spiritual one."[17] The Beat Generation, he wrote, was "the first generation in several centuries for which the act of faith has been an obsessive problem, quite aside from the reasons for having a particular faith or not having it. It exhibits on every side, and in a bewildering number of facets, a perfect craving to believe." (*Nothing,* 113).

In this, the role played by Neal Cassady was crucial, particularly for Ginsberg and Kerouac.[18] Cassady exemplified both hip distrust for convention and that "wild self-believing individuality" Kerouac associated with an earlier America. Cassady was a Westerner. He had grown up on the streets and in the poolhalls of Denver, and to Ginsberg and Kerouac, whose backgrounds were comparatively conventional, he exemplified freedom; he seemed to have found a way out of the darkness Holmes saw at the end of the road. "Neal had answered questions Jack couldn't answer for himself, or so Jack fancied it," Holmes said (Tytell, "Holmes," 161). Cassady could apparently do what he wished and not, like Cannastra, have to pay for it. Cassady was, of course, the impeccable driver who became Dean Moriarty in *On the Road,* and it may have been he whom Holmes had in mind when he wrote that "the giggling nihilist, eating up the highway at ninety miles an hour, and steering with his feet, . . . invites death only to outwit it. He is affirming the life within him in the only way he knows how, at the extreme" (*Nothing,* 19). In effect what Cassady did in his life, the Beats tried to do in their poetry and fiction.

In one manner or another, all of the Beats pushed their work to extremes. Each began in the claustrophobic, oppressive world of the hipster and then moved out, testing words as Cassady tested a car to see how fast it could take a corner. There were two kinds of hipsters, "cool" and "hot," as Kerouac reported in *The Subterraneans* (1958). The former is suggested by Burroughs's restrained, neutral tone in *Junky* and *Queer.* With *Naked Lunch* (1959), however, he began writing a more extreme language, testing boundaries of diction and expression much as Ginsberg did in "Howl." Corso too learned to write with similar expressive power in such works as "Elegiac Feelings American" (1970). "Most Beat Generation artists belong to the hot school," Kerouac wrote, add-

ON THE SUBJECT OF...

LUCIEN CARR

"The father of the Beat Generation was not Jack Kerouac or Allen Ginsberg or William Burroughs," declared Aaron Latham. "It was Lucien Carr. He was the one who brought the others together." Like Herbert Huncke, Carr is a liminal Beat figure who is often overlooked in studying the origins of the movement. It was while attending Columbia University that Carr met and befriended Burroughs, Kerouac, and Ginsberg; to the budding authors he was a charismatic and seasoned guide to the New York City Bohemian scene. The classmates formulated the "New Vision," a kind of literary manifesto. Inspired by the writings of Dostoyevsky, the New Vision sought knowledge through experience, especially experience from the underside of life. While such ideas propelled Ginsberg, Kerouac, and Burroughs to experiment with drugs and other aspects of the New York underground, the credo took on a lethal manifestation when Carr murdered David Kammerer. Kammerer, a one-time friend of Carr's, became obsessed with Carr, followed him everywhere, and reportedly made unwanted sexual advances toward him. Kerouac and Ginsberg were subsequently held as material witnesses in the case. While the Beat writers were not guilty of any crime, their association with the Kammerer case had a powerful negative influence on the public's—and Columbia University's—perception of them. Carr served two years in prison and, upon his release, took a job as a reporter with United Press. It is rumored that the scroll upon which Kerouac typed *On the Road* came from Carr's teletype machine at the Press. Carr had a long, successful career with the United Press, and married and divorced Francesca von Hartz, with whom he had a son, Caleb, in 1955. Caleb Carr became an author, penning the bestselling novel *The Alienist.*

Introductory quote is taken from the following source: Latham, Aaron. "The Columbia Murder That Gave Birth to the Beats." *New York Magazine* (19 April 1976): 41.

ing that he was originally "a hot hipster . . . who finally cooled it in Buddhist meditation" ("Origins," 363).

Although the hipster's enemy was the materialistic American, even the "cool" hipster was rarely so ascetic or austere as to cut him or herself totally off from the world. Hip culture was itself in some ways deeply commercial (or commercialized) and materialistic. Holmes saw that his generation was obsessed with spiritual questions but depended on the capitalistic economy it despised in order to spread the new ideas and values. Records, radios, cars, clothes, and books were all ways in which the hipster could express his or her ethic and identify those who shared it. The popular response to the beat writers may have in part been due to the fact that by the time "Howl" and *On the Road* were published, the ethic and attitudes they advocated had in some ways already pervaded America.

The first journal to popularize hip culture was Jay Landesman's *Neurotica,* begun in 1948. A friend who had been reading W. H. Auden's *Age of Anxiety* told Landesman, "He's got his finger on the pulse of the times. The new look is going to be the anxious look." The hipster was certainly anxious, and *Neurotica* became a major journal for hip culture. The second issue included a story by John Clellon Holmes, which Landesman thought may have been "the first piece of published fiction that utilized the language of the hipster."[19] *Neurotica* dealt with much more than hip culture, and although some of its contributors, such as Chandler Brossard, rejected the hip world, Landesman's journal was important in preparing readers for the sort of literature they were soon to get from Kerouac, Ginsberg, and Holmes.

Although widely circulated, *Neurotica* was read by a relatively small, but sophisticated, group of Americans. Anyone could get something of the hip style, however, simply by going to the movies, where the hipster's mannerisms were incorporated into the acting styles of Marlon Brando, Paul Newman, Montgomery Clift, and James Dean. Hipster culture was the subject of such popular films as *Young Man with a Horn* (1950) starring Kirk Douglas, *The Man with the Golden Arm* (1956) featuring Frank Sinatra, and *All the Fine Young Cannibals* (1959) with Robert Wagner. *Film noir* also incorporated the hipster's paranoid view of civilization.

One could also find hip culture and attitudes by listening to Symphony Sid's all-night jazz program on the radio in New York or the weekly broadcasts from Manhattan's Birdland. This kind of jazz, bepob or just bop, as it was called, would have a major influence on rhythms in Corso's, Ginsberg's, and particularly Kerouac's work. Bop arose in the early 1940s, although its great popularity did not arrive until the middle of the decade. In 1942, as part of an action against licensing agencies, the musicians' union banned its members from making recordings. The ban lasted more than two years during which bop musicians were able to go their own way without having to acquiesce to the public's taste. Before 1942, jazz was determined very much by the big bands, which, because of their size, left little room for spontaneity or improvisation. The arranger and the band's leader (sometimes the same person) dominated the music. But bop was performed by small groups in which improvisation was encouraged. This music, with its emphasis on the individual, was quintessentially hip, and such record companies as Blue Note and Contemporary made the music of Charlie Parker, Dizzy Gillespie, and other bop musicians widely available.[20]

Beat poetry and fiction were rooted in hip culture, but they also drew from literary traditions which encouraged personal and spontaneous styles. Rimbaud and Whitman were among their principal forerunners. Among twentieth-century predecessors, Ginsberg pointed specifically to French Surrealists and Gertrude Stein (*Composed,* 88). Stein was especially important, for both her fiction and poetry were major contributions to expressionist aesthetics, and the Beats were strongly indebted to the expressionist tradition.

The word *expressionism,* as R. S. Furness wrote, "has to cover so many disparate cultural manifestations as to be virtually meaningless," yet it is conventionally identified with "self-expression, creativity, ecstatic fervour and a ruthless denial of tradition." Expressionism implies the discovery of meaning which no objective analysis or consensus can reach and which is found within the self rather than through a study of society or history. Expressionist writing is, although subjective, not solipsistic (or so the writer claims), for it achieves a level of experience and understanding that is not merely personal but common, or at least potentially common, to all readers. According to Henry Miller, the artist "recreates [the universe] out of his own experience and understanding of life."[21]

Expressionism in American literature has its roots in Ralph Waldo Emerson, who asserted in his essay "The Poet" that "the Universe is the externization of the soul," but the great expressionist poet was Walt Whitman, who in one of the finer humorous and arrogant moments in *Song of Myself* identified the voice of his poem as "Walt Whitman, a kosmos, of Manhattan the son." He meant that literally, of course: both a man in the city and "a kosmos." "In all people I see myself," he said in another comic but at the same time utterly serious moment, "none more and not one a barleycorn less."

American expressionism as it developed from Whitman should be distinguished from German Expressionism, which is a related but quite separate movement, and the romantic search for transcendent moments when the division between the self and the universe was seemingly eclipsed.[22] For the romantic, those sublime moments occurred at best sporadically; there were discrete occasions of sudden illumination. For the American expressionist, however, the most personal, even ordinary occasion had its universal character. As Michael McClure wrote, "I did not fear obscurity in my poetry because I had come to believe that the way to the universal was by means of the most intensely personal. I believed that what we truly share with others lies in the deepest, most personal, even physiological core—and not in the outer social world of speech that is used for grooming and transactions."[23]

The expressionist has a particular mission when realism and materialism are dominant. For the realist, language is at best transparent, designating a reality separate from itself, and the author is in the extreme instance, therefore, not visible in the work. Expressionist writing can be personal and autobiographical, but it does not have to be. It may draw on personal experience, may indeed be deeply confessional, but it has the potential to do much more than celebrate the private self. Perhaps few expressionists would make as large a claim as Whitman's—"In all people I see myself"—but the expressionist aesthetic gave William Saroyan, for example, permission to speak for Armenian-Americans and William Faulkner permission to speak for the South.

Gertrude Stein, in a review of Sherwood Anderson's *A Story Teller's Story*, pointed out that what he did in his work was "express life" rather than document or "embroider" it.[24] He was, that is, not a writer in those realistic and naturalistic traditions with which he had often been (and occasionally still is) mistakenly associated. Anderson had listened to his father tell stories and found that his father's success depended on the manner of telling rather than on matters of character and plot. The story's real subject, in other words, was

the narrator. Taking that as a starting point, Anderson's usual approach was to locate an episode and a narrator, bring them together, and let the story go wherever the occasion indicated—an intuitive rather than a traditional or formalist approach. His stories are spoken narratives depending directly on the rhythms of spoken English for their effects, much as Mark Twain's had been.

Anderson's disciples in the 1920s and 1930s included William Faulkner, Ernest Hemingway, Thomas Wolfe, and William Saroyan. Kerouac cited the last three as major influences on his work, and one of his early novels, *Pic* (not published until 1971 although written in 1951), was obviously inspired by Faulkner. At first Kerouac tried to imitate surface elements of other expressionists. He wrote stories, as he put it in *Vanity of Duluoz*, "in the Saroyan-Hemingway-Wolfe style" and modeled the prose in *The Town and the City* on Thomas Wolfe's. But the true expressionist cannot merely imitate or borrow surface characteristics from other works. The writer must find a language and a rhythm which allows him or her to speak directly from the self. The book in which Kerouac first did that was *On the Road*, the principal draft of which was written in three weeks and so required a direct, improvisatory style: there was no time to imitate.

According to Allen Ginsberg, there is "a tradition of prose in America, including Thomas Wolfe and going through Kerouac, which is personal, in which the prose sentence is completely personal, comes from the writer's own person—his person defined as his body, his breathing rhythm, his actual talk."[25] This was what Kerouac discovered in writing *On the Road*, perfected in *Visions of Cody*, and named "spontaneous prose."

Ginsberg spoke of "a tradition of prose," but expressionism is of equal significance in American poetry in general and beat poetry in particular. The principal source is certainly Whitman, but D. H. Lawrence, particularly in *Birds, Beasts and Flowers* (1923), may have had greater influence on Kenneth Rexroth and William Everson, among other American poets in the generation immediately preceding the Beats. Other essential influences include Rimbaud, Stein, and the Surrealists.

Holmes noted that at the end of World War II, "man was seen as a victim, either of toilet training [Freud] or his place in society [Marx], but he was determined from the outside. That conception of man we all found, quite independently because we all have different backgrounds, to be increasingly inadequate" (Tytell, "Holmes," 165). Expressionism gave the Beats an aesthetic that avoided the rationalism of both Freudians and Marxists. There were also quasi-religious implications as Ginsberg recognized when he asserted that "poetry is the record of individual insights into the secret soul of the individual—and, because all individuals are One in the eyes of their Creator, into the soul of the World."[26]

By the time the Beats appeared, expressionist writing (unless it was a *cause célèbre* like Miller's *Tropic of Cancer*) seldom received a sympathetic hearing in established literary journals or in the universities. Saroyan had been dismissed, Wolfe was considered a writer for adolescents, and Lionel Trilling, rereading Anderson's works, found that he liked them "even less" than he remembered. R. P. Blackmur, preferring "objective" to "expressive" form, felt that the latter was a "heresy" and a "plague."[27]

Under these circumstances, it is not surprising that the conservative critic Norman Podhoretz could dismiss Kerouac's "conception of feeling [as] one that only a solipsist could believe in" and could argue that he and Ginsberg shared with juvenile delinquents a "resentment against normal feeling and the attempt to cope with the world through intelligence." Nor is it surprising that the formalist poet John Ciardi could insist that beat writing had "been systematically vitiated by [the] insistence on the holiness of the impromptu and by the urge to play the lunatic." Ciardi concluded that Kerouac was "basically a high school athlete who went from Lowell, Massachusetts, to Skid Row, losing his eraser en route."[28]

The first friendly attempts to discuss the Beats came from writers rather than from professional or academic critics.[29] The first sympathetic work was Holmes's novel *Go* (1952), in which the term *Beat Generation*, which Kerouac had proposed in 1948, appeared in print for the first time. *Go* is not an expressionistic work, and Holmes was critical about much that he and his friends did (his portrait of a misogynistic Cassady is particularly unattractive). In both style and sensibility, *Go* is the work of an outsider—a man who wanted to be hip but who, as the novel reveals, was too constrained and conservative. He was, however, a close observer and knew Ginsberg, Kerouac, Cannastra, Ansen, Cassady, and other members of the early beat group very well. *Go* is in effect a history of their lives from 1948 to 1950. As Holmes reported in his introduction to a 1980 reprint, the

novel is "almost literal truth," even reporting "whole conversations . . . verbatim."[30]

The principal figures in the novel are Ginsberg (David Stofsky), Kerouac (Gene Pasternak), Cassady (Hart Kennedy), Huncke (Albert Ancke), Cannastra (Agatson), and Holmes (Paul Hobbes). As the name Hobbes suggests, Holmes portrayed himself as crippled or "hobbled" by the world and his own values, yet he does share with Stofsky and Pasternak a discontent bordering on desperation and a sense that traditional values have become pointless. To be hip or "beat" is one way to respond, but Hobbes has to will himself to act that way, while it is natural to others.

Hobbes is self-conscious in a way Pasternak and Stofsky are not and as a result does not share "their thirsty avidity for raw experience, their pragmatic quest for the unusual, the 'real,' the crazy" (*Go*, 35). Stofsky decides that he "wants a break-through into the world of feeling" and has "decided to believe in God." "All systems," he says, "are just mirrors, mirrors. You look into them and see only your self, with the world as the dim background" (*Go*, 65). In fact, Hobbes's marriage is a mirror of his own narrow ethics and imagination, but he never quite realizes that.

"Everyone I know," says Pasternak, "is kind of furtive, kind of beat. . . . And it's happening all over the country, to everyone; a sort of revolution of the soul . . ." (*Go*, 36). For Holmes, as for Kerouac, this new generation was typified by Neal Cassady (Hart Kennedy). Although Kennedy is far more callous than Kerouac's Cody Pomeray, Holmes still saw Cassady as gifted with great energy and independence and, therefore, able to resist pressures to conform. Agatson has equally great energy and can be "possessed by a demon of fantastic anarchy" (*Go*, 269), but his death leads Hobbes to realize how desperate life has become for his circle of friends. Trapped in his pointless marriage, he has at the end of the book "a vision of unending lovelessness" and believes that this same vision "must have entered [Agatson] like a germ and corrupted his heart and mind." A person in that circumstance would lose hope, be "outraged, violated, raped in his soul," and be left in the end with "the consuming desire to jeer, spit, curse, smash, destroy" (*Go*, 310).

Holmes said of his generation that "their own lust for freedom, and the ability to live at a pace that kills, (to which war had adjusted them), led to black markets, bebop, narcotics, sexual promiscuity, hucksterism and Jean-Paul Sartre. The beatness set in later" (*Nothing*, 111). Here, as in *Go*,

Holmes was speaking as a traditional, perhaps even Victorian, moralist, believing that America, having lost its values, could cure its discontents only by going faster—a solution that in its obvious pointlessness only exposed further the underlying desperation. To stop running would be to face the "vision of unending lovelessness" and the solitude it implied. Since Holmes's generation, as he saw it, had no fundamental values, it had no adequate cure for the predicament in which it was caught. Melville, of course, had made similar observations. Only by keeping busy and involved with his work could the narrator of *Bartleby the Scrivener* prevent himself from having to confront the fact that in his success he was as isolated as Bartleby.

For Holmes, Bartleby, and Melville's narrator, solitude and "unending lovelessness" are the penalties for "wild self-believing individuality." For Holmes the collapse of Hobbes's marriage was a terrible thing, but that Holmes should have felt that way is a measure of how conservative a moralist he was. American heroes from Natty Bumppo to Huck Finn to Nick Adams fled exactly what Holmes seeks. The price for freedom (Ishmael's, Hester Prynne's, Huck Finn's, Thoreau's, Pasternak's, Kennedy's, Agatson's) may be "unending lovelessness," but that never deterred heroes in American myth and literature.

Insisting, in McClure's words, that "the way to the universal was by means of the most intensely personal," expressionism provided a solution to "unending lovelessness." Holmes was a fairly conventional writer and not an expressionist, but other Beats found in the expressionist aesthetic an escape from the solitude that cursed Agatson. "Whitman all along had said that private consciousness *is* public consciousness," wrote Ginsberg (*Composed*, 72).

Although the deterioration of Hobbes's marriage is the central tragedy in *Go*, none of the principal characters aside from Hobbes and his wife is affected by it. Holmes is not suggesting merely that Hobbes's tragedy is a private matter; he is suggesting that marriage itself and traditional relationships between men and women have no place in the new world he is describing.

Marriage in fact had little significance in the beat world. Ginsberg in his journal in 1954 recorded a dream in which he received a letter from Holmes saying, "The social organization which is most true of itself to the artist is the boy gang," to which Ginsberg himself added, "not society's perfum'd marriage."[31]

Women have little place in most beat writings. There are few women in Ginsberg's work outside of such poems as "Kaddish" and "White Shroud," which concern his mother and other women in his family. Corso's "Marriage" is one of two well known mid-century poems attacking its subject, and various early poems by him involve grotesque images of women, particularly mothers. In *Visions of Cody* Kerouac wrote, "As far as young women are concerned I can't look at them unless I tear off their clothes one by one."[32]

Burroughs's fiction can be severely misogynistic, but as Jennie Skerl has noted, "his attacks upon women in general are attacks upon women's roles within a certain social structure."[33] In this he followed that conspicuous American literary tradition which characterizes men as renegades and advocates of freedom and women as defenders of decorum, domesticity, and the status quo. It is the distinction between Becky Thatcher and Huck Finn in which the woman is (unless a comic figure) the antithesis of Kerouac's "wild self-believing individuality." Not surprisingly Burroughs called the family a "formula" that had to be dissolved. "'Women,'" he said, quoting a character in Conrad's *Victory*, "'are a perfect curse.'"[34]

"I realize I am widely perceived as a misogynist," Burroughs wrote in an essay entitled "Women: A Biological Mistake?" But in fact, he continued, he would suggest androgyny, "the sexes fusing into an organism," as "the next step" in evolutionary development. The real villain he remarked in an interview, is romantic love: "love is a fraud perpetrated by the female sex." Sexual relations between men do not involve "love, but rather what we might call *recognition*."[35] What Burroughs would choose, as his novels repeatedly make clear, is sexuality unencumbered by illusions or sentiment—and that was not the way relations between men and women were conceived when the Beats began to write.

All that changed radically in the 1960s and 1970s, of course, and "the boy gang" very quickly became anachronistic. The hipster values the Beats promoted did not disappear, however. The Beats, as Gregory Stephenson wrote, were concerned with "knowledge of the Self, and the discovery or recovery of a true mode of perception"—objectives obviously equally important to feminists.[36] Younger women writers learned much from Burroughs, Corso, Ginsberg, and Kerouac, and if the second generation of the Beats included such important male writers as Ed Sanders, Clark Coolidge, and Sam Shepard, it also included many highly regarded women poets such as Diane di Prima, Anne Waldman, and Alice Notley as well as Patti Smith, Laurie Anderson, and other popular singers and performers.

Notes

1. Paul O'Neil, "The Only Rebellion Around," *Life* 47 (30 November 1959): 115.

2. Donald Allen, ed., *Off the Wall: Interviews with Philip Whalen* (Bolinas, CA: Four Seasons, 1978) 62.

3. Parkinson identifies the specifically local roots of the San Francisco Renaissance in "Phenomenon or Generation," *A Casebook on the Beat* (New York: Crowell, 1961) 276-90.

4. Inger Thorup Lauridsen and Per Dalgard, *The Beat Generation and the Russian New Wave* (Ann Arbor: Ardis, 1990) 67-68; James McKenzie, "Moving the World an Inch" (interview with Gary Snyder), *The Beat Vision*, ed. Arthur and Kit Knight (New York: Paragon, 1987) 2; Lauridsen and Dalgard, 135.

5. Lauridsen and Dalgard, 115.

6. Daniel Odier, *The Job: Interviews with William S. Burroughs* (New York: Grove, 1974) 43.

7. Michael Andre, "An Interview with Gregory Corso," *Unmuzzled Ox* 22 (Winter 1981): 123.

8. He was born in 1914; Kerouac was born in 1922, Ginsberg in 1926, Corso in 1930.

9. Norman Mailer, "The White Negro," *Advertisements for Myself* (New York: Putnam's, 1959) 339.

10. Mailer, 339. Gerald Nicosia discusses differences between Mailer's view of the hipster and Kerouac's in *Memory Babe: A Critical Biography of Jack Kerouac* (New York: Grove, 1983) 206.

11. John Tytell, "An Interview with John Clellon Holmes," *Kerouac and the Beats*, ed. Arthur and Kit Knight (New York: Paragon, 1988), 166. Subsequent references are given parenthetically in the text.

12. Jack Kerouac, "The Origins of the Beat Generation," *On the Road: Text and Criticism*, ed. Scott Donaldson (New York: Viking, 1979), 362. Subsequent references are given parenthetically in the text.

13. Jack Kerouac, *Desolation Angels* (New York: Coward-McCann, 1965) 319.

14. Jack Kerouac, *The Town and the City* (New York: Harcourt, Brace, 1950) 451.

15. John Clellon Holmes, "This Is the Beat Generation," *Nothing More to Declare* (New York: Dutton, 1967) 110. The article originally appeared in 1952. Subsequent references are given parenthetically in the text.

16. Allen Ginsberg, *Composed on the Tongue* (Bolinas, CA: Grey Fox, 1980) 71. Subsequent references are given parenthetically in the text.

17. John Clellon Holmes, "Crazy Days, Numinous Nights: 1948-1950," *The Beat Vision*, ed. Arthur and Kit Knight, 86.

18. The only biography of Cassady to date is William Plummer's *The Holy Goof* (Englewood Cliffs, NJ: Prentice-Hall, 1981). Cassady's published writings are collected in *The First Third* (San Francisco: City Lights, 1971).

19. Jay Landesman, *Rebel Without Applause* (New York: Paragon, 1990) 45, 55.

20. On connections between bop, on the one hand, and hipsters and the Beats, on the other, see Roy Carr, Brian Case, and Fred Dellar, *The Hip: Hipsters, Jazz and the Beat Generation* (London: Faber and Faber, 1986).

21. R. S. Furness, *Expressionism* (London: Methuen, 1973) 1, 14; Henry Miller, "An Open Letter to Surrealists Everywhere," *The Cosmological Eye* (New York: New Directions, 1939) 193.

22. Sherrill E. Grace traces parallels between German Expressionism and works by Canadian writers and such American writers as Eugene O'Neill in *Regression and Apocalypse: Studies in North American Literary Expressionism* (Toronto: University of Toronto Press, 1989). American expressionists like Sherwood Anderson, Henry Miller, Thomas Wolfe, and William Saroyan derived their aesthetics ultimately, however, from Whitman rather than from German writers such as Gottfried Benn, Alfred Döblin, and Ernst Toller.

23. Michael McClure, *Scratching the Beat Surface* (San Francisco: North Point, 1982) 26.

24. Gertrude Stein, Review of *A Story Teller's Story*, in *Sherwood Anderson: A Collection of Critical Essays*, ed. Walter B. Rideout (Englewood Cliffs, NJ: Prentice-Hall, 1974) 86.

25. Allen Ginsberg, *Allen Verbatim: Lectures on Poetry, Politics, Consciousness*, ed. Gordon Ball (New York: McGraw-Hill, 1974) 153.

26. Allen Ginsberg, "Poetry, Violence, and the Trembling Lambs," *The Poetics of the New American Poetry*, ed. Donald Allen and Warren Tallman (New York: Grove, 1973) 331.

27. Lionel Trilling, "Sherwood Anderson," *The Liberal Imagination* (Garden City, NY: Anchor Books, 1953) 21; R. P. Blackmur, *The Expense of Greatness* (New York: Arrow Editions, 1940) 190; *The Double Agent* (New York: Arrow Editions), 105.

28. Norman Podhoretz, "The Know-Nothing Bohemians," *On the Road: Text and Criticism*, ed. Donaldson, 353, 355; John Ciardi, "Epitaph for the Dead Beats," *Dialogue with an Audience* (Philadelphia: Lippincott, 1963) 304.

29. The first major critical book by an academic was *Casebook on the Beat* (1961), Thomas Parkinson's collection of works by and about the Beats, but Parkinson was himself a respected poet, associated early in his career with Jack Spicer, William Everson, Robert Duncan, and Kenneth Rexroth.

30. John Clellon Holmes, *Go* (New York: New American Library, 1980) xvii-xviii. Subsequent references are given parenthetically in the text.

31. Allen Ginsberg, *Journals: Early Fifties Early Sixties* (New York: Grove, 1977) 80. This reference came to my attention through Catharine R. Stimpson, "The Beat Generation and the Trials of Homosexual Liberation," *Salamagundi* 58/59 (Fall/Winter 1982-83): 373-92.

32. Corso's "Marriage" is discussed in chapter four. The other poem, also entitled "Marriage," is by Marianne Moore; Jack Kerouac, *Visions of Cody* (New York: McGraw-Hill, 1972) 23.

33. Jennie Skerl, *William S. Burroughs* (Boston: Twayne, 1985) 4.

34. Odier, *The Job*, 42, 110.

35. William S. Burroughs, "Women: A Biological Mistake?" *The Adding Machine* (New York: Seaver, 1986) 126; Odier, *The Job*, 112.

36. Gregory Stephenson, "The 'Spiritual Optics' of Lawrence Ferlinghetti," in *Beat Indeed!*, ed. Rudi Horemans (Antwerp: EXA, 1985) 117.

Work Cited

Charters, Ann, ed. *The Beats: Literary Bohemians in Postwar America*, 2 volumes. Detroit: Gale, 1983. Good introductions to beat writers and others associated with them.

THE BEAT GENERATION AS A SOCIAL PHENOMENON

KINGSLEY WIDMER (ESSAY DATE 1970)

SOURCE: Widmer, Kingsley. "The Beat in the Rise of the Populist Culture." In *The Fifties: Fiction, Poetry, Drama,* edited by Warren French, pp. 155-73. Deland, Fla.: Everett/Edwards, Inc., 1970.

In the following essay, Widmer analyses Beat writing with respect to its impact on the cultural, literary, and political climate of the 1960s.

I. The Rebellious Movement

Few commentators on the "Beat Generation," as it was formally called in the 50s, saw it as part of an enduring cultural movement. But in the 70s they should be able to recognize the Beats as parcel as well as part of much that was to come— and much, no doubt, still to come. For by the early 60s there was the worldwide figure of the "Beatnik," almost as evident on the Spanish Steps, Rome, and in the coffee houses of the Midlands, England, as in the beach shacks of Venice West, Los Angeles, and on the streets of the East Village, New York. The defiantly outcast costumes and manners and sensibility were continued and enlarged in the mid-60s with the successor Hippies. By the late 60s there were many variations, such as the politicized Yippies and the religiocized hip communes. From post-World War II ex-GI-Bohemians of the late 40s—their military leftovers set the first styles of dressing down, of marginal living and of revulsion against authority—through the Beats, the Beatniks, the Hippies, the Yippies and others, and seeping into faddish adolescent "teenieboppers" and fashion-exploiting adult "swingers," we can find a minority sensibility expanding through and beyond the "underground" of Western culture.

By the late 60s, cultural symposia and literary moralizers were finally recognizing all of this as a vast though rather amorphous rebellious movement. Often called "the youth culture," though both its youthfulness and artistic culturation were in some doubt, it evidently involved millions with their communal ways and public festivals, with their distinctive communications (underground papers) and entertainment (folk, blues and rock groups), and with their own costuming and commerce, manners and morals. The bizarre personal decoration, ritualistic use of marijuana, and polymorphous sexuality merely provided the more obvious signs of a large para-community of the dissident. Though the evidence is quite clear that all of this has been developing for some decades, the mass media hireling commentators still treat it, as they did the Beats, as a "generational" problem, as a temporary malaise of late-adolescent delinquency. Righteously focusing on the "pot" mystique (developed by marginal groups in the thirties), the preachers of middle-class manners (and the pretenders to "social science") often reduce the movement to "the drug culture." The Beats and their successors have defiantly taken up the metaphor and made drugs into sacrament and magic and pot into poetry and politics. Also, since the under-Bohemians—the Beats and the Hippies—have emphasized their disenchantment with American competitive patterns and disaffiliation from the controlling institutions, they often get labeled the "drop-out culture." At least one hostile commentator condemns the erotic openness of the movement (obscene language and gesture, nudity, homoeroticism, and other mixed libidinal ways as well as rejection of the anxious nuclear family of the suburbs) as the "porno culture." A more disinterested observer would simply grant that it must be a large cultural movement, not to be reduced to a single sick attribute. The denigrations and dismissals by the custodians of the "straight" (formerly called "square") culture largely express the resentment of those identifying with social domination.

On one side, the movement towards a countering culture can hardly be separated from the blues-folk-rock musics, which in the past decade have considerably transformed popular entertainment, and from the increased impetus toward communal and immediate arts (happenings, new modes of decoration, participatory theatre, etc.). On another side, the counter-culture can hardly be separated from dissenting social action, including "civil rights," peace-protest, campus rebellion, utopian communalism, and many other ways of dissent which both adapt and inform the cultural movement. Movement it must be since in three decades it has grown from artistic coteries and deviant grouplets to a collective social and cultural process of large proportions. While the life-styles are quite evident that come out of this, the movement was, and is, characteristically American in being too various, elusive and often vague to be contained in a single artistic or religious or social doctrine. It cannot adequately be defined by its leaders since none of its better known figures seem to have achieved the roles of heroic prophets, nor by its creative works since none of these seem recognizable as masterpieces. Both culture heroes and art works remain secondary to communal styles of responding and living. Since the Bohemian-Beat-Hippy-deviant-underground-dissident movement goes beyond its social dimensions to a popular and protesting tradition of feeling and style, I suggest seeing it as a new populist culture based, like its predecessors, on a revolt against apathetic decorum as well as against social and political legitimacy.

The Beat should now be recognized as but one phase in this development. By way of definition, *beatness* might be analogized as social alienation, vagrant religious beatitude, a mode of humble moral resistance, a confession-spontaneity aesthetic, and the historical under-Bohemianism of the fifties. Possibly, we could include in *beatness* some of the ecstatic-melancholy beat of the blues, enthusiastically admired by most of the Beat litterateurs and then in process of transformation to popular rock music. Additional slang overtones might not be irrelevant: "beat-up" could describe the usual costuming (jeans, work shirts, boots, "war-surplus" jackets, etc.); "beat-out" suggests some of the a-political and a-intellectual disenchantment; and "to-beat-it" points to the mobility, the wandering outsiderness, which marked the movement. All of these carry a conscious revulsion, a wary disaffiliation, from a competitively repressive and blandly dehumanizing mass technological civilization.

Some years ago I wrote at tendentious length in *The Literary Rebel* on the parallels between the Beats and analogous earlier social-cultural rebels, including the Greek Cynics, certain Christian heretics, some figures of the Taoist movement, the Medieval Goliard poets, Bohemian vagrants, Thoreauvian individualists, American hobos, and the moral *enragés* of modernist art. The literary role of the Beat was in good part a recognizable variation on the anti-academic one that runs from Walt Whitman through Henry Miller. But the movement was a melange which included orientalism and avant-gardist aesthetic experimentation, Western America populist folk motifs and nostalgic political dissent (a considerable number of the beat pace-setters were children of Leftists of an earlier period), and a broad recrudescence of antinomian, utopian and deviant styles. The Beat movement and its successors belong to a long minority social, religious and artistic history. Perennially, something similar blooms in late-urbanized and post-religious civilizations marked by counterfeit and exploitative culture, such as ours, and would seed a revolutionary change in sensibility.

Since these movements would change consciousness and lifestyles, art—at least in the "high culture" senses—usually subordinates to personal and communal needs. We should hardly expect, and we rarely get, complexly subtle art from such a movement. Its thrust works against the specialized craftsmanship and elite-class connoisseurship which provides the conditions of "high art." For the Beats, "creativity," when not a rather forced religious euphemism for states of feeling, was a defensive definition of their unemployed, irregular and outcast state. It bulwarked them against the pressures of the Protestant work ethic and our religiosity of competitive aggrandizement. Art also served as a recognized rationalization for deviance. This in several senses. The high proportion of identifiable homosexual writers and of obsessional homoerotic motifs in the literary works not only uses art as a justification but would undermine the compulsive American "he-man" sensibility. As a British poet-critic recently noted, minority cultural movements in America tend to flaunt "feminine" qualities, from long hair through sexual inversion to emotionality and tenderness, as defiance of the narrow and repressive masculinity held as the standard of character. The working out of homoerotic problems may have given them an exaggerated place, though it also points to the therapeutic role that dominated so much Beat activity as well as, perhaps, new bi-sexual ways.

Since marginal life styles and communities provide a haven for various deviancies, especially in our highly rejecting society, the proportions of such people run high, and so do the therapeutic expectations for art. Thus confessional modes dominate. By need as well as defiant ideology, subjectivist and narcissistic emphases encourage an anti-formalist aesthetic. Beat poetry pushed a mystique of loose poetics: anti-iambic ("the breath unit"), refusing established patterns, heavy on colloquial and obscene and mixed dictions, depending on progressions by association to the extreme of surrealist disjunctions, and generally insisting on expressive irregularity and openness. The more purely verbal poetic functions—the chant, the curse, the celebratory shout, the prayer—played a major role.

Beat prose was usually autobiographical, with personal awkwardness and fragmentation taken as expression of social reality as well as of individual sincerity. Many of the writers pontificated on not being "literary" and "intellectual" but personal and direct. Social rebelliousness encouraged parody and burlesque of the officially received forms. With wearisome insistence, taboo indicated literary subject—a quickly self-defeating direction of much of post-modernist writing—and so most accounts are of sexual inversion, drug addiction, pathology, and other outcastness. Since initially the movement was quite self-consciously a dissident literary minority, coterie allusion and other personal reference runs heavy. For the same reason, cultish exoticism, in the jargon of addiction and Buddhism (and, to lesser extent, of Amerindian lore, the Beat foreign circuit, nostalgic pop culture, antique Leftism, and the San Francisco Bay Area) received elaborate play. The cultism, of course, got justifications as essential to psychic transformation and enlarged awareness. A major social function of Beat literature was to "witness" to changes of consciousness, or at least of cultural and social allegiances. The assumed audience usually seems to be other dissidents, or potential dissidents, especially the young. In that direction, it had a considerable, if sometimes rather opportunistic, success.

In its largest ambitions, Beat literature presents a personal entree into the process of apocalyptic vision. It prophesies and demonstrates, by idiosyncrasies and hysterias, against a dehumanizing and exploitative technocratic civilization—bomb-ridden, consumer-compulsive, competitively anxious, sensually confused, mass-media warped, institutionally boxed, politically mad—and therefore incapable of simplicity and contemplation and intense experience and tenderness and community and love. And surely doomed!

II. Soft and Hard Confessions
Probably two of the best as well as most influential Beat novels are Louis-Ferdinand Céline's *Journey to the End of the Night* and Henry Miller's *Tropic of Cancer*. Though written in the early 30s, a full generation before the Beat mode

became a populist movement, they contain much of what was to come, and remain largely unsuperseded. Miller, rewriting his fragmented and self-glorying Whitmanian autobiography in Paris when he enthusiastically read Céline's *Journey,* adapted some of that hard and rancorous outcast view to his bumptious innocence and surreal expressionism. The mad French doctor's bitter burlesque and nihilistic perceptiveness about his wanderings through twentieth-century war, colonialism, industrial America, Parisian suburbs, alleys and asylums, and other human rottenness, carried far. Allen Ginsberg, Jack Kerouac, William Burroughs, and other Beats, highly praised, and drew from, Céline. Curious, since American genres of sentimental confession and hobo documentary would seem to be more appropriate to what is usually recognized as Beat fictions.

Yet central to Beat writers, though little noticed, is the desperate flight from lower middle class life and its culture of anxiety. The unredeemable horrors of petit bourgeois meanness and restriction combine, as also in Céline's *Death on the Installment Plan,* with dissociated child fantasy, savage forbodings, and strange moments of tenderness. This characterizes most of the Beat confessions. Kerouac's lyrical-ruminative documentaries of his anxious *wanderjahrs*—*On the Road* (1958), *The Dharma Bums* (1959), the travel sketches not masquerading as fiction such as *The Lonesome Traveller* (1960) and his later imitations of his earlier work (such as *Big Sur*)—depend essentially on the softness of the child in flight from a petty order. This is not only the guilty-ecstatic adolescent romanticism and its poignant muddle (and its artistic correlative of the inability to realize character and scene other than in ragged detail and forced private mood—in the Thomas Wolfe manner) but the yearning for the return to innocence, both of the self and the American order. Identifying his wanderings with the quest for freedom, from that of Zen monks and American hobos through the prophetic outcasts ("Jesus was a strange hobo who walked on water"), hardly modifies the personal pathos.

Kerouac touches at moments on the existential intensity and profundity of the traditional wanderer: the defiant separateness, the sharp moral comment of a life denuded of surplus, the suspension of time by those wedded to motion, and the outcast's brilliant perceptions of most of what passes for humane order and meaning. But childishness usually takes over. On looking at the lights in the night, Kerouac comments: "I wish I was a little child in a crib in a little ranch style sweet house." In similar forlorn need, and incisive prose, he describes "kid dreams," juvenile ideas and adolescent tastes. As he notes of his "gang" of rather over-aged "boys," "We sorta wander around like children." The ideal is to return to "the happy life of childhood again." The style corresponds, with inflated and run-on sentences (perhaps an attempt to give a literally breathless heightening) and cute expletives ("comfy," "heavenly," "raving great," "glady," and the catatonic "Wow!"). The insights show similar quality, it being a great revelation of Kerouac that everybody walks around with a "dirty behind," or that most people are "crazy," or that buddies are "great," or that America is a "nutty" place. Of course there is a rather burbling charm about intensifying the commonplace, such as eating a hot dog or hungering for home. LIFE is unalterably "sad" or "fun," we are regularly told. Recurrent paranoid episodes, the guilty sexual fears, the eager and then disillusioned identifications with more manly or purposive buddies, and a constant anxious inadequacy block any more incisive ordering of experience. Yet intermittently Kerouac's kid-world, as heightened by a series of trips across America in the late 40s and middle 50s, opens into some suggestive responsiveness of a rebel on the road, junior division.

Kerouac's aesthetic, if such we can call a widespread quasi-art ideology of salvational self-expression, claims rebellion against intellectualized literature and thought. This generally comes out as free-associational confession but also, as with Ginsberg, includes efforts to "spiritualize" the flight from American lower middle class sensibility. While the material of *On the Road* mostly consists of some of the history of the coterie which became publicly identified as the Beat Generation, the novel attempts something more. Focusing on a touchingly flamboyant psychopath, Dean Moriarity (the late Neal Cassidy), it presents him as profound wanderer and "HOLY GOOF," the wild pilgrim. To achieve romantic apotheosis in an otherwise blandly repressive society, Kerouac exalts a delinquent intensity, an amoral posture and personality without much specific content. Awe, more adolescent than sacred, covers "the ones who are mad to live, mad to talk, mad to be saved, desirous of everything at the same time, the ones who never yawn or say a commonplace thing, but burn, burn, burn, like fabulous roman candles exploding like spiders across the stars and in the middle you see the blue centerlight pop and everybody goes 'Awww!'"

The fireworks hardly light up the intellectual and social vagueness, any more than do the temporary Buddhist trappings put on in *Dharma Bums*. There the hero-narrator is the outdoors American boy turned contemplative, with Japhy (Gary Snyder) providing Kerouac's pattern for a religious-therapeutic summer in the mountains and woods. The mystagoguery, and an excess of reportage on fatuous Bohemianism in the Bay Area, muddle an interesting larger theme—a call for a style of "rucksack wanderers," "Dharma bums," American Don Quixotes of tenderness who refuse to be imprisoned in a system of pointless work, forced consumption, and control by the "Master Switch" in a wired-up civilization. That moving ideal is still with us, still a leading edge of the "youth culture" in its perceptive disaffiliation and poignant vagary.

The interest of Kerouac's writings is mostly documentary. Sometimes they give apt details, hardly ever developed, about the American scene, when not obscured by "real straight talk about souls." While the trips start in earnest zest and pursue romantic intensification, they rest on an elegiac sense of lost dream and innocence. "Isn't it true that you start your life a sweet child believing everything under your father's roof? Then comes the day of the Laodiceans, when you know you are wretched and miserable and poor and blind and naked." The sense of disinheritance of the outcast child—really the American lack of community which encourages both resentment and generosity—leads to a moral awareness with a sympathy for "the great fellahin people of the world." Though in Kerouac this sense of suffering and injustice is mostly sentimental, here is part of the change in sensibility which resulted in the Civil Rights and New Left Movement of the sixties. In Kerouac's repeated and desperate "wishing I were a Negro," or a Mexican, or almost anything other than a "disillusioned" American defeated in responsiveness and wholeness because of "white ambitions," we find fragmented dramatization of the Lawrencean revulsion at willful and anxious "white consciousness." Kerouac's "deliriums" of outcast otherness sound plaintive cries for holistic feeling and life.

On the Road ends with a frenzied journey in Mexico with glimpses of what is taken to be a more real and primordial life; *Dharma Bums* ends with the trip down Desolation Mountain with glimpses of what is taken to be a primal therapy and spiritual transformation. Somewhere on those journeys, the author hopes, he has rediscovered life as it has eternally been, and will be again after the "Apocalypse" willful and arbitrary and mad American civilization is inevitably creating.

In spite of the childishness of much of the writing and thinking, Kerouac's yearning flights show us something about the American scene of the time with its harshly alienating places and lavishly fraudulent order and forlornly dissociated young. The "road is life," we are told with typical sententiousness and repetition of an old American metaphor, but it leads to both a vaguely visionary sense of a different life, "the ragged and ecstatic joy of pure being," and a "senseless nightmare road," in which even an inadequate sensibility recognizes our existential failures and foresees the collapse of the old culture.

In John Clellon Holmes' *Go,* a somewhat more analytical fiction about the same material as *On the Road,* which helped define the movement, the rebel-delinquents group motive is developed as "an inability to believe in anything . . . and the craving for excess which it inspired." However, the "youth culture," from orientalizing Beats through occultizing Hippies, equally shows a frenzied willingness to believe in almost anything so as to escape the existential perplexities. Perhaps the religiosity and the disenchantment, the disaffiliation from mainstream America and the fanciful nostrums which become fads out of the underculture, provide simply variant expressions of the deepest inability to believe in the American culture because it doesn't merit acceptance.

The soft rebellion in sensibility of a Kerouac, the All-American boy as Beat cynosure of the spiritual vagrant, melts away. Jack Kerouac went on in the 60s to mere idiosyncratic legendizing of himself (books about his own ancestry and dreams) and further pathetic withdrawal. The literature, like the figure, seems mostly symptomatic. So, I would also argue, with the more artful and arduous, and genuinely excessive, sensibility of William Burroughs. That demonic father-figure of some in the Beat coteries helped pattern a certain style of hard extremity, of drug experiment and addiction, of marginal living in New York and Mexico and Tangiers, and of paranoid and pastiched excremental vision.

Naked Lunch (first published in Paris in the late 50s), and its continuation in *The Soft Machine* and *Nova Express,* and some related literary experiments of cut-up and fragmented writing, display a peculiarly destructive anti-art which in other forms became fashionable in the sixties. *Naked Lunch,* for example, is the excreta of the drug-addict's consciousness. But the self-hating author, in order to counter the sick compulsions which dominate the work, willfully shatters plot, character, even page sequence, and other usual signs of order. This ambivalently plays with addiction's fragmentation and nausea; the art becomes homeopathic, with verbal disintegration and revulsion to counter that of consciousness. Method and madness conflict. Paranoid fantasies receive a science-fiction cast and claim to prophesy a police state implicit in our society. An ostensible attack on addiction becomes a loving catalogue of its nausea and cultish expertise. Amidst fantasies of sadistic pederasty and naturalistic treatments of addiction and poetic-obscene meditations, the positive impetus seems the most outrageous: the defense of cooperatives and the arguments for reform of cruel laws, the hortatory call for spirituality and passion, and even the simple flashes of human suffering ("Last night I woke up with someone squeezing my hand. It was my other hand."). The hated addiction, and its loving account, confirms Burroughs' major, and libertarian, insight that domination of people can never lead to the good, control *"can never be a means to anything but more control."*

Some of the ingeniously nasty fantasies of scientistic destruction aim at fairly specific satire of doctors, modern technology, cops who are really criminals, and the willful national character: "Americans have a special horror of giving up control, of letting things happen in their own way. . . . They would like to jump down into their stomachs and digest the food and shovel the shit out." But Burroughs' very style depends on just such willfullness, on such delighted shoveling from the gut. So, too, control and destruction fascinate him and take over the art. In spite of claims to exposing himself because he wishes to reveal the underside, his "prophetic mutterings" don't really leave the excrement and control and destructiveness which he excoriates. Following the logic of Celinish revulsion, the victim demands the torturing civilization. The author, too, is one of the "Citizens who want to be utterly humiliated and degraded—so many people do nowadays, hoping to jump the gun." The harsh personal confession claims to be representative of what is happening underneath our civilization, an apocalyptic awareness of the future forming. Burroughs exploits his own dissociations and perversities and pathologies in the attempted downward path to illumination. Thus redemption becomes a metabolic drug problem, anal rending opens up a greater reality, bodily discharges provide ecstatic colorations, until "we see God through our assholes."

Burroughs' best fragments come forth as surreal comic rhetoric ("mail order whorehouse," "osteopaths of the spirit," etc.), as pieces of caricature of junkie and police and technologue types—aren't they really all one type?—and as intermittent burlesque of usual claims to goodness and beauty and sense. But the excremental obsessions, the pedantry about drugs, the forced poeticism with addict analogies (a mystic search for "connections" which contradicts his basically positivistic bent), and the willful fracturing of the material reduce the suggestiveness to the merely artful. This is melodrama, not only an insistence on degradation so to be *the* bottomside moralist but also literary wickedness. For homoerotic and addict flagellation of the flesh are not, in fact, the evil of our time, not the horrendously banal dehumanization and destruction which we must struggle to comprehend. The confessional author indulges in rather than enlarges the personal nausea which provides the dominant tone, and tedium, of *Naked Lunch*. We are force-fed literary excrement in the name of a truthful diet, an interesting effort, but most of it turns out to be a private snack.

The confessions of Kerouac and Burroughs, and a good many imitations of these soft and hard, adolescent and pathological, artistic manners, don't really produce major literary experience. Both writers make righteous claims of going beyond literary "intellectuals" and "entertainers." Indeed they do, but then their proper effort is no longer intelligent literature. They do not succeed, and perhaps one cannot, in having it both ways. Apocalyptic confession has been better done before, by such as hard Celine and soft Miller, who managed to confess more reality with more art. Nor do Kerouac and Burroughs, and the many others, allow us to fully transcend literary judgment; we can hardly see them as saints of the present and therefore prophets of the new culture.

III. The Art of Poetic Saintliness

The Beat movement encouraged, and practiced, public performances of poetry—coffee house readings, poems recited in bars to a jazz beat, group word-fests of those high on pot or wine, as well as more *outré* (and sometimes nude, mystical or belligerent) use of the poetic. Those who did not see these sometimes quite effective performances can recognize from the published remains that the real effort was not towards what we usually consider the literary object but to the half-verbal occasion for ritualism, therapy, curse, exhibition or celebration. Valid activities in their own right, we should not expect them to also produce the precious artifacts, conventionally bound in small volumes or academic anthologies and used for private meditation, that we usually call poems. The words of prayer, rage and festival do not gain from printed permanency. They depend on the physical situation and communal spirit and therapeutic function, far more than on verbal craft and formal order, and so are not "literature" in the academic or modernist senses. The Beats enlarged and spread the uses of the poetic, though the purely literary results tend to be thin and unartful.

No doubt some of the self-identified Beat poets thought, and some of the careerist ones still think, they were being Artists in the "high culture" senses. Mostly they were not. Separated from the group or occasion, the poetry is no more high art than the lyrics of blues or rock separated from the musical performance. Probably the poetic impetus that moved the Beat littérateurs is more generally found now amongst the creative performers at musical festivals. There would seem to be considerable continuity between the poets chanting at The Place in North Beach, San Francisco, in the mid-50s and the composers singing at the massive Peace and Art Festival near Woodstock, New York in 1969. A decade later than the literary Beats, their progeny, the Hippies, more fully recognized the communal focus of their artistry in ritual and celebration. By the late 60s, those in the underculture far less often practiced unconscious parody of the high culture in claiming officious careers as Artists. But in the 50s even many of the most dissident still treated the Man of Letters as culture hero and aspired to Poet or Novelist as justification for marginal life style as well as self-sanctification of sensitivity.

Before noting some other characteristics of the Beat poetic role, we might ask what text we should use. With the one main exception of Allen Ginsberg, it is hard to identify major progenitors of Beat poeticism. As with the New Left political movement developing slightly later, and as with the Hippies of the 60s, there were exceptional persons (frequently not the most celebrated ones) but an essentially egalitarian tone and truly anarchical quality which does not allow us to fully identify one, or several, figures as *the* movement or the sufficient personification of its characteristics. In revolt against hierarchies of values as well as persons, much of the endurance of the underculture depends on its amorphousness—a temper and style fluid, tolerantly various, loosely grouped, anonymously carried by persons more than publications, and unprogrammatic and unstructured. In short, libertarian in social reality as well as in literary imagination. Surely, too, the movement, and its continuation, shift and change in resistance to the co-optation by the mainline cultural institutions which, empty and cannibalistic, desperately seek new material for titillation and profit. Thus an unauthoritarian cultural revolution attempts, with only partial success (the Beats served much in fad and fashion), to evade a hostile and counterfeiting order.

Many of the writings linked to the Beat movement seem more accidentally than essentially so. Even one of the better known figures, Lawrence Ferlinghetti, denies much relation to the Beats, except as publishing friend. His own poetry, as in *A Coney Island of the Mind,* at its best shows an urbanely comic cast hardly in accord with the usual tone of the movement. So, too, with Ferlinghetti's political broadsides. Propinquity also accounts in considerable part for some confusing the Beat writers with the "Black Mountain school" of poets. Though there is some overlap, the latter is a much more restricted, rather cultish, poetic experimentation linked to the charismatic figure of Charles Olson. His fervently idiosyncratic writings (*The Maximus Poems*), and his synthetically narrow and flat verbal aesthetic, considerably contrast with the free surrealism and communal therapeutic common to the Beat movement. Various other writers loosely connected with the Beats relate by time and place and only secondarily by some loosely common sense of dissidence from American social and cultural orthodoxies. Many of these were simply figures present in the 50s as part of long-time Bay Area Bohemia: the mannerist-proletarian Kenneth Rexroth, the religionized Jeffers, Brother Antoninus, and others such as Robert Duncan, Philip Whalen, Jack Spicer, Robin Blazer, etc.—hardly of one style or aesthetic or prophetic role. Perhaps second best known in the 50s as a Beat poet was the nasty-clever gamin Gregory Corso (*Bomb* and *Gasoline*) who came up with cute-Dadaist verbal flourishes, such as "fried shoes." There were quite a number of them. With more moral than literary appropriateness, some social-religious spokesmen also identified themselves as poets with the Beats. Perhaps the best known of these, Gary Snyder (*Riprap* and *Myths and Texts*) had, and has, serious interests in natural living and Buddhism, which, unfortunately, do not much improve his poetic

quaintness and flat writing. There are others who may merit discussion as minor poets or prophets, though not especially because of their role in the Beat movement. But there could hardly be a *good* anthology of Beat poetry as such.

Allen Ginsberg, because of his central and continuing role as well as representativeness, merits fuller discussion. I think it should be granted from the start that he is not much of a poet in most usual literary senses, though he may well be an admirable and important practitioner of poetic saintliness. Carefully going again through his three volumes of published poetry covering the 50s (*Howl and Other Poems, Kaddish and Other Poems 1958-60,* and *Reality Sandwiches 1953-60*), I find three pieces that could well bear rereading as poems: 'Howl," "America," and "Death to Van Gogh's Ear!" Other pasages here and there give a curious surreal twist, or are informative of matters mostly Ginsbergian, such as the bitter-bathetic physical description of his mad mother in the elegy-prayer "Kaddish," or maybe of some other non-literary interest. But most of it is poorly realized, pastiches of awkward language which many a poet could rewrite into more consistent style and apprehendable experience. The stuff of it seems more often unmade than crafted, and it is patent that Ginsberg never quite found a literary style of his own. Much of what he published as poems can better be considered pre-poems, fitting his own categories of "notes" and "nightmares" (including the drug "visions") and "musings." He is less writing poems than awkwardly adumbrating a personal and public "spiritual" mission. He adapts poetic methods to "widen the area of consciousness" and, while translating personal therapy as public revelation, hopes that the reader will "taste my mouth in your ear."

Certainly Ginsberg displays considerable ambivalence about his poetic role, but finally degrades the writer to justify the seer. Though posing sometimes as a *naif* who wants a visceral poetry of direct screams and obscenities—a stance partly contradicted by his public as well as private acts of charm and intelligence and charity—he is also highly, probably excessively, literary, full of commemorative allusions to his whole tradition from Blake through Whitman to Apollinaire and his own contemporaries. In the provocative surrealist styled poem, "Death to Van Gogh's Ear!" he uses disparate images of the "mad" visionary poets, such as Mayakovsky and Crane, set against more truly insane public leaders and their order of "Money" and "Owners" and "vanishing Selfhood!" He suggests a government cabinet of mad poets, an anarchic cultural order in place of a repressive political one. With wry aptness, he comments within the poem on what he is doing: "History will make this poem prophetic and its awful silliness a hideous spiritual music."

Not so silly, with its vivacious disjunctures, wit, and (for once) meshing of syntax and sense, it sweepingly extends that most basic theme of modernist art, the culture against the society. This can also be said about the burlesque "America." Though ending with a comic pledge of allegiance ("America I'm putting my queer shoulder to the wheel."), he lashes out at an exploitatively false and insensitively technological civilization. "Your machinery is too much for me. / You made me want to be a saint." This conversion, though hardly realized as poetry, runs through all. Apparently central is that night in New York when he had a Blakean vision of eternity: "my eyes were opened for one hour / seeing in dreadful ecstacy / the motionless buildings of New York rotting / under the tides of Heaven." This intensity he desperately seeks to recapture in drugged and mythic and other gropings which don't quite translate into mere words.

The terms, the needs, of the conversion experience may be found in exacerbated awareness of loneliness, cruelty, madness and death. Their scene serves as equally important, the placement in the marginal ugliness of industrial-urban America and the indifferent skidrow human dumps of an aggrandizing society. The homely Jewish invert from the wastelands of New Jersey ("My Sad Self" and the recurrent images of his own ugliness) wants to transcend his unsatisfactory self and world, transform all not only into "one moment of tenderness" but into that which will sustain it: "A MAGIC UNIVERSE." Of course he sees the absurdity of it, the grotesque effort to put "a flower in the ass." But "It's hard to eat shit, without having visions."

To love all, even one's ugly, perverted, inadequate self, requires the largest effort, beyond mere art, beyond the sophisticated whimper, then, to the "Howl." In that poem's run-on of fractured details (Part I) of the cold, junky, mean, loveless misorder forced upon marginal and outcast men, we find the bitter images which demand conversion. The semi-hysterical chant against such a world's false gods (Part II), against "Moloch," whose "mind is pure machinery," and the Molochs of stone and government, of war and oil, of blindness and antennae, of abstractions and money, denounces the loss of human sensitivity

and "natural ecstacy" that leave us "lacklove and manless in Moloch!" Therefore one can only choose union (Part III) with the sensitive mad, the lost visionaries, and chant the dirge "I'm with you in Rockland [New York State Mental Hospital]." One ends, one hopes, transformed, endlessly praying ("Footnote to Howl"), in hip fractured variations on Blake's penultimate aphorism of *The Marriage of Heaven and Hell,* "Everything is holy!" Nothing less than the anguished sacramental sense of life will restore us.

"Howl" serves as one of the best known poems of our time, though not in the schoolteacher anthologies and literary racketeering. Or perhaps it would be more accurate to say that its anguished view of contemporary life and yearning for tender poeticization of existence provide the most influential saintly gesture for a generation. Ginsberg's effort to spiritualize the self in a destructive order of commercial and technological domination— quite consciously a social-political as well as literary-religious rebellion—provides essential style for the underculture. It is poetry mostly because the poet is priest of the confession-conversion-protest. For this, it seems, the traditions of modernist poetic culture provide a better discipline than does theology and ritual, or ideology and politics. It is from modernist culture that he finds the delineations of sensibility in revolt against a commercial—technological order and the grounds for a consciousiness that can include delight and death, sensitivity and sodomy, far-out drugs and fractured myths, Dadaist disjunctions and libertarian perceptions. Modernism, then, may finally result less in poetry than in saintliness, including a good bit of holy foolishness.

The later Ginsberg, dressed in denims, beard and indulgently ethereal smile, silencing on television the abstract Rightist rant of William Buckley by chanting an erotic imitation of Wordsworth, or the half naked, bead-draped, sutra-chanting Saint Allen leading a circle of dancing kids in the middle of a massive war-protest march, carries on, with proper Surrealist decorum, the poetic saintliness. That is the imagery that we, along with a whole populist culture, should focus on. The society needs it, the culture exists by it, and that is the real art and imagination of Allen Ginsberg.

IV. The Reverberating Beat

The Beats appear to have had a considerable, perhaps even disproportionate, effect on American sensibility and life styles. Or at least we see them that way because, willy nilly, they provide as well as represent much of the rebellious mode of the time. While their most significant effects belong to a larger social and cultural movement which goes quite beyond them, and the 50s, they also seem to have had considerable literary significance, less individual than as a movement. Beat writings were not the only but were certainly one of the largest and most influential refusals of the academic baroque and "little magazine" neoclassicism which dominated post-World War II serious writing. In both poetry and prose, the Beat impetus gave considerable "freeing," opening up subject matters and loosening forms. In style, the Beats carried the recurrent Romantic return to more direct and intense language. The "obscenity" and colloquial spontaneity and, less positively, the argot (such as that of the addict sub-culture) certainly spread widely from the Beats and related writers. Beat use of surrealist disjunctions and visionary metaphors and Dadaist burlesques and nihilist mockeries gave new life to such imagery even though varied writers, including Henry Miller and Kenneth Patchen and Nathanael West, employed it a generation before. More broadly, the Beats helped regenerate the cultural rebellion and allied social dissidence which the hot-and-cold-war cultural nationalism of the preceding decade and a half had muted in literary and social awareness.

Probably cultural movements, like ideologies, show more import in their climatic effects than in their own ideas and arts. While "fictions" such as those of Kerouac and Burroughs may help us understand the byways of a larger movement of sensibility—of the movement itself they tend to be more signs and symptoms than players and prophets—their art is less interesting than other works only peripherally related to them. For example, Norman Mailer's *Advertisements for Myself* aggrandizingly utilizes the confessional and extremist ways of the Beats (just as Mailer had previously imitated the naturalistic War Novel, the Ideological Melodrama, and the Hollywood Novel). He then took on from the Beat weather the obscenity, the therapeutic and drug postures, the rhetoric of rage, the magic, the glorification of the psychopath ("The White Negro"), and the stance of exacerbated revolt against American civilization. Some things, such as the adolescent egotism, he already had; others, such as simple living and orientalism and the return to nature, were quite alien to the New York ideologue. Adding tough-guy bluster, and considerable intellectual adroitness, Mailer came out with his own version of Beatness. Mailer, of course, was manipulating, as usual, and passing through to something

else, yet another Mailerism. But that sophisticated ambivalence, which makes him a rather exploitative public figure, adds some intriguing and perceptive richness to his writing—more than with the simpler, and no doubt more sincere and honest, Beat literary cynosures. As rebel-pretender and prophetic posturer, Mailer displays the alter-ego of much of what he attacks. But because he is partly a genuine fraud, he is truly responsive to much of what is happening in American culture, as he was with the Beats and his own pose of Hipsterism, and makes up in artful perception for his moral dubiousness. Or almost.

In another direction, the most delightful novel of the 50s may well be J. P. Donleavey's *The Ginger Man*. Apparently a once-only achievement (his later works are coy and sentimental), *The Ginger Man* carries out, at an artful distance, the mocking and tender wanderings and the intense and disenchanted life-hungerings we find in the Beats. This comic and bawdy picaresque of an Irish-American student abroad may have no direct relation to the Beats (though it apparently comes out of some of the same sources), and in amorality belongs outside any movement, yet in longer historical perspective it may reasonably appear as the best artistic ordering of much of the Beat sense of life in that time.

A later exceptional novel, considerably and directly influenced by William Burroughs' *Naked Lunch,* especially by his paranoid metaphors and vision of control by a technological-psychiatric bureaucracy, may most fully realize in fiction the rebellious side of the Beat movement: Ken Kesey's *One Flew Over the Cuckoo's Nest* (1962). Its defiant and wandering rogue-hero becomes the therapeutic-sacramental martyr in modern society's microcosm of a mental hospital—a Western version of "I'm with you in Rockland." *Cuckoo's* McMurphy provides the most persuasive image of the Beat hero, the brilliant psychopath fighting the system unto saintliness. Kesey, of course, also famously carried on outside of literature the rebel-saint role established by the Beats, and, therefore, provides proper completion to our sense of the movement. He gave up mere novel writing to become a psychedelic guru in the Bay Area, far-out holy leader of the drug-and-rock Merry Pranksters, frenzied wanderer across the American landscapes (even with some of the same people who were in earlier Beat pilgrimages), and major founder of redemptive Hippy communalism. The Beat poetic saintliness continues.

Thus the main significance of the Beat movement of the 50s, I believe, was not literary but cultural in a far broader sense. In attempting to change the bland bureaucratic-technological society by transforming sensibility and trying to radically revitalize a false order by creating a different life-style, the movement was toward a cultural revolution. The new populist culture contained considerable malaise: adolescent addiction—and addictive adolescence—but also rather synthetic religiosity, morality replaced by relativistic muddle, a decline in artistic craftsmanship in the name of self-expression, and an often naively ineffective politics of rebelliousness and tenderness. But the movement itself, and our need for it, remains considerably greater than its obvious failings. Whether the final result will be a new religion, a full social revolution, or merely a quaint phase of cultural history, we cannot yet be sure. In the meantime, we can feel with the reverberations of the Beats many more of the deficiencies of our culture and society. Not least, we should more fully recognize that art is not a remote elitist creation of artifacts to be preserved but the often desperate and poignant expression of a way to live and the attempt to re-create human community. That is the beat of it.

JOHN TYTELL (ESSAY DATE 1999)

SOURCE: Tytell, John. "The Frozen Fifties." In *Paradise Outlaws: Remembering the Beats,* pp. 44-64. New York: William Morrow and Company, Inc., 1999.

In the following essay, Tytell examines the rise of the Beat Generation in the context of contemporary political events, using several examples of Beat writing to trace their mutual impact.

From time to time there occurs some revolution, or sudden mutation of form and content in literature. Then, some way of writing which has been practised for a generation or more, is found by a few people to be out of date, and no longer to respond to contemporary modes of thought, feeling, and speech. A new kind of writing appears, to be greeted at first with disdain and derision; we hear that the tradition has been flouted, and that chaos has come. After a time it appears that the new way of writing is not destructive but re-creative. It is not that we have repudiated the past, as the obstinate enemies—and also the stupidest supporters—of any new movement like to believe, but that we have enlarged our conception of the past and in the light of what is new we see the past in a new pattern.

—T. S. Eliot, *"American Literature and Language"*

I The Syndrome of Shutdown

Those with a certain literary rectitude may find it odd to consider Eliot's remarks in the context of the Beat Generation. Kerouac, after all, in a manifesto he called "The Origins of Joy in

Poetry," complained about Eliot's "dreary negative rules," about his "constipation" and the "emasculation of the pure masculine urge to freely sing."

While it is correct to assume that the openheartedness of many of the Beats was directly opposed to the calculated set of disguises and the elaborated "personae" informing Eliot's modernism, all writers have ancestors and spiritual fathers; they all exist in historical moments that can be measured and that motivate them to see their own past, as Eliot put it, "in a new pattern."

More than a half century ago, when the writers who would form the Beat Generation were establishing their first friendships in New York City, the United States was collectively about to win the largest-scale international conflict ever. Curiously, the individualism that had characterized the American way through the nineteenth century seemed threatened by new forces.

The historian Hannah Arendt, in the tradition of George Orwell's *1984,* declared that the postwar era was marked by the insidious emergence of faceless power, of "Rule by Nobody," as she put it. During the Truman administration, millions of Americans were investigated because of their imagined ideological sympathies. Allen Ginsberg called it the "Syndrome of Shutdown," the time of the closed society when the crucial decisions—shall we build thousands of nuclear devices, shall we inject nicotine into cigarettes?—would be made in secret.

Revisionist historians will argue that the Cold War and the threat of nuclear holocaust were primarily a means of maintaining and even accelerating an unprecedented rate of war production that had resolved all the economic issues perpetuating the Great Depression of the 1930s. From 1950 to 1953, defense spending tripled in the United States, and the country's major growth industry had become the production of sophisticated weapons systems. Disarmament meant recession, as the economy seemed inextricably tied to an armaments industry, and we began supplying the rest of the world with military hardware.

At the same time, military lobbyists and some politicians maintained that we lagged behind the Russians in attack capability. The Soviet invasion of Hungary in 1956, the erection of the Berlin Wall, and the launch of the Sputnik satellite in 1957, all seemed a confirmation of what the lobyists had been saying.

The correlation between the defense budget and an unprecedented affluence was clear, though it would hardly have been politically correct to point it out in the 1950s. Affluence seems most compatible with denial, which by the 1950s had become endemic in the United States. This, of course, was the historical moment when big business merged with bureaucratic government, when the former heads of Procter & Gamble assumed control of the Food and Drug Administration.

The denial was also encouraged by a political climate of psychic terrorism, the so-called Red Menace dramatized by the trials of Alger Hiss and the Rosenbergs. As the novelist E. L. Doctorow noted in his brilliant fiction *The Book of Daniel,* based on the Rosenbergs, a spirit of fierce partisanship and recrimination dominated the postwar years, which he attributed "to the continuance beyond the end of the war of the war hysteria. Unfortunately, the necessary emotional fever for fighting a war cannot be turned off like a water faucet. Enemies must continue to be found. The mind and heart cannot be demobilized as quickly as the platoon. On the contrary, like a fiery furnace at white heat, it takes a considerable time to cool."

Actually, during the affluent fifties, the United States was being physically transformed. Seven million men had returned to make babies and build supermarkets, malls, and four-lane highways all over the country. Suddenly, radio had been replaced by television with its potential to condition us all into more efficient and insatiable consumers. Whereas our Puritan ancestors had taught Americans that borrowing money was ungodly, that excessive interest was usurious, postwar capitalism seized Keynes's notion of infinite credit for nations and applied it to the suburban family.

As a sign of the new comfort zones on the American horizon, the air conditioner could transform a fetid summer afternoon and remove the sweat from a man's brow. This innovation was reflected in the rapid development of Arizona and the Southwest, just as it became the title of Henry Miller's jeremiad *The Air-Conditioned Nightmare,* a book denouncing the changes Miller saw on his return to the United States during the war years after a decade of expatriation.

For most, the new technology was a convenient distraction from any political costs to freedom in the United States. The Cold War hysteria was accelerated by Senator Joseph McCar-thy's allegations of traitors in the State Department, and the House Un-American Activities Committee witch-hunts in academia and Hollywood.

The gossip columnist Hedda Hopper's remark that those suspected of disloyalty were best interned in concentration camps is a touchstone of the irresponsible dimensions of political rage at that time. Soon the enormous inquisitional terror of a federal HUAC was replicated state by state by similar committees intent on declaring what it meant to be an American.

The right-wing persecution was not entirely without precedent or basis. The first Red Scare had occurred during the First World War, when the Russian Bolsheviks withdrew from the battlefield and were seen as deserting the Allied cause. In the United States, as Warren Beatty's film *Reds* suggests, there was considerable fear that workers and their unions would be organized by Communists loyal only to Moscow.

This same fear was prevalent after the Second World War. The war had brought Americans together and made them suspicious of questioning and dissent. Some of McCarthy's victims were involved in espionage, some had been active in left-wing causes, some did have associations with Communists. The American Communist Party was dependent on Soviet financing, which meant Soviet control. Party members, who were after all members of a secret society, accepted the dogma of the Party line. I remember students at CCNY in the late 1950s who naively still revered Stalin and Mao as gods who could not fail and refused to admit that these men had butchered and sacrificed millions of their own countrymen for the sake of expedience.

The repercussions of the Red Scare were enormous, from the suicide of Harvard scholar F. O. Matthiesson—author of *American Renaissance,* the classic study of American transcendentalism—to the dismissal of sixty professors at the University of California at Berkeley in 1951 for refusing to sign loyalty oaths. There are thousands of other examples. The poet Gary Snyder, a young man working for the U.S. Forest Service early in the 1950s, was discharged as a security risk—a case of the poet preaching to the trees?—because of radical associations as an undergraduate at Reed College. Allen Ginsberg's companion Peter Orlovsky was reading a book by psychiatrist Erich Fromm at boot camp in West Virginia in 1953, which caused an army lieutenant to call him a Communist. Orlovsky was transferred to a San Francisco hospital, where he completed his military service as a medic.

The magazine *Red Channels* caused a blacklisting of intellectuals who may have signed a petition two decades earlier, of artists and writers with leftist or progressive perspectives. The FBI used illegal wiretaps and created the Security Index, a list of millions of citizens who might require detention in the event of national emergency. These attempts to poison the atmosphere with fear and to enforce conformity at all costs succeeded in debilitating and marginalizing all progressive programs from disarmament to civil rights.

One register of the psychic contamination during the Korean War period in the early 1950s was recalled by the poet Michael McClure in his book *Scratching the Beat Surface*:

> My self-image in those years was of finding myself—young, high, a little crazed, needing a haircut, in an elevator with burly, crew-cutted, square-jawed eminences staring at me like I was misplaced cannon fodder. We hated the war and the inhumanity and the coldness. The country had the feeling of martial law. An undeclared military state had leapt out of Daddy Warbucks' tanks and sprawled over the landscape. As artists we were oppressed.

One major symptom of the repression was a culture of informing—actually what the Communists had effected in postwar China and Russia—so at Harvard one Henry Kissinger, a teaching fellow in the early 1950s, was accused of opening his fellow students' mail and passing some of it to the FBI. Ronald Reagan, president of the Screen Actors Guild, had been an FBI informant since the early 1940s.

The American Puritans had imagined pagan frolics in the woods and guilt by association with Satan. The new informers intoned the names of the guilty before secret committees. Some of the informers, like the failed novelist Whittaker Chambers, were drunkards with powerful imaginations and the novelistic ability to spin a good story. Others were seeking advancement. Informers were rewarded in many ways, but the most shocking aspect of the matter is that J. Edgar Hoover, director of the FBI, insisted that the informant's identity had to be shielded. It was enough to be named to be considered guilty, and this represented a profound reversal of what had been considered an essential American liberty.

The paternal, benevolently benign presence overseeing the political repression of the 1950s was Dwight D. Eisenhower, the Supreme Allied Commander during the Second World War, and a representative figure who helps explain his era. His radiant grin seemed derived from a Grant Wood painting or a Sherwood Anderson story. In her novel *The Bell Jar*, the poet Sylvia Plath aggressively compared Eisenhower's bald head and blank stare to a "foetus in a bottle," but her harsh image underestimated the attraction of his placating but firm charm. Ike's rounded face suggested a placid contentment and a beguiling innocence, a heartland look Americans associated with an old-fashioned optimism and courage.

As the most popular American of his time, Eisenhower could be used by fund-raisers, whether for Columbia University, which was his apprenticeship in civilian administration, or the Republican Party. He delegated his authority freely, to men like the Dulles brothers in matters of foreign policy and espionage, and to Charles Wilson, his Secretary of Defense, who insisted that whatever was good for General Motors was good for the country. That sentiment became the unspoken ideology of the fifties, and the utility of corporate profits the ultimate value. Only a very select group of artists and intellectuals could see that to succeed, the mercantile mind—what Ginsberg called "Moloch"—would even sacrifice the environment for the sake of the profit motive. Of course, such rapacity was not traditionally associated with democratic governance, which was supposed to exist for the good of the people.

Although Eisenhower was an uninspiring speaker, he became an icon of confident victory in a new kind of war. Eisenhower was the presiding figure during the 1950s, a moment when notions of personal responsibility were being subsumed by the values caused by an unprecedentedly sophisticated technology and corporate largeness, when the future was being mortgaged to the Pentagon, when the industrial oligarchy that Eisenhower warned us of in his farewell address was perpetuating the power of the police state.

II The Control State

I think this fear of arbitrary authority relates to an important part of the Beats' prophecy. In the preface to Barry Miles's 1986 edition of the facsimile *Howl*, Allen Ginsberg remarks that in writing the poem "I was curious to leave behind after my generation an emotional time bomb that would continue exploding in U.S. consciousness in case our military-industrial-nationalist complex solidified into a repressive police bureaucracy." This was a shared, central Beat sentiment.

For example, in one of the rare political moments in *On the Road,* Sal Paradise, Dean Moriarty, and a few friends arrive in Washington, D.C., on the day of Truman's inauguration for his second term. Driving down Pennsylvania Avenue, Kerouac observed that "great displays of war might" lined the street: "B-29's, PT boats, all kinds of war material that looked murderous in the snowy grass."

In the next scene, after being stopped for speeding and harassed by police because of their appearance, Kerouac observed, "The American police are involved in psychological warfare against those Americans who don't frighten them with imposing papers and threats. It's a Victorian police force; it peers out of musty windows and wants to inquire about everything, and can make crimes if the crimes don't exist to its satisfaction."

One such "criminal" was William S. Burroughs, who in 1947 was growing marijuana secreted between rows of alfalfa on his farm in New Waverly, Texas. He was trying to grow opium, which doesn't grow north of the Rio Grande, but didn't he anticipate a multibillion-dollar business that the government ultimately could not control? Control, of course, is very much to the point: "*You see, control,*" Burroughs tells us in italics in *Naked Lunch, "can never be a means to any practical end. . . . It can never be a means to anything but more control. . . . Like junk . . .*"

In Texas, Burroughs observed how the agricultural bureaucracy conspired to provide migrant labor for the big farmers at peon's wages. Actually, the federal bureaucracy tripled under Truman, and that had to trouble so arch an individualist as Burroughs, who, when I interviewed him in 1974, even denied belonging to the Beat movement. Burroughs would later relentlessly parody bureaucrats and authority figures in *Naked Lunch,* his nightmarish vision of a society in a state of entropy that develops a perspective so nihilistic as to believe in nothing, certainly not in any organized system.

Burroughs's discontinuity—his microcosmic focus on what frequently appear to be unrelatable experiences—is part of a similar attempt to deny the organic unities of nineteenth-century structure in poetry and fiction. Burroughs's use of the "cut-up" method—an arbitrary juxtaposition of randomly selected words and phrases—is part of an attempt to restructure the grammar of perception; the new linguistic order that Burroughs invents initiates the Beats' assault on the conditioning influences of language.

Burroughs takes the motif of the Unreal City from *The Waste Land* and compounds it with a nauseating imagery of hideous physical disintegration and degradation that promises a state of future plague. His hanged-men episodes in *Naked Lunch* are grotesque parodies of the talismanic material Eliot himself parodied with the grail legend in *The Waste Land.*

Burroughs presents these horrors with an unsettling calm, a cold earnestness reminiscent of Swift, a view of the psychological transformations latent in fantasy close to Kafka. His view of man as helpless victim reminds us of Sartre, Beckett, and Genet. Entering the absolute nadir of existence, Burroughs's fiction defines a purgatory of endless suffering—Beat in the sense of beaten, oppressed, and dehumanized.

If there is a political center in *Naked Lunch,* it is the equation of cancer and bureaucracy:

> The end result of complete cellular representation is cancer. Democracy is cancerous, and bureaus are its cancer. A bureau takes root anywhere in the state, turns malignant like the Narcotic Bureau, and grows and grows, always reproducing more of its own kind, until it chokes the host if not controlled or excised. Bureaus cannot live without a host, being true parasitic organisms. (A cooperative on the other hand *can* live without the state. That is the road to follow. The building up of independent units to meet needs of the people who participate in the functioning of the unit. A bureau operates on opposite principle of *inventing* needs to justify its existence.) Bureaucracy is wrong as a cancer, a turning away from the human evolutionary direction of infinite potentials and differentiation and independent spontaneous action, to the complete parasitism of a virus.

William Burroughs's identification of bureaucracy as the cancer in democracy may seem offensive, though it is characteristic of the apocalyptic urgency of the Beats. I have taught the novel to undergraduates for two decades, and this is a book that more profoundly than any other violates the nerve endings and offends.

Of course, what was most threatening about *Naked Lunch* from the establishment's point of view was not its predictive warning of the drug plague that would sap the support systems of Western civilization but its detailed, "factualist" accounting of bizarre sexual rituals, the cannibalistic mutilations and orgasmic death hangings that seem related, however loosely, to the

Mayan practices that fascinated Burroughs when he studied at Mexico City College in the early 1950s.

Burroughs described the factualist style in a letter to Ginsberg dated November 9, 1948: "All arguments, all nonsensical considerations as to what people 'should do' are irrelevant. Ultimately, there is only fact on all levels, and the more one argues, verbalizes, moralizes, the less he will see and feel of fact." For Burroughs, "factualism" meant that the writer had to suspend any moral evaluation, which since Fielding and the first stirrings of the novel as a form had been an obligatory priority.

It is difficult for us now to imagine the radical depth of Burroughs's suspension of moral judgment. The 1950s were an era when any public discussion of sexual matters in the United States was taboo, when masturbation was seen as a cause of insanity and premarital sex as immoral, when half of American women were married by the age of nineteen, oral sex was considered sheer perversion, and adultery and homosexuality were regarded as criminal acts. In 1950, a group of Republican senators accused the Truman administration of being rife with homosexuals, and one of President Eisenhower's first executive orders made homosexuality grounds for disbarment from any form of federal employment.

So lines like "Gentle reader, we see God through our assholes in the flash bulb of orgasm"—which Burroughs wrote in Tangier in the mid-1950s—were considered as intolerable (certainly in Boston, at least, where the courts had to decide whether the book could be sold) as the fact that Dr. Alfred Kinsey, an obscure investigator of gall wasps from Indiana University, had amassed some eighteen thousand sexual case histories, many in the Times Square area and three of them with Burroughs, Ginsberg, and Kerouac.

I see Kinsey's sexual explorations as a parallel to Freud's curiosities about the mind, although when *Sexual Behavior in the Human Male* appeared in 1948 and the subsequent report on women in 1953, these studies were viciously attacked by psychiatrists and psychoanalysts for reporting data rather than making judgments. In other words, psychiatists, like the Victorian novelists of an earlier era, were expected to enforce social controls, to condemn, vilify, or declare medically abnormal what the power elite could not publicly condone.

Incidentally, many of these same psychiatrists vigorously proposed electroshock therapy for depression even though it effectively erased memory and was so crudely barbarous as a technique patients had to be strapped down during convulsions. After shock treatments the patient—take, for example, Carl Solomon, to whom *Howl* is dedicated—was placed on a permanent lifetime diet (or is the word "addiction"?) of drugs like Thorazine, drugs that lead us to Prozac or Huxley's prediction of the soma that would control us all.

III Derelicts

Each of the Beats turned to writing because of a psychic wound: Burroughs had his childhood nightmares and the murder of his wife, Kerouac was four when his older brother Gerard died of rheumatic fever, Ginsberg suffered with his troubled mother, Naomi.

It is illuminating, in this connection, to note that the catalyst figures for each of the Beats—Solomon for Ginsberg, Huncke for Burroughs, and Neal Cassady for Kerouac—were all wounded figures as well, perennial outsiders who had enormous difficulty living within what they called "the system." Solomon spent eight years in mental hospitals, and ended his life working as a messenger. Like Huncke and Cassady, he was a talker, and he told me he had talked his way into the bin, which made him an American "untouchable." Both Huncke and Cassady were untouchables as well because they had been to prison for theft, although Cassady's incarceration was in a reform school for having stolen the Denver district attorney's car on a dare. All three relied on drugs, Solomon on Thorazine, Cassady on amphetamines and marijuana—he was known as the Johnny Appleseed of the West Coast—and Huncke on an entire pharmacology of opiates.

But even more important than their outlaw status was the fact that each aspired to write, Solomon with his pithy essays, Huncke with his stories of circus life and the hustler's road, Cassady with the awkward story of his childhood on the Denver bowery. While these men were sympathetically accepted as "dumbsaints," to use Kerouac's term—and the crucial point of the entire Beat enterprise was exactly this sympathetic encouragement—they were shunned by the rest of the world as crazy deviants or con men.

No wonder the postwar years seemed to artists to be an imperiled period of profound powerlessness. This was true on a general scale—not just true of the writers I am discussing here. The novelist William Styron claimed his generation had been "cut to pieces" by the trauma of the war and the "almost unimaginable presence of the bomb." In *The Prisoner of Sex,* Norman Mailer wondered how he survived those years without losing his mind. The Abstract Expressionist painter Adolph Gottlieb remembered painting with "a feeling of absolute desperation." His generation "felt like derelicts," Gottlieb maintained. "Everything felt hopeless and we had nothing to lose."

Gottlieb's word "derelict" is on the same wavelength as Herbert Huncke's "beat," the term that led Jack Kerouac to name a generation. Jack Kerouac defined "beat" as the state of a spirit that had been so defeated, so beaten down by experience, that the writer could honestly confess his deepest, most personal feelings without inhibition or shame because there was nothing to lose.

Beat begins with a sense of cultural displacement and disaffiliation, a distrust of official "truth," an awareness that things are often not what they seem to be, which is a fundamental point of departure for writers. Kerouac would later extend his definition by relating Beat to beatitude, a state of bliss achieved through jazz, sex, meditation, writing, or any other intense experience in which the sense of self is obliterated. The object was to open the individual through the doors of feeling, to leave him vulnerable, sympathetic, and receptive.

I have too much respect for Kerouac's fiction to suggest that it was self-consciously philosophical or in any sense a programmatic exposition. But the famous characters in *On the Road,* with their sometimes frenetic searches for the next visionary epiphany, their mad, ecstatic conversations, and their cross-country journeys, are in flight from an American they found too cold-hearted—so they found it difficult to breathe in an atmosphere of envy, fear, competition, and suspicion. At the same time—forming a central tension in the novel—it is a flight in pursuit of an American warmth for which Kerouac yearned and which suffused his fiction, a quality that made some of his critics condemn him for sentimentality.

The reviewers misread the novel almost without exception, finding it incoherent, unstructured, unsound as art, and unhappy as prophecy. Instead of seeing Dean Moriarty as a genuine picaresque center, and thereby a source of unity in a novel about turbulence, the reviewers attacked the sensibility of nihilism.

It is, perhaps, easier to see Dean today as a remarkable fusion of desperation and joy, as the "ragged and ecstatic joy of pure being," to borrow Kerouac's description, an utterly rootless individual who careens from coast to coast on sudden impulse, a man whose incredible energy makes a mockery of the false idol of security.

Dean is drawn in the tradition of Huckleberry Finn but is untainted by Miss Watson's puritanism; as a result he is without guile or guilt. The sign of Dean's freedom is his infectious laughter, a token of spirit representing a life force. Merely to laugh at the world, like the existentialist ability to say no, becomes a valuable source of inspiration for Kerouac. Dean has been in jail and reads Proust; but his defining quality is speed—in conversation, in a car, in his lifestyle.

Kerouac, depicting Dean as a function of speed, has saliently tapped the distinguishing strain of American life in the second half of the twentieth century. This speed is reflected in an extraordinary hyperactivity that determines the atmosphere of the novel: "the only people for me are the mad ones, the ones who are mad to live, mad to talk, mad to be saved, desirous of everything at the same time, the ones who never yawn or say a commonplace thing but burn, burn, burn like fabulous yellow roman candles exploding like spiders across the stars."

Kerouac himself, through the figure of his narrator, Sal Paradise, tried to offer a check on Dean's exuberant anarchism; indeed, one of the bases for scenic organization in the novel is the way in which other characters find fault with Dean. And Sal is inevitably drained by the momentum of experience, always aware of growing older and saddened by this; like Kerouac, he is an outsider, an imperfect man in an alien world, brooding, lonely, seized by moments of self-hatred. The refrain in *On the Road* of "everything is collapsing" is a reminder of the effects of disorder, of Kerouac's own vision of uncontained release, on himself. Clearly, the endless celebrations, the pell-mell rushing from one scene to the next, create a hysteria that makes Sal want to withdraw from the world.

IV The Great Divide

Early in the 1950s, as a student in the New York City public schools, I experienced the kind of endemic powerlessness in the face of Big Government that provoked the Beats, and that in a full swing of the historical pendulum caused the sustained challenge to authority of the 1960s. I refer to the humiliations of what were called Civil Defense drills, when sirens would suddenly wail and we would all cower under our tiny desks in tense, almost fetal anticipation, or file into dark basement shelters that even we knew offered no protection, no relief for the dread that was being fostered in us.

Nelson Rockefeller, a scion of Standard Oil who didn't need more income, and governor of New York State, had defended the importance of such drills and started a company for the fabrication of shelters. In New York State, participation in Civil Defense drills was mandatory.

When Judith Malina of The Living Theatre joined Dorothy Day of the Catholic Worker movement to defy mandatory compliance, in June of 1955 in the park outside New York's City Hall, Malina was remanded to Bellevue by a judge who decided such protest was a sign of insanity. In elementary and junior high school, where we began our day by pledging allegiance, none of us were free enough to scream out that these drills were a farce. Later, these drills seemed paradigmatic, semaphores for the frozen fifties and its emphasis on conformity at all costs.

Preposterously, in 1954, *Walden* had been removed from all United States Information Agency libraries because of its alleged "socialism." In October of that year, the postmaster of Los Angeles refused to deliver a little magazine called *One,* the first consequential gay magazine, on the grounds of obscenity. We must remember that in 1956, *Howl* would be confiscated by the San Francisco customs police on the same grounds, and that the right to publish *Naked Lunch* would have to be established in the courts.

The world was quite different then. In 1955, interracial marriage was still banned in thirty states, and the Democratic Party ballot in Alabama was headed by the slogan "White Supremacy." The struggle for civil rights was often linked to subversion, seen as part of a left-wing attempt to weaken the social fabric. When the Supreme Court in its historic *Brown* decision voted to end segregation, Senator Sam Eastland of Mississippi declared the judges to be brainwashed victims of a Communist plot.

There were subtle sounds of change evident in the mid-fifties. In California, the Pacifica Foundation started broadcasting on radio station KPFA. In New York, critic Irving Howe began *Dissent* and Norman Mailer helped found the *Village Voice* in 1955. A disc jockey symbolically named Allan Freed changed the format of his program from rhythm and blues to rock and roll, playing Chuck Berry, Fats Domino, Bo Diddley, Little Richard, and then Elvis Presley.

This great divide was the beginning of the culture wars. An early sally was provided by Frank Sinatra, testifying before a congressional committee. In a spirit of malicious self-interest, he claimed that rock music "was the most brutal, ugly, desperate, vicious form of expression it has been my misfortune to hear" and that "by means of its almost imbecilic reiterations and sly, lewd, and in plain fact dirty lyrics, manages to be the martial music of every sideburned delinquent on the face of the earth."

V An Emotional Time Bomb

When I began college in 1957, there was already the shared sense that the cultural climate could change if enough of us resisted. That was a seething and fertile period for New York City, and I shared in it, attending avant-garde concerts at Columbia University's McMillan Theater, some of the Abstract Expressionist shows, and almost all of the plays being done by The Living Theatre at its Fourteenth Street location.

Part of the liberating headiness of that moment—an antidote to the poisonous contaminations of the Cold War—was the aesthetic thunderbolt of works like *Howl, On the Road,* and *Naked Lunch,* all of which I read as an undergraduate. These works were signifiers of a new consciousness, although it would take a few decades for that to be appreciated on a broad cultural level.

In Pound's tradition of "Make It New," each of these books proposed something fundamentally new about form and perspective. In *Howl,* the first of these works to appear, the dithyrambic rhythm and length of Ginsberg's line, the surging locomotion and momentum of the strophes, were an attempt to hypnotize the reader into a realization of what was crippling and wrong about America. *Howl* defined a new sensibility in its rush of raw feeling, and its hyperbole was a way to rouse what Robert Lowell had called the tranquilized fifties. The rhapsodic rant of the "Holy! Holy!" near the end of the poem was a Whitmanesque cry of identification with human suffering.

The goal of complete self-revelation, of nakedness, as Ginsberg put it, was in *Howl* based on a fusion of bohemianism, psychoanalytic probing, and Dadaist fantasy that dragged the self through the slime of degradation to the sublime of exaltation. While the idea of self is a Beat focal point, it represents only a beginning, an involvement to be transcended. The movement in Ginsberg's poetry is from an intense assertion of personal identity to a merger with larger forces in the universe. The ensuing tension between the proclamation of self—evident in a poem like "America"—and an insistence upon man's eternal place in time creates a central opposition in Ginsberg's poetry.

Believing that consciousness is infinite, and that modern man has been taught to suppress much of his potential awareness, Ginsberg attempted to exorcise the shame, guilt, and fear that he saw as barriers to self-realization and total being. Ginsberg's work, generally, is an outgrowth of the tradition begun by Blake and Coleridge: an effort to search for the source of dream, to release the unconscious in its pure state (avoiding literary simulation), to free the restraints on imagination so as to feel the potency and power of the visionary impulse.

Ginsberg saw his poetry as transmitting a sacred trust in human potentials, and he spoke in a *Paris Review* interview of how his mystical encounter with Blake in 1948 revealed the nature and direction of his own search as a poet. Ginsberg, then living in New York's East Harlem, suddenly heard a voice reciting Blake's "Ah! Sunflower" and "The Sick Rose." The resulting feeling of lightness, awe, and wonder catalyzed him as a poet, making him see that his role would be to widen the area of consciousness, to open the doors of perception, to transmit messages through time that could reach the enlightened and receptive.

Ginsberg's poetry is characteristic of the Beat desire *to be,* affirming existence as a positive value in a time of apathy. The quest for experience is as obsessive and all-consuming in "Howl" as in *On the Road.* Whether these experiences are destructive or not is of less importance than the fact of contact, of the kind of experience that allows an individual to discover his own vulnerability, his humanness, without cowering.

As Gary Snyder has argued in his essay "Why Tribe," to follow the grain of natural being "it is necessary to look exhaustively into the negative and demonic powers of the Unconscious, and by recognizing these powers—symbolically acting them out—one releases himself from these forces." This statement points to the shamanistic implications of Beat literature; "Howl," like *Naked Lunch,* is an attempt to exorcise through release. While Burroughs's novel futuristically projects into fantasy, "Howl" naturalistically records the suffering and magnanimity of a hipster avant-garde, a group that refuses to accept standard American values and materialism as permanent.

The experiences in "Howl," certainly in the opening part of the poem, are hysterically excessive and frantically active. It is the sheer momentum of nightmare that unifies these accounts of jumping off bridges, of slashing wrists, of ecstatic copulations, of purgatorial subway rides and longer journeys, a momentum rendered by the propelling, torrential quality of Ginsberg's long line, a cumulative rhythm, dependant on parallelism and the repetition of initial sounds that is biblical in origin.

Ginsberg's poetry ranges in tone from joy to utter despair, soaring and plunging from one line to the next, confident, paranoid, always seeking ways to awaken us in the somnambulism of our denial, to regain the ability to *feel* in numbing times, always insisting on a social vision that stresses transcendence and the need for spirit in the face of a materialistic culture.

VI Wildfire

These three writers were not simply arguing rebellion. As Allen Ginsberg remarked in a letter to his father dated November 30, 1957, rebellion was a minor element:

> What we are saying is that these values are not really standard or permanent, and we are in a sense I think ahead of the times. . . . When you have a whole economy involved in some version of moneymaking—this just is no standard of values. That it seems to offer a temporary security may be enough to keep people slaving for it. But meanwhile it destroys real value. And it ultimately breaks down. Whitman long ago complained that unless the material power of America was leavened by some kind of spiritual infusion we would wind up among the "fabled damned." It seems we're approaching that state as far as I can see. Only way out is individuals taking responsibility and saying what they actually feel—which is an enormous human achievement in any society. That's just what we as a group have been trying to do. To class that as some form of "rebellion" in the kind of college-bred social worker doubletalk . . . misses the huge awful point.

And just as the Beat Generation was not simply about rebellion, it was not exclusively about the work of Ginsberg, Kerouac, and Burroughs. A generational recognition spreads like wildfire, and in this case it included at least a hundred other writers such as Gary Snyder, Lawrence Ferlinghetti, Gregory Corso, and Michael McClure, and it continued into a succeeding generation.

The extent to which the Beat Generation existed on a national level in the 1950s, also, has not been fully appreciated, and outposts existed in cities like Chicago with the literary magazine *Big Table,* and in Kansas City and New Orleans.

The best-documented instance of the immediate flowering of Beat culture is in the San Francisco Bay area. Kerouac acknowledged in *Desolation Angels* that San Francisco "tugged at your heart" like New York City, and both places—promontories into the sea, really—represented traditional escapes from Main Street, U.S.A.

The poet Philip Lamantia, whose family emigrated to San Francisco from Italy at the beginning of the twentieth century, has remarked that after World War II, the North Beach area was buoyed by a euphoric energy as it filled with conscientious objectors, anarchists, and "poet-orientalist-surrealist-majic-jazzed-out-alchemy heads." These newcomers were regarded with suspicion by the local Italians, who as a group were slow to assimilate and would not tolerate demonstrations of sexual freedom or racial mixing on the street.

A key figure was Kenneth Rexroth, the paterfamilias of the West Coast Beats, who began poetry readings with jazz musicians in the Fillmore area. Rexroth had the idea for the famous Six Gallery reading where Ginsberg first read "Howl," which became the defining moment of what was called the San Francisco Renaissance.

Rexroth had organized the Libertarian Circle, an anarchist discussion group that held weekly meetings, evolving into a sort of bohemian salon. The conversations continued during the week at cafés with a distinctly European flavor—like the intellectual hangout Vesuvio's; the Cellar; the Black Cat Café; the Co-Existence Bagel Shop, where Richard Brautigan would read; and the Hungry i (for "id"), where comedians like Woody Allen, Mort Sahl, Bill Cosby, Mike Nichols, and Elaine May performed, and where Lenny Bruce was arrested.

The poets whose voices animated this floating salon attended Ruth Witt-Diamant's poetry series at San Francisco State (Ginsberg met McClure at Auden's reading in 1954), and some of them studied with Robert Duncan. They started a number of small magazines that continued the energy. *Circle Magazine* in Berkeley published Anaïs Nin and Henry Miller (then living a few hundred miles to the south in Big Sur). Some of these magazines were very fluid: *Inferno* became *Ark,* which became *Ark Moby* when McClure edited it in 1956. The editorship of a mimeographed publication called *Beatitude* was passed from poet to poet (although it was mostly run by Bob Kaufman), prompting Lawrence Ferlinghetti to call it a "floating crap-game," even though it was a successful demonstration of anarchism.

Another crucial part of this literary scene was the magazine *City Lights,* named, after Chaplin's film, by Peter Martin, who taught at San Francisco State and who was the son of an assassinated Italian anarchist named Carlo Fresca. In 1953, Ferlinghetti joined Martin to form the first paperback bookstore in America and a publishing company, both called City Lights, to disseminate anarchist and Beat writing.

Some of the Beats, or their cousins, are still relatively unknown, like Judith Malina and Julian Beck, who formed The Living Theatre, the most radical, dynamic theatrical group of our time. Writing my history of The Living Theatre, which Grove Press published in 1995, I read Julian's journal accounts of meeting Jack Kerouac at Horace Mann in 1939, and of reading "Howl" to Judith when that great poem first appeared in 1956. I told the story of The Living Theatre, incarnate heroes or martyrs of Beat underground culture, only quite recently, and my point here is that the history of the Beat movement has only begun to be transcribed. The huge Whitney Museum 1995 exhibit "Beat Culture and the New America," the show of Burroughs's paintings and collages at the Los Angeles County Museum of Art in 1996, the Viking Press publication of Burroughs's letters in 1993, Kerouac's letters in 1995, and *Some of the Dharma* in 1997, and William Morrow's publication of *The Herbert Huncke Reader* in 1997 are clear signs of mounting interest in the Beat legacy.

William Burroughs told me in 1972 that the Beats were primarily a cultural rather than a literary force, and I argued then, as I do now, that any genuine literature ultimately helps to shape the culture and gives it some of its aspiration. The Beats may be one trigger for the sixties, but I think their influence goes far beyond that decade. The Beat message will become even more prominent in the twenty-first century as the powers assumed by political states are concentrated, as such threats as biological warfare encourage the employment of technological means to control populations, as bureaucracy compromises and corrodes the concept of human rights everywhere.

Selected Bibliography

Burroughs, William S. *Junky: Confessions of an Unredeemed Drug Addict.* New York: Ace Books, 1953.

———. *Naked Lunch.* New York: Grove Press, 1959.

————. *The Job: Interviews with William Burroughs.* Ed. Daniel Odier. New York: Grove Press, 1972.

————. *Cities of the Red Night.* New York: Holt, Rinehart and Winston, 1981.

————. *The Letters of William S. Burroughs, 1945-1959.* Ed. Oliver Harris. New York: Viking, 1993.

Ginsberg, Allen. *As Ever: The Collected Correspondence of Allen Ginsberg and Neal Cassady.* Ed. Barry Gifford. Berkeley: Creative Arts, 1977.

————. *Allen Verbatim: Lectures on Poetry, Politics, Consciousness.* Ed. Gordon Ball. New York: McGraw-Hill, 1974.

————. *Collected Poems: 1947-80.* New York: Harper & Row, 1984.

————. *Howl: Original Draft Facsimile Transcript and Variant Versions.* Ed. Barry Miles. New York: Harper & Row, 1986.

————. *Journals Mid-Fifties: 1954-1958.* Ed. Gordon Ball. New York: Harper-Collins, 1995.

Huncke, Herbert. *The Herbert Huncke Reader.* Ed. Benjamin Schafer. New York: Morrow, 1997.

Kerouac, Jack. *On the Road.* New York: Viking, 1957.

————. *The Subterraneans.* New York: Grove Press, 1958.

————. *Scattered Poems.* San Francisco: City Lights Books, 1971.

————. *Visions of Cody.* New York: McGraw-Hill, 1972.

————. *The Portable Jack Kerouac.* Ed. Ann Charters. New York: Viking, 1995.

————. *Selected Letters: 1940-1956.* Ed. Ann Charters. New York: Viking, 1995.

Kinsey, Alfred C. *Sexual Behavior in the Human Male.* Philadelphia: W. B. Saunders, 1948.

McClure, Michael. *Scratching the Beat Surface.* San Francisco: North Point Press, 1982.

————. *Selected Poems.* New York: New Directions, 1986.

Snyder, Gary. *The Back Country.* New York: New Directions, 1968.

————. *Earth House Hold: Technical Notes & Queries to Fellow Dharma Revolutionaries.* New York: New Directions, 1969.

————. *Mountains and Rivers Without End.* Washington, D.C.: Counterpoint, 1996.

DRUGS, INSPIRATION, AND THE BEAT GENERATION

WALTER HOUSTON CLARK (ESSAY DATE 1969)

SOURCE: Clark, Walter Houston. "Historical Notes: The Harvard Incident." In *Chemical Ecstasy: Psychedelic Drugs and Religion*, pp. 44-62. New York: Sheed and Ward, 1969.

In the following excerpt, Clark briefly recounts early experiments in the psychedelic drug movement, including an account of Timothy Leary's dismissal from his position as a lecturer at Harvard University.

The Modern Phase of the Use of the Psychedelics

The modern phase of the investigation and use of the psychedelics began in 1938, when the brilliant Swiss biochemist, Albert Hofmann, discovered and synthesized what he christened "d-lysergic acid diethylamide tartrate-25" (LSD for short) as the result of research with the products of fermented rye. Several years later he discovered its psychoactive properties by accidentally ingesting a tiny portion of the drug, perhaps not more than 50 millionths of a gram, which gives an indication of its potency. From the beginning, Hofmann was aware of the religious potentialities of LSD. Most scientists and physicians, not much interested in religion, saw in it chiefly a means of producing temporary madness and began to call this class of drugs "psychotomimetic."

At the same time some psychotherapists began to see it, not so much as a means of creating mental illness, as of treating it. With this purpose in mind, the late Max Rinkel, M.D., introduced it in the United States and encouraged its scientific study.

During the fifties, Canadian scientists became interested. The best known among them were Abram Hoffer and Humphry Osmond. The latter coined the term "psychedelic" in response to his observation that subjects often discovered sensitivities and capacities within themselves that they never would have suspected had it not been for the influence of the drugs. Hoffer and Osmond did important pioneer work on the use of LSD in the rehabilitation of alcoholics, and discovered, to their surprise, that the key to its effectiveness seemed to reside in its religious properties. I will describe this work in a later chapter.

Another fascinating chapter in psychedelic discovery was written through the hobby of a New York banker and his wife, Gordon and Valentina Wasson, amateur mycologists. Their interest in mushrooms led them from one species to another until they encountered the sacred mushrooms of Mexico. In June, 1955, they journeyed to the Sierra Mazateca in Oaxaca, and were probably the first outsiders to eat the mushroom as part of the mushroom rite. Their religious experiences and subsequent insights into, and interest in, the religious significance of the mushrooms have been discussed under several scholarly titles.[1] This interest led to collaboration with the French mycologist, Roger Heim, and the subsequent synthesis of the active principle of the mushrooms, psilocybin, the drug with which Dr. Timothy Leary later began his researches.

In the fifties, Aldous Huxley, who had an interest in the mystical consciousness and had written several volumes touching on it, also tried this direct method of studying it. In May, 1953, he "turned on" with four-tenths of a gram of mescaline. His publication in 1954 of an account of his experiences in *The Doors of Perception* constituted something of a literary event.[2] For the first time, large numbers of the educated public became aware of the phenomenology of one of the psychedelic drugs and of their relationship to religious experience. Having become convinced that the visionary and mystical forms of religion alone had power to change and shape personality at a deep level, Huxley advocated the use of mescaline as a safe and nonaddictive way to effective religious life. In this connection, he cited J. S. Slotkin's research about the peyote cult. Along with the theologian-scientist, Gerald Heard, and the writer, Alan Watts, he became associated with a group which has largely turned away from western forms of religion in favor of the eastern faiths with their greater emphasis on mysticism and the nonrational aspects of the religious life.

The Harvard Incident

Perhaps the most highly publicized, single happening in the history of the psychedelic drug movement was the summary dismissal of Dr. Timothy Leary from his post as lecturer at Harvard University. Its repercussions are not likely to be stilled during the present generation. Behind the scenes burned a whole complex of charges and countercharges, passionate loyalties and vicious meanness, painfully arrived at administrative decisions, ambitions thwarted and fulfilled, passions, rumors, jealousies, gossip, wisdom, and folly. It will be impossible to do complete justice to the intricacies of this witches' brew. I will confine myself to the barest outline of the facts as I knew them and carefully checked them, together with such interpretations as seem compatible with a responsible, but necessarily subjective, judgment of such controversial matters.[3]

From February, 1960, Dr. Leary held a position as lecturer in psychology in Harvard's Department of Social Relations. During the summer of 1960, with other scholars and friends, he tested the effect of the sacred mushroom of Mexico on himself. Almost immediately he saw the revolutionary possibilities of its active principle, psilocybin, and later LSD, for psychotherapy and religion.

After coming to Harvard, he continued to experiment with growing interest, involving some Harvard students as subject volunteers. Gradually,

modestly funded research projects were developed, including the very promising pilot project for the rehabilitation of convicts at the Concord Prison, to be described later. Soon the use of student subjects aroused criticism and apprehension among Dr. Leary's colleagues and the Harvard administration. It was indicated to him that parents were objecting, and the effect of his research on public relations was pointed out more than once. Consequently, he and his faculty associate in the work, Richard Alpert, agreed to confine experimentation to graduate students only. Finally, Dr. Leary consented to entrust his supply of the drugs to Dr. Dana Farnsworth, Director of Harvard Health Services, with the understanding, at least on Dr. Leary's part, that they would be readily available for appropriate research.

Shortly after, when Dr. Walter Pahnke, with Leary's approval, desired access to these chemicals for the Good Friday Experiment, they were unavailable. Since the experiment had been sanctioned by Dr. Pahnke's faculty-appointed Harvard doctoral committee, Dr. Leary felt that Dr. Farnsworth had broken faith with him, if he had not deliberately tricked him. Dr. Farnsworth had been made aware of serious problems among some students using the drugs, and from these cases he had inferred high danger from psychedelic substances. He was in no way equipped as an expert in the sense that he had tried them on himself, observed any sessions from beginning to end or systematically followed up a randomly selected population of those who had been given the drugs. But he felt that to release the drugs for human experimentation would be irresponsible. Furthermore, guidelines for the use of the drug had not yet been worked out among all interested parties at Harvard, according to Dr. Farnsworth. The historic Good Friday Experiment was saved from being cancelled at the last minute only because Leary had previously given a supply of psilocybin to a researcher in a nearby city, who made enough available for the experiment.

The esteem of colleagues for Dr. Leary's work is indicated, not only by his being called to Harvard in the first place, but by offers of recommendation for tenure by two of his superiors, if he would only "lay off drugs" for a year or two. But by this time the Timothy Leary, brought to Harvard as a social scientist, was beginning to turn into a mystic and a poet with a prophetic sense of mission to change others as he had been changed through profound religious experience. As he has said, Harvard was no place to carry on research on visionary experience.[4] The process of mutual disenchantment had begun, and he whose adventurous course

> . . . with no middle flight intends to soar
> Above the Aonian mount, while it pursues
> Things unattempted yet . . .[5]

began to conceptualize the bold project of bringing what he now saw as an almost Promethean gift to a world, which seemingly has lost its way in materialism, greed and strife. His destiny became clearer to him with every hour. The Harvard "establishment" seemed to see only stubbornness and fanaticism. A drama of failure to communicate, so tragically constant in the history of conscientious men in authority with points of view different from the mystic and the prophet, was about to be played once again. One can only speculate what mistakes, on both sides, could have been avoided through mutual understanding. But this perception would have required of those making the administrative decisions some empathic discernment of the profound religious experience that had taken Timothy Leary captive. There was little evidence that they possessed this type of wisdom. Furthermore, for reasons that are at least partially clear, they were unwilling to take the risks involved in acquiring such wisdom by trying the drugs themselves.

The axe fell just a few weeks before Leary's contract was to expire. Toward the end of the academic year 1961-62, Dr. Leary had been informed that, despite his contract, he was to teach only part-time and was to be paid accordingly. He was listed in the catalog as teaching only in the spring semester of 1962-63. He asked his immediate superior, Professor David McClelland, permission to do all his teaching in the fall semester so that he could go to Mexico in March or April to set up a project for the International Federation for Internal Freedom. This request was granted, according to Dr. Leary. Professor McClelland, however, denies any recollection of the agreement. That there was nothing in writing was quite characteristic of Dr. Leary's habitual ways of dealing with people. Dr. McClelland asserts that his first awareness of Leary's absence came when a reporter in Los Angeles phoned to check on the authenticity of a report by Dr. Leary that he had been fired. McClelland states that this antedated the action of the Harvard Corporation on April 30, and that Leary could have avoided dismissal even then by returning to Cambridge.

When the spring semester of 1962-63 had begun, Dr. Leary assumed that his duties had been discharged. However, he consented to supervise the field work of two students at Bridgewater State Hospital. The students were informed that he intended leaving Cambridge in March. Actually, it was about the middle of April before he left. The fact of his absence was brought to the attention of the Harvard administration, and on May 6, 1963, the Harvard Corporation passed the following vote:

> Voted: Because Timothy F. Leary, Lecturer on Clinical Psychology, has failed to keep his classroom appointments and has absented himself from Cambridge during term time without permission, to relieve him from further teaching duty and to terminate his salary as of April 30, 1963.

The Corporation viewed his action as a clear violation of faculty rules and, therefore, not subject to a hearing,[6] although their decision was clearly contrary to principles governing Academic Tenure, Section 4, drawn up by representatives of the American Association of University Professors, and of the Association of American Colleges in 1940, and subscribed to officially by both Associations in 1941. Section 4 reads in part:

> . . . dismissal for cause of a teacher previous to the expiration of a term appointment, should, if possible, be considered by both a faculty committee and the governing board of the institution. In all cases where the facts are in dispute, the accused teacher should be informed before the hearing in writing of the charges against him and should have the opportunity to be heard in his own defense by all bodies that pass judgment upon his case.

These principles were reprinted in the summer, 1963, issue of the AAUP *Bulletin*, shortly after Dr. Leary's dismissal.

Whether Dr. Leary could have obtained a hearing, had he requested it at the time, will never be known, since he did not do so. He felt that even previous to this action he had been treated in an unfair and arbitrary manner. He had made up his mind that the work so important to him could not be done at Harvard, and had expected no extension of his contract beyond June 30, 1963. To have engaged in an altercation with Harvard over a few months' salary seemed to him a waste of his energies and a possible disservice to friends who were working with him.

There were some who felt that Harvard's action was a body blow to the principles of academic freedom. If Harvard, with its reputation as a defender of these principles and a bellwether of the academic flock, could dismiss a teacher *for any cause* without a hearing, then any institution could do the same. These people felt that the Harvard chapter of the AAUP should have called for an investigation of the case in the interest of academic freedom in general, whether Dr. Leary wished it or not.

But whatever the rights and wrongs of Harvard's or Dr. Leary's actions, there were certain clear, practical consequences bearing on the investigation and use of the psychedelic drugs. Whatever the technical reasons for the dismissal of Dr. Leary, and of his colleague, Dr. Richard Alpert, about the same time but on different grounds, the public and most of the Harvard community considered the controversy over the use of the drugs to be the basic factor. Though there were many on the faculty and elsewhere who accepted Dr. Farnsworth's judgment of the danger of the drugs, there were others who differed, and who believed that investigation of their effects on human beings should go forward. The dismissal effectively frightened many who might have pursued controlled study of the drugs at Harvard and elsewhere. Few wished to risk loss of reputation or position. Many of Leary's former friends dropped him. The Massachusetts Mental Health Center, partly under Harvard's direction, afterward pursued some carefully controlled research with psilocybin under the direction of Dr. Walter N. Pahnke and others. However, even this was soon stopped by order of the trustees.

The damage done to the principles of academic freedom cannot be calculated, but there is no doubt that they were considerable. I am reporting just a few cases of pressure that I happen to know about. A professor of psychology, known to be interested in the drugs, was summoned before the president of his institution's board of trustees (not Harvard) and threatened with summary dismissal unless he promised to stop all experimentation and never to mention the drugs again in his classes. A Harvard student who had been associated with Dr. Leary in his research with convicts, narrowly escaped dismissal from his field work position by the respected director of a Boston mental health agency. Another graduate associate, who had received high recommendations from his Harvard professors for a teaching appointment elsewhere, was immediately dropped from consideration when his research with psychedelic drugs was discovered.

But Dr. Leary's rejection by the Harvard community had another more subtle result. He felt that they treated him in an unsympathetic, unjust and inhumane way. It seemed that Harvard had been afflicted with a failure of nerve. When the chips were down, institutional preservation prevailed over open-mindedness and the search for truth. The inhumanity of the method of his dismissal completed his disenchantment with the establishment in general, and the academic establishment in particular. This helps to explain his radical appeal to the youth of America, the only segment of society that seems to him sufficiently courageous to experiment on themselves with the psychedelics, and sufficiently free from prejudice to consider the truths with which the visionary experience confronted them. Hence his advice, "Don't trust anyone over thirty!" and "Turn on, Tune in and Drop out!"

If some with grey hair and a liking for their entrenched power of position and faith in the affluent and achieving society, deplore the ways of Leary's followers, they may well ask themselves whether the situation they deplore is not in large part a product of the failure in communication within the Harvard community, and the abrupt action of dismissal. I have heard it estimated by a public relations expert that the dismissal, with an able assist by the U. S. government, which subsequently arrested Leary, was worth several millions of dollars of free publicity. If Harvard's aims were to disseminate Dr. Leary's views as widely as possible among young and old, it could hardly have performed more superbly.

This is not a judgment between Dr. Leary and Harvard, nor a pretense that Harvard made all the mistakes, and that Dr. Leary made none. He can see mistakes he regrets, and he is not unsympathetic with the dilemma of those who forced his rejection. Furthermore, Harvard has made some amends by throwing fewer obstacles in the way of his subsequent lecturing on the campus than other less secure universities do. But there is no doubt that, if Harvard had weathered the storm for the few remaining weeks of his contract, fewer young people would now be engaging in rebellious and frivolous experimentation with the drugs. And the free academic marketplace with respect to ideas about these drugs would be less restricted. For one example, it is a shameful impoverishment of the debate on the drugs that so few institutions are willing to hear the views of Dr. Leary himself, who probably has had more varied experience with the psychedelics than anyone in the world, and whose intuitions about them are penetrating.

Since leaving Harvard, Dr. Leary's history has included a series of harassments of himself and his family. About a year later, he was arrested on the charge of "smuggling" when a small amount of marihuana was found on his daughter. Apparently, he was framed by collusion of Mexican and United States customs agents on the Texas border. His sentence of thirty years in federal prison and a $30,000 fine was reversed by the United States Supreme Court in May, 1969. About this time he incorporated the League for Spiritual Discovery as a religious institution with headquarters at Millbrook, N.Y. The League maintained its constitutional right to use drugs religiously. A posse of fifteen police agents raided the premises in the dead of night, wakened his guests and undressed the women in the search for evidence. Inconsequential amounts of marihuana, unknown to Leary, were found on a visiting couple. Leary was handcuffed and arrested. A few weeks later the charges were dropped. But more recently, at the instigation of the townspeople, he was again arrested; his son was abused by the police and he was forced to close down. Most recently, in the fall of 1968, he was arrested by the police in Laguna Beach, California for double-parking. The occupants of his car were searched, and marihuana was found on his son. Again he was arrested and now faces charges.

A Clue to the Personality of Dr. Leary

I cannot resist the desire to comment on this attractive enigma, Timothy Leary. A clue to his personality will also be a clue to many an "acid head" and, therefore, a step toward understanding the drug movement and its significance, which may be crucial to our society. The clue I have in mind is in William James' chapter on saintliness in his *Varieties*. James does not give the conventional picture of the saint but relies on his original intuitions. Had his spirit been invoked at Harvard during the Leary controversy, it would almost certainly have spoken on Leary's side.

James speaks of the saint having "a feeling of being in a wider life than that of this world's selfish little interests; and a conviction, not merely intellectual, but as it were sensible, of an Ideal Power."[7] To most of Leary's academic associates no goal can be imagined higher than achieving a full professorship at Harvard, with tenure and the emoluments, tangible and intangible, that go with such achievement—unless it be more of the same type of reward. To them, any person who would knowingly pass up such an opportunity must truly be mad. It was behavior of this type that won for the psychedelic drugs the reputation for warping the judgment of those who ingested them. Nevertheless, most of those who tried them did glimpse that wider world in which Timothy Leary lives.

James quotes Henry Drummond's phrase, "the expulsive power of a higher affection."[8] It is this headlong force of the "higher affection" that marks the saint and makes nonsense of all the lesser values of sober society. The ordinary Christian can tolerate church only because he can close his ears to the invitation to saintliness. He can ignore Jesus' call to leave father and mother, son and daughter, to cast aside his nets and business—in modern terms to "drop out"—and follow him. Similarly, Socrates was reproved by his neighbors for living a life of idleness, "corrupting the youth" of Athens. The citizens of Assisi closed their doors to the ragged band of "hippies" who scrounged food and practiced poverty with Francis. The sober, unimaginative, hard-working and conscientious citizen should not be despised any more than should the conscientious Harvard administrator or department head, who is responsible for the welfare of many students. Circumscribed by values that they understand, they perform the necessary chores of serving society. In doing so, they must also obey their inhibitions and say, "No, no!" instead of "shifting the emotional centre towards loving and harmonious affections, towards 'yes, yes' where the claims of the non-ego are concerned." In James' view, this is another mark of the saint.

Timothy Leary exhibits this absolute commitment also, for he is nothing if not a permissive and hospitable man, although he can be stubborn when one man imposes his standards on another. He calls this "tyranny." One senses "the friendly continuity of the ideal power" with his own life, the "surrender to its control" and the "immense elation and freedom" of which James speaks. Leary's equanimity, keenness of mind, his sense of humor, empathy and compassion under misfortunes, which would crush ordinary men, would be impossible were it not linked to some source of strength in that wider life James also connects with "strength of soul."[9]

This freedom from conventional values has opened the eyes of the despised and rejected to the virtues of saintliness more often than it has convinced respectable men. Jesus was depreciated for mingling with publicans and sinners, and the outcasts and lepers followed Francis long before his respectable neighbors in Assisi listened to him. So with Leary. He knowingly welcomed ex-convicts to his house. Two of them, to the alarm of the neighbors, lived with him. An armed robber told me that Dr. Leary was the first man he had ever met who was, he felt, unequivocally on his side. Another robber said that, in his thirty-odd years of a life of crime, Leary was the only man he had ever known about whom convicts never had a critical word. Of course, it could be claimed that both of these men were prejudiced, for in an experiment on the use of psilocybin, Dr. Leary had psychologically and spiritually raised them from the dead!

All this is not to say that Timothy Leary is a second Jesus Christ, Socrates, or Francis of Assisi. He is only a first Timothy Leary. He is a human being who has made his share of mistakes. He is a complex man to whom I have offered merely one clue. For a definitive picture, we must wait a long time.

In terms of the "wider life," of which James has spoken, the perspective of time is required to bring out true spiritual greatness or the lack of it. Time will tell whether Timothy Leary is a pied piper or one of the perceptive prophets of the age. His aims, his personality and the sources of his insights and energies dictate that he be judged by the criteria James describes in his discussion of saintliness.

William Ernest Hocking once spoke of the true mystic or authentic prophet as one man in a thousand. He agrees with James in seeing saintliness as the best thing that history has to show. But here, he says, nature makes a thousand failures to one success.[10] I do not know whether Timothy Leary represents a failure or a success. But if I had to gamble on one or the other, I would wager on success!

The Development of Psychedelic Churches

If the type of religion uncovered by the psychedelic drugs is ever to influence the main stream of western religious life, it will probably have its rise, like most vigorous religious movements, outside the main line religious institutions. Historically this has nearly always been the case, for fresh movements seem radical to the average institutional observer. In addition, the nonrational energies which they release, if they are powerful enough to "redeem" human nature, may occasionally cause personal breakdowns and unsettling confusion. These considerations, combined with a multitude of vested interests, make the religious institutions a hard nut to crack. Consequently, it is not surprising that any experience so powerful and so esoteric as that released by the psychedelic drugs should be kept at arm's length by the orthodox churchmen who will scornfully refer to the "psychedelic churches" as "cults." I

use the term "cult" in a descriptive, not judgmental, sense. In some ways the term is interchangeable with the word "church." The "psychedelic churches" *are* churches, at least in an embryonic sense.

I have already referred to the Native American Church, the most clearly defined and the most traditional of the psychedelic churches or cults. Its membership is restricted almost wholly to Indians. But there are a number of religious organizations that have been formed with the idea of making the psychedelic sacrament a central or very important element in worship. There is a tendency in many of these to form a community, a not untraditional aspect of the beginnings of many religious movements, such as the early Christians, monastic orders or Hasidic communities.[11]

One of the most visible of the psychedelic churches is the League for Spiritual Discovery formed by Dr. Leary. I have already spoken of its harassment by neighbors and the police, again a not untraditional experience for cultic groups. A second example is the Neo-American Church, founded by the Reverend Arthur Kleps, who calls himself Chief Boo Hoo of the Church. Many people, including some judges, hardly know whether to take him as a religious leader or a professional funny man. However, in an appearance before the Special Senate Judiciary Subcommittee on Narcotics in Washington on May 25, 1966, Mr. Kleps left no doubt that he considered the religious use of the psychedelic drugs a right which the Constitution confers on any citizen, and which he and his followers intend to exercise.

There have been reports of an open Neo-American communion service in a Washington, D.C., park on Easter Sunday, April 6, 1969, with peyote the sacramental element. This attempt to test the constitutionality of the drug laws was frustrated by the refusal of the police to make any arrests. However, on the following day, Mr. Kleps invaded a public building where he could not be ignored and the arrest followed.

In justification of his somewhat jocular treatment of his own church, Mr. Kleps points out that through the ages the church institution has been the great enemy of the interior religious spirit. To refuse to take himself and his own church organization seriously is to build in a protection against institutionalization. To do him justice, it must be said that occasionally he has refused to depart from this principle even when his church seemed to have something temporal to gain by doing so. I do not necessarily approve of all the practices of the Neo-American Church. But I see no reason to doubt that Arthur Kleps is a religious man. At the very least, in company with Erasmus and Dean Swift, he is a keen ecclesiastical satirist.

A third organization within this growing movement is the more conservative Church of the Awakening, incorporated as a religious institution in Socorro, New Mexico, in 1963. The founders are two retired physicians, Doctors John and Louisa Aiken, who had often administered both peyote and mescaline sacramentally before the spate of punitive legislation against any use of the psychedelics. This group is a fellowship dedicated to the religious quest by any effective means, of which the psychedelic sacrament is not only important but essential. Membership does not preclude membership in other religious bodies. So far, the church has stayed within the law as a matter of policy and has applied, so far unsuccessfully, to the Bureau of Narcotics and Dangerous Drugs of the Justice Department for permission to use peyote for sacramental purposes. When all legal recourse has been exhausted, the church intends to resort to a test case.

Other similar institutions include Naturalism, Incorporated, headed by Mr. George Peters of Chicago, another psychedelic leader recently jailed. Naturalism maintains a free service for helping people on "bad trips" and guiding users to distinguish the addictive drugs, like heroin and alcohol, from the nonaddictive psychedelics. Still another body, according to reports, is the Church of the Clear Light on the West Coast. In addition to those bodies that are incorporated, there are any number of nonincorporated psychedelic bodies and communities of greatly varying quality and levels of responsibility.

With the passage of time there seems to be a tendency for these bodies to rely on psychedelic drugs less rather than more. The successful groups have seen the necessity for a discipline to govern household management and to set at least implicit standards of personal behavior. Nearly all members of such psychedelic communities use marihuana freely and have used the more potent drugs like LSD at least once. One very rarely finds anyone, whether a member or nonmember, or one who has given up the drugs, who is sorry that he took them in the first place.[12]

Notes

1. See R. G. & V. Wasson, *Mushrooms, Russia, and History* (privately printed, 1957); R. G. Wasson, "The Hallucinogenic Fungi of Mexico," *Psychedelic Review,* 1, No. 1 (1963), pp. 27-42.

2. Aldous Huxley, *The Doors of Perception* (New York: Harper and Row, 1954).

3. Valuable information of events leading to, but not including the dismissal controversy itself, may be found in T. Leary, *High Priest* (Cleveland: World Publishing, 1968). My personal knowledge of the events consisted of participation in seminars organized for professors and scholars of religion by Dr. Leary dating from late 1961; involvement as an organizer and director in the affairs of the International Federation for Internal Freedom; assistance with the Good Friday Experiment; extensive follow-up of the Concord Prison Project, and warm personal friendship and respect for Dr. Leary, which I still retain. At one time or another I have been swayed by and weighed all of the conflicting positions aroused by the controversy. Recently I have taken the trouble to review the facts with Dr. Leary, as well as with certain involved representatives of other positions. I have found him amazingly without rancor in his judgments of Harvard and helpful in aiding me to clarify in my own mind for this book the picture of the whole situation. My own approach to the drugs, which may differ from his, can be judged by comparing this volume with his writings. We concur in the desire for a continuation of the study of the drugs in order to maximize their value to religion.

4. T. Leary, *High Priest*, pp. 2, 20. Leary's *Psychedelic Prayers* (Kerhonkson, N.Y.: Poets Press, 1966) reveals genuine poetic insight and gift of expression, which the reader may check for himself.

5. John Milton, *Paradise Lost,* Part 1.

6. I received this information from the office of the President of Harvard University in a letter dated February 9, 1967, which was a response to my inquiry. Dr. Farnsworth and Professor McClelland, in particular, very kindly took time to discuss their recollections of the Leary incident with me, and I have tried to present their positions as fairly as I can. Their views naturally differ from my own. Dr. Farnsworth was good enough to supply the following statement relative to his position on the Good Friday Experiment:

"By arrangement between the Dean of Harvard College and Mr. Leary and his associates, the total supply of psilocybin in their possession was to be given to me for safekeeping until the proper procedures surrounding such research were worked out. Presumably, all interested groups (Department of Social Relations, University Health Services, Office of the Dean of Students, etc.) would be involved in developing such procedures. When, a few days later, I was asked to release the drug before policies governing its use had been worked out, I did not do so for obvious reasons. When I heard a few days later that the Good Friday experiment at the Boston University Chapel had been carried out on schedule, I was left to draw my own conclusions. Not until this year did I learn the source of the psilocybin that was used."

In Leary's book, *The Politics of Ecstasy* (New York: G. P. Putnam's Sons, 1968), p. 237, a lecture at Central Washington State College states, "This is my last lecture as a college teacher to a college audience. . . ." The note states that the lecture was delivered a week before he was fired from Harvard. Its title was, "American Education as an Addictive Process and its Cure."

It may have been this statement, or a similar one at Los Angeles, that prompted the phone call from the reporter to Dr. McClelland.

7. William James, *The Varieties of Religious Experience*, p. 292.

8. *Ibid.*

9. *Ibid.*

10. William Ernest Hocking, *The Meaning of God in Human Experience* (New Haven: Yale University Press, 1912), p. 349.

11. See W. H. McGlothlin, *Hippies and Early Christianity* (Institute of Government and Public Affairs, MR-101, University of California, Los Angeles, 1967).

12. In one hundred replies to a questionnaire I have circulated among psychedelic drug users, only one has stated he was sorry to have taken psychedelics in the first place, though he specifically stated that they had done him no harm. This has confirmed my more informal impressions covering some two hundred additional drug users. So far there is *not one* who has not described some element of religious experience on the questionnaire.

ROBERT C. FULLER (ESSAY DATE 2000)

SOURCE: Fuller, Robert C. "Psychedelics and Metaphysical Illumination." In *Stairways to Heaven: Drugs in American Religious History*, pp. 51-89. Oxford: Westview Press, 2000.

In the following excerpt, Fuller studies the impact of drugs on the spiritual and literary consciousness of intellectuals in the 1950s and 1960s, including Timothy Leary, Huston Smith, Allen Ginsberg, Alan Watts and others.

Prophet of a New Spiritual Consciousness

The year 1960 turned out to be a critical one in the social history of psychedelics in the United States. Prior to this time, LSD—while legal—was for the most part confined to the laboratories of a handful of pharmaceutical and psychological researchers. Yet larger social forces were at work that were destined to implicate LSD in a major cultural revolution. The transformation of LSD from laboratory alkaloid to cultural icon is a fascinating story in American history. And like most good stories, this one centers around a main character of mythic proportions. In the summer of 1960, Timothy Leary took a vacation to Mexico before beginning his new job at Harvard's Center for the Study of Personality. A Berkeley psychologist, Frank Barron, had told Tim about the psilocybin mushrooms (*teonanacatl*, the "flesh of the gods") that had played such an important role in classic shamanism. Leary, who later described himself as someone who had never met a drug he didn't like, purchased a few of these sacred mush-

rooms and gave them a try. "The journey lasted a little over four hours," he wrote. "Like almost everyone who had the veil drawn, I came back a changed man."[1]

When Leary assumed his duties that fall at Harvard he found that he had little interest in the relatively boring field of personality assessment. Statistical analyses of questionnaire responses paled by comparison to the wonders unleashed by the psilocybin, mescaline, and LSD he was experimenting with on a nearly daily basis. Leary and his colleague Richard Alpert shifted their research interests in a way that allowed them to turn their favorite hobby into a full-time occupation. Within months they had managed to become the directors of what they christened the Harvard Psychedelic Drug Research Project. During the next four years, Leary and Alpert managed to "arrange transcendent experiences" for over 1,000 persons. Their subjects included students, writers, artists, convicts, and sixty-nine members of the clergy. Also notable for their participation in Leary's investigations were Aldous Huxley, Allen Ginsberg, Alan Watts, and Huston Smith. Although Leary was the most charismatic prophet of the psychedelic gospel, these latter individuals were among the most able apostles.

Leary and Alpert focused principally on studying the ways in which "set" and "setting" influenced the nature of an LSD trip. Their studies indicated that when the setting was supportive but not explicitly spiritual, between 40 and 75 percent of their test subjects nonetheless reported life-changing religious experiences. Yet when the set and setting emphasized spiritual themes, up to 90 percent reported having mystical or illuminating experiences.

Leary was only an advisor and experimental subject in the most famous of these studies on psychedelic spirituality. In the spring of 1962, a graduate student in the Philosophy of Religion program at Harvard Divinity School approached Leary about an exciting project. Walter Pahnke was an M.D. and a minister. He now wanted to earn a degree in religion by conducting an empirical test of the categories scholars use to describe the mystical experience. Pahnke enlisted the help of twenty theology students who gathered on Good Friday at Boston University's Marsh Chapel. The test was a controlled, double-blind experiment in which he divided the twenty subjects into five groups of four students each. Ninety minutes before the Good Friday service began, Pahnke administered identical capsules to each subject. Half of the capsules contained thirty milligrams of psilocybin. The other half contained two hundred milligrams of a vitamin that causes feelings of warmth and tingling but has no effect on the mind. The subjects then attended a two-and-a-half-hour religious service consisting of organ music, prayers, and personal meditation. The subjects were later interviewed and asked to fill out a 147-item questionnaire designed to measure phenomena related to a typology of mystical consciousness. Of note is the fact that nine of the ten students who had taken the psilocybin reported having religious experiences, while only one of the subjects who had been given a placebo reported any such sensations.[2] Pahnke maintained that psychedelics extinguish the "empirical ego" and assist individuals in transcending the subject-object dichotomy of ordinary rational consciousness. His study concluded that LSD occasions every major characteristic of "authentic" mystical experience (e.g., sense of unity, transcendence of space and time, alleged ineffability, paradoxicality, and subsequent elevation of mood). One of Panhnke's group leaders, Walter Clark, surmised that the miracle of Marsh Chapel was "the most cogent single piece of evidence that psychedelic chemicals do, under certain circumstances, release profound religious experience."[3]

Leary and Alpert believed that discoveries such as these were about to usher in a new era in human spiritual consciousness. They believed that they were on the verge of reducing centuries of theological abstractions down to a simple chemical formula. Their studies indicated that if the proper training and setting could be provided, nearly everyone was capable of achieving a sense of mystical oneness with God. Yet much to their surprise and dismay, the world did not run to embrace the implications of their research. Scorn, not praise, met their psychedelic gospel. Part of this disapproval was theological. Already scholars were contending that the "nature mysticism" engendered by LSD was not true or authentic mysticism. However, the central objection to Leary's seemingly indiscriminate advocacy of psychedelics was concern over widespread licentiousness, particularly among youth. The use of LSD was spreading across the country. Easily synthesized in makeshift chemistry labs (and legal until late 1966), the availability of LSD and other psychedelics escalated while the price continued to drop. Chemical euphoria was instantly accessible to the emerging "hippie" culture. Leary frequently warned against misuse and hoped that psychedelics would be restricted to the philosophical elite. But if his words cautioned discretion, his overall

demeanor and actions fostered chemical promiscuity. Harvard had made Leary and Alpert pledge not to use undergraduate students in their "research." They never complied. Reports of ribald partying and sexual dalliance in Leary's office swept across campus. Harvard officials had no recourse but to remove both Leary and Alpert from the faculty and shut down their center for psychedelic research.

For a short time, Leary became a rebel without an expense account. His colleague, Richard Alpert, later ventured to India, where he took up the practice of yoga meditation and changed his name to Ram Dass. Alpert had found that the psychedelic experience ultimately led nowhere. Now, in the transformed incarnation of Ram Dass, he continued to believe that psychedelics were of value in helping a person break out of their restricted consciousness. But Ram Dass maintained that such an awakening is only the beginning of an authentic spiritual life. Thus while never renouncing the possibility that drugs might introduce persons to spiritual dimensions of reality, Alpert shifted the focus of his countercultural ministry to Hindu-style meditation and spiritual discipline.[4]

Leary, however, was more determined than ever to advance the cause of psychedelics. Believing that he could generate sufficient income from his writings, speaking fees and donations, Leary organized the International Federation for Internal Freedom (IFIF) in 1963 for the purpose of continuing his psychedelic research. After being expelled from the organization's original headquarters in Zihuatanejo, Mexico, Leary was offered the use of an estate located in Millbrook, New York. The Millbrook estate provided the perfect setting in which to engage in outlandish behaviors that ranged from serious research to bacchanalian debauchery. For about four years Millbrook was a monastery, school, research laboratory, religious commune, and opium den all rolled into one. The sixty-four-room manor was home not only to the IFIF (subsequently renamed the League for Spiritual Discovery, and finally the Castalia Foundation in reference to the monastery in Hermann Hesse's *The Glass-Bead Game*) but also to a constantly revolving door of visitors who came for drugs, sex, and stimulating conversation. Leary even turned Millbrook into a weekend getaway for those with discretionary income to spend on "consciousness-expanding" retreats. All the while Leary was taking notes on his and others' experiences in an attempt to create a map of the previously unexplored regions of the mind.

Leary and others were increasingly persuaded that LSD was giving Westerners access to regions of the mind that practitioners of Eastern meditation systems had known for centuries. For this reason he hoped that Eastern texts might be of great value in his attempt to create a cartography of inner space. Leary first adapted the verses of the *Tao Te Ching* in a book he called *Psychedelic Prayers*. Then, in 1962, he, Ralph Metzner, and Richard Alpert created a psychedelic variation on the Buddhist scholar W. Y. Evans-Wentz's translation of *The Tibetan Book of the Dead*. *The Tibetan Book of the Dead* is an ancient Buddhist meditation manual that purports to explain the realties (termed *bardos*) into which one travels following physical death. It was originally designed to be read to those near death in order to prepare them for the next stage of their metaphysical journey. Leary, Metzner, and Alpert titled their version *The Psychedelic Experience*. They were convinced that the dissolution of the ego afforded by LSD permitted entry into the same realms of consciousness described in Buddhist metaphysics. *The Psychedelic Experience* blended the esoteric terminology of Eastern mystical thought with buzzwords then current in popular American psychology. In this way the Millbrook pundits helped steer their readers to the insight that psychedelic research had at last uncovered the fundamental truths uniting East and West. This volume eventually went through sixteen editions and was translated into seven languages, giving it a long-lasting influence upon subsequent understandings of the realities disclosed by a psychedelic adventure.

Catastrophes had a way of following Leary. His obvious wit and the constant twinkle in his eyes endeared him to many. But his theatrical excess and cavalier ways frightened others. Drugs were beginning to destroy the lives of a good many young people, and Leary was an obvious target for blame. Leary himself had been arrested in 1965 for possessing marijuana as he attempted to cross the Mexican border. Despite his argument that marijuana had a legitimate religious use and thus the arrest violated his First Amendment rights, he was convicted by a Texas jury. The conviction was eventually overturned, but in the meantime Millbrook was itself raided by G. Gordon Liddy (who was destined to become a symbol and spokesperson for conservative American culture when the Watergate scandal thrust him into national prominence). Liddy, then the assistant district attorney of Dutchess County, led a small troop of law enforcement officials in a midnight raid with the hopes of finding Leary

with his pants down and his head turned on. Just what was going on at Millbrook when the police came busting through the doors is still a matter of dispute. Ironically, Liddy and Leary eventually reunited as friends and colleagues on the college lecture circuit and turned their conflicting accounts of the event into entertaining repartee. One thing was clear, however: Government toleration of psychedelics was nearing an end. By 1967 California made the manufacture or possession of LSD illegal. Leary's never-ending attacks upon "the system" were drawing a response. And in 1970, Leary was again convicted of drug possession and sentenced to a minimum security prison in San Luis Obispo. Leary managed to escape from prison and live in exile outside the United States for several years before being caught and returned to prison. Finally released in 1976, Leary continued to promote the psychedelic cause until his death in 1996 (his ashes were sent up in a satellite to orbit earth, which seemed a somewhat apt transition from navigating inner space to orbiting outer space).

Following his 1970 arrest, Leary never quite regained the peculiar role he had achieved in advocating a new, drug-enhanced spirituality. Yet by this time he had already succeeded in spreading his psychedelic gospel throughout the country. The Haight-Ashbury district of San Francisco had surfaced as the Vatican of the Acid Church as early as 1965, giving the psychedelic cause a geographical and symbolic foothold in the terrain of a newly emerging segment of American culture. No one ever quite rivaled Timothy Leary as the High Priest of America's new spiritual consciousness; he and his apostles had spread the psychedelic gospel far and wide.

Turning On

Leary was well suited for his role as self-appointed spokesperson for the growing hippie movement. The word hippie, probably derived from the forties and fifties jazz terms hep and hepcat, suggests a desire to be "with it."[5] And if any one in the United States was possessed by the conviction that he knew what it meant to be "with it," it was Tim Leary. Furthermore, Leary was able to condense his message into a crisp, catchy slogan: "Turn on, tune in, and drop out." Leary's slogan was multivalent, carrying different messages to different people in different settings. In this way it helped piece together the disparate elements of the sixties counterculture. Leary's genius was to synthesize otherwise contrary impulses into a mantra of common aspiration.

Turning on was the fun part. Psilocybin, mescaline, LSD, methedrine, and later STP were the "major hallucinogens" of the hippie movement. Marijuana and alcohol were its "minor hallucinogens." Although the official rhetoric was that these substances were simply *upaya* (the Sanskrit term for "skillful means," which Ram Dass used to explain the value of psychedelics for opening consciousness past the restrictive ego), most users were probably content with the emotional rush. Even Millbrook usually resembled an opium den or upscale fraternity party more than a research facility. Jay Stevens offered the apt description of as "a house party of unparalleled dimensions."[6] The weekend marathons of drugs and sex at Millbrook set the tone for what turning on was all about to a good many who dabbled in the sixties and seventies hippie counterculture. Leary chided the Puritan or antipleasure strain in American culture. He argued that the hedonistic pursuit of pleasure is a basic human right, perhaps even a moral duty. Leary's point was that we should take full advantage of the pharmaceutical breakthroughs that will allow us to "design one's life for pleasure through chemical turn-ons and turn-offs."[7]

Sense and sensuality are natural sacraments in Leary's view. Turning on, then, is a form of nature religion. Much as earlier Americans such as Henry David Thoreau or John Muir had turned attention to the sacredness of forests, Leary was turning attention to the sacred sensations to be found in our own natural constitution. What Leary discovered was that God is infused in every life-generating emotion, including sexual desire: "I was awed and confused by the sexual power [of turning on]. It was too easy. I was too much an Irish Catholic, too prudish to deal with it. Too Western Christian to realize that God and Sex are one, that God for a man is woman, that the direct path to God is through the divine union of male-female."[8]

Turning on also meant more than hedonistic pleasure. It had to do with ecstasy, with expanding consciousness. As the Episcopal priest turned psychedelic messiah, Alan Watts, wrote, "ecstasy is a legitimate human need—as essential for mental and physical health as proper nutrition, vitamins, rest, and recreation."[9] Leary went even further, likening himself to a religious prophet, a revolutionary seer whose message concerning spiritual ecstasy was slightly ahead of his time. He insisted that psychedelics open up the metaphysical vistas glimpsed by Moses, Mohammed, Blake, Boehme, Shankara, and St. John of the Cross. In

his psychedelic gospel, experience and message were one and the same: "Listen! Wake up! You are God! You have the Divine plan engraved in cellular script within you. Listen! Take this sacrament! You'll see! You'll get the revelation! It will change your life! You'll be reborn!"[10]

Tuning In

Tuning in had a slightly more esoteric ring to it. The mid- to late sixties was also the time of the human potential movement. Figures such as Abraham Maslow and Fritz Pearls were among the many "third force" or humanistic psychologists whose writings attracted a broad following. Humanistic psychologists were proposing an extremely optimistic view of human nature based largely on the view that the unconscious mind has unlimited energies that can be tapped for self-realization. Many human potential writers saw psychedelics as a way of tuning in to the "higher" energies of the unconscious.

Those who studied the psychedelic experience went out of their way to draw attention to the remarkable personal growth observed in their research subjects. For example, Sidney Cohen extolled LSD for stimulating "super-conscious bursts" of knowing.[11] Robert Mogar, summarizing the current status of LSD research in 1965, suggested that the principal use of LSD in the future would be to serve as a catalyst for rapid personal growth.[12] When R. E. Masters and Jean Houston wrote their oft-cited *The Varieties of Psychedelic Experience* in 1966, they took it for granted that "psychedelic (mind-manifesting) drugs afford the best access yet to the contents and processes of the human mind."[13] In their professional opinion, psychedelics pointed the way to the next step in human evolution. The work being done in this field was destined "to result in eventually pushing human consciousness beyond its present limitations and on towards capacities not yet realized and perhaps undreamed of."[14] Not to be overlooked was their bold hint that among these "undreamed of capacities" are the abilities for telepathy, ESP, and other paranormal phenomena. Masters and Houston, like a good many other apostles of the psychedelic message, could not resist making broad hints that psychedelic research was on the verge of documenting humanity's unexplored potentials for extrasensory perception.

Tuning in had other connotations, too. Psychedelic researchers were not interested in limiting their work to the development of a new psychological model of the human mind. When Albert Hofmann suggested that LSD adjusted the "wavelength" setting of the receiving self, he was arguing that our ordinary consciousness fails to apprehend all that there is to reality. Almost all psychedelic researchers agreed. It was argued that psychedelics do not distort reality but disclose dimensions or levels of existence that are otherwise screened by the rational ego. Psychedelics didn't just help us tune into previously untapped levels of our own mind; they also helped us tune into previously unrecognized dimensions or levels of reality.

Tuning in, then, sought to do more than enhance the kinds of mental processes that psychology already dealt with. Leary's psychology aimed at ecstasy, not normalcy. His own experience with LSD had all the hallmarks of a shaman's death-rebirth initiatory rite. It followed "that the religious-ontological nature of the psychedelic experience was obvious to me, and any secular discussion about psychedelic drugs—creativity, psychiatric treatment, etc.—seemed irrelevant."[15] What was relevant was helping persons to tune into the Kingdom of God residing deep within themselves.

Psychedelic researchers faced a major difficulty in pressing LSD sessions into the service of religious metaphysics. The data didn't completely justify their metaphysical claims. Few subjects actually had experiences that substantiated the hybrid of Eastern mysticism and Western occultism nurtured by the likes of Leary, Huxley, Watts, and Smith. Only about 3 percent of Alpert's and Leary's subjects ever "tuned in" to such metaphysical realities.[16] Masters and Houston put the figure at about 5 percent.[17] Psychedelic researchers were convinced, however, that these relatively small percentages could be accounted for. It was argued that subjects who failed to have an appropriate mystical experience might have brought the wrong set (personality, belief structure) to the session. Others might not have been afforded the right kind of supportive setting. Yet another possibility was that the dose might not have been high enough or the subject just clung too rigidly to his or her ego rather than letting the experience unfold on its own.

By 1966 Masters and Houston provided a neat typology for explaining such discrepancies between experimental findings and the claims that the researchers wanted to make on behalf of their newly found stairways to metaphysical illumination. They contended that there are four distinct levels of psychedelic experience. Each is successively "deeper" than its predecessor. Not every person moves easily through all levels, however,

any more than every person can rapidly progress through the levels of musical or athletic performance. All of their subjects who used LSD were able to attain the first level, the level of enhanced sensory awareness. At this level of experience, subjects report seeing colors more intensely, sensing an extraordinary beauty residing in things, and witness an endless flow of dancing geometrical forms. Masters and Houston noted that many, but not all, subjects were able to progress to the second level of psychedelic experience, which they referred to as the recollective-analytic. At this level, subjects become acutely aware of their mental and emotional processes. Memories of past events surface, and insight is gained into the psychological effect they have had. The third level, attained by even fewer subjects, is the symbolic level. Here the subject experiences primal, universal, and recurring themes of human experience. This level affords insight into the rites of passage, initiations, and other archetypal experiences we all go through. Masters and Houston called the fourth, and deepest, level the integral level. The integral level is mystical in nature. It affords individuals a vivid sensation of being "one" with the deepest level of reality. Unfortunately, only 11 of their 206 subjects had reached the deep integral level. Those who did described a feeling of oneness with God. Masters and Houston note that their subjects' descriptions of God do not exactly match conventional religious language. Rather than describing God in biblical terms, they utilized words more reminiscent of Paul Tillich's definition of God as the Ground of Being. As Masters and Houston explained, "When we examine those psychedelic experiences which seem to be authentically religious, we find that during the session the subject has been *able to reach the deep integral level* wherein lies the possibility of confrontation with a Presence variously described as God, Spirit, Ground of Being, Mysterium, Noumen, Essence, and Ultimate or Fundamental Reality."[18]

Another and more elaborate version of this typology was advocated by Stanislav Grof. Grof began conducting research into psychedelic drugs in his native Czechoslovakia in 1956. In 1967 he came to the United States and resumed his investigations at the Research Unit of Spring Grove State Hospital in Baltimore, Maryland. By 1973 Grof had conducted over 2,500 psychedelic sessions (each lasting a minimum of five hours), giving him the largest data base of any researcher in the field. His subjects were drawn from various groups, including terminally ill patients, severe psychoneurotics, alcoholic patients, graduate students, nurses, psychologists, artists, and theologians. Grof, too, proposed that there are four major levels of psychedelic experience.[19] He labeled the first level "abstract and aesthetic experiences." The second level was "psychodynamic experiences," which he claimed so closely manifested the kinds of psychosexual dynamics that Freud described that this level of psychedelic experience might be seen as an empirical confirmation of Freud's hypotheses. The third level varied somewhat from Masters and Houston's symbolic level. Grof called this the "perinatal" level, since his subjects frequently relived the trauma of birth and uterine existence. Jungian archetypes, death/rebirth imagery, and even visions of wrathful deities accompany these spontaneous impressions of perinatal existence. He wrote, "Everyone who has *reached these levels* develops convincing insights into the utmost relevance of the spiritual and religious dimensions in the universal scheme of things."[20] Grof termed the final level that of "transpersonal experiences." Those of his subjects who reached the deepest level spontaneously exhibited a variety of experiences that suggested that their conscious functioning was no longer restricted to the sensory plane or to the restrictive activities of the socially constructed ego. Subjects found themselves reliving earlier moments in the earth's evolutionary history, having instances of clairvoyance or precognition, enjoying out-of-body experiences, or conversing with suprahuman spiritual entities.

Grof's model, like that constructed by Masters and Houston, appealed to many. A major part of the spiritual awakening of the sixties and seventies was the excitement of "discovery." People were discovering new aspects of themselves. They were discovering new worldviews that told of other realms or levels of existence awaiting our exploration. Psychedelics contributed to the excitement of this discovery process. Even for those who didn't take them, psychedelics seemed to lend experimental confirmation to the kinds of metaphysical claims being made by those attracted to Eastern religions, the Western occult traditions, and the new human potential psychologies. That is, the results of psychedelic research were understood to have substantiated the claim that there are whole new worlds awaiting to be discovered right within ourselves. Tuning in, then, was the key to enlightenment.

Perhaps no one's life was more affected by tuning in than Huston Smith's. Smith was a professor of philosophy at MIT when he first learned about Timothy Leary's investigations. On New Year's Day, 1961, Smith visited Leary's home and accepted his host's kind invitation to try some mescaline. Smith's philosophical outlook on life was never the same. It was but a moment before he realized what Bergson had meant about the brain's role as a reducing agent. Free of the ego's restrictions, Smith now saw deeply into the mysteries of the cosmos. Perhaps most striking was his insight into "the metaphysical theory known as emanationism, in which, beginning with the clear, unbroken and infinite light of God or the Void, the light then breaks into forms and decreases in intensity as it diffuses through descending degrees of reality."[21] Smith's psychedelic illumination enabled him to see that Light was in all, all was in Light. All levels of existence are connected with one another. He further realized that the "power" of being flows continuously from higher levels to lower ones. It followed that the key to genuine spirituality is learning to become receptive to this spiritual inflow.

Smith became increasingly fascinated with what he called the common vision of the world's religions—the vision of this emanationist cosmology. His lectures, workshops, and prolific publications all promoted the "perennial philosophy" that he was quite literally turned on to while visiting Timothy Leary. In *Forgotten Truth: The Common Vision of the World's Religion,* the book that most clearly summarizes his own worldview, Smith appended a brief essay titled "The Psychedelic Evidence."[22] Smith held that the data collected by Stanislav Grof provided empirical evidence supporting the claims of the perennial philosophy: The self exists on many levels; the levels of self (or consciousness) correspond to levels of the cosmos that are ordinarily obscured from human view; enlightenment is reached by finding a means of circumventing the ego and having a direct experience of the deeper levels of the cosmos.

Even Huston Smith acknowledged that such metaphysical illuminations are probably not for the masses. The uninitiated must rely on the exoteric teachings of institutional religion. But for the initiated, the one who has turned on and tuned in, the esoteric teachings of the perennial philosophy were now being understood as objects of direct, immediate perception.

Dropping Out
Dropping out also had multiple meanings. Some were political. Others were social. And still others were religious. When Aldous Huxley first

opened the doors of perception in 1953, most Americans were too busy building a brave new world to step back and evaluate it. The postwar economy was booming. The good life was there for the taking. Supermarkets, affordable automobiles, and an expanding freeway system symbolized a nation in hot pursuit of material paradise. The terms of economic, social, and technological progress were all well defined. It was only up to individuals to conform to those terms and then work for the success that would be theirs. Only a few middle-class Americans seemed interested in questioning, let alone dropping out of, the American way of life.

By the mid-1960s things had obviously changed. Pockets of discontent couldn't be overlooked or contained at the periphery. Racial unrest broke out from Harlem to Watts. But the biggest source of discontent was to be found in America's youth. Although seemingly poised to inherit an economic paradise, college-age youth seemed restless, yearning for something that was somehow more authentic, freer, more pure. In his *The Making of a Counter Culture,* Theodore Roszak emphasized the importance of the period's antitechnology sentiment.[23] People were balking at regimentation, the loss of individuality in a world of mass merchandising. There was something more at work, however. This was an age of what religious historian Robert Ellwood called a "New Romanticism."[24] The cultural mood swung toward a celebration of childhood, an endorsement of individuality, and an embracing of the "new epistemology" of the supernatural, as found in ESP, astrology, and Eastern meditation. As Ellwood aptly put it, the 1960s witnessed a dramatic cultural shift away from modernism to postmodernism. And the psychedelic movement was both a contributing cause and a symptomatic effect of this cultural shift.

What Ellwood refers to as modernism was the intellectual and cultural expression of rationalistic science. Intellectually, modernism affirms the existence of single, universal truths that can be discerned through disciplined rational inquiry. Psychologically, modernism posits the unity of the self, asserting the existence of a true or essential self lurking behind the various identities that society imposes on us. And culturally, modernism assumes the inevitability of material progress. In contrast, postmodernism embraces relativism and what physicists call the uncertainty principle. Although postmodernism means different things to different people, it is commonly understood as a philosophical outlook that distrusts the subject-object dichotomy of conventional rationality. It is skeptical of universal, general truths and finds value instead in multiple perspectives and conversations. And if modernism emphasizes the "distance senses," such as viewing, reading, or hearing, postmodernism embraces the "proximity senses" of touching, tasting, or—in the words of the sixties—just happening. Postmodernism sees the self as plural, capable of being many identities without any conflict or necessary incompatibility.

The use of psychedelics turned the logic behind modernism upside down. The point here is not that psychedelics were alone responsible for the major ideological reorientations of the sixties and early seventies. Many arrived at new philosophical outlooks without ever using mind-altering substances; and many who did use psychedelics never changed their fundamental way of viewing life. But the use of psychedelics, in conjunction with exposure to the philosophical themes of the era's youth culture, provided tens—maybe hundreds—of thousands of Americans with an experiential template for arriving at a new spiritual outlook that might be characterized by such words as pluralism, postmodernism, and religious eclecticism.

Psychedelic experiences were thought to have exploded the pretensions of rationalistic science to understand the totality of existence. As James would have put it, they proved that normal rational consciousness is but one special type of consciousness. They also brought the proximity senses to the forefront of experience and discovery. Under the influence of mind-manifesting drugs, what is felt or experienced is valued more than rational abstractions. Psychedelic experience focused upon immediate bodily sensations. It seemed to show that the universe was no one, single thing but rather altered with changes in subjectivity and awareness. At a cultural or intellectual level, then, psychedelics challenged the modern intellectual paradigm.[25] At a personal level, the use of psychedelics initiated persons into a new stance toward the world; the psychedelic trip was a rite of passage into a distinct counterculture. For thousands of Americans, the use of psychedelic drugs was thus the first step toward dropping out of a worldview that had framed middle-class American life for decades.

Dropping out became a slogan for the era's reappraisal of middle-class values. It meant attempting to stand back and undo one's social conditioning, to reassess the value of almost everything that fifties America assumed it fully understood: the relative importance of such things as a job, sex, conformity, material acquisition, technology, and church. Jay Stevens suggested that drugs provided the emerging counterculture with a "deconditioning agent." In a matter of seconds, psychedelics quite literally dismantled the whole cognitive repertoire that society had programmed into individuals. And although the dismantling was only temporary, it gave vivid insight into how arbitrary our "normal waking state" actually is. In their foreword to Alan Watts's psychedelic masterpiece *The Joyous Cosmology*, Timothy Leary and Richard Alpert argued that the freedom to use drugs in order to liberate our minds from the tyranny of social conditioning is a basic American freedom: "Thus appears the fifth freedom—freedom from the learned, cultural mind. The freedom to expand one's consciousness beyond artifactual cultural knowledge. The freedom to move from constant preoccupation with the verbal games—the social games, the game of self—to the joyous unity of what exists beyond."[26]

It is interesting in this context to remember that learning how to "stop the world" was the principal theme of Carlos Castenada's works. Readers turned to Castenada's books hoping to learn how they might disentangle themselves from—and evolve beyond—the seemingly oppressive nature of middle-class society. The allure of Don Juan's teachings was that some combination of psychedelics and Native American wisdom might prove helpful in the quest of "stopping" the power of social conditioning. A surprising number of Americans wanted to learn how they might peel away the layers of socialization and somehow uncover other layers of consciousness that were more pristine, genuine, and teeming with creative potential.

Aldous Huxley devoted a great deal of attention to how psychedelics give new perspectives on the relationship between the individual and culture. In an article appearing in *Playboy*, Huxley maintained that drugs give access to "culturally uncontaminated" levels of thought.[27] Huxley's point was that drugs can bypass the utilitarian thought processes that strip reality of its sacredness. In this way drugs can help recapture an awareness of the divine ground of all being. To be sure, most of this philosophical reasoning was lost on a good many of the entrants into hippie life. Instead, most of the era's youth probably turned to drugs for the emotional thrills. What drugs most allowed them to do was to drop out of the world defined by parental and school authorities.

Indeed, Marlene Dobkin de Rios has discerned that one of the most common themes of drug use across world cultures is their implicit and explicit challenge to authority. By prompting individuals to feel that a true, experientially based authority can be found within, drugs make institutional authorities—secular and religious—appear irrelevant.[28]

Dropping out became ever more fashionable as the 1960s progressed. Clothing trends, hair length, music, and everyday jargon all reflected the implicit admiration of the hippie movement. By 1967 there may have been as many as 200,000 full-time hippies across the United States, let alone the multiples of that number who adopted elements of the hippie lifestyle.[29] Wherever they resided or whatever the degree of their affiliation with the movement, they all knew that the counterculture had a geographical center: the Haight-Ashbury district of San Francisco. The Haight-Ashbury district is a section of San Francisco that butts up against Golden Gate Park. Its handsome Victorian homes and proximity to the park had made it a favorite hangout for students and youthful drifters. But in the mid-sixties the Haight-Ashbury district became the Mecca of all things counterculture, including the heavy use of drugs. Upwards of 15,000 young men and women rented space in the adjacent houses and created what Warren Hinkle described as "a tribal, love-seeking, free-swinging, acid-based type of society."[30] In those years it was a favorite haunt of the famed author, Ken Kesey. Kesey, who had traveled the nation in a multicolored bus with his cavalier cohort known as the Merry Pranksters, became a self-appointed emissary of the psychedelic experience. Kesey had been "into" acid since 1960 and delighted in promulgating the psychedelic cause by staging public happenings he called "Acid Tests."

Haight-Ashbury developed to the point where it appeared that dropping out might be a self-sustaining way of life.[31] Coffee shops such as the Blue Unicorn and I/Thou popped up, with chessboards, sewing kits, secondhand clothes boxes, and space for social and intellectual gathering. Later, the Psychedelic Shop opened to sell metaphysical books, incense, marijuana paraphernalia, paisley fabrics, and Indian art. The quintessential expression of Haight-Ashbury's drop-out lifestyle, however, was the so-called "Be In." Predating Woodstock by a few years, the first Be-In at Haight-Ashbury was part rock concert, part political rally, part art fair, and part orgy. Top rock groups such as Quicksilver and the Grateful Dead

"Further," the psychedelic bus in which the Merry Pranksters traveled on a cross-country trip in 1964.

performed. Between sets Timothy Leary, Gary Snyder, Allen Ginsberg, and Alan Watts wholeheartedly encouraged their followers to experiment with alternative lifestyles ranging from the most esoteric of Eastern mystical practices to the daily use of mind-expanding drugs. And everywhere could be had the latest batch of LSD synthesized by famed Bay-area "chemist" Owsley Stanley. These Be-Ins were also referred to as "gatherings of the tribes." And gather they did. Particularly important was the way in which Be-Ins gathered together both the more politically active and the more spiritual wings of the counterculture. As Charles Perry has chronicled, the expressed purpose of these gatherings or Be-Ins was to show that "the hippies and radicals were one, their common aim being to drop out of 'games and institutions that oppress and dehumanize' . . . and to create communities where 'new values and new human relations can grow.'"[32]

Dropping out was also an act of religious affirmation. Several short-lived churches emerged that made drugs the center of their otherwise amorphous theologies. The Shiva Fellowship Church, the Psychedelic Venus Church, the Fellowship of the Clear Light, the American Council of Internal Divinity, and the Psychedelic Peace Fellowship were among the groups hoping to legitimize the religious elements of the psychedelic

experience.[33] In the late 1990s, Gordon Melton could find evidence that only about a half dozen of these "dope-related churches" were still functioning, with a combined membership estimated to be under six hundred persons.[34]

It is difficult to assess the sincerity of the motives that prompted persons to affiliate with these "dope churches." For some it was no doubt a matter of momentary impulse. The rhetoric of spiritual discovery lent an aura of respectability to the random hedonism that often characterized the hippie movement. Yet others were surely serious about their quests for ecstasy. A retired physician by the name of John Aiken formed the Church of the Awakening in 1963, advocating the use of drugs "as an aid in meditation." Art Kleps, a friend and associate of Timothy Leary, organized the Neo-American Church that mixed cynicism, satire, and the hope of using drugs with the full legal protection of the First Amendment. Timothy Leary reorganized his International Federation for Internal Freedom under the nomenclature of the League for Spiritual Discovery. In his own words, "We're not a religion in the sense of the Methodist church seeking new adherents. We're a religion in the basic primeval sense of a tribe living together and centered around shared spiritual goals. . . . In our religion the temple is the human body, the shrine is the home, and the congregation is a small group of family members and friends."[35] Leary failed to add that his League for Spiritual Discovery (LSD) might also provide a smoke screen under which persons could use drugs without government prosecution.

Most persons connected with the hippie movement never really elevated drugs to the point where they were themselves the object of religion. Instead, drugs were heralded as catalysts or "skillful means" for obtaining religious experience. Psychedelics were said to be vehicles to spiritual authenticity, not authenticity in and of themselves. But one thing was for sure. As vehicles, psychedelics were traveling in a direction opposite of the churches in which the hippie generation had been raised.

The mostly white, middle-class youth who were attracted to the counterculture came from fairly staid religious backgrounds. A significant percentage of the hippie movement had attended college. There they had been exposed to secularizing influences that made it impossible to embrace Sunday-school teachings in any straightforward way. Evolutionary biology, analytic philosophy, and the perspectives on either cultural conditioning or cultural relativism taught by the social sciences had their toll on individuals' allegiance to their parents' churches. Even more critical were the increasingly popular courses in academic departments of religion. Modern scholarship on the Bible provided students with irrefutable perspectives on the human—and hence culturally tainted—authorship of the scriptures they had formerly thought to be delivered from the mouth of God. Courses in comparative religion became the most popular courses on campuses across the nation. Exposure to Hinduism, Buddhism, and Taoism intrigued a new generation who demanded a more experiential approach to religion. In his book on *The Hippies and American Values,* Timothy Miller summarized the counterculture's religious outlook by noting that

> the hippies tended to take unusual (by traditional American standards) approaches to religion, often emphasizing Eastern spiritual teachings, and they were often syncretistic, pursuing a sort of religiosity that combined elements ranging from Hindu mysticism to Neopaganism to Ouija boards. It's a fair guess that most hippies would not have been very welcome in most churches; for their part, the hippies were not interested in getting active in any conventional religious body.[36]

It is thus easy to see why a significant number of Baby Boomers looked to the apostles of the psychedelic revolution for spiritual direction. Alan Watts, Huston Smith, Allen Ginsberg, and Richard Alpert/Ram Dass were homegrown gurus.

Watts was the embodiment of metaphysical illumination. A former Episcopal priest, Watts had been introduced at an early age to Theosophy and other metaphysical vocabularies that mingled Hindu Vedantism with Western occult traditions. His knowledge of Taoism and Zen Buddhism further set him apart as a guide to the mysterious yet uncharted spiritual territories that American reading audiences were eager to explore. When Watts converted to psychedelic enlightenment, he gave the movement its most gifted writer.

Huston Smith, meanwhile, was the movement's closest link to academic respectability. Smith was one of the few psychedelic pundits who was able to retain his academic stature. Writing in calm and understated fashion, it was Smith who did the most to get a fair hearing for the claim that drugs have religious significance.

Ginsberg, on the other hand, was quite possibly the most outrageous of the group; and that's a significant claim in a list that includes Timothy Leary. Ginsberg's connections with the literary and artistic communities preserved the psychedelic movement's ties with the Beat generation that preceded it. Up until his death in 1997, Ginsberg continued to promulgate Eastern perspectives through his own theatrical lecture/Be-Ins.

Ram Dass, meanwhile, was a living symbol that West can go East and return as a self-actualized sage. His message was that we must learn to go beyond conceptual structures. And although he has acknowledged that he still takes drugs from time to time, Ram Dass has dedicated his life to showing others a number of spiritual practices that can make ecstasy a sustained reality rather than a one-shot experience.

Watts, Smith, Ginsberg, and Ram Dass were all more capable religious thinkers than Leary. Whereas Leary encouraged persons to drop out, the others provided at least some broad hints about where persons might drop "in." All four turned Americans' attention to Asian mysticism and the perennial philosophy long connected with the Western occult tradition.

It was Leary, however, who made the clearest case for not needing to be attached to any kind of formal religion at all. A real religious experience, according to Leary, is "the ecstatic, incontrovertibly certain, subjective discovery of answers to four basic spiritual questions."[37] The four basic spiritual questions, according to Leary, are the Power Question ("What is the ultimate power of the universe?"), the Life Question ("What is life? Why and where did it start?"), the Human Destiny Question ("Whence did humans come and where are we going?"), and the Ego Question ("What am I? What is my place in the grander plan?"). In Leary's view, everything outside of these questions—rituals, dogmas, liturgical practices—is completely divorced from spirituality and is best seen as caught up in the corruptions of human institutions. The implication is that true spirituality is inward and personal. The "outer" aspects of religion are separable from true spirituality. Authentic spirituality, therefore, necessitates dropping out of institutional religion. This logic, whether expressly stated or not, permeated the psychedelic literature. A sizable number of Baby Boomers followed the logic to its conclusion and drifted away from the churches. And most never came back.[38] This is not to say, however, that they had turned their backs upon religion altogether. Instead, they had arrived at an alternative, and more personally compelling, spiritual awakening.

Ecstasy and Spiritual Awakening

By the early 1960s it became abundantly clear that a significant ideological revolution was beginning to take shape in American religious and cultural life. Literally millions felt they were searching for something more than they were finding in the established churches. Their intellectual curiosity made it difficult to settle for a one-size-fits-all form of mainline religion. Many also hungered for the spiritual excitement that comes from personal religious experience. This spiritual restlessness gave rise to what historian William McLoughlin termed the "fourth great awakening" in American religious life. By "awakening" McLoughlin means a significant moment in a nation's religious life in which a great many people undergo an alteration and revitalization in their religious thoughts or feelings. In McLoughlin's terms, awakenings "are periods of cultural revitalization that begin in a general crisis of beliefs and values and extend over a period of a generation or so, during which time a profound reorientation in beliefs and values takes place."[39] Such reorientations had happened three previous times in American life: one just prior to the Revolutionary War, a second during rapid western expansion in the early nineteenth century, and a third during rapid urbanization in the late nineteenth and early twentieth centuries. Each of these, however, had happened largely within the established, consensus churches. And each was dominated by the ascetic pole of religion, culminating in the subordination of the intellect and will to biblical authority.

Unlike previous awakenings of American spirituality, however, the awakening that began in the early 1960s occurred largely among those opting for an unchurched or alternative form of spirituality. Robert Ellwood has suggested that the major themes of this reorientation were (1) a shift from mainline to nonconformist religion, (2) a rediscovery of natural rather than revealed religion, (3) a new appreciation for Eastern religious thought, and (4) a new Romanticism that accords spiritual importance to certain nonrational modes of thought and perception.[40] In general, this represented a shift from seeking God in the church to seeking God in the depths of nature (including the depths of our own psychological nature). The spiritual awakening of the sixties was committed to the belief that the sacred is already implanted in the human heart and the natural world. The essence of personal spirituality, in this view, is to seek out new avenues for discovering the point of connection with this immanent divinity. American authors such as Emerson, Whitman, and James surely provided clues. So, too, did the mystical writings of Hinduism and Buddhism. And not to be overlooked were the kinds of metaphysical illumination made possible with the help of mind-manifesting drugs.

Psychedelics were, without doubt, one of most important factors in the spread of spiritual change in the 1960s and early 1970s. Members of the Baby Boom generation used these substances in settings that implicitly connected them with the very themes Ellwood discerns in the spiritual unrest of the 1960s: the shift from mainline to nonconformist religion, the rediscovery of natural religion, a new appreciation for Eastern thought, and a new Romanticism. Drugs induced an experiential ecstasy that lent an aura of mystical authority to the changes taking place in many Americans' orientation to religious issues. This was true not only for those who ingested drugs but also for a good many of those who never used them at all.

For those who used them, psychedelics provided an experience-based rite of passage to the "new Romanticism." As we noted earlier, they elicited an emotional ecstasy based not on the "distance senses" of reading and hearing but rather on the "proximity senses" of touch, taste, and bodily sensation. Psychedelics provided new configurations of the world based not upon reflective reason but upon dream-like free association and idiosyncratic impressions. Psychedelics deconstructed the world of waking rationality and temporarily transported the initiate into a whole new mode of thinking and feeling. This new mode was charged with excitement, mystery, and intrigue. And although this new mode of awareness gave rise to insights that were ineffable upon return to the normal waking state, it nonetheless left the lasting impression that the world is surrounded by a higher order of Being. In this way the use of psychedelics—and the literature describing this use—meshed perfectly with the era's growing interest in writers such as Robert Heinlein, Hermann Hesse, Mircea Eliade, Carl Jung, and Joseph Campbell. All reinforced American reading audiences' desire to imagine new ways of thinking about themselves and their relationship to nonvisible realities.

Drug use was also a springboard to fascination with extraordinary states of consciousness. Aldous Huxley, Timothy Leary, Richard Alpert, Alan Watts, Huston Smith, and Allen Ginsberg were perhaps the closest thing to shamans that middle-class America has ever known. With the help of psychedelics, they made ecstatic flights into other metaphysical dimensions. And when they returned, they were prepared to instruct others concerning the kinds of thoughts and actions that would best align individuals with a higher, spiritual reality. In an article on "Psychedelics and Religious Experience," Alan Watts reported that "I myself have experimented with five of the principal psychedelics: LSD-25, mescaline, psilocybin, DMT, and cannabis. I have done so, as William James tried nitrous oxide, to see if they could help me in identifying what might be called the 'essential' or 'active' ingredients of the mystical experience."[41] His experiments proved most successful. They yielded a variety of insights that were crammed into several best-selling books and hundreds of lectures on college campuses. We can only assume that such proselytizing by the likes of Watts, Smith, Ginsberg, and Leary prompted others to explore the essential and active ingredients of the mystical experience for themselves.

This fascination with extraordinary states of consciousness in turn led to interest in Eastern religions, whose meditation practices struck Americans as perfectly suited to their own new spiritual convictions. Psychedelics were understood to be cleansing the very doors of perception opened through Hindu and Buddhist meditation systems. The role of psychedelics was so important to the growth of Americans' interest in Eastern religions that in the fall of 1996 a major Buddhist journal devoted an entire issue to the topic. One American-born practitioner of Buddhism noted that "many who took LSD, mushrooms, and other psychedelics, often along with reading from The Tibetan Book of the Dead or some Zen texts, had the gates of wisdom opened to a certain extent." Opening these gates gave them vivid insight into the fact that "their limited consciousness was only one plane and that there were a thousand new things to discover about the mind."[42]

For thousands of Americans, then, psychedelics and interest in Eastern religious practices went hand in hand. The statistics are staggering. A recent poll of over 1,300 Americans engaged in Buddhist practice showed that 83 percent had taken psychedelics.[43] Some, of course, had eventually decided that the two were incompatible. But 59 percent responded that psychedelics and Buddhism do mix, and 71 percent believed that psychedelics can provide a glimpse of the reality to which Buddhist practice points. Ram Dass, a.k.a. Richard Alpert, was interviewed in this issue and admitted that he still took drugs as a supplement to his other spiritual practices. He offered that "from my point of view, Buddhism is the closest to the psychedelic experience, at least in terms of LSD. LSD catapults you beyond conceptual structures. It extricates you. It overrides your habit of identifying with thought and puts you in a nonconceptual mode very fast."[44]

Drug-induced states of consciousness appealed to many Baby Boomers who yearned for an experientially based spirituality. As one researcher put it, psychedelics serve "as a kind of phase through which we pass when we're trying to become more truly who we are, more authentic, and more genuine."[45] The ecstatic nature of drug-induced states of consciousness lent charisma or authority to the claims made by psychedelic pundits. In this sense they provided a higher authority that legitimated the transition from "consensus" to "alternative" religion. Cultural anthropologist Marlene Dobkin de Rios pointed out that to the extent that firsthand experience is considered the true way to knowledge, drugs will be considered with awe and respect: "In those societies where plant hallucinogens play a central role, one learns that the drug user believes that he or she can see, feel, touch, and experience the unknown."[46] The various social settings in which Baby Boom Americans used drugs tended to foster precisely this conviction that drugs are one means of seeing, feeling, and experiencing a metaphysical reality. There was, of course, a concurrent tendency for these persons to view established religious institutions as a secondhand or less authentic form of spirituality. And thus the use of psychedelics helped accelerate a shift away from mainline to nonconformist religion among those Baby Boomers who were most caught up in the "ideological revolution" of the sixties and seventies.

The psychedelic movement also influenced the spirituality of millions who never used drugs at all. Psychedelics were a cultural icon; they symbolized an orientation to the world that was embraced by those who never even saw a mushroom or tab of LSD. The books and public lectures by the major gurus of the psychedelic revolution spread their message to almost every bookstore and college campus in the nation. Rock music, too, carried the major themes of this movement into American life and thought. The multisensory nature of the psychedelic experience was replicated on album covers, in lyrics, and in the light shows that accompanied live concerts. Rock concerts were their own Be-Ins. And as Woodstock proved, they had a powerful influence in transmitting both the best and worst elements of the counterculture's philosophy. It shocked no one to learn that Paul McCartney, John Lennon, and George Harrison of the Beatles had all tried LSD. Their albums, particularly "Sgt. Pepper's Lonely Hearts Club Band," increasingly communicated the exotic and alluring qualities of an altered state of mind. And when they became interested in Hinduism and Eastern metaphysics, the world was almost obligingly forced to recognize this as a normative spiritual quest.

Even those pursuing a scholarly approach to understanding religion were forced to consider the possibility that drugs constituted a legitimate and genuine path to metaphysical illumination. The highly respected scholar Huston Smith, for example, argued that psychedelics provide an "empirical metaphysics." Smith argued that the extensive data collected by Leary, Masters and Houston, and Grof provided impressive evidence in favor of a worldview that proclaims humanity's inner connection to a wider spiritual universe. In this way Smith, Watts, Leary, and others whose writings often found their way into college courses helped create a bridge linking academe, the use of psychedelics, and the counterculture's advocacy of such themes as individuality, nonrational modes of thinking, multisensory experiences, and the inner divinity of every person.

One example of the connection between the use of psychedelics and the larger awakening occurring within American religious life was the way in which psychedelic experiences helped put new understandings of God into popular circulation.

Psychedelic literature hastened the period's trend away from identifying God solely in biblical terms and instead defining God in more monistic and even pantheistic ways. For instance, Alan Watts claimed that psychologists were "studying peculiar states of consciousness in which the individual discovers himself to be one continuous process with God, with the universe, with the Ground of Being, or whatever name he may use by cultural conditioning or personal preference for the ultimate reality."[47] Huston Smith, meanwhile, claimed that LSD research substantiated a very different view of God than is found in the Bible. As he put it, "the God who is almost invariably encountered [while under the influence of psychedelics] is so removed from anthropomorphism as to elicit, often, the pronoun 'it.'"[48] A theological student writing in the mid-1960s witnessed that under the influence of LSD he, as an individual, "ceased to exist, becoming immersed in the ground of Being, in Brahman, in God, in 'nothingness,' in Ultimate Reality."[49] The religious experiences connected with the use of psychedelics were thus powerful testimony to the era's yearning for a religious vocabulary grounded in our own personal existence and experience. And, again, even many who never used psychedelics were confirmed by these accounts in the legitimacy of their growing interest in new and unchurched forms of spirituality.

All in all, then, psychedelics led a good many Americans down the road toward a more Romantic, postmodern, and unchurched form of spiritual thinking. Even among those who didn't use them, psychedelics were a symbol of the metaphysical illumination available to all who venture past the narrow confines of consensus religion. They demonstrated in the most vivid of ways that normal waking consciousness is but one special type of consciousness, parted by the filmiest of screens from unsuspected other worlds of Being. Psychedelics opened the doors separating these otherwise discrete worlds of consciousness, allowing passage back and forth. The ecstatic adventure was nothing short of a metaphysical illumination. And that illumination provided the key symbols and metaphors for a great deal of the unchurched spirituality that has flourished in the late twentieth century.

Notes

1. Timothy Leary, cited in Rick Fields, "A High History of Buddhism," *Tricycle: The Buddhist Review* (Fall 1996): p. 47. Readers interested in Leary's storied career should read his two autobiographical accounts, *High Priest* (New York: World Publishing, 1968), and *Flash-*

backs (Los Angeles: Tarcher, 1983). See also Jay Stevens's *Storming Heaven;* Robert Ellwood, *The Sixties Spiritual Awakening* (New Brunswick, NJ: Rutgers University Press, 1994), pp. 82-85, 151-153; and Robert S. DeRopp's entry on "Psychedelic Drugs," in Mircea Eliade, ed., *Encyclopedia of Religion,* vol. 12 (New York: Collier Macmillan, 1987), pp. 53-55.

2. See Walter Pahnke, "Drugs and Mysticism: An Analysis of the Relationship Between Psychedelic Drugs and the Mystical Consciousness (Unpublished doctoral dissertation, Harvard University, 1966). See also Walter N. Pahnke and William A. Richards, "Implications of LSD and Experimental Mysticism," *Journal of Religion and Health* 5 (1966): 175-208; and Walter Pahnke, "The Mystical and/or Religious Element in the Psychedelic Experience," in D. H. Salman and R. H. Prince, eds., *Do Psychedelics Have Religious Implications?* (Montreal: R. M. Bucke Memorial Society, 1967), pp. 41-56. Leary's account of the Marsh Chapel experiment can be found in his *High Priest,* pp. 291-318. An excellent overview of the psychological study of the religious dimensions of psychedelic drug use can be found in David Wulff, *Psychology of Religion* (New York: John Wiley & Sons, 1991).

3. Walter Clark, *Chemical Ecstasy: Psychedelic Drugs and Religion* (New York: Sheed & Ward, 1969), p. 77.

4. Ram Dass, *Remember. Be Here Now* (San Cristobal, NM: Lama Foundation, 1971). This unusual book contains an autobiographical account of Alpert's introduction to Leary and their subsequent collaboration prior to his spiritual metamorphosis.

5. See Ellwood, *The Sixties Spiritual Awakening,* p. 193. Ellwood suggests that the word hippie was popularized by the March 1967 article in *Ramparts* by Warren Hinckle, "The Social History of the Hippies."

6. Stevens, *Storming Heaven,* p. 208.

7. Timothy Leary, cited in Timothy Miller, *The Hippies and American Values* (Knoxville: University of Tennessee Press, 1991), p. 19. See the discussion of this same point in Ellwood, *The Sixties Spiritual Awakening,* p. 314.

8. Leary, *High Priest,* p. 154.

9. Alan Watts, *Cloud-Hidden, Whereabouts Unknown* (New York: Random House, 1973), p. 35.

10. Leary, *High Priest,* p. 285.

11. Sidney Cohen, *The Beyond Within: The LSD Story* (New York: Atheneum, 1965), p. 60.

12. Robert E. Mogar, "Current Status and Future Trends in Psychedelic (LSD) Research," *Journal of Humanistic Psychology* 2 (1965): 147-166.

13. Masters and Houston, *The Varieties of Psychedelic Experience,* p. 3.

14. Ibid., p. 316.

15. Leary, *High Priest,* p. 296.

16. Ram Dass, *Remember. Be Here Now.*

17. Masters and Houston, *The Varieties of Psychedelic Experience,* p. 148.

18. Ibid., p. 266.

19. The most succinct of Stanislav Grof's books is his *Realms of the Human Unconscious: Observations from LSD Research* (New York: Viking Press, 1975). Other important books include his *Beyond the Brain: Birth, Death, and Transcendence in Psychotherapy* (Albany: State University of New York Press, 1985), and his book with Joan Halifax, *The Human Encounter with Death* (New York: E. P. Dutton, 1978).

20. Grof, *Realms of the Human Unconscious,* p. 95.

21. Huston Smith, "Empirical Metaphysics," in Ralph Metzner, ed., *The Ecstatic Adventure* (New York: Macmillan, 1968), p. 72.

22. Huston Smith, *Forgotten Truth: The Common Vision of the World's Religions* (New York: HarperCollins, 1976).

23. Theodore Roszak, *The Making of a Counter Culture* (Garden City, NY: Doubleday, 1969).

24. See Ellwood, *The Sixties Spiritual Awakening,* pp. 10-15.

25. Spokespersons for the psychedelic or "altered states of consciousness" field of research frequently engaged in philosophical critique of Western scientific paradigms. Perhaps the most representative of these comes in Charles Tart's *States of Consciousness* (New York: Dutton, 1975).

26. Richard Alpert and Timothy Leary, in the foreword to Alan Watts, *The Joyous Cosmology* (New York: Vintage Books, 1965), p. x.

27. Aldous Huxley, article originally appearing in *Playboy,* reprinted as "Culture and the Individual," in David Solomon, ed., *LSD: The Consciousness Expanding Drug* (New York: G. P. Putnam's Sons, 1964), p. 32.

28. Marlene Dobkin de Rios, *Hallucinogens: Cross-Cultural Perspectives* (Albuquerque: University of New Mexico Press, 1984), p. 203.

29. Lewis Yablonsky, *The Hippie Trip* (New York: Pegasus, 1968), p. 35.

30. Warren Hinckle, "The Social History of the Hippies," cited in Ellwood, *The Sixties Spiritual Awakening,* p. 196.

31. See Charles Perry, *The Haight-Ashbury: A History* (New York: Random House, 1984).

32. Ibid., p. 122.

33. See Timothy Miller's discussion of "dope churches" in his *The Hippies and American Values,* pp. 31-34.

34. J. Gordon Melton, *The Encyclopedia of American Religions,* 5th ed. (Detroit: Gale Research, 1996), pp. 145ff.

35. Timothy Leary, quoted in Miller, *The Hippies and American Values,* p. 32.

36. Ibid., p. 19.

37. Timothy Leary, "The Religious Experience: Its Production and Interpretation," *Journal of Psychedelic Drugs* 1 (1967): 7.

38. In his *A Generation of Seekers,* Wade Clark Roof provides a segmented analysis of the spirituality of Baby Boomers by their degree of "exposure to the '60s." The greater the degree of exposure to the '60s counterculture, the greater the likelihood that individuals will describe themselves as "spiritual" rather than "religious." Exposure to the '60s is negatively correlated with putting value on "sticking to a faith," whereas it is positively correlated with valuing an

ongoing "exploration of teachings." Furthermore, the greater the degree of exposure to the '60s, the less likely individuals are to embrace conventional views of God and the more likely they are to embrace pantheistic or Eastern religious views.

39. William McLoughlin, *Revivals, Awakenings, and Reform* (Chicago: University of Chicago Press, 1978), p. xiii.

40. See the concluding chapter ("Final Reflections on the Sixties") of Robert Ellwood's *The Sixties Spiritual Awakening*, pp. 326-336.

41. Alan Watts, "Psychedelics and Religious Experience," in Bernard Aaronson and Humphry Osmond, eds., *Psychedelics* (Garden City, NY: Doubleday, 1970), p. 132. An article appearing in Timothy Leary's *Psychedelic Review* also reported the use of psychedelics to explore the nature of mystical experience. John Blofeld ingested one-half gram of mescaline to test Huxley's claim that mescaline can induce yogic experiences of a higher order. Blofeld reported that psychedelics can indeed enable us to discard our illusory egos and elicit bliss. His mescaline experience gave him (1) an awareness of undifferentiated unity, (2) a sense of unutterable bliss, and (3) a vivid awareness that all things are devoid of own-being as implied in the Buddhist doctrine of "dharma." See his "A High Yogic Experience Achieved with Mescaline," *Psychedelic Review* 3 (1966): 27-32.

42. Jack Kornfield, interview in *Tricycle: The Buddhist Review* (Fall 1996): 35.

43. Magazine and Web poll, reported in *Tricycle: The Buddhist Review* (Fall 1996): 44.

44. Ram Dass, interview in ibid., p. 102.

45. Joan Halifax, interview in ibid.

46. Dobkin de Rios, *Hallucinogens: Cross-Cultural Perspectives*, p. 203.

47. Watts, "Psychedelics and Religious Experience," p. 131.

48. Smith, *Forgotten Truth*, p. 168.

49. John Robertson, "Uncontainable Joy," in Metzner, ed., *The Ecstatic Adventure*, p. 86.

A. ALVAREZ (ESSAY DATE FALL 2001)

SOURCE: Alvarez, A. "Drugs and Inspiration." *Social Research* 68, no. 3 (fall 2001): 779-93.

In the following essay, Alvarez focuses on the impact of drugs on the creation of literature, particularly in the writings of the Romantics and the Beats.

I want to discuss two periods in English literature when drugs and inspiration seemed to go together. The first was the Romantics' furtive flirtation with opium around the close of the eighteenth century; the second was in the 1950s and 1960s, when the Beatniks became infatuated with what they optimistically called "mind-enhancing" drugs. The writers' attitudes to drugs, the way they used them, and the effect their habits had on their work were all very different, but the most basic difference was in the legality of the drugs themselves. For the Romantics, opium was ethically neutral; it was just another medicine with unexpected side effects. For the Beats, the ultimate charm of dope was that it was a "controlled substance," and to use it was a political statement, a gesture of defiance.

I

In her fascinating book, *Opium and the Romantic Imagination,* Althea Hayter explains, in great detail, that the use of opium as a painkiller and soporific is literally as old as the practice of medicine: "In an Egyptian medical treatise of the sixteenth century B.C., Theban physicians were advised to prescribe opium for crying children just as, three and a half millennia later, Victorian babies were dosed with the opiate Godfrey's Cordial by their nurses to keep them quiet" (Hayter, 1968: 19). Opium was used by doctors in classical Greece and ancient Rome; Galen prescribed it, Virgil mentioned it in the *Aeniad* and the *Georgics*; Arab physicians used it—Avicenna is said to have been an addict—and the Crusaders picked it up from them and brought it back to Europe, where it became a standard medicine. It is mentioned not only famously by Shakespeare in *Othello*—"Not poppy nor mandragora / Nor all the drowsy syrups of the world / Shall ever medicine thee to that sweet sleep / Which thou owedst yesterday"—but also by Chaucer, Sir Thomas Browne, and Robert Burton. Hayter quotes a slightly dotty Doctor John Jones who published a book in 1700 called *The Mysteries of Opium Reveal'd* in which he claimed it could cure or relieve "gout, dropsy, catarrh, ague, asthma, fevers of all kinds, travel sickness, stone, colic, measles, rheumatism, and even plague, as well as psychological troubles like hypochondria and insomnia. He listed the different preparations of opium then in use: Venice Treacle, Mithridate, Sydenham Laudanum, Dr. Bate's Pacific Pill, London Laudanum, and so on" (Hayter, 1968: 25).

In other words, two centuries ago, opium was generally available as a cure for everything. It was like aspirin; every household had some, usually in the form of laudanum—that is, mixed with alcohol—and used it as an analgesic for aches and pains, for hangovers, toothache, and hysteria. Shelley drank laudanum to calm his nervous headaches, Keats used it as a painkiller, Byron took an opium-based concoction called Kendal Black Drop as a tranquilizer; even Jane Austen's sedate mother prescribed it for travel sickness. Wordsworth—not surprisingly—seems to have been the only major English Romantic poet never to have touched the stuff. It was also classless and cheap, so cheap that factory workers in the earliest "dark satanic mills" swilled laudanum on Saturday nights because it cost less than booze, even in the days of Gin Lane when you could get "drunk for a penny, dead drunk for tuppence." When Marx called religion "the opiate of the masses," the masses would have known what he meant.

Naturally, the general availability of opium and the medical profession's enthusiasm for it helped create addicts, some of them very famous: Clive of India, for example, and William Wilberforce, the great emancipator. Among the literary addicts, Coleridge and De Quincy were the best known, but they also included that most sober poet, George Crabbe. (Oddly enough, William Blake, the hippies' hero, was not an opium-eater; but then, he was so eccentric that he started where opium left off.) All, however, were addicts despite themselves, not by design but by mistake, by misfortune, by chance. At a time when doctors had no concept of addiction, there was nothing to alert their patients to the dangers of the patent medicines they prescribed or to prepare them for the side effects. As a result, there was no more stigma attached to the opium habit than to alcoholism; it was an unfortunate weakness, not a vice.

It also fitted in with the Romantics' newfound absorption in the inner world. To simplify grossly, the Romantic movement began around the time of the French Revolution and, like the revolution, it was founded on an idea of freedom—a freedom to feel, to react in a personal and unpredictable way, without reference to classical precedent. When Pope, for example, talked about "the World" he meant polite society; for Shelley the world usually meant untamed nature with a shivering sensibility at its center. I am talking about a profound shift of focus, away from established Augustan certainties and toward subjective experience. Genius as we now understand it is a wholly Romantic concept: not just a great artist but a great artist who has embarked on an inner journey and makes his own rules as he goes—Beethoven rather than Haydn, Rousseau rather than Dr. Johnson, Rimbaud rather than Pope.

The essence of Romantic genius is revelation and the exultation and certainty that go with it. (Think of Wordsworth at *Tintern Abbey,* Keats and the *Grecian Urn,* or even "stout Cortez" gazing out over the Pacific with "a wild surmise.") But revela-

tion cannot be willed or worked for; it is more like a blessing, something that might happen to you if you live right. Hence Coleridge's curiously passive image in "Dejection: An Ode" of the poet as an Aeolian harp blown upon by forces beyond his control. This is inspiration in the most literal sense and, if it cannot be deliberately ordered up, it can at least be provoked and encouraged. Hence the opium. Hence, too, the preoccupation with dreams (think of "La Belle Dame sans Merci") or rather, with nightmares. All young Romantics, good and bad, gifted and foolish, were besotted with what Shelley called "the tempestuous loveliness of terror." Goya said "the sleep of reason breeds monsters" and the Romantics went to great lengths to wake those monsters. For example, the painter Fuseli guzzled platefuls of raw meat and rotting food late at night in order to provoke nightmares; so did Anne Radcliffe, who wrote *The Mysteries of Udolpho,* one of the most famous of all Gothic novels; so did many other lesser figures. The artists gave themselves bad dreams and indigestion in the name of inspiration in the same hopeful masochistic spirit as the young women of the time tortured themselves in the name of High Romance: they drank vinegar and sucked lead pencils to make their faces pale and melancholy, dilated their pupils with belladonna for luminous eyes, starved themselves and wore iron corsets for a sylphlike figure—all because they wanted to look like the heroines of the Gothic novels they devoured.

This was the sensationalist side of Romanticism, more to do with fashion than creativity, a sad parody of the serious artist's belief that dreaming and poetic creation were parallel and interchangeable worlds, intimately linked. Although the word "unconscious" had not yet entered the language in its modern sense, poets believed that a hotline to their dream life was a necessary part of their professional equipment. Especially Coleridge, who was a lifelong martyr to nightmares so terrible that he was afraid to sleep and often woke up screaming. These nightmares had started when he was a small child and no doubt, like other small children at the time, he was dosed with some opium-based snake oil to calm him down. So when he began taking laudanum again 20 years later, to cure an agonizing eye infection, he would have recognized the landscape. This was in 1796, when he was 24, unhappily married and suffering from a bad dose of the writer's sickness that C. K. Ogden called "hand-to-mouth disease"—lack of money, deadlines, printer's errors, anxiety about the next book. From then on, he gradually became addicted to opium, which duly changed and intensified the nightmares. Coleridge was always a wonderfully subtle observer and interpreter of his own states of mind—both a psychoanalyst and an *analysand avant la lettre*—and part of his genius was his ability to use his underlife—his dreams and anxieties, and also his prodigious learning—not just for images but as a source of poetry, as a way of re-creating the strangeness of the inner world. Out of his addict's pains of sleep he created—implicitly, though not formally—a new aesthetic. In other words, for intellectual and highly self-aware writers like Coleridge, altered states of consciousness were a source of fresh artistic inspiration and they had aesthetic consequences.

In the early stages of addiction the link was obvious and fruitful. Coleridge's famous description of the genesis of "Kubla Khan" is at once a paradigm of Romantic inspiration and also, incidentally, a most seductive come-on for the use of drugs as a shortcut to creativity:

> In consequence of a slight indisposition, an anodyne had been prescribed, from the effects of which he fell asleep in his chair at the moment when he was reading the following sentence . . . in "Purchas's Pilgrimage": "Here the Kubla Khan commanded a palace to be built, and a stately garden thereunto. And thus ten miles of fertile ground were enclosed with a wall." The Author continued for about three hours in a profound sleep, at least of the external senses, during which time he has the most vivid confidence, that he could not have composed less than from two to three hundred lines; if that indeed could be called composition in which all the images rose up before him as things, with a parallel production of the correspondent expression, without any sensation or consciousness of effort. On awakening he appeared to have a distinct recollection of the whole, and taking his pen, ink, and paper, instantly and eagerly wrote down the lines that are here preserved
>
> (Coleridge, 1957: 296).

The resulting poem is a prime example of what Freud called "dream work": condensation and elision, thoughts expressed as "things," thinking acted out dramatically as in a charade, all of it dredged up from the unconscious and drenched with feeling and significance. As I wrote in my book *Night,* an old-fashioned Freudian could have a field-day with the "caverns measureless to man" and the "sunless sea," the walled paradise garden, "that deep romantic chasm" with a "mighty fountain" spurting from it, the "demon lover" and "ancestral voices." But the primal scene was not, I think, the only creativity Coleridge had (even unconsciously) in mind. The landscape of "Kubla

Khan" sounds, instead, very like the poetic imagination as he later described it in the famous chapters of his *Biographia Literaria:* as a river, a living force that "dissolves, diffuses, dissipates, in order to re-create" or, as he depicted Shakespeare's genius, as two rivers, his creative powers and his intellectual energy, "that, at their first meeting within narrow and rocky banks, mutually strive to repel each other and intermix reluctantly and in tumult; but soon finding a wider channel and more yielding shores blend, and dilate, and flow on in one current and with one voice." In other words, in the same way as dreams are often about themselves and the process of dreaming, "Kubla Khan" can be read as a dream poem about poetry and the poetic imagination (Alvarez, 1995: 184-5).

Although "Kubla Khan" was a one-off phenomenon, Coleridge learned from it and it had a profound effect on the two great poems that followed. "The Ancient Mariner" and "Christabel" are steeped in hallucination and dreams: nightmare shifts of focus like the swift, secret, chilling transformation of the face of "the lovely lady Geraldine" into a serpent's ("One moment—and the sight was fled!"), or of the ocean into a putrid pond ("The very deep did rot: O Christ! / That ever this should be! / Yea, slimy things did crawl with legs / Upon the slimy sea."); also hallucinatory distortions of time and place, such as the Mariner's eternity becalmed, then his seemingly overnight flit from the Pacific to England. Coleridge's notebooks are full of shrewd comments on "the language of Dream = Night [and] that of Waking = Day," and he had a genius for using his experiences under opium to fuse together what he called the ego diurnus and the ego nocturnus, the day-self and the night-self. The result was a genuinely altered state of aesthetic consciousness, a precursor of the systematic deregulation of the senses that Rimbaud talked about later.

These three great poems were written during the relatively blissful honeymoon period when opium was still a source of inspiration for Coleridge, an enabler of his imagination. The dreams that came later, when he was seriously addicted, were altogether more threatening and unforgiving, like those described by De Quincy in *The Confessions of an English Opium-Eater.* The habit had killed what Coleridge called his "shaping spirit of imagination"—his emotional energy, his delight in poetry, his appetite for life. He wrote one great poem, "Dejection," about the inner desolation that drug addiction creates, then, despite reams of indifferent verse, he turned mostly to prose. But he knew precisely what he had lost. In 1815, with all his great poems behind him, he wrote in his notebook, "If a man could pass thro' Paradise in a Dream & have a flower presented to him as a pledge that his Soul had really been there, and found that flower in his hand when he awoke—Aye! and what then?" I think the paradise he was talking about was the period of seemingly effortless opium-fueled inspiration and the great poems he produced in his youthful prime. And the flower in his hand was a poppy.

II

To repeat: Because opium-based medicines were commonplace at the end of the eighteenth century, they came without moral baggage; like alcohol, the stigma was in the excessive use, not in the drugs themselves. Coleridge may have ended up as an addict but only by accident and he was not initially interested in opium in or for itself. Like any writer, of course, he was enraptured by the idea of blissful, effortless inspiration, but he was interested even more in the states of mind drugs produced—insights, images, hallucinations, and all the other strange mental disjunctions that were part of the mystery of the self the Romantics, at the end of the classical eighteenth century, were suddenly free to explore.

The Beatniks attitude to drugs was altogether different. It had not much to do with aesthetics and a great deal to do with politics, though maybe not quite as we now remember them. We think of the 1960s as the decade when drugs became the common cause that separated the young from the old, but this is neither strictly nor historically true. The Beatniks helped create the drug culture that climaxed during the latter stages of the Vietnam War, but the Beat generation itself took off in the previous decade, during the placid, prosperous years of Eisenhower's presidency, when the domestic issue that provoked greatest anxiety among intellectuals was conformism. In Mary McCarthy's words, "We are a nation of 20 million bath tubs, with a humanist in every tub" (McCarthy, 1962: 18). I do not happen to believe that the time was as conformist as it was said to be. I myself remember it—at least in New York, if not at Oxford—as a period of intense intellectual excitement and argument. But at the height of the Cold War and McCarthyism, politics was a no-go area, so the argument had shifted from politics to literature, from Marxism to the New Criticism.

The tone of voice, however, was very similar. The New Critics saw themselves as being in opposition to the old appreciators. William Empson put it best: "Critics as 'barking dogs' . . . are of two sorts: those who merely relieve themselves against the flower of beauty, and those, less continent, who afterwards scratch it up" (Empson, 1949: 9). Instead of throwing up their hands and saying "Magic!" when confronted with great literature, they tried to talk rationally about the irrational and intensely subjective experience of reading, to find reasons why these lines were better than those, to explain how they worked, and why they were—or were not—so moving. They valued sensibility but refused to believe that it precluded intelligent argument.

This was far too intellectual for the Beat writers. They were in revolt against the high-minded '50s—determinedly anti-intellectual, anti-aesthetic, anti-everything the New Critics and the great Modernists they revered, like Eliot and Joyce, believed in. That, I think, is why Ginsberg chose to write like Whitman. Philip Rahv had written a famous essay about the two opposing groups of American writers, "Paleface and Redskin" he called them, the aesthetes and the wild men, Boston and the frontier, patrician and plebeian, "the drawing-room fictions of Henry James and the open air poems of Walt Whitman" (Rahv, 1957: 1). So to write in the bardic style of Whitman or William Blake's *Prophetic Books* at a time when most other poets were struggling with the inheritance of John Donne and T. S. Eliot was a gesture of defiance. As gestures went, however, it was too restricted, too literary and academic. Ginsberg had been brought up among Bohemian Marxists—his father was a poet and a socialist, his schizophrenic mother was a communist—and he called himself "a political [poet] or a visionary activist" (Ginsberg, 1996: 339). In 1958, when the Beat Generation was grabbing the headlines, Norman Mailer remarked, "The beatnik—often Jewish—comes from the middle-class, and 25 years ago would have joined the YCL" (Mailer, 1960: 335). Since the Young Communist League was no longer an option and, with Joe McCarthy on the prowl, capitalism was a touchy subject, the next best target was highbrow art, and the equivalent of radical politics was dope. "Howl" famously begins, "I saw the best minds of my generation destroyed by madness, starving hysterical naked, / dragging themselves through the negro streets at dawn looking for an angry fix. . . ." (Ginsberg, 1987: 126). I remember someone remarking at the time, "It makes you wonder whom he met." In fact, Ginsberg studied at Columbia under Lionel Trilling, so he must have known plenty of clever people, but they were not the ones who interested him. He preferred "angelheaded hipsters burning for the ancient heavenly connection to the starry dynamo in the machinery of night." He reinvented the addicts and misfits who were his friends as a new proletariat, a spiritual proletariat with a taste for Eastern mysticism: "Dreamers of the world unite. You have nothing to lose but your karma."

It is impossible to overestimate the anti-intellectualism of the Beat Generation. They were know-nothings in revolt against the know-alls and in their war against their highbrow enemies dope was the perfect weapon. They regarded it as way of cutting through inhibitions at a peculiarly inhibited time, but I suspect this mattered less than distancing themselves from square society.

Because drugs were "controlled substances," when those angelheaded hipsters turned on, tuned in, and dropped out they were putting themselves outside the law. More important, drugs do not agree with the intellectual life. To the impartial observer outside the stoned circle, the most obvious feature of most drugs is that they are thought constricting rather than mind expanding. Dope may make you feel good but it kills the conversation stone dead. John Berryman, a chronic alcoholic but a fierce intellect, wrote in one of his guilt-drenched "Dream Songs," "This is not for tears; / thinking." But you cannot think when you are stoned. You cannot, in fact, register anything much except vague goodwill. Similarly, what comes across most strongly in Joan Didion's wonderful report on the hippies of San Francisco, "Slouching Towards Bethlehem," was her dismay at the mindlessness and sentimentality of Beatnik existence as it was played out on the streets of San Francisco (1974: 78-110). Like the sad pseudo-Romantics who devoured Gothic novels a century and a half earlier, the lost children of Haight Ashbury hankered after spiritual drama and significance, but lacked the talent, patience, and application art requires, and so had to make do with fancy dress and a pose.

Most Beat literature is equally mindless. Ginsberg has plenty of so-called drug poems with rifles like "Mescaline," "Lysergic Acid," and "A Methedrine Vision in Hollywood," but all they have in common is slackness. Writing under the influence means never having to bother with punctuation. The roll call of images may be a little loopy and the connections between them haphazard, but the tone of voice is curiously monotonous: chanting, self-absorbed, yet paradoxically lacking in inwardness.

I am not suggesting that experiences under drugs have not inspired some extraordinary modern writing. The novels of Robert Stone, for instance, who was a paid-up member of the '60s drug scene and even spent time on Ken Kesey's notorious bus, are full of eerie dope-induced visions and are narrated in the sardonic, edgy style, bristling to the point of paranoia, of someone who has taken one bad trip too many. But Stone is an artist; he is not simply reporting on his drug experiences or using them to give his work unearned significance: he is expressing them as allusively, vividly, and dispassionately as he can—using them, that is, to create works of art in which some of the characters are afflicted with a dazed, drug-induced fecklessness that has real consequences in a real and unstoned world. No doubt terrible things happened to Stone as they happened to Coleridge, but both artists try to make sense of them, give them form and significance, and thereby make them aesthetically acceptable.

Artistic objectivity was not a concept that interested the Beats. For them, the personality taking the drug always mattered more than any work of art, even when the personality's overwhelming interest is the elimination of personality. Consider the case of William Burroughs, whom Ginsberg and Kerouac genuinely revered because he had really done what they mostly posed at doing. Burroughs, for his part, although he had a brief crush on Ginsberg, seemed in other ways contemptuous of the group's juvenile antics: "Perhaps weed does affect the brain with constant use, or maybe tea heads are naturally silly. . . . Tea heads are a sociable lot. Too sociable for my liking" (Burroughs, 1977: 18). That comes from *Junky,* Burroughs' autobiographical book about his years as a heroin addict. It is an extraordinary piece of writing—cold-eyed, cold-blooded, clear-headed, full of detailed, slow-motion descriptions of the rituals of drug taking and the pleasures and griefs that accompany it—all of it done without a flicker of emotion, apart from a deadpan relish in the underworld he inhabited.

Opium allowed Coleridge to touch imaginative and emotional depths that were otherwise mostly out of his reach. For Burroughs, heroin seems to have reinforced what he already was. "Death," he writes, "is absence of life" (1977: 106) and that is what his style is about, although it is not clear if the made the style out of his addiction or if the absence of life came naturally to him—that is, the psychopath's lack of affect was something he was born to and the junk echoed it, gave it meaning, gave it a literary voice. He was by any standards, especially those of the 1950s, an unusually nasty piece of work—a drug-addict, accidental wife-killer, and predatory homosexual with a taste for very young boys. In *Junky*, his documentary record of the lower depths he swam in, he has the courage of his psychopathology. He does not sentimentalize, he does not excuse himself; he simply describes how it was, and that gives his writing a strange, affectless purity.

Burroughs claimed he was doing the same in *The Naked Lunch*, which deals with same subject as *Junky* and reworks the same material, sometimes word for word. To emphasize its objectivity the novel duly comes with a learned appendix—an article by Burroughs, reprinted from the *British Journal of Addiction* (vol. 53, no. 2), in which he lists the many different drugs he has used, reports on their characteristics and effects, and how best to break the various addictions. It is all done in a strictly impersonal scientific manner, like a researcher writing up a series of experiments in which he himself happened to be the laboratory animal.

According to Burroughs, "*The Naked Lunch* is a blueprint, a How-To Book . . . Black insect lusts open into vast, other planet landscapes . . . Abstract concepts, bare as algebra, narrow down to a black turd or a pair of ageing cojones" (1964: 222). In practice, however, he seems far less interested in the blueprint than in the turds, the cojones, and his junk-inspired, science-fiction vision of another planet, with its bad smells, ectoplasmic presences, and insect lusts. The result is a novel that is suitably shocking in a childish way—scatological, vicious, paranoid—but has nothing like the power or purity of the autobiography. In other words, *Junky* is the original blueprint and a genuine work of art, and Burroughs himself downgraded it into a strip cartoon version called *The Naked Lunch*.

The key word is "downgrade." I think downgrading is a process inherent in the highly political attitude to drugs of the original Beatniks and the aesthetics, such as they were, that followed from them. I do not happen to rate Ginsberg as a poet, but that is not the point. The point is his legacy, what he helped do to the arts. I once attended a reading he gave at SUNY Buffalo in 1966. The audience was too large for a lecture hall, so he gave it in the basketball gym. The p.a. system was not working, so you could not hear him, and the clouds of pot smoke were so thick you could scarcely see him. Even so, the kids were having a wonderful time. He tinkled his bells and chanted his poems and the audience responded with a kind of collective "Wow!" It was not about com-

munication, it was about communion—everyone joined by a sense of vague well-being, more like a religious ceremony or a political rally than a poetry reading. And that suited the verse just fine. There's no way you can read a Ginsberg poem on the page and get much pleasure from it. It has to be declaimed, performed. Poetry of this kind is not a private experience, it is a public phenomenon, a happening, and—most important of all—it is democratically available to everyone regardless of creative imagination, intelligence, and technical ability. And that, I think, was the secret of Ginsberg's appeal: he made the audience feel that they, too, were bards like him, initiates of the same hip clan. All that was required was to be there, mellowed out on weed or tripping on LSD, and everyone could be a poet, no matter whether or not they ever got words down on the page.

The irony of all this is that mind and consciousness were in fact very much the concern of the best artists in a century that began, after all, with Freud's *Interpretation of Dreams*. That is why the Modernists were preoccupied with experiment, because experiment, in the arts, always involves an element of inner or psychic exploration. You want to make it new not for novelty's sake but because the style at hand is not adequate to what you have to express. But drugs were not part of this aesthetic equation and the kind of experiments undertaken, first by the great Modernists in the first quarter of the twentieth century, then, after World War II, by the abstract expressionist painters and by poets like Lowell, Berryman and Plath, involved an inward journey in which intelligence, artistic skill, and discipline were supremely important: "This is not for tears; thinking." This attitude toward creativity was altogether sterner and more demanding than the free-associating "confessional" style of the Beatniks who let it all hang out any old way and basked in the applause. I think Ginsberg and Company literally meant what they said when they talked about the "counterculture": they were truly counter—that is, against—culture, and we are now living with the aesthetic consequences of their antics: poetry as public entertainment, novels as strip cartoons. The silly and sociable teaheads, whom Burroughs looked down on, were not ultimately as harmless as they seemed. Instead, they turned out to have been precursors of the larger process of dumbing down, by which, during the twentieth century, high art was gradually reduced to just another form of show biz where reputations depend less on talent than on self-promotion and marketability, and drugs are not just a shortcut to inspiration but a substitute for it.

Works Cited

Alvarez, A. *Night: Night Life, Night Language, Sleep, and Dreams.* New York: Norton, 1995.

Burroughs, William. *The Naked Lunch.* London: John Calder, 1964.

———. *Junky.* London: Penguin, 1977.

Coleridge, Samuel Taylor. *Poems.* Oxford: Oxford University Press, 1957.

Didion, Joan. *Slouching towards Bethlehem.* Harmondsworth: Penguin, 1974.

Empson, William. *Seven Types of Ambiguity.* London: Chatto and Windus, 1949.

Ginsberg, Allen. *Collected Poems, 1947-1980.* London: Penguin, 1987.

———. *Journals.* London: Penguin, 1996.

Hayter, Althea. *Opium and the Romantic Imagination.* London: Faber, 1968.

Mailer, Norman. *Advertisements for Myself.* New York: Signet, 1960.

McCarthy, Mary. *On the Contrary.* London: William Heinemann, 1962.

Rahv, Philip. *Image and Idea.* New York: New Directions, 1957.

RELIGION AND THE BEAT GENERATION

THEODORE ROSZAK (ESSAY DATE 1969)

SOURCE: Roszak, Theodore. "Journey to the East . . . and Points Beyond: Allen Ginsberg and Alan Watts." In *The Making of a Counter Culture: Reflections on the Technocratic Society and Its Youthful Opposition,* pp. 124-54. Garden City, N.Y.: Doubleday & Company, Inc., 1969.

In the following essay, Roszak examines the importance of Zen teachings, religion, and spirituality to writers such as Ginsberg and Watts, noting that their attraction to Zen stemmed at least in part from their opposition to the increasingly technological society of which they were a part.

On October 21, 1967, the Pentagon found itself besieged by a motley army of anti-war demonstrators. For the most part, the fifty thousand protestors were made up of activist academics and students, men of letters (among them, Norman Mailer leading his "armies of the night"), New Left and pacifist ideologues, housewives,

doctors . . . but also in attendance, we are informed (by *The East Village Other*), were contingents of "witches, warlocks, holymen, seers, prophets, mystics, saints, sorcerers, shamans, troubadours, minstrels, bards, roadmen, and madmen"—who were on hand to achieve the "mystic revolution." The picketing, the sit-down, the speeches, and marches: all that was protest politics as usual. But the central event of the day was a contribution of the "superhumans": an exorcism of the Pentagon by long-haired warlocks who "cast mighty words of white light against the demon-controlled structure," in hopes of levitating that grim ziggurat right off the ground.[1]

They did not succeed—in floating the Pentagon, that is. But they did manage to stamp their generation with a political style so authentically original that it borders on the bizarre. Is the youthful political activism of the sixties any different from that of the thirties? If the difference shows up anywhere, it reveals itself in the unprecedented penchant for the occult, for magic, and for exotic ritual which has become an integral part of the counter culture. Even those protestors who did not participate in the rite of exorcism took the event in stride—as if they understood that here was the style and vocabulary of the young: one had simply to tolerate its expression. And yet how strange to see the classic rhetoric of the radical tradition—Marx, Bakunin, Kropotkin, Lenin—yielding place to spells and incantations! Perhaps, after all, the age of ideology is passing, giving way to the age of mystagogy.

An eclectic taste for mystic, occult, and magical phenomena has been a marked characteristic of our postwar youth culture since the days of the beatniks. Allen Ginsberg, who has played a major part in fostering the style, professes the quest for God in many of his earliest poems, well before he and his colleagues had discovered Zen and the mystic traditions of the Orient. In his poetry of the late forties, there is a sensitivity for visionary experience ("Angelic raving," as he was to call it), which suggested even then that the social dissent of the younger generation would never quite fit the adamantly secular mold of the Old Left. Already at that point, Ginsberg speaks of seeing

all the pictures we carry in our mind
images of the Thirties,
depression and class consciousness
transfigured above politics
filled with fire
with the appearance of God.

These early poems[2] contrast strongly and significantly in style with Ginsberg's more widely read later work. They are often brief, tightly written affairs, done in a short, well-ordered line. We have nothing of the familiar rambling and ham-fisted Ginsberg line (based, as he puts it, on "Hebraic-Melvillian breath") until the 1949 poem *Paterson*. But the religiosity is already there, giving Ginsberg's poetry a very different sound from the social poetry of the thirties. From the outset, Ginsberg is a protest poet. But his protest does not run back to Marx; it reaches out, instead, to the ecstatic radicalism of Blake. The issue is never as simple as social justice; rather, the key words and images are those of time and eternity, madness and vision, heaven and the spirit. The cry is not for a revolution, but for an apocalypse: a descent of divine fire. And, already in the later forties, we have the first experiments with marijuana and chiliastic poems written under the sway of narcotics.

In some respects, these early poems, modest as they are, are superior to anything Ginsberg has written since—or so I find. Without compromising their lurching power, and without by any means becoming finely wrought, they possess a far greater sense of control and structure than the work that was later to give him his reputation. There is the willingness to be brief and to the point—and then to break off before the energy has been dissipated. By the early fifties, however, Ginsberg has abandoned these conventional literary virtues in favor of a spontaneous and un-checked flow of language. From this point on, everything he writes has the appearance of being served up raw, in the first draft, just as it must have come from mind and mouth. There is never the trace of a revised line; there is, rather, another line added on. Instead of revision, there is accumulation. As if to revise would be to rethink, and hence to doubt and double back on the initial vision. For Ginsberg, the creative act was to be a come-as-you-are party and his poems would arrive unshaven and unwashed, and maybe without pants on, just as they happened to be lying around the house. The intention is clear: lack of grooming marks the poems as "natural," therefore honest. They are the *real* thing, and not artifice.

There is a good deal of Charlie Parker's improvisation in Ginsberg's work, as well as the spirit of the action painters. Jackson Pollack worked at a canvas with a commitment never to erase, or re-do, or touch up, but to add, add, add . . . and let the whole finally work itself out into a unique pattern appropriate to *this* man at *this* moment of his life. The same sense of haste and total self-absorption clings to Ginsberg's poetry, the same

eagerness to project the unvarnished imaginative impulse—though it seems all too clear that such improvisation is much less at home in literature than in music or painting. The intention of his poetry of the middle fifties was, says Ginsberg, "to just write . . . let my imagination go, open secrecy, and scribble magic lines from my real mind." Two of his best-known poems of these years were written without either forethought or revision: the long first part of *Howl* was typed off in one afternoon; *Sunflower Sutra* was completed in twenty minutes, "me at desk scribbling, Kerouac at cottage door waiting for me to finish." Of *Howl*, Ginsberg says, "I'd had a beatific illumination years before during which I'd heard Blake's ancient voice and saw the universe unfold in my brain," and this served as the inspiration for the later outburst.[3] In a similarly improvisatory manner, Jack Kerouac was to come to the point of typing off his novels nonstop onto enormous rolls of paper—six feet per day—with never a revision.

That this improvisatory style of writing produces a great deal that is worthless as art is, for our purposes here, less important than what this choice of method tells us about the generation that accepted Ginsberg's work as a valid form of creativity. What we have here is a search for art unmediated by intellect. Or rather, since it is the application of intellectual control that makes art of impulse, it is an effort to extract and indulge the impulse, regardless of the aesthetic quality of the product.

Far from being an avant-garde eccentricity, Ginsberg's conception of poetry as an oracular outpouring can claim an imposing genealogy that reaches back to the rhapsodic prophets of Israel (and beyond them perhaps to the shamanism of the Stone Age). Like Amos and Isaiah, Ginsberg aspires to be a *nabi,* a mutterer: one who speaks with tongues, one who permits his voice to act as the instrument of powers beyond his conscious direction. If his work falls short of the highest aesthetic standards of this great tradition, he can scarcely be denied the virtue of having complied with the demands of his calling in what is perhaps a far more important respect. Ginsberg has committed himself totally to the life of prophecy. He has allowed his entire existence to be transformed by the visionary powers with which he conjures and has offered it as an example to his generation. It is as if, initially, Ginsberg set out to write a poetry of angry distress: to cry out against the anguished state of the world as he and his closest colleagues had experienced it in the gutters and ghettos and mental institutions of our society.

Lenore Kandel, 1932-.

What came of that suffering was a howl of pain. But at the bottom of that howl Ginsberg discovered what it was that the bourgeois god Moloch was most intent upon burying alive: the curative powers of the visionary imagination.

In making that discovery, Ginsberg uncovered at the heart of the poem what every artist has found in the creative process, to one degree or another. But what distinguishes his career is the project that followed upon that discovery. Having once experienced the visionary powers, Ginsberg found himself driven to reach beyond literary expression to a total life style. More than a poet, he has become, for the disaffiliated young of America and much of Europe, the vagabond proselytizer whose poems are but a subsidiary way of publicizing the new consciousness he embodies and the techniques for its cultivation. At poetry readings and teach-ins, he need not even read his verses: he need only appear in order to make his compelling statement of what young dissent is all about. The hair, the beard, the costume, the mischievous grin, the total absence of formality, pretense, or defensive posturing . . . they are enough to make him an exemplification of the counter cultural life.

There is something more that has to be observed about the visionary impulse in Ginsberg's poetry. The ecstatic venture to which Ginsberg

and most of the early beat writers have been drawn is unexceptionally one of immanence rather than transcendence. Theirs is a mysticism neither escapist nor ascetic. It has not led them, like the ethereal quest of T. S. Eliot a generation earlier, into a rose garden far removed from the corruptions of the flesh. Instead, it is a this-worldly mysticism they seek: an ecstasy of the body and of the earth that somehow embraces and transforms mortality. Their goal is a joy that includes even (or perhaps especially) the commonplace obscenities of our existence. As Ginsberg put it in one of his early poems:

> This is the one and only
> firmament . . .
> I am living in Eternity.
> The ways of this world
> are the ways of Heaven.

Or, even more powerfully:

> For the world is a mountain
> of shit: if it's going to
> be moved at all, it's got
> to be taken by handfuls.

William Carlos Williams, commenting on the poems of the young Ginsberg, observed in them "a beat that is far removed from the beat of dancing feet, but rather finds in the shuffling of human beings in all the stages of their life, the trip to the bathroom, to the stairs of the subway, the steps of the office or factory routine, the mystical measure of their passions."[4] The observation holds true for much of the work of the beat writers and is one of their defining features as a group: an appetite for ecstasies that have been buried and forgotten beneath the nitty-gritty scatological and sexual rubbish of existence.

For Ginsberg, who tells us he did not find the Zen satori until 1954, this salvaging of enchantment from the very dross of daily life served to resolve the acute personal tension one of the early poems reflects:

> I feel as if I am at a dead
> end and so I am finished
> All spiritual facts I realize
> are true but I never escape
> the feeling of being closed in
> and the sordidness of self,
> the futility of all that I
> have seen and done and said.

The way out of this corner was to arrive at a vision of sordidness and futility that made of *them* "spiritual facts" in their own right. The world might then be redeemed by the willingness to take it for what it is and to find its enchanting promise within the seemingly despiritualized waste. At least, in Ginsberg's development, some such psychic strategy seems to have been involved in his break from the stark pathos of the early poems. It is certainly a striking feature of his personal growth that, as time goes on, he moves further and further from the despondency of these early efforts, through the impassioned outburst of *Howl*, toward a poetry of gentleness and charitable acceptance. Ginsberg, who went through the hell of our mental institutions, finishes by telling us that he can find only tears of pity for the madness of a Lyndon Johnson and for all the wrong-headed men of power who sacrifice their lives for debased objectives; but the sorrow does not grind down Ginsberg's wise and impish sense of humor. As time goes on, he progressively reverses Wordsworth's dictum.

> We poets in our youth begin in gladness;
> But thereof come in the end despondency and
> madness.

Whatever the explanation for Ginsberg's liberating enlightenment, what we have in the kitchen-sink mysticism to which the early poetry leads is a remarkable anticipation of the Zen principle of the illuminated commonplace.

If we can believe the account Jack Kerouac gives us in *The Dharma Bums* (1956)—the book which was to provide the first handy compendium of all the Zen catch phrases that have since become more familiar to our youth than any Christian catechism—it was from the West Coast poet Gary Snyder that he and Ginsberg learned their Zen upon coming to San Francisco in the early fifties. Snyder had by that time already found his way to a Zen-based pattern of life dedicated to poverty, simplicity, and meditation. He was soon to undertake formal Zen studies in Japan and to become, of all the early beats, the most knowledgeable practitioner of the tradition—as well as the poet whose work seems to express the pregnant calm of Zen most gracefully. But along with Snyder there was Alan Watts, who had recently begun teaching at the School of Asian Studies in San Francisco after leaving his position as an Anglican counselor at Northwestern University. By the time he had reached San Francisco, Watts, who was only thirty-five years old in 1950, had behind him at least seven books dealing with Zen and mystical religion, dating back to 1935. He had, in fact, been a child prodigy in his chosen field of study. At nineteen he had been appointed editor of *The Middle Way*, an English journal of Buddhist studies, and at twenty-three, coeditor of the English "Wisdom of the East" series. Along with D. T. Suzuki, Watts, through his televised

ON THE SUBJECT OF...

LENORE KANDEL

Lenore Kandel's fame is largely based on her authorship of *The Love Book,* a volume of sexually themed poems seized by the San Francisco police in 1966 for its purportedly obscene content. The incident resulted in instant notoriety for Kandel. For many, she is revered as a teacher and leading advocate of lovemaking. While her published poems deal with a variety of subjects both within and outside of the Beat spectrum, it is for her poems celebrating the power of love, particularly physical love, that she has received the most recognition. Kandel is also the author of the poetry collections *A Passing Dragon* (1959) and *Word Alchemy* (1967).

lectures, books, and private classes, was to become America's foremost popularizer of Zen. Much of what young America knows about the religion traces back to one or the other of these two scholars and to the generation of writers and artists whom they have influenced.

Of the two, I think it is Watts whose influence has been the more widespread, for often at the expense of risking vulgarization, he has made the most determined effort to translate the insights of Zen and Taoism into the language of Western science and psychology. He has approached his task with an impish willingness to be catchy and cute, and to play at philosophy as if it were an enjoyable game. It is a style easily mistaken for flippancy, and it has exposed him to a deal of rather arrogant criticism: on the one hand from elitist Zen devotees who have found him too discursive for their mystic tastes (I recall one such telling me smugly, "Watts has never experienced satori"), and on the other hand from professional philosophers who have been inclined to ridicule him for his popularizing bent as being, in the words of one academic, "The Norman Vincent Peale of Zen." It is the typical and inevitable sort of resistance anyone encounters when he makes bold to find a greater audience for an idea than the academy or any restricted cult can provide—and it overlooks the fact that Watts' books and essays include such very solid intellectual achievements as *Psycho-*

therapy East And West. Too often such aristocratic stricture comes from those who have risen above popularization by the device of restricting themselves to a subject matter that preserves its purity only because it has no conceivable relevance to anything beyond the interests of a small circle of experts.

There is a sense, however, in which it would seem to be impossible to popularize Zen. Traditionally, the insights of the religion have been communicated directly from master to student as part of an extremely demanding discipline in which verbal formulations play almost no part. Zen is neither a proselytizing creed nor a theology, but, rather, a personal illumination that one may have to be tricked into experiencing while intellectually off guard. Thus the best way to teach Zen, so it would seem, is to talk about anything but Zen, allowing the enlightening spark to break through of its own unpredictable accord—which is rather the way the composer John Cage, one of Suzuki's students, uses his music. Similarly, I have watched one of Watts' colleagues in San Francisco try to bring students around to the key experience by way of what purported to be rehearsals of a drama, but a drama that was never intended to reach production. Much the same intention seems to underlie the sensory awareness classes of Charlotte Selver, with whom Watts often works.[5] Watts himself is best at employing these outflanking strategies as part of his private courses, rather than as part of his writing or public lecturing.

Now, if this sort of psychic jiujitsu is the essence of Zen, then it may very well be that, on the religion's own terms, all the youthful confabulation with Zen over the past decade or so has been less than useless. "Those who know do not speak; those who speak do not know"—and I would have to leave it to the Zen adepts to decide whether anything that deserves to be called authentic has actually taken root in our culture. It is indisputable, however, that the San Francisco beats, and much of our younger generation since their time, *thought* they had found something in Zen they needed, and promptly proceeded to use what they understood of this exotic tradition as a justification for fulfilling the need. The situation may be rather similar to Schopenhauer's attempt to elaborate his limited knowledge of the Upanishads into a philosophy that was primarily an expression of his generation's Romantic *Weltschmerz.*

What was it that Zen offered or seemed to offer to the young? It is difficult to avoid feeling that the great advantage Zen possesses (if it can be called an advantage) is its unusual vulnerability to what I have called "adolescentization." That is to say: Zen, vulgarized, dovetails remarkably with a number of adolescent traits. Its commitment to a wise silence, which contrasts so strongly with the preachiness of Christianity, can easily ally with the moody inarticulateness of youth. Why do Zen masters throw their disciples into a mud puddle, asks Kerouac's Sal Paradise in *The Dharma Bums.* "That's because they want them to realize mud is better than words." A generation that had come to admire the tongue-tied incoherence of James Dean and which has been willing to believe that the medium is the message, would obviously welcome a tradition that regarded talking as beside the point. Similarly, Zen's commitment to paradox and randomness could be conveniently identified with the intellectual confusion of healthily restless, but still unformed minds. Perhaps above all, Zen's antinomianism could serve as a sanction for the adolescent need of freedom, especially for those who possessed a justified discomfort with the competitive exactions and conformities of the technocracy. There could very well be a subtle, subterranean connection between the discovery of Zen by some young American writers in San Francisco of the early 1950s and the placards that appeared on the walls of the beleaguered Sorbonne in May 1968 proclaiming, "It is forbidden to forbid." As Lewis Mumford suggests:

> Since ritual order has now largely passed into mechanical order, the present revolt of the younger generation against the machine has made a practice of promoting disorder and randomness . . .[6]

The amorality of Zen, as one might imagine, was rapidly given special emphasis where sex is concerned. And in this respect, the latest European-American journey to the East *is* a new departure. The Vedantism of the twenties and thirties had always been severely contemplative in the most ascetic sense of the term. One always has the feeling in looking through its literature that its following was found among the very old or very withered, for whom the ideal swami was a kindly orientalized version of an Irish Jesuit priest in charge of a pleasant retreat. The novels of Hermann Hesse, which are now once more so popular among the young, convey this ethos of ethereal asexuality. But the mysteries of the Orient we now have on hand in the counter culture have broken entirely from this earlier Christianized interpretation. In fact, nothing is so striking about the new orientalism as its highly sexed flavor. If there was anything Kerouac and his colleagues found especially appealing in the Zen they adopted, it was the wealth of hyperbolic eroticism the religion brought with it rather indiscriminately from the *Kamasutra* and the tantric tradition. Again, this looks very much like postwar middle-class permissiveness reaching out for a religious sanction, finding it, and making the most of it. As Alan Watts observed in a widely circulated critique of 1958, a great deal of "Beat Zen" was a "pretext for license . . . a simple rationalization." Kerouac's brand of modish Zen, Watts gently criticized, ". . . confuses 'anything goes' at the existential level with 'anything goes' at the artistic and social levels." And such a conception of Zen runs the risk of becoming the banner of

> the cool, fake-intellectual hipster searching for kicks, name-dropping bits of Zen and jazz jargon to justify disaffiliation from society which is in fact just ordinary, callous exploitation of other people. . . . Such types are, however, the shadow of a substance, the low-level caricature which always attends spiritual and cultural movements, carrying them to extremes which their authors never intended. To this extent beat Zen is sowing confusion in idealizing as art and life what is better kept to oneself as therapy.[7]

Even if Zen, as most of Ginsberg's generation have come to know and publicize it, has been flawed by crude simplifications, it must also be recognized that what the young have vulgarized in this way is a body of thought which, as formulated by men like Suzuki and Watts, embraces a radical critique of the conventional scientific conception of man and nature. If the young seized on Zen with shallow understanding, they grasped it with a healthy instinct. And grasping it, they bought the books, and attended the lectures, and spread about the catch phrases, and in general helped to provide the ambiance within which a few good minds who understood more deeply could speak out in criticism of the dominant culture. Perhaps what the young took Zen to be has little relationship to that venerable and elusive tradition; but what they readily adopted *was* a gentle and gay rejection of the positivistic and the compulsively cerebral. It was the beginning of a youth culture that continues to be shot through with the spontaneous urge to counter the joyless, rapacious, and egomaniacal order of our technological society.

This is another way of saying that, after a certain point, it becomes little better than pedantic to ask how authentically Buddhist a poem like Ginsberg's "Sunflower Sutra" (1955) is. Perhaps not very. But it *is* a poem of great tenderness, expressing an unashamed wonder for the commonplace splendors of the world. It asserts a sensibility that calls into question the anthropocentric arrogance with which our society has gone about mechanizing and brutalizing its environment in the name of progress. And it is a commentary on the state of what our society regards as its "religion" that the poet who still commands the greatest attention among our youth should have had to cast about for such an exotic tradition from which to take inspiration in expressing these beautifully humane sentiments.

The same holds true for Ginsberg's more current Hinduism. It is, at the very least, a fascinating Odyssey of the contemporary spirit that takes a young Jewish poet from Paterson, New Jersey, to the banks of the Ganges in order to make of him America's greatest Hindu guru. But is his Hinduism the real thing? I suggest the question is beside the point. What is far more important is his deeply felt necessity to turn away from the dominant culture in order to find the spirit for such remarkable poems as "The Wichita Vortex Sutra" and "Who Be Kind To"—both such compelling expressions of humanity and compassionate protest. Even more important is the social fact: Ginsberg the mantra-chanting Hindu does not finish as an isolated eccentric, but rather as one of the foremost spokesmen of our younger generation. Following Ginsberg, the young don cowbells, tuck flowers behind their ears, and listen entranced to the chants. And through these attentive listeners Ginsberg claims a greater audience among our dissenting youth than any Christian or Jewish clergyman could hope to reach or stir. (Perhaps the one exception to this might be the late A. J. Muste in the last years of his life. But then it was always Muste's practice to keep his ministerial identity as unobtrusive as possible.)

Indeed, we are a post-Christian era—despite the fact that minds far more gifted than Ginsberg's, like that of the late Thomas Merton, have mined the dominant religious tradition for great treasures. But we may have been decidedly wrong in what we long expected to follow the death of the Christian God; namely, a thoroughly secularized, thoroughly positivistic culture, dismal and spiritless in its obsession with technological prowess. That was the world Aldous Huxley foresaw in the 1930s, when he wrote *Brave New World*. But in the 1950s, as Huxley detected the rising spirit of a new generation, his utopian image brightened to the forecast he offers us in *Island*, where a nonviolent culture elaborated out of Buddhism and psychedelic drugs prevails. It was as if he had suddenly seen the possibility emerge: what lay beyond the Christian era and the "wasteland" that was its immediate successor might be a new, eclectic religious revival. Which is precisely what confronts us now as one of the massive facts of the counter culture. The dissenting young have indeed got religion. Not the brand of religion Billy Graham or William Buckley would like to see the young crusading for—but religion nonetheless. What began with Zen has now rapidly, perhaps too rapidly, proliferated into a phantasmagoria of exotic religiosity.

Who would have predicted it? At least since the Enlightenment, the major thrust of radical thought has always been anti-religious, if not openly, defiantly atheistic—perhaps with the exception of the early Romantics. And even among the Romantics, the most pious tended to become the most politically reactionary; for the rest, the Romantic project was to abstract from religion its essential "feeling" and leave contemptuously behind its traditional formulations. Would-be Western revolutionaries have always been strongly rooted in a militantly skeptical secular tradition. The rejection of the corrupted religious establishment has carried over almost automatically into a root-and-branch rejection of all things spiritual. So "mysticism" was to become one of the dirtiest words in the Marxist vocabulary. Since Diderot, the priest has had only one thing the radical wanted: his guts, with which to strangle the last king. Shaw, writing in 1921 on the intellectuals of what he called the "infidel half-century" (he was dating from the time of Darwin), summarized the situation thus:

> We were intellectually intoxicated with the idea that the world could make itself without design, purpose, skill, or intelligence: in short, without life. . . . We took a perverse pleasure in arguing, without the least suspicion that we were reducing ourselves to absurdity, that all the books in the British Museum library might have been written word for word as they stand on the shelves if no human being had ever been conscious, just as the trees stand in the forest doing wonderful things without consciousness.

> The first effect was exhilarating: we had the runaway child's sense of freedom before it gets hungry and lonely and frightened. In this phase we did not desire our God back again. We printed the verses in which William Blake, the most religious of our great poets, called the anthropomorphic idol Nobodaddy, and gibed at him in terms which the printer had to leave us to guess from his blank spaces. We had heard the parson droning that God is not mocked; and it was great fun to mock Him to our hearts' content and not be a penny the worse.

> (From the preface to *Back to Methuselah*.)

When he wrote these words, Shaw had himself long since abandoned the crusading skepticism of his generation's intelligentsia in favor of a species of Vitalism, convinced that it was destined to become the new religion. Instead, it became only another of the enclaves from which alienated artists, eccentric psychiatrists, and assorted cranks could do no more than snipe at the secularized mainstream culture. Only the debased mysticism of the fascists, as the ideology of an aggressive war machine, has seriously troubled the scientized intellectual consensus of the twentieth century. Even so, the *Schwärmerei* of fascism, as I have remarked, really served as the facade behind which one of the most formidable technocracies of the age was consolidated.

But now, if one scans any of the underground weeklies, one is apt to find their pages swarming with Christ and the prophets, Zen, Sufism, Hinduism, primitive shamanism, theosophy, the Left-Handed Tantra. . . . The Berkeley "wandering priest" Charlie (Brown) Artman, who was in the running for city councilman in 1966 until he was arrested for confessing (quite unabashedly) to possession of narcotics, strikes the right note of eclectic religiosity: a stash of LSD in his Indian-sign necklace, a chatelaine of Hindu temple bells, and the campaign slogan "May the baby Jesus open your mind and shut your mouth." Satanists and Neo-Gnostics, dervishes and self-proclaimed swamis . . . their number grows and the counter culture makes generous place for them. No anti-war demonstration would be complete without a hirsute, be-cowbelled contingent of holy men, bearing joss sticks and intoning the Hare Krishna. An underground weekly like *The Berkeley Barb* gives official Washington a good left-wing slamming on page one, but devotes the center spread to a crazy mandala for the local yogis. And in the back pages, the "Servants of Awareness . . . a unique group of aware people using 136 symbols in their meditation to communicate directly with *Cosmic Awareness* . . ." are sure to take out a four-column ad. The San Francisco *Oracle* gives us photos of stark-naked madonnas with flowers in their hair, suckling their babies . . . and the effect is not at all pornographic, nor intended to be so.

At the level of our youth, we begin to resemble nothing so much as the cultic hothouse of the Hellenistic period, where every manner of mystery and fakery, ritual and rite, intermingled with marvelous indiscrimination. For the time being, the situation makes it next to impossible for many of us who teach to carry on much in the way of education among the dissenting young, given the

fact that our conventional curriculum, even at its best, is grounded in the dominant Western tradition. Their interests, when not involved with the politics of revolution, are apt to be fathoming phenomena too exotic or too subterranean for normal academic handling. If one asks the hip young to identify (a) Milton and (b) Pope, their answers are likely to be: (a) Milton *who?* and (b) *which* Pope? But they may do no mean job of rehearsing their kabbala or *I Ching* (which the very hip get married to these days) or, of course, the *Kamasutra.*

What the counter culture offers us, then, is a remarkable defection from the long-standing tradition of skeptical, secular intellectuality which has served as the prime vehicle for three hundred years of scientific and technical work in the West. Almost overnight (and astonishingly, with no great debate on the point) a significant portion of the younger generation has opted out of that tradition, rather as if to provide an emergency balance to the gross distortions of our technological society, often by occult aberrations just as gross. As often happens, one cultural exaggeration calls forth another, which can be its opposite, but equivalent. In the hands of a Herman Kahn, science, logic, and the precision of numbers have become their own caricatures as part of the black arts of mass murder. But Kahn and his like are massively subsidized out of the public treasury and summoned to the corridors of power. Even official Washington calls its Sino-Soviet advisors "demonologists"—and the designation is scarcely a wisecrack. So mumbo jumbo is indeed at the heart of human affairs when so-called scientific decision-making reveals itself as a species of voodoo. "A communion of bum magicians," as Ginsberg has called it. What, then, does "reason" count for?

Expertise—technical, scientific, managerial, military, educational, financial, medical—has become the prestigious mystogogy of the technocratic society. Its principal purpose in the hands of ruling elites is to mystify the popular mind by creating illusions of omnipotence and omniscience—in much the same way that the pharaohs and priesthood of ancient Egypt used their monopoly of the calendar to command the awed docility of ignorant subjects. Philosophy, the hardheaded Wittgenstein once said, is the effort to keep ourselves from being hexed by language. But largely under the influence of logicians and technicians, and with the supposed purpose of dehexing our thinking, we have produced the scientized jargon which currently dominates official

parlance and the social sciences. When knowledgeable men talk, they no longer talk of substances and accidents, of being and spirit, of virtue and vice, of sin and salvation, of deities and demons. Instead, we have a vocabulary filled with nebulous quantities of things that have every appearance of precise calibration, and decorated with vaguely mechanistic-mathematical terms like "parameters," "structures," "variables," "inputs and outputs," "correlations," "inventories," "maximizations," and "optimizations." The terminology derives from involuted statistical procedures and methodological mysteries to which only graduate education gives access. The more such language and numerology one packs into a document, the more "objective" the document becomes—which normally means the less morally abrasive to the sources that have subsidized the research or to any sources that might conceivably subsidize one's research at any time in the future. The vocabulary and the methodology mask the root ethical assumptions of policy or neatly transcribe them into a depersonalized rhetoric which provides a gloss of military or political necessity. To think and to talk in such terms becomes the sure sign of being a certified realist, a "hard research" man.

Thus to bomb more hell out of a tiny Asian country in one year than was bombed out of Europe in the whole Second World War becomes "escalation." Threatening to burn and blast to death several million civilians in an enemy country is called "deterrence." Turning a city into radioactive rubble is called "taking out" a city. A concentration camp (already a euphemism for a political prison) becomes a "strategic hamlet." A comparison of the slaughter on both sides in a war is called a "kill ratio." Totaling up the corpses is called a "body count." Running the blacks out of town is called "urban renewal." Discovering ingenious new ways to bilk the public is called "market research." Outflanking the discontent of employees is called "personnel management." Wherever possible, hideous realities are referred to by cryptic initials and formulalike phrases: ICBM, CBR, megadeaths, or "operation" this, "operation" that. On the other hand, one can be certain that where more colorful, emotive terms are used— "the war on poverty," "the war for the hearts and minds of men," "the race for space," "the New Frontier," "the Great Society"—the matters referred to exist only as propagandistic fictions or pure distraction.

Such is the technocratic word magic Ginsberg rails against in his *Wichita Vortex Sutra:*

The war is language,
   language abused
     for Advertisement,
   language used
  like magic for power on the planet
Black Magic language,
   formulas for reality—
    Communism is a 9 letter word
     used by inferior magicians
with the wrong alchemical formula for
   transforming earth
into gold
    funky warlocks operating on guesswork,
     handmedown mandrake terminology . . .

Governments have no doubt always resorted to such linguistic camouflage to obscure realities. Certainly the vice is not limited to our own officialdom. Marcuse has shrewdly shown how the Soviet Union's endlessly reiterated verbal formulae—"warmongering capitalist imperialism," "the people's democratic" this or that, always the same adjective hitched to the same noun—use the Marxist lexicon to produce the same ritualistic obfuscations.[8] But the special irony of our situation is the employment of what purports to be a clinically objective vocabulary of technologisms for the purpose of hexing intelligence all over again.

When science and reason of state become the handmaidens of political black magic, can we blame the young for diving headlong into an occult Jungian stew in search of "good vibrations" that might ward off the bad? Of course, they are soon glutted with what they find. They swallow it whole—and the result can be an absurdly presumptuous confabulation. Whole religious traditions get played with like so many baubles. A light-show group in Detroit names itself The Bulging Eyeballs of Gautama and the Beatles become the contemplative converts of a particularly simple-minded swami who advertises his mystic wares in every London underground station—only to drop him after a matter of months like a *passé* fashion.

No, the young do not by and large understand what these traditions are all about. One does not unearth the wisdom of the ages by shuffling about a few exotic catch phrases—nor does one learn anything about anybody's lore or religion by donning a few talismans and dosing on LSD. The most that comes of such superficial muddling is something like Timothy Leary's brand of easy-do syncretism: "somehow" all is one—but never mind precisely how. Fifty years ago, when Swami Vivekananda first brought the teachings of Sri Ramakrishna to America, he persuaded a clique of high-society dilettantes to believe as much. The

results were often as ludicrous as they were ephemeral. Yet things are just beginning in our youth culture. In the turgid floodtide of discovery, sampling, and restive fascination, perhaps it would be too much to expect disciplined order of the young in their pursuit—and surely it would be folly to try to deduce one from their happy chaos. They have happened upon treasure-trove long buried and are busy letting the quaint trinkets spill through their fingers.

For all its frequently mindless vulgarity, for all its tendency to get lost amid the exotic clutter, there is a powerful and important force at work in this wholesale willingness of the young to scrap our culture's entrenched prejudice against myth, religion, and ritual. The life of Reason (with a capital R) has all too obviously failed to bring us the agenda of civilized improvements the Voltaires and Condorcets once foresaw. Indeed, Reason, material Progress, the scientific world view have revealed themselves in numerous respects as simply a higher superstition, based on dubious but well-concealed assumptions about man and nature. Science, it has been said, thrives on sins of omission. True enough; and for three hundred years, those omissions have been piling up rather like the slag tips that surround Welsh mining towns: immense, precipitous mountains of frustrated human aspiration which threaten dangerously to come cascading down in an impassioned landslide. It is quite impossible any longer to ignore the fact that our conception of intellect has been narrowed disastrously by the prevailing assumption, especially in the academies, that the life of the spirit is: (1) a lunatic fringe best left to artists and marginal visionaries; (2) an historical boneyard for antiquarian scholarship; (3) a highly specialized adjunct of professional anthropology; (4) an antiquated vocabulary still used by the clergy, but intelligently soft-pedaled by its more enlightened members. Along none of these approaches can the living power of myth, ritual, and rite be expected to penetrate the intellectual establishment and have any existential (as opposed to merely academic) significance. If conventional scholarship does touch these areas of human experience, it is ordinarily with the intention of compiling knowledge, not with the hope of salvaging value.

When academics and intellectuals arrogantly truncate the life of the mind in this way, we finish with that "middle-class secular humanism" of which Michael Novak has aptly said,

It thinks of itself as humble in its agnosticism, and eschews the "mystic flights" of metaphysicians, theologians and dreamers; it is cautious and remote in dealing with heightened and passionate experiences that are the stuff of great literature and philosophy. It limits itself to this world and its concerns, concerns which fortunately turn out to be largely subject to precise formulations, and hence have a limited but comforting certainty.[9]

I think we can anticipate that in the coming generation, large numbers of students will begin to reject this reductive humanism, demanding a far deeper examination of that dark side of the human personality which has for so long been written off by our dominant culture as "mystical." It is because this youthful renaissance of mythical-religious interest holds such promise of enriching our culture that one despairs when, as so often happens, the young reduce it in their ignorance to an esoteric collection of peer-group symbols and slogans, vaguely daring and ultimately trivial. Then, instead of culture, we get collage: a miscellaneous heaping together, as if one had simply ransacked The Encyclopedia of Religion and Ethics and the *Celestia Arcana* for exotic tidbits. For example, one opens the underground *International Times* of London and finds a major article on Aleister Crowley. The exuberant treatment goes no further than the sensational surface—and how much further does such a figure allow one to go? It is the simple principle of inversion which too often dominates the underground press: the straight papers would have said "scandalous"; *we* say "marvelous." But understanding gets no further. One does not seek to discriminate, but only to manipulate: don't ask questions about the subject; just put it on a stick and wave it like a flag. It is at this point that the young, who are offering us, I feel, a great deal that is good to work with, need the help of mature minds, in order that enduring distinctions can be drawn between the deep and the shallow, the superstitious and the wise.

For what they are groping their way toward through all their murky religiosity is an absolutely critical distinction. The truth of the matter is: no society, not even our severely secularized technocracy, can ever dispense with mystery and magical ritual. These are the very bonds of social life, the inarticulate assumptions and motivations that weave together the collective fabric of society and which require periodic collective affirmation. But there is one magic that seeks to open and vitalize the mind, another that seeks to diminish and delude. There are rituals which are imposed from on high for the sake of invidious manipulation; there are other rituals in which men participate democratically for the purpose of freeing the imagination and exploring self-expression. There are mysteries which, like the mysteries of state, are no better than dirty secrets; but there are also mysteries which are encountered by the community (if such exists) in a stance of radical equality, and which are meant to be shared in for the purpose of enriching life by experiences of awe and splendor.

A presidential convention or campaign filled with phonied-up hoopla is an obvious example of a debased ritual meant to cloak disreputable politicking with a democratic sanction. Similarly, modern war fever, manufactured out of skillfully wrought propaganda and playing upon hysterical frustrations, is a perverted blood ritual. It is a throwback to the rite of human or animal sacrifice, but now so highly regimented that it is lacking in the immediate and personal, if ugly, gratifications of its primeval original. It therefore requires not one, but millions of victims: anonymous populations that are known only as stereotypes in the mass media. The blood of the killed is never seen and touched, either in dread or strong satisfaction. Instead, a warrior, perhaps reluctantly conscripted, drops a bomb from on high or triggers a remote control—and somewhere far off an entire city dies in agony. The deed has been mechanistically precise, objectively planned by headquarters, and accomplished in cold blood. The society participates even in the life and death of war by passively reading the statistics of genocide in the newspaper. As Paul Goodman has commented, our wars get more murderous and less angry all the time—or perhaps one should say less *authentically* angry, for the anger is a managed and inculcated emotion that attaches itself to concocted images and abstract ideological issues—like those Big Brother provides for the citizens of 1984.

Compare these empty alienative rituals with such rites as our hippies improvise for themselves out of potted anthropology and sheer inspiration, and the distinction between good and bad magic should be clear enough. The tribalized young gather in gay costume on a high hill in the public park to salute the midsummer sun in its rising and setting. They dance, they sing, they make love as each feels moved, without order or plan. Perhaps the folklore of the affair is pathetically ersatz at this point—but is the intention so foolish after all? There is the chance to express passion, to shout and stamp, to caress and play communally. All have equal access to the event; no one is misled or manipulated. Neither kingdom, nor power, nor glory is desperately at stake. Maybe, in the course of things, some even discover in the commonplace sun and the ordinary advent of summer the inexpressible grandeur that is really there and which makes those who find it more authentically human.

It would be easy to dismiss such merry displays as so much marginal *joi de vivre,* having no political relevance. But I think this would be a mistake. Here, in such improvised rituals, there is something postulated as sacred—and it is something worthy of the designation: the magnificence of the season, the joy of being this human animal so vividly alive to the world. And to this something sacred which stands above all men, causes, regimes, and factions, all are allowed equal access. Could this not be the ultimate expression and safeguard of a participative democracy, without which the popular control of institutions might always be corrupted by partisan interest or deference to expertise? These embryonic rituals may very well be an approximation of the "no-politics" Norman Brown speaks of. For what might this "no-politics" be, if not a politics that doesn't *look* like politics at all, and which it is therefore impossible to resist by conventional psychic and social defenses?

Ginsberg has made his own contribution to this bizarre strategy. In 1966 he wrote a poem titled *How to Make a March/Spectacle,* an effort too long and particularly awful to merit quotation.[10] The poem has, however, either influenced or summarized the character of much of the demonstrating the young have been doing ever since. Its thesis is that demonstrations should lay aside their usually grave and pugnacious quality in favor of a festive dancing and chanting parade that would pass out balloons and flowers, candy and kisses, bread and wine to everyone along the line of march—including the cops and any Hell's Angels in the vicinity. The atmosphere should be one of gaiety and affection, governed by the intention to attract or seduce participation from the usually impassive bystanders—or at least to overcome their worst suspicions and hostilities.

An eccentric notion—and yet is there not a certain crafty wisdom to it? How many demonstrations have there been over the years: angry, vituperative, morally fervent displays which have been compounded of morbid breast-beatings and fierce denunciations . . . and which have won not a soul to the cause who was not already converted? What *is* the purpose of such activity? On what conception of human psychology is it

based? Where unconvinced people hear harsh slogans and see massed ranks of grim faces, their defenses are well rehearsed: they grimace and shout back and become, before the sensed threat, more entrenched in their opposition. How many people are ever won over by being harangued or morally bullied? And winning over is a dissenting minority's only alternative to acts of factional violence.

In contrast, Ginsberg invokes the Zen principle of catching the opponent off guard, of offering no resistant target at which he can strike back. The cause of the happy parade is clearly anti-war (and that simple sentiment is really as much as *any* peace demonstration ever gets across anyway)—but it is declared without self-congratulatory indignation or heavy, heady argument. Instead, the effort is to create a captivating mood of peaceableness, generosity, and tenderness that may melt the rigidities of opponents and sweep them along despite their conscious objections. Perhaps most important, the Ginsberg stratagem suggests that the demonstrators have some idea of what innocence and happiness are . . . which is supposed to be what good political principles aim for.

In a somewhat better poem than Ginsberg's, Julian Beck, director of the Living Theater, catches the spirit of the enterprise:

it is 1968
i am a magic realist
i see the adorers of che

i see the black man
forced to accept
violence

i see the pacifists
despair
and accept violence

i see all all all
corrupted
by the vibrations

vibrations of violence of civilization
that are shattering
our only world
                    . . . . .

we want
to zap them
with holiness

we want
to levitate them
with joy

we want

to open them
with love vessels

we want
to clothe the wretched
with linen and light

we want
to put music and truth
in our underwear

we want
to make the land and its cities glow
with creation

we will make it
irresistible
even to racists

. . . . .

we want to change
the demonic character of our opponents
into productive glory[11]

Over the past few years, while the demonstrations of the New Left have increased in conventional militancy, politicking of this gentler spirit has also proliferated among the young. New York hippies have invaded the Stock Exchange to tear up and scatter dollar bills like so much confetti; San Francisco hippies have staged "strip-ins" in Golden Gate Park—in both cases with every appearance of thoroughly enjoying the exercise. Are these such inappropriate ways of taking issue with the economic and sexual hang-ups of our society? Would handing out leaflets on the subjects be a more effective challenge? The style easily carries over into a form of theater—such as that of the New York Bread and Puppet Theater or R. G. Davis' San Francisco Mime Troupe, both of which have toured the country giving street-corner and public park performances attacking the Vietnam war and racial injustice. In England, too, protests have taken on the form of street theater. In 1968, an anarchist group called the Cartoon Archetypal Slogan Theater (CAST) staged, as one of its many demonstrations, the "capture" of a Fleet Street monument by actors dressed like U.S. soldiers. The players claimed the monument for the American Government and then comically set about recruiting everybody on hand who supported the war in Vietnam for the American Army. They finished by delivering a giant-sized draft card bearing Prime Minister Wilson's name to No. 10 Downing Street.

"Revolutionary festivals," "revolutionary carnivals," "revolutionary playgrounds" . . . actors instead of speakers, flowers instead of pamphlets, enjoying instead of reviling—these are no substitute certainly for the hard work of community organizing (which is the New Left's best

and most distinctive form of politics); but they are, I think, a significant revision of the art of demonstrating. Still, old-style radicalism frowns on such antics. For surely politics is not a thing to be enjoyed: it is a crusade, not a carnival; a penance, not a pleasure. No doubt many a "revolutionary festival" will degenerate into a mere mindless frolic—even as the militancy of "serious" demonstrations has been known to degenerate into fistfights . . . and then nobody convinces anybody of anything. But before we decide that the strategy of "no-politics" cannot possibly work, with its recourse to indirection, involvement by seduction, and subliminal persuasion, let us be honest about one thing. If violence and injustice could be eliminated from our society by heavy intellectual research and ideological analysis, by impassioned oratory and sober street rallies, by the organization of bigger unions or lobbies or third parties or intricate coalitions, by "the flat ephemeral pamphlet and the boring meeting," by barricades or bombs or bullets . . . then we should long since have been living in the New Jerusalem. Instead, we are living in the thermonuclear technocracy. Given the perfectly dismal (if undeniably heroic) record of traditional radicalism in America, why should the dissenting young assume that previous generations have much to tell them about practical politics?

Notes

1. *The East Village Other's* report appears in the issue of November 1-15, 1967, p. 3.

2. They are collected in the volume *Empty Mirror: Early Poems* (New York: Totem Press, 1961).

3. Ginsberg's statement on aesthetics appears in Donald M. Allen, ed., *The New American Poetry 1945-1960* (New York: Grove Press, 1960), pp. 414-18.

4. From Williams' preface to *Empty Mirror: Early Poems.*

5. An exposition of Charlotte Selver's work can be found in "Sensory Awareness and Total Functioning," *General Semantics Bulletin* Nos. 20 and 21, 1957, pp. 5-16. Miss Selver's system is a forerunner of all the many tactile and self-expressive therapies that have now become the stock in trade of hip spas like California's Eselen.

6. Lewis Mumford, *The Myth of the Machine* (New York: Harcourt, Brace & World, 1967), pp. 62-63. But Mumford warns that this style of revolt can also turn into "a ritual, just as compulsive and as 'meaningless' as the routine it seeks to assault."

7. Alan Watts, "Beat Zen, Square Zen, and Zen," in *This Is It, and Other Essays on Zen and Spiritual Experience* (New York: Collier Books, 1967).

8. Marcuse, *Soviet Marxism: A Critical Analysis,* p. 88.

9. Michael Novak, "God in the Colleges: The Dehumanization of the University," in Cohen and Hale, *The New Student Left,* pp. 253-65.

10. The poem appears in *Liberation,* January 1966, pp. 42-43.

11. Julian Beck, *Paradise Now, International Times* (London), July 12-25, 1968. The Becks, Julian and Judith, have, during their years of European exile from America (they were hounded from New York by the Internal Revenue Service in 1964) become the foremost impresarios of revolutionary theater. "Paradise Now" is also the title of one of their audience-participation drama rituals, intended to "envelope the audience in churchly communion" and to finish with "a call for a non-violent revolution right now." (I quote from their program notes for the production.) Perhaps inevitably, the more therapy and tribal ritual such efforts offer, the less dramatic art one can expect of them.

CARL JACKSON (ESSAY DATE SPRING 1988)

SOURCE: Jackson, Carl. "The Counterculture Looks East: Beat Writers and Asian Religion." *American Studies* 29, no. 1 (spring 1988): 51-70.

In the following essay, Jackson analyzes the Beat attraction to Eastern spirituality, noting that this was the first time that America's cultural focus shifted from Europe to other sources, including Asia.

It has become customary to date the birth of the so-called "Beat Generation" to an evening in March 1955, marked by an unforgettable poetry reading at the Six Gallery in San Francisco. The postcard announcement of the watershed event proclaimed:

Six poets at the Six Gallery, Kenneth Rexroth, M.C. Remarkable collection of angels all gathered at once in the same spot. Wine, music, dancing girls, serious poetry, free satori. Small collection for wine and postcards. Charming event.[1]

The promise of an experience marked by inspired poetry, uninhibited pleasure, and easy enlightenment would become identifying marks of the new generation. Though the emphasis on "free satori" would alarm serious students of Zen Buddhism, the reference may be seen as an early indication of one of the Beat Generation's major preoccupations. Asian thought was an essential element in the Beat view of the world.[2]

Like many other such designations, the term "Beat Generation" has been badly misused. Rather than a generation, it might be better applied to a small group of poets and writers active in the late 1940s and 1950s in New York and San Francisco, whose countercultural lifestyles and denunciations of American culture caught the eye of the media. The names include Jack Kerouac, Allen Ginsberg, William Burroughs, Lawrence Ferlinghetti, Gary Snyder, Philip Lamantia, Gregory Corso, Philip Whalen, Brother Antonius (William Everson), Peter Orlovsky and Michael McClure—to mention only the best known. The movement was surprisingly brief: intruding into the public's consciousness in the later 1950s as the result of the national sensation created by Kerouac's *On the Road* and the publicity surrounding the obscenity suit brought against Ginsberg's *Howl,* the movement had already dispersed by the early 1960s. Writing in 1963, Seymour Krim would lament that the group had "splintered and broken up" with its writers in jail, in India, or in Paris. "I never dreamed it would come and go so quickly . . . ," he sighed.[3]

Obviously, the Beat movement may be approached from a number of perspectives—most narrowly, as a literary rebellion which championed "spontaneous prose," a neo-Romantic spirit and a rejection of academic literature. From a broader outlook, it may be seen as the beginning of a generational revolt, marking the emergence of a post-World War II generation which would repudiate both the old-style radicalism of the 1930s and the new-style conservatism of the 1950s. Still again, the Beats may be considered the vanguard in a significant shift in post-World War II American religious consciousness, marked by rejection of institutional religion, a questioning of Christian values, and an affirmation of the possibility of new religious meaning to be found through mystical experience, hallucinogenic drugs and Asian religions. The last perspective, and in particular the attraction to Eastern spirituality, will dominate the succeeding remarks.[4]

First emerging in the nineteenth century, American interest in the Asian religions has grown spectacularly since World War II and today affects the lives of large numbers of Americans. Some have dismissed the phenomenon as a fad, while others hail (or denounce) the growth of interest in Eastern spirituality as the beginning stages of a shift in religious consciousness that will profoundly alter the religious view of future Americans. There is not sufficient space here to analyze the reasons for the appeal of Asian religion, but it does seem evident that interest represents both rejection and attraction. Rejecting the standardized, lowest-common-denominator religion presented in many of today's churches, increasing numbers of Americans seem to be attracted to the novel teachings and emphasis on direct religious experience offered by the Asian traditions. In fact, restless twentieth-century Americans are not only turning to Eastern spirituality, but also to new forms of Christianity. The particular choice seems to depend in part upon level of education and social class. Where the less well-educated seem to embrace charismatic and fundamentalist Christianity, increasing numbers of the more educated seem to prefer some form of Hinduism, Buddhism, or Zen Buddhism. At one level, the Beat writers may be seen as early leaders in the post-World War II "turn to the East," whose attitudes and use of Asian religious thought provide important insight into the impact of the East on modern American religious beliefs.

But Beat interest in the Asian religions should also be considered from a cultural perspective. Traditionally, American writers and intellectuals have looked to Europe for their inspiration and sense of identity. In view of America's parent-child relationship, such an identification with European civilization was inevitable. Throughout most of its history American writers and thinkers concerned with creating a distinctive national culture have juxtaposed their views to those inherited from Europe. Positively as well as negatively, European ideas were central to America's search for identity. Obviously, the situation has changed as Asia has increasingly impinged upon the consciousness of Americans. The growing number of significant American writers and thinkers who are now looking to Asian thought represent a major shift in cultural attitude. Going back to the 1890s, the names include Ernest Fenollosa, Lafcadio Hearn, Irving Babbitt, Paul Elmer More, Ezra Pound, Kenneth Rexroth, Thomas Merton—to mention only a few of the best-known cases. If Europe remains central, increasing numbers of Americans now look to the East as well as the West for inspiration. In the post-World War II period, Beat writers did more than any other literary group to shift America's cultural focus toward the East. The ways in which the Beats utilized and distorted Asian conceptions reveal both the rewards and dangers of turning to non-European sources.

The nearly simultaneous publication in 1958 of a special Zen number of the *Chicago Review* and of Jack Kerouac's novel, *The Dharma Bums,* first alerted the public to Beat interest in Asian thought. In addition to pieces from such respected Zen Buddhists as D. T. Suzuki and Nyogen Senzaki, the special issue featured Kerouac's "Meditation in the Woods," a selection from *The Dharma Bums;* Philip Whalen's Zen poem "Excerpt: Sourdough Mountain Lookout"; and Gary Snyder's description of meditation in a Japanese monastery, "Spring Sesshin at Shokoku-ji." Well-known Zen popularizer Alan Watts introduced the issue with a provocative essay on "Beat Zen, Square Zen, and Zen," in which he sought to define the differences between traditional Zen and the newer "Beat Zen."[5] (Most commentators have overlooked Watts' critical reservations concerning the Beats' view of Zen, as well as his preference for the original Zen of Chinese masters.) Meanwhile, the appearance of Kerouac's *The Dharma Bums* celebrated a new American Zen hero, Japhy Ryder, whose actions suggested that Buddhism need not be dull. Commenting on these unusual developments, *Time* magazine observed, "Zen Buddhism is growing more chic by the minute."[6]

In succeeding months a flurry of articles denounced, dismissed, and, occasionally, even tried to understand the Beat attraction to Zen. Looking back several decades later, it is clear that commentators exaggerated the American appeal of Zen, which never touched more than a few thousands.[7] One of the legacies of media coverage is the myth that, insofar as they looked toward the East, the Beats restricted themselves to Zen Buddhism. In fact, Zen was only one and, indeed, with the exception of Gary Snyder and Philip Whalen, a passing concern of most Beat writers. The assumption that the Beats were fascinated by Zen has obscured recognition of a much wider and more profound interest in Asian thought.

Several qualifications may be noted before proceeding. First, not all Beat writers responded to the attraction of Asian thought. If Kerouac, Ginsberg, Snyder and Whalen expressed strong positive reactions, Ferlinghetti seems to have felt only passing interest, Burroughs preferred Scientology (for a time) to Asian spirituality and Brother Antonius opted for Catholic Christianity.

Second, one must remember that Eastern conceptions were always only one influence among many that nurtured Beat thought. Though critics, led by Norman Podhoretz, have dismissed the Beats as "Know-Nothing Bohemians,"[8] in fact most were college-educated and well-read. Ferlinghetti held a Ph.D. from the Sorbonne; Snyder did graduate work at Indiana and Berkeley; Burroughs completed a B.A. with Honors at Harvard; and Ginsberg and Kerouac attended Columbia. (Though Kerouac dropped out, Ginsberg eventually graduated in 1948.) Other important influences on the Beats besides Asian thought include such writers as Walt Whitman and Ezra Pound and such movements as Romanticism and Existentialism.

Third, examination of the Beat interest in Asian thought will be restricted to Kerouac, Ginsberg and Snyder, and will be extended well beyond the 1950s to their later careers. The decision to concentrate on three writers is due to limitations of space; the choice of these three arises from the prominence of Asia in their thought. In following the three men's subsequent development, one may more fully evaluate the influence of Asian interests taken up during the Beat years. Though there were admittedly important changes after 1960, the three remained Beat writers long after the Beat movement had dispersed.

i

Much of the violent condemnation and unfortunate distortion that has been focused on Beat writers may be traced to the tortured personality of Jack Kerouac. On the surface his was a Horatio Alger success story: the talented son of obscure French Canadian parents who grew up in the industrial town of Lowell, Massachusetts, he won a football scholarship to Columbia University and went on to achieve international fame as a celebrated author. In reality, however, his career was punctuated by repeated traumas and personal tragedies that pursued him throughout his life. These included the childhood loss of his beloved brother Gerard; uncertainty about his own sexuality, which led to a series of broken marriages and homosexual encounters; addiction to alcohol and other drugs; and psychological dependence on his mother Gabrielle, which eventually led him to break with all his old associates. The messy disorder of his life has made it easy for unsympathetic critics not only to ignore his obvious talent, but also to dismiss the Beats generally.

In flight from deep personal and psychological problems, it is clear that much of Kerouac's adult life was spent in the search for a religious answer to slay his private demons. Following the enormous success of his novel *On the Road,* the Beat writer became a media attraction. Asked by a television interviewer: "This beat generation has been described as a 'seeking' generation. What are you looking for?" Kerouac responded without hesitation: "God. I want God to show me His face."[9] Raised in a traditional Roman Catholic home, he regularly attended mass and went to confession. He quit attending mass in high school, and in later years drifted further and further away from the church's moral teachings. His subsequent interest in Asian spirituality surely arose in part as a response to the need to fill the religious void in his life.

Kerouac's first hazy awareness of Asian thought probably dawned in 1943, as a result of the suggestion of Professor Raymond Weaver, who taught literature at Columbia. Sought out by Ker-

ouac, Weaver recommended a reading list, including the Egyptian *Book of the Dead,* Jacob Boehme, and, in all probability, the *Tibetan Book of the Dead* and several Zen classics. However, it would be at least a decade before Kerouac followed up on Weaver's suggestions. In 1953 Ginsberg stumbled upon Zen Buddhism at the New York Public Library, and seems to have transmitted his enthusiasm to his friend. By the end of the year Kerouac was proclaiming himself a "big Buddhist" and spending much of his time reading the sacred writings of that tradition.[10]

Kerouac began to read Buddhism in earnest in January 1954, after moving in with Neal and Carolyn Cassady, who were then living in Oakland, California. Neal, the model for the legendary Dean Moriarity, hero of *On the Road,* had recently become a follower of Edgar Cayce, the American mystic and occultist. Confronted in nightly discussions by Cassady's enthusiastic advocacy of Cayce's ideas, Kerouac counter-attacked with arguments from Buddhism. In order to defend his position, he began to spend every afternoon in the San Jose Public Library boning up on Buddhism. During February he read the *Diamond Sutra,* skimmed other Buddhist scriptures, and moved on to Lao-Tzu, the *Vedas,* Confucius, and Patanjali's *Yoga Precepts*—comprising what Ann Charters has described as a "mammoth dose of Eastern Studies."[11]

Inspired by his reading in the San Jose library, Kerouac characteristically launched not one but a series of works on Buddhism. As he read, he scribbled notes and rephrased the texts in his own words; the eventual result was a manuscript of several hundred pages of extracts, reflections, aphorisms, and *haiku* which he entitled "Some of the Dharma." In the same period he also began a life of the Buddha, "Wake Up," and compiled a collection of Tibetan Buddhist texts to be entitled "Buddha Tells Us," an English translation of the French translation of the original Tibetan.[12] It may be fortunate that none of the projects were ever completed.

The Beat position seemed to demand action; it was axiomatic that while the middle-class "square" conformed, the Beat rebelled. In the case of Kerouac's Buddhism, it is apparent that he not only studied the teachings, but also sought to practice them. He made repeated efforts to meditate—a serious problem because knee injuries incurred as a football player made it impossible for him to assume the lotus position. Refusing to be discouraged, he wrote his friend Allen Ginsberg that he was on his way to becoming a *bodhi-*

sattva and that when they next met he would instruct him in Buddhist teachings. For a time he read the *Diamond Sutra* every day.[13]

Forced at first to rely solely on his reading for knowledge of Asian thought, in 1955 Kerouac met Gary Snyder, who immediately became a model and Buddhist hero to the aspiring Beat *bodhisattva*. Snyder did all the things that Kerouac dreamed of doing: he read Chinese and Japanese, meditated regularly, and, most exciting, planned to sail to Japan to enter a Zen monastery. They became fast friends, with Snyder encouraging Kerouac's Asian interests and introducing him to wilderness hiking.

A full analysis of Kerouac's intellectual and religious interests would require perusal of all his published works. Though presented in novelistic form (with names changed), practically every character and event described in his works represents a fragment of the author's personal experience. His interest in Asian religion was mainly concentrated in the years 1954-56 and may be followed in four works: *Mexico City Blues, The Dharma Bums, The Scripture of the Golden Eternity,* and *Desolation Angels.* Each will be briefly described.

Mexico City Blues (1959), written in a three-week burst in Mexico City during the summer of 1955, documents Kerouac's active interest in Buddhism already before his critical meeting with Gary Snyder in November of the same year. Seeking to put Buddhist doctrine into Beat language, the volume includes a sizeable number of offbeat, humorous Buddhist stanzas in its 242 choruses; among these, the 2nd, 6th, 15th, 66th, 111th, 113th, 132nd, and 190th Choruses reveal clear indebtedness to Buddhism. Drawing on his recent reading of the *Diamond Sutra,* he playfully recast the teaching:

> Dharma law
> > Say
> All things is made
> > of the same thing
> > which is nothing
>
> All nothings are the same
> > as somethings
> > the somethings
> > are no-nothings
> > equally blank[14]

The lines focus on the Buddhist concept of *Sunyata,* or Nothingness, conceived as Ultimate Reality. The paradoxical note he associated with Buddhism is struck again and again.

The Dharma Bums (1958) offers a thinly disguised account of Kerouac's Buddhist adven-

tures following his departure from Mexico and his critical meeting with Gary Snyder. Assuming a Buddhist persona, Kerouac describes himself at the beginning of the novel as an "oldtime bhikku in modern clothes," and he proclaims his intention to turn the "wheel of the True Meaning, or Dharma" to "gain merit for myself as a future Buddha. . . ."[15] Though narrated by Ray Smith (Kerouac), the book's hero is Japhy Ryder (Gary Snyder). In the course of the work Japhy introduces Ray to "yabyum," a Tibetan Buddhist practice involving sexual yoga; and, in the climactic final section, the two friends undertake a difficult mountain climb, culminating in a mystical experience in which Smith comes to understand that the "mountains were indeed Buddhas and our friends. . . ."[16] Though there is a good deal of reference to Zen in the novel, it is evident that Kerouac mistakenly equated it with spontaneity and non-conformist behavior. The need for rigorous discipline, regular instruction by a spiritual master and long hours of meditation, characteristic of authentic Zen Buddhism, are notable by their absence. *The Dharma Bums* provides the most overt, most detailed record of Kerouac's involvement with Asian religion.

The Scripture of the Golden Eternity, a philosophic poem written in 1956 but not published until 1960, was Kerouac's attempt to synthesize his Buddhist reading with other religious traditions to form a modern scripture. Gary Snyder's remark, "All right, Kerouac, it's about time for you to write a sutra," apparently aroused his desire to undertake the project.[17] Unlike *Mexico City Blues* and *The Dharma Bums* which were dashed off at breakneck speed with little attempt at revision, Kerouac composed *The Scripture of the Golden Eternity* quite deliberately: "In pencil, carefully revised and everything, because it was a scripture." "I had no right to be spontaneous,"[18] he explained, a telling comment from the inventor of "spontaneous prose." Although meant to present a universal view, the *Scripture* is strongly Buddhist in tone. Thus, the deity is portrayed as an impersonal, undifferentiated reality, while the world is envisioned as nothing but mind—conceptions that strongly hinted his recent reading of the *Lankavatara Sutra.*[19]

Desolation Angels, published in 1965, records Kerouac's often confused thoughts and lonely experiences during two fateful months in 1956 when he sought to live a life of solitude and Buddhist commitment as a fire-spotter in the Cascades. Appearing in the novel as Jack Duluoz, he confessed as he set out for the top of Desolation

Peak that he expected to "come face to face with God or Tathagata" and to "find out once and for all" the meaning of existence.[20] He discovered instead that he was not suited for the religious life. Though he experienced moments of intense sweetness, fantasizing a coming Buddhist "rucksack revolution" in which "millions of Dharma Bums" would abandon society for the hills, much of the time he found himself longing for the very sensual distractions that he had fled. "I'd rather undo the back straps of redheads dear God and roam the redbrick walls of perfidious samsara than this rash rugged ridge full of bugs . . . ," he sadly confessed. His disenchantment with nature's solitude seems also to have diminished his enthusiasm for Buddhism. Soon after descending to the fleshpots of San Francisco, the Beat poet would lament: "O I'm not a Buddhist anymore—I'm not anything anymore!"[21]

After 1960 Kerouac's attention to Buddhism declined precipitously. In the nine remaining years of his life, he rediscovered and exulted in his Lowell roots, French Canadian ancestry, American patriotism and Catholic upbringing, while increasingly repudiating his former Beat associates, countercultural values and intellectual enthusiasms. Near the end of *Big Sur* (1962), Jack Duluoz is lying exhausted in bed, wracked by days of excessive drinking, poor eating and fitful sleep. Suddenly, the image of the cross breaks in upon his feverish dreams, and he awakens mumbling, "I'm with you, Jesus, for always, thank you." Dazed, he wonders "what's come over me"; years of Buddhist studies and of meditation on emptiness had seemingly had no effect.[22] By the time he undertook a pilgrimage to Brittany in 1965 to search out the records of his French ancestors, Kerouac was proclaiming: "But I'm not a Buddhist, I'm a Catholic revisiting the ancestral land. . . ."[23]

What may one conclude concerning Kerouac's interest in Eastern thought? One important point is that he was primarily attracted not to Zen, but to a broad, non-sectarian Buddhism. Though he reveals some indebtedness to Zen—to haiku and to such poets as Han Shan, for example—the Beat writer is surprisingly critical toward that religion. In *The Dharma Bums* Ray Smith complains that Zen "didn't concentrate on kindness so much as on confusing the intellect. . . ."[24] Clearly, Kerouac regarded Zen as too intellectual—despite the fact that, more than other religions, it rejected intellectual inquiry as the path to enlightenment. Asked the year before his death about the influence of Zen on his work, he replied: "What's really influenced my work is the Mahayana Bud-

dhism, the original Buddhism of Gotama Sakyamuni, the Buddha himself. . . ." While recognizing some indebtedness to Zen Buddhism, he claimed that "my serious Buddhism" traced back to India, embracing such teachings as compassion, brotherhood, charity, "don't step on the bug" and the "sweet sorrowful face of the Buddha."[25]

Buddhism's obvious attraction was its special emphasis on human suffering, which Kerouac knew so well. In addition to his personal sorrows and disappointments, he was chronically plagued by the pain of old football injuries and attacks of phlebitis. He surely spoke from the heart when Ray Smith declares that his sole interest in Buddhism is in the first of Buddha's four noble truths, *"All life is suffering,"* and to a lesser extent the third, *"The suppression of suffering can be achieved. . . ."*[26] The superiority of Buddhism over other religions was its very simple yet precise explanation of the cause and cure of pain. The elimination of ego, cessation of conflict and achievement of detachment offered by Buddhism promised the inner peace that Kerouac so yearned for.

It is intriguing that during the period he looked to Buddha, Kerouac did not repudiate Jesus. He repeatedly emphasized the point in the years before his death. Asked in an interview in 1968 why he had written about Buddha, but never Jesus, he responded incredulously, "I've never written about Jesus? . . . All I *write about* is Jesus." Questioned further, "What's the difference between Jesus and Buddha?" he responded, "There is no difference."[27] Raised a Roman Catholic, he never entirely turned his back on Christianity, even in his most Buddhistic phase.

Philip Whalen, a friend and fellow Beat writer who knew a good deal about Asian religion, questioned whether the author of *The Dharma Bums* ever really understood Buddhism. Kerouac, he suggested, was more drawn to Buddhism's "extravagant language" and "cosmic ideas" than its deeper message.[28] A close acquaintance of Kerouac's, he should have known. Most scholars have concurred with the judgment. While such a conclusion is valid enough, in a sense it misses the point, since Kerouac's ultimate significance as a student of Buddhism is likely to be not the depth of his knowledge, but his influence in stimulating interest in Asian religion. Whatever his ultimate literary reputation—and his standing seems again to be rising—his books were extremely popular and he was a cult hero to many young people. It may well be that *The Dharma Bums* did more to spark American interest in Zen Buddhism in the late 1950s than all the excellent Zen studies authored in the years before 1958 by the great Japanese Zen scholar, D. T. Suzuki.

ii

Unlike his close friend who dropped Buddhism after only a few years, Allen Ginsberg has become more and more deeply committed to Asian religion with the passage of time. The exact moment at which the Beat poet discovered Asian thought may be documented with unusual specificity. Writing to Neal Cassady on May 14, 1953, he described a "new kick" which he had just taken up two weeks earlier. Browsing in the fine arts room of the New York Public Library, he had accidentally stumbled across a series of volumes on Chinese painting. Remarking that he had only the "faintest" idea that China possessed so rich a cultural heritage, he confessed that since the discovery he had spent all his free time "leafing through immense albums of asiatic imagery."[29] Interest in Chinese art soon carried over to Asian religion, with exploratory reading on Zen Buddhism. Putting his discoveries to good use, he repeated several Zen anecdotes and explained *satori*, based on D. T. Suzuki's *Introduction to Zen Buddhism*; he ended by urging Cassady to look eastward as well. Though his interest soon diverted to other fascinations, including drugs and Hinduism, he never attacked Zen Buddhism as did his friend Kerouac. In 1971 he would remark that although he had done some formal Zen meditation, "I'm not a specialist in Zen. . . ."[30] The Japanese religion's impact on Ginsberg was that it led him to a more serious investigation of other forms of Asian religion.

Ginsberg's subsequent explorations in Asian spirituality unquestionably owed much to a profound 1948 mystical experience awakened by reading the great English poet William Blake, which he henceforth dated as the turning point in his life. The unforgettable moment had come upon him without warning: in his bedroom with Blake's *The Sunflower* open before him, he had suddenly undergone an incredibly intense experience, climaxed by a "deep earthen grave voice," which he immediately recognized as the English poet's. The result was a profound awakening, which he described as a "sense of cosmic consciousness."[31] Though the resulting euphoria soon dissipated, he became obsessed with again achieving such a state of higher consciousness; he has subsequently referred to Blake as his guru.[32]

In 1962, accompanied by Peter Orlovsky, Ginsberg traveled to India to seek Eastern spirituality at its source. He arrived in low spirits, depressed by a feeling of personal drift. "What's to be done with my life which has lost its idea?" he confided to his journal. "I don't even have a good theory of vegetarianism."[33] Random and unsystematic, the poet's earlier readings in Eastern philosophy as well as occasional encounters with Asian teachers encouraged, but failed to satisfy, his desire to know more about Asia's religious teachings. He would later describe the Indian journey as rescuing him from the "corner I painted myself in with drugs."[34]

In many instances Western travelers have come to India filled with romantic illusions about the country and its people, only to react with dismay and even flight when confronted by its swarming streets, alien customs and Third World economic conditions. It is evident that while Ginsberg approached India with great expectation ("I'm deliriously happy, it's my promised land," he would remark in anticipation of the journey),[35] he did not shun contact with its darker realities. Indeed, his *Indian Journals* record frequent interaction with Hindus of all types; he also spent a good deal of time visiting burning ghats where corpses were being cremated.

Though he did not achieve the rebirth he sought ("I wanted to be a saint," he confided in his journal),[36] he did pursue the possibilities of spiritual growth as never before. Meditation proved surprisingly difficult. "There is no direction I can willingly go into without strain—nearest being lotus posture & quiet mornings, vegetarian breathing before the dawn," he wrote in his journal; "I may never be able to do that with devotion." Joanne Kyger, who accompanied Ginsberg and Orlovsky for part of the journey, complained: "Allen keeps talking about Meditating [*sic*] while he is on drugs. That is the only time, he says that he can sit still long enough to 'meditate.'"[37] The restless American poet sought out a number of India's holy men for advice, with some success. Swami Sivananda, founder of the Divine Life Society in Rishikesh and exponent of a broad Yoga-Vedanta message, proved especially helpful, advising him, "Your own heart is your guru." Several holy men urged the need to come to terms with his body, or, in Ginsberg's words, "getting *in* the body" rather than "getting out of the human form." The Beat poet supplemented his travels with wide reading on Asia's history and religions.[38]

The climax to his Asian pilgrimage came suddenly in 1963, when, speeding by train in Japan, he underwent a second deep mystical experience that marked a new turning point in his life. Describing the epiphany in his highly charged poem, "The Change: Kyoto-Tokyo Express," dated July 18, 1963, he wrote: "Tears alright, and laughter / alright / I am that I am—"[39]/ Apparently, he had finally come to terms with himself. After this seering event, his dependence on drugs sharply diminished, and he abandoned his former obsession with escaping his body. The result was the end of a long cycle and the realization that he must put the past behind him:

> My energies of the last . . . oh, 1948 to 1963, all completely washed up. On the train in Kyoto having renounced Blake, renounced visions. . . . There was a cycle that began with the Blake vision which ended on the train in Kyoto when I realized that to attain the depth of consciousness that I was seeking . . . I had to cut myself off from the Blake vision and renounce it. Otherwise I'd be hung up on a memory of an experience. Which is not the actual awareness of now, now.[40]

Though the Beat movement had largely disintegrated by the early 1960s, opening the way for the subsequent Hippies and Flower Children, Ginsberg continued to be a leading actor and, in many ways, *the* countercultural hero of the 1960s.

Meanwhile, the poet's interest in Asian religion has continued to deepen, while evolving in new directions. He had begun the chanting exercises of Mantra Yoga in India under the direction of Swami Sivananda; and he continued to receive spiritual instruction after returning home from Swamis Bhaktivedanta and Satchitananda of New York and from Roshi Suzuki (no relation to D. T. Suzuki), Zen master of the San Francisco Zen Temple.

Between 1963 and 1968 Ginsberg revealed particular interest in Hindu mantra chanting, a traditional method of concentrating the mind through repetition of sacred syllables. He experimented with a variety of chants, including the familiar Hare Krishna mantra. He often accompanied the chants with finger cymbals or the harmonium. In addition to mantra chanting, following his Indian pilgrimage, Ginsberg also concentrated more seriously on meditation. He had tried "sitting" on a number of occasions, but without much success. A turning point was 1963, when he visited Gary Snyder in Kyoto, Japan and participated in a four-day *sesshin* at the Zen temple. Apparently, he has meditated on a regular basis since that time; in an interview in 1974 he remarked that he spends an hour every morning "sitting cross legged, eyes closed, back straight, observing my consciousness. . . ."[41] The result

has been a significant change in outlook. Daily meditation persuaded him that regular sitting rather than a sudden mystical breakthrough was the true path to spiritual growth.[42]

Where Kerouac had pursued wisdom on his own and eventually created his own canon (*The Scripture of the Golden Eternity*), Ginsberg accepted the need for outside help and traveled to India to find a guru. His long search seemed to end in 1971 when he encountered Chogyam Trungpa, a Tibetan teacher, who now became his spiritual advisor. Fleeing his native country after the Chinese invasion of Tibet in 1959, Trungpa eventually had settled in Boulder, Colorado in the 1970s, where his Naropa Institute has been a dynamic center of Tibetan Buddhism ever since. In a number of ways, the charismatic lama must have seemed the Tibetan incarnation of the "Zen lunatic" originally celebrated by Kerouac and Ginsberg years before. Contemptuous of conventions, the Tibetan teacher ate what he wanted, drank alcohol freely and smoked; in addition, he was a poet. Under Trungpa's direction, Ginsberg began advanced meditation (*vipasyana*) and in 1973 undertook a grueling three-month, ten-hour-per-day meditational retreat at the movement seminary in Wyoming.[43] With his Tibetan master's encouragement, in 1974 Ginsberg and Anne Waldman founded the wonderfully named "Jack Kerouac School of Disembodied Poetics," which offers classes each summer at the Naropa Institute. Attracted to Zen Buddhism in the 1950s and Hinduism in the 1960s, the American poet finally found his refuge in Tibetan Buddhism in the 1970s.

In sum, it is clear that Asian religion has influenced Ginsberg much more profoundly than his friend Kerouac. Nearly all his published volumes reveal deep immersion in Asian thought. To be sure, the early collections of poems such as *Empty Mirror* (1961) and *Howl* (1956) make no reference to the East, but they already indicate a religious concern which led to Asian spirituality. Beginning with explicit references to Buddhism in *Kaddish* (1971), the evidence of Asian influence may be encountered everywhere in subsequent publications, including *Planet News* (1968), *Ankor Wat* (1968), *The Fall of America* (1972), and, of course, most pervasively, in *Indian Journals* (1970).

Asian thought has also exerted a powerful influence on Ginsberg's literary career. Indeed, his very conception of poetry reveals the indebtedness. In 1971, he spoke of the "function of poetry" as "a catalyst to visionary states of being"; he further remarked that he looked upon writing "as a form of meditation or introspective yoga. . . ."[44]

At its best, he believed that a poem, like hallucinogenic drugs or Asian spiritual methods, could be the means of reaching ultimate truth. *Haiku* was one important Asian influence, which may be seen in the poet's emphasis on spontaneity and highly compressed, juxtaposed images, in such works as *Mind Breaths*. His use of ellipses, the gap between two images which leads to a flash of awareness (*sunyata*), also suggests the impact of *haiku*.[45]

If *haiku* and Zen Buddhism were early literary influences, his later writing reveals the impact of Hindu mantra-chanting. An emphasis on oral delivery had, of course, been an identifying characteristic of Beat poetry from the beginning; thus, his discovery of chanting merely confirmed and strengthened earlier preferences. A growing emphasis on the importance of breath in his poetry also reflected Hindu influence, an impact that may be seen in such works as *First Blues* (1975). Asked whether his experiments with mantra-chanting had influenced his poetry, Ginsberg replied: "Yeah a lot, *now*."[46] Hindu chanting supplied a tradition and body of practices to justify prior preferences.

iii

Much less well-known in the 1950s than Kerouac or Ginsberg, Beat poet Gary Snyder has increasingly come to be viewed by many as the movement's most accomplished writer. While other Beats were savagely attacked and contemptuously dismissed, he won the approbation both of his fellow poets and of academic critics. Raised in the Pacific Northwest, Snyder's original interest in Asia had been kindled as a child of eleven or twelve when he discovered the Chinese landscape paintings at the Seattle art museum. Following graduation from Reed College, he had attended Indiana University for a year before shifting to the University of California to study Chinese and Japanese. By the time he reached Berkeley he had already read Ezra Pound's and Arthur Waley's translations of Chinese poetry, the *Tao Te Ching*, Confucius, the *Upanishads, Bhagavad-Gita,* and "most of the classics of Chinese and Buddhist literature."[47]

The entries in his "Lookout's Journal," originally jotted down during stints as a fire lookout in the Cascades during the summers of 1952 and 1953, document his developing Asian preoccupation. On July 9th, 1952 one finds the entry: "Reading the sutra of Hui Neng"; on August 3rd "—study Chinese until eleven"; and on August 10th, "First wrote a haiku and painted a haiga for

it; then repaired the Om Mani Padme Hum prayer flag. . . ." The most tantalizing entry is dated August 15, 1952: "Almost had it last night: *no identity*. One thinks, 'I emerged from some general, non-differentiated thing, I return to it.' One has in reality never left it. . . ."[48] Although he has subsequently denied ever undergoing a mystical experience, he seemed that summer day to teeter on the edge of such an illumination.

Just as the Beat movement was beginning to attract national attention, Snyder left the country to commence Zen Buddhist studies in Japan, a commitment that would stretch over the next seven years (1956-57 and 1959-65), interrupted by periodic returns to the United States. D. T. Suzuki's works had made him aware of Zen's attractions and the possibility of studying its disciplines in Japan.[49] Supported by a scholarship from the First Zen Institute of America, founded by fellow American Ruth Fuller Sasaki, Snyder began formal Zen study in Kyoto under the direction of Miura Isshu. After a year, he transferred allegiance to Roshi Oda Sesso, head abbot of the Zen temple at Daitokuki, who remained his spiritual teacher until the abbot's death in 1965.[50]

The decision to undertake formal instruction in a Zen temple was a radical step in the 1950s. (Indeed, it would still be regarded as unusual today.) It seems clear that one major reason for Snyder's decision was his cool, even hostile, view of Christianity. In no area did he and Kerouac differ more sharply. In a revealing conversation with Dom Aelred Graham, prior of the Benedictine order's house at Portsmouth, Rhode Island, Snyder confessed that he had felt alienated from his native religion almost from the first. "I was never able to accept Christianity as a child," he recalled, explaining that on the two or three occasions when he had attended Sunday school he had "raised the question about the future of animals" only to be informed that "animals didn't have souls." "I wasn't able to accept that . . . ," he explained.[51] When an interviewer suggested in 1977 that some of his poems seemed to negate Christianity, he rejoined: "I was never a Christian, so I never negated it."[52] In later years the American poet has repeatedly criticized Christianity for its puritanical view of sex and anti-ecological emphasis on man's domination of nature.

Thanks to his Japanese training, Snyder could claim to be a real Zen Buddhist. The training was quite demanding, particulalry during *sesshins,* times of round-the-clock meditation scheduled for eight days twice each year. As Snyder reported in "Spring Sesshin in Shokoku-ji," the day began at 3 a.m. and extended to 11 p.m. The Zen novice devoted most of his time to sutra-chanting and meditation under the vigilant eyes of a head monk, who might smack and even knock a student off his meditation cushion for nodding. Carefully regulated spaces for food, work, clean-up, lectures and *sanzen* (face-to-face interviews with the roshi) completed the long days.[53]

During the first year Snyder attempted to live the life of a Zen monk completely, but in subsequent years, he adopted the life of a lay disciple, dividing his time between the temple and working outside the monastery.[54] Though he spent many hours on the outside, he still saw his roshi almost daily. Janwillen ven de Wetering, a Dutchman who entered the temple in 1958, was greatly impressed by Snyder's dedication: "His self-discipline was beyond reproach: even if he was running a temperature he would arrive in the morning, or at night, park his motorcycle near the gate and visit the master, trembling with physical misery."[55]

If attracted by Zen's strict discipline and precise methods of meditation, Snyder was critical of its hierarchy and institutional rigidities. (Indeed, he brought such objections against all organized religions.) With some exceptions, he was unimpressed by Zen priests, complaining that "Too many are just duds at present." He exempted his master Roshi Oda Sesso from such criticisms, impressed by his spiritual director's subtle teaching and gentle manner.[56] Looking back on his Japanese experience almost twenty years later, he had obviously forgotten all doubts:

> I spent a few years, some time back, in and around a training place. It was a school for monks of the Rinzai branch of Zen Buddhism, in Japan. The whole aim of the community was personal and universal liberation. In this quest for spiritual freedom every man marched strictly to the same drum in matters of hours of work and meditation. . . . The training was traditional and had been handed down for centuries—but the insights are forever fresh and new. The beauty, refinement and truly civilized quality of that life has no match in modern America.[57]

While aware of its limitations, Snyder clearly believed that Zen still had much to offer the West.

Where his friend Kerouac tried to meditate on several occasions and, unable to assume the lotus position, soon gave up the effort, Snyder took up "sitting" almost effortlessly. He originally taught himself to meditate from books, remarking to Father Aelred Graham that, "You get the posture and breathing without too much difficulty just by experimentation." In a recent interview he disclosed that he has continued to meditate for more than twenty years.[58] His approach has always been practical: denying ever undergoing "any great enlightenment experiences," he has insisted that meditation is as normal as walking or breathing. At the same time that he has sought to eliminate its mystery and exoticism, he has emphasized that meditation is crucial. "The point of it is to sit cross-legged and do meditation. That's all I can say, ZAZEN, that's what Buddhism's about. . . ."[59] For Snyder Buddhism *is* meditation.

Examination of Snyder's published works makes it clear that years of residence in Japan as well as decades of reading in Eastern literature have profoundly molded his thought and writing. Indeed, he has become so familiar with Buddhism, Chinese poetry, and *haiku* that he has increasingly dropped references to these traditions in later works, internalizing the Buddhist and Zen Buddhist perspective.

Like other Western writers including Ezra Pound, Amy Lowell, and Kenneth Rexroth, Snyder approached Asian thought through translation, as seen in his first work, *Riprap* (1965). In addition to a selection of his own poems, *Riprap* presented translations of twenty-four of poet Han Shan's "Cold Mountain Poems." Translation made it possible to explore the riches of Chinese literature while still improving his language skills. The choice of Han Shan, a seventh-century A. D. T'ang dynasty poet whom Snyder described as a "mountain madman in an old Chinese line of ragged hermits," could hardly have been accidental.[60] Han Shan's love of wild nature and solitude as well as his Buddhism and Taoism corresponded very closely to Snyder's preferences.

Upon closer examination, Snyder's translations suggest that his personal identification with the legendary Chinese poet may have been too close. In a fascinating analysis based on a line-by-line comparison with the original Chinese texts, scholar Ling Ching has recently concluded that the American "imbued the poems" with "his own experience of the wilderness in Northern America."[61] Of some three hundred surviving poems, the twenty-four the American poet chose to present avoid those poems dealing with mundane life and Buddhist doctrine in favor of those describing his experience on Cold Mountain. Citing the ninth poem as an example, Ling Ching argues that the American has interpolated words throughout, conveying roughness or adversity and in which man is pitted against nature, in place of the original more tranquil mood conveyed in the original text. Snyder's difficulties were hardly unique; every Westerner who has ventured to translate Chinese poetry has found it necessary to sacrifice literal transcription in the search for greater clarity and artistic effect.

Snyder's subsequent publications point to both a widening acquaintance and deepening commitment to Asian religious concepts. *The Back Country,* published in 1968, presents poems grouped into four sections: "Far West," "Far East," "Kali," and "Back." The "Far East" poems present Snyder's impressions of Japan, while "Kali" includes poems based on travels in India in 1962. (Unlike Ginsberg's very confessional poetry, Snyder's poems are descriptive and largely bare of personal comment, making them difficult to analyze.) The volume concludes with a translation of eighteen free-verse poems by Japanese poet Kenji Miyazawa (1896-1933), whose focus on nature and Buddhism obviously attracted Snyder.[62] Sub-titled "Technical Notes & Queries to Fellow Dharma Revolutionaries," *Earth House Hold* (1969) is surely Snyder's most revealing work. In addition to an assortment of book reviews, journal selections, translations and essays, it includes journal entries from the 1956-57 residence in Japan, a detailed description of Zen meditation and an account of a visit to Swami Sivananda's ashram in India. Three of the volume's essays, "Buddhism and the Coming Revolution," "Passage to More Than India" and "Poetry and the Primitive," are particularly significant, presenting his most systematic statements on Asian religion.[63] Among publications since the 1960s, mention may be made of *Turtle Island* (1974) and *The Old Ways* (1977), both emphasizing his later tendency of merging his interests in Asian thought, the American Indian and ecology.

Though he has maintained strong ties to the Far East, and to Japan particularly, marrying a Japanese woman in 1967, Snyder has clearly chosen to live out his life and write his books in America. (He has insisted that he never had any other intention.) In an earlier generation Lafcadio Hearn, who also spent years in Japan and married a Japanese woman, became so completely immersed in his new life that he never returned. By contrast, Snyder's years in the East seem, in some ways at least, to have reawakened his identification with his native land. In 1971 he began construction of a home in the Sierras of northern California, where he has since resided.

He has also come home intellectually, as revealed by the increasing prominence of American Indian and wilderness values in his thought. However, he has not repudiated earlier loyalties.

Rather than rejecting Eastern spirituality, he has increasingly championed both Asian and American Indian values; he contends that the two traditions embody a single, primordial teaching. Queried about their connection in 1977, he observed, "Oh, it's all one teaching. There is an ancient teaching, which we have American Indian expressions of, and Chinese, Tibetan, Japanese, Indian, Buddhist expressions of."[64] At the same time, he believes that each tradition might contribute an element missing in the other. The modern need is to combine the profound philosophic insights of the Asian religions with the nature-connected lifestyles of the Indian.

Though a champion of Asian thought, Snyder has not been its uncritical apologist. This may be best seen, perhaps, in his "Buddhism and the Coming Revolution." Hailing Buddhism's profound understanding of human nature and of the roots of human unhappiness, at the same time he laments its insensitivity to historical and social conditions. "Historically," he declares, "Buddhist philosophers have failed to analyze out the degree to which ignorance and suffering are caused or encouraged by social factors. . . ."[65] He particularly castigates "institutional Buddhism" for its willingness to ignore or make its peace with oppressive political systems. Aware of the danger of stagnation, Snyder has also insisted on the need for adaptation in the movement of Asian religion to the West; Zen Buddhism in America must be different from Zen Buddhism in Japan. He once defined the goal as "Making contact with local spirits. . . ."[66]

iv

Responding in 1972 to inquiries concerning his personal beliefs, William Burroughs remarked that he had "always drawn very much of a blank" on yoga. He continued: "It's questionable in my mind whether these Eastern disciplines do have very much to offer. I mean, after all these thousands of years, where is India?"[67] Obviously, not all writers associated with the Beat movement looked upon Asian thought as favorably as Kerouac, Ginsberg and Snyder. Nevertheless, the role of Asian religion must be considered in any full analysis of the Beats. Their rebellion against middle-class values extended to middle-class religious preferences. Rejecting acceptance of the ethic of success, they championed the "hip" lifestyle of black people; rejecting the conventional Christianity of traditional believers, they frequently proclaimed the superiority of the Asian religions. This is to say that the Beat conception of Eastern religion was countercultural. Eastern ideas and techniques were seen as instruments for breaking through normal consciousness to higher consciousness.

Interest in Asian thought at the beginning of the twentieth-century had been largely confined to well-educated representatives of the upper-middle class such as William Sturgis Bigelow, Percival Lowell and Henry Adams, who had the time, education and income needed for such cosmopolitan explorations. If unorthodox in intellectual taste, such men were for the most part conventional in lifestyles and values, and would have been horrified by the excesses of the Beat generation. Representatives of a "genteel" tradition, they tended to approach the Asian religions as the expressions of ancient, highly refined civilizations needed to balance the modern excesses of a Western civilization increasingly dominated by technology. For Percival Lowell, as for other representatives of genteel culture, Asia held out the hope of balancing a "masculine" West by the "feminine" East.[68] By contrast, the Beat writers viewed the Asian religions as a means of transcending Western civilization's institutional and psychological barriers to achieve higher consciousness. For the Beats, Asian spirituality provided a path to ecstasy and liberation rather than to order and harmony. Their discovery and championing of Eastern religion obviously influenced the Hippies and many other Americans in the decades since the 1950s.

Notes

1. Reprinted in Bruce Cook, *The Beat Generation* (New York, 1971), 63.

2. Too obvious to ignore, the influence of Asian thought is mentioned in nearly all scholarly studies; however, few accounts offer more than a superficial description. An exception is James Whitlark, "The Beats and their Tantric Goddesses: A Study in Erotic Epistemology," *Literature East and West,* 21 (January-December, 1977), 148-60, which emphasizes the impact of Tantric Buddhism.

3. Seymour Krim, ed., *The Beats* (Greenwich, Connecticut, 1963), 12.

4. See Charles Y. Glock and Robert N. Bellah, eds., *The New Religious Consciousness* (Berkeley, 1976); Robert Wuthnow, *Experimentation in American Religions: The New Mysticism and their Implications for the Churches* (Berkeley, 1978); and Jacob Needleman, *The New Religions* (New York, 1972).

5. See *Chicago Review,* 12 (Summer 1958), 3-11.

6. "Zen, Beat and Square," *Time,* 72 (July 21, 1948), 49.

7. Ned Polsky, "The Village Beat Scene: Summer 1960," *Dissent,* 8 (Summer, 1961), 353.

8. Norman Podhoretz, "The Know-Nothing Bohemians," *Partisan Review,* 25 (Spring, 1958), 305-11, 313-16, 318.

9. Quoted in Krim, *The Beats,* 14.

10. Gerald Nicosia, *Memory Babe: A Critical Biography of Jack Kerouac* (New York, 1983), 451. See William Blackburn, "Han Shan Gets Drunk with the Butchers: Kerouac's Buddhism in *On the Road, The Dharma Bums,* and *Desolation Angels,*" *Literature East and West,* 21 (January-December, 1977), 9-22.

11. Ann Charters, *Kerouac* (New York, 1974), 192.

12. *Ibid.,* 195, 220-21.

13. *Ibid.,* 218.

14. Kerouac, *Mexico City Blues* (New York, 1959), 66.

15. Kerouac, *The Dharma Bums* (New York, 1958), 6.

16. *Ibid.,* 57.

17. Quoted in Ann Charters, *A Bibliography of Works by Jack Kerouac* (Rev. ed.; New York, 1975). 34.

18. *Ibid.,* 35.

19. Kerouac, *The Scripture of the Golden Eternity* (2nd ed.; New York, 1970).

20. Kerouac, *Desolation Angels* (New York, 1965), 4.

21. *Ibid.,* 62, 63, 187.

22. Kerouac, *Big Sur* (New York, 1962), 205.

23. Kerouac, *Satori in Paris* (New York, 1966), 69.

24. Kerouac, *Dharma Bums,* 13.

25. Ted Berrigan, ed., "The Art of Fiction XLI: Jack Kerouac," *Paris Review,* 43 (Summer, 1968), 84, 85.

26. Kerouac, *Dharma Bums,* 12.

27. *Paris Review,* 43 (Summer, 1968), 85, 86.

28. Donald Allen, ed., *Off the Wall. Interviews with Philip Whalen* (Bolinas, California, 1978), 55-56.

29. Barry Gifford, ed., *As Ever. The Collected Correspondence of Allen Ginsberg and Neal Cassady* (Berkeley, California, 1977), 140.

30. Ginsberg, *Allen Verbatim. Lectures on Poetry, Politics, Consciousness,* Gordon Ball, ed. (New York, 1974), 9.

31. Thomas Clark, "The Art of Poetry VIII: Allen Ginsberg. An Interview," *Paris Review,* 10 (Spring 1966), 36, 38.

32. Alison Colbert, "A Talk with Allen Ginsberg," *Partisan Review,* 38, 3 (1971), 292.

33. Ginsberg, *Indian Journals. March 1962-May 1963. Notebooks, Diary, Blank Pages, Writings* (San Francisco, 1970), 11.

34. Clark, "Allen Ginsberg," *Paris Review,* 47.

35. Ginsberg, *Indian Journals,* 5.

36. *Ibid.,* 11.

37. *Ibid.,* 10. Joanne Kyger, *The Japan and India Journals 1960-1964* (Bolinas, California, 1981), 190. She was then married to Gary Snyder.

38. Clark, "Allen Ginsberg," *Paris Review*, 48, 49. For a list of works read, see Ginsberg, *Indian Journals*, 71-72.

39. Ginsberg, *Planet News. 1961-1967* (San Francisco, 1968), 55.

40. Clark, "Allen Ginsberg", *Paris Review*, 50-51.

41. James McKenzie, "An Interview with Allen Ginsberg," *The Beat Journey (The Unspeakable Visions of the Individual)*, 8 (1978), 5; "Craft Interview with Allen Ginsberg" in William Packard, ed., *The Craft of Poetry: Interviews from the New York Quarterly* (New York, 1974), 61.

42. See Ginsberg's remarks in Ekbert Faas, ed., *Towards a New American Poetics: Essays and Interviews* (Santa Barbara, California, 1978), 274-76.

43. For Ginsberg's most detailed discussion of his involvement with Tibetan Buddhism, see "An interview with Allen Ginsberg," reprinted in Paul Portuges, *The Visionary Poetics of Allen Ginsberg* (Santa Barbara, California, 1978), 134-63.

44. "Craft Interview with Ginsberg," *New York Quarterly*, 6 (Spring, 1971), 31, 19.

45. Clark, "Allen Ginsberg," *Paris Review*, 29-30 and Faas, *Towards a New American Poetics*, 270.

46. Ginsberg, *Composed on the Tongue*, Donald Allen, ed. (Bolinas, California, 1980), 36.

47. Peter B. Chowka, "The *East West* Interview," reprinted in Gary Snyder, *The Real Work: Interviews & Talks, 1964-1979*, William S. McLean, ed. (New York, 1980), 93-95.

48. Snyder, *Earth House Hold. Technical Notes & Queries to Fellow Dharma Revolutionaries* (New York, 1969), 2, 6, 8, 10.

49. Graham, *Conversations: Christian and Buddhist. Encounters in Japan* (New York, 1968), 59. Visiting Japhy Ryder's shack in 1955, Ray Smith noted that Ryder's Oriental library included Suzuki's complete works. See Kerouac, *Dharma Bums*, 17.

50. See David Kherdian, *A Biographical Sketch and Descriptive Checklist of Gary Snyder* (Berkeley, California, 1965), 11-12.

51. Graham, *Conversations*, 59.

52. Rebecca A. Pickett, "Interview with Gary Snyder," in Pickett, "Gary Snyder and the Mythological Present," Ph.D. Diss., University of Nebraska, 1981, Appendix I, 1.

53. Snyder, "Spring Sesshin at Shokoku-ji," *Chicago Review*, 12 (Summer, 1958), 41-49.

54. "Interview: Gary Snyder" in Faas, *Towards a New American Poetics*, 114.

55. Janwillem ven de Wetering, *The Empty Mirror. Experiences in a Japanese Zen Monastery* (Boston, 1974), 58. Snyder is identified only as "Gerald."

56. Donald Allen, ed., *I Remain. The Letters of Lew Welch & the Correspondence of his Friends*. Volume One: *1949-1960* (Bolinas, California, 1980), 113; Snyder, *The Real Work*, 97-98.

57. Snyder, *Turtle Island* (New York, 1974), 104.

58. Graham, *Conversations*, 59; Faas, *Towards a New American Poetics*, 115.

59. "An Interview with Gary Snyder," *Road Apple Review*, 1 and 2 (Winter 1969/Spring 1970), 51-52; Kherdian, *A Biographical Sketch*, 13.

60. Snyder, *Riprap & Cold Mountain Poems* (San Francisco, 1965), 33. Italicized in the original.

61. Ling Ching, "Whose Mountain Is This?—Gary Snyder's Translation of Han Shan," *Renditions*, 7 (Spring, 1977), 93, a very important article.

62. Snyder, *The Back Country* (New York, 1968), 113-28.

63. For the three essays, see Snyder, *Earth House Hold*, 90-93, 103-12, and 117-30.

64. Paul Geneson, "An Interview with Gary Snyder," *Ohio Review*, 18 (Fall, 1977), 84-85.

65. Snyder, "Buddhism and the Coming Revolution," *Earth House Hold*, 90.

66. Nathaniel Tarn, "From Anthropologist to Informant: A Field Record of Gary Snyder," *Alcheringa*, 4 (Autumn, 1972), 113.

67. Robert Palmer, "The Rolling Stone Interview: William Burroughs," *Rolling Stone* 108 (May 11, 1972), 53.

68. See the author's *The Oriental Religions and American Thought: Nineteenth-Century Explorations* (Westport, Connecticut, 1981), 201-21.

STEPHEN PROTHERO (ESSAY DATE APRIL 1991)

SOURCE: Prothero, Stephen. "On the Holy Road: The Beat Movement as Spiritual Protest." *Harvard Theological Review* 84, no. 2 (April 1991): 205-22.

In the following essay, Prothero examines the beginnings of Beat spirituality, noting its influence on future movements of spiritual and literary resistance.

For the beat generation of the 1940s and 1950s, dissertation time is here. Magazine and newspaper critics have gotten in their jabs. Now scholars are starting to analyze the literature and legacy of the beat writers. In the last few years biographers have lined up to interpret the lives of Jack Kerouac, Allen Ginsberg, and William Burroughs, and publishers have rushed into print a host of beat journals, letters, memoirs, and anthologies.[1] The most recent *Dictionary of Literary Biography* devotes two large volumes to sixty-seven beat writers, including Neal Cassady, Herbert Huncke, Gary Snyder, Gregory Corso, John Clellon Holmes, Lawrence Ferlinghetti, Philip Lamantia, Peter Orlovsky, Michael McClure, and Philip Whalen.

Historical writing on relatively recent subjects tends to get bogged down in issues raised by early critics, and recent scholarship on the beat generation is no exception to this rule. From the pages of *Life* and *Partisan Review*, contemporary scholars have inherited two key interpretive lines that I want to call into question here: first, the tendency to view the beat movement rather narrowly as a literary or cultural impulse; and second, the inclination to judge this impulse negatively, as a *revolt against* rather than a *protest for* something.

Although there was a smattering of early critical acclaim for the beat writers,[2] neither their literature nor their movement fared well with the critics. One reviewer called William Burroughs's *Naked Lunch* "a prolonged scream of hatred and disgust, an effort to keep the reader's nose down in the mud for 250 pages."[3] Kerouac's *On the Road* was said to distinguish itself from true literature by its "poverty of emotional, intellectual, and aesthetic resources, an ineptitude of expression, and an inability to make anything dramatically meaningful."[4] What bothered the critics most about the beats was their negativity. *Life* claimed they were at war with everything sacred in Eisenhower's America—"Mom, Dad, Politics, Marriage, the Savings Bank, Organized Religion, Literary Elegance, Law, the Ivy League Suit and Higher Education, to say nothing of the Automatic Dishwasher, the Cellophane-wrapped Soda Cracker, the Split-Level House and the clean, or peace-provoking H-bomb."[5] The *Nation* dismissed the beats as "naysayers"; even *Playboy* called them "nihilists."[6]

This interpretation reached its rhetorical heights in a 1958 *Partisan Review* review of *On the Road* by Norman Podhoretz. While *Life* had compared the beats with communists and anarchists, Podhoretz grouped them with Nazis and Hell's Angels. "The Bohemianism of the 1950s is hostile to civilization; it worships primitivism, instinct, energy, 'blood,'" he wrote. "This is a revolt of the spiritually underprivileged and the crippled of soul."[7] In a follow-up note in the next issue, Podhoretz asked those who wrote in to defend the beat writers, "Where is the 'affirmation of life' in all this? Where is the spontaneity and vitality? It sounds more like an affirmation of death to me."[8]

The beats responded to this critical chorus with one voice. "Beat," Kerouac asserted, stood not for "beat down" but for "beatific." "I want to speak *for* things," he explained. "For the crucifix I speak out, for the Star of Israel I speak out, for the divinest man who ever lived who was German (Bach) I speak out, for sweet Mohammed I speak out, for Buddha I speak out, for Lao-tse and Chuang-tse I speak out."[9] To those who called "Howl," a "howl against civilization," Ginsberg replied that his signature poem was a protest in

the original sense of "pro-attestation, that is testimony in favor of Value."[10] He too described his protest in religious terms. "'Howl' is an 'Affirmation' by individual experience of God, sex, drugs, absurdity," he explained.[11] "The poems are religious and I meant them to be."[12]

Apologies of this sort have convinced most scholars of American literature that the beat movement amounted to something rather than nothing. Beat literature is, as a result, edging its way into the American literary canon. But exactly what (and how much) beat poems and novels amount to remains a matter of debate. Few interpreters now ignore entirely the obvious spiritual concerns of the beats' work. But the tendency among literary scholars is to see those concerns as tangential rather than constitutive.[13]

Surprisingly, historians of American religion have demonstrated even less interest in beat spirituality. The beats are conspicuously absent from standard surveys of the field and from recent monographs on American religion in the postwar period.[14] Historians of American religion who have explored beat spirituality have tended to focus almost exclusively on the beats' engagement with Zen and then to dismiss that engagement as haphazard. Thus Carl T. Jackson, echoing Alan Watts's earlier contention that "beat Zen" is "phony zen,"[15] contends in a recent article that the beats (with one exception) deviated from some hypostatized "authentic" Zen and therefore fail to qualify as "real" Zen Buddhists.[16] While such judgments may do something to safeguard Zen orthodoxy (whatever that may be), they tend, perhaps unintentionally, to render beat spirituality illegitimate even while informing us about it.

Forty years ago Perry Miller contended that transcendentalism, which had previously been interpreted largely in literary terms, was essentially a "religious demonstration" and as such deserved a prominent place not only in American literature but also in American religious history.[17] This article presents an analogous, if somewhat more modest, argument for the beat movement. My thesis is that the beats were spiritual protesters as well as literary innovators and ought, therefore, to be viewed at least as minor characters in the drama of American religion. If, as Miller argues, transcendentalism represented a religious revolt against "corpse-cold" Unitarian orthodoxy, the beat movement represented a spiritual protest against what the beats perceived as the moribund orthodoxies of 1950s America.

A "New Vision"

The beat movement began with the meeting of Kerouac, Burroughs, and Ginsberg in New York in 1944, coursed its way through the San Francisco poetry renaissance of the 1950s, and spent itself sometime in the early 1960s. It was led by three main figures—a working-class French-Canadian Catholic from Lowell, Massachusetts (Kerouac), a middle-class Russian-American Jew from Paterson, New Jersey (Ginsberg), and an upper-class Anglo-American Protestant from St. Louis (Burroughs)—and included a large supporting cast of novelists, poets, and hangers-on. What united these men (and the vast majority of them were men[18]) was a "new consciousness" or a "new vision."[19]

Like any spiritual innovation, this new vision included a rejection of dominant spiritual norms and established religious institutions. Neither of the two most popular spiritual options of the early postwar period—the new evangelicalism of Billy Graham and the mind cure of Rabbi Joshua Liebman's *Peace of Mind* (1946), Monsignor Fulton J. Sheen's *Peace of Soul* (1949), and the Rev. Norman Vincent Peale's *The Power of Positive Thinking* (1952)—seemed viable to the beats in the light of the long postwar shadow cast by the Holocaust, the bomb, and the cold war. Thus Burroughs, Kerouac, and Ginsberg joined neo-orthodox theologians H. Richard and Reinhold Niebuhr in rejecting any easy return to normalcy and in damning the evangelical and mind-cure revivals as vacuous at best. For this beat trio, neither positive thinking nor evangelical Christianity could make sense of God's apparent exodus from the world. But somehow Oswald Spengler's *The Decline of the West*, a book the beats studied and discussed in the late 1940s, could.

Inspired by Spengler's apocalypticism, the beats announced the death of the tribal god of American materialism and mechanization. ("There is a God / dying in America," Ginsberg proclaimed.) But in keeping with Spengler's cyclical view of history, they prophesied that a new deity was arising from the wreckage. (Ginsberg called it ". . . an inner / anterior image / of divinity / beckoning me out / to pilgrimage.")[20]

In 1938, two years after his graduation from Harvard, William Burroughs wrote a humorous yet foreboding short story entitled "Twilight's Last Gleamings."[21] Loosely based on the sinking of the Titanic, this cynical satire is a dark allegory on the fall of America and the refusal of Americans to accept the inevitability of their own deaths and the demise of their civilization. Burroughs's characters are Neros with urban savvy: con men conning, robbers robbing, preachers preaching as the ship goes down. The moral of this story is well expressed in a later poem by Lawrence Ferlinghetti:

The end has just begun
I want to announce it
Run don't walk
to the nearest exit.[22]

Along with this preoccupation with America's eschaton, the theme of individual suffering and death looms in beat writing. Unlike Liebman, Sheen, and Peale, who resolved to will into existence a "placid decade," the beats devoted their lives and their literature to understanding and explicating the private hells of those who remained on the margins of postwar prosperity. Burroughs's first four books—*Junkie, Queer, Naked Lunch,* and *Yage Letters*—document in factualist style the horrors of addiction to "junk" in its many forms (drugs, sex, power). Much of Ginsberg's work, including "Howl" and "Kaddish," explores madness and death. Three of Kerouac's novels—*Maggie Cassady, The Subterraneans,* and *Tristessa*—are odes to lost loves; and his *Big Sur* depicts his own alcohol-induced breakdown.

If the beats had stopped here, critics' categorization of their work and thought as morbid or mad might have been accurate. But like the Lutheran preacher who hits her congregation with sin only to smother them with grace, the beats sought to move beyond predictions of social apocalypse and depictions of individual sadness to some transcendental hope. "The Beat Generation is insulted when linked to doom, thoughts of doom, fear of doom, anger of doom," Ginsberg, Corso, and Orlovsky protested in 1959.[23] "It exhibits on every side, and in a bewildering number of facets," John Clellon Holmes added, "a perfect craving to believe . . . the stirrings of a quest."[24] Thus the beats' *flight from* the churches and synagogues of the suburbs to city streets inhabited by whores and junkies, hobos and jazzmen never ceased to be a *search for* something to believe in, something to go by.

From the perspective of *Religionswissenschaft*, the beats shared much with pilgrims coursing their way to the world's sacred shrines. Like pilgrims to Lourdes or Mecca, the beats were liminal figures who expressed their cultural marginality by living spontaneously, dressing like bums, sharing their property, celebrating nakedness and sexuality, seeking mystical awareness through drugs and meditation, acting like "Zen lunatics" or holy fools, and perhaps above all stressing the chaotic sacrality of human interrelatedness or *communitas* over the pragmatic functionality of social structure. The beats, in short, lived both on the road and on the edge. For them, as for pilgrims, transition was a semipermanent condition. What distinguished the beats from other pilgrims, however, was their lack of a "center out there."[25] The beats shared, in short, not an identifiable geographical goal but an undefined commitment to a spiritual search. They aimed not to arrive but to travel and, in the process, to transform into sacred space every back alley through which they ambled and every tenement in which they lived. Thus the beats appear in their lives and in their novels not only as pilgrims but also as heroes (and authors) of quest tales, wandering (and writing) *bhikkhus* who scour the earth in a never fully satisfied attempt to find a place to rest. This commitment to the spiritual quest is expressed by Burroughs in *Naked Lunch:*

> Since early youth I had been searching for some secret, some key with which I could gain access to basic knowledge, answer some of the fundamental questions. Just what I was looking for, what I meant by basic knowledge or fundamental questions, I found difficult to define. I would follow a trail of clues.[26]

On the trail that Kerouac, Ginsberg, and Burroughs followed after the war, one important clue was provided by Spengler: the suggestion that the solution to their individual crises of faith (and to America's crisis of spirit) might lie outside western culture and civilization, in the Orient and in the "fellaheen" or uprooted of the world.[27]

A Preferential Option for the Fellaheen

Inspired by a populism akin to contemporary Latin American theologians' preferential option for the poor, the beats looked for spiritual insight not to religious elites but to the racially marginal and the socially inferior, "fellah" groups that shared with them an aversion to social structures and established religion. Hipsters and hoboes, criminals and junkies, jazzmen and African-Americans initiated the beats into their alternative worlds, and the beats reciprocated by transforming them into the heroes of their novels and poems.

Shortly after Kerouac, Ginsberg, and Burroughs teamed up in New York in 1944, their circle of acquaintances expanded to include "teaheads from everywhere, hustlers with pimples, queens with pompadours . . . the unprotected, the unloved, the unkempt, the inept and sick" who hung out at the penny arcades, peep shows, and jazz clubs in the Bowery, Harlem, and Times Square.[28] Kerouac described them in his first novel, *The Town and the City,* like this:

> soldiers, sailors, the panhandlers and drifters, the zoot-suiters, the hoodlums, the young men who washed dishes in cafeterias from coast to coast, the hitch-hikers, the hustlers, the drunks, the battered lonely young Negroes, the twinkling little Chinese, the dark Puerto Ricans, and the varieties of dungareed young Americans in leather jackets who were seamen and mechanics and garagemen everywhere. . . . All the cats and characters, all the spicks and spades, Harlem-drowned, street-drunk and slain, crowded together, streaming back and forth, looking for something, waiting for something, forever moving around.[29]

Recalling Dostoevsky's "underground men," Ginsberg dubbed these characters "subterraneans." Kerouac, assigning them a place a little closer to heaven, christened them "desolation angels."

Of all these fallen angels, the beats were especially enamored of Herbert Huncke, who according to Ginsberg "was to be found in 1945 passing on subways from Harlem to Broadway scoring for drugs, music, incense, lovers, Benzedrine Inhalers, second story furniture, coffee, all night vigils in 42nd Street Horn & Hardart and Bickford Cafeterias, encountering curious & beautiful solitaries of New York dawn."[30] Huncke embodied for the beats both marginality and spirituality.

> In his anonymity & holy Creephood in New York he was the sensitive vehicle for a veritable new consciousness which spread through him to others sensitized by their dislocations from History and thence to entire generations of a nation renewing itself for fear of Apocalyptic Judgement. So in the grand Karma of robotic Civilizations it may be that the humblest, most afflicted, most persecuted, most suffering lowly junkie hustling some change in the all-night movie is the initiate of a Glory transcending his Nation's consciousness that will swiftly draw that Nation to its knees in tearful self-forgiveness.[31]

Initiated by Huncke into this "holy Creephood," Ginsberg, Kerouac, and Burroughs now identified with the beat-up and the beat-down. Kerouac dropped out of Columbia, and the same university expelled Ginsberg. Burroughs began what would turn into a life of participant-observation of the netherworlds of gangsters, addicts, and hustlers. Kerouac explored the jazz clubs and marijuana bars of Harlem. Ginsberg investigated the lives of the working class in Paterson, New Jersey. All three men attempted to transform their experiences into literature worthy of Rimbaud or Baudelaire. By venerating Huncke (who according to beat lore was the first to use the term "beat") as a saint, the beats risked transforming their "new vision" into an amoral, nihilistic apocalypticism. What prevented this outcome, at least for Ginsberg and Kerouac, was the arrival in New York in 1947 of Neal Cassady.

The "secret hero" of Ginsberg's "Howl" and the inspiration for the ecstatic Dean Moriarty of Kerouac's *On the Road*, Cassady was born, quite literally, on the road (in a rumble seat in Salt Lake City while his mother and father were making their way to Hollywood). His parents separated when he was six years old, so he was raised by an alcoholic father in western pool halls, freight yards, and flophouses. While a teenager, Cassady supposedly stole over five hundred cars and seduced nearly as many women. He did six stints in reformatories before landing in San Quentin in the late 1950s.[32]

Kerouac and Ginsberg celebrated and romanticized Cassady as a "holy goof." Kerouac, who by 1947 had grown tired of the apocalyptic intellectualism of Burroughs, greeted the lusty Cassady as a "long-lost brother." Contrasting Cassady to Huncke, Kerouac observed that "his 'criminality' was not something that sulked and sneered; it was Western, the west wind, an ode from the Plains, something new, long prophesied, long a-coming (he only stole cars for joy rides)."[33] Ginsberg also embraced Cassady, who soon became his lover, in mythic terms—as "cocksman and Adonis of Denver."[34] Burroughs, however, dissented, dismissing Cassady as a con man. Thus Cassady's arrival precipitated a split of sorts in the nascent beat movement. The pro-Huncke Burroughs persisted in a more absurdist and apocalyptic reading of the "new vision" (beat as beat down) while Ginsberg and Kerouac attempted to incorporate in their new, pro-Cassady consciousness some redemptive force or transcendental hope (beat as beatitude).

Cassady redeemed the beatific beats' "new vision" by pointing the way to what would become two major affirmations of Kerouac's and Ginsberg's spirituality: the sacralization of everyday life and the sacramentalization of human relationships. If Dean Moriarty preaches a gospel in *On the Road*, it is that every moment is sacred, especially when shared with friends. And if he incarnates an ethic, it is that since all human beings are of one piece, every person must share in every other person's sorrow just as surely as all people will be delivered to heaven together in the end. Thus Cassady personified for Kerouac and Ginsberg the sacred connections of *communitas*. While Huncke symbolized the misery of lonely individuals suffering and dying in dark Times Square bars, Cassady symbolized the splendor of cosmic companions digging the open road.

Shortly after their initial encounter in 1947, Ginsberg and Cassady bowed down together at the edge of an Oklahoma highway and vowed always to care for one another. Seven years later Ginsberg and Peter Orlovsky agreed to "explore each other until we reached the mystical 'X' together" and promised "that neither of us would go into heaven unless we could get the other one in."[35] Such covenants expressed ritualistically Ginsberg's credo "that we are all one Self with one being, one consciousness."[36] They represented an attempt to routinize the group's *communitas*, to incarnate Whitman's vision of "fervent comradeship" in a spiritual brotherhood of beatific monks.

Cassady inspired in this way a shift in the beatific beats' writing from the pessimistic, Dreiserian realism that would mark Burroughs's work to a more optimistic, even transcendental realism: literature as "a clear statement of fact about misery . . . *and* splendor [my emphasis]."[37] Like Burroughs, Ginsberg and Kerouac would continue to depict the suffering of the fellaheen, but unlike him they would insist that such suffering was both revelatory and redemptive. Thus Ginsberg transformed the profanity of working-class life in Paterson into a hierophany:

> The alleys, the dye works,
> Mill Street in the smoke,
> melancholy of the bars,
> the sadness of long highways,
> negroes climbing around
> the rusted iron by the river,
> the bathing pool hidden
> behind the silk factory
> fed by its drainage pipes;
> all the pictures we carry in our mind
>
> images of the thirties
> depression and class consciousness
> transformed above politics
> filled with fire
> with the appearance of God.[38]

And thus Kerouac insisted that while authors must "accept loss forever," they should nonetheless "believe in the holy contour of life."[39]

Turning East

If the beats followed Spengler's clue in looking to fellaheen like Huncke and Cassady for spiritual insight, they also followed his lead in steering their spiritual quest toward Asia. While other Americans were forging Protestant-Catholic-Jewish alliances during Eisenhower's presidency, the beats were moving toward a far more radical ecumenism. In addition to the Catholicism of Kerouac, the Protestantism of Burroughs, and the Judaism of Ginsberg, the beats studied gnosticism, mysticism, native American lore, Aztec and Mayan mythology, American transcendentalism, Hinduism, and especially Buddhism.

This religious eclecticism was epitomized by Jack Kerouac who, though born a Catholic, practiced Buddhist meditation and once observed the Muslim fast of Ramadan. When asked in an interview to whom he prayed, Kerouac replied, "I pray to my little brother, who died, and to my father, and to Buddha, and to Jesus Christ, and to the Virgin Mary."[40] His pluralism reached still farther in this creedal chorus from *Mexico City Blues*:

> I believe in the sweetness
>   of Jesus
> And Buddha—
>   I believe
> In St. Francis
>   Avaloki
> Tesvara,
>   the Saints
> Of First Century
>   India A D
> And Scholars
>   Santivedan
> And Otherwise
>   Santayanan
>   Everywhere.[41]

Only Ginsberg, a self-styled "Buddhist Jew," approached Kerouac's eclecticism. In a poem entitled "Wichita Vortex Sutra" he invoked a litany of gods:

>   million-faced Tathagata gone past suffering
> Preserver Harekrishna returning in the age of
>   pain
> Sacred Heart my Christ acceptable
>   Allah the Compassionate One
>   Jaweh Righteous One
>   all Knowledge-Princes of Earth-man,
>   all
> ancient Seraphim of heavenly Desire, Devas,
>   yogis
>   & holyman I chant to—[42]

Clearly the beats were not wed exclusively to any one religious tradition. One religion, however, did inspire more of them more deeply than any other, namely, Buddhism, especially the Zen and Yogacara formulations of the Mahayana school. Though Burroughs had introduced them through Spengler to Asian thought in 1945, Kerouac and Ginsberg did not begin to study Buddhism in earnest until 1953. In that year a reading of Thoreau's *Walden* inspired Kerouac to learn more about Asian religious traditions. He began his investigation by reading Ashvagosa's biography of Gautama Buddha. Struck by the Buddha's injunction to "Repose Beyond Fate," Kerouac sat down to meditate. He then experienced what he later described as "golden swarms of nothing."[43] Immediately he left to go to San Jose to enlighten Neal Cassady. But Cassady had already found his own prophet in the person of Edgar Cayce, whose strange brew of Christian metaphysics, clairvoyance, reincarnation, and karma had whetted his eclectic appetite. While in San Jose, Kerouac began to study Mahayana Buddhist scriptures, especially the Diamond Sutra, the Perfection of Wisdom Sutra, and the Sutra of the Sixth Patriarch, as they appeared in Dwight Goddard's *A Buddhist Bible*.

Buddhism attracted Kerouac because it seemed to make sense of the central facts of his experience (suffering, impermanence) and to affirm his intuition that life was dreamlike and illusory. Perhaps more importantly, by locating the origin of suffering in desire, the Buddhist sutras seemed to offer a way out. In the summer of 1954 Kerouac wrote to Burroughs, who was now living in Tangier, about his discovery of Buddhism and his vow to remain celibate for a year in an attempt to mitigate his desire and thus his suffering. Burroughs wrote back, urging Kerouac not to use Buddhism as "psychic junk." "A man who uses Buddhism or any other instrument to remove love from his being in order to avoid suffering has committed, in my mind, a sacrilege comparable to castration," he wrote. "Suffering is a chance you have to take by the fact of being alive." Interestingly, Burroughs wrote a letter that same summer to Ginsberg, urging him to "dig" Tibetan Buddhism if he had not yet done so. Burroughs was opposed not to Buddhism itself but to its use in the West as some sort of "final fix."[44]

Ginsberg took Burroughs's advice, and by mid-decade the novels and poems of Kerouac and Ginsberg were filled with references to Buddhism. In one eighteen-month period between 1954 and 1956 Kerouac meditated daily and still found the time to write five books with a decidedly Buddhist bent. Three of these works, *Some of the Dharma* (a thousand-page personal meditation), *Buddha Tells Us* (an American version of the Surangama Sutra), and *Wake Up* (a life of the Buddha) have never been published. A book of Buddhist poems, *Mexico City Blues,* and a beat sutra entitled *The Scripture of the Golden Eternity* appeared in 1959 and 1960 respectively.

In 1955 Ginsberg and Kerouac met Gary Snyder, a mountain poet and Zen initiate, who contributed greatly to their understanding of Buddhism and their commitment to it. Just as Neal Cassady appeared as Dean Moriarty, the hero of *On the Road,* Snyder was immortalized as Japhy Ryder, the thinly veiled protagonist of *Dharma*

Bums. Although Kerouac was clearly intrigued by
Snyder and by Zen, he devoted a good portion of
Dharma Bums to arguments between Ray Smith
(himself) and Ryder (Snyder) and to criticisms of
Zen. Smith, who presents himself not as a Zen
Buddhist but as "an old fashioned dreamy hi-
nayana coward of later mahayanism," clashed
with Ryder and his Zen on a number of occasions.[45] One of Smith's arguments was that showing compassion (*karuna*) was more important
than achieving insight (*prajna*). Smith was especially critical of the violence that sometimes attended uncracked Zen koans. "It's mean," he
complained to Ryder, "All those Zen masters
throwing young kids in the mud because they
can't answer their silly word questions." "Compassion," Smith contended, "is the heart of Buddhism."[46] Unlike Ryder who had no use for
Christianity, Smith revered not only Avalokites-
vara, the bodhisattva of compassion, but also Jesus
Christ. "After all," he explained, "a lot of people
say he is Maitreya [which] means 'Love' in Sanskrit
and that's all Christ talked about was love."[47]

Despite such disputes, Kerouac, Snyder, and
Ginsberg agreed on a few crucial points that they
shared with Buddhism (especially the Mahayana
tradition's Yogacara school). They believed, for
example, that life is characterized by suffering
(*dukkha*) and impermanence (*anicca*). Yet they
also believed that this world, at least as it appears
to our senses, is ephemeral and illusory. "Happiness consists in realizing that it is all a great
strange dream," Kerouac wrote in *Lonesome Traveler*.[48] And he echoed the sentiment (albeit in
decidedly biblical grammar) in *Dharma Bums*:
"Believe that the world is an ethereal flower, and
ye live."[49]

This shared awareness of what Ginsberg called
"the phantom nature of being" was tremendously
liberating for the beatific beats. It enabled them
both to confront suffering and death as major
obstacles in this relative world of appearances and
to see their ultimate insignificance from the
absolute perspective of heaven or nirvana. It
empowered them, moreover, to deny the absolute
reality of the material world even as they affirmed
enthusiastically our spiritual experiences in it. Out
of such paradoxes came the this-worldly joy of
statements like "This is it!," "We're already there
and always were," "We're all in Heaven now,"
"The world has a beautiful soul," "The world is
drenched in spirit," "everything's all right."

There is a constant tension in beat literature,
therefore, between misery and splendor, between
an overwhelming sadness and an overcoming joy.

"The world is beautiful place / to be born into,"
Lawrence Ferlinghetti observed, "if you don't
mind happiness / not always being / so very much
fun / if you don't mind a touch of hell now and
then."[50] In the beat cosmos God is both absent
and everywhere. Dualisms between sacred and
profane, body and soul, matter and spirit, nirvana
and samsara do not hold. Thus Ginsberg's celebrated encounter with the poet William Blake in
Harlem in 1948 incorporated both a vision of
death ("like hearing the doom of the whole
universe") and a vision of heaven ("a breakthrough from ordinary habitual quotidian consciousness into consciousness that was really seeing all of heaven in a flower").[51] And so one of
Ginsberg's most profane poems, "Howl," contains
his boldest affirmation of the sacred camouflaged
in the profane:

> Holy! Holy! Holy! Holy! Holy! Holy! Holy! Holy!
>   Holy! Holy! Holy! Holy! Holy! Holy! Holy!
>   Holy! Holy! Holy! Holy!
> The world is holy! The soul is Holy! The skin is
>   holy! The nose is holy! The tongue and cock
>   and hand and asshole holy!
> Everything is holy! everybody's holy! everywhere
>   is holy! everyday is in eternity! Everyman's
>   an angel![52]

Conclusions

After the beat generation graduated from
young adulthood to middle age in the 1960s, beat
writers went in different directions. Following an
extended stint at the wheel of the bus of Ken Kesey's Merry Pranksters, Cassady collapsed along a
railroad track and died of exposure in Mexico in
1968. Kerouac's seemingly endless cycles of exile
and return to his mother's home in Lowell ended
in 1969 when he died an alcoholic's death of cirrhosis of the liver. Burroughs, perhaps the least
likely of beats to make it past middle age, is alive
and well and enjoying the acclaim of European
critics. Ginsberg too has survived even his transmi-
gration from literary rebel to de facto poet laureate of the United States. In this way beat writers
have earned a place in the history of American
letters.

What I have argued here is that the beats also
deserve a place in American religious history. More
than literary innovators or bohemian rebels, the
beats were wandering monks and mystical seers.
They went on the road—from New York to San
Francisco to Mexico City to Tangier—because they
could not find God in the churches and synagogues of postwar America. They venerated the
poor, the racially marginal and the socially inferior
because they saw no spiritual vitality in the

celebrated postwar religious revival of mainstream white preachers. And they experimented with drugs, psychoanalysis, bisexuality, jazz, mantra chanting, Zen meditation, and new literary forms in an attempt to conjure the gods within.

Like the transcendentalists who inspired them, the beats were critics of "corpse-cold" orthodoxies; they were champions of spiritual experience over theological formulations who responded to the challenge of religious pluralism by conjuring out of inherited and imported materials a wholly new religious vision. Like Emerson, the beats aimed to make contact with the sacred on the nonverbal, transconceptual level of intuition and feeling, and then to transmit at least a part of what they had experienced into words. Like Thoreau, they insisted on the sanctity of everyday life and the sainthood of the nonconformist. And like George Ripley and his associates at Brook Farm, they aimed to create a spiritual brotherhood based on shared experiences, shared property, shared literature, and an ethic of "continual conscious compassion."[53] With transcendentalists of all stripes, the beats gloried in blurring distinctions between matter and spirit, divinity and humanity, the sacred and the profane.

The beats diverged from their transcendentalist forebears (and toward their neo-orthodox contemporaries), however, in maintaining a more sanguine view of the problems of human existence and the possibility of social progress. In the beat cosmos, society is running toward apocalypse; individuals are doomed to suffer and die, and perhaps to endure addiction or madness along the way. But in the beatitudes according to Kerouac and Ginsberg, those who suffer are blessed, and the sacrament of friendship can redeem a portion of that suffering. In the last analysis, "The bum's as holy as the seraphim!" and everyone—junkies and criminals, beats and squares, Catholics and Buddhists, culture-peoples and fellaheen—is raised up from the dreamworld of our quotidian existences and "buried in heaven together."[54]

On the question of whether this is a compelling spiritual vision, reasonable people can and will disagree. All I argue here is that the vision is in fact spiritual and, as such, warrants the scrutiny of scholars of American religion. Precisely how such scrutiny might alter our understanding of American religion and culture I cannot say. But I suspect greater attention to beat spirituality will open up at least one avenue of revision.

Traditional accounts of American religion and culture in the 1950s have tended toward consensus rather than dissension. Social critics and historians have described early postwar America as a "one-dimensional" society in which "organization men" produced a mass culture consumed by "lonely crowds." Religious historians too have depicted the decade as placid rather than contentious—an age in which a general anxiety was rather effectively relieved by a generic faith in a Judeo-Christian God and the American Way of Life.[55] From this perspective the 1960s appear as something of a historiographic non sequitur. Thus, according to religious historian Sydney Ahlstrom, the sixties represent "a radical turn" in America's religious road, a crossroads between a more consensual Protestant (or Judeo-Christian) America and a more conflictual "Post-Protestant America."[56]

While this article does not directly engage this prevailing thesis, it does support recent scholarly work underscoring continuities rather than discontinuities between the 1950s and 1960s.[57] While the ostensibly radical religious pluralism of the sixties may not seem inevitable to students of beat spirituality, it comes as far less of a surprise. A decade before the death-of-God movement in theology and the eastward turn in religion the beats were announcing the death of the gods of materialism and mechanization and looking to Buddhism for spiritual insight. And nearly two decades before the rise of black and Latin American liberation theologies the beats incorporated the socially down and the racially out in their radically inclusive litany of the saints. To study the beats alongside Graham, Peale, Liebman, and Sheen is to glimpse the existence of countercurrents of spiritual resistance coursing around (if not through) the placid religious mainstream.

Notes

1. See Gerald Nicosia, *Memory Babe: A Critical Biography of Jack Kerouac* (New York: Grove, 1983); Dennis McNally, *Desolate Angel: Jack Kerouac, the Beat Generation, and America* (New York: McGraw Hill, 1979); Barry Miller, *Ginsberg: A Biography* (New York: Simon & Schuster, 1989); Ted Morgan, *Literary Outlaw: The Life and Times of William S. Burroughs* (New York: Henry Holt, 1988). Notable memoirs include Carolyn Cassady, *Off the Road: My Life with Cassady, Kerouac and Ginsberg* (New York: William Morrow, 1990); and Joyce Johnson, *Minor Characters* (Boston: Houghton Mifflin, 1983).

2. On 5 September 1957, *New York Times* literary critic Gilbert Millstein hailed the appearance of Jack Kerouac's *On the Road* as "a historic occasion" comparable to the publication of Hemingway's *The Sun Also Rises*. Millstein's review is reprinted in Barry Gifford and

Lawrence Lee, *Jack's Book: An Oral Biography of Jack Kerouac* (New York: Saint Martin's, 1978) 238. During the "Howl" obscenity trial of 1957, Kenneth Rexroth praised Ginsberg's work as "probably the most remarkable single poem published by a young man since the second world war" (J. W. Ehrlich, ed., *Howl of the Censor* [San Carlos, CA: Nourse, 1961] 64).

3. John Wain, "The Great Burroughs Affair," *New Republic,* 1 December 1962, 21.

4. Norman Podhoretz, "letter to the editor," *Partisan Review* 25 (Summer 1958) 476.

5. Thomas Parkinson, ed., *A Casebook on the Beat* (New York: Thomas Y. Crowell, 1961) 232.

6. Ibid., 255.

7. Norman Podhoretz, "The Know-Nothing Bohemians," *Partisan Review* 25 (Spring 1958) 307-8, 316.

8. Norman Podhoretz, "letter to the editor," *Partisan Review* 25 (Summer 1958) 479. Podhoretz renewed his attack on the occasion of the opening of a Kerouac memorial in Lowell, MA in 1987. See, e.g., his "Spare Us a Revival of Kerouac and the Pied Pipers of Despair," *Los Angeles Times,* 8 January 1987, sec. 1.

9. Jack Kerouac, "The Origins of the Beat Generation," *Playboy,* June 1959, 31-79.

10. Allen Ginsberg, *To Eberhart from Ginsberg* (Lincoln, MA: Penman, 1976) 11.

11. Ibid., 21.

12. Ibid., 32.

13. Notable exceptions include James Whitlark, "The Beats and their Tantric Goddesses: A Study in Erotic Epistemology," *Literature East and West* 21 (1977) 148-60; and Paul Portuges, *The Visionary Poetics of Allen Ginsberg* (Santa Barbara: Ross-Erikson, 1978).

14. I refer to Sydney Ahlstrom's otherwise exhaustive *A Religious History of the American People* (New Haven: Yale University Press, 1972) and George Marsden's self-consciously pluralistic *Religion and American Culture* (San Diego: Harcourt Brace Jovanovich, 1990) as well as Robert Wuthnow, *The Restructuring of American Religion: Society and Faith since World War II* (Princeton: Princeton University Press, 1988) and Mark Silk, *Spiritual Politics: Religion and America since World War II* (New York: Simon & Schuster, 1988). The beats do receive careful, if divided, attention in Robert S. Ellwood, *Alternative Altars: Unconventional and Eastern Spirituality in America* (Chicago: University of Chicago Press, 1979) and Rick Fields, *How the Swans Came to the Lake: A Narrative History of Buddhism in America* (Boston: Shambala, 1986).

15. Alan Watts, *Beat Zen, Square Zen and Zen* (San Francisco: City Lights, 1959) 16.

16. Carl T. Jackson, "The Counterculture Looks East: Beat Writers and Asian Religion," *American Studies* 29 (1988) 51-70.

17. Perry Miller, ed., *The Transcendentalists: An Anthology* (Cambridge, MA: Harvard University Press, 1950) 8. See also William R. Hutchison's extension and refinement of Miller's thesis in *The Transcendentalist Ministers: Church Reform in the New England Renaissance* (New Haven: Yale University Press, 1959).

18. By the reckoning of the *Dictionary of Literary Biography,* only nine of sixty-seven beat writers were women. Very few female characters appear in Kerouac's books, Burroughs's novels, or Ginsberg's poems. Those that do flitter through like phantoms, appearing here for sex and there to fix a cup of coffee. According to Joyce Johnson, whose aptly titled *Minor Characters* remains one of the most revealing insider accounts of the beats, "The whole Beat scene had very little to do with the participation of women as artists themselves. The real communication was going on between the men, and the women were there as onlookers. . . . It was a very masculine aesthetic" (quoted in Gifford and Lee, *Jack's Book,* 235-36). Exclusion of women veered into blatant misogyny in Burroughs and Cassady and into a near-paranoid distrust of women in Kerouac. See, e.g., Daniel Odier, *The Job: Interview with William Burroughs* (London: Jonathan Cape, 1969) 113; Barry Gifford, ed., *As Ever: The Collected Correspondence of Allen Ginsberg & Neal Cassady* (Berkeley: Creative Arts Book Company, 1977) 36.

19. References to a "new vision" and a "new consciousness" abound in beat literature. See, e.g., "The New Consciousness," in Ginsberg, *Composed on the Tongue* (Bolinas, CA: Grey Fox, 1971) 63-93.

20. "Siesta in Xbalba," in Allen Ginsberg, *Collected Poems, 1947-1980* (New York: Harper & Row, 1984) 105-6. Excerpts from *Collected Poems 1947-1980* [copyright ©1984 by Allen Ginsberg] are reprinted by permission of HarperCollins Publishers.

21. Burroughs wrote this piece with a friend named Kells Elvins in 1938. It was finally published as "Twilight's Last Gleamings," *Paris Review* 109 (Winter 1988) 12-20.

22. Ferlinghetti, "Junkman's Obbligato," in idem, *A Coney Island of the Mind* (New York: New Directions, 1968) 63-64; reprinted by permission of the publisher.

23. Gregory Corso, Allen Ginsberg, and Peter Orlovsky, "Reply to Symposium," *Wagner Literary Magazine* (Spring 1959) 30.

24. John Clellon Holmes, "This is the Beat Generation," *New York Times Magazine,* 16 November 1952.

25. I am borrowing here from Victor Turner, especially *The Ritual Process: Structure and Anti-Structure* (Ithaca, NY: Cornell University Press, 1969); idem, "The Center Out There: Pilgrim's Goal," *HR* 12 (1973) 191-230; and idem with Edith Turner, *Image and Pilgrimage in Christian Culture: Anthropological Perspectives* (New York: Columbia University Press, 1978). Turner makes this connection between liminality, *communitas,* and the beats explicit in *The Ritual Process,* 112-13.

26. William Burroughs, *Naked Lunch* (New York: Grove, 1962) 6. Consider also John Clellon Holmes's 1950 journal entry: "Our search is, I firmly believe, a spiritual one. . . . Our search is for the Rose that we insist must dwell, or at least become visible, after the end of the night has been reached" (Arthur and Kit Knight, eds., *The Beat Vision: A Primary Sourcebook* [New York: Paragon House, 1987] 86).

27. In *The Decline of the West* (trans. Charles Atkinson; 2 vols.; New York: Knopf, 1939) that the beats read and debated in the late 1940s, Oswald Spengler argued (2. 169) that cultures and peoples arise and decline in grand cycles in which "primitives" yield to "culture-peoples" as cultures expand and then to "fellaheen"

as cultures degrade. The fellaheen, who exist at the *limina* of cultures, are from the perspective of culture-builders useless "waste-products" who endure the slings and arrows of history without changing events or being changed by them, who identify with all human beings rather than with their nation only (2. 186). A spiritual people, their "second-religiousness" is marked by "a deep piety that fills the waking-consciousness . . . the naive belief . . . that there is some sort of mystic constitution of actuality" (2. 311). According to Spengler, fellaheen in every age follow the lead of "world-citizens, world-pacifists, and world-reconcilers . . . who withdraw themselves out of actuality into cells and study-chambers and spiritual communities, and proclaim the nullity of the world's doings . . . timeless, a-historic, literary men, men not of destiny, but of reasons and causes, men who are inwardly detached from the pulse of blood and being, wide-awake thinking consciousnesses" (2. 184-85). The beats clearly sympathized with the fellaheen, whose lives Spengler described as "planless happening[s] without goal or cadenced march" (2. 170-71). And at least some of the beats saw themselves as the prophesied "literary men" who would lead the fellaheen into a revolution of the soul.

28. Allen Ginsberg, "A Version of the Apocalypse," in Knights, *The Beat Vision*, 190.

29. Jack Kerouac, *The Town and the City* (New York: Harcourt Brace, 1950) 361-62. Excerpts from *The Town and the City* copyright 1950 by John Kerouac, and renewed 1978 by Stella S. Kerouac, reprinted by permission of Harcourt Brace Jovanovich, Inc.

30. Allen Ginsberg, "On Huncke's Back," *The Unspeakable Visions of the Individual* 3 (1973) 20-21; reprinted by permission of the publisher.

31. Ibid.

32. See Neal Cassady, *The First Third* (San Francisco: City Lights, 1981); William Plummer, *The Holy Goof: A Biography of Neal Cassady* (Englewood Cliffs, NJ: Prentice-Hall, 1981); and Carolyn Cassady, *Off the Road.*

33. Jack Kerouac, *On the Road* (New York: Viking, 1957) 10, 11.

34. Allen Ginsberg, "Howl," in idem, *Collected Poems*, 128.

35. Allen Ginsberg, *Gay Sunshine Interview* (Bolinas, CA: Grey Fox, 1974) 23.

36. Allen Ginsberg, *Allen Verbatim: Lectures on Poetry, Politics, Consciousness* (Gordon Ball, ed.; New York: McGraw-Hill, 1974) 5.

37. Allen Ginsberg, "A Prefatory Letter," *The Gates of Wrath: Rhymed Poems, 1948-1952* (Bolinas, CA: Grey Fox, 1972).

38. Allen Ginsberg, "A Poem on America," in idem, *Collected Poems*, 64.

39. Jack Kerouac, "Belief & Technique for Modern Prose," *Evergreen Review* 2 (Spring 1959) 57.

40. Jack Kerouac, *Mexico City Blues* (New York: Grove, 1959) 65; reprinted by permission of the publisher.

41. Ibid., 15.

42. Allen Ginsberg, *Planet News* (San Francisco: City Lights, 1968) 127; reprinted by permission of Harper-Collins Publishers.

43. Jack Kerouac, "The Last Word," *Escapade* (October 1959) 72.

44. Both of Burrough's letters can be found in William Burroughs, *Letters to Allen Ginsberg: 1953-1957* (New York: Full Court, 1982) 48, 56-58.

45. Jack Kerouac, *Dharma Bums* (New York: Viking, 1957) 13.

46. Ibid., 105.

47. Ibid., 159.

48. Jack Kerouac, *Lonesome Traveler* (New York: McGraw-Hill, 1960) 34-36.

49. Jack Kerouac, *Dharma Bums*, 108.

50. Ferlinghetti, *A Coney Island of the Mind*, 88.

51. Clark Thomas, "The Art of Poetry VIII," *Paris Review* 37 (Spring 1966) 36-37.

52. Allen Ginsberg, "Footnote to Howl," in idem, *Collected Poems*, 134.

53. Jack Kerouac, "The Art of Fiction LXI," *Paris Review* 43 (Summer 1968) 85.

54. Nicosia, *Memory Babe*, 277, 513.

55. Classic formulations include David Riesman, *The Lonely Crowd: A Study of the Changing American Character* (New Haven: Yale University Press, 1950); Will Herberg, *Protestant-Catholic-Jew* (Garden City, NY: Anchor, 1955); William H. Whyte, *The Organization Man* (New York: Simon and Schuster, 1956); Martin Marty, *The New Shape of American Religion* (New York: Harper & Row, 1959); Daniel Bell, *The End of Ideology: On the Exhaustion of Political Ideas in the Fifties* (New York: Collier, 1960); Herbert Marcuse, *One-Dimensional Man* (Boston: Beacon, 1964).

56. Ahlstrom, *A Religious History of the American People*, 1079-96. See also his "The Radical Turn in Theology and Ethics: Why It Occurred in the 1960s," *Annals of the American Academy of Political and Social Science* 387 (1970) 1-13.

57. See, e.g., W. T. Llamon, *Deliberate Speed: The Origins of a Cultural Style in the American 1950s* (Washington, DC: Smithsonian Institution Press, 1990). Llamon argues that the 1950s belonged at least as much to an "oppositional culture" of method actors, action painters, beat writers, and civil rights activists as to Marcuse's "one-dimensional man."

WOMEN OF THE BEAT GENERATION

BRENDA KNIGHT (ESSAY DATE 1996)

SOURCE: Knight, Brenda. "Joan Vollmer Adams Burroughs: Calypso Stranded (1924-1951)." In *Women of the Beat Generation: The Writers, Artists and Muses at the Heart of a Revolution*, pp. 49-56. Berkeley, Calif.: Conari Press, 1996.

In the following essay, Knight discusses Joan Vollmer Adams Burroughs's seminal role in the evolution of the Beat Generation.

I went back to Mexico City
and saw Joan Burroughs leaning
forward in a garden chair, arms
on her knees. . . .
—Allen Ginsberg, "Dream Record," June 8, 1955

Joan Vollmer Adams Burroughs was seminal in the creation of the Beat revolution; indeed the fires that stoked the Beat engine were started with Joan as patron and muse. Her apartment in New York was a nucleus that attracted many of the characters who played a vital role in the formation of the Beat; those who gathered there included Bill Burroughs, Jack and Edie Kerouac, and Herbert Huncke. Brilliant and well versed in philosophy and literature, Joan was the whetstone against which the main Beat writers—Allen, Jack, and Bill—sharpened their intellect. Widely considered one of the most perceptive people in the group, her strong mind and independent nature helped bulldoze the Beats toward a new sensibility.

Joan paid dearly for her refusal to live within the boundaries of the social mores of forties' and fifties' America, ultimately dying in a horrible accident at the hand of her common-law husband, author William Burroughs. There is no denying, however, that Joan hastened the new consciousness that the Beats espoused in her short time with them. Joan was not an artist or writer, but Bill and others credit her with being a powerful inspiration for their work.

Joan Vollmer grew up in Loudonville, New York, a suburb of Albany. Her father, David Vollmer, managed a large plant and worked hard to provide his family with the best of everything. Joan grew up in an economically privileged world, but wished for a sense of self that money could not buy. She fought with her mother constantly and chafed at the constraints of the household. As soon as she could, she eagerly departed the ritzy world of her family for New York City and Barnard College.

A handsome woman who constantly questioned the status quo, Joan read constantly and enjoyed discussing a wide range of topics, usually while in the bathtub. Her appetite for books was rivaled only by her appetite for men, and she married law student Paul Adams soon after arriving in New York, more an act of defiance than of love. After her marriage, Joan spent her evenings prowling bars like the West End, looking for the company of strangers; Paul had been drafted and was stationed in Tennessee.

Late one night, Joan met a kindred spirit, Edie Parker, during one of her rambles at the West End

Bar and the two soon moved into an apartment at 421 West 118th Street. This was the first in a series of apartments that would provide an open forum for the exchange of new ideas and attitudes, with Joan at the center, a strong and magnetic presence.

Joan and Edie's apartment became a haven for a bunch of Columbia students who were disillusioned with all the starched-collar conservatism of the forties. Edie's boyfriend, Jack Kerouac, who had forsaken a football scholarship at Columbia to pursue his writing, lived there when he was not shipping out with the merchant marines. One of Joan's lovers, a sixteen-year-old Columbia student named John Kingsland, also moved into the apartment, as did Hal Chase, a graduate student from Denver. The atmosphere was both intellectual and chaotic—a nonstop salon with both discourse and dalliance.

Columbia student Lucien Carr began coming around with his girlfriend, Celine Young. He also brought over a Columbia hallmate named Allen Ginsberg. Allen found the open exchange of ideas at Joan's place reassuring, for at the time he was grappling with his sexual identity.

Lucien decided that Allen's mind was ripe for an awakening and brought him downtown one day to meet a friend from St. Louis named William Burroughs. The heir to the Burroughs adding-machine fortune, William Burroughs had graduated from Harvard University in 1936. Allen was bowled over by the enigmatic Bill, a man who dressed in a suit, quoted Shakespeare in a nasal voice, and enjoyed skewering people with his dry wit. With a $200 monthly stipend from his parents, Bill enjoyed exploring the seedy Times Square area for kicks.

Bill started coming up to Joan's place and, although predominantly homosexual, he was intrigued by her quicksilver intellect and love of stirring people up. Joan was attracted to Bill for his brilliant mind, outrageous proclamations, and vaguely sinister air. Bill moved in and the two began their curious marriage of minds.

Bill brought with him a collection of hustlers, petty criminals, and drug dealers, and the uptown and downtown coalesced into an even stranger tableau. Joan and Jack were introduced to Benzedrine by a neighborhood prostitute named Vickie Russell, and Bill started his longtime addiction to heroin. Eventually, Bill and others were arrested for drug use, and Joan ended up in Bellevue, speed-addled and in need of help.

Bill arranged Joan's release from the hospital and they conceived a child soon after. Although never married in a ceremony, the two were never parted again. They moved to New Waverly, Texas, to escape the legal problems that had been plaguing them back in New York. Bill bought a farm—the plan was to make lots of money growing marijuana. Mostly thought, they entertained guests, including their old New York Beat crony Herbert Huncke, who came to "sharecrop," do drugs, and play with guns.

Joan and Bill had a special psychic connection which, friends said, seemed to transcend the normal—Joan had the uncanny ability to receive images that Bill sent to her telepathically. They would sit across the room from each other for hours, playing this psychic game and startling visitors with their amazing associative talent.

Later that year, Joan and Bill were caught in flagrante delicto by a notoriously vigilant sheriff, who charged Bill with drunk driving and public indecency. Rather than deal with more potential problems in the Lone Star state, they moved to New Orleans; Joan had plenty of Benzedrine to fuel her attempts to rake the lizards out of the trees in her new front yard. New Orleans was fine for a while, but once again a drug bust prompted another move. This time they moved to Mexico City to ensure that there would be no more reckoning with U.S. authorities.

Bill enjoyed Mexico because the boys and the heroin were cheap and plentiful; two hundred dollars went considerably farther than it had in the States. Also the *federales* were always willing to overlook a problem if there were some money in it for them. Joan could no longer get Benzedrine and made do with cheap tequila instead. She looked terrible and hinted to friends that her days were numbered.

On September 6, 1951, Joan and Bill were at a party. Everyone had been drinking gin for hours when Bill announced that it was time for the William Tell act. Joan put a water glass on her head and turned her face, saying that she couldn't stand the sight of blood. Bill, a crack shot, took aim from about six feet away. She died instantly, not yet thirty years old.

Bill was able to keep himself out of too much trouble with the help of a good lawyer and spent only thirteen days in jail. But he would forever be haunted by Joan's ghost. He maintained years later that it was an accident, but has also said that there is no such thing as an accident. In either case, he has always maintained that it was Joan's death which has motivated him to write ever since.

Burroughs was not the only Beat to be inspired by Joan. Allen Ginsberg's opus "Howl" was written after a dream of Joan in 1957.

BRENDA KNIGHT (ESSAY DATE 1996)

SOURCE: Knight, Brenda. "Eileen Kaufman: Keeper of the Flame (1922-)." In *Women of the Beat Generation: The Writers, Artists and Muses at the Heart of a Revolution*, pp. 103-14. Berkeley, Calif.: Conari Press, 1996.

In the following essay, Knight reflects on Eileen Kaufman's function as muse and inspiration to her husband, poet Bob Kaufman, an influential leader within the Beat Generation.

"I knew all the Beat writers and artists. Bob was so gregarious that he had friends everywhere. We were like an extended family from coast to coast and all thru Europe and certain grapevine isles and countries throughout the world. It was a joyful time of communication with kindred souls that only was extended when the hippie movement came in. We were precursors of that community, and we were happy to have influenced their loving feeling."

—Eileen Kaufman

As the wife of San Francisco poet Bob Kaufman, Eileen Kaufman passionately took on the role of lover, wife, muse, mother, and personal archivist, a position she maintains to this day. Eileen was an up-and-coming journalist, heading to the top of her profession when she dropped everything to fully embrace the Beat philosophy, poetics, and lifestyle—a decision that changed and still informs her writing.

Revered in Europe as the "black Rimbaud," Bob Kaufman was a shamanic figure, a street bard, and an anarchist. Eileen married him in 1958. "In those early days," she recalls, "I'd accompany Bob and Jack Kerouac to those infamous Blabbermouth Nights in North Beach. There was a bottle of champagne for the winner—the best poet to stand up and improvise—and since either Bob or Jack always won, I always knew I'd be drinking champagne that night."

When Allen Ginsberg, Gregory Corso, Jack Kerouac, Philip Whalen, and Gary Snyder eventually all departed San Francisco, Bob Kaufman remained, becoming the guiding light of the North Beach Beat scene. In the spring of 1959, Eileen, Bob, and Allen founded *Beatitude*, a magazine devoted to unpublished poets, which lasted a year but had a tremendous impact on the poetry community. City Lights first published Bob in a broadside, "Abomunist Manifesto" in 1959, and in 1965 New Directions published his first collection of poems, *Solitudes Crowded With Loneliness.* But more than his writing, it was the force of Bob's presence that had such an impact on the San Francisco poetry scene. A true street poet, Bob was the Diogenes who vigilantly moved through the North Beach corridor seeking fakes to expose and spouting poetry. And Eileen was right by his side, transcribing his oral poems into written form.

By the time his first book appeared, however, Bob had little to do with it. In 1963, in the wake of the Kennedy assassination, he took a vow of silence that lasted ten years, during which time he was sometimes referred to as "the silent guardian of the center." Eileen left with their four-year-old son, Parker, for Mexico, where she prepared *Solitudes* for publication.

Upon her return, Eileen started writing for the *Los Angeles Free Press,* covering the Monterey Pop and Jazz Festivals, and was instrumental in drawing attention to Janis Joplin, Jimi Hendrix, the Doors, and the Grateful Dead. Her articles on the rock-and-roll revolution appeared in the Los Angeles *Oracle, Billboard* magazine, and *Music World Countdown.*

With the election of Richard Nixon, she once again left the country with her son, this time for Europe, where she stayed for four years before returning to San Francisco. In 1973, Bob emerged from his prolonged silence, New Directions published his book *The Ancient Rain,* and in 1976 he and Eileen reunited in a ceremony on Mt. Tamalpais in Marin County.

Ultimately, the Kaufmans separated again. Bob remained in San Francisco, and Eileen left with Parker for Los Angeles, where she worked for a time as a copywriter. In 1980, she moved back to San Francisco, and Bob began his courtship anew. They remained together, on and off, for the next five years.

In 1985, Eileen flew to Paris, where she presented Bob Kaufman's body of work up to 1980 to the Bibliotec Archives at the Sorbonne; the rest of Bob's work that Eileen transcribed is in the Mugar Museum and Library of the Letters section of Boston University. In January 1986, Bob Kaufman died of emphysema. In 1987, Mayor Dianne Feinstein proclaimed "Bob Kaufman Day," and a small street in San Francisco, Harwood Alley, is now called Bob Kaufman Street. Eileen remains, in her words, "the keeper of the flame," traveling the world for Bob Kaufman celebrations, reading both his work and her own.

BRENDA KNIGHT (ESSAY DATE 1996)

SOURCE: Knight, Brenda. "Ruth Weiss: The Survivor (1928-)." In *Women of the Beat Generation: The Writers, Artists and Muses at the Heart of a Revolution,* pp. 241-56. Berkeley, Calif.: Conari Press, 1996.

In the following essay, Knight offers an overview of ruth weiss's life and career.

"A fine funkiness: Beat Generation goddess ruth weiss (she launched the jazz-poetry readings at The Cellar) and trumpeter Cowboy Noyd will have their first reunion since what John Ross calls 'the bad old days' . . ."
—February 15, 1993 item in Herb Caen's column
in the *San Francisco Chronicle*

Austria, 1938. Amid political strife and religious genocide, some Jewish families managed to escape the horror of the Nazi regime. One was ten-year-old ruth weiss, born in Berlin in 1928, who in 1933 escaped with her parents to Vienna, where she began her schooling and wrote her first poem at the age of five. In 1939, on the last train allowed to cross the Austrian border, they fled to Holland to board ship for the United States. Though her immediate family survived, most of ruth's relatives perished in the Nazi concentration camps.

The family's first years in New York were far from their comfortable life in Berlin. ruth's parents, struggling with a new language and long hours with low wages, placed her in a children's home to prevent her from wandering the city streets alone. Even though ruth was eleven at the time, she was so small that she passed for eight, the maximum age for the housing facility. Her parents visited on weekends.

Eventually ruth's family settled in Chicago, where she graduated eighth grade from a Catholic boarding school. During high school, ruth felt alienated from her classmates; she kept to herself and studied hard, graduating in the top 1 percent of her class with high grades in every subject—including all *A*'s in Latin, solid geometry, and English. In 1946, she and her family left their upper-middle-class Jewish neighborhood to return to Germany, where her parents worked as American citizens with the Army of Occupation. She then spent two years in Switzerland at the College

ruth weiss, 1928- .

of Neuchatel, hitchhiking and bicycling through the countryside, learning French, learning to drink, and, as she recalls, "learning little else." ruth wrote several short stories during this period and kept a journal, which she later destroyed. This was to be the only time she ever destroyed her writing.

ruth returned to Chicago with her parents in 1948. This time, she moved into the Art Circle, a rooming house for artists on the Near North Side, where she gave her first reading to jazz in 1949. Shortly thereafter, ruth began her Bohemian wandering, which led to New York's Greenwich Village and the French Quarter in New Orleans. In 1952, she hitchhiked again, this time from Chicago to San Francisco's North Beach, moving into 1010 Montgomery, later occupied by Allen Ginsberg and his last girlfriend, Sheila. ruth wrote poetry in the Black Cat, a bar two blocks away, and she entered the all-night jazz world across town in the Fillmore at Bop City and Jackson's Nook.

Haiku has long been a favorite form of ruth's, and there have been many exhibits of her watercolor haiku. In the early 1950s, when she was living at the Wentley Hotel, Jack Kerouac would stop by. "You write better haiku than I do," he'd say. After a night of writing, talking, and sharing haiku, Neal Cassady would show up, insisting they join him in a drive to Portrero Hill to see the sunrise. ruth fondly recalls the wild ride down "that one lane two-way zig-zag street."

Through a piano player she knew from New Orleans, ruth met many jazz musicians in San Francisco and jammed in their sessions with her poetry. When three of these musicians, Sonny Nelson, Jack Minger, and Wil Carlson, opened The Cellar in North Beach in 1956, ruth joined them onstage, performing her poetry to jazz accompaniment, creating an innovative style whose impact would reverberate throughout the San Francisco art scene.

During this time, ruth published in the majority of the early issues of *Beatitude,* one of the first magazines to give voice to the Beat Generation. Wally Berman also included her in the Mexican issue of *Semina,* a Beat art-and-poetry magazine.

In 1959, ruth returned from traveling the length of Mexico with her first husband, having completed her journal *COMPASS,* which includes an excerpt of her memorable meeting with two close San Francisco friends in Mexico City—poet and photographer Anne McKeever and poet Philip Lamantia. After talking all night in a cafe, they decided to climb the Pyramid of the Sun in the Mayan ruins outside Mexico City and catch the sunrise. Neither guides nor other tourists were there in the predawn chill. The climb to the top of the pyramid was easy, but ruth, paralyzed by a fear of heights, had to be carried all the way down.

That same year, ruth published a book, *GALLERY OF WOMEN,* poem-portraits that included poets Aya (born Idell) Tarlow, Laura Ulewicz, and Anne McKeever, written out of "my respect and admiration for these women with whom I felt a kind of sisterhood."

ruth's first marriage was to artist Mel Weitsman, who studied with artist Clyfford Still. They met in 1953, lived together for a year, split up for a while, and then married in 1957. In 1963, their lives moved in separate directions and they parted as friends. Weitsman went on to become a Zen priest, and ruth kept on with poetry as the central focus of her life. ruth's second marriage, to sculptor Roy Isbell in 1966, lasted less than a year; Roy, imprisoned on a drug charge, was later murdered in prison by guards.

North Beach has always been "home turf" for ruth. Here, in 1967, she met her life partner—artist Paul Blake—at the Capri, a classic North Beach watering hole. During the Vietnam War, Paul was a conscientious objector, and he and ruth went to Los Angeles while he worked his alternative service for two years as an attendant in the psychiatric ward at Los Angeles Country General Hospital. During this time, ruth expanded her artistry beyond the written form and worked with San Francisco artist and filmmaker Steven Arnold, playing major roles in all of his films. Their collaboration received international attention when Arnold's film *Messages Messages* premiered at the Cannes Film Festival in 1969. In the early sixties, ruth, excited by the new wave of films coming out of France, Italy, Sweden, and Japan, began a series of filmpoems and plays, including *FIGS, NO DANCING ALOUD,* and *THE 13TH WITCH.*

Throughout the decades, to support her poetry career, ruth worked at part-time jobs that included waitress, chorus girl, gas station attendant (even though ruth doesn't know how to drive), postal employee, museum cashier, and accountant. Mostly, she worked as a model, sitting for artists and students. In the early 1970s, she tended bar at the Wild Side West, a lesbian bar in San Francisco's Bernal Heights where she did Sunday afternoon poetry readings with her long-time friend, Madeline Gleason. ruth also ran various poetry series in San Francisco, including Minnie's Can-Do Club, Intersection, and a poetry theater, *Surprise Voyage,* at the Old Spaghetti Factory, connecting with many of the younger poets.

In 1981, ruth and Paul moved to Inverness, fifty miles north of San Francisco. A year later, after a flood threatened their lives and their life's work, they moved further north to the small town of Albion in the coastal redwoods. The peaceful surroundings have been good for ruth, and these later years have been some of her most productive. In 1990, ruth won the Bay Area "Poetry Slam" and released *Poetry & Allthatjazz,* volumes 1 and 2, on audio and videocasette, collected from her live performances.

ruth weiss is finally getting the attention she has long deserved. In 1996, *The Brink,* the 1961 film that ruth wrote, directed and narrated with jazz, was screened at The Whitney Museum of American Art during their exhibit *Beat Culture and the New America, 1950-1965,* by the Bancroft Library at the University of California Berkeley's Pacific Film Archive, and at the Venice Biennale Film Festival. The San Francisco Main Public Library held a three-month exhibition of ruth's and Paul's individual work and collaborations over

ON THE SUBJECT OF...

RUTH WEISS

Often referred to as the matriarch of the Beat Generation, ruth weiss has achieved prominence as a poet, playwright, and performance artist in California's San Francisco Bay Area. Unlike many women writers working within the Beat milieu, weiss was viewed as a peer by many of her male counterparts. *Desert Journal,* perhaps her best-known work, contains forty numbered poems, each representing a day's journal entry; the poems were written between 1961 and 1968 and published in 1977. weiss also wrote, directed and narrated the motion picture *The Brink.* The film was screened at the Whitney Museum's 1996 exhibit *Beat Culture and the New America, 1950-1965.*

the past twenty-five years; her work is also in over fifty special collections at universities and libraries across the United States.

And ruth continues to perform. Since their heyday in the fifties, ruth is one of the few Beat poets to have continued reading poetry live in North Beach, proving how she has honed her craft to become one of our finest living poets. She and her jazz collaborators are at The Gathering Caffé on Grant Avenue on the last Monday of every month. For anybody who missed out on the Beat scene the first time around, this is a rare and wonderful opportunity to experience one of the original Beat poets firsthand. To hear ruth weiss read her poetry in a dimly lit coffeehouse in San Francisco's North Beach is to understand why our fascination with the Beat Generation will never die.

As poet Jack Hirschman said, "No American poet has remained so faithful to jazz in the construction of poetry as has ruth weiss. Her poems are scores to be sounded with all her riffy ellipses and open-formed phrasing swarming the senses. Verbal motion becoming harmonious with a universe of rhythm is what her work essentializes. Others read *to* jazz or write *from* jazz. ruth weiss *writes* jazz in words."

JOYCE JOHNSON (ESSAY DATE 1999)

SOURCE: Johnson, Joyce. "Beat Women: A Transitional Generation." In *Beat Culture: The 1950s and Beyond*, edited by Jaap van der Bent, Mel van Elteren, and Cornelis A. van Minnen, pp. 211-19. Amsterdam: VU University Press, 1999.

In the following essay, Johnson provides a first-hand account of the experiences of women—and discusses the various roles they played—as part of the Beat Generation.

In 1922, my nineteen-year-old mother Rosalind Ross went on the road. For nearly a year, in her family's effort to improve her marital prospects, she was shipped from cousin to cousin—from Cleveland, Ohio to Baton Rouge, Louisiana; from Baton Rouge to Little Rock, Arkansas; from Little Rock to Los Angeles, California. She was the youngest and prettiest of three sisters, a proud and withdrawn girl who dreamed of singing Schubert on the stage of Carnegie Hall. My aunts, who were in their early thirties still lived with their mother in Bensonhurst; one was a bookkeeper, the other a stenographer. They had no prospects whatsoever. "Stay away as long as you can," my mother's eldest sister Anna wrote her. "There's nothing for you here." My mother saw the Grand Canyon and posed for a snapshot outside the gates of the Fox Pathé studio, but she returned to Brooklyn without a proposal. She gave up her voice lessons and became a secretary. Ten years later she married my father, an auditor in a tobacco firm. In 1935, when I was born, her brother Uda wrote her: "At last you have something of your own!"

After my mother died, I found a small manuscript typed on onion skin among her papers. It was a record one of my childless aunts had kept of entertaining episodes from my earliest years. I was interested to learn that at age four, I had developed an adventurous streak and had persistently agitated to be allowed to cross our street on my own and go to the candy store on the opposite corner. My mother's response to me, which my aunt also jotted down, seemed so characteristic that I had the sensation of recalling it word for word: "Why would you want to do that? There's nothing there." It seemed to epitomize our lifelong conflict. My need for experience that inescapably involved risk; her need to insist there was nothing out there in order to keep me tied to her.

My mother chose the all-girls schools I attended in New York City—Hunter High School and Barnard College. In the late forties and early fifties, they were rather grim institutions in which bright girls were rigorously educated in ironic preparation for limited futures. Except for an aged elevator operator, not one male was visible inside the grey Gothic building that housed Hunter High. Within the conventlike precincts, however, there were adolescent nonconformists. Red diaper babies who marched in Mayday parades, lesbians who were having affairs with their teachers. Audre Lorde and Diane DiPrima, two sixteen-year-old poets who would later make their mark, were running *Argus,* the Hunter literary magazine, where I published my first story. Diane was then writing imitative rhymed verse, but Audre wowed us all in that era of Bomb consciousness with her daring riposte to T. S. Eliot: "This is how the world ends. / Not with a whimper but with a BANG!"

My rebellion began at thirteen with my first sip of that forbidden beverage coffee in a diner two blocks from Hunter. Soon I was sneaking off to Greenwich Village on Sunday afternoons with my classmate Maria Meiff. We played the guitar and sang folksongs in Washington Square Park with a bohemian crowd that was much too old for us, but actually quite harmless. We peered in the windows of bars like the San Remo and Fugazzi's, which were hangouts of Allen Ginsberg, Jack Kerouac, and other subterraneans at the time. We seemed condemned to be observers, shielded from what we considered "real life" by our embarrassing jailbait status. Yet we had inklings that real life could be a scary proposition. A black ex-convict named Billy became obsessed with Maria, who looked seventeen; Maria was rather fascinated by the situation, but refused to go out for coffee with him in the Waldorf cafeteria unless I came along for protection. One Sunday Billy started following us when we left Washington Square; we gave him the slip by ducking into Minetta Lane. There we saw a man bashing another man's head against the curb; blood was everywhere. We ran away to the uptown subway as fast as we could, but I knew that what we had just seen was good material. I wrote up the fight in a paper for my English class and got a C. "Write about what you know," the teacher reprimanded me in red ink.

What did "real life" mean to a middle-class adolescent girl in 1950? I yearned for it and thought I would recognize it when I saw it, but could not quite define it. I was sure real life was sexual, though my ignorance of sex was profound. Since no information could be extracted from grownups, and my friends knew little more than I did, I pursued my forbidden research in the dictionary and in the steamy passages of historical novels, trying to connect the dots. At fifteen, I probably knew less than the average eight-year-old of today. Until I entered Barnard College in 1951 and took a freshman course called Modern Living, I did not have a very clear idea of how babies were born, nor did many of my classmates. I would meet Jack Kerouac only six years later.

The postwar period was an age of enforced innocence in America. Ground that women had won in the Jazz Age and during the war years was suddenly gone, as if society had deliberately contracted amnesia. Women who had worked were now relegated to the home, and girls were sent to college to get their Mrs. Sexual intercourse was reserved for married couples. It was unusual in the early fifties for a young woman to get her own apartment, and if she did, it was a sign that she would be up to no good there. The only proper way for a girl to achieve independence from her family was to put herself under the protection of a husband.

In a journal entry written in September of 1951, when she was a sophomore at Smith College, Sylvia Plath voiced the despair and frustration that many rebellious young women felt:

> . . . I have come to the conclusion that I *must* have a passionate physical relationship with someone—or combat the great sex urge in me by chastic means. I chose the former answer. I also admitted that I am obligated in a way to my family and to society (damn society anyway) to follow certain absurd and traditional customs—for my own security they tell me. I must therefore confine the major part of my life to one human being of the opposite sex. . . .

For unmarried young women sex was more than adventure, more than a broadening of experience; it was a high risk act with sometimes fatal consequences, given the inadequacy of birth control. To get a diaphragm in those days from the Margaret Sanger Clinic, an unmarried woman would have to appear wearing a wedding ring (purchased at the Five and Ten) and be prepared to fill out a form detailing the number of times a week she had intercourse with her fictitious husband. "Don't discuss your marriage with your classmates," a friend of mine who married at nineteen was warned by a dean at her college.

For fifties women, all this repression made sex a very charged and anxious thing. You were breaking the rules. You could lose your place in the world, you could even lose your life. With so much at stake, feelings became very heightened. In contrast, relationships between young people in the nineties seem so easily entered into and so casually ended, that the novel of love, as Vivian Gornick has noted, is dying out.

The neighborhood around Columbia University and Barnard College was the birthplace of the Beat Generation, the meeting ground in the early forties of Jack Kerouac, Allen Ginsberg, William Burroughs, and Lucien Carr. The group included two unusually adventurous young women—Edie Parker, Kerouac's first wife, and Joan Vollmer Adams, who had a common-law marriage with Burroughs. As I would be in the next decade, both were drawn to charismatic men who lived the larger lives denied to women, and offered them little in the way of security or protection. Edie was from an affluent Grosse Pointe, Michigan, family; when her mother discovered that her daughter and Kerouac were living in sin in Joan Adams's apartment, Edie's checks from home were cut off. Determined to stay on in New York with Jack come what may, Edie worked as a longshoreman for eighteen months loading Liberty ships; after that she worked as a cigaret girl in Twenty-one, earning $27.50 a week. Some of her earnings went to supporting Jack and other early members of the Beat circle who crashed in Joan Adams's famous apartment.

When Edie Parker was nineteen and Kerouac was away at sea, she discovered she was pregnant. Edie knew Jack's fear of familial responsibility, so she had a horrendous abortion by forced labor at five months in the kitchen of a Bronx apartment; the baby, a perfectly formed boy, was dropped into a bucket. Edie survived, but was never able to have children. Joan paid even more heavily for the chances she took. She went too willingly where Burroughs led her—she accepted his homosexuality, followed him into experimentation with drugs and became addicted to benzedrine; she died in 1951, when her husband attempted to shoot a cocktail glass off her head and missed. Like Carolyn Cassady, who later married Kerouac's friend Neal, these forties women seemed content to define themselves as wives of geniuses. Although Joan was said to be brilliant and could hold her own in intellectual discussions with the men, she left behind no writings of her own.

Edie Parker did not read any of Kerouac's novels until after his death in 1969; she was surprised to find bits of herself all through his work—from *The Town and the City* through *Vanity of Duluoz*. She remained married to Kerouac in her mind even years after they had split up. When she looked me up in the eighties, she told me that she believed Jack would have ultimately returned to her and that the annulment of their marriage in 1945 had never been valid. "Do you know who you look like?" she asked me, as we sat in the

Chinese restaurant where we had agreed to meet. "Didn't Jack ever tell you? You look just like Joan!"

Like Edie and Joan before us, Elise Cowen and I were a disaffected duo, neither of us quite fitting in at Barnard. We both found the austere, rather militaristic brand of feminism preached by Dean Millicent McintoshQuite useless and unappealing. The dean made much of the fact that she had been a commander of the Waves during the war. She inveighed against promiscuity and sexual experimentation. Women were to remain chaste until marriage, and if they worked at a job, no allowances were to be made for any special needs they might have. For those who were especially ambitious to prove they could do a man's job, the Waves had a recruiting office right on campus. McIntosh's success as a superwoman seemed unduplicatable—dean of Barnard, married to a medical specialist, mother of five. In her freshman orientation course, Modern Living, she somehow neglected to tell us about the household help she must have had, the boarding schools her children were sent to.

Like me, Elise had hung around in the Village and was attracted to what we then called bohemianism. I had entered college at sixteen; Elise was two years older. The summer before her freshman year, she had actually gone all the way with a boy she was crazy about, who had rejected her soon after—a pattern in Elise's relationships. Nice young men found Elise offputting. She was too intellectual, too intense; eruptions of acne flared on her face like evidence of her seething emotions. Elise cared little about making herself pretty. She would stand in a corner at a freshman dance defiantly rolling her own cigarets. The aspirations she had, she kept to herself. She was obsessed with T.S. Eliot, but majored in psych. I would show her the stories I was writing, but she would never show me her poems. "I'm a *mediocre*," she told me, pronouncing the word in an odd hollow French way.

The Beats have often been accused of having no respect for creative women. But in truth this lack of respect was so pervasive in American culture in the postwar years that women did not even question it. One exception was Elizabeth Hardwick, who wrote in "The American Woman as Snow Queen," an essay published in *The Prospect Before Us* in 1955, about the contempt of male intellectuals for what she called "the culture-hungry woman." In his posthumous memoir, *When Kafka Was the Rage,* the critic Anatole Broyard, a contemporary of Kerouac's who was very jealous of the Beat writers' success, complained

about girls "who wore their souls," like "negligées they took off." No wonder an intellectual young woman like Elise felt so little confidence.

I felt surer than Elise about what I wanted to be. Certainly I would write—it was the only thing I was good at—though my belief in my powers could momentarily be deflated by a cutting remark from a man. "Quite the little existentialist, aren't we?" a male professor wrote sneeringly on one of my papers. Another teacher, John Kouwenhoven, who had just made his reputation as a critic of popular culture, told a roomful of girls that if they really wanted to be writers, they would not even be enrolled in his class—they would be out in America hopping freight trains. Since it was inconceivable in 1953 that a young woman would open herself up to such experience, and since all we had to write about was what Kouwenhoven called our "boring little lives," there was obviously no hope for us. I remember feeling angry and confused, yet the notion of challenging the professor's remark seemed unthinkable. A few years later, during my relationship with Kerouac, I found an unexpected source of encouragement when I showed him the novel I was working on. Jack was critical only of the way I was arranging my life. Instead of wasting so much of my time on the dreary secretarial jobs that supported me, why did not I go for broke the way he had—see the world, put all my energy into writing, try to become great. I could not respond to his question; the answer was too humiliating: Because I was a woman. Because I did not see how I could survive without a safety net. Yet, oddly enough, I never expected that a man would provide me with one.

In some important ways my upbringing had been rather unconventional. My mother had grown up in a fatherless household; her sisters had gotten their first jobs when they were in their teens. She always told me I would have to make my own way in the world. My mother mistakenly believed I would eventually write musical comedies that would be produced on Broadway and advised me to defer marriage (in other words, to continue living under her thumb) until I had established this career. Meanwhile I might have to work in offices, so she enrolled me one summer in a secretarial course where I learned typing and shorthand. These were the skills that later kept me afloat. My mother did not realize that she had equipped me to leave her, that I was only biding my time.

By nature I was rebellious but innately cautious, never questioning the need for a safety net of my own making. Elise proved to be more like Kerouac—unable to find one, not even really trying to.

It was Elise who eventually led me to the Beats, first by introducing me to her experimental psychology instructor Donald Cook, who had been a classmate of Allen Ginsberg's. Donald had a shabby groundfloor apartment near Columbia where the door was always open—interesting people who later became literary figures kept passing through: John Hollander, Richard Howard, Robert Gottleib, Allen Ginsberg, even William Burroughs. The phonograph played jazz and Mahler. There were trips to Birdland, solemn experimentation with smoking grass. Elise began sleeping with Donald, painfully accepting the fact that he was not hung up on her. But she would soon fall in love much more deeply with Allen Ginsberg—at last she had found someone who could read her soul. She would remain in love with Allen—a one-sided passion—until her suicide in 1962. Allen who was still painfully working out his sexual identity saw in Elise a resemblance to his mother Naomi that both attracted and disturbed him.

In 1952, Elise and I read John Clellon Holmes's article "This Is the Beat Generation" with great excitement, recognizing the name John Kerouac that we had heard in Donald's apartment, and finding a stirring affirmation of our own sense of being outsiders.

"There are those who believe that in generations such as this," wrote Holmes, "there is always the constant possibility of a great new moral idea, conceived in desperation, coming to life. Others note the self-indulgence, the waste, the apparent social irresponsibility, and disagree. But its ability to keep its eyes open, and yet avoid cynicism; its ever-increasing conviction that the problem of modern life is essentially a spiritual problem; and that capacity for sudden wisdom which people who live hard and go far, possess, are assets and bear watching."

We too were going to "live hard and go far." Surely this Beat Generation was the one we really belonged in, not the grey, bottled-up Silent one. Soon we read Holmes's novel *Go*, fascinated by the Dostoevskian intensity generated by Holmes's "boy gang," but we were incapable of asking ourselves why Holmes's female characters were always relegated to the back seat. That sort of analysis would have to wait until the next decade.

For some doctrinaire feminists in our own time *On the Road* has been a deceptively easy target. Choosing to ignore the social context in which *On the Road* was written, they deplore the *macho* posturing of Dean and Sal and the way Kerouac depicts their transient, totally irresponsible sexual relationships with women. Reading Kerouac now, they find nothing in his work that speaks to female readers. Yet, in 1957 when *On the Road* was published, thousands of fifties women experienced a powerful response to what they read. *On the Road* was prophecy, bringing the news of the oncoming, unstoppable sexual revolution—the revolution that would precede and ultimately pave the way for women's liberation. It was a book that dared to show that men too were fed up with their traditional roles. It suggested that you could choose—choose to be unconventional, choose to experiment, choose to open yourself up to a broad range of experience, instead of simply duplicating the lifestyle of your parents.

Kerouac seemed to realize how mired in the status quo women were; he saw the intrinsic sadness in lives of quiet desperation. "What do you want out of life?" Sal Paradise asks the pretty little waitress Rita Bettencourt who is "tremendously frightened of sex." "'I don't know,' she said. 'Just wait on tables and try to get along.' She yawned. I put my hand over her mouth and told her not to yawn. I tried to tell her how excited I was about life. . . ." Later Sal asks the same question of a country girl in Michigan. "I wanted to take her and wring it out of her. She didn't have the slightest idea what she wanted. She mumbled of jobs, movies, going to her grandmother's for the summer, wishing she could go to New York and visit the Roxy, what kind of outfit she would wear. . . . She was eighteen and most lovely and lost."

When I read these passages in late August of 1957, I thought of my mother and her sisters, but Kerouac's lost girls did not remind me of myself and it was Sal with his passionate impatience with the status quo whom I identified with.

By then I had begun my relationship with Kerouac, but even before that, I had had my immersion in real life. I had defied my parents to have a painful affair with Donald Cook, left home, broken with my family, found jobs, had an abortion and had my first taste of despair. Still, I would not have turned back if given the choice. At twenty-one I felt I had gone to the bottom and floated up; I had the lightness of feeling there was nothing left to lose, so I had let Kerouac come home with me the first night I met him. Quite the little existentialist, as my Barnard professor once wrote. Or perhaps my state of mind approached the original definition of Beat.

"Come on down, I'm waiting for you," Jack had written to me from Mexico City that July. "Don't go to silly Frisco. First place, I have this fine earthquake-proof room for 85 cents a night for both of us, it's an Arabic magic room with tiles on the walls and many big round whorehouse sexorgy mirrors (it's an old 1910 whorehouse, solid with marble floors)—we can sleep on the big clean double bed, have our private bath . . . it's right downtown, we can enjoy city life to the hilt then when we get tired of our Magian inwardness sultan's room we can go off to the country and rent a cottage with flowerpots in the window— Your money will last you 5 times longer & in Frisco you wouldn't be seeing anything *new & foreign & strange*—Take the plane to Mexico City (bus too long, almost as expensive too), then take a cab to my hotel, knock my door, we'll be gay friends wandering arm-in-arm. . . ."

How could I resist such an invitation? I immediately quit my secretarial job at Farrar, Straus and Cudahy and gave up my apartment. Jack and I were going to live forever on the five-hundred dollar advance I had just gotten from an editor at Random House for my first novel, but unfortunately I did not move fast enough. By the time I was ready to leave for Mexico City, Jack, too depressed and shaky to stay alone in that sultan's room, was on his way to his mother's house in Florida. From there he wrote me asking for a loan of thirty dollars, so that he could take a bus to New York in time for the publication of *On the Road*. Being a witness to Jack's collision with sudden, unexpected fame would soon turn into one of the most profoundly educational experiences of my life.

Looking at Beat women in a paper she read at the 1994 Beat Conference at New York University, Alix Kates Shulman saw merely passivity, pathos and victimization. Of course, she did not take into consideration the heady excitement of taking part in the cultural revolution ushered in by the Beats. Nor did she acknowledge the courage required to venture into what was then new territory for women. As Hettie Jones put it succinctly in her memoir *How I Became Hettie Jones*, "Sex hadn't made us *bad*." Hettie had dared to cross the color line to marry the poet LeRoi Jones. Her family considered her dead. Like Elise, Hettie would become my comrade and close friend; years before the concept of sisterhood became fashionable, we found in each other the emotional support we could not get from our men or our parents. "We shared what was most important to us," Hettie

wrote, "common assumptions about our uncommon lives. We lived outside, as if. As if we were men? As if we were newer, freer versions of ourselves?"

In our downtown scene in the East Village there was an interesting role reversal going on— women were often the breadwinners so the men would be free to pursue their creative work. I had a taste of this the first night I met Kerouac, when I bought him frankfurters and beans at Howard Johnson's because he was absolutely broke. I had never done such a thing before. Interestingly enough, it did not make me feel exploited but strangely grown-up. During our relationship whenever he passed through New York, each of the three apartments I lived in from 1957 through 1958 served as a base for him. Homelessness had become Jack's way of life; even the house he bought in 1958 with his royalties from *On the Road* was more his mother's than his.

In the LeRoi Jones household, it was Hettie who paid the rent. Her small salary from her job as editorial assistant at *Partisan Review* not only supported her husband, but fed numerous other young writers who hung out at their apartment in Chelsea, which rapidly turned into a Beat salon. On what was left over, Hettie and LeRoi published the literary magazine *Yugen*.

"It's perfectly possible to live with a male chauvinist and not be oppressed," Joanna McClure, whose husband Michael was one of the leading figures in the San Francisco Renaissance, observed in 1982 on a women's panel at the Kerouac Conference in Boulder, Colorado. It all came down to what kind of male chauvinist you were with. The men Hettie and I found suffocating were the bourgeois, conventional ones. Men like LeRoi and Jack somehow gave us the breathing space we needed. "You'll end up in Mamaroneck with Marjorie Morningstar," a lawyer boyfriend of Hettie's had once predicted. "What unforeseen catastrophe would send me up the river," she had wondered, "to decorate a home in Westchester?"

"But you *suffered*!" I can imagine a feminist critic like Shulman interrupting accusingly. "Don't forget that!" Yes indeed we suffered. We were poor, sometimes even hungry; we had holes in our black stockings and wore thrift shop clothes; whenever Consolidated Edison turned off the electricity, we were plunged into darkness. At times we were frightened. We had orphaned ourselves by becoming "bad women," so we had no one to fall back on. We took terrible chances with our bodies when we had illegal abortions. We were afraid our restless men would leave us, and usually they did, even when we tried to put up with their affairs. Most of us never got the chance to literally go on the road. Our road instead became the strange lives we were leading. We had actually *chosen* these difficult lives for good reasons; we had not fallen into them by default, or been kidnapped into fifth-floor walkups in the East Village. We could not take on the task of transforming relationships between men and women because it took such an overwhelming amount of effort to come as far as we had; our most consuming struggle was the break with the mores of our parents' generation. We experienced the thrill of being part of a movement that changed life in America, and we endured the hard times that came with making something new. Many of us discovered we were tougher and more resilient than we had imagined we could be.

Would Hettie have become a writer herself if her marriage had not broken up? How long would I have lasted as Mrs. Jack Kerouac, coping with Jack's heartbreaking alcoholism and his jealous *mémère*? Sometimes the unhappy endings of love stories turn out to be the right ones.

The subject of Beat women is currently rather fashionable. Two anthologies of the women's writings have recently been published, and I keep hearing about scholars who are working on papers. There is particular attention paid to Elise Cowen, but too much of it is morbidly centered upon her suicide, as if she is the prime victim even the admirers of Beat Women have been looking for. In *Women of the Beat*, Brenda Knight improves upon the victim story by coming up with a fictitious detail: in her version, Elise jumps *through* a locked window in her parents' living room as if simply jumping out that window were not enough.

Elise was remarkable because of her intellect, her absolute honesty and her capacity for devoted friendship. The poems she left behind are rough and unfinished but have the power that comes when a writer holds nothing back. Elise's obsessive love for Allen Ginsberg set her on an impossible course—as if she had to prove herself worthy of him by living as he did. She even emulated him sexually—entering into an affair with a Barnard classmate when Allen became involved with Peter Orlovsky. I remember feeling very worried about her in 1957 when she set off for San Francisco on a Greyhound bus with only a few dollars in her pocket. As usual she was unable to hold a job. She

ended up in a skidrow hotel in North Beach and came to grief when she found she needed an abortion and could not afford one. By the time she found a psychiatrist who signed the papers permitting her to have a clinical abortion, she was six months pregnant. The operation was traumatic for her.

Elise had been subject to depression even back when I first met her and had slit her wrists when we were in our junior year at Barnard. She had a toxic relationship with her parents, especially with her father who was far too emotionally involved with her. She began taking speed around 1960 and deteriorated very quickly. Her parents had her committed to a mental hospital and then had her released in their custody even though she was far from stable. In our last conversation, she spoke of radios listening in on her; her parents were planning to take her to Miami Beach, of all places. A few weeks later, I heard about her death.

"I wonder how I'll wear my hair when I'm thirty," I remember Elise saying. But she never found out. I have often thought Elise was born too soon. In a time with more tolerance for nonconformist behavior in women she might even have survived. Elise could never conceal what she was. She could never put on a mask as I did and pass in and out of the straight world.

When I was writing my memoir *Minor Characters*, I went, for research purposes, to the twenty-fifth reunion of my Barnard class of 1955. Few of the renegades I had known were there. Most of the women present had followed the traditional fifties path, marrying soon after or even during college, becoming housewives in the suburbs. Some, judging by their nametags, had married two or three times. Now with their children grown, they were wondering how to get into the job market. They had difficulty describing themselves—"I live in Scarsdale," they would say, or "I have a son at Yale." One of them went up to one of the few members of the class who had never married, peered at the single name on her nametag, and said, "What's the matter? Didn't anyone *like* you?" These women looked old to me. How had vibrant girls turned into these matrons? I felt grateful that I had escaped this fate.

I thought of Elise as I stood on the Barnard lawn drinking punch. When the 1955 yearbook was passed around, I looked for her picture. I found a blank rectangle with her name printed underneath.

FURTHER READING

Criticism

Campbell, James. "The Birth of the Beatnik." In *This is the Beat Generation: New York-San Francisco-Paris*, pp. 245-71. London: Secker & Warburg, 1999.

Discusses the commercialization of the Beat Generation.

Clark, David K. "Knowledge of Reality." In *The Pantheism of Alan Watts*, pp. 49-64. Downers Grove, Ill.: Inter-Varsity Press, 1978.

Explains the satori, *or insight into mystical experience, in the context of Alan Watts's interpretation of Zen beliefs.*

Cook, Bruce. "Beatniks and Hipsters." In *The Beat Generation*, pp. 91-101. New York: Charles Scribner's Sons, 1971.

Traces the development of the Beat Generation, focusing particularly on the reception Beat writing received in traditional media.

Davidson, Michael. "From Margin to Mainstream: Postwar Poetry and the Politics of Containment." *American Literary History* 10, no. 2 (summer 1998): 266-90.

An analysis of the relationship between Beat poets and their writing and the American cultural mainstream.

Eburne, Jonathan Paul. "Trafficking in the Void: Burroughs, Kerouac, and the Consumption of Otherness." *Modern Fiction Studies* 43, no. 1 (1997): 53-92.

Examines Burrough's Naked Lunch *and Kerouac's* The Subterraneans *as examples of Beat literature that challenged notions of censorship and social norms in contemporary America.*

Ellwood, Robert S., Jr. "Zen Journeys to the West." In *Alternative Altars: Unconventional and Eastern Spirituality in America*, pp. 136-66. Chicago: University of Chicago Press, 1979.

Provides an overview of Zen Buddhism and its impact on several intellectuals of the Beat Generation, including Jack Kerouac and Alan Watts.

Ferguson, Robert. *Henry Miller: A Life.* New York: W. W. Norton, 1991, 391 p.

Biography of Henry Miller.

Gilmour, Peter. "Blessed are the Beatniks." *U.S. Catholic* 64, no. 3 (March 1999): 7.

Explains the meaning of the term beatitude *and provides an overview of Kerouac's* On the Road.

Gottesman, Ronald, ed. *Critical Essays on Henry Miller.* New York: G. K. Hall & Co., 1992, 411 p.

Collection of critical essays on the life and work of Henry Miller.

Harries-Jones, Peter. *A Recursive Vision: Ecological Understanding and Gregory Bateson.* Toronto: University of Toronto Press, 1995, 358 p.

Full-length critical study of Bateson's work.

Harris, Oliver. "Queer Shoulders, Queer Wheel: Homosexuality and Beat Textual Politics." In *Beat Culture: The 1950s and Beyond*, edited by Cornelis A. van Minnen, Jaap van der Bent, and Mel van Elteren, pp. 221-40. Amsterdam: VU University Press, 1999.

Recounts the role of homosexuals and homosexuality in relation to both the Beat Generation and American politi-

cal ideology during the Cold War; in addition, he examines the different literary approaches to homosexuality taken by Ginsberg, Kerouac, and Burroughs.

Hays, Peter L. "The Danger of Henry Miller." *Arizona Quarterly* 27, no. 3 (autumn 1971): 251-8.

Outlines the limitations and contradictions of Henry Miller's work.

Hynes, Sam. "The Beat and the Angry." *Commonweal* (29 August 1958): 559-61.

Explores reasons for the rise of the Beat Generation, identifying it as a phenomenon that is more static than rebellious.

Kimball, Roger. "A Gospel of Emancipation." *New Criterion* 16, no. 1 (September 1997): 4-11.

Characterizes the Beat Generation as an unconventional rebellion that evolved into an established movement of opposition and chaos.

Lardas, John. Introduction to *The Bop Apocalypse: The Religious Visions of Kerouac, Ginsberg, and Burroughs*, pp. 3-32. Urbana: University of Illinois Press, 2001.

Traces the social, political, and historical reasons that set the stage for the emergence of the Beat connection with religion and spirituality.

Leary, Timothy and Bill Moseley. "Still Crazy after All These Years." *Psychology Today* 28, no. 1 (January-February 1995): 30ff.

Interview with Timothy Leary in his Beverly Hills home.

Lott, Tim. "A Guru for Those Who Doesn't Trust Guru's." *New Statesman* 128, no. 4451 (30 August 1999): 24.

Brief overview of Alan Watts's life, work, and philosophy.

Mahoney, Stephen. "The Prevalence of Zen." *Nation* (1 November 1958): 311-15.

Review of Kerouac's The Dharma Bums *and Watts's* Nature, Man, and Woman.

May, Rollo. "Gregory Bateson and Humanistic Psychology." In *About Bateson*, edited by John Brockman, pp. 75-99. New York: E. P. Dutton, 1977.

Considers Bateson's contribution to the theory of humanistic psychology.

Maynard, John Arthur. Introduction to *Venice West: The Beat Generation in Southern California*, pp. 1-21. New Brunswick, N.J.: Rutgers University Press, 1991.

Chronicles the rise of the Beat Generation in southern California, especially the area around Hollywood and Los Angeles.

McWilliams, Wilson Carey. "The Beats." In *The California Dream*, edited by Dennis Hale and Jonathan Eisen, pp. 293-7. New York: Collier Books, 1968.

Commentary on the Beat Generation.

Phillips, Rod. "Introduction: 'Forest Beatniks' and 'Urban Thoreaus.'" In *"Forest Beatniks" and "Urban Thoreaus": Gary Snyder, Jack Kerouac, Lew Welch, and Michael McClure*, pp. 1-27. New York: Peter Lang, 2000.

Ppresents an overview of the Beat counterculture in the context of their impact on environmental issues, tracing these concerns in their writing and poetry.

Polsky, Ned. "The Village Beat Scene: Summer 1960." In *Hustlers, Beats, and Others*, pp. 150-85. Chicago: ALDINE, 1967.

Offers an account of Greenwich Village and its surroundings during the height of the Beat Generation.

Prebish, Charles C. "Beat Zen." In *American Buddhism*, pp. 22-7. North Scituate, Mass.: Duxbury Press, 1979.

Overview of the Zen Buddhist movement in America during the 1950s.

Riedlinger, Thomas J. "Existential Transactions at Harvard: Timothy Leary's Humanistic Psychotherapy." *Journal of Humanistic Psychology* 33, no. 3 (summer 1993): 6-18.

Synopsis of Leary's research in the field of existential-transactional psychotherapy.

Roszak, Theodore. "The Counterfeit Infinity: The Use and Abuse of Psychedelic Experience." In *The Making of a Counter Culture: Reflections on the Technocratic Society and Its Youthful Opposition*, pp. 155-77. Garden City, N.Y.: Doubleday & Company, Inc., 1969.

Questions the authenticity of the scientific gains made by psychedelic and hallucinogenic experiments during the 1950s.

Smith, Richard Cándida. "The Beat Phenomenon: Masculine Paths of Maturation." In *Utopia and Dissent: Art, Poetry, and Politics in California*, pp. 145-71. Berkeley: University of California Press, 1995.

Investigates Kerouac and Ginsberg's works in light of their interpretation of gender roles in society.

Snyder, Gary. "Buddhism and the Possibilities of a Planetary Culture." In *Beat Down to Your Soul: What Was the Beat Generation?* edited by Ann Charters, pp. 524-8. New York: Penguin Books, 2001.

Overview of Mahayana Buddhism.

Stuart, David. "The Quality of Gravity." In *Alan Watts*, pp. 225-31. Radnor, Pa.: Chilton Book Company, 1976.

Appraisal of Alan Watts's continuing influence on and teaching of Zen.

Tytell, John. "The Beat Generation and the Continuing American Revolution." *American Scholar* 42, no. 2 (spring 1973): 308-17.

Proposes that the writers of the Beat Generation offered a humanistic ideology that formed the basis of American writing in the 1960s and later.

———. "The Beat Legacy." *Beat Culture: The 1950s and Beyond*, edited by Cornelis A. van Minnen, Jaap van der Bent, and Mel van Elteren, pp. 269-74. Amsterdam: VU University Press, 1999.

Traces the impact of specific Beat Generation figures and their literature on later works and events.

———. "Allen Ginsberg and the Messianic Tradition." In *Naked Angels: The Lives and Literature of the Beat Generation*, pp. 212-57. New York: McGraw Hill Book Company, 1976.

Detailed analysis of Ginsberg's poetry.

van der Bent, Jaap. "'Holy Amsterdam Holy Paris': The Beat Generation in Europe." *Beat Culture: The 1950s and Beyond*, edited by Cornelis A. van Minnen, Jaap van der Bent, and Mel van Elteren, pp. 49-60. Amsterdam: VU University Press, 1999.

Examines the reactions of French, English, German, and Dutch writers to the Beats.

van Elteren, Mel. "The Culture of the Subterraneans: A Sociological View of the Beats." *Beat Culture: The 1950s and Beyond*, edited by Cornelis A. van Minnen, Jaap van der Bent, and Mel van Elteren, pp. 63-92. Amsterdam: VU University Press, 1999.

Examines the social behavior of the Beats, which stressed primitivism, spontaneity, and unconventionality.

———. "The Subculture of the Beats: A Sociological Revisit." *Journal of American Culture* 22, no. 3 (fall 1999): 71-100.

An overview of Beat culture, including a historical and sociological summary of Beat practices and influence.

Watts, Alan. "Beat Zen, Square Zen, and Zen." *Chicago Review* 42, no. 3-4 (1996): 48-55.

Watts explains the difficulty faced by Anglo-Saxons in absorbing the principles of Zen.

THE BEAT "SCENE": EAST AND WEST

The settings in which the formative events of the Beat Generation took place included coffeehouses, bars, colleges, and nightclubs of New York City and San Francisco. These were the establishments where students—aspiring artists, poets, and writers—from Columbia University, the University of California at Berkeley, Portland's Reed College, and North Carolina's Black Mountain College gathered to meet other writers and artists, formulating the ideas and philosophies that would form the basis of the post-World War II American countercultural landscape. It was in such intimate venues as the San Remo bar, the Peace Eye Bookstore, and St. Mark's Church in New York City, as well as the Cellar Bar, the Coffee Gallery, the Poetry Center, and the City Lights Bookstore in the North Beach section of San Francisco, that influential friendships were forged, ideas were exchanged, and poetry readings were performed. Soon the movement began to spread to other regions, and the life-styles and values espoused in the poetry and fiction of the Beat Generation began to appear in mainstream American art and music.

The bohemian communities of San Francisco's North Beach area and New York City's Greenwich Village were already well established by the time the quintessential Beats Allen Ginsberg, William Burroughs, and Jack Kerouac became acquainted at Columbia University in 1944. The post-World War II culture of Harlem, New York, recalling the Harlem Renaissance of the 1920s, spawned a new society of black citizens known as "hipsters." These African Americans sought to intentionally differentiate themselves from white Americans rather than seeking to imitate them to gain acceptance and status. Soon white musicians, such as Mezz Mezzrow, who became familiar with the world of the "hipster" through their associations with black jazz musicians, began "talking jive" and smoking marijuana with other culturally marginalized, white musicians and artists. Mezzrow's 1946 autobiography, *Really the Blues,* was popular among New York City-area college students (including Ginsberg, Kerouac, and Burroughs) and is credited with introducing the "hipster culture" to those outside of the world of jazz music. Malcolm X, in his *Autobiography of Malcolm X,* recalled that "A few of the white men around Harlem, younger ones whom we called 'hippies,' acted more Negro than Negroes."

On the opposite coast of the United States, in San Francisco, was a thriving community of radical politics and counterculture sensibilities. San Francisco had historically served as a haven for conscientious objectors and other anti-war activists; during World War II, the Bay area was home to active, well-supported chapters of the War Resisters League and the Fellowship of Reconciliation. Within this culture of civil disobedience, Ruth Witt-Diamant established the Poetry Center at San Francisco State College, drawing some of the country's most innovative poets, including

Kenneth Rexroth, Robert Duncan, Lew Welch, and Philip Lamantia. Eventually other, like-minded literary figures sought out the Bay area, including William Everson (a known radical political activist, who began writing columns for *Catholic World* under the pseudonym Brother Antoninus), Michael McClure, Philip Whalen, Gary Snyder, and Lawrence Ferlinghetti, founder of City Lights Bookstore and publishing firm. Visual artists, such as Jay DeFeo, Joan Brown, Wallace Berman, and Bruce Conner, also thrived in this community. The setting for their creative pursuits had been established by Jackson Pollock and other abstract artists, as well as Douglas MacAgy, Ansel Adams, and Edward Corbett, who made the California School of Fine Arts a hub of abstract-expressionist art in America.

While attending Columbia University in New York City during the 1940s, Ginsberg and Burroughs were introduced to each other by their mutual friend Lucien Carr, who had also introduced Burroughs to Kerouac. Burroughs then introduced Kerouac and Ginsberg, and the group quickly forged a close friendship that served as the basis of what was to become the Beat Generation. The group immersed themselves in the bohemian lifestyle, using these experiences—including experimenting with drugs, psychoanalysis, collaborations with jazz musicians, and scholarly study of the works of such writers as Arthur Rimbaud, Franz Kafka, William Butler Yeats, and Andre Gide—to inform and enhance their own literary and artistic pursuits. In 1947 Kerouac's former roommate at Columbia, Hal Chase, introduced him to Neal Cassady, a friend he had met in his childhood home in Denver. Cassady, who was known for his relentless, unceasing energy, as well as an affinity for repairing cars and driving them at dangerously high speeds, took the group on wild, extensive road trips around the United States and Mexico, introducing them to the Bay area scene. In 1952 Ginsberg and Kerouac moved to Berkeley and became acquainted with Rexroth and other poets from the Poetry Center. Their association with area writers, artists, and activists grew steadily, and eventually a definitive Beat presence in the Bay area was established. The visual artists and literary figures of the Bay area during this time worked closely together, collaborating in much the same manner as the jazz musicians and poets of Greenwich Village. In 1955, at the Six Gallery owned by Bay area artist Wally Hedrick, a momentous gathering of Beat poets and artists was held. All of the key Beat figures were present, including Allen Ginsberg,

who generated a feverish excitement among those assembled with his highly-charged reading of "Howl" at the close of the gathering. "Howl" was published shortly thereafter and thrust the Beats into the public spotlight when it spawned an obscenity trial and a national debate over the issue of censorship and freedom of speech. In *The Dharma Bums* (1958), Kerouac called this gathering at the Six Gallery and Ginsberg's reading "the birth of the San Francisco Poetry Renaissance."

The coining of the term "beatnik" is ascribed to *San Francisco Chronicle* columnist Herb Caen, who likened the Beats to the Russian satellite *Sputnik*, because in his mind both were "equally far out." Nevertheless, by the late 1950s, "beatniks" were widely known among mainstream Americans as strangely dressed, unshaven, slovenly hedonists whose art and literature made little sense and garnered only superficial curiosity outside of their small, bizarre counterculture. Gradually, however, fascination with the "rebel" archetype grew, particularly among teenagers and young adults, most of whom merely adopted the superficial trappings of Beats—smoking marijuana, wearing berets and dark, shabby clothing, and attending poetry readings—but some of whom became genuinely interested in the literary, artistic, political, and spiritual ideals espoused in Beat literature and art. By the early 1960s, a beatnik character—Maynard G. Krebbs—was featured on one of America's top-rated situation comedies, *The Many Loves of Dobie Gillis*. The character, portrayed by actor Bob Denver, was a watered-down, ineffectual, representation of a "beatnik" that has been regarded as a reassurance to midstream Americans that Beats were incapable of exacting any significant radical changes to their way of life. For most of America, the Beat "scene" remained an abstract concept well into the 1960s, but the physical and cultural landscapes of the San Francisco and New York City areas were significantly, and in some cases, permanently, altered by the actions of the members of the Beat Generation.

REPRESENTATIVE WORKS

William S. Burroughs

Junkie: The Confessions of an Unredeemed Drug Addict [as William Lee] (novel) 1953; republished as *Junky* 1977

The Naked Lunch (novel) 1959; also published as *Naked Lunch*, 1962; restored text edition 2001

Gregory Corso
The Vestal Lady on Brattle and Other Poems (poetry) 1955

Gasoline (poetry) 1958

The Happy Birthday of Death (poetry) 1960

Robert Duncan
Medieval Scenes (poetry) 1950; revised edition 1978

Caesar's Gate Poems 1949-1950 (poetry) 1955; revised edition 1972

Selected Poems (poetry) 1959

The Opening of the Field (poetry) 1960

William Everson
Triptych for the Living (poetry) 1951

An Age Insurgent [as Brother Antoninus] (poetry) 1959

The Crooked Lines of God: Poems 1949-1954 [as Brother Antoninus] (poetry) 1959

Lawrence Ferlinghetti
Pictures of the Gone World (poetry) 1955; enlarged edition 1995

A Coney Island of the Mind (poetry) 1958

Her (novel) 1960

Allen Ginsberg
Sunflower Sutra (poetry) 1955

Howl and Other Poems (poetry) 1956

John Clellon Holmes
Go (novel) 1952

"This Is the Beat Generation" [published in *New York Times Magazine*] (newspaper article) 1952

The Horn (novel) 1958

Jack Kerouac
On the Road (novel) 1957

The Dharma Bums (novel) 1958

Mexico City Blues (poetry) 1959

Norman Mailer
The White Negro: Superficial Reflections on the Hipster (essays) 1957

Advertisements for Myself (short stories, verse, essays) 1959

Michael McClure
Passage (poetry) 1956

Peyote Poem (poetry) 1958

Dark Brown (poetry) 1959

For Artaud (poetry) 1959

Hymns to St. Geryon, and Other Poems (poetry) 1959

Mezz Mezzrow
Really the Blues (autobiography) 1946

Hilda Morley
To Hold in My Hand: Selected Poems 1955-83 (poetry) 1984

Kenneth Rexroth
A Bestiary for My Daughters Mary and Katherine (poetry) 1955

One Hundred Poems from the Japanese [translator] (poetry) 1955

Thou Shalt Not Kill: A Memorial for Dylan Thomas (poetry) 1955

Gary Snyder
Riprap (poetry) 1959

The Back Country (poetry) 1968

Earth House Hold (essays; reviews; journal entries) 1969

William Carlos Williams
Paterson (poetry) 1946-63

PRIMARY SOURCES

JACK KEROUAC (NOVEL DATE 1958)

SOURCE: Kerouac, Jack. "Chapter 2." In *The Dharma Bums*, pp. 10-16. New York: Viking, 1958.

In this excerpt from Kerouac's 1958 novel, the author fictionalizes the historic Six Gallery reading. He gave the actual participants fictional names, rendering Ginsberg as Alvah Goldbook; Gary Snyder as Japhy Ryder; Philip Whalen as Warren Coughlin; Michael McClure as Ike O'Shea; Kenneth Rexroth as Rheinhold Cacoethes; and Philip Lamantia as Francis DaPavia.

It was a great night, a historic night in more ways than one. Japhy Ryder and some other poets (he also wrote poetry and translated Chinese and Japanese poetry into English) were scheduled to give a poetry reading at the Gallery Six in town. They were all meeting in the bar and getting high. But as they stood and sat around I saw that he was the only one who didn't look like a poet, though poet he was indeed. The other poets were either hornrimmed intellectual hepcats with wild black hair like Alvah Goldbook, or delicate pale handsome poets like Ike O'Shay (in a suit), or out-of-this-world genteel-looking Renaissance Italians like Francis DaPavia (who looks like a young priest), or a bow-tied wild-haired old anarchist fuds like Rheinhold Cacoethes, or big fat bespectacled quiet booboos like Warren Coughlin. And all the other hopeful poets were standing around, in various costumes, worn-at-the-sleeves corduroy jackets, scuffly shoes, books sticking out of their pockets.

. . . . .

Anyway, I followed the whole gang of howling poets to the reading at Gallery Six that night, which was, among other important things, the night of the birth of the San Francisco Poetry Renaissance. Everyone was there. It was a mad night. And I was the one who got things jumping by going around collecting dimes and quarters from the rather stiff audience standing around in the gallery and coming back with three huge gallon jugs of California Burgundy and getting them all piffed so that by eleven o'clock when Alvah Goldbook was reading his, wailing his poem "Wail" drunk with arms outspread everybody was yelling "Go! Go! Go!" (like a jam session) and old Rheinhold Cacoethes the father of the Frisco poetry scene was wiping his tears in gladness. Japhy himself read his fine poems about Coyote the God of the North American Plateau Indians (I think), at least the God of the Northwest Indians, Kwakiutl and whatall. "Fuck you! sang Coyote, and ran away!" read Japhy to the distinguished audience, making them all howl with joy, it was so pure, fuck being a dirty word that comes out clean. And he had his tender lyrical lines, like the ones about bears eating berries, showing his love of animals, and great mystery lines about oxen on the Mongolian road showing his knowledge of Oriental literature even on to Hsuan Tsung the great Chinese monk who walked from China to Tibet, Lanchow to Kashgar and Mongolia carrying a stick of incense in his hand. Then Japhy showed his sudden barroom humor with lines about Coyote bringing goodies. And his anarchistic ideas about how Americans don't know how to live, with lines about commuters being trapped in living rooms that come from poor trees felled by chainsaws (showing here, also, his background as a logger up north). This voice was deep and resonant and somehow brave, like the voice of oldtime American heroes and orators. Something earnest and strong and humanly hopeful I liked about him, while the other poets were either too dainty in their aestheticism, or too hysterically cynical to hope for anything, or too abstract and indoorsy, or too political, or like Coughlin too

incomprehensible to understand (big Coughlin saying things about "unclarified processes" though where Coughlin did say that revelation was a personal thing I noticed the strong Buddhist and idealistic feeling of Japhy, which he'd shared with goodhearted Coughlin in their buddy days at college, as I had shared mine with Alvah in the Eastern scene and with others less apocalyptical and straighter but in no sense more sympathetic and tearful).

Meanwhile scores of people stood around in the darkened gallery straining to hear every word of the amazing poetry reading as I wandered from group to group, facing them and facing away from the stage, urging them to glug a slug from the jug, or wandered back and sat on the right side of the stage giving out little wows and yesses of approval and even whole sentences of comment with nobody's invitation but in the general gaiety nobody's disapproval either. It was a great night. Delicate Francis DaPavia read, from delicate onionskin yellow pages, or pink, which he kept flipping carefully with long white fingers, the poems of his dead chum Altman who'd eaten too much peyote in Chihuahua (or died of polio, one) but read none of his own poems—a charming elegy in itself to the memory of the dead young poet, enough to draw tears from the Cervantes of Chapter Seven, and read them in a delicate Englishy voice that had me crying with inside laughter though I later got to know Francis and liked him.

. . . . .

Between poets, Rheinhold Cacoethes, in his bow tie and shabby old coat, would get up and make a little funny speech in his snide funny voice and introduce the next reader; but as I say come eleven-thirty when all the poems were read and everybody was milling around wondering what had happened and what would come next in American poetry, he was wiping his eyes with his handkerchief.

DIANA TRILLING (ESSAY DATE SPRING 1959)

SOURCE: Trilling, Diana. "The Other Night at Columbia: A Report from the Academy." *Partisan Review* 26, no. 2 (spring 1959): 214-30.

In the following essay, Trilling recounts her early association with Allen Ginsberg, including a reminiscence of a poetry reading Ginsberg held at Columbia University.

The "beats" were to read their poetry at Columbia on Thursday evening and on the spur of the moment three wives from the English department had decided to go to hear them. But for me, one of the three, the spur of the moment was not where the story had begun. It had begun much farther back, some twelve or fourteen years ago, when Allen Ginsberg had been a student at Columbia and I had heard about him much more than I usually hear of students for the simple reason that he got into a great deal of trouble which involved his instructors, and had to be rescued and revived and restored; eventually he had even to be kept out of jail. Of course there was always the question, should this young man be rescued, should he be restored? There was even the question, shouldn't he go to jail? We argued about it some at home but the discussion, I'm afraid, was academic, despite my old resistance to the idea that people like Ginsberg had the right to ask and receive preferential treatment just because they read Rimbaud and Gide and undertook to put words on paper themselves. Nor was my principle (if one may call it that) of equal responsibility for poets and shoe clerks so firm that I didn't need to protect it by refusing to confront Ginsberg as an individual or potential acquaintance. I don't mean that I was aware, at the time, of this motive for disappearing on the two or three occasions when he came to the house to deliver a new batch of poems and report on his latest adventures in sensation-seeking. If I'd been asked to explain, then, my wish not to meet and talk with this troublesome young man who had managed to break through the barrier of student anonymity, I suppose I'd have rested with the proposition that I don't like mess, and I'd have been ready to defend myself against the charge, made in the name of art, of a strictness of judgment which was intolerant of this much deviation from respectable standards of behavior. Ten, twelve, fourteen years ago, there was still something of a challenge in the "conventional" position; I still enjoyed defending the properties and proprieties of the middle class against friends who persisted in scorning them. Of course, once upon a time—but that was in the '30's—one had had to defend even having a comfortable chair to sit in, or a rug on the floor. But by the '40's things had changed; one's most intransigent literary friends had capitulated by then, everybody had a well-upholstered sofa and I was reduced to such marginal causes as the Metropolitan Museum, after-dinner coffee cups, and the expectation that visitors would go home by 2 A.M. and put their ashes in the ashtrays. Then why should I not also defend the expectation that a student at Columbia, even a poet, would do his work, submit it to

his teachers through the normal channels of classroom communication, stay out of jail, and then, if things went right, graduate, start publishing, be reviewed, and see what developed, whether he was a success or failure?

Well, for Ginsberg, things didn't go right for quite a while. The time came when he was graduated from Columbia and published his poems, but first he got into considerable difficulty, beginning with his suspension from college and the requirement that he submit to psychiatric treatment, and terminating—but this was quite a few years later—in an encounter with the police from which he was extricated by some of his old teachers who thought he needed a hospital more than a prison. The suspension had been for a year, when Ginsberg had been a Senior; the situation was not without its grim humor. It seems that Ginsberg had traced an obscenity in the dusty windows of Hartley Hall; the words were too shocking for the Dean of Students to speak, he had written them on a piece of paper which he pushed across the desk: "F - - - the Jews." Even the part of Lionel that wanted to laugh couldn't, it was too hard for the Dean to have to transmit this message to a Jewish professor—this was still in the '40's when being a Jew in the university was not yet what it is today. "But he's a Jew himself," said the Dean. "Can you understand his writing a thing like that?" Yes, Lionel could understand; but he couldn't explain it to the Dean. And anyway he knew that the legend in the dust of Hartley Hall required more than an understanding of Jewish self-hatred and also that it was not the sole cause for administrative uneasiness about Ginsberg and his cronies. It was ordinary good sense for the college to take therapeutic measures with Ginsberg.

I now realize that even at this early point in his career I had already accumulated a fund of information about young Ginsberg which accurately forecast his present talent for self-promotion although it was surely disproportionate to the place he commanded in his teacher's mind and quite contradicted the uncertain physical impression I had caught in opening the door to him when he came to the apartment. He was middling tall, slight, dark, sallow; his dress suggested shabby gentility, poor brown tweed gone threadbare and yellow. The description would have fitted any number of undergraduates of his or any Columbia generation; it was the personal story that set him acutely apart. He came from New Jersey where his father was a school teacher, or perhaps a principal, who himself wrote poetry too—I think for the *New York Times*, which would be as good a way as any of defining the separation between father and son. His mother was in a mental institution, and, off and on, she had been there for a long time. This was the central and utterly persuasive fact of this young man's life; I knew this before I was told it in poetry at Columbia the other night, and doubtless it was this knowledge that underlay the nervous irritability with which I responded to so much as the mention of Ginsberg's name. Here was a boy to whom an outrageous injustice had been done: his mother had gone mad on him, and now whoever crossed his path became somehow responsible, guilty, caught in the impossibility of rectifying what she had done. It was an unfair burden to put on those who were only the later accidents of his history and it made me more defensive than charitable with this poor object of her failure. No boy, after all, could ask anyone to help him build a career on the terrible but gratuitous circumstance of a mad mother; it was a justification for neither poetry nor prose nor yet for "philosophy" of the kind young Ginsberg liked to expound to his teacher. In the question period which followed the poetry-reading the other night at Columbia, this matter of a rationale for the behavior of Ginsberg and his friends came up: someone asked Ginsberg to state his philosophy. It was a moment I had been awaiting and I thought: "Here we go; he'll tell us how he's crazy like a daisy and how his friend Orlovsky is crazy like a butterfly." I had been reading *Time* magazine; who hadn't? But, instead, Ginsberg answered that he had no philosophy; he spoke of inspiration, or perhaps it was illumination, ecstatic illumination, as the source of his poetry and I was more than surprised, I was curiously pleased for him because I took it as a considerable advance in self-control that he could operate with this much shrewdness and leave it, at least for this occasion, to his audience to abstract a "position" from his and his friends' antics while he himself moved wild, mild, and innocent through the jungle of speculation. Back in the older days, it had always been my feeling that so far as his relationship with his teacher was concerned, this trying to formulate a philosophy must reveal its falseness even to himself, so that his recourse to it insulted his intelligence. Two motives, it seemed to me, impelled him then: the wish to shock his teacher, and the wish to meet the teacher on equal ground. The first of these motives was complicated enough, involving as it did the gratifications of self-incrimination and disapproval, and then forgiveness; but the second was more tangled still. To talk with one's English

professor who was also a writer, a critic, and one who made no bones about his solid connection with literary tradition, about one's descent from Rimbaud, Baudelaire or Dostoevsky was clearly to demonstrate a good-sized rationality and order in what was apparently an otherwise undisciplined life. Even more, or so I fancied, it was to propose an alliance between the views of the academic and the poet-rebel, the unity of a deep discriminating commitment to literature which must certainly one day wipe out the fortuitous distance between boy and man, pupil and teacher. Thus, Ginsberg standing on the platform at Columbia and refusing the philosophy gambit might well be taken as an impulse toward manhood, or at least manliness, for which one might be grateful.

But I remind myself: Ginsberg at Columbia on Thursday night was not Ginsberg at Chicago—according to *Time,* at any rate—or Ginsberg at Hunter either, where Kerouac ran the show and a dismal show it must have been, with Kerouac drinking on the platform and clapping James Wechsler's hat on his head in a grand parade of contempt—they were two of four panelists gathered to discuss, "Is there such a thing as a beat generation?"—and leading Ginsberg out from the wings like a circus donkey. For whatever reason—rumor had it he was in a personal crisis—Kerouac didn't appear on Thursday night, and Ginsberg at Columbia was Ginsberg his own man, dealing with his own history, and intent, it seemed to me, on showing up the past for the poor inaccurate thing it so often is: it's a chance we all dream of but mostly it works the other way around, like the long-ago story of Jed Harris coming back to Yale and sitting on the fence weeping for a youth he could never re-write no matter how many plays of Chekhov he brought to Broadway, no matter how much money he made. I suppose I have no right to say now, and on such early and little evidence, that Ginsberg had always desperately wanted to be respectable, or respected, like his instructors at Columbia, it is so likely that this is a hindsight which suits my needs. It struck me, though, that this was the most unmistakable and touching message from platform to audience the other night, and as I received it, I felt I had known something like it all along. Not that Ginsberg had ever shown himself as a potential future colleague in the university; anything but that. Even the implied literary comradeship had had reference, not to any possibility of Ginsberg's assimilation into the community of professors, but to the professor's capacity for association in the community of rebellious young poets. Still, it was not just anyone on the campus to whom Ginsberg had come with his lurid boasts which were also his confession; it was Lionel, it was Mark Van Doren; if there was anyone else he would very likely be of the same respectable species, and I remember saying, "He wants you to forbid him to behave like that. He wants you to take him out of it, else why does he choose people like you and Mark to tell these stories to?" To which I received always the same answer, "I'm not his father," with which there could of course be no argument.

And yet, even granting the accuracy of this reconstruction of the past, it would be wrong to conclude that any consideration of motive on Ginsberg's part was sufficiently strong to alter one's first and most forceful image of Ginsberg as a "case"—a gifted and sad case, a guilt-provoking and nuisance case but, above all, a case. Nor was it a help that Lionel had recently published a story about a crazy student and a supposedly normal student in which the author's affection was so plainly directed to the former; we never became used to the calls, often in the middle of the night, asking whether it wasn't the crazy character who was really sane. Ginsberg, with his poems in which there was never quite enough talent or hard work, and with his ambiguous need to tell his teacher exactly what new flagrancy he was now exploring with his Gide-talking friends at the West End Café had at any rate the distinction of being more crudely justified in his emotional disturbance than most; he also had the distinction of carrying mental unbalance in the direction of criminality, a territory one preferred to leave unclaimed by student or friend.

Gide and the West End Café in all its upper-Broadway dreariness: what could the two conceivably have in common except those lost boys of the '40's? How different it might have been for Ginsberg and his friends if they had come of age ten or fifteen years sooner was one of the particular sadnesses of the other evening, it virtually stood on the platform with them as the poets read their poems whose chief virtue, it seemed to me, was their "racial-minority" funniness, their "depressed-classes" funniness of a kind which has never had so sure and live a place as it did in the '30's, the embittered fond funniness which has to do with one's own awful family, funniness plain and poetical, always aware of itself, of a kind which would seem now to have all but disappeared among intellectuals except as an eclecticism or a device of self-pity. It's a real loss; I hadn't quite realized how much I missed it until Thursday night when Ginsberg read his poem, "The Ignu,"

and Corso read his poem, "Marriage" (a compulsive poem, he called it, about a compulsive subject) and they were still funny in that old racial depressed way but not nearly as funny and authentic as they would have been had they been written before the Jews and the Italians and the Negroes, but especially the Jews, had been crammed down their own and everyone else's throat as Americans-like-everyone-else instead of outsiders raised in the Bronx or on Ninth Avenue or even in Georgia. The Jew in particular is a loss to literature and life—I mean the Jew out of which was bred the Jewish intellectual of the '30's. For a few short years in the '30's, as not before or since, the Jew was at his funniest, wisest best; he perfectly well knew the advantage he could count on in the Gentile world, and that there was no ascendancy or pride the Gentile comrades could muster against a roomful of Jewish sympathizers singing at the tops of their voices, "A SOCialist union is a NO good union, is a COM-pan-y union of the bosses," or against Michael Gold's mother who wanted to know did her boy have to write books the whole world should know she had bedbugs. If Ginsberg had been born in an earlier generation it would surely have been the Stewart Cafeteria in the Village that he and his friends would have hung out at instead of the West End, that dim waystation of undergraduate debauchery on Morningside Heights—and the Stewart Cafeteria was a well-lighted place and one of the funniest places in New York; at least, at every other table it was funny, and where it was decadent or even conspiratorial, this had its humor too, or at least its robustness. As for Gide—the Gide of the '30's was the "betrayer of the Revolution," not the Gide of the *acte gratuite* and homosexuality in North Africa. One didn't use pathology in those days to explain or excuse or exhibit oneself and one never had to be lonely; there was never a less lonely time for intellectuals than the Depression, or a less depressed time—unless, of course, one was recalcitrant, like Fitzgerald, and simply refused to be radicalized, in which stubborn case it couldn't have been lonelier. Intellectuals talk now about how, in the '30's, there was an "idea" in life, not the emptiness we live in. Actually, it was a time of generally weak intellection—so many of us who put our faith in Marx and Lenin had read neither of them—but of very strong feeling. Everyone judged everyone else, it was a time of incessant cruel moral judgment; today's friend was tomorrow's enemy; whoever disagreed with oneself had sold out, God knows to or for what, maybe for $10 more a week; there was little of the generosity among intellectuals which nowadays dictates the automatic "Gee, that's great" at any news of someone else's good fortune. But it was surely a time of quicker, truer feeling than is now conjured up with marijuana or the infantile cameraderie of *On The Road*. And there was paradox but no contradiction in this double truth, just as there was no contradiction in the fact that it was a time in which the neurotic determination of the intellectual was being so universally acted out and yet a time in which, whatever his dedication to historical or economic determinism, personally he had a unique sense of free will. In the '30's one's clinical vocabulary was limited to two words—escapism and subjectivism—and both of them applied only to other people's wrong political choices.

Well, the "beats" weren't lucky enough to be born except when they were born. Ginsberg says he lives in Harlem, but it's not the Harlem of the Scottsboro boys and W. C. Handy and the benign insanity of trying to proletarianize Striver's Row; their comrades are not the comrades of the Stewart Cafeteria nor yet of the road, as Kerouac would disingenuously have it, but pick-ups on dark morning streets. But they have their connection with us who were young in the '30's, their intimate political connection, which we deny at risk of missing what it is that makes the "beat" phenomenon something to think about. As they used to say on 14th Street, it is no accident, comrades, it is decidedly no accident that today in the '50's our single overt manifestation of protest takes the wholly non-political form of a bunch of panic-stricken kids in blue jeans, many of them publicly homosexual, talking about or taking drugs, assuring us that they are out of their minds, not responsible, while the liberal intellectual is convinced that he has no power to control the political future, the future of the free world, and that therefore he must submit to what he defines as political necessity. Though of course the various aspects of a culture must be granted their own autonomous source and character, the connection between "beat" and respectable liberal intellectual exists and is not hard to locate: the common need to deny free will, divest oneself of responsibility and yet stay alive. The typical liberal intellectual of the '50's, whether he be a writer for *Partisan Review* or a law school professor or a magazine or newspaper editor, explains his evolution over the last two decades—specifically, his present attitude toward "co-existence"—by telling us that he has been forced to accept the unhappy reality of Soviet strength in an atomic world, and that there is no

alternative to capitulation—not that he calls it that—except the extinction of nuclear war. Even the diplomacy he invokes is not so much flexible, which he would like to think it is, as disarmed and, hopefully, disarming, an instrument of his impulse to surrender rather than of any wish to dominate or even of his professed wish to hold the line. Similarly docile to culture, the "beat" also contrives a fate by predicating a fate. Like the respectable established intellectual—or the organization man, or the suburban matron—against whom he makes his play of protest, he conceives of himself as incapable of exerting any substantive influence against the forces that condition him. He is made by society, he cannot make society. He can only stay alive as best he can for as long as is permitted him. Is it any wonder, then, that *Time* and *Life* write as they do about the "beats"—with such a conspicuous show of superiority, and no hint of fear? These periodicals know what genuine, dangerous protest looks like, and it doesn't look like Ginsberg and Kerouac. Clearly, there is no more menace in *Howl* or *On The Road* than there is in the Scarsdale PTA. In the common assumption of effectlessness, in the apparent will to rest with a social determination over which the individual spirit and intelligence cannot and perhaps even should not try to triumph, there merge any number of the disparate elements of our present culture—from the liberal intellectual journals to Luce to the Harvard Law School, from Ginsberg to the suburban matron.

But then why, one ponders, do one's most relaxed and non-square friends, alongside of whom one can oneself be made to look like the original object with four sides of equal length; why do one's most politically "flexible" friends, alongside of whom one's own divergence from dominant liberal opinion is regularly made to look so ungraceful, so like a latter-day sectarianism, even a fanaticism, feel constrained to dispute Columbia's judgment in giving the "beats" a hearing on the campus and my own wish to attend their poetry-reading? Why, for instance, the dissent of Dwight MacDonald, whom I happened to see that afternoon; or of W. H. Auden, who, when I said I had been moved by the performance, gently chided me, "I'm ashamed of you"; or of William Phillips who, although he tells me yes, I may go ahead with this article, can't hide his puzzlement, even worry, because I want to give the "beats" this kind of attention? In strict logic, it would seem to me that things should go in quite the other direction and that I, who insist upon at least the assumption of free will in our political

Allen Ginsberg, Jack Kerouac, and William Burroughs, as well as other Beat Generation writers, first became acquainted through their common ties at Columbia University, shown here in May, 1959.

dealings with Russia, who insist upon what I call political responsibility, should be the one to protest a university forum for the irresponsibles whereas my friends whose politics are what I think of as finally a politics of victimization, of passivity and fatedness, should be able to shrug off the "beats" as merely another inevitable, if tasteless, expression of a *Zeitgeist* with which I believe them to be far more in tune than I am. I do not mean, of course, to rule out taste, or style, as a valid criterion of moral judgment. A sense of social overwhelmment which announces itself in terms of disreputableness or even criminality asks for a different kind of moral assessment than the same emotion kept within the bounds of acceptable social expression. But I would simply point to the similarities which are masked by these genuine moral differences between the "beats" and my friends who would caution us against them. Taste or style dictates that most intellectuals behave decorously, earn a regular living, disguise instead of flaunt whatever may be their private digressions from the conduct society considers desirable; when they seek support for the poetical

impulse or ask for light on their self-doubt and fears, they don't make the naked boast that they are crazy like daisies but they elaborate a new belief in the indispensability of neurosis to art, or beat the bushes for some new deviant psycho-analysis which will generalize their despair without curing it. And these differences of style are of course important, at least for the moment. It is from the long-range, and no doubt absolute, view of our immediate cultural situation, which bears so closely upon our continuing national crisis, that the moral difference between a respectable and a disreputable acceptance of defeat seems to me to constitute little more than a cultural foot-note to history.

But perhaps I wander too far from the other night at Columbia. There was enough in the evening that was humanly immediate to divert one from this kind of ultimate concern. . . .

It was not an official university occasion. The "beats" appeared at Columbia on the invitation of a student club—interestingly enough, the John Dewey Society. Whether the club first approached

Ginsberg or Ginsberg initiated the proceedings, I don't know, but what had happened was that Ginsberg in his undergraduate days had taken a loan from the university—$200? $250?—and recently the Bursar's office had caught up with him in his new incarnation of successful literary itinerant, to demand repayment. Nothing if not ingenious, Ginsberg now proposed to pay off his debt by reading his poetry at Columbia without fee. It was at this point that various members of the English department, solicited as sponsors for the operation, had announced their rejection of the whole deal, literary as well as financial, and the performance was arranged without financial benefit to Ginsberg and without official cover; we three wives, however, decided to attend on our own. We would meet at 7:45 at the door of the theater; no, we would meet at 7:40 at the door of the theater; no, we would meet no later than 7:30 across the street from the theater: the telephoning back and forth among the three women was stupendous as word spread of vast barbarian hordes converging on poor dull McMillin Theater from all the dark recesses of the city, howling for their leader. The advance warnings turned out to be exaggerated; it was nevertheless disconcerting to be associated with such goings-on, and the fact that Fred Dupee, at the request of the John Dewey Society, had consented to be moderator, chairman, introducer of Ginsberg and his fellow-poets, while it provided the wives of his colleagues with the as-surance of seats in a section of the hall reserved for faculty, was not without its uncomfortable reminder that Ginsberg had, in a sense, got his way; he was appearing on the same Columbia platform from which T. S. Eliot had last year read his poetry; he was being presented by, and was thus bound to be thought under the sponsorship of, an important person in the academic and liter-ary community who was also one's long-time friend. And indeed it was as Dupee's friend that one took a first canvass of the scene: the line of policemen before the entrance to the theater; the air of suppressed excitement in the lobbies and one's own rather contemptible self-consciousness about being seen in such a crowd; the shoddiness of an audience in which it was virtually impos-sible to distinguish between student and camp-follower; the always-new shock of so many young girls, so few of them pretty, and so many dreadful black stockings; so many young men, so few of them—despite the many black beards—with any promise of masculinity. It was distressing to think that Dupee was going to be "faculty" to this rabble, that at this moment he was backstage with

Ginsberg & Co., formulating a deportment which would check the excess of which one knew them to be capable, even or especially in public, without doing violence to his own large tolerance.

For me, it was of some note that the audito-rium smelled fresh. The place was already full when we arrived; I took one look at the crowd and was certain that it would smell bad. But I was mistaken. These people may think they're dirty inside and dress up to it. Nevertheless, they smell all right. The audience was clean and Ginsberg was clean and Corso was clean and Orlovsky was clean. Maybe Ginsberg says he doesn't bathe or shave; Corso, I know, declares that he has never combed his hair; Orlovsky has a line in one of the two poems he read—he's not yet written his third, the chairman explained—"If I should shave, I know the bugs would go away." But for this occa-sion, at any rate, Ginsberg, Corso and Orlovsky were all clean and shaven; Kerouac, in crisis, didn't appear, but if he had come he would have been clean and shaven too—he was at Hunter, I've inquired about that. And anyway, there's nothing dirty about a checked shirt or a lumber-jacket and blue jeans, they're standard uniform in the best nursery schools. Ginsberg has his pride, as do his friends.

And how do I look to the "beats," I ask myself after that experience with the seats, and not only I but the other wives I was with? We had pulled aside the tattered old velvet rope which marked off the section held for faculty, actually it was trail-ing on the floor, and moved into the seats Du-pee's wife Andy had saved for us by strewing coats on them; there was a big grey overcoat she couldn't identify: she stood holding it up in the air murmuring wistfully, "Whose is this?"—until the young people in the row in back of us took account of us and answered sternly, "*Those* seats are reserved for faculty." If I have trouble unravel-ing undergraduates from "beats," neither do the wives of the Columbia English department wear their distinction with any certainty.

But Dupee's distinction, that's something else again: what could I have been worrying about, when had Dupee ever failed to meet the occasion, or missed a right style? I don't suppose one could witness a better performance than his on Thursday evening; its rightness was apparent the moment he walked onto the stage, his troupe in tow and himself just close enough and just enough re-moved to indicate the balance in which he held the situation. Had there been a hint of betrayal in his deportment, of either himself or his guests—naturally, he had made them his guests—the whole evening might have been different: for instance, a few minutes later when the overflow attendance outside the door began to bang and shout for admission, might not the audience have caught the contagion and become unruly too? Or would Ginsberg have stayed with his picture of himself as poet serious and triumphant instead of succumbing to what must have been the greatest temptation to spoil his opportunity? "The last time I was in this theater," Dupee began quietly, "it was also to hear a poet read his works. That was T. S. Eliot." A slight alteration of inflection, from irony to mockery, from condescension to contempt, and it might well have been a signal for near-riot, boos and catcalls and whistlings; the evening would have been lost to the "beats," Dupee and Columbia would have been defeated. Dupee transformed a circus into a classroom. He himself, he said, welcomed the chance to hear these poets read their works—he never once in his remarks gave them their name of "beats" nor alluded even to San Francisco—because in all poetry it was important to study the spoken accent; he himself didn't happen especially to admire those of their works that he knew; still, he would draw our attention to their skillful use of a certain kind of American imagery which, deriving from Whitman, yet passed Whitman's use of it or even Hart Crane's. . . . It was Dupee speaking for the Academy, claiming for it its place in life, and the performers were inevitably captive to his dignity and self-assurance. Rather than Ginsberg and his friends, it was a photographer from *Life,* exploding his flashbulbs in everybody's face, mounting a ladder at the back of the stage the more effectively to shoot his angles, who came to represent vulgarity and disruption and disrespect; when a student in the audience disconnected a wire which had something to do with the picture-taking, one guessed that Ginsberg was none too happy but it was the photographer's face that became ugly, the only real ugliness of the evening. One could feel nothing but pity for Ginsberg and his friends that their front of disreputableness and rebellion should be this transparent, this vulnerable to the seductions of a clever host. With Dupee's introduction, the whole of their defense had been penetrated at the very outset.

Pity is not the easiest of our emotions today; now it's understanding that is easy, and more and more—or so I find it for myself—real pity moves hand-in-hand with real terror; it's an emotion one avoids because it's so hard; one understands the cripple, the delinquent, the unhappy so as not to have to pity them. But Thursday night was an oc-

casion of pity so direct and inescapable that it left little to the understanding that wasn't mere afterthought—and pity not only for the observed, the performers, but for us who had come to observe them and reassure ourselves that we were not implicated. One might as readily persuade oneself one was not implicated in one's children! For this was it: these *were* children, miserable children trying desperately to manage, asking desperately to be taken out of it all; there was nothing one could imagine except to bundle them home and feed them warm milk, promise them they need no longer call for mama and papa. I kept asking myself, where had I had just such an experience before, and later it came to me: I had gone to see O'Neill's *Long Day's Journey into Night* and the play had echoed with just such a child's cry for help; at intermission time all the mothers in the audience were so tormented and anxious that they rushed in a body to phone home: was the baby really all right, was he really well and warm in his bed; one couldn't get near the telephone booths. A dozen years ago, when Ginsberg had been a student and I had taxed Lionel with the duty to forbid him to misbehave, he had answered me that he wasn't the boy's father, and of course he was right. Neither was Mark Van Doren the boy's father; a teacher is not a father to his students and he must never try to be. Besides, Ginsberg had a father of his own who couldn't be replaced at will: he was in the audience the other night. One of the things Ginsberg read was part of a long poem to his mother who, he told us, had died three years ago, and as he read it, he choked and cried; but no one in the audience tittered or showed embarrassment at this public display of emotion, and I doubt whether anyone thought, "See, he has existence: he can cry, he can feel." Nor did anyone seem very curious when he went on to explain, later in the evening, that the reason he had cried was because his father was in the theater. I have no way of knowing what Ginsberg's father felt the other night about his son being up there on the stage at Columbia (it rather obsesses me), but I should guess he was proud; it's what I'd conclude from his expression at the end of the performance when Ginsberg beat through the admirers who surrounded him, to get to his father as quickly as he could: surely that's nice for a father. And I should suppose a father was bound to be pleased that his son was reading his poems in a university auditorium: it would mean the boy's success, and this would be better than a vulgarity, it would necessarily include the chairman's critical gravity and the fact, however bizarre, that T. S. Eliot had been the last poet in this place before him. In a sense, Orlovsky and Corso were more orphans than Ginsberg the other night, but this was not necessarily because they were without fathers of their own in the audience; I should think it would go back much farther than this, to whatever it was that made them look so much more armored, less openly eager for approval; although they were essentially as innocent and childlike as Ginsberg, they couldn't begin to match his appeal; it was on Ginsberg that one's eye rested, it was to the sweetness in his face and to his sweet smile that one responded; it was to him that one gave one's pity and for him one felt one's own fullest terror. Clearly, I am no judge of his poem, "Lion in the Room," which he announced was dedicated to Lionel Trilling; I heard it through too much sympathy, and also self-consciousness. The poem was addressed as well as dedicated to Lionel; it was about a lion in the room with the poet, a lion who was hungry but refused to eat him; I heard it as a passionate love-poem, I really can't say whether it was a good or bad poem, but I was much moved by it, in some part unaccountably. It was also a decent poem, it now strikes me; I mean, there were no obscenities in it as there had been in much of the poetry the "beats" read. Here was something else that was remarkable about the other evening: most of the audience was very young, and Ginsberg must have realized this because when he read the poem about his mother and came to the place where he refered to the YPSLs of her girlhood, he interposed his only textual exegesis of the evening: in an aside he explained, "Young People's Socialist League"—he was very earnest about wanting his poetry to be understood. And it wasn't only his gentility that distinguished Ginsberg's father from the rest of the audience; as far as I could see, he was the only man in the hall who looked old enough to be the father of a grown son; the audience was crazily young, there were virtually no faculty present, I suppose they didn't want to give this much sanction to the "beats." For this young audience the obscenities read from the stage seemed to have no force whatsoever; there was not even the shock of silence, and when Ginsberg forgot himself in the question period and said that something or other was bull-shit, I think he was more upset than his listeners; I can't imagine anything more detached and scientific outside a psychoanalyst's office, or perhaps a nursery school, than this young audience at Columbia. Of Corso, in particular, one had the sense that he

mouthed the bad word only with considerable personal difficulty: this hurts me more than it hurts you.

Obviously, the whole performance had been carefully devised as to who would read first and what, then who next, and just how much an audience could take without becoming bored and overcritical: it would be my opinion we could have taken a bit more before the question period which must have been an anti-climax for anyone who had come, not as a tourist, but as a fellow-traveller. I've already reported how Ginsberg dealt with the philosophy question. There remains, of the question period, only to report his views on verse forms.

I don't remember how the question was put to Ginsberg—but I'm sure it was put neutrally: no one was inclined to embarrass the guests—which led him into a discussion of prosody; perhaps it was the question about what Ginsberg as a poet had learned at Columbia; but anyway, here, at last, Ginsberg had a real classroom subject: he could be a teacher who wed outrageousness to authority in the time-honored way of the young and lively, no-pedant-he performer of the classroom, and suddenly Ginsberg heard himself announcing that no one at Columbia knew anything about prosody; the English department was stuck in the nineteenth century, sensible of no meter other than the old iambic pentameter, whereas the thing about him and his friends was their concern with a poetic line which moved in the rhythm of ordinary speech; they were poetic innovators, carrying things forward the logical next step from William Carlos Williams. And now all at once the thing about Ginsberg and his friends was not their social protest and existentialism, their whackiness and beat-upness: suddenly it had become their energy of poetic impulse that earned them their right to be heard in the university, their studious devotion to their art: Ginsberg was seeing to that. Orlovsky had made his contribution to the evening; he had read his two whacky uproarious poems, the entire canon of his work, and had won his acclaim. Corso had similarly given his best, and been approval. The question period, the period of instruction, belonged to Ginsberg alone, and his friends might be slightly puzzled by the turn the evening had taken, the decorousness of which they suddenly found themselves a part—Corso, for instance, began to look like a chastened small boy who was still determined, though his heart was no longer in it, to bully his way through against all these damned grown-ups—but they had no choice except to permit their companion his deviation into high-mindedness. (Rightist opportunism?) Thus did one measure, finally, the full tug of something close to respectability in Ginsberg's life, by this division in the ranks; and thus, too, was the soundness of Dupee's reminder, that there is always something to learn from hearing a poet read his poems aloud, borne in on one. For the fact was that Ginsberg, reading his verse, had naturally given it the iambic beat: after all, it is the traditional beat of English poetry where it deals with serious subjects as Ginsberg's poems so often do. A poet, one thought—and it was a poignant thought because it came so immediately and humanly rather than as an abstraction—may choose to walk whatever zany path in his life as a man; but when it comes to mourning and mothers and such, he will be drawn into the line of tradition; at least in this far he has a hard time avoiding respectability.

The evening was over, we were dismissed to return to our homes. A crowd formed around Ginsberg; he extricated himself and came to his father a few rows ahead of us. I resisted the temptation to overhear their greeting. In some part of me I wanted to speak to Ginsberg, tell him I had liked the poem he had written to my husband, but I didn't do it: I couldn't be sure that Ginsberg wouldn't take my meaning wrong; after all, his social behavior is not fantasy. Outside, it had blown up a bit—or was it just the chill of unreality against which we hurried to find shelter?

There was a meeting going on at home of the pleasant professional sort which, like the comfortable living-room in which it usually takes place, at a certain point in a successful modern literary career confirms the writer in his sense of disciplined achievement and well-earned reward. I had found myself hurrying as if I were needed, but there was really no reason for my haste; my entrance was an interruption, even a disturbance of the attractive scene. Auden, alone of the eight men in the room not dressed in a proper suit but wearing his battered old brown leather jacket, was first to inquire about my experience. I told him I had been moved; he answered that he was ashamed of me. I said, "It's different when it's a sociological phenomenon and when it's human beings," and he of course knew and accepted what I said. Yet as I prepared to get out of the room so that the men could sit down again with their drinks, I felt there was something more I had to add—it was not enough to leave the "beats" only as human beings—and so I said, "Allen Ginsberg read a love-poem to you, Lionel. I liked it very

ON THE SUBJECT OF...

MEZZROW ON THE ORIGINS OF JIVE
I first heard the jive language in its early stages, when I was hanging around the South Side in Chicago. It was the first furious babbling of a people who suddenly woke up to find that their death-sentence had been revoked, or at least postponed, and they were stunned and dazzled at first, hardly able to believe it. . . . That was the first real jive—the lingo of prisoners with a temporary reprieve. When I got to Harlem I found it had spread to the East, and really come of age. These Harlem kids had decided they wouldn't be led back to jail nohow. They spieled a mile a minute, making that clear.

Mezzrow, Mezz. From *Really the Blues*, with Bernard Wolfe, p. 217. New York: Random House, 1946.

much." It was a strange thing to say in the circumstances, perhaps even a little foolish. But I'm sure that Ginsberg's old teacher knew what I was saying, and why I was impelled to say it.

ALLEN GINSBERG (INTERVIEW DATE 1978)

SOURCE: Ginsberg, Allen. Interview in *Jack's Book*, by Barry Gifford and Lawrence Lee, pp. 198-9. New York: St. Martin's Press, 1978.

In the following excerpt, Ginsberg recalls when he and fellow Beat writers gathered for the "6 Poets at 6 Gallery" reading held at Wally Hedrick's art gallery in San Francisco.

The Six Gallery reading had come about when Wally Hedrick, who was a painter and one of the major people there, asked Rexroth if he knew any poets that would put on a reading. Maybe Rexroth asked McClure to organize it and McClure didn't know how or didn't have time. Rexroth asked me, so I met McClure and Rexroth suggested I go visit another poet who was living in Berkeley, which was Gary. So I went right over to Gary's house and immediately had a meeting of minds with him over William Carlos Williams, 'cause I had written *Empty Mirror* at that time and he had begun *Myths and Texts*, or *The Berry Feast*, or something, and he told me about his friend Philip Whalen who was due in town the next day. And I told him about my friend Kerouac who was in town that day, and within three or four days we all met. . . .

Jack and I were coming from Berkeley, and had just arrived in San Francisco at the Key System Terminal, the bus terminal there, and we met right out on First and Mission, by accident. Gary was with Phil and I was with Jack, and we all went off immediately and started talking. And then Philip Lamantia was in town, whom I'd known from '48 in New York, and then there was Michael Mc-Clure. So there was a whole complement of poets. Then Gary and I decided we ought to invite Rexroth to be the sixth—sixth poet—to introduce at the Six Gallery, be the elder, since he had linked us up.

OVERVIEWS

ELIAS WILENTZ (ESSAY DATE 1960)

SOURCE: Wilentz, Elias, ed. Introduction to *The Beat Scene*, pp. 8-15. New York: Corinth Books, 1960.

In the following essay, Wilentz provides an overview of the Beat literary scene and defines what it meant to be a Beat writer.

John Clellon Holmes says he named it and it is a jazz term. Jack Kerouac says he started it and it means "beatitude." Norman Mailer traces it all to the cool hipster who went awry. Whatever the beginnings or shadowy meanings, the Fifties will go down in our literary history as the Beat Decade.

Ironically, the attachment of this vivid label is largely due to the double-handed efforts of *Life* and *Time* who, early in the game, picked up the "beats" as the great American rebellion of our youth and our times. This they lampooned in their stylish language of rhetorical deceits. Instead of the anticipated burst balloon, lying limp in the street to be kicked aside into the gutter until the next rebellion came along, "beat" found an echo in our ferocious times and has continued to sound through the nation.

The term lost any significance of meaning, assuming it ever had a specific one, and broke down to a physical type—a kid with beard, rumpled clothes, sandals, bongo drum, jazz records and a copy of *Howl*. Hints of sexual immoralities and use of drugs added a perverted glamor. The "beats"—whether in Venice, California or Green-

wich Village, New York—were lumped together in the same mattress on steel spring bed. With more and more name calling came less and less clarity until the word assumed mythic proportions and the Beat Generation had arrived. This might be called typical for America which would rather catalogue people than attempt to understand them.

In titling this book, an obvious dilemma developed which was finally resolved by accepting the popularization as at least readily recognizable even if of questionable pertinence. For the intent here lies beyond the narrow though confused castigations inflicted by ignorant journalists for whom everyone in this gathering is easily labeled as "beat." To the point, the "beats" are those who identify themselves with the ideas of Allen Ginsberg, Jack Kerouac, Gregory Corso and Peter Orlovsky. The others are whatever they might call themselves—"underground," "Black Mountain," "abomunist," or simply poets and writers. There are also the numerous amorphous cliques that tend to cluster around a particular "little" magazine—*Exodus, Big Table, Yugen, Chelsea, Birth,* etc.—or a "little" press—*City Lights, Jargon, Totem, Auerhahn,* etc.

All are Bohemians but all have been labeled as "beat." Certainly it is a different Bohemianism than the cool hipsterism of seven years back, different too from the McCarthy time conformists of ten years ago when almost the only Bohemianism around was that still practiced by the "old-timers" of the Twenties and Thirties who had never given it up. Possibly the present Bohemians should revel in the popular "beat" label instead of resenting it. This pigeonholing by the soothsayers, whether University academics or Rockerfeller Center journalists, sunders any possible tie of identity with an H-Bomb world of Four Seasons steaks. The cutting of such an umbilical cord establishes the seat of reason and what matters the name calling.

Without presuming to be all-inclusive, the attempt here is to show the new young literary world of New York's Greenwich Village—its writers, its parties, its readings, its *scene*. Before World War II, the Village—then America's only Bohemia—was a vaguely defined geographic area centering around Washington Square, extending north to Fourteenth Street, west to the Hudson River and south to Houston Street. The subsequent housing shortage pushed the young writers in search of inexpensive flats to Chelsea, the East Side, Brooklyn Heights and even further outlaying areas of the city. But the Village is still their haven and center and over ninety per cent of Fred Mc-

Darrah's photographs were taken there. The writers, too, who appear here are all "Villagers" or, at least, visitors to this home of Bohemia which has clearly established branches throughout the country especially on the West Coast where the "beat" movement initially started and reached its most outstanding proportions. The selection of contributions attempts to illustrate the chief currents presently evident among these writers.

This Bohemia of social, political and artistic outcasts is deeply rooted in America. Over a hundred years ago, Herman Melville in *Pierre* saluted its presence and perfectly described its qualities: "They are mostly artists of various sorts; painters or sculptors, or indigent students, or teachers of languages, or poets, or fugitive French politicians, or German philosophers. Their mental tendencies, however heterodox at times, are still very fine and spiritual on the whole; since the vacuity of their exchequers leads them to reject the coarse materialism of Hobbes, and incline to the airy exaltations of the Berkleyean philosophy. . . . These are the glorious paupers from whom I learned the profoundest mysteries of things; since their very existence in the midst of such a terrible precariousness of the commonest means of support, affords a problem on which many speculative nut-crackers have been vainly employed. Yet let me offer up three locks of my hair to the memory of all such glorious paupers who have lived and died in this world. Surely, and truly I honor them—noble men often at bottom—and for that very reason I make bold to be gamesome about them; for where fundamental nobleness is, and fundamental honor is due, merriment is never accounted irreverent. The fools and pretenders of humanity, and the imposters and baboons among the gods, these only are offended with raillery. . . ."

Now in the mid-twentieth century, at a time of the country's greatest economic prosperity, has come again the Bohemian discovery of the insignificance of wealth. The Bohemian lives by his ideas and emotions which while easily convertible to money are not then left intact. Poverty, moreover, becomes desireable by freeing a person's attachment to the physical niceties of living beyond, as Walt Whitman said, "the easy dollars that supply the year's plain clothing and meals." This, they would argue, liberates the spirit for the joyful intensities of the human condition.

Accept the idea of the unimportance of money except to provide the necessities and you destroy the foundation of the prevailing American concept of the good life. Neglect wealth, social position and security and you reject the frenzied whirl that has possessed the age. In this social sense, today's Bohemia can be said to be in "revolt" and "revolutionary" with clear political implications. The shape of such politics depends on the emphasis placed on the concept of the role of the individual. There are those for whom the duty is purely personal sensuality and possibly William Burroughs best expresses it. At the other side are those believing the individual to be found only in his life with other people; and here one might place Lawrence Ferlinghetti.

Arguments have been made that the "beats" are neo-fascist in spirit because there is apparent in some of the writings an anti-humanist element, a mystical withdrawal to the inner life, a glorification of individual sensibilities, a denunciation of social responsibilities, use of drugs and the applauding of sexual immorality. It is never possible to avoid this political argument. We have seen in our own time Ezra Pound reading Fascist speeches from Rome and his disciple, John Kasper, leading racist mobs in our southern states; Celine on the side of anti-semitism and the Nazis; Hamsun welcoming Hitler's armies; Hesse's early books—*Steppenwolf* and *Demian*—used cult-like by young SS officers.

Who can question this? But the presence of others must not be forgotten: Sartre and Camus in the French underground, Kenneth Patchen's ardent pacifism, Hemingway's *For Whom the Bell Tolls,* Garcia Lorca murdered in Spain, Auden and Spender—all speaking for the humanistic, democratic spirit.

You can't lump all writers together—not even the Bohemians. And if you mean just the "beats," do you mean *Life* magazine "beat," Ginsberg "beat," Kerouac "beat," or Norman Mailer "beat"? Each should have to be examined separately to make conclusions—whether aesthetic, political or moral. Such variety is the nature of the human; the artist probably more than any other reflects and projects this spectrum of impulses driving people's emotions and thoughts deciding their minds. The writer is no better (though critics think they should be) and no worse (though philosophers tend to allege) than other people. The reader has the choice of agreeing or disagreeing. This is the common ground of all social life and in the field of human expression—of art—there is just as much responsibility for the observer as for the artist. Each has his own and it serves no purpose to state that neither has any, as though that were possible.

Of explicit political attitudes, a deep suspicion and distrust of all state operations and participation dominates a rejection of both armed camps—communist and capitalist. Its configuration is the mushroom shape of the nuclear bomb and the holes dug in the salt mines to circumvent the abolition of national suicide. It spews anti-politics if politics must mean the acceptance of "practical" man hugging shibbeloths of moralities that would countenance non-moral deceits, lies, cheating, distrust, violence, self-agrandissement and national political life aimed at bigger rockets to the moon. If a label is desired, perhaps that of Thoreau is most suited—the Thoreau who envisioned, to alter slightly, "a world at last which can afford to be just to all men, and to treat the individual with respect as a neighbor; which even would not think it inconsistent with its own repose if a few were to live aloof from it, not meddling with it, nor embraced by it, who fulfilled all the duties of neighbors and fellow men. A world which bore this kind of fruit, and suffered it to drop off as fast as it ripened, would prepare the way for a still more perfect and glorious world. . . ."

Along with the rediscovery of the human—the individual—has come the resurgence of poetry as a means of expression. Poetry, assumedly, always functioned this way but the peculiar turn it had taken in America in the previous twenty years had obscured its potency. Poetry had largely become smothered with explication and obscurantism to the extent of poets writing set pieces about minimal fragments of life and reaching a small coterie who alone could decipher the symbols. Prose had fallen into the hands of journalists or literary stylists. Creativity had become tongue-tied by language and art. Walt Whitman's cry was again raised, "What I experience or portray shall go from my composition without a shred of my composition. You shall stand by my side and look in the mirror with me."

The aesthetic problem assumes interest in this current Bohemia in direct relation to the individual writer's view of the role of art. There is the ever-evident denunciation of Academies though in this everchanging Bohemia there are already discernible "schools" forming as aesthete followers group around appointed "leaders." The battles of form vs. content are again waged round the clock and it is questionable if the Ivory Tower of Art is a crushed rubble lying buried off Cape Cod with the radioactive waste of atomic plants. Aesthetic influences range far and wide—Walt Whitman, William Carlos Williams, Ezra Pound—

Rimbaud, Apollinaire, Valery—Lorca, Brecht, Mayakovski—Hoelderlin, Smart, Blake—and not only the Western writers but also those of Far East. There are neo-dadaists, neo-surrealists, and neo-romantics. There is no want of aesthetic theories. Contemporary European writers such as Beckett, Ionesco, Genet, and Artaud exert enormous influence. The less well known Americans, Robert Creeley and Charles Olson, are playing an important role in the shaping of current poetics; both were teachers at the avant-garde Black Mountain College, North Carolina, which was forced to close in the early Fifties.

The dominating concern, though, would appear to be more typically with philosophical questions. This finds particular emphasis in religious quests inextricably bound up in the popular mind with the bursting interest in Zen Buddhism. To Japanese Zen, they look for the ecstasy of experiencing the momentary as against the usual Western view of counting one's enjoyments as pieces of a larger way of life. In Zen, they seek to penetrate beyond the logical aspects of the mind into the core of the human spirit to bring fruition to this "truly human reality."

Alternately, there is the appeal of primitive Christianity—"what Christ really meant"—to which they turn for a humanist, rational, social tradition. In not quite rejecting the nonpurposeful life, they would see in the Sermon on the Mount, the "beatitudes," a pure statement of by what a man should live. This used to be called primitive communism but today is linked more closely with philosophical anarchism. Moreover, God, instead of being dumped, is assuming the proportions of a Revival.

In this litany of influences the atheistic Existentialism developed by Jean Paul Sartre cannot be overlooked especially as it was modified in the writings of Albert Camus. This mixed vision of life, a brew of Zen, Christ, Camus, is clearly reflected in the recent joint statement by Ginsberg, Orlovsky and Corso who sought to define the Beat Generation: ". . . there are six thousand stars at night; but there are billions and billions of unseen stars. Six thousand you can actually count. The sun is a star. But earth isn't a star. You know how many earths can fit into a star, let's say our star the sun? I bet a thousand or more. So there. How does that make you feel? Insignificant? Cheap? Terrible? Envious? Contemptuous? That's why there's a Beat Generation, not because doom hovers over earth manmade doom, doom (destruction) was here before we were born, there's no escape, so why worry about that, destruction is a distraction, there are other things to consider, wondrous things; the Beat Generation is insulted when linked to doom, thoughts of doom, fear of doom, anger of doom. The Beat Generation is because truth rests on the contradictory rattans of the soul. . . . All is endless, limitless, infinity is a dog sitting at its own feet. The BG is a climax, therefore it's as insignificant as anything man can mouth, for what has the BG to do with the dromedaries of the solar system? . . . Nothing means nothing. Cows, radiator soup, mother's death, war documents, Alcman's Maiden Song, Greeks wearing shorts, Smith College; only the wonders of sunset mean anything. . . . Yet starless things would deprive the BG of its illusions. Why? Because they, the starless, don't believe in clairvoyant abstraction, that's why. They really believe that man is, that man exists, how sad, how absurd! Man does not exist, man is just an invention of God; a senseless invention in this great movement of insensibility. . . . So don't listen to what earth has to say, earth is jealous of heaven. Jealous because it knows it's not even a star. The truth is thick in the fleeted loom. Mutinous substance! The truth is deep, the truth is sickening, the truth is relatively safe; everything but the BG stands amid the ordeals of lie. . . ."

While Jack Kerouac's novel *On the Road* launched "beat" in the public eye, it was brought more into focus by Allen Ginsberg's slim book of poetry, *Howl.* Most academics, university professors, critics and established poets made it absolutely clear what they thought of *Howl*—it stank. In America's literary past, there was another comparable to-do when Walt Whitman brought out *Leaves of Grass* exactly a hundred years earlier. Ginsberg had William Carlos Williams, the respected elder of American poets, to champion his cause and Whitman had Ralph Waldo Emerson who wrote him enthusiastically, "I greet you at the beginning of a great career."

Emerson began a one-man crusade for Whitman, sending copies to his friends and insisting to others that they buy and read it—"Have you read that wonderful book . . . ," he kept asking.

Now look at the reactions. Charles Eliot Norton acknowledged some good points but ". . . passages of intolerable coarseness—not gross & licentious, but simply disgustingly coarse. The book is such, indeed, that one cannot leave it about for chance readers, and would be very sorry to know that any woman had looked into it past the title page. . . ." James Russell Lowell when queried; "No, no, the kind of thing you describe won't do. When a man aims at originality, he acknowledges himself consciously unoriginal, a want of self-respect, etc." J. P. Lesley, friend of Emerson; ". . . had examined the 'profane and obscene' *Leaves of Grass* and thought the author a pretentious ass without decency. . . ."

The *Boston Intelligence* roared: "The beastliness of the author is set forth in his own description of himself, and we can conceive of no better reward than the lash for such a violation of decency. The author should be kicked from all decent society as below the level of the brute. He must be some escaped lunatic raving in pitiable delirium."

But Emerson stuck with him and Thoreau championed him and Walt Whitman kept on with poetry.

Here are the echoes today. Philip Rahv pronounces, "I have looked over the stuff and it seems pretty vacuous to me." Lionel Trilling: "I have no admiration for the 'beat' literature—except for a few lines or sequences of lines in some of the poems I have read—and my only interest in the whole 'beat' movement is in the quasi-religous aspect of the phenomenon." William Troy: "Any absurdity pushed far enough may lead to a rediscovery of order and grace." Marius Bewly: "I imagine by this time all decent Americans are opposed to fall-out and Eisenhower, but I fail to see why protest against the age should extend to good manners and creased trousers."

Walt Whitman managed through self-effort to sell or give away a thousand or so copies of *Leaves of Grass* in the first few years; *Howl* sold over 50,000 copies in the same span. It had the initial notoriety of a California Court case where local police sought to suppress the City Lights edition. This has largely been forgotten as more recent such cases as *Lady Chatterly's Lover* have taken this public spotlight. But *Howl* keeps selling. Seemingly, every college freshman must be buying it for this ever new and young audience would appear to be the source of continuing readership.

Ferlinghetti's *Coney Island of the Mind* is also having a sensational sale for poetry in America. New Directions, the publishers, have sold tens of thousands and at one time were hard pressed getting copies from the printers to meet the demand. This is extraordinary because a volume of so-called "good" poetry hovers around the 800 sales mark and rarely gets beyond 2,000 except for established poets such as Auden, Moore and Cummings. At University readings, Ginsberg packs thousands into staid halls. In coffee shops throughout the nation, young writers read to a seemingly ever increasing audience. On statistics alone, it is clear that this new literature is speaking for an important part of its generation.

PAUL S. GEORGE AND JEROLD M. STARR (ESSAY DATE 1985)

SOURCE: George, Paul S., and Jerold M. Starr. "Beat Politics: New Left and Hippie Beginnings in the Postwar Counterculture." In *Cultural Politics: Radical Movements in Modern History*, edited by Jerold M. Starr, pp. 189-233. New York: Praeger, 1985.

In the following essay, George and Starr trace the rise and spread of the Beat Generation in New York and San Francisco, characterizing it as a "countercultural rebellion" that arose in opposition to the conformity and consumerism of contemporary society.

Modern bohemia can be traced to the production of Victor Hugo's play *Hernani* in Paris in 1830. Amid shouts of "shock the bourgeoisie," "Hugo's 'romantic army' of wild-haired, funkily-dressed artists was born." These first bohemians had rejected their bourgeois families to make art and live freely among the city's poor. The bourgeoisie called them *buozingo*—a derogatory reference to their fondness for booze.

In the late 1840s Henri Murger wrote several stories about four bohemian comrades that he called *Scènes de la vie bohème.* The lines include: "Where will we eat today? We'll know tomorrow." In 1849 he put them together into a surprisingly popular play, and in 1896 the play became the opera *La bohème,* by Puccini. All of this notoriety "drew young people aspiring to the life, along with bourgeois voyeurs" (Miller 1977, pp. 44-58; Graber 1958). Malcolm Cowley (1951, p. 13) credits Murger with creating the myth of bohemia as a territory and a way of life.

Through the years bohemian communities have grown up at different times all over the world. San Francisco, a lusty, brawling city immersed in the feverish California gold rush and settled recently by "lunatic miners, whores, pirates, Latins and Asians," became an early haven for bohemians (McNally 1979, p. 201). An explosion of interest in the arts in the 1880s gave the city the claim to be America's first true bohemia. From the turn of the century through the 1920s, New York and Chicago also had flourishing bohemias. They were located in older, poorer neighborhoods where food and lodging were inexpensive. Bistros and restaurants served as important social centers (Howard 1974, p. 181).

Wherever they lived, bohemians expressed certain Romantic ideals in their art and life-styles.

These included the notion that every human's potential should be allowed to develop freely; adoration of the "primitive"; the celebration of fraternity; the beauty of nature; wanderlust and the lure of the exotic; the transformative power of art; free love; the quest for intense experience; and, above all, living uncorrupted by bourgeois materialism and unrestrained by bourgeois convention (Mannheim 1971; Gouldner 1973).

The materialist and nationalist preoccupations of the Great Depression and World War II proved inhospitable to the survival of a bohemian alternative in the United States. By the end of the war none was visible. Soon after, however, small numbers of dissident artists and intellectuals began seeking escape from bourgeois society in New York's Greenwich Village and San Francisco's North Beach.

Over the next several years, American society became increasingly militarized. For the first time in its history, the federal government forced its young men into peacetime military training. It raced with the Soviet Union to develop and stockpile nuclear weapons even larger than those which had leveled Hiroshima and Nagasaki. And it sacrificed 50,000 lives in Korea in what it called a "police action."

On the home front, patriotic conformity was enforced by the carrot of Madison Avenue consumerism and the stick of McCarthyite repression. The principles of Nuremberg were left to the Existentialist philosophers. In the midst of all this, those few bohemian alternative communities grew rapidly, each in its own way. In the early 1950s, some of the New York bohemian writers traveled to San Francisco and made contact with their brothers. Within the next five years, they started a countercultural rebellion. The Beat Generation was born.

Hipsters Beget Beats

The tone of New York bohemian life after World War II was profoundly influenced by the cultural rebellion in the black ghetto. Recalling the spirit of the Harlem Renaissance of the 1920s, many residents sought to re-create the culture of their community. Renouncing Uncle Tomism, they declared their independence of whites through a new language, dress, and music. A restrained "cool," referred to these days as "style," replaced the earlier image of a child-like, excitable "darkie" who humbled himself before whites.

These new blacks, aggressively independent, were called "hip." Some claimed the term referred to someone who lived dangerously and carried "a bottle or bankroll or, more likely, a gun on his hip" (Miller 1977, pp. 238-39). Others suggested the term came from "a much earlier phrase, 'to be on the hip,' to be a devotee of opium smoking—during which activity one lies on one's hip" (Polsky 1969, pp. 145-46). In either case, the term "hip" was associated with drugs, violence, and crime. Daring and defiant, the "hipster" was a person "who could take care of himself in any situation."

The patois of the hipster, called "jive" talk, was a secret code language, laced with poetic metaphor to conceal illegal drug traffic. For music, the hipsters "dug" blues or hot jazz that gave expression to the sorrow of their oppression and the transcendent joy of their togetherness (McNally 1979, p. 82; Mailer 1969).

As early as the late 1920s, white big-band musicians, such as Mezz Mezzrow and Bix Beiderbecke, were smoking marijuana and talking jive with their black brothers (Nuttall 1968, pp. 3-9; Miller 1977, pp. 237-38). By the 1940s other disaffiliated whites used drugs and took up the outlaw life-style of the black hipster. In recalling his youth in the 1940s, Malcolm X reflected, "A few of the white men around Harlem, younger ones whom we called 'hippies,' acted more Negro than Negroes" (Miller 1977, p. 239).

The Central Characters

It was on the edge of Harlem, around Columbia University, that the New York wing of the Beat Generation first formed. Around Christmas of 1944, Lucien Carr introduced his fellow Saint Louisan Bill Burroughs to Allen Ginsberg, whom he had met in his Columbia dormitory the previous year. Carr also had introduced Jack Kerouac, another Columbia undergraduate, to Burroughs, and it was Burroughs who brought Ginsberg, then a sophomore, and Kerouac together (Cook 1971, pp. 40-41).

Ginsberg was very impressed with Kerouac, who had come to Columbia four years earlier on a football scholarship. "I remember being awed by him, because I'd never met a big jock who was sensitive and intelligent about poetry." Kerouac was at first less taken with Ginsberg, who was five years his junior and had a reputation as a mad genius who would argue any position for the sport of it. Before long, however, Kerouac was charmed by Ginsberg's passion for ideas and total candor (Cook 1971, pp. 40-41).

Within a year the three grew to be close friends. Ginsberg was 21; Kerouac, 26; and Burroughs, 32. Ginsberg and Kerouac were impressed with Burroughs, who put them on a reading regimen of literary works by such "renegades of high culture" as Céline, Rimbaud, Spengler, Kafka, Gogol, Yeats, and Gide (McNally 1979, p. 66; Kostelanetz 1970). Burroughs also conducted psychoanalysis with each, on the couch in his back room, for about a year (Cook 1971, p. 41).

By that time Burroughs was addicted to heroin. He introduced Ginsberg and Kerouac to one of his friendly connections, Herbert Huncke. A homosexual, drug addict, intellectual, and part-time researcher for the original Kinsey Report, Huncke was "an authentic professor of hip" (Tytell 1976, pp. 37-40). He led the three on a personal tour of the hipster underworld of Times Square, turned them on to several drugs, and introduced them to "a steady succession of petty and not-so-petty criminals, sex deviates and desperate men" (Cook 1971, p. 42). From these experiences Ginsberg and Kerouac saw that there were others, like themselves, who were different, and came to identify with the defiance of the outlaw rather than the shame of the outcast (Tytell 1976, p. 57).

Around the beginning of 1947, Kerouac met Neal Cassady through former roommate Hal Chase. Cassady and Chase were both from Denver and knew each other through their common mentor, high school teacher Justin Brierly. Chase called Cassady "a self aware representative of the American underclass, a reform school punk with an eye for poetry." Soon after meeting Cassady, Kerouac introduced him to the group in New York. All of them were impressed with young Neal, who had served time in prison and also wrote poetry (McNally 1979, pp. 89-93; Gifford and Lee 1979, p. 85).

Cassady was a skillful, tireless automobile driver and mechanic with a passion for speed. Referred to in print as "Superman," the "fastest-manalive," and "the Holy Goof," Cassady is fictionalized as "Hart Kennedy" in the first Beat novel, John Clellan Holmes's *GO*, as "Dean Moriarty" and "Cody Pomeray" in Kerouac's *On the Road* and *Visions of Cody*, and as "Hicks" in Robert Stone's *Dog Soldiers* (later made into a film called *Who'll Stop the Rain*).

Cassady was a man of enormous energy, a nonstop talker, handsome, muscular, and bursting with intelligent curiosity. He had affairs with countless women and also with Allen Ginsberg and a few other men, apparently as part of his insatiable quest for new experience.

Many considered Cassady to be the most authentic Beat of all because he never acquired money or national reputation from the movement (Hills 1979; Cook 1971, p. 198). Yet in the late 1960s Kerouac was to claim: "I'm not afraid to admit that Neal made me a better writer. His letters, his philosophy, his whole existence was a treasure to me. Neal Cassady was the greatest writer of the bunch. Better than Ginsberg, Holmes, Corso" (Jarvis 1973-74, p. 132; Gifford and Lee 1977, p. 115).

It was Cassady who put the Beat's Romantic wanderlust in high gear. By the summer of 1947, with Cassady behind the wheel, Kerouac, Burroughs, Huncke, and Ginsberg crisscrossed the continent in search of adventure. Burroughs' homes in Louisiana and, later, Mexico were frequent stops, as were Denver and San Francisco.

Despite their limited success—none of the Beats really made any money from their writing until 1957—all of them thought of themselves as men of letters. In his introduction to Burroughs' autobiography, *Junky*, Ginsberg admits that, by the beginning of the 1950s, both he and Kerouac considered themselves "poet/writers in Destiny" (Burroughs 1979, p. v).

According to Ginsberg, "it was Kerouac who encouraged Burroughs to write," first involving him in a "big detective book" in which they alternated chapters, imitating the style of Dashiell Hammett (Clark 1970). By the beginning of the 1950s, Burroughs had completed *Junky* and Ginsberg "began taking it around to various classmates in college or mental hospitals who had succeeded in establishing themselves in Publishing—an ambition which was mine also, frustrated; and thus incompetent in wordly matters, I conceived of myself as a secret literary agent" (Burroughs 1979, p. vi). At the time, Ginsberg also was carrying around "Kerouac's Proustian Chapters from *Visions of Cody* that later developed into the vision of *On the Road*." He met Carl Solomon, a poet and bohemian celebrity, while both were patients at the New York Psychiatric Institute. Soloman later became an editor under his uncle at Ace Books, and Ginsberg persuaded him to publish *Junky* and advance Kerouac $250 for a prose novel (Burroughs 1979, p. vii; Clark 1970, p. 133).

Although many interesting women passed through their lives, they all were kept outside of this tight circle of "junkies and geniuses" who met frequently to discuss literature, philosophy, and social change, experiment with drugs, and party raucously. Carr believed the circle was creating a "New Vision," a heightened awareness of man and society (McNally 1979, pp. 62-67; Gifford and Lee 1979, p. 45; Kramer 1968, p. 77).

The Generational Vision

Kerouac has left a fascinating account of the emergence of this postwar counterculture. Toward the end of the war, he observed hipsters around Times Square who "looked like criminals" and spoke a language sprinkled liberally with such phrases as "crazy, man" and "man, I'm beat" (Kerouac 1959). He also heard them articulate "long lines of personal experience and vision, nightlong expressions full of hope that had become illicit and repressed by War, stirring rumblings of a new soul" (Plummer 1979). "Rising from the underground," Kerouac (1957, p. 46) wrote in *On the Road*, was "the sordid hipster, a new beat generation that I was slowly joining."

Kerouac told John Clellan Holmes (1958) of a vision he had of crazy, illuminated hipsters roaming America. In a conversation with Cassady in 1951, he pictured an America where at "a Ritz Yale Club party [which he attended] . . . there were hundreds of kids in leather jackets instead of big tuxedo Clancy millionaires . . . cool, and everybody was smoking marijuana, wailing in a new decade in one wild crowd." According to Kerouac (1972, pp. 36-37), this second generation of hip replaced the original black hipsters, who, by 1950, had "vanished into jails and madhouses, or were shamed into silent conformity. . . ." This new, post-Korean War "Beat Generation" consisted of white youth who slouched around in T-shirts and jeans, wore long sideburns, took drugs, "dug" bebop, and talked like the original hipsters.

The term "Beat" was taken from the jive talk of the jazz musicians. It was introduced to Kerouac by Huncke, who used it to describe a person "exhausted, defeated, depressed, but full of internal conviction" (Kramer 1968, p. 77). In the first Beat novel, *Go*, author John Clellan Holmes (1967, p. 107) quotes Kerouac's definition of Beat:

> It's a sort of furtiveness, like we're a generation of furtives. You know, with an inner knowledge there's no use flaunting on that level, the level of the "public," a kind of beatness—I mean being right down to it, to ourselves, because we all really know where we are—and a weariness with all the forms, all the conventions of the world. . . . It's something like that. So I guess you might say we're a beat generation.

Holmes added that the "Beats" felt like Negroes caught in a square world that wasn't enough for them.

San Francisco Beat

In 1952 Ginsberg and Kerouac moved to Berkeley, where they met Kenneth Rexroth and, over the next three years, many young San Francisco poets. By the time Kerouac and Ginsberg arrived, San Francisco had been a center for political and cultural radicalism for years. During World War II the War Resisters League and Fellowship of Reconciliation were actively supported. San Francisco was within hitchhiking distance of all of the conscientious objectors' camps in America; most passed through and many stayed. Rexroth recalls:

> All of this led immediately after the war to the founding of the Anarchist Circle, a very important group while it lasted. Talk about your intellectual fellowship—well, you really could sense it in those meetings . . . you could say damned near anything there and not get sneered at or put down. It was all open in a way that real political discussion never is. This was ideas beyond factions and politics.
>
> (Cook 1971, p. 60)

In 1947 Ruth White founded the San Francisco Poetry Center. Along with Rexroth, Philip Lamantia, Robert Duncan, and Lew Welch gathered there regularly. A radical conscientious objector named William Everson came to town and started writing poems for *Catholic World* under the name of Brother Antoninus. Michael McClure came from the Midwest, Philip Whalen and Gary Snyder from the Northwest, and Lawrence Ferlinghetti from New York. Ferlinghetti established the City Lights Bookstore, perhaps the first paperback bookstore in the country. It became a favorite hangout for many local poets and, at their urging, Ferlinghetti started the City Lights Press in 1956 to publish their works.

Ginsberg introduced Kerouac to poet Gary Snyder, who had a profound impact on the Beat movement. First, he introduced the Beats to a love of nature and more natural ways of living (Seelye 1974). A student of the American Indian, Snyder was deeply concerned about the destruction of the environment. In his collection *Earth House Hold*, Snyder (1969, p. 90) writes: "The conditions, The Cold War, has turned all modern societies—Communist included—into vicious distortions of man's true potential. . . . The soil, the forests, and all the animal life are being consumed by these cancerous collectivities; the air and water of the planets are being fouled by them."

Snyder's second major contribution to the Beats consisted of "his anecdotes and poems of the wandering Zen Buddhist monks," which "gave a sense of intellectual, even religious justification to the beats' deep natural impulse to freedom, their wish to stay unattached and on the move" (Cook 1971, p. 29).

Under Snyder's influence Kerouac learned to camp in the mountains and commune with nature. He abandoned the desperate activity of his previous escapes from boredom and began an inward search for his roots. Written in 1956, *The Dharma Bums* "replaces the hysteria of *On the Road* with quietly contemplative retreat toward meditation" (Tytell 1976, p. 25).

The philosophy of Zen Buddhism enjoyed widespread popularity through the 1950s. Polsky (1969, p. 172) calls it perhaps the first major bohemian cultural importation in America that traveled from west to east. Many of its themes were compatible with the Beats' Romantic, bohemian outlook, including the focus on inner consciousness and the fleeting present, the political quietism, the idea of the wandering quest, the holiness of the personal impulse, and the significant role of the Zen lunatic, the holy madman.

The Ideology of Beat

Kerouac's encounter with Zen reinforced the Catholic mysticism of his youth. Snyder chided him, "You old son of a bitch. You're going to end up asking for the Catholic rites on your death bed" (Cook 1971, p. 84). And, in fact, it was in a church in Lowell in 1954 that Kerouac had had the religious experience that led to his redefinition of "Beat": "I went one afternoon to the church of my childhood (one of them), Ste. Jeanne d'Arc in Lowell . . . and suddenly with tears in my eyes I had a vision of what I must have really meant with "Beat" anyhow when I heard the holy silence in the church . . ." (Rigney and Smith 1961, pp. 34-35).

When *On the Road* was published in 1957, it contained a new definition of Beat: "He was BEAT—the root, the soul of Beatific." In other comments Kerouac disavowed the label of bohemian for the Beats and emphasized the religious dimension of their philosophic quest. In a 1958 article, "The Philosophy of the Beat Generation," Holmes concurred with Kerouac: "The Beat Generation is basically a religious generation . . . [it] means beatitude, not beat up." In May 1959 several North Beach poets launched a magazine that they called *Beatitude* (Rigney and Smith 1961, p. 32).

On the other hand, while "a few of the beats" studied by Rigney and Smith (1961, pp. 34-38) in North Beach "professed to be Orientalists, the majority were 'irreligious' avowedly professing no belief in anything." Neither did many see themselves as Beat "in the sense of beatitude or 'holiness' or mysticism." Instead, they saw themselves as "beaten down" but not "entirely 'out'" (Rigney and Smith 1961, p. 28). Through the years both the black/hipster and the religious meanings of Beat persisted, the former more compatible with the New Left of the early 1960s, the latter with the New Age movement of the early 1970s.

The Social Psychology of Ideology

In *Young Man Luther,* Erikson (1959) applies Freudian theory to the analysis of Martin Luther's biography in order to identify the psychological sources of his religious ideology. In Erikson's view, it was Luther's intense need "to be justified" in relation to his father that drove him to his revolutionary work. His historical success was due to the fact that, in working through his personal problems on the symbolic level, he developed an ideological solution to historical problems confronting vast numbers of his contemporaries. Thus, he was able "to lift his individual patienthood to the level of a universal one and to try to solve for all what he could not solve for himself alone" (Erikson 1959, p. 67).

The personal lives of the original Beats were marked by conflict, deprivation, failure, and disorder. They all suffered miserable early childhoods and, throughout life, found normal institutional regimentation an impossible burden to bear. As a consequence they became gifted misfits—refusing to fit into what they perceived to be an unfit fitness. Through the years they never stopped believing in their destinies as great writers. They burned with the need to justify themselves to the world and, through their writings, they gave voice to many others.

Ginsberg's mother, Naomi, a schoolteacher and Communist Party worker, suffered numerous nervous breakdowns, beginning in 1919, even before Allen was born. As Allen and his brother Eugene grew up,

> They watched her deteriorate before their eyes. One breakdown followed another, put her in and out of hospitals, and left her in a more or less permanent state of paranoia. . . . Her feelings of persecution were tied in the most twisted knots to her background in radical politics. Nothing was clearcut. Everyone was against her.
>
> (Cook 1971, pp. 113-14)

Allen and Eugene lived with their mother separately for extended periods of time. Ginsberg was certain that his homosexuality had roots in his adolescent repulsion toward his mother. His profoundest memories of that period "are of his mother's gross carnal reality—dresses hitched to the hips, pubic hair exposed, the smells of the body. Yes, always the body, her body" (Cook 1971, p. 114). All of this is revealed in his poem "Kaddish." A later poem, "The Change," resolves this conflict. In Cook's view, "The Change" should be read "as the missing final movement of 'Kaddish,' Resolution: To forgive the body that Naomi had made him hate was to forgive the body principle, woman, Naomi herself" (Cook 1971, p. 116).

Perhaps Naomi influenced Allen's politics, from his sustained opposition to all establishments to his later preoccupation with a mammoth drug ring conspiracy involving the CIA, the police, and organized crime (for which, it must be said, more than a little evidence exists). However, given the complexities of human character, Ginsberg's politics might better be considered an expression of his personality. Dickstein (1977, p. 20) comments:

> In his *Playboy* interview, Ginsberg described how his homosexuality . . . contributed to his political consciousness by making him sensitive to the element of hyper-masculinity and aggressiveness in the American mentality. He revived Whitman's version of a society whose communal ties are based on a renewal of personal tenderness. And of course he was delighted at the "reappearance in the form of long hair and joyful dress of the affectionate feminine in the natural Adamic man, the whole man, the man of many parts."

Although a brilliant student, Ginsberg had numerous confrontations with the dean of Columbia College "due to his sloppy appearance and eccentric behavior" (Cook 1971, p. 41). It sometimes took the intervention of such an esteemed Columbia scholar as Lionel Trilling and Mark Van Doren to get him off the hook with the Columbia administration. All of this must have made some impression, however, because the dean later got Ginsberg out of a threatening criminal situation by intervening with District Attorney Frank Hogan, a Columbia graduate (Tytell 1976, p. 94).

From 1945 to 1955 Ginsberg made five separate attempts at psychoanalysis. The first was with Burroughs; the second, for three months, with "a Reichian who is no longer a Reichian." In 1950 his association with Huncke, caught leaving Ginsberg's apartment with stolen merchandise, landed him in the New York State Psychiatric Institute for eight months with "dreary Freudians." This was followed by two and a half years with a doctor formerly attached to the institute. His final bout with therapy was his most successful. In 1955 Ginsberg spent a year with a follower of Harry Stack Sullivan in San Francisco. This doctor "urged Ginsberg to abandon the square life of a market researcher for Peter [Orlovsky], poetry, and pleasure," advice that apparently brought him greater peace of mind (Kostelanetz 1970).

Kerouac was born Jean Louis Kerouac, the son of French-Canadian parents in the old New England mill town of Lowell, Massachusetts. His alcoholic father died of stomach cancer when Jack was twenty-four. His mother was protective and domineering. In early childhood Jack witnessed the death of his brother Gerard of rheumatic fever. Gerard was the family saint, and he made a lasting impression on Jack both in life and in death. Charles Jarvis, an English professor, Lowell neighbor, and biographer of Kerouac, claims that Kerouac's glorification of his "holy brother" Neal Cassady in *Visions of Cody* and *On the Road* has roots in his spiritual longing for Gerard (Jarvis 1973-74, p. 128). Indeed, in *On the Road*, Kerouac (1957, p. 10) says Dean (Cassady) "reminded me of some long-lost brother." Five years after *Visions of Cody*, Kerouac wrote *Visions of Gerard*.

According to Jarvis, Kerouac grew up "sexually inhibited" and "very straight as a kid." He endeared himself to his gang of friends by his remarkable ability to recall the intimate details of their escapades, a service he was later to perform for the Beats. In Lowell they called him "memory babe" (Jarvis 1973-74, pp. 142-43, 162).

Kerouac's college career started with great promise. A star running back in high school, he received a scholarship to play football at Columbia. Within two years he had broken his leg during a game, decided to drop football, lost his scholarship, and enlisted in the navy. It was 1942, but the navy soon discharged him as "a schizoid personality," and he drifted into the merchant marine. In 1944 he got married during one of his weeks in port. He took his wife back to Columbia, determined to "get himself an education and become a great writer. But neither marriage nor his pass at education lasted long. His wife left him after six months, and shortly afterward he dropped out of Columbia" (Cook 1971, p. 41). He underwent psychoanalysis with Burroughs at the same time as Ginsberg, but it apparently failed to give him peace of mind.

In Jarvis' (1973-74, p. 208) view, Kerouac "was a man at war with himself. If his Beat novels shriek for the desire to burn, burn, burn, his Lowell novels lament for a lost innocence, an unfulfilled grace." While his Beat novels strove to achieve absolutely unedited spontaneity, his Lowell novels were censored so as not to offend his mother. Tytell (1976, p. 24) describes him as "brooding, lonely, seized by moments of self-hatred."

Visions of Cody was written between the fall of 1951 and the spring of 1952, while Kerouac lived with Neal Cassady and shared the affections of his wife, Carolyn. In her sentimental account of that period, Carolyn Cassady says she has "never known a man with such a tender heart, so much sweetness." However, he "was far too moody, his feelings too touchy, too wrapped up in himself." Although he was a brilliant observer, Kerouac's efforts to participate fully in life around him were "generally disappointing; he felt threatened and alone." Even his lovemaking "had an air of apology. I didn't feel that he ever gave or received completely." Only 31 at the time, Kerouac already "was never far from a bottle of wine." His alcoholism grew progressively worse (Cassady 1976, pp. 116-17). Kerouac vigorously denied being a "fag," but his association with Ginsberg, Burroughs, and Huncke caused rumors that disturbed him. (The most publicized was Gore Vidal's boast of having seduced him.) After two bad marriages and the shock of his sudden celebrity in the late 1950s, Kerouac returned to Lowell to marry a high school girlfriend and take care of his widowed mother. He remained a recluse during the final years of his life, his mother turning away the visits of Ginsberg, Burroughs, and others, until he succumbed to cirrhosis of the liver in 1969, at the age of 47 (McNally 1979, pp. 322-24, 344; Charters 1973, pp. 362-67).

Kerouac's companion Neal Cassady grew up in poverty in Denver. His father, a skid row alcoholic, separated from his mother when Neal was just a toddler. As early as age six, Neal remembers living with his father in flophouses, taking his meals at a nearby mission, begging his father to stop drinking, and riding the rails east to Kansas City and west to Los Angeles. His mother had nine children from her two marriages and was "simply too much harassed" to show him "her affection adequately . . . I still can't remember her ever kissing me." Still, he recalled her as "the kindest and most gentle of women" (Cassady 1971, p. 53).

Two older stepbrothers, as strapping adolescents, used to beat his father bloody when he came home drunk every Saturday night and, after his separation from their mother, whenever their paths crossed. Another stepbrother, a few years older and larger than Neal, was a jealous, sadistic bully who enjoyed beating him and imprisoning him inside a wall bed for hours on end.

A compulsive car thief, Cassady refers, in a letter to Kerouac dated July 3, 1949, to already having been arrested 10 times, and convicted 6 times, and to having served 15 months (Cassady 1971, p. 129). Some of these arrests may have been for marijuana, which brought him a two-year sentence on a California prison farm in 1957-58 (Cook 1971, p. 198). Shortly thereafter, he met Ken Kesey and over the next few years became one of Kesey's Merry Pranksters, graduating from pot and peyote to LSD and speed. In the mid-1960s he drove Kesey's Dayglo colored bus up and down the California coast and across the country (Wolfe 1968).

Cassady's father disappeared sometime during Neal's youth. As late as age 24, while on the road with Kerouac, Neal still searched for him, but in vain. Despite his awesome manic energy, Cassady has been described as unhappy, even suicidal, for most of his adult life (Berriault 1972). He was married three times, but was alone at the end. He died of exposure in rural Mexico in February 1968, rumored to have been depressed at growing old. He was 42.

William Burroughs was born to wealthy parents in St. Louis in 1914. His father owned and ran a lumber business. His grandfather had started the Burroughs machine empire and left him a trust fund that provided $150 per month for life. Still, life was anything but easy for young Bill. In his autobiography, *Junky,* Burroughs confesses that his "earliest memories are colored by a fear of nightmares. I was afraid to be alone, and afraid of the dark, and afraid to go to sleep because of dreams where a supernatural horror seemed always on the point of taking shape." Even when awake, Burroughs suffered from recurring hallucinations (Burroughs 1979, pp. xi-xvi).

Burroughs went to a "progressive school," where he was "timid with the other children and afraid of physical violence." In high school he became a "chronic malingerer" with fantasies of a life of crime, given to acts of petty vandalism to combat the "dullness of a Midwest suburb where all contact with life was shut out" (Burroughs 1979, p. xii). One episode cost him his only friend, and he then found himself "a good deal alone," drifting into "solo adventures" of breaking into private homes (but not taking anything) and reckless driving.

At Harvard, Burroughs "knew no one," "was lonely," "hated the University," and "hated the town it was in." For a time he associated with "some rich homosexuals of the international queer set," but decided they were "jerks" and went his own way. However, his desire for young males was now established. He was graduated from Harvard "without honors" and "drifted around Europe for a year or so."

Back in the United States, Burroughs underwent three years of psychoanalysis that "removed inhibitions and anxiety" regarding his homosexuality. Somewhere along the line he was put into a "nut house" and diagnosed "schizophrenic, paranoid" after cutting off a finger joint as a gesture of love for a friend. This record was sufficient to have him released from military service after a short stint during the war.

Burroughs then drifted along, holding a variety of jobs, such as private detective, exterminator, bartender, factory worker, and office worker, also engaging in occasional petty crime. Burroughs writes, "It was at this time and under these circumstances that I came in contact with junk, became an addict, and thereby gained the motivation, the real need for money I had never had before" (Burroughs 1979, p. xi). His nightmarish addiction to heroin was to last for 15 years. Married for many years, he accidentally killed his wife, Peggy, while demonstrating his prowess with a pistol. Urged on by friends, although too drunk to aim straight, he missed the apple and put a bullet through her head.

The last of the principal New York Beats to join the circle was Gregory Corso. Ginsberg met Corso at a bar in 1950. Corso had grown up a street kid, his Italian immigrant father a hazy figure of his childhood and his mother having died young. He spent some time in the children's observation ward at Bellevue Hospital and was in and out of trouble. At 16 he was sentenced for robbery and spent the next three years in prison. Corso, just released, had written some poems while in prison that he showed to Ginsberg at his urging. He soon became the "bad boy" of the Beats, a role he gloried in (Cook 1971, pp. 133-49).

In sum, all of the Beats suffered childhoods troubled by parents who were disturbed, alcoholic, domineering, or unloving, or siblings who were jealous and sadistic. Whatever resources they developed within themselves to cope with these situations somehow rendered them unfit for conventional life. They had confrontations with school authorities or the law, they dropped out, were imprisoned, placed in an asylum, or became addicted to heroin. None of them desired any vocation in life other than writing, so they took only temporary jobs to support their literature. They lived in barely furnished, run-down apartment buildings, in neighborhoods that trafficked in all sorts of crime. They wore old clothes and made most of their own entertainment. They were shunned by the "square" world and scorned by many of the prominent critics of their day as untalented "know nothings."

What distinguished them from ordinary deviants or malcontents was their talent, their inner conviction, and the historical circumstances that made it possible for them to communicate with the growing constituency of youth and bohemians they came to represent. In so doing, they turned their stigma into a blessing, their shame into defiance. In the process they set the pattern for the black, youth, women's and gay revolutions to follow. Each of these groups stopped trying to justify its failure to meet white, adult, middle-class male standards, and instead accepted the dominant stereotype of themselves and declared it superior. They inverted the values by which such judgments were made and such prestige hierarchies sustained. The Beats were the first to put down the "squares," ridicule the authorities, debunk the myths, expose the hypocrisies, and, thus, delegitimate the culture of domination. Writing about Cassady (Dean Moriarty) in *On the Road,* Kerouac (1957, p. 11) declares, "His 'criminality' was not something that sulked and sneered; it was a wild yea-saying overburst of American joy. . . ."

Beat Writing: The Romantic Challenge

The main characteristics of Beat writing are the juxtaposition of opposites, presenting a picture of the world in all its beauty and terror; a sense of the absurd; the importance of the clown or holy fool; and insistence on the nonrational as a way of knowing (Lipton 1959, pp. 238-44). This orientation is reflected in the Beat writers' lists of their favorite poets and authors: almost entirely nineteenth-century French and English Romantics and American transcendentalists such as Hugo, Baudelaire, Rimbaud, Blake, Shelley, Keats, Byron, Thoreau, and Whitman (Kostelanetz 1970; Clark 1970).

Ginsberg and Kerouac, in particular among the Beats, attempted to achieve Romantic form in their writing. In Ginsberg's view, the "trouble with conventional form is it's too symmetrical, geometrical, numbered and pre-fixed unlike my own

Rick Allmen's Cafe Bizarre on West Third Street in Greenwich Village, circa 1959.

mind which has no beginning and end, nor fixed measure of thought [of speech writing] other than its own cornerless mystery" (Kostelanetz 1970).

Kerouac's challenge was to break down the distinction between the frank content of personal conversation between friends and the formality of conventional literary subject matter. Ginsberg comments,

> That was Kerouac's great discovery in *On the Road.* The kinds of things that he and Neal Cassady were talking about, he finally discovered were *the* subject matter for what he wanted to write down. That meant, at that minute, a complete revision of what literature was supposed to be.
>
> (Clark 1970, p. 135)

The special form the Beats attempted to effect in their writing was that of black urban bebop jazz. Bebop was first played in a Harlem nightclub called Minturn's Playhouse in 1942. The group consisted of Thelonious Monk (piano), Dizzie Gillespie (trumpet), Charles Christian (guitar), and Kenny Clark (drums), and featured Charlie Parker (saxophone) (Hodeir 1956, p. 99). It carried jazz radically further in its movement away from the tight symphonic arrangements of the white "swing" bands and toward group and solo improvisation and an emphasis on rhythm and feeling (Hodeir 1956, pp. 99-104; Willener 1970, pp. 231-32; Bjorn 1980). Bebop was played everywhere in the post-World War II period.

The Beats embraced jazz with a passion. Holmes (1958, p. 38) stated:

> In the arts, modern jazz is almost exclusively the music of the Beat Generation . . . because jazz is almost exclusively the music of the inner freedom, of improvisation, of the creative individual rather than the interpretative group. It is the music of a submerged people, who *feel* free, and this is precisely how young people feel today.

Lipton (1959, p. 212) added, "To the Beat generation, jazz is also a music of protest. Being apolitical does not preclude protest. There are other solutions besides political solutions."

Ginsberg's poems "Howl" and "Kaddish" are said to be "saxophone inspired" (Nuttall 1968, p. 110). Indeed, in his Paris interview Ginsberg explains that his "organic" approach to poetry allows the source of the meter to come "from a source deeper than the mind," from "the breathing and belly and the lungs" (Clark 1970, p. 130). Ginsberg says the organization used in "Howl," "a recurrent kind of syntax," is based on the "myth of Lester Young as described by Kerouac, blowing 89 choruses of *Lady Be Good* say, in one night, or my own hearing of Illinois Jacquet's *Jazz at the Philharmonic* Volume 2; I think *Can't Get Started* was the title" (Clark 1970, p. 131).

Kerouac was the Beat most obsessed with the jazz ethos. Cook (1971, p. 221) writes, "It was not just in the occasional scene that Kerouac would try to inject something of the jazz feeling; he attempted rather, to infuse all his work with the urgency and continuous flow of music." It was the "furious abandon and overwhelming spontaneity of Charlie Parker" that for Kerouac "became the model for unfettered, immediate creativity . . . Kerouac wanted to let go into an almost biological form of writing—to write spontaneously, outwards from a burning center, until details and words pile up into a fluid frenzy of notes and rhythms."

His method was to type his prose onto a continuous roll of teletype paper (provided by Lucien Carr), writing as fast as possible, never stopping to choose the "proper" word, concentrating only on the subject in his imagination, and never revising: to seek "deep form, poetic form, the way consciousness *really* digs everything that happens" (Cook 1971, p. 74). In this manner the original manuscript of *On the Road* was completed in three weeks of almost nonstop typing. Ginsberg called it "spontaneous bop prosody" (Cook 1971, p. 221; Tytell 1976, p. 17).

Most literary critics were hostile to the Beats. Writing in *Partisan Review*, Norman Podhoretz

(1960) called the Beats "know nothing bohemians" who were "hostile to civilization." In fact, the Beats aroused such intense antipathy from some of the gatekeepers of high culture that Cook (1971, p. 87) commented, "There were people who made a career out of attacking the Beats."

The reaction was predictable. The literary scene in the 1950s was dominated by the New Critics of the colleges and universities and those New York intellectuals, like Podhoretz, known as the *Partisan Review* crowd. The former were academic elitists who delighted in making small points. For them, a poem was to be analyzed as an object that was independent of the author's life and background, an object that employed particular means to achieve particular effects (Bush 1978, p. 167). The latter were political polemicists. Thus, the norms were either classicism or abstract political moralizing. Neither approached literature in a spirit of play (Cook 1971, pp. 11-12).

Needless to say, the aggressively Romantic Beats loomed as a wild, shaggy menace to these establishments. Seymour Krim observed that the New Criticism started out as a "worthy effort" to "lift American experience and intellectual standards, but had become enslaved by its own criteria" until it became just an effort "to impose European standards on American experience." As such, "the Beat thing was healthy, organic, unstoppable. It had to happen" (Cook 1971, pp. 52-53).

Beat Comes of Age and Becomes the Rage

In 1955 the interaction of the New York and San Francisco Beats began to give off sparks. In the words of Rexroth, Ginsberg "was impatient for the revolution to begin" (Cook 1971, p. 62). Sensing the time was right for the inaugural event, he organized a reading at the Six Gallery in San Francisco, bringing together the area's best young poets for a full evening of poetry. Participants included Philip Lamantia, Michael McClure, Gary Snyder, Lew Welch, Philip Whalen, and Ginsberg himself. Writing about the reading in *The Dharma Bums*, Kerouac called it "the birth of the San Francisco Poetry Renaissance."

The climax of the evening was Ginsberg's half-drunk, wildly rhythmic recitation of "Howl." He had written the poem two weeks earlier, "during a long weekend spent in his room under the influence of various drugs—peyote for visions, amphetamine to speed up, and Dexedrine to keep going." Ginsberg's delivery electrified the audience, bringing forth chants of "Go! Go! Go!" (Cook 1971, p. 64). Later, Rexroth was to say, "It was different from anything he had done up until then—hell, it was different from what anyone had done until then" (Cook 1971, p. 61).

"Howl" begins with an allusion to the hipster experience that has become one of the most widely quoted passages in American poetry:

> I saw the best minds of my generation, starving hysterical naked, dragging themselves through the negro streets at dawn looking for an angry fix, angelheaded hipsters burning for the ancient heavenly connection. . . .
>
> (Ginsberg 1956, p. 3)

It concludes with a series of indictments of the corporate America of the 1950s that seethe with controlled rage:

> Moloch . . . whose love is endless oil and stone! Moloch whose soul is electricity and banks! Moloch whose poverty is the specter of genius! Moloch whose fate is a cloud of sexless hydrogen. . . .
>
> (Ginsberg 1956, p. 27)

In 1957 Ferlinghetti's City Lights Books published the poem in a collection entitled *Howl and Other Poems.* Publication was blocked immediately by an obscenity suit. Ferlinghetti noted that the trial was "not only a forum on the meaning of obscenity and the right of free speech but also a platform for ideas that would be of widespread concern" in the years to follow (Cherkovski 1979, p. 109). The trial brought the book widespread notoriety and the judge upheld the defendants' rights of free press. Ginsberg' scathing denunciation of materialism, militarism, and conformity, his adulation of the primitive, and his tribute to sex, drugs, and other taboo literary subjects would be read.

Ginsberg soon found his public. Within a dozen years the City Lights edition of *Howl* sold over 150,000 copies in 20 printings (Kostelanetz 1970). The most immediate impact was on the hundreds of kindred bohemian souls who migrated to North Beach, Venice West, and Greenwich Village in those last three years of the decade.

With the publication of Kerouac's *On the Road,* also in 1957, the movement gained national attention. Based on the adventures of Kerouac (Sal Paradise) and Cassady (Dean Moriarty), who rambled around the country in the late 1940s and early 1950s, *On the Road* is filled with vivid vignettes of the underside of affluent America. The novel became an instant best seller, especially among the restless young, for whom Dean Moriarty became a modern romantic hero.

Gilbert Millstein (1957), writing in the *New York Times,* hailed its publication as a "historic occasion" and predicted that just as *The Sun Also Rises* was a testimonial to the Lost Generation, so would *On the Road* become a monument to the "Beat Generation." *On the Road,* Millstein concluded, was "the most beautifully executed, the clearest and most important utterance yet made by the generation Kerouac himself named 'beat' . . ." For Holmes (1958) the Beats were a generation "groping toward faith out of an intellectual despair and moral chaos in which they refuse to lose themselves."

The popularity of *On the Road* triggered a wave of national publicity for the Beat Generation. Kerouac, Ginsberg, and Corso were interviewed by representatives from all the mass media. The term "beatnik" was fastened to members of the movement by *San Francisco Chronicle* columnist Herb Caen, who explained that he had invented it in the wake of Sputnik because beatniks were "equally far out" to him (McNally 1979, p. 253; Cook 1971, p. 199).

Holmes believed the Beat Generation was an international phenomenon, sharing many traits with Britain's Teddy Boys, Japan's Sun Tribers, and even some underground youth in Russia. At a party to celebrate the publication of *The Beats,* editor Seymour Krim proclaimed, "It's a posture of rebellion. It's for anybody unwilling to put up with the older compromises" (*New Yorker* 1960a).

Obviously there were many such rebels in waiting because, as Cook (1971, p. 10) reports, the movement "attracted thousands—tens of thousands—of young people in a very short time." Beat symbols and styles found a fertile climate in the burgeoning college campuses of affluent America. After World War II and through the 1960s, the number of college students grew to encompass over half of the 18- to 21-year-old cohort. Such youth represented a new social category created by a number of factors, including the need to delay the assimilation of the "baby boom" cohorts into the economy, the growing reliance of private industry on universities for low-wage, high-skill labor (graduate students) for research and development, larger federal subsidies to higher education (especially through the military), a credential inflation in the job market, and rising status competition in the expanding middle class (Starr 1980; 1981).

All of these factors resulted in a delayed entry into marriage and the labor market, a prolongation of adolescence into what had been young adulthood (Starr 1981). Erikson's (1953) popular *Childhood and Society* introduced his concept of the "identity crisis." Through the decade many youth learned to conceptualize "their quite understandable anxieties about an uncertain future" as a problem of "identity." According to this developmental norm, one is obliged to continue "searching for" one's identity "until one's commitments to and immersion in family, community, and career result in the disappearance of the identity problem—whereupon one may be told that the identity crisis has been resolved" (Berger 1971, p. 90).

The appeal of the Beats to such youth obviously resided in their burning existential quest. As Holmes (1957-1958, p. 17) insisted:

> Everywhere the Beat Generation seems occupied with the feverish production of answers . . . to a single question: how are we to live? . . . This generation cannot conceive of the question in any but personal terms, and knows that the only answer it can accept will come out of the dark night of the individual soul.

In a short time dress and grooming among the young reflected the new style: beards, blue jeans, sandals, berets, and sweatshirts for the men; long hair, beads, and leotards or black stockings for the women. From the late 1950s until the mid-1960s, there were Beat coffeehouses in every city of over 100,000 population (Cook 1971, p. 92). As an important consequence poetry, jazz, and Abstract Expressionist art gained new followings.

The major centers—Greenwich Village, North Beach, and Venice West—were all studied by social scientists. Titillated by their reports, "squares" crammed into buses offering tours of the bohemian sections. Motion picture and television producers moved quickly to capitalize on public interest in the beatniks. Kerouac's *The Subterraneans*, a 1953 novel about his unhappy love affair with a black Indian woman (he loses her to Corso), was made into a movie. The insipid cinema version claimed to tell the shocking "truth" about the sex, drugs, and music of the new bohemians. A television producer approached Kerouac about writing episodes for a weekly series based on *On the Road*. Kerouac declined, but the series went on the next year under the title "Route Sixty-Six." It featured Martin Milner and a young actor, named George Maharis, who bore a close resemblance to Kerouac (Cook 1971, pp. 72-73). Perhaps the most famous beatnik was Maynard G. Krebs, the scrawny, shaggy sidekick of television's "Dobie Gillis."

The publicity given to the Beats was quite mixed. The Luce publications made the movement sound both ridiculous and dangerous (Cook 1971, p. 91). Paul O'Neil (1959) of *Life* magazine dismissed the Beats as dirty, noisy rebels. *Time* denounced them as "mendicants of marijuana and mad verse" and "oddballs who celebrate booze, dope, sex, and despair." Ginsberg later returned the compliment by calling *Time* "the whore of Babylon" (*Time* 1959a; 1959b).

Growth of the Beat Colonies

Despite, or perhaps because of, the criticism of the conservative media, young people migrated in large numbers to expand the Beat colonies in North Beach and Greenwich Village. As mentioned, social scientists soon showed up on the scene to record their views. Rigney and Smith (1961) sampled 51 out of an estimated 180 to 200 Beats living in North Beach, and Polsky (1969) did in situ interviews with an estimated 300 Beats in the Village.

The Rigney and Smith sample consisted of 33 men, whose average age was 27 years, and 18 women, whose average age was 24 years. Most had come to North Beach from big cities like New York, Los Angeles, or Chicago. Less than a fifth came from rural areas. Two-thirds came from middle-to-upper-middle-class homes, in contrast with only about one-third in the general population. Polsky's estimates are quite comparable: about 5 percent upper-class, 60 percent middle-class, and 35 percent lower-class.

More than 70 percent of the North Beach Beats started college, most going for two years and about a fifth graduating. Three had master's degrees in music. However, only about half a dozen Beats (less than one in eight) had white-collar jobs. Over a third were dependent on the government, partners, or parents as their primary means of support. Most Beats worked at low-paid clerical, sales, or personal service jobs that required little formal education or training and offered very limited opportunities for advancement. Less than half had steady employment of any kind.

Polsky reported that the anti-work ethic was so strong that many took jobs away from the scene so as not to be seen by other Beats. Some would have preferred to starve rather than take work they considered demeaning. In Polsky's view, this refusal was ideological: "Sensible of America's inequitable distribution of income *and* its racial injustices *and* its Permanent War Economy, the Beats have responded with a Permanent Strike" (Polsky 1969, pp. 159-60). Goodman (1960, p. 68) points out that the humble jobs taken by the Beats could be justified in that they perform useful service, "no questions asked and no beards have to be shaved." They were jobs that were easily taken and left, jobs that fit a life committed to art and movement.

Of the 51 Beats surveyed by Rigney and Smith (1961, p. 178), 46 said they had "some sort of artistic outlet." These included two composers, two jazz men, three painters, one writer, and four poets (altogether about one-fourth of the sample) who were considered "better than 'good,' even near 'great'" by their peers. Polsky (1969), much more critical, estimated only one-sixth were "habituated to reading" and less than one-tenth were concerned with writing. While this latter proportion compares with that of earlier bohemias, Polsky complained it was "godawful stuff," marred by anti-academicism, anti-historicism, and a consequent lack of technical skills.

Goodman (1960, p. 68) also denigrated the Beats' lack of standards, doubted they really cared about the bomb, and suspected that their rejection of competition and achievement was just a defense against a deeply felt sense of inferiority and fear of failure. Nevertheless, Polsky and Goodman both conceded that aesthetic values occupied a much more important place in the Beat community than in "square" society. Indeed, Goodman (1960, p. 179) observed that "everybody engages in creative acts and is likely to carry a sketchbook." He acknowledged that "such creative activity sharpens the perceptions, releases and refines feelings, and is a powerful bond."

Of course, there were occasions when Beats would compromise their principles of eschewing money and "squares." Ted Joans, a black Village poet, rented himself out as a Beatnik for "square" parties so that he could make enough money to take a cruise around the world. Around the same time a Beat woman contacted a "Rent-a-Beatnik" agency in the Village for work similar to Joans's. She insisted that she found the idea of displaying herself at a "square" party "faintly nauseating" but she needed the "bread," and "for that, almost anything is worth it . . ." (Millstein 1960, pp. 3, 28, 30).

Such instances can fit within the Beat ethic if one distinguishes between a "gig" (gainful employment) and a "hustle" or "scuffle." The latter involves deceiving, swindling, or, in these two cases, putting somebody on. In putting on the timid "squares," Beats provided a cheap thrill, kept

their cool, and remained in control of the situation (Rigney and Smith 1961, pp. xiii-xvii).

About half the North Beach Beats were single. A fourth were married, and another fourth were divorced. Ten had children. Although there was no gay subculture in North Beach, 12 of the 33 men had had homosexual experiences. However, all but one of the 12 considered themselves actively bisexual. Although many failed "to establish deep and lasting sexual relationships," there was a "very high tolerance of sex-role ambiguity" (Polsky 1969). Sexual freedom for Beats on both coasts included liaisons with blacks, typically between black men and white women, although these were not approved by all.

Many in the North Beach group had emotional problems. Seven had been in mental hospitals, five were undergoing psychotherapy, and five were taking medication regularly. However, Rigney and Smith (1961, p. 39) cautioned that sickness certainly was "not a requirement for membership in the group." Many were emotionally stable. What was distinctive about the community was its tolerance for eccentric behavior based on an appreciation of a common humanity that was missing in polite bourgeois society.

All the North Beach Beats experimented with a wide variety of drugs. Four-fifths had tried marijuana, half had taken peyote, and a fourth had used heroin. Of the 13 who had tried heroin, 7 had become addicted, but 5 had kicked the habit before coming to North Beach. The favorite drug in North Beach was alcohol. Almost all had taken a drink, and eight (about one in six) had become addicted. Polsky reported marijuana, hashish, peyote, synthetic mescaline, and heroin use among the Village Beats. He estimated that while about 10 percent of the Beats over 20 years of age were heroin addicts, about 90 percent were marijuana users.

Drugs were advocated to overcome one's cultural conditioning, to liberate the mind from false concepts and the body from deeply implanted self-repression. To get high, one had to suspend one's rational defenses and submit to the total experience. Once launched on one's inner trip, one could search for the holy primitive within, the authentic nature that had been repressed and distorted by the demands of bourgeois society.

Drugs also were used as aids to creativity. A North Beach painter claimed that peyote helped him to see "new colors hidden from my conscious mind" (Rigney and Smith 1961, p. 39). In Venice

West a Beat insisted that he "never really *heard* the music until (he) started listening with pot" (Lipton 1959, p. 172).

Thus, in social background, current circumstances, and ideology, these Beats closely resembled the original New York group. Many came to North Beach because they viewed it as a retreat from "square" society where they could devote themselves to art. Other enticements included low rents, inexpensive food, friendly bistros, and the area's reputation for tolerance.

The Politics of Romanticism: Radical and Conservative Beats

As pointed out in the introduction to this volume, Romanticism can lead in antagonistic political directions. Both versions reject bourgeois Rationalism with its abstract analysis and positivistic-utilitarian philosophy. Instead, they champion holistic thinking, personal intuition, devotion to higher principles, and individual heroism.

The rejection of any objective method or standard of truth soon leads to the problem of order. One solution is to reject a common order and allow each person his or her individual expression. Another is to invest all authority in a charismatic leader with claims to a higher truth. One solution offers freedom but threatens chaos; the other offers security but threatens repression. Thus, one version of Romanticism is radically progressive, extending the democratic imperative toward anarchism. The other version is reactionary, reaching back to an idealized premodern past, exalting the virtues of blood and soil, patriarchal religion, patriarchal family, and nationalism—that is, neofascism.

As long as Romanticism is confined to culturally radical expression, its implicit political foundations may not be apparent. Because the Beats avoided politics through the 1950s, differences in philosophy remained covert. As Michael Harrington (1972, p. 100) reflected on the late 1940s bohemia around the University of Chicago: "As long as there was an iconoclastic regard for standards and a contempt for a middle class utilitarianism, Bohemia could assimilate any content, the revolutionary as well as the conservative, the romantic and realist. . . ."

The dynamics of this ideological diversity can be illustrated vividly by tracing the public careers of the original Beat brothers, Allen Ginsberg and Jack Kerouac, as the politics of the 1960s brought them to a fork in the long and winding road they had traveled together. In 1960 Ginsberg began to get involved in radical politics. He signed ads in support of the pro-Castro Fair Play for Cuba Committee and traveled to Cuba to view the revolution first hand. The following year he pronounced Beat "dead" and left America for spiritual study in India, which took up most of the next four years (Dickstein 1977, p. 8).

While in New York in 1964, Ginsberg joined with many other Lower East Side poets to protest the *New York Daily News* editorial attacks on the Mobilization for Youth program. A writer covering the event asked: "Is it not possible that the same Poet-prophet who warned us with a terrible negation of our emptiness—might now be one, if not *the* one, to find us a challenge of spiritual and social affirmation? . . ." (Hahn 1966, pp. 293-94).

Ginsberg became an active participant in many pro-pot demonstrations. He served as a witness at congressional hearings and wrote "one of the most elegantly written pro-pot polemics in print, 'The Great Marijuana Hoax.'" The essay was published in *Atlantic Monthly* and reprinted in *The Marijuana Papers* (Kostelanetz 1970). During the period 1964-66 Ginsberg also supported the activities of a free-love cult called Kerista, seeing "political overtones" in the new family structures and life-styles (Gruen 1966, p. 54).

As he surveyed the radical movement in the mid-1960s, Ginsberg saw the political radicals as having a "real vision of the material and social ills of the society," but little insight into personal consciousness. His objection to confrontational tactics was that "certain kinds of political action deform the agent more than they change society" (Dickstein 1977, p. 21). He was seeking a creative synthesis of means and ends, a strategy of oppositional politics that would liberate the participants as it effected change in the system. A proven publicist, he felt that any attempt to change public opinion would have to involve the mass media.

From 1966 to 1968, Ginsberg emerged as a major public figure, a patient, charming, and conciliatory "guru to the new generation" who lent "his magnetic spiritual presence to so many of the most obscene and solemn moments of the 1960s" (Dickstein 1977, p. 6; Cook 1971, p. 205). Wherever he went, he preached his new philosophy of cultural politics, a radical synthesis to achieve the final transformation.

Ginsberg's ideological solution was to advocate a "politics of exorcism, celebration and public joy rather than violent confrontation," to seduce rather than debate those undecided or opposed

(Dickstein 1977, p. 22). In 1966 he wrote a poem called "How to Make a March/Spectacle" that advised demonstrators to "lay aside their usually grave and pugnacious quality in favor of a festive dancing and chanting parade that would pass out balloons and flowers, candy and kisses, bread and wine to everyone along the line of march—including to the cops and any Hell's Angels in the vicinity" (Roszak 1969, p. 150).

Ginsberg's approach restored the affirmative implicit in the original meaning of protest—to "witness for" something. It allowed for a demonstration of radical cultural values as a basis for radical politics. It showed peace and love.

In January 1967, Ginsberg joined with Gary Snyder to stage "A Gathering of Tribes for a Human Be-In" on the polo fields of Golden Gate Park. The "Be-In" was partly a demonstration of solidarity with Haight-Ashbury Beat/hippies weary from their community battles with "square"/straight adversaries and partly an elaboration on the Free Fairs put on by the Artists Liberation Front and the Trips Festivals sponsored by Ken Kesey and the Merry Pranksters (Wolfe 1968, pp. 13-14; Cook 1971, pp. 199-201; Kramer 1969, pp. 189-91; Cherkovski 1979, p. 184-85). Also participating in the event were a diverse group of hipsters and radicals, including Dizzie Gillespie, Dick Gregory, Jerry Rubin, and Tim Leary. Called to celebrate the New Age, the "Be-In" attracted widespread media coverage, created the myth of the hippie, and triggered the migration of 100,000 youths to San Francisco for the "Summer of Love" (Miller 1977, p. 251).

In 1968 Ginsberg attended the Democratic National Convention in Chicago as a correspondent for the now defunct *Eye* magazine. As commotion raged on the convention floor, where Mayor Daley controlled all the microphones, Ginsberg chanted mantras from the balcony—apparently hoping to calm the multitude and chase the evil vibrations from the convention. He was picked up by the Chicago police, and the Secret Service took his press pass away. Ginsberg commented later, "Every reporter got the same treatment. The police were working hand in hand with the government men, Daley and Hoover . . . I suddenly realized that I was living in a police state then and there." In Ginsberg's view it was all done to keep Eugene McCarthy from being nominated because he also was afraid of the authoritarian police state (Cook 1971, p. 242).

By the end of the decade, Ginsberg spoke hopefully about the political possibilities of the themes of the 1967 "Be-In." He insisted that "anything communal is thus political," that the genesis of political movement lies in communal energy. He felt that the "one sort of spontaneous movement" that had come out of the commune movement was "the sudden awareness of the menace to ecology" (Cook 1971, p. 240). This, he felt, was facilitated by the new world view of the 1960s generation, "a cosmic consciousness, an awareness of being in the middle of the cosmos instead of this town or that valley or city" (Cook 1971, p. 243). And this cosmic consciousness was nurtured by LSD: "It was necessary and inevitable in a highly rigid and brainwashed civilization such as ours to help us find what was always there. To us the LSD thing was just as important as the trip to the moon. LSD equals the moon in terms of the expansion of human possibilities" (Cook 1971, p. 245).

In Ginsberg's view, the intellectual heart of the Beat movement was "the return to nature and the revolt against the machine," and the "getting out from under the American flag and marching to a different drummer in the Thoreauvian sense that one can find one's own self here," that is, Romantic anarchism (Cook 1971, p. 104). In 1969, looking back on the last quarter-century, Ginsberg saw "many elements of continuity from the Beats to the present," "including the first serious experimentation with altered states of consciousness," the "movement from jazz and rhythm and blues in *On the Road* to rock today," the "whole rediscovery of the Body of the Land," and "the Eastern elements that interest young people today" (Cook 1971, p. 104).

On the other hand, the road Kerouac traveled in the 1960s took him far away from Ginsberg and his Beat comrades. In fact, "as his friends gained widespread recognition as radicals, he raged at them for not being like him, American Patriots." Through the decade Kerouac denounced Ginsberg for his "socialist ideals," Holmes for his "leftism," and Ferlinghetti and Lipton as "Communists." He put down liberalism as a sham for the middle class and adamantly declared his support for William F. Buckley, Jr., the leading spokesman for the Romantic conservative Libertarian right (Charters 1973, p. 344; Tytell 1976, p. 62).

Kerouac was vehemently critical of black militants, the politicized evolution of his early hipster heroes. In conversation one evening, Corso challenged his attitude toward blacks, reminding him of the passage in *On the Road* that reads: "At lilac evening I walked with every muscle aching among the lights of 27 and Welton in the

Denver section, wishing I were a Negro, feeling that the best the white world offered was not enough ecstasy for me, not enough life, joy, kicks, darkness, music, not enough night" (Kerouac 1957, p. 148).

> Kerouac protested, "Nobody is going to tell me how to live, or come into my house, or insult my own people because they're not Negro."
> CORSO: "Ah, then that's where it's at, Jackie. How could you mean what you wrote when you feel that way?"
> KEROUAC: "I felt that way, then, *that night.*"
> CORSO: "But you weren't looking inside the Negro. You weren't seeing him, his misery, his isolation."
> KEROUAC: "I wanted to have a good time, the way the Negroes can."
> CORSO: "But they didn't really feel that way. They didn't want to be that way."
> KEROUAC: "I will never take back one poetic statement I've ever written."
> (Jarvis 1973-74, pp. 157-58)

Kerouac also rejected the hippies. He had been willing to break down conventional literary and social barriers in his quest for authenticity, but he was shocked and repelled by the blatancy of those who carried the movement forward. Jarvis (1973-74, p. 106) reports, "In my talks with him about hippies, he kept coming back to one term, 'loud-mouthed fags.' He had no use for them, said they were assuming a stature they had not earned, said they were playacting, said they hadn't produced any real literature and never would."

Looking back on his Beat days, Kerouac denied that he was trying "to create any kind of consciousness or anything like that. We didn't have a whole lot of abstract thoughts. We were just a bunch of guys who were out trying to get laid" (Cook 1971, p. 89). Indeed, in *On the Road,* Kerouac finds Cassady, the mad conman, superior to the "tedious intellectualness" of all his other friends. Kerouac (1957, p. 11) adds, "Besides, all my New York friends were in the negative, nightmare position of putting down society and giving their tired bookish or political or psychoanalytical reasons, but Dean just raced in society, eager for bread and love. . . ." Later in the novel, Kerouac observed with contempt, "The arty types were all over America, sucking up its blood."

In Cook's (1971, p. 85) view, those who knew Kerouac in the old days weren't surprised by his later conservatism. Michael McClure "recalls that he shocked all his friends in San Francisco in 1956 by insisting that if he were voting that year he would vote for Eisenhower. 'It just seemed a weird idea to us then,' he said. 'Not voting we could

understand, but *wanting* to vote for Eisenhower!'" Burroughs explains, "His father was a real old French peasant anti-Semite, Catholic rightist, and Jack got a lot of his basic attitudes from him. And his mother! Talk about your old peasant types!" (Cook 1971, p. 181).

It seems clear that Kerouac's strong Catholic and smalltown roots were the basis for his Romanticism. At one point in *On the Road* Kerouac (1957, p. 82) goes with a Mexican woman and her son and becomes a migrant worker, picking cotton for very low pay until his fingers bleed. Still, he rejoices, "I was a man of the earth, precisely as I had dreamed I would be." In Jarvis' (1973-74, p. 193) view, Kerouac preferred a "romanticized America which, in the context of current events, makes him an arch conservative." "Few men," Jarvis (1973-74, p. 99) states, "loved America as Jack Kerouac did; and in this abiding love there was no room for criticism—especially of its political institutions." Tytell agrees, characterizing Kerouac's Romantic visions as nostalgia for the rural frontier, the rugged individualist, the outlaw (Tytell 1976, pp. 52, 63, 65, 140-42, 160-61). With its rolling landscapes and boozathons, *On the Road* is much more the romance of a trucker than an artist or intellectual, a good ol' boy on the run, a melancholy Rabelais on wheels.

When confronted by Cook in 1968, Kerouac insisted that his politics had not changed, explaining: "Everybody just assumed I thought the way *they* wanted me to think. What really bothered me a lot, though, was the way a certain cadre of leftists among the so-called beats took over my mantle and twisted my thoughts to suit their own purpose" (Cook 1971, p. 88).

The misrepresentation of Kerouac's private convictions in his public image wasn't due solely to the company he kept. In any literary movement there may emerge commentators who succeed in shaping its political meaning and, perhaps, its public effects. One common strategy to influence public perception of a movement is to attribute certain unspoken intentions to the author(s) of certain works or events. The role of hip commentator on the Beats was played by none other than Norman Mailer. In 1957 Mailer wrote an essay called "The White Negro," published in *Dissent.* The essay begins with references to the Holocaust, the bomb, and the "collective failure of nerve" that paralyzes American life. Mailer (1969, pp. 198-99) introduces his savior thus:

> . . . the American existentialist—the hipster, the man who knows that if our collective condition is

to live with instant death by atomic war . . . or with a slow death by conformity with every creative and rebellious instinct stifled . . . then the only life-giving answer is to accept the terms of death, to live with death as immediate danger, to divorce oneself from society, to exist without roots, to set out on that uncharted journey into the rebellious imperative of the self.

In America, Mailer wrote, "The source of Hip is the Negro, for he has been living on the margin between totalitarianism and democracy for two centuries." As such, in certain places, such as Greenwich Village, the black, the juvenile delinquent, and the bohemian have come together around marijuana, jazz, and the special argot of hip to form a common culture. Because there were whites who had come to embrace so much of black culture, they are best described as "white Negroes."

Mailer's essay created a stir and, when the Beats gained sudden popularity that year, he put himself forward as their public supporter. Mailer argued that the Beats, as well as all those who were alienated or angry, embodied an authentic critique of bourgeois society. In attempting to impose this interpretation on Kerouac, Mailer provided perhaps the most amusing example of such ideological reinterpretation:

> There is a sort of instinctive sense in them that they should stay away from politics—or make their remarks on politics surrealistic. For example, when Kerouac says, "I like Eisenhower, I think he's a great man. I think he's our greatest president since Abraham Lincoln." Well, you know that's not a serious political remark at all. I don't think he even believed it, except, perhaps when he said it. It's a surrealistic remark. He's mixing two ideas that have absolutely no relation to each other—one of them is greatness and the other is Eisenhower.
>
> (Cook 1971, p. 96)

Of course, Kerouac had twisted his own thoughts to serve his purpose by redefining Beat from beat-up to beatific. But while the beatific was related to Kerouac's roots in Catholic mysticism, this didn't stop Ginsberg from appropriating the new term for the acid hippie movement of the late 1960s. In a 1969 interview with Cook he stated, "LSD equals the moon in terms of expansion of human possibilities. The moon thing is a technological manifestation of cosmic consciousness. . . . It was what we meant when we used to tell them that Beat was short for Beatific" (Cook 1971, p. 245). Moreover, despite Kerouac's obviously superficial understanding of blacks, Corso credited him with predicting the black revolution in his novel *The Subterraneans* (*Newsweek* 1963).

Neither could Kerouac escape having his thoughts twisted to others' purpose long after he left the Beats—indeed, even after his death.

In 1968, after Kerouac had slipped deep into alcoholism, pledged himself to Jesus, returned to Lowell, married his high school sweetheart, become outspokenly archconservative, and refused to see his former Beat buddies, Ginsberg still commented, "It seemed that he was so horrified by the police state he saw taking shape around us that he decided to stay as far away from it as possible. He practically went underground! So in a way he took it more seriously than any of us" (Cook 1971, p. 85). Even in death, Kerouac's public image was fashioned to fit the new radicalism. In Corso's poetic eulogy he was joined finally with the hippies he held in such profound contempt:

> And you were flashed upon the old and darkling day a Beat Christ-Boy . . . bearing the gentle roundness of things
> Insisting the soul was round not square and soon . . . behind there came
> A-Following
> the children of flowers.
>
> (Corso 1970)

Romanticism does have a Janus face. Mussolini was able to harness the Futurists' muddled anarchism to his program of fascism (Wohl 1979; Shapiro 1976). Such co-optations are more common than what befell Kerouac. Perhaps turnabout is fair play.

In the final analysis, the movements of the 1960s embodied the principles of both of these men. Certainly, the Romanticism they shared was widely in evidence. Kerouac's themes of alienation and the search for identity, fraternity, travel, and adventure described the orientation of the youth generation. And, certainly, active sexuality, drugs, wanderlust, mysticism, openness, freedom, and spontaneity were countercultural values they both could claim (Spates 1971; Ebner 1972; Hodges 1974, p. 509).

The Relation Between Cultural and Political Radicalism

Like Kerouac and Ginsberg in earlier days, Beats in the 1950s rejected electoral politics. Lipton (1959, p. 306) noted, "All the vital decisions [the Beats] will tell you, are beyond the control of the electorate, so why go to the polls?" For most Beats the ballot was meaningless because it did not represent "such vital issues as war and peace to the voter." Other Beats insisted that all political parties used lies and manipulations: "Elections are rigged . . . the whole political game is a big shuck, the biggest shuck of all." Polsky said the Beats were not just apolitical but "anti-political," because they rejected not only the major political parties but the opposition movements as well. As Romantics, most Beats did not believe it possible for one person to represent another.

On the other hand, Goodman (1960, pp. 187-88) proposed that the very existence of the Beat community constituted an important political statement: *"People can go it on their own,* without resentment, hostility, delinquency, or stupidity better than when they move in the organized system and are subject to authority." Indeed, Willener (1970, p. 259) has distinguished "two senses" in which "the notion of politics may be understood: (a) institutional/organizational, or explicit; and (b) cultural, a latent force of conservation or transformation." Politics of the latter type would include creating a bohemian counter to bourgeois culture.

Berger has discriminated political from cultural radicalism according to the ends pursued—whether change is sought in the structure of political and/or economic institutions or in the practice of life-styles and the arts. Of course, this leaves open the possibility that political radicals may employ cultural innovation as one means to achieve their ends and that, conversely, cultural radicals may employ overtly political tactics in order to achieve their ends.

The latter is most likely to occur when the liberty to practice life-style and artistic innovation is denied by state intervention. Such intervention may take various forms, such as police raids on parties, drug busts, harassment of interracial couples and gays, or the shutting down of important community institutions (such as coffeehouses or communes) by agencies of the state (such as the fire department, the zoning commission, or the liquor control commission) (Hahn 1966, pp. 266-68; Smith and Luce 1976, p. 80; Rigney and Smith 1961, pp. 5-10).

In their ongoing "war" with bourgeois society, Beats frequently found their social life, art, and morals the target of state regulation and police violence. In the late 1950s and early 1960s, many Beats abandoned their disengagement to commit themselves to the struggle for cultural freedom. They responded with rallies, demonstrations, legal challenges, and other weapons of political protest (*San Francisco Chronicle* 1960a; Rigney and Smith 1961, p. 164).

Until the media "discovered" North Beach in 1957, the Beats there lived in virtual anonymity. Soon sensational stories of alleged Beat orgies, depravity, and violence brought seemingly endless invasions of tourists, youthful adventurers, and police. Especially damaging to the North Beach colony were three exposés in the Hearst-owned *San Francisco Examiner* in May 1958, which caused more police to be sent to the area. Called "distorted" and "sensational" by many, these articles were soon followed by the accidental death of a young man from Chicago who fell from the roof of a Beat bistro while drunk, and the murder of his girlfriend that same evening by an "alcoholic, drug addicted Negro seaman out near Golden Gate Park." Neither the murderer nor the victims were locals or even Beats, but the *Examiner* featured front-page coverage of the "beatnik deaths," and the "police crackdown" on what Police Captain Charles Borland had now decided was a "notorious problem section" (Rigney and Smith 1961, pp. 159-60; Hahn 1966, pp. 267-68).

Public outcry led to police raids on Beat hangouts. Many were arrested on charges of drunkenness and vagrancy. When some protested that they were being denied their constitutional rights, they were slapped with additional charges of "obscenity," "resisting arrest," or "interfering with justice." Several arrests were accompanied by name-calling, shoving, handcuffing, and brutality. A cop asked one club owner, "Why do you allow so many commies and jigs to patronize this place? After all, if you give 'em an inch, they'll take a mile." In another incident, a policeman called a white woman with a black man a "nigger-lover." She was threatened with a vagrancy arrest usually reserved for suspected prostitutes and warned: "Don't let us catch you around here again with a Negro . . . [or] we'll run you in" (Rigney and Smith 1961, pp. 161-64).

In February 1959 several Beats organized the North Beach Citizens' Committee with the charge to fight police harassment, explain their civil rights to members of the colony, and provide bail and instruction on how to behave when arrested. One member announced: "Our job will be to protect our group from the police" (Rigney and Smith 1961, pp. 165-66). Beats began watching the police, hanging around during interrogations, bearing witness to misconduct.

Relations between Beats and police worsened. In August 1959 black poet Bob Kaufman had to have his toenail removed after police stomped on it while arresting him. Kaufman's experience is described in his subsequent "Jail Poem" (Rigney and Smith 1961, pp. 164-65). In January 1960 there were several marijuana raids, including one in which police destroyed books on Communism and ripped paintings off the walls while arresting all of the occupants of a Beat "pad."

One week after the raid, the Beats held a rally in North Beach's Washington Square that drew 325 persons, including a reported 25 plainclothes cops. North Beach Beats accused police of violating their civil rights, blamed the area's newspapers for increasing tensions, and criticized members of their own group for failing to defend themselves against these assaults. Chester Anderson, editor of *Beatitude* and *Underhound* (*sic*), exhorted the audience to use every legal means available to protect themselves. "If you are falsely arrested," he shouted, "say so and sue. If you are roughed up by the police, say so and sue. Don't cover up. Fight back in every legal way" (*San Francisco Chronicle* 1960a).

Jerry Kamstra, bearded owner of a book and art shop in North Beach, shouted that he was "'tired of being persecuted for not supporting any razor company . . . tired of being persecuted for not sharing the same social point of view as [the police].'" Kamstra equated police "repression" in North Beach with Nazi Germany. Kaufman complained that he had "'spent World War II fighting for democracy'" and now received only "'2% of it [in North Beach].'" One unidentified speaker declared that the rally was the beginning "'of a great American general strike.'" She called for an alliance of artists and writers with the "'workingmen who have no democracy'" (*San Francisco Chronicle* 1960a).

By the fall of 1959, many Beats had left embattled North Beach for Greenwich Village. After publication of Lawrence Lipton's study of Venice West, another 500 to 1,000 Beats moved there. The sudden immigration divided the Venice West community. Many protested. One irate resident complained: "They're a dirty bunch of people. They drink and are every night in debauchery. They make free love practically in the streets, play bongo drums, and none of us can get any sleep after 2 AM." In contrast, sympathetic residents organized the Venice Citizens and Property Owners Committee for Cultural Advancement to support the Beats, stressing their potential cultural and commercial contributions to the community (*Newsweek* 1959).

The North Beach pattern was repeated in Venice West and Greenwich Village. As each community grew, media coverage became more sensational, bringing citizen pressure upon city officials to constrain Beat activities. After Venice officials closed the Gas House, a popular coffeehouse, the community's bohemians contacted the local chapter of the American Civil Liberties Union for assistance (*Newsweek* 1959; *Time* 1959b).

In 1960 Village Beats marched in demonstration after the fire department closed two prominent coffeehouses for purported violation of department regulations. One was allowed to reopen at half of its former capacity. A committee of several coffeehouse owners was organized to conduct a legal defense against the closing and to rally community support for their businesses (*New York Times* 1960a; 1960b). The manager of the Figaro coffeehouse proclaimed with proud defiance: "We don't permit the weekend tourist beatnik in here. Our beatniks are the real, true, old-fashioned wonderful bohemians" (*New Yorker* 1960b).

In Fort Worth, Texas, concern with community protection and improvement led Beats to try electoral politics. Two bearded coffeehouse poets and helpers ran for two Democratic Party precinct chairmanships under the slogan "Kick the Cows out of Cowtown and Let the Cats in to Swing." Their program called for cleaning up government, slum clearance, and better flophouses for winos (*Life* 1960).

Beat involvement in community politics finally led to collaboration with political radicals. A few months after the Beat rally in Washington Square, hundreds of students and Beats protested outside San Francisco's city hall against the House Committee on Un-American Activities (HUAC) hearings on subversives in the Bay area. Jerry Kamstra was arrested and dragged away from the building after attempting to gain entry to the hearing (*San Francisco Chronicle* 1960b). Police turned fire hoses on seated demonstrators, dragged many all the way down the steep concrete steps, and arrested 68. In response, some 5,000 showed up to picket city hall the next day.

This event received tremendous publicity over the next year and has often been cited as a milestone in the founding of the New Left. In its zeal HUAC impounded enough television news film to produce a highly biased and inflammatory film, entitled *Operation Abolition,* which claimed that the students had provoked the violence and were Communist dupes in a plot to discredit HUAC. For the next year and a half, the film "was a staple item on the rightwing banquet and camp meeting circuit." The Bay Area Student Committee for the Abolition of HUAC was formed in response and

> . . . sent speakers and literature around the country pointing out the distortions and inaccuracies in the film. The American Civil Liberties Union made a film of its own, supporting the student version and calling for the Committee's abolition. On campuses where both sides of the story were heard, the Berkeley students emerged a clear winner.
>
> (O'Brien 1968, pp. 3-4)

"Local Committees to Abolish HUAC were organized in many areas," and a "federation of local civil liberties and anti-HUAC student groups was organized which provided speakers and literature to local groups, and coordinated the showing of films on campuses throughout the country." These civil liberties campaigns "laid the groundwork for more widespread and politically focused activities" (Altbach 1974, pp. 181-82).

Beat political activism in the early 1960s was almost always anarchist in orientation. Except for a brief flirtation with the Fair Play for Cuba Committee following Castro's successful revolution, we have not been able to find any instances of Beats supporting socialist causes. Even in this case, it is worth noting that Ginsberg was expelled from Cuba for protesting Castro's discrimination against homosexuals. This same issue provoked his expulsion from Czechoslovakia in 1965, reinforcing his conviction, expressed in his 1960 poem "Death to Van Gogh's Ear," that there is "no human answer" in "dogmatic Leninism-Marxism."

As cultural radicals, Beats condemned power as inherently corrupting of the individual spirit. They were not interested in seizing the state to promote equality, especially if such a program required the bureaucratic regulation of social life. On the contrary, they were concerned with opposing the state in order to maximize individual liberty. Their anarchist ideology was consistent with causes like draft resistance, repeal of drug restrictions, and freedom of speech and the press. Robert McGrath, a Beat artist and one of the few who ignored his draft summons in 1960s, charged that military service was degrading to the human personality and the state had no moral authority to induct him against his will. He was given a one-year jail sentence (Adams 1980; Ross 1961).

Whatever their intention, the Beats had a powerful impact on the politics of the 1960s. Michael Harrington (1972-1973, p. 137) reflects, "It seemed obvious enough that the cultural rebellion in North Beach and the political beginnings

at Berkeley [late 1950s] were of a piece." In Jessica Mitford Treuhaft's (1961) view, "The beats may have helped crystallize for students a concept of what they are against." Altbach (1974, pp. 216, 219) proposes that the Beats and their hippie followers "helped to infuse the student community with a certain style of activism through their attacks against the achievement orientation of the broader society and a concomitant emphasis on noncompetitive values and experiments with new life styles." Jacobs and Landau (1966, p. 13) describe some of the flavor of that new style:

> As the apolitical "beats"—almost alone as symbols of protest in the 1950s—turned their concern to concrete issues of racial equality and peace, their style, dress and decor affected the activists. Arguments about politics began to include discussions of sexual freedom and marijuana. The language of the Negro poet-hipster premeated analyses of the Cuban Revolution. Protests over the execution of Caryl Chessman ultimately brought together students and some bohemians—the loose and overlapping segments of what was to become known as The Movement.

Beat enclaves, typically located near urban college campuses, provided many recruits for protest causes in the early days of the New Left Movement (Jacobs and Landau 1966, p. 13; O'Neil 1959; Altbach 1974, pp. 112, 115, 210). Yippie leader and Chicago 8 defendant Abbie Hoffman was one of those clubbed by police in the anti-HUAC protest in San Francisco. He promptly joined the ACLU tour of college campuses calling for the abolition of HUAC. Also, in 1960 Robert Allen Haber (1966, p. 49), cofounder of the Students for a Democratic Society, acknowledged that "the Movement has drawn heavily, if not always reliably," on the Beat group. Haber's SDS cofounder, Tom Hayden, revealed in his 1972 *Rolling Stone* interviews that his political education started only in 1960, at which time he "was an editor, very influenced by the Beat Generation. My thing was to hitchhike all over the country in different directions—the Latin Quarter of New Orleans and Miami and New York, Greenwich Village . . ." (Findley 1972, p. 38). Bob Dylan, a balladeer of the protest movement in the early 1960s, recalls that after reading the Beats, he realized "there were other people out there like me" (McNally 1979, p. 307). In fact, the style of Dylan's early protest songs clearly reflects the influence of his friend Allen Ginsberg.

By the late 1960s, there were millions of youth "out there" like Dylan, practicing life-styles and supporting causes introduced by the small circle of New York and San Francisco bohemian artists whose own youth was long past. Ironically, the retreatist, apolitical Beats played a critical role in the rise of both the hippies and the New Left, movements that together significantly altered a society most Beats believed was beyond redemption.

Bibliography

Adams, William R. 1980. Interview with Paul S. George. St. Augustine, Fla., Sept. 7.

Altbach, Philip. 1974. *Student Politics in America: A Historical Analysis.* New York: McGraw-Hill.

Ball, Gordon, ed. 1977. *Allen Ginsberg, Journals: Early Fifties, Early Sixties.* New York: Grove Press.

Berger, Bennett. 1971. *Looking for America: Essays on Youth, Suburbia and Other American Obsessions.* Englewood Cliffs, New Jersey: Prentice-Hall.

Berriault, Gina. 1972. "Neal's Ashes." *Rolling Stone,* Oct. 19, pp. 32, 34, 36.

Bjorn, Lars. 1980. "The Evolution of Jazz—The Artist's Effects." Paper Presented at American Sociological Association Meeting, New York.

Brown, Bernard O. 1968. "An Empirical Study of Ideology in Formation." *Review of Religious Research* 9: 79-87.

Burroughs, William S. 1979. *Junky.* New York: Penguin Books.

Bush, Douglas. 1978. "Literature, the Academy, and the Public." *Daedalus* 107, no. 4 (Fall): 165-74.

Cassady, Carolyn. 1976. *Heartbeat: My Life with Jack and Neal.* New York: Pocket Books.

Cassady, Neal. 1971. *The First Third and Other Writings.* San Francisco: City Lights Books.

Charters, Ann. 1973. *Kerouac.* New York: Warner Paperback Library.

Cherkovski, Neeli. 1979. *Ferlinghetti: A Biography.* New York: Doubleday.

Clark, Thomas. 1970. "Interview with Allen Ginsberg: 'The Art of Poetry.'" In *The Radical Vision: Essays for the Seventies,* edited by Leo Hamalian and Frederick R. Karl, pp. 129-65. New York: Thomas Y. Crowell.

Cook, Bruce. 1971. *The Beat Generation.* New York: Charles Scribner's Sons.

Corso, Gregory. 1970. "Elegiac Feelings American (for the dear memory of John Kerouac)." In *Elegiac Feelings American,* edited by Gregory Corso. New York: New Directions: 3-12.

Cowley, Malcolm. 1951. *Exile's Return.* New York: Viking Press. Reprinted in *Writers at Work: The Paris Review Interview,* edited by Malcolm Cowley, pp. 279-320. New York: Viking Press, 1967.

Dickstein, Morris. 1977. *Gates of Eden: American Culture in the Sixties.* New York: Basic Books.

Ebner, David Y. 1972. "Beats and Hippies: A Comparative Analysis." In *Society's Shadow: Studies in the Sociology of Countercultures,* edited by Kenneth Westhues. Toronto: McGraw-Hill.

Erikson, Erik H. 1959. *Young Man Luther.* New York: W. W. Norton.

———. 1953. *Childhood and Society.* New York: W. W. Norton.

Findley, Tom. 1972. "Tom Hayden: Rolling Stone Interview, Part I." *Rolling Stone,* Oct. 26, pp. 38-39.

Fromm, Erich. 1941. *Escape from Freedom.* New York: Avon Books.

Gifford, Barry, ed. 1977. *As Ever, The Collected Correspondence of Allen Ginsberg and Neal Cassady.* Berkeley: Creative Arts Book Co.

Gifford, Barry, and Lawrence Lee. 1979. *Jack's Book: An Oral Biography of Jack Kerouac.* New York: Penguin Books.

Ginsberg, Allen. 1956. *Howl and Other Poems.* San Francisco: City Lights Press.

Goodman, Paul. 1960. *Growing up Absurd: Problems of Youth in the Organized Society.* New York: Vintage Books.

Gouldner, Alvin. 1973. "Romanticism and Classicism: Deep Structures in Social Science." In *For Sociology: Renewal and Critique in Sociology Today,* edited by Alvin Gouldner, pp. 324-53. New York: Basic Books.

Graber, David. 1978. "Bohemia in Revolt." *Human Behavior,* June, p. 8.

Gruen, John. 1966. *The New Bohemia: The Combine Generation.* New York: Grosset and Dunlap.

Haber, Robert. 1966. "From Protest to Radicalism: An Appraisal of the Student Movement." In *The New Student Left: An Anthology,* edited by Mitchell Cohen and Dennis Hale, pp. 41-49. Boston: Beacon.

Hahn, Emily. 1966. *Romantic Rebels: An Informal History of Bohemianism in America.* Cambridge, Mass.: Riverside Press.

Harrington, Michael. 1972-73. *Fragments of the Century.* New York: Simon and Schuster.

———. 1972. "We Few, We Happy Few, We Bohemians." *Esquire,* Aug., pp. 99-103, 162-64.

———. 1962. "The American Campus: 1962." *Dissent,* Spring: 164-68.

Hills, Ruts. 1979. "Introduction." In Ken Kesey, "The Day After Superman Died." *Esquire,* Oct., pp. 42-44.

Hodeir, André. 1956. *Jazz: Its Evolution and Essence.* New York: Grove Press.

Hodges, Harold, Jr. 1974. *Conflict and Consensus: An Introduction to Sociology,* 2nd ed. New York: Harper & Row.

Holmes, John C. 1967. *Nothing More to Declare.* New York: Dutton.

———. 1958. "The Philosophy of the Beat Generation." *Esquire,* Feb., pp. 35-38.

———. 1952a. *GO.* New York: Charles Scribner's Sons.

———. 1952b. "This Is the Beat Generation." *New York Times Magazine,* Nov. 16, pp. 10, 19, 20, 22.

Howard, John. 1974. *The Cutting Edge: Social Movement and Social Change in America.* New York: Lippincott.

Jacobs, Paul, and Saul Landau. 1966. *The New Radicals: A Report with Documents.* New York: Vintage Books.

Jarvis, Charles. 1973-74. *Vision of Kerouac.* Lowell, Mass.: Ithaca Press.

Kerouac, Jack. 1972. *Visions of Cody*. New York: McGraw-Hill.

———. 1959. "The Origins of the Beat Generation." *Playboy*, June, pp. 31-32, 42, 79.

———. 1957. *On the Road*. New York: Signet.

Kostelanetz, Richard. 1970. "Allen Ginsberg: Artist as Apostle, Poet as Preacher." In *Representative Man: Cult Heroes of Our Time*, edited by Theodore L. Gross, pp. 257-75. New York: The Free Press.

Kramer, Jane. 1969. *Allen Ginsberg in America*. New York: Random House.

———. 1968. "Profiles: Allen Ginsberg." *New Yorker* 44 (Aug. 24): 77-79.

Life. 1960. "Politics: Beat in the Hip of Texas." Mar. 7, pp. 48-51.

Lipton, Lawrence. 1959. *The Holy Barbarians*. New York: Julian Messner.

Mailer, Norman. 1969. "The White Negro: Superficial Reflections on the Hipster." In *Voices of Dissent*, pp. 197-214. Freeport, N.Y.: Books for Libraries Press. Originally published in *Dissent* 4 (1957): 276-93.

McNally, Dennis. 1979. *Desolate Angel: Jack Kerouac, the Beat Generation and America*. New York: Random House.

Mannheim, Karl. 1971. "Conservative Thought." In *From Karl Mannheim*, edited by Kurt Wolff, pp. 132-222. New York: Oxford University Press.

Miller, Richard. 1977. *Bohemia: The Protoculture Then and Now*. Chicago: Nelson-Hall.

Millstein, Gilbert. 1960. "Rent a Beatnik and Swing." *New York Times Magazine*, Apr. 17, pp. 26, 28, 30.

———. 1957. "Books of the Times." *New York Times*, Sept. 5, p. 27.

Myerhoff, Barbara. 1972. "The Revolution as a Trip: Symbol and Paradox." In *The New Pilgrims: Youth Protest in Transition*, edited by Philip Altbach and Robert Laufer, pp. 251-66. New York: David McKay.

Newsweek. 1963. "Bye Bye Beatnik." July 1, p. 65.

———. 1959. "Heat on the Beatniks." Aug. 17, p. 36.

New Yorker. 1960a. "The Talk of the Town: Movement Party to Celebrate Publication of *The Beats*." Apr. 16, pp. 36-37.

———. 1960b. "Life Line: The Figaro in Greenwich Village." Aug. 6, pp. 21-23.

New York Times. 1960a. June 11, p. 23.

———. 1960b. June 13, p. 32.

Nuttall, Jeff. 1968. *Bomb Culture*. New York: Delacorte Press.

O'Brien, James. 1968. *A History of the New Left, 1960-1968*. Boston: New England Free Press.

O'Neil, Paul. 1959. "Only Rebellion Around." *Life*, Nov. 30, pp. 114-16, 119-20, 123-24, 126, 129-30.

Plummer, William. 1981. *The Holy Goof: A Biography of Neal Cassady*. Englewood Cliffs, N.J.: Prentice-Hall.

———. 1979. "The Beat Goes on." *New York Times Magazine*, Dec. 30, p. 41.

Podhoretz, Norman. 1960. "The Know Nothing Bohemians." In *The Beats*, edited by Seymour Krim. Greenwich, Conn.: Fawcett. The essay originally appeared in *Partisan Review* 25 (Spring 1958): 111-24.

Polsky, Ned. 1969. *Hustlers, Beats, and Others*. Garden City, N.Y.: Anchor Books.

Richardson, Derek. 1979. Review of *Desolate Angel*. *In These Times*, Dec. 5-11, p. 12.

Rigney, Francis, and Douglas Smith. 1961. *The Real Bohemia*. New York: Basic Books.

Ross, Tim. "Rise and Fall of the Beats." *The Nation*, May 27, pp. 456-58.

Roszak, Theodore. 1969. *The Making of a Counterculture: Reflections on the Technocratic Society and Its Youthful Opposition*. Garden City, N.Y.: Doubleday/Anchor.

San Francisco Chronicle. 1960a. Jan. 31, p. 1.

———. 1960b. May 15, pp. 1, 4.

Schjeldahl, Peter. 1976. Review of John Tytell's *Naked Angels: The Lives and Literature of the Beat Generation*. *New York Times Book Review*, May 9, p. 4.

Seelye, John. 1974. "The Sum of '48." *The New Republic* 171 (Oct. 12): 23-24.

Shapiro, Theda. 1976. *Painters and Politics: The European Avant-Garde and Society*. New York: Elsevier.

Siske, John P. 1959. "Beatniks and Tradition." *Commonweal*, Apr. 17, pp. 75-78.

Smith, David E., and John Luce. 1976. *Love Needs Care: A History of San Francisco's Haight-Ashbury Free Medical Clinic and Its Pioneer Role in Treating Drug Abuse Problems*. Boston: Little, Brown.

Snyder, Gary. 1969. *Earth House Hold*. New York: New Directions.

Spates, James. 1971. "Structure and Trends in Value Systems in the 'Hip' Underground Counterculture and the American Middle Class, 1951-1957, 1967-1969." Ph.D. dissertation, Boston University.

Starr, Jerold. 1981. "Adolescents and Resistance to Schooling: A Dialectic." *Youth and Society*, Dec., pp. 189-228.

———. 1980. "New Directions in the Study of Youth and Society." *Current Sociology*, Winter, pp. 341-72.

Time. 1959a. "Manners and Morals, Fried Shoes." Feb. 9, p. 16.

———. 1959b. "Bang, Bong, Bing." Sept. 7, p. 80.

Treuhaft, Jessica Mitford. 1961. "The Indignant Generation." *The Nation*, May 27, pp. 451-56.

Tytell, John. 1976. *Naked Angels: The Lives and Loves of the Beat Generation*. New York: McGraw-Hill.

Willener, Alfred. 1970. *The Action-Image of Society: On Cultural Politicization*. New York: Pantheon Books.

Wohl, Robert. 1979. *The Generation of 1914*. Cambridge, Mass.: Harvard University Press.

Wolfe, Tom. 1968. *The Electric Kool-Aid Acid Test*. New York: Farrar, Straus and Giroux.

THE BEAT SCENE IN THE EAST

SUSAN EDMISTON AND LINDA D. CIRINO (ESSAY DATE 1976)

SOURCE: Edmiston, Susan, and Linda D. Cirino. "The Lower East Side." In *Literary New York*, pp. 111-46. Boston, Mass.: Houghton Mifflin Company, 1976.

In the following essay, Edmiston and Cirino delineate how the locales in and around East Greenwich Village in New York City served as the settings for the activities of the Beat Generation.

In the early fifties, as rents rose ever higher in Greenwich Village, writers began to find homes on the Lower East Side. Although Allen Ginsberg, Jack Kerouac and Norman Mailer drank in the San Remo on Bleecker Street or the White Horse on Hudson, they went home to the region east of Third Avenue. Gradually the migration into the area north of Houston and south of 14th Street swelled until the neighborhood came to be known as the East Village. Its tenement-lined streets, where rents were among the cheapest in the city, provided an incubating ground for the writers of the "Beat Generation." Later, in an outcast tradition exemplified by these writers, the East Village became the center of the counterculture of the sixties, producing its most avant-garde poetry and theater and representing its lifestyle at its most extreme.

Much of the East Village was originally the farm of Peter Stuyvesant, which stretched from Broadway to the river and from 5th to 17th streets. In the early nineteenth century the land was broken into lots, and prosperous New Yorkers lived in the brick houses that still stand on 10th Street, Stuyvesant Street, St. Mark's Place and other blocks on the area's western edge. Washington Irving lived in historic Colonnade Row at 428 to 434 Lafayette Street (the Astor Place Theatre now occupies 434), in 1836; and James Fenimore Cooper rented 6 St. Mark's Place in 1834. Later the tenements Henry Roth described were built farther to the east. More recently the area has been a patchwork of ethnic enclaves—Poles, Ukrainians, Italians, Puerto Ricans and Jews living in clusters side by side—and it was not until the arrival of the Beats that it began to take on the literary dimension it has today.

The Beat Generation is sometimes said to have been made up of four people—Allen Ginsberg, Jack Kerouac, William Burroughs and Gregory Corso. Although Ginsberg, Kerouac and Burroughs had met around Columbia University and Ginsberg traces the birth of the Beat sensibility to an apartment on 115th Street and Morningside Drive, they came to be most strongly associated with the Lower East Side. It is tempting to link the "beatness" of the movement with the current desolation of the neighborhood, but Ginsberg says there is no connection. "New York was Charlie Chaplin-land then," he said. "You'd walk around the city hearing 'Rhapsody in Blue' in your head."[1]

The term *Beat* referred to a certain sensibility rather than a physical state or surroundings. It was Kerouac who gave it a name. In an article called "The Origins of the Beat Generation," he wrote, "John Clellon Holmes . . . and I were sitting around trying to think up the meaning of the Lost Generation and the subsequent existentialism and I said, 'You know, this is really a beat generation' and he leapt up and said 'That's it, that's right.'"[2] According to Holmes, who also wrote an article on the subject, Kerouac described Beat as meaning "being right down to it, to ourselves, because we all *really* know where we are—and a weariness with all the forms, all the conventions of the world."[3] Whatever Beat may have meant exactly—Kerouac later said it was "beatific"; Holmes likened it to Kierkegaardian rather than Sartrean existentialism; and Ginsberg and Kerouac had originally heard the term from a Times Square junkie named Herbert Huncke—it came to represent a revolt against both the political and literary establishments in favor of a glorification of spontaneous, personal and mystical, rather than academic, experience.

Ginsberg was the first of the Beats to move to the Lower East Side. He had been hanging out in Village bars since 1948 and in 1951 took an apartment at 206 East 7th Street, which rapidly became an outpost for his friends. Here he regularly received letters from Burroughs, who was in South America and Mexico. In 1953, two years after Burroughs accidentally killed his wife (he tried to shoot a glass off her head in an imitation of William Tell) he came back to New York and moved in with Ginsberg. Burroughs assembled his letters as two books—*The Yage Letters* and *Queer*—and Ginsburg, in one of the first of his endless activities as agent, publicist, promoter, mediator and exchange bureau for poets and writers, set out to get them published. Earlier, he had been successful with *Junkie*, which he sold to his friend Carl Solomon at Ace Books. (Ginsberg had met Solomon, to whom he later dedicated *Howl*, when both were patients at Columbia Psychiatric Institute.) *Junkie*, set in part in a tenement apartment on the Lower East Side, told the story of Burroughs's addiction to morphine and heroin. It was originally published as *Junkie* by "William Lee." Meanwhile, Ginsberg was writing the first three poems of *Reality Sandwiches.*

Jack Kerouac often stayed at the 7th Street apartment and it was there that he met the woman he would depict as Mardou Fox in *The Subterraneans.* The relationship that ensued was more intense than his generally superficial affairs with women. For two months he spent a great deal of time in her apartment at 501 East 11th Street, a glorified tenement building with an inner courtyard known to the Beats as "Paradise Alley." After the affair was over, Kerouac went home to Queens and wrote *The Subterraneans* in "three full moon nights" of October 1953, typing at his mother's kitchen table.[4]

Like all of Kerouac's books, *The Subterraneans* is a barely disguised retelling of his own experience. Kerouac is Leo Percepied, Allen Ginsberg is Adam Moorad, William Burroughs is Frank Carmody and Gregory Corso is Uri Gligoric. Kerouac shifts the scene from Paradise Alley to a fictional Heavenly Lane in San Francisco. But the novel is an exact description of the Lower East Side scene of the time, with its parties, jazz and drugs. He describes

> the Pierre-of-Melville goof and wonder of it, the dark little beat burlap dresses, the stories you'd hear about great tenormen shooting junk by broken windows and starting at their horns, or great young pads with beats lying high in Rouault-like saintly obscurities, Heavenly Lane the famous Heavenly Lane where they'd all at one time or another the beat subterraneans lived . . . seeing it for the first time . . . the wash hung over the court, actually the back courtyard of a big 20-family tenement with bay windows, the wash hung out and in the afternoon the great symphony of Italian mothers, children, fathers Be-Finneganing and yelling from stepladders, smells, cats mewing, Mexicans, the music from all the radios whether bolero of Mexican or Italian tenor of spaghetti eaters or loud suddenly turned-up KPFA symphonies of Vivaldi harpischord intellectuals performances boom blam the tremendous sound of it . . .[5]

In invoking the "Pierre-of-Melville" comparison, Kerouac makes the link the Beats frequently did between themselves and other writers once outcast and in disrepute like Melville and Whitman. John Clellon Holmes, in an essay on Kerouac called "The Great Rememberer," draws a direct parallel: "Melville, armed with the manuscript of *Typee,* must have struck the Boston Brahmins in much the same way.[6] Stocky, medium-tall, Kerouac had the tendoned forearms, heavily muscled thighs and broad neck of a man

who exults in his physical life." And Ginsberg, like Kerouac, compares life on the Lower East Side in the fifties with the society of poets and outcasts Melville had depicted in *Pierre* a hundred years earlier. "Like *The Subterraneans,*" said Ginsberg, "*Pierre* depicts the gnostic, garbage culture of its time." With the Lower East Side experience, Beat broadened its dimensions. Said Ginsberg: "This was the loam or soil out of which a lot of it grew . . . the apocalyptic sensibility, the interest in the mystic arts, the marginal leavings, the garbage of society . . . the beginning of Department of Sanitation culture."[7]

Beat, therefore, was a social stance first—an attitude of protest against the establishment. It was a protest, again, as a literary movement—the Beats stood in opposition to the writing and criticism of the academy in favor of the literature drawn from their own spontaneous experience. Seymour Krim reduces it to the simplest terms: "The real thing to remember is that they were people . . . who had respect for their own experience and wanted to write from it."[8]

Technically, William Carlos Williams was the Beats' major poetic influence. They took his dictum, "No ideas but in things," as a starting point ("Williams' precise real images are such a relief after affected iambics," said Ginsberg) and learned from his use of the natural breath in the poetic line.[9] But they went on from there to develop a kind of prosody that Ginsberg has sometimes compared to jazz and called "spontaneous bop prosody," the syntax and rhythms arising out of the attempt to "transcribe the thought all at once so that its ramifications appear on the page."[10]

And there was always the extraliterary influence of drugs. Burroughs's *Naked Lunch* was written on cannabis; Kerouac did virtually all his work on benzedrine; Ginsberg wrote *Howl* on peyote for visions. Later, there would come experimentation with the altered states of consciousness, which Ginsberg recorded in a series of poems named for the drugs under which they were produced, like "Lysergic Acid" and "Mescaline."

In the third poem in *Reality Sandwiches,* "The Green Automobile," Ginsberg wrote: "If I had a Green Automobile/I'd go find my old companion/in his house on the Western ocean."[11] The poem was addressed to Neal Cassady, who had been Ginsberg's lover and who was the hero of Kerouac's *On the Road.* Cassady occupied a rather mythic position in the Beat pantheon, both as hero and as muse, and it was he rather than any literary scene that drew Ginsberg and Kerouac to California. There were, however, a number of poets living in the San Francisco area—Michael McClure, Gary Snyder, Philip Whalen, Philip Lamantia and, from an older generation, Kenneth Rexroth—and Ginsberg's great organizational energies and publicity instincts catalyzed what was to be called the San Francisco Renaissance. In 1955, two years after arriving in California, Ginsberg organized a reading of six poets and there first read "Howl." The poem, which launched the Beat poets in the public mind, recalled the Lower East Side experience of those

> who ate fire in paint hotels or drank turpentine
> in Paradise Alley, death, or purgatoried their
> torsos night after night
> with dreams, with drugs, with waking
> nightmares, alcohol and cock and endless
> balls . . .[12]

While the Beats were in California, Norman Mailer was living out another Lower East Side experience. In 1951, after returning to New York from Hollywood, he had moved to a simple, cold water flat on Pitt Street, "way over on the Lower East Side beneath the Williamsburg Bridge, a grim apartment, renovated in battle-ship gray," as he described it in *Advertisements for Myself*.[13] He was trying to write stories for magazines, without much success, and at the same time thinking disconnectedly about a long novel. One morning he woke with the plan in his mind for a prologue and eight-book work concerning the adventures of a mythical hero named Sergius O'Shaughnessy. Mailer plunged into part one, *The Deer Park*, and when he finished the first draft decided to forget the eight-novel concept. *The Deer Park*, said to be about Mailer's second wife, Adele Morales, draws on his experience in Hollywood and ends with its protagonist living in a "hole in New York, a cold-water flat outside the boundary of the Village."[14]

Mailer's next address was 39 First Avenue, the top floor of a five-story red brick tenement. Dan Wolf, who later founded the *Village Voice* with Mailer and Ed Fancher, lived on the top floor of the house next door and would walk over the roof to visit. "There was a kosher brewery or winery on the ground floor and its odor permeated the building," recalled Wolf.[15] Mailer's next address was a huge loft on Monroe Street—"you needed a bicycle to go from one end to another," says Wolf. Here Mailer held enormous parties attended by hundreds of people, some of them celebrities. "It was a very rough neighborhood, and at one of the parties—I remember Montgomery Clift was there that night," said Dan Wolf, "a bunch of toughs came in.[16] They began hitting Norman over the

head with a hammer. It was the stunned and silent fifties and nobody rose to the occasion and helped him." After this experience Mailer left the Lower East Side for the more civilized East Fifties.

In 1957, with his essays "The White Negro" and "Reflections on Hip," Mailer charted his own variant of Beat, which he called "hip." Later he differentiated between the two attitudes in "Hipster and Beatnik." "The Beat Generation," he wrote, "is probably best used to include hipsters and beatniks . . . Still, it must be said that the differences between hipsters and beatniks may be more important than their similarities, even if they share the following general characteristics: Marijuana, jazz, not much money, and a community of feeling that society is the prison of the nervous system."[17] Mailer went on to distinguish between the hipster as coming out of "a muted rebellion of the proletariat" and the beatnik as coming from the middle class and choosing not to work as a "sentence against the conformity of his parents." While hipster and beatnik agreed on "the first tenet of the faith: that one's orgasm is the clue to how well one is living," their bodies were not the same: the hipster moves like a cat and dresses with chic while the beatnik is slovenly and has less body with which to lift himself by his sexual bootstraps. For a time, Mailer allied himself with the hipsters and classified Ginsberg and Kerouac in a hybrid group, the "hipniks and beatsters."

In 1957 Allen Ginsberg and Jack Kerouac came back east and found, like prophets who leave their own countries and achieve recognition, that California had made them famous. Strangely, they were now referred to as "San Francisco poets," which both they and the true San Franciscans found insulting. But success was finally theirs. *Evergreen Review* published a special issue on the San Francisco Renaissance, which included *Howl* and a piece by Kerouac. Malcolm Cowley, one of Kerouac's early supporters, had finally aroused enough enthusiasm at the Viking Press for the publication of *On the Road*, and *The Subterraneans* was scheduled for publication by Grove Press. *Howl* was sold out at the Eighth Street Bookshop and the Gotham Book Mart. The *Village Voice* heralded the writers' arrival with an article headlined WITLESS MADCAPS COME HOME TO ROOST. But they did not roost long. Kerouac, Ginsberg, Corso and Peter Orlovsky, whom Ginsberg had met in San Francisco, all left for Tangier to visit William Burroughs.

Kerouac was back in New York within three months but Ginsberg and Orlovsky spent two years in Europe. In 1959 they returned to the Lower East Side and moved into Apartment 16 at 170 East 2nd Street, a red brick building with white stone trim one notch above a tenement. The apartment is the setting for Ginsberg's "I beg you come back & be cheerful," which captures the mixed Spanish-Jewish quality of the neighborhood.

> Tonite I got hi in the window of my apartment
> chair at 3 : AM
> gazing at Blue incandescent torches
> bright-lit street below
> clotted shadows loomin on a new laid pave
> —as last week Medieval rabbiz
> plodded thru the brown raw
> dirt turned over—sticks
> & cans
> and tired ladies sitting on spanish
> garbage pails—in the deadly heat . . .[18]

Here Ginsberg wrote "Kaddish" and edited Burroughs's *Naked Lunch* (the title was originally *Naked Lust* but Kerouac misread it and Burroughs liked his version better). Ginsberg found himself at the center of the scene, which had expanded to include such writers as Diane di Prima, Tuli Kupferberg, Seymour Krim, LeRoi Jones and Hubert Selby. The Cedar Street Tavern at 24 University Place between 8th and 9th streets,[19] which had been a hangout for abstract expressionist painters like Jackson Pollock, Franz Kline and Willem de Kooning, who had studios and galleries on the Lower East Side, also became the watering place of the Beats. "Who was there?" asked Seymour Krim.[20] "Well, everybody you might expect—Holmes, Ginsberg, Corso and occasionally Kerouac and then others that might be thought of more as the Black Mountain crowd—[Hubert] Selby, Gilbert Sorrentino, and for a while Robert Creeley."

Also "there" was the poet Frank O'Hara, who linked painters and writers through his work as an associate curator of the Museum of Modern Art. "John Ashbery, Barbara Guest, Kenneth Koch and I, being poets," he wrote, "divided our time between the literary bar, the San Remo, and the artists' bar, the Cedar Tavern.[21] In the San Remo we argued and gossiped: in the Cedar we often wrote poems while listening to the painters argue and gossip. So far as I know nobody painted in the San Remo while they listened to the writers argue." In 1957 O'Hara moved downtown to 90 University Place, an old three-story gray brick building. The apartment appears in one of what he called his "'I do this I do that' poems":

> I live above a dyke bar and I'm happy.
> The police car is always near the door

> in case they cry
> or the key doesn't work in the lock. But
> he can't open it either. So we go to
> Joan's
> and sleep over,
> Bridget and Joe and I.
> I meet Mike for a beer in the Cedar as
> the wind flops up the Place, pushing the leaves
> against the streetlights . . .[22]

In 1959 O'Hara moved deep into the East Side to 441 East 9th Street. This apartment was "a tenement dump, a two-room flat," said Patsy Southgate, poet, translator and close friend of O'Hara's.[23] "Frank preferred to spend his money on cabs, restaurants, liquor, cigarettes, rather than living quarters." Among O'Hara's close friends were Ginsberg, Koch and LeRoi Jones. "People just dropped by," said Southgate. "They drank at his house and then went out to a restaurant to eat—Il Bambino, El Charro, John's on East Tenth Street and Second Avenue, Joe's, Angelina's or the Cedar bar. Once at Ninth Street and Avenue A I spent a whole evening trying to convince LeRoi that James Baldwin had a point and wasn't really so radical. LeRoi had nothing but white friends."

In 1964 O'Hara moved to 791 Broadway, across from Grace Church. "The apartment was a sort of elegant big loft facing the rose window of the church. It was all painted white, including the floor," said Patsy Southgate.[24] "There were paintings by De Kooning, Frankenthaler, Motherwell, Franz Kline, Mike Goldberg and Joan Mitchell. It was his first sort of 'grand lodgings.' Usually the TV set would be on and Frank would be on the phone and probably the record player would be on and the icebox would be empty. I never saw anything in it except orange juice for making screwdrivers and maybe a prune whip yoghurt."

One night O'Hara, Jones and the painter Larry Rivers were to be on a television panel together. "LeRoi turned up at Frank's with a lot of blacks and all of a sudden fought with Frank over a glass," remembered Southgate.[25] "When we got to the TV program he gave his famous speech in which he said 'the only good white man is a dead white man.' Then he moved up to Harlem."

LeRoi Jones, now known as Amiri Baraka, had lived first in a one-and-a-half-room apartment on the top floor of 7 Morton Street in the West Village, where he and his wife, Hettie, put out a magazine called *Yugen*, financed on her salary as manager of the *Partisan Review*. The magazine, which published many of the Beat writers, was named for a Zen term that meant "flower of the miraculous." Hettie prepared the magazine on an old IBM electric typewriter. "The people in San

Francisco said 'Oh, it's such a messy thing,'" she recalled.[26] "No one had considered amateurism before. We didn't have any money but we thought these things were valuable to put out." At one point a controversy regarding the nature of poetry between those Hettie Jones called "the crazy faction—Allen, Gregory, Peter and Jack" and "the Black Mountain plus New York people—Frank, Kenneth Koch, John Ashbery" raged over several issues. During its course O'Hara wrote "Personism: A Manifesto" in which he stated that the poem should be "between two persons instead of two pages." In writing, "you just go on your nerve. If someone's chasing you down the street with a knife you just run, you don't turn around and shout, 'Give it up! I was a track star for Mineola Prep' . . . As for measure and other technical apparatus, that's just common sense: if you're going to buy a pair of pants you want them to be tight enough so everyone will want to go to bed with you."[27]

At this time the Joneses also published books in collaboration with Eli Wilentz of the Eighth Street Book Shop under the imprint of Totem Books. The most important of these was Charles Olson's *Projective Verse,* in which he outlined the concepts that would dominate the poetry of the sixties. There were three main principles: "A poem is energy transferred from where the poet got it . . . by way of the poem itself to, all the way over to, the reader. FORM IS NEVER MORE THAN AN EXTENSION OF CONTENT. And, ONE PERCEPTION MUST IMMEDIATELY AND DIRECTLY LEAD TO A FURTHER PERCEPTION."[28]

In the fall of 1958, the Joneses moved to 402 West 20th Street and then in 1960 to 324 East 14th Street—the parlor floor of a Victorian house that has since been radically remodeled. "It was huge, baronial and a bitch to clean," said Hettie.[29] "This home soon became a center for people who would stay overnight, like Joel Oppenheimer who lived in the Bronx and Gilbert Sorrentino who lived in Brooklyn or those like John Wieners and Gary Snyder who came from out west and stayed longer." There were immense parties: "I could feed hundreds on one pot of spaghetti."

By the sixties, said Hettie, "the Lower East Side had become a 'scene.' There was the Cedar bar, happenings and the beginning of black bohemia." The writers also hung out at the Five Spot, where owner Iggy Tormini let musicians like Billie Holiday perform without cabaret cards, and writers and artists listen without paying. On July 17, 1959, on reading of the death of Billie Holiday in the newspaper, O'Hara wrote "The Day Lady Died," which ended with the lines:

then I go back where I came from 6th Avenue
and the tobacconist in the Ziegfeld Theatre and
casually ask for a carton of Gauloises and a
     carton
of Picayunes, and a NEW YORK POST with her face
     on it
and I am sweating a lot by now and thinking of
leaning on the john door in the 5 SPOT
while she whispered a song along the keyboard
to Mal Waldron and everyone and I stopped
     breathing . . .[30]

In the winter of 1962 the Joneses moved again, this time to 27 Cooper Square. They installed heating in what had previously been a "cold-water flophouse for bums with upward mobility" and here LeRoi wrote *Blues People* before moving uptown to Harlem.[31]

Unaffiliated with Beat, hip or any of their variants, W. H. Auden lived quietly on the Lower East Side from 1953 to 1972 at 77 St. Mark's Place, where Trotsky had printed *Novy Mir* in the basement. Auden's ties were with the academics and West Side intellectuals whom the Beats opposed. In fact, one evening at the Trillings', Auden chided Diana Trilling for having been moved by a Ginsberg reading. A visitor described Auden's second-floor walkup as it was in 1971: "Auden writes on a new portable typewriter ('the best money can buy') in his small, windowless living room, which is cluttered with books, phonograph records and manuscripts. Off the living room are a sleeping alcove with a rumpled bed, a kitchen where he cooks gourmet meals . . . for himself and his friends and another room, also cluttered, which overlooks St. Mark's Place."[32] Although not a presence on the neighborhood poetry scene, Auden was a parishioner at his local church, the historic St. Mark's-in-the-Bouwerie, and a familiar figure to local shopkeepers.

In 1963, when Allen Ginsberg and Peter Orlovsky returned after traveling in South America, Europe and India, they found the Lower East Side in full swing. The media had discovered the area's intense poetic activity and made it the subject of a publicity explosion. Poetry readings had begun in 1960 at the 10th Street Coffee-House, owned by Mickey Ruskin. On Mondays there were open readings and on Wednesdays a guest poet was invited. In 1961 Ruskin bought Les Deux Megots [sic] Coffeehouse on East 7th Street and the poetry readings moved there. At the end of '62 Ruskin gave up Les Deux Megots and the readings were re-established in the winter of 1963 at the Café Le Metro. Generally 125 people would be allowed in and another twenty-five or fifty waited outside.

During 1964, readings held on radio, in bars, theaters, art galleries and churches diversified and proliferated.

There were many little magazines and a number of important subcommunities. One of these was a group of black poets called the Society of Umbra, which set up its own workshop and magazine. Among those originally involved were Calvin Hernton and David Henderson. *Umbra* was still publishing as recently as 1970-71, when Larry Neal, Ishmael Reed, Toni Cade, LeRoi Jones, Langston Hughes and Nikki Giovanni were among the writers represented in an issue edited by David Henderson.

Another group formed around Diane di Prima and Alan Marlowe's American Theatre for Poets, which presented happenings, dance programs and a series of new one-act plays, including works by Diane di Prima, Robert Duncan, LeRoi Jones, Frank O'Hara, and Michael McClure. Di Prima, who lived at 31 Cooper Square, also published a large and varied selection of books through the Poet's Press, which she founded, and *The Floating Bear*, a magazine that she had cofounded with LeRoi Jones in February 1961.

Although he was not involved with the East Village scene, one of the most important figures in the experimental theater lived for several years on the Lower East Side. Jack Gelber had come to New York from San Francisco in 1955 and found a "rundown smelly apartment" at 435 East 5th Street.[33] He paid $11.20 a month for the place, which he shared with a saxophone player whose acquaintances were constantly coming and going. Next he went to live at 11 Pitt Street, where he wrote the *Connection*, based mostly on San Francisco experiences but set in a "shooting gallery" that had something of the atmosphere of his 5th Street apartment.

After the Le Metro poetry readings ended in 1965, the Lower East Side "community climate," as poet and editor Allen de Loach called it, began to ebb. Strangely enough, it was only after it was all over that one of the foremost Beats, Gregory Corso, came to live in the area. In 1967 he lived on 5th Street and Avenue C, "right in the heart of the horror," as he described it.[34] "Oh how oppressive it was!" In the late sixties, in a mass fulfillment of the Beat ethos, the Lower East Side became New York headquarters of the psychedelic counterculture. For a brief period the East Village was a colorful center of rock music and hippie life; ethnic dance halls became discotheques and Yiddish theaters were transformed into rock auditoriums. But the runaways who flocked to the area from all over the country were unprepared for the harshness of tenement life. Today many of the poets, of necessity, still live on the Lower East Side—many others have moved to Westbeth in the West Village—and regular poetry readings at St. Mark's-in-the-Bouwerie maintain the tradition. But the increasing viciousness of the neighborhood has created an atmosphere inhospitable to the vital communal scene that existed in the sixties. Of the major figures only Ginsberg, truly indifferent to material comfort, has remained in the neighborhood. He and Peter Orlovsky lived in the East 10th Street apartment they took in 1965 until 1975 and then moved several blocks away.

Notes

1. "New York was Charlie . . ." Interview with Allen Ginsberg, December 21, 1971.

2. "John Clellon Holmes . . ." Jack Kerouac, "The Origins of the Beat Generation," *Playboy*, June 1959, reprinted in *A Casebook on the Beat*, edited by Thomas Parkinson (New York: Thomas Y. Crowell Co., 1961), p. 70.

3. "being right down to it . . ." John Clellon Holmes, "The Philosophy of the Beat Generation" in *The Beats*, edited by Seymour Krim (Greenwich: Gold Medal Books, Fawcett Publications, 1960), p. 15.

4. "three full moon nights . . ." Bruce Cook, *The Beat Generation* (New York: Charles Scribner's Sons, 1971), p. 79.

5. "the Pierre-of Melville goof . . ." Jack Kerouac, *The Subterraneans* (New York: Grove Press, 1958), p. 15.

6. "Melville, armed with the manuscript . . ." quoted in Cook, *The Beat Generation*, p. 45.

7. "Like *The Subterraneans* . . ." Interview with Ginsberg, Winter 1971.

8. "the real thing to remember . . ." Cook, *The Beat Generation*, p. 51.

9. "Williams' precise real images . . ." Jane Kramer, *Allen Ginsberg in America* (New York: Random House, 1969), p. 174.

10. "transcribe the thought . . ." Kramer, *Allen Ginsberg in America*, p. 171.

11. "If I had a Green Automobile . . ." Allen Ginsberg, *Reality Sandwiches* (San Francisco: City Lights Books, 1963), p. 11.

12. "Who ate fire . . ." Allen Ginsberg, *Howl* (San Francisco: City Lights Books, 1965), p. 9.

13. "Way over on the lower . . ." Norman Mailer, *Advertisements for Myself* (New York: New American Library, A Signet Book, 1960), p. 139.

14. "hole in New York . . ." Norman Mailer, *The Deer Park* (New York: Berkley Publishing Corporation, A Berkley Medallion Book, December 1970), p. 300.

15. "There was a kosher brewery . . ." and subsequent quotations this paragraph, interview with Dan Wolf, Spring 1971.

16. "It was a very rough neighborhood . . ." Interview with Dan Wolf.

17. "The Beat Generation . . ." Mailer, *Advertisements for Myself*, p. 334.

18. "Tonite I got hi . . ." Ginsberg, *Reality Sandwiches*, p. 77.

19. The Cedar, its original building torn down to make way for an apartment house, moved up the street to 82 University Place.

20. "Who was there? . . ." Cook, *The Beat Generation*, p. 51.

21. "John Ashbery, Barbara Guest . . ." Frank O'Hara, "Larry Rivers: A Memoir," in *The Collected Poems of Frank O'Hara*, edited by Donald Allen, with an introduction by John Ashbery (New York: Alfred A. Knopf, 1971), p. 512.

22. "I live above a dyke bar . . ." Allen, *The Collected Poems of Frank O'Hara*, p. 286.

23. "a tenement dump . . ." and subsequent quotations this paragraph, interview with Patsy Southgate, April 29, 1971.

24. "The apartment was . . ." Interview with Patsy Southgate.

25. "LeRoi turned up . . ." Interview with Patsy Southgate.

26. "The people in San Francisco . . ." Interview with Hettie Jones, May 17, 1971.

27. "You just go on your nerve . . ." Allen, *The Collected Poems of Frank O'Hara*, p. 498.

28. "A poem is energy . . ." Cook, *The Beat Generation*, p. 121.

29. "It was huge, baronial . . ." Interview with Hettie Jones.

30. "then I go back . . ." Allen, *The Collected Poems of Frank O'Hara*, p. 325.

31. "cold-water flophouse . . ." Interview with Hettie Jones.

32. "Auden writes on a new . . ." Judson Hand, *The New York Daily News*, January 13, 1971.

33. "rundown smelly . . ." Interview with Jack Gelber, September 18, 1974.

34. "right in the heart . . ." Interview with Gregory Corso, April 1971.

RONALD SUKENICK (ESSAY DATE 1987)

SOURCE: Sukenick, Ronald. "Bleecker Street." In *Down and Out: Life in the Underground*, pp. 87-122. New York: Beech Tree Books, 1987.

In the following essay, Sukenick describes several of the important places and people in Greenwich Village in the 1950s and 1960s.

It was beautiful because they loved one another. There was no money involved yet, or not much, and the only kind of success in view was limited to clique, cult, and coterie. In-groups huddling in enclaves as here, now, in the dead point of the fifties the youthful patrons of Tulla's coffeehouse in Cambridge, Massachusetts, huddle against the draft, the cold war, and the windiness of academe. One day you are surprised to find this daring bridgehead of Bohemia opening its door to tweedy Harvard Square, at a time when a cappuccino is a symbol of subversive sophistication. Of the couple who run the place, the guy looks wasted by sin, and the woman, vaguely Viennese, ready to waste you with it.

In the mid-fifties the New York Jewish Intellectual Establishment is moving to Brandeis University at a rapid rate, but Waltham, where Brandeis is located, thirty minutes away from Cambridge, is far too blue collar for intellectual tastes, even socialist intellectual tastes. Brandeis is the Ellis Island of academe, funneling the first large influx of Jewish intellectuals, with and without academic degrees, into the American university system. But nobody wants to live on Ellis Island. Despite a certain condescension toward the new school and even hints of a genteel anti-Semitism emanating from the Harvard establishment, noted by Irving Howe, then a Brandeis professor, in *A Margin of Hope*, the faculty shuttles from Brandeis to the academic mainland of Cambridge, or at least to the Belmont, Newton, or Back Bay suburbs of Harvard, Radcliffe, and MIT.

Drawn to Brandeis by the prospect of laying claim to what I consider my intellectual patrimony from proponents of it like Howe, Herbert Marcuse, and Philip Rahv, co-editor of *Partisan Review*, I assume the identity of a grad student. I see Brandeis as a short cut to the underground of intellectual resistance that seems the best alternative to an oppressive middle-class culture. One day in January, 1958, I stroll over to violinist Arnold Fournier's furniture rental shop at 47 Mount Auburn Street not far from Harvard Square to pay an installment on my furniture, and I find that Fournier is no longer the proprietor of the shop. Fournier is no longer there at all, instead the premises are occupied by another coffee shop started by two recent Brandeis graduates that will feature jazz, opening with a trio including still another Brandeis product, Chuck Israels, on bass. I keep the furniture.

Shortly, after being closed by the cops, the coffee shop reopened as a club, Club Mount Auburn 47, featuring folk music. If Tweedsville was proving attractive to the intellectuals after their years of sneering at academe—by a strange coincidence at the very moment that academe is opening its arms to them—the intellectuals and their style were also making an impact on Harvard Square. Tulla's was definitely not derived from the prep school mentality, and Club 47—with its tweedy-rebel and leather-jacket crowd and its barefoot madonna and major discovery, Joan Baez, giving a new voice to folky pieties—was distinctly not "shoe," as they used to say. Baez's first public appearance in Cambridge was an impromptu at Tulla's. Someone was strumming a guitar and Joan, sitting there with her family, started "one of those 'whoo-haa' things in the background, and it just went all over Cambridge. The place froze," according to the guy managing it. "Everybody was staring. What is this singing?"

The influence of Club 47 on the subsequent New Left can be seen in a 1979 statement by folk singer Bobby Neuwirth, habitué of the club, later an intimate of Bob Dylan and, still later, one of the inner circle at Max's Kansas City and companion of Warhol "Superstar" Edie Sedgwick: "Cambridge was one of the navels of the cultural period, and a lot of influence came out of it. It put a lot of intelligence into the guitar movement, and the guitar movement was the forerunner of the peace movement. It made people aware enough to allow the peace movement to enter people's consciousness. Between Elvis Presley and the folk singers, the guitar movement enabled kids to believe in youth and the correctness of their own thinking. So when the peace movement started, they didn't buckle under at the first signs of parental authority—the people who said, 'You're Communists. Shut up and crawl under a rock.'"

By the mid-fifties, middle-class kids were already listening to white rock'n' roll—"blue-eyed soul." Elvis Presley was getting on national television by 1955-56. "Suddenly white people are feeling things that they didn't feel before. Rock'n' roll takes off as a rebellious sound," says rock'n' roll archivist Mitch Blank. "You have people who are rebelling against the normal, everyday concept of what's right and what's wrong, how I should feel."

"Did that have trouble getting air time?" I ask.

"Absolutely. It was race music. White people shouldn't be singing that. Certainly white people shouldn't be listening to that."

Allen Freed's rock'n' roll revues were traveling all around the country and you started getting interracial audiences. Buddy Holly was the first white act ever to play Harlem's Apollo Theater. But by 1959 Elvis had been drafted, Buddy Holly

was killed in an airplane crash and Chuck Berry was in jail on the Mann Act.

"This really knocks the guts out of rock'n' roll," says Blank. "So instead of these creative people you have synthetic rock'n' roll—Frankie Avalon, Fabian. They cleaned up rock'n' roll." So you got Pat Boone and Chubby Checker, both "cover" artists for more authentic musicians, even Chubby Checker's name a rip-off of Fats Domino. At the end of the fifties there was a void, and while the middle class was dancing the twist to Chubby Checker, a lot of youthful, rebellious energy was starting to be expressed through folk music.

Other things were cooking in Cambridge besides folk music and movements emanating from Brandeis. A little earlier Harvard had produced a group of poets destined to be a major influence on literary developments through the fifties and sixties that came to be known as the New York School, oddly, since its first generation was from Harvard and its second from the Midwest. Frank O'Hara, John Ashbery, and Kenneth Koch, plus fiction writer and Parisian exile Harry Mathews, were the main figures who, with James Schuyler, made up one of the most important of the literary elements that would come together and ignite in 1960's New York. The Cambridge Poets' Theater was producing adventurous plays. Gregory Corso, whose book of poems *The Vestal Lady of Brattle Street* was the first significant volume of Beat poetry to be published, was hanging out in the Harvard dorms, cadging money, and sitting in one classes. A more notorious Cambridge development was the experiments of Harvard professors Leary and Alpert, a little later, with LSD. William Burroughs, who visited them at a late stage of the Harvard episode, expresses disappointment with their level of scientific seriousness.

"I stayed with Leary in Newton, Massachusetts," recalls Burroughs, "and I went to his classes, and they were going great guns in seersucker suits just like regular professors. And very shortly afterwards they were discredited and the whole thing collapsed. They thought they had the fix in at the time and they didn't at all. It turned out they weren't into experimentation in a long time—they were, I suppose, fooling around. The man who turned on the world!" snorts Burroughs, his W. C. Fields accents almost breaking into a whinny of nasality.

In 1955 when future activist Abbie Hoffman got to Brandeis as an undergrad, he was living in a dorm, playing poker, a jock. "I come out of that culture from Wooster, the street culture, the bowling alleys, the pool halls, the sports, anti-intellectual. I was smart but I was a troublemaker." In fact, Hoffman looks a lot like a diabolical Dead End Kid, though the devilish quality turns out to be an irrepressible energy and good humor that's evident as he talks. Among Brandeis students, Hoffman was famous for starting a sub sandwich service in the dorms.

But by the second half of the fifties America was about ready for revival. Conversion. Salvation. It has happened before in our history and it will happen again. Henry Adams has written that his ancestors "viewed the world chiefly as a thing to be reformed, filled with evil forces to be abolished, and they saw no reason to suppose that they had wholly succeeded in the abolition." This is a strain in American culture that is not confined to Adams's New England. In addition, the culture will soon be engulfed by the tidal wave of flesh and hormones known as the baby boom, which will ineluctably generate its own needs, ask its own questions. The experience providing the answers could be triggered by opening a book, by hearing a song, by turning on to acid. It could even be triggered inadvertently by a professor taken too much at his word. There will be, no doubt, more than a few professors at Brandeis appalled by the fruition of their abstractions in figures like Abbie Hoffman and Communist Angela Davis. Most students cannot be expected to have the history of often painful struggle with social attitudes and one's own sanity that lends ballast to those who have evolved a creative style or an intellectual position. The situation had become volatile, and the touch on the trigger did not need to be very heavy.

James Dean, whose role as the rebel without a cause carried over to his public image, in the movie can no longer live with the disastrous mendacity and compromise of his parents. There is a scene in the film in which he comes close to patricide. "Kill your parents," Jerry Rubin would say in the sixties. In California, Kansas, Boston, New York, kids were disaffected with the dad in the gray flannel suit. New role models miraculously appeared to answer the need, not that they hadn't been around before, but it was as if there were an imperceptible click and the culture suddenly moved into a new gear. The culture heroes of previous generations had been most influential on a relatively small community of creative people and their hangers-on. All that was about to change. Culture was about to be democratized, and was about to inherit the problems of democracy. There was an older, more self-contained underground that had been quietly accumulating cultural capital for years. Writers like Kenneth Patchen, forerunner and probably superior of Kerouac in the rebellious freedom of his style in poetry and fiction, and poet Kenneth Rexroth, after Langston Hughes and with Patchen largely responsible for the beginnings of the jazz/poetry-reading movement picked up by the Beats, were either bypassed or felt bypassed and turned angrily on the youth wave. So also did the leftist intellectuals who were used to being regarded as the vanguard of the antiestablishment band.

Maybe if you were an older artist and famous, or dead, you were safe—Pollock, Parker, Dylan Thomas—but Kerouac, after years of not even being able to get his books published, was suddenly notorious for reasons so irrelevant to his talent they were impossible for him to deal with. And even among the older and famous there was a high rate of suicide and self-destruction. The times required new role models and, so much the worse for them, this did not necessarily require a very substantial understanding of what made those models important. A flash of recognition would do, at least for a start.

"And then I started to get turned on by some of these teachers," says Hoffman about Brandeis, "and listening to Pete Seeger come and sing songs. And Martin Luther King, I remember, he came that first year, right after the Birmingham boycott. Our cultural life was in Harvard Square. We were influenced by the Beat Generation and their life style and their political outlook and their literature. Of course I went to readings there, and Joan Baez, I remember her riding around on the back of a motorcycle in a leather jacket then around 47 Mount Auburn Street, singing free concerts, Phil Ochs going through. There was a Brandeis connection, that's why we went over there."

"Was your father right to blame everything you got into on Brandeis?"

"I was programmed, trained, encouraged by some of the best minds of the time," says Hoffman of the intellectuals and activists he encountered at Brandeis. "Maslow one, Marcuse second."

"Howe?" I ask.

"No, Howe was the kind of guy that said don't go read the Beats because they're dirty, they're vile. So of course I ran out and read them. Most of these people, by the way, except for Marcuse, would turn against what we were doing in the sixties. Then there were the people that would pass through. Dorothy Day, Martin Luther King, Saul

Alinsky, those were three people who had a tremendous effect on me even though I heard them speak only once."

Around college campuses from Cambridge to Kansas students were finding their uncertain, sometimes difficult paths to Bleecker Street. If you were already there and connected with the underground that was continuous with the old Village Bohemia and had risen to prominence with Abstract Expressionism and the cult success of Be-bop, life in the second half of the fifties could be a gas. "New York, in 1956, was the wildest, greatest city anywhere," writes Fielding Dawson in his short story "Pirate One." "American painting had just been taken seriously for a first in history, and the city was the art center of the world. Europe was as jealous as all hell, and it was wonderful. You could walk along 10th Street and stop and say a few words with Philip Guston, go into the Colony on the corner there, at 4th Avenue, have a beer with de Kooning, walk over to the Cedar and have a few with Creeley, Dan Rice, or Kline, and that night fall by the Riviera or Romero's and then cross up to the Vanguard on 7th Avenue, dig Getz and Brookmeyer, and then walk down to the Cafe Bohemia, and get your head torn off by Miles, and around one, fall by the Cedar, and pick up some friends and go over to the 5 Spot and completely flip over Cecil Taylor, then afterwards go to Riker's for breakfast, and around dawn head home, maybe with a chick. It was really great. You could feel the exuberance, you could see and hear the dedication."

If you were a little younger, though, if you didn't have connections to the established Village underground and you were living in a tenement on the Lower East Side or in one of the slummier areas up around Hell's Kitchen, things looked a little different. "The affluent post-Korean war society was settling down to a grimmer, more long-term ugliness. At that moment, there really seemed to be no way out," writes Diane di Prima in *Memoirs of a Beatnik.*

"As far as we knew, there was only a small handful of us—perhaps forty or fifty in the city—who knew what we knew; who raced about in Levis and work shirts, smoked dope, dug the new jazz, and spoke a bastardization of the black argot. We surmised that there might be another fifty living in San Francisco, and perhaps a hundred more scattered throughout the country: Chicago, New Orleans, etc., but our isolation was total and impenetrable. . . . Our chief concern was to keep our integrity (much time and energy went into defining the concept of the 'sellout') and to keep

our cool: a hard, clean edge and definition in the midst of the terrifying indifference and sentimentality around us—'media mush.'" The ongoing underground concern about "selling out," however negative and merely reactive to the dominant culture, nevertheless indicates a sustained commitment to alternative values despite the fact that there seemed to be "no way out."

Then, one evening, someone arrives to "thrust a small black and white book into my hand. . . . I took it and flipped it open idly, still intent on dishing out beef stew, and found myself in the middle of *Howl* by Allen Ginsberg. . . . I was too turned on to concern myself with the stew. I handed it over to Beatrice and, without even thanking Bradley, I walked out the front door with his new book. Walked the few blocks to the pier on Sixtieth Street, and sat down by the Hudson River to read, and to come to terms with what was happening. The phrase "breaking ground" kept coming into my head. I knew that this Allen Ginsberg, whoever he was, had been breaking ground for all of us, though I had no idea yet what that meant, how far it would take us. . . . I sensed that Allen was only, could only be, the vanguard of a much larger thing. All the people who, like me, had hidden and skulked, writing down what they knew for a small handful of friends . . . all these would now step forward and say their piece. Not many would hear them, but they would, finally, hear each other. I was about to meet my brothers and sisters. . . . I was high and delighted. I made my way back to the house and to supper, and we all read the poem, I read it aloud to everyone. A new era had begun."

Blond, blue-eyed Ed Sanders looks like a Hollywood model of the all-American boy instead of the scatological rebel, underground bard, and anti-nuke-sub protest jailbait that he turned out to be. "I was born in Kansas City," says Sanders. "I was just a regular American kid, you know, I mean I was a Boy Scout, I was in my high-school choir, I went to Sunday school, it was the whole American panoply. I mean I was an all-American guy. And then, I was browsing at the University of Missouri book store in the fall of 1957, and there was the first edition of *Howl*, which I still have, and *Evergreen Review* number one and number two. There was a whole panoply of writers that I got exposed to in one five-dollar purchase, the fifty cents for *Howl*, two-fifty for the two issues of the *Evergreen Review*, and I was ready to go. I absorbed all that information and, you know, that was it. My life changed overnight.

"This street here we're sittin' on," he says as we sit talking in the Café Figaro on Bleecker and MacDougal, "was where I first experienced the concept of poetry readings. There was a place called the Scene where the Café Borgia is now in 1958 that had poetry readings, and there was the Gaslight where all the Beats read in early '58, there were other places along here, but mainly the Gaslight and the Scene where there were readings all the time."

"Did you start reading at them right away?"

"Oh, no. I was so shy, I would have never approached. . . . I remember once my future wife and I were sitting in the Figaro almost at this table and it was around 1959, and Ferlinghetti walked by and pressed his nose against the glass. Little did I know that a few years later Ferlinghetti would be my publisher and we'd be friends, but I mean this deity pressed his nose against the pane of glass, oh wow. I used to go to these readings and I'd see Kerouac and Edward Dahlberg, and I was too shy to think I had anything. . . . I mean I used to hang out, I would never have made myself known to these people, my God."

But whether as participant or voyeur, Sanders found the Figaro in those days a great place to take in the scene. "I spent many an hour staring in this place," he says. "This was stare headquarters for me. My wife used to come in here and she had this leather vest and Alan Block sandals laced up to her knees, oh man, in a black turtleneck sweater. This was the woman I was later to marry, she was nineteen years old, from Queens, determined to look like a Village woman, you know, not a girl from Queens, with the black kohl around her eyes and straight blond hair and a tight skirt, oh man. We'd sit in here, that table there, trying to figure out where we could go to fuck."

"I thought *Howl* was the cat's pajamas," says Tuli Kupferberg, who was later to be Sanders's partner in the Fugs. "I guess because of its range, you know. It was political and it was personal and it seemed to free the forms up. It was certainly what was needed at the time. It really came like a great cleansing shower, something that opened up everything again."

And not only in America. In Europe, *Howl* had a similar impact, and Yevtushenko, now Russia's most visible poet, told me recently that in the early sixties Ginsberg and other Beat writers hit Russian poets with much the same effect.

America in the fifties had large numbers of people in what today would be called internal

Diane di Prima reads selections from her first published book of poetry, *This Kind of Bird Flies Backward,* at the Gas Light Cafe in New York City, circa 1959. Copyright © by Fred W. McDarrah.

exile, a condition creating a kind of subversive sensibility maybe best described by the title Herb Gold refused to relinquish, *The Man Who Was Not With It.* In this mode, even screwing up became a form of resistance. It was the heyday of the antihero and the *schlemiel.* Given the fifties, the emergence of a Woody Allen was unavoidable. If you happened to be one of these inadvertent subverts, your career inevitably turned out to be a painful comedy, psychological slapstick pitting your real self against your official cover identity. I was at Brandeis in disguise, presumably to earn a doctorate I had no intention of getting. Actually I was there because my teaching fellowship both supported me and spared me for two years from the military efforts of an inimical regime, and, more important, because this academy was dominated not by academics, but precisely by the intellectuals I assumed were the vanguard of the underground, and whom I took to be in tune with my real self.

Unfortunately, the Brandeis intellectuals don't recognize my real self. Or if they do, they don't like it. Much to my surprise it develops that what they would like is for me to become a good academic. Yes, they know that my ambition is to become a writer, but they've come across young men with this ambition before. And besides, as I am advised by Irving Howe and poet-scholar J. V. Cunningham on one occasion when I announce my intention to drop out, why give up the chance for a successful career in the university system? A writer's life is precarious. Why not choose security and do both? And besides, what are you going to do in New York? Write ad copy? Become an editor? Write reviews for *Time*? Howe shakes his head. He's tried this stuff, there's no future in it. He argues at me like a shrewd East European Talmud scholar brought up on the spinach of American secular life. The option of withdrawing to the underground and living cheap doesn't even exist. When I finally do this a few years later, Cunningham gets the impression I must be rich since I have no visible means of support.

At stake here was that vague homunculus I chose to call my real self, independent of middle-class definitions of success and failure. This was the phenomenon vulgarized at the time as "identity crisis," but it was a real issue and it will remain a real issue. Is the American personality simply the sum of success-driven responses to the network of cultural pressures? Or is it the stubborn assertion of a virtuous independence, however unexamined? Horatio Alger or the Lone Ranger? Is there such a thing as a real self, and if there isn't, what makes life worth living? Consumption of products? Liberty and justice for clones? Social welfare for pods?

One day in the faculty dining room, Philip Rahv grumbles to me that a young writer, Philip Roth, is pestering him to publish his stories. He claims that Roth's work is at odds with itself. "I told him you can't be Scott Fitzgerald and Franz Kafka at the same time," he grumbles. Everything Rahv says in his rumbling East European mumble sounds grumbling, when you can understand it at all. His speech is as heavy as his bearish figure. The only thing agile about him is his mind.

The difference between Fitzgerald and Kafka is the same difference as that between Horatio Alger and the Lone Ranger at another level. If Kafka, who had a mind so fine that anything could violate it, had an allergy to entering his mantic projections in the public discourse by publishing them, for Fitzgerald success in that discourse was everything. In the schizoid dialogue of the American psyche, the real self is Emersonian, passive, innocent, and spontaneous, while the public self needs to be aggressive, power oriented, and politic. Part of the implicit strategy of the Beats was to reintroduce the real self into the public arena

while the intellectuals, with their consciousness of *Realpolitik,* were still expressing themselves in terms of the power play of polemic. Pre-Vietnam America was still learning about the limits of power, and the idea that it's sometimes better to be negatively capable than positively impotent was still news unless you happened to be a certain kind of artist.

The pervasive intellectual tone at Brandeis was European, and the fact that the original building and center of campus life was an imitation castle seemed a symbolic coincidence. Many of the academics, rather than being narrow specialists, were intellectuals of broad range in the European tradition and there were many professors who were in fact émigrés from a wide variety of European countries. The lingua franca of the Brandeis old guard seemed to be Yiddish. Howe tells of being interviewed for his job there in Yiddish. Any lingua franca helped. At times it was hard to understand the polyglot accents of English spoken by some of the faculty. This communication problem was symptomatic of Brandeis's privileged isolation at the time. It was an exceptional Europhile enclave within American culture. That's why I liked it. That's also why I didn't like it.

The "Permanent Crisis" crisis, which effectively ends my efforts to make a satisfactory connection at Brandeis, involves a public reading of that story—which was later to become the initial story in my first book of stories—to the Brandeis literati. The story, my first real story, is written in one long sentence, a device that can be traced to the circumstance of my studying Faulkner intensively with Howe. Its take is to express a political situation at the level of personal experience, a strategem certainly on the wavelength of Howe's *Politics and the Novel,* which I admire. I realize that the faculty is dominated by professors whose taste for innovation ends with the great Moderns of yesteryear, at best, but I figure Faulkner, politics—Irving will really like this one. When I'm done reading Irving doesn't even say anything to me. Instead he goes and yells at the grad student organizing the readings for allowing this kind of thing to go on at a college gathering. Howe does not intend to be an adversary, and this is undoubtedly a fit of temper, i.e., he means it. If I ever have any illusions that the intellectual's turf is the territory I should be lighting out for, I know right there that I'm making a big mistake.

I did not know yet that in America artists and intellectuals are necessarily different sorts of critters, committed to the schizy split that pits the real self against the public self, even when the two selves are part of the same psyche. Art is impelled by the anarchic force of eros, and pleasure can be experienced spontaneously only by a real self. A public self, insofar as it is divorced from the emotional life, which it puts to one side in the interests of calculation, policy, and power, can register feeling of any kind only in a limited way. In such a situation, the creative arts will always have a potentially subversive force, the more so the more they are innovative and unassimilated at the public level. The effect of such art can be disruptive and without regard to received ideas of what is right and good, as conservative critics and authoritarian regimes are well aware. American intellectuals have tended to be sociopolitical in orientation, and do their best to redirect the erotic force of art toward their concerns with good and bad, right and wrong. Furthermore, from the perspective of form, which is necessarily that of the artist, art does not operate on the ethical plane in so direct a way.

One day Alfred Kazin, another intellectual big shot with whom I expect to connect, comes to give a lecture, yet when I ask some innocent question at the end of his speech he takes off on this five-minute tirade about academics, beginning with "You graduate students," leaving me in a state of confusion and Howe furious. But sometimes it's good to get kicked in the face, because that bit of nastiness exposes to me once and for all my terminally false position. When I get an offer to begin my academic career teaching at a good Midwestern school, despite the urging of my advisers—"So what if you don't like the Midwest," says Irving, "you get a student claque, you publish your book, you stay for three years and find another job"—I turn it down without a second thought, and leave for New York.

When I finally come back to Brandeis a few years later to take my doctoral exams, it's probably more than chance that the night before the exams I fall in with a sexy lady in a black dress who keeps me up all night dancing, drinking, and screwing. The next morning I find myself confronting a day of exams on no sleep and a terrible hangover. Somehow I manage to bumble through and pass, wondering why I do this kind of thing to myself. I did them as assertions of identity, however foolish, against an encroaching and alien mentality. No regrets.

New York quickly confirmed my sense that Bleecker Street and environs was where it was at. A lot of things were opening up in New York toward the end of the fifties, and not only because of poetry. Izzy Young of the Folklore Center on

MacDougal Street and Howard Moody, pastor of the Judson Church, an underground culture center on Washington Square, organized and ran the Sunday folk music protests in the Square. There was a city ordinance out that prohibited music in Washington Square Park, which had been a center for folk singers from all over New York. It was an early attempt at gentrification. The protests were "one of the first battles in America where the outs beat city hall," says Howard Smith. "The thing got bigger every week. Each week it drew more and more people. It was huge, it was really heavy."

"Did people get beaten up by the cops?"

"Very badly. Real, heavy riots. And all over should musicians be allowed to play in the park."

"The cops had wanted us to leave," recalls Tuli Kupferberg. "We had sat down in the circle. Izzy had said, 'Let's leave,' and just as he says, 'Let's leave,' the cops come charging in and beating people up. Because they had gotten the command five minutes before. . . . The guys who were beating us had heard Izzy say that too, they could have disobeyed orders, but no. I think, you know, some of them might have gotten a thrill. Anyway, that was the classical example of police stupidity. They had got what they wanted, and then they beat everyone up anyway."

"Was that the final big demonstration?"

"Yeah, I think permission was given to sing in the park. Somehow the singers won most of what they wanted."

"That was one of the first highly-publicized-all-over-America battles against city hall where city hall backed down," continues Smith. "The next one was when Robert Moses tried to put the highway right through Washington Square Park. And we won that one. Women laying down with their babies in front of the bulldozers. The *Voice* was very instrumental in beating that one, and the Village Independent Democrats. The Village was changing, and a lot of people who were willing to stand up, really stand up for what they believed were moving in. The next big demonstration years later was the Julian Beck-Judith Malina over not taking shelter [in A-bomb drills]. And the first few of those were held in Washington Square Park. . . . There were only maybe fifteen or twenty of them, that's all you could see other than police anywhere. And they did arrest them. But by the sixth or seventh demonstration they filled Times Square. Each one got bigger. And I would say that those were three very important stepping-stones toward later militancy and around the country that gave people the idea that you could fight city hall. That was literally how it was always written about, as an example that if citizens got together in a community feeling, you could win."

The fact that the Village was swinging by the time Sanders, myself, and others like us got there was partly because of the receptivity of a handful of promoters and club owners to what was happening in the new scene. These included Izzy Young, who booked folk singers into Mike Porco's club—which, after being taken over by Porco himself, became well known as Gerde's Folk City, where many famous folksters got their start—as well as Art D'Lugoff, who owned the Village Gate. But most important were Tom Ziegler and especially John Mitchell. Mitchell was the original owner of the Figaro, and Ziegler, who was his manager, took it over from him. Mitchell owned the Gaslight on MacDougal and later the Fat Black Pussycat.

Mitchell ran the Gaslight "with a shotgun," according to Ted Joans. "He literally had a shotgun, he had a single-shot shotgun, and he used to have a sign above the door, 'No, your goddamn friends are not in here.' Because you walk to the door, instead of paying the dollar, you said, 'Well, I'm looking for a friend,' you know. A lot of people used to do that shit. And then they'd come in and wouldn't come out. And then he had a shotgun to back it, and he was training his dog to be mean, but his dog, if you had some food the dog would no longer be mean." When Mitchell left the Village he went to Torremolinos, outpost of Bohemia in southern Spain, where, according to Howard Smith, he opened a Fat Black Pussycat that became the center of the expatriate community there.

One day around 1980, an old friend of Smith, Kristina Gorby, an avant-garde dress designer from the sixties married to painter Jules Olitski, calls Smith and says, "You wouldn't believe who's sitting here in my house. John Mitchell." Mitchell had actually built the original Figaro, before it moved to the corner of Bleecker and MacDougal, and then, in the seventies, to Beverly Hills, then later reopened in the Village at the same corner location. But the original Figaro "was a few doors down from the San Remo on Bleecker," says Smith. "He built it and then Tom Ziegler stole Royce, his girlfriend, that's what I always heard." Then she had an auto accident in Spain. "She came back paralyzed and mentally retarded from the accident and Tom took care of her for the rest of her life. She was not quite a vegetable but wasn't pleasant. She was very well liked by everybody and was beautiful, and they had long since

split up. As soon as that happened he went right over, got her, and took care of her, as weird as he was, with all of his girlfriends, right to the end he took care of her.

"Tom and Mitchell were always bitter, vicious, nasty enemies from the day they saw each other. Both are macho, aren't afraid of fist fights with people. So anyway, so I went over to Kristina's house and there was John Mitchell, he was always a small little wiry guy but the type that you wouldn't want to fight with because he looked like he'd kill you. Over anything—if you had an argument over this napkin he'd kill you. And there he was, half his teeth gone, very drunk, a chronic alcoholic as was Tom Ziegler, and really fucked up, and as usual with one of the most beautiful girls I'd ever seen, all of about twenty-one, French, but exquisite, a French model is what she looked like. Totally devoted, 'Oh, John!' and he was a mess, a wreck. He always had that touch. I think Kristina's theory was that he was so dangerous, certain types are very masochistic, beautiful women are attracted to men that they think might kill somebody, might kill them. I don't know, who knows, he was always with incredible beautiful women. Tom Ziegler always was, but was a real ladies' man and was very good looking. John Mitchell was this little swamp rat.

"There were always a lot of fights at the Figaro. The Figaro was famous as a fighting place. Ziegler would beat people up. None of his friends, but if a customer pinched a waitress and the waitress said, 'That guy's really annoying me,' Tom would go over and knock him out."

"He became a karate expert after he moved the Figaro to Los Angeles, Mickey Ruskin told me," I add. Ruskin, owner of Max's Kansas City, was an admiring rival of Ziegler in that both the Figaro and Max's had excellent competing softball teams.

"He didn't even need that. Tom said the best karate is hit the guy before he thinks you're gonna hit him. We used to pull him off of a lot of people. There were a lot of fights there but not over issues, it was like against outsiders, or Tom wanting to let off steam, things like that."

By the late fifties, the influence of books like *Howl* and *On the Road,* and media coverage of the life style that produced them, was such that the Village belonged to the Beats. Within a couple of years Mike Wallace would be interviewing people at the Gaslight for a special on the Beat Generation.

The action in the coffee shops was a big change from the bar scene in the Village, partly reflecting a switch from booze to drugs among younger subterraneans, and partly the fact that it was cheaper and easier to start a coffee shop than a bar. But whether they served alcohol or coffee, the café explosion in the Village provided gathering places and performance spaces for a new generation of writers and musicians, especially folk singers. At the Figaro, Ziegler opened a basement for music, but since he didn't have the right city permit for the kids who came to dance, he devised a solution whereby the kids were strapped in their seats to prevent any spontaneous violations. Some of the places on the circuit were Rick Allmen's Café Bizarre; the Café Rafio, in front of which its manager was shot by a tenant in the building; the Rienzi, started by five or six writers and painters, above which Ted Joans would hold rent parties in his apartment; and the Limelight.

Poet and intermedia artist Dick Higgins's old route for poetry readings, which they used to call "the Elephant Walk," ended west of Second Avenue in the days before the East Village blossomed. "I used to read in the coffee shops with the Beat poets. I never knew how the Elephant Walk got its name, it wasn't my name. It was a circuit, and it started at S and G Corner, Sodom and Gomorrah Corner, which was the corner of Sixth Avenue and Eighth Street, where a lot of the hustlers hung out, so that's how it got its name, and then one used to walk in on Eighth Street, go along MacDougal Street past the old Meat Rack—which was more strictly homosexual—on the Park, it was the metal railings that used to be cruising grounds. And then you'd get into MacDougal Street proper, the coffee houses, and particularly the folk coffee houses. For example Leonard Cohen used to read, that was the City Lights, that was quite a strong coffee house, it had quite a following. And then when you hit Bleecker Street it would turn east again to the Epitome coffee shop," which was managed by painter Larry Poons and had art exhibitions. There they held readings and "sort of miniature performances, what we would call art performances today. That was the center, that was where we hung out for about two years, about '58 and '59. Poons got involved for a while with Dick Bellamy, who had the Green Gallery, and had his first big shows there. The Elephant Walk ended where West Broadway and Bleecker Street met, which is what's now called La Guardia Place. Past that, there were no coffee shops, there was like a no-man's-land between those areas and the Second Avenue scene."

"The Limelight, remember where the Limelight was a few years ago over on Seventh Avenue South?" asks Howard Smith. It was opened by Helen Gee. "No liquor license. One of the reasons she didn't want a liquor license, she didn't want the Mafia to give her trouble. She had never run a place. The only reason she opened it as a coffee shop-restaurant, she was obsessed with photography. Those were in the days when one of the biggest arguments hanging out in the bars and coffee shops was, was photography an art or wasn't it? There'd be fist fights over that. I remember vicious, all-night battles, groups, people screaming at each other."

"It was a big hang-out, the Off-Broadway crowd especially hung out there, the actresses, actors, all the photographers who were anybody hung out there. Jean Shepherd eventually did his radio show live from there. The Mafia tried to get control of her place many, many times and she eventually sold it years later. She kept her photo collection going, and in recent years her collection's been shown in many museums all over the world. She's now worth a lot of money, because eventually those photos were worth a fortune—Westons and Ansel Adams. I think she told me once the most expensive photo she ever bought was twenty-five dollars. Her place was one of the most intellectual of all the hang-outs. People who weren't just full of shit but really did things. There was a little of everything, writers, actors, a lot of the *Voice* people."

One of the more interesting places to open in the second half of the fifties was Johnny Romero's, because it was a sign of changing times. Romero was a West Indian, and his bar was a racially mixed scene—that is, Black guys and white girls. It had its happy side and its sinister side. "It was the first bar, the only bar that I knew of in the Village that had interracial dating," says David Behrens. "And it had a calypso jukebox and it was probably the most happy place in the Village. I think to put it into perspective also is that Harry Belafonte was new that year, I mean that was the year that calypso was big in New York. I think that there were a lot of people who went there who were very proud to be there. It was a place you went to to support, I mean I remember feeling that way. You were glad that this was what was happening in America. Although it wasn't happening anywhere else in America. It became a political gesture to go there."

I first meet Romero in Paris, I think with Ishmael Reed, years after his place has closed. Then another time I recognize him in Rue Saint-André-des-Arts in the Latin Quarter and catch up with him in a little *tabac*. I want to talk to him about his bar and how much I enjoyed it in the old days. Ishmael has told me that he's a strange, bitter guy. Romero doesn't want to talk about it. He's sullen and offish. Maybe he thinks I'm a cop. Or maybe he doesn't like white people, especially if they're Americans. At the time I don't know the story about what happened to his bar.

Romero's was in Minetta Lane, a narrow alley that runs between Bleecker and Sixth Avenue. Fielding Dawson describes it in one of his stories. "The jukebox was to the left of the door, and beyond it was a small rectangular wooden table, which fit into a small corner, fitted with an L-shaped bench, and beyond that on the left still, were a lot of posters most of Negro guys and women. . . . The bar ran the length of the place, opposite the jukebox." There was a small garden out back with three or four tables. "Most white cats including myself spoke a spade musician's lingo and it was (embarrassing) strange, me talking to some spade cat imitating his jive. Hi man, gimme some skin! . . . What not many people knew was Romero's was an essentially middle-class place. Black guys and their chicks drove downtown in their big cars, or their sports cars . . . especially on weekends. It was the downtown place to go. I guess there were black gangsters and black detectives, too. . . . People were friendly. . . . It was Johnny's effect. He was a popular guy. Everybody liked him; he was very friendly. . . . The black guys who went there were *big*, big guys, and some of them must have been prize fighters." Dawson mentions meeting Roberto Clemente there.

Howard Smith's take catches the other side of Romero's.

"Do you know the story about Johnny Romero?" I ask him.

"Yeah."

"What was it?"

"That was one of the weirdest places I had ever been in in my life. Those were the days when the Village was a little known for interracial relationships but very few, I mean it was still dangerous for a Black guy to walk with a white girl in the South Village, he'd get beaten up. Johnny Romero was known on the scene as somebody who only went with white girls, and word went around that he'd opened this incredible place, like something you'd read about in novels about Paris in the twenties. I went to the place, I'll tell you it looked like the real McCoy to me. I'd never been in a place up to that point in my life that looked more dangerous. Wooo! Especially to an innocent Jew-

ish kid from New Jersey, I'll tell you. And the Black guys in there did not look like they were fooling around, either. I mean they looked like they'd just as soon cut you up. They looked like guys fresh out of Harlem who heard that you could get white girls and they were there, but they didn't care about the Village, reading books, they didn't care about anything, they were there for poontang. That's what they were there for. And that was one of the few places that I saw where people smoked joints out in the open. In those days you didn't even smoke a joint out in the open at a party. You remember those days. It was real weird, some nights there'd be almost no one in it, and the next night it would be packed to the walls. I never felt safe in there. But like everyone else I was drawn to it because this was really different from any other place."

"And then there were rumors around that he was going out with Carmine de Sapio's daughter. That was the story. And that word went around and everybody said, God, they'll kill him. What are they gonna do? They're gonna kill him. Carmine de Sapio was a national political power, and certainly in the Village, my God. He almost made Harriman president. He and Richard Daley had equal power in backroom Democratic politics, and when the conventions would come around reporters from all over the country would ask de Sapio what he thought. We in the Village all felt he was a Mafia crook. So when everybody heard this it was like, what is he, crazy? You don't fool around with that. And then there were stories that they threatened him, that he was shot at, and then all of a sudden the place would close for a week or two, then it would be open again, and rumors would fly, what was going on? And all of a sudden it was closed, never to open again, nobody knew where he was, and then the rumors started that what they did was that they warned her, they warned him, they threatened him with everything possible, and finally they basically said, 'If you don't leave immediately this country, not the city, this country, and never see her again, you're dead.' And God knows what else they threatened him with. And also there was a story they also paid, they also gave him money. And he split. And that was the end of the relationship and it was the end of the place. That's the story."

De Sapio, who had been a Tammany liberal in his time and whose power base had been the old Italian Village and, supposedly, its mob connections, was later forced out of power by the new sophisticated gentry of the Village led by the Village Independent Democrats in a reform movement that helped launch Ed Koch's career. It's probably no accident that the man now Mayor Koch's chief adviser, Dan Wolf, was co-founder of *The Village Voice.* Some of us who were hot-under-the-collar reform sympathizers in those days now look back at de Sapio with a certain nostalgia.

Around the same time the underground began drifting over to the Lower East Side, subterraneans began to occupy old industrial lofts in significant numbers. There had always been a certain amount of loft life, especially among the painters, who needed the space. The lofts were scattered in various locations downtown, from Chelsea to East Tenth Street to Canal Street. Bond Street had some "very, very rudimentary lofts," says Gloria, "I mean but so rudimentary like, I mean Tony Frusella was staying with some people that had a loft in one of those buildings on Bond Street. It was really a junky loft. They had a fire place with huge gigantic logs and no furnishing at all and the sanitation and the plumbing was rudimentary if at all. Stanley Gould moved to a loft on Second Avenue over the Anderson Theater, below Eighth Street, there were lots of early lofts in those buildings. Romey Beardon used to live on Canal Street, that was the other loft scene. Romere Beardon, he's a painter and he's showing a lot now, he's a Black painter. That was kind of the beginning of the SoHo thing. Louise Nevelson had a loft on Third Street," as did Gloria's friend Chuck Mangrovite, who was building Wilhelm Reich's orgone boxes. A bit later, when the loft scene began to get a little more homey, the lofts provided the space for often enormous parties, which writer George Dennison used to refer to as "parties that changed people's lives." Westbeth, the low-rent creative artists' residence in the West Village, eventually came out of the loft movement when the painters finally got organized in response to loft harassment by landlords and the city.

Gloria's loft in Chelsea, one of the areas the subterraneans moved into, cost $51.75 a month for a whole floor, fireplace, and use of the roof for sunbathing. Other economies were possible. "Chuck had showed me how to turn the gas meter facing the wall so that it would tick backwards. One day the guy came to read the meter and it was facing the wall, and I panicked, I thought I was going to be thrown in jail. And he goes in the back and my heart is thumping, really it was like total panic. And like he looks at me and I'm panic stricken and he says, 'You know, there's something very funny I notice a lot on this block, the meter is facing the wall where it's very hard to read. Do you have a mirror I can use?'"

While the Beat style was coalescing and spreading through the bars and coffee houses of the Village, another style was being promoted by Norman Mailer, through his role in the early *Village Voice,* as well as through his writing and what might be called his socioliterary behavior. Mailer, in the mid-fifties, set about trying to shape his life as another might shape a novel. "If Mailer the failed novelist could not move the culture with his fictional imagination," according to Hilary Mills, his biographer, "he would make his own life a story that others would have to follow. It would inspire the underground army of similar souls which Mailer suddenly envisioned around him."

For Mailer, the *Voice,* which he helped start, was a public platform in an ideological campaign. "Norman felt that we were much too conservative on an ideological level," says Ed Fancher. "They wanted a straight paper that was going to make some money," says John Wilcock of Wolf and Fancher, "and Mailer was too far out for them." Mailer's break with the *Voice,* however, came ostensibly on a writer's issue—a typo that distorted a sentence in one of his columns.

But if Mailer was too radical—or maybe just too erratic—for the newspaper business, it was evidently as much in the direction of the political intellectuals as in that of the creative artists. Mailer spoke the language of the intellectuals as well as that of the artists, was in an intellectual as well as a creative tradition, which possibly helps explain why Mailer never attracted the animosity that the Beat writers did, and continues as the aberrant darling of critics and intelligentsia. Back at Brandeis, for example, Philip Rahv keeps urging Mailer's *Barbary Shore* on me enthusiastically. So finally I go read the novel, fail to be thrilled, and ask Rahv what's so good about it. Rahv looks miffed. "It's written in a secret code," he answers evasively, referring to the Trotsky allusions in the book, thereby invoking an intellopol lingua franca I supposedly don't understand. But it's not that I don't understand. It doesn't turn me on.

If Mailer gets plenty of flak from those who consider themselves in an adversary relation to the establishment, in part it's because he is so easily indulged by it. How many times have I heard, on asking one of Mailer's intellectual acquaintances about something foolish he's done, the comment, delivered with a shrug, that "Mailer is Mailer"? As if he were the exception that proves—what? That smart Jewish boys can be just as crazy as macho goys? "The secret language of the dirty little secret of success," writes Norman Podhoretz in his autobiographical *Making It,* "as I was discovering from the images in which my own fantasies of failure, renunciation, and salvation were spontaneously cast, was the language of Christianity." It's fascinating that Podhoretz, editor of the Jewish *Commentary* magazine, yet whose career, if one is to believe his autobiography, seems to have been driven by a flight from Jewishness, originally wanted to write, instead of an autobiography, a biography of Mailer.

There has to be an element of self-contempt in the admiration of intellectuals and academics for Mailer's daring to be what they are not, could not be, and in many cases would not want to be. Podhoretz considers Mailer's pursuit of money and celebrity in addition to intellectual influence a noble public "experiment," rather than the normal behavior of an American who has bought into the familiar Horatio Alger syndrome. Mailer "would 'settle for nothing less,'" asserts Podhoretz, "than making a revolution in the consciousness of his time, *and* earning millions of dollars, *and* achieving the very types of American celebrityhood." Mailer's exercise of ambition may be illuminating for the unworldly, but is hardly a brilliant spiritual adventure.

"Norman has enormous ambivalence," says Ed Fancher of Mailer. "First of all, he's in opposition. Second of all, he's a multimillionaire. . . . He's very interested in money. He's very money oriented, he goes crazy." Let Mailer be Mailer. He is compelling because of his ambivalence as he enacts for us a painful duality in our culture, expressing tensions between intellectual excellence and ambition, between justice and success. Because of this Mailer, as an artist, is able to become one of those figures whose vices are also their virtues. And in opposing so emphatically the underground cult of failure with the middle-class cult of success, he has inadvertently called into question the legitimacy of both.

In a "footnote" to "The White Negro," called "Hipster and Beatnik," he explains of the Hipster, "that in a time of crisis, he would look for power, and in the absence of a radical spirit in the American air, the choices of power which will present themselves are more likely to come from the Right than the moribund liberalities of the Left." Mailer is a Hipster, as he conceives the term. It is easy to see how, "in a time of crisis," he might gravitate to the right. "One is a rebel or one conforms," writes Mailer, "one is a frontiersman in the Wild West of American night life, or else a Square cell, trapped in the totalitarian tissues of American society, doomed willy-nilly to conform

if one is to succeed." Mailer is both a frontiersman and a conformist, both an explorer of the Wild West and trapped in the tissues of American society and its compulsion to success.

In fact, in the dialectic Mailer sets up, the frontiersman must become the settler, the Lone Ranger must become Horatio Alger, because the loner, the outsider, the explorer, is always doomed to fail, dooms himself to fail in conformist terms. And the one thing Mailer absolutely cannot do is fail. Poet William Carlos Williams, in his account of American history, *In the American Grain,* describes a type of outsider, doomed to failure, Columbus, Daniel Boone, who nevertheless is essential to the ongoing discovery of America. "It is my earnest desire," wrote Melville during the composition of *Moby Dick,* "to write those sort of books which are said to 'fail.'" In failure Melville was a brilliant success. Mailer's ambition is not of that kind. He insists on the claim of talent to mainstream success.

"I was just reading Kerouac's *The Subterraneans,*" I remark to Judith Malina, talking in her Paris apartment. "And it gets very annoying finally, the business about who's saintly and who isn't saintly and how saintly he, Kerouac, is, especially in that book where there are some unpleasant sexist sides. And just after that I read Norman Mailer's book *Armies of the Night* and the thing that I then noticed is that he insists on the fact that he is not innocent, that he likes sin and assumes a diabolical pose, and after Kerouac it was a kind of relief."

"I'm a moralist," responds Malina, a stagy magnetism and emphasis evident even as she talks informally. "I think morality is really it. I think saintliness is the thing that we want. . . . I'm a Gandhian in that sense. I think that there is purity and I think it is available to us and I think we should strive for it every single second including this one. And I think Kerouac was brave and good to say it. I *despise* Mailer for his male cowardice, his fear of goodness, his fear of purity, his distrust of honesty and honor, I despise him because he's a coward. He thinks he's such a brave macho man, he stabs his wife and he's proud of it, he defends murder as murder—not to defend the murderer, of course I approve—but to defend murder as justifiable, to defend toughness of attitude, to defend hardheartedness, I mean I find him a pathetic devil's advocate, I don't think he can help himself."

"Mailer once said in my presence," says Seymour Krim in a café in the West Village, "that he loved Allen Ginsberg but he thought he was a damn fool. In other words, by being so exposed, and so bizarre." Krim's granny glasses and considered phrases give him the air of an intellectual Bohemian, a role that, in his writing, he has rebelled against as out of step with American culture. Krim's influential 1959-60 essay "Making It!" is the classic, if ironic, sneer at the underground cult of failure: "Middle-class ideals of success once curled the lip of the intellectual; today he grins not, neither does he snide. . . . You've got to move, hustle, go for the ultimate broke or you'll be left with a handful of nothing. . . . *Baby, that world went up in the cornball illusions of yesterday!* . . . The only enemy today is failure, failure, failure, and the only true friend is—success!" But what Krim perceived with irony, Mailer acted out in his career.

"I think the Beat Generation offered new possibilities to Mailer but he would never adopt that style," Krim tells me. "It was just alien to him, it seemed naïve. It seemed like Moondog on Broadway wearing a big blanket. Norman would never do that. . . . I think he regarded them with a twinkle in his eye. He was always interested in money. And that kind of idealism, rank idealism, I think was something he couldn't relate to."

"What about selling out?" I ask. "Was that a concept that would have meant anything to him?"

"After *The Naked and the Dead,* unlike the rest of us, he was always conscious of having been a best-selling writer, and will always be conscious of it. It became some kind of standard for him. I mean you could talk literature all you wanted but he was very conscious of the power, of the reality of that, which does not come to most literary writers. So he always wanted to straddle those two worlds."

It is not surprising that Beat attitudes would be alien to Mailer as White Negro Hipster. Despite Herb Gold's 1960 contention that a Beatnik "is the hipster parodied and packaged as a commercial product," and promoted by his Columbia schoolmate Allen Ginsberg, "the greatest publicist for literary fashion since Ezra Pound," there are important differences between Hip and Beat. Not that Gold's quip that the Beatnik "bears the same relation to the hipster as the cornflake does to a field of corn," is completely off the wall. Noting the commodity component of the Beat movement, its association with the promo techniques of the advertising world, in which Ginsberg briefly worked—as of course did another art publicity genius, Andy Warhol—is not unjust. But there is more to the Hip-Beat distinction than that.

"Kerouac," says Allen Ginsberg of the Hipster, as opposed to Beat, underground, "thought that the cool element, especially Mailer's interpretation as a psychopathic knifer, and John Clellon Holmes' as a juvenile delinquent, was an idiot misinterpretation of a yea-saying, Dostoyevskian, healthy colossus like Neal Cassady. Kerouac was warm. Warmth, tenderness. Burroughs was very tender-hearted. Kerouac was really strong about that view, from Lawrence Lipton's *Holy Barbarians* on, that the ideologization of the Beatnik thing diverted it entirely from the open mind and universal intelligence, Shakespearian intelligence, Burroughsian intelligence, to an angry and violence-prone, antifamily, anti-middle-class attack, and demeaned the whole scene, and diverted all the energy into materialistic fighting and arguments and anger, whereas there should have been a much more angelic and lamby politics all along. With the introduction of Mailer's 'White Negro' he was praising psychopathy instead of the Holy Lamb and the second religiousness, the psychopath who was sticking a knife into the white middle class. So that white-middle-class contempt wasn't from Kerouac, that was from Mailer. And it was only a phase for him, I think. I don't know if that was his term, it might be unfair, but the notion of emotionless rather than emotional, as cool, the Hipster being cool, that's the Mailer-Anatole Broyard branch. Then that developed through Lawrence Lipton's book, interpreting it as holy barbarians from a Marxist point of view, which Kerouac *hated,* see, and to try and take what we were doing and make it into political aggression, till by the time 1968, Chicago, he said, 'Those Jews Ginsberg, Hoffman, and Rubin, all they're doing is finding new reasons for spitefulness.'

"The demonstration in the park [at the 1968 Chicago Democratic convention] was supposed to have been a festival of life. It would have been great if they had done that but instead they sabotaged it. Wolf Lowenthal the first day was teaching karate when he should have been teaching t'ai chi. He's now teaching t'ai chi and he says, 'Oh what a mistake, my God, who sent that signal out?' . . . Revolutionary aggression fantasies. I went there and I complained to Tom Hayden and Rennie Davis about a month before the thing, because we had started, Ed Sanders and Davis and Dellinger and Rubin and Hoffman and myself and a couple of others, the original signers of the Yippie manifesto, and made the press conference that announced, quote, 'festival of life.' And it was supposed to be rock'n' roll bands and present something that would overjoy people compared to the drag of the war convention. And the political radicals by then were interested in confrontation to show how bad the fascism was."

It's fairly obvious that Kerouac's point of view, with its stress on poverty, antimaterialism, fellow feeling—"the fact that everybody dies makes the world kind"—and pacifism, with its insistent imagery of saints and angels, with its pervasive visions, is deeply allied with a primitive Christianity, which may partly account for its apparently instinctive populist appeal. Populism and primitive Christianity intersect in the sanctity of the common man. Kerouac once described the ambience of the Beat state of mind as "the strange talk we'd heard among the early Hipsters of the end of the world and the Second Coming, stoned-out visions and even visitations, or believing, all inspired and fervent and free of bourgeois Bohemian materialism, such as Philip Lamantia being knocked off his chair by the angel in his vision of the books of the fathers of the church and of Christ crashing through time, Gregory Corso's visions of the devil and celestial heralds, Allen Ginsberg's visions of Harlem and elsewhere of the tearful divide in love, William Burroughs' reception of the word that he is the one prophet, Gary Snyder's Buddhist visions of the vow of salvation, peyote visions of all the myths being true, Philip Whalen's visions of the mellific flashes and forms of the roof flying off his house, Jack Kerouac's numerous visions of heaven, the golden eternity, bright light in the night woods, Herbert Huncke's geekish vision of Armageddon experienced in Sing-Sing, Neal Cassady's visions of reincarnation under God's will . . ."

But Kerouac's view also has ties with classic nineteenth-century American Transcendentalism. "Beat" for Kerouac meant, as he has written, "characters with a special spirituality who didn't gang up but were solitary Bartlebys staring out of the dead window of our civilization." Whether you take the withdrawn hero of Melville's "Bartleby the Scrivener" as a parody or celebration of the Transcendentalist character, the reference is both clear and appropriate. The split between the politicos and the Beats on the question of activism is much like a similar schism concerning the Transcendentalists that can be found in Emerson himself, and reminds one of the perhaps apocryphal exchange between Emerson and Thoreau when the former went to visit the latter, who was in jail for civil disobedience. "Henry, why are you

there?" Emerson was supposed to have asked. Thoreau supposedly responded, "Why are you not here?"

Throughout the sixties, with the increasing tempo of activism, of the cultural-pacifist variety that Ginsberg favored as well as of the hard-edged ideological-political kind, Kerouac became increasingly conservative, anti-Semitic, withdrawn, and alcoholic. You have to wonder, why was Jack not there?

If Kerouac seems to have been the inspirational spirit of the Beat movement, in death he has become the Holy Ghost to Ginsberg's Apostle Paul and a multiplying series of gospel accounts. Ginsberg likes to stress Kerouac's gentleness and the view that the antagonism surrounding the Beats was initiated by the hostility of those reacting to them. "I wasn't interested in working in the system or outside of the system," Ginsberg tells me. "I didn't think that was the point at all. That's a Marxist-ideological-conceptual thing. The whole idea of Us and Them is obsolete. One, it's vanity and self-righteousness, and two, it polarizes unnecessarily."

What the Beat shared initially with the Hipster was withdrawal from the political and cultural struggle as defined ideologically by contemporary intellectual polemicists. John Clellon Holmes, introducing the Beat Generation in the mass media, wrote that even in "the wildest hipster, making a mystique of bop, drugs and the night life, there is no desire to shatter the 'square' society in which he lives, only to elude it." It will be Norman Mailer, both in ideological essays like "The White Negro" and in his media persona, who will repoliticize the Hipster, reengaging him in a hostile way with society and, paradoxically, putting his mystique at the service of social and economic ambition. But as there are differences between Mailer and Kerouac, so Kerouac and Ginsberg evolved in different ways.

"What was *Howl*," asks Nat Hentoff, speaking to me on the phone about Ginsberg, "but, in a very powerful, distilled way, an indictment of what was going on in the flat fifties—not only the end of ideology, but the end of real feeling. It was quite a howl then, and so of course was *On the Road* . . . as a rebuttal, or as an indictment of the kind of conformity, you know. . . . These were political attitudes, as I understand politics. Because on the other hand you have people like Daniel Bell, and Norman Podhoretz at the end of the fifties writing that collection of essays in which he essentially said what Bell had been saying—you don't need much ideology anymore, because, he was saying, we've solved all of our problems pretty much. And what Ginsberg and Kerouac were saying, and they weren't radicals politically in the sense that we use the term, but they were looking at things radically, getting to the root of things and saying the root, my God, is diseased, it's so shrunken as to have no feeling. It wasn't so much a call to action as a call to consciousness. And whatever Allen says now, he certainly was against the establishment. My God, the establishment in those days thought of him as some kind of crazy, homosexual idiot, or somebody who had burned his brains out."

"Y'know the ball game they put on him?" says Corso, referring to Ginsberg in the fifties Remo. "The so-called early Hipsters? Him and Kerouac, this is what they laid on these two guys. Me and Allen or Jack would have heated, loving conversations. Their so-called sharp hip talk was this: 'Dig that aggression.' Can y'imagine that, they called us aggressive because of the way we talked. Maybe they were right."

Though Ginsberg denies that *Howl* is an angry poem, making a distinction between anger and "wrath," maybe part of the thrust of the Beat movement was that it released aggression suppressed by the cool of the Hipsters and by the general withdrawal of the underground as an adversary movement. Maybe it is Ginsberg's willingness to confront the commercial culture, immerse himself in impurity, and "turn shit to gold" that distinguishes him from the later, declining Kerouac. Maybe Mailer's ideologized, politicized, hostile version of the Hipster is in some ways not so different from Ginsberg's "angelic and lamby politics" in its release of subterranean aggression, permitting the underground once more to grapple with the system, even if—far more than Ginsberg's approach—on the terms of the system. Besides, Ginsberg is not universally considered angelic and lamby even by those who admire him. Some talk about his apparent need for recognition, his desire to be universally liked and admired. "He's very competitive," says poet and photographer Ira Cohen. "I don't think that I know a more competitive person. Anyway, what's the big deal? Allen Ginsberg is a very complicated subject, and depending on my mood I could say almost anything about Allen, and I think that's one of the things that's probably in the end the most provocative and interesting thing about Allen." After all, Ginsberg's Beat angelicism and Mailer's Hip

diabolism are both part of the same Christian mythology, and the first primitive Christians were all maverick Jews.

In any case, how far is Mailer's conception of "advertisements for myself" from the billboard advertisement *Evergreen Review* ran in the subway, of Ginsberg in an Uncle Sam hat with the caption, "Join the underground"? And how far from there to the thriving business developed by underground photographer Fred McDarrah, called "Rent-a-Beatnik"? While there were differences in intent in these three phenomena of the late fifties and early sixties, they all portended a movement away from the isolation of the underground and its cult of failure, using the methods of the mainstream business culture for its own ends, and even adapting some of the ends of that culture to its own needs. Suddenly the Bohemian need to keep a critical distance from the establishment seemed to be evaporating, and the ideological distinctions on which that distancing had been based were becoming irrelevant both to the Beats and to their bitter polemical opponents like Norman Podhoretz, once Ginsberg's fellow student at Columbia.

"It was McDarrah's idea, it was McDarrah's business. McDarrah needed a poet that could communicate with the bourgeois, so that was Ted Joans," says Ted Joans. We're talking about Rent-a-Beatnik in his Latin Quarter apartment, five flights up on Rue Montagne Sainte-Geneviève. "Because he had heard me read, he watched me in those coffeehouses, how the people responded, so he said, 'Ah ha, this guy, along with the Beatniks I pick up on MacDougal Street, will be perfect.'"

"Yeah, but this was merchandising, right?"

"You see now, Corso was against me to be involved in the Fred McDarrah thing. He was talking about 'Look, you got to read to creeps and squares. . . .' But I told him, I said, 'Take it to the enemy.' I said, 'For example, Christ. Did he just preach to the Christians?' I said, 'It'd be a drag. They'd say, "Yeah, we know that, man, you preached that last week, we all hear that, you know. Shit, we all right. Lay it on people who don't know."' I said, 'When I was brought up, a guy was in this church, a preacher, the preachers that travel around from church to church, he'd say, "All of you here that've seen Christ raise your hand." He's disappointed if all those hands were all up.' I said, 'But he was glad when he saw a whole bunch that were not up, cause that was the reason the church brought him in, brought him in to get those who couldn't raise their hand up.' You see, so that's it. In other words, to get to the so-called squares."

"Was Rent-a-Beatnik successful, by the way?"

"It was successful till the Internal Revenue stepped in, and that was the end of it. Because money was coming in. I don't know what Fred was making, but I know what he was paying me, and I know what he paid some of the Beatniks. They got something like five dollars an hour. Five dollars an hour was a lot of money. Five dollars an hour and all they could eat and transportation there and back. And I would receive from seventy-five up to two, three hundred dollars."

In Paris, eighty years before the Bleecker Street café scene started attracting a large enough middle-class audience to make an enterprise like Rent-a-Beatnik successful, there was a development in Bohemian circles similar enough to be instructive. Till the end of the 1870's, the Bohemian cafés were meeting places for creative artists, serving them as, in the words of historian of the café scene Georges Bernier, "rallying points, ideological workshops, springboards from which their artistic concepts spread." The most important café at the time was La Nouvelle Athènes, of which writer George Moore could say, "I did not go to either Oxford or Cambridge, but I went to La Nouvelle Athènes." But at about that time, a handful of clever entrepreneurs started a series of Bohemian cabarets whose function was basically to vend Bohemia to the middle class. The most famous of these were Le Chat Noir and Aristide Bruant's Le Mirliton, cabarets of the sort that in fact, to this day, provide the dominant image of Parisian Bohemia through the work of Toulouse-Lautrec. But contrary to those who prefer to think that such adversary movements are predestined to be assimilated by the bourgeoisie, the artists' meeting places did not disappear. La Nouvelle Athènes continued for years as an important Bohemian rendezvous, and other such cafés evolved elsewhere.

In the Village also there were artists' bars and cafés that proved durable, but the merchandising that was taking place along Bleecker Street pushed creative people toward the Lower East Side, if for no other reason than that the influx of middle-class money forced up prices. Art is the avant-garde of real estate, writer Andrei Codrescu has quipped. And real estate in Bohemia seems to follow an ineluctable evolution from artists to gays to the middle class. "Julius's was a big hang-out and I remember the night it turned gay," recalls Howard Smith. "They turned it gay in one night. You remember Julius's, it's still there. Sawdust on the floor. It was famous for its hamburgers, it was a big Bohemian hang-out on the corner of Waverly and Tenth Street, and it was a bar we all hung out in. There were very few hang-outs. The scene was so much smaller. There were maybe five bars and you'd make the circuit during the night, a few coffee shops and a few bars. So I remember one night we went into Julius's, there were four of us, myself and a friend and both of us had girlfriends, and we walked up and there was this bouncer at the door. They'd never had a bouncer at the door, and he said"—Smith assumes a gravelly baritone—"'Where are you goin'?' We said, 'We're going in, what do you mean?' He said, 'No, we don't want youse in here anymore.' 'Whaddaya mean, we been hanging out here for the past two years, every night, whaddaya mean?' And he said, 'I don't think youse wanna come in here anymore.' We said, 'Well, why not, what's the problem?' He said, 'All right, one a ya, c'mere.' He grabbed me and said, 'Take a look.' I took a look. It was gay. They had hired gay bartenders, they had decided to make it a gay bar. That was the first time I'd ever seen that happen to a bar. We couldn't believe what was happening. That was the talk of the Village."

Some years later, in 1965, in a gesture that came to symbolize the surfacing of the underground, Bob Dylan, one of the many descending from Woody Guthrie's radical minstrelsy, turned his back on the ambience of Club 47, the Gaslight, and Gerde's Folk City, and at the Newport Folk Festival went electronic. Dylan's "band got onstage and started to play," says one who was onstage at the time. "All of the old folk mafia were saying, 'Get them offstage! This is a violation of what this festival is all about! This is pop music! This can't happen!' . . . Pete Seeger was livid. He ran back somewhere and came back with an ax, and he said, 'I am going to chop the power cables if you don't take them off the stage right now!' . . . There was a fight going on at the sound board where they were mixing, over the volume, trying to cut off Dylan. The first song was 'Maggie's Farm.' A lot of people were booing. The second song was 'Like a Rolling Stone.' Half were applauding, half booing."

Dylan, says Nat Hentoff, "is such a hustler, and has been since he first came to New York, and I knew him pretty early on. He's like some underworld people I know, who has been lying and hustling and playing parts for so long that it may be, and I think in his case, it finally did come to be, though I can't prove it, that he doesn't know who the hell he is anymore, that the masks keep coming off and on and whatever the thing is down at the last one below the final mask, I think he's lost that entirely. I don't believe anything he says anymore. At one point he told me back in the sixties that all the stuff that really got him catapulted into renown because he was riding the *Zeitgeist*—'The Masters of War,' you know, the initial songs, the civil rights songs—he said, 'I just made those up because I knew people wanted to hear it and I figured that would be the quickest way to make some money.' Now I don't think that's true. I don't think it was true at the time. He may well now believe it was true."

"Do you think he was putting you on?" I ask

"He could have been, I mean he's a master of that. My guess is he went electric the same way Miles Davis went electric. When Miles, I guess it was the early seventies, saw that there was this large rock audience, not only here but around the world, and he didn't see why he shouldn't have some of it, and he knew he couldn't do it with his regular instrumentation. And people said that Miles had sold out then too. I think that Dylan was after the biggest possible audience he could get, and he saw where rock was going and he too wanted to be part of it."

"So by the standards of Seeger this would be a sell-out," I say, "even though the music might, in fact I think in Dylan's case the music did, get better."

"I think it did get better. He really was of another generation. Pete could never be electric, so if Pete and the others made it an ideological or a virtue-testing thing, they were wrong on the face of it. The motivation was simply that Dylan always wanted a big audience. And anybody who knew Dylan should have known that. And Pete certainly did."

Allen Ginsberg goes further in support of Dylan, praising his changes as a paradigm of fluidity in contrast to the crippling ideological rigidity of the old radical left. Selling out, says Allen, is "one of those cornball ideas that people who didn't have anything to do got hung up on. I wouldn't have minded doing it if I could find what to sell out to. Geniuses don't sell out, in the sense that genius bursts the bounds of either selling out or not selling out. When somebody has real inspiration like Dylan, the move to electric is just simply the expansion of his genius into more forms, wilder forms. He's got that sense of negative capability being able to go all the way in, without

necessarily losing himself. Committing himself and at the same time doing it like a poet, landing like the cat with nine lives."

In 1962, Ted Joans, a painter friend helping him move, went down to the Brooklyn docks "where I put my things on a Yugoslavian freighter and headed for Africa. And what did he move me in? An old, obsolete Cadillac hearse. Ha ha ha ha ha!" Ted guffaws—hilarious. "Isn't that great, to leave America in a Cadillac hearse? You know, alive! Alive too, alive. You know, it was a old big white one too. That's it." Ted, who ended up in Timbuctou, didn't come back till '68.

By the time Joans leaves for Africa, I've already been living on the Lower East Side for two years. It's cheap and it's peaceful, but grinding, and the changes have been coming fast. The neighborhood is starting to jump. In the old bar across the street, on Twelfth and Avenue B, you can find almost as many subterraneans now as local Polacks, and if you go there every afternoon as I do, you're on talking terms with Stanley, the owner. But there was a movement abroad between 1958 and '62, led once more by the Beats, who eventually settled in their now-famous grungy hotel off Place Saint-Michel in Paris around the same time as my first European trip. I think everybody felt the need for a break somewhere in there, a chance to cool out, feeling lucky to get out alive. I leave for Europe about the same time as Ted for Africa. In Torremolinos, southern Spain, sometime in 1963, I find such a dense colony of hip Americans that when I ask someone for the location of a place I'm thinking of renting, she tells me, "Oh, that's over in Spanish Town." And some guy tells me he's just gone through New York, and the Lower East Side is *the* scene. Especially this old bar on Twelfth and B that's so jammed wall to wall with Beatniks every night, you have to fight to get in. He's talking about Stanley's place.

ALLEN GINSBERG (ESSAY DATE 1991)

SOURCE: Ginsberg, Allen. Foreword to *Out of This World: An Anthology of the St. Mark's Poetry Project, 1966-1991*, edited by Anne Waldman, pp. xxiv-xxx. New York: Crown Publishers, 1991.

In the following essay, Ginsberg chronicles the valuable contributions that St. Mark's Church in New York City made to the development of the Beat Generation by hosting poetry readings.

St. Mark's has always been a culture church, and as a venue for poetry it has an old history. I first went to a poetry reading at St. Mark's in the

ON THE SUBJECT OF...

JANINE POMMY VEGA
It was while living in Greenwich Village during the early 1960s that Pommy Vega befriended Gregory Corso, Allen Ginsberg, Jack Kerouac, and Peter Orlovsky. Her brief marriage to Peruvian painter Fernando Vega, who died of a drug overdose, led to the writing and publication of her first book, *Poems to Fernando* (1968), by City Lights. After various temporary relocations from San Francisco to Woodstock, New York, Pommy Vega traveled to Columbia and Peru, settling at Lake Titicaca. It was after settling in the Lake community that she wrote *Journal of a Hermit* (1974) and *Morning Passage* (1976).

thirties with my father, Louis, who was once secretary of the Poetry Society of America. W. H. Auden was a member of the congregation in the fifties, but long before that Isadora Duncan had danced there, Frank Lloyd Wright had lectured, Houdini'd given a magic show. There had been jazz in the late fifties, even theater.

Our postmodern era began with a series of open readings that took place in a basement, formerly a rare gay place, the Macdougal Street Bar, renamed The Gaslight Café by owner John Mitchell in '58 or '59—with LeRoi Jones, Gregory Corso, Ray Bremser, myself and Peter Orlovsky, José Garcia Villa, others. These were predated by a year by readings given by Jack Kerouac, Philip Lamantia, Howard Hart, Steve Tropp, and others at Circle in the Square, as well as at various lofts and parties. Initial events were so extraordinary that readings sprang up all along Macdougal Street, with Café Wha?, Café Figaro, Rienzi's; the first Gaslight Café reading was such an unheard-of event that it made the front page of the New York *Daily News*. In a way, it was an imitation of the San Francisco scene, supposedly brought west from Existentialist Paris, maybe ancient Rome.

The late 1950s New York readings, ignited by the San Francisco Renaissance readings, in turn continued the traditions of the "Berkeley Renaissance." The latter wave crested in 1948, with Jack Spicer, Tom Parkinson, Kenneth Rexroth, Robert Duncan, Philip Lamantia, Robin Blaser—a group of poets, an elite (not alienated, but an elite)—reading to one another in private houses, an intimate Buddhist anarchist hermetic circle that prepared the way for later generations. Grad psychologist Timothy Leary and hermetic artist-filmmaker Harry Smith were present, same community, same era. In 1955, our "famous" Gallery Six reading was held in a very small venue, an art gallery that was formerly a garage—maybe 150 people could fit in. The readings were thereafter carried on by the San Francisco State College Poetry Center.

Thus, the genealogy extends from San Francisco through the Gaslight to St. Mark's Church in New York. After the Gaslight, poets floated from joint to joint—from Circle in the Square to a couple of small cafés up and down the Lower East Side, then over to the Seven Arts Café on Ninth Avenue and 43rd Street, near Times Square. Seven Arts flourished for about a year and a half, with Ray Bremser, Janine Pommy-Vega, myself, Gregory and Peter, LeRoi, Jack Kerouac, Diane di Prima, Ed Sanders—and many other poets. As the "Beatnik" era ended, around 1963 or so, we wound up at The Metro, which was the final surge before the St. Mark's Poetry Project. The Metro was attended by everybody: Paul Blackburn was around, di Prima, Ted Berrigan, Frank O'Hara and Jackson Mac Low attended, and readings were for a long while organized by Allen DeLoach, who started a little "ditto" magazine, *Poetry at the Metro*. Later Ted Berrigan hosted the readings. Bob Dylan came once, I remember, to listen; regulars like Ishmael Reed, David Henderson and the Umbra group, A. B. Spellman, Steve and Gloria Tropp came to read. There had been an era of good feeling between blacks and whites, 1958-1962, when one literary center was LeRoi Jones's house with his wife Hettie Cohen. *The Floating Bear* magazine, an early mimeo edited by LeRoi and Diane di Prima, had circulated, as well as LeRoi's omniscient *Yugen*. *Evergreen Review* was flourishing and *Chicago Review* had begun printing Burroughs, Kerouac, Corso; after censorship troubles, the latter went independent as *Big Table* and fought Post Office censorship successfully in 1959.

The Metro suffered through two crises, which continue to this day, in one form or another. You had to have a "cabaret license" to have so-called "entertainment." In those days, the crucial questions concerned cost: forty, fifty, sixty thousand dollars, not to mention all the bureaucratic problems attached to a cabaret license—you had to put in an extra fire escape or an extra fire door, as well. The Metro was not a place with liquor, it was just a coffee shop with poets, and the real and legal point was freedom of speech.

Someone also wanted to hold a poetry reading in Washington Square Park. The police said no and refused to allow it; we defied the police and held the reading one Sunday. There were lots of European and Japanese camerapeople there, and the image of poets declaiming in the grass went all over the world. So-called "profanity" seemed the underlying problem—but again, the real issue was freedom of speech. This was the early sixties, but city regulations still insisted there could be no entertainment in the parks without a license, and bureaucrats said this was "entertainment," so you had to get a license. It was a classic First Amendment case. The ACLU intervened and said no, it's not "entertainment," it's public speech, free speech, soapbox.

Now, the cabaret-licensing problem was a hangover from a Draconian dope law that said that anybody who'd been busted, had any kind of conviction—misdemeanor or felony—couldn't get a cabaret license to play at a New York City café. That barred geniuses like Charlie Parker, Thelonious Monk, and Billie Holliday from performing in New York clubs for decades. We abolished the poet's cabaret-license requirement through intervention of the City Council—by that time, we'd organized a public committee. Central to it was Ed Sanders, who then edited his elegant *Fuck You: A Magazine of the Arts.*

A New York City District Attorney, one Richard Kuh, had been prosecuting D. H. Lawrence's *Lady Chatterley's Lover,* Henry Miller's *Tropic of Cancer,* Jean Genet's *Our Lady of the Flowers,* and finally William Burroughs's *Naked Lunch.* By 1962, that censorship was broken by the courts, but Kuh went on to prosecute Lenny Bruce for his Greenwich Village nightclub act, and there was a strong literary reaction to that prosecution.

All at once came the emergence of underground films, synchronous with attempts at literary censorship, cabaret card licensing, Lenny Bruce persecution, underground newspapers like *The East Village Other* (which carried poetry) and *The Village Voice,* more or less at its height as a crusading bohemian paper. The literary, musical, and cinematic avant-garde, as well as civil rights, censorship, and minority problems, all came together at one point, one spot in time, in the early sixties. So it was a glorious ferment, as the old-fashioned littérateurs say, good as anything in the thirties or twenties. Race problems arose with

the Metro proprietors, so we moved to St. Mark's Church—led by Joel Oppenheimer and Paul Blackburn.

St. Mark's has become my church, my religion place. I've been living nearby on the Lower East Side for thirty-five years. Certainly by the sixties it was my church in the sense that that's where my community was, my Sangha, my peers. I could pass out information, find out the latest gossip, what's new, follow the latest art spurt. It was part of my education, part of my resources. Networking in that open community was intricately involved with private and public life. High-school kids coming to the church could enter a very sophisticated atmosphere and get an education they wouldn't get in grammar schools or even colleges: education in the advanced standards of Bohemia.

Officially, The Poetry Project began in 1966. According to Anne Waldman, the sociologist Harry Silverstein applied for the founding grant, through the New School for Social Research across town. Money came through the Office of Economic Opportunity (OEO) under Lyndon Johnson, for a pilot program to help "alienated youth" on the Lower East Side. So the church started housing the Black Panthers' breakfast program, the Motherfuckers' dinner program. Anne remembers "huge pots always cooking"; there was a child-care project too. The Lower East Side hadn't any counterculture center, and given the alienation of different minority groups, some center was needed with sensitive antennae for white, black, brown, and hippie post-Beat groups.

One interesting fringe benefit of this gathering was the margin of old bohemians left over from the thirties and forties still living on the Lower East Side and in the Village—antique "delicatessen intellectuals." Politically, there were remnants of the Old Left among the poets. Another node on the Lower East Side at that time, older than The Poetry Project, was the War Resisters' League. The war was central to everybody's preoccupations in the sixties. Many of the poems of the time expressed outrage or sympathy or violence or fright or grief. Primarily grief or fear. So there was a community, a forum where people could articulate their relationship to the big national problem of the Vietnam War and the hyper-militarization of Whitman's America. Questions of ecology had also entered into poetry through the 1950s San Francisco Renaissance; Kerouac and Gary Snyder and Lew Welch used their verse as a vehicle for expressing fright or shock or information for all mankind on the planet. Sixties

St. Mark's Church in New York City provided an early venue for Beat poetry readings, and ultimately became home to the St. Mark's Poetry Project.

mouths could meet people who had been pacifists in World War I, people who knew Catholic worker saint Dorothy Day. You got a taste of prior eras, prior movements, prior communities and their moments of glory: publications, parties, social activities, and love affairs, decades old.

For a person without an extended family in New York—my brother was living on Long Island, my father in New Jersey, and my mother was dead—St. Mark's served as immediate neighborhood community and family. "Rootless cosmopolitans," urbanized, sophisticated artists and writers gathered at The Poetry Project. It served and still serves to formulate local public opinion. Barriers were removed between inner and outer, between subjective worlds and objective social worlds. Here was space where people could proclaim to society what they wanted—and in a church, which lent their address proper dignity.

Liberation of the word. Liberation of minority groups, questions of race. The famous "sexual revolution." The celebrated women's liberation—women writing and reading brilliantly, led by poets Anne Waldman and Diane di Prima, Alice Notley, Maureen Owen, Denise Levertov, Joanne Kyger, also Diane Wakoski and Rochelle Owens and Carol Bergé, others. At least in my circle these were among the stars who gave expression to new independence. There were angry denunciations, manifestos, gay liberation performance pieces; there was romantic love poetry, there were prose poetry journals like Taylor Mead's excellent *Diary of a New York Youth* (Kerouac liked Mead's free style and frankness). *The World* mimeo publications were acknowledging the changed role of sex, and all these themes could be expressed—even put to music. None of this was particularly "committed" poetry, *engagé* in the old Marxist or newer Existentialist sense. Put simply, the mode of poetry was subjective, so that any rumination that might engage you alone in bed would enter your poetry, and that could include what you read in *The New York Times* or saw on television or heard on the radio or thought in bathtub solitude or saw on the streets if you were tear-gassed. Very often, while making national pronouncements in poetry,

I wondered if the FBI sat in the audience listening (as they did later in Chicago in '68).

Beginning with Great Society sixties Johnson policies, followed by Carter's, the government spent a great deal of money on the arts through OEO, as it had through the 1930s WPA. In 1966-68, money was spent on art. With that came some democratization of the intelligentsia, and some local poverty workers became intelligentsia. Everyone realized that heretofore this subsidy money for the arts had been going to institutional millionaires who operated symphonies and museums. Suddenly, small, decentralized, individual community projects could be subsidized by the government. There was a big push for minority and multicultural arts, bohemian arts, for individual arts, for poetry readings around the country, poetry in the schools, little magazines with their Coordinating Councils, and a number of strong provincial centers of poetic activity.

Monday-night readings at St. Mark's were open to everyone. And then, for bardic soapbox stars of their own romance, subjectivity, passions, and political prophecy, you had the Wednesday-night readings. On New Year's Day readings, everybody in the community would come out, perhaps two or three hundred people, to do a one-, two-, three-, or four-minute shot—maybe their most intense perception of the year, or the one piece they'd prepared that they could show off to the entire community, and that would include everybody from John Cage up to Grand Master Xylophone. Yoko Ono came once, completely dressed in white, and breathed into the microphone with her "Formula in Awe of the Air"—was that it?—a piece mostly of silence. The audience was, and is, a regular community, unlike those at university readings—this audience had been going to the same place to hear readers for ten, twenty years, so accumulated much granny wisdom about poetry, familiarity, and gossip. The audience, totally attuned, might know prior work from prior readings. Let's say Robert Creeley comes and reads a special poem dedicated to René Ricard, or I read an epilogue to "Kaddish" in the form of "White Shroud," hearers know these texts resonate with old history, because everyone's familiar with earlier texts and styles.

In later years, St. Mark's became a cradle for some higher rock'n' roll, New Wave, and performance language. Patti Smith, Jim Carroll, William Burroughs, Laurie Anderson, Lou Reed, Philip Glass, Steven Taylor—all were at one time either apprentice poets at St. Mark's or participated in year-round activities or performed occasional

work. So it had tremendous impact on the centralized progression of rock'n' roll intelligentsia. Interestingly enough, St. Mark's was only ten blocks away from CBGB's, the bedraggled punk mecca of the early eighties.

With the age of Reagan, a deliberate, Federal concerted anti-democratic attack on small, individualistic, community-led arts groups began. The present attack on the NEA is an attack on decentralized initiative and diversity. "Why should the general public support, with taxpayers' money, dirty poems, anti-American poems, 'immoral' poems?" Kill the classic U.S. avant-garde that helped with the Cold War in Eastern Europe! "What good is this avant-garde? Why should the public be forced to pay for it?" This is the voice of the demagogue bureaucrat and can be answered simply:

The avant-garde has a healthy role to play in any culture. The Green Revolution and notions of ecology were proclaimed by the avant-garde in America before scientific popular notions of ecology became part of majority opinion. The green movement was fostered in 1950s poetry by savants like Gary Snyder and Michael McClure. More poignantly, it was the avant-garde, the very same artists who would be censored by the so-called "anti-Communist" fundamentalists in America, who were censored in totalitarian Eastern Europe. Deconstruction of the German, Czechoslovakian, Hungarian, Bulgarian, and Romanian Communist bureaucracies was spearheaded by members of the literary avant-garde who were allied, historically and by personal connection, to the very same avant-garde here in America censured by neo-conservatives. Ed Sanders and his band, the Fugs, with their "Coca-Cola Douche" or "Police State Blues," would never be subsidized under the demagogue censor's 1990s NEA new rules, nor would The Mothers of Invention, led by Frank Zappa, or Andy Warhol's Velvet Underground, Lou Reed, Dylan, Burroughs, Kerouac be approved—though all are heroes now in free Czechoslovakia. For myself, my own poetry has been chilled off public broadcast in parallel censorship by the Federal Communications Commission.

The age of Reagan-Bush, then, cracked down on the liberation of the Word, lowering St. Mark's NEA grants funds as well as diminishing funds previously granted to other decentralized arts groups, including Intersection for the Arts in San Francisco. In 1989, St. Mark's funds were reduced to $5,000, not enough to pay one person to move chairs for a year. Neo-con politicians are talking as if they had a monopoly on God, with gas-bag "moral majority" and "born-again" political groups hyping money off airwaves for promotion of what the American Founding Fathers denounced: the domination of State policy by an intolerant Church. These neo-con cults try to make the nation legislate parochial Church morality, aiming to restrict political humor and liberty of expression. The Bush Era's permissive manipulation of fundamentalist political mania has already led to withdrawal of appropriate subsidy and encouragement for the spiritual liberation that the St. Mark's Poetry Project manifests. Either way poets rather than fundamentalist betrayers of the spirit will win the world, because the planet needs imagination, the avant-garde spirit of poetry, to survive.

BRIAN CONNIFF (ESSAY DATE MARCH 1993)

SOURCE: Conniff, Brian. "Reconsidering Black Mountain: The Poetry of Hilda Morley." *American Literature* 65, no. 1 (March 1993): 117-30.

In the following essay, Conniff considers the status of Hilda Morley in the pantheon of Black Mountain Poets.

For a place so committed to innovative pedagogy and experimental art, so consumed by vitriolic debate and—at least in its last few years—so dedicated to the destruction of hierarchies, Black Mountain College has been transformed into a literary "movement" of surprisingly predictable and comfortable dimensions. From the moment he first took up residence, Charles Olson set out to undermine any stable tradition derived from "the great Greeks," any valuation of "forms as extricable from content."[1] Those who were accustomed to using such a tradition to authorize their own writing sensed the imminent danger, and by the late 1960s "Black Mountain poetry" was widely misrepresented and simplified. George Butterick and Paul Bové have documented the many misreadings of Olson's poetry, by rival poets and New Critics, in terms that ignored his deconstruction of "the very word 'tradition'" and obscured his assault on all "mystified centers."[2] More recently, in an examination of the various readings of Olson's "The Kingfishers," Burton Hatlen has described the pervasive tendency to find in such poems a static "sequence of images or symbols" rather than "a *verbal action,* a kinetic event."[3]

But for Olson, Robert Creeley, Robert Duncan, Ed Dorn, Denise Levertov, and all the other writers associated with the last years of Black Mountain College, the attempt to restore poetry's kinesis—both in the sense of the poem as a verbal action and in the sense of writing as an act of constant redefinition—has always been fundamental. In his own attempt to describe the creation of a Black Mountain "movement," Duncan said that his "life work" began in the period from 1952 to 1956—the years in which Olson was most fully engaged in writing *The Maximus Poems* and most activating to the writers around him. Then, in Duncan's words, "it's, as Charles would say, a vector."[4] Duncan's remarks are typical. In the Olson years the writers at Black Mountain College were undoubtably devoted to the rhetoric—and usually to the practice—of forward impetus, "implosion," "propulsion," and cultural resistance. Such "vectors" inevitably destroy the systems meant to contain them—or leave the systems behind to sustain themselves.

It is not so surprising, then, that in the past ten years the innovative writing of "Black Mountain poets"—by now perhaps best considered Black Mountain offshoots or, Olson might say, "projectiles"—has distanced itself more and more from the scant scholarly discussion still devoted to it. In 1984 Dorn told an interviewer that the entire movement had already been reduced to a state of "constant rehash," a "pro forma" set of received connections. "Nobody," Dorn would say, "*thinks* about Black Mountain anymore."[5] As recently as 1987 Francine du Plessix Gray could write that even Olson—in whose monumental shadow the "Black Mountain School" has invariably been cast—was still consigned to an "understimated place in American letters." More importantly, she could add that still less attention had been given to his "legacy," his influence "beyond" his own published texts.[6] After a 1987 conference at Bard College on "Poetry at Black Mountain College"—an event that might have been devoted to reappraisal and redirection—Robert Richman concluded, "If it weren't for a glancing reference to AIDS, a mention of Nicaragua, and Albert Cook's slap at today's young formalists ('traditionalists-come-lately,' he called them), one could very easily have come away from the conference thinking the last twenty years had never occurred."[7]

What is most startling about this process of calcification is the speed and apparent ease with which it has taken place. After all, it is still only fourteen years since Robert von Hallberg published the first major study of Olson's poetry and helped introduce to academic criticism one of the most confrontational and influential voices in post-World War II poetry. The other major studies of

Olson—by Bové, Paul Christensen, Thomas Merrill, Sherman Paul, and Don Byrd—all appeared by 1982 and were still trying to give some kind of basic outline to Olson's career.[8] Taken together, these studies managed to "open space" of truly imposing dimensions in the study of contemporary poetry—to borrow another piece of Olson rhetoric—but they also struggled, understandably enough, with the breadth and resistant idiosyncracy of Olson's scholarship, from Mayan civilization to quantum mechanics. Von Hallberg did provide a brief but significant discussion of Olson's influence on Dorn and Amiri Baraka, and Christensen devoted his final chapter to a wider understanding of "The Black Mountain Poets," including some of those on the "outer fringe" of the movement like Baraka, Gilbert Sorrentino, Ed Sanders, and Paul Carroll. But these discussions were sketchy, almost by necessity, and the other studies of Olson mentioned the work of his colleagues—even Creeley, in many respects the closest to him—only in passing. More importantly, in the years that have followed, no one has tried to consider the "movement" in any broader, truly contemporary context.

One reason for this stagnation is that the seemingly inevitable treatment of Olson as the "central" figure of the movement has slanted the reading of the few recognized "Black Mountain" writers and—as is just now becoming apparent—has helped preclude consideration of many others. Partly for this reason, writing that might be considered most distant from Olson's—especially that which did not reach its culmination until after the Olson boom of the late 1970s and early 1980s, like Duncan's H.D. book, or Oppenheimer's domestic lyrics, or Creeley's latest sequences—has attracted remarkably little attention. This neglect not only emphasizes the need to reconsider Black Mountain but also suggests a method of escaping the most crudely pro forma generalizations. To restore some of Black Mountain's kinetic energy—as Olson would write, "its usableness, in practice"—it is helpful, in a very practical sense, to try to establish some kind of legitimate poetic distance from Olson's writing and from that work of Duncan and Creeley most often associated with him.[9] At the same time, it is necessary to keep in sight the "movement"'s fundamental preoccupations—especially its deconstruction of "tradition."

For such a reconsideration, the poetry of Hilda Morley is particularly useful. Morley spent four years at Black Mountain during the Olson era. In fact, she was there for those same four years, 1952 to 1956, in which Creeley began to assimilate into his poetry Olson's anti-metaphysical "stance toward reality," in which Duncan claims his significant work began, and in which Olson tried most desperately to turn the decline of the college into the birth of a "movement." Morley wrote throughout most of this period and then, to use Duncan's figure of speech, went on to become her own version of a poetic "vector," with a career that has continued to move and accelerate in a direction of its own. Yet she is never mentioned in any of the critical studies of Olson, and she is never included in any of the long lists of Black Mountain's "writers," "artists," or otherwise impressive people. To put it in the spatial terms by which movements are made to appear static, Olson has almost always been placed at the "center"—rightly or wrongly, for better or for worse—while Morley has always been relegated to the most distant periphery, beyond even Christensen's "outer fringe." If from the moment Olson arrived at Black Mountain he became "an immediate cult-figure" and the college's dominant presence—as Martin Duberman writes in *Black Mountain: An Exploration in Community*—then Morley just as immediately became invisible.

In Duberman's book, which remains not only the most thorough study of the college itself but also one of the most powerful shaping forces in later discussions of "Black Mountain" poetry, Morley is mentioned only once. Her introduction suggests that she is little more than a piece of luggage brought along by her husband, the composer Stefan Wolpe. "He and his wife, the poet Hilda Morley, arrived at the start of the summer session in 1952," Duberman writes, "he to teach composition, she to offer courses on literature and Hebrew. Wolpe and Olson—both dynamic, vital men—hit it off immediately."[10] At the very moment the "cult-figure" and the composer hit it off, the teacher of literature and Hebrew disappears. The only other evidence Duberman provides of Morley's four years at Black Mountain is a photograph taken on the occasion of a farewell party given for her and Wolpe. There she stands, smiling, between her husband and Olson. Both of these "dynamic, vital men" seem to have an arm around her and, mostly due to Olson's size, they just about surround her. When a larger group is assembled for another photo, she has vanished again. Duberman later explains that "Wolpe left the community for good in 1956," but this time he does not even mention that Morley went along.[11]

Tom Clark's recent biography of Olson provides little additional information about Morley. Clark mentions (parenthetically, no less) that when Olson decided in the fall of 1952 to extend his leave of absence in Washington, claiming he needed "further restoration as a writer and educator," his temporary substitute as writing teacher was "poet Hilda Morley, the wife of Stefan Wolpe."[12] Strangely, Morley's role as the "writing teacher"—at this college so often characterized, at least since the 1950s, by and for its writers—is never again mentioned, as Clark goes on to survey Olson's marital tribulations, his sexual uncertainties, and his grant applications. Later, when Olson's first wife leaves him, Morley finds her only other place in Clark's account, not as a poet or a teacher but, once again, as the "wife of Stefan Wolpe." Morley and Wolpe took part in the "domestic arrangements" somehow made necessary by Olson's separation. In particular, they participated in the "dinner rotation" devised to feed "the hungry but helpless rector"—that is, until one evening when Olson "sternly pointed out a stray fragment of Brillo pad in his serving of Morley's *paella*."[13]

Clark never seems to suspect that the Brillo pad fragment might have been placed there intentionally, but, in any case, Morley did leave Black Mountain with Wolpe, and she continued writing, most productively in the years following his death in 1972. But until 1983 her poetry was never noticed by the critical mainstream, except for one brief review of her small volume *A Blessing Outside Us*. Then, out of nowhere it seems, Stanley Kunitz chose Morley's *To Hold in My Hand: Selected Poems, 1955-1983* as the first winner of the Capricorn Award, sponsored by the Writer's Voice of the West Side YMCA in New York City and "given annually to a poet over forty in belated recognition of excellence."[14] Even though some of the poems in this volume were already almost thirty years old—the earliest having been written during Morley's years at Black Mountain—Kunitz wrote in his introduction that "the bulk of Hilda Morley's work has remained in manuscript or available only in a scattering of mostly esoteric periodicals."[15] Nonetheless, *To Hold in My Hand* is in itself testimony to a long, remarkable, and still pretty much undiscovered career. The terms of the Capricorn Award could hardly have been more appropriate: seldom has recognition been at once so deserved, so belated, and so brief.

Kunitz suggested one possible cause of this neglect. Perhaps Morley "felt that there was room for only one genius in the family and that one had to be her husband, the avant-garde composer Stefan Wolpe, a magnificently bright, rare, and"—here borrowing an adjective from one of the poems Morley wrote to Wolpe—"ebullient spirit." Kunitz supposed that the poet must have chosen to "give herself" to the advancement of the composer's "difficult career" until, with his death, she was at once "devastated" and "liberated." Considering the often hostile sexual politics surrounding writers associated with Black Mountain, this notion of the "family" genius hardly seems as benign as Kunitz's introduction implies. Even a brief consideration of Olson's career—with his proclivity for manifestos, his macho posturing, his "great man" approach to teaching, his tendency to construct militant counter-canons, and his often excessive attempts to influence his protegés—makes it seem just about inevitable that women's voices would be silenced in the construction of a Black Mountain canon. Such an idea needs to be considered in a context that accounts for the misogyny that sometimes appears in the writings of Olson and Baraka, the homosexual subculture that surfaces only briefly in the writing of Michael Rumaker and Fielding Dawson, the homophobia with which writers like John Crowe Ransom responded to some of Duncan's early publications, and the usually reluctant consideration of Levertov as a token woman in (or out) of the movement.[16]

In the case of Morley, this notion of the "family genius" has unusually direct implications, mainly because she is determined not to allow Olson to have the kind of authority in the realm of poetry that Wolpe seems to have assumed in her family. In her elegy "Charles Olson (1910-1970)," she begins by presenting Olson as a kind of poetic, almost spiritual master whose immensity can barely be fathomed. Looking back, the speaker of the poem suggests that she was only able to overcome his death through a kind of ritual that—as she now realizes—had to be followed almost blindly:

> The night I heard that you'd died & I
> just beginning to see you whole
>   I lit a candle
> without knowing why
>   I burned the sandalwood
> Wong May had given me
>   The sticks curled
> downward crumpling   powdered away
>   sharpening
> the air
> Fire in its advance will condemn & judge
>   all things says Heraclitus.
>
>   (23)

But the voice of this poem, which starts out dutiful, if not worshipful, keeps modulating until the jagged half-lines open into a space more harsh and revealing than any of the written words, a visual analog to the couple of seconds of silence following the disintegration and immediate dispersal of the sandalwood. After this silence, the quotation from Heraclitus is ominously conclusive, half-tribute and half-invocation. Olson might have enjoyed the thought of being posthumously immolated in the fire of his favorite pre-Socratic philosopher, a fire that scorches the imposing past to ashes and "sharpens" the air. In this sense, the passage is a kind of tribute to Olson's poetic style and to his philosophical devotion to the common world, his belief that actuality is ceaselessly active. But the poem sounds less like Olson, and less dutiful, as it goes on. The master is all too readily immersed in the flux of "all things." In the act of writing the poem, Morley has prepared herself to judge him and to condemn him—as his own poetics demand—much in the way that Nietzsche's critical historian judges and condemns the past. Her memory of Olson, like his poetics, must serve the needs of the present.

Five years later, in a poem written after the death of Olson's first wife, "For Constance Olson (January 1975)," Morley recalls her own years at Black Mountain. But by the time she writes this poem she no longer needs to invoke the master's Heraclitean fire; by now, she has fully recognized that the past is always, immediately, judged by life. Even though this later poem also begins in recollection, its voice is far more comfortable with its immersion in time and in time's transformations. If the fire is no longer completely consuming, that is because it has been generated by her own body:

                    & the 4 of us—
                        you & Charles
                        Stefan & myself
                            I only
        am alive.
                        What is remembered
        piles itself, thread onto thread,
                            fragment
        along fragment,
                    phrase over phrase,
                        sentence,
        image joined to each other,
                            delicately
        so a breath might topple,
                        a spark of anguish
        blast them to ashes,
                    the heat my body trembles with
        this moment perhaps sufficient
                        in warmth
        to shelter them.

                                        (41)

Compared to her elegy for Charles Olson, "For Constance Olson (January 1975)" is more repre-

sentative of the poems Morley would write throughout the late 1970s and the 1980s, especially those published in her recent volume, *Cloudless at First.*[17] The anguish of loss always gives way, immediately and without any numbing ritual, to a self-sufficiency that is tenuous, as any human relation to the actual world of process must always be, yet complete in its commitment. A phrase like "the heat my body trembles with" is, in this case, both fearful and ecstatic. Moreover, this passage demonstrates Morley's most characteristic use of the kinetic formula Olson adopted from Edward Dahlberg: "One perception must immediately and directly lead to another perception."[18] As the rush of perceptions accelerates, her poetry "blasts" apart the delicate conjunction of images, phrases, and rhythms that constitute memory—and shelters the fragments that remain in the "sufficient" moment of the present.

Such a combination of care and irreverence for the past is more than just enervating; it is also liberating. Just as she uses the poetic line to assail the carefully aligned phrases with which the above passage begins—"you & Charles / Stefan & myself"—Morley always uses her poetry to remove herself from any enclosed position, personal or poetic, between Wolpe and Olson or within any other arrangement of masterful figures. No matter how "gentle" the voice of these poems might sometimes sound, Morley realizes that any use of language is a struggle for power on the most primal level, a struggle traced in her poems by a "projective" line that fractures and decenters:

        Finding the names of birds here,
        of flowers, important, I say I must
        know them, name them,
                    to be able
        to call upon where their magic
        resides for me: in naming them
        myself—to lay hold upon whatever
        quivers inside the bird-calls,
                        the dripping
        of tail of wing—
                    to know it
        inside my hand where power
        of that sort lives
                        & in my fingers
        wakes and becomes
                    an act of
        language.

                                        (78)

This centrifugal use of the line brings epistemology to the level of sensation. She is so intent upon discovering the common world, an "active" reality much like the one Olson came to understand by studying Alfred North Whitehead, that the knowledge she achieves is always at once tenuous and physical: "to lay hold upon whatever / quivers inside the bird-calls, . . . to know it / inside my hand where power / of that sort lives."

Olson once told Francine du Plessix Gray, when she was a student in his writing seminar at Black Mountain, that for ten years she should only write in a journal and not try to publish anything. She obeyed, but in doing so she kept her emotions "and the power of their expressions . . . at maximum intensity." Eventually, under such pressure, her writing began "to explode."[19] Only much later did she realize that this explosiveness was part of the "bittersweet paradox" of being a woman writer under Olson's influence. For her, Olson was both a censor and a liberator, both a sham and a prophet.[20] Morley's poetry shows all the signs of having been written under similar pressures.

Still, Olson's overwhelming presence is not the main cause of Morley's anonymity. More crucial is another kind of belatedness, separate from problems of discipleship and inherent in her own poetics. Even the poems written in her early days at Black Mountain move so strongly toward a testing of the immediate physical environment that assertion inevitably gives way to sensation, conclusion to fragmentation, and affiliation to self-definition—until the surrounding silence seems to be just as significant as the moments of speech. The result is certainly not the sort of poetry that would easily place its author in a stable, well-defined "movement," let alone a greater "tradition." Unlike Olson, who never wanted to accept delay for himself, no matter how forcefully he might sometimes have tried to impose it on others, Morley often views delay as providential, so long as it is part of a larger process in which attention is directed to the common world, as when she writes of the narcissus:

> That hiding
> all winter was worth it—
> to offer such grace,
> 　　　　such whiteness,
> awareness of being vulnerable—
> faintness of perfume.
>
> 　　　　　　　　(9)

This kind of delay can suspend the egotistical will long enough to allow her to recognize, in another, the potential for self-definition, as when she writes of the dancer, La Belle Otero:

> Being one of those who postponed
> her real self so much,
> 　　　　　　letting
> others lead me　　(or not)

> 　　　　　　　being loved
> & loving so much,　　touching what I could
> in the dark,　　it is
> the life of La Belle Otero
> entertains me—a woman who used
> her capacities to the full,
> 　　　　　　from
> the beginning.
>
> 　　　　　　　　　(19)

Morley repeatedly writes that all those years in which she "postponed" her "real self" might best be considered an extended prelude to these moments of unfettered, unforeseen fulfillment. In the terms of this poetry, questions of literary "influence" or domination are never quite appropriate: she can simply choose to let others lead her, or not. She can direct her attention to whomever or whatever "entertains" her. Even conventional notions of "development," of a career progressing toward some inevitable end, make no real sense: from the "beginning," as she has learned from studying the life of La Belle Otero, capacities can be used "to the full." Yet postponement, too, is an art.

To Hold in My Hand ends with a pair of poems that reconceive the artist's postponement by subsuming it into a vision of life as a continuously creative act. In the next-to-last poem, "Second Spring," Morley writes of the cyclamen, a flower of a "delicacy / so confident" that she always thought it was "invulnerable." And in the same poem she writes of George Seferis, who speaks of the cyclamen "often / (over and over)" simply "because it consoles him / for the burden of the ruins" (211). What matters in the writing of the Greek poet is not the attainment of consolation but his commitment to an endless search among the ruins. Immediately following, the volume's final poem, "The Last Rehearsal," describes the moments before a concert in language that recalls the growth and blossoming of the cyclamen following September rains in the Mediterranean's "second spring." To use an image that appears in both of these poems, Morley is concerned with the process by which the "bare bones" are covered with flesh, "made invisible" by being incorporated into the living world. Like "Second Spring," "The Last Rehearsal" culminates in a multiplication of beginnings:

> Where something is being made is
> where joy is,
> 　　　　　where something
> begins—
> 　　　the bare bones
> before flesh has covered it
> 　　　　　or the innards

of the body where things begin to
work,
    where the cell begins
to stretch itself, the nucleus
to multiply.
    It is a scaffolding,
but one that trembles.

(212)

Many of Morley's recent poems aspire to this condition: "the beginning / of the last rehearsal," a final refusal to "conclude," the book's last page on which all sense of beginning and end is destroyed. What matters most about writing—or any other art—is not a masterful performance with its sense of finality but the joy of preparation. Everything about poetry—the writing and the silence, the sense of burden and the search for consolation, the multiplication of beginnings and the refusal to end—is really nothing more than a seamless "run-through," the necessary activity of a life committed to the work "behind the scenes."

It is not surprising, then, that the main preoccupation of Morley's "early" poetry—that is, the thirty years' worth finally collected in *To Hold in My Hand*—is a constant revision of the figure of the artist. A poem dedicated to George Oppen, which alludes to a bust of Verdi, is followed by the poem about La Belle Otero, which alludes to a photograph of Wolpe. These are followed by poems beginning with quotations from Norbert Wiener and André Malraux, dedicated to Charles Olson and Emma Raphael. And these, in turn, are followed by poems involving Tolstoy, Cézanne, Goethe, and Matisse. The overall effect is directly opposed to the stability usually expected from a "canon": by altering the figure of the artist for each occasion, in the full awareness that the next moment will require a new revision, Morley always avoids a self-debasing, self-defeating worship of heroic masters.

Instead, every nuance of artistry is put into practice in the very act of exploration. Among the few recurrent examples are Matisse and Cézanne, who are exemplary most of all for their ability to translate an ordinary vision of space into a sense of motion:

What is delightful in *The Red
Studio* is that air of suspended
space moving in unbroken
curves with the eye travelling
as Matisse wished it
        around
and free in a continual
flight   but at the same time with
an assurance nothing
can shatter

What is free here is not
the eye only
      not space only, but our-
selves swerving & shifting.

(33)

This meditation on the figure of "the artist" suspends the poetic self, which Olson called "the lyrical interference of the individual as ego," to allow for a free-play of self-revision.[21] It is much like the meditation of Wallace Stevens's Penelope, constantly recreating herself as she reflects on an imagined Ulysses: "She has composed, so long, a self with which to welcome him, / Companion to his self for her, which she imagined."[22]

Taken together, all of Morley's writers, painters, dancers, and musicians do not constitute anything like a "tradition," because her revisionary poetics will admit no static assumptions about the artist and no stable boundaries. She also writes about Joan of Arc, who chose as her patron Saint Catherine, "guardian / of prisoners, the patron of getaways" and who perfected the habit of saying "there's no mistake" (4-5). And Morley writes about Saint Theresa, "who cried to her / novice nuns 'Look only, / I ask you / to learn to look'" (128). But perhaps the most consummate artist of all is La Belle Otero, who once danced the fandango on a table at Maxim's and at every moment "made life fit her needs completely—those concrete / gross, material needs" (20).

So it might be that the best way to complicate the suddenly comfortable sense of "Black Mountain Poetry" is to consider the case of Hilda Morley, how it has happened that she—who has been all along as intelligently preoccupied as anyone with the most insistent preoccupation of the "movement," the provisional redefinition of the artist within the common world—could still be completely excluded from even the most "definitive" literary criticism. If the movement were to be given, for a moment, stable dimensions, it could even be argued that Morley's writing is more "central" than Olson's. But the more fundamental lesson to be learned from her career is that the Black Mountain movement has no center. After all, much of the writing associated with Black Mountain has primarily been devoted, like Morley's, to the destruction of any stable tradition, no matter how reconstituted. This writing is better considered, as Duncan put it, in terms of "vectors," moving outward. Or in terms closer to Morley's poetry, it is better considered the kind of endless rehearsal that prevents literary history from ever becoming static.

Notes

This paper was originally presented at the 1991 meeting of the Mid-Atlantic Popular Culture Association/ American Culture Association.

1. Charles Olson, *Selected Works,* ed. Robert Creeley (New York: New Directions, 1966), 55, 61.

2. Paul Bové, *Destructive Poetics: Heidegger and Modern Poetry* (New York: Columbia Univ. Press, 1980). See also George Butterick, "Foreword" to Paul Christensen's *Charles Olson: Call Him Ishmael* (Austin: Univ. of Texas Press, 1979), vii-xi.

3. Burton Hatlen, "Kinesis and Meaning: Charles Olson's 'The Kingfishers' and the Critics," *Contemporary Literature* 30 (1989): 546-72.

4. "An Interview with Robert Duncan," conducted by John R. Cohn and Thomas J. O'Donnell, in *Interviews with Contemporary Writers: Second Series, 1972-1982,* ed. L. S. Dembo (Madison: Univ. of Wisconsin Press, 1983), 236.

5. "An Interview with Edward Dorn," conducted by Tandy Sturgeon, *Contemporary Literature* 27 (1986): 1-2.

6. Francine du Plessix Gray, "Charles Olson and an American Place," *Yale Review* 76 (1987): 352.

7. Robert Richman, "Black Mountain Comes to Bard," *New Criterion* 6 (1987): 88.

8. See Robert von Hallberg, *Charles Olson: The Scholar's Art* (Cambridge: Harvard Univ. Press, 1978); Sherman Paul, *Olson's Push: Origin, Black Mountain, and Recent American Poetry* (Baton Rouge: Louisiana State Univ. Press, 1978); Paul Christensen, *Charles Olson: Call Him Ishmael;* Don Byrd, *Charles Olson's Maximus* (Urbana: Univ. of Illinois Press, 1980); Thomas Merrill, *The Poetry of Charles Olson, a Primer* (Newark: Univ. of Delaware Press, 1982).

9. Olson, 17.

10. Martin Duberman, *Black Mountain: An Exploration in Community* (Gloucester, Mass.: Peter Smith, 1988), 347.

11. Duberman, 407.

12. Tom Clark, *Charles Olson: The Allegory of a Poet's Life* (New York: Norton, 1991), 229.

13. Clark, 243.

14. Stanley Kunitz, "Where Joy Is," prefatory note to Hilda Morley's *To Hold in My Hand* (New York: Sheep Meadow, 1983). Citations for Morley's poetry are from this volume and will be included parenthetically within the text.

15. Kunitz, "Where Joy Is."

16. See Fielding Dawson, *The Black Mountain Book* (New York: Croton, 1970); and Michael Rumaker, "Creeley at Black Mountain," *boundary 2* 6 (1978): 137-77. As early as 1973, Catharine Stimpson mentioned a "domineering patriarchal bias" in Olson's writing. Nonetheless, as Robert O'Brien Hokanson has very recently pointed out, "Few critics have addressed, let alone examined in detail, this fundamental role gender plays in his work" ("Projecting Like a Man: Charles Olson and the Poetics of Gender," *Sagetrieb* 9 [1990]: 169).

17. Hilda Morley, *Cloudless At First* (Mt. Kisco, N.Y.: Moyer Bell Limited, 1988).

18. Olson, 17.

19. Du Plessix Gray, 349.

20. Du Plessix Gray, 352.

21. Olson, 24.

22. Wallace Stevens, *The Collected Poems* (New York: Vintage, 1982), 521.

BARRY MILES (ESSAY DATE 1993)

SOURCE: Miles, Barry. "The Beat Generation in the Village." In *Greenwich Village: Culture and Counterculture,* edited by Rick Beard and Leslie Cohen Berlowitz, pp. 165-79. New Brunswick, N.J.: Rutgers University Press, 1993.

In the following essay, Miles delineates specific events among Beat Generation figures that took place within the bohemian culture of Greenwich Village from the 1940s to the early 1960s.

American bohemianism is said to have started with Edgar Allan Poe, who, in his endless search for cheap lodgings, often found himself living in Greenwich Village. America's first Latin Quarter, New York's Montmartre, forever associated in the public mind with artists and bohemians—it was obvious that the stereotypical beatniks of the late fifties, with their bongos, flasks of cheap Chianti, berets, and sandals, would live in the Village. The original Beat Generation—Kerouac, Burroughs, Ginsberg, Corso, et al.—who were active in the forties and fifties, met in the Village bars and coffee shops, but the Village was already too expensive for them actually to live there.

In December 1943, a few days before Christmas, seventeen-year-old Allen Ginsberg, a freshman at Columbia, wrote to his elder brother Eugene: "Saturday I plan to go down to Greenwich Village with a friend of mine who claims to be an 'intellectual' and knows queer and interesting people there. I plan to get drunk Saturday evening, if I can. I'll tell you the issue."

His guide on this, his first visit, was Lucien Carr, a friend from St. Louis who lived on his floor at Union Theological Seminary, which was being used for student housing during the war. Carr first took Ginsberg to visit a hometown friend, David Kammerer, who had a room at 44 Morton Street, off Seventh Avenue. To Ginsberg, who grew up in Paterson, New Jersey, and had traveled little, the simple act of walking among the garbage cans and piles of dirty snow on those legendary streets was an exciting experience, made doubly so because he was aware of his homosexuality but had not yet revealed it to anyone, yet here he was "going down to the Village where all the fairies were. It was both romantically glorious and at the same time frightening and frustrating." After introductions had been made, they headed out, edging their way gingerly over the icy sidewalk of Minetta Lane to the Minetta Tavern—in those days one of the main bohemian watering holes in the Village—for Ginsberg's first drink in Greenwich Village.

A few days later Ginsberg and Carr again took the subway down to Christopher Street, but this time Kammerer was out. Undaunted, Carr led Ginsberg around the corner to 69 Bedford Street, where lived another hometown friend: William Seward Burroughs. He had one room on the second floor with French windows overlooking a small yard. Upstairs lived a lesbian friend of his named Louise. Burroughs liked Louise because, in his words, she was "straightforward, manly and reliable." (She eventually appeared as Agnes in the unpublished William Burroughs-Jack Kerouac collaborative novel *And the Hippos Were Boiled in Their Tanks*.) Ginsberg was delighted; the Village was proving to be everything he had hoped.

Littered with books but little else, Burroughs's room contained an old settee and an upturned log that served as both coffee table and chair. Carr told them about a fight he had been involved in after getting drunk at the Minetta Tavern with Kammerer. They had gone on to the studio of a gay portrait painter he knew, but the visit developed into a brawl that had demolished most of the painter's studio, and Carr had bitten off part of the painter's earlobe as well as sinking his teeth into Kammerer's shoulder. Recalling the event, Ginsberg said: "I thought it was pretty shocking and amazing. I never heard of *anything* like that because I was from East Side High School in Paterson, New Jersey. I didn't know people went around getting drunk and biting people's ears off!" The Village, even in wartime, lived up to its reputation.

Burroughs and Kammerer frequented the San Remo and Chumley's, as well as the Minetta Tavern, sometimes with novelist Chandler Brossard, then a reporter for *The New Yorker*'s "Talk of the Town" column, who lived in Kammerer's building. Burroughs, whose grandfather had invented the adding machine and founded the Burroughs Corporation, was working as a bartender at the time, even though he was receiving an allowance of two hundred dollars a month from his parents in St. Louis. For someone like Burroughs, the Village was a refuge where he

could live as he wished without encountering the disapproval of his fellow citizens.

Through Lucien Carr, Ginsberg also met Jack Kerouac, a merchant seaman living with his girlfriend, Edie Parker, near the Columbia campus. Parker was still at college, but Kerouac, who had attended Columbia on a football scholarship, had argued with the coach and left the college under less than agreeable conditions. He was officially "unwelcome on the campus."

Ginsberg, Kerouac, and Carr were romantic idealists, inspired by Yeats's "A Vision" and concerned with creating a "new vision" of their own—an inchoate version of what would become known as the philosophy of the Beat Generation. They read Paul Verlaine, Charles Baudelaire, Arthur Rimbaud, Jean Cocteau, and Percy Bysshe Shelley as well as the works of Samuel Taylor Coleridge, Edward Fitzgerald, and the Marquis de Sade. Sitting in the West End Bar, across from the Columbia campus, they created their own *vie de bohème*: Their Pernod became absinthe; shabby Broadway, the Boulevard St. Germain. Whenever possible, they made the trip downtown, where Greenwich Village provided the same artistic and tolerant atmosphere they imagined had existed on the Left Bank before the war.

David Kammerer was a homosexual who had become obsessed with Carr while teaching him in a grade-school play group. Although Carr was not gay, Kammerer pursued him relentlessly. Carr left St. Louis and attended Bowdoin College in Maine and several other schools, including the University of Chicago, but Kammerer followed him everywhere to pester him and demand his friendship. One night, while Carr and Kammerer were sitting in Morningside Park after the West End Bar had closed, matters came to a head: Kammerer threatened to harm Carr's girlfriend and lunged at him. "Dave wanted Lucien to stab him," says Burroughs, and that was what happened. Defending himself with a Boy Scout knife, Carr stabbed Kammerer twice through the heart, killing him. Jailed for two years, after his release, Carr kept a certain distance, at least in public, from the others. This "honor killing," as it was labeled by the newspapers, brought an end to the first phase of the Beat Generation.

· · · · ·

The poet Harold Norse remembers meeting Ginsberg in 1944, on his way home to the Village on the subway at 3:00 A.M. There was one other person in the car, a young man wearing a red bandanna who was reciting French poetry to himself, aloud. The noise of the train prevented Norse from hearing what was being said until, at one stop, he caught enough to identify "The Drunken Boatman" and called out: "Rimbaud!"

"You're a poet!" exclaimed Ginsberg. Getting into conversation, they went to Norse's tiny apartment on Horatio Street near the meat market, where they read their poems to each other. "I found him sexy and appealing but had no idea of his poetic capacities," Norse recalls. "The poems he showed me were slight four-liners, and he seemed even shyer than I was." In Norse's autobiography, *Memoirs of a Bastard Angel*, he wrote: "For Allen, as for all of us, the Village was an oasis in the puritan desert, a watering place for the soul. The Village offered freewheeling sex. The closet cases of America were drawn to the bars and hangouts of Bohemia, longing to fulfill their secret desires."

The Beats first began experimenting with drugs, mostly morphine and benzedrine, in 1945, when Kerouac, Burroughs, Ginsberg, and several other friends shared an apartment on West 115th Street. Following Burroughs's lead, they explored the Times Square area, where the prostitutes, hustlers, junkies, jazz musicians, servicemen, jazz clubs, all-night bars, and Automats made it the most exciting place in the city. The twenty-four-hour neon lighting held a particular attraction for them, probably associated with the amphetamine they were using. Burroughs was thirty, but the others were still very young: Ginsberg was a teenager, Kerouac only twenty-three.

Slowly their ideas for a new society developed, and they began to meet like-minded people. The dropping of A-bombs on Japan and the revelation of the horrors of the concentration camps combined with the petty puritanism of bourgeois America to cause widespread disillusion with the established values of society and to lead them to seek another direction, away from hypocrisy toward honesty, truthfulness, and, they hoped, a new spirituality. Burroughs's particular interest in drugs led him to the society of petty criminals and hoodlums, among whom he met Herbert Huncke, the man who provided the key word *beat* for the sobriquet Beat Generation and the Times Square hustler who had first introduced Burroughs to morphine. (Burroughs tells the full story in his autobiographical novel *Junky*.) Burroughs left New York to grow marijuana in Texas in June 1946, after a drug bust at the 115th Street apartment. From Texas he moved to New Orleans, where he

again ran into trouble with the law. He continued south to Mexico City and did not return to New York until 1953.

Shortly after Burroughs left a young car thief from Denver named Neal Cassady appeared on the scene. Both Kerouac and Ginsberg were enchanted by him. Ginsberg fell in love and began a long-drawn-out, torturous relationship with him. Kerouac worshiped just as avidly, and spent much of the late forties journeying back and forth across the United States with Cassady at the wheel, later casting him as the hero, Dean Moriarty, in *On the Road*. When not in San Francisco or Denver with Cassady, Kerouac stayed at home with his mother in Ozone Park, living off her wages from the shoe factory where she worked. He had no apartment of his own.

In the late forties the most likely place to meet Ginsberg, Kerouac, and their circle of friends was the San Remo, at 93 MacDougal Street, on the northwest corner of Bleecker. A typically dark and smoky New York bar with a loud jukebox and crowded tables, the San Remo stayed open until 4:00 A.M. The alcoholic poet Max Bodenheim could often be found propping up the bar—above which hung a photograph of him in his younger days. Among its regulars were James Agee, Larry Rivers, Paul Goodman, John Cage, Merce Cunningham, W. H. Auden, Chester Kallman, Harold Norse, and virtually everybody associated with Judith Malina and Julian Beck's newly launched Living Theatre. Jackson Pollock, Willem de Kooning, Franz Kline, and many other abstract expressionists also hung out there when they weren't at the Cedar Street Tavern over on University Place.

"The only people for me," says Sal Paradise, Jack Kerouac's narrator in *On the Road*, "are the mad ones, the ones who are mad to live, mad to talk, mad to be saved, desirous of everything at the same time, the ones who never yawn or say a commonplace thing, but burn, burn, burn like fabulous yellow roman candles exploding like spiders across the stars."

This could easily have been a description of Bill Cannastra, a madcap Italian American lawyer, who despite poor attendance had managed to graduate from Harvard Law School. (He was also drunk when he took his bar examinations.) A regular at the San Remo, Cannastra was a friend of both Kerouac and Ginsberg, the leader of a large group of talented friends, most of whom were writers or artists of some sort, and one of the main players in the late forties Village scene. He lived three doors from Lucien Carr at 125 West Twenty-first Street, the site of frequent parties. Cannastra's many exploits were later featured in Alan Harrington's *The Secret Swinger,* in which he appears as Bill Genovese.

Cannastra enjoyed scaring his friends and passers-by by dodging through busy traffic and was knocked down on a number of occasions. Another trick was to lie down in the middle of an avenue before advancing traffic just as the lights changed a block away. A favorite party piece was to cavort drunkenly along the unrailed parapet on the roof of his building, taking greater and greater risks the more his friends pleaded with him to come down. He would encourage guests to take part in a competition to see who could hold his or her head the longest in the oven with the gas on and at parties he would dance barefoot across broken glass. Although he was mostly self-destructive, Cannastra sometimes turned his violence on others, once attempting to set fire to a friend who had passed out in a drunken stupor.

Alan Harrington's novel described the scene: "Genovese's loft was sometimes strewn with broken glass. People made love in the bathroom (often, without realizing it, for a circle of spectators looking down from the skylight). They made love on the fire escape and on the roof. . . . The loft was divided into sections by translucent hanging screens, and there were unmade beds and cots everywhere. The light of a bare bulb shone in the kitchen by the fire escape, but as you moved into the loft's interior smaller amounts of light filtered through the screens, until at the far end it was a dark place. Here young philosophers sat on a window ledge. Clutching dirty coffee cups filled with Tallyho beer, or drinking blended whiskey from old jelly glasses, they looked out over the low roofs of Chelsea, and back into the room where shadowy people were cutting their feet on glass fragments, and Bill Genovese ate glass and music roared out of the dark."

The broken glass also featured in Ginsberg's poem *Howl:* "(who) danced on broken wineglasses barefoot, smashed phonograph records of nostalgic European 1930s German jazz finished the whiskey and threw up groaning into the bloody toilet." To Ginsberg, Cannastra was another of the "best minds" of his generation, "destroyed by madness." Gerald Nicosia's biography of Kerouac, *Memory Babe,* says that "practically every gathering at the loft was planned to end as a sexual occasion. As much as these orgies gratified Cannastra's voyeurism, there was probably a deeper motivation involved, for a large part of Cannastra's life was a struggle to feel less like an outsider,

to blend in with everybody else and relax. . . . At any rate, after getting thoroughly drunk, people climbed on top of one another on the beds, everyone groping everyone else. Actual sex acts when they occurred were virtually meaningless."

Between 1948 and 1950, Cannastra's alcoholism overcame him. He lost his job with a New York law firm, and his friends began to desert him. He was bisexual, and though his sexual preference seems to have been for men, in 1950 he was living with a twenty-year-old woman called Joan Haverty, who shared his enthusiasm for pranks and happily joined him in his escapades. Together they would roam the fire escapes, peering unseen into people's apartments and commenting on their mundane lives. Cannastra was fond of spying on people and had drilled peepholes into the wall of his bathroom so that he could watch his guests use it.

Just after midnight on the morning of October 12, 1950, Cannastra was out on the town with a group of friends who were making their way to Carr's loft to borrow some money. They boarded the northbound Lexington Avenue IRT local train, heading for Twenty-third Street. At the Bleecker Street stop one of the party mentioned Winnie, the black bartender at the Bleecker Tavern, a favorite haunt. The doors closed and the train began to pull out of the station when Cannastra, as a joke, jumped to his feet and lunged out of the window on the platform side as if he meant to go to the bar. He misjudged his leap and found himself unbalanced, with his head and shoulders hanging too far out of the window. His friends rushed to save him, grabbing at his clothing, but his coat tore away in their hands. His shoulders were too far out of the window for them to reach. The train picked up speed, and he began to scream in terror but it was too late. As the train entered the tunnel, there was a thud and he was snatched from their hands, out of the window and onto the tracks. Someone pulled the emergency cord, but he was dragged for fifty-five feet before the train came to a halt. He was pronounced dead on arrival at Columbus Hospital.

After Cannastra's death Jack Kerouac devoted a tremendous amount of attention to Joan Haverty, Cannastra's girlfriend, who was still living in the loft. She was deeply impressed by the twenty-seven-year-old Kerouac. Within a few days he had moved into the apartment, and then to everyone's surprise, on November 17, 1950, only a month after Cannastra's death, Jack and Joan married. Afterward there was a party for two hundred at the loft. Attended by all the San Remo regulars, it was strangely subdued despite Kerouac's attempts to liven things up.

The marriage was doomed. Although in the early days it seemed to be a marriage based on love, Kerouac's views on marriage were old fashioned, even for 1950. Joan was not allowed to accompany him when he went visiting his friends, because Kerouac thought wives belonged at home with the dishes. She was not allowed to hold any opinions but those that Kerouac espoused; her role was to wash, cook, and clean for him as well as to keep them both from her earnings as a dressmaker. To earn extra money she took a job in a department store during the busy Christmas season, but Kerouac was lonely sitting at home writing and insisted that they give up the loft and move in with his mother in Queens. The move was a disaster: Kerouac and his mother spoke French together most of the time so that Joan was unable to understand them, and Kerouac spent a lot of his time going to parties and hanging out with his friends. Kerouac made her hand over her wage check to his mother each week, and Mrs. Kerouac regarded her as little more than a slave provided by her son to do all the housework.

It took only a few weeks for Joan to deliver an ultimatum: She was returning to Manhattan. Kerouac could either live with her or stay home with his mother. In January 1951 she found a new job and took an apartment at 454 West Twentieth Street, in the beautiful Greek Revival row that forms the south side of Chelsea Square between Ninth and Tenth avenues. She was at work when the moving men collected her things, but during her lunch break she went over to West Twentieth to see how the move was progressing. Sitting outside the building on his rolltop desk was Kerouac, his slippers in his hand. She took him in.

Among the items Joan had salvaged from Cannastra's loft was a pile of twenty-foot rolls of Japanese writing paper that provided the solution to one of Kerouac's problems. He did not believe in correcting his writing—a system he called "spontaneous prose"—and although he was a fast, accurate typist, he always felt stymied by the need to keep feeding his typewriter with paper. (A word processor would have suited him admirably.) Early in April 1951 he taped the rolls of paper together and fed one end into his typewriter. Writing continuously, often with little sleep, he had already written 34,000 words by April 9. By April 20 his masterpiece, *On the Road*—consisting of one long paragraph with little punctuation—was almost finished, with more than 86,000 words on a 120-foot roll. The latter part of the manuscript was written at Lucien Carr's Twenty-first Street loft, where one of the hazards was Carr's dog, who ate the last four feet of the roll.

Unfortunately his marriage to Joan had not been much improved by the move back to Manhattan. Jack's meanness—he wouldn't even share his cigarettes with Joan—his infidelities, and the fact that she was still a domestic slave at home after working all day at Stouffer's as a waitress, placed intolerable pressure on the relationship. Despite the fact that Jack often slept at Carr's loft, Joan managed to get pregnant, something that they had been trying hard for in the earlier days of their brief marriage. Now, as they were separating, Kerouac reacted with fear and anger at the news. She had revenged herself for his affairs by bringing a fellow worker at the restaurant home to her bed. Kerouac felt cuckolded and, despite his Catholicism, demanded that she get an abortion, claiming that the baby was not his. Joan refused and threw him out. After living at Carr's for a few weeks, he returned to live with his mother.

Jan Kerouac was born on February 16, 1952, but despite her uncanny physical likeness to her father, Kerouac denied paternity and went into hiding in California rather than pay child support. His daughter grew up desperately impoverished during the years of his greatest success. By the age of fourteen she was a heroin addict, selling herself on the streets to get a fix. She later recorded her experiences in *Baby Driver* and *Trainsongs*, two painfully honest autobiographical volumes of hippie life in the sixties.

. . . . .

Of the original members of the Beat Generation, Gregory Corso had the greatest claim to a Greenwich Village connection, having had the good fortune to be born above the funeral parlor on the southwest corner of Bleecker and MacDougal streets. In 1930, when he was only six months old, his eighteen-year-old mother returned to her home in Italy. Thereafter his father boarded him with foster parents for most of his childhood. By the age of twelve he was out on the streets, where he was caught stealing food and sent to the Tombs. After his release the next year, he was arrested again almost immediately—having nowhere to go, he had broken into a youth center to sleep—and was returned to the Tombs. The next time he hit the streets he was fifteen and streetwise.

His conviction for organizing a robbery using walkie-talkies resulted in his spending the years

1947 to 1950 in Clinton Prison, at Dannemora, New York, near the Canadian border. It was there he learned to be a poet, reading his way through the prison copy of a 1905 standard dictionary, reveling in the obscure and archaic words. He studied history and, not knowing where to start, began with the Greeks. When he was released, just before his twentieth birthday, he had the beginnings of a classical education.

It was not long after he got out of prison that he met Allen Ginsberg. Corso was sitting at a table in the Pony Stable, a lesbian bar on Third Street at Sixth Avenue, enthusiastically telling some new acquaintances what a great poet he was. He had with him a sheaf of professionally typed poems. Ginsberg immediately recognized how good they were and soon introduced Corso to Jack Kerouac, Lucien Carr, and Ginsberg's other friends. The young poet quickly became the final member of the original Beat group.

The constant mobility of the Beats meant that whoever had an apartment invariably had many of the other members of the group staying with him. Kerouac, for instance, never had an apartment of his own. Throughout his entire life, he either stayed with friends or lived with his mother. Ginsberg was the only member of the group who actually took regular jobs for a living, working as a copyboy, typist, and for six years as a market researcher. Having a job meant that he had an apartment, and there was a time in 1953 when Burroughs, Corso, and Kerouac were all staying with him. Ginsberg moved into his first apartment near the Village, an eighteen-dollar-a-month, two-room attic with dormer windows at 346 West Fifteenth, between Eighth and Ninth avenues, in December 1951. It is still there, a nondescript brownstone dwarfed by the huge bulk of the Port Authority warehouse, which occupies the entire block on the north side of Fifteenth Street. His feelings about the place are expressed in the poem "Walking Home at Night," which ends: "Remembering / my attic I reached / my hands to my head and hissed / 'Oh God how horrible!'" While he was there he worked on many of the poems that later appeared in his book *Empty Mirror*.

Ginsberg was using his marketing skills in another direction. While in Texas and Mexico City, Burroughs had written a novel about his experiences as a heroin addict in New York, New Orleans, and Mexico City that Ginsberg had been trying to sell for him. After seeing virtually every editor in town, he turned to his friend Carl Solomon, who worked at his uncle's paperback publishing company, Ace Books. Solomon was enthusiastic about the idea of publishing something other than the usual run of westerns and whodunits, and Burroughs was enthusiastic about a paperback original. Out of concern that they might be advocating the use of drugs by publishing a junkie's memoirs, Ace hesitated before finally putting *Junky* on the newsstands in the summer of 1953. It had a lurid cover of a woman in a red dress struggling with a man for possession of a hypodermic syringe, and was bound back-to-back with *Narcotic Agent*, by Maurice Helbrant, described as "a gripping true adventure of a T-man's war against the dope menace." Burroughs published the book under the pseudonym of William Lee because he didn't want his parents to read it and cut off his allowance.

Kerouac was not having comparable luck in getting his books into print. His first book, *The Town and the City*, a conventional Thomas Wolfean novel, had been published in 1950 but had not set the world on fire. No one wanted the more radical *On the Road* or his subsequent books *Dr. Sax* and *Maggie Cassady*. Ginsberg managed to get an advance for him from Ace for *On the Road*, but the text as Kerouac presented it, though no longer on one long roll of paper, was still too far out for them, and they dropped their option.

Kerouac had written *Dr. Sax* while staying with Burroughs in Mexico City. It was unfinished when he returned to New York, where he and Ginsberg had finally come up with an ending while leaning on a fence in the Village at West Fourth Street and Sixth Avenue in the summer sunshine. *Dr. Sax* is a novel of awakening youth based on Kerouac's upbringing in Lowell, Massachusetts. It explores the demons and monsters of his fantasy-ridden adolescent world. Memories and dreams give way to an apocalyptic vision of a huge snake emerging from the center of the earth, but Kerouac did not know how to go on. Ginsberg proposed a Shakespearian solution: "Ah! 'twas a husk of doves," suggesting that the snake, representing all the evil in the world, was nothing but a dry husk surrounding a flock of beautiful doves. Kerouac liked the idea and wrote: "His Snake would not destroy the world but merely be a great skin of doves on coming-out day." Years later Ginsberg arranged for *Dr. Sax* to be published by Grove Press.

By October 1952 Ginsberg was earning enough money as a free-lancer in market research to enable him to move to a bigger apartment on the Lower East Side, an area in which he has lived ever since. Located at 206 East Seventh Street, between Avenues B and C, a half block from

Tompkins Square Park, Ginsberg's apartment was, as usual, a gathering point where the other, more itinerant Beats could stay. Gregory Corso was the first to move in. In the summer of 1953 Ginsberg took a forty-five-dollar-a-week job as copyboy at the *New York World-Telegram,* which offered shorter hours than his job in market research in the Empire State Building. Corso lived off his wages, but Ginsberg did not complain because he enjoyed having Corso around. Kerouac, who had been living in California with Neal Cassady, now returned to his mother and made frequent visits to the city to stay with them.

They hung out at the San Remo, still largely populated by a collection of Village types Ginsberg referred to as "subterraneans." Kerouac later appropriated the name for his book about the bohemian scene in Greenwich Village and the Lower East Side around 1952-1953. Although certain unconvincing cosmetic changes were made in the published text to relocate the book in San Francisco to avoid charges of libel, the book is peopled by many of the same characters that appeared in Burroughs's *Junky* and Ginsberg's *Howl.* One of them, Adam Moorad (Ginsberg's name in the book), is credited with inventing the name. "The subterraneans," wrote Kerouac, "is a name invented by . . . a poet and friend of mine who said, 'They are hip without being slick, they are intelligent without being corny, they are intellectual as hell and know all about Pound without being pretentious or talking too much about it, they are very quiet, they are very Christlike.'"

In the summer of 1953 William Burroughs, who had returned to New York City for the first time in seven years while en route to Tangier, displaced Corso from Ginsberg's apartment. While Burroughs was in New York, he was mildly addicted to Dolophine, an early form of methadone and the pill of choice to replace junk in the early fifties. His habit did not trouble him at all, because he could always score "dollies" at Joe's Luncheonette on Cornelia Street, the subterraneans' favorite place to eat.

Ginsberg and Burroughs did a great deal of work while Burroughs was in town. Burroughs had been on an expedition to South America in search of the telepathic, hallucinogenic *yage,* and his letters from there were filled with anecdotes, routines, and hilarious descriptions of his tribulations. Together they assembled the material into the third book in a projected trilogy—*Junky, Queer,* and *Yage*—and hired Alene Lee, Jack Kerouac's new girlfriend, to type it up. Sections from all three books were later incorporated into a text

known as *Interzone,* which for a time had the working title of *Naked Lunch. Yage* was never published as conceived in 1953, but many of the letters were used in *The Yage Letters,* a volume of correspondence City Lights Books published in 1963. It was a creative period for Burroughs, and many of the ideas that appeared later in *The Naked Lunch* were first thought of at East Seventh Street. The futuristic vibrating city of Interzone, with its levels connected by a web of catwalks, was inspired by the fire escapes and washing lines in Ginsberg's backyard.

The mid-1950s was a time of exodus for the Beats. Burroughs left New York in December 1953 for Tangier. Apart from a short stay in 1965, he did not live in the United States again for more than twenty years, returning as a prodigal son in 1974 when he felt the atmosphere was finally amiable enough for him to live here peaceably. Kerouac continued to shuttle back and forth across the country, spending most of his time in California or Mexico City. He made a brief trip to Tangier in 1957 but did not like it and was back in New York for the publication of *On the Road.* Corso moved on to Cambridge, Massachusetts, where his first book, *The Vestal Lady on Brattle,* was published. Then he joined Ginsberg in San Francisco, traveled with him to Mexico City and from there on to Paris.

Ginsberg also left the city for an extended period. Apart from a four-month stopover en route to Tangier, he did not return to the city until August 1958. He first explored the jungles of Chiapas, Mexico, for six months before spending almost three years in San Francisco. Thereafter he toured Europe before living with Burroughs and Corso for a year or so in the Beat Hotel in Paris. When Ginsberg returned to New York City, he found that everything had changed. The publication of *On the Road* in September 1957 had made Kerouac famous and much in demand for television talk shows and interviews. Kerouac's sojourn in Europe had been short, and he was living with his girlfriend, Joyce Glassman, at her midtown apartment when the book came out and became an immediate best-seller. His unsuccessful attempts to handle the resultant fame and media attention are related very effectively in her autobiography, *Minor Characters.*

Kerouac used the money from *On the Road* to set up house with his mother in suburban Northport, Long Island, but she refused to return from Florida, where she was then living, unless Ginsberg and Burroughs were banned from the house. Kerouac's preference for his mother over his friends and literary associates effectively ended his participation in the group, although he often came into New York for drunken weekends until his death from alcoholism in 1969. Kerouac covered his shyness by drinking, but alcohol made him loud and sometimes belligerent, often resulting in bar-room scuffles and fights.

On the Road caught the public imagination, and Greenwich Village began to fill with "weekend beatniks," a term coined by Herb Caen of the *San Francisco Chronicle* when writing about North Beach, San Francisco. But the original Beats had long gone. A decade had passed since the events chronicled in *On the Road* and *Howl*. Some of the players were already dead or had moved to the country. Others, like Burroughs and Corso, were expatriates, and the small-time gangsters and hoodlums Burroughs had hung out with in the forties were never part of the Greenwich Village scene. Herbert Huncke stuck to an uptown beat. The hero of *On the Road,* Neal Cassady, lived in California and had always made only short visits to New York. California was also the home of most of the second-generation Beats: Gary Snyder, Philip Whalen, Lawrence Ferlinghetti, Bob Kaufman, and the other heroes of Kerouac's books.

New York had a few home-grown second-generation Beats of its own, most notably LeRoi Jones (now Imamu Amiri Baraka) and Diane diPrima, two poets influenced by Ginsberg. But Ginsberg's own favorite New York poets were Ed Marshall and Frank O'Hara. Ginsberg made contact with all these new poets when he and his lover, Peter Orlovsky, passed through New York on their way to Europe in the winter of 1956-1957. They returned in August 1958 and found an apartment on the Lower East Side, between Avenues A and B at 170 East Second Street, overlooking an all-night Jewish bakery. Ginsberg enjoyed the sound of the noisy trucks coming and going all night, collecting fresh bagels and rye bread. The bakery also had a big clock in its front window, which was useful since Ginsberg didn't own one. It was here that Ginsberg wrote his greatest work, *Kaddish,* an elegy for his dead mother.

The poem had its inspiration in an all-night visit with his friend Zev Putterman, who lived on the corner of West Fourth and West Tenth streets— one of those anomalous Village addresses that so confuse tourists. They sat up talking, playing Ray Charles records, and taking morphine and Methedrine, a form of amphetamine new to Ginsberg. As the night wore on, Ginsberg chanted the verses of Shelley's *Adonais*. Then Putterman produced his old bar-mitzvah book of Hebrew ritual, and together they read aloud the central passages of the Kaddish, the Jewish prayer for the dead. Morning came and Ginsberg left, walking home to the Lower East Side.

He reached Seventh Avenue and walked south, through all the surreal empty streets, past all the familiar clubs and bookstores, groceries and delis, all closed and shuttered. The rhythms of the Kaddish rang in his head, and on reaching home, he sat down to write. *Kaddish* was written in one long thirty-hour session, beginning with an account of its genesis: "Downtown Manhattan, clear winter noon, and I've been up all night, talking, talking, reading the Kaddish aloud, listening to Ray Charles blues shout blind on the phonograph . . . / I go out and walk the street, look back over my shoulder, Seventh Avenue, the battlements of window office buildings shouldering each other high, under a cloud, tall as the sky."

. . . . .

By the end of 1958 the Village was being overrun by weekend beatniks. Ginsberg reported to his publisher, Lawrence Ferlinghetti: "God, reporters all over, all asking the same questions and no end in sight, it's getting stranger and stranger, life. Beginning to get invites from TV programs but have been holding out for scene where I can read poetry rather than discuss Beatnikism. The world is really mad."

The Village streets were filled with tourists and weekend beatniks in beards and berets. Beatnik cartoons appeared in *The New Yorker,* television companies made documentaries, and poet Ted Jones and photographer Fred McDarrah set up Rent-a-Beatnik, charging the squares steep fees to have their parties attended by a scruffy beatnik carrying bongo drums and a sheaf of bad poetry. The *New York Post* ran a twelve-part series on beatniks, and *Life* and *Time* worried whether America would survive this attack on its moral values. The situation was summed up very succinctly by Ted Jones in his poem "Let's Play Something":

> Let's play something. Let's play anything. Let's play bohemian, and wear odd clothes, and grow a beard or a ponytail, live in the Village for 200.00 a month for one small pad and stroll through Washington Square Park with a guitar and a chick looking sad.

Corso fled back to Europe, first to Athens and then to Paris, where he was joined in 1961 by Ginsberg and Orlovsky, who were slowly making their way to India. Kerouac moved to Florida with his mother. Burroughs remained in Tangier. The transition from Beat to beatnik was complete, and it would not be long before the tolerant streets of Greenwich Village and the Lower East Side were filled with a new crop of bohemians: the hippies.

THE BEAT SCENE IN THE WEST

PAUL PERRY (ESSAY DATE 1990)

SOURCE: Perry, Paul. "Origins." *On the Bus*, pp. 3-39. New York: Thunder's Mouth Press, 1990.

In the following excerpt, Perry discusses the genesis of the use of LSD as a means of enhancing artistic and literary creativity that was embraced by Ken Kesey and The Merry Pranksters.

Where did the "psychedelic revolution" begin? Certainly not with Ken Kesey and his Merry Band of Pranksters. Their role was to experiment in public and record it while it was happening, trailblazing a new frontier that attracted others. They didn't invent psychedelic drugs, they only used what was released from Pandora's box.

Science Discovers a Revolutionary New Headache Cure

To see where the psychedelic revolution really started, we have to go back to April 16, 1943, when LSD's creator, Albert Hofmann, mixed a batch of the stuff that he had synthesized from rye fungus five years earlier. He was hoping to find a cure for the common migraine and decided to do more research with a substance he called "LSD-25." While mixing it up, a small amount was absorbed through his fingertips. Notes in his diary record history's first acid trip:

> [What overcame me was] a remarkable but not unpleasant state of intoxication . . . characterized by an intense stimulation of the imagination, an altered state of awareness of the world. As I lay in a dazed condition with eyes closed there surged up from me a succession of fantastic, rapidly changing imagery of a striking reality and depth, alternating with a vivid, kaleidoscopic play of colors. This condition gradually passed off after about three hours.

Three days later Dr. Hofmann continued his solo experiment, taking 250 micrograms, and bicycling home through the streets of Zurich, Switzerland. That small dose had a large effect on the chemist:

> I had great difficulty in speaking coherently. My field of vision swayed before me, and objects appeared distorted like images in curved mirrors. I

had the impression of being unable to move from the spot, although my assistant told me afterwards that we had cycled at a good pace. Occasionally I felt as if I were out of my body. . . . I thought I had died. My ego was suspended somewhere in space and I saw my body lying dead on the sofa.

> (*LSD: My Problem Child*, New York: McGraw-Hill, 1980)

By accident, Dr. Hofmann had discovered the kind of experience that mystics patiently search for for years, an encounter with altered, fresh perception. He didn't see it that way, however. When asked about LSD, Hofmann often referred to it as his "problem child."

Like many people with problem children, Hofmann was proud of his offspring. He saw many therapeutic applications for LSD and was happy to see it being used by scientists interested in how the mind works.

Still, LSD offered too many enticements to the spy community, mystics, and fun-seekers to keep it in the lab with common psychiatric drugs. Before long, the Central Intelligence Agency became interested in the possibilities of LSD as a mind control drug. Aroused by the scientific work of Dr. Werner Stoll (son of Sandoz president Arthur Stoll) the CIA began experiments of their own into uses of LSD.

They experimented on convicts, soldiers, the general populace, and even each other, in a research program known as ARTICHOKE. They tested many substances in this program, including morphine, mescaline, and even ether. But LSD was their favorite, perhaps because of the enormous effects that could come from so small a dose.

There was considerable experimentation being done outside the CIA, too. It seemed as though everyone was trying to figure out what to do with LSD.

One of these was Captain Alfred Hubbard, a wealthy, former World War II Army intelligence officer, whose enthusiastic sharing of the substance with members of his influential circle led him to be known as the "Johnny Appleseed of LSD". A unique character even for the surveillance community, he was a speculator in uranium mining, a one-time arms dealer, and a friend to industrialists and artists. He was what would eventually be called an "acid head," and he claimed to have seen his own conception while on acid, right down to his own parents having sex.

> It was the deepest mystical thing I've ever seen. I saw myself as a tiny mite in a big swamp with a

spark of intelligence. I saw my mother and father having intercourse. It was all clear.

(Martin A. Lee and Bruce Shlain, *Acid Dreams: The CIA, LSD and the Sixties Rebellion,* New York: Grove Press, 1985.)

In his search for people interested in this drug, he met and befriended Dr. Humphry Osmond, a psychiatrist at Weyburn Hospital in Saskatchewan, Canada, who was studying LSD's effect on the mentally ill. Dr. Osmond's writings would broaden the LSD community still further by reaching an influential author who would write a classic treatise on the psychedelic experience.

The "Miracle of Naked Existence"

Aldous Huxley's book-length essay, *The Doors of Perception,* was, for many, a literary door into the realm of psychedelics, that defined, perhaps as far as words can, the psychedelic experience. Huxley's own interest in psychedelics arose from reading a report on LSD written by Dr. Osmond. Fascinated, he offered himself as a guinea pig to the researcher, who in 1953, gave the author of *Brave New World* a healthy dose of LSD. The experience led the enthusiastic and articulate Huxley to expound on the marvels of the drug. In both *The Doors of Perception* and in public, the author discussed brain function, the ability of psychedelic drugs to open the mind's screening process to a virtual torrent of sensation, and the general "beatific" experience of it all. He didn't find that psychedelic drugs imitated psychosis, but instead that they opened the mind to a world of fresh perceptions.

> What Adam had seen on the morning of creation—the miracle, moment by moment, of naked existence . . . flowers shining with their own inner light and all but quivering under the pressure of the significance with which they were charged. . . . Words like 'grace' and 'transfiguration' came to mind.
>
> (*The Doors of Perception,* New York: Perennial Library, 1970)

Later, Huxley had an LSD experience with Captain Hubbard. It is said that Hubbard was so well-connected that the Vatican allowed him to administer LSD as part of the Catholic faith. Indeed, a newsletter item dated December 8, 1957, from Reverend J.E. Brown, a Catholic priest at the Cathedral of the Holy Rosary in Vancouver, seems to confirm that. From Reverend Brown's letter:

> We humbly ask Our Heavenly Mother the Virgin Mary, help of all who call upon Her to aid us to know and understand the true qualities of these psychedelics, the full capacities of man's noblest faculties and according to God's laws to use them for the benefit of mankind here and in eternity.

Years before Jerry Garcia began to lead Dead heads in celebration, the irrepressible Captain Al Hubbard served as the original "Captain Trips."

Tripping Draws Admirers: Life Magazine, Christopher Isherwood and Clare Boothe Luce . . .

By the mid-1950s, LSD was being used socially by intellectuals, scientists, and artists, such as Aldous Huxley, Dr. Humphry Osmond, philosopher Alan Watts and others in a Los Angeles social circle acquainted with Captain Hubbard. All became vigorous advocates of LSD's benefits. Huxley and Osmond were especially interested in challenging the prevailing belief that LSD induced insanity. While people who had repeatedly come close to insanity (alcoholics with delirium tremens, for instance) described that experience in awful terms, they usually spoke glowingly of their LSD experiences.

At this time, word of mouth began to draw others to sample the drug, for example, Henry Luce, the president of Time/Life, and his wife Clare Boothe Luce, had dropped acid with Huxley and the novelist Christopher Isherwood. LSD caused Luce to experience a vision of God while out on the golf course, and led him to "hear" heavenly music in a cactus garden while visiting the American West. Luce's *Life* Magazine soon showed editorial sympathies toward the psychedelic experience, publishing a seventeen-page article on "magic" mushrooms (written by R. Gordon Wasson, a vice-president of J.P. Morgan and Company) that is a virtual love song to the visions they induce:

> We were never more awake, and the visions came whether our eyes were opened or closed. . . . They began with art motifs, angular such as might decorate carpets or textiles or wallpaper or the drawing board of an architect. They evolved into palaces with courts, arcades, gardens—resplendent palaces all laid over with semi-precious stones. . . . Later it was as though the walls of our house had dissolved, and my spirit had flown forth, and I was suspended in mid-air viewing landscapes of mountains, with camel caravans advancing slowly across the slopes, the mountains rising tier above tier to the very heavens. . . . The thought crossed my mind: could divine mushrooms be the secret that lay behind the ancient Mysteries?
>
> ("Seeking the Magic Mushroom," *Life,* May 27, 1957)

The article caused hundreds of people to head for Mexico in search of psychedelic bliss. Among those eventually lured to mushrooms by Wasson's article was Dr. Timothy Leary.

Dr. Leary Takes an Interest

Although head of clinical research and psychology at the Kaiser Foundation Hospital in Oakland, California, Leary was ready to devote his life to something entirely new. His first wife had committed suicide, he was divorced from his second one, and the thought of spending a lifetime in academia wasn't as appealing to him as it had once been.

On a trip to Mexico he took some magic mushrooms and had "the deepest religious experience of my life."

He returned to join Harvard University and establish a psilocybin research project. With him in this endeavor was Richard Alpert, an assistant professor of psychology. Alpert later became known as Baba Ram Dass, and is the India-mystic influenced American spiritual leader who is widely-known for his autobiographical book dealing with spirituality and enlightenment, "Be Here Now."

LSD as a Government Weapon

Through all of this, the CIA had a growing interest in LSD. Relatively small doses of the psychedelic could potentially affect the populations of whole cities, a capacity the CIA was interested in developing during the new era of cold war. They believed, for instance, that a dose properly introduced into a public water system might render a city helpless; that a smear of acid on a government official's drinking glass could make him act like a fool in public; that LSD given to a prisoner of war could erase his reluctance to talk.

There were many possible uses for LSD and other psychedelic drugs in the world of espionage. To explore these, the CIA financed the MK-ULTRA program in 1953, its purpose being to examine the mind-control possibilities of psychedelics.

MK-ULTRA experimenters tested LSD on each other as well as on unsuspecting fellow CIA employees. They dosed people during coffee breaks, Christmas parties, dinners, lunches, official retreats, at times administering these drugs when convenient, or simply interesting to do so.

Among the results: One CIA agent wept as he described his trip, saying he didn't want to leave the beautiful place that LSD took him to. An MK-ULTRA report said that the drug had made him "psychotic." Another fellow agent, it was reported, "Couldn't pull himself together." He said that his

LSD trip was like a bad dream that wouldn't stop, one in which there was a monster out to get him in each car that passed.

These surreptitious experiments, practiced under the institutional respectability of government authority, backfired when a group of army technicians were dosed by CIA personnel at an informal work conference in the Maryland woods. A doctor slipped LSD into the dinner drinks of everyone present and then announced what he had done. It made for an evening of laughter and unintelligible talk and appeared to be a good time for everyone except Dr. Frank Olson, a biological warfare researcher.

There are certain people for whom LSD brings internal conflicts to the surface which might otherwise be surpressed, particularly if they are unprepared for the experience as Dr. Olson was. In the weeks following his unexpected LSD trip, he became unhappy, confused, and convinced that he was hearing voices and being harassed by the CIA. He became so despondent that he offered his resignation. In an attempt to undo some of the damage they had caused, CIA officials tried to get Dr. Olson counseling and they sent him to New York City accompanied by an agent. The CIA brought Olson to see Dr. Harold Abramson at Columbia University, who was one of their chief LSD researchers. He advised that Olson should receive psychiatric help, claiming that he was stuck in "a psychotic state . . . with delusions of persecution . . . crystallized by the LSD experience." Plans were made to send the dosed doctor to a sanitarium in Maryland.

But before that could happen, Olson died by hurtling through a closed, tenth-story Manhattan hotel window. His death was determined to be a suicide.

Without taking responsibility for his death, the CIA paid Olson's widow a full government pension. They were able to cover up the incident for twenty years, until it was uncovered by a Senate investigation of the agency's covert activities.

Still, CIA experimentation continued. A CIA operative set up a "safe house" in San Francisco and then paid prostitutes $100 a night to bring men to the apartment and dose them with LSD before having sex. The operative watched from behind a two-way mirror as dozens of men had sex with prostitutes under the influence of psychedelic drugs.

Military units were given LSD and asked to perform basic tasks like marching in formation, driving jeeps, and reading radar scopes. These experiments were filmed and shown later to demonstrate the incapacitating effects of LSD. By the mid-1960s, the U.S. Army alone had tested LSD on nearly 1500 soldiers.

You have to keep this all in mind before considering Ken Kesey and the Merry Pranksters. They didn't bring psychedelic drugs into the world. They merely helped make public what the CIA, the U.S. Army, Albert Hofmann, Aldous Huxley, Timothy Leary, and Clare Boothe Luce already knew: LSD re-opens doors of perception that modern life has closed.

Our Story Begins

For Ken Kesey those doors opened in 1959.

He came to Stanford University in 1958 after winning a Woodrow Wilson Fellowship, which was designed to help graduate students who had an interest in becoming college teachers. While at Stanford, Kesey opted to try out for the Stanford Writing Program using a football novel he was writing at the time as an entree into the department that novelist Wallace Stegner had built.

Kesey and his wife Faye found a house on Perry Lane, the bohemian section of Palo Alto. This was an entirely new environment for Kesey, a powerfully built 24-year-old country boy from Eugene, Oregon who had been a collegiate wrestler and drama student as an undergraduate at the University of Oregon.

Perry Lane was a literary world that was set apart even from Stanford University itself. Here Kesey found a suburban California bohemia, and friends such as Jane Burton, Ed McClanahan, Chloe Scott, Gurney Norman, and Ken Babbs, who would all later take part, to various degrees, in his Merry Prankster adventures. It was on Perry Lane that Kesey grew a beard and began playing folk songs on a guitar, here that Kesey ate his first marijuana brownie and got drunk for the second time (the first being his wedding day). It was also here that Kesey quit working on the football novel and started work on *Zoo*, a novel about a rodeo rider's son who moves to North Beach in San Francisco, where he experiences the communalism of the Beat generation. Ken Babbs was with him on many of his research trips to North Beach and recalls:

One of the places we went to in North Beach was a coffee house called "The Place." Every Tuesday they had Free Speech Night. They had a balcony there and anyone who wanted to could get up and rant and rail about anything they wanted. I loved it. The same guys would always be in there,

drinking coffee and beer and wine and listening to the new speeches. They would sit there, never crack a smile or anything. They were the regulars, assessing new talent as it came in.

As part of the classroom experience, Kesey and the other Stanford writing students, who included Robert Stone and Larry McMurtry, read their works-in-progress to the rest of the class. But this year, 1959, Kesey was reading from *Zoo*, which didn't quite have the edge of his later work. Although it was largely responsible for getting him a graduate school scholarship, it remains unpublished, a student work that helped him develop the immense talent that was soon to reach fruition. A year later, after working in a mental hospital and taking part in drug experiments, Kesey would be reading unforgettable work that became *One Flew Over the Cuckoo's Nest*.

Drug Experiments Lead to the Writing of Cuckoo's Nest

Perry Lane and Stanford University were eye-openers for Kesey. In this academic setting he was exposed to literary disciplines that were new to him, just as he was exposed to people who broadened his world view. It was also here that Kesey elected to become one of the guinea pigs in what later proved to be part of the MK-ULTRA program. The CIA farmed out this top-secret program to a number of researchers, among them Dr. Leo Hollister at the Veterans Hospital in Menlo Park.

They were offering small cash stipends (under $100) for anyone who would partake of psychedelic drugs while researchers questioned, observed, and tested them. When Vic Lovell, a Perry Lane resident and psychology student, found out about the offer he convinced Kesey to enter the experimental program with him. Lovell had introduced Richard Alpert to marijuana and was himself curious about the effects of psychedelic drugs on the mind.

Over the next few weeks Kesey was given a variety of psycho-active drugs—from psilocybin and mescaline to LSD and the amphetamine IT-290. Some of it, he later told friends, was real bad, some real good, and some downright inspirational. But he believed that all would be better suited to use in a non-institutional setting.

In a short time, LSD found its way to Perry Lane, where Kesey and others were able to take this psychedelic drug in a more relaxed setting, where they could look at the world through these "doors of perception" without a hospital staff of white-coated researchers supervising the experience.

ON THE SUBJECT OF...

ANDY CLAUSEN

Andy Clausen is often described as a poet of the common man, a writer whose works examine human experience on personal, familial, and national levels. Clausen's work has been both influenced and praised by such notable Beats as Lawrence Ferlinghetti, Allen Ginsberg, Gregory Corso, and Jack Kerouac. He has described his own poetry as "sentence movies." Clausen has been an active performer and organizer of public readings, maintaining that full appreciation of poetry can only be achieved through oral presentation. He has performed his verse so frequently that some critics assert that his work has been heard far more than it has been read. Among his collections are *Extreme Unction* (1974), *Shoe Be Do Be Ee-op* (1975), and *Austin, Texas, Austin, Texas* (1981). Clausen founded and began editing the underground *Renegade* magazine in 1977. He also taught at the Naropa Institute's Jack Kerouac School of Disembodied Poetics in 1980.

He discussed this fresh perspective drugs offered with the *Peninsula Times Tribune,* a Bay Area newspaper, in 1964:

> With these drugs, your perception is altered enough that you find yourself looking out of completely strange eyeholes. All of us have a great deal of our minds locked shut. And these drugs seem to be the key to open these locked doors.

In 1960, he took a summer job as a psychiatric aide at the Veterans Hospital. There he worked the graveyard shift, mopping floors, and talking to nurses and patients.

The Veterans Hospital afforded some of the best material for a novel that Kesey had ever seen. He was allowed to bring a typewriter to the nurses' station and write when his duties were completed. His experience in the hospital engaged his sympathies for the mentally ill, or people designated as such by the system and provided the theme of his first published work.

The characters in *One Flew Over the Cuckoo's Nest* were largely drawn from the patients and nurses surrounding him. But one night, after taking a dose of peyote, Kesey envisioned Chief Bromden, the schizophrenic Native American who narrates this incredible book about individuality and the system's desire to squash it flat.

Peyote helped Kesey discover the narrator (he admits to never having known such a character) just as it helped him clearly see the story line of man versus machine. As Kesey wrote in his Prankster anthology collection *Garage Sale*:

> [It] was after choking down eight of the little cactus plants that I wrote the first three pages. These pages remained almost completely unchanged through the numerous rewrites the book went through, and from this first spring I drew all the passion and perception the narrator spoke with during the ten months writing that followed.

The next ten months were extraordinary ones for Kesey. He worked hard at *Cuckoo's Nest,* often writing at night when he could be totally alone and then reading his work in class at Stanford. For much of the semester Kesey's writing professor was Malcolm Cowley, who had discovered Jack Kerouac and who had edited the works of William Faulkner and Ernest Hemingway. Cowley insisted on a supportive atmosphere in class, reminding his students not to become too cut-throat with their peers lest they have their throats cut in retribution. He also is responsible for this maxim, intended to help maintain a constructive atmosphere of respect, among students: "Remember, it is just as hard to write a bad novel as it is a good one."

This was the best environment that a young novelist like Kesey could hope for. Bearing testimony to this was the subsequent success of his classmates in the program, who included novelists Larry McMurtry, Ed McClanahan, Gurney Norman, Peter Beagle, Ken Babbs and Robert Stone. With supportive friends, an intellectual community, good material to draw from, and LSD to help him see it more clearly, his talent soon began to flourish.

JOHN ARTHUR MAYNARD (ESSAY DATE 1991)

SOURCE: Maynard, John Arthur. Introduction to *Venice West: The Beat Generation in Southern California,* pp. 1-21. New Brunswick, N.J.: Rutgers University Press, 1991.

In the following essay, Maynard investigates the role of Venice, California, in Beat culture and history.

Venice, California, has seldom been an entirely respectable place. Founded in 1905 as a genteel retreat for esthetically-minded Los Angeles businessmen, it quickly became the Coney Island of the West—and image-wise, at least, things have been all downhill from there. Although its property values are higher than they used to be, so is the price of everything else that fronts on the Pacific Ocean; recent crackdowns may have chased some of the drug dealers and squatters away from the beach, but there is still a fundamental raunchiness to the Venice Ocean Front that only the bulldozers will ever do away with completely.

The outward symbol of the boardwalk's economy is the mom-and-pop t-shirt stand; the outward signs of its culture include buskers, panhandlers, skaters, bodybuilders, esoteric healers, aspiring musicians, chainsaw jugglers, badly weathered murals, dirty-mouthed comedians and guitar-playing Sufi mystics on skates. There is something faintly threatening about it all, an energetic gutter craziness that no one really claims to have under control. Venice has always been a place where meanness and creativity run too close together for comfort. If there are no plaques dedicated to the poets and artists who made it famous as an enclave of the Beat Generation in the late fifties—no memorials to Stuart Perkoff, Charles Foster, Alexander Trocchi, "Mad Mike" Magdalani, or even the man who introduced "Venice West" to the world, Lawrence Lipton—it is because if they were still around in force, respectable people would undoubtedly be making plans to chase them away.

But there are signs that they and their culture were there. Not on the bookshelves, certainly; few of their works, with the exception of Trocchi's *Cain's Book,* were or ever will be published. At the height of their notoriety, when there seemed to be no end to the public's appetite for things "beat," the poets of Venice West congratulated themselves on sharing the "greatest drive for nonrecognition in the history of literature." (This book may be read as their collective recognition.) Even the Ocean Front's lone bookstore—the local counterpart to San Francisco's City Lights—lacks a section devoted to the Beat Generation, let alone to Venice West. No, most of the hints are subtle, and there is something conspiratorial about being able to recognize them. A hand-lettered sign in an apartment window reads "BIRD LIVES;" another quotes a line from the beat poet, Bob Kaufman: "Charlie Parker was an electrician. He went around wiring people." A small art gallery now occupies the storefront slot that once housed the Venice West Café, while a few blocks away, a single cast-iron column, towering above the Promenade like the mast of a sunken ship, marks the site of the Gas House, where the Beat Generation of Venice West briefly tried to take its case to the people. Across the lawn at the Pavilion, where the spray-painters come to write at night, it is sometimes possible to find the closest thing to a monument that the Venice beats are likely to get.

Graffiti may or may not have the high cultural significance that is sometimes claimed for it, but since it is a form of nobudget advertising, a few simple conclusions can sometimes be drawn from it. One of these is that it meant something to the writer; another is that the writer expected it to be understood more or less instantaneously by some imagined reader. That lends a shabby but defiant significance to the fact that every now and then, in place of the usual obscenities, passages from Revelation and threats to kill members of rival gangs, someone takes the time to draw a cartoon figure labeled "Maynard G. Krebs" on the wall of the Venice Pavilion. Almost thirty years ago, when "The Many Loves of Dobie Gillis" was one of the most popular comedies on television, almost any American would have recognized Dobie's beatnik sidekick, Maynard. Not one of Max Shulman's original characters, he is said to have been written into the show for the express purpose of capitalizing on an improbable national obsession with the exotic, "poetry-spouting" bohemian subculture of the late fifties and very early sixties. The show is back in syndication on some of the cable networks, but that hardly explains why, after more than thirty years, the old image, in the words of a Venice poet, still "makes a bridge to the eye."

But oddly enough, the cartoon figure seldom looks anything like the TV character. As played by Bob Denver, Maynard G. Krebs looked only marginally different from anyone else, except that he wore shirts with no collars and had the faintest hint of a goatee (but not a mustache, of course; that would have been too "masculine," and ineffectuality was the essence of his character). By contrast, the figure on the Pavilion wall is rather menacing, and brings to mind the unlikely fact that in his own time, the "beatnik," like any other "weirdo," tended to be laughed at in preference to being feared.

Like the cartoon character of the 1990s, the standard beatnik stereotype of the late 1950s was generally represented as a sly, knowing, physically unimpressive (read: weak and unathletic) young man, usually bearded, who dressed shabbily, wore his sunglasses indoors, went around in sandals all year long, and never seemed to do much of anything. A cigarette dangling from his mouth and a floppy beret on his uncombed head, he was almost never depicted without either a knowing grin or a hostile smirk pasted across his face. He was smug, inscrutable, rather silly, and utterly convinced of his own intellectual superiority; he spoke, whenever possible, in vague, smokey hip talk or rhyming couplets, and it was just as easy to see through his pretentions as it would have been to pull the "shades" away from his eyes. He seemed to embody two middle-class prejudices at once: the old one against intellectuals, and the even older one against "people who don't work." Since it was taken for granted that the beatnik "didn't wash," he was also an affront to the modern mania for going about with no more personal scent than a piece of china.

His female counterpart was the beat chick, who was equally silly but portrayed as considerably sexier. She tended to wear bulky sweaters, black stockings, and lots of eye makeup. Her hair could be long or short, but always out of fashion—no home perms or hairspray for the beat chick. Since she was principally a male fantasy, it was assumed that she was "available," although how she ever connected with a eunuch like the stereo-typical male beatnik was a good question. What she probably needed, in the eyes of most observers, was a "real man." She was weird and spacey, sitting in coffeehouses all night with no expression on her face at all, so it was easy to imagine that she had never met one.

These may be laughable images, but they correspond to the ones presented in all seriousness by *Reader's Digest* in the illustration that accompanied Paul O'Neil's article, "Life Among the Beatniks," in the April 1960 issue. A line drawing, the picture was a collage of all the standard beat clichés—a pretty, tousle-haired, and obviously neurotic girl staring straight at the reader; an earnest-looking young man with a goatee reading poetry; a group of bearded, sweatshirted men playing chess late at night in a coffeehouse. Though certainly among the more innocuous scenes in the history of shock literature, they were meant to be disturbing, or at least lamentable, and *Reader's Digest* seldom miscalculated. Its readers knew the beats represented a kind of low-grade warfare being conducted against their way of life—a war all the more perplexing because it was pointless. It would have been bad enough if the beatniks were communists, out to abolish the good life for everyone; instead, they attacked the good life by refusing to acknowledge it as good. This was war on common sense. What was so bad about being

normal? Or, as O'Neil himself asked, "What have we done to deserve this?"

Nor was this all. From these images there emerged a pair of sub-stereotypes, one "good," one "bad." The "good" beatnik was a harmless, funny fellow like Maynard G. Krebs—loyal, good-hearted and honest, but naive and given to panic at the thought of "work!" The "bad" beatnik, on the other hand, figured in crime story after crime story, especially after the San Francisco Police Department initiated a heavily publicized crackdown on the beat enclave in North Beach in the summer of 1958. The "bad" beatnik smoked marijuana and, by some accounts, took heroin, which automatically put him in the same category with another stock figure in fiction and crime reporting: the hopped-up, withdrawal-crazed dope addict. More often, however—since the broadcast media had strict guidelines about the representation of drugs, even in crime dramas, and the comics could not mention them at all—the "bad" beatnik was represented as a social misfit, perhaps a psychopath, but certainly a man who had rejected conventional society because he was incapable of succeeding in it.

In every one of its manifestations, the image of the beatnik posed the same question: why would anyone want to *be* like that? While for most Americans it was a question of how he could be so "wrong," it was inevitable that some should wonder whether or not he was "right," or at least right enough to teach them something about their own options in life. Even among those who rejected everything he stood for, there was just enough seductive power in the stock figure of the beatnik to make him an attractive nuisance. The best part about the temptation was that it could be indulged, if only in fantasy, on any number of levels. That was what Norman Podhoretz and other public-spirited intellectuals were afraid of, and they were right to fear it.

Behind the silly, opportunistic images, there were, of course, real people with real beliefs and a powerful and tenacious commitment to them. But perhaps because it is so hard to separate them from the trivialized images that linger from their own time, few historians have paid much attention to them. Allen J. Matusow presents a standard, and characteristically brief, description of them in *The Unraveling of America* (1984):

> By the late 1950s, a fully developed beat subculture had emerged not only in North Beach but also in Venice West (near Los Angeles), New York's Greenwich Village, and a few other hip resorts in between. The beats possessed deviant tastes in

language, literature, music, drugs, and religion. Profoundly alienated from dominant American values, practicing voluntary poverty and spade cool, they rejected materialism, competition, the work ethic, hygiene, sexual repression, monogamy, and the Faustian quest to subdue nature. There were, to be sure, never more than a few thousand fulltime beats, but thanks to the scandalized media, images of beat penetrated and disconcerted the middle classes. Beats, like hula hoops, were a fad.

They were more than a fad, of course; they were a direct reproach to the consumer society around them, and since the people who laughed at them also understood this, it would be a mistake to dismiss their influence on the basis of the silly sensationalism that actually helped to spread it. But that is largely what has happened. Thirty-three years after the publication of Jack Kerouac's *On the Road,* the beats are still a historical sideshow, studied in hagiographic detail by specialists but ignored at little peril. Scholarship about them tends to take the form of literary criticism, biography, or background material for studies on the events of the sixties. Thus there is a growing body of work on the poems and novels themselves, on the lives of Jack Kerouac, Allen Ginsberg, William Burroughs, and their friends, and on the beats' contributions to the better-publicized and more attractively photographed movements that came after them. Even the historians who do take them seriously tend to show them the same sort of appreciation usually given to a good opening act at a rock concert: not bad at all, guys, and thanks for warming up the crowd.

As already noted, Allen Matusow is one historian who does take the beats seriously, although his admiration for the counterculture in general is fairly restrained. He identifies the beats as the vanguard of a revolution in the relationship of mind to body, or, more precisely, of the libido to the rational mind. Applying Norman O. Brown's mid-sixties concept of the Dionysian ego ("a new ego, a body ego . . . overflowing with love, knowing no limits, affirming life") to the bohemians who had helped to make Brown's ideas acceptable, Matusow sees them as the founders of a latter-day paganism whose exaltation of the nonrational has pushed its way into everyday life. "The creation of the Dionysian ego, the ego in service of liberated Eros," he writes, ". . . was a project millions of mothers would soon understand implicitly and fear with good reason." Lawrence Lipton, the self-appointed "Shaman" of Venice West, would have been happy to endorse his conclusion that by the end of the following decade, "Dionysus had been absorbed into the dominant culture and domesticated, and in the process routed the Protestant ethic." Since his primary concern in *The Unraveling of America* is with liberalism and public policy, Matusow does not explain this transformation in detail, but he comes close to seeing the Venice beats, at least, in the way they saw themselves.

The cultural historian William O'Neill seems more concerned with the momentum and direction of the counterculture than with its origins. He does give the beats credit for contributing to the movement its uniform and its marching order:

> Even in the 1950's and very early sixties, when people still worried about conformity and the silent generation, there were different drummers to whose beat millions would one day march. The bohemians of that era (called "beatniks" or "beats") were only a handful, but they practiced free love, took drugs, repudiated the straight world, and generally showed which way the wind was blowing.

O'Neill concludes this observation with an astonishing throwaway line: "When the bohemian impulse quickened, dropouts knew what was expected of them." Why should nonconformists need to know what is expected of them? For that matter, why should millions of young people in the late sixties have expressed their individuality by making themselves look almost exactly like one other? O'Neill acknowledges conformity as a conservative force but neglects its role as a force for raising hell. Despite his tendency to equate popularity with validity, he overlooks one of the most interesting differences between the beats and the hippies: the beats instinctively distrusted publicity, while the hippies, raised in the age of television and saturation advertising, seemed to think it proved they were right.

In *The Fifties: The Way We Really Were,* Douglas T. Miller and Marion Nowak contribute more substantially to an understanding of the beats in their own time, and especially in relation to their critics. Although their book is weakened by an all-too-obvious loathing for the tastes and aspirations of ordinary people—as well as an over-eagerness to define middle-class culture only by its excesses—Miller and Nowak do a convincing job of explaining why the mainstream intellectuals of the late fifties felt justified in using strong-arm, or, as the authors put it, "McCarthyist" tactics against the beats. That was the way of intellectual power struggles in an era of consensus. The intellectuals' exaggerated hostility made it "all right" for others to attack the beats, just as their acquiescence had made it easier for conservatives to put the Old Left out of business. Miller and Nowak also believe the media chose to focus on the beats because other, more significant manifestations of dissent might have been harder to ridicule; by calling them "the only rebellion around," Paul O'Neil implied in *Life* that rebellion itself was childish and inconsequential.

On the other hand, I think Miller and Nowak have failed to recognize the extent to which the media acted against the presumed interests of mainstream society—or succeeded in having it both ways. For example, where they see "bland journalese" in a *Life* article contrasting bohemian life in Venice West with middle-class life in Hutchinson, Kansas, *I* see carefully crafted language that made it possible to promote the one while pretending to uphold the other. The fact is that despite its celebration of middle-class values, the essential message of the commercial media, then as now, was not "you never had it so good," but "you're *missing* something." Why would anyone spend good advertising money on a medium calculated to make people satisfied with what they have? Can such a massive engine of dissatisfaction always be assumed to be fully under control?

As for the beats themselves, Miller and Nowak consider them an important step, but also a dead end. They see in the beat fad a sign of mass dissatisfaction which called for political action, not artistic withdrawal. Their epitaphs for the fifties are drawn from C. Wright Mills, H. Stuart Hughes, and Paul Goodman. The new day they see dawning in the closing pages of their book is one of a "radicalized," decidedly elitist political consciousness. This interpretation "works," by the airtight logic of the New Left, but it denies any independent power to the beats' own persuasive brand of illogic. I suggest that not to explore that illogic is to ignore a great deal.

In *The Making of a Counterculture* (1969), Theodore Roszak tends to treat the intuitive and antipolitical aspects of the sixties counterculture in exactly the same way. But much of the counterculture was not about political consciousness at all; it was about the possibility of a completely transcendant state of mind. To dismiss the beats, as Roszak does, for "failing" to do their political duty is not only to write history in terms of a desired ending, but to ignore most of what they themselves said they were trying to do. It also ignores the possibility that there *are* more forms of power than are yet accounted for in political theory.

There is certainly no denying that the beats arrived on the scene at a time when middle-class culture seemed triumphant—and when most

Americans, regardless of what kind of work they did, are generally agreed to have thought of themselves as middle class. While a good many middle-class Americans felt insulted by the diet of ideas they were served—by high-pressure commercials, low comedy, and questionable moral standards—few would deny that most of the books, phonograph records, films, magazines, newspapers, radio programming, and television shows of the fifties were intended for mass consumption and professed, at least, to celebrate middle-class values. As Miller and Nowak demonstrate, popular culture made a point of telling the majority of Americans that they were good, honest people who worked hard and deserved everything they got as a result. In return, middle-class Americans were expected to spend more of their earnings than they had dared to part with in the past. That was not all. Mass culture also served the more arcane purpose of helping the nation's intellectuals define what they were *not* and simultaneously reaffirm their claim to the moral and esthetic leadership of the big, boorish, clumsy, tasteless country from which they felt so isolated.

The leadership issue helps to explain why professional thinkers like Norman Podhoretz, Diana Trilling, and even one early ally and sponsor, Kenneth Rexroth, reacted so violently to the literature of the Beat Generation. It was one thing to condemn materialism and crassness in American life; it was another to do so without the slightest sign of respect for those who normally worked that side of the street.

As Miller and Nowak point out, most American intellectuals had reconciled themselves to approving of their country in at least a ritual way—so long as it conceded them their status as a cultural elite, and not a very friendly one at that. "Until the day dawns when a democratic elite will be welcomed and listened to in this country," Bernard Iddings Bell wrote in 1952, "the American who would escape from slavery to crowd culture must expect to have a difficult time of it." The beats hated crowd culture and consumer values as much as Bell did, but in claiming to find the alternative in the untaught human mind, belly, heart, and crotch, they also threatened to put their cultural betters out of business. Who needed a cultural elite when the purest poetry and fiction sprang out of the typewriter with the spontaneity of thought itself?

Jack Kerouac, it must be said, was extremely proud of having gotten an "A" in English from Mark Van Doren at Columbia, and Allen Ginsberg was just as pleased when his friend William Carlos Williams (who never found his medical practice an impediment to writing poetry) contributed the foreword for *Howl and Other Poems.* Few of the beats really rejected literary tradition as ferociously as the keepers of that tradition rejected the beats. The real source of the quarrel was that both parties, the beats and the mainstream intellectuals, believed strongly enough in literature to fight over it. The intellectuals thought of the beats as charlatans and barbarians; the beats thought of *them* as members of a worn-out cultural gentry who had held power for so long that they had forgotten what to do with it. After John Ciardi, James Dickey and John Hollander wrote devastating attacks on *Howl and Other Poems* (1956), for example, Allen Ginsberg responded with the same cordiality: "Poetry has been attacked by an ignorant and frightened bunch of bores who don't understand how it's made, and the trouble with these creeps is they wouldn't know poetry if it came up and buggered them in broad daylight."

To its credit, the Southern California literary establishment was initially friendlier. It was mainly the Venice beats' association with the writer Lawrence Lipton that turned them into pariahs—as the Malibu poet Curtis Zahn called them, "the Great Ungifted." The principal local reviews, *California Quarterly* and *Coastlines,* usually made a point of endorsing all serious literary efforts in the area. Lipton himself had once spent a great deal of energy getting himself accepted into this harried little inner circle of writers, which included Lawrence Spingarn, Thomas McGrath, and James Boyer May—after a lifetime of writing potboilers for large sums of money. Once accepted into the literary fraternity, Lipton seemed determined to get himself thrown out—and when he finally succeeded, he took his Venice protégés with him, effectively cutting them off from any hope of acceptance. Time and Lipton's death have healed some of the damage, but Venice West still represents something of an outlaw strain in Southern California letters. The poet Stuart Perkoff's editor, Paul Vangelisti, draws a hard line between the writer he admired and the tradition he considered pure moonshine.

Where the general public was concerned, it was certainly nothing that the Venice beats wrote or painted that made them the objects of ridicule and even fear. Nor was bohemianism really the issue; if the beats had merely been eccentric, they might have slid along. The Southern California "nut," with a bottle of goat's milk and sign predicting the end of the world, was already a well-established stock figure, and the Los Angeles basin had a long tradition of congeniality to the odd and unconventional. Vedanta, Theosophy, Rosicrucianism, spiritualism, New Thought, and the Self-Realization Fellowship had all found homes there, right along with Krishnamurti, Paramahansa Yogananda, Ernest Holmes, and Aimee Semple MacPherson. Nudism, spiritualism, bodybuilding, ethical vegetarianism, Theocracy, and homeopathy all coexisted more or less amiably with circus-tent revivalism, militant atheism, the Nation of Islam, and the Church of Wicca. The city's older, pre-Forest Lawn-era cemeteries were studded with crypts bearing the sun disk, wings, and cobras of ancient Egypt, while the vast industrial complex collectively known as "Hollywood" housed three of the most powerful crypto-religions of modern times, the American motion picture, television, and record industries.

For more than fifty years, Hollywood had been the world's great channeler and shaper of mass fantasy, with its own inscrutable doctrines of beauty, perfection, reward, punishment and deification. Though not particularly systematic about it, the industry tended to emphasize the marks of virtue that showed in pictures—material goods were easy to photograph, inner peace somewhat trickier—and because of its presence, the fabrication of dreams and beliefs was as calmly accepted in Los Angeles as the harvesting of cotton in Fresno County.

Paradoxically, none of this made Los Angeles a really tolerant city. It was not an easy place to defy convention; it simply tolerated a great many odd conventions. As late as 1959, local authorities were still trying to root communist teachers out of the public schools, and the police department had acquired a national reputation for persecuting homosexuals. But personal eccentricity, if not political or sexual unorthodoxy, was a long-standing tradition, and much that was culturally foreign, cranky, and strange routinely slipped into the realm of tolerated behavior before the gates, as gates will, slammed shut.

The gates slammed hard on the Venice beats. It was one thing to harbor strange ideas; it was another, in the language of the theater, to "kid the show." In Southern California, the show was economic growth—and the unquestioning belief in its goodness. From 1953 to 1963, the Los Angeles metropolitan area added 300,000 new residents a year, or not quite one thousand per day—and there was a reason why people were coming. Between 1950 and 1957, at least 15,000 new single-family houses were built each year in the city alone; in the same time frame, manufacturing jobs in what had been an overwhelmingly service economy more than doubled, growing twice as fast as the population itself. In adjacent counties, housing-tract construction made possible by state and Federal veterans' benefits from two wars swallowed up prime agricultural land. Communities with names like Dairyland, Dairy City, and Dairy Valley incorporated valiantly to save themselves, only to vanish. By 1960, the "Southland" held seven and a half million people, and there was no reason for most people to think it would ever end. Growth was nature's way, and the best thing about it was that there seemed to be something in it for everybody.

That makes it particularly ironic that the Venice beats, preaching the virtues of having nothing in a place where everyone expected to have more tomorrow, should be left out of most accounts of the Beat Generation. They were the movement's point men where the attitudes it challenged were strongest, and yet the inference seems to be that they were not "real" beats—just amateurs from the no-class end of California who never did anything but attract publicity. They certainly attracted plenty of that, but, then, so did that born-again marketing researcher, Allen Ginsberg.

The fact is that the Beat Generation as a whole enjoyed a curious relationship with its own hype. It was always the cultural equivalent of that old science-fiction standby, the cyborg—part human, part manufactured, and no one, least of all the creature itself, quite able to say where the organism left off and the contraption began. It also included more than one biological generation. Kerouac, Ginsberg, and Burroughs were old enough to have served in World War II, and Charlie Foster was a combat veteran. Most of the original Venice beats were Korean War-era enlisted men (except for Stuart Perkoff, who resisted the draft in 1948). The beatniks who flocked to North Beach, Greenwich Village, and Venice West in 1959 and 1960, however, tended to be very young people who had read about the revolution and wanted to join it. Kerouac's biographers usually treat the publicity, the hangers-on, and the rebellion's worshipful younger recruits either as aberrational (Jack never meant *this*!) or as a skewed confirmation of his power to inspire. While that was certainly true from Kerouac's point of view, it avoids the issue of who and what the Beat Generation really was—let alone explain its pull on the public's imagination.

As the "third" beat community—third, that is, after North Beach and Greenwich Village, which continue to draw most of the scholarly attention because of the "star system" that necessarily characterizes literary history—Venice West may supply some fresh answers. In its own time, it actually provided the detail-hungry public with most of what it thought it knew about the beat way of living. Even if nobody knew the names of its artists and poets, everyone seemed to be aware of what they wore, how they talked to each other, and what strategies they used to support life without holding jobs. That was Lawrence Lipton's doing—and the mass media, with their preference for eye-catching symbols and explanations of twenty-five words or less, decided to run his version of the story. Lipton's book, *The Holy Barbarians* (1959), became the outsider's handy one-volume guide to the beat scene, complete with photographs, capsule biographies, transcribed conversations, a ready-made historical context, and even a glossary of beat jargon in the back. It was a distorted picture but a vivid one, and it has stuck.

That is one reason for studying the Venice beats. Whatever else it may have been, the phenomenon of which they became a part was an example of something real merging with something fabricated to produce something totally unforeseeable: a new branch of popular culture dedicated to the *rejection* of popular culture. Its life cycle was interrupted and transformed by public awareness, and the effects of that awareness are more easily seen in the story of Venice West than in any accounts of the two better-known beat enclaves. Long before the beats, San Francisco and Greenwich Village had well-established traditions of cultural revolt and experimentation; Venice had only a local reputation for cheap thrills and oddness. Yet its tiny community of dropouts was living the "beat" life long before Lawrence Lipton pulled that label out of the headlines and forced his neighbors to wear it for the rest of their lives. Though his book was an honest attempt to describe a simpler and perhaps truer way of living, his street barker's instincts prevailed. No one actually did more to sell the Beat Generation to the American people—and when something is sold, it becomes a commodity.

The fact that Lipton was telling an essentially true story is another reason to look closely at Venice West. Before "the book," Larry's neighbors were genuinely dedicated to a code of ethics, ideals, and behavior they had largely invented for themselves. If they were trying to measure up to anyone, it was Charlie Parker, not Kerouac's hero, Dean Moriarty. They lived on subsistence incomes in the shabbiest part of Southern California's

Beats hold a peaceful demonstration on a walking tour of downtown San Francisco in 1958.

tackiest beach town, held jobs no longer than they had to, and considered the sacrifice worth it if it freed them from the false values and phony satisfactions of conventional life. They used illegal drugs to draw themselves even farther away from respectable society, and even closer to each other. Instead of amassing possessions and staring into the television set, they wrote poetry, painted pictures, made collages, and tried to burrow into each other's minds through endless hours of self-revelatory talk.

Their contempt for middle-class people and their values was the equal of any New York intellectual's, and they cheerfully paid a higher price for it—complete and voluntary obscurity. By their own transmuted version of the Puritan ethic, a fully realized human being was one who lived for art, friendship, love, and candor, and whose devotion was expressed through undistracted, unrelenting, unrewarded work. They even agonized about the temptations of fame within their own closed circle. All of this was hard enough to bring off in isolation, when the outside world neither knew nor cared, but when the eye of the public turned their way, in 1959 and 1960, the results were both

cruel and bizarre, if occasionally heroic. Their history is one of struggle—to survive and create in a materialistic society; to imagine, construct, and sustain a competing version of reality; and to keep faith with each other despite the worst that publicity, notoriety, the herd instinct and their own self-destructive tendencies could do to them.

This study devotes most of its attention to the beats themselves, and inevitably invites comparison to a pair of well-known books on pre-World War I Greenwich Village, Arthur Wertheim's *The New York Little Renaissance* (1976) and Robert E. Humphrey's *Children of Fantasy* (1978), focusing, as they do, on the lives of key individuals. It is not, strictly speaking, a community study, since Venice West was not a community. It was, like Humphrey's prewar Villagers, an "island of art and freedom surrounded by a hostile world of crass materialism and hypocritical respectability"—or at least a collection of like-minded rebels who tried to make it so.

There were, of course, crucial differences between the Little Renaissance and Venice West. In the first years of the century, Greenwich Village lay within easy striking distance of the literal center of American culture, popular as well as elite. Small but determined intellectual guerrillas could choose their targets, strike, and fall back to the relative safety of an established, tolerated bohemian community. The Venice beats, by contrast, lived near but tried to ignore Hollywood, and in the end, it was Hollywood that pounced on them. Nor did Venice, that embarrassing stepchild of Los Angeles, offer them any support; after 1959, its solid citizens were always trying to drive them away. If the Village of Max Lerner and Floyd Dell was the perfect staging area for guerrilla raids on the dominant culture, Stuart Perkoff's Venice was an untenable place to retreat from it. Besides, the Village rebels really expected to transform American civilization; the Venice beats did not. They dreamed about changing people's consciousness through art, but they knew the people better than that. What they really wanted to do was to write their poems, paint their paintings, take their drugs, love their friends, and keep from getting busted by the police.

The prewar Villagers were also extremely well-connected. They were, in fact, elitists who never doubted their own superiority. They had studied at first-rate universities and often remained close to their professors. Unless they were "excessively eccentric or uncouth," they were as much at home in Mabel Dodge's strategically located salon as in their own romantically shabby rooms and cheap bars. They had that much in common, moreover, with the better-known members of the Beat Generation—Kerouac and Ginsberg had studied at Columbia; Burroughs was a Harvard man and a member of the business-machine family; Gary Snyder had been steeped in a new kind of elitism at Reed College; and even Gregory Corso eventually got himself "adopted" at Yale. Kenneth Rexroth, who initially shared his literary connections with Ginsberg and his friends, was connected to practically everybody in the literary world, especially the influential East Coast journals through which he later denounced his protégés. By comparison, the Venice beats were complete outsiders. Tony Scibella was a housepainter's son who chose poetry in preference to "the lunch box forever;" John Thomas was a computer programmer who hated computers; Stuart Perkoff was a dedicated misfit who seldom got anything right except his poetry. Lawrence Lipton, who willed the myth of Venice West into existence, was a hack writer, an obscure novelist and poet, and an immigrant from Tsarist Poland. Of all the Venice beats, only Charlie Foster started out with any

substantial advantages in life, and he spent his whole life making sure they would do him no good.

The Village rebels also tended to go on to bigger and better things—Walter Lippman to the deanship of American journalism, Eugene O'Neill to near-godhood in the American theater, John Reed to a grave at the foot of the Kremlin Wall. They could plausibly claim to have "helped change the entire course of twentieth-century American painting and literature"—not only by producing art and literature, but by decisively influencing those who bought, exhibited, and published it. The Venice beats, for the most part, remain unpublished and unhung. The best of them were very good indeed, but that is almost beside the point. What they really contributed to the culture of the fifties was their example of lives based on art, poverty, and a separate arrangement with reality, at a time when that amounted to an assault on common sense.

But millions of Americans did find them irresistible, if only as an alluring source of consternation. This was not entirely Lawrence Lipton's doing. From 1948 through at least 1962, Henry Luce, that staunch upholder of Protestant values in Asia, was in the habit of receiving a fortnightly briefing paper on the activities of the avant-garde throughout America, prepared for him and his senior editors by a shrewd and very canny researcher named Rosalind Constable. Ms. Constable, who apparently had no other responsibility (and was also said to be the only person at Time-Life with an office, Room 2221, but no title), regularly scanned some 160 obscure publications, including *Contact, Evergreen Review,* several English and French journals, and the *Village Voice* (whose columnist John Wilcock obtained a copy of one briefing in 1962). The purpose of her report, as she herself wrote, was to "draw attention to the more off-beat events, sometimes the very ones that are causing such consternation among the critics. . . . And the weirder the better, if there is reason to believe that the author knows what he is doing. It is just possible (as history has sometimes proved) that he is inventing a new language which takes most people, including most critics, time to learn." It is therefore not surprising that the relationship between the Luce Publications and the Beat Generation should have been as close and often perverse as that of, say, Robert Capa and the wars of the twentieth century—although what *Time, Life,* and their close competitors chose to make of the beats is a more complex issue.

It is also interesting to note that while everyone seemed to have an opinion about the beats' mental stability, no one seemed to take much notice of the only formal psychological study ever devoted to the issue: Francis J. Rigney and L. Douglas Smith's unpretentious little book, *The Real Bohemia.*

Dr. Rigney, a San Francisco psychotherapist, had spent every night from October 1958 through January 1959 in the Grant Street section of North Beach, getting to know the people and persuading them to take a battery of standard psychological tests. Fifty-one bohemians cooperated fully, out of a total beat population he estimated at between 180 and 200 persons. While his standards of sickness and health were understandably skewed in favor of conventional society—one was, or was not, able to "function" within it, and was therefore healthy or not healthy—Dr. Rigney found much to intrigue him and to admire among the Grant Street bohemians.

Yes, he said, many of them were "sick":

Sickness stalks the Beach. The largest number in our group were found to be lonely, depressed, anxious, only ocasionally *able* to work despite, in the cases of some, real gifts. . . . But unlike many communities, they do not *conceal* these problems. . . . These Bohemians have created a combined artistic and therapeutic community whose inhabitants are trying to help themselves, but only in their own way.

While the beats scored high on the parts of the tests which indicated "psychic and physical distress," they also showed a strong capacity for "self-acceptance." While Dr. Rigney certainly felt it was better to be cured than to stay sick, he also came close to saying that the beats' psychic troubles and their honesty about them tended to balance each other out, especially in comparison with members of ordinary society.

He did note a certain hostility to women, who were viewed by the men as an "encumbrance" and a "source of problems for man." Few of the men expected anything but sex out of a relationship with a woman, and most had trouble imagining one that was "warm and enduringly human." As for drug addiction, or what we would now call substance abuse, he found that while there was more of it among the beats than in the general population, it was still a "minority phenomenon," and the chief difference was that the beats still treated the addicts among them as human beings. Besides, the real destroyer among them was, of all things, alcohol.

What did "real" beats look like? What did they wear? Despite the general impression that there was a beatnik "uniform"—beards, grubby clothes, and sandals for the men, leotards, bulky sweaters and basic black for the women—Dr. Rigney found no evidence of it among his subjects. Of the thirty-three men he studied, nineteen were consistently clean-shaven, four had mustaches, and ten had beards; twelve went about in sandals much of the time, but fourteen, or nearly half, wore ordinary business suits practically every day. Twelve of the eighteen women were seen to wear black stockings "more than once," and seven wore black dresses on a fairly regular basis; but only six wore leotards. Three were "very chic"; the rest "varied," with eight described as "very neat" and only five as "shabby to sloppy." This, of course, was in the winter of 1958-59; it would have been interesting to see what the costume mix was like one year later, after the real media blitz and the publication of the *The Holy Barbarians,* but Rigney was interested in committed bohemians, not worshipful seekers who had practiced in front of mirrors in San Leandro, Daly City, or Bakersfield.

But where had the beatnik come from? While the stereotype contained no hint of his social and economic background, it was never suggested of him, as it would be of the stereotypical hippie, that he felt free to defy convention because he had been born with privileges that he could not imagine losing. Perhaps because the beatnik was, by definition, a failure, it hardly occurred to anyone to ask how far he had fallen. On the other hand, since he was also, by definition (*Partisan Review*'s as well as *Time*'s), unlettered, some of his hostility toward the prevailing culture had to be presumed to have sprung from envy. *Of course* he rejected high art and middle-class morality—what did he know of either one? Yet 16 percent of Dr. Rigney's subjects were the sons and daughters of "professionals and big entrepreneurs," compared to a national average of 2.7 percent; 20 percent came from "educated semiprofessional" backgrounds, compared to 9.8% percent of the general population; 30 percent described their parents as "white collar," as opposed to the standard 18.9 percent; 28 percent were of "blue collar" origin, despite the fact that fully 48 percent of the people answered to that description. While the government still counted a fifth of the nation as "unskilled" or unemployed, only 4 percent of Rigney's beatniks came from such a background.

What did Rigney's findings mean? At the very least, they meant that the stereotypical beatnik was a repository of fantasy. On the one hand, he represented the absurdity of arguing with "real life"; on the other, he offered a way out, if only in the imagination. That was probably why the popular media, which were perfectly capable of getting their facts straight about Amazonian Indians, trapdoor spiders, and the Battle of El Alamein, preferred exploiting the comic-strip beatnik to finding out about the real one.

"Why this interest?" Dr. Rigney wrote. "Why this simultaneous fascination and repugnance?" He thought the answer lay with the onlooker. His subjects' behavior represented only an "exaggerated and prolonged" version of the "dynamics common to everyone." But if everyone went through the same "search for identity and contact," especially in adolescence, why all the fuss? "It is the intensity—real or fancied," he wrote, "which disturbs the onlooking outsider. The open sexual or angry material that threatens the stabilized attitude systems and defenses of those ordinarily *hiding their own own such impulses.*"

He hastened to add: "But the ability to hide problems is not synonymous with health."

The beats of Venice West, as already noted, tended to come from a little further down the social ladder and to look a little more like the stereotype. But, then, Larry Lipton had essentially fashioned the stereotype around them. The fact is that the public liked and, as Dr. Rigney suggests, probably needed the fantasy image. By the time *The Real Bohemia* appeared, of course, the fad phase of America's relationship with the Beat Generation was largely over; the beatnik had become a part of the national folklore, if not its demonology. The interesting thing is that even at its high-water mark, only one social scientist seems to have cared enough about the truth behind a popular obsession to find out how much of it was based on fact.

The immediate result of Larry Lipton's book, on the other hand, was an influx of tourists, reporters, photographers, criminals, law enforcement officials, and would-be beatniks that overwhelmed Venice, anticipating San Francisco's Summer of Love by nearly a decade. Among the long-term results of the beat mania, in turn, were the installation of the far-out artist as a durable and extremely influential fixture in twentieth-century popular culture—and of the dropout life as an ever-present option for the younger members of the middle class. The beats, of course, can hardly claim all the credit for making alienation the presumed attitude of the young—or the preferred means of packaging things to sell to them. Part of the significance of the Beat Generation was that it proved rebellion sells, and Venice West, even without its cooperation, helped provide one of the earliest examples of how the culture of perpetual dissatisfaction could be profitably turned back on itself.

On the other hand, the Venice beats were real rebels whose message of personal revolt survived its exploitation by friend and enemy alike. Most of them remain unknown because they refused to cash in on themselves; even Larry Lipton, a man seemingly born with commercial genes, never allowed the fad he helped create make him rich—notorious, yes, but not rich. And while *Time, Life, Look, Newsweek, Reader's Digest,* the sagging movie industry, and the hungry television networks all borrowed his ready-made clichés to exploit the beats as clowns, they also succeeded in spreading the beat message of art, community, simplicity, spiritual independence, and freedom from possessions to a vast and surprisingly receptive audience. It was an assault on the American way of life promoted by the same people who manufactured its images. The irony was that it could only have been done in the course of selling soap, since, as the early fifties had clearly demonstrated, there were laws against trying to subvert the Republic on purpose.

"Where there's smoke," John F. Kennedy is reported to have said, "there is usually a smoke-making machine." This book can be read, in part, as a case study in the relationship of the smoke to the machine, and as a suggestion that the two often work together in ways more complicated, perverse, and ungovernable than most of us prefer to imagine. On the other hand, there was far more to Venice West than sensationalism and manufactured images. It really *was* a collective attempt to live outside the way of life other Americans considered normal, if not divinely inspired. To a surprising extent, it succeeded. Many of its founders died young, and nearly all of them allowed themselves to be driven away from Venice, but few of them lost their faith in what they had tried to do. Most of the ones who survive, in fact, are still trying to do it.

Accordingly, *Venice West* takes the form of a collective biography, with the narrative intentionally written, for the most part, as if nothing similar had ever happened before. In the fullest sense, nothing like it had. The significance of Venice West lies less in its artistic achievements—although there were quite a few—than in the audacity of its people in trying to live for art *and nothing else* in a city that adored, and still adores, its status as the world's biggest, gaudiest, and wildest symbol of material success. In its high-floating, quirky visions and stubborn, off-handed poverty, Venice was a brave and deliberate affront to an American Dream that worked.

In a sense, the beats served as a kind of spiritual Rorschach test for their fellow Americans. Intellectuals and middle-class working people alike tended to see their worst fears for society confirmed in them. Both sets of fears were based on the still greater fear that the beats and their approach to life might prevail. To mainstream intellectuals, they were childish, irresponsible, barbaric, self-indulgent and unworthy of moral leadership. To the coalescing New Left, they were childish, irresponsible, barbaric, self-indulgent, and incapable of revolutionary action. To millions of people who harbored traditional values, they were deviants who "don't work." Not only did they not work, they got away with not working because they had no desire for the things other people worked to get. In each case, what the beats did with their own lives was probably less important than the doubt their example cast on the validity of life as lived by others. In each case, the underlying fear was the same: "If the beats are right, we and all we strive for are nothing at all."

To which the beats themselves might have answered: "No, perhaps not. Why not start over?"

HERBERT GOLD (ESSAY DATE 1993)

SOURCE: Gold, Herbert. "When North Beach Made an Offer, Old Bohemia Couldn't Refuse." In *Bohemia: Where Art, Angst, Love, and Strong Coffee Meet*, pp. 24-39. New York: Simon & Schuster, 1993.

In the following essay, Gold reminisces about the Beat era in North Beach, an enclave of San Francisco.

Thank the gods that protect writers from the obligation to write: the phone just rang. It's an old acquaintance from North Beach days whom I haven't seen since breakfast at the Trieste Caffe this morning. We Bohemians in our red-lined satin capes and berets believe in mystic synchronicities.

Ffrank Ffollet (don't forget the extra f's, to differentiate him from the bogged-down Irish one-f Francises) is writing his own version of *Roots*—in this case, the roots of a Welshman, since Dylan Thomas just didn't have enough genius to do the job right. You need *spark*. You need *fire*. You need *Ffrank Ffollett*.

But now my friend's wife has been laid off from her job as a teacher's aide, and the IRS says

he owes $623 in taxes from four years ago when he briefly sold out to the military-industrial-bucketshop complex and took a job selling circus tickets by phone for the Firemen's Alzheimer's Benefit. Those bastards were supposed to forget to report his earnings, but you can't count on the boojwah to do it right by not doing it, despite the promise that their brains have turned to tofu.

Since Ffrank owes such a small amount, the whole force of the government was coming down on him in a strike force of attack helicopters filled with auditors from the Federal Building. It makes him nervous. Even after three double espressos, his stomach is still jumpy. How can a person sing the truth of the Welsh race, their sagas, their kings in fur hats, under such pressure? As a member of an ethnic group myself, can I dig what he's saying, brother?

That's his story. And since I bought a pair of circus tickets from him, I'm partly to blame.

"Okay," I said, "I'll lend you a hundred. Come and pick up the check."

"Jeez," he said, "couldn't you meet me at the Puccini? I'm pretty busy right now, got to make a couple more calls, but I could take a break in an hour. Can I lay a cappuccino on you, pal?"

Ffrank qualified. The Christmas Alzheimer's circus ticket salesman and Welsh epic poet knows I won't change my mind. He's got other trapezes to fly. And I'm a sucker for a free cappuccino.

Among my early memories of San Francisco's Old Bohemia, then bivouacked in a North Beach concentration so dense that one strategic bomb could have wiped out most of the nation's resources of unrhymed verse, are the even older Bohemians of the late fifties and early sixties, complaining, "I remember the *real* Bohemia of the thirties . . . Wobblies, anarchists, jug wine toters, poets, and you could get a big dollar dinner for seventy-nine cents. There were giants in those days, young feller."

Well, when I roamed North Beach with Allen Ginsberg in 1957—hadn't yet come to live in San Francisco, but was scouting the terrain—the prix fixe dinners at the Hôtel du Midi (upstairs Basque), Ripley's (sort of French), the Pisa (definitely Italian), and a half dozen other all-you-can resorts cost in the neighborhood of a buck seventy-five, red wine a quarter extra. Allen preferred the New Cup Café (Chinese) because it was less expensive. But we are all artists here, our heads in the clouds; let's not emphasize vulgar inflation. The young whippersnapper eventually becomes an old whippersnapper.

Surely the Bohemians of the twenties and thirties ran into garrulous veterans at the Black Cat or in their studios in the Monkey Block, now buried under the TransAmerica Building, who remembered the carefree, romantic, and sexy pre-earthquake San Francisco Bohemia described by Frank Norris in his novel *Blix*. This picture of lazy young would-bees buzzing over the seven, count 'em, well maybe nine hills of the Bay was published in 1899, the same year as his better-known *McTeague*, a gritty story of Zolaesque misfortune on Polk Street. One of the miracles of my early discovery of San Francisco was to find that Polk Street, adapted into Eric von Stroheim's great and doomed film *Greed*, was psychically intact—still very much as Norris described it, even with the hint of homosexuality discreetly foreshadowed nearly a hundred years ago.

When *Greed* was shot, von Stroheim used a corner apartment on Columbus in North Beach to represent the Polk Street dentist's office. When I used to visit, it was the house and studio of a cigarette-addicted abstract-expressionist painter who moved out from New York after one of his lungs was removed. "If I'm gonna die," he said, "might as well have some fun before I go."

It was a time of great fun in North Beach. We watched Officer Bigaroni enter the life of poetry by rousting poets guilty of interracial marijuana smoking. (A bar on Upper Grant had a swinging outdoor sign which announced: HEADQUARTERS FOR ETHNICS.) The black Jewish abominist poet Bob Kauffman wrote his "Notes Found at the Tomb of the Unknown Draft Dodger." We broke sourdough together at the old Pisa (it was called the New Pisa) and melted with feeling as that Japanese opera troupe arose after the family-style dinner to sing "Oh! Susanna" in Japanese. We should have suspected, when they took over Stephen Foster, they would move next into the automobile industry.

The San Francisco Renaissance, nationally celebrated and therefore validated by Grove Press in a special issue of the *Evergreen Review,* laid waste the terrain, reciting to jazz and pillaging, shooting paint onto canvas, smoking, and attacking New York while Kenneth Rexroth beamed and Zen pioneers learned how to pronounce Om. Heroes arrived from Manhattan by thumb, by driveaway car, and by prop plane, as brave in their hearts as Cortez, Richard Henry Dana, Robert Louis Stevenson, and Fatty Arbuckle, who made the trip to San Francisco a little earlier by . . . was it covered wagons?

Allen Ginsberg recited "Howl," with its famous results in destroying the very fabric of western civilization.

The Circle Gallery dropped the scales from our eyes.

Michael McClure snarled, growled, snuffled, and purred his beast poems in front of my fireplace, scaring my young woman friend, who spoke only English and French, not Beast.

Ron Boise's *Kama Sutra* instruction sculptures were arrested, jailed by the police, and ultimately acquitted. I have a mug shot of a cast-iron couple caught in flagrante and tagged: BOOKED. S.F.P.D. One gaunt erotic enigma stood for years on the roof of the Anchor Steam Beer factory, where it was visible from the freeway, improving the sex life of commuters, until Fritz Maytag took over the native brew.

Katharine Ross, later to star in *The Graduate* and *Butch Cassidy and the Sundance Kid,* was a lovely young understudy in Actor's Workshop productions. She lived upstairs of a grocery on Stockton near Filbert; she stood nude on stage in a daring version of Jean Genet's *The Balcony.* When I lent her my prewar Citroën gangster getaway car—it had running boards—she wisely used convenient parking in front of her building. When I returned from a trip to Saint-Germain-des-Prés, the North Beach of Paris, I found that she had collected one fire hydrant parking ticket for each day I had been obviously dreaming at the Flore, the Deux Magots, and the Bonaparte.

She had the bedrock solidity of a true North Beach believer. Everything was for the best in the best of all possible worlds if you remember to tuck the tickets neatly into the glove compartment . . . especially if you look like Katharine Ross. The first time I was ever comp'd for a meal was at Cho-Cho, the Japanese restaurant near City Lights Bookstore, when Jimmy, the proprietor, said: "You come in with a person who looks like her, you don't ever have to pay."

I'll tell you how long ago that was: sushi hadn't yet made it past Hawaii, crossing the Pacific. California cuisine meant Hangtown fry. Natural foods were Bird's-eye frozen instead of Libby's canned peas.

My excuse for moving to San Francisco—the excuse that paid my child support—was a grant to do a play at the Actor's Workshop. If I took kindly, sweet-tempered, high-cheekboned Katharine Ross to dinner, you see—the logic should be clear to any other pure soul—it was only because we needed to exchange hints on success in show business. In the great tradition of noncommercial theater, my play was not performed here because I wouldn't consent to the director's wish to cast his wife in a role for which she was of the wrong generation. The play was later given an undeserved run in Los Angeles.

Katharine was itching to get away from Vesuvio's. When she returned to Adler Alley, now called Jack Kerouac Street, it was with makeup personnel, trailer, canvas chair with her name stenciled on it, and a full crew. The ghost of Kathie Past haunted this set. I watched in the crowd of gawkers, along with Jimmy from Cho-Cho, who said, "Just as pretty. Just as pretty."

Across from City Lights and Vesuvio's ("We Are Itching to Get Away from Portland, Oregon") there used to be the Bodega, flamenco dancing, cans of tomato sauce over rice at night, guitar lessons during the day. A psychiatrist's ex-wife told me that her guitar would never betray her as her husband did. (He lied to her, like a banjo.) Where there is now an "adult" screening room-bookshop there was then an art cinema and a restaurateur who liked to relax by wearing spike heels during his at-home hours. Kenneth Anger, film collagist of *Scorpio Rising*, lived upstairs with his fan magazines and his leather collection. At Vesuvio's, another psychiatrist's ex-wife, author of *I'm Sorry, Darling*, the story of premature ejaculation, sat patiently for two years, analyzing her divorce. She

said everything many times, like a balalaika. The Discovery Bookshop, a treasure trove presided over by Frederick Roscoe, rhymemaster, world champion in the Indoor Olympic Doggerel Competition, gave employment to such clerks as David Meltzer, who now teaches poetry at New College in the Mission, and Peter Edler, a German beatnik known as "the Hip Hun" because he had been expelled from the Hitler Youth for talking in class. He later married a Swedish woman, ran a child-care service in Marin, and moved to Stockholm when she came into her inheritance.

Prominent vegetarians and the founder of Breatharianism, which taught people how to nourish themselves without eating, a recipe using the native chlorophyll in their skins plus a dash of the sunlight over the miracle church of Peter & Paul, hung out in the Bermuda triangle of Grant, Broadway, Union, and Columbus. The geometry might suggest a rectangle to some, but at least it's not square. The prophet of Breatharianism sat at the bar of the Washington Square Bar & Grill, tossing popcorn and pretzels into his mouth while he promised to reveal the secrets of foodless feeding to anyone who bought him a brandy. "That cognac is pure sunlight, it's a known fact," he explained. A friend remembers Joan Baez crooning softly on a bench in front of the church while an admirer brushed her long, dark, glossy hair. It was a scene of peace and love until Joan said to her fan, "Get your sticky fingers the fuck away from my guitar." Peace, Sister.

The spike-heeled restaurant owner on Columbus near the Hungry i entertained his patrons by singing and dancing "Tiptoe through the Tulips." His ambition was to grow up to be Tiny Tim, but twinkletoes was stilled, due to murder by his late-night busboy. An occasional crime of passion is part of the Bohemian tradition called Going Too Far. Later there was another musical tragedy, the case of the killer piano which crushed a bouncer who happened to be embracing a lady after hours at the Condor. It crushed him against the *ceiling*. Some prankster pressed the button that raised this traditional platform on which Paderewski and Carol Doda cavorted, and in his ardor the lover failed to notice that the earth was moving toward heaven. The couple lay pinned together until cleaning folks arrived in the morning. The woman survived but, wishing to change her karma, departed North Beach for North Dakota.

Did the Vesuvio's psychiatrist's wife, author of *I'm Sorry, Darling*, preoccupied with sexual persistence, lean on the button? History cannot tell us everything; that's why we need rhetorical questions.

Mort Sahl used to get his exercise sprinting to the bank when it opened to cash his paychecks from Enrico Banducci's Hungry i. Other employees were often ahead of him in line, rubbing the sleep from their eyes and praying. Enrico was an entrepreneur with ample soul but loosely wrapped accounting skills. The one-legged hooker at his bar entertained seekers of oddness, including Alvah Bessie, the Hollywood Ten blacklisted writer who came to work the nightclub's light and sound system after he was released from prison. I walked out on Barbra Streisand because she sang too loud; I blushed for Woody Allen, who panicked on stage and forgot his lines. The next day we drove to Berkeley because he said he needed to get over his trauma by viewing "girls with major hair."

When Lenny Bruce thought he was a bird and flew out a window of the Swiss-American Hotel on Broadway, near Enrico's Coffee House, which provided an outdoor office for entertainers, mobsters, financial-district employees, and sixties grokkers and groovers—also Vietnam service people on R& R—Ralph Gleason, jazz and rock critic, stood by taking notes. The medical emergency crew that came to carry Lenny to the hospital taped his mouth shut because the disappointed bird was using language not in the vocabulary of your average fallen eagle. "Is there anything I can do?" I asked Gleason.

"There's nothing anyone can do now," intoned the philosopher.

The Hip Hun strolled past in his medal-bedecked caftan, which looked like a ball gown. The wife of a stage manager at The Committee offered me a fuzzy capsule from her private stash. What's this? I asked her. "A dream of truth," she said. "Try it."

The ambulance went sirening off, carrying a bird with his wing broken and his mouth taped.

Old cities are better than rapidly evolving new communities at offering enclaves and backwashes in which Bohemians can set down their lightly packaged roots. In the late nineteenth and early twentieth centuries, Montparnasse and Montmartre in Paris, Soho in London, Greenwich Village in New York—and the ancient inner cities of Rome, Athens, even such buttoned-up places as Geneva, Switzerland, and less buttoned-up Stockholm, Copenhagen, Buenos Aires—discovered that gypsylike strangeness could sprout in alleyways like the ailanthus tree in my native Cleveland. Some-

times a college neighborhood helped to provide the necessary cheap eats, lodging, and companionship. San Francisco's street ambling, its site as a hilly port, as destination for Latin folks, its speculative fervor, its early prosperity, its newness and oldness, gave it unique advantages. This city has studied hard how to entertain itself and others. Mark Twain came for the gold rush; Ambrose Bierce, Joaquin Miller, Bret Harte, Isadora Duncan, and the Emperor Norton were famous beatniks and hippies before the words. The Emperor Norton wore flowers, dressed like a burning bush, printed his own currency; now street poets hawk their wares in North Beach and at the Café Picaro in the Mission—still living off the yearning for distraction a Mediterranean, forever-springtime climate helps to nurture.

Even businesses with a sordid criminal aroma elsewhere assume a genuinely playful form where the yerba buena grows. The Mitchell brothers, Artie and Jim, hippie filmmakers out of San Francisco State University, were official pornographers-in-chief, avuncular sex-show operators. They followed their bliss. The outdoor mural at their erotic world headquarters in the Tenderloin propagandizes for the rain forest; the one it replaced dealt in nymphs and myths. Unfortunately the brothers, intimate friends and fishing companions, raising a flock of children together, seem to have had a falling out and Jim shot Artie to death. Naughtiness crossed the edge to violence in the real world of money, power, and fraternal rivalries.

Pure naughtiness has always had a central position in San Francisco Bohemia, in keeping with the city's tradition of taking its frivolity seriously. The Barbary Coast and the International Settlement, archaeological remnants of which can still be found in the bidets and outdoor erotic murals not yet extirpated on the Jackson Square area, specialized in drink, sex, and the genial spending of money. This was a port, after all. The Sexual Freedom League, sponsored by the Reverend Jefferson Fuck Poland in the sixties and early seventies, hasn't been heard from lately. The Kerista Commune, a group marriage, men and women who share everything, including children, used to provide me with house-cleaning service, arriving in a group marriage of three, one sanitary expert carrying a snakelike vacuum cleaner draped like a Jungian symbol about his upper body. In response to my application to visit their commune as research for this report, they said they would take a vote. They discussed; they voted. "We've consensussed," one of them responded by telephone, and the answer came to my request: they noed.

Margo St. James started the first hooker's union, Call Off Your Old Tired Ethics (COYOTE), in North Beach. "Since I didn't find a nice old man, preferably an invalid, to support me, I went into business," she explained. "I like giving shampoos."

Another enterprising young woman, a nurse from Boston, started the Golden Gate Foundation to guide libidinous men back toward karmic tranquility. She thrived for a few years. A receptionist used to say to the waiting clients, "The therapist will see you now, big boy."

I was invited to the Christmas party given at a popular North Beach restaurant by a woman I might call Ilse von Braunschlofer (not her real name, if you plan to look her up in the S&M yellow pages), whose business was the constant care of men devoted to leather and severe discipline. Like hay fever, this seems to require regular visits for skin tests and prickly inoculation. Aside from me, the other male guests were clients. The disciplinarians were schoolteachers, parole officers, motorcycle-repair ladies, except for one who told me she was a nuclear physicist. "Aw," I said, "you look more like a molecular biologist."

"Caught again," she exclaimed, snapping her fingers. "Hey, promise you won't tell my mother?"

What in other climates might be called prostitution came to be a slightly eccentric work-study program in San Francisco. A young woman who took showers with visitors at the Mitchell brothers' emporium ("Take a Shower with a Feminist") was a graduate student in clinical psychology. "We're pioneering in the safe-sex field," she said. Another groundbreaker was my friend Judy Roe, author of *The Same Old Grind*, writer, stripteaser, set designer, costume maker, now retired to full-time authorship and the occasional painting of "Nymphs from Hell" backdrops for an erotic live show. When I asked why she corresponded with me before we met, she said, "Because you're the only stranger I know."

My sons keep asking me, "Dad, were you alive before there was AIDS and herpes?"

There were giants in those days, my boys.

Besides the ever-popular sex adventurers, chafing at the limits, there are San Francisco's Bohemian stockbrokers, lawyers, physicians (Dr. Flash Gordon, the motorcycle specialist, for example), even real estate speculators. A Zen Center musician from Green Gulch Farm leaned on my shoulder, crossing Upper Grant, muttering, "The punk monk is drunk." Part-time, many try for Bohemianism, and the nice thing is, all can succeed. Why not? The rules are generous in San Francisco, unlike the rules for major-league basketball, where you have to be tall.

One of the less benign elements of the sixties flower epoch was the discovery of drugs as a shortcut to satori, nirvana, dream therapy, relief from parental nagging, esthetic fulfillment, preparing for final exams, and foreplay. Bad drugs came into the mainstream. Thank you, Dr. Leary, Dr. Alpert, and the other Dr. Feelgoods. A poet-filmmaker-cabdriver-stand-up comedian named Chris preached his new discovery, chanting: "If coffee, tea, or Ovaltine don't do it, try Meth." He had a way of injecting friends so that he would be murmuring, "Now don't you feel . . ." and just as the speed hit their bloodstreams, he would utter the lyrical word *"bettah?"*

It was magic. He had a gig as a stand-up comic at the Hungry i, he charmed everyone, he made a prizewinning film, and within a couple of years he gave himself a Methedrine lobotomy. His IQ went from something near genius to moron and below. He became nearly blind. He wandered North Beach and panhandled and pretended he still knew me. "Chris, remember we first met at the Crystal Palace in St. Louis? Remember Gaslight Square?"

"Yeah man. Yeah man."

Bohemia promises eventual performance; not everyone fakes it very well (Ffrank Ffollet and his telephone solicitation for the charities of his choice). Another poet saw me with Allen Ginsberg on Grant a few years ago, and said, "Hey, how's it feel to be the eastern establishment?"

Allen looked quizzical, he looked bemused. He was worried about a friend's upset stomach and was heading for a store to buy a roll of Tums.

"Back east," muttered the young middle-aged poet of the Golden West, "they just don't understand the post-Ginsbergian revolution."

"Pardon?"

"They're Eurocentric. Gender chauvinists. Deconstruction is a hegemony racket, man."

The 12 Adler Place poet gave me high fives and slapped my palm. Power to the post-Ginsbergians! Down with the *Paris Review*!

A hyphen and overlap between my old Bohemia and the even older Bohemia of a previous generation is exemplified by William Saroyan, whom I met by accident as he was boisterously touring the San Francisco Museum of Modern Art, explaining matters to his son and daughter. He came to visit my flat on Russian Hill above North Beach—Charles Reich, author of *The Greening of America,* and also the sculptor who did the fakes for William Randolph Hearsts's San Simeon have been my neighbors. Saroyan, a lover of Strange, adored the fresh plaster smells when newly minted Renaissance masterpieces were moved onto the sidewalk out of the defunct artist's studio after the sculptor's untimely death. When I introduced Saroyan to Reich, the two gentlemen stared at each other and said, like gentlemen: "Good day."

In the early sixties, since I was five or ten years younger than I am now, I had the right to a young woman friend (called "girlfriend" in those dear dead days beyond recall). She had a roommate who admired William Saroyan. We decided to . . . please recall this quaint Mickey Rooney language . . . "double-date." The two young women arrived at my apartment and I lit a fire. Saroyan arrived and a burning crate leapt out of the fireplace, due to the draft of his entrance. "That's the tiger in the fireplace," he explained, as we ran about, stifling the conflagration.

The evening had begun nicely: warm hearts and singed rug. But Saroyan decided, to her great disappointment, that his date was too young for more than avuncular attention. He gave us a tour of his—an earlier—North Beach Bohemia, Barbary Coast, International Settlement. We had dinner at the Brighton Express. He asked the cook if she would like to be God in his new play. She giggled prettily, wiped her hands on her apron, and said she might consider the job if it didn't conflict with her schedule for making mud pies, the ice cream dessert she had invented.

The question of the existence of God resolved, Saroyan took us to Earthquake McGoon's to hear Turk Murphy, the great Dixieland horn player, another old San Francisco Bohemian from that border where North Beach fades into the waterfront, the longshoreman's union of Harry Bridges, and the spiritual link of two raffish ports, San Francisco and New Orleans.

Late that night, we said our prayers with an Irish-coffee ritual on the terrace at Enrico's, where a famous pair of call girls used to cruise in their jointly owned Thunderbird. They parked in the no-parking zone reserved for taxis, callperson Thunderbirds, Zen real estate showoffs, and close personal friends of Enrico Banducci, and then strolled over for an exchange of sociability in the 2:00 A.M. damp. The outdoor heaters sizzled. Saroyan peered with his ardent dark eyes into their faces and began to discuss their ethnic heritages "because such things are *very interesting.*" And when they left, he reminisced about the call girls of yore, who didn't drive Thunderbirds.

Our young women were charmed by this contact with the literature of the thirties. And then, ever courtly, Saroyan doffed his fedora to his date, the deep Saroyan scholar, said goodnight (her eyes were gleaming with pride and frustration), and began to trudge across town to his sister's house. The scholar was thankful for a glimpse of "The Daring Young Man on the Flying Trapeze," that great early story about a starving writer in San Francisco. She remembered that his Pulitzer Prize play, *The Time of Your Life,* was inspired by Izzy Gomez's saloon nearby on Pacific. "That's cool, Herb, I can make do with insight," she said, "even if he's gotten kind of lazy."

When I see my friend of thirty years ago, she still sometimes recalls that evening and says, "Poor Debbie. She thought Saroyan would be more . . . Bohemian. But she said the same thing about a wing of the Jefferson Airplane and a vice president of Merrill Lynch."

North Beach was still a place for seekers who came seeking. The working artists couldn't stay up all night, liked to tuck themselves in at closing time.

Bohemians are not what weekend visitors, bridge and tunnel folks, think they are. Bohemians may look like outcasts and scapegoats, cultivators of private gardens, but in fact, they want to run things, define the taste, preach the theories, support the arts, make the music, write the literature, and drink the coffee and wine that keeps society jumping, vigorous, and fun. Even Bohemian deadbeats and panhandlers help give body to the soup.

A CBS producer and I strolled around North Beach, he carrying a tape recorder while I chatted with the turbulent Bohemian masses, which include few actual artists, of course, but many profound lumpens living off the land. I interviewed Lawrence the Young Poet, who hoped people would confuse him with Lawrence Ferlinghetti.

At City Lights, Mad Alex, a handsome, tall, black street rapper, said to us by way of introduction: "I got the bucket if you got the water."

What could be a better, more mysterious, yet strangely coherent description of the marginalized performers who enact our street theater?

America needs to match up the buckets and the waters. I'll drink to that.

Hube the Cube, retired dope dealer to the beat generation—"Hey, man, *Jack Kerouac* bought from him!"—later peddled the early streets edition of the San Francisco *Chronicle* to the folks on the terrace of Enrico's, audience and actors in the hundred-and-fifty-year-long operetta. In 1957, when Allen Ginsberg introduced me to Mad Alex at the Co-Existence Bagel Shop on Upper Grant, he acknowledged my presence with bucket and water riddles. Alex returned from some kind of forced vacation to stand in front of City Lights, haggard, gaunt, white haired, but still reciting his paradoxes. Bob Kauffman, our Rimbaud, our champion of doom, took a vow of silence except for harrowing croaking demands for rent or food money. A toothless novelist and poet whose exercise consisted of hiking to City Lights to pick up his mail, whom I used to invite to Enrico's for hot chocolate—all he could chew—met a schoolteacher from Sacramento, married her, and grew teeth. Henri Lenoir, ballet dancer, proprietor of Vesuvio's, patron of the beat painters, permanent honorary mayor of North Beach, came in his retirement to the meals offered him by Enrico Banducci. Occasionally he raised cash by selling off part of his art collection. At the Hôtel du Midi, a prix fixe Basque restaurant, I met temporary true love in the early sixties. Richard Brautigan, suddenly the rage in his Confederate general disguise, handed out free poetry:

I give her an A + for long blond hair . . .

and curtseyed winsomely when college women asked for his autograph. Later he shot himself.

The hum and whir of the late fifties, early sixties mimeograph machines, churning out beat poetry, deafening me as I walked down North Beach alleys, grew still. The preeminence of rock'n' roll slowed poetry production to a torrent. The Reverend Pierre de Lattre, the Congregational minister who founded the Bread & Wine Mission to the beats, hoping to convert them to Christianity, was instead converted himself and now lives and writes in New Mexico.

The Black Cat, a link with ancient North Beach Bohemia, became a gay bar and then closed. There was another dark side here, too. Bunny Simon, the stately New Orleans Creole

City Lights Bookstore in San Francisco, founded by Lawrence Ferlinghetti and Peter Martin.

gentleman who owned The Anxious Asp, moved his bar to Haight Street. "Some folks in North Beach didn't want a man of color doing business," he told me. Officer Bigaroni, who harassed the beats, flailing with his club, ran into his own troubles with fraud charges during his retirement. As Bohemia made North Beach chic, rents became confiscatory, driving out theaters, cheap restaurants, artists, and the old radicals. Greenwich Village and Saint-Germain-des-Prés followed the same pattern, the iron grip of real estate speculation closing upon the graceful swan necks.

Irascible Fred Roscoe, rhymemaster with his Santa Claus beard and pinkness, closed Discovery Bookshop and moved to San Anselmo. Enrico Banducci lives with his son back east in Virginia. A few grizzled veterans still hang out at Gino & Carlo's, remembering grand old poets, grand old pool-cue fights. A few stubborn radicals like Jack Hirschman still sell their verse and their manifestos at 12 Adler Place. The countercultural physicist Jack Sarfatti, Ph.D., preaches the corkscrew shape of time to his permanent seminar at the Trieste. "Things that haven't happened yet can cause events in the past."

I know, I know, Jack.

Occasionally, I still see Lawrence the Young Poet on the bus. He's retired from seeking patronage up and down Columbus, Broadway, and Grant. A young poet who was once five-seven years old, then six-seven, eventually gets to be eight-zero.

A few cafés, bars, restaurants, bookshops still keep the faith. Beautiful Clara Bellino, actress, poet, and founder of the rock group The Flying Monkeys, stands at the microphone with her delicate pale face and leather miniskirt, singing her tender lyric to some lucky lover:

> You're lying on a cloud My lipstick on your ass . . .

An occasional brave entrepreneur prevents North Beach from becoming a Bohemia theme park, a kind of Beatnikworld. Recently Rumors, on the corner across the street from boarded-up Enrico's, has been trying to put together the right ingredients—cheap food, warm hearts, a hospitable eccentric proprietor in the form of James Swim, a Chinese-speaking former U.S. Army intelligence expert. There were blabbermouth nights, occasional fits of reggae, waitresses with metal decor pinned through haphazard parts of their lovely countenances, whispered conferences among pursuers of beauty and truth, an easy layabout atmosphere, and most basic of all . . . *Cheap Pasta*. In North Beach today, this miracle makes a person weep with gratitude and nostalgia. The sourdough bread was baked on the premises. It's not gourmet dining; this was comfortable, adequate feeding in a world of congenial loafing. Eureka, we can go home again. I met Ffrank Ffollet there in the company of a daughter by a marriage he had forgotten. They explained that they had just happened to notice each other, found something familiar in their faces, and realized . . . "Hey, Dad? Is that you?"

"Fflorence?"

The miracle of a third-generation Bohemian meeting a second-generation beatnik.

I blessed them and found my own table under a light in the corner. A tall fellow, the ghost of Mad Alex, pale, with a fragile beard, introduced himself. "My name is Wo," he said.

"That's funny, you don't look Chinese. How'd you get that name?"

"Because Wo is me," he said. "Now will you buy one of my poems?"

MICHAEL KOWALEWSKI (ESSAY DATE 1995)

SOURCE: Kowalewski, Michael. "Jack Kerouac and the Beats in San Francisco." In *San Francisco in Fiction: Essays in a Regional Literature*, edited by David Fine and Paul Skenazy, pp. 126-41. Albuquerque: University of New Mexico Press, 1995.

In the following essay, Kowalewski suggests that San Francisco's "international flavor and its continuing receptiveness to social iconoclasm and strong-willed personalities rendered it a particularly apt setting for Beat life and artistry."

At the beginning of his fine study of the San Francisco Renaissance, Michael Davidson remembers an older "bohemian" student in 1959 loaning him a copy of Lawrence Ferlinghetti's translations of the French surrealist poet Jacques Prévert. The book's small format and stapled binding (in the Pocket Poet series put out by City Lights Books) intrigued Davidson as much as "the clandestine way" that his friend handed him the book on a schoolbus.

> Like many other teenagers of my generation, I followed the book to its lair, taking the yellow Key Line train across the Bay Bridge . . . to North Beach, where "it" was happening. I'm not sure I knew then what "it" was, but one thing was certain: It wasn't what was happening in my middle-class neighborhood in Oakland. North Beach was a perpetual theater where all sorts of unpredictable things were going on. People dressed "differently" and spoke the exotic argot of the hipster. In those days, underaged youths could get into clubs (at least those that served food) and hear jazz at The Cellar or The Place [and] folk music at the Coffee Gallery, . . . not to mention poetry readings at a number of galleries and bars. My friends and I could sit around Beat shrines like Cafe Trieste or City Lights Books or Dante's (Mike's) Billiard Parlor and forget the fact that we were kids with crewcuts from the suburbs.[1]

That same year, 1959, *Playboy* magazine sought to understand "The Origins of the Beat Generation" by turning to the movement's chief chronicler. Jack Kerouac was not only the author of popular and (to some) notorious novels such as *On the Road* (1957) and *The Dharma Bums* (1958), he was also quick to admit his centrality to the Beat phenomenon: "I *am* the originator of the term [Beat Generation], and around it the term and the generation have taken shape."[2] The movement was not new, Kerouac insisted. Its emergence more than a decade before in the mid-forties was being forgotten in the wake of fatuous clichés inspiring "evil movies . . . where innocent housewives are raped by beatniks."[3] The Beat phenomenon, Kerouac complained, was being taken up "by everybody, press and TV and Hollywood borscht circuit" to include everything from a "bunch of fools marching against the San Francisco Giants protesting baseball" to "beatnik routines on TV . . . with satires about girls in black and fellows in jeans with snapknives and sweatshirts and swastikas tattooed under their armpits."[4] Whereas "the word 'beat' originally meant poor, down and out, dead-beat, on the bum, sad, sleeping in subways," Kerouac said, the term was now being stretched "to include people who do not sleep in subways but have a certain new gesture, or attitude, which I can only describe as a new *more*.

'Beat Generation' has simply become the slogan or label for a revolution in manners in America."[5]

As various critics have suggested, the antecedents of certain Beat attitudes can be found in Lost Generation writers (less Hemingway and Fitzgerald than, say, Hart Crane and Eugene Jolas), in thirties proletarian writing, in hipsterism, and in surrealism.[6] In San Francisco, the character of Beat life and writing was further indebted to previous bohemian movements in Northern California (in Carmel, Big Sur, and Berkeley), and to various figures associated with them (Jack London, George Sterling, Henry Miller, and Kenneth Rexroth). San Francisco's international flavor and its continuing receptiveness to social iconoclasm and strong-willed personalities rendered it a particularly apt setting for Beat life and artistry. "From the Barbary Coast days . . . to the North Beach of the 1950s," Davidson says, "San Francisco inspired certain 'unhampered types' to think of themselves as unhampered—and to provoke others elsewhere to think of the same as provincial."[7]

Yet for all their precursors and antecedents, the Beat Generation formed a distinct phenomenon, "a native and intuitive response," as Gregory Stephenson puts it, "to the particular artistic, social, and spiritual climate of midcentury America." The Beat authors (who ranged in age from twenty to fifty) were too individualistic to be easily classified. Beat aesthetics were expressed less in manifestos and commonly shared beliefs than in what Stephenson calls "mutual sympathy . . . and a sense of kinship in personal and artistic matters," especially those concerned with self-knowledge and "true" perception.[8]

The event that brought together many of these maverick minds and that seemed best to epitomize the Beat spirit was a poetry reading on October 13, 1955, at the Six Gallery (a small artspace in the Marina district named for its six founders). Allen Ginsberg, Michael McClure, Gary Snyder, Philip Whalen, and Philip Lamantia all read from their work, after being introduced by Kenneth Rexroth. Jack Kerouac, who was enthusiastically in attendance, chronicled the evening in his novel *The Dharma Bums*:

Anyway I followed the whole gang of howling poets to the reading at Gallery Six that night, which was, among other important things, the night of the birth of the San Francisco Poetry Renaissance. Everyone was there. It was a mad night. And I was the one who got things jumping by going around collecting dimes and quarters from the rather stiff audience standing around in the gallery and coming back with three huge gallon jugs of California Burgundy and getting them

all piffed so that by eleven o'clock when Alvah Goldbook [Ginsberg] was reading his, wailing his poem "Wail" ["Howl"] drunk with arms outspread everybody was yelling "Go! Go!" (like a jam session) and old Rheinhold Cacoethes [Rexroth] the father of the Frisco poetry scene was wiping his tears in gladness.[9]

After "all the poems were read and everybody was milling around wondering what had happened and what would come next in American poetry," Kerouac and the poets retire "to Chinatown for a big fabulous dinner . . . with chopsticks, yelling conversation in the middle of the night in one of those free-swinging great Chinese restaurants of San Francisco" (16).

Poetry tended to overshadow fiction for most of the Beat writers in San Francisco. Kerouac was the significant exception, though his fiction typically approximated poetry (which he also wrote) in the form of free-swinging "spontaneous prose."[10] Kerouac's fiction generally takes the form of thinly veiled autobiography, with many characters so recognizably modeled on actual people that scholars have compiled "character keys" to *The Duluoz Legend*, a sequence of twelve novels Kerouac published between 1950 and 1968.[11] Kerouac's fiction exemplifies the fact that Beat aesthetics, as Davidson says, "were inextricably confused, in the public perception as well as in the minds of its participants, with matters of lifestyle."[12]

The autobiographical feel of Kerouac's work, however, springs not simply from correspondences between characters and actual people but from a more general sense of lived urgency in his writing, a poetics of immediacy and ragged yearning that testified to intensely lived experience. While Kerouac and other Beat writers openly challenged middle-class mores about work, sexuality, big business, and the American Dream, their radical literary experiments relied less on social activism than on the expression of individual experience. They insisted upon the primacy of personal sensibility and spiritual pilgrimage over imperatives for social change. Or rather, social change would emerge, they felt, from the spiritual transformations of individuals. The Beats felt alienated from a society shadowed by the nightmare of nuclear annihilation and awash in consumerism, suburban conformity, and McCarthyesque intolerance. But unlike political radicals before them, as Stephenson says, the Beats "proposed a revolt of the soul, a revolution of the spirit.[13] "Kerouac's protagonists reject the materialist-rationalist assumptions of their culture, together with the concomitant imperatives of competition and acquisitiveness, and they cultivate instead of the nonrational as a mode of knowledge [and] the unconscious as a source of wisdom and guidance."[14]

Kerouac stated that the term "beat" also meant "beatific." But his conception of spiritual vision and reorientation was never far removed from the initial sense of "beat" as meaning down-and-out. He emphasizes this duality in his essay for *Playboy*. "There is no doubt about the Beat Generation, at least the core of it, being a swing-ing group of new American men intent on joy" and "wild selfbelieving individuality," he ex-plains.[15] But joyous self-assertion formed only one side of Beat psychology and behavior. Kerouac goes on in the *Playboy* article:

> today . . . there are two distinct styles of hipster-ism: the cool today is your bearded laconic sage, or schlerm, before a hardly touched beer in a beatnik dive, whose speech is low and unfriendly, whose girls say nothing and wear black: the "hot" today is the crazy talkative shining eyed (often in-nocent and openhearted) nut who runs from bar to bar, pad to pad looking for everybody, shout-ing, restless, lushy, trying to "make it" with the subterranean beatniks who ignore him. Most Beat Generation artists belong to the hot school, naturally since that hard gemlike flame needs a little heat. In many cases the mixture is 50-50. It was a hot hipster like myself who finally cooled it in Buddhist meditation, though when I go in a jazz joint I still feel like yelling "Blow baby blow!" to the musicians.[16]

Part of Kerouac's tone—especially his use of the term "beatnik"—is tongue-in-cheek.[17] Still, his very description of competing behavioral styles here implicitly enacts what it argues for. By mix-ing references to jazz, bars, and Buddhism with an allusion to Walter Pater ("burning with a hard gemlike flame"), Kerouac blurs the line between "high" and "low" culture. Kafka, Blake, and Krazy Kat all share the page in his fiction. T'ang dynasty poets are as easily invoked as the Three Stooges when a character shops for undershirts in an Oakland Army Navy store. The Beats were accused by critics like Irving Howe of merely mirroring the anti-intellectualism of the middle-class mass society they opposed. But as Davidson says, the Beats "did not presume to stand above or beyond that society and judge from some 'higher' cultural vantage. . . . Rather, they acted out or celebrated certain alternative mythic possibilities already present in American life—the alienated James Dean hero, the Huck Finn adventurer, the op-pressed Negro, the fast-talking Jewish comic."[18] This "acting out" of alternative possibilities is readily apparent in Kerouac's fiction, which presents not a unified aesthetic front but a mercu-rial, improvisatory set of "50-50" impulses that fluctuates between exuberance and gloom, buoy-ancy and depression, withdrawn observation and spontaneous action.

None of Kerouac's novels is set exclusively in San Francisco or Northern California, though vari-ous works include sections set there. By examin-ing images of the region that emerge from three works—his prose sketch "The Railroad Earth" and his novels *On the Road* and *The Dharma Bums*—it becomes apparent that Kerouac's "images" are often more auditory than visual. His impres-sionistic evocation of place in San Francisco depended as much upon the musical fluency and momentum of his prose as upon its visual coordi-nates. This should come as small surprise given his interest in jazz and spontaneous composition in expressing what he called "the speed and ten-sion and ecstatic tomfoolery of the age." He distrusted "slow, painstaking, and-all-that-crap craft business." "FEELING is what I like in art," he declared, "not CRAFTINESS":

> jazz and bop, in the sense of a, say, a tenor man drawing a breath and blowing a phrase on his saxophone, till he runs out of breath, and when he does, his sentence, his statement's been made . . . that's how I therefore separate my sentences, as breath separations of the mind. . . . there's the raciness and freedom and humor of jazz instead of all that dreary analysis and things like "James entered the room, and lit a cigarette. He thought Jane might have thought this too vague a ges-ture . . ." You know the stuff.[19]

Perhaps nothing better catches the racy, free auditory status of Kerouac's writing—its tendency to play to the ear with its "breath separations of the mind"—than "The Railroad Earth." Written in the fall of 1952, when Kerouac was a breakeman for the Southern Pacific railroad, the sketch evokes his shifting impressions of San Francisco and the California towns he passes through. There is, for instance, this response to the quiet residential suburbs he traverses while riding a train south of San Francisco:

> I wish I was a little child in a crib in a little ranch-style sweet house with my parents sipping in the livingroom with their picture window pointing out on the little backyard of lawning chairs and the fence, the ranchstyle brown pointed full fence, the stars above, the pure dry golden smelling night, and just beyond a few weeds, and blocks of wood, and rubber tires, bam the main line of the Ole SP and the train flashing by, toom, tboom, the great crash of the black engine, the grimy red men inside, the tender, then the long snake freighttrain and all the numbers and all the whole thing flashing by, gcrachs, thunder, the world is going by all of it finally terminated by the sweet

little caboose with its brown smoky light inside where old conductor bends over waybills and up in the cupolo the rear man sits looking out once in a while and saying to himself all black, and the rear markers, red, the lamps in the caboose rear porch, and the thing all gone howling around the bend to Burlingame to Mountain View to the sweet San Joses of the night the further down Gilroys Carnaderos Corporals and that bird of Chittenden of the dawn, your Logans of the strange night all be-lit and insected and mad, your Watsonvilles sea marshes your long long line and mainline track sticky to the touch in the midnight star.[20]

Kerouac said he wanted this writing "to clack along . . . like a steam engine pulling a 100-car freight with a talky caboose at the end,"[21] and that is certainly part of its effect. The narrative voice as well as the train picks up momentum as the speaker looks first out at suburban tranquillity and then in at the smoky compartments of "the long snake freighttrain" howling around the bend. No reconciliation of these "inside" and "outside" perspectives seems necessary because they all simply run together. They all share the same unpunctuated, alliterative rhythm that does not wait for precise visualization. The writing serves to dramatize a mood of yearning rather than depict a specific scene. The list of names at the end of this sequence—"the sweet San Joses of the night"—becomes a rhythmic segment all by itself in this traveling music. The *sound* of these town names, as much as any direction one might trace with a finger on a map, is meant to convey Kerouac's Whitmanesque vision of "the great metaphysical passage of iron traffics of the rail" (p. 75).

"Kerouac's San Francisco," Davidson says, "is valued for its embodiment of a certain type of pulsating American energy that both enlivens and alienates at the same time."[22] The "railroad earth" is an image of technological intersection and urban motion. Whether on or off the train, Kerouac provides a kinetoscope whir of class images from "neat-necktied producers and commuters of America and Steel civilization" (p. 37) to Mexican farm laborers and winos vomiting in backalleys. He identifies with the beaten, wearied life of marginal street-people (hobos, poor blacks, day laborers, homosexuals), but not for the purpose of social reform. Instead, as John Tytell says, Kerouac's identification with the downstrodden "omits the deprivation [and] humiliation, the hopelessness and victimization that a writer like James Baldwin would magnify, [in order] to emphasize a romantic sense of brotherly community and joy in simple pleasures."[23] So too the speaker wanders the hills of the city, making no

attempt to reconcile its past—its "immense ugly gargoyle Frisco millions fronts of other days" (p. 43)—with the futuristic feel of the Oakland Bay Bridge, "like radar machine of eternity in the sky" (p. 43). The city becomes a spectacle so varied as to defeat conclusive action or representation. Kerouac fells both exhilarated by and slightly afraid of the urban panorama that moves around him: "my whole soul . . . looking out on this reality of living and working in San Francisco with that pleased semi-loin-located shudder, energy for sex changing to pain at the portals of work and culture and natural foggy fear" (p. 46).

The image of San Francisco as a "portal" or an opening to another realm is one that recurs throughout "The Railroad Earth." San Francisco is presented as a liminal site, a place where America runs out of continent and running room. The result is an "end of land sadness" (p. 38), one associated with the kind of wasted, despairing Tenderloin nightlife Oedipa Maas will later encounter in her night journey through San Francisco in Thomas Pynchon's *The Crying of Lot 49* (1966). But the melancholy also seems somehow postcoital, associated with a crystalline, seawashed beauty—"the clarity of Cal to break your heart" (p. 38)—that should be consoling rather than saddening.

San Francisco is presented not merely as a place where a westering impulse runs out of speed, but as a place receptive to influences from the Far East. James D. Houston has noted the ways in which the notion of "Continent's End" (in Robinson Jeffers's terms) has been replaced in California writing by the image of the Pacific Rim, of "a great wheel of peoples who surround the Pacific Basin" that includes California not as an ultimate destination but as one point, albeit a significant one, on a vast continental rim.[24] Kerouac voices this idea of influences from the East in "The Railroad Earth," but in a vaguely ominous and threatening way. Rather than "the keenpure lostpurity lovelyskies of old California" (p. 61), he looks west and sees "huge fogs milking furling meerolling in without a sound,"

the oldfashioned dullmasks mouth of Potato Patch Jack London old scrollwaves crawling in across the gray bleak North Pacific with a wild fleck, a fish, the wall of a cabin, the old arranged wallworks of a sunken ship, the fish swimming in the pelvic bones of old lovers lay tangled at the bottom of the sea like slugs no longer discernible bone by bone but melted into one squid of time, that fog, that terrible and bleak Seattleish fog that potatopatch wise comes bringing messages from Alaska and from the Aleutian mongol, and from the seal, and from the wave, and from the smiling porpoise, that fog at Bayshore you can see waving in and filling in rills and rolling down and making milk on hillsides and you think, "It's hypocrisy of men makes these hills grim."

(p. 60)

Interestingly, the fog brings with it not an Asian presence but an Alaskan and Aleutian one. The fog soundlessly blots out vision or drives it underwater into images of disintegrating human identity and the "squid of time." In a parallel moment in *On the Road,* Sal Paradise stands on a promontory overlooking the Pacific in a more upbeat mood asking "Oh where is the girl I love?" But once again, despite the vaguely beckoning beauty of the "blue and vast" ocean, the fog drifting in "a great wall of white" throws Sal back on "the great raw bulge and bulk of my American continent; somewhere far across, gloomy, crazy New York was throwing up its cloud of dust and brown steam. There is something brown and holy about the East; and California is white like washlines and emptyheaded—at least that's what I thought then."[25]

There is a moment late in *The Dharma Bums,* when the narrator Ray Smith is hitchhiking alone between Crescent City and Grant's Pass, Oregon, that continues this imagistic pattern. Smith walks a mile into the woods and takes a nap "right in the heart of the Siskiyou Range," only to wake up "feeling very strange in the Chinese unknown fog" (p. 218). This might seem an aberrant image in this novel, for just a few pages earlier, Japhy Ryder (Gary Snyder) looks out over the Pacific from Stimson Beach and tells Smith, "Look at all that water out there stretching all the way to Japan" (p. 211). Ryder is about to leave on a freighter to study Buddhism in Japan and Smith has a dream the night before that Ryder will become "a little seamed brown unimaginable Chinese hobo," "the Han Shan ghost of the Orient mountains and even the Chinese'll be afraid of him he'll be so raggedy and beat" (p. 208). The continuing "unimaginability" of Chinese culture for Kerouac has bothered subsequent figures, such as Wittman Ah Sing, himself a Kerouacian character, in Maxine Hong Kingston's *Tripmaster Monkey* (1989).[26] Nevertheless, the importance of Asian spirituality in the form of Buddhism represents the single most significant difference between "The Railroad Earth" and *The Dharma Bums.*

In the latter work—set in 1955-56, three years after "The Railroad Earth"—Kerouac imagines San Francisco not as a city receiving cold fogs from the north but as a point on an "immense triangular arc of New York to Mexico City to San Fran-

cisco" (5). Kerouac's imagination—and travels—tended south rather than west from California, and Smith arrives in the city after hopping trains north from Mexico City and Los Angeles. He is a scruffy spiritual vagabond or "Dharma bum," a rucksack pilgrim cooking pork and beans on the beach, avoiding railroad cops, and searching for the Buddhist principle of Dharma or the Path of Truth. Critics have tended to find the novel a little thin and poorly structured, and not without reason. Smith's trip back to North Carolina in the middle of the book scatters the focus of the novel; the suicide of Rosie Buchanan, the girlfriend of Cody Pomeroy (Neal Cassady), is only fleetingly presented; and Smith's stint as a fire watcher on Mt. Desolation in Washington seems somewhat sketchy and anticlimactic. Nevertheless, the novel has remained one of Kerouac's most popular works and this undoubtedly has to do with the presentation of Smith's friendship with Japhy Ryder.

What fascinates Smith is the "West Coast" nature of Ryder's lifestyle. Disciplined, practical, healthy, and at peace with himself, Ryder immediately impresses him with a sense of focused spirituality:

> A peacefuller scene I never saw than when, in that rather nippy late red afternoon, I simply opened his little door and looked in and saw him at the end of the little shack, sitting crosslegged on a Paisley pillow on a straw mat, with his spectacles on, making him look old and scholarly and wise, with book on lap and the little tin teapot and procelain cup [of tea] steaming at his side.

(p. 19)

The life of Zen serenity, brewing tea on his "noisy gasoline primus" (p. 24), represents only one side of Ryder, however. A former fire lookout and logger, Ryder grew up in the wet woods of the Northwest. His clothes are all hand-me-downs or Goodwill/Salvation Army specials except for a pair of expensive lightweight hiking boots: the true sign of a mountain-climbing connoisseur. Ryder is a kind of poet woodsman who exemplifies both practicality and spirituality for Smith: "What hope, what human energy, what truly American optimism was packed in that neat little frame of his!" (p. 209).

Ryder also has an inspired spontaneity and an unembarrassed lack of inhibition Smith envies. He is perfectly happy hiking in the Sierras in only a jockstrap and he introduces Smith to a form of tantric group sex known as "yabyum." Smith, who says he is "still afraid to take my clothes off . . . especially with men around" (p. 29), gradually participates while Ryder sits naked and crosslegged, rolling a Bull Durham cigarette and proclaiming, "I distrust any kind of Buddhism or *any* kinda philosophy or social system that puts down sex" (p. 30). Ryder, as Tytell says, is "an avatar of a change in consciousness whose impact on American life would only be realized in the sixties."[27] He freely participates in an uninhibited sexuality that fascinates Smith but that also makes him feel at times like an insecure voyeur. At Ryder's going-away party, people start undressing, but "nobody seemed to mind."

> In fact I saw Cacoethes [Rexroth] and Arthur Whane [Alan Watts] well dressed standing having a polite conversation in the firelight with the two naked madmen, a kind of serious conversation about world affairs. Finally Japhy also got naked and wandered around with his jug. Every time one of his girls looked at him he gave a loud roar and leaped at them and they ran out of the house squealing. It was insane. I wondered what would ever happen if the cops in Corte Madera got wind of this and came roarin up the hill in their squad cars. . . . Nevertheless it was strangely not out of place to see the bonfire, the food on the board, hear the guitar players, see the dense trees swaying in the breeze and a few naked men in the party.
>
> I talked to Japhy's father and said "What you think about Japhy bein naked?"
>
> "Oh I don't give a damn, Japh can do anything he wants far as I'm concerned. Say where's that big old tall gal we was dancin' with?"
>
> (pp. 196-97)

Kerouac dramatizes his alter-ego's need to invoke a more conservative sense of social protocol in wondering how the police would react and in looking to a member of an older generation for a moral judgment he doesn't deliver. Yet however out of place Ray Smith feels at the party—alone in his sleeping bag or playing "bongo drums on inverted cans" (p. 193)—it is clear that the open sexuality he associates with Japhy Ryder characterizes Kerouac's vision of alternative lifestyles in Northern California more generally. After arriving in Marin from his cross-country trip, Smith contemplates "a royal table of wine and hamburgers and pickles and [his host] lit a big bonfire and took out his two guitars and it was really a magnificent kind of way to live in Sunny California" (p. 178). "It was so pleasing," Smith says, "to meet so many Buddhists after that harsh road hitchhiking" (p. 176).

The Dharma Bums evokes the Bay Area as a haven for unconventional behavior. It is a place where Ryder can envision "a world full of rucksack wanderers, Dharma Bums refusing to subscribe to the general demand that they . . . work, produce, consume, work, produce, consume, . . . [and] going up to mountains to pray" (p. 97) or where one can listen to the wacky dialogue of Henry Morley. Morley, an eccentric mountain-climber/librarian in Berkeley, accompanies Smith and Ryder on their trip to the Matterhorn in the Sierras, delivering "brilliant inanities with a complete deadpan" (p. 42):

> "Sure," says Morley wheeling the car around increasing curves, "they're boarding reindeer Greyhound specials for a pre-season heart-to-heart Happiness Conference deep in Sierra wilderness ten thousand five hundred and sixty yards from a primitive motel. It's newer than analysis and deceptively simple. If you lost the roundtrip ticket you can become a gnome, the outfits are cute and there's a rumor that Actors Equity conventions sop up the overflow bounced from the Legion. Either way, of course, Smith" (turning to me in the back) "and in finding your way back to the emotional wilderness you're bound to get a present from . . . someone. Will some maple syrup help you feel better?"
>
> "Sure, Henry."
>
> (p. 43)

Morley's special brand of surrealistic talk entrances Ray Smith: "I couldn't understand what kind of strange secret scholarly linguistic clown he really was under these California skies" (p. 42).[28] Morley's zany thinking and private obsessions (unlike the Zen adept Ryder, he insists upon bringing a bulky inflatable air mattress on the hike) prefigure many of the odd characters in later novels either about or partially set in Northern California. Richard Brautigan's *A Confederate General from Big Sur* (1964) and *Trout Fishing in America* (1967), Rudolf Wurlitzer's *Nog* (1969), Tom Robbins's *Another Roadside Attraction* (1971), Jerry Kamstra's *The Frisco Kid* (1975), Anne Steinhardt's *How to Get Balled in Berkeley* (1976), Jim Dodge's *Fup* (1983), Thomas Pynchon's *Vineland* (1990): these and other novels hark back, whether stylistically or thematically, to Kerouac's vision in *The Dharma Bums* of San Francisco as the scene of offbeat impishness and spiritual self-searching.

The suicide, bitterness, depression, and erotic tension that reside only in the shadows of this novel increasingly characterize subsequent images of San Francisco in Kerouac's later novels like *Big Sur* (1962) and *Desolation Angels* (1965). In the latter novel, seeing the Golden Gate Bridge actually makes the narrator Duluoz "*shudder with horror. The bottom drops out of my soul. Something about that bridge, something sinister . . . like the forgotten details of a vague secanol nightmare.*"[29] Yet like Kerouac's personal withdrawal in the face of the sixties' counterculture, this later darkening of his vision cannot substantially diminish his initial receptiveness to the fresh possibilities of Beat writing and living in San Francisco.

Along with other diverse literary personalities like Allen Ginsburg, Gary Snyder, Lawrence Ferlinghetti, Jack Spicer, Robert Duncan, Philip Whalen, Diane DiPrima, and Michael McClure, Kerouac drew national attention to San Francisco's prominence in the Beat movement. The attention, especially in the popular media, often distorted and trivialized the work the Beat writers produced. But it couldn't detract from Kerouac's ability to evoke both the tender sadness and the simple joys of his own experience. Whether his characters discuss Buddhism over salami, cheese, and Ry-Krisp on a Pacific beach or tread "soft as ghost the indented hill sidewalks of Ah Me Frisco all in the glitter night,"[30] Kerouac evokes a rich, kinetic sense of place in his writings about Northern California. And he evokes it most memorably when his writing itself approximates Ray Smith's turn for a final look up the trail as he's hiking down from the Matterhorn by moonlight in *The Dharma Bums*:

> I thanked everything up that way. It had been like when you're a little boy and have spent a whole day rambling alone in the woods and fields and on the dusk homeward walk you did it all with your eyes to ground, scuffling, thinking, whistling, . . . like a little girl pulling her little brother home on the sled and they're both singing little ditties of their imagination and making faces at the ground and just being themselves before they have to go in the kitchen and put on a straight face again for the world of seriousness.
>
> (p. 88-89)

Notes

1. Michael Davidson, *The San Francisco Renaissance: Poetics and Community at Midcentury* (New York: Cambridge University Press, 1989), ix-x.

2. Jack Kerouac, "The Origins of the Beat Generation," *Playboy* (June 1959); rpt. in Thomas Parkinson, ed., *A Casebook on the Beat* (New York: Thomas Y. Crowell, 1961), 70.

3. Ibid., 76

4. Ibid., 75, 76.

5. Ibid., 73. One can already hear Kerouac bristling at phoney bohemianism in a way that would lead him, late in his life, to denigrate the 1960s counterculture. "They've even started crucifying chickens in happenings," he protested in 1968. "What's the next step? An actual crucifixion of a man. . . . I'm pro-American and the radical political involvements seem to tend elsewhere. . . . As for LSD, it's bad for people with incidence of heart disease in the family." Jack Kerouac, "Interview: The Art of Fiction XLI," *Paris Review*, 43 (Summer 1968): 102-3.

6. On precursors of the Beats, see Davidson, 1-59 and Gregory Stephenson, "Introduction," in Gregory

Stephenson, ed. *The Daybreak Boys: Essays on the Literature of the Beat Generation* (Carbondale: Southern Illinois University Press, 1990), 1-16.

7. Davidson, *The San Francisco Renaissance*, 8.

8. Stephenson, *Daybreak Boys*, 7, 8.

9. Jack Kerouac, *The Dharma Bums* (1958; rpt. New York: Vintage, 1986), 13-14. Subsequent references are cited parenthetically in the text.

10. See Jack Kerouac, "Essentials of Spontaneous Prose" (1958) and "Belief and Technique for Modern Prose" (1959) in *A Casebook on the Beat*, 65-68.

11. See the "Character Key" in Barry Gifford and Lawrence Lee's *Jack's Book: An Oral Biography of Jack Kerouac* (1978; rpt. Penguin, 1979), 322-34.

12. Davidson, *The San Francisco Renaissance*, 2.

13. Stephenson, *Daybreak Boys*, 6.

14. Gregory Stephenson, "Circular Journey: Jack Kerouac's *Duluoz Legend*, in *The Daybreak Boys*, 23.

15. Kerouac, "Origins," 70, 72.

16. Ibid., 73.

17. Thomas Albright notes that "after Soviet Russia's Sputnik was launched in 1957, *Chronicle* columnist Herb Caen began using -nik with maddeningly comic virtuosity, and with 'Beatnik' the affix stuck." *Art in the San Francisco Bay Area, 1945-1980* (Berkeley: University of California Press, 1985), 81.

18. Davidson, *The San Francisco Renaissance*, 25.

19. Kerouac, "Interview," 65, 66, 83-84.

20. Jack Kerouac, "The Railroad Earth," *Lonesome Traveler* (1960; rpt. New York: Grove Press, 1970), 64. Subsequent references are cited parenthetically in the text. Kerouac slightly revised "The Railroad Earth" from two pieces that were published in *Evergreen Review*, "October in the Railroad Earth" (1957) and "Conclusion of the Railroad Earth" (1960). Both are reprinted in *A Casebook on the Beat*, 31-65.

21. Kerouac, "Interview," 65.

22. Davidson, *The San Francisco Renaissance*, 14.

23. John Tytell, *Naked Angels: The Lives and Literature of the Beat Generation* (New York: McGraw-Hill, 1976), 166.

24. James D. Houston, "From El Dorado to the Pacific Rim: The Place Called California," *California History* 68 (Winter 1989/90): 177.

25. Jack Kerouac, *On the Road* (New York: Signet, 1957), 66-67.

26. See Maxine Hong Kingston, *Tripmaster Monkey: His Fake Book* (1989; rpt. New York: Vintage, 1990), 69-70.

27. Tytell, 171. For a perceptive discussion of Snyder's presence in the novel, see David Robertson, "Real Matter, Spiritual Mountain: Gary Snyder and Jack Kerouac on Mt. Tamalpais," *Western American Literature* 27, no. 3 (November 1992): 209-26.

28. Henry Morley was based on John Montgomery, who himself wrote a memoir of Kerouac: *Kerouac West Coast* (Palo Alto: Fels & Firn, 1976).

29. Jack Kerouac, *Desolation Angels* (New York: Coward-McCann, 1965), 353.

30. Kerouac, "The Railroad Earth," 47.

JAMES J. PARSONS (ESSAY DATE JANUARY 1996)

SOURCE: Parsons, James J. "'Mr. Sauer' and the Writers." *Geographical Review* 86, no. 1 (January 1996): 22-41.

In the following essay, Parsons investigates the influence of Carl Sauer on the Black Mountain Poets, especially Charles Olson.

The close ties and personal friendship of Carl Ortwin Sauer (1889-1975) with many of the major intellectual figures of his generation, so well reflected in a vast, unpublished correspondence in the University of California's Bancroft Library, remind us that Sauer was much larger than his chosen field. We geographers, especially those of the historical-cultural persuasion, tend to think of him—"Mr. Sauer" or "the Doc" to most who knew him—as our own. "Culture history" was Sauer's shorthand term for his distinctive approach to a venerable subject, defined as concern with the agency of humankind in using, modifying, and shaping the earth's surface through time. Representing a main current within twentieth-century academic geography long before environmental history was named or in vogue, Sauer was at the same time an articulate and influential contributor and critic within the larger field of American scholarship. It is the awesome breadth of his inquiring mind, his gentle wisdom, the originality of his insight, the magic in his turn of phrase, the enduring quality of his humanity that admirers continue to celebrate.[1]

One group far removed from conventional academic geography took Sauer to its bosom with particular enthusiasm in the Berkeley geographer's later years. They were those avant-garde writers and poets who gravitated to Black Mountain College, an intense, experimental community in the Appalachian Mountains of western North Carolina founded by disaffected university teachers and staffed by an unmatched collection of painters, composers, architects, sculptors, writers, and other visionary artists who despaired of effecting what they understood as "education" in institutionalized places of higher learning (Duberman 1972). The Black Mountain project was powerfully influenced by the complex and ambiguous figure of Charles Olson (1910-1970), rector of the college from 1952 until its demise in 1956, who has been widely heralded as one of the major poets of our era.

The Black Mountain School—students and disciples of Olson—became pivotal figures in the late 1950s, when in the streets and cafés of San Francisco what was increasingly recognized as a spiritless modernist literature was entirely recast into something novel and emphatically distinct—loosely known then as the Beat Generation but since described as a key and especially intellectual part of the San Francisco Renaissance and as a cornerstone of the New American Poetry (Allen 1960; Davidson 1989; Snyder 1995a, 1995b). Even among those in this group who never attended Black Mountain, Olson's influence is apparent. The relationship of this circle of postmodern poets with Sauer has been echoed most directly to geographers through Bob Callahan (1942-), the personable Irish American author and publisher who headed up the Turtle Island Press in Berkeley in the early 1970s (Callahan 1975, 1977, 1978).[2]

These writers were strongly attracted to American cultural and environmental history over a time span reaching back to the earliest occupation of the New World. They found an exhilarating model and source of inspiration in Sauer's insistence on the immutable link between history and geography and in the concreteness and authenticity of his pungent, vigorous expression, his identification with people living close to the land, and his sensitivity to the aesthetic values in the humanized landscape. There have been geographers since Sauer whose work is embraced by fashion-setters in social science, but there is no geographer who has ever attained such a following in arts, prose, or poetry. It was a relationship that has not yet palled.

At the time, Sauer himself seems to have been baffled and even a bit unnerved by this attention, bordering on adulation, from so unexpected a quarter. But if these strangers often seemed to be speaking in tongues, it was of people and places and their history, themes dear to his heart. Charles Olson insisted, in his Black Mountain "A Bibliography on America for Ed Dorn," that students should read "Sauer . . . all the way back to his first job" (Olson 1974, 11). Bob Callahan, who became aware of Sauer through reading Olson, heralded the geographer to friends as "the finest historical intelligence of the twentieth century" and as "the one person you would read before any other on pre-historic America" (Callahan 1978, 25). Stewart Brand, the freewheeling Marin County editor and publisher, called him a major influence on American poets, "a man so routinely correct about matters so fundamental that a popular following never caught up with him!" (Brand 1976, 48).

Searching for the Roots

Charles Olson, an idiosyncratic latter-day Ezra Pound with a passion for engagement, was a central figure in the postmodern revolution that energized poetry in the United States after World War II (Olson 1983, 1987). Although Olson's poetry is sufficient legacy, his influence has been far larger. In a pivotal essay on "Projective Verse," Olson argued for severing poetry from strict metric form, allowing poets and their material much greater leeway in appearance and structure (Olson 1966a; Davidson 1980; McPheron 1986, 386-387).

For his followers, Olson assumed the status of guru, a combination of teacher, culture theorist, and critic, exemplifying what Gary Snyder termed, "a combination of the highest activity of trained intellect and the deepest insight of the intuitive, instinctive, or emotional mind" (Snyder 1995a, 14). No longer was a romantic sensibility and elegant phrasing sufficient for poets—a scholar's knowledge of history, geography, and engagement with them in prose were needed. Today, more than twenty years after his death, Olson's literary heirs are reaching back to the maestro's roots, seeking among other things to learn more about the man Sauer and his geography that so intrigued and influenced their mentor.

The Olson-inspired literature is enormous and still growing. William McPheron of the Stanford University Library's English language and literature division has recorded and annotated chronologically (if only through 1983) more than 1,600(!) critical responses and critically significant biographical accounts of the brilliant but eccentric poet Olson and his work (McPheron 1986). This lode of commentary scans some thirty years of literary critiques of the iconoclastic New Englander who "pushed American poetry beyond the self-conscious aestheticism of New Critical Orthodoxy into the open ranges of unmediated experience" (McPheron 1986, xiii). The index to these capsule accounts includes nineteen references to Carl Sauer.

For the respected English critic, the late Donald Davie (1928-1995), who taught at Stanford and Vanderbilt Universities in the course of his distinguished career, Olson's best known work, *The Maximus Poems,* a metaphorical history of Gloucester, Massachusetts, and its fishing community written over a period of twenty years,

"enacts the general principle of Sauer's geography" as represented in Sauer's 1925 "The Morphology of Landscape" (Olson 1983; McPheron 1986, 81). Olson's effort to map his hometown in this multi-volume epic, like his earlier emphasis on the Pacific Ocean in *Call Me Ishmael* (1947), a strikingly original interpretation of Herman Melville and *Moby Dick,* is seen by Davie as evidence of the "desperate seriousness" with which Olson regards geography and the matter of geographical location (Davie 1977a, 182).

Another critic, Oliver Ford, then of Massachusetts State College, Lowell, found that although Sauer's 1948 essay "Environment and Culture During the Last Glaciation" (Sauer 1963e) provides Olson with his entrance into the remote past, "The Morphology of Landscape" is more germane to his poetry, because it offers a method of study based on the content of particular places (Ford 1973-1974; McPheron 1986, 178). Sherman Paul, in the *Iowa Review,* refers to Olson's adoption of Sauer's "investigative method" to recover the "fresh, naked perception of America's beginning" (Paul 1975, 86; McPheron 1986, 204). Another English critic, Graham Clarke,[3] saw Sauer's geography as a "poetic methodology for restoring man's original intimacy with nature" (Clarke 1977; McPheron 1986, 236). It is almost as though a grounding in the history of locality and attachment to place is something new, something that Sauer and his geography had for the first time laid bare and authenticated, an unsuspected vein to be mined and exploited.

McPheron's bibliographical guide to Charles Olson's work includes extensive references to the poet-essayist Donald Davie's collected essays, *The Poet in the Imaginary Museum* (1977c). In the introduction that volume's editor, Barry Alpert, recalls how the geographer Sauer implicitly invited artists, Davie among them, to enter his physical realm when, in "The Morphology of Landscape," he wrote: "A good deal of the meaning of area lies beyond scientific regimentation. The best geography has never disregarded the aesthetic qualities of landscape, to which we know no other approach than the subjective" (Sauer 1963a, 344; Alpert 1977, xviii). In a 1968 essay entitled "Landscape as Poetic Focus" Davie is seen to have accepted Sauer's invitation, with the geographer being described as the guiding spirit behind some of Davie's first verse. Where Davie turns his literary-historical attention to the New World, Alpert writes, "it is mediated by the presence of Sauer and those American poets who saw Sauer's worth, Charles Olson and Edward Dorn" (Alpert 1977, xix; Davie 1977b).

In "Landscape as Poetic Focus" Davie argues that good poetry may legitimately originate in response to landscape. He observes how Olson's *Maximus* poems "aspire to give in language a *map, a map of one place*, the town of Gloucester" (Davie 1977a, 166). In some cases, Olson's linkages between form and content were literal, and a poem would literally take the form of its subject. To be sure, among Olson's students, poems might often incorporate much of the history of the place mapped, but so did the ancient geographies of Herodotus. And so did some of the best writings of Carl Sauer.

Davie, searching for the roots of the Olson-Sauer linkage, noted approvingly Alexander von Humboldt's remark, footnoted by Sauer, that "in classical antiquity the earliest historians made little attempt to separate the description of lands from the narration of events the scene of which was in the areas described. For a long time physical geography and history appear attractively intermingled" (Sauer 1963a, 318 n. 5; Davie 1977a, 166). But the English critic believed that some of Olson's veneration of Herodotus and what he professed was more probably derived from Sauer who, in "The Morphology of Landscape," observed that "the *historia* of the Greeks with its blurred feeling for time relations had a somewhat superior appreciation of areal relations and represented a far from contemptible start in Geography" (Sauer 1963a, 318; Davie 1977a, 166-167).

"Its Tone Is Militant"

Sauer's writings, as seen especially in the collection of his papers edited by John Leighly (1963) under the title *Land and Life,* were commended by Davie as "exceptionally instructive for poets and students of twentieth-century poetry" (Davie 1977a, 167). Although Davie noted Leighly's observation that Sauer later withdrew in good part from the exposed and extreme position taken up in his early essay on "The Morphology of Landscape," Davie insists that "However this may be for professional geographers, it is the statement of 1925 that will have readiest appeal for poets. Its tone is militant" (Leighly 1963, 6; Davie 1977a, 167). He again quotes Sauer:

Area or landscape is the field of geography because it is a naively given, important section of reality, not a sophisticated thesis. Geography assumes the responsibility for the study of areas because there

exists a common curiosity about that subject. . . . The subject existed long before the name was coined. The literature of geography in the sense of chorology begins with parts of the earliest sagas and myths, vivid as they are with the sense of place and of man's contest with nature.
(Sauer 1963a, 316, quoted in Davie 1977a, 167)

In the same paper Davie cites the *Shorter Oxford English Dictionary* definition of chorology as "the scientific study of the geographical extents or limits of anything" (Davie 1977a, 167). So Sauer in 1925 was recalling geography to its ancient roots, away from the "overweening divagations" (Davie 1977a, 167) to which it had earlier lent itself, especially as the discipline embraced environmental causation. Reference to Humboldt's use of "physiognomy" as a category employed to accommodate subjective responses to landscape recalled in Davie's mind Sauer's essay in 1941 on "The Personality of Mexico," reprinted in the *Land and Life* collection. Perhaps it was the essay's beginning that most caught the poet Davie's attention:

For, whatever the problems of the day may be that claim the attention of the specialist and which result in more precise methods of inspections and more formal systems of comparison, there remains a form of geographic curiosity that is never contained by systems. It is the art of seeing how land and life have come to differ from one part of the earth to another. This quality of understanding has interested men almost from the beginning of human time and requires restatement and reexamination for each new generation.
(Sauer 1963c, 104)

Davie concludes his 1968 essay with an elegant dovetailing of Sauer and the new writers he so admires: "It begins to seem as if a focus on scenery, upon landscape and areas, relations in space, are a necessary check and control upon the poets' manipulation of the historical record. If this is what Olson and Dorn have discovered, all honour to them. And any poet who seeks to follow them cannot do better than to read with instructive excitement this volume [*Land and Life*] of the writings of Carl Ortwin Sauer" (Davie 1977a, 169; Sauer, 1963h).

Ed Dorn (1929-), Robert Creeley (1926-), and Robert Duncan (1919-) are the best known of the numerous protégés of Charles Olson (Fox 1989), but his influence radiated out through a much larger community of poets, including Ed Dahlberg, William Carlos Williams, Kenneth Rexroth, Ken Irby, Paul Metcalf, and LeRoi Jones. The link with the San Francisco Beats, such as Allen Ginsberg, Jack Kerouac, and Gary Snyder, was rather more tenuous, but the San Francisco Renaissance clearly kept many of Olson's ideas in circulation (Davidson 1989). Dorn, Creeley, and Duncan were closely associated with Black Mountain College and the *Black Mountain Review* (1953-1957).

It was especially Ed Dorn, with his deep western North American roots and his concern for the artistic forms of cultural landscapes, who found inspiration from Sauer through Olson (Dorn 1980; McPheron 1988). From the fall of 1965 on Dorn was for some years a visiting lecturer at the newly chartered University of Essex, where Donald Davie was vice chancellor. The interaction can be imagined. In Olson's "A Bibliography on America," a revealing syllabus constructed for Dorn's education at Black Mountain, Sauer is repeatedly mentioned as the pivotal figure (Olson 1974, 81). For all the evident affection and the stylistic singularities in the "Bibliography," Olson was very much engaged in describing a serious methodology of study and knowledge. "The results of historical study are not 'how much one knows but in what field of context it is retained and used,'" Michael Davidson has written, quoting Charles Olson's instructions to Dorn. "For [Dorn] this meant studying the West in terms of its exploitation. Landscape, he learned from Carl Sauer, is contingent upon man's uses of it; the ultimate meaning of barbed wire lies in attitudes of containment and proprietorship which extent into the culture at large" (Davidson 1980, 170-171).

Dorn took Olson's exhortations to heart in his sizable body of poetry and prose.[4] The titles of his numerous published collections suggest a common ground: *Geography* (1965), with its long narrative "Idaho Out"; *The Shoshoneans* (1966, in collaboration with African American photographer LeRoy Lucas); *The North Atlantic Turbine* (1967); *Recollections of Gran Apachería* (1974b); *Mesozoic Landscape* (1974d); *Slinger* (1975); and *Hello, La Jolla* (1978). Underlying much of Dorn's writing is the belief that because the North American continent offers the poet a new set of materials, a fresh set of possibilities becomes available. Dorn's work is eminently geographical in taste, scholarship, and sensibility. It is waggishly so in a part of "Idaho Out":

>   no
> the sky
>   is not
> bigger in Montana. When
> for instance you come
> from Williston
> there seems at the border a change

> but it is only because man has
> built a tavern there.
>
>   (Dorn 1975a, 115)

A more emphatic geography appears in Dorn's *The North Atlantic Turbine*, a poetic study of mercantilism and its role in the formation of a global economy (Dorn 1967). Michael Davidson argues that "The theme of the poem, like that of Olson's *Maximus* series, is the displacement of man by the 'turbine' of the global dollar. . . . From the rum and slave trade to munitions sales to the war in Vietnam, the swirling force of North Atlantic mercantilism widens; its ultimate result is the transformation of man" (Davidson 1980, 170):

> †note: Natural resources have been
>   the first way men
>   have been put down:
>   to exploit the immediate surroundings
>   and then have themselves at large, and if
>   resources have been absent
>   the unlucky have had to settle
>   for a moral lesson: *buy* or *die*.
>   Since the original design of the earth
>   left no area lacking in *some*
>   resource deprivation has always
>   meant "lack of machinery."
>   Natural resources generate the unnatural—
>   (not the "super" natural,
>   which is creative)
>   is a basic paradox.
>
>   (Dorn 1975b, 192-193)

At the beginning of "Idaho Out" Dorn makes Carl Sauer's words a declaration of his own conviction: "The thing to be known is the natural landscape. It becomes known through the totality of its forms" (Sauer 1963a, 337; Dorn 1975a, 115). In discussing this meditation upon a round trip between Pocatello, Idaho, and Missoula, Montana, critic Sherman Paul noted that Dorn's three conspicuous references are Olson, Sauer, and LeRoi Jones, with Olson and Sauer "conjoined in what Dorn calls 'earth-writing'" (Paul 1981, 104). "Idaho Out" and much of Dorn's other work relates the trauma involved in wresting the land from a "gathering" people, a habit or lifeway "not to be broken in a few generations by official declaration or harassment" (Paul 1981, 104), as in "The Slipping of the Wheel," from *Recollections of Gran Apachería*:

> They were sentenced to observe
> the destruction of their World
> The revolutionary implications
> are interesting
>
> They embody a state
> which our still encircled world
> looks toward from the past
>
>   (Dorn 1974c; unpaginated)

This, Sherman Paul notes, "is what Sauer's *Man in Nature: America Before the Days of the White Men* [the 1939 grade-school primer] is about, the incredible human achievement of habituation of the land, that long habituation of place that makes an Indian unwilling to forsake it, set against the implicit consequences of what every child already knows: *after the days of the white man*. After history, as Lévi-Strauss tells in *Tristes Tropiques*" (Paul 1981, 131). Behind *The North Atlantic Turbine*, Paul suggests, was "perhaps Sauer's *Northern Mists*, the Sauer of the West, like Dorn, having turned East? The meanness of not just Americans; it belongs to Western Civilization, originating in the imperialism fostered by the opening up of the seas" (Paul 1981, 141). As early as 1957, with the publication of Dorn's "C.B.& Q." in the *Black Mountain Review*, the influence of Sauer was evident. "Like Carl Sauer and Charles Olson before him," wrote the critic William Lockwood, "Dorn has earned a distinctive and distinguished place among the great geographers of the North American soul" (Lockwood 1978, 79).

At its most austere, Dorn's poetry shares Sauer's intuition for fact, direct and astringent, as in his assay of the fate and history of the Apache of the North American Southwest:

> The most absolute of the predatory tribes
> Apache policy was to extirpate
> Every trace of civilization
> From their province.
>
> (Dorn 1974a, unpaginated)

But in Dorn's writing there can be moments of equal lightness and grace. These fill his epic *Slinger*, with its allusions to an elusive Howard Hughes, Claude Lévi-Strauss, Truth or Consequences, New Mexico, an ongoing (and never consummated) pilgrimage to Las Vegas, Nevada, and a whole range of in-jokes:

> But now, over the endless sagey brush
> the moon makes her silvery bid
> and in the cool dry air of the night
> the winde wankels across the cattle grid.
>
> (Dorn 1975c, [144])

It was not, however, solely Dorn and Olson who took Sauer's ideas to heart. The larger sensibility that Olson praised, so much embodied in Sauer's feeling for the past and for the human exploitation of the larger world, came to be part of the poetry of many writers, especially those who called the American West their home. Of these, perhaps Gary Snyder may be the clearest example.[5] Snyder shares Sauer's deep appreciation for the longer reaches of human time and its value for teaching us now. Whereas Olson turned to

Gloucester and Dorn looked to the arid Southwest of the United States for much of his grounding in place, Snyder is the poet of California and the Pacific Slope. He is arguably the leading—certainly the best known—proponent of a bioregionalist ethic, with its insistence that localities matter and that we turn away from them only at great personal and spiritual cost (Parsons 1985). An essayist and Zen disciple, Snyder is also among the most explicitly geographical of American writers. From *Regarding Wave* (1970), one of Snyder's poems is titled "What You Need to Know to Be a Poet," and the advice is succinct:

> all you can about animals as persons
>   the names of trees and flowers and weeds
>   names of stars, and the movements of the planets
>   and the moon.
>   your own six senses, with a watchful and
>   elegant mind.
>
> (Snyder 1970, 40)

Although Sauer might not have embraced the whole of the sentiments of these poets and writers, there could be little doubt that the geographer would appreciate their drift.

The Contact

It was clearly Charles Olson who "discovered" Sauer and from whom enthusiasm for him and his geography radiated outward through this segment of the postmodern literary community.[6] By all accounts Olson was a charismatic if elusive figure who was impossible to ignore, not simply because of his mountainous size and his mental brilliance but also because of the way he disposed himself. The two men first met in 1947, when Olson came to Berkeley's Bancroft Library in search of materials on the Gold Rush. Sauer would have known something of the New Englander through his fellowship applications to the Guggenheim Foundation, for which the geographer long served on the selection committee. (Olson was a Guggenheim Fellow in 1939 and again in 1948.) At this first meeting Olson was immediately overwhelmed, according to Callahan (1975), with the geographer's knowledge of American space. But if Sauer saw in Olson a most unusual and interesting mind, "a powerhouse and genius of some order," he also found his conversation and unconventional writing "difficult and frequently incomprehensible" (Callahan 1975, [13]).

A fitful exchange of letters took place during the next dozen or so years (Callahan 1979), with Olson repeatedly expressing admiration and affection for the professor, before whom he seems to

ON THE SUBJECT OF...

STUART Z. PERKOFF

For the West Coast Beats, particularly the writing community located in Venice, California, Stuart Z. Perkoff was one of the most respected poets of the Beat era. Eyewitnesses describe his readings with almost religious fervor, and celebrities such as Groucho Marx and Steve Allen considered Perkoff the quintessential Beat (he was a frequent guest on their respective television shows). Despite such reverence, Perkoff never achieved a widespread readership. A contributing factor to his relative anonymity was his tendency toward addiction; from books to heroin, Perkoff's passions overwhelmed other aspects of his life and career. Numerous stories circulated among his friends and admirers about the great number of unpublished poems that vanished during Perkoff's erratic career. Testimonies abound of brilliant work lost in countless moves, arrests, and confiscations of property. His relatively small body of published work—from 1956's *Suicide Room* to *Alphabet* (1973), to the last collection before his death in 1974—is all the tangible evidence that remains of Perkoff's legacy. But for the artists and followers of the Beat scene, he occupied a place of almost exemplary importance. In short, he is, as many called him, a "pure" or "poet's poet."

have stood in uncharacteristic humility. "It doesn't matter that you are an impossible correspondent," he wrote with warmth and familiarity, "I still love you. But why don't you put me on some minor mailing list so that I can get your notices to members of your department or such?" He sought persistently to pick Sauer's brain on questions such as "How long had man been herbivorous?" "What was the first flesh he ate?" "How did earlier man understand the juxtaposition of the position between the Sun and the She-Boss?" or "What to read for the latest on the tradition of pre-Columbian Chinese voyages to the New World?" (Callahan 1979, 136-139).

"But there you are," Olson wrote on 20 October 1949, "too many miles away and you won't

talk. I can't even get a correspondence course out of you." On 25 October 1950 he wrote to Sauer, "You are one of the rare and native forces. . . . I am hungry for all Carl Sauer says in print. Please, please! I don't know of a man whose work I want more to keep abreast of." Somewhat later came a letter from Campeche, Mexico, expressing a profound sadness over the death by his own hand of young Robert Barlow (1918-1951), the reserved but accomplished Nahuatl scholar and poet who Sauer had enthusiastically supported and recommended to Olson, described by the latter as "so much fine wood your own hand had worked" (Callahan 1979, 140-148 ff).

Black Mountain College

Soon after the Mexican sojourn, which had produced his *Mayan Letters* (1953), Olson went to Black Mountain College near Asheville, where, for the next five years, he was the presiding spirit, at the height of his powers of persuasion and intellect (Duberman 1972). Early in his tenure Olson sought unsuccessfully to lure Sauer to head up an institute at the school to be devoted to "the geographical and biosciences as proper gates for an attack upon man" (Duberman 1972, 478). Sauer in reply had suggested the British ecologist Frank Fraser Darling (1903-1979) or the architect and author Roderick Seidenberg (1910-1973) as possibilities. Concluding with an expression of hope for a favorable outcome of Olson's application to the Viking Fund for financial support, he subtly added, "But you can write quite difficult language you know" (Callahan 1979, 152).

For Black Mountain students and friends alike, Olson's recommended bibliography on America included many names familiar to geographers: Francis Parkman, Bernard DeVoto, Walter Prescott Webb, Armin Lobeck, Harvard historian Frederick Merk, and the botanist Edgar Anderson, but especially, in Olson's own words (clearly delivered from imperfect memory), "Carl Sauer, from 'Environment & Culture in the Last Deglaciation' all the way through 'Road to Cíbola,' back to his first job, for the State of Illinois handbook (1915?) on the new State park at Starved Rock, [and including] Sauer doing job on Indian agriculture" (Olson 1974, 11).

Sauer's reluctance to become too involved with the enigmatic poet-historian is evident from the correspondence, which is dominated by Olson's pleas for attention. Of the twelve letters that have been retrieved and published (Callahan 1979), nine are from Olson. Olson's last (14 July 1960), noting despondently that his funds were exhausted, asked for a complete bibliography of Sauer's publications (Callahan 1979, 166). It was Professor Sauer's secretary who replied, stating that he had forgotten the request and had instructed her to send it as he was departing on an extended trip. When Olson visited the Berkeley campus in 1965 for what must have been a most raucous reading at the Berkeley Poetry Conference, there is no record of his having attempted to contact Sauer (Olson 1966b).

The relationship that Olson seems to have hoped for did not develop. Just before he died he somewhat timorously made a cross-country telephone call to Sauer, then more than eighty years old and to whom he had not written or spoken for many years. He expressed surprise and delight at the warmth of the response at the other end of the line ("How are you, Charles?") after all that time (Boer 1975, 68; Callahan, 1979, 168). The subject of the conversation can only be surmised. He was quite possibly seeking Sauer's assistance on another application for funding or perhaps some esoteric bit of information on the distant American past that so preoccupied him.

As is so often chronic with poets, financial problems were recurrent. Olson recognized Sauer's influence with the major foundations but found himself reluctant to use him. "My ace is Sauer," he wrote to his friend Robert Creeley, "but one plays one's ace carefully. . . . One has to weigh all moves now against what may happen 3-5 years ahead and I hold back on Sauer until I have something solid. I respect him so much. . . . He is the best backer I could turn to in such work as this, the most open, and one wants to offer the most" (Butterick 1980b, 88).

In an unpublished paper prepared for a seminar at Berkeley some months after Sauer's death, Bob Callahan wrote:

> Most of the major writers that have emerged from Black Mountain [or been associated with it] have found the work of Carl Sauer on their required reading lists, and this includes some of the greatest American writers practicing the craft to this day. . . . It is not . . . because of some abstract linguistic ability that these writers continue to read Sauer—but rather that they feel that they can tell an original mind at work when they come across one.

(Callahan 1975, [13-14])

They have been equally impressed, Callahan continues, with Sauer's studies of the origins and diffusion of agriculture and of frontier life in early America:

> These writers have been drawn to Sauer's studies of colonial conditions as the ancient world of the American Indian and its long-standing traditions . . . came to clash with the New World of the Europeans and then Euro-Americans. As Americans this clash between these two worlds is still the biggest story we have and our writers, don't forget, are still our appointed story makers and story-tellers. The relationship between Carl Sauer and Charles Olson, and the continuing & growing awareness of Sauer by students of American Literature is, I think, always renewed on these grounds. Born on this continent the American writer has finally learned that he has as much if not more to learn from the Zuni Farmers of the Southwest as he does from the Cathedral Makers of France, and to a great extent he realizes & continues to learn from both Charles Olson and Carl Sauer [and to thank them] for providing this opening.

(Callahan 1975, [14])

Except for Callahan, who developed a close personal relationship with Sauer in the geographer's last years (Callahan had been urged by friends to look up Sauer on his move to the Bay Area), the familiarity of the Black Mountain folk with Sauer derived almost entirely from their readings of Sauer's work. Olson, especially, was concerned with the importance of landscape and space early in his historical ruminations and found in Sauer, for whom history was so fundamental for his own discipline, a congenial spirit. At the time of their first encounter the fiercely energetic and unorthodox Olson had just completed his much heralded if convoluted *Call Me Ishmael*, which he saw as a literal account of the whaling industry rewritten as tragedy under the influence of Shakespeare. In it Pacific whaling is viewed as the fateful extension of America's pioneer effort. Its opening paragraph marked the author as a "born geographer" in the mold of Carl Sauer: "I take SPACE to be the central fact to man born in America, from Folsom Cave to now. I spell it large because it comes large here, large and without mercy. It is geography at bottom" (Olson 1947, 11).

Many of the central figures in Olson's works, especially in the convoluted *Maximus* poems, are also present in Sauer's writings—the Vikings, Columbus, Juan de la Cosa, Cabeza de Vaca, Captain John Smith. The year after the two men first met, Olson traveled beyond the border to Lerma, a few miles south of Campeche on the Yucatán coast. His extended researches, documented in his *Mayan Letters*, make the debt to Sauer apparent. He was fascinated by this "glyph world" and its mysteries and was especially interested in Sauer's speculation that the Mayan push into the lowlands of Yucatán may in some way have been associated with a dietary need for the protein and fat that coastal fishing would have provided.

Time and again Olson, widely credited in literary circles with transforming the shape and practice of poetry since 1945, lavished praise on Sauer before his friends and associates. In 1954 he named the Berkeley geographer to the Black Mountain College Advisory Board, along with such luminaries as Albert Einstein, Carl Jung, Norbert Weiner, the painter Franz Kline, and William Carlos Williams. The appointment was no more than a sinecure, a kind of window dressing, perhaps even made without Sauer's knowledge or permission. At a proposed Institute of the New Sciences Olson had envisioned "Sauer talking about place, England's Christopher Hawkes on culture and Carl Jung on mythology" (Clark 1991, 233). Another time Olson had bracketed Sauer with Victor Bérard (the French *Ulysses* scholar), Josef Strzykowski (the Austrian art historian), Leo Frobenius (the German anthropologist), and Owen Lattimore (the geographer-sinologist) as "the boys who taught me something" (Duberman 1972, 374; Butterick 1980b, 129). In his last years Olson came up with another list of the major influences on his life, judging himself to have had four fathers in addition to his natural one: his Wesleyan College teacher Wilbert Snow, the Gloucester fisherman Lou Douglas, Ezra Pound, and Carl Sauer (Boer 1975).

In a checklist of the books and papers owned, read, and consulted by Charles Olson in the course of his literary career (Butterick 1976; Maud 1996), only Pound, D. H. Lawrence, and Olson's beloved Melville are cited more frequently than is Carl Sauer, for whom there are twelve entries. Olson, no less than Melville, seems to have "read to write," doing so prodigiously. His writings clearly reflect an insuperable appetite for the riches of the written word. One is struck in perusing the extensive checklist by both the scope of Olson's interests (the parallel with Sauer is evident) and what a major poet of our time felt he needed to know.

The Enduring Attraction of Sauer

The surprising attraction of the innovative and influential Olson, with many other writers of his genre, to Sauer seems explainable on at least five grounds. First, Sauer and Olson each had strongly developed interests in beginnings, in the entire span of human history on American soil and the problems associated with the origin and diffusion of culture and culture traits, including possible pre-Columbian linkages between the Old World and the New World. Sauer's writings on early man and his insistence on pushing human history back to dates well beyond those of more conventional scholars strongly appealed to Olson and to at least some of his followers. It made, of course, for a great story. Anxious to get away from what one described as "the Westernism of Greek culture," this new generation of poet-historians looked directly and reverentially to the American experience. Sauer's "Environment and Culture During the Last Deglaciation" (1948), "The End of the Ice Age and Its Witnesses" (1957), and similar, often speculative, Sauer papers relating to the first sedentary fishing communities, the origin of agriculture, and human ecological dominance through the use of fire were accepted as gospel. Sauer's *Northern Mists* (1968), which explored early Viking and Irish voyages to the New World, was seen by Olson as a gold mine. And so on. To Olson's regarding eyes the circle of Sauer's interests, so rich with imagery, appeared without boundaries. So did his authority.

Second, they found congenial Sauer's championing of direct observation, of hands-on knowledge, of the "eye-view." His concept of the cultural landscape and its morphological study—the study of the form and content of a specific locale—was to them a refreshing spring. It was from eyewitness accounts of the sixteenth- and seventeenth-century explorers and chroniclers, as in *The Early Spanish Main* (1966), *Sixteenth Century North America: The Land and People as Seen by Europeans* (1971), and *Seventeenth Century North America* (1980), that Sauer drew many of his ideas and inferences regarding the conditions of land and life at the time of contact. His own observations about the Middle West of his boyhood, and later in Latin America, which informed so much of his writing, honored the local. We recall his advice to field-workers that "locomotion should be slow, the slower the better" and how he decried the betrayal of geography by the increasing numbers of younger practitioners who, refusing to use their eyes, knew little and cared less for the real or natural world (Sauer 1963f, 400).

Third, accompanying this was Sauer's emphasis on labeling, on identification, on "unadorned facts." He wrote to a student:

> The pleasure of geographical description [a term to be used with respect] is in proper identification. I suspect and hope (!) that this is a pleasure that those who work with numbers miss. . . . My great dictum for the day is that identification comes through seeing (and recording).
>
> (Sauer 1962)

As a geographer, Sauer recognized the critical importance of binomial nomenclature in the biological world, of the correct identification of rocks, of clouds, of places on the map, and of culture traits from pottery styles to house types, and he found pleasure in such knowledge. This was not a form of pedantry but a way to elevate observations on the matter at hand to their broader implications. The Black Mountain poets' appreciation of names, of words, was perhaps based as much on aesthetics as on a desire to deepen understanding, but they recognized a friend when they spotted one.

Fourth, the emphasis on space and the running of time, on location, extension, position, and distribution (mapping), was central to the ways of both Sauer and the Olson school and congenial to their temperaments. Process and change, especially the impact of humankind on the land, as exemplified by the Sauer-inspired Princeton conference in 1956 on Man's Role in Changing the Face of the Earth, lay at the heart of Sauer's historical geography (Sauer 1963b; West 1981; Williams 1983, 1987). This inevitably brought into play the data of archeologists and anthropologists, especially those who were receptive to early dates for humans in the New World. This paleogeography or archeology was not static. Olson, at times as much historian as poet, wrote from the limestone lands of Yucatán in 1951 of "process as the most important fact . . . the overwhelming one, how it works" (Butterick 1980b). Sauer's Middle West and Olson's Gloucester were of a kind, places remembered fondly but ever changing, not always for the better.

Finally, Sauer's flair for metaphor and evocative expression, the earthiness of his resolutely American conversational language, the ingenuity of his hypotheses, inevitably struck a favorable chord among writers who were familiar with his work. The larger the synthesis the more powerful. The *Village Voice*, periodical of record for Manhattan's Bohemian quarter, had described his *Man in Nature: America Before the Days of the White Men* (1939), as "insinuating the white man's villainy (in the dispossession of Indian America) in a tone more elegiac than angry" (Village Voice 1976, 29). Olson, no mean judge of such matters despite his own telegraphic, "free form writing style,"[7] referred glowingly to Sauer's prose as "too much for novelists to match" (Butterick 1980a, 60). The writing was, as Callahan put it, "spare, very direct and pragmatic . . . clear-headed, wonderfully personal, eccentric, always humane," the best Sauer essays having "the rhythm and lucidity of

long symphonic poems" (Callahan 1976, 52). And again, "The good doctor, as people are wont to say, could sure pack it in" (Callahan 1976, 52).[8],[9]

Conclusion

Carl Sauer and the Black Mountain poets, along with their followers, studied and wrote of the past because they liked it. They not only had a certain nostalgia for early American values, they found much to admire in the continuity represented by generations reaching back numerous millennia. Yet they were at the same time alert to the world around them and concerned about its uncertain fate. For Charles Olson and his literary heirs, at least, historical geography—especially as represented by the vision and the written word of Carl Sauer—seems to have opened new and challenging horizons. Many contemporary poets know of Sauer and have read him appreciatively. The critical literature is replete with references to this relationship. Such attention from so unexpected a quarter brings welcome further validation and vindication for the branch of our discipline that perhaps promises the closest and most rewarding linkages with the humanities and the world of letters (Meinig 1989). Cultural and historical geographers are not drifting alone in that vast sea of creative endeavor, unnoticed and unappreciated. The linkages described here with even so seemingly remote a group as these postmodern poets reminds us of the interdisciplinary attraction and centrality of what interests us and what we do, at least when we do it well. For that, Carl Sauer will ever stand as a model and inspiration.

Notes

1. Certainly Sauer has had his detractors. Some have dismissed his work as "shabby, parochial and unintelligent" (Gould 1979, 140). Others have targeted him for a purported narrow-mindedness (Pred 1984). Either view represents a fringe position within geography.

2. Turtle Island Press (2845 Buena Vista Way, Berkeley, California 94708) published Carl Sauer's 295-page *Seventeenth Century North America* (1980) and his 391-page *Selected Essays 1963-1975* (edited and with an introduction by Bob Callahan; 1981) and reprinted the school text *Man in Nature: America Before the Days of the White Men* (1939) and *Northern Mists* (1968).

3. The 1977 Ph.D. dissertation of Graham Clarke, "Landscape and Geography: Approaches to English and American Poetry with Specific Reference to Charles Olson," University of Essex, has not been available. It would appear to relate closely to the theme of this essay.

4. Dorn's debt to Sauer is underscored both by the poet himself and in numerous critical essays on his works, of which *Gunslinger* (a.k.a. *Slinger*) and "Idaho Out"

have attracted the most attention. The poet, most recently on the faculty of the University of Colorado, expounded on both the nature of geography and the man who brought him to it in a series of interviews:

> I got interested in Sauer because he was the first one, especially in that "Morphology of Landscape," who spoke to me with that love of the formation of the land which was beyond what I could see as an aesthetic, as an alternative. Superior to an aesthetic because it was like the constituents, the bones of America.
>
> (Dorn 1980, 21-22)

And:

> There are systems of knowledge that the University wouldn't actually reproduce on its own, with its stamp. For instance, the kind of transmission across the frontiers of Geography that Sauer made. That involved a lot of people who weren't geographers, or even poets. There seem to be small universities that have grown like buds on the [larger] University, and they are really interdisciplinary.
>
> (Dorn 1980, 68)

And, more specifically, of geography as a humanizing discipline:

> I don't feel that geography itself or a human preoccupation with the geography or a concern with the aesthetic properties of landscape and so forth necessarily leads anywhere at all and in fact most of that material is more or less interesting perhaps but inert. Until it is infused with the whole dynamism of human movement I think its meaning is trivial. After all, the appreciation of landscape and geography is a human involvement.
>
> (Dorn 1980, 44-45)

5. The connection between Snyder and Olson involves more than circuitous Black Mountain ties; they had also some interesting mutual friends. When Snyder was studying Zen in Kyoto, a frequent contact there was the poet, translator, and publisher Cid Corman (Eshleman 1991, 235-236). It was Corman who, in the 1950s, had resurrected the then-moribund periodical, *Origin,* which became a main publishing venue for Charles Olson and Robert Creeley (Evans 1987; Clark 1991, 181).

6. It has been noted (Hoover 1994, xxv) that Olson used the word "postmodern" as early as 20 October 1951, in a letter from Black Mountain to Robert Creeley (Butterick 1980c, 72). Over the years the term has received increasing acceptance in all areas of culture and the arts. Applied to the period following World War II it suggests, in Paul Hoover's words, "an experimental approach to composition as well as a worldview that sets it apart from mainstream culture. Postmodernist poetry is the avant-garde poetry of our time. It has reshaped and recharged poetry through new, but initially shocking, strategies" (Hoover, 1994, xxv). There is a certain irony that Sauer and Olson, two figures so fundamentally conservative and yet creative, should turn out to be the figureheads of postmodern innovation.

7. One critic described Olson "at his most irritating [as] like a computer overloaded with modern thought and ancient culture. He simply spews out citations, translations, beliefs" (Stimpson 1973-1974, 151). A former Black Mountain student noted his "militant insistence on subjectivity, self expression, and self exposure" and that "he emanated an awesome oracular majesty (in part shrewdly cultivated) which one only associates with the most seasoned shamans" (Gray 1990, 301).

8. Callahan concludes a later lyrical essay, an overarching historical review that reaches deep into the American past, with his own bit of "symphonic poetry," based on Sauer's "A Geographic Sketch of Early Man in America" (Sauer 1963d), in which, he observes, the geographer

> so warms to the detail of his reconstruction that the prose, with mild rearrangement, can almost be heard as song:
>
> The route of dispersal south
>   along the eastern base of the Rockies, south-
>   east
>   into the forest in pursuit of old world mam-
>   mals,
>   musk ox, giant elk, mammoth, bison burn-
>   ing ahead
>   the plains
>   transformed, wooded areas turning into
>   grasslands
>   down past St. Louis
>   the winding Pleistocene river, melted, reaches
>   the rich mesothermal woodland of lower
>   Missouri:
>   groves of nut trees growing
>   in the new, loess-covered, upland soil
>   walnut, hickory, pecan in the flood plain
>   stands of oaks of many kinds, some with
>   sweet acorns,
>   grapes, black cherry, persimmon, pawpaw,
>   Virginia deer, opossum, turkey, quail, wood-
>   cock.
>
> Here the flight of migrant waterfowl
>   converged in the fall, scattered
>   in the spring to northern breeding grounds
>   river bluffs & Ozark hills, limitless
>   supply of superb chert, suitable for tools,
>   and salt licks marked the outcroppings of
>   shale beds,
>   creeks
>   and river bluffs, cut into Paleozoic rocks of
>   varying
>   resistance,
>   formed snug coves and shelter at last
>   away from the western winde.
>
> (Callahan 1977, 107-108)

Callahan continues on Sauer:

> In still another essay, *The End of the Ice Age and Its Witnesses,* he spells out the character of these cultures and their central cultural traits—the old bison and elephant hunters of the southern plains, the early basketmaker cultures centered in and around what is now Nevada, and the ancient miller cultures of southern California. In still a third, and possibly the most famous essay, *Environment & Culture During the Last Deglaciation,* he extends his survey to note in passing the evidence of an old Fishing Culture, a "Pro-

gressive Fishing Folk" as he puts it, and goes on to suggest a connective link between the first people and the people who will create the American Neolithic. Let us not be timid about this contribution, for too much caution takes the soul out of imagination: Let us see these essays as they are—notes toward an American Book of Genesis, the rediscovery of the very first New World.

(Callahan 1977, 108)

Thanks to William Denevan, emeritus Carl Ortwin Sauer Professor of Geography, University of Wisconsin, Madison, for pointing out this felicitous tribute.

9. The spirit of place and a sensitivity to the local is, of course, widely reflected in the field of modern American literature (Lutwack 1984). It is a sensitivity increasingly inspired by recognition that the environment is being radically changed and degraded by more and more powerful and pervasive technologies. Among other nonacademics who have recently paid tribute to the geography of Sauer as a guiding force in their writing are Barry Lopez (*Crossing Open Ground* [1988]) and Michael Parfit (*Chasing the Glory* [1988]).

Works Cited

Alpert, B. 1977. Introduction. In D. Davie, *The Poet in the Imaginary Museum,* edited by B. Alpert, ix-xxi. New York: Persea Books.

Allen, D. C., ed. 1960. *The New American Poetry: 1945-1960.* New York: Grove Press.

Boer, C. 1975. *Charles Olson in Connecticut.* Chicago: Swallow Press.

Brand, S. 1976. Untitled editorial introduction accompanying reprint of Sauer's "Themes of Plant and Animal Domestication in Economic History." *Co-Evolution Quarterly* No. 10: 53.

Butterick, C., ed. 1976. Olson's Reading: A Preliminary Report. *Olson, the Journal of the Charles Olson Archives* [Storrs: University of Connecticut] 5: 85-86.

———. 1980a. *Charles Olson and Robert Creeley: The Complete Correspondence.* Vol. 1. Santa Barbara, Calif.: Black Sparrow Press.

———. 1980b. *Charles Olson and Robert Creeley: The Complete Correspondence.* Vol. 5. Santa Barbara, Calif.: Black Sparrow Press.

———. 1980c. *Charles Olson and Robert Creeley: The Complete Correspondence.* Vol. 8. Santa Barbara, Calif.: Black Sparrow Press.

Callahan, B. 1975. Untitled report to a seminar on Carl Sauer's contribution to Latin American studies, Department of Geography, University of California, Berkeley, 14 manuscript pages.

———. 1976. A Carl Sauer Checklist. *Co-Evolution Quarterly* 10: 52-53.

———. 1977. Carl Sauer (The Migrations). *New World Journal* [Berkeley, Calif.] 1 (2-3): 94-111.

———. 1978. Bob Callahan on Turtle Island: An Interview with Michael Helm. *City Miner* [Berkeley, Calif.] 3 (3): 24-26, 33-39.

———. 1979. The Correspondences: Charles Olson & Carl Sauer. *New World Journal* [Berkeley, Calif.] 1 (4): 136-168.

Clark, T. 1991. *The Allegory of a Poet's Life.* New York and London: W. W. Norton.

Clarke, G. 1977. Landscape and Geography: Approaches to English and American Poetry with Specific Reference to Charles Olson. Ph.D. diss., University of Essex.

Davidson, M. 1980. Archeologist of Morning: Charles Olson, Edward Dorn, and Historical Method. *ELH [English Literary History]* 47 (1): 158-179.

———. 1989. *The San Francisco Renaissance: Poetics and Community at Mid-Century.* Cambridge, England: Cambridge University Press.

Davie, D. 1977a [1968]. Landscape as Poetic Focus. In *The Poet in the Imaginary Museum,* edited by B. Alpert, 165-176. New York: Persea Books.

———. 1977b [1970]. The Black Mountain Poets. In *The Poet in the Imaginary Museum,* edited by B. Alpert, 177-190. New York: Persea Books.

———. 1977c. *The Poet in the Imaginary Museum.* Edited by B. Alpert. New York: Persea Books.

Dorn, E. 1965. *Geography.* London: Fulcrum Press.

———. 1967. *The North Atlantic Turbine.* London: Fulcrum Press.

———. 1974a. Dress for War. In *Recollections of Gran Apachería,* unpaginated. Berkeley, Calif.: Turtle Island Press.

———. 1974b. *Recollections of Gran Apachería.* Berkeley, Calif.: Turtle Island Press.

———. 1974c. The Slipping of the Wheel. In *Recollections of Gran Apachería,* unpaginated. Berkeley, Calif.: Turtle Island Press.

———. 1974d. *Mesozoic Landscape.* [Kent, Ohio:] Kent State Arts Festival.

———. 1975a [1965]. Idaho Out. In *The Collected Poems 1956-1974,* 107-122. Bolinas, Calif.: Four Seasons Foundation.

———. 1975b [1967]. A Theory of Truth, The North Atlantic Turbine. In *The Collected Poems 1956-1974,* 186-195. Bolinas, Calif.: Four Seasons Foundation.

———. 1975c. *Slinger* [previously published serially as *Gunslinger I, II, III,* and *The Cycle*]. Berkeley, Calif.: Wingbow Press.

———. 1978. *Hello, La Jolla.* Berkeley, Calif.: Wingbow Press.

———. 1980. *Interviews.* Edited by D. Allen. Bolinas, Calif.: Four Seasons Foundation.

Dorn, E., and L. Lucas. 1966. *The Shoshoneans: The People of the Basin-Plateau.* New York: William Morrow.

Duberman, M. 1972. *Black Mountain: An Exploration in Community.* New York: E. P. Dutton.

Eshleman, C. 1991. Imagination's Body and Comradely Display. In *Gary Snyder: Dimensions of a Life,* edited by J. Halper, 231-242. San Franciso, Calif.: Sierra Club Books.

Evans, G., ed. 1987. *Charles Olson and Cid Corman: Complete Correspondence 1950-1964.* Orono, Maine: National Poetry Foundation, University of Maine.

Ford, O. J. 1973-1974. Charles Olson and Carl Sauer: Towards a Methodology of Knowing. *Boundary 2* Fall and Winter 2 (1-2): 145-150.

Fox, W., III. 1989. *Robert Creeley, Edward Dorn and Robert Duncan: A Reference Guide.* Boston: G. K. Hall.

Gould, P. 1979. Geography 1957-1977: The Augean Period. *Annals of the Association of American Geographers* 69 (1): 139-151.

Gray, Francine du Plessix. 1990. Black Mountain: The Breaking (Making) of a Writer. In *Black Mountain College: Sprouted Seeds,* edited by M. Lane, 300-311. Knoxville: University of Tennessee Press.

Hoover, P., ed. 1994. *Postmodern American Poetry: A Norton Anthology.* New York: W. W. Norton.

Leighly, J., ed. 1963. *Land and Life: A Selection from the Writings of Carl Ortwin Sauer.* Berkeley, Los Angeles, and London: University of California Press.

Lockwood, W. J. 1978. Ed Dorn's Mystique of the Real: His Poems for North America. *Contemporary Literature* 19 (1): 59-79.

Lopez, B. 1988. *Crossing Open Ground.* New York: Charles Scribner's Sons.

Lutwack, L. 1984. *The Role of Place in Literature.* Syracuse, N.Y.: Syracuse University Press.

McPheron, W. 1986. *Charles Olson, A Critical Reception 1941-1983. A Bibliographic Guide.* New York and London: Garland.

———. 1988. *Edward Dorn.* Boise, Idaho: Boise State University.

Maud, R. 1996. *Charles Olson's Readings: A Biography.* Carbondale and Edwardsville: Southern Illinois University Press.

Meinig, D. W. 1989. The Historical Geography Imperative. *Annals of the Association of American Geographers* 79 (1): 79-87.

Olson, C. 1947. *Call Me Ishmael.* New York: Reynal and Hitchcock.

———. 1953. *Mayan Letters by Charles Olson.* Edited by R. Creeley. Palma de Mallorca [Spain]: Divers Press.

———. 1966a [1950]. Projective Verse. In *Selected Writings of Charles Olson,* edited by R. Creeley, 15-30. New York: New Directions.

———. 1966b. *Charles Olson Reading at Berkeley.* Transcribed by Z. Brown. San Francisco: Coyote Books [City Lights].

———. 1974 [1964]. A Bibliography on America for Ed Dorn. In *A Bibliography on America for Ed Dorn, Proprioception, and Other Notes & Essays,* edited by G. F. Butterick, 3-14. Bolinas, Calif.: Four Seasons Foundation.

———. 1983. *The Maximus Poems.* Edited by G. F. Butterick. Berkeley, Los Angeles, and London: University of California Press.

———. 1987. *The Collected Poems of Charles Olson, Excluding the Maximus Poems.* Edited by G. F. Butterick. Berkeley, Los Angeles, and London: University of California Press.

Parfit, M. 1988. *Chasing the Glory: Travels across America.* New York: Macmillan.

Parsons, J. J. 1985. On "Bioregionalism" and "Watershed Consciousness." *Professional Geographer* 37 (1): 1-6.

Paul, S. 1975. In and about *The Maximus Poems. Iowa Review* 6 (1): 118-130; 6 (3): 74-95.

———. 1981. *The Lost America of Love: Rereading Robert Creeley, Edward Dorn, and Robert Duncan.* Baton Rouge: Louisiana State University Press.

Pred, A. 1984. From Here and Now to There and Then: Some Notes on Diffusion, Defusions and Disillusions. In *Recollections of a Revolution: Geography as Spatial Science,* edited by M. Billinge, D. Gregory, and R. Martins, 86-103. New York: St. Martin's Press.

Sauer, C. O. 1939. *Man in Nature: America Before the Days of the White Men. A First Book in Geography.* New York: Charles Scribner's Sons.

———. 1962. Letter, C. O. Sauer to M. W. Mikesell, 14 February. Sauer Papers, Bancroft Library, University of California, Berkeley.

———. 1963a [1925]. The Morphology of Landscape. In *Land and Life: A Selection from the Writings of Carl Ortwin Sauer,* edited by J. Leighly, 315-350. Berkeley and Los Angeles: University of California Press.

———. 1963b [1941]. Foreword to Historical Geography. In *Land and Life: A Selection from the Writings of Carl Ortwin Sauer,* edited by J. Leighly, 351-379. Berkeley and Los Angeles: University of California Press.

———. 1963c [1941]. The Personality of Mexico. In *Land and Life: A Selection from the Writings of Carl Ortwin Sauer,* edited by J. Leighly, 104-118. Berkeley and Los Angeles: University of California Press.

———. 1963d [1944]. A Geographic Sketch of Early Man in America. In *Land and Life: A Selection from the Writings of Carl Ortwin Sauer,* edited by J. Leighly, 197-245. Berkeley and Los Angeles: University of California Press.

———. 1963e [1948]. Environment and Culture During the Last Deglaciation. In *Land and Life: A Selection from the Writings of Carl Ortwin Sauer,* edited by J. Leighly, 246-270. Berkeley and Los Angeles: University of California Press.

———. 1963f [1956]. The Education of a Geographer. In *Land and Life: A Selection from the Writings of Carl Ortwin Sauer,* edited by J. Leighly, 389-404. Berkeley and Los Angeles: University of California Press.

———. 1963g [1957]. The End of the Ice Age and Its Witnesses. In *Land and Life: A Selection from the Writings of Carl Ortwin Sauer,* edited by J. Leighly, 271-288. Berkeley and Los Angeles: University of California Press.

———. 1963h. *Land and Life: A Selection from the Writings of Carl Ortwin Sauer.* Edited by J. Leighly. Berkeley and Los Angeles: University of California Press.

———. 1966. *The Early Spanish Main.* Berkeley and Los Angeles: University of California Press.

———. 1968. *Northern Mists.* Berkeley and Los Angeles: University of California Press.

———. 1971. *Sixteenth Century North America: The Land and People as Seen by Europeans.* Berkeley and Los Angeles: University of California Press.

———. 1980. *Seventeenth Century North America.* Berkeley, Calif.: Turtle Island Press.

———. 1981. *Selected Essays 1963-1975.* Edited by B. Callahan. Berkeley, Calif.: Turtle Island Press.

Snyder, G. 1970. What You Need to Know to Be a Poet. In *Regarding Wave*, 40. New York: New Directions.

———. 1995a [1960]. The New Wind. In *A Place in Space: Ethics, Aesthetics, and Watersheds*, 13-18. Washington, D.C.: Counterpoint.

———. 1995b [1960] Notes on the Beat Generation. In *A Place in Space: Ethics, Aesthetics, and Watersheds*, 7-13. Washington, D.C.: Counterpoint.

Stimpson, C. R. 1973-1974. Charles Olson: Preliminary Images. *Boundary 2* Fall and Winter 2 (1-2): 151-172.

Village Voice. 1976. [Review]. *Village Voice* [New York, New York] 2 August, 21 (31): 28.

West, R. C. 1981. The Contribution of Carl Sauer to Latin American Geography. *Proceedings of the Conference of Latin Americanist Geographers* 8: 8-21.

Williams, M. 1983. "The Apple of My Eye," Carl Sauer and Historical Geography. *Journal of Historical Geography* 9 (1): 1-21.

———. 1987. Sauer and "Man's Role in Changing the Face of the Earth." *Geographical Review* 77 (2): 218-231.

FURTHER READING

Bradshaw, Steve. "Neon Jukes, Heavenly Blue." In *Café Society: Bohemian Life from Swift to Bob Dylan*, pp. 180-90. London: Weidenfeld and Nicolson, 1978.

Emphasizes the importance of Greenwich Village coffeehouses to Beat culture.

Charters, Ann. "Beat Poetry and the San Francisco Poetry Renaissance." In *The Columbia History of American Poetry*, edited by Jay Parini, pp. 581-604. New York: Columbia University Press, 1993.

Differentiates the Beat Generation and the San Francisco Poetry Renaissance.

Ferlinghetti, Lawrence, and Nancy J. Peters. *Literary San Francisco: A Pictorial History from Its Present Day.* San Francisco: City Lights Books, 1980, 254 p.

Overviews the significant literary landmarks in San Francisco.

McDarrah, Fred W., and Gloria S. McDarrah. *Beat Generation: Glory Days in Greenwich Village.* New York: Schirmer Books, 1996, 286 p.

Summarizes the significant people, places, and occurrences in Beat-era New York City.

Shoemaker, Steve. "Norman Mailer's 'White Negro': Historical Myth or Mythical History?" *Twentieth-Century Literature* 37, no. 3 (fall 1991): 343-60.

Places Norman Mailer's work, especially his seminal essay "The White Negro," in the context of the Beat movement.

Tashjian, Dickran. "William Carlos Williams." In *Skyscraper Primitives: Dava and the American Avant-Garde, 1910-1925*, pp. 91-115. Middletown, Conn.: Wesleyan University Press, 1975.

Discusses William Carlos Williams as a Dadaist.

Watson, Steven. *The Birth of the Beat Generation: Visionaries, Rebels, and Hipsters, 1944-1960.* New York: Pantheon Books, 1995, 387 p.

Listing of major events, places, and people associated with the Beat movement.

BEAT GENERATION PUBLISHING: PERIODICALS, SMALL PRESSES, AND CENSORSHIP

The Beat writers faced a significant obstacle to publication: their lifestyle and the writing that reflected it flew in the face of convention and thus distanced them from the conservative publishing establishment. Writers frustrated by the lack of acceptance by larger publishers created their own underground or "little" magazines and small presses. For many writers of the Beat era, publication in magazines such as Robert Creeley's *Black Mountain Review*, Gilbert Sorrentino's *Neon* magazine, or LeRoi Jones's *Yugen* was the first appearance of their work in print. The major small presses devoted to publishing works by these writers were City Lights (started by Lawrence Ferlinghetti, founder of City Lights bookstore), Grove Press (purchased in 1951 by Barney J. Rosset, Jr.), and New Directions (started by James Laughlin).

The Beat Generation saw the resurrection of an earlier Bohemian spirit defined, on the one hand, by a suspicion of wealth and social position as delineators of worth, and, on the other, by an affirmation of the value of ideas and emotions, especially as expressed in artistic form. According to Sorrentino, the magazines catering to the Beat writers did not serve as catch-all publications for those who simply "wished to express themselves," but instead had "a definite literary bone to pick, and . . . set themselves up not as mere *alternative* press but as a press that considered its criteria to be correct."

The Beats were not the first group of writers to depend on small literary presses. As Sally Dennison points out, "Blake, Shelley, Byron, and many other writers owe much to alternative publishing" and a number of American writers published their own works. In addition to books, small presses often published poetry broadsides—single-sheet, unbound renderings of poetry that were often illustrated. Broadsides were also self-published by individuals and groups in the 1960s and 1970s as a result of technological changes that made inexpensive printing and copying techniques available to more people.

Access to mimeograph machines, inexpensive offset printing, and letterpress made it possible for anyone to become a publisher. In only a few days, a small run of a magazine could be produced, and the appearance of independent bookstores provided a distribution outlet. As a whole, this came to be known as the "mimeograph revolution" and gave rise to the San Francisco Renaissance, the New York Poets, and in some ways the Beat Generation itself. Steven Clay and Rodney Phillips cover the history of this revolution and provide a comprehensive chronology of the events, including the publication of seminal works and the birth of the little magazines in the introduction to their book *A Secret Location on the Lower East Side*.

In his introduction to *Black Mountain Review*, Creeley notes the advice and encouragement he received from Ezra Pound and William Carlos Williams and describes the purpose of the magazine and Black Mountain Press as "a place wherein we might make evident what we, as writers, had found to be significant." *Kulchur* magazine was founded in 1960 by Marc Schleifer and was instrumental in bringing the literature and commentary of Beat writers to a wider East-coast audience than those in attendance at their readings and public demonstrations, while *City Lights, Evergreen Review,* and *Beatitude* reached out to audiences on the West coast. Poet Jack Spicer published his own journal called *J* in 1959, and inspired Joe Dunn to start the White Rabbit Press in 1957 to publish the literary works produced by Spicer and other writers who congregated at a North Beach area bar called The Place. *Neurotica,* a magazine published beginning in 1948 by gallery owner Jay Landesman, was—according to Landesman's statement published in the first issue—designed "to draw an analog to this observation and the plight of today's creative 'anxious' man. We are interested in exploring the creativeness of this man who has been forced to live underground." Decidedly unconventional, *Neurotica* published articles dealing with drug addicts, prostitution, sadism, and was the first magazine with a national circulation to publish Allen Ginsberg's work.

Quite often, alternative publishing venues were created by or supported by alternative authors and poets, among them City Lights Books, Jones's *Yugen* magazine, and Winston Leyland's Gay Sunshine Press. Jones, in an interview with David Ossman, discusses *Yugen,* its publication of writers who were unable to publish elsewhere, his views on poetry, and the effect that being an African American has had on his work. Robert Dana's in-depth interview of Ferlinghetti, covers, among other topics, his life, his time abroad studying art, his writing, and his publication of Allen Ginsberg's *Howl and Other Poems,* which brought about a landmark obscenity case in the California courts. When asked whether he had, in fact, sent a copy of *Howl* to the ACLU (American Civil Liberties Union) before publication, Ferlinghetti responded: "Yeah. We knew exactly what we were doing. We figured we might very well get busted for it, but in those days it was important to take a stand on the question of censorship. This was the McCarthy Era." Leyland also took a stand, as outlined in his "self-interview." Leyland discusses his study and ordination as a Catholic priest, his subsequent realization of his gay identity and abandonment of the priesthood, and

his work with *Gay Sunshine* newspaper and journal and the birth of the Gay Sunshine Press. *Gay Sunshine* was published between 1970 and 1982, and, according to Allen Ginsberg, was continually "reliable in its presentation of literary history hitherto kept in the closet by the academies."

In the first of several legal battles over attempted censorship of the works of Beat writers and publishers, Ginsberg's *Howl and Other Poems* was contested in the courts of the state of California as obscene. Ferlinghetti, as publisher of the book, was put on trial. Judge W. J. Clayton Horn found Ferlinghetti not guilty on October 3, 1957. In declaring that *Howl* was not obscene, Horn cited *Roth v. United States,* a 1957 U.S. Supreme Court decision in another obscenity case, and argued that unless "the book [was] entirely lacking 'in social importance' it [could] not be held obscene."

REPRESENTATIVE WORKS

Wallace Berman
Semina [publisher and editor] (journal) 1955-64

William Burroughs
Junkie: The Confessions of an Unredeemed Drug Addict [as William Lee] (novel) 1953; republished as *Junky* 1977

The Naked Lunch (novel) 1959; also published as *Naked Lunch,* 1962; restored text edition 2001

Cid Corman
Origin [publisher and editor] (journal) 1951-82

Robert Creeley
Black Mountain Review [editor] (journal) 1954-57

Joe Dunn
White Rabbit Press [publisher] 1957-c.81

Lawrence Ferlinghetti
City Lights [editor, with Peter Martin, and others] (journal) 1952-c.55

City Lights Publishers [publisher] 1953-

A Coney Island of the Mind (poetry) 1958

Back Roads to Far Places (poetry) 1971

Jeff Giles
Mother [editor with Lewis MacAdams, and Duncan McNaughton, David Moberg, and Peter Schjeldahl] (journal) 1964-68

Allen Ginsberg
Howl and Other Poems (poetry) 1956

Kaddish and Other Poems, 1958-1960 (poetry) 1961

David Haselwood
Auerhahn Press [publisher] 1958-66

Robert Hawley
Oyez Press [publisher] 1963

LeRoi Jones (Imamu Amiri Baraka)
Yugen [editor and publisher] (journal) 1958-62

Bob Kaufman
Beatitude [editor, with Lawrence Ferlinghetti, William J. Margolis, John Kelly, Kenneth Rexroth, Allen Ginsberg, and others] (journal) 1959-76

Jack Kerouac
On the Road (novel) 1957

Book of Dreams (diaries) 1961

Jay Landesman
Neurotica [publisher and editor] (journal) 1948-52

James Laughlin
New Directions Press [publisher] 1936-c.91

New Directions in Prose and Poetry [editor] (periodical) 1948-91

George Leite
Circle [editor] (journal) 1944-46, 1948

Winston Leyland
Gay Sunshine [editor] (periodical) 1970-73; name changed to *Gay Sunshine Journal*, 1973-82

Gay Sunshine Press [publisher] 1975-

Harold Norse
Bastard Angel [editor] (journal) 1972-74

Charles Plymell
Mikrokosmos [editor] (journal) 1959

Poet's Corner [editor] (journal) 1959

Now [editor] (journal) 1963-65

Irving Rosenthal and Paul Carroll
Big Table [editors] (journal) 1959-60

Barney J. Rosset, Jr.
Grove Press [publisher] 1951-85

Evergreen Review [editor] journal 1957-73; editor of online version, c. 1998-

Foxrock [publisher] 1994-

Edward Sanders
Fuck You: A Magazine of the Arts [editor] 1962-65

Investigative Poetry (poetry) 1975

Marc Schleifer
Kulchur [editor, with Lita Hornick] (periodical) 1960-66

Gilbert Sorrentino
Neon [editor] (journal) 1956-60

Jack Spicer
J [publisher and editor, with Fran Herndon, George Stanley, and others] (journal) 1959-60

Anne Waldman and Lewis Warsh
Angel Hair [editors] (journal) 1966-69

PRIMARY SOURCES

ROBERT CREELEY (ESSAY DATE 1954)

SOURCE: Creeley, Robert. Introduction to *"Black Mountain Review": Volume 1, 1954*, pp. iii-xiii. New York: AMS Press, 1969.

In the following essay, Creeley provides an overview of the creation of his journal Black Mountain Review.

In hindsight it is almost too simple to note the reasons for the publication of the *Black Mountain Review*. Toward the end of 1953 Black Mountain College—a decisive experimental school started in the early thirties by John Rice and others in Black Mountain, North Carolina—was trying to solve a persistent and most awkward problem. In order to survive it needed a much larger student enrollment, and the usual bulletins and announcements of summer programs seemed to have little effect. Either they failed to reach people who might well prove interested, or else the nature of the college itself was so little known that no one quite trusted its proposals. In consequence a summer workshop in pottery, which had among its faculty Hamada, Bernard Leach, and Peter Voulkos, found itself with some six rather dazzled persons for students. Whatever the cause—and no doubt it involves too the fact that all experimental colleges faced a very marked apathy during the fifties—some other means of finding and interesting prospective students had to be managed, and so it was that Charles Olson, then rector of the college, proposed to the other faculty members that a magazine might prove a more active advertisement for the nature and form of the college's program than the kind of announcements they had been depending upon.

This, at least, is a brief sense of how the college itself came to be involved in the funding of the magazine's publication. The costs, if I remember rightly, were about $500 an issue, so that the budget for a year's publication would be about $2000—hardly a large figure. But the college was in such tight financial condition that it could not easily find any money for any purpose, and so its support of the magazine, most accurately the decision of the faculty to commit such an amount to that purpose, is a deeply generous and characteristic act. Too, it's to be acknowledged that Olson's powers of persuasion were considerable.

The nature of the magazine itself, however, and the actual means of its publication, that is, literally its printing, are of another story which is really quite separate from the college itself. In the late forties, while living in Littleton, N.H., I had tried to start a magazine with the help of a college friend, Jacob Leed. He was living in Lititz, Pennsylvania, and had an old George Washington handpress. It was on that that we proposed to print the magazine. Then, at an unhappily critical moment, he broke his arm, I came running from New Hampshire—but after a full day's labor we found we had set two pages only, each with a single poem. So that was that.

What then to do with the material we had collected? Thanks to the occasion, I had found excuse to write to both Ezra Pound and William Carlos Williams. I didn't know what I really wanted of them but was of course deeply honored that they took me in any sense seriously. Pound very quickly seized on the possibility of our magazine's becoming in some sense a *feeder* for his own commitments, but was clearly a little questioning of our *modus operandi*. What he did give me, with quick generosity and clarity, was a kind *rule book* for the editing of any magazine. For example, he suggested I think of the magazine as a center around which, "not a box within which / any item." He proposed that verse consisted of a constant and a variant, and then told me to think from that to the context of a magazine. He suggested I get at least four others, on whom I could depend unequivocally for material, and to make their work the mainstay of the

magazine's form. But then, he said, let the rest of it, roughly half, be as various and hogwild as possible, "so that any idiot thinks he has a chance of getting in." He cited instances of what he considered effective editing, *The Little Review* and the *Nouvelle Revue Francaise* when its editor gave complete license to the nucleus of writers on whom he depended 'to write freely what they chose.' Williams in like sense gave us active support and tried to put us in touch with other young writers, as Pound also did, who might help us find a company. But with our failure to find a means to print the magazine, it all came to an abrupt end. I remember Pound's consoling me with the comment that perhaps it was wise for "the Creel" to wait for awhile before "he highflyz as editor," but things seemed bleak indeed.

Happily, there was what proved to be a very significant alternative. Cid Corman, then living in Boston and having also a weekly radio program there called "This Is Poetry," had come to be a friend. I had heard the program, by some fluke, in New Hampshire, wrote him, was not long after invited by him to read on the program, and soon after we were corresponding frequently, much involved with senses of contemporary writers and writing. It was Cid, in fact, who got me in touch with Olson, by way of their mutual friend, Vincent Ferrini—who sent me some of Olson's poems, with his own, for possible use in the magazine that had not yet collapsed. In returning Olson's poems to Vincent, I made the somewhat glib remark that he seemed to be "looking for a language," and got thereby my first letter from Olson himself, not particularly pleased by my comment and wanting to discuss it further, like they say. The letters thus resulting were really my education just that their range and articulation took me into terms of writing and many other areas indeed which I otherwise might never have entered. But the point now is that Cid, once Jake Leed's and my magazine was clearly dead, undertook himself to publish a magazine called *Origin*. Significantly enough its first issue includes some of the material I had collected—for example, Paul Blackburn's, whom I had come to know through Pound's agency—and features the work of Charles Olson, specifically the first of the *Maximus* sequence as well as other poems and prose.

Origin was, in fact, the meeting place for many of the writers who subsequently became the active nucleus for the *Black Mountain Review*. More than any other magazine of that period, it undertook to make place for the particular poets who later came to be called the "Black Mountain

School." In its issues prior to 1954, and continuingly, it gave first significant American publication to Denise Levertov, Irving Layton, Robert Duncan, Paul Carroll, Paul Blackburn, Larry Eigner, myself and a number of others as well. Although I had, for example, published stories in *Kenyon Review* and the *New Directions Annual,* neither place could afford me the actual company nor the range of my own work that *Origin's* second issue provided. For me it was an acknowledgement I had almost begun to think impossible, and I am sure that Cid's consistent support of our writing has much to do with what became of it.

The point is that we felt, all of us, a great distance from the more conventional magazines of that time. Either they were dominated by the New Critics, with whom we could have no relation, or else they were so general in character, that no active center of coherence was possible. There were exceptions certainly. *Golden Goose,* edited by Frederick Eckman and Richard Wirtz Emerson, was clearly partisan to myself and also to Olson, and published my first book, *Le Fou,* and would have published a collection of Olson's, *The Praises,* but for a misunderstanding between him and the editors, when the book was already in proof. Both men were much involved with Williams, and made his example and commitment the center for their own. There were also other, more occasional magazines, as *Goad*—whose editor, Horace Schwartz, involved me in a useful defense of my interest in Ezra Pound, just that it helped clarify my own terms of value.

But, with the exception of *Origin,* and possibly *Golden Goose* also, only two magazines of that time, the early fifties, had finally either the occasion or the sense of procedure, which served as my own measure of the possibility. One, *Fragmente,* edited and published in Freiberg, Germany, by Rainer Gerhardt—whose acquaintance I was also to make through Pound's help—was an heroically ambitious attempt to bring back into the German literary canon all that writing which the years of the Third Reich had absented from it. Rainer and his wife, living in great poverty with two young sons, were nonetheless able to introduce to the German context an incredible range of work, including that of Olson, Williams, Pound, Bunting, and myself. I was its American editor but its literal activity was completely the effort of Rainer and Renate. Their conception of what such a magazine *might* accomplish was a deep lesson to me. They saw the possibility of *changing* the context of writing, and I think myself that this magazine, and also the small paperbacks they were able to publish, effectually accomplished this for present German poetry—despite the bitter fact of Rainer's early death.

In like sense, a group of young writers of various nationalities centered in Paris was of great interest to me. They were led by a lovely, obdurate and resourceful Scot, Alexander Trocchi, and included the British poet, Christopher Logue, and the brilliant American translator, Austryn Wainhouse. Others too were of equal interest, Patrick Bowles, for example, who translated the first of Beckett's French novels into English—and Richard Seaver, who was later to become a decisive editor for Grove Press. Again, what these men proposed to do with their magazine, *Merlin,* and the books which they also published with the help of the Olympia Press as Collection Merlin, was to change the situation of literary context and evaluation. I've given a brief, personal sense of my relation to Trocchi in a novel, *The Island,* where he figures as "Manus," and I was also invited by them to be an associate editor on the magazine—but by that time the funds necessary to continue publication of the magazine were not obtainable. But their translation of Genet and Beckett's work as well as their brilliant critical writing, which extended to political thinking as well as literary, made them an exceptional example of what a group of writers might do.

By 1954 my wife and I were already much involved with a small press called the Divers Press. We had moved from France to Mallorca, and had become close friends with a young English couple, Martin Seymour-Smith and his wife, Janet. It was Martin who first interested us in publishing books, since, as he pointed out, printing costs were exceptionally cheap on the island and so much might be done on a shoestring. But our initial venture together, the Roebuck Press, came a cropper because Martin's interests were not really decisively my own nor mine his. We did publish a selection of his poems, *All Devils Fading,* but our center was finally in writers like Olson (*Mayan Letters*), Paul Blackburn (*Proensa* and *The Dissolving Fabric*), Irving Layton (*In The Midst Of My Fever*), Douglas Woolf (*The Hypocritic Days*), Larry Eigner (*From The Sustaining Air*), and, though he comes a bit later, Robert Duncan (*Caesar's Gate*). We also published Katue Kitasono's *Black Rain,* and it is a design of his that is used for the covers of the first four issues of the *Black Mountain Review* as well as another on the credits page. What I felt was the purpose of the press has much to do with my initial sense of the magazine also. For me, and the other writers who came to be involved, it was

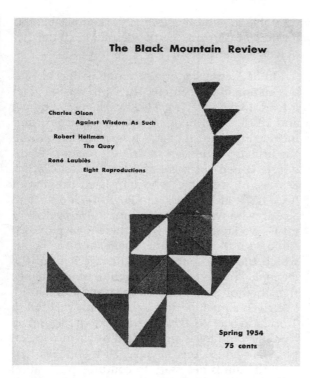

The Black Mountain Review

Charles Olson
    Against Wisdom As Such

Robert Hellman
    The Quay

René Laubiès
    Eight Reproductions

Spring 1954
75 cents

Cover of the Spring, 1954 edition of the *Black Mountain Review.*

a place defined by our own activity and accomplished altogether by ourselves—a place wherein we might make evident what we, as writers, had found to be significant, both for ourselves and for that world—no doubt often vague to us indeed—we hoped our writing might enter. To be published in the *Kenyon Review* was too much like being "tapped" for a fraternity. It was too often all over before one got there, and few if any one's own fellow writers came too. Therefore there had to be both a press and a magazine absolutely specific to one's own commitments and possibilities. Nothing short of that was good enough.

Origin had already done, in some sense, as much as one could hope for, and I remember having doubts about either the use or the practicality of simply another magazine more or less "like" it. I certainly didn't want to compete with Cid. But one possibility did seem to me lacking in *Origin,* despite occasional notes and reviews, and that was the *ground* that an active, ranging critical section might effect. I wasn't thinking of criticism finally as judgement of whether or no this or that book might be deemed "good" or "bad." What I hoped for, and happily did get, was critical writing that would be, in Olson's sense, "prospective," a kind of writing that would break down habits of "subject" and gain a new experience of context

generally. If I have any disappointment in the magazine in retrospect, it's only that this part of it does not extend as far as I had hoped. Still, Jung's "The Mass & The Individual Process" (in the 5th issue)—which I remember he sent to "The Black Mount Review," which pun, unintentional I assume, was a delight—and Borges' "Three Versions of Judas" (in the 7th issue)—which I read with absolute seriousness, not realizing it was a "fiction"—are some instance of what I was after. But, and here I was much influenced by Olson, the possible *range* of such writing as we conceived of it was never fully demonstrated.

There have been various comments and summaries published with respect to the Black Mountain Review's activity as a little magazine. Most lively and helpful, I think, is Paul Blackburn's account which appears in *Kulchur* (Vol. 3, No. 10, Summer 1963), called "The Grinding Down." Among other things, he identifies the initials used by reviewers in the first four issues, and also the pseudonyms used for signature in some other instances. Too, Kent State University Library, in one of its bulletins, provides an accurate and useful bibliography together with a brief note by myself. But now I think it best that the pseudonyms stay pseudonyms, and that initials, if not recognized (I used three sets, for example), be part of the present reader's experience. Often I, or some friend I could quickly get hold of, had to fill blank pages, to manage our length of sixty-four pages, or subsequently the longer format of two hundred and twenty plus. I at times had nightmares of having to write the whole thing myself.

The contributing editors listed in the first issue conform to that sense Pound had earlier made clear: get a center of people you can depend on for consistently active contributions, elsewise you'll have nothing to build with. Olson was to prove that center almost single-handedly, but Blackburn was also very helpful, with all manner of support including legwork around New York to get the magazine into stores as well as much sympathetic and practical handholding. Layton I had come to know through a Canadian mimeographed magazine, *Contact,* which many of us had been involved with as its contents will show. He had an intensive energy and obviously was restless with what was then the Canadian literary milieu. His brother-in-law, John Sutherland, editor of the *Northern Review,* no longer invited him to literary parties because Irving's conduct was so irascible. So he was an unequivocal cohort and wrote, happily, voluminous amounts of verse. If I remember rightly, I also asked others as well—in particular Paul Goodman, who answered he'd prefer being just a contributor, since his other commitments very possibly would not give him time to do more. Rexroth generously agreed although we had little information of each other beyond his own public figures. Less happily, by the time he'd read the first issue, he had realized his error and his withdrawal (as well as that of Paul Blackburn, whose reasons were happily less adamant) is noted at the back of the Fall 1954 issue along with a defensive comment by myself.

Many of the writers who became very decisive to the magazine are not so listed, however. Robert Duncan is very much one of these. His first contribution, sent at Olson's suggestion, was a poem I in turn suggested we print a section of—and Duncan's response was to the effect that if he *had* wanted a section of the poem printed, he *would* have sent it—and I learned much from him also. There was one very amusing confusion involved with a poem of his I did print, in the Fall 1954 issue, "Letters for Denise Levertov: An A Muse Ment." Apparently Denise, for some reason, took it as a parody on her own way of writing, and was thus hurt. And Olson too thought is was some kind of attack on him. I think that poor Duncan and myself were the only ones unequivocally to enjoy it, and it remains for me an extraordinary summary and *exempla* of contemporary possibilities in poetry.

Denise herself, Louis Zukofsky (whom I found thanks to Edward Dahlberg and also Duncan), Jonathan Williams, and Robert Hellman (a close friend first in France, who subsequently came to teach briefly at Black Mountain), all were of great help to me in that they were there to be depended on, for specific writing but equally, for a very real sense of the whole act's not being merely a whistling in the dark but something making a way. God knows one often doubted it. Holding to Pound's sense of letting at least part of the magazine seem wide open, I know I printed work at times that any of them must have been puzzled by. Some things I just liked, for example, Gautier's "The Hippopotamus," which appears in the 5th issue. I still do. However, I've never found anyone to share my pleasure in "The Goat Man" by Harold Lee Drake, in the 6th issue. He wrote, to put it mildly, extraordinary prose—including one piece involved with masturbating by the seashore, which the condition of censorship in the fifties never permitted me to print. He was one of the contributors who came out of nowhere, and unhappily seems to have returned there, since I've never seen his work printed again.

Of contributors generally, I've defined, I think, the character of one group clearly evident throughout the magazine's publication. These are writers who have either come together earlier, in *Origin,* or who are "found" by the same nature of attention that *Origin*'s preoccupations had effected. Louis Zukofsky would be one of these latter as would be also Edward Dahlberg. There are also "occasional" contributors, as Paul Goodman, and those who simply appear with no previous or necessarily continuing sense of relationship, like James Purdy. I think we were, possibly, the first magazine to print his work in America, and that was surely a pleasure. He had found us somehow, submitted the story, and I printed it. The same is true of Sherry Mangan's story (a curious echo from the twenties) in the 7th issue, or of Alfred Kreymborg's "Metaphysical Ballad" printed there as well.

But two other kinds of contributor were particularly significant. Thus far the relation to the college itself must seem the fact that it was paying for the magazine's publication, and that Olson was the rector of the college. Although Hellman, Duncan, and myself were briefly on the faculty, this was somewhat after the fact because the nature of the magazine was determined otherwise and really prior to that fact. But if those contributors are noted who were either students at the college at the time, or had recently been so, then a relation of the college to the magazine, and particularly to Olson's influence as a teacher, becomes very clear. First there is Jonathan Williams—who is certainly not a "student" at this point, but who is much interested in the college and in Olson particularly, as his own publishing (*Jargon*) makes clear. Look at the advertisements for his press in the various issues of the magazine, for further instance. Then there is Joel Oppenheimer, who had left the college not long before the publication of the first issue and so comes into its activity by that fact. Then Fielding Dawson—also absent at this point from the college, in the army in Stuttgart, but again much involved by relation to the college and so to the magazine also. Then there are those literally there: Edward Dorn, Michael Rumaker, and Tom Field. Dorn had published one poem in *Origin,* in an issue edited by Denise Levertov, and his story in the *Black Mountain Review* is, I think, his first published prose—and clear example of what is to be his extraordinary ability in that mode as well as in poetry. Michael Rumaker has his first publication of any kind in the magazine, with two stories I feel to be as fine as ever were published—in fact, "The Pipe" I think as exceptional a piece of writ-

ON THE SUBJECT OF...

ROBERT CREELEY

Throughout the 1950s, Robert Creeley was associated with the "Black Mountain Poets," a group of writers that included Denise Levertov, Ed Dorn, Fielding Dawson, and others connected with Black Mountain College, an experimental, communal college in North Carolina. Creeley edited the *Black Mountain Review* and developed a close and lasting relationship with Charles Olson, who was the rector of the college. The two engaged in a lengthy, intensive correspondence about literary matters that has been collected and published in ten volumes as *Charles Olson and Robert Creeley: The Complete Correspondence* (1980-96). Creeley was a leader in the generational shift that veered away from history and tradition as primary poetic sources and gave new prominence to the ongoing experiences of an individual's life. Because of this emphasis, the major events of his life loom large in his literary work. Creeley's marriage to Ann McKinnon ended in divorce in 1955. The breakup of that relationship is chronicled in fictional form in his only novel, *The Island* (1963), which drew upon his experiences on the island of Mallorca, off the coast of Spain, where he lived with Ann and their three children in 1953 and 1954. After the divorce Creeley returned to Black Mountain College for a brief time before moving to San Francisco, where he became associated with the writers of the Beat Generation.. Creeley's work appeared in anthology *The New American Poetry: 1945-1960,* edited by Donald Allen.

ing as any of any time. Then, finally, Tom Field—actually a painter, but whose writing struck me usefully, though it has not proven of major interest to himself. But think of it—that a college having an enrollment of about *twenty* people as average during the time the magazine is published should have such gifted men as Dorn, Rumaker, Dawson, Oppenheimer and Williams have so

proven themselves to be. Hopefully, it makes excuse for the kind of eulogy these comments must now seem.

The college closed in the spring of 1956 and at that point Jonathan Williams became the ostensible publisher of the last issue—on the cover of which he put a little sticker to make this fact clear. There was hope we might continue. Some material for the next issue was in hand, some photos of Frederick Sommer for one thing, and some essays of Edward Dahlberg's. But the last issue itself was almost impossible to manage. I had left Black Mountain, had been briefly in San Francisco, and was now living in New Mexico. The printer, of course, was still in Spain, and the delays in proofing, or even getting the initial printing begun, was almost impossible to manage. However, the last issue—with the addition of Allen Ginsberg as contributing editor—defines the last group of contributors who have particular relevance. Ed Dorn had moved to San Francisco with his family after leaving Black Mountain the year previous. I was in restless state, having separated from my wife, and being really at odds with much in my life. I wanted a new condition and so went west, where I'd never been, to see if that might be an answer. So I was also in San Francisco, in the spring of 1956—and for a writer there was really no place that could have been quite like it, just at that time. The contents pages of the 7th issue will make this much clearer than I can—Ginsberg, Kerouac, Whalen, McClure, Burroughs (Lee), Snyder—and another man I was deeply pleased to include, albeit from the east, Hubert Selby, Jr. It was unequivocally a shift and opening of the previous center, and finally as good a place as any to end. Other magazines had appeared as well, with much the same concerns, among them *Big Table* and the *Evergreen Review.* Whatever battle had been the case did seem effectually won.

A last note, briefly, about the divers reproductions and photographs that appear in the various issues, as well as the covers for the last three . . . I valued these especially, in that they freshened everything when otherwise things seemed almost too dense. It was a particular honor to include Franz Kline, Philip Guston, Aaron Siskind, and Harry Callahan, because all had been teachers at the college, and, even more than that, had each made so actively clear a new way of seeing in their art. John Altoon I can never thank enough for so much it would be specious to try to list it—and he also has made very evident how extraordinary a painter he is. Dan Rice, a close friend of those days and first met at the college—the same. Edward

Corbett I met while I was editing the last issue in New Mexico, and though I'm sure he thought I was simply hysterical, his cover as well as other generosities is a lovely fact of his concern. As for Laubies—he saw it all.

So it's finally all well in the past, either as one's own experience of something, or else the communal fact of what the writers of that situation and time seemed to have had in mind. I don't think it can ever be very different. You want to do something, to see it happen, and apparently it can't or at least can't with what then exists as possibility. So you try to change it, and you do or don't as proves the case. What really now delights me is that a magazine having a usual printing of some five to seven hundred and fifty copies, about two hundred of which ever got distributed, could have made any dent whatsoever. That should cheer us all.

LAWRENCE FERLINGHETTI (ESSAY DATE 1957)

SOURCE: Ferlinghetti, Lawrence. "Horn on *Howl*." In *On the Poetry of Allen Ginsberg*, edited by Lewis Hyde, pp. 195-9. Ann Arbor: University of Michigan Press, 1984.

In the following essay, which was first published in Evergreen Review *in 1957, Ferlinghetti details the censorship trials centering on the publication of* Howl and Other Poems.

Fahrenheit 451, the temperature at which books burn, has finally been determined not to be the prevailing temperature at San Francisco, though the police still would be all too happy to make it hot for you. On October 3 last, Judge Clayton Horn of Municipal Court brought in a thirty-nine-page opinion finding Shigeyoshi Murao and myself not guilty of publishing or selling obscene writings, to wit Allen Ginsberg's *Howl and Other Poems* and issue 11 & 12 of *The Miscellaneous Man*.

Thus ended one of the most irresponsible and callous police actions to be perpetrated west of the Rockies, not counting the treatment accorded Indians and Japanese.

When William Carlos Williams, in his Introduction to *Howl*, said that Ginsberg had come up with "an arresting poem" he hardly knew what he was saying. The first edition of *Howl*, Number Four in the Pocket Poets Series, was printed in England by Villiers, passed thru Customs without incident, and was published at the City Lights bookstore here in the fall of 1956. Part of a second printing was stopped by customs on March 25,

1957, not long after an earlier issue of *The Miscellaneous Man* (published in Berkeley by William Margolis) had been seized coming from the same printer. Section 305 of the Tariff Act of 1930 was cited. The San Francisco *Chronicle* (which alone among the local press put up a real howl about censorship) reported, in part:

> Collector of Customs Chester MacPhee continued his campaign yesterday to keep what he considers obscene literature away from the children of the Bay Area. He confiscated 520 copies of a paperbound volume of poetry entitled *Howl and Other Poems*. . . . "The words and the sense of the writing is obscene," MacPhee declared. "You wouldn't want your children to come across it."

On April 3 the American Civil Liberties Union (to which I had submitted the manuscript of *Howl* before it went to the printer) informed Mr. MacPhee that it would contest the legality of the seizure, since it did not consider the book obscene. We announced in the meantime that an entirely new edition of *Howl* was being printed within the United States, thereby removing it from customs jurisdiction. No changes were made in the original text, and a photo-offset edition was placed on sale at City Lights bookstore and distributed nationally while the customs continued to sit on the copies from Britain.

On May 19, book editor William Hogan of the San Francisco *Chronicle* gave his Sunday column to an article by myself, defending *Howl* (I recommended a medal be made for Collector MacPhee, since his action was already rendering the book famous. But the police were soon to take over this advertising account and do a much better job—10,000 copies of *Howl* were in print by the time they finished with it.) In defense of "Howl" I said I thought it to be "the most significant single long poem to be published in this country since World War II, perhaps since T. S. Eliot's *Four Quartets*." To which many added "Alas." Fair enough, considering the barren, polished poetry and well-mannered verse which had dominated many of the major poetry publications during the past decade or so, not to mention some of the "fashionable incoherence" which has passed for poetry in many of the smaller, avant-garde magazines and little presses. "Howl" commits many poetic sins; but it was time. And it would be very interesting to hear from critics who can name another single long poem published in this country since the war which is as significant of its time and place and generation. (A reviewer in the *Atlantic Monthly* recently wrote that *Howl* may well turn out to be *The Waste Land* of the younger generation.) The central part of my article said:

. . . It is not the poet but what he observes which is revealed as obscene. The great obscene wastes of "Howl" are the sad wastes of the mechanized world, lost among atom bombs and insane nationalisms. . . . Ginsberg chooses to walk on the wild side of this world, along with Nelson Algren, Henry Miller, Kenneth Rexroth, Kenneth Patchen, not to mention some great American dead, mostly in the tradition of philosophical anarchism. . . . Ginsberg wrote his own best defense of "Howl" in another poem called "America." Here he asks:

> What sphinx of cement and aluminum bashed
>   open their skulls and ate up their brains and
>   imagination?
> Moloch! Solitude! Filth! Ugliness! Ashcans and
>   unobtainable dollars! Children screaming
>   under the stairways! Boys sobbing in armies!
>   Old men weeping in the parks!
>   [The lines are taken from the second part of
>   "Howl," not from "America."—Ed.]

A world, in short, you wouldn't want your children to come across. . . . Thus was Goya obscene in depicting the Disasters of War, thus Whitman an exhibitionist, exhibiting man in his own strange skin.

On May 29 customs released the books it had been holding, since the United States Attorney at San Francisco refused to institute condemnation proceedings against *Howl.*

Then the police took over and arrested us, Captain William Hanrahan of the juvenile department (well named, in this case) reporting that the books were not fit for children to read. Thus during the first week in June I found myself being booked and fingerprinted in San Francisco's Hall of Justice. The city jail occupies the upper floors of it, and a charming sight it is, a picturesque return to the early Middle Ages. And my enforced tour of it was a dandy way for the city officially to recognize the flowering of poetry in San Francisco. As one paper reported, "The Cops Don't Allow No Renaissance Here."

The ACLU posted bail. Our trial went on all summer, with a couple of weeks between each day in court. The prosecution soon admitted it had no case against either Shig Murao or myself as far as *The Miscellaneous Man* was concerned, since we were not the publisher of it, in which case there was no proof we knew what was inside the magazine when it was sold at our store. And, under the California Penal Code, the willful and lewd *intent* of the accused had to be established. Thus the trial was narrowed down to *Howl.*

The so-called People's Case (I say so-called, since the People seemed mostly on our side) was presented by Deputy District Attorney Ralph McIntosh whose heart seemed not in it nor his mind on it. He was opposed by some of the most formidable legal talent to be found, in the persons of Mr. Jake ("Never Plead Guilty") Ehrlich, Lawrence Speiser (former counsel for the ACLU), and Albert Bendich (present counsel for the ACLU)—all of whom defended us without expense to us.

The critical support for *Howl* (or the protest against censorship on principle) was enormous. Here is some of what some said:

Henry Rago, editor of *Poetry* (Chicago):

. . . I wish only to say that the book is a thoroughly serious work of literary art. . . . There is absolutely no question in my mind or in that of any poet or critic with whom I have discussed the book that it is a work of the legitimacy and validity contemplated by existing American law, as we know it in the statement of Justice Woolsey in the classic *Ulysses* case, and as we have seen it reaffirmed just recently by the Supreme Court in the Butler case. . . . I would be unworthy of the tradition of this magazine or simply of my place as a poet in the republic of letters . . . if I did not speak for the right of this book to free circulation, and against this affront not only to Allen Ginsberg and his publishers, but to the possibilities of the art of poetry in America. . . .

. . . *Howl and Other Poems,* according to accepted, serious contemporary American literary standards, is a dignified, sincere and admirable work of art. . . .

Robert Duncan and Director Ruth Witt-Diamant of the San Francisco (State College) Poetry Center:

. . . *Howl* is a significant work in American poetry, deriving both a spirit and form from Walt Whitman's *Leaves of Grass,* from Jewish religious writings. . . . It is rhapsodic, highly idealistic and inspired in cause and purpose. Like other inspired poets, Ginsberg strives to include all of life, especially the elements of suffering and dismay from which the voice of desire rises. Only by misunderstanding might these tortured outcryings for sexual and spiritual understanding be taken as salacious. The poet gives us the most painful details; he moves us toward a statement of experience that is challenging and finally noble.

Thomas Parkinson (University of California):

. . . *Howl* is one of the most important books of poetry published in the last ten years. Its power and eloquence are obvious, and the talent of Mr. Ginsberg is of the highest order. Even people who do not like the book are compelled to testify to its force and brilliance. . . .

James Laughlin (New Directions):

I have read the book carefully and do not myself consider it offensive to good taste, likely to lead youth astray, or be injurious to public morals. I feel, furthermore, that the book has considerable distinction as literature, being a powerful and artistic expression of a meaningful philosophical attitude. . . .

Kenneth Patchen:

The issue here—as in every like case—is not the merit or lack of it of a book but of a Society which traditionally holds the human being to be by its very functional nature a creature of shameful, outrageous, and obscene habits. . . .

Eugene Burdick (novelist and critic):

The poem "Howl" strikes me as an impressionistic, broadly gauged, almost surrealistic attempt to catch the movement, color, drama, and inevitable disappointments of life in a complex, modern society. "Howl" is a pessimistic, and indeed, almost a tragic view of life. . . . It is my impression that the total impact of the poem is far from lascivious or obscene. It is depressing, but not licentious or extravagant in its use of harsh words. . . .

Northern California Booksellers Association:

It may or may not be literature but it does have literary merit. . . . The proposition that adult literature must meet the standards of suitability for children is manifestly absurd. . . . To quote Supreme Court Justice Frankfurter in a similar case—". . . the effect of this is to reduce the adult population to reading only what is fit for children . . . surely this is to burn the house down to roast the pig."

Barney Rosset and Donald Allen, editors of the *Evergreen Review* (in which "Howl" was reprinted during the trial):

The second issue of *Evergreen Review,* which was devoted to the work of writers in the San Francisco Bay Area, attempted in large part to show the kinds of serious writing being done by the postwar generation. We published Allen Ginsberg's poem "Howl" in that issue because we believe that it is a significant modern poem, and that Allen Ginsberg's intention was to sincerely and honestly present a portion of his own experience of the life of his generation. . . . Our final considered opinion was that Allen Ginsberg's "Howl" is an achieved poem and that it deserves to be considered as such. . . .

At the trial itself, nine expert witnesses testified in behalf of *Howl*. They were eloquent witnesses, together furnishing as good a one-sided critical survey of *Howl* as could possibly be got up in any literary magazine. These witnesses were: Mark Schorer and Leo Lowenthal (of the University of California faculty), Walter Van Tilburg Clark, Herbert Blau, Arthur Foff, and Mark Linenthal (all of the San Francisco State College faculty), Kenneth Rexroth, Vincent McHugh (poet

and novelist), and Luther Nichols (book editor of the San Francisco *Examiner*). A few excerpts from the trial transcript:

DR. MARK SCHORER: The theme of the poem is announced very clearly in the opening line, "I saw the best minds of my generation destroyed by madness, starving hysterical naked." Then the following lines that make up the first part attempt to create the impression of a kind of nightmare world in which people representing "the best minds of my generation," in the author's view, are wandering like damned souls in hell. That is done through a kind of series of what one might call surrealistic images, a kind of state of hallucinations. Then in the second section the mood of the poem changes and it becomes an indictment of those elements in modern society that, in the author's view, are destructive of the best qualities in human nature and of the best minds. Those elements are, I would say, predominantly materialism, conformity and mechanization leading toward war. And then the third part is a personal address to a friend, real or fictional, of the poet or of the person who is speaking in the poet's voice—those are not always the same thing—who is mad and in a madhouse, and is the specific representative of what the author regards as a general condition, and with that final statement the poem ends. . . .

MR. MCINTOSH: (*later in cross-examination*): I didn't quite follow your explanation to page 21, "Footnote to Howl." Do you call that the second phase?

MARK SCHORER: I didn't speak about "Footnote to Howl." I regard that as a separate poem.

MR. MCINTOSH: Oh, I'm—

MARK SCHORER: It is not one of the three parts that make up the first poem. It's a comment on, I take it, the attitude expressed in "Howl" proper, and I think what it says—if you would like my understanding of it—is that in spite of all of the depravity that "Howl" has shown, all of the despair, all of the defeat, life is essentially holy and should be so lived. In other words, the footnote gives us this state in contradistinction to the state that the poem proper has tried to present.

MR. MCINTOSH (*later*): Did you read the one in the back called "America"? . . . What's the essence of that piece of poetry?

MARK SCHORER: I think that what the poem says is that the "I," the speaker, feels that he has given a piece of himself to America and has been given nothing in return, and the poem laments certain people who have suffered at the hands of—well, specifically, the United States Government, men like Tom Mooney, the Spanish Loyalists, Sacco and Vanzetti, the Scottsboro boys and so on.

MR. McINTOSH: Is that in there?

MARK SCHORER: That's on page 33. In other words, that is the speaker associating himself with those figures in American history whom he regards as having been martyred. He feels that way about himself.

MR. McINTOSH: Well, "America" is a little bit easier to understand than "Howl," isn't it? . . . Now [referring to shorter poems in the back of the book]—you read those two? You think they are similar, in a similar vein?

MARK SCHORER: They are very different. Those are what one would call lyric poems and the earlier ones are hortatory poems.

MR. McINTOSH: What?

MARK SCHORER: Poems of diatribe and indictment, the mood is very different, hortatory.

MR. McINTOSH: That's all.

DR. LEO LOWENTHAL: In my opinion this is a genuine work of literature, which is very characteristic for a period of unrest and tension such as the one we have been living through the last decade. I was reminded by reading "Howl" of many other literary works as they have been written after times of great upheavals, particularly after World War I, and I found this work very much in line with similar literary works. With regard to the specific merits of the poem "Howl," I would say that it is structured very well. As I see it, it consists of three parts, the first of which is the craving of the poet for self-identification, where he roams all over the field and tries to find allies in similar search for self-identification. He then indicts, in the second part, the villain, so to say, which does not permit him to find it, the Moloch of society, of the world as it is today. And in the third part he indicates the potentiality of fulfillment by friendship and love, although it ends on a sad and melancholic note actually indicating that he is in search for fulfillment he cannot find.

KENNETH REXROTH: . . . The simplest term for such writing is prophetic, it is easier to call it that than anything else because we have a large body of prophetic writing to refer to. There are the prophets of the Bible, which it greatly resembles in purpose and in language and in subject matter. . . . The theme is the denunciation of evil and a pointing out of the way out, so to speak.

That is prophetic literature. "Woe! Woe! Woe! The City of Jerusalem! The Syrian is about to come down or has already and you are to do such and such a thing and you must repent and do thus and so." And "Howl," the four parts of the poem— that is including the "Footnote to Howl" as one additional part—do this very specifically. They take up these various specifics seriatim, one after the other. . . . And "Footnote to Howl," of course, again, is Biblical in reference. The reference is to the Benedicite, which says over and over again, "Blessed is the fire, Blessed is the light, Blessed are the trees, and Blessed is this and Blessed is that," and he is saying, "Everything that is human is Holy to me," and that the possibility of salvation in this terrible situation which he reveals is through love and through the love of everything Holy in man. So that I would say, that this just about covers the field of typically prophetic poetry. . . .

HERBERT BLAU: The thing that strikes me most forcefully about "Howl" is that it is worded in what appears to be a contemporary tradition, one that did not cause me any particular consternation in reading, a tradition most evident in the modern period following the First World War, a tradition that resembles European literary tradition and is defined as "Dada," a kind of art of furious negation. By the intensity of its negation it seems to be both resurrective in quality and ultimately a sort of paean of possible hope. I wouldn't say that the chances for redemption or chances for salvation in a work of this kind are deemed to be very extensively possible but, nonetheless, the vision is not a total vision of despair. It is a vision that by the salvation of despair, by the salvation of what would appear to be perversity, by the salvation of what would appear to be obscene, by the salvation of what would appear to be illicit, is ultimately a kind of redemption of the illicit, the obscene, the disillusioned and the despairing. . . .

VINCENT McHUGH: In this case . . . we have a vision of a modern hell. Now, we have certain precedents for that, for example, the book that it makes me think of, or the work of literature that it makes me think of offhand, the work of literature which is ferociously sincere in the same way, is Mr. Pound's—some of Mr. Pound's Cantos, especially Canto XIV and Canto XV. These, for example, in turn derive certainly from Dante and from the famous so-called cantos in Dante, and Dante, in turn, derives from the Odyssey, and so on into all the mythologies of the world. . . .

The prosecution put only two "expert witnesses" on the stand—both very lame samples of academia—one from the Catholic University of San Francisco and one a private elocution teacher, a beautiful woman, who said, "You feel like you are going through the gutter when you have to read that stuff. I didn't linger on it too long, I assure you." The University of San Francisco instructor said: "The literary value of this poem is negligible. . . . This poem is apparently dedicated to a long-dead movement, Dadaism, and some late followers of Dadaism. And, therefore, the opportunity is long past for any significant literary contribution of this poem." The critically devastating things the prosecution's witnesses could have said, but didn't, remain one of the great Catholic silences of the day.

So much for the literary criticism inspired by the trial. Cross-examination by the prosecutor was generally brilliant, as in the following bit:

Mr. McIntosh: Does Mr. Ferlinghetti attend your poetry writing workshop?

Dr. Mark Linenthal: He does not.

Mr. McIntosh: Do you attend his?

Dr. Linenthal: I do not.

Mr. McIntosh: You haven't been over there hearing him read poetry?

Dr. Linenthal: No, I haven't.

(etc.)

Legally, a layman could see that an important principle was certainly in the line drawn between "hard core pornography" and writing judged to be "social speech." But more important still was the court's acceptance of the principle that if a work is determined to be "social speech" the question of obscenity may not even be raised. Or, in the words of Counsel Bendich's argument:

> The first amendment to the Constitution of the United States protecting the fundamental freedoms of speech and press prohibits the suppression of literature by the application of obscenity formulae unless the trial court first determines that the literature in question is utterly without social importance."
>
> (Roth v. U.S.)

> . . . What is being urged here is that the majority opinion in Roth requires a trial court to make the constitutional determination; to decide in the first instance whether a work is utterly without redeeming social importance, before it permits the test of obscenity to be applied. . . .

> . . . The record is clear that all of the experts for the defense identified the main theme of Howl as

social criticism. And the prosecution concedes that it does not understand the work, much less what its dominant theme is.

Judge Horn agreed, in his opinion:

> I do not believe that Howl is without even 'the slightest redeeming social importance.' The first part of "Howl" presents a picture of a nightmare world; the second part is an indictment of those elements in modern society destructive of the best qualities of human nature; such elements are predominantly identified as materialism, conformity, and mechanization leading toward war. The third part presents a picture of an individual who is a specific representation of what the author conceives as a general condition. . . . "Footnote to Howl" seems to be a declamation that everything in the world is holy, including parts of the body by name. It ends in a plea for holy living. . . .

And the judge went on to set forth certain rules for the guidance of authorities in the future, [including] . . . :

> In considering material claimed to be obscene it is well to remember the motto: Honi soit qui mal y pense (Evil to him who thinks evil).

At which the Prosecution was reliably reported to have blushed.

Under banner headlines, the Chronicle reported that "the Judge's decision was hailed with applause and cheers from a packed audience that offered the most fantastic collection of beards, turtlenecked shirts and Italian hairdos ever to grace the grimy precincts of the Hall of Justice." The decision was hailed editorially as a "landmark of law." Judge Horn has since been reelected to office, which I like to think means that the People agree it was the police who here committed an obscene action.

THE NATION (ARTICLE DATE 9 NOVEMBER 1957)

SOURCE: "New Test for Obscenity." The Nation 185 (9 November 1957): 314.

In the following brief article, the critic commends Judge Clayton Horn's decision in the 1957 Howl *obscenity trial.*

The obscenity case against Allen Ginsberg's Howl was closed last month when Judge Clayton W. Horn of the San Francisco Municipal Court found Lawrence Ferlinghetti, a local bookseller, not guilty of a misdemeanor for having sold the book. Judge Horn's decision followed the general line of enlightened opinion in this area—words are not obscene in themselves, an author's intent must be given full consideration, "good taste" and conventional mores are not binding on a writer who wishes to comment persuasively on sections of society where such restraints are not recognized. The judge, however, added one important concept to the country's judicial opinion about obscenity. He stated that for material to be judged obscene in California, it must present a "clear and present danger of inciting to anti-social or immoral action." By applying Holmes's famous test in the area of obscenity, Judge Horn effectively blocks the zealous district attorney who inveighs against a book because it might conceivably move some peculiarly susceptible individual to reprehensible behavior.

OVERVIEW

STEVEN CLAY AND RODNEY PHILLIPS (ESSAY DATE 1998)

SOURCE: Clay, Steven, and Rodney Phillips. "A Little History of the Mimeograph Revolution." In *A Secret Location on the Lower East Side: Adventures in Writing, 1960-1980*, pp. 13-54. New York: The New York Public Library and Granary Books, 1998.

In the following essay, Clay and Phillips provide a history of American little magazines and small presses beginning in 1929 with the earliest piece of mimeographed literature.

There was no more significant poetry anthology in the second half of the twentieth century than *The New American Poetry, 1945-1960,* edited by Donald M. Allen and published by Grove Press in 1960. Poised almost at mid-century, it provides a summing up of a very particular situation in poetry as it looks back to the achievements of the 1950s and ahead to the possibilities of the 60s.

Allen's anthology was a self-conscious counter to *New Poets of England and America,* edited by Donald Hall, Robert Pack, and Louis Simpson and published by Meridian in 1957. It was to prove prophetic (the two anthologies have not one poet in common) and to serve as both a calling for and a permission to younger writers. The goal, according to Allen, was to present poetry that "has shown one common characteristic: a total rejection of all those qualities typical of academic verse. Following the practice and precepts of Ezra Pound and William Carlos Williams, it has built on their achievements and gone on to evolve new conceptions of the poem. These poets have already created their own tradition, their own press, and their public. They are our avant-garde, the true continuers of the modern movement in American poetry."[1]

Allen's anthology was prophetic in another way. It assigned poets to large overall groupings that have persisted for nearly forty years and have entered the critical nomenclature: Black Mountain, San Francisco Renaissance, Beat Generation, and New York Poets—as well as identifying a group of younger poets "who have been associated with and in some cases influenced by the leading writers of the preceding groups" (p. xiii). Allen was circumspect to a fault concerning his classifications: "Occasionally arbitrary and for the most part more historical than actual, these groups can be justified finally only as a means to give the reader some sense of milieu . . ." (p. xiii).

When the Allen anthology came out, several of the featured poets had barely been published. Of necessity, they existed on the margins, outside mainstream publication and distribution channels. Of necessity, they invented their own communities and audiences (typically indistinguishable), with a small press or little magazine often serving as the nucleus of both.

Direct access to mimeograph machines, letterpress, and inexpensive offset made these publishing ventures possible, putting the means of production in the hands of the poet. In a very real sense, almost anyone could become a publisher. For the price of a few reams of paper and a handful of stencils, a poet could produce, by mimeograph, a magazine or booklet in a small edition over the course of several days. Collating, stapling, and mailing parties helped speed up production, but, more significantly, they helped galvanize a literary group. The existence of independent bookstores meant that it was actually possible to find these publications in all their raw homemade beauty. In several instances (for example, Wallace Berman's *Semina* and LeRoi Jones and Diane di Prima's *The Floating Bear*), the magazines were available only to a mailing list; they were produced for a community of kindred spirits as a literary newsletter—a quick way to get new work out. And they were the cutting edge of new explorations in and through language. As Ron Loewinsohn noted, "[M]ore important than the quality of their contents was the fact of these magazines' abundance and speed. Having them, we could see what we were doing, as it came, hot off the griddle. We could get instant response to what we'd written last week, & we could respond instantly to what the guy across town or across the country had written last week."[2]

At the other pole were magazines like *Evergreen Review,* which published equally subversive material—but with the financial backing and distribution of a large publishing house. Comparatively slick and "professional," it helped to bring new writing and new thinking to a much larger and geographically diverse audience.

These extremes of production quality and availability are comfortably subsumed under the concept of the "mimeo revolution," the unprecedented outpouring of poetry books and magazines that took place roughly between 1960 and 1980; the writing and publishing with which this survey is concerned are those which emerged precisely at the point at which the New American Poetry met the mimeo revolution. The "mimeo revolution," as a term, is a bit of a misnomer in the sense that well over half the materials produced under its banner were not strictly produced on the mimeograph machine; however, the formal means of production are not as important in identifying the works of this movement as is the nature of their content. Looking back at them now, the books and magazines of the mimeo revolution appear imbued with a vivid purity of intention which it is nearly impossible to conceive of creating in today's publications. Although the earliest mimeographed literary item we have been able to identify is Yvor Winters's *Gyroscope* (published for his classes at Stanford in 1929 and early 1930), we'll start our story in 1943 in the conscientious objectors' camp at Waldport, Oregon. There, William Everson published poems in an unofficial newsletter, *The Untide,* and helped run the mimeograph machine to produce his own *X War Elegies,* among other small volumes. The last book produced at the Untide Press in Waldport was Kenneth Patchen's *An Astonished Eye Looks Out Of the Air,* which Everson printed via letterpress in 1945 as the war was ending. Everson was soon to move down to Berkeley and purchase a Washington hand press to continue his printing. His poems from this period, including those originally written in Waldport, were collected by James Laughlin and published by New Directions in 1948, as *The Residual Years.*

In 1947, the first issue of *The Ark,* strongly committed to literary and political writings influenced by anarchist and pacifist principles, appeared in San Francisco. Contributors included Kenneth Rexroth, Richard Eberhardt, Paul Goodman, and William Everson. Another contributor was Robert Duncan, whose essay "The Homosexual in Society," published in Dwight MacDonald's *Politics* in August 1944, had occasioned John Crowe Ransom to renege on publishing Duncan's previously accepted "African Elegy" in *The Kenyon Review.* Despite his feeling that the

ON THE SUBJECT OF...

CHARLES PLYMELL

Poet Charles Plymell lived with Ginsberg and Neal Cassady in San Francisco during the early 1960s. His association with the Beats greatly influenced his writing, which was published in Beat journals and by Ferlinghetti's City Lights imprint. As an editor and publisher of journals such as *Poet's Corner, Mikrokosmos,* and *Now,* Plymell was responsible for disseminating the work of many Beat figures, including Ginsberg, Burroughs, and Herbert Huncke. Younger than the first wave of Beat writers, Plymell is often categorized as part of the movement's second generation. His collections include *Apocalypse Rose* (1966), for which Ginsberg wrote the introduction, and *The Last of the Moccasins* (1971).

article was courageous, Ransom felt the poem was a "homosexual advertisement." On a sojourn to the East Coast, Duncan had co-edited with Sanders Russell *The Experimental Review*—a formal beginning to his long experience with small presses and little magazines. In California, he produced two issues of *The Berkeley Miscellany* (in 1948 and 1949), as well as his own *Poems 1948-1949* under the imprint of Berkeley Miscellany Editions. In the two issues of the magazine, Duncan published his own work as well as that of Mary Fabilli, Jack Spicer, and Gerald Ackerman.

Spicer, like Duncan and Robin Blaser, was then a student at the University of California at Berkeley. These three were the center of the "Berkeley Renaissance," a group heavily influenced by the study of medieval and Renaissance culture. The Duncan-Spicer-Blaser circle created "a spiritual and artistic brotherhood out of shared homosexual experience, occultism, and the reading of modern literature."[3] The Berkeley group held regular meetings for discussions and readings influenced in part by Kenneth Rexroth's evenings in San Francisco. Spicer went on to produce his own magazine, *J,* in 1959, and was influential on Stan Persky's beginning *Open Space* in 1964. Both of these magazines were produced via mimeograph in San Francisco. In 1957, Spicer conducted the Poetry as Magic Workshop attended by, among others, John

Wieners, then in the middle of producing his own little magazine, *Measure*. The Berkeley group consolidated important shared tendencies and were to exert a considerable force as they moved to San Francisco in the early 1950s.

Meanwhile, across the bay in San Francisco, the commingling of several activities helped to prepare the ground for the remarkable literary explosion that was soon to take place. The Libertarian Circle held regular literary events; poet members included Kenneth Rexroth, Muriel Rukeyser, William Everson, Robert Duncan, Jack Spicer, and Thomas Parkinson. Rexroth also ran a literary program on KPFA, the country's first listener-sponsored radio station. Madeline Gleason (assisted by Rexroth and Duncan) founded the San Francisco Poetry Center, housed at San Francisco State College and managed by Ruth Witt-Diamant. The magazines *Circle, Ark, City Lights, Goad, Inferno,* and *Golden Goose* helped to consolidate the growing literary underground.

The famous reading at Six Gallery on Fillmore Street was publicized by Allen Ginsberg (via a hundred mailed postcards and a few flyers) thus: "6 POETS AT 6 GALLERY Philip Lamantia reading mass. of late John Hoffman—Mike McClure, Allen Ginsberg, Gary Snyder & Phil Whalen—all sharp new straightforward writing—remarkable collection of angels on one stage reading their poetry. No charge, small collection for wine and postcards. Charming event. Kenneth Rexroth, M.C. 8 PM Friday Night October 7, 1955 6 Gallery 3119 Fillmore St. San Fran." On October 7, 1955, in a room measuring 20 x 25 feet with a dirt floor, Ginsberg "read *Howl* and started an epoch."[4] Gary Snyder, Philip Lamantia, Michael McClure, and Philip Whalen shared the bill and, by all reports, also read brilliantly. Aside from Rexroth and Whalen, all the readers were in their twenties. Again, in the words of Kenneth Rexroth, "What started in SF and spread from there across the world was public poetry, the return of a tribal, preliterate relationship between poet and audience."[5]

These events, along with the flourishing of Lawrence Ferlinghetti's City Lights Bookshop and publishing house, helped to inaugurate and consolidate what has become known as the San Francisco Renaissance. City Lights published *Howl* in 1956 (Ferlinghetti asked Ginsberg for the manuscript the same night it was read at the Six Gallery) as Number Four in the Pocket Poets Series. (It had been preceded by an extremely rare mimeographed edition, typed by Martha Rexroth and mimeographed by none other than Robert Creeley. Ginsberg's *Siesta in Xbalba* had been mimeo-

graphed by the man himself on a freighter in the Alaskan Ocean.) Among the audience members that night was one who added his own chant, the young novelist Jack Kerouac, whose *On the Road,* published in 1957, was to make this reading and its readers legendary.

It was also in 1957 that Charles Olson, rector of the experimental Black Mountain College, visited San Francisco and gave a series of lectures on Alfred North Whitehead at the Portrero Hill home of Robert Duncan and his companion, the painter Jess Collins. Among the attendees at the lectures were, of course, Duncan himself, but also Michael McClure, Gary Snyder's Reed College friend Philip Whalen, Jack Spicer, and Richard Duerden. The same year saw the "San Francisco Scene" issue of *Evergreen Review*. Poet Helen Adam's flamboyant 1961 ballad opera, entitled *San Francisco's Burning,* epitomized the time, outrageous both aesthetically and socially. Other writers associated with the San Francisco Renaissance included James Broughton, Lew Welch, Ron Loewinsohn, Madeline Gleason, David Meltzer, Kirby Doyle, and Lenore Kandel.

Experimentation with forms of literature and lifestyle had long been an attractive characteristic of life in San Francisco. But the tolerance felt in Northern California was not as evident in Los Angeles. In 1957, an exhibit of work by assemblage artist Wallace Berman at the Ferus Gallery was closed by the Los Angeles Police Department, and Berman was jailed on charges of exhibiting "lewd and lascivious pornographic art." Found guilty (by the same judge who ruled against Henry Miller), Berman and family left L.A. for San Francisco that year. Berman edited and published a fascinating assemblage magazine called *Semina*. After the raid of his exhibit at Ferus, he announced in *Semina* 2 that "I will continue to print Semina from locations other than this city of degenerate angels." Berman's friend, artist George Herms, designed his own books and provided the artwork for others, including Diane di Prima. Herms had likewise found the political climate in L.A. intolerable and had preceded the Bermans to Northern California.

In the mid-1960s, John Martin's Black Sparrow Press began publishing broadsides and booklets and has, over the years, published a wide variety of experimental and alternative poetry and prose, including work by Duncan, Olson, Spicer, and Creeley among very many others. Black Sparrow continues to publish in 1998 from Santa Rosa, California.

Because of the previous associations of house printer/designer Graham Mackintosh, Black Sparrow is linked to earlier literary small presses of Northern California, particularly White Rabbit Press (at the urging of Jack Spicer, Mackintosh resurrected the press in 1962, printing Spicer's own *Lament for the Makers*); Robert Hawley's Oyez Press (Mackintosh had printed its first book in 1963); and Dave Haselwood's Auerhahn Press, which flourished during the 1960s and early 70s in San Francisco. Auerhahn published a wide variety of well-designed books, including *The Exterminator,* an early example of William S. Burroughs and Brion Gysin's cut-up technique, in 1960. Auerhahn also published John Wieners's first book, *The Hotel Wentley Poems.* Oyez published many memorable volumes including Philip Lamantia's *Touch of the Marvelous.* Joe Dunn's White Rabbit Press, which had begun publishing in 1957 with Steve Jonas's rough work *Love, the Poem, the Sea & Other Pieces Examined,* produced books somewhat less elegant than Auerhahn's or Oyez's but with a beauty all their own.

The editorial genius behind White Rabbit was the irrepressible Jack Spicer, who published his own remarkable mimeographed magazine, *J.* Spicer emphasized the inclusion of writers who were not well published elsewhere, and accepted contributions for consideration in a box that was kept in one of three bars in the North Beach area of San Francisco. *J* is representative of the best of the mimeograph revolution: an uncompromising editorial stance combined with a playful, even colorful, formal character thanks to Fran Herndon, who edited the artwork for the magazine. Spicer's model for *J* was *Beatitude,* which had begun publication in San Francisco slightly before *J.* And a recalcitrant model it was, since Spicer was not a fan of the Beats and carried on a running war against Ferlinghetti in particular. He imagined Ferlinghetti had become commercial and financially successful, thereby, in Spicer's mind, "selling out" to the establishment. Magnificently consistent with his principles, Spicer never copyrighted his own work, anticipating the "no copyright, no nuthin" statements of Tom Clark's London-based *Once* series. The performative aspects of Spicer's poetics as well as his personality also prefigured the rise of poetry readings in the 1950s, particularly those sponsored by the Poetry Center at San Francisco State, which featured mimeographed programs and booklets printing selections from the poets who were reading, among them, Charles Olson, Denise Levertov, and Louis Zukofsky.

Although Spicer's *J* didn't publish the works of "established" poets, Spicer did include the work of Robert Duncan in four issues of his magazine. Duncan and Jess Collins (whose work adorned the cover of many magazines and books of the period, including *Open Space, Caterpillar,* and *The Floating Bear*) were important influences on the literary and artistic scene in San Francisco in the 60s. Duncan's early work was published in Berkeley or North Carolina (his *Song of the Borderguard* was published by the Black Mountain College Press with a cover by Cy Twombly in 1952). Other earlier works were multilithed (*Fragments of a Disordered Devotion* in San Francisco in 1952) or mimeographed (the first hundred copies of *Faust Foutu* were mimeographed by Duncan himself, and the next 150 or so of one act of the play were multilithed by Joe Dunn of White Rabbit Press at his place of employment, the Greyhound Bus offices in San Francisco). The multilithed third edition of *Faust Foutu,* although also produced by Dunn, was published under Duncan's own imprint, Enkidu Surrogate, of Stinson Beach. Duncan's work was published by an amazing variety and number of publishers, including Oyez, Auerhahn, White Rabbit, Black Sparrow, Divers Press, Jargon, Perishable Press, City Lights, Grove Press, New Directions, and Scribners.

Slightly outside the Spicer circle (although some of his own poems were published in *J*) was Donald Allen, who, after the publication of *The New American Poetry, 1945-1960* and before his removal to New York, established the Four Seasons Foundation in San Francisco, which published the work of a number of the writers from the anthology, including Charles Olson, Ed Dorn, Ron Loewinsohn, Philip Lamantia, Michael McClure, Joanne Kyger, Robin Blaser, and Robert Creeley. Among the early Four Seasons publications were two important works by poet Gary Snyder (the Reed College roommate of Lew Welch and Philip Whalen and the "Japhy Ryder" of Kerouac's *The Dharma Bums*): *Six Sections from Rivers and Mountains Without End* and *Riprap and Cold Mountain Poems,* both published in 1965. *Riprap,* it should be noted, was originally published in 1959 as a booklet by Cid Corman's Origin Press. Snyder's *Myths and Texts* was published in 1960 by Corinth Books. Snyder was out of the country on an extended stay in Japan, and the text used for the Corinth publication was probably from a manuscript that LeRoi Jones had hand-copied from one that Robert Creeley had received from Snyder in 1955 or 1956. Snyder's poetry was extremely popular in the 60s and was often used as text for broadsides by small presses, particularly those whose owners were ecologically minded. For instance, Snyder's poem "Four Changes" was published in 1969 by Earth Read Out, a Berkeley environmental protection group, as four mimeographed pages, as well as in a folded, printed version in 200,000 copies by environmentalist Alan Shapiro for free distribution to schools and citizens' groups.

Literary scenes with strong affiliations to the New American Poetry were in evidence elsewhere in California—most notably Bolinas in the 1970s, when that somewhat remote hippie village north of San Francisco became home to many poets. In particular, the transplanted easterner and Poetry Project veteran Bill Berkson and his press Big Sky flourished there in the decade, publishing both a magazine and a series of books. Bolinas residents of the period also included Robert Creeley, Bobbie Louise Hawkins, David Meltzer, Lewis Warsh, Tom Clark, Lewis MacAdams, Philip Whalen, Aram Saroyan, Joanne Kyger, Jim Carroll, and Duncan McNaughton, among others. Ted Berrigan, Alice Notley, and Joe Brainard were among many occasional visitors, with Joe Brainard's *Bolinas Journal* providing an interesting record of one such extended stay.

Poetry conferences at Vancouver (1963) and Berkeley (1965) were significant events that brought together and introduced a range of poets from diverse locations and temperaments. Warren Tallman was the man behind the conference in Vancouver, an event Robert Creeley described as "landmark" in that it brought "together for the first time, a decisive company of then disregarded poets such as Denise Levertov, Charles Olson, Allen Ginsberg, Robert Duncan, Margaret Avison, Philip Whalen and myself, together with as yet unrecognized younger poets of that time, Michael Palmer, Clark Coolidge and many more." The conference at Berkeley in July of 1965 further galvanized the gains made by the Allen anthology and the Vancouver event. Mostly organized and emceed by Thomas Parkinson and Robert Duncan, it featured readings and lectures by, among many others, Charles Olson, Jack Spicer, Allen Ginsberg, Gary Snyder, Ed Dorn, Robert Creeley, John Wieners, Ed Sanders, Ted Berrigan, Joanne Kyger, Lew Welch, Ron Loewinsohn, John Sinclair, and Victor Coleman. For the senior poets, the Berkeley conference was at once a triumphant victory and the beginning of the end. In the years immediately following the conference, a general emigration of spirits took place. Jack Spicer's lecture on poetry and politics was to be his last

public appearance; he died a month later. Within the next couple of years, a great many of the participants in the San Francisco Renaissance had moved from the area or passed away. Yet for many of the younger poets in attendance, the Berkeley Poetry Conference was the flash point of the mimeo revolution, the place from which much of the writing and publishing just ahead was to locate its identity and its momentum.

Among those writers at the 1955 reading at the Six Gallery in San Francisco were, of course, both Allen Ginsberg and Jack Kerouac. Both were to become literary idols of a generation, and both were heavily connected to life in the West. Ginsberg's poem *Howl* had been written on Montgomery Street in San Francisco, where he was to meet his lover and companion Peter Orlovsky. Kerouac's most famous books all deal in one way or another with the myth of the West and its place in the American imagination. However, Kerouac and Ginsberg, who, with William S. Burroughs and Gregory Corso, were to form the nucleus of the Beat writers, had met in the 1940s in New York City, where they had begun their writing as well. New York was to become a Beat capital in the 1950s, with its plethora of coffeehouses and jazz bars, where poetry was occasionally performed, with or without musical accompaniment. One enterprising young man, Dan Saxon, collected the manuscripts that poets read in the East Seventh Street coffeehouses and published an early mimeographed magazine, *Poems Collected at Les Deux Mégots,* and its continuation, *Poets at Le Metro,* directly reproducing the original handwritten manuscript or typescript. In 1960, Corinth Books published the defining anthology, *The Beat Scene,* edited by Eli Wilentz, with spectacular and intimate photographs by Fred McDarrah. That same year, Corinth also published (sometimes in association with Totem Press) Jack Kerouac's *The Scripture of the Golden Eternity,* Philip Whalen's *Like I Say,* and Gary Snyder's *Myths and Texts.* In 1961, Corinth published Diane di Prima's *Dinners and Nightmares,* Ginsberg's early poems in *Empty Mirror,* and LeRoi Jones's breakthrough *Preface to a Twenty Volume Suicide Note.*

LeRoi Jones started the little magazine *Yugen* in 1958 with Hettie Cohen, and its pages were full of writings by core Beat writers, including Kerouac, Burroughs, Orlovsky, Snyder, and Whalen, as well as Jones himself. In 1961, Jones and Diane di Prima started the mimeo magazine *The Floating Bear,* early issues of which were typed up by di Prima and produced on the mimeograph machine at Robert Wilson's Phoenix Bookstore in New York

Campus of Black Mountain College in North Carolina.

in exchange for finished copies of the magazine. Jones and di Prima intended their "newsletter" to be an engine for quick and informal communication, particularly for younger and unpublished experimental poets who practiced "the open and implied rebellion—of form and content." *The Floating Bear* 9 (October 1961) was apparently a little *too* rebellious for the authorities, as it contained an excerpt from Jones's *The System of Dante's Hell* and Burroughs's *Routine*. Jones was arrested and charged with sending obscene material through the U.S. mails. But he was not indicted by the grand jury, who listened patiently to his reading great literature of all types, once deemed obscene. *The Floating Bear* had a bold and colorful editorial style, and a simple design. It emphasized the publication of new work from a variety of sources, be they Black Mountain, Beat, San Francisco Renaissance, or New York School.

BLACK MOUNTAIN

Among the several streams which made up the New American Poetry was a group known as the Black Mountain poets, so named for the experimental college in North Carolina where many of them taught or attended classes in the 1950s. The most prominent of these poets were of course Charles Olson, rector of the college in its last five years, and Robert Creeley, who edited *The Black Mountain Review*. The work of both has exerted an extraordinary influence on the course of American poetry in the latter half of this century. Closely allied with many of the Black Mountain writers, but especially influential on Creeley, were the poets occasionally known as the Objectivists, such as Louis Zukofsky, George Oppen, and Charles Reznikoff, who were in fact too individualistic to be part of any school. Still, the spare lyricism, historical knowledge, and social conscience found in all three poets were highly regarded in the camps of the New American Poetry.

Those who taught or listened at Black Mountain constitute a veritable roll-call of the American avant-garde; among those most relevant to our literary purposes are John Cage, Merce Cunningham, Fielding Dawson, Ed Dorn, Robert Duncan, Buckminster Fuller, Basil King, Joel Oppenheimer, M. C. Richards, Michael Rumaker, John Wieners, and Jonathan Williams. *The Black Mountain Review* was founded to supplement allied magazines such as *Origin* (Olson succinctly described the importance of *Origin* when he told editor Cid Corman, "The thing is, because *Origin* exists, I write better, I write more . . .")[6] and attempted to extend this work by creating a critical grounding for the new writing through the publication of theoretical writings. The magazine also acted as a bridge to writers outside the Black Mountain milieu, publishing work by Lorine Niedecker, James Purdy, Allen Ginsberg, Hubert Selby, Jr., and Jack Kerouac, among others. Jonathan Williams returned from San Francisco to his home-state to study photography with Aaron Siskind and Harry Callahan at Black Mountain College. Williams's nascent Jargon Society flourished in part as a result of his stay at the college—books published during and just after this period include Olson's *The Maximus Poems,* Creeley's *A Form of Women,* Louis Zukofsky's *Some Time,* Larry Eigner's *On My Eyes,* Duncan's *Letters,* Denise Levertov's *Overland to the Islands,* Paul Metcalf's *Genoa,* and Williams's own *Empire Finals at Verona* (illustrated by Fielding Dawson), to name just a few. *The Black Mountain Review* had a distinctive squat format and was very well produced. Published in part as an attempt to draw attention to the college in a last-ditch effort to increase enrollment, the edition size never exceeded 750 copies.

The bringing together of unusual talents from diverse arts in the cloistered setting at Black Mountain played a crucial role in the development of postmodernism later in the 1960s. Having the likes of Buckminster Fuller, John Cage, Merce Cunningham, Robert Rauschenberg, Willem de Kooning, David Tudor, Stephen Volpe, Paul Goodman, and Cy Twombly (along with the poets mentioned above) under one roof pinpoints the location of one of several influential force fields in America that surely extended the boundaries of the various arts into new kinds of expression and new ways of making art.

INTERMEDIA

New York in the late 1950s saw the emergence of radical changes in dance, painting, film, sculpture, and theater as well as in writing. Indeed, writing or "text" was foregrounded in much of the new art. Language was newly seen as a material form, and could thus be worked with as one would work with paint or movement or sound. Concrete and sound poetry flourished. Conceptual and minimal artists began publishing their works in the form of books (later to be called "artists' books")—Edward Ruscha's early published book-

lets (for example, *Twenty-six Gasoline Stations*) were important extenders of the book as an art form. Other artists, such as Dan Graham, Adrian Piper, Sol LeWitt, Vito Acconci, Lawrence Weiner, and Carl Andre, were publishing both artists' books (i.e., books as works of art) as well as poetry and other writings, sometimes in the same places as those writers most easily identified as poets. Painter Carolee Schneemann was (and continues to be) crucial in highlighting the value of the ecstatic body as a source of knowledge. Her early performances and films are the source books for much of the performance art that followed in the 70s. *Parts of a Body House Book,* published by Beau Geste Press in 1972, connects text and image to ritual, performance, and dream and links her work to that of the writers working in ethnopoetics.

John Cage's influence, in part disseminated through his class in "Composition of Experimental Music" at the New School for Social Research, was crucial in the development of both Happenings and Fluxus. In the summer of 1958, class members included Dick Higgins, Jackson Mac Low, Jim Dine, Allan Kaprow, and George Brecht. Cage's collection of lectures and writings, entitled *Silence,* was published in 1961 by Wesleyan University Press. George Maciunas met La Monte Young in Richard Maxfield's New School class in electronic music. In early 1961, Young and Maciunas hosted a series called "Literary Evenings and Musica Antiqua et Nova" at the latter's AG Gallery. Participants included Trisha Brown, Yvonne Rainer, Jackson Mac Low, Dick Higgins, and Ray Johnson. In 1960, Young was invited to guest edit an issue of *Beatitude East* focusing on performance and poetry. The project for *Beatitude East* was canceled but was resurrected as *An Anthology of Chance Operations,* edited by Young, designed and produced by Maciunas, and published by Young and Mac Low in 1963. The anthology, a collection of music and performance scores, essays, stories, and poems, included work by Emmett Williams, George Brecht, Henry Flynt, Robert Morris, Terry Riley, Yoko Ono, Simone Forti, Jackson Mac Low, and others. Mac Low's own work as a writer dates to 1937; he stands, in the words of Jerome Rothenberg, alongside John Cage as "one of the two major artists bringing systematic chance operations into our poetic & musical practice since the Second World War."[7] His first book, *The Twin Plays,* was mimeographed in 1963, and was soon followed by *The Pronouns* in 1964, which was mimeographed at the Judson Memorial Church.

The year 1964 saw the founding of one of the most interesting presses of the period: Dick Higgins's Something Else Press. As an editor, Higgins seemed to be interested in everything having to do with the new arts—his interest in and knowledge of the history of bookmaking, printing, design, and typography helped him to accomplish something very few of the previously mentioned publishers ever managed to achieve: distribution. One of the most radical achievements of the Something Else Press was to slip avant-garde content into what looked like "regular books" and then to get those books into bookstores and libraries around the world. The list of titles published by Something Else in its regular series as well as the series of Great Bear Pamphlets is astonishing for its range and depth. A few examples are Daniel Spoerri's *An Anecdoted Topography of Chance, Notations* by John Cage with Alison Knowles, *An Anthology of Concrete Poetry,* edited by Emmett Williams, *Breakthrough Fictioneers,* edited by Richard Kostelanetz, *Store Days* by Claes Oldenburg, and *Stanzas for Iris Lezak* by Jackson Mac Low. It is interesting to note that Higgins's own first book, *What Are Legends,* was published by Bern Porter in 1961. Porter, himself an important writer and visual artist, also published the first books of Philip Lamantia and Robert Duncan.

THE DEEP IMAGE AND ETHNOPOETICS

In the late 50s and early 60s, another group important to the New American Poetry was emerging, primarily in New York. They were a sort of "in-between" generation—younger than most of the poets in the Allen anthology but older than the second-generation New York School or the Language poets. This group began publishing in magazines such as *Some/thing, Poems from the Floating World, Trobar, Matter,* and *Caterpillar.* Poets most closely allied with this group include Jerome Rothenberg, Robert Kelly, Clayton Eshleman, Diane Wakoski, David Antin, Paul Blackburn, Frank Samperi, Armand Schwerner, and George Economou. The basic sense of deep image poetry, as distinct from Imagism, was, according to Robert Kelly, to "generate a kind of poetry not necessarily dominated by the images, but in which it is the rhythm of images which forms the dominant movement of the poem."[8] Jerome Rothenberg would later describe the "deep image" as "a power, among several, by which the poem is sighted & brought close." Investigations into deep image existed alongside and resonated with work in translation, performance, and an awareness of earlier avant-gardes and poetry from "those anonymous tribal & subterranean predecessors." Consequently, these poets were keenly aware of the need to build on the insights and discoveries

of Dada and Surrealism. Ethnopoetics developed, in part, out of a growing awareness "that we weren't just doing something new (which we were) but were getting back in our own terms to fundamental ways of seeing & languaging from which we (the larger 'we' of the Western enterprise) had long been cut off."[9] Thus, Ethnopoetics is a recognition of the "primitive" as a way to ease ourselves into the future. *Alcheringa: Ethnopoetics,* "a first journal of the world's tribal poetries," edited by Jerome Rothenberg and Dennis Tedlock, published five numbers in its first series (1970-1973) and continued forward with a second series in 1975. Several of the issues contained phonograph records, including readings by Jaime de Angelo, Jackson Mac Low, and Anne Waldman. *New Wilderness Letter* (edited primarily by Jerome Rothenberg but with the help of co- and guest editors) extended the ethnopoetics project into an exploration of the relation between old and new forms of art-making across the full spectrum of arts. One of the most interesting issues was *New Wilderness Letter* 11 (1982), entitled *The Book, Spiritual Instrument,* which Rothenberg co-edited with anthropologist/poet David Guss. A significant contribution to the ethnopoetic project is to be found in the collection of anthologies edited by Rothenberg, including *Technicians of the Sacred, Shaking the Pumpkin, America: A Prophecy* (with George Quasha), and *A Big Jewish Book.*

The New York School really began, strangely enough, in Cambridge, Massachusetts, at Harvard University where several of its most famous members were students along with other postwar poets Robert Bly, Robert Creeley, Donald Hall, Adrienne Rich, and Richard Wilbur. It was at Harvard that Kenneth Koch met John Ashbery and that John Ashbery published Frank O'Hara, later meeting him in the flesh at an opening of a show of Edward Gorey's watercolors (Gorey was Ashbery's roommate). All three eventually ended up in New York City, where they became involved with each other and with a number of painters, including Jane Freilicher, Nell Blaine, Larry Rivers, and Fairfield Porter.

Everyone, it seems, wrote for *Art News* or worked at the Museum of Modern Art, except for Koch who taught and pioneered the teaching of poetry to children. The poetry and art worlds were deeply intertwined, and collaboration between visual artists and writers continues to be a salient characteristic of the New York School. In 1953, for instance, John Bernard Myers of the Tibor de Nagy Gallery published O'Hara's *Oranges* in an edition of about twenty mimeographed copies. Issued in gray "three-clasp binders," some of the copies contained oil paint sketches by Grace Hartigan (the publication was in fact to accompany the exhibition of her work at the gallery). In 1952, Myers had produced, somewhat more "professionally," O'Hara's *A City Winter,* with some copies containing drawings by Larry Rivers. This was followed in 1953 by Koch's *Poems,* with prints by Nell Blaine, and Ashbery's *Turandot,* with plates by Jane Freilicher. These volumes were all printed letterpress with decorative covers. In 1969, Myers published an anthology, *The Poets of the New York School,* which included O'Hara, Koch, and Ashbery as well as James Schuyler, Barbara Guest, Joe Ceravolo, Kenward Elmslie, Frank Lima, and Tony Towle. James Schuyler, whose *May 24th or So* was published (unaccompanied by art) by Tibor de Nagy in 1966, had arrived on the scene (he was to become one of the most famous of the residents of New York City's Chelsea Hotel) and, in 1972, had published the mimeographed anthology *49 South.* His *Freely Espousing* was published by Paris Review Press in 1969 with a jacket by Alex Katz, and *Hymn to Life, The Crystal Lithium,* and *The Morning of the Poem* were all published by Random House with covers by Fairfield Porter.

All the major figures of the New York School were to find commercial publishers, but continued to provide work to the small presses and mimeograph magazines (Barbara Guest, for instance, appeared in several issues of *"C"* magazine, and Ashbery's *The New Spirit* was published by Larry Fagin's Adventures in Poetry). In 1970, *An Anthology of New York Poets,* edited by Ron Padgett and David Shapiro (with a cover by Joe Brainard), was published by Vintage. It featured work by Schuyler, Koch, Ashbery, and O'Hara scattered throughout the book, which also included Clark Coolidge, Kenward Elmslie, Ted Berrigan, Harry Matthews, Tony Towle, Tom Clark, Tom Veitch, Lewis MacAdams, Frank Lima, John Giorno, Joe Ceravolo, Jim Brodey, John Perrault, Bill Berkson, Michael Brownstein, Ed Sanders, Peter Schjeldahl, Aram Saroyan, Ron Padgett, Dick Gallup, Bernadette Mayer, Edwin Denby, and David Shapiro.

Some of the great New York-based magazines were *"C", Fuck You, a magazine of the arts, Mother, Angel Hair, The World, 0 to 9, Lines,* and *Adventures in Poetry,* all born in the turbulent literary and social atmosphere of the East Village in the 1960s.

Ed Sanders came from Kansas to study classics at NYU. Poet, editor, publisher, bookstore owner (Peace Eye), singer/songwriter (founding member of the Fugs), political activist, and relentless archivist, Sanders founded *Fuck You, a magazine of the arts* in 1962. Unabashed and unashamed on every front, *Fuck You* reveled in an attitude best described by William Blake 150 years before: "Energy is eternal delight." *Fuck You* published the likes of Charles Olson, Lenore Kandel, Carol Bergé, Ted Berrigan, Tuli Kupferberg, W. H. Auden, and Ezra Pound. The energy and ethos of the magazine is vividly expressed in the following statement: *"Fuck You: A Magazine of the Arts* is edited, published, zapped, designed, freaked, groped, stomped, & ejaculated by Ed Sanders at a secret location in the lower east side, New York City, U.S.A." Almost forty years later, it is still completely original and a total delight.

Mother was edited by several different poets including David Moberg, Jeff Giles, Peter Schjeldahl, Lewis MacAdams, and Duncan McNaughton from such diverse locations as Northfield, Minnesota; Galesburg, Illinois; New York City; and Buffalo, New York. Yet it was always associated with the New York School and published work by such poets as John Ashbery, Bernadette Mayer, Ed Sanders, John Wieners, Tony Towle, Kenneth Koch, and Joe Ceravolo, and artwork by many including Les Levine, Andy Warhol, and Joe Brainard. Issue 7 included the infamous interview with John Cage conducted by Ted Berrigan. Actually, Berrigan was responsible for both questions *and* answers, most of which were appropriated from other sources, a circumstance that caused some embarrassment when the interview was honored with a cash award from *The National Literary Anthology.*

Ted Berrigan, in many ways the focal point of the East Village literary outburst, arrived in New York from Tulsa in late 1960 (or early 1961), having completed his Master's thesis on G. B. Shaw. While in the army, he had learned to operate the mimeograph machine, a skill that would serve him well. The first issue of *"C"* was published by Lorenz Gude in May 1963—the contributors were editor Berrigan and his three best friends, all from Tulsa: Ron Padgett, Dick Gallup, and Joe Brainard. *"C"* was preceded by the one and only issue of a mimeographed magazine entitled *The Censored Review,* which published poems by Berrigan ("I Was Born Standing Up"), Jonathan Cott, Dick Gallup ("Ember Grease"), Nancy Ward, and David Omer Bearden, and the very long and anonymous "Eli's Story" about a group of characters who were "All orbits in Brian Benedict's universe." In 1963, *"C"* published the Edwin Denby issue with its cover by Andy Warhol. Berrigan's breakthrough book, *The Sonnets,* was mimeographed and published by "C" Press in 1964. Ron Padgett edited the work and typed the stencils.

Among the other early mimeograph publications of the East Village were several collaborations: *Some Things* (a collaboration late in 1963 between Berrigan, Padgett, and Brainard) and *Seventeen* (plays by Ted Berrigan and Ron Padgett, and by the two in collaboration, 1964). In the early years, Berrigan and Padgett were the best of friends, and their combined talents were crucial ingredients in the emerging scene. Padgett's high school experience in Tulsa editing the *White Dove Review* proved invaluable. His wisdom and learning mixed with Berrigan's enthusiasm and energy to provide an atmosphere of friendly competition and collaboration that inspired and encouraged other poets and writers throughout the 60s.

Lines was edited by Aram Saroyan and, like *0 to 9* (edited by Bernadette Mayer and Vito Acconci), published works somewhat more visually and conceptually based than many of the other literary magazines of the period. *The World*, the magazine of The Poetry Project, was first published in 1967. Mimeographed at St. Mark's Church-in-the-Bowery, it has long been a cohesive, unifying element in the downtown New York literary scene and has always been identified with a broad range of new and interesting writing. Remarkably, *The World* is still publishing in 1998. Angel Hair was born at Robert Duncan's reading at the Berkeley Poetry Conference, where Anne Waldman and Lewis Warsh first met. They edited six issues of the magazine and a series of books. Larry Fagin moved to New York from San Francisco where he was associated with the Spicer circle. His eclectic Adventures in Poetry published both the magazine and a series of books.

It is interesting to note that, at least for a short while, trade publishers in New York and elsewhere did take considerable interest in the new writing. A great many anthologies of new and experimental poetry were published, including *The World, Another World, An Anthology of New York Poets,* and *Naked Poetry,* to name a few. Also, a significant number of books by individual writers—including Anne Waldman, Tom Clark, Carol Bergé, Joel Oppenheimer, Clark Coolidge, Lewis MacAdams, Michael Brownstein, Ron Padgett, and Dick Gallup—were published in the late 60s and early 70s by the likes of Bobbs-Merrill and Harper & Row.

The third generation of New York School writers emerged at roughly the same time that the poets associated with language writing began to be identified as a group. The magazine *United Artists* served to a great extent as a bridge between the generations, publishing many of the newcomers to the scene alongside the more established members of the St. Mark's school. *United Artists* was also in many ways the apotheosis of the mimeograph magazine, spectacular in its simple design (the first twelve covers were simply tables of content) and adventuresome in its combination of the personal and the experimental, pioneering in the publication of journal and diary entries. The third generation was largely based at The Poetry Project, and much influenced by teachers there such as Ted Berrigan, Alice Notley, Lewis Warsh, and Bernadette Mayer. In the mid- to late 70s and early 80s, East Village magazines and presses such as *Mag City,* Frontward Books, *4, 3, 2 Review, KOFF, Tangerine, Ghandhabba, Ladies Museum,* and *Dodgems* published writings by Greg Masters, Ed Friedman, Eileen Myles, Susie Timmons, Tom Weigel, Michael Scholnick, Maggie Dubris, Jeff Wright, Simon Schuchat, Elinor Nauen, and Gary Lenhart, among others who identified with and extended the heritage of the New York Schools. A similar scene developed in the Los Angeles area with the Beyond Baroque reading series in Venice, and many of its trends can be seen in the magazine *Little Caesar,* which further blurred the lines between literature, music, and the visual arts.

In 1982, two literary journals as disparate as *Ironwood* and *The Paris Review* both featured collections of language writing. Ron Silliman, in his introduction to the collection in *Ironwood,* traces a kind of "anti-history" back to the early 70s with the publication of two important journals, *Tottel's* and *This.* Silliman makes the important point that the phenomenon is based on a created audience and that language writing is most significantly identified as community based, with almost all its practitioners sharing "the responsibility of creating the institutions through which the work can be made public." He goes on to say that "the project of this writing is the discovery of a community."[10] In his introduction to the selection of language writing published in *The Paris Review,* Charles Bernstein offers the useful hint that this is a "writing that takes as its medium, or domain of intention, every articulable aspect of language."

Although language writing surely flourished in the 1980s, a fact amply demonstrated by several anthologies (such as *In the American Tree: Language Realism Poetry,* edited by Ron Silliman, and *"Language" Poetries: An Anthology,* edited by Douglas Messerli) and critical works (*Code of Signals,* a special issue of *Io* edited by Michael Palmer; Barrett Watten's *Total Syntax*, Charles Bernstein's *Content's Dream*; Bernstein and Bruce Andrew's *The L=A=N=G=U=A=G=E Book*; and Ron Silliman's *The New Sentence*), it was, from its beginnings in the early 70s, an influential and always controversial presence in the poetry community at large. At first, the lines between the soon-to-be-identified language poets and various other vaguely defined schools or groups were not so clearly drawn. For instance, Barrett Watten's first book, *Opera-Works*, was published by Bill Berkson's New York School—identified Big Sky, and *Roof* magazine, an important New York-based outlet for language writing, was born at Naropa Institute in 1976. Its early issues included both Beat and New York School poets. The second small anthology of language writing appeared in the ethnopoetics journal *Alcheringa* in 1975—but by the end of the 70s, those associated with language writing had thoroughly established their presence and made visible their various unique and shared tendencies through an incredible network of magazines, presses, and reading and talk series located primarily in San Francisco and New York, with a smaller group active in Washington, D.C. Magazines and presses such as *L=A=N=G=U=A=G=E*, *This*, *A Hundred Posters*, *E pod*, *Hills*, *Vanishing Cab*, *Miam*, *Roof*, *Sun & Moon*, The Figures, Asylum's, Tuumba, *The Difficulties*, *Poetics Journal*, and others served as venues for writing (poetry as well as critical prose) by Ron Silliman, Charles Bernstein, Lyn Hejinian, Bruce Andrews, Barrett Watten, Robert Grenier, Steve Benson, Rae Armantrout, Bob Perelman, Nick Piombino, Diane Ward, Carla Harryman, Alan Davies, and Johanna Drucker, among many others.

Other Places (Chicago, Michigan, Ohio, Rhode Island, Iowa, and Beyond)

CHICAGO

The literary climate in the Midwest began to heat up in 1958 when *The Chicago Review*, as its Spring number, presented an issue devoted to the San Francisco Renaissance. This included a chapter from the then-unpublished *Naked Lunch* by the notorious William S. Burroughs, as well as work by Duncan, Ginsberg, Ferlinghetti, McClure, and others. Editors Irving Rosenthal and Paul Carroll gathered and published more such "Beat" material in the Autumn 1958 issue. As they prepared the Winter issue, the *Chicago Daily News* published an article entitled "Filthy Writing on the Midway"; as a consequence, that issue was suppressed by a cowardly administration, galvanizing and energizing the literary underground.

Carroll and Rosenthal, along with a half dozen other editors, resigned from *The Chicago Review*. With the suppressed material they founded *Big Table* (so named by Jack Kerouac in a telegram: "CALL IT BIG TABLE"). The first issue, which featured Kerouac, Dahlberg, and Burroughs, was impounded by the U.S. Post Office. The ACLU challenged the Post Office in a hearing presided over by Judge Julius S. Hoffman, who later presided over the Chicago Seven conspiracy trial. Judge Hoffman followed Judge Woolsey's decision regarding Joyce's *Ulysses*, and *Big Table* continued publishing through five issues. The aura, even the glamour, of censorship helped to increase its distribution, and its audience consequently grew significantly. Like *Evergreen Review*, *Big Table* was crucial in bringing the underground to those of us waiting in the wings in small-town America.

(Three editors of the geographically distant *Northwest Review* at the University of Oregon, in Eugene, were to face this same issue later, when their publication was suspended by the university after the publication of eight poems by Philip Whalen and work by Antonin Artaud in its Fall 1963 issue. Also included were an interview with Fidel Castro and a portfolio of photographs of contemporary Cuba. Like their fellows in Chicago, the group, led by editor Edward Van Aelstyne, started their own periodical, entitled *Coyote's Journal*, which in its first three issues used material gathered for the *Northwest Review*.) Other important Chicago periodicals and presses of the 1960s and 70s included Alice Notley's *Chicago*, Art Lange's *Brilliant Corners* (which, in addition to poetry, printed writings on improvisational jazz), the Surrealist/anarchist/leftist-oriented Black Swan (still in operation), Yellow Press, and *Milk Quarterly*, principally edited by Darlene Pearlstein with Bob Rosenthal, Peter Kostakis, and Richard Friedman. Interestingly, some of the poets in Chicago were taught how to use the mimeograph machine in the 1960s and 70s by Ted Berrigan on one of his visits to Chicago or during teaching stints at Northwestern.

MICHIGAN, OHIO, AND RHODE ISLAND

Other activities in the Midwest included the Artists' Workshop Press in Detroit, which published (often in broadside format) work by such poets as George Tysh, John Sinclair, and John Wieners. The use of colored "construction" papers (of the sort favored by grade school teachers) was a particularly distinctive characteristic of this press, which also cultivated a sort of hard-core working-class aesthetic. Dudley Randall's Broadside Press of Detroit was very important for the

Black Arts Movement during the late 60s and 70s and published a great many writers including Gwendolyn Brooks, Sonia Sanchez, and Sterling Brown. Ken and Anne Mikolowski's The Alternative Press, also of Michigan, has published an avalanche of interesting work over the past thirty years, most of which has taken the form of broadsides, postcards, bookmarks, bumperstickers, and other ephemera. In 1971, they began to issue annual packets of printed matter by subscription, the announcement for which carried the slogan "Art Poetry Melodrama." Artists and writers published include Faye Kicknosway, John Sinclair, Ted Berrigan, Allen Ginsberg, Robert Creeley, Jerome Rothenberg, Lewis Warsh, Tom Clark, George Tysh, William Wantling, Joel Oppenheimer, Robert Bly, Philip Guston, and others. Burning Deck Press (as in "the boy stood on the") began as a literary magazine in Ann Arbor in 1961. Three issues were published in Michigan before editors Keith and Rosmarie Waldrop moved to Durham, Connecticut, where the fourth issue came out. Material for a fifth issue was gathered but never published. In 1968, the editors moved to Providence, Rhode Island, the city where Clark Coolidge had earlier co-published his influential magazine *Joglars*. Burning Deck has published over 200 books and broadsides, primarily by younger writers, and is generally recognized as one of the most important and interesting literary presses publishing in English. Its books are often designed and printed by the editors by letterpress. It is interesting to note that letterpress, previously the mark of more upscale publishing with a distinctly main-stream flavor, was then in the process of undergoing its own revolution. As photo-offset became the standard in commercial printing, the letterpress machines became available for next to nothing. Poets like the Waldrops picked them up cheaply and produced works very much in the spirit of those working with mimeo, thus transforming letterpress aesthetics into the service of the revolution. The Waldrops are both accomplished writers and translators with wide-ranging tastes. Over the years they have published works from John Heath-Stubbs, Bruce Andrews, X. J. Kennedy, Rochelle Owens, Mark Strand, Ron Silliman, Edwin Honig, Lisa Jarnot, Marcia Southwick, William Bronk, Lyn Hejinian, and Barbara Guest, among others.

465: An Anthology of Cleveland Poetry published the work of T. L. Kryss, Russell Atkins, Grace Butchert, d. a. levy, and others. d. a. levy was an important catalyst in Cleveland on several fronts. His aptly named Renegade Press (later 7 Flowers Press) produced some fifty volumes of levy's work, much of which takes the form of amazingly beautiful and prescient concrete poetry (see, for example, *Fortuitons Motherfucer, Zen Concrete,* and *The Tibetan Stroboscope*). levy also edited several anthologies, serials, and magazines including *The Buddhist 3rd Class Junkmail Oracle* and the *Marrahwannah Newsletter*. As Ed Sanders later said of Ted Berrigan and Paul Blackburn, levy "lived it 24 hours a day" and he paid a heavy price. levy was arrested and jailed along with Jim Lowell (proprietor of the great Asphodel Bookshop, a welcoming home for new poetry for over thirty years) on charges of distributing obscene material. One of the truly unique and authentic spirits of the mimeo revolution, levy became famous as the poetry world gathered in his support, but in 1968, at the age of twenty-six, he committed suicide.

Ray DiPalma began publishing, among others, writers associated with scenes in Iowa City and around The Poetry Project in New York in his magazine *Doones* in 1969 out of Bowling Green, Ohio. A considerable range of poets such as Ted Berrigan, Merrill Gilfillan, Ted Greenwald, Darrell Gray, Anselm Hollo, Robert Kelly, James Tate, Bill Knott, Ron Silliman, and Larry Fagin published in *Doones* as well as in DiPalma's series of booklets and one-shot "supplements" such as *Painted Horses* and *Shelter*. DiPalma moved to New York in the mid-70s. He has been associated with language writing since the beginning and has published many impressive volumes of his own work under such imprints as Sun & Moon, Segue, and Burning Deck.

IOWA

Whether because or in spite of the University of Iowa Writers' Workshop, a vibrant literary scene developed in Iowa City during the late 60s and early 70s. Ted Berrigan and Anselm Hollo were both in residence as teachers at the famous workshop for a spell, but probably wielded greater influence in the bars and cafes off campus. More than thirty small presses and magazines sprouted up during the period. Among the most interesting were *This, Toothpaste* (later *Dental Floss*), *Gum, Hills, Matchbook,* Search for Tomorrow, Blue Wind, *Poetry Comics,* and *The Spirit That Moves Us*. A genuine "movement" evolved, and Darrell Gray's articulate and rousing manifesto of "Actualism" appeared in *Gum 9* (January 1973). It begins, "Actuality is never frustrated because it is complete." And ends, "Why belabor the impossible?" *The Actualist Anthology* appeared in 1977. *Toothpaste* was edited by poet and printer Allan Kornblum, who is now the director of its direct descendant, The Coffee House Press. Dave Morice (a.k.a. Dr. Alphabet, a.k.a. Joyce Holland) has been an important poet and teacher in Iowa City since the mid-60s. His magazines and books continue to stretch the limits of language (and publishing) in subtle ways. *Matchbook,* for instance, was a magazine of oneword poetry, and each copy was stapled to the inside of a found matchbook. "Joyce Holland" edited *The Alphabet Anthology* in 1973. Contributors to this anthology of one-letter poetry include Bruce Andrews ("O"), Larry Eigner ("e"), and Bernadette Mayer ("n"). Dave Morice began publishing his *Poetry Comics* in 1979, and Simon & Schuster later published (and then remaindered) a collection of this excellent work.

BEYOND

Interesting magazines and presses flourished throughout the country as a network of literary publications kept far-flung poets and writers in contact with one another. Fine work could be found in *Margins* (which published reviews and writings on poetics), *Grist* (established in Kansas in 1964 by John Fowler, *Grist* is now publishing online at http://www.thing.net/~grist/), *Quixote, The Wormwood Review, Io, Truck, Suck-Egg Mule, Duende, Wild Dog, The Fifties, The Sixties,* and *The Outsider. The Outsider* represents an extreme act of publishing and deserves special mention. Edited and published in New Orleans by Jon Edgar and Louise "Gypsy Lou" Webb, *The Outsider* was lavishly (one imagines even maniacally) produced by letterpress with a wide range of interesting and unusual materials. Yet in spite of its formal sophistication, it still manifests the indomitable spirit of the mimeo revolution by virtue of its devotion to such writers as Charles Bukowski and Kenneth Patchen, both of whom were recipients of the "Outsider of the Year" award. Other contributors to this "book periodical" were Robert Creeley, Douglas Woolf, Gary Snyder, Larry Eigner, William S. Burroughs, Michael McClure, and Barbara Moraff.

Canada, England, Scotland, Europe, and Australia

Of course, kindred acts of experimental writing and publishing were committed around the world. For a time, in the 60s and 70s, Toronto might well have boasted the largest number of avant-garde poets per capita of any city on the face of the earth. The great Coach House Press has been a vortex for innovative writing and publishing since its inception in 1966. Among the many Coach House titles are Michael Ondaatje's *The Dainty Monsters, Journeying and the Return* by bp

Nichol, *Excellent Articles of Japan* by David Rosenberg, *The Great Canadian Sonnet* by David McFadden and Greg Curnoe, *Neil Young* by Tom Clark, *Ow's Waif* by Steve McCaffery, *Bill Jubobe* by Bob Cobbing, and Nicole Brossard's *A Book,* to mention only a few of the works published during its first decade. Throughout Canada, writers, editors, performers, publishers—instigators-at-large—worked through such presses and magazines as *Contact, blewointment,* Coach House Press, the *Ant's Forefoot, Tish,* Periwinkle Press, Intermedia, Talonbooks, Very Stone House, Ganglia Press, Oberon, *grOnk, Open Letter,* and *Weed.* A great deal of memorable work, particularly in the realms of concrete and sound poetry, emanated from Canada (especially Toronto and Vancouver) during the period. bp Nichol's presence and example were an inspiration for many, and his untimely death in 1988 was a great tragedy.

A quick sketch of presses and magazines operating in other parts of the world would have to include, in England, *My Own Mag,* Aloes, *Stereo Headphones,* Fulcrum Press, Coracle Press, *Aggie Weston's,* Writers' Forum, Beau Geste Press, Gaberbocchus, and Cape Goliard/Grossman; in Scotland, *Poor. Old. Tired. Horse.* (and the work of its editor, Ian Hamilton Finlay, in general); in the Netherlands, *Kontexts;* in Germany, Edition Hansjörg Mayer; in France, *Merlin* and *OU;* and in Australia, *The Ear in a Wheatfield.*

Women's and Feminist Writing

Great strides were made in the development of women's and feminist writing during the late 60s and through the 70s. Ron Silliman observed in 1982 that "the single most significant change in American poetry over the past two decades is to be seen in the central role of writing within feminist culture, which in 1982 is (for good reason) the largest of all possible verse audiences."[11] Important developments among women and feminist poets run parallel to the New American Poetry but rarely intersect during the 1960-1980 period, except perhaps as they relate to the creation of independent poet-operated women's presses. The establishment, for example, of Judy Grahn's The Women's Press Collective in Oakland in 1969 and Alta's Shameless Hussy Press in Berkeley were crucial in providing a venue for women's literary voices to speak out. These writers (with significant exceptions) felt self-consciously apart from the more experimental side of poetry and determined that their concerns might perhaps be more directly served through populist modes of expression. The example of work by such writers as Adrienne Rich, Judy Grahn, Pat Parker, Ntozake Shange, and Susan Griffin, among many others, was important in defining and foregrounding issues particular to women and feminists that would be further explored over the next two decades. It is no coincidence that the magazine *HOW(ever)*, edited by Kathleen Fraser and first published in May 1983, opens with the questioning "And what about the women who were writing experimentally? Oh, were there women poets writing experimentally? Yes there were, they were." Fraser, working with contributing editors Frances Jaffer, Beverly Dahlen, Rachel Blau DuPlessis, and Carolyn Burke (and later with Susan Gevirtz, Chris Tysh, Myung Mi Kim, Meredith Stricker, Diane Glancy, and Adalaide Morris), published sixteen issues (in six volumes) between 1983 and 1992. Unlike many other feminist magazines, *HOW(ever)* was framed in a literary context and traced its history to include Emily Dickinson, Gertrude Stein, Virginia Woolf, and Dorothy Richardson. Thus, *HOW(ever)* set out to be, as Jaffer expressed it in the first issue, "A vehicle for experimentalist poetry—post-modern if you will, to be thought of seriously as an appropriate poetry for women and feminists." Contributors and topics include Norma Cole, Karen Riley, Kathy Acker on humility, Lyn Hejinian, Caroline Burke on Mina Loy, Johanna Drucker on canon formation, a group of writings on Barbara Guest, Laura Moriarty, Joan Retallack, Gail Scott, and the various editors, among many others.

African American Writing

African American literary magazines of the years 1960-1980 were rarely devoted exclusively to literary concerns—more often they presented a mix of cultural expression and political commentary in an ongoing effort to battle the racism, oppression, and violence that characterized the era. The history of the African American little magazine runs rich and deep, and a beginning look would include such publications as *Freelance, Confrontation, Callaloo, Soulbook, Umbra,* the *Journal of Black Poetry,* and *Hambone,* among many others. As with feminist writing, third-world writing, and writing by people of color in general, the trajectory of African American poetry charts a somewhat different course than that of the New American Poetry and nearly always speaks to its own audience of its own issues and on its own terms. One fascinating and eclectic example is *Yardbird Reader.* Edited by Ishmael Reed, Al Young, Shawn Wong, Frank Chin, and William Lawson,

it ran for five volumes, from 1972 to 1976. A vast range of writing from many cultures was presented, including African Americans, Asian Americans, Colombians, Puerto Ricans, Filipino-Americans, Franco-Americans, Anglo-Americans, North Africans, Kenyans, and Caribbeans. *Y'Bird,* edited by Ishmael Reed, continued the work after the demise of *Yardbird Reader.* In 1978, Grove Press published a collection of work from *Yardbird Reader* entitled *Yardbird Lives!* Dudley Randall's Broadside Press in Detroit was a prominent venue for the Black Arts Movement, and during the late 60s and throughout the 70s published such writers as June Jordan, Lucille Clifton, Raymond Patterson, Etheridge Knight, Audre Lorde, Dudley Randall, Alice Walker, and Sonia Sanchez, among many others. LeRoi Jones and Larry Neal edited the provocative *Black Fire: Anthology of Afro-American Writing,* published in 1968.

Conclusion

In 1982, Grove Press published *The Postmoderns: The New American Poetry Revised.* Edited by Donald Allen and George Butterick, this anthology confirms the prophecy of its predecessor. In the opening sentence of its introduction, it boldly proclaims its intention "not to deal comprehensively with the full range of recent American poetry but with that poetry written in America since the Second World War which, by its vitality alone, became the dominant force in the American poetic tradition." It is this vitality which is the unifying element in all the various intertwined and tangled schools and movements described above. In the heyday of the mimeo revolution it was called "the indomitable spirit," and it is our hope that this collection will serve as a vivid reminder for those who were there, and as a source of inspiration for poets and publishers now and of the future. As William Carlos Williams reminds us,

> It is difficult
> to get the news from poems
>   yet men die miserably every day
>   for lack
> of what is found there.

Notes

1. Donald Allen, *The New American Poetry* (New York: Grove Press, 1960), p. xi.

2. Ron Loewinsohn, "Reviews: After the (Mimeograph) Revolution," *TriQuarterly* 18 (Spring 1970): 222.

3. Michael Davidson, *The San Francisco Renaissance: Poetics and Community at Mid-century* (New York: Cambridge University Press, 1989), p. 40.

4. Kenneth Rexroth, *American Poetry in the Twentieth Century* (New York: Herder and Herder, 1971), p. 141.

5. Ibid.

6. Sherman Paul, *Olson's Push: Origin, Black Mountain and Recent American Poetry* (Baton Rouge: Louisiana State University Press, 1978), p. 32.

7. Jerome Rothenberg, Pre-Face to Jackson Mac Low, *Representative Works: 1938-1985* (New York: Roof, 1986), p. v.

8. *The Little Magazine in America: A Modern Documentary History,* edited by Elliott Anderson and Mary Kinzie (Yonkers, N.Y.: Pushcart Press, 1978), p. 400.

9. Jerome Rothenberg, *Pre-Faces and Other Writing* (New York: New Directions, 1981), pp. 52, 139.

10. Ron Silliman, ed., "Language Writing," *Ironwood* 20 [vol. 10, no. 2] (Fall 1982): 64.

11. Ron Silliman, ed., "Language Writing," *Ironwood* 20 [vol. 10, no. 2] (Fall 1982): 68.

BEAT PERIODICALS: "LITTLE MAGAZINES"

IMAMU AMIRI BARAKA (LEROI JONES) AND DAVID OSSMAN (INTERVIEW DATE FALL 1963)

SOURCE: Ossman, David. "LeRoi Jones: An Interview on *Yugen. TriQuarterly* 43 (fall 1978): 318-23.

In the following interview, originally published in 1963, Ossman talks with LeRoi Jones about his magazine Yugen.

LeRoi Jones did not adopt the name Imamu Amiri Baraka until the late sixties. After the middle of that decade, he turned away from his literary interests and toward black theater and black politics in Newark. (He ran for community council office there in 1968 to oversee slum rehabilitation, but lost the election.) From that time on he increasingly departed from the white world, favoring even "a mathematics which would have no whiteness in it."

In 1960, when David Ossman conducted this interview, LeRoi Jones had edited his magazine *Yugen,* along with the Totem Press, for two years (*Yugen* ran until 1962). It was later in 1960 that he visited Cuba to demonstrate support for Fidel Castro. His poem *Preface to a Twenty-Volume Suicide Note* was published by Corinth Books in 1961, the same year that he became an instructor at the New School for Social Research and a contributing editor to Diane di Prima's *The Floating Bear.* In 1962 he took the post of music editor for *Kulchur* and continued to write his columns on jazz until 1964. It was during these years that LeRoi Jones was writing his first important plays—*Dutchman, The Toilet,* and *The Slave* (all first produced in 1964).

Yours seems to be one of the three or four "clique" magazines around today, in that it publishes a fairly restricted group of so-called "Beat," "San Francisco," and "New York" writers. Why do you publish this group—this "stable" of writers?

Well, it does seem to fall that way. But for a long time Dr. Williams couldn't get into the *Hudson Review,* and several other mature, older poets like Kenneth Patchen were never admitted there, or in magazines like the *Partisan Review* or *Sewanee.* If those editors had a literary point of view in excluding their work, then I feel I have as much right, certainly, to base my choice on my literary taste. If it seems like a coterie—well, it turns out to be that way. There are other reasons—but that's the simplest explanation, actually.

The writers that I publish are really not all "Beat" or "San Francisco" or "New York." There are various people who could also fit into other groups—for instance, the people who went to Black Mountain College—and others not affiliated with any real group. But they have some kind of affinity with the other so-called groups—their writing fits into a certain kind of broad category.

Many of the same names appear regularly in Yugen, Big Table, Evergreen . . .

It's a little different though. Most of the people whom, say, Paul Carroll prints, he wouldn't have printed if it hadn't been for a magazine like *Yugen.* And *Evergreen Review,* to a great extent, has picked up on things that I've done already and that have appeared in magazines like the *Black Mountain Review* and *Neon.* They pick them up. As a matter of fact, in Paul Carroll's case, I know of at least two poets who appear in his magazine only because of various things he saw in *Yugen* and in an essay I wrote. He said he picked up some things in that essay that enabled him to understand, or become more sympathetic with, certain people's work.

I'd like to have your thoughts on a kind of contemporary writing that could be illustrated by Frank O'Hara's "Personal Poem" in Yugen 6. In it he describes his thoughts before and after having lunch with one "LeRoi." With its highly and specifically personal references, it seems to be more an anecdote of interest to future scholars than something partaking of the heightened qualities of a more traditional poetic nature. What is the validity in this kind of writing?

I didn't especially think that there was any charted-out area in which the poetic sensibility had to function to make a poem. I thought that anything—anything you could grab—was fit material to write a poem on. That's the way I think about it. Anything in your life, anything you know about or see or understand, you could write a poem about if you're moved to do it. I'm certain that if they have to footnote what the House of Seagrams was in his poem, or who the LeRoi was, that will only be of interest to academicians and people doing master's theses. Anybody who is concerned with the *poem* will get it on an emotional level—or they won't get it at all. Certainly, if I didn't like it, I wouldn't go through any book to look up those names with the hope that I would feel moved once I knew where the building was or who LeRoi was. I don't think that means anything at all. I don't think that has anything to do with the *poem,* actually. What the poem means, its function, doesn't have to do with those names—that's just part of it. It doesn't seem to me to be the same kind of stupidity that's found when you have to go to Jessie Weston's book to find out what a whole section of "The Waste Land" means. The House of Seagrams is certainly less obscure than certain Celtic rites. And I don't see what makes it any less valid because it's a casual kind of reference or that it comes out of a person's life, rather than, say, from his academic life.

I'd say that if a poem, as a whole *poem, works, then it's a good poem. . . .*

Right. . . .

You once wrote that, "MY POETRY is whatever I think I am. I make a poetry with what I feel is useful and can be saved out of all the garbage of our lives." Would you like to develop that a little more fully?

Well, it's part of what you mentioned about "traditional" poetic areas. I believe that the poet—someone with a tempered sensibility—is able, or should be able, to take almost any piece of matter, idea, or whatever, and convert it, if he can, into something really beautiful. I don't mean "beautiful" the way Bernard Berenson means it—but into something moving, at least.

And I don't think that there are any kind of standard ideas or sentiments or emotions or anything that have to be in a poem. A poem can be made up of anything so long as it is well made. It can be made up out of any feeling. And if I tried

ON THE SUBJECT OF...

AMIRI BARAKA/LEROI JONES
LeRoi Jones (he changed his name to Amiri Baraka in 1968) was an influential figure among the literary avant-garde of New York's Greenwich Village and the lower East Side during the late 1950s and early 1960s. A poet, music critic, essayist, dramatist, novelist, and political activist, Jones came to prominence in 1964 when his play *Dutchman* established him as an outspoken commentator on race relations. Jones played a key role in the establishment of East Coast Beat culture; his apartment was a frequent gathering place for many New York Beats. Jones also edited the journal *Yugen,* in which the works of many Beat authors appeared.

One of Jones's first published statements was a defense of the Beat Generation. In the Summer 1958 issue of the *Partisan Review* (a publication for which his wife was the advertising and business manager), Jones wrote a rebuttal to critic Norman Podhoretz's article, "The Know-Nothing Bohemians." In the article, Jones stated his aesthetic allegiance to Beat literature, aligning himself with the literary innovations of Kerouac and Ginsberg while attacking Podhoretz as an example of the entrenched cultural and literary values the Beats challenged. Beat literature, Jones wrote, was "less a movement than a reaction against . . . fifteen years of sterile unreadable magazine poetry" Turning to Podhoretz's contention that "Bohemianism . . . is for the Negro a means of entry into the world of whites," Jones argued: "Harlem is today the veritable capital city of the Black Bourgeoisie. The Negro Bohemian's flight from Harlem is not a flight from the world of color but the flight of any would-be Bohemian from what Mr. Podhoretz himself calls 'the provinciality, philistinism, and moral hypocrisy of American life.'"

For more information on Jones/Baraka's life and works, see *Contemporary Literary Criticism,* Volumes 1, 2, 3, 5, 10, 14, 33, and 115.

to cut anything out of my life—if there was something in my life that I couldn't talk about . . . it seems monstrous that you can tell almost anything about your life except those things that are most intimate or mean the most to you. That seems a severe paradox.

You've mentioned your influences as including Lorca, Creeley, and Olson. What from Lorca—a surrealist approach?

Yes, that, but at the time I got hold of Lorca, I was very much influenced by Eliot, and reading Lorca helped to bring me out of my "Eliot period" and break that shell—not so much *Poet in New York,* which is the more surreal verse, but the early *Gypsy Ballads*—that kind of feeling and exoticism.

What about the Black Mountain people, and Williams?

From Williams, mostly how to write in my own language—how to write the way I *speak* rather than the way I *think* a poem ought to be written—to write just the way it comes to me, in my own speech, utilizing the rhythms of speech rather than any kind of metrical concept. To talk verse. Spoken verse. From Pound, the same concepts that went into the Imagists' poetry—the idea of the image and what an image ought to be. I learned, probably, about verse from Pound—how a poem should be made, what a poem ought to *look* like—some little inkling. And from Williams, I guess, how to get it out in my own language.

Is there a middle ground between natural speech and formal metrics?

Oh, yes. I don't mean that I write poems completely the way I'm talking now, although I'm certain that a great deal of my natural voice rhythm dominates the line. For instance, my breathing—when I have to stop to inhale or exhale—dictates where I have to break the line in most cases. Sometimes I can bring the line out longer for effect—you learn certain tricks, departures from a set method. But mostly it's the *rhythms* of speech that I utilize, trying to get closer to the way I sound *peculiarly,* as opposed to somebody else.

Does your being a Negro influence the speech patterns—or anything else, for that matter, in your writing?

It could hardly help it. There are certain influences on me, as a Negro person, that certainly wouldn't apply to a poet like Allen Ginsberg. I couldn't have written that poem "Kaddish," for instance. And I'm sure he couldn't write certain things that have to deal with, say, Southern Baptist church rhythms. Everything applies—everything in your life. Sociologically, there are different influences, different things that I've seen, that I know, that Allen or no one knows.

I asked that because I don't find in your work the sense of "being a Negro" that occurs, say, in the poetry of Langston Hughes. . . .

That may be part of, like they say, his "stance." You have to set up a certain area in which you're going to stand and write your poems, whether you do it consciously or not. There has to be that stance. He is a Negro. It doesn't lessen my feeling of being a Negro—it's just that that's not the way I write poetry. I'm fully conscious all the time that I am an American Negro, because it's part of my life. But I know also that if I want to say, "I see a bus full of people," I don't have to say, "I am a Negro seeing a bus full of people." I would deal with it when it has to do directly with the poem, and not as a kind of broad generalization that doesn't have much to do with a lot of young writers today who are Negroes. (Although I don't know that many.) It's always been a separate section of writing that wasn't quite up to the level of the other writing. There were certain definite sociological reasons for it before the Civil War or in the early part of the twentieth century, or even in the 30s, but it's a new generation now, and people are beset by other kinds of ideas that don't have much to do with sociology, per se.

I'm always aware, in anything I say, of the "sociological configuration"—what it *means* sociologically. But it doesn't have anything to do with what I'm writing at the time.

LITA HORNICK (ESSAY DATE FALL 1978)

SOURCE: Hornick, Lita. "*Kulchur*: A Memoir." *TriQuarterly* 43 (fall 1978): 281-97.

In the following essay, Hornick, a long-time editor and publisher of Kulchur, *discusses the magazine's birth and some of the notable writers published therein.*

Kulchur was founded in 1960 by Marc Schleifer, who published and edited the first two issues. I became the publisher in February 1961, and formed Kulchur Press, Inc. I shall not deal with the two issues with which I had no contact, as this essay is conceived as a personal memoir. In the first three issues under my ownership, I was not involved in any editorial work, but devoted myself to the business end of the magazine, struggling to find a national distributor and to build a subscription list.

Schleifer edited *Kulchur* 3, and then took off for Cuba without telling me where he was going or how long he would be gone. That issue was more political than literary in orientation, but nevertheless contained some notable pieces. Most important of all, perhaps, was "In Search of Yage," letters to Allen Ginsberg by William Burroughs, recounting his search for the drug in South America. There were poems by Charles Olson and Diane di Prima and "sound scores" by George Brecht. (The printing of scores and articles on music was a tradition which was to be continued in later issues of *Kulchur*.) Joel Oppenheimer wrote a very interesting piece on the obscure poet Samuel Greenberg, LeRoi Jones an essay called "Milneburg Joys (or, Against 'Hipness' as Such)," and Julian Beck an article on "The Life of the Theatre." "A Second Look at Pornography" by Donald Phelps was noteworthy. There were also reviews of art exhibitions, books, films, and records—a feature of the magazine that was to be continued.

Before Schleifer left, he appointed Gilbert Sorrentino guest editor of *Kulchur* 4, and I persuaded Gil to go ahead with the issue. Number 4 was much more concerned with literature and poetics than were previous issues, and was much more to my taste. Gil had the honor to introduce Robert Duncan into the magazine; he contributed a very important essay, "Ideas on the Meaning of Form." Characteristically, Duncan relates the poetic imagination to the forces of the cosmos and scorns conventional inorganic form. Ed Dorn, also new to the magazine, contributed an important essay, "What I See in the *Maximus* Poems (1)." His writing on poetry was the furthest thing in the world from the New Criticism, and this was what *Kulchur* was later to strive to feature: comment by poets on poetry in a vein far different from that of the academic quarterlies. Ron Loewinsohn, for example, contributed an essay on his poetics called "A Credo Sandwich."

Besides these notable essays on poetry and poetics, the issue contained a hard-hitting essay on brutality in mental hospitals by "Harry Black," pseudonym of Hubert Selby. LeRoi Jones's article on the history of African and Afro-American music was a learned piece that was never pedantic. Although Jones is known today chiefly as a black political revolutionary, the actual range of his intellect can be quickly estimated from the pages of *Kulchur*. Last but not least among the essays in *Kulchur* 4 was the first appearance in the magazine of the great but then neglected poet Louis Zukofsky, writing here on the art of Charlie Chaplin. The issue closed with reviews of books and films

but none of art exhibitions or records—the only areas later featured in the magazine that did not appear in this issue.

Not having heard from Schleifer, I invited Gil Sorrentino to edit *Kulchur* 5, but he declined. Marian Zazeela (now married to the eminent composer La Monte Young, but then married to Schleifer) appointed Joel Oppenheimer as editor, with my acquiescence. Joel continued the policy of publishing Louis Zukofsky—including "Little Baron Snorck," an account of a child violin prodigy, based on the childhood of Zukofsky's son Paul. Charles Olson contributed a poem, and Kenneth Koch a hilarious parody of Pound. Jones's piece, "Tokenism: 300 Years for 5 Cents," was one of his key works and prophetic for 1962. Gilbert Sorrentino continued the tradition of literary comment with "Reflections on 'Spring and All.'" Most notable of all, perhaps, were Louis and Celia Zukofsky's translations of Catullus.

Comment on music fell to A. B. Spellman with "The Next to the Last Generation of Blues Singers." Lawrence Kornfeld, a great director who has never received the recognition he deserves, provided the theater article, "A Director's Search for a Stage." The pièce de résistance was *Kulchur*'s first "Art Chronicle" by Frank O'Hara, which I solicited. It included an account of the Abstract Expressionists and Imagists show at the Guggenheim, a defense of that controversial Frank Lloyd Wright building, and an appreciation of Claes Oldenburg's exhibition, The Store, which contradicts the commonly held opinion that Frank O'Hara hated all pop art. He also spoke well of the Rauschenberg show at the Leo Castelli Gallery. Film and book reviews followed.

Still not having heard from Marc Schleifer, I undertook the editing of *Kulchur* 6 myself. This issue presented the first publication of Louis Zukofsky's great play *Arise, Arise*. It also had a cover and picture portfolio on the Living Theatre and an essay by Julian Beck titled "Broadway and Living Theatre Polemic." The so-called "deep image poets" made their initial appearance here in *Kulchur*—the first of my continuing efforts to broaden the base of contributors and cover the whole avant-garde scene. "Deep Image" was represented by Jerome Rothenberg in an exchange of letters with Robert Creeley on the subject of poetics, and by Robert Kelly in the poem "Staccato for Tarots: I." (Of course Creeley did not belong to this group, but was receptive to Rothenberg's argument.)

An essay by Denise Levertov on current English poets was also included in number 6; it had been solicited by Joel Oppenheimer, but he had decided against printing it in *Kulchur* 5. Comment on music was presented in Morton Feldman's "Liner Notes," his first appearance in the magazine, and comment on film consisted of an article by Donald Phelps on Parker Tyler's film criticism. Frank O'Hara's second "Art Chronicle" dealt enthusiastically with the Nakian sculptures at the Loeb Study Center and at the Egan gallery, Alex Katz's cutouts at Tanager, and the Gorky exhibitions at Janis and Anderson. Film reviews by Fielding Dawson closed the issue.

When *Kulchur* 6 was in page proof, Marc Schleifer returned from Cuba and resigned from the magazine to take off for parts unknown. At that time he persuaded me to buy his back-issue inventory of *Kulchur* 1 and 2 so that I might fill the needs of new subscribers who wanted a full set.

After the resignation of Marc Schleifer, I appointed an editorial board composed of LeRoi Jones, Gilbert Sorrentino, Frank O'Hara, Joe Le Sueur, Bill Berkson, and myself. This group held together roughly from *Kulchur* 7 through *Kulchur* 12. *Kulchur* 7 was notable for the reprinting of Louis Zukofsky's "Five Statements for Poetry," which I had solicited. Two of these statements, "Program: Objectivists' 1931" and "Sincerity and Objectification," were first printed in *Poetry*'s historic objectivist issue in 1931.

Ed Dorn's "Notes More or Less Relevant to Burroughs and Trocchi" continued the precedent of unorthodox comment on literature. Bill Berkson, at Frank's request, provided the "Art Chronicle." Joe Le Sueur wrote the first of *Kulchur*'s "Theatre Chronicles," which dealt with, among other things, a fine production of Beckett's "Happy Days." LeRoi provided another of his essays on black music, "Introducing Bobby Bradford."

Issue 7 was rich in reviews. LeRoi edited his first jazz record review section, written by himself and A. B. Spellman. The book review section, edited by Gil, dealt chiefly with small-press books, which went unnoted by other magazines at the time and are scarcely noted today. *Kulchur* continued to review them throughout its duration. Perhaps the most important contribution to this section was Paul Blackburn's review of Robert Kelly, "The American Duende."

At Frank O'Hara's request, the issue was dedicated to the late Franz Kline, and a reproduction of one of his paintings, "Cardinal," graced

the cover. Reproductions of paintings by De Kooning and Guston were also included.

Kulchur 8 continued the reprinting of Zukofsky's "Five Statements for Poetry" with "Poetry for My Son When He Can Read." Cid Corman, in his first appearance in the magazine, contributed an important essay on Creeley's "For Love." Paul Zukofsky, Louis's gifted musician son, presented us with an essay on the musical setting of one of his father's poems. Another first appearance was Michael McClure in an essay on Anglo-Saxon words called "Phi Upsilon Kappa"; the title was supposed to be "Fuck" spelled in Greek. At that time (winter 1962), I feared that if "Fuck" appeared as the title the Post Office would impound the issue, so McClure rather humorously agreed to "spell it in Greek."

Joe Le Sueur's always interesting "Theatre Chronicle" contrasted the Eric Bentley and Living Theatre productions of Brecht's *A Man's a Man,* and offered an appreciation of Joseph Papp's productions of Shakespeare in the Park. Gil wrote, to my way of thinking, an ill-considered attack on pop art, "Kitsch into Art: The New Realism," but unfortunately there was no "Art Chronicle." Anselm Hollo provided a report on the somewhat gloomy state of poetry and jazz in England.

A long and solid jazz review section, edited by LeRoi and written by Spellman, Jon Rappaport, and Jones himself, was included. The creditable book review section, again edited by Gil, unfortunately did not feature small-press books, but did contain reviews of important avant-garde writers such as Kerouac, McClure, and Olson, written by Sorrentino, Dorn, and Richard Barker.

Kulchur 9 was a special drama issue edited by Joe Le Sueur. Larry Rivers did the cover on which, in his own words, he "put Shakespeare behind the eight ball." Although our usual chronicles and reviews were included, there were no essays, only plays. The issue was most notable for the first publication of LeRoi's famous and savage play "The Toilet," later produced off Broadway to much acclaim. Michael Smith wrote an amusing satire of a mother and son in an oedipal situation. Arnold Weinstein contributed a two-page absurdist trifle. Douglas Woolf, a too little appreciated writer, sent us a poignant play, "The Love Letter," and Ruth Krauss a charming little poem-play. Kenward Elmslie's contribution, "The Aleutians," was written in the author's well-known witty manner, and Diane di Prima's "Murder Cake" was a beautiful and funny fantasy that included such characters as Childe Harold, Richard Lovelace, and Dante. Barbara Guest contributed a short poem-play.

Frank's third and last "Art Chronicle" appeared in this issue. He only wrote three for *Kulchur,* contrary to other information: Donald Allen, in the biographical notes to his edition of Frank O'Hara's *Collected Poems,* states that Frank wrote an "Art Chronicle" for every issue of *Kulchur!*

Instead of editing a book review section for *Kulchur* 9, Gil wrote a "Poetry Chronicle," which was in most respects excellent. I was embarrassed by his attacks on Jerry Rothenberg and the "four young lady poets"—Rochelle Owens, Diane Wakoski, Carol Bergé, and Barbara Moraff—but of course he had the right to speak as he saw fit. The first of Bill Berkson's three "Film Chronicles" appeared, and the music section, in addition to LeRoi's and A. B.'s jazz reviews, included a review of a Günther Schuller concert by Morty Feldman.

Kulchur 10 featured the wonderful essay by Edwin Denby, "Balanchine Choreographing," with cover and picture portfolio from the New York City Ballet, all obtained by Frank. The issue was also rich in comment on poetry by poets, always the core of the magazine. George Oppen covered a good deal of modern poetry in his essay "The Mind's Own Place." Paul Blackburn contributed an important piece on literary magazines, and Louis Zukofsky his historic essay on poetics, "A Statement for Poetry (1950)." Michael Rumaker also sent us a piece on Melville's "Bartleby the Scrivener," and Larry Eigner a piece on Gertrude Stein's *Three Lives.*

There were three essays on music: La Monte Young's "Excerpts from 'Lecture 1960,'" Martin Williams' "Thelonious Monk: Prelude to Success," and Gil's "Remembrances of Bop in New York 1945-1950." Joe Le Sueur's "Theatre Chronicle" covered "The Milk Train Doesn't Stop Here Anymore" by Tennessee Williams, "Natural Affection" by William Inge, "Who's Afraid of Virginia Woolf?" by Edward Albee, and "Lorenzo" by Jack Richardson. Bill Berkson contributed his second "Film Chronicle." The book reviews were written by LeRoi, Gil, Charles Olson, and Donald Phelps, and the jazz reviews by A. B. and Joe Early. The issue also included a letter to the editors by Anselm Hollo attacking Gil for his roasting of Rothenberg, Owens, Wakoski, Bergé, and Moraff and Hollo's own translations of Russian poets, "Red Cats." For the first time, *Kulchur* became an arena for a diversity of opinion. Gil resigned as an editor after this issue, and I took over the editing of the book

review section myself, striving thereafter to cover as many small-press books as possible. The reasons for his resignation were never very clear to me, but I doubt that they had anything to do with Anselm's letter. He told me he didn't like the direction in which the magazine was going, but agreed to stay on as a contributing editor.

Kulchur 11 featured a brilliant piece by W. S. Merwin, modeled on Swift's "A Modest Proposal," suggesting ways in which the mutants produced by nuclear explosions might be put to service in the army. Robert Duncan sent us a story, entitled "Love." Comment on literature was provided by Zukofsky's great essay on Pound. Ed Dorn also contributed a valuable appreciation of Douglas Woolf, and Anselm Hollo an appreciation of Jerome Rothenberg.

Musical scores and a brief essay by Morty Feldman were included. Joe's "Theatre Chronicle" was devoted to a rave notice of the Living Theatre's production of "The Brig" by Kenneth H. Brown, which Joe saw as a realization of Artaud's "theatre of cruelty." Bill Berkson's third and last "Film Chronicle" appeared, and there were book reviews by Sorrentino, Kenneth Irby, Jones, and Saul Gottlieb. Most notable was the review of Rochelle Owens' *Futz* by Saul Gottlieb, at that time unknown and unproduced and only recently published by Hawk's Well Press. The jazz reviews were written by LeRoi and A. B., and the issue concluded with a letter to the editors by Jerry Rothenberg, refuting Gil's criticism of him in *Kulchur* 9. Bill Berkson then went off for an extended stay in Europe; he never wrote for the magazine again, though he never formally resigned. However, in a recent conversation Bill told me he never formally resigned because the relationship among the editors at that time was so *casual.* This, I think, was entirely true.

Kulchur 12 was originally planned as a special issue devoted entirely to civil rights, but not enough material on the theme was submitted. As it finally turned out, the civil rights section extended only from page 2 to page 32, containing contributions from Jones, Spellman, Robert Williams, Sorrentino, Dorn, Oppenheimer, Donald Windham, and Denise Levertov. The rest of the issue contained the sort of material usually featured in *Kulchur.*

Undoubtedly the most important piece was Robert Kelly's long analysis of Zukofsky's "A 1-12." LeRoi contributed another important article, "Expressive Language," about the social implications of speech, especially black American speech.

Film was covered by William S. Pechter's essay on Frank Capra. There was no "Theatre Chronicle" by Joe, but Kenward Elmslie contributed a "Chronicle of Musicals," which dealt with *How to Succeed in Business Without Really Trying, A Funny Thing Happened on the Way to the Forum, Oliver, Stop the World—I Want to Get Off, Mr. President, Hot Spot, Little Me, Tovarich,* and *She Loves Me.* Ed Dorn sent us an enigmatic little story called "Clay," and LeRoi provided a smashing post-assassination poem called "Exaugural Address (for Jacqueline Bouvier Kennedy, who has had to eat too much shit)."

The book review section included a review of John Rechy's *City of Night* by Frank O'Hara, the last thing he was to write for the magazine, and reviews of four small-press books: *Reality Sandwiches* by Allan Ginsberg, reviewed by LeRoi; *The Wake* by Andrew Hoyem, reviewed by Gil; *Residence on Earth* by Pablo Neruda (translated by Clayton Eshleman), reviewed by Gil, and *City Lights Journal #1*, reviewed by Allan Kaplan. Jazz reviews by LeRoi, A. B., and Marion Brown concluded the issue.

After *Kulchur* 12, I wrote to Frank, Joe, and LeRoi, telling them I would hold no more editorial meetings but would edit the magazine myself thereafter, inviting them at the same time to continue as contributing editors for as long as they desired. I listed them as editors on the masthead for one more issue, but the credits in *Kulchur* were never a very accurate indication of who was doing the work—more often than not only a courtesy. There was no unpleasantness between us. I was motivated merely by the fact that the poets' own work drew them increasingly away from the magazine, whereas *Kulchur* was my only interest at that time. It became more and more difficult to get them to write the chronicles they had agreed to write, to solicit material, or to read manuscripts. Therefore the last eight issues of the magazine, numbers 13 through 20, were edited by me, although LeRoi continued to handle the jazz section through number 15. After that, there was no more jazz section.

Kulchur 13 boasted a cover and picture portfolio by Andy Warhol, from his film *The Kiss.* Comment on literature was provided by two Canadian poets, hitherto unpublished in *Kulchur*: George Bowering on William Carlos Williams and Warren Tallman on Robert Creeley. Gil contributed a very important piece on "The Art of Hubert Selby." Allen Ginsberg sent me a poem, "The Change: Kyoto-Tokyo Express July 18, 1963," and Ed Dorn a story, "Rest Stop." Richard Brautigan, then a relatively unknown writer, contributed a characteristic piece of fiction called "The Post Offices of Eastern Oregon." Joe sent me his last "Theatre Chronicle," as well as some brilliant film reviews by Pauline Kael. A brief essay on music by Peter Hartman was included and, much to my satisfaction, twenty pages of book reviews covering a wide variety of opinion. The reviewers were Allan Kaplan, Joe, Jerry Rothenberg, Kenneth Irby, George Economou, and LeRoi. Jazz reviews by Martin Williams, A. B., Marian Brown, Kenneth Irby, John B. Litweiler, and James Brody completed the issue.

Kulchur 14 had a cover by the wonderful young artist and writer Joe Brainard. The issue was originally planned as a Zukofsky number, but only three writers contributed pieces on L. Z.: Creeley, Jonathan Williams, and Charles Tomlinson. Clayton Eshleman's translations of Vallejo, sent to me by Gil, were, I felt, among the best things I had ever published. There was also a remarkable story, sent to me by LeRoi: "The Fable of Orby Dobbs" by Mack Thomas. Michael McClure reappeared in the magazine with his essay on "Reason" (though I cannot help thinking it was more about instinct than reason). Kenneth H. Brown, author of *The Brig,* proved in his piece "My Seed Grows Wilder" that he really could write and that *The Brig* was not merely a director's play. The extensive book review section included four small-press books: *The Moderns,* edited by LeRoi and reviewed by Gil; *Twenty Poems of César Vallejo,* reviewed by Clayton Eshleman; *Her Body Against Time* by Robert Kelly; *El Corno Emplumado,* reviewed by Kenneth Irby; and *The World of the Lie* by Ron Lowenstein, reviewed by Irby. John B. Litweiler was the only jazz reviewer.

Kulchur 15 contained the first piece on art to be published in the magazine since Frank had ceased to write his chronicles—a long and brilliant essay on Robert Rauschenberg by the eminent art critic Nicolas Calas. The Leo Castelli gallery provided the Rauschenberg cover and an eight-page picture portfolio. George Bowering contributed an important essay on prosody. Charles Boultenhouse, the distinguished underground filmmaker, appeared as our new film chronicler with a piece on film time and its relationship to real time which commented extensively on the art of cutting. Donatella Manganotti, the most devoted scholar of the works of William Burroughs, sent a very solid essay. Music and musical theory were covered by Barney Childs in "The Beginning of the Apocalypse?"; the article was a refutation of a piece by Leonard B. Meyer in the *Hudson Review.* Also published in this issue was an interesting story, "To Lie Down in Negritude," by an unknown writer, Rush Greenlee.

The book review section had the distinction of introducing Gerard Malanga and Ted Berrigan to the magazine for the first time. The other reviewers were Gil and Rochelle Owens, and four small-press books were reviewed. The last jazz review section that LeRoi edited appeared in this issue, with reviewers John B. Litweiler, Joe Early, Frank Busto, and Mack Thomas. The issue closed with the "Hungrealist Manifestos," statements on poetry, the short story, and politics by a group of young writers in India who were very much turned on by the American avant-garde.

Kulchur 16 was graced with a cover by the distinguished artist Al Held, and a picture portfolio of his drawings, but unfortunately there was no article to accompany them. The issue opened with two of LeRoi's poems, "A Western Lady" and "Correction." These were followed by Charles Tomlinson's important interview with Creeley in which, as might be expected, the subjects dealt with were Pound, Williams, Zukofsky, Olson, the *Black Mountain Review,* and some of the action painters at Black Mountain College. Jack Hirschman contributed a very interesting essay, "Constellations," primarily concerned with Mallarmé's *"Un Coup de dés"* but ranging over a broad field of contemporary poetry and music. Nicolas Calas' brief "Exercises" was followed by Gerard Malanga's interview with Andy Warhol, in which Andy answered questions in his usual cool and cryptic manner. Martin Williams contributed an article on television and Charles Boultenhouse wrote a "Theatre Chronicle" instead of a "Film Chronicle" for this issue. This was supplemented by Wallace Thurston's essay on "The Films of Charles Boultenhouse." "Elga's Incantation," a work in progress by Rochelle Owens, was an early rendering of this gifted writer's now famous style.

The issue concluded with John Keys's interesting "Letter to Robert Kelly," which was more general philosophy than poetics, and with the book review section, which comprised reviews by Economou, Bowering, Carolyn Kizer, Allan Kaplan, Berrigan, Malanga, Irby, and Ron Padgett in his first appearance in the magazine.

Kulchur 17's startling cover was a reproduction of Robert Indiana's painting *DIE,* one of several illustrations accompanying Carl Belz's article, "Pop Art, New Humanism and Death." It is uncertain whether the many deathly images in pop art, such as Warhol's electric chairs and auto crashes, represent a criticism of our society or mere deadpan cool. Nicolas Calas, a literary as well as art critic, contributed an essay on the poetic image. A poem by LeRoi, "Corregidor," was his last contribution to the magazine. Much to my satisfaction, Clayton Eshleman contributed some more of his brilliant translations of Vallejo. Ron Padgett's hilarious takeoff of some solemn discussions of poetic form struck a new and refreshing note.

The inside front cover carried an announcement that I would publish a poetry anthology edited by LeRoi, first projected as a book and later as the contents of *Kulchur* 20. Unfortunately LeRoi never did this, having by that time become completely involved in black politics.

The next three issues were to see the introduction of a whole new group of writers, who might have contributed much to the magazine had my time and energies permitted me to continue as editor. Number 17 was concluded with Charles Boultenhouse's "Film Chronicle," Matthew Andrews' "Theatre Chronicle," and the book review section, where Irby, Berrigan, Padgett, Malanga, and David Meltzer reviewed, among other things, eight small-press books.

The opening piece in *Kulchur* 18 was Morgan Gibson's interview with Paul Goodman. Charles Boultenhouse contributed his last and most important piece about film, an essay on Stan Brakhage's "The Art of Vision." Charles and I watched the film together for five hours at the Film-Makers' Cinemathèque (then near the Brooklyn Bridge), nourished by brandy and sandwiches. Margaret Randall, the distinguished poet and editor of *El Corno Emplumado,* sent me "Thoughts on the Poetic Line." Another important comment on literature was the first part of a long essay on Wallace Stevens by Armand Schwerner. Music was covered by Robert Ashley's interview with Morty Feldman.

"Poem-Plays" by Ruth Krauss was one of the delights of the issue; famous as a writer of children's books, Ruth had not yet attained recognition as a writer for adults. Joe Brainard's story "Sunday, July the 30th, 1964," was a landmark for the magazine. Felix Pollak's "Soirées" was a satire on Denise Levertov which in retrospect seems to me too harsh. At that time, however, I was interested in making *Kulchur* an arena for a diversity of opinion and anxious to prevent it from becoming a coterie magazine.

The notable "Art Chronicle," by David Antin, was his first published piece of art criticism and

ON THE SUBJECT OF...

SEYMOUR KRIM

Essayist Seymour Krim began his writing career in New York City in the late 1940s and early 1950s. His early work was comprised of literary criticism for such periodicals as *Partisan Review* and *Commentary*. His writing changed significantly following a psychological breakdown in the mid 1950s. From this point Krim became allied with the Beat Generation, and he began attacking the traditional literary establishment for its detachment from the experiences of everyday life. While continuing his contributions to journals and periodicals, Krim expressed his opinions in three essay collections: *Views of a Nearsighted Cannoneer* (1961); *Shake It for the World, Smartass* (1970); and *You and Me* (1974). During the early 1960s he helped to publish the writing of other nonconformist authors through his work as an editor at *Swank* and *Nugget* magazines; he also edited the important 1960 anthology titled *The Beats.* By the late 1970s, Krim's articles were published in the *New York Times, Harper's,* and *Commentary*. Krim stated that his goal was to bring his Beat-inspired views before a broad spectrum of conformist American society. Krim taught writing at numerous universities, including Iowa, Pennsylvania State, and Columbia. A few years before his death (an apparent suicide in 1989) he received a Fulbright grant to travel to Israel, where he taught at the University of Haifa.

dealt mainly with Duchamp. The "Theatre Chronicle" was by Matthew Andrews. The book reviews were by Fielding Dawson, Berrigan, Randall, Padgett, and John Sinclair. Ron Padgett's review of Joe Ceravolo's unpublished manuscript, "Wild Flowers Out of Gas," was included.

Kulchur 19 was distinguished by a variety of brilliant and funny contributions from the group of then-emerging young writers who are now sometimes called the second generation New York School, though none of them like the appellation. There was Ron Padgett's mad story "Bill" and Ted Berrigan's account of an academic poet on a reading tour, "A Boke." Tom Vietch's "Yoga Exercises" was hilarious and obscene. So was Ron's picture story, "Pere Ubu's Alphabet," derived from Jarry and Bonnard. Ted's "Art Chronicle" was witty and outrageous, and the illustrations were the funniest I have ever seen. Two scenes from Dick Gallup's much admired play "The Bingo" were an important contribution, while the second part of Armand Schwerner's essay on Stevens provided more sober comment on literature. The "Theatre Chronicle" by Matthew Andrews and the "Film Chronicle" by Yale M. Udoff followed. Book reviewers were Berrigan, Sinclair, Margaret Randall, Eshleman, Malanga, Bowering, Morgan Gibson, Aram Saroyan, Douglas Blazek, and Irby. This section covered a wide range of often conflicting ideas, including Ted's review of Harold Rosenberg, which was shocking to some people.

Though I don't think I was wholly aware of it at the time, looking back through the issues of *Kulchur* I realize that number 19 may have seemed to reflect a surprising change in editorial perspective. There was really no reason for this except that I felt I wanted to do something different. I was excited by the new writers' work and felt the emphasis of the modern cultural scene had shifted. I wanted the magazine to reflect that change.

In *Kulchur* 20 Ted and Ron continued their wildly funny writing with a series of letters, "Big Travel Dialogues." This was later reprinted in *Bean Spasms,* a book by them that I published after I had ended the magazine and switched to publishing books. Gerard contributed an interview with the dancer James Waring, accompanied by a cover photograph and picture portfolio, and Ron and Joe had a poem-picture series entitled "Go Lovely Rose." A selection from Ted's wonderful "Sonnets" was included and a long poem by Armand, "Prologue in Six Parts." Comment on literature was covered in an essay on Creeley by Ellen Maslow, comment on art in David Antin's second "Art Chronicle," dealing with current art criticism, and comment on film by Yale M. Udoff's review of *Girl with the Green Eyes* and Margaret Randall's poem "The Ritual, Antonioni." The book review section, which included six reviews of small-press books, again presented a wide variety of opinion, provided by Fielding Dawson, David Meltzer, Margaret Randall, George Bowering, David Ross, Ted Berrigan, Tom Clark, and Ronald Caplan.

This last issue of *Kulchur* appeared while it was still at its height. There was no reason to feel that the magazine's energies were depleted and that it had to end; it was only *my* energies which were depleted. After editing eight issues myself, with quarterly deadlines, I found I had no time for my husband and children. I decided to switch to publishing Kulchur Press books, producing only two books a year and working with only one author at a time. I also felt that, after five years of publishing a magazine which focused mainly on criticism, I would like to change to publishing poetry. Since then I have published twenty-four books. My decision may have seemed confusingly abrupt to some, since *Kulchur* 20 bore an announcement promising great things for *Kulchur* 21. I'm afraid it *was* rather abrupt, but little-magazine editors have never been known for their reasonableness.

GILBERT SORRENTINO (ESSAY DATE FALL 1978)

SOURCE: Sorrentino, Gilbert. "*Neon, Kultur, Etc.*" *TriQuarterly* 43 (fall 1978): 298-316.

In the following essay, Sorrentino provides a first-hand account of the publication of "little magazines" from the mid-1950s to the mid-1960s.

The decade between the mid-fifties and the mid-sixties, a singularly rich one for American writing, appears, on reflection, to be complex in the extreme as far as the little magazine is concerned. It seems to me that, although there were fewer magazines in evidence at any given time during that ten-year period than there are at present, many if not most of those magazines were oddly interdependent; this gave them a presence and an influence far exceeding their numbers. Those that were involved in publishing what may be called the "new writing"—if that is not too pompous and shopworn a phrase—were possessed by a passion to print what their editors took to be writing that quite literally had no place else to go. Not surprisingly, it fell out that the bulk of this writing was done by a rather small group of writers, so that many little magazines drew on essentially the same authors as contributors. There slowly evolved a kind of network of magazines acting as a general clearinghouse for new methods, techniques, and ideas of literary composition and criticism.

I think two things should be made clear immediately. The magazines I speak of were not academic or scholarly, and had little to do with what are called quarterlies; nor were they open to anything at all, refuges for writers who wished to "express" themselves—in other words, they were

not what might be termed bohemian publications. On the contrary, they had a definite literary bone to pick, and they set themselves up not as a mere *alternative* press but as a press that considered its criteria to be correct. At this remove, I sometimes detect the wild eye of the fanatic staring out from these defunct journals; yet by and large they were not fanatical, but revolutionary in a conscious, controlled, and planned way. To call them, even now, "alternative" or "experimental" smacks of the academic patronization that, not so many years ago, was made manifest as contempt, hatred, and even fear. If this seems farfetched, the reader is urged to peruse, at his leisure, the reams of nonsense written, for instance, on the "Beat generation" in the popular, slick, and academic journals of the late fifties. The new writing was bitterly maligned and insulted by all those who, as Robert Creeley has noted, "were dominant in their insistence upon an *idea* of form extrinsic to the given instance." A critical-academic structure that rigidly excluded such writers as Williams and Zukofsky did not know what hit it in the fifties.

In 1953 I was discharged from the Army and began work on a novel, the first extended piece of writing I had ever done. Concurrently I wrote poetry, which I had begun to write while in college in 1949. It became clear as time passed that there were few, if any, magazines interested in publishing the kind of work that I was doing. I don't mean to imply that my work was first-rate; on the contrary, it was the work of an apprentice, one who was casting about to find some form into which he could work his experience. Yet the writing in the magazines I read at the time seemed to be singularly stale, even though it was presented as a model of excellence. *Partisan Review, Hudson Review, Poetry,* and others were publishing writers who, for some reason, seemed to me to be people who lived at another time in another country. The poetry I read might as well have been written in a foreign language. I had begun to read Pound and had just discovered Williams; in a half-baked way I knew that what these poets had discovered and championed had not been acted upon by the poets who were at that time critically acclaimed. The concerns of the latter seemed to be those of a polite and official intellectualism. Lowell, Roethke, Berryman, Wilbur, Eberhart, Shapiro, Viereck, Schwartz, et al.—I read them all. And the more I read them, the more I wallowed in confusion. Their poetic concerns seemed oddly fossilized and rigid, and my own poems, in their crudity and ignorance, "floated," as it were, as I belligerently refused to use the poems of my celebrated masters as models. My slow understanding of Williams' work exhilarated and depressed me—the former since I saw in his writing a method of anchoring my work sans stuffiness and dullness, the latter because I realized that Williams was not a peer; there was something that I "heard" that Williams did not. How was one to transcribe that sound? Was there anyone who was trying to do the same thing? In brief, who and where were my peers? Did they publish anything? If so, where?

All this seems quite extraordinary to me now, almost as if it did not happen that way, but I assure you that it did. In 1955 I returned to college, for want of something better to do. I was still almost totally ignorant of my peers, but I had, as they say, glimmerings, although I knew no other writers. At Brooklyn College I met some young men as dissatisfied as I, who also had begun, in one way or another, to write. We read each other's work; we complained of the insubstantiality of the literary establishment; we decided, in time-honored fashion, to begin our own little magazine, to be called *Neon*. (The title referred both to the ubiquitous city lights and the meaning of the word in Greek: "new thing.") I don't think any of us knew what we were doing, only that we wanted to publish our work together, to make a statement of sorts. The friends involved with *Neon* were Sam Abrams, John Richardson, Jack Freiwald, Alfred Siegel (a dedicated Poundian), and Hubert Selby, who had, as I recall, just begun to write. We were, it goes without saying, hopeful and naive. Somehow, through Hugh Kenner, Siegel had put me in touch with Pound, and I wrote to ask if he would be interested in contributing to the magazine. To my absolute amazement, he replied to me by postcard, giving me the names of two Australians, Noel Stock and William Fleming, both of whom were affiliated with an Australian magazine, *Meanjin*. Whereupon I wrote to them and they responded with poems.

At about this time, early 1956, I met Williams. I had sent him, with misgivings, a short impressionistic sketch I had written while in the Army in 1951. He replied cordially, and subsequently invited me to Rutherford for dinner. As it turned out, he wanted my permission to use a piece of the sketch in *Paterson Five*, which he was then in the process of composing. I of course granted him permission, and we began a correspondence. In the course of it, I asked him for a poem for *Neon*, but he declined, writing, as I recall, that it would be much better for us to go it alone with a first issue.

Some time in February or March, the mimeograph stencils were cut for *Neon* 1, in Jack Freiwald's basement apartment in Brooklyn. The bill was paid by Alfred Siegel, and toward the end of March we had 250 copies of the first issue in hand, with work by Abrams, Richardson, Freiwald, Stock, Fleming, and myself. The price was a quarter.

Copies were placed in the Eighth Street Book Shop, Gotham, a Bleecker Street shop called the Make It New, operated by John Kasper and William Horton more as a dissemination point for right-wing political propaganda than as a bookshop, and City Lights in San Francisco. As I remember, the Make It New manager, a young woman and a rabid follower of Pound's politics and economics, seemed to think that *Neon*, perhaps because of the inclusion of "Pound's people," Stock and Fleming, was or soon would be a political broadside. At all events, the store soon closed—what happened to the copies of *Neon* that they had taken I don't know. The rest of the copies were given to contributors and friends, and a few were sold by mail.

I'm afraid that after the publication of *Neon* 1 things happened so fast—and it seems, all at once—that I doubt if I can set them down here in any true chronology. I had by this time discovered the *Black Mountain Review, Origin,* the *Chicago Review* (under Irving Rosenthal), and other magazines. *On the Road* had been published, and I had read Ginsberg, Corso, McClure, et al. Then *Neon* 2 was ready; it included Selby's first published story, "Home for Christmas," Williams' "To My Friend Ezra Pound," which he had sent me because of his pleasure in the first issue of the magazine, and some poems by Paul Goodman, whom Selby had met and requested work from. Selby paid for this issue, which was multilithed. I believe we sold it out, perhaps on the strength of Williams' poem. *Neon* 2 was much more sophisticated than the first number, since we had discovered an entire world of writers that we had not known existed just two years earlier. Everything indeed seemed to be happening at once: I had just read Creeley's poems in the *Black Mountain Review,* his book *All That Is Lovely in Men,* and in *Origin,* and began a correspondence with him; unsolicited poems were coming in to the magazine, many of them from Southern California (I was still almost completely ignorant of the writers of the San Francisco area); we had, by some means, obtained a mailing list and the magazine was beginning to receive subscriptions; and Jack Freiwald, who had moved to the West Coast, had found a printer who said he would do *Neon* 3 for a reasonable price.

Toward the end of 1957 Selby completed a story called "Love's Labor's Lost," which would later be the first part of "The Queen Is Dead." Since his first story he had worked almost constantly at his prose, writing hundreds of drafts that were then revised, rewritten, torn apart. I don't know another writer who so swiftly mastered his statement as Selby. In any event, when I read "Love's Labor's Lost" I was certain that he was well on his way to becoming an extremely powerful and important writer. I badly wanted to publish the story in *Neon* 3, which was still in gestation, but something had happened to my financial plans insofar as the West Coast printer was concerned and Jack Freiwald was looking about for another one. I suggested to Selby that he send the story to Williams for his comment, which he did. Williams replied, almost immediately, that the story had absolutely stunned him but that it was, as far as he could see, quite unpublishable, given the subject matter and language. However, Williams went on, if *anyone* would publish it, it would be the men who edited the *Black Mountain Review* and he had taken the liberty of sending the story to Jonathan Williams.

Jonathan read it and sent it on to Creeley, who was at the time in New Mexico, and Creeley scheduled the story for what was to be the final number of the *Black Mountain Review*; the college had closed and there were funds only for that last issue.

Neon 3 was finally published, an ill-starred attempt on my part to partially represent in the magazine what I took to be the "California writers." As I look at the issue now, it seems fuzzy, unfocused, hardly cogent, although some individual pieces stand out as having merit—they are lost, however, in this issue, which is, quite candidly, an aberration. God knows how long I had waited for the publication of *Neon* 3, but in the meantime I had almost completed assembling *Neon* 4 and, once again, was looking around for a printer that I could afford—or, I should say, could afford to be in debt to. Before I write of *Neon* 4, and the circumstances of its publication, it might be useful to try to make clear to the reader the ambience that existed in New York at that time (1958).

I suppose what is fondly called by literary historians a "ferment" was occurring in the arts at this time—most of it, it seems to me, quite accidental. That is to say, a number of very diverse things all happened at the same time, all of them linked together, however tenuously, and all of them serving to create what I might call, with some misgivings, an avant-garde community in New York that had cultural and artistic ties to other communities in other parts of the country. At the risk of boring the reader with dry notation, here are a few of the things that occurred in the last three years of the fifties—none of them in itself remarkable, yet together serving to consolidate what had begun as a scattered movement. Black Mountain College had closed, its students and faculty settling in New York and San Francisco, with Creeley temporarily anchored in New Mexico, where his friends were Max Finstein and Judson Crews, among others. The Beat writers—Ginsberg, Kerouac, Corso, et al., after "electrifying" the Bay Area, had begun moving back to New York, whence they had originally come. Don Allen's "San Francisco Scene" issue of the *Evergreen Review* (number 2) had acquainted East Coast writers with McClure, Spicer, Duncan, Brother Antoninus, Rumaker. The writers who were later to initiate the "New York School"—Koch, O'Hara, Ashbery, Field, Schuyler, Guest—had come together in New York as a loosely affiliated group. Ashbery and O'Hara were deeply involved with painting and the other plastic arts as critics and general commentators (O'Hara was a curator at the Modern), and associated with painters and sculptors in a natural and easy way. This had not previously been the case in New York, where the abstract painters formed a group *sui generis*. And among the younger artists were such men as Dan Rice and John Chamberlain and Robert Rauschenberg, all of whom were alumni of Black Mountain College. Paul Blackburn had returned from France to settle in New York. And everyone—painters, sculptors, poets, and writers—used the Cedar Bar in Greenwich Village as a headquarters, base of operations, and home away from home. It was an incredible stew out of which was to come an American literature that by 1960 could no longer, even by the most benighted, be called "fanatic," "ignorant," "vapid," or "puerile." By the most curiously unintentional means, as I have said, the scattered elements of this movement became unified.

By late 1958 *Neon* 4 was in the process of being printed, but it would be a whole year until I received finished copies. Early in that year Jonathan Williams had written to Joel Oppenheimer to tell him of Selby, and they arranged to meet. Through Joel Oppenheimer, Selby met Fielding Dawson and then introduced both men to me, as the editor of a magazine that might possibly take on many of the writers who had been affiliated with the *Black Mountain Review*. Through Oppenheimer I met Max Finstein, just arrived from New Mexico, and a little later, I met Jonathan Williams, in New York for a visit. *Neon* 4 had contributions from Finstein, Oppenheimer, and a collage cover by Dawson; at the time when I met these men I had begun to read what little there was available by Louis Zukofsky, and wrote to ask him for a contribution, which he sent, telling me at the same time to write to Lorine Niedecker, Cid Corman, and Robert Duncan. The fourth issue was rapidly being filled, and contributions also came in from William Carlos Williams, Paul Goodman, and Selby, who gave me a story called "Double Feature." There were many other writers in *Neon* 4, plus a section of translations of the Chinese ideograms in *The Cantos* by Alfred Siegel.

While the issue was being made up, I received in the mail one day the first issue of *Yugen,* edited by LeRoi Jones (Amiri Baraka) and Hettie Cohen. *Yugen*'s early issues focused on Beat writers—Ginsberg, Corso, Bremser—and also printed work by Phil Whalen and local Greenwich Village writers. I subsequently met Jones, and we became fast friends; through him I got to know "his" writers, and through me he got to know "mine." LeRoi Jones had a magnetic and powerful personality, and his magazine immediately began to flourish—so much so, in fact, that the poets and writers who contributed to it and who were drawn to Jones's apartment (first on West 20th Street in Chelsea and later on East 14th Street) became known as the "*Yugen* crowd." Jones had informal gatherings in his apartment for readings, discussions, talk, and drinking, and often these gatherings would turn into all-night parties. A not at all atypical party at Jones's would include Selby, Rumaker, Kerouac, Ginsberg, Bremser, Corso, Rosenthal, Oppenheimer, Finstein, and, when they were in New York, Wieners, George Stanley, Dorn, and Burroughs. There was often music played by Ornette Coleman, Archie Shepp, Wilbur Ware, and Don Cherry. About 1960 or so, Frank O'Hara, Koch, Bill Berkson, and other people of the New York School also began to frequent Jones's place. It assumed the character of a freewheeling and noisy salon.

By the time *Neon* 4 was off the press, Jones had just published *Yugen* 4. Dawson did a drawing for *Yugen,* black on white—his collage for *Neon* had been white on black—and he had suggested to Jones that his drawing be printed as a negative, so that it too would be white on black and the two magazines could therefore be displayed in bookshops as "sisters." Jones did this, and the magazines were displayed, at least in the Eighth Street Book Shop, side by side.

Some months earlier, I had complained to Dawson about the ridiculous length of time I had been waiting for *Neon* 4. Many people, incidentally, thought that *Neon* had folded, and some subscribers had canceled their orders. Dawson suggested that we do, jointly, a supplement to the magazine, to be given to subscribers as a sign of good faith and a kind of bonus. We decided to call it *Supplement to Now.* It was to be small, both in number of pages and format, and Dawson arranged to have it printed at the plant of the *Kirkwood Messenger,* his Missouri hometown newspaper, for sixty dollars. Its theme was to be, as the title implies, "now." As I look back at the magazine, the theme seems thin, tenuous at best, but it provided a hook on which we hung a number of excellent pieces. The issue had Charles Olson, Robert Creeley, Max Finstein, Hubert Selby, Jonathan Williams, Dawson, and myself. The cover, a drawing of a linotype machine by Dawson, was especially fitting. *Supplement to Now* appeared at the end of 1958 and was immediately mailed to subscribers free of charge; it was sold in bookshops for fifty cents, and has become, so I am told, a collector's item, one that is very scarce.

Neon, after the appearance of its fourth issue and the supplement, entered a period of extreme financial difficulty. Numbers 3 and 4 had been printed on the West Coast—a situation that had become impossible. There was no way to oversee the printing, there were no proofs, and the low production costs were offset by the freight bills that had to be paid upon delivery. *Neon* 5 was ready by this time, and what I needed was a New York printer who would do the issue in a month or so and at a reasonable price. LeRoi Jones had found a small printing company in East New York, the Orion Press, and used it to do a reprint of Olson's "Projective Verse" as a Totem Press chapbook (Totem was a *Yugen* book imprint). Nothing turned out well with *Neon* 5, however, and it was all I could do to get my deposit on the printing bill back from the company. I was very disappointed, since *Neon* 5 was to have included work by Duncan, McClure, and Loewinsohn, the first time that the magazine was to have Bay Area writers represented in its pages.

At this point I was just about ready to give up on the magazine. There was never enough money to bring issues out on a fairly regular basis, but, more depressing, the issues always seemed to be too slender to have any adequate selection of prose among their contents. I wanted to print

Selby, Rumaker, and Douglas Woolf—I also had begun to think that it was time to use the magazine as a place in which nonfiction—criticism and reviews—might appear as a regular feature. There seemed to be no hope of doing this, and in 1960, with a gift of money from Tony Weinberger, I put together a final issue of the magazine, *Neon Obit*. Again it was to have a unifying theme—this one on dead Americans who had made a great impact on this country, or on dead currents of behavior and thought that were still in the air. The contributors were Dawson, Jones, Selby, Weinberger, Early, Oppenheimer, Loewinsohn, Olson, Finstein, and myself. The cover drawing was again by Dawson, of a Curtiss Robin that had gone out of production during the depression. If I remember rightly, 300 copies of the issue were sold out immediately.

In the same year, Jones began to run critical articles in *Yugen*. His feeling about them was much the same as mine; that is, the new writers had been appearing in magazines for about a decade, and it was time for the establishment of a critical position vis-à-vis these writers. The reader must know that, to my knowledge, not one so-called major critic had ever written a word on any of the writers I have here mentioned; indeed it was a cause for utter astonishment to be shown a review, however mindless, of one of their books. If anything did appear in print about any of them, it was usually in the nature of a jeremiad against "the destroyers of letters and culture," etc., etc., ad nauseam. It was quite apparent to Jones and to me as well (and to many others) that the writers of this new movement should have at least one outlet for their own critical commentary on their peers. It also seemed incumbent upon us to begin a counterattack against those who had set themselves up as the guardians of letters and arts. *Neon* was, for all purposes, dead, and the avant-garde community in New York had only *Yugen* as a medium for expression. And *Yugen* simply did not have the room to print anything more than short critiques.

While this was going on, a young journalist, Marc Schleifer, brought out the first issue of a magazine called *Kulchur*, with Jones as one of the contributing editors. (The others were John Fles, Charles Olson, Donald Phelps, and Martin Williams.) *Kulchur* was exactly what we had been looking for—a magazine of criticism and comment, dealing with literature, politics, art, jazz, and popular culture. Through Jones, I met Schleifer and accepted his invitation to write for the magazine, which looked as if it might indeed become that catholic yet eclectic publication

which was needed. The problem, as always, was financial: Schleifer had to pay for the printing of *Kulchur* as best he could, and it seemed as if it would collapse almost before it got started. One night, Jones, Schleifer, and I sat talking in the Cedar, and discovered that Schleifer had somehow met a wealthy woman who was interested in the arts, Lita Hornick. She offered to pay for *Kulchur*, oversee its distribution, and assure its appearance, right on time, every three months. Most agreeably, she wanted nothing to do with the editorial policy of the magazine, nor did she wish to exercise editorial judgment concerning its contents. It was absolutely too good to be true. If I am not mistaken, it was on this same night that we decided to bar all poetry and fiction from the magazine and devote its pages to criticism and commentary. (In later issues this policy was relaxed, but never to the extent that unsolicited poetry and fiction were considered.)

It is probably quite unfair of me to say so, but I always thought of *Kulchur* as the critical wing of *Yugen*; that is to say, *Kulchur* seemed to me to be what *Yugen* might have become had Jones had the money to continue it. The nucleus of the magazine, from the beginning, was made up of those writers who had been affiliated with *Yugen* and *Neon*, and, further back, with the *Black Mountain Review*. (Ultimately, it became the official voice of the entire new movement. Although I haven't the issues at hand, it seems to me that every nonacademic writer of value in this country either appeared or was discussed in its pages.)

At all events, *mirabile dictu*, we had a magazine of our own, one that we did not have to worry about funding. I became the poetry editor with, I believe, number 3, and then book editor. My function was to be responsible for all articles and reviews on writing and books and to contribute regularly to the magazine.

Kulchur published, over a five-year period, twenty issues. I believe it must be considered one of the great magazines of the twentieth century, an authoritative voice, as important as The Little Review, *The Dial, transition, The Criterion,* and *Contact.* It had a clear point of view, an unmistakable position, and its range of commentary was simply staggering. It was a perfect argument against the idea that a magazine is a hodgepodge of good pieces by good writers. The articles in each issue complemented and buttressed each other and lent weight and depth to the articles in every other issue. It had, in a word, a tone that was unique to itself—*Kulchur* simply did not read like any other magazine before or since.

The editors all wrote for almost every issue, so that the voice of the magazine was coherent and *located*. The regular reader knew where the editors stood, and hence their criticism made sense; it had roots. Interestingly, *Kulchur* evolved a review style that, for better or worse, has persisted in little-magazine writing to this day. It was personal, colloquial, wry, mocking, and precisely vulgar when vulgarity seemed called for. It was also "careless," by which I mean that it wore its learning lightly, was witty and, as they say, irreverent. Although in its twenty issues at least a dozen brilliant essays were printed, not one of them had the miasmal aura of the "think piece." Most pointedly, perhaps, the *Kulchur* "style" expected the reader to know what was occurring in the avant-garde community in New York; nothing was ever explained, the writing was elliptical, casual, and obsessively conversational. We had wanted a flashing, brilliant magazine that had nothing to do with the academic world and we had got one.

By 1961 Marc Schleifer, because of an increasing concern with politics, had begun to lose interest in the magazine, or perhaps he no longer had the time to edit it—it came to the same thing. He asked Mrs. Hornick for a leave of absence and requested that I be guest editor for *Kulchur* 4. I accepted, and went to work on the issue. I asked Zukofsky (whom I badly wanted to begin to use the magazine for an outlet), Duncan, Ron Loewinsohn, and Selby for contributions, and they all responded. Zukofsky gave me "Modern Times," a beautiful essay on Charlie Chaplin, written in 1936 and never before published; Duncan sent his matchless "Ideas of the Meaning of Form"; Loewinsohn sent "A Credo Sandwich," a piece on poetics that complemented Duncan's; and Selby, writing as "Harry Black," submitted "Happiness House," a bitter assault on New York State mental institutions. Jones, as an editor, gave me a chapter from his as yet unpublished book, *Blues People*, and I asked Edward Dorn if I might reprint his "What I see in the *Maximus* Poems," originally published in Gael Turnbull's *Migrant*. Paul Goodman sent a comment on material that had appeared in number 3. An oddly curious Freudian study of L. Frank Baum, and in particular the Oz books, came in unsolicited from Osmond Beckwith, of whom I have never again heard, and seemed to me exactly right for the issue. The reviews were by Dawson, Jones, Cid Corman (on Zukofsky), Oppenheimer (on Dorn), and Walter Lowenfels, who sent a review of *Tropic of Cancer*, written in Paris on the appearance of Miller's novel in 1933 and previously unpublished. Marian Zazeela, Marc Schleifer's wife, gave me a snapshot of Kerouac and Burroughs taken in Paris about 1955, and that became the cover: the title page identifies it as a photograph of Inspector Maigret and Sam Spade.

Joel Oppenheimer was the guest editor for number 5. He printed a group of the Zukofskys' Catullus translations and a chapter from Louis Zukofsky's novel *Little* (from this point on, Zukofsky was a regular contributor to *Kulchur*, all of his "Five Statements for Poetry" appearing in later issues). And he "commissioned" the first of Frank O'Hara's art chronicles, which were to become a regular feature of the magazine.

After the appearance of *Kulchur* 6, the editorial staff was set. Schleifer had not returned, and the magazine, instead of having a single editor to oversee everything, had an editorial board, each member of which had absolute autonomy in his field. Lita Hornick was listed as the managing editor; the music editor was Jones; Frank O'Hara was art editor; Joseph Le Sueur, theater editor; Bill Berkson, film editor; and I was book editor. The contributing editors were Diane di Prima, A. B. Spellman, Charles Olson, and Donald Phelps. I should mention that *Kulchur* 9 was a special theater issue of short plays, edited by Le Sueur.

By the end of 1963 my editorial relationship with the magazine was becoming strained, mostly because of editorial differences between me and Mrs. Hornick. Increasingly, she had begun to take a hand in editorial decisions affecting the contents of *Kulchur*. Pieces appeared without having been seen or approved by any editor. Writers who had very little to do with the tone or position of the magazine were asked, by Mrs. Hornick, for contributions. *Kulchur* began to assume the look and feel of just another little magazine; it rapidly began to lose its singularity, and the excellent pieces that still appeared were weakened or lost within the context of these diffuse issues. Mrs. Hornick had become not only an editor, but *the* editor.

One incident that occurred at this time stands out in my memory. Donald Phelps, as a contributing editor—one of the original contributing editors of the magazine—had sent in a film review that Mrs. Hornick rejected, I cannot remember on what grounds. I protested, as did some of the other editors, pointing out that as a contributing editor he was expected regularly to contribute to *Kulchur*, and that if his work was to be rejected, what was the point of carrying him as an editor? Mrs. Hornick did not see it that way, and by issue

11 I had asked to be relieved of my editorial duties and listed as a contributing editor. By issue 14, all the editors had been metamorphosed into contributing editors, and the masthead of number 20, the final issue, carries only Mrs. Hornick's name and represents the total change that had come over *Kulchur*. Of the old contributors, only Fielding Dawson was left.

All this happened very gradually, over a period of a year and a half or so. On reflection, it seems unfortunate to me, since I think that *Kulchur* might have gone on for at least another half-dozen issues had it retained its original focus. At precisely that moment at which the magazine found itself in the position of being without peers, it became fuzzy, off-center, and fashionable. I suspect that the reason for this was that Mrs. Hornick wanted to discover her *own* writers, and ranged all over to get them. So the magazine died—having, at its end, less energy and verve than it displayed in its first tentative issue. *Kulchur* was a remarkable publication because its strength came from the fact that its editorial position was rooted in a true artistic community, and that community was rooted in a great city. It was not the organ of a precious and isolated "artists' colony," nor was it—horror of horrors—the journal of an academic milieu's rebels. The contributors were asked to submit work on the basis of what the editors took to be relevance to the magazine's overall position, not because they were fashionable or well known. (In later issues this changed.) It was alive because it grew out of a *specific* modern movement and because it was necessary to that movement's cohesion. Williams told me, just before *Neon* began, that a little magazine's only rationale is its editor's belief that the writers he prints must be presented as a group. Anything else is just a collation of pages. I have always believed this, and the experience of the past twenty years has shown that the magazines that never really come to life are always those that reveal themselves to be little anthologies of anything at all (as long as it's "good").

I should mention, before I close, another publication that was circulated concurrently with the last issues of *Yugen* and throughout the life of *Kulchur*. This was *The Floating Bear*, edited by LeRoi Jones and Diane di Prima. I was not directly involved with it but contributed to it on an irregular basis, often under pseudonyms (the only one I can remember being "Abe Harvard"). The *Bear* was a mimeographed newsletter of about 15 to 20 pages, and distributed solely by a mailing list, free of charge. It can best be explained by the fact that its first fifteen or twenty numbers contained all the material that could have just as easily gone into *Kulchur* had that magazine been a monthly. In other words, it had "hot news"—reviews of movies, plays, recitals, jazz clubs, and the like. It also contained poems, essays, letters to the editors, buyer's guides, notes on trashy paperbacks, reading lists, and an enormous amount of New York "inside" gossip. Hundreds of people contributed to it. It was, at its best, fresh, arrogant, and funny. After 1965 or so, it continued under, I think, the sole editorship of Diane di Prima until about 1973, appearing less and less frequently. Its last issues were almost all gossip and deeply involved in an alternative politics.

The reader will have by now seen that my own view of the little magazine of the fifties and sixties is necessarily narrow, being severely restricted to my knowledge of the workings of my own magazine, *Neon*, Jones's *Yugen*, and the magazine we both worked for over a four-year period, *Kulchur*. There were many other magazines that appeared at about the time *Kulchur* was entering its last year of publication, among them *Trobar, Poor.Old.Tired.Horse., Poems from the Floating World, Some/Time*, etc. Many of them were outlets for those poets who at that time had embraced the theory, if you will, of the "deep image." I am essentially ignorant of these magazines and never appeared in any of them. Although I rarely agreed with any of those poets on anything, the magazines that presented them were *absolute*; i.e., they too had a bone to pick, and articulated a position doggedly.

When I consider *Neon, Yugen*, and *Kulchur*, they seem to me almost of a piece. I often cannot recall what pieces I contributed to which of them. The three of them performed a particular function at a particular time, and died, one might suppose, when they were no longer needed. *Kulchur* most definitely reflected the close of a literary era that had begun in about 1950 and found its first voice in the *Black Mountain Review* and *Origin*. By the time it ceased publication, in the winter of 1965, that era was over and the community from which it had sprung no longer existed—it had become something else. By that time, most of the writers who appeared in these magazines were known, and some of them were beginning to be treated with at least a measure of respect; they were no longer considered ignorant beatniks by the great majority of critics and academics.

A final note. I suspect that a new magazine—perhaps even one of "criticism and comment," like *Kulchur*—will soon be necessary. The generation that had just begun to write and publish in the mid-sixties has been around more than a decade. Although the writers of this generation have published in many magazines (and published many books as well) and founded many others, they have been curiously and inexplicably uncritical of each other and of everybody else; everyone seems to like everyone else's work. The situation is oddly passive, and many of the magazines in which these writers appear read like the later issues of *The Floating Bear*—all charm, gossip, and news notes. These younger writers have never established a critical position for themselves; it seems to be beneath them. Perhaps it is. Maybe they are too close to my generation to assault it—certainly they were born, as it were, into an era that was kind to them. In comparison to the fifties, it was an era of light, air, and acceptance or, as Frank O'Hara might put it, of girls, grapes, and snow. If the next generation sees this present one as dull and empty. I'm certain we will see the birth of another literary movement that will view the present generation of younger writers as the establishment, and launch its own rebellious magazines.

LAWRENCE FERLINGHETTI AND NANCY J. PETERS (ESSAY DATE 1980)

SOURCE: Ferlinghetti, Lawrence, and Nancy J. Peters. *Literary San Francisco: A Pictorial from Its Beginning to the Present Day*, pp. 163-88. San Francisco: City Lights Books and Harper & Row, 1980.

In the following excerpt, Ferlinghetti and Peters provide an overview of City Lights, Evergreen Review, *and* Beatitude *magazine.*

City Lights was founded in June 1953 by Peter D. Martin and Lawrence Ferlinghetti, the former an English instructor at San Francisco State College. It was Martin's brilliant idea to open the first all-paperback bookstore in the United States and thus pay the rent for the second-floor editorial offices of his magazine, *City Lights,* an early pop-culture little magazine. *City Lights* featured the first film criticism by Pauline Kael plus pieces by Grover Sales and others with titles like "The Sociological Significance of Moon Mullins" and poems by Robert Duncan, Philip Lamantia, and Jack Spicer.

Martin, who now runs the New Yorker Bookstore in Manhattan, is the son of Carlo Tresca, Italian anarchist who was assassinated in 1943. (City Lights itself is generally in an anarchist, civil libertarian, antiauthoritarian tradition. Martin named his magazine and the bookstore after the

film by Chaplin, whose Little Man has always been a symbol of the subjective man against the world. Some of the bookstore's first customers were old Italian anarchists in derbies buying *L'Adunata* and *L'Humanità Nova.* One was on the local garbage truck and would run in to buy his anarchist paper as the truck passed.)

Within a year of the bookstore's opening, Martin departed for New York, and Shigeyoshi Murao became manager and eventually co-owner with Ferlinghetti. In the tradition of great literary bookstores on the East Coast and especially in Europe, City Lights began publishing its own books in 1955 and now has about a hundred books in print, none federally financed by grants from the National Endowment of the Arts. (Its editors, in the Anarchist/Surrealist tradition, like it that way.)

. . . . .

[The back cover of *Evergreen Review,* No. 2, published by the Grove Press in 1957, edited by Donald M. Allen and Barney Rosset,] spoke of

the exciting phenomenon of a young group in the process of creating a new American culture. With what the *New Yorker* calls "a pervasive desire to get out into the open in order to breathe fresh, creative air . . . looking for some large poetic form that can accommodate anything and everything—including ordinarily rejected and suspect material," a vigorous new generation of writers, painters and musicians in the Bay Area is revolting against the sterility of American "academicians." Brought together here for the first time are the leading figures of the "San Francisco Renaissance."

Contributors included Kenneth Rexroth, Brother Antoninus (William Everson), Robert Duncan, Lawrence Ferlinghetti, Henry Miller, Michael McClure, Josephine Miles, Jack Spicer, Michael Rumaker, James Broughton, Gary Snyder, Philip Whalen, Jack Kerouac, and Allen Ginsberg. There were also critical articles by Ralph J. Gleason on the "San Francisco Jazz Scene" and New York art critic Dore Ashton's "Eastern View of the San Francisco School" (of painting).

This New York-oriented review made the eastern U.S. connection in painting and poetry. (Ginsberg, Kerouac, Ferlinghetti, Rumaker, and Gregory Corso on the set in San Francisco were all from the eastern seaboard.) It ignored some San Franciscans vital to the movement—notably Philip Lamantia (leading American Surrealist), black-Jewish poet Bob Kaufman (whose early broadsides were second only to Ginsberg's *Howl* as seminal influences), and figurative painter James Weeks (whose paintings of jazz musicians in session were closer to San Francisco "jazz poetry" than any paintings mentioned by Ashton).

Ashton's essay, linking New York abstract expressionism to early non-objective paintings in San Francisco by Clyfford Still, Rothko, Hans Hoffman, and others associated with the California School of Fine Arts (Hassel Smith, Elmer Bischoff, Walter Kuhlman, Frank Lobdell, John Saccaro) made a connection in print with the San Francisco poets. In reality, such a liaison hardly existed. In New York some of the same poets, together with New Yorkers Frank O'Hara and Kenneth Koch, did indeed intimately associate with painters and art critics. In San Francisco this happened on only a very limited scale in the 1950s. James Weeks, John Saccaro, and Canadian Ronald Bladen were among the few who communicated directly with some poets or showed any awareness of the new poetry and its possible affinities with what the painters were doing. (Hubert Crehan, as editor of *Arts Digest* in New York, hired Ferlinghetti to write a monthly San Francisco Letter in which he reviewed Hassel Smith, Ronald Bladen, Jay DeFeo, and William Wulf. Sculptor Beniamino Buffano collaborated in print with Ferlinghetti on one later occasion.)

It was some time later that younger artists like Wallace Berman, Bruce Conner, George Herms, and Jordan Belson began to work with poets and "jumped around from painting to collage and film to poetry" (as art critic Thomas Albright later described them). Separate from them in North Beach in the 1970s were the powerful young visionary painters Michael Bowen, Michael Mc-Cracken, Arthur Monroe, and Wilfried Satty. And Peter Leblanc began a career of portraying poets and Buddhist themes in silkscreen and etching. In 1979 Wallace Berman had a posthumous show at the University Art Museum in Berkeley, including a poetry reading by his old friends Michael Mc-Clure, David Meltzer, and Diane di Prima.

Including Henry Miller among the San Francisco insurgent writers was gratuitous. (Given the New Yorker's mental map of what lay beyond the Hudson, it was natural to assume Miller's Big Sur was a part of San Francisco.) A hundred and seventy miles to the south, Miller remained aloof from the beat in San Francisco, even though his *Tropics* were underground classics for most poets and he was their immediate forebear as a dissident writer. (The title of Ferlinghetti's *Coney Island of the Mind* was taken from a Miller book.) When the young Allen Ginsberg wrote to Miller asking if

ON THE SUBJECT OF...

HAROLD NORSE

Believing boredom to be the greatest of all sins, Harold Norse has traveled the world and spent years in search of rational evidence for the absurdity in all human existence. He spent fifteen years (1953-1968) in self-imposed exile wandering Europe, North Africa, and the Near East. Norse was in Paris in 1959 when Corso introduced him to Burroughs, who suggested Norse move into the hotel at 9, rue Git-Le-Coeur. In 1960 Norse moved into what became known as the Beat Hotel (so nicknamed because of the famous Beat writers who stayed there at one time or another). During the three years he lived there, he witnessed the first cut-up technique work of Burroughs, Brion Gysin, Corso, and Sinclair Beiles. He later wrote of the famous residence in his 1975 book *The Beat Hotel*. Upon his return to America in the late 1960s, Norse settled in San Francisco and founded a short-lived magazine titled *Bastard Angel*. Despite only producing three issues, the periodical boasted contributions from such notable figures as Burroughs, Ginsberg, Ferlinghetti, and Charles Bukowski. Norse chronicled the magazine's brief, notable life, as well as his own, in *Memoirs of a Bastard Angel* (1989).

he could drop in while visiting Big Sur, Miller wrote back a card: "Dear Friend—Please do not drop in." The dissident sound of San Francisco writers found no answering echo in Miller until the publication of Kerouac's *Subterraneans*.

Miller later invited Kerouac for dinner at Ephraim Doner's house in Carmel Highlands. Kerouac never made it, having delayed leaving Vesuvio's bar in North Beach until well past dinnertime, with at least a three-hour drive down the coast. He finally did arrive in a wilder part of Big Sur in the dark hours of the morning, in a taxi. It was a canyon where Ferlinghetti had a cabin. Kerouac, weaving about with his brakeman's lantern, couldn't find the cabin and fell asleep in a meadow, where Ferlinghetti found him at dawn. (The event is documented in Kerouac's *Big Sur* and in various Kerouac biographies.) Kerouac and Miller never did meet.

. . . . .

Beatitude magazine's first issue was printed at the Bread and Wine Mission, Greenwich and Grant Avenue, April 1959. . . . *Beatitude,* its title embodying Kerouac's original definition of beat, has been like a floating crapgame during the twenty years of its funky existence, edited by whatever resident visionary happened to want to do an issue. "Edited & produced on a kick or miss basis" by anarchists, "neo-existentialists, beggars, winos, freuds, wordmen, brushmen, axemen & other habitués & gawkers of the North Beach scene," the production was generally Xerox or mimeo, limited in run by the durability of the paper plates.

While big literary magazines like *Contact* and *Evergreen Review* came and went, *Beatitude* survived, and an extraordinary twentieth-anniversary issue was published in late 1979, edited by Neeli Cherkovski and Raymond Foye. Solid with new work by new and old writers (as well as unknown texts by Edgar Allan Poe, Fernando Pessoa, and Samuel Greenberg), this issue showed *Beatitude* to be still more alive than most big quarterlies, moribund in academe, and Little Magazines, breast-fed by the National Endowment of the Arts and Humanities, a far cry indeed from the rambunctious independence of the early *Argonaut* and *Overland Monthly.*

JAMES CAMPBELL (ESSAY DATE 1999)

SOURCE: Campbell, James. "Behind the Beat: *Neurotica.*" In *This Is the Beat Generation: New York-San Francisco-Paris,* pp. 93-6. London: Secker and Warburg, 1999.

In the following excerpt, Campbell explores the early Beat magazine Neurotica.

The Beat Generation writers are unusual among literary gangs in never having had a little magazine of their own, through which to distribute their early work. At the beginning of 1950, Ginsberg had still to publish in anything other than a student journal; Kerouac, though he had a novel waiting to come out, had to date published nothing of a literary nature at all, while Burroughs, age thirty-five, did not even consider himself a writer.

The closest there was to a beat magazine (though it could only be seen that way in retrospect) in the late 1940s and early 50s was a

slim, eccentric journal whose contributors moved among the bases of art, sex and neuroticism. *Neurotica* was owned and edited by a young gallery owner from St Louis, like Burroughs, called Jay Landesman. In the first issue, Spring 1948, he set out the magazine's aims:

> *Neurotica* is a literary exposition, defense and correlation of the problems and personalities that in our culture are defined as 'neurotic'.
>
> It is said that if you tie a piece of red cloth to a gull's leg its fellow-gulls will peck it to pieces: and *Neurotica* wishes to draw an analog to this observation and the plight of today's creative 'anxious' man.
>
> We are interested in exploring the creativeness of this man who has been forced to live underground . . .

The magazine's most prolific contributor was a maverick psychologist called Gershon Legman, described by John Clellon Holmes, who was a friend of Landesman and provided the conduit for beatness, as a 'small belligerent facsimile of Balzac'. The general theme of Legman's articles for *Neurotica* was that the American public's increasing appetite for violence and sadism in fiction (Legman did not condescend to study film) stemmed directly from the puritanical suppression of the libido in everyday life.

Legman made his debut in *Neurotica* 3, with 'The Psychopathology of the Comics', which examined the aggressive nature of children's comic-books. In the next issue he published 'Institutionalized Lynch: The anatomy of a murder-mystery'. In three separate columns, he listed the instances of 'Sadism', 'Sadism and Sex' and 'Sex' as they occurred in the action of a bestselling novel, *The Strange Woman* (1941), by Ben Ames Williams. Legman worked on the principle that, as the law tolerated no general description of sex, the result was the 'mundane substitute for sex'—i.e., sadism.

> Murder having replaced sex in the popular arts, the glorification of one requires the degradation of the other . . . so that we are faced in our culture by the insurmountable schizophrenic contradiction that sex, which is legal in fact, is a crime on paper, while murder—a crime, in fact—is, on paper, the bestseller of all time.

Taking a fifty-page sample of *The Strange Woman,* Legman found ten examples of 'Sadism' ('Woman listens "with pent breath" to details of whipping a man . . . "Did he bleed?"' etc), ten examples of 'Sadism and Sex' ('her knotted fists beat at him in passionate ecstasies'), and a single evocation of 'Sex', that being a 'nebulous description of a coitus'.

The early issues of *Neurotica* contained articles which combined a serious intellectual tone with a tendency to titillate, such as a piece on prostitution as a force for social good, by Rudolph Friedmann (in the way that books on spanking and bondage were often written by someone with a medical practitioner's initials after his or her name, Friedmann was said to have 'worked in connection with educational activities in London'), another on homosexuals who marry, by Nathaniel Thornton ('Professor Thornton teaches abnormal psychology'), and others on fetishists such as 'Jack the Snipper', who secretly cuts off locks of ladies' hair in cinemas, and on the bar as a pick-up place. In *Neurotica* 2, there was a very short story, 'Tea for Two', by Holmes (signed simply 'Clellon Holmes'), a limbering-up exercise for the novel he was planning to write about the scene, and the first appearance in the pages of the magazine of a writer defined (even self-defined) as 'beat':

> This is a local fable and the boy is Beeker. This guy was a Pekoe-man, and he blew himself out of the coils of a trumpet every night. He came on for culture, not for loot; so he passed the marihuana to his cohorts when the need was near. This tea-dispensing on the cuff brought in enough for bills, and the lad was living in a new era.

There were few journals in 1948 which were willing to publish a sympathetic portrait of a drug-pusher, and there were even fewer editors who would risk confrontation with the law by printing the word 'fuck', which appeared in *Neurotica* 5 (Autumn 1949) and led to the banning of the issue by the Post Office. The same issue included an article by Marshall McLuhan, in which he wrote that '*Time*, *Life* and *Fortune* (the *New Yorker* can be thrown in with them) are the American Bloomsbury, our psychological bureaucracy, inhabited by well-paid artist-apes'.

Ginsberg's first contribution to a magazine with a nationwide circulation appeared in *Neurotica* 6, Spring 1950, by which time the magazine had adopted a furtive beat identity. Ginsberg's brief 'Song: Fie My Fum' was not likely to advance by much the editor's avowed cause of describing 'a neurotic society from the inside'; nevertheless, it was the right kind of verse for the venue, with its playful sexual content:

> Say my oops,
> Ope my shell,
> Roll my bones,
> Ring my bell . . .

The contributor's note informed readers that 'Allen Ginsberg recently recovered from a serious illness'. There was also an article on homosexuality and art, a dissertation on 'Afro-Cuban rumba' by the white Negro Anatole Broyard, and a short piece on literary parties by the up-and-coming novelist Chandler Brossard, who was soon to set himself up as Broyard's nemesis, exposing him as a black man passing for white. The longest and most serious contribution to *Neurotica* 6 was 'Report from the Asylum: Afterthoughts of a shock patient' by Carl Goy, the pseudonym of Ginsberg's new friend in the Columbia PI, Carl Solomon:

> The testimony that follows is that of an eye-witness, one who has undergone insulin shock treatment and has slept through fifty comas . . .

> Upon being strapped into my insulin bed, I would at once break off my usual stream of puns and hysterical chatter. I would stare at the bulge I made beneath the canvas restraining sheet, and my body, insulin-packed, would become to me an enormous concrete pun with infinite levels of association, and thereby a means of surmounting association with things, much as the verbal puns had surmounted the meaning of words . . .

> Each coma is utterly incomparable to that of the previous day. Lacking a time-sense and inhabiting all of these universe at one and the same time, my condition was one of omnipresence, of being everywhere at no time.

Neurotica published only three more issues, before coming to an end in another battle with the law, over an article by Legman on—what could be more fitting?—the castration complex.

ANNE WALDMAN (ESSAY DATE MARCH 2002)

SOURCE: Waldman, Anne. "*Angel Hair* Feature." *Jacket* (online magazine), <www.jacketmagazine.com/16/ahl-wald.html> (March 2002).

In the following essay, the introduction to Jacket *magazine's special issue devoted to* Angel Hair, *Waldman describes the birth of her magazine and her personal and professional relationship with cofounder Lewis Warsh.*

I met Lewis Warsh at the Berkeley Poetry Conference [in 1965] and will always forever after think we founded *Angel Hair* within that auspicious moment. Conflation of time triggered by romance adjacent to the glamorous history-making events of the conference seems a reasonable explanation. Perhaps *Angel Hair* was what we made together in our brief substantive marriage that lasted and had repercussions. And sped us on our way as writers. Aspirations to be a poet were rising, the ante grew higher at Berkeley surrounded by heroic figures of the New American Poetry. Here was a fellow New Yorker, same age, who had also written novels, was resolute, erudite about contemporary poetry. Mutual recognition lit us up. Don't I know you?

Summer before last year at Bennington where I'd been editing *SILO* magazine under tutelage of printer-poet Claude Fredericks, studying literature and poetry with Howard Nemerov and other literary and creative faculty, I was encouraged by Jonathan Cott—comrade I'd known since high school—to visit radical Berkeley and check out the poetry convention. It was certainly going to be more experimental than what I was exposed to at Bennington. A few students had been making queries about why no one taught Williams, Pound or Gertrude Stein, let alone H. D. I was trying to get the school to invite Allen Ginsberg to read. Jon and I had been exchanging work, he'd sent copies of Ted Berrigan's *C* magazine jamming my little rustic p.o. box. He'd known Ron Padgett at Columbia University. We were on to the *New American Poetry* and the poetry net was widening, inviting.

My mother's connection to poet Anghelos Sikelianos—he was her father-in-law over a decade—had decidedly informed my upbringing and aspirations to poetry. Frances was part of the utopian Delphic Ideal community in Greece in the 1930s spearheaded by Eva Palmer Sikelianos with links to Isadora Duncan, Jose Clemente Orozco, others, that had a humanistic brave notion that art, and Greek drama in particular, could 'save mankind.' There was encouragement in our bohemian household towards any act of poetry.

I wrote stories and plays and e. e. cummingsesque poems in high school, and sent them uneventfully off to *The Village Voice* and *The Evergreen Review,* to which I loyally subscribed. The night Lewis and I took lysergic acid diethylamide at a friend's apartment on Nob Hill, first time, I hallucinated a lineage tree, an arbor vitae (prevalent archetypal 'acid' icon)—resonant with what you visualize in particular Buddhist practices—that included all the people I'd ever known: family, friends, their families, friends. Also heroes, heroines, cultural figures, saints, poets, ballplayers, actors, movie stars, singers, many others—bad guys, enemies even. Animals, trees, plants, lakes, mountains, and so on. All gathered in my brain in witness motif, gazing at one another and then up at the sky waiting for an impulse to get something 'going.' Or make use of their precious time 'on earth.' Of course all these folk were already busy, that wasn't the point. It was my yearning to be part of it all, a blueprint for community, for *sacre conversatione.* More like a fifties Sci Fi movie?

And yet the desire to belong, and to 'lead 'had a naive, albeit egotistical, purity.

Back on the relative level, clearly Lewis and I were bonded and destined to 'do something' together. Certainly meeting on the West Coast and having a sense of those poetry communities helped define or keep expansive the aesthetic of our magazine and press. Also the perspective of an alternative to the official verse culture so clearly manifest at Berkeley was appealing. We were already drawn to underground 'autonomous zones,' tender beauties of small press production. White Rabbit books were sacred objects Lewis turned me towards. Later *Locus Solus, Art & Literature, The Floating Bear* and Ed Sanders' *Fuck You: A Magazine of the Arts* were also galvanizing for their intimacy and immediacy.

I had met Diane di Prima in 1963 when she was in situ at the Albert Hotel with children and entourage and books on alchemy. Back in Vermont I'd been working on *SILO* with printer Ronnie Ballou, who printed grocery lists and menus for livelihood. He was a taciturn New Englander, rarely smiled, but pleased with the new venture. This was not fine letterpress printing but a modest and cheaper substitute. We ordered out for the elegant Fabriano cover paper.

The first *Angel Hair* cost less than $150 to print. A large page size (9" x 12") gave ample space around the works. Simple type for our title—from Jon Cott's provocative line 'Angel hair sleeps with a boy in my head'—felt consummately luxurious. The denouement issue was pristine in its own way, sporting George Schneeman's black line drawing of a couple sailing off in their roadster convertible. I had wanted a different look and texture from other magazines we'd encountered. We weathered complaints from bookstores about the magazine being 'oversized' but made no compromise. We sent *Angel Hair* I out to a range of family, friends, poets, other folk, receiving back modest support, Ann and Sam Charters being among the first subscribers.

By the time I moved back to New York City into 33 St. Marks Place the magazine had been launched. Word came late summer 1966 I'd been hired at The Poetry Project at a salary in the range of $6000 a year which would help supplement, along with Lewis's job at the Welfare Department, our budding publishing venture. The Project would be a continuation of alternative poetry and an active and engaged literary community.

Our skinny floor-through 'railroad' apartment became a veritable salon. First regulars (Ted Berrigan, Dick Gallup, Michel Brownstein, many others) then huge crowds would spill into the premises after readings at the Church [St. Mark's Church in the Bowery, home of the Poetry Project.] Plethora of stories. The night Kenneth Koch stripped down, shocking my mother who later made the remark that the New York School got 'Beat' below 14th Street. The cranky lady next door often called the police as decibels mounted. Occasionally some of the Velvet Underground and Andy Warhol crowd would show up. Many nights we'd hop over to Max's Kansas City or take a taxi to 42nd Street to an all-night movie theater.

Although confirmedly inspired by our generation's music, fashion, drugs, attitudes, politics and being caught up and shaken by the devastating events of our times—the war in Viet Nam, assassinations of Bobby Kennedy and Martin Luther King—we didn't think of ourselves as hippies. Too occupied being writers and publishers, and in my case, an infrastructure (arts administrator) poet. Ted Berrigan jokingly called us the 'A' students for our industriousness. After the activity would subside we'd often stay up the rest of the night working, occasionally spotting W. H. Auden out our window (he lived on the next block) in his University of Michigan sweatshirt as he took his early morning 'constitutional,' a London *Times* under his arm. Then we'd sleep a few hours and get ready for the next round of work, art, conversation.

When we decided to publish books and pamphlets we wanted texts enhanced by the work of the artists who had come into our lives, particularly Joe Brainard (also a writer we were to publish) and George Schneeman. Each book had its own reality. Shape and size weren't confined by an 8½" x 11" stapled format, although plenty of those we published had charming distinctions. Bright colored tissue endpapers often enclosed the body of the work. Decisions were made based on budgetary concern or expediency. Early productions (Charles Stein, Gerard Malanga, Lee Harwood) made use of elegant cover papers. Frank O'Hara and John Wieners's work inspired cottage industry George Schneeman drawings for covers with mimeo insides.

To get something ready in time for a reading or a birthday could be a push. John Giorno's *Birds* was timed for a reading. *Giant Night* with silk-screened Schneeman of a window with holly spring was a Christmas production. Bill Berkson had ceremoniously invited Lewis and me to meet Philip Guston and his wife Musa in Woodstock which resulted in a generous friendship and Phil-

ip's cover for Clark Coolidge's *ING,* and later a cover for Alice Notley's *Incidentals in The Day World,* both stunning black and white drawings. Alex Katz's astute graphic drawing was a perfect match for Bill Berkson's *Shining Leaves.* When Jim Dine responded with understated cover art for Ron Padgett and Tom Clark's *Bun,* wittily making use of a photo of a bagel, we got nervous about getting the background (burnt almond?) right. Ditto, Jim Rosenquist's psychedelic cover for Peter Schjeldahl's *Dreams.*

Sometimes serious errors in the runs. Kenward Elmslie's *Girl Machine* was mis-bound and upside-down. Back to the shop. Donna Dennis's mysterious cover for Lewis's *Moving Thru Air* was printed on limp cover stock, losing all edge and clarity. Re-do. We had standards. The most important thing was pleasing the poets and artists themselves. I mistakenly had Joe Brainard's cover drawing for Lee Harwood's *Man With Blue Eyes* (our very first venture) printed on blue paper. Joe had assumed it would be printed on white but in typical Joe-fashion was gracious (and amused) about it.

Photographs were often an option. A cover designed by Donna Dennis for *3 American Tantrums* by Michael Brownstein features an emaciated yogin. Photographs of Joe Brainard at various stages of childhood grace the serialized *I Remember, I Remember More* and *More I Remember.* Limited signed editions were a point of pride.

My own writing was undergoing shifts of attention and intention. Many writers of my generation were hybrids feeding off the branches of the *New American Poetry.* My earliest poems are confessional, soulful, questioning of American values. They move around the page. Poems from my last year at Bennington fashioned into a manuscript for graduation were denser, ponderous, ambiguous—sprung from dream, hints of relationship but distanced from palpable experience. Excessively muted in tone and atmosphere, they seem remote now, as if filtered through gauze. Serial poems of Spicer and Blaser were an influence. Yeats and Stevens, Pound's 'Cathay' still haunted the premises. 'The DeCarlo Lots' felt genuine—a steadier hand and sound moving in there. Then Ted Berrigan burst in haranguing, breaking the narratives, taking issue with 'message.' Look to the painters. Words were things as Gertrude Stein proclaimed. It was easy for me to fall in love with Frank O'Hara's poetry. Philip Whalen's. The Surrealist antics were a kick to late-night collaborations, *corps exquis.*

The education continued along, to paraphrase Whalen. I got looser, dumber, more playful, writing down things I overheard, read, names of people, places, snippets from the radio, the street. O'Hara's 'Personism' manifesto was affecting as an antidote to Charles Olson's 'Projective Verse,' which was potent as well. Cut-up à la Burroughs. Berrigan's *Sonnets*. I was also reading the work of all my new poetry friends who were regularly walking into the living room any hour of the day or night. Also giving readings, organizing and running countless poetry events which hosted many elders, being drawn more and more into oral/aural performative possibilities for myself, inventing 'modal structures,' experimenting with tape cut-ups, using music and film with readings, and had begun some tentative musical collaboration. (I was an early—though brief—student of Lamonte Young's in 1970.)

By the late sixties the Viet Nam War had escalated. An estimated 550,000 troops were in Southeast Asia by 1969. The Tet offensive was a serious setback, discrediting the American government's optimistic and false reports. By the time of Nixon's illegal bombing of Cambodia in 1970, the Mai Lai Massacre, and gruesome casualties all around, the anti-war movement was at its height of engagement. St. Mark's was a hotbed of political activity that many of us became more consumed by in the late 60s/early 70s.

I began working with John Giorno on various provocative 'cultural interventions 'including street works, dial-a-poem. Several of us, in cahoots with the Yippies, participated in cultural activism around the Chicago Seven trial. Allen Ginsberg and I started our demonically active 'spiritual marriage' (as he called it) which began by chanting Hindu mantras in Daley Park in Chicago and resulted in the founding of the Jack Kerouac School of Disembodied Poetics at Naropa Institute (now University) in Boulder, Colorado, in 1974. I had visited the Tail of The Tiger Tibetan center in Vermont in 1970 and begun Tibetan Buddhist practice.

Life and focus were already changing by the time Lewis left for the West Coast in 1970. We were able to keep the press going in spite of our separation, stayed friendly, mutually supportive, and consulted one another concerning our continuing Angel Hair productions, now literally from two coasts. We spawned further publishing ventures with new partners and situations: United Artists, Songbird Editions, Rocky Ledge, Erudite Fangs. Obviously a major consequence of Angel Hair's publishing debut books and pamphlets and other items was the launching of an array of young experimental writers, including ourselves, onto the scene and into the official annals as second-generation New York School poets. A handy moniker, it doesn't cover the entire territory. Of course the magazine was a project of friendships, artistic collaboration, which are defining qualities of 'New York School.' Yet our project mixed up East and West coast scenes and juxtaposed them in an unusual and appealing context. We were also making up on the spot, stumbling along improvisationally.

In retrospect, *Angel Hair* seems a seed syllable that unlocked various energetic post-modern and post-New American Poetry possibilities, giving a younger generation cognizance that you can take your work, literally, into your own hands. You don't have to wait to be discovered. And so-called ephemera, lovingly and painstakingly produced, have tremendous power. They signify meticulous human attention and intelligence, like the outline of a hand in a Cro-Magnon cave.

Yet with the overwhelming availability of information—everything known, nothing concealed—that we have today through more and more complex technologies, I wonder if Lewis and I would go about our press now in quite the manner. With the same naive enthusiasm and optimism? I like to think so. We gave away our magazine and books, sent them out into the void. We saw little income from bookstores, many of which never even responded. But how much more pleasurable to visit Donna Dennis in her studio, discuss collage versions for Jim Carroll's *4 Ups & 1 Down*, than generate computer art at a solitary 'work station.' Or vie and hustle constantly in the competitive world of grants.

When we published a pamphlet it was a grand occasion. We celebrated all week when Ted Berrigan's *The Sonnets* was picked up by Grove Press. It would seem in the new millennium poets have to hide their successes from one another. Envy, literary 'politics,' who's in, who's out—concerns seemingly tangential to the work itself cloud the atmosphere. The early years were magical. Unself-conscious about who we were and what we were doing, we were our own distraction culture.

We weren't thinking about career moves or artistic agendas. We weren't in the business of creating a literary mafia or codifying a poetics. There were no interesting models for that kind of life. We talked about poetry constantly, wrote a lot, worked nonstop on the magazine and press. It was the most interesting and smartest thing we could be doing. We created a world in which we were purveyors, guardians, impresarios of a little slice of poetry turf, making things, plugging in our youth, offering the gift of ourselves to help keep the ever-expanding literary scene a lively place. And it was.

BEAT PUBLISHING: SMALL PRESSES

LAWRENCE FERLINGHETTI AND ROBERT DANA (INTERVIEW DATE 1986)

SOURCE: Ferlinghetti, Lawrence, and Robert Dana. "Lawrence Ferlinghetti." *Against the Grain: Interviews with Maverick American Publishers,* pp. 87-112. Iowa City: University of Iowa Press, 1986.

In the following interview, Ferlinghetti discusses his life and literary career, including the creation and history of City Lights bookstore and publishing company.

Lawrence Ferlinghetti, in a brief partnership with Peter Martin, founded City Lights bookstore and publishing company in San Francisco in 1953. The publication of Allen Ginsberg's *Howl,* and the trial of City Lights on obscenity charges, resulted in a landmark judicial ruling against censorship, and in national prominence for the publisher and the writers of the so-called Beat Generation.

In addition to Ginsberg, Gregory Corso, and Jack Kerouac, City Lights authors include Kenneth Patchen, Malcolm Lowry, Edward Dahlberg, Julian Beck, and Antonin Artaud.

Mr. Ferlinghetti was educated at the University of North Carolina and holds an M.A. in art from Columbia and a *Doctorat de l'Université* in art from the Sorbonne. In July 1981, the loft offices of City Lights Bookstore, where this conversation took place, were hung with more than a dozen of the publisher's canvases, some of them very recent. A well-known poet, Ferlinghetti is also the author of more than a dozen books, including *Pictures of the Gone World, A Coney Island of the Mind,* and *The Populist Manifestos.*

[Dana]: *You said, when I talked to you earlier on the phone, that you're "on leave." What's that mean?*

[Ferlinghetti]: Well, I'm painting. See, these are all my paintings.

I noticed them on my way in. Does that mean you're giving yourself more to painting these days than to publishing? Or writing?

Oh yeah.

Why is that?

I have a co-editor here, Nancy Peters. The one that did the *Literary San Francisco* book. She's the main editor here. She's the brains of the outfit.

Is there some reason that you're moving away from publishing?

Well, there are just a lot of other things I want to do. The business doesn't leave time enough to do them all, so . . .

When did you get interested in painting? Didn't you do an M.A. at . . . ?

The paintings on this wall are from the fifties. I've been painting a long time.

You did an M.A. at Columbia on Ruskin and Turner, didn't you?

Yeah.

How did that all start? The interest in painting.

Well, I was on the GI Bill in Paris at the Sorbonne, and I was going to an art school at night, and two, three days a week. That little black and white one there, I did in those days.

Does your move toward painting reflect the discontent with American poetry expressed in your manifestos recently?

Well, no, I think it's the other way around. The manifestos really enunciate what I wanted to happen with the Pocket Poets series.

What you wanted to happen with the Pocket Poets series?

Yeah. Well, it's what we're still *trying* to make happen. There can't be a revolution when there isn't one. For instance, in the fifties, when we published the Beat writers first, there was this whole group of writers that no one was publishing. Now, if J hadn't been in India . . .

James Laughlin?

Yeah. If he hadn't been in India in the fifties, he probably would have picked up on all these properties. Like Ginsberg had sent Laughlin poems before *Howl.*

Oh, he had?

And when I published *Howl,* JL wrote me and said, "Ginsberg suddenly got good." Well, I mean this is strictly *my* point of view. I don't know if J will agree with me or not, but he was in India editing *Perspective USA.* He left New Directions in the hands of other people. I mean he was still the owner, but he had other editors there while he was away. I think they sort of had different tastes than he did. I've never discussed this with him, and I don't know whether this is true or not.

All I know is that in the fifties there was this hiatus when no one was publishing this hot group of writers. Grove Press didn't exist yet. This was, say, 1953. So that's when we rushed into the gap. And New Directions was always my model and ideal as a publisher. JL is the greatest of the contemporary publishers. Of the publishers of the avant-garde, or of belle-lettres, or the modern classics. There's no one else that can compare with him.

Well, you're going to come pretty close.

The quality of his list, you know. And I never dreamt that I would ever get published by New Directions.

How did you happen to get published by New Directions?

Well, *A Coney Island of the Mind* was a book that I wrote sort of all at once. I didn't even have time to submit any of them to magazines. I never had submitted any poems to magazines, and that's unusual. Usually an unknown poet gets his first book published by getting poems in separate magazines, and then he goes to some book editor and says, "Look here, this poem has been published in *Harper's,* and this one's been published in the *Podunk Review,* and . . ."

That's right, ". . . and I've got a lot of boilerplate."

And so that makes it something you can list on your title page and blah, blah, blah. *Coney Island* I just . . . New Directions had always been my ideal when I was a kid in New York, so there was no question in my mind where to send it.

Did you know Laughlin at all at the time? You'd never met him?

I was just an unknown. One of the thousand unknown poets, ten thousand . . . and he'd just gotten back from India not long before. This was 1958, '57 sometime.

That's not long after you started the bookstore.

We started the bookstore in June of '53. And we published our first books in '54. I published my own first book as number one in the Pocket Poets series, *Pictures of the Gone World.* And then we did Kenneth Rexroth, Kenneth Patchen, and *Howl* was number four. Then there was *True Minds,* by Marie Ponsot, who is now being published by Knopf.

When you published your own first book, did you think you were launching a publishing company or your career as a poet, or both?

Well, yeah. When I started the bookstore with Peter Martin—Peter Martin is a book dealer in New York. He has the New Yorker bookstore. It was really his idea to have the first all-paperbound bookstore in the country. There weren't any trade paperbacks then. There was no place to get quality pocket books. They were merchandised like toothpaste in the drugstore, and the people didn't know what they had.

Right.

You could get Avon books and Penguins and Signet, and that's about all there was. European publishers have always had a paperback. You could read books in paperback for modest prices. But in this country paperback publishing didn't start until the mid-fifties. There was Penguin, but Doubleday Anchor was the first quality paperback, in about '54, '53, somewhere in there. And New Directions didn't go into paperback until late in the fifties.

Well, New Directions did have that Poet-of-the-Month series they farmed out to small presses in the late fifties.

But mainly all New Directions books were hardcover 'til about '57? '56?

Yes, even the New Classics series were hardback.

I was very surprised when I heard right back from them in '58. He said, "I was just writing to you, and then I found your manuscript on my desk." And I sent it in cold without any introduction by anybody, no letter of recommendation. I didn't know anybody.

Well, that's the way it's supposed to happen, right?

I have a suspicion that Kenneth Rexroth was advising Laughlin at that time. Because I know that when Laughlin was out of the country Rexroth was hollering and screaming about what was happening here.

In San Francisco?

Yeah. And trying to get New York interested, get the East Coast establishment interested. We were doing poetry and jazz at The Cellar, and Kenneth was sounding off about, "Hey, there's a lot happening here and no one's paying any attention," and he must have written Laughlin about it.

When you started the bookstore, did you think you were going into the book business or the publishing business, or both?

Both.

So you really knew you were going into publishing?

Right from the beginning. My partner had no idea of that. In fact, he sold out and went to New York after the first year. He had published a little magazine, sort of an early pop-culture magazine focused on films. It was called *City Lights* magazine. It was . . . they didn't call it Xerox in those days, it was something-o-graph.

Multigraph.

There were about four or five issues of just a small pamphlet stapled together. But he wasn't interested. He was very surprised when, after he'd left, he found out we were publishing books. That's what I had in mind, because I'd come from Europe, where the bookstores and the publishers are often the same company. The big publishers in France—I'm not sure whether they're bookstores or publishers first, like Gallimard. And in Italy it's the same way.

So did you have that in mind when you came back from Europe?

Yeah.

Why did you want to go into publishing?

Well, it's hard to say.

I know while you were in high school you did some work in a printshop in Bronxville.

Oh yeah, I did. I got involved with printing at a very early age, and I always liked printing.

Was that because your foster-father had a big library?

Oh yeah, he had a classical library. Half of it was in Latin, some in Greek. He was a self-educated classical scholar in the old Southern tradition. Old families in the South would send their children to France to be educated, and so forth. By the time he came along, the family was fairly impoverished, but the classical tradition still existed in his family. All the books were in his house. This was in Natchez, Mississippi. Well, it's all in that biography of mine by Neeli Cherkovski.

But did he do anything or say anything that led you to . . . ?

Oh, yeah, he was a big influence on me to general literacy.

General literacy?

It was like *The Autocrat of the Breakfast-Table.* Oliver Wendell Holmes. When you came to the dinner table or the breakfast table, you were supposed to be able to converse intelligently and even wittily.

Then one had to have some source material.

He was liable to say, "Young man, you've been to school, . . ." Later, "Young man, you've been to college. Who was Demosthenes?" Or something like that. Or, "What did Horatius say when he was crossing the bridge?" Oh, and he used to give me silver dollars for memorizing poems, which I would have to recite at the dinner table.

Well, some people would say that should have turned you off of poetry and off of literature.

No. I would meekly pipe up with some line—say, I was about nine years old—and he would say, "No, no, young man." Then he would launch forth in his historinic recitations like Mark Twain. In fact, Mark Twain was his hero. He dressed like Mark Twain. He was not from Missouri, but he was sort of like Mark Twain, same style of man, very handsome. It's hard to impart this tradition to a generation today. Kids are not interested.

But he never said to you what Pound said to Laughlin: "Go home and start a publishing house." Or "Go out and be a poet."

Oh no. But he always wanted to be a writer himself. He never made it because he had to . . . I don't know. He got involved in making money, I guess.

That's a big diversion.

You can't do both. Our publishing company really doesn't make money and never set out to make money. It's survived, and broken even all these years, but it's always . . .

How much money did you put into the publishing end of it when you started?

Five hundred dollars.

Five hundred dollars?

I had five hundred dollars, and Peter Martin had five hundred dollars. That's what we started the store on.

So did you buy mostly books or . . . ?

Yeah.

Well, how did you finance a first book out of that?

We couldn't get the door closed. As soon as we got the place open, it was open 'til midnight seven days a week right from the beginning. It still is. There was no place to buy paperback books them. Now, of course, there are thousands of paperback bookstores.

Another thing about the publishing end . . . I read that a successful publisher, like some of the big publishers, not necessarily big ones, but usually in their history they had a big hit in one of their very first books. And that was the case with *Howl*, which was the fourth book we published. Luckily, we were busted by the police, who gave us all this free national publicity.

You sent that book out of the country to be printed, didn't you?

It was printed in England, yeah. In those days, the exchange was such that it was much cheaper to get books printed in England.

Did you start out printing them in England?

Yeah.

Your own book was printed in England? The first one?

No. My very first one was set here locally by a printer named David Ruff, and it was printed here. Set and printed by hand. But after the first one, they were all printed at Villiers Publications in London.

So Howl *was not the first one to be printed abroad?*

No. I think it was the third one. No one bothered the Patchen and the Rexroth and the Marie Ponsot. Then Customs first seized *Howl* as an obscene book, and then the local police raided the bookstore.

Cherkovski says in his biography that you sent a manuscript of Howl *to the ACLU before you printed it, is that correct?*

Yeah.

You did?

Yeah. We knew exactly what we were doing. We figured we might very well get busted for it, but in those days it was important to take a stand on the question of censorship. This was the McCarthy Era.

So, in a sense, you deliberately started out to challenge the law.

Sure. Well, it wasn't so much that. We wanted to publish what we wanted to publish, and if they wanted to make something of it we were willing to . . .

You were willing to challenge the law.

Yes. But we took the precaution of making sure the ACLU would defend us—ahead of time. That's why we submitted it to them.

Well, this is an academic question . . .

See, we wanted to make sure that they would defend us, because if you didn't have the ACLU to defend you, a little business like ours couldn't have made it.

Would you not *have published . . . ?*

That was one of McCarthy's main tactics, and the tactics of the government in persecuting the underground press in the sixties, the counterculture press in the sixties—one of the main tactics was to involve them in legal proceedings and make them go broke from the cost of the legal defense.

What would you have done if the ACLU had said, "No, we won't"?

Well, I don't know. Hard to say. Obviously, we didn't have any money at all to hire a lawyer. As it turned out, we not only had the ACLU, but we had Jake Erlich, who was a famous criminal lawyer who smelled the amount of publicity he could get out of the case and rushed to the defense.

How long did the case run?

Oh, it ran about three weeks one summer. The summer of '55, I guess it was. There's a whole book on the subject called *Horn on 'Howl.'* Horn was the name of the judge.

How did you feel about it by the time it was over?

That opened up the whole set of questions which Grove Press was later able to use for publishing D. H. Lawrence and Henry Miller. It established the legal precedent that a work had to have redeeming social significance, and if it did have redeeming social significance, then the question of obscenity could not even be raised, according to the judge.

Do you think that principle's in danger at present?

Yeah, it's quite possible. It's a continuing battle. It's a continuing battle in every age, whether it's . . . It's a battle against the police mentality, which is a continuing thing the world over. It's a little bit like what they say about ecology: "Every victory is temporary. Every defeat is permanent." Well, it's not necessarily permanent. There can always be another court case. But, yeah, today, it seems to me . . . Well, the newest book we just published, *UnAmerican Activities,* it's a history of government subversion of the underground press in the sixties and seventies, and it brings it up to date with the Reagan administration's latest attempts to water down the restrictions on wiretapping and search-and-seizure regulations, making it easier to do those things without telling anybody. All those things can be done very quietly without anyone realizing you've done it. Just change a little administrative rule here and there, and you can have another McCarthy pretty easy.

Yes. The rules the game is played by can make a lot of difference.

They sure do.

Can we go back to France for a moment?

Yeah.

Is it true you found a Prevert poem on a paper tablecloth?

Oh, sure. I was in the Normandy invasion in the navy. And then I was in Brittany, along the coast, after the invasion. I was in a few towns along the coast, like St. Brieuc and St. Malo. I was in Cherbourg. And I remember finding part of a Prevert poem on one of those paper tablecloths, the kind they always had in the cheap cafes?

How did you know it was his? Or did you not know it was his?

Oh, I didn't know it was his at the time.

It was just a poem in French that interested you.

Yeah. See, he had been an underground poet, really, during the German occupation, and people passed his poems around. The French passed them around. Before they were ever printed in a book. And then I got ahold of one of his books during that same month. But I remember I lost that one, and it wasn't 'til I got back to France several years later on the GI Bill that I got the book again. By then there were something like 300,000 in print.

Did you then meet Prevert?

No, I never met him. I wrote him a lot of letters, and he never answered.

How old was he then?

Oh, he died about ten years ago now. I think he was . . . He couldn't have been more than forty-five at the end of the Second World War, in the late forties. Maybe he was forty years old. He did write me a postcard from the Riviera many years later.

Was this after you had published Paroles?

Yeah. He sent me a two-line postcard.

What did it say?

I remember he had an American friend who had taken care of one of his children, and she had translated a lot of his poems, and he was always insisting that she be his translator, except they were absolutely atrocious translations.

Well, I won't ask who she was, then.

I don't know what her name was. I don't know whether she was an ex-mistress of his or what. Probably a typical literary situation, if she was.

And when Penguin wanted to publish the same book—in fact they did, they took our City Lights edition and made it a Penguin. The chief editor of Penguin was Tony Godwin in those days, and he was very enthusiastic about it, and when . . .

Now, you did those translations, right?

Yeah. And when Prevert insisted that they use his friend's translations, Penguin said, "Well, we'll just drop the whole project. We're not going to *deal* with *those* translations." So then Prevert said, okay, use mine.

What attracted you in that poem you found on the tablecloth, that stuck by you all those years?

Generally, Prevert's poetry is very visual, which is really maybe the most obvious characteristic in my own poetry. It's super-visual poetry. Later, I think he got a little bit too superficial; he really didn't develop. He became more and more musical. A lot of his poems were made into songs, and he became very popular, but he didn't grow as a poet. He became lighter instead of more profound.

Instead of denser?

His later books really didn't interest me very much. It was just the one book called *Paroles*.

Later, on your second trip to France, you seemed to have picked up on a group of writers, including Artaud.

I started reading Artaud in '63. The translator is here in North Beach still. Jack Hirschman. He was the translator of our volume. Just saw him up the street.

Out of all the people you could've picked from that group of French writers, why did you choose to publish Artaud?

Well, he was not my type of writer, but he's a very important revolutionary writer. I don't think New Directions would have published Artaud. He was too . . .

Probably not.

For one thing, he's a junkie, or he was. Heavy on drugs, and quite a madman. Of course, when you've spent many, many years in an insane . . . in a mental institution . . . obviously . . . This book was the first Artaud in this country, the first Artaud published in America.

Then you must have thought his revolution was . . .

It was very important to the French theatre and to French poetry in general. It happens the translator . . . even looks like Artaud. He sits up in the Puccini Cafe all day long.

What did you think that Artaud might introduce into . . . ?

Have you read Artaud?

Very little.

Well, I mean you can't ask me a question like that if you haven't read any Artaud. I mean it's like trying to . . . Am I supposed to give a three-hour lecture on Artaud to tell you what he's all about?

No, about a five-minute . . .

That's impossible.

. . . statement about what you saw there back in 1963.

Why do you pick on this Artaud book? Why not any of the other seventy-five books?

I don't know. The Artaud is a special thing.

Well, all books are special. What about Julian Beck? Do you know Living Theatre?

No, I don't.

Living Theatre was in New York City for many years before it was run out of the country by the Internal Revenue Service. They padlocked the Living Theatre in lower New York. Living Theatre went to live in Europe, consequently. And between these two books you have the most important things that were happening in American theatre or in international theatre in the fifties and sixties, I'd say. They both had an enormous influence on American avant-garde theatre.

Are you referring to breaking down the walls between audiences and players?

Artaud was one of the direct and most powerful influences on the Living Theatre. It's a madman's vision, but it's not. I'm calling him a madman, but that's just from a straight point of view. What he's saying is what some of the psychiatrists

in the sixties were saying; it's not the poets that are mad but the society that's mad. And this would be one of Artaud's main messages. So he may seem to you to be a raving madman, but he's actually . . . because he doesn't conform, he's much saner than the person working in the bank or on the railroad.

You're talking about the . . .

I mean, this is the tradition of the outsider which Colin Wilson outlined in his book. Going back to François Villon, Baudelaire, and Edgar Allan Poe. Whitman considered himself an outsider. Ginsberg, the outsider. The poet as the alienated bearer of Eros. I have that in one of the *Populist Manifestos.*

When you started City Lights, did you have that clear a perspective on . . . ?

You see, another aspect is Artaud as an anarchist, politically. And the poet as anarchist is an old and honorable tradition. As the bearer of Eros, he represents the free individual, the free spirit, so the State is his natural enemy. Any repression by the State or by anyone is the enemy of the poet. This naturally puts the poet in the alienated position.

When you started City Lights, did you think of yourself as an anarchist press?

Of course. It still is. Did you read this *Literary San Francisco* book? You ought to get a copy, because a lot of these questions you're asking are in there.

Well, it's one thing to read things, it's another to hear you say them.

Well, it's written better than I can say it off the top of my head. The whole history of our publishing and bookstore is in that book, so you can get a lot of facts out of it.

Who's had the greatest influence on City Lights besides yourself, directly or indirectly?

J Laughlin. And Rexroth, indirectly. J's never advised us to publish such and such a book or suggested we publish such and such a book. Generally, I saw his press as a model.

But Laughlin says, "Well, yes, I listened to Kenneth Rexroth. I listened to Gary Snyder when he said publish so and so." Did Ginsberg, for example, ever suggest people to you?

Oh yeah, definitely. Allen tends to proselytize his whole gang. "Publish me, publish all my friends."

Is it true you turned down Kerouac's On the Road *once?*

No, I never had a chance at *On the Road,* unfortunately. Jack was way ahead of me. We were much too small for his possibilities, even at that time. No, I never had a chance at *On the Road.* He offered me *other* books. We did *Book of Dreams.* Later we did *Poems,* and I have an unpublished Kerouac manuscript, over a hundred pages, called "Poems All Sizes." The original manuscript.

Are you going to publish it soon?

His widow won't allow us to publish it.

Oh.

But I won't send it to her, either. I've got the only copy.

Well, it's a standoff.

Yes.

Who else besides Ginsberg had any direct influence on what you published?

Well, Ginsberg didn't *have* very much influence on what we published, because I've never published across the board. We've never wanted to be known as exclusively the publisher of the Beat poets. I didn't publish the Beat poets across the board. I turned down the manuscript of *The Naked Lunch.* That's the one that I did have a chance at. Burroughs' *Naked Lunch.*

Why did you turn it down?

Naked Lunch is about this junkie. And the heroin addict is a particularly Burroughs consciousness, which sees no love in the world, no joy. And it's really a very fierce consciousness which, at the time, I wasn't much interested in. As you see Burroughs' later works, you see how this first book fits in in his great worldview, which is something else. But, at the time, having just the first book to go by, and even then it was only scattered pages which Ginsberg had assembled, there was just this junkie's story, this junkie consciousness, and it's a matter if you like to eat shit or not. That's what . . . I mean that's what they call junk, and if you like to, if you have a taste for that, fine, but at the time I wasn't interested.

If the book came to you now would you publish it?

Well, by hindsight, when you see the body of work around it now, that's different.

Suppose it came in, just as an isolated item, would you still turn it down?

It's possible. I don't know.

You once wanted to do a sampler of Marianne Moore's work.

She was willing to go along with it, but her publisher, Viking, wouldn't let her.

Oh, that's what happened.

Yeah. I had the selection all made and everything and spent a lot of time corresponding with her publisher, I think it was Viking, but they wouldn't let her do it.

Marianne Moore seems like an odd choice for City Lights.

Well, no. She's a very important poet. Her language is a great influence on a lot of modern poets.

But, philosophically she would be at an extreme from somebody like, say, Ginsberg.

She likes baseball. That's what I mean. I wasn't publishing in the Pocket Poets series just one type of poetry.

You were looking for a range of interesting writers.

I mean, *True Minds.* Did you ever see *True Minds,* by Marie Ponsot?

No.

Well, this is Catholic poetry. She's a Catholic with a capital "C." Her new book is just coming out from Knopf. It's her first book since *True Minds.* It's around here somewhere. It's called *Admit Impediment,* which comes from the same Shakespearean line as the title of the first book: "Let me not to the marriage of true minds admit impediment."

"Let me not to the marriage of true minds admit impediment." This is as far as you can get from Ginsberg. I mean, . . . In fact, that was sort of the principle of . . . I wanted to do that, have a very wide-ranging, catholic list. Small "c" catholic.

Right.

For instance, in the bookstore there, right below you, we'll have the *National Review* sitting right next to the publications of the Communist Revolutionary party. Or we'll have *Time* magazine right next to a Marxist journal, or something like that.

I see.

So what else in the Pocket Poets series? I mean Ginsberg was not very interested in a poet like Prevert. For one thing, so much of the Ginsberg school is homosexual. He's not much interested in heterosexual poets.

Among his close friends that he always pushed, I never published a book of poetry by Gary Snyder with Philip Whalen. I didn't publish any books of poetry by either of them, even though we had some separate poems by Whalen in the *City Lights* journal. I never felt like publishing a book of their poems. I did publish Gary's prose. And that's the way it went. *I* never published whatever *he* proposed.

It sounds as though you were "cautiously resistant" to that influence.

The trouble is, with most small presses, they publish one clique, like "Our Gang." You could say that's what Don Allen does. It's all one school of poetry.

Or, as we used to say, "a stable," with poets as horses.

That's usually what lowers the political position of the press. Because it lowers its credibility, it seems to me.

But it also has the effect of insuring, for a certain period, the flow of a particular group's work, right?

Oh, sure. Well, another thing, J Laughlin has a principle that when he takes an author, he'll publish *everything* that author produces. Since he published my *Coney Island,* he's published ten or eleven books of mine. Whatever I offered, . . . he has done the judicious editing, . . . he went ahead with it. He really backs up the authors that he picks. He backed them up, right for their whole career. I've never done that. Ginsberg's the only one where I've published every book. I've turned down books by a lot of other authors who wanted us to publish a second book of theirs.

Do you think that . . . ?

Well, for one thing, New Directions is a much bigger operation than ours. I realized in the sixties that there was room for a West Coast-type New Directions, or a West Coast Grove Press. There's a big vacuum that still exists out here for such a press.

But it would have been a matter of becoming a full-time businessman, a full-time editor, and not doing anything else. I could have had a big press or a big, long list like Grove Press by now. I didn't feel like spending that much time on it and . . .

Richard Kostelanetz in a recent article criticized you for not being experimental enough.

Me personally?

The press, City Lights.

Well, Richard Kostelanetz will criticize anyone that will make a sensation. If he can make a sensation by criticizing the pope for wearing his beanie backwards, he'll do it.

Are you saying he's wrong?

Well, no, not necessarily. Why doesn't he send me these great experimental works he wants me to publish. I just haven't run across them. It's hard to publish a book without having the manuscript.

Are you saying that poetry seems to you now generally less experimental?

No. It isn't less experimental. But whether it's great or not, that's something else. I mean, for instance, there's plenty of experimental poetry being written in the techniques of Ginsberg's style. I don't know, have you read any of his books on poetics?

I try not to read too much about what he says about poetics.

Oh, it's very important. A very important body of beautiful theory on poetry.

Well, I have my own ideas about critical theory.

In other words, you don't know what I'm talking about.

I think I know what you're talking about.

What?

I just read what you had to say about his . . . what is it? The Disembodied School of Poetics and their interiority and the relationship between one's interior self and breath and what did you call it in French? Not laissez-faire, but . . . ?

Well, there's a very important book down there called *Improvised Poetics,* and it's worth reading. The trouble with Ginsberg's followers, . . . mainly you could say it's the Graphic Consciousness School of Poetry, where the form is defined as a graphic consciousness. So you have a lot of practitioners in the Ginsberg school that define the poem in that manner. Like Philip Whalen and Gary Snyder, for instance. Philip Whalen will have a poem which will be titled "Take 7-21-81," and it will be what ran through his mind at a certain moment on that date. And you may have "Take 2" for the same date. And maybe he spoke it into a tape recorder. Or maybe he wrote it down. Anyway, that's the take, and that's a poem set on the page as a poem. Usually with slant lines, and with *cd* as an abbreviation for *could* or *wd* for *would.* Just the mannerisms that Robert Creeley developed, for instance. The poem as a graphic consciousness. It's a very valid concept. It assumes that consciousness is basically poetic, which is not necessarily so.

But, besides that point, if you have a genius mind and a really interesting consciousness setting down what's going through his mind, transcribing as directly as he can what comes from his consciousness that moment, then you get a very interesting piece of writing. Because when mind is comely, what mind says is going to be comely or interesting.

And so with Ginsberg. Ginsberg has this omnivorously packrat intelligence. It consumes information omnivorously, and whatever comes out of his mind is very interesting because he's got a very unusual consciousness. Whereas when younger followers of Ginsberg use the same technique, not having interesting minds in the first place, what comes out isn't very interesting. So you get enormous, dreary amounts of modern poetry following this technique.

Well, you're almost talking about the law of the computer: Garbage in, garbage out.

No. It's not necessarily garbage, but I wish Kostelanetz would send me some of these great experimental works that I refuse to publish. If you see him, tell him to send them.

Another thing I would never answer . . . I get a lot of attacks not only in the press but on my own poetry. I think the best rule is never to answer a critic unless he's right.

Can we talk about the National Endowment? What do you think its influence has been on the small-press scene?

I think it's compromised practically every small press in the country. It's a matter of what Albert Camus called "guilt by complicity." Including you're going to get this story published in the *American Poetry Review* . . . ?

Not necessarily.

. . . which, I believe, in the past has been supported by grants from the National Endowment for the Arts.

Yes, it has.

And this is compromising to any publisher, to let itself be subsidized by *any* source, particularly government. When Albert Camus talked about "guilt by complicity," he was talking about under the German occupation. Who collaborated with the Germans, or who didn't collaborate but didn't say anything. Let's say like the good German who didn't say anything under Hitler.

Collaboration by omission.

I mean, you went along with it. Like, if you go along with Ronald Reagan's new rationalization for supporting countries who have no human rights, then you're guilty by complicity. So if the small press takes money from the U.S. government, say, under Reagan, by complicity you're guilty of supporting this policy which ignores human rights around the world. To go back to the Vietnam days, so many little presses I knew, supposedly dissident presses and writers, took money from the National Endowment for the Arts, a branch of the U.S. government, which with its other hand was killing millions of people overseas in the middle of the war.

So you're not talking about the quality of a press's production, but its moral and political quality.

Yeah! I don't care what they publish with that money, it's . . . George Hitchcock was a good case in point. George Hitchcock had a press, what was it called now . . . ?

You're talking about Kayak Press?

Kayak. He received several grants from the National Endowment for the Arts, and George was a communist in the thirties. He was an anarchist. I don't know about the communist part. That was before I got here, but he was very radical. He was an anarchist who made his living as a gardener. And when the House Un-American Activities Committee came to San Francisco in its last visit, in the late fifties—no, in the sixties—he was called up in front of the committee and they asked him what he did and he said he worked underground. Then later he said, "with roots." He was a gardener, and he told 'em to fuck off, and he wouldn't answer a single question. In fact, it was at the San Francisco City Hall, and that's what all the witnesses told the committee more or less, and the committee never came back. They were really sort of laughed out of town.

But now George, ten years later, took these grants from the NEA. And he justified one grant by offering a five-hundred-dollar prize for the best poem on Fidel Castro. He was publishing radical literature financed by the government, which is one argument for taking the money and running. Take the money and run. Or you could take the money and build bombs to blow up the johns at the University of California, which another grantee did. That's the revolutionary argument for taking the money. That's an opportunist, pragmatic rationalization, whereas from the strictly moral point of view or the point of view of Albert Camus, you're compromising your press.

In fact, I'm always very conscious of my connections with particularly French and some Italian intellectuals who might read in some American publication that City Lights Press just received a grant from the NEA. They wouldn't see all the rationalizations and the fact that we were allowed to publish anything we wanted with that money. All they would see is that City Lights Press took government money, which is the same government that is carrying on an imperialist foreign policy around the world, et cetera.

So, as far as you're concerned, it doesn't matter how many small presses come into existence as a result of government grants or how many go out of existence as a result of the loss of government grants. You don't think that money has, by and large, had any positive effect.

Well, I know editors who did very well on it. I know some local editors who put out some of the most soporific issues you could imagine who lived very well for a number of years on these grants.

In your view, it's been largely a kind of gravy train?

Sure. No doubt about it.

With negative moral and political implications.

And people have gotten fat. Maybe that's why there isn't any poetry with any real heart to it being published these days. I mean it's the same in the other arts. It's the same in painting. It's the same in sculpture.

What about a press like Blue Wind over in Berkeley?

I don't know Blue Wind.

They've been publishing people like Anselm Hollo, for example, who did Red Cats *for you years ago.*

What's revolutionary about that?

I didn't say it was revolutionary. I just said, "What about that?"

He's a real competent translator and poet, but he's been in the university world all these years. I wouldn't say that was publishing someone new and . . . He's a real nice man, but he was very much originally influenced by the American Beat poets and is continuing in that line. I don't see it as anything new, even though he's a very fine poet. If you're citing him as an example of the new and exciting works that Blue Wind Press is publishing, I don't know whether that's any argument for anything.

Well, they're publishing other poets too, members of the so-called Actualist group.

Well, I've read some of what you might call Actualist poetry, but I really didn't see very much exciting going on in it. It's a term that really doesn't mean anything. It's a very dumb term, actually.

What are your future plans for City Lights as a publishing house?

We have too many books lined up. We have a new version of Neil Cassady's *The First Third*. The authentic manuscript has finally turned up. Fawn Cassady, Neil Cassady's widow, recently sent me the version that should have been published in the first place, but which was lost for many years. So we have to reset Cassady's *First Third* completely. It'll be a completely new book. We have a lot of books on the back burner.

How many books, on the average, would you say you're publishing a year now?

Six to eight.

Six to eight a year?

Yeah.

Is that down from what you published in the past?

No, it's about what it always was. We're putting out a new journal starting this winter, called *Free Spirits*. Basically, it's a surrealist publication. It's going to be edited by American surrealists. Nancy Peters and Phil Lamantia are the West Coast editors. The editor in Chicago is Franklin Rosemont. He publishes a surrealist magazine called *Arsenal*. And then there's an East Coast editor named Paul Buell. And this *Free Spirits* will be an amalgam of surrealism, anarchism, and socialism. The subtitle of the magazine is going to be *Annals of the Insurgent Imagination*. It's a very politically committed magazine, but politics isn't the main thing.

Well, do you think there's something new in surrealism today that wasn't there twenty years ago?

Well, what American surrealists have you read?

Almost every poet you read employs surreal effects.

Oh, well, we're not talking about that.

So you're looking for a pure American surrealist?

Well, I'm not a member of the surrealist group myself. I was when I was in Paris when I wrote *Her*. *Her* was a surrealist novel. That was years ago.

Who are the chief American surrealist writers?

Philip Lamantia is the best known.

Then, in your view, you're still looking for the new and the revolutionary to publish.

Well, I mean, you don't want to publish the old. I'm not gonna publish Theocritus and Virgil at this point. If they had a new translation that was better than the old translation, I'd publish it.

Isn't it true that all revolutions finally grind down and become currency?

Well, I don't really use this word "revolutionary." You won't find it in any of our jacket blurbs or in this sheet here. I mean you really have to stay away from throwing a word like that around, because "revolutionary" can mean so many things to so many people.

What would you mean if you used it?

Well, I'm not using it.

Okay, how about "new"?

"Make it new." That's what Ezra Pound said.

How would you know the new if you saw it? Or where do you think the new will come from, if there is another round of newness?

That's an absurd question. It's like saying, "What's going to happen tomorrow?"

But there are contexts in which that would not be an absurd question, right?

Well, there are a lot of people who can answer it. Say "What's new?" and they'll give you a definition of new, but what's wrong with the dictionary definition?

I don't know.

I mean this is absurd. I mean what's going to happen tomorrow? First off, let's get rid of Reagan. You need a form of world socialism, with a central planned economy which has nothing to do with national boundaries. Ecologically planned economy, because capitalism is the most wasteful system that's ever been devised. Wasteful ecologically. It's wasted the face of the earth. It has to be nontotalitarian, supernationalistic central planning for the world's restructuring of the economy in general. Everyone laughs at Mitterand and thinks that Mitterand isn't going to have a chance, that the French economy can't possibly survive the transition to socialism under Mitterand. But I think they may be wrong. I certainly hope they're wrong, because I think Mitterand is right and Reagan's wrong.

So you're talking about a sort of world federalism.

Well, federalism is still a pretty mellow term, except it's based on national states. I mean nationalisms themselves have to go. Nationalism is certainly a barbaric hangover from earlier times. It's like states' rights had to go. It was part of the Civil War in this country to abolish states' rights. So that now it's the national rights that have to go. We're going to have world civil war unless the national rights go.

Boy, we're a hell of a long way from that, aren't we?

I mean, I don't have to pledge allegiance to the American flag. I feel just as much allegiance to the French flag or to the ecology flag or to the Buddha flag . . .

Well, a lot of countries don't share that view.

. . . or to the Marilyn Monroe flag.

So you think that literature and art can't change until some of these other changes occur? Or is it a two-way street?

That's what people publish for. They hope they're going to be able to change the consciousness enough to make things in the world better.

MICHAEL DUFF (ESSAY DATE AUGUST 1990)

SOURCE: Duff, Michael. "Manning the Barricades: City Lights Booksellers and Publishers." *Small Press: The Magazine and Book Review of Independent Publishing* (August 1990): 15, 20.

In the following essay, Duff discusses City Lights bookstore and press.

Almost a contradiction in terms, City Lights bookstore and press are successful business operations run by subjective anarchists and social libertarians. The bookstore, once the haunt of the Beat writers in the fifties and sixties and now a mecca for migrating tourists looking for the place where it all happened, has grown from a tiny one-room storefront—formerly a florist's shop—to an expanded three-room light-filled aerie for intellectuals. The bookstore opened its doors for the first time in June 1953 and in 1988 celebrated its thirty-fifth anniversary with a rollicking party in the Beat-Dionysian tradition of yore which spilled out of the bookstore and engulfed three nearby hallowed cafes—also made famous in the fifties: Vesuvio's, Tosca, and Specs. Heavily weighted to social theory, the bookstore has excellent fiction, poetry, and film sections. The press, started in 1955, has approximately one hundred titles in

ON THE SUBJECT OF...

NORMAN MAILER

An outspoken, controversial intellectual and celebrity, Norman Mailer is highly regarded for his prodigious ability as a novelist and social critic. Mailer's writing attempts to engage and reenact the major crises of the modern world to affect greater understanding of self and society, and is mirrored in reality by his active participation in national events. Mailer achieved sudden fame with his first novel, *The Naked and the Dead* (1948), still considered among his finest accomplishments along with the award-winning nonfiction novels *The Armies of the Night* (1968) and *The Executioner's Song* (1979). With Daniel Wolf and Edwin Fancher he cofounded the leftist newspaper *The Village Voice,* for which he wrote a regular column beginning in 1956. In "The White Negro," a frequently anthologized essay first published in 1957 by City Lights Press and later included in *Advertisements for Myself* (1959), Mailer considers African Americans, whom he views as capable of placing the needs of the self over those of society, as a model for the American hipster, a sinister character immune to traditional institutions of social control. An independent thinker who eschews identification with literary and political circles, Mailer has given forceful expression to the voice of alienation and disillusionment in postwar American society.

print today and includes such big sellers as Sam Shepard, Charles Bukowski, Jack Kerouac, and of course, the writer who put City Lights on the map, Allen Ginsberg.

Lawrence Ferlinghetti and coeditor Nancy Peters oversee this contemporary empire of the intellect from their offices above the bookstore. There are five members of the publishing staff. In addition to Ferlinghetti and Peters, there is acquisition editor Bob Sharrard and editor Amy Scholder as well as production designer Patricia Fujii. The bookstore, managed by Richard Berman, has half a dozen more employees (the bookstore hours are from 10:00 a.m. to 11:30 p.m.). From the beginning, the idea was to have a symbiotic relationship between the bookstore and the press. "The idea of the bookstore/publisher was conceived by Lawrence on the European model like Gallimard in France," Peters stated. "For the publisher it's helpful to have the store because then we are familiar with what readers want." Ferlinghetti believes that the press is an effective marketing tool for the bookstore and vice versa. "I have never understood why more bookstores didn't publish," he said. "Some years the bookstore carries the press; others, the press the bookstore." The radical social theory of symbiosis is paying off in simple capitalistic terms: The bookstore is thriving and the press is strong, issuing between ten and twelve books a year, with print runs of 2,000 to 5,000.

Even though City Lights is more successful today than ever before, it is still best known for what occurred more than thirty years ago. On March 25, 1957, copies of Allen Ginsberg's *Howl,* which City Lights was publishing and having printed in England, were seized by United States Customs as obscene. A few days later, Lawrence Ferlinghetti and his bookstore manager, Shigeyoshi Murao, were arrested. The ensuing trial with its attendant publicity catapulted an obscure poet, a very small press, and a tiny bookstore located in the heart of San Francisco's Italian North Beach neighborhood into the national headlines. Overnight that obscure poet became the spokesman for an alienated generation. City Lights Publishers became the house organ for the emerging Beat writers, and the bookstore became a haven for nonconformists of every persuasion.

As with countless other publishing houses, City Lights had been founded first as a small literary magazine, published by Peter D. Martin, an instructor at San Francisco State University. Ferlinghetti, who saw "The little Chaplin man as a pure anarchist, a subjective anarchist," was attracted by the magazine's title as well as its pop cultural contents. He submitted his translations of several Jacques Prévert poems (Ferlinghetti attended the Sorbonne after World War II on the GI Bill. His dissertation was on "The City as a Symbol in Modern Poetry"). Martin published the translations and the two men became friends. "It was Martin's idea to start this little pocket bookshop—there weren't any at the time. You couldn't find any [paperbacks] except at newsstands or drugstores where the operators didn't know a tube of toothpaste from a book," Ferlinghetti said. The two men hoped that the profit from the bookstore would enable them to continue to publish the magazine. Each partner put up $500 which, in those days, was enough to stock a bookstore. For the next couple of years, both magazine and bookstore struggled but managed to survive. Ferlinghetti wanted to expand the publishing end of the operation by issuing a Pocket Poets Series of books. In 1955 Ferlinghetti bought out Martin and became the sole proprietor of City Lights. Ferlinghetti's first publication was of his own poetry book, *Pictures of the Gone World,* number One in the Pocket Poets Series. Kenneth Rexroth and Kenneth Patchen were numbers Two and Three. *Howl* was number Four, and to date is the biggest seller with 700,000 copies in print, even though in recent years, as Sharrard pointed out, Ginsberg's sales have leveled off. Other writers of note in the Pocket Poets Series are Bob Kaufman, Diane Di Prima, Denise Levertov, William Carlos Williams, and Philip Lamantia, to name a few.

The group of outlaw dissenters, anarchists (subjective or otherwise), pacifists, and conscientious objectors now memorialized as the Beat Generation would not have been a generation at all, it could be argued, without Ferlinghetti and City Lights. As often happens with such success, however, what starts a press can later stop it. The label once affixed is hard to remove. The City Lights logo is now a part of pop culture iconography, attesting to the press and the bookstores' widespread recognition. Nonetheless, by the late seventies charges were made against City Lights that it was out of date, provincial, irrelevant—a press and bookstore whose importance was eclipsed by new attitudes and writing movements. Sharrard concurs that there has been a problem. "It was difficult to surmount our reputation as a Beat publisher. Our heroic era was in the fifties, but a press has to have a future." Ferlinghetti maintains that the criticisms are less than based on reality. "For instance," he noted, "we have never done a San Francisco-only anthology." Much of City Lights' list today is dedicated to foreign writers and writers from the minority communities in the United States. It is no longer the exclusive bastion of anglo males. Now-classic titles include *Memoirs of a Woman Doctor,* a novel by Egyptian writer Nawal El Saadawi, which reveals a woman's struggle for equality in a Muslim country; *Resistance,* by Russian writer Victor Serge, which chronicles, in poetry, a writer's exile under Stalin's repressive regime; *Clamor of Innocence:*

Stories from Central America, edited by Barbara Paschke and David Volpendesta; and a book of seventeen tales by Moroccan writer Mohammed Mrabet (translator Paul Bowles) entitled *The Boy Who Set the Fire.* Karen Finley's forthcoming *Shock Treatment* is a collection of her writing from performance art appearances that includes her notorious monologues. Charles Henri Ford's selected poems *Out of the Labyrinth* will present a retrospective of his work (plus new poems) that reflects his activism in the gay liberation movement. The same wide range of voices can be found in *City Lights Review,* whose fourth issue will appear this fall.

Though the City Lights writers are varied, there are certain themes and attitudes that bind them together. "Philosophical anarchism was a founding philosophy behind City Lights," Nancy Peters explained, "and threads of that can be found in what we are publishing today. We are attracted to writers of conscience. What we publish is about radical social change . . . ecological issues, the freedom of the individual against incursions of bureaucracy."

The disestablishmentarianism of City Lights is an absolute constant in the bookstore and the press. City Lights publishers never applied for a federal grant. Ferlinghetti feels very strongly about not accepting money from the government, but his caveat doesn't extend to state governments "because the state doesn't murder 100,000 people overseas."

The financial independence and the independence of vision that City Lights exhibits is a paradigm for small presses. Not everyone agrees with City Lights' philosophy; but that should not stop other presses from learning from its example. City Lights' commitment to the individual voice in a period of mass homogenization is unswerving. It believes in publishing as a free and unfettered enterprise outside the strictures of a lumbering bureaucracy, and it strongly supports the small, autonomous bookseller against the encroachment of faceless bookstore chains. The City Lights ideology is not mainstream. It is advance-guard; some would say, self-consciously advance-guard. Criticism of this type does not deter Ferlinghetti, who at seventy-one is still manning the barricades. When asked what is the single greatest problem confronting him as a writer, publisher, and bookseller, he responded, "That there hasn't been a revolution!"

STEVEN CLAY AND RODNEY PHILLIPS (ESSAY DATE 1998)

SOURCE: Clay, Steven, and Rodney Phillips. "J" and "White Rabbit Press." *A Secret Location on the Lower East Side: Adventures in Writing, 1960-1980*, pp. 58-9, 62-3. New York: The New York Public Library and Granary Books, 1998.

In the following excerpt, Clay and Phillips discuss Jack Spicer's journal J *and some of the books published by Joe Dunn's White Rabbit Press.*

"His parents were professional bridge players from Southern California."

—Josephine Miles on Jack Spicer, from an unpublished manuscript in the collections of the Bancroft Library, University of California, Berkeley

In many ways the most beautiful of all the mimeo magazines, *J* had an eight-issue run. The first five issues were edited from North Beach bars by Jack Spicer with Fran Herndon as art editor. Spicer, who embodied the spirit of poetry in the Bay area, collected pieces for his magazine from a box marked "J" in The Place, a bar at 1546 Grant Avenue in San Francisco. A refugee from Los Angeles with two degrees from Berkeley, he had been a student of Josephine Miles there in the mid-1940s. They became close friends, and Spicer participated in the Friday afternoon poetry readings in Wheeler Hall during the late 1940s as well as the readings organized with Rockefeller money by Ruth Witt-Diamant at the new Poetry Center at San Francisco State. Into the cauldron of poetic politics surrounding Miles, Kenneth Rexroth, Robert Duncan, Lawrence Ferlinghetti, and others, Spicer introduced his freest of spirits, sometimes more Caliban than Ariel. Spicer lived for words (even making his living as a research assistant on a lexicographical project at Berkeley). He could be found most evenings in one of the North Beach bars or coffeehouses leading the discussion on poetry, poetics, myth, linguistics, and other mysteries. Like Blake and Yeats (with the help of Mrs. Yeats), Spicer attempted to clear his mind and open himself to "dictation" from other sources, which he devotedly pursued. Spicer also believed wholeheartedly in the necessity of human beings' helping each other through communication, which he confronted in the editorship of *J*, a little newsletter of the poetic spirit. Donald Allen acted as *J*'s distributor in New York ("New York Contributions are not forbidden. But quotaed"), selling copies for Spicer to the Wilentz brothers of the Eighth Street Book Shop. In an early letter to Spicer, Allen eagerly wondered "what your editorial policy may be. Seduction by print."

The first book of the White Rabbit Press was Boston poet Steve Jonas's *Love, the Poem, the Sea & Other Pieces Examined*, published in 1957 with a cover by San Francisco artist Jess Collins. It was followed closely by poet Jack Spicer's breakthrough book *After Lorca* in the same year ("Things fit together. We knew that—it is the principle of magic."). The press was owned by Joe Dunn, who started it to print the work of the group who surrounded Spicer at The Place in North Beach, a bar owned by Leo Krikorian, an alumnus of Black Mountain College. Dunn, who worked for Greyhound Bus Lines in San Francisco, took a secretarial course at Spicer's insistence and learned to operate a multilith machine. He produced the first ten or eleven titles of the press at work, squeezing out time here and there. Among the books he produced were Denise Levertov's *5 Poems*, with a cover by Jess Collins, Richard Brautigan's *The Galilee Hitch-hiker*, Helen Adam's *The Queen o' Crow Castle*, George Stanley's *The Love Root*, Charles Olson's *O'Ryan 2, 4, 6, 8, 10*, and Ebbe Borregaard's *The Wapitis*, with a cover drawn by Robert Duncan. These pieces were all uniformly lithographed from typescripts or even manuscripts provided by the authors, and each book was sized 8½ by 6½ inches. In many ways they are perfect examples of the printing of poetry. After Joe Dunn's relationship with methamphetamines ended in tragedy, the presswork at White Rabbit was taken over in 1962 by a close friend of Spicer's, Graham Mackintosh, dubbed "the ruffian printer" by the elegant San Francisco pressman Robert Grabhorn. As a graduate student at Berkeley in 1961, Mackintosh had worked closely with Spicer on *The Linguistic Atlas of the Pacific Coast*. His first experience in printing was Spicer's *Lament for the Makers,* for which he also provided the collage cover. Mackintosh, who was Robert Duncan's favorite printer, went on to print books for Oyez and to design and print, along with Saul Marks of the Plantin Press, the first few books of the Black Sparrow Press.

BEAT BATTLES WITH CENSORSHIP

J. W. EHRLICH (ESSAY DATE 1961)

SOURCE: Ehrlich, J. W., ed. Introduction and "The Decision." In *Howl of the Censor*, pp. vii-xiv, 114-27. San Carlos, Calif.: Nourse Publishing, 1961.

In the following essay, Ehrlich provides an introduction to the court decision in the California censorship case involving Lawrence Ferlinghetti's publication of Allen

Ginsberg's Howl and Other Poems. *The introduction is followed by the text of the decision handed down by Judge Horn.*

This is the history of a trial. In the *Howl of the Censor* I have given the actual court proceedings, after some editing of the testimony and the arguments on the law. But first, some information about censorship and its origins as well as some of its history through the years.

In ancient Rome, appointed censors were arbiters of the political and social position of every freeman. Judicial functions, and the control of morals, fashion and speech, which we associate with censorship flowed naturally from that part of the functions of the two Roman censors which had to do with their establishment of standards of conduct for Roman citizens.

The modern theory of censorship assumes that established institutions of authority and the beliefs and customs which support them are essentially good. Individual liberty of self-expression must not be allowed to jeopardize the existing mores of the community.

Authoritarians believe that men are innately weak, full of sin, and prone to error. The masses must therefore be guided, controlled and restrained in their ideas and behavior and forced to respect the established morality, property rights, and constituted authority.

Libertarians agree that the state has the right to control behavior in the interests of the national group, but believe free discussion to be of inestimable value to the community. That with such freedom there is little danger of special interest groups using the power of legal authority to suppress freedom of expression. Liberals, in general, oppose censorship.

When the church ruled, heresy was warred against. With the advent of Victorian morality, sex became the target. According to Tacitus, Emperor Augustus was the first ruler who undertook to punish spoken or written words. He ordered the works of Labienus, who criticized the Government, to be burned. The historian Corus, who was too outspoken to please Tiberius, was left to starve to death, and his books were burned. Thinking himself libeled, Emperor Domitian ordered that Hermogenes, and all those who had circulated his writings, be crucified.

The English Crown forbade all printing except by royal license. Presses were maintained under close governmental supervision, and were subject to the decrees of the Star Chamber. In 1557 the Stationer's Company of London received the exclusive privilege of printing and publishing in the English dominions. In 1586, each university was allowed one printing press. Queen Elizabeth demanded that all books be read and passed by loyal bishops and councillors before publication. In the same year, the Star Chamber decreed that all works be examined in manuscript and licensed by the Archbishop of Canterbury. Penalties, such as the cropping of ears, the branding of foreheads, and the slitting of noses, were prescribed for violators. Precensorship of the press continued until it was abolished in 1695.

In 1637 Thomas Morton of the Plymouth Plantation wrote a book called The New English Canaan, printed in Amsterdam, in which he attacked the conduct of the authorities at the plantation. He was imprisoned for a year. Subsequently Philip Ratcliff was convicted "of most foul scandalous invective against our churches and government, was sentenced to be whipped, lose his ears, and be banished from the plantation, which was presently executed."

Political and religious control of books preceded sex censorship by hundreds of years. The English common law was slow to recognize the crime of obscenity. The works of Chaucer, Smollette, Sterne, Fielding, and Swift, however forthright in matters of sex, circulated without legal hindrance. This immunity apparently extended even to pornography unrelieved by literary quality. In 1708 Lord Holt ruled that the notorious *Fifteen Plagues of Maidenhead* would not support an indictment. As late as 1733 there was a like ruling on the salacious poems of the Earl of Rochester.

Queen Victoria ushered in an era which witnessed an unprecedented drive for the purification of literature. Shelley's "Alastor" was attacked as offensive, and Shakespeare was bowdlerized. The morality drive which flourished in England found its counterpart in America. Hawthorne's, *The Scarlet Letter,* was called a "brokerage of lust," and Walt Whitman was discharged from the U. S. Department of the Interior because of *Leaves of Grass. Huckleberry Finn* was banned as "trash and suitable only for slums" because Mark Twain had prefaced the book with the waggish warning that persons attempting to find a moral in it would be banished.

In 1688 England ordered Governor Thomas Dongan not to allow any printing press in New York. In 1754, Daniel Fowle, a Boston publisher, was jailed because it was suspected he had printed remarks derogatory to the members of the Colonial Assembly. It was doubtless this background that prompted the inclusion of the guaranty of free speech and press in almost all state constitutions, and in the first amendment to the Federal Constitution.

The early days of the republic witnessed an era of political calumny rarely paralleled in the history of the world. Bitter rivalry prevailed in politics; defamation was seized upon as an effective weapon for demolishing opponents in public life. The partisan fury culminated in the Sedition Act of 1798. The Federalists, assailed by the Jeffersonians and fearful of losing power, rushed through a law which in effect forbade any criticism of the government on pain of severe penalties. Federalist judges and officials were free to use the statute to oppress their political foes, and they did not hesitate to do so. The Sedition Act cut perilously near the root of freedom of speech and of the press. It doomed the Federalist Party forever.

Colonial America took no legal precautions to ward off the taint of sex. The early Presidents read and apparently liked the bawdy and outspoken works of the early English novelists. Chancellor Kent himself, a dour and strait-laced man, confessed he enjoyed Fielding. Yet obscenity laws sprang up in a few states before the middle of the 19th century; one in Vermont (1821), another in Connecticut (1834), and a third in Massachusetts (1835). The Federal Comstock Laws were enacted in 1873 and forbade the mailing, as well as the interstate transportation and importation of obscene matter.

The uplift movement flourished and spread, Elizabeth Barrett Browning's *Aurora Leigh* was denounced as "the hysterical indecencies of an erotic mind." In 1888 Henry Vizetelly was fined for publishing Emile Zola's "La Terre"; a year later he was fined again and sent to jail for reissuing Zola's "pernicious literature." Thomas Hardy's *Jude the Obscure* encountered trouble in 1895; and when H. G. Wells's *Ann Veronica* appeared in 1909, a group of influential editors and publishers asked the Home Secretary to suppress it. The repeated confiscation of D. H. Lawrence's works, some claim hastened his death. During recent years many other books, among them *The Well of Loneliness* and *Sleeveless Errand* have been suppressed by the authorities in England.

The list of prose works banned during past and present centuries includes Homer's *Odyssey*, Cervantes' *Don Quixote*, La Fontaine's *Fables*, Defoe's *Robinson Crusoe*, Swift's *Tale of Tub* and

Gulliver's Travels, Voltaire's *Candide*, Fielding's *Pasquin*, Richardson's *Pamela*, Casanova's *Memoirs*, Goethe's *Faust* and *Sorrows of Werther*, Gibbon's *Decline and Fall of the Roman Empire*, Sterne's *Sentimental Journey*, Andersen's *Fairy Tales*, Balzac's *Droll Stories*, Flaubert's *Madame Bovary*, Maupassant's *Une Vie* and *L'Humble Vérité*, Stowe's *Uncle Tom's Cabin*, Hawthorne's *The Scarlet Letter*, Eliot's *Adam Bede*, George Moore's *Flowers of Passion*, Zola's *Nana*, Hardy's *Tess of the d'Urbervilles*, Upton Sinclair's *Oil*, Cabell's *Jurgen*, Lawrence's *Woman in Love*, Sinclair Lewis' *Elmer Gantry*, and Remarque's *All Quiet on the Western Front*, Dante's *La Commedia* and *DeMonarchia*, Shelley's *Queen Mab*, Rossetti's Poems, *Baudelaire's Fleurs de Mal*, Whitman's *Leaves of Grass*, Elizabeth Barrett Browning's *Aurora Leigh* and Swinburne's *Poems and Ballads*.

Hundreds of the disciples of Confucius were buried alive for disseminating their master's beliefs. Roger Bacon, whose treatises on alchemy and optics expressed unorthodox views, was accused of witchcraft and imprisoned for ten years. Sir Thomas Malory's *Morte d'Arthur* was attacked as no more than "bold adultery and wilful murder." The church branded Moliere a demon in human flesh for writing *Tartuffe*, a satire on religion. Andre Chenier went to the guillotine for *Iambes* and *Jeune Captive*. Almost every book setting forth new themes, unfamiliar ideas, or protests against social, economic or religious abuses, met with instant reprisal—Montaigne's *Essays*, Descartes' *Meditations*, Montesquieu's *L'Esprit des Lois*, Swedenborg's *Principia*, Rousseau's writings, Kant's *Philosophy*, Galileo's study of the Ptolemaic and Copernican theories, Francis Bacon's works, Darwin's *Origin of Species*, Machiavelli's *The Prince*, Jefferson's pamphlets, the political works of Thomas Paine and John Stuart Mill, the Koran, the writings of Savonarola, Erasmus, Luther, Tyndale and Calvin. The Bible itself was not immune. Versions of it were suppressed by Emperor Justinian, the synod of Canterbury, Cardinal Wolsey, the Inquisition, and Queen Mary. In 1525 Tyndale's translation of the New Testament was denounced by the church as "pernicious merchandise" and 10 years later Tyndale was burned at the stake with his books.

It is ironic that the suppressed books in one age in many cases become part of the accepted literature or even the venerated classics of the next. Sometimes the metamorphosis requires generations, sometimes only a few years. Gautier's *Mademoiselle de Maupin* was shocking enough in the middle of the 19th century to deprive him of the wreath of the Academy; in 1922 the highest New York court could find nothing offensive in it. Schnitzler's *Casanova's Homecoming* was suppressed in 1923; it was fully vindicated in 1930. In 1928 a customs court held that Joyce's *Ulysses* was filled with obscenity; in 1934 a higher court found it to be a serious work of art.

The studies of the troublesome Havelock Ellis, once rigorously prosecuted, are now considered standard in the field of sex psychology. Theodore Roosevelt called Tolstoy "a sexual and moral pervert," and the Post Office Department barred his *Kreutzer Sonata* from the mail in 1890; today it is on the shelves of the public libraries.

There are official and semi-official censors. Official censors are those empowered by law to exercise powers of supervision and suppression. They include judges (despite their oft-repeated declarations that it is not the function of the courts to exercise censorship); and administrative officials such as the Postmaster General, the Collector of Customs and licensing authorities. Administrative bodies and officials purport to operate under specific statutes which outline their powers and prescribe the procedure they must follow. The judges interpret and apply the law in cases that come up before them, as where the seller of an "obscene," libelous or seditious book is prosecuted criminally.

Some idea of the activities of official censors may be gleaned from the fact that in 1922, a bookseller was fined $1,000 for placing a copy of the *Decameron* in the mails; that the highest court in the State of New York upheld a conviction based on Arthur Schnitzler's *Reigen*; that the post office has at various times and places denied the use of the mails to such widely differing works as Ovid's *Metamorphoses*, ancient Chinese manuscripts imported by the Field Museum, Swedenborg's *Amor Conjugalis* and the official report of the Vice Commission of the City of Chicago. The customs authorities have sought to bar from our shores Aristophanes' *Lysistrata*, Defoe's *Moll Flanders*, the *Arabian Nights*, the *Satyricon* of Petronius, the *Golden Ass* of Apuleius, Rousseau's *Confessions*, Gauguin's *Journals*, and Krafft-Ebing's *Psychopathia Sexualis*.

The semi-official censors are groups that have no specific powers under the law, but have been organized for the express purpose of "moral uplift." The New York Society for the Suppression of Vice, fathered by Anthony Comstock, the Boston Watch and Ward Society, and the Clean Amusement Association of America, belong in this category. Some of these agencies possess limited police powers. They work in cooperation with the authorities, ferret out alleged violations, act as complaining witnesses, and prod the police and the district attorneys. The New York Society claimed that it was responsible for the confiscation of nearly 200,000 books and other printed material running into millions of copies.

Under the system of government in the United States certain spheres of activity are under national control, and others are left to the states. The federal government has exclusive jurisdiction over the mails and interstate and foreign commerce. The Postmaster General sees to it that the mails are not contaminated, and the Customs Bureau bars from our shores whatever material may be thought to imperil the morals of the American people. On the other hand, whatever happens within the confines of a particular state is regulated by the state itself. The line of demarcation between federal and state censors, while clear-cut in theory, is not sharply observed in practice. A book banned at the customs is effectively kept from the people of the states; the decisions of the federal courts on books, plays and films are usually followed by the state courts, and vice versa.

Censorship, in the historic sense, means prelicensing, that is to say, the submission of material to an official person or agency for approval (imprimatur) in advance of publication or presentation to the public. The licensing of motion pictures by state boards of review is an example of this kind of surveillance.

There is a greater peril to books today than at any other time since the invention of the printing press. The peril does not flow from sex censorship, but from the rise of authoritarian power and the attendant regimentation of thought and opinion. If the world turns totalitarian, there may be a holocaust in books beside which Savonarola's Florentine bonfires will pale into utter insignificance. Hitler's Germany lighted the fires of its destruction when it fanned the flames of burning books.

It was my good fortune to have in association during the trial two men of great legal ability; Mr. Speiser and Mr. Bendich.

In his summation Mr. Speiser struck heavy blows for the right of man to portray in words, that which he saw and felt. Mr. Bendich argued the right to speak freely under the Constitution of the United States and its Amendments.

Both arguments are not included solely because of space. Their value nevertheless did much to impress the Court with our position.

The Decision

Horn, Clayton W., J. The defendant is charged with a violation of Section 311.3 of the Penal Code of the State of California. Defendant pleads Not Guilty. The complaint alleged that the defendant did wilfully and lewdly print, publish and sell obscene and indecent writings, papers and books, to wit: *Howl and Other Poems.*

It is to be noted that the statute requires proof of criminal intent, namely, that the defendants did wilfully and lewdly commit the acts specified. It should also be noted that no reference to minors is made in the statute.

It must be borne in mind that the prosecution has the burden of proving beyond a reasonable doubt and to a moral certainty two things: first, that the book is obscene and, second, that the defendants wilfully and lewdly committed the crime alleged. It is elementary that where a statute makes a specific intent an element of an offense, such intent must be proved. The proof may be circumstantial; but if so, the circumstances must be such as reasonably to justify an inference of the intent.

The prosecution has advanced the theory that the word "indecent" means something less than obscene.

In their broadest meaning the words indecent and obscene might signify offensive to refinement, propriety and good taste. A penal statute requiring conformity to some current standard of propriety defined only by statutory words would make the standard in each case, ex post facto.

Unless the words used take the form of dirt for dirt's sake and can be traced to criminal behavior, either actual or demonstrably imminent, they are not in violation of the statute. Indecent as used in the Penal Code is synonymous with obscene, and there is no merit in the contention of the prosecution that the word indecent means something less than obscene.

The evidence shows that *Howl* was published by the defendant and therefore it remains to be seen whether said book is obscene and if so, whether this defendant wilfully and lewdly published it. The prosecution contends that having published the book defendant had knowledge of the character of its contents and that from such knowledge a lewd intent might be inferred.

The mere fact of knowledge alone would not be sufficient. The surrounding circumstances would be important and must be such as reasonably to justify an inference of the intent. To illustrate, some might think a book obscene, others a work of art; with sincere difference of opinion. The bookseller would not be required to elect at his peril. Unless the prosecution proved that he acted lewdly in selling it, the burden would not be met.

Written reviews of *Howl* were admitted in evidence on behalf of the defendants, over the objection of the District Attorney. One was from *The New York Times Book Review,* dated September 2, 1956; one from the *San Francisco Chronicle,* dated May 19, 1957, which included a statement by Ferlinghetti; one from the *Nation* dated February 23, 1957. All of the reviews praised *Howl.*

The practice of referring to reviews in cases of this nature has become well established. Opinions of professional critics publicly disseminated in the ordinary course of their employment are proper aids to the court in weighing the author's sincerity of purpose and the literary worth of his effort. These are factors which, while not determining whether a book is obscene, are to be considered in deciding that question.

Over the objection of the prosecution the defense produced nine expert witnesses, some of them with outstanding qualifications in the literary field. All of the defense experts agreed that *Howl* had literary merit, that it represented a sincere effort by the author to present a social picture, and that the language used was relevant to the theme. As Professor Mark Schorer put it: *Howl,* like any work of literature, attempts and intends to make a significant comment on, or interpretation of, human experience as the author knows it.

The prosecution produced two experts in rebuttal, whose qualifications were slightly less than those of the defense. One testified that *Howl* had some clarity of thought but was an imitation of Walt Whitman, and had no literary merit; the other and by far the most voluble, that it had no value at all. The court did not allow any of the experts to express an opinion on the question of obscenity because this was the very issue to be decided by the court.

Experts are used every day in court on other subjects and no reason presents itself justifying their exclusion from this type of case when their experience and knowledge can be of assistance.

The court also read many of the books previously held obscene or not for the purpose of comparison.

In determining whether a book is obscene it must be construed as a whole. The courts are agreed that in making this determination, the book must be construed as a whole and that regard shall be had for its place in the arts.

The freedoms of speech and press are inherent in a nation of free people. These freedoms must be protected if we are to remain free, both individually and as a nation. The protection for this freedom is found in the First and Fourteenth Amendments to the United States Constitution, and in the Constitution of California, Art. I, sec. 9 which provides in part:

> "Every citizen may freely speak, write, and publish his sentiments on all subjects, being responsible for the abuse of that right; and no law shall be passed to restrain or abridge the liberty of speech or of the press . . ."

The Fourteenth Amendment to the Federal Constitution prohibits any State from encroaching upon freedom of speech and freedom of the press to the same extent that the First Amendment prevents the Federal Congress from doing so.

These guarantees occupy a preferred position under our law to such an extent that the courts, when considering whether legislation infringes upon them, neutralize the presumption usually indulged in favor of constitutionality.

Thomas Jefferson in his bill for establishing religious freedom wrote that "to suffer the Civil Magistrate to intrude his powers into the field of opinion, and to restrain the profession or propagation of principles on supposition of their ill tendency, is a dangerous fallacy which at once destroys all religious liberty . . . it is time enough for the rightful purposes of civil government for its officers to interfere when principles break out into overt acts against peace and good order."

The now familiar "clear and present danger" rule represents a compromise between the ideas of Jefferson and those of the judges, who had in the meantime departed from the forthright views of the great statesman. Under the rule the publisher of a writing may be punished if the publication in question creates a clear and present danger that there will result from it some substantive evil which the legislature has a right to proscribe and punish.

Mr. Justice Brandeis maintained that free speech may not be curbed where the community has the chance to answer back. He said: "those who won our independence by revolution were not cowards. They did not fear political change. They did not exalt order at the cost of liberty. To courageous, self-reliant men, with confidence in the power of free and fearless reasoning applied through the processes of popular government, no danger flowing from speech can be deemed clear and present, unless the incidence of the evil apprehended is so imminent that it may befall before there is opportunity for full discussion. If there be time to expose through discussion the falsehood and fallacies, to avert the evil by the processes of education, the remedy to be applied is more speech, not enforced silence. Only an emergency can justify repression. Such must be the rule if authority is to be reconciled with freedom. Such, in my opinion, is the command of the Constitution. It is therefore always open to Americans to challenge a law abridging free speech and assembly by showing that there was no emergency justifying it.

"Moreover, even imminent danger cannot justify resort to prohibition of these functions essential to effective democracy, unless the evil apprehended is relatively serious. Prohibition of free speech and assembly is a measure so stringent that it would be inappropriate as the means for averting a relatively trivial harm to society—the fact that speech is likely to result in some violence or in destruction of property is not enough to justify its suppression. There must be the probability of serious injury to the State. Among free men, the deterrents ordinarily to be applied to prevent crime are education and punishment for violations of the law, not abridgment of the rights of free speech and assembly."

The authors of the First Amendment knew that novel and unconventional ideas might disturb the complacent, but they chose to encourage a freedom which they believed essential if vigorous enlightenment was ever to triumph over slothful ignorance.

I agree with the words of Macaulay who finds it difficult to believe that in a world so full of temptations as this, any gentleman, whose life would have been virtuous if he had not read Aristophanes and Juvenal, will be made vicious by reading them.

I do not believe that *Howl* is without redeeming social importance. The first part of *Howl* presents a picture of a nightmare world; the second part is an indictment of those elements in modern society destructive of the best qualities of human nature; such elements are predominantly identified as materialism, conformity, and mechanization leading toward war. The third part presents a picture of an individual who is a specific representation of what the author conceives as a general condition.

"Footnote to Howl" seems to be a declamation that everything in the world is holy, including parts of the body by name. It ends in a plea for holy living.

The poems, "Supermarket," "Sunflower Sutra," "In the Baggage Room at Greyhound," "An Asphodel," "Song" and "Wild Orphan" require no discussion relative to obscenity. In "Transcription of Organ Music" the "I" in four lines remembers his first sex relation at age 23 but only the bare ultimate fact and that he enjoyed it. Even out of context it is written in language that is not obscene, and included in the whole it becomes a part of the individual's experience "real or imagined," but lyric rather than hortatory and violent, like "Howl."

The theme of "Howl" presents "unorthodox and controversial ideas." Coarse and vulgar language is used in treatment and sex acts are mentioned, but unless the book is entirely lacking in "social importance" it cannot be held obscene. This point does not seem to have been specifically presented or decided in any of the cases leading up to Roth v. United States.

No hard and fast rule can be fixed for the determination of what is obscene, because such determination depends on the locale, the time, the mind of the community and the prevailing mores. Even the word itself has had a chameleon-like history through the past, and as Mr. Justice Cardozo said: "A word is not a crystal, transparent and unchanged. It is the skin of living thought and may vary greatly in color and content according to the circumstances and the time in which it is used." The writing, however, must have a substantial tendency to deprave or corrupt its readers by inciting lascivious thoughts or arousing lustful desires.

The effect of the publication on the ordinary reader is what counts. The Statute does not intend that we shall "reduce our treatment of sex to the standard of a child's library in the supposed interest of a salacious few. This test, however, should not be left to stand alone, for there is another element of equal importance—the tenor of the times and the change in social acceptance of what is inherently decent.

The modern rule is that obscenity is measured by the erotic allurement upon the average modern reader; that the erotic allurement of a book is measured by whether it is sexually impure—i.e., pornographic, "dirt for dirt's sake," a calculated incitement to sexual desire—or whether it reveals an effort to reflect life, including its dirt, with reasonable accuracy and balance; and that mere coarseness or vulgarity is not obscenity.

Sexual impurity in literature (pornography, as some of the cases call it) is any writing whose dominant purpose and effect is erotic allurement; a calculated and effective incitement to sexual desire. It is the effect that counts, more than the purpose, and no indictment can stand unless it can be shown.

In the Roth case no question of obscenity was involved or considered by the court. The sole question was whether obscenity as such was protected by the constitution and the court held it was not. In the appeals involved the material was obviously pornographic, it was advertised and sold as such. The United States Supreme Court refers to the various rules on obscenity by stating that: "sex and obscenity are not synonymous. Obscene material is material which deals with sex in a manner appealing to prurient interest. The portrayal of sex, e.g., in art, literature and scientific works is not itself sufficient reason to deny material the constitutional protection of freedom of speech and press."

The following instruction, given in the Alberts case, is approved in Roth: "The test is not whether it would arouse sexual desires or sexual impure thoughts in those comprising a particular segment of the community, the young, the immature or the highly prudish, or would leave another segment, the scientific or highly educated or the so-called worldly-wise and sophisticated indifferent and unmoved. The test in each case is the effect of the book, picture or publication considered as a whole, not upon any particular class, but upon all those whom it is likely to reach. In other words, you determine its impact upon the average person in the community. The books, pictures and circulars must be judged, as a whole, in their entire context, and you are not to consider detached or separate portions in reaching a conclusion. You judge the circulars, pictures and publications which have been put in evidence by present-day standards of the community. You may ask yourself does it offend the common conscience of the community by present-day standards. In this case, ladies and gentlemen of the jury, you and you alone are the exclusive judges of what the common conscience of the community is, and in determining that conscience you are to consider the community as a whole, young and old, educated and uneducated, the religious and the irreligious—men, women and children."

Mr. Chief Justice Warren, concurring in the result in the *Roth* case, stated: "I agree with the result reached by the court in these cases, but the line dividing the salacious or pornographic from literature or science is not straight and unwavering, the personal element in these cases is seen most strongly in the requirement of scienter. Under the California law, the prohibited activity must be done 'wilfully and lewdly.'"

There are a number of words used in *Howl* that are presently considered coarse and vulgar in some circles of the community; in other circles such words are in everyday use. It would be unrealistic to deny these facts. The author of *Howl* has used those words because he believed that his portrayal required them as being in character. The People state that it is not necessary to use such words and that others would be more palatable to good taste. The answer is that life is not encased in one formula whereby everyone acts the same or conforms to a particular pattern. No two persons think alike; we were all made from the same mold but in different patterns. Would there be any freedom of press or speech if one must reduce his vocabulary to vapid innocuous euphemism? An author should be real in treating his subject and be allowed to express his thoughts and ideas in his own words.

In *People v. Viking Press,* the court said: "The Courts have strictly limited the applicability of the statute to works of pornography and they have consistently declined to apply it to books of genuine literary value. If the statute were construed more broadly than in the manner just indicated, its effect would be to prevent altogether the realistic portrayal in literature of a large and important field of life. . . . The Court may not require the author to put refined language into the mouths of primitive people," and in *People v. Vanguard Press,* the court observed: "The speech of the characters must be considered in relation to its setting and the theme of the story. It seems clear that use of foul language will not of itself bring a novel or play within the condemnation of the statute. As I have indicated above, all but one of these books are profoundly tragic, and that one has its normal quota of frustration and despair. No one could envy or wish to emulate the characters that move so desolately through these pages. Far from inciting to lewd or lecherous desires,

which are sensorially pleasurable, these books leave one either with a sense of horror or of pity for the degradation of mankind. The effect upon the normal reader, *l'homme moyen sensuel* (there is no such deft precision in English), would be anything but what the vice hunters fear it might be. We are so fearful for other people's morals; they so seldom have the courage of our own convictions."

In *Commonwealth v. Gordon*: the test for obscenity most frequently laid down seems to be whether the writing would tend to deprave the morals of those into whose hands the publication might fall by suggesting lewd thoughts and exciting sensual desires. The statute is therefore directed only at sexual impurity and not at blasphemy or coarse and vulgar behavior of any other kind. The word in common use for the purpose of such statute is "obscenity." The familiar four-letter words that are so often associated with sexual impurity are, almost without exception, of honest Anglo-Saxon ancestry, and were not invented for purely scatological effect. The one, for example, that is used to denote the sexual act is an old agricultural word meaning "to plant" and was at one time a wholly respectable member of the English vocabulary. The distinction between a word of decent etymological history and one of smut alone is important; it shows that fashions in language change as expectably as do the concepts of what language connotes. It is the old business of semantics again, the difference between word and concept. But there is another distinction. The decisions that I cite have sliced off vulgarity from obscenity. This has had the effect of making a clear division between the words of the bathroom and those of the bedroom; the former can no longer be regarded as obscene, since they have no erotic allurement, and the latter may be so regarded, depending on the circumstances of their use. This reduces the number of potentially offensive words sharply.

"The law does not undertake to punish bad English, vulgarity, or bad taste, and no matter how objectionable one may consider the book on those grounds, there is no right to convict on account of them. The dramatization of the song 'Frankie and Johnnie' caused much furor, but the court there held that 'the language of the play is coarse, vulgar and profane; the plot cheap and tawdry. As a dramatic composition it serves to degrade the stage where vice is thought by some to lose "half its evil by losing all its grossness." That it is indecent from every consideration of propriety is entirely clear' but the court is not a censor of plays

ON THE SUBJECT OF...

BARNEY J. ROSSET, JR.

A firm believer in freedom of the press, Barney Rosset has long waged a war against censorship. In 1959, as the owner and publisher of Grove Press, he went to court and won the right to publish and distribute the unexpurgated version of D. H. Lawrence's *Lady Chatterley's Lover.* Later he fought for the right to publish Henry Miller's *Tropic of Cancer,* which had been banned for twenty-seven years by U.S. Customs officials. As editor of the *Evergreen Review* from 1957 to 1973, Rosset provided a public forum for new writers. The *Evergreen Review* began as a paperback book in 1957 and evolved into a bimonthly magazine. In 1968 it became a monthly. The early issues of this avant-garde journal featured Beat writers like Allen Ginsberg, Jack Kerouac, and Lawrence Ferlinghetti, and since its inception, the works of such diverse writers as Edward Albee, Carlos Fuentes, Jean-Paul Sartre, William Burroughs, Jorge Borges, Friedrich Duerrenmatt, and Susan Sontag have appeared in its pages. The *Evergreen Review* became known for its graphic depictions of sex and radical politics. The *Evergreen Review* regularly featured the commentary of such controversial political figures as Che Guevara, Malcolm X, and Ho Chi Minh. Like the *Evergreen Review,* Grove Press—during Rosset's tenure as editor, which ended in 1985—published a wide variety of works, including *The Autobiography of Malcolm X,* Frantz Fanon's *The Wretched of the Earth,* and Abbie Hoffman's *Steal This Book.* In 1994 Rosset became publisher of Foxrock publishing, named after a suburb of Dublin where Samuel Beckett was born. Foxrock's inagural title was *Eleutheria,* Beckett's first and previously unpublished play; since then the company has published the works of such authors as Kenzaburo Oe, Marguerite Duras, Michael McClure, Ghislaine Dunant, and Sushi Asano. Rosset also serves as editor-in-chief of the online version of *Evergreen Review.*

and does not attempt to regulate manners. One may call a spade a spade without offending decency, although modesty may be shocked thereby. The question is not whether the scene is laid in a low dive where refined people are not found or whether the language is that of the bar room rather than the parlor. The question is whether the tendency of the play is to excite lustful and lecherous desire."

To determine whether a book falls within the condemnation of the statute, an evaluation must be made of the extent to which the book as a whole would have a demoralizing effect on its readers, specifically respecting sexual behavior. Various factors must be borne in mind when applying the judicially accepted standards used in measuring that effect. Among others, these factors include the theme of the book, the degree of sincerity of purpose evidenced in it, its literary worth, the channels used in its distribution, contemporary attitudes toward the literary treatment of sexual behavior and the types of readers reasonably to be expected to secure it for perusal.

Material is not obscene unless it arouses lustful thoughts of sex and tends to corrupt and deprave *l'homme moyen sensuel* by inciting him to anti-social activity or tending to create a clear and present danger that he will be so incited as the result of exposure thereto.

If the material is disgusting, revolting or filthy, to use just a few adjectives, the antithesis of pleasurable sexual desires is born, and it cannot be obscene.

In *United States v. Roth,* a footnote to the concurring opinion of Judge Frank is of interest: "The very argument advanced to sustain the statute's validity, so far as it condemns the obscene, goes to show the invalidity of the statute so far as it condemns 'filth,' if 'filth' means that which renders sexual desires 'disgusting.' For if the argument be sound that the legislature may constitutionally provide punishment for the obscene because, anti-socially, it arouses sexual desires by making sex attractive, then it follows that whatever makes sex disgusting is socially beneficial.

"To date there exist, I think, no thoroughgoing studies by competent persons which justify the conclusion that normal adults reading or seeing of the 'obscene' probably induces anti-social conduct. Such competent studies as have been made do conclude that so complex and numerous are the causes of sexual vice that it is impossible to assert with any assurance that 'obscenity' represents a ponderable causal factor in sexually deviant behavior. Although the whole subject of obscenity censorship hinges upon the unproved assumption that 'obscene' literature is a significant factor in causing sexual deviation from the community standard, no report can be found of a single effort at genuine research to test this assumption by singling out as a factor for study the effect of sex literature upon sexual behavior. What little competent research has been done, points definitely in a direction precisely opposite to that assumption."

While the publishing of "smut" or "hard core pornography" is without any social importance and obscene by present-day standards, and should be punished for the good of the community, since there is no straight and unwavering line to act as a guide, censorship by Government should be held in tight reign. To act otherwise would destroy our freedoms of free speech and press. Even religion can be censored by the medium of taxation. The best method of censorship is by the people as self-guardians of public opinion and not by government. So we come back, once more, to Jefferson's advice that the only completely democratic way to control publications which arouse mere thoughts or feelings is through nongovernmental censorship by public opinion.

From the foregoing certain rules can be set up, but as has been noted, they are not inflexible and are subject to changing conditions, and above all each case must be judged individually.

1. If the material has the slightest redeeming social importance it is not obscene because it is protected by the First and Fourteenth Amendments of the United States Constitution, and the California Constitution.

2. If it does not have the slightest redeeming social importance it may be obscene.

3. The test of obscenity in California is that the material must have a tendency to deprave or corrupt readers by exciting lascivious thoughts or arousing lustful desire to the point that it presents a clear and present danger of inciting to anti-social or immoral action.

4. The book or material must be judged as a whole by its effect on the *average adult* in the community.

5. If the material is objectionable only because of coarse and vulgar language which is not erotic or aphrodisiac in character it is not obscene.

6. Scienter must be proved.

7. Book reviews may be received in evidence if properly authenticated.

8. Evidence of expert witnesses in the literary field is proper.

9. Comparison of the material with other similar material previously adjudicated is proper.

10. The people owe a duty to themselves and to each other to preserve and protect their constitutional freedoms from any encroachment by government unless it appears that the allowable limits of such protection have been breached, and then to take only such action as will heal the breach.

11. I agree with Mr. Justice Douglas: I have the same confidence in the ability of our people to reject noxious literature as I have in their capacity to sort out the true from the false in theology, economics, politics, or any other field.

12. In considering material claimed to be obscene it is well to remember the motto: *"Honi soit qui mal y pense."* (Evil to him who evil thinks.)

Therefore, I conclude the book *Howl and Other Poems* does have some redeeming social importance, and I find the book is not obscene.

The defendant is found not guilty.

Bibliography of the Argument and the Decision

California Constitution, Art. I, sec. 9.

45 Calif. L. Rev. 70.

California Penal Code, sec. 311.

Commonwealth v. Gordon, 66 Pa. D. & C. R. 101.

Commonwealth v. Isenstadt, 62 N. E. 2nd 840.

People v. Creative Age Press, 79 N.Y.S. 2d 198.

People v. Vanguard Press, 192 N.Y. misc. 127.

People v. Viking Press, 147 N.Y. misc. 813.

People v. Vogel, 46 Cal. App. 2d Supp. 959.

People v. Wepplo, 78 Cal. App. 2d Supp. 959; 178 P. 2d 853.

Roth v. United States, 354 U.S. 476.

Sweezy v. State of New Hampshire, 354 U.S. 234.

United States Constitution, First and Fourteenth Amendments.

United States v. Roth, 237 Fed. 2d 796 (C.C.A.).

Watkins v. United States, 354 U.S. 178.

Yates v. United States, 354 U.S. 298.

MAURICE BERGER (ESSAY DATE 1995)

SOURCE: Berger, Maurice. "Libraries Full of Tears: The Beats and the Law." In *Beat Culture and the New America: 1950-1965*, by Lisa Phillips et al., pp. 123-37. New York: Whitney Museum of American Art, 1995.

In the following essay, Berger outlines the polarization between the Beats and traditional society, tracing the conflict via several attempts to censor writing and poetry during the 1950s.

America when will you be angelic?
When will you take off your clothes?
When will you look at yourself through the
   grave?
When will you be worthy of your million
   Trotskyites?
America why are your libraries full of tears?
   Allen Ginsberg, "America," from *Howl and Other
                                 Poems* (1956)

At the risk of sounding melodramatic, one could argue that our present-day culture wars actually began on May 21, 1957. For it was on that day that two plainclothes police officers entered the City Lights Bookstore in San Francisco and declared war on a brilliant, albeit marginal, homosexual poet whose only offense was to speak out against what he believed was the repressiveness of American society. The story has been recast many times in recent years: cultural figure creates work that is sexually explicit, homoerotic, and/or outspoken and incurs the wrath of moralizing, right-wing zealots. The central character in their primal scene of cultural repression was Allen Ginsberg; the alleged crime was the publication and sale of his first book, *Howl and Other Poems*.

Lawrence Ferlinghetti, the publisher of *Howl* and owner of City Lights who was arrested along with store clerk Shigeyoshi Murao, had anticipated that the book's four-letter words and references to gay sex and drugs might catch the eye of censors. He submitted the manuscript to the American Civil Liberties Union. He also reluctantly agreed to a demand by his printer that several words in the text be replaced with asterisks. The city's law enforcement community, however, would not be appeased. In March 1957, 520 copies were seized by the San Francisco office of the US Customs, an action that was reversed only after the Washington, DC, office, aware that many intellectuals and artists across the country were outraged, recommended that the case be dropped. Within a few months, perhaps with the intention of compensating for the failure of earlier attempts to suppress the book, the municipal police department moved in on the City Lights Bookstore.[1]

The much-publicized trial of Murao and Ferlinghetti in the summer of 1957 set off a collision of legal and literary forces in a "dreadful mismatch."[2] Assistant district attorney Ralph McIntosh, a hard-line censorship advocate, moralized about Ginsberg's references to homosexuality and the use of such words as "cock," "fuck," and "balls," while the experienced ACLU defense team, headed by noted criminal lawyer Jack Ehrlich, produced an impressive barrage of testimony and letters affirming the social and literary merits of the work. On October 3, 1957, Judge W. J. Clayton Horn, a conservative jurist known for his Sunday school Bible classes, found Ferlinghetti not guilty. (Charges against Murao had earlier been dismissed on the grounds that as an employee he might not have known the actual contents of the book he sold to undercover cops.) Echoing the logic of *Roth* v. *United States,* a landmark obscenity decision handed down four months earlier by the US Supreme Court, Horn concluded that unless "the book [was] entirely lacking 'in social importance' it [could] not be held obscene."[3] In effect, the judge found that while Ginsberg's message was neither entirely convincing nor civil, it was a legitimate expression of social protest that merited constitutional protection.[4]

While Judge Horn's decision underscored the degree to which the legal definition of obscenity was narrowing by the late 1950s, the thorny question of what constituted obscene speech remained unsettled.[5] Within the next decade a number of prominent personalities of the Beat generation found themselves entangled in battles to protect their work from suppression. Despite a series of landmark anti-censorship rulings by the Supreme Court in the mid-1960s, the threat against freedom of cultural expression in the United States exists to this day. Thirty years after the last of these trials, religious fundamentalists and conservative politicians continue to call for the suppression of artists and their supporters. For this reason, there are a number of lessons to be learned from reexamining the persecution of Beat culture—lessons that proffer great insight into the how, and more important, the why of our own present-day reign of repression.

As recent history suggests, the imperative to declare representations obscene and thus illegal inevitably stirs up a torrent of political danger. Well beyond the desire to eliminate offending words and images, these repressive campaigns have easily veered into the realm of ideological manipulation.[6] Ambitious public officials and zealous religious leaders, searching for scapegoats to offer a public angry and frustrated about difficult social and moral problems, have argued that radical or provocative art is "immoral," "obscene," or "blasphemous," that it threatens deeply held political and religious values. This moralistic targeting of words and images can be an effective, even devastating means of social manipulation and control. In selecting particularly provocative depictions that are highly disturbing to conservative elements of the community and whose controversial or elitist nature makes them difficult for their supporters to defend, manipulative politicians and religious leaders have been reasonably successful in gaining public support for repressive actions that might otherwise be seen as questionable or unconstitutional. Even if the First Amendment prevails and efforts at prosecution fail (as is often the case), the resultant chill effect can stifle dissent. In the end, writers, artists, and performers and the institutions that represent them will often turn to self-censorship rather than risk the possibility of public humiliation or bankruptcy.

The Beats' representation of homosexuality, bisexuality, and interracial liaisons, their advocacy of free sex and drugs, and their expressed desire to test the limits of cultural acceptability made them as vulnerable to censorship as any artists of this century. Despite their marginal status, the Beats were constantly the focus of newspaper and magazine articles, radio and television shows, and other mass-media outlets. Their odd manner of dress, stream-of-consciousness rants, and general nonconformity made them fair game for any number of sycophants, satirists, and paranoid cold warriors. The widely reported Beat prosecutions also paralleled and contributed to the gradual liberalization of moral and sexual attitudes then taking place, during a period when district attorneys regularly prosecuted *Playboy* magazine and young innocents could still be scandalized by the sight of Elvis' gyrating hips.[7]

The polarization between the "Beats" and "straights" that occurred in public discussion, as historian Richard Cándida Smith observes, "ritually enacted interior conflicts over the limits of freedom"—an artificial dichotomy between hedonism and chastity promoted by both sides through reductive symbols and stereotypes.[8] In September 1959, for example, *Life* published a photo-essay comparing two "extremes" of American society: the God-fearing citizens of Hutchinson, Kansas, and the "seedy" beatniks of Venice, California.[9] The piece centered around Lawrence Lipton, leader of the Venice Beat community, and the three bored adolescent girls from "squaresville" who invited him and his friends to teach them

about the beatnik who "throbs with rebellion . . . ridicules U.S. society . . . and talks a strange language."[10] The meeting was canceled after the girls were publicly admonished by community leaders for their thoughtless invitation and a police spokesman hinted that the Beats might be arrested for vagrancy if they showed up in Hutchinson. The contrasting shots of clean-as-a-whistle, God-fearing Americans and scruffy, work-fearing beatniks were accompanied by a text that predicted, somewhat ominously, that Beat communities would soon rise across the United States. "We know Beatniks aren't good," teenager Luetta Peters ruefully acknowledged of the lesson she had learned, "but we thought they just dressed sloppy and talked funny. Now we know that they get married without licenses and things like that."[11]

Not surprisingly, the young Miss Peters and her brave protectors pointed to alleged or imagined instances of criminality to justify their disdain for the Beats. Indeed, district attorneys, politicians, clerics, and even prominent intellectuals worked hard to associate Beat culture with criminality. "The spirit of the beat generation," wrote the literary critic Norman Podhoretz, "strikes me as the same spirit which animates the young savages in their leather jackets who have been running amuck in the last few years with switch-blades and zip guns. . . . [I] believe that juvenile crime can be explained partly in terms of the same resentment against normal feeling and the attempt to cope with the world through intelligence that lies behind Kerouac and Ginsberg."[12] When Beat behavior transgressed the threshold of the patently felonious—for example, Lenny Bruce's arrests for narcotics possession in the early 1960s—such associations were even easier to turn into generalizations. Nevertheless, Podhoretz's vague equation between Beat hipsterism and juvenile delinquency became one of the most durable stereotypes of the entire Beat generation.

For the most part, however, law enforcement officials bent on harassing the Beats had little choice but to resort to obscenity charges. Their zeal was often relentless: Barney Rosset, publisher of Grove Press, for example, had to sell off property in order to afford the exorbitant legal fees necessary to defend several of his books in scores of prosecutions, including Henry Miller's *Tropic of Cancer* and *Tropic of Capricorn* and William Burroughs' *Naked Lunch*. In New York City, small Off Broadway theaters, movie houses, and coffeehouses periodically found their licenses revoked or suspended. One institution in particular, the Living Theater, and its directors Julian Beck and

Judith Malina, were repeatedly harassed by federal agents. And in San Francisco and Berkeley in the mid-1960s, productions of Michael McClure's play *The Beard*—a lustful and passionate confrontation between two icons of American popular culture, Billy the Kid and Jean Harlow, which culminated in an explicit recreation of heterosexual cunnilingus—were continually hounded by police and prosecutors: over a period of three years, both McClure and the cast were arrested more than twenty times on pornography charges, including arrests on nineteen consecutive nights during the show's Los Angeles run.[13]

The psychological and financial effects of these repeated prosecutions were often devastating. During a twenty-year career in which he challenged what he felt was the hypocrisy of organized religion and other political and social institutions, Lenny Bruce was arrested nearly twenty times on obscenity charges.[14] The rigors of these arrests and prosecutions and the devastating publicity and canceled performances that followed ultimately destroyed Bruce's career. Once able to command more than $3,500 per week, the demoralized comedian was forced to declare bankruptcy in October 1965. Less than a year later, he would die of a morphine overdose at the age of forty.

Wallace Berman, too, was shattered after his arrest and conviction in 1957 for exhibiting "pornographic" work at the Ferus Gallery in Los Angeles. After receiving several complaints about Berman's exhibition—a group of three, mixed-media assemblages replete with mystical symbols, Latin and Hebrew inscriptions, and photographs and drawings of genitalia and heterosexual intercourse—the LA vice squad telephoned the gallery and offered the artist the option of removing the offending work. Berman was defiant. So foreign was his art to the arresting officers that they had trouble determining what, in the end, was even obscene. Trial judge Kenneth Halliday, who had earlier found Henry Miller guilty of obscenity, refused a defense motion to present testimony affirming the work's artistic merits, remarking that "we have no need to have an expert tell us what is pornographic."[15] During the trial and its aftermath, Berman received little public support. Judge Halliday's guilty verdict left the artist depressed and unable to [open] . . . his studio for weeks. He retreated further into a "highly personal, hermetic language, arcane even to those who knew him"— although the trial itself may not have been the sole cause of the evolution in his sensibility.[16] As critic John Coplans surmised in 1963, Berman had learned a new and complex means of survival: the

construction of a vision so internal that it would confound even the most zealous censor.[17]

These narratives of suppression tell another, more revealing story about the deep and abiding anxieties provoked by radical culture in the fifties and early sixties. American attitudes toward unconventional styles and behavior was, of course, more complex than cold war stereotypes might suggest: a national survey on conformity conducted in 1953, for example, reported that participants ranked academics, writers, and artists higher than business leaders or politicians in social stature because of the "assumed propensity of intellectuals to question things most people took for granted."[18] Even public opinion on obscenity was less than intransigent: in a controversial and much publicized campaign that centered on the issue of obscenity, Justice Horace Wilkie of the Wisconsin Supreme Court was reelected in 1964 after his opponent bitterly and continually attacked his earlier, tie-breaking vote to free Henry Miller's *Tropic of Cancer* for sale in the state. In this contest, which became a referendum on conservative Christian values versus the right to free speech, a slim majority of the voting public sided with Wilkie, agreeing with the idea expressed by a number of newspapers across the state that "we do not want right-wingers. . . . setting themselves up as the arbiters of what we and the rest of Wisconsin can read."[19] By this time, the remnants of an entrenched, mostly straight, white, male status quo, people already in command of the legal apparatus necessary to ween out unwanted words and images, could not shake a deeper, unspoken fear: that the power to control the sensibility and limits of culture was slipping from their grasp.

Cold war America was teeming with cultural watchdogs—members of church committees and parent-teacher associations, Daughters of the American Revolution and American Legionnaires, district attorneys and city councilmen—who prowled the artistic landscape in search of the abnormal, the maladjusted, and the nonconformist. Thus, Congressman George A. Dondero warned of a foreign enemy that wreaked of "all the isms of depravity, decadence and destruction." He continued:

> Cubism aims to destroy by design disorder. Futurism aims to destroy by a machine myth. Dadaism aims to destroy by ridicule. Expressionism aims to destroy by aping the primitive and insane. . . . Abstractionism aims to destroy by the denial of reason. . . . Abstractionism, or non-objectivity . . . was spawned as a . . . Communist product. . . . Who has brought down this curse upon

us; who has let into our homeland this horde of germ carrying art vermin?[20]

Driven by such paranoid and reactionary logic, rhetoric reminiscent in both tone and content of the Nazi campaigns against "degenerate" art, the legal moralists of the day conscripted the Beats to represent any number of social and cultural ills: to the Massachusetts Supreme Court, they were "brutal, obscene and disgusting."[21] To a judge in Boston, they were fornicators who "portrayed unnatural acts."[22] To the New York Bureau of Narcotics, they were drug pushers.[23] To J. Edgar Hoover, they were violent enemies who had to be reformed, reined in, set straight.[24] Thus it is not surprising that upon Ginsberg's release from Columbia Presbyterian Psychiatric Institute in 1950, where he had been hospitalized for eight months for depression, he was encouraged to "try harder to conform to American norms . . . [to] go straight, get a job, get married."[25]

Of all the crimes against nature and God, homosexuality was perhaps the most egregious. The homophobia of the 1950s, like the pervasive homophobia of today, often served as a useful tool for discrediting the cultural enemies of the day. Although homosexual sex, through a multitude of local sodomy laws, was (and frequently still is) illegal in many states, obscenity prosecutions against the Beats were not about acts but representations. Yet the innate association between criminality and homosexuality was often used to cast doubt on any words or images that represented gay sexual behavior. It is for this reason that prosecutors in the trials of Burroughs, Bruce, Ginsberg, and others strategically cited passages on gay fellatio and anal sodomy in court in order to prove that the work in question was illegal and dangerous.

Anti-gay hatred was so insidious that even offending artists who weren't homosexual were transformed by censors into handmaidens of the gay conspiracy. When Michael McClure and the cast of The Beard were arrested in San Francisco in 1966, for example, the district attorney's office charged them, among other things, with lewd and dissolute conduct in a public place, the "charge most frequently used against homosexuals arrested in men's rooms."[26] Lenny Bruce recounted that during his first obscenity arrest, over the use of the word "cocksucker," the police officer reminded him that the word signified a "favorite homosexual practice" and was against the law to say in public. During the March 1962 trial in San Francisco, Bruce's attorney, Albert Bendich, attempting to prove that community standards

already sanctioned a gay and even homoerotic presence, asked the officer about other clubs he patrolled in the neighborhood. While Bruce had never performed in Finocchio's, a well-known gay hangout, his attorney had the officer describe the club's ever-present coterie of scantily clad transvestites. In effect, Bendich understood the underlying juridical subtext, one that fought hard to equate criminal depravity with homosexuality; he successfully fought back by reminding the court that while some communities would prefer to banish homosexuals, others welcomed them with open arms.[27]

Perhaps the most tragic aspect of the crusade against gays, and the greatest testament to the power of the censor to do considerable political and psychic damage, was the extent to which homophobia was internalized by artists under fire. In a number of instances, prosecutors were able to coax defendants and their witnesses into conceding that homosexuality was in some way immoral or unhealthy. Ginsberg, testifying at the trial of Naked Lunch in Boston Superior Court in 1963, for example, attempted to appease prosecutors by citing several examples of how he felt Burroughs exposed the homosexual tendency "to control other people," an impulse he later analogized to Nazism.[28] Similarly, in the Howl trial, the chief defense witness observed that Ginsberg's references to homosexuality indicated a "corrupt sexual act" that contributed to the "picture which the author is trying to give us of modern life as a state of hell."[29]

The ideological need to rid society of gay and lesbian imagery is, in part, motivated by an awareness that these representations, continually announcing, and hence to some extent regularizing, the homosexual presence, are important forces for cultural and political enfranchisement.[30] As anthropologist Carole Vance observes:

> Diversity in images and expression in the public sector nurtures and sustains diversity in private life. When losses are suffered in public arenas, people for whom controversial or minority images are salient and affirming suffer a real defeat. Defending private rights—to behavior, to images, to information—is difficult without a publicly formed and visible community. People deprived of images become demoralized and isolated, and they become increasingly vulnerable to attacks on their private expression of nonconformity, which are inevitable once sources of public solidarity and resistance have been eliminated.[31]

That people deprived of this access to self-representation and self-expression become demoralized and isolated, an observation borne out by

Allen Ginsberg reads his poem, *Howl,* outside the U.S. Court of Appeals in Washington, D.C.

some of the stories of Beat artists under fire, points to the terroristic power of censorship. The censor, wanting to engender a chilling cultural climate that literally scares artists into submission, exercises immense political power by attempting to forcibly take away the voices of the targets—a reality eloquently challenged by Berman who, after Judge Halliday's guilty verdict was read, mutely walked over to the courtroom blackboard and scrawled the words "There is no justice. There is just revenge."[32]

When it comes to gay men and lesbians and other contested minority groups, it may be muteness (denying the power to represent) rather than physical repression (preventing the act itself) that is the goal of the censor. There is a kind of parallelism between the desire to censor and the need to deny oppressed peoples a voice. The courts have usually interpreted open (i.e., voiced) homosexuality, for example, as dangerous to society's well-being; only when it is closeted (i.e., unspoken) does it have a reasonable chance of falling within the boundaries of legality.[33] The legal permission to proclaim materials "obscene" is also built on the desire to render them speechless, to drive them into a kind of juridical closet. Thus, there is a fine line between the authorized, official power to regulate "obscene" materials and

the extralegal power to coerce people into hiding their ideas, their emotions, and even their personal identities.[34]

The idea that censorship often goes hand in hand with an underlying desire to deny minority peoples a voice is underscored by another anxiety about the Beats: their proximity to African-American culture. If the denial of homosexual rights was one of the most overtly stated desires of the Beat censor, the fear of African-American power and of the burgeoning civil rights movement was perhaps the most hidden and unconscious. Unlike homosexuality, drugs, or "obscene" or pornographic representations, being black in the United States in the 1950s was not a crime, despite the vicious realities of segregation and racism. Even miscegenation, an issue strangely central to the Beat ethos, was no longer illegal in most states. Anxieties about race were therefore rarely ever part of obscenity prosecutions; instead, they lay subtly at the margins and below the surface of much hostility toward the Beats.

African-American jazz, styles, and cultural sensibilities were pervasive in the Beat milieu, associations that contributed to numerous critical misreadings. Norman Mailer, in his widely read essay "The White Negro," saw African-Americans as the positive archetypes for Beat bohemianism and juvenile delinquency, an analogy that was both retrograde and racist.[35] "Blacks supplied the argot," writes Richard Pells of Mailer's reasoning, "the worship of 'abstract states of feeling' (nourished by marijuana), and the knowledge of what it meant to live with perpetual danger. Insofar as the hipster had absorbed the 'existentialist synapses' of the blacks, he was in effect a white Negro . . . his 'intense view of existence' matched the experience of most adolescents, and reinforced their own 'desire to rebel.'"[36]

Mailer's skewed reasoning, deemed "well intentioned but poisonous" by Ginsberg and rejected by most other Beat artists, nevertheless inflected much of the critical thinking about the movement.[37] Podhoretz, dismissing an interracial love affair in Jack Kerouac's *The Subterraneans* as "one long agony of fear and trembling over sex . . . very primitive, very spontaneous, very elemental, very beat," concluded that it represented one more example of the Beats' romanticized view of interracial love and friendships.[38] To some degree confusing primary texts with Mailer's romanticized interpretation, Podhoretz complained that while blacks and whites "associate freely on a basis of complete equality and without a trace of racial hostility" in the Beat milieu of social defiance, there is in the end only "adulation for the happy, true-hearted, ecstatic Negroes of America."[39] The Beat's love of blacks, he reasoned, was tied to a fetishization of the primitive rather than any real social commitment to civil rights, a sensibility that represented "an inverted form of keeping the nigger in his place."[40]

On one level, Podhoretz's argument is not entirely unfounded. The scarcity of prominent African-Americans in the Beat movement suggests an appropriative, hierarchical, and sometimes disingenuous relationship to black culture. Often, too, the African-American presence in Beat literature and art signified negative or generalized values that rarely considered the complexity of black culture. The association of the "negro streets" as a haven for drug addicts in the opening lines of "Howl" represents a rather typical example of this phenomenon. Yet Podhoretz strategically misses another level of social meaning: in a period galvanized by fears of the mingling of the races (*Brown* v. *Board of Education I* and *II*, the US Supreme Court's landmark and controversial school desegregation rulings, were handed down in 1954 and 1955, respectively), the Beats were advocating an open, interracial culture. Indeed, the Beat milieu was relatively integrated in contrast to virtually all other white-identified avant-gardist movements in the twentieth century.[41] While African-American music, literature, and art did not need validation from whites (except as a means of entering the cultural mainstream), associations with African-American culture helped spur the Beat's own, sometimes socially astute attitudes toward race and racism. In an analysis of Burrough's *Naked Lunch* at the Boston trial, for example, Ginsberg maintained that a passage singled out by the court as "grossly offensive" (despite its relatively mild language) was, in fact, a "brilliant and funny" satire of the "monstrous speech and thought processes" of the "anti-Negro . . . anti-Northern, anti-Semitic . . . Southern, white racist bureaucrat."[42] Such satires and commentaries appeared in the work of a number of other Beat figures, including Ginsberg, Bruce, and LeRoi Jones—writing that often associated racism with the provincialism, philistinism, hypocrisy, and conformity of American life that the Beats so fervently rejected.[43]

Lenny Bruce, for example, often joined Jewish and black idioms in his act as a means of "symbolizing his rejection of a WASP-controlled society that he considered lacking in honesty, decency, mercy, and morality."[44] Incorporating improvisational techniques, slang, and phrases drawn from black jazz culture (as well as attacking anti-black stereotypes in Hollywood, the anti-Communist indifference to the lack of freedom for blacks in the United States, and de facto segregation in liberal communities), Bruce attempted to bring "Jewish ethical and social values to bear on the black movement for civil rights."[45] But the end of Jim Crow segregation was followed by a particularly virulent conservative backlash. That such associations were threatening to reactionary forces in the United States was confirmed by Ginsberg's investigation in the 1970s of extralegal operations of government agencies designed to undermine dissident groups during the cold war period.[46] "In sum," wrote Ginsberg, "there *was* a vast bureaucratic conspiracy to brainwash the public . . . separate the generations, project obnoxious images of youth, divide black and white citizens, abort and blackmail . . . [the] social leadership of black citizens, set blacks on each other, provoke whites to murderous confusion, confound honest media, infiltrate, prevaricate and spy on reformist multitudes, becloud understanding and community, and poison public consciousness."[47] There is no doubt that censorship contributed to these repressive goals; reading between the lines of both popular and juridical texts of the day, one intuits the reactive fear of homosexual, black, and erotic bodies then seemingly poised to overtake the power of white, heterosexual, bourgeois men.

Over the past decade, the United States has witnessed a remarkable escalation of censorious actions—aggressive campaigns built on the very apprehensions about homosexuality, race, eroticism, drugs, nonconformity, and the unification of minority voices that fueled the censorship of the Beats forty years ago. Works like filmmaker Marlon Riggs' *Tongues Untied*, a documentary on black, gay men, Andres Serrano's *Piss Christ*, a photograph of a crucifix suspended in urine, performance artist Karen Finley's feminist allegory in which she smeared herself with chocolate, and photographer Robert Mapplethorpe's explicit, homoerotic photographs of African-American men are powerful representations of minority interests expressed through defiant, multiple, and convergent identities. Their direct opposition to the "hegemonic model of straight, white, bourgeois male identity traditionally privileged in Western art history"—has produced a fire storm of vehement, even vitriolic protest.[48]

But as the censorious campaigns of the fifties and early sixties prove, it remains unclear where public opinion actually lies with regard to such issues as "family values," obscenity, or censorship.

After Patrick Buchanan proclaimed in a series of articles, speeches, and an address at the 1992 Republican National Convention that America was in the midst of a "cultural war," public opinion polls indicated that he had gone too far in allowing the venomous bigotry of the far-right to slip out in full view of the nation. Like the crazed Joseph McCarthy at the end of his reign of terror or the hysterical diatribes of Congressman Dondero, one could detect a bit of desperation in Buchanan's sneering screed: "As with our rivers and lakes, we need to clean up our culture: for it is a well from which we all must drink. Just as poisoned land will yield up poison fruits, so a polluted culture, left to fester and stink, can destroy a nation's soul."[49]

If there is one difference between the zealots of the 1950s and contemporary fundamentalists, however, it is that the latter tend to artfully conceal their desire to censor behind an anti-elitist rejection of government funding for the arts. Nevertheless, both hone in on similar issues of sexuality, blasphemy, and obscenity: religious leaders of the Christian right, such as the Rev. Donald Wildmon and his American Family Association, willfully manipulate the public into rechanneling its fears about the Communist menace toward a post-cold war homosexual monster who threatens our children and our moral standing. Hatred for gay men and lesbians consumes conservative social critics—disturbed individuals who, like *Washington Times* writer Richard Grenier, yearn for the moment when they might "set fire to . . . Mapplethorpe['s body], and not just as a self-expression, but as *performance art*."[50] And others, such as *New Criterion* editor Hilton Kramer, struggle to shore up the cultural status quo against the tide of a presumed multiculturalist erosion of standards and quality.

Within this cultural context, it should not be surprising that more than thirty years after his first confrontation with the law, the radical, outspoken, and openly gay Allen Ginsberg would once again be silenced. In 1988, a reading of "Howl" was bumped off the air, the victim of a Federal Communications Commission regulation intended to ban "indecency" from radio broadcasts. A year later, a still angry Ginsberg wrote to arch-conservative Jesse Helms, protesting the senator's sponsorship of an infamous and draconian "Arts-Control" amendment: "These hypocrite scoundrels have muscled their way into museums already, and plan to extend their own control-addiction to arts councils, humanities programs, universities. How long will Congress,

the Public & Arts be held hostage to this cultural Mafia?"[51] If the events of the past forty years are any indication, it may well be that we will always be cultural hostages. For when it comes to the suppression of artistic words and images, there is a tragic propensity for history to repeat itself, the howl of the censor growing louder and more menacing with each assault.

Notes

1. For more on these events, see J. W. Ehrlich, ed., *Howl of the Censor: The Four Letter Word on Trial* (San Carlos, California: Nourse, 1961); Lawrence Ferlinghetti, "Horn on HOWL," *Evergreen Review*, 4 (1957), pp. 145-58; J. G. Fuller, "Trade Winds: Ginsberg Trial," *Saturday Review*, 40 (October 5, 1957), pp. 5-7; and Michael Schumacher, *Dharma Lion: A Critical Biography of Allen Ginsberg* (New York: St. Martin's Press, 1992), pp. 254-55.

2. Schumacher, *Dharma Lion*, p. 260.

3. Horn, as quoted in Edward de Grazia, *Girls Lean Back Everywhere: The Law of Obscenity and the Assault on Genius* (New York: Random House, 1992), p. 337. Associate Justice William Brennan, writing in *Roth*, reasoned that sex, rather than "utterly without redeeming social importance," has "indisputably been a subject of absorbing interest to mankind throughout the ages." Although the Supreme Court ruled that obscenity per se was not protected by the Constitution, it nevertheless attempted to decide what constituted obscenity. As such, it offered a test based on whether the "average person, applying contemporary standards, [would conclude that] the dominant theme of the material taken as a whole appeals to prurient interests." The Court's muddled reasoning—notions of the average person or prurience are always variable and subjective—may have been intentional. By keeping such definitions hazy, the Court left room for juries and judges to protect sexual representations tied to social or cultural content. For more on the case, see Albert B. Gerber, *Sex, Pornography, and Justice* (New York: Lyle Stuart, 1965), pp. 125-33, and Marjorie Heins, *Sex, Sin, and Blasphemy: A Guide to America's Censorship Wars* (New York: The New Press, 1993), pp. 20-21, 30.

4. Horn concluded: "The answer is that life is not encased in one formula whereby everyone acts the same or conforms to a particular pattern. . . . An author should be real in treating his subject and be allowed to express his thoughts and ideas in his own words"; quoted in De Grazia, *Girls Lean Back Everywhere*, p. 338.

5. While the wording of the First Amendment—"Congress shall make no law . . . abridging the freedom of speech"—would appear to suggest an absolute right to free speech, certain exceptions have always been sanctioned by society and the courts: libel, slander, threats, extortion, perjury, fraud, "fighting words," and, at least since the mid-nineteenth century, "obscenity." For the juridical and societal constructions of obscenity and censorship, see Heins, *Sex, Sin, and Blasphemy*, pp. 1-14.

6. Recently, the concept of what is censorious has grown even more complicated. Advocates of minority groups, for example, arguing that bigoted words and images

can wound and endanger already vulnerable minds, have recently called for codes against hate speech. And some feminists, theorizing that degrading images of women can engender misogynist or sexually violent behavior in men, have supported more stringent anti-pornography laws.

7. Through radio and television interviews and trial reports in major newspapers and national magazines—including *Life*, *Saturday Review*, *The Nation*, *New Republic*, and *Newsweek*—the *Howl* prosecution attained national media standing. Ironically, Ferlinghetti's legal problems boosted sales. By the end of the trial, the book was in its fourth printing, and thousands of mimeographed copies were also in circulation.

8. Richard Cándida Smith, *Utopia and Dissent: Art, Poetry, and Politics in California* (Berkeley and Los Angeles: University of California Press, 1995), p. 157.

9. "Squaresville U.S.A. vs. Beatsville," *Life*, September 21, 1959, pp. 31-37.

10. Ibid., p. 31.

11. Ibid., p. 37.

12. Norman Podhoretz, "The Know-Nothing Bohemians," *Partisan Review*, 25 (Spring 1958), p. 318.

13. In another important and harsh application of obscenity laws, Jonas Mekas was prosecuted in 1964 for showing the film *Flaming Creatures* by Jack Smith. For further discussion of this incident, see John Hanhardt's essay, p. 216 below.

14. The judge in the Chicago case, one of several that actually went to trial, imposed such an exorbitant punishment (Bruce was sentenced to a $1,000 fine and a year's imprisonment) that the case was appealed. The Supreme Court of Illinois in 1964 refused to reverse the conviction, basing its decision on a tape recording of Bruce's act in which he joked about Jimmy Hoffa as a Christ figure, the vows of celibacy taken by Catholic priests and nuns, and condoms in toilet vending machines. Less than a week later the US Supreme Court further undercut local obscenity laws with its landmark *Jacobellis* decision. Following the Court's lead, the Illinois judges unilaterally moved to vacate their earlier decision, reasoning that Bruce's "entire performance was [now] immunized" from the possibility of an obscenity conviction because it contained material of "social importance." Another unsuccessful trial in New York became a national media event, with an imposing array of cultural stars testifying for the defense—from newspaper columnist Dorothy Kilgallen (who described Bruce as a brilliant social satirist and "moral man") to Episcopal minister Sidney Lanier (who maintained that Bruce's nightclub act was "in some ways helpful, even healing"). For more on the Bruce prosecutions, see Gerber, *Sex, Pornography, and Justice*, pp. 219-26.

15. For an account of the trial, see Smith, *Utopia and Dissent*, pp. 225-31.

16. Ibid., p. 231.

17. Ibid.

18. Ibid., p. 157.

19. Editorial, *Capital Times*, March 16, 1964; quoted in E. R. Hutchison, *Tropic of Cancer on Trial: A Case History of Censorship* (New York: Grove Press, 1968), p. 229.

20. George A. Dondero, "Modern Art Shackled To Communism," speech given in the US House of Representatives, August 16, 1949, *Congressional Record*, First Session, 81st Congress. I would like to thank Donna De Salvo for directing me to this material.

21. *Attorney General* v. *A Book Named "Naked Lunch,"* Supreme Court of Massachusetts, July 7, 1966; reprinted in Williams S. Burroughs, *Naked Lunch*, Black Cat Edition (New York: Grove Weidenfeld, 1966), p. viii.

22. "Excerpts from the Boston Trial of *Naked Lunch*," in Burroughs, *Naked Lunch*, p. xxiv.

23. In 1965, the Bureau, inspired by Allen Ginsberg's call for the legalization of marijuana and his well-publicized narcotics use, decided that Ginsberg was a drug dealer and launched a harassment campaign; see Schumacher, *Dharma Lion*, p. 449.

24. Ibid., for Hoover's file on Ginsberg.

25. De Grazia, *Girls Lean Back Everywhere*, p. 329.

26. See Smith, *Utopia and Dissent*, pp. 338-39.

27. For the arrest and trial, see Lenny Bruce, *How to Talk Dirty and Influence People: An Autobiography* (New York: Fireside, 1992), pp. 104-28.

28. "Excerpts from the Boston Trial of *Naked Lunch*," in Burroughs, *Naked Lunch*, pp. xxviii-xxix. Burroughs' lurid and graphic novel became embroiled in a number of repressive crusades, including two major obscenity prosecutions, after its US publication in 1962: a 1965 trial in Los Angeles, in which the book was cleared of charges, and a less successful one in Superior Court in Boston in 1963. Despite defense testimony from such expert witnesses as Norman Mailer, Allen Ginsberg, and John Ciardi, the Boston court ruled against Burroughs. On July 7, 1966, the Massachusetts Supreme Court, finding that *Naked Lunch* had not been "commercially exploited for the sake of prurient appeal, to the exclusion of other values," reversed the earlier decision and thus eliminated the threat of a statewide ban; see *Attorney General* v. *A Book Named "Naked Lunch,"* p. ix.

29. Mark Schorer, quoted in Schumacher, *Dharma Lion*, p. 261.

30. There are, of course, a number of other reasons for the imperative to impugn homosexuality. Conservative campaigns to restore traditional social arrangements (or, in present-day parlance, "family values") innately view gay men and lesbians as suspect because they don't reproduce "normal" family life; they are thought to be childless and employed in "frivolous" and economically marginal fields. On these issues, see Allan Sekula, "Gay Bashing as an Art Form" (1989), in Richard Bolton, ed., *Culture Wars: Documents from the Recent Controversies in the Arts* (New York: The New Press, 1992), pp. 118-20.

31. Carole Vance, "The War on Culture" (1989), in Bolton, *Culture Wars*, p. 111.

32. See Smith, *Utopia and Dissent*, p. 227.

33. In *Doe* v. *Casey*, the plaintiff was dismissed from his job as a CIA agent after he voluntarily revealed his homosexuality to a CIA security officer. A federal appeals court, denying that Doe could be stigmatized by his dismissal, reasoned that "the real stigma imposed

by [the employer's] action . . . is the charge of homosexuality." The court, taking a typical "don't ask, don't tell" position, argued that Doe, seeing nothing scandalous in his own homosexuality and thus having no "liberty interest" in evading its consequences, was in some sense to blame for his legal problems. Thus, a self-identified homosexual in government, in order to retain a legally self-protective interest in his or her job, "must (1) subjectively regard his or her homosexuality as degrading and (2) hide it." For more on the case, see Janet E. Halley, "The Politics of the Closet: Legal Articulation of Sexual Orientation Identity," in Dan Danielson and Karen Engles, eds., *After Identity: A Reader in Law and Culture* (New York and London: Routledge, 1995), pp. 33-34.

34. To a great extent, the epistemic violence of censorship can be analogized to the physical violence frequently directed at homosexuals, women, and people of color. If such violence "aims to deform, and often utterly, to destroy, its targets," as Kendall Thomas suggests, censorship results in a kind of representational murder, wherein offending images and words are obliterated. Like the legal structures for outlining and enacting censorious acts, homophobic violence, for example, can also be understood as a kind of coercive "institution," as Thomas has recently argued, a social construction "structured by rules that define roles and positions, powers and opportunities, thereby distributing responsibility for consequences." Thus, the objective and result of violence against lesbians and gays is the "social control of human sexuality through the regulation of the erotic economy of contemporary American society and the enforcement of the institutional and ideological imperatives of what Adrienne Rich has termed 'compulsory heterosexuality.'" Insofar as homophobic assault is motivated by the desire to prevent actual or imagined deviations from heterosexual acts and identities by creating a kind of chill effect, it mimics the imperatives of censorship; both are undeniably powerful tools for undermining homosexual rights by discouraging gay men and lesbians from coming out and reinforcing the negative impression of homosexuality in the public sphere. See Kendall Thomas, "Beyond the Privacy Principal," in Danielson and Engles, *After Identity*, p. 290, and Claudia Card, "Rape as a Terrorist Institution," in R. G. Frey and Christopher W. Morris, eds., *Violence, Terrorism, and Justice* (Cambridge, England: Cambridge University Press, 1991), pp. 297-98.

35. Norman Mailer, "The White Negro: Superficial Reflections on the Hipster," *Dissent*, 4 (Summer 1957), pp. 276-93.

36. Richard Pells, *The Liberal Mind in a Conservative Age: American Intellectuals in the 1940s and 1950s* (New York: Harper & Row, 1985), p. 209.

37. Allen Ginsberg, quoted in Schumacher, *Dharma Lion*, p. 341.

38. Podhoretz, "The Know-Nothing Bohemians," p. 310.

39. Ibid.

40. Ned Polsky, quoted by Podhoretz, ibid., p. 311.

41. I would like to thank Lisa Phillips for pointing out to me this usually misunderstood aspect of the Beat movement.

42. Ginsberg, "Excerpts from the Boston Trial of *Naked Lunch*," in Burroughs, *Naked Lunch*, pp. xxx-xxxi.

43. See, for example, LeRoi Jones, "Correspondence: The Beat Generation," *Partisan Review*, 25 (Summer 1958), p. 473.

44. Frank Kofsky, *Lenny Bruce: The Comedian as Social Critic and Secular Moralist* (New York: Monad Press, 1974), p. 90.

45. Ibid., p. 98.

46. These agencies included the FBI, CIA, Bureau of Narcotics, and the Drug Enforcement Administration; see Schumacher, *Dharma Lion*, pp. 624-25.

47. Ginsberg, quoted in ibid., p. 625.

48. See Kobena Mercer, "Skin Head Sex Thing: Racial Difference and the Homoerotic Imaginary," in *Welcome to the Jungle: New Positions in Black Cultural Studies* (New York and London: Routledge, 1994), p. 191. For the censorship battles of recent years, see Bolton, *Culture Wars*; Maurice Berger, "Too Shocking To Show," *Art in America*, 80 (July 1992), pp. 37-39; and Brian Wallis, "Bush's Compromise: A Newer Form of Censorship?" *Art in America*, 78 (November 1990), pp. 57-63, 210.

49. Patrick Buchanan, "How Can We Clean Up Our Art Act?" *The Washington Post*, June 19, 1989, quoted in Vance, "The War on Culture," p. 109.

50. Richard Grenier, "A Burning Issue Lights Artistic Ire," *Washington Times*, June 28, 1989, reprinted in Bolton, *Culture Wars*, p. 44.

51. Ginsberg, letter to Jesse Helms, August 14, 1989, reprinted in Bolton, *Culture Wars*, p. 92.

PETER B. LEVY (ESSAY DATE 1999)

SOURCE: Levy, Peter B. "Beating the Censor: The 'Howl' Trial Revisited." In *Beat Culture: The 1950s and Beyond*, edited by Cornelis A. van Minnen, Jaap van der Bent, and Mel van Elteren, pp. 107-16. Amsterdam: VU University Press, 1999.

In the following essay, Levy highlights the Beat Generation's impact on Americans' constitutional right to freedom of speech by examining the 1957 Howl *obscenity trial.*

Students of American history have often characterized the 1950s as a claustrophobic period, one of muted political and cultural criticism. In contrast, they have cast the 1960s as a time in which all authorities were challenged and a counterculture flourished. Standard discussions of the process whereby cultural conformity gave way to youth rebellion generally mention the role the Beats played, especially their effect on the arts and on many budding new leftists who were starved for role models outside the mainstream. While no one should deny that the Beats played this role, a more sophisticated understanding of their significance must also take into account the impact they had on politics, broadly defined, especially on the law. Even though we tend to perceive the Beats as isolated rebels who recklessly and often spontaneously defied authority, they were willing and able to engage themselves in political and legal battles, as they did when they defended their constitutional right to write, publish and distribute their works in series of criminal trials. Indeed, their greatest legacy may be the long-term impact they had on one of the most fundamental freedoms, that of freedom of speech.[1]

This paper will explore this subject by revisiting the "Howl" trial of 1957, the case in which San Francisco authorities unsuccessfully sought to prohibit the publication and sale of Allen Ginsberg's signature poem. The case pit a conservative San Francisco prosecutor and police commander, bent on crushing the Beats and other deviants, against Lawrence Ferlinghetti, the owner of City Lights Bookstore and publisher of "Howl." To Ferlinghetti's defense came a loose network of left-liberals, most notably the American Civil Liberties Union (ACLU). The case demonstrated that the Beats, often seen as foes of tradition, used conventional means to pursue their ends. By framing the dispute in legalistic terms, as one which involved constitutional rights, the Beats won the support of many Americans who otherwise tended to agree with the conservative critique of the artistic and literary creations of the Beats. Ironically, as contemporaries observed, by seeking to censor "Howl," conservatives added greatly to the Beats' fame and influence. The trial transformed "Howl" from an obscure poem into a best-seller and the Beats from a minor artistic movement into defenders of democracy.[2]

Put differently, the "Howl" trial allows us to better understand the dialectic process of change that marked the 1950s and 1960s. By drawing on primary and secondary sources, including the transcript of the trial, contemporary news coverage, biographies and autobiographies, published letters and private papers, we will see how conservatives created the opportunity for a small collection of avantgarde artists to expand the meaning of freedom of expression in the United States of America. Partly as a result of the "Howl" trial, much of what was deemed illegal and obscene prior to the trial, is now commonly expressed in all sorts of media, from television and radio, to poetry and prose.

While the story of the "Howl" trial has been told elsewhere, it is worth reviewing.[3] Immediately following Ginsberg's famous public reading of "Howl," at the Six Gallery in San Francisco, Lawrence Ferlinghetti, who had only recently opened the City Lights Bookstore, wrote a brief letter to Ginsberg, in which he quoted the famous words Ralph Waldo Emerson had written upon reading Walt Whitman's *Leaves of Grass*, "I greet you at the beginning of a great career." Ferlinghetti added, "When do I get the manuscript?" Shortly after accepting Ferlinghetti's proposal to publish his poems in the newly launched "Pocket Poet Series," Ginsberg sent a copy of "Howl" to his father, also a poet. Although Ginsberg's father generally praised the poem, he also expressed misgivings about some of its language. "There is no need for dirty, ugly, words," Ginsberg's father declared. If he did not edit out these words, Ginsberg senior warned, he could expect "entanglements" with the law. In spite of, or perhaps because of his father's warnings, Allen Ginsberg chose not to edit out the poem's racier sections. On the contrary, he seemed to relish the prospect of a fight with the censor, responding to his father's plea that he was "almost ready tackle the U.S. Govt. out of sheer delight." (Allen Ginsberg also replied that the open expression of some writers, like Henry Miller and Genet, posed a "real threat to society," a somewhat underhanded criticism of his father, a life-long socialist.)[4]

Meanwhile, suspecting that "Howl" might lead to legal troubles, Ferlinghetti submitted a copy of the poem to the ACLU even before he sent it to Villiers, the English printer he had chosen to ready the first edition. As a result, when Chester McPhee, the U.S. collector of Customs, seized 520 copies of the book in late March 1957, deeming the writing "obscene," and declaring that "you wouldn't want your children to come across it," Ferlinghetti was prepared to defend the book in a court of law. (Even though written in America and published under the City Lights logo, the book came under the custom office's jurisdictions because it was technically imported from abroad.)[5] On 3 April, the ACLU notified McPhee that it would contest the seizure. In addition to the ACLU, other liberals helped Ferlinghetti make his case that McPhee and other censors, not Ginsberg, were the real threat to American values. William Hogan, a prominent columnist at the *San Francisco Chronicle*, lent Ferlinghetti his space in the 19 May Sunday edition of the *Chronicle*. Ferlinghetti used the opportunity to lambast McPhee. "It is not the poet but what he observes which is . . . obscene. The great obscene wastes of HOWL are the waste of the mechanized world, lost among atom bombs and inane nationalisms." Linking Ginsberg to a long tradition of censored artists, Ferlinghetti also sarcastically thanked McPhee for making "Howl" famous. Ten days after Ferlinghetti's column appeared, McPhee released the books and the U.S. attorney in San Francisco announced that the federal government would not prosecute the Beat publisher.[6]

Not knowing that the federal government would drop the case, Ferlinghetti printed a separate edition of "Howl" and placed it for sale at City Lights Bookstore. Identical to the original text, it lay outside the jurisdiction of customs officials, since it was printed in San Francisco, rather than England. Shortly after this edition of Ginsberg's writing appeared, Captain William Hanrahan, commander of the Juvenile Division of the San Francisco Police Department, who had a reputation as a "zealous smut hunter," proclaimed he hoped "Howl" would "open the door for a host of book seizures he wanted to initiate." In early June two of Hanrahan's officers purchased a copy of "Howl" at the City Lights Bookstore. Later that same day, city officials notified Shig Murao, the bookstore's clerk, and Ferlinghetti that they were being charged with printing and selling lewd and indecent material, and ordered the two men to come to the Hall of Justice to be booked and fingerprinted. Reacting to their arrest, one San Francisco newspaper wrote: "The Cops Don't Allow No Renaissance Here." Ginsberg, who was in Tangier, Morocco, when he received news of Ferlinghetti's arrest, displayed a bit less enthusiasm for doing battle with the government than he had in the past. Still he never considered appeasing authorities by changing the language of the poem. Certainly, his fellow Beat writer, William Burroughs, who was with Ginsberg in Tangier at the time, never suggested that he change some of the language of the poem so as to make it more acceptable to the American pallet.[7]

The ACLU, which bailed Ferlinghetti and Murao from jail, quickly assembled a top team of defense attorneys, including Lawrence Spieser and Albert Bendich, ACLU's lead trial counsel and staff counsel, and J. W. "Jake" Ehrlich, a prominent criminal attorney who had been in practice in San Francisco since the 1920s and who had recently gained fame by defending death row inmate Caryl Chessman. Assistant District Attorney Ralph McIntosh, who had a long record of successfully prosecuting publishers and producers of nudist publications and pornographic movies (including *The Outlaw,* starring Jane Russell), represented the state. The case was assigned to the court of Judge Clayton Horn, a Sunday School teacher, who had gained notoriety by sentencing a woman convicted of shoplifting to view *The Ten Commandments* and write an essay on its "moral lesson."[8]

With the help of Ferlinghetti, Ehrlich readied an assortment of well-respected expert witnesses, including Mark Schorer and Leo Lowenthal, both professors at the University of California, Berkeley, Kenneth Rexroth, a renowned San Francisco poet, Mark Linethal, Walter Van Tilburg, Arthur Foff, and Herbert Blau, all professors at San Francisco State College, and Vincent McHugh, a novelist and prominent book reviewer. Almost every one of these expert witnesses had taught at top colleges and universities, including Harvard, Stanford and Columbia, and served as book reviewers and on the editorial boards of prominent newspapers and magazines, ranging from the *New York Times* and *San Francisco Chronicle* to the *New Yorker* and the *Nation*. In many ways, they represented the liberal literary establishment of the time. For instance, Mark Schorer, Ehrlich's first expert witness, chaired the graduate studies program in English at the University of California at Berkeley, had taught at the University of Wisconsin, Dartmouth College and Harvard University, and had already had published three novels, about seventy-five short stories, innumerable pieces of literary criticism, magazine articles and book reviews.[9]

After arguing that the court had to judge "Howl" in its entirety, rather than just looking at individual words to determine if Ginsberg's poems were obscene, a position lent weight by the Supreme Court's recent ruling in the *Roth* case (1957), Ehrlich steered his experts into demonstrating that "Howl" was a serious work of art. Schorer testified that the poem "attempts and intends to make a significant comment on or interpretation of human existence as the author knows it." Rexroth, who had presided over the initial reading of "Howl" in 1955, stated that it was "probably the most remarkable single poem published by a young man since the end of the second world war." Others similarly praised the literary value of "Howl" and the other poems published alongside it by Ferlinghetti.[10]

During cross-examination, Assistant District Attorney McIntosh sought to focus the court's attention on the poem's most ribald sections. Yet, by arguing that the poem's slang and sexual language added to its literary value, that the particular words Ginsberg chose were central to the tone he sought to create, one expert witness after another deflected McIntosh's attempt to paint "Howl" as obscene. For example, after reading the following passage: "Who blew and were blown by those human seraphim, the sailors, caresses of Atlantic and Caribbean love," McIntosh asked if "*those* [my emphasis] words are necessary." Professor Schorer responded: "The essence of the poem is the impression of a world in which all sexuality is confused and corrupted. These words indicate a corrupt sexual act. Therefore, they are part of the essence of the picture which the author is trying to give us of modern life as a state of hell." After reading another passage replete with slang and sexually suggestive language, McIntosh exploded: "Couldn't that have been worded some other way? Do they have to put words like that in there?" Ehrlich quickly objected to McIntosh's question on the grounds that the expert could not testify as to whether the author "could have used another term or not." More to McIntosh's dismay, not only did Judge Horn uphold Ehrlich's objection, he commented, "it is obvious that the author *could* [my emphasis] have used another term; whether or not it would have served the same purpose is another thing; that's up to the author."[11]

McIntosh called only two expert witnesses, David Kirk and Gail Potter. In contrast to those called by the defense, neither Kirk nor Potter were leading figures in the field of literary criticism. Kirk was a doctoral student at Stanford and an assistant professor of English at the University of San Francisco. Potter had taken some graduate courses but had no advanced degree and she was employed only as a part-time teacher. Kirk testified that "Howl" had "negligible literary merit." Potter agreed. During cross examination Kirk acknowledged that he knew little about modern American literature—his speciality was seventeenth century English literature. Ehrlich also got Kirk to praise works by Walt Whitman, Voltaire and others, which, Ehrlich then informed the court, had once been censored as obscene. Ehrlich did not even bother cross examining Potter, whose main complaint was that Ginsberg's poem made her feel like she was "going through the gutter." Potter did not help the prosecutor when she "assured" the court that she had not "lingered long" on the meaning of the poem.[12]

In his summation, McIntosh appealed to the court's sense of propriety. "I would like you to ask yourself, your Honor, in determining whether or not these books are obscene, would you like to see this sort of poetry printed in your local newspaper, that is to say, be read by your family, that type of thing?" Or, McIntosh rhetorically inquired, "would you like to have this poetry read over the air on the radio . . . ? In other words, your Honor, how far are we going to license the use of filthy, vulgar, obscene and disgusting language? How far can we go?" Ehrlich countered by emphasizing the dangers posed by state censorship. He bolstered his argument by citing several federal court rulings, including Judge Learned Hand's opinion in the case of *Gordon versus the Commonwealth of Pennsylvania,* in which the court had freed James Joyce's *Ulysses* from the grips of the censor. "That numerous long passages in *Ulysses* contain matter that is obscene under any fair definition of the word cannot be gainsaid," Hand had written, Ehrlich reminded the court. "Yet," still citing Hand, Ehrlich stated, "they are relevant to the purpose of depicting the thoughts of the characters and are introduced to give meaning to the whole, rather than to promote lust or portray filth for its own sake." To temper McIntosh's alarm over the slang terms included in Ginsberg's writing, Ehrlich established that Christopher Marlowe, one of Shakespeare's influences, had used the word "fuck." "I don't think that the mere use of one word is going to destroy anyone's morals or cause them to embrace that which is base and unworthy of an intellectual decency," Ehrlich asserted. "Impure sexual thoughts or prurient interest is self-generated by a desiring mind which is disposed to lewdness and impure sexual thoughts."[13]

Citing the *Roth* case (1957) and several other relatively recent federal court decisions, Judge Horn issued a clear, concise and unambiguous ruling. "While the publishing of 'smut' or 'hard core pornography' is without any social importance and obscene by present-day standards, and should be punished for the good of the community," Horn maintained, "since there is no straight and unwavering line to act as a guide, censorship by the Government should be held in tight reign. To act otherwise," Horn declared, "would destroy our freedoms of free speech and press." Invoking Justice William Douglas's dictum: "I have the same confidence in the ability of our people to reject noxious literature as I have in their capacity to sort out the true from the false in theology, economics, politics, or any other field," Horn ruled that *Howl and Other Poems* had "some redeeming social importance" and thus were "not obscene." Accordingly, he concluded, "the defendant [was] not guilty."[14]

The audience in the packed courtroom, which one observer described as "the most fantastic collection of beards, turtle-necked shirts and Italian hair-dos ever to grace the grimy precincts of the Hall of Justice," gleefully responded to the Horn's ruling. The *San Francisco Chronicle* approvingly called the decision a "landmark of law." While Ferlinghetti did not issue a public statement at the time, he subsequently wrote an article for the

Evergreen Review, an artistic magazine given life by the decision in the "Howl" trial, entitled "Horn on Howl," in which he thanked a wide variety of writers, academics and organizations, from Thomas Parkinson, of University of California at Berkeley, to the Northern California Bookseller's Association, for their support. Ferlinghetti also noted that the re-election of Judge Horn, in 1958, demonstrated that the citizens of San Francisco agreed that "it was the police who were committing an obscene action." Ginsberg, who was still abroad at the time of the verdict, linked the decision to the civil rights outburst taking place in Little Rock, Arkansas, as a symbol of a new mood in America.[15]

Since most commentators have portrayed the Beats as subaltern rebels divorced from traditional politics and cast them as fore-runners, rather than as the actual agents of sweeping political and cultural change, the "Howl" trial has received little serious attention. One recent Pulitzer Prize winning work on the post-World War II era, literally relegates the trial to the status of a footnote, indicating that the incident was insignificant in terms of understanding the Beats or more importantly the main currents or themes of the recent past. This historian should not be blamed for portraying the Beats in this way, as he builds his interpretation on the works of tens of other scholars and writers who have treated the Beats, and more specifically the "Howl" trial, in a similar manner.[16]

Yet, the "Howl" trial should not be viewed as a mere footnote of history nor as a minor coincidental incident in the history of the Beats. Arguing counter factually, if Judge Horn had ruled against Ferlinghetti and/or if the ACLU and other liberals had not come to his defense, then the Beats might have been snuffed out as a literary movement. By Ferlinghetti's own reckoning, City Lights Bookstore and the pocketbook series of which "Howl" was one, would have been quashed by a guilty verdict. In addition, McIntosh would have been encouraged by a guilty verdict to pursue other "indecency" cases. Instead, the not guilty verdict inspired many other small presses and literary magazines to form. These small presses and magazines published even more daring writings and artwork, which themselves oftentimes resulted in censorship cases that further expanded the legal definition of permissible speech or expression.[17] For instance, in 1959, Federal District Court Judge Julius Hoffman, who later earned notoriety as the judge in the "Chicago Seven trial," ruled that passages of William Bur-

roughs's *Naked Lunch,* published in *Big Table,* a tiny literary journal, were not obscene. Even Ferlinghetti had chosen not to publish these writings by his fellow Beat writer, although he had supported and helped students from the University of Chicago launch the journal and get Burroughs' consent to publish sections of his novel. The same year, encouraged by several recent rulings, including the "Howl" case, Grove Press published the first "unexpurgated" edition of D. H. Lawrence's *Lady Chatterley's Lover* and readied *Naked Lunch,* in its entirety, for publication.[18]

Put differently, let me suggest that "Howl" played a role similar to that played by the *Brown* decision. Scholars of the civil rights movement have noted that the *Brown* decision alone did not result in the desegregation of public education. Rather *Brown* was part of a continuum of battles. It was preceded and succeeded by countless battles in communities across the nation that first prodded the Supreme Court to overturn *Plessy* versus *Ferguson* (1896) and then compelled federal and state authorities to enforce the decision. Similarly, the "Howl" trial was one of many other battles involving "Beat" figures, from the Boston trial of *Naked Lunch* to the harassment, arrest and trials of comedian Lenny Bruce, playwright Michael McClure, artist Wallace Berman, Grove Press publisher Barney Rosset, director Julian Beck, and political-activist writer LeRoi Jones. Taken together these legal fights transformed the meaning and practice of freedom of speech in America. They made real the views expressed by the Supreme Court in the *Roth* case and several other landmark first amendment cases. Indeed, initially the ACLU felt it had lost the *Roth* case. Only in retrospect did it recognize through decisions in the "Howl" and other cases, that Justice William Brennan's opinion in *Roth* had opened the way for a much more free society.[19]

In most of these cases, key Beat figures did not just happen to become involved in the fight to expand the legal definition of freedom of speech. Rather their participation in these legal challenges grew out of and was consistent with their general commitments. This was especially true for Ferlinghetti. In 1953, Ferlinghetti had defended artist Anton Refregier, a leftist whose works were attacked by the American Legion and the Veterans of Foreign Wars. In an article in *Art Digest,* he proclaimed that Refregier's murals symbolized the "latest battleground of intellectual and artistic censorship" and he urged other artists to defend Refregier. At a time when many feared associating themselves with leftist causes, Ferlinghetti joined the Committee for the Defense of Re-fregier's murals. Ferlinghetti also befriended Kenneth Rexroth and other independent leftists who had a tradition of political activism. After the "Howl" trial, Ferlinghetti's commitment to political causes deepened further. In 1958 he wrote his first full-fledged political poem, "A Tentative Description of a Dinner to Promote the Impeachment of President Eisenhower," which was published in *Liberation,* an independent left-wing magazine headed by A. J. Muste. (Other activists associated with *Liberation* were Dave Dellinger, Staughton Lynd and Bayard Rustin.) In 1959, Ferlinghetti and Ginsberg attended a writers' conference in Chile sponsored by the Communist Party. The following year Ferlinghetti wrote an ode to Fidel Castro, which he delivered at a Fair Play for Castro Rally in San Francisco. During the 1960s, Ferlinghetti was politically active in the antiwar movement and in the drive to impeach Nixon.[20]

While Ginsberg chose to pursue a relatively apolitical course in the 1950s, as a son of old leftists he was well aware of the historical struggle for freedom of speech that an assortment of socialists and anarchists had waged throughout American history. He explicitly paid homage to Tom Mooney, Sacco and Vanzetti, and the Scottsboro boys, all icons of the left, in "America," one of the "other" poems published alongside "Howl" in the City Lights Books' "Pocket Poet Series." He testified as an expert witness in support of Burroughs in the obscenity trials involving *Naked Lunch.* Furthermore, while some of the of Beats disdained the political antics of the New Left, Ginsberg actively participated in the movement of the 1960s.[21]

It seems to me that we can use the "Howl" trial to help us better understand several of the main themes of postwar America, especially the reach and strength of liberalism in the latter half of the 1950s and the relationship between the Beats and liberals. If not for the ACLU, which represented Ferlinghetti free of charge, it is unlikely that "Howl" would have withstood the challenge of the censor. The ACLU consisted of and was nurtured by a broad array of liberals, from its top attorneys to its anonymous financial supporters. Numerous academics and independent artists, from Mark Schorer to Kenneth Rexroth, strengthened the ACLU's case by testifying as expert witnesses and by publicly condemning the federal government and then the assistant District Attorney McIntosh for attempting to muzzle "Howl." It needs to be added that while today the ACLU is considered far to the left in its commit-

ment to civil liberties, at the time the ACLU was much more centrist, having equivocated in its defense of communists and steered clear of anything smelling of gay rights during the 1940s and early 1950s. Sympathetic newspaper and magazine columnists and writers, and their editors and publishers, from William Hogan, who lent Ferlinghetti his column, to John Fuller, who approvingly described the Beats' fight in the *Saturday Evening Post,* rallied around the cause of freedom of speech as well.[22]

In many ways David Perlman's "How Captain Hanrahan Made 'Howl' a Best-Seller," published in the *Reporter,* embodied the liberal reaction of the time and suggested that the reach of 1950s conservatism had been overestimated. In a lengthy article, Perlman described the seizure of "Howl," the arrest of Ferlinghetti, the trial itself, as well as the verdict and the public reaction to it. Overall, he characterized McIntosh as a zealot, Ferlinghetti and Ginsberg as serious artists, and Horn as a defender of the constitution. Perlman was not a radical; nor was the *Reporter.* Rather both represented a segment of the population, tolerant of artistic dissent and alarmed by right-wing zealots. Articles in the *New Republic, The Nation,* and other liberal journals took a very similar approach. Only Norman Podhoretz expressed great alarm over the work of the Beats (as opposed to the actions of the censor), and Podhoretz focused on Kerouac's *On the Road* in his widely-read jeremiad.[23]

Lastly, the "Howl" trial allows us to better understand the timing and nature of the political and cultural shift that took place during the postwar era. Too many students of recent America have adopted an overly simplistic view of the recent past; they conceive of the 1950s as a conservative decade and the 1960s as a radical one. Yet, as the "Howl" trial suggests, the lines between the two decades were never so clearly drawn. Chronologically, as Ginsberg observed, the "Howl" trial paralleled the birth of black New Left, namely the modern civil rights movement. Well before the Free Speech movement at the University of California at Berkeley in 1964, or the reinvigoration of the Students for a Democratic Society (SDS), the traditional birth dates given to the New Left, "something was happening" (to borrow the words of a popular 1960s rock tune). One of the things that was happening was that a loose network of men and women, from black clergymen in the South to avant-garde artists on the coasts were engaged in a struggle to enlarge the meaning of freedom, from freedom of speech and freedom of association to the right to vote. In other words, rather than conceiving of the Beats as a marginalized movement, cut off from a broader spectrum of left-liberals, the "Howl" trial suggests that the Beats were part of a movement that emerged in the latter part of the 1950s, blossomed in the early 1960s, and reached its zenith toward the close of the decade. Conversely, many of the same forces that assembled in opposition to the New Left and counterculture, and many of the arguments made to counter "the movement," were evident in the 1950s; they did not emerge simply as part of a backlash against the excesses of the New Left, but had been there all along, part of a long-standing tradition that favored restricting individual liberties to maintaining social order. But of course, a discussion of this topic must await another occasion.

Notes

1. See for example William O'Neill, *Coming Apart: An Informal History of America in the 1960s* (Chicago: Quadrangle, 1971); David Halberstam, *The Fifties* (New York: Villard, 1993), James T. Patterson, *Grand Expectations: The United States, 1845-1974* (New York: Oxford University Press, 1998). One typical interpretation is John Patrick Diggins, *The Proud Decades: America in War and Peace, 1941-1960* (New York: W. W. Norton, 1988). He writes that the Beats were "antipolitical" artists who "preferred to rejoice to the end rather than try to find the basis for a new beginning," 267. Likewise, Todd Gitlin, *The Sixties: Years of Hope, Days of Rage* (New York: Bantam, 1987), states: "Living in the rubble of a once-confident old left, they didn't want to change society so much as sidestep it. . . . Politics they declared was yet another boring, pointless sub-assembly in the grotesque machinery of Moloch. Their clubbiness echoed the general withdrawal from political activity," 51.

2. J. W. Ehrlich, *Howl of the Censor* (San Carlos, CA: Nourse, 1961), x-xii. In his introduction to the transcript of the trial, lead defense attorney J. W. Ehrlich linked Ginsberg to a long line of great writers whose works had once been banned, including Homer, Cervantes, Voltaire, Swift, Goethe, Dante, Balzac, Zola and Flaubert. "Ironically," Ehrlich declared, "the suppressed book in one age in many cases becomes part of the accepted literature or even the venerated classics of the next."

3. For summaries of the trial see: Barry Silesky, *Ferlinghetti: The Artist in His Time* (New York: Warner Books, 1990); Neeli Cherkovski, *Ferlinghetti: A Biography* (New York: Doubleday, 1979); Edward de Grazia, *Girls Lean Back Everywhere: The Law of Obscenity and the Assault on Genius* (New York: Random House, 1992), chapter 7; Maurice Berger, "Libraries Full of Tears: The Beats and the Law," in Lisa Phillips, ed., *Beat Culture and the New America: 1950-1965* (Paris and New York: Whitney Museum of Modern Art/Flammarion, 1995), 123-140; City Lights, "A History of Howl," http://www.citylights.com/howl.html.

4. Louis Ginsberg to Allen Ginsberg, 29 February 1956, and Allen Ginsberg to Louis Ginsberg, March 1956, both in Barry Miles, ed., *Howl: Original Draft Facsimile,* *Transcript & Variant Versions, Fully Annotated by Author, With Contemporaneous Correspondence . . .* (New York: Harper and Row, 1986), 150-151.

5. McPhee quoted in Silesky, *Ferlinghetti,* 69.

6. Lawrence Ferlinghetti, "Horn on Howl," *Evergreen Review* (Winter 1957); Lawrence Ferlinghetti, *San Francisco Chronicle* (19 May 1957): 35.

7. Neeli Cherkovski, *Ferlinghetti,* 101-102; Lawrence Ferlinghetti, "Horn on Howl," in Miles, *Howl,* 152. A week after the trial began charges against Murao were dropped because the state could not prove that he had actually read the book or been aware of its "obscene" content.

8. Silesky, *Ferlinghetti,* 71.

9. Ehrlich, *Howl of the Censor,* 23-25.

10. Ibid., 26-27, 61-65.

11. Ibid., 34.

12. Ibid., 94.

13. Ibid., 99, 105-106.

14. Ibid., 127.

15. Miles, *Howl,* 165-166; Silesky, *Ferlinghetti,* 78; Ferlinghetti, "Horn on Howl."

16. Patterson, *Grand Expectations,* 409.

17. Larry Smith, *Lawrence Ferlinghetti: Poet-at-Large* (Carbondale: Southern Illinois University Press, 1983); Ferlinghetti, "Horn on Howl."

18. De Grazia, *Girls Lean Back Everywhere,* chapter 7; William S. Burroughs, *Naked Lunch* (1959; reprint, New York: Grove Press, 1990). This edition includes excerpts from the Boston trial of *Naked Lunch.* Among those testify as expert witnesses were Norman Mailer and Allen Ginsberg.

19. Ibid.; Berger, "Libraries Full of Tears." On the *Brown* decision see Richard Kluger, *Simple Justice: The History of Brown v. Board of Education and Black America's Struggle for Equality* (New York: Random House, 1975); Harvard Sitkoff, *The Struggle for Black Equality* (New York: Hill and Wang, 1993); Charles Eagles, ed., *The Civil Rights Movement in America* (Jackson: University of Mississippi Press, 1986); De Grazia, *Girls Lean Back Everywhere.*

20. See especially Silesky, *Ferlinghetti,* 58-60, 83, 107-108; Richard Candida Smith, *Utopia and Dissent: Art, Poetry and Politics in California* (Berkeley: University of California Press, 1985), chapter 2.

21. Allen Ginsberg, "America," in *Howl and Other Poems* (San Francisco: City Lights Books, 1956); Barry Miles, *Ginsberg: A Biography* (New York: Simon and Schuster, 1989); Norman Podhoretz, "Where Is the Beat Generation Going?" *Esquire* (December 1958): 148-150. Podhoretz argued that the Beats represented "a revolt of all the forces hostile to civilization itself," "a movement of brute stupidity and know-nothingness that is trying to take over the country from the middle class which is supposed to be the guardian of civilization but which has practically dislocated in its eagerness to throw in the towel. . . . [W]hat juvenile delinquency is to life, the San Francisco writers are to literature."

22. Samuel J. Walker, *In Defense of American Liberties: A History of the ACLU* (New York: Oxford, 1990).

23. David Perlman, "How Captain Hanrahan Made 'Howl' a Best-Seller," *The Reporter* 17.10 (12 December 1957): 37-39; Richard Pells, *The Liberal Mind in a Conservative Age: American Intellectuals in the 1940s and 1950s* (New York: Harper and Row, 1985).

FURTHER READING

Bibliographies

"Beatitude" Anthology. San Francisco: City Lights Books, 1960, 111 p.

 A selection of material from the first sixteen issues of Beatitude *magazine, which began publication in May 1959.*

Hickey, Morgan. *The Bohemian Register: An Annotated Bibliography of the Beat Literary Movement.* Metuchen, N.J.: Scarecrow Press, 1990, 252 p.

 Bibliography of Beat writers and topics.

Lawlor, William. *The Beat Generation: A Bibliographical Teaching Guide.* Lanham, Md.: Scarecrow Press, 1998, 357 p.

 A bibliography for teaching Beat generation topics.

Morgan, Bill. *Lawrence Ferlinghetti: A Comprehensive Bibliography to 1980.* New York: Garland, 1982, 397 p.

 A bibliography devoted to Lawrence Ferlinghetti.

———. *The Works of Allen Ginsberg, 1941-1994: A Descriptive Bibliography.* Westport, Conn.: Greenwood Press, 1995, 456 p.

 Bibliography covering the works of Allen Ginsberg.

———. *The Response to Allen Ginsberg, 1926-1994: A Bibliography of Secondary Sources.* Westport, Conn.: Greenwood Press, 1996, 505 p.

 A bibliography of writings about Allen Ginsberg.

Criticism

Clay, Steven, and Rodney Phillips. *A Secret Location on the Lower East Side: Adventures in Writing, 1960-1980.* New York: The New York Public Library and Granary Books, 1998, 350 p.

 Based on a 1998 exhibition at the New York Public Library; focuses on small press publishing in New York and San Francisco in the 1960s and 1970s and provides detailed descriptions of over eighty magazines and presses that operated during this period.

Dennison, Sally. "The Handmaiden of Literature." In *[Alternative] Literary Publishing,* pp. 193-221. Iowa City: University of Iowa Press, 1984.

 Discusses the fact that little magazines and small presses have historically represented vehicles for writers whose work is outside the mainstream of contemporary literature.

Ferlinghetti, Lawrence, and Nancy J. Peters. *Literary San Francisco: A Pictorial History from Its Beginnings to the Present Day.* San Francisco: City Lights Books and Harper & Row, 1980, 254 p.

 Provides a historical look at the personalities, small presses, and magazines of the Beat generation.

Leyland, Winston, ed. *Orgasms of Light: The Gay Sunshine Anthology.* San Francisco: Gay Sunshine Press, 1977, 264 p.

 An anthology of poems that appeared in the Gay Sunshine *journal or in one of the chapbooks published by Gay Sunshine Press.*

———, ed. *Gay Roots: Twenty Years of "Gay Sunshine."* San Francisco: Gay Sunshine Press, 1991, 704 p.

 Provides information on Leyland's life, the development of the Gay Sunshine press and journal. Also provides general context of gay history, politics, and culture in San Francisco.

Montag, Tom. "The Little Magazine Press Connection: Some Conjectures." *TriQuarterly* 43 (fall 1978): 575-93.

 Deals with what Montag views as the neglect of the small literary press in literature studies.

Rosset, Barney, ed. *"Evergreen Review" Reader: 1967-1973.* New York: Four Walls Eight Windows, 1998, 543 p.

 An anthology of material printed in Evergreen Review, *including contributors such as Allen Ginsberg, Lawrence Ferlinghetti, Jack Kerouac, and Michael McClure.*

Sullivan, James D. *On the Walls and in the Streets: American Poetry Broadsides from the 1960s.* Chicago: University of Illinois Press, 1997, 206 p.

 A study of American poetry broadsides and their cultural influence and importance.

Watson, Steven. *The Birth of the Beat Generation: Visionaries, Rebels, and Hipsters, 1944-1960.* New York: Pantheon Books, 1995, 387 p.

 A chronicle of Beat writers such as William Burroughs, Allen Ginsberg, and Jack Kerouac that explores their lives and works.

PERFORMING ARTS AND THE BEAT GENERATION

While the works of Jack Kerouac, Allen Ginsberg, and William S. Burroughs garnered considerable public attention, they were not necessarily the first advocates or practitioners of the artistic philosophy that came to be associated with Beat writers. The notoriety of the Beats—particularly following Ginsberg's premiere of "Howl" at the Six Gallery reading in San Francisco in 1955—in many respects eased the path for other unconventional artists to garner attention. Artists who had been working outside the mainstream saw in the Beats a validation of their own efforts, and as Beat style passed into the mainstream, the audience for other nontraditional artists's work also grew. Like the Beat writers, contemporary artists in other disciplines—music, theatre, and film—wanted to convey an immediacy of experience, to break out of academic standards of artistic value, and to connect "high" art with the most mundane, unremarkable, and even unappealing aspects of ordinary people's lives.

Beat writers acknowledged that music was one of their most important influences—particularly the jazz that was played in clubs where white patrons often were not welcome. Beat authors such as Kerouac or Lawrence Ferlinghetti were not necessarily great connoisseurs of jazz, and some later critics have suggested that their celebration of jazz was in part based on their misunderstanding of the art form. For some white writers from wealthier backgrounds, the seeming freedom and unhindered celebration of supposedly "less-civilized" blacks appealed to their interest in the exotic and their desire to shed all inhibitions. The free form of jazz seemed to embody an artistic lawlessness that nonetheless coalesced into something meaningful and beautiful. Particularly influential was the Bebop style of music popularized during the 1940s by Charlie Parker and Dizzy Gillespie. Both Kerouac and Ginsberg admired these musicians intensely and modeled their efforts at creating a new style of prose and poetry on their music, using a syncopated rhythm and dashes to indicate breath pauses between improvisational bursts. San Francisco poets Ferlinghetti and Kenneth Rexroth began staging poetry readings with jazz accompaniment and also wrote poems specifically to be read to jazz music—two strategies for bringing poetry to the masses. Beat writers made ample use of the musical style, but there is no evidence that jazz was in turn transformed in any lasting way by its connection with the short-lived Beat movement. By contrast, folk and folk-rock music may owe some of their increased popularity during the early 1960s to the earlier work of the Beats, which paved the way for poetry and political engagement in popular culture. A crucial figure in this development was singer-songwriter Bob Dylan, who came to be recognized as a poet as much as a musician. Dylan's artistic sensibility resonated well with that of other Beats, including his friends Michael Mc-Clure, a San Francisco Beat poet, and Ginsberg.

Among the most widely discussed mergers between Beat literature and other media is that of film—both films in the Beat style and films about the Beats. The first real Beat film was *Pull My Daisy* (1959) a dramatization of an unfinished play by Kerouac based on an event in the life of Kerouac's friend and literary inspiration, Neal Cassady, and Cassady's wife, Carolyn. Photographer Robert Frank coproduced the film, which featured Ginsberg and poet Gregory Corso, among others in Beat society, with Kerouac providing semi-improvised narration throughout the picture. The independent film was not a great success financially or artistically, but it reflects the sensibilities of Beat writers in its experimental and spontaneous approach. One of the first major movies about the Beats was based on Kerouac's novel *The Subterraneans,* which MGM studios transformed into a romance ornamented by Beat stylings. Fascination with Beat culture did not end in the 1960s; films of the late twentieth century also demonstrate the lasting appeal of Beat figures as both authors and curiosities, and several documentaries have attempted to capture and illuminate the era on film. In terms of artistic influence, however, a significant connection between Beat writing and filmmaking is reflected in the work of David Cronenberg, whose debt to Burroughs was clear even before his 1991 adaptation of Burroughs's *Naked Lunch.* As a motion picture by a major Hollywood director, *Naked Lunch* drove critics and scholars to reflect anew on the sympathies and antipathies between film and literature. Not unlike *The Subterraneans* of 1960, *Naked Lunch* struggled with portraying the grotesque images Burroughs had incorporated into his works and attempted to capture on film the prose style that made Beat literature unique. Many critics felt the film failed to adequately capture the vivid images and abstract prose of the original, arguing that less direct connections between Beats and films tended to yield better results.

Although films have continued to be fascinated with the Beats and their philosophy as subjects in the years since the 1960s, during the Beat era itself, mainstream Hollywood was beset by the federal government's initiative to investigate and weed out Communism. This, coupled with audience demands following the end of the Second World War, necessitated films that did little to challenge ideas of mainstream America as openly as the Beats did. Nonetheless, the work of such filmmakers as Douglas Sirk presents loose

parallels to themes explored by Beat authors like Kerouac and Ginsberg. Similarly, other filmmakers, including Abraham Polonsky, Nicholas Ray (*Rebel without a Cause,* 1955) and Robert Aldrich, also used their works to highlight the sociocultural issues that were being explored by the Beats. In addition to these films, the 1940s also saw the emergence of the *film noir* genre, dark-toned works that focused on the most important issues of the day for Beats and other artists—the lack of public honor, the loss of personal integrity, and the place of art in society. Science fiction movies of the period bear a striking resemblance to issues being explored by artists in other genres, openly exploring issues such as the cold war and apprehension about new developments in science and technology. The films of the era that explored the seedy underbelly of post-World War II American life also resonate strongly with the Beat desire to expose alienation, moral corruption, and anger to the light of day. Late-twentieth-century filmmakers such as Jim Jarmusch have incorporated Beat aesthetics into their works. Films such as *Down by Law* (1986) and *Strangers in Paradise* (1984) employ familiar Beat themes such as travel, world-weariness, and lawless, though charming, protagonists.

REPRESENTATIVE WORKS

David Amram
Pull My Daisy (music for film) 1959

Offbeat: Collaborating with Kerouac (nonfiction) 2002

Art Blakey and the Jazz Messengers
Art Blakey and the Jazz Messengers (music) 1953

Blakey with the Jazz Messengers (music) 1954

At The Cafe Bohemia, Volume 1 [live recording] (music) 1955

At The Cafe Bohemia, Volume 2 [live recording] (music) 1955

At The Cafe Bohemia, Volume 3 [live recording] (music) 1955

Art Blakey's Jazz Messengers with Thelonious Monk (music) 1957

John Coltrane
Blue Train (music) 1957

A Love Supreme (music) 1964

Jim Dine
Car Crash (performance art) 1960

Bob Dylan
Bob Dylan (music) 1962

The Freewheelin' Bob Dylan (music) 1963

Highway 61 Revisited (music) 1965

Robert Frank and Albert Leslie
Pull My Daisy (film) 1959

The Fugs [Tuli Kupferberg, Ed Sanders, and Ken Weaver]
The Village Fugs (music) 1965

The Fugs (music) 1966

Tenderness Junction (album) 1968

Charles Haas
The Beat Generation (film) 1959

Jim Jarmusch
Stranger than Paradise (film) 1984

Down by Law (film) 1986

Ranald MacDougall
The Subterraneans (film) 1960

Charles Mingus
Charles Mingus Quintet + Max Roach at the Cafe Bohemia (music) 1955

Pithecanthropus Erectus (music) 1956

The Clown (music) 1957

Mingus Ah Um (music) 1959

Mingus Dynasty (music) 1959

Thelonius Monk
Brilliant Corners (music) 1956

Thelonius Monk with John Coltrane (music) 1957

Ken Nordine
Word Jazz (poetry and music) 1957

Gary Walkow
Beat (film) 2000

The Weavers [Ronnie Gilbert, Lee Hays, Fred Hellerman, and Pete Seeger]
The Weavers at Carnegie Hall [live recording] (music) 1956

Traveling on with The Weavers (music) 1959

The Weavers at Carnegie Hall, Volume 2 [live recording] 1960

Tom Waits, Robert Wilson, and William Burroughs
The Black Rider (film) 1990

Chuck Workman
The Source (film) 1999

PRIMARY SOURCES

KENNETH REXROTH (ESSAY DATE 29 MARCH 1958)

SOURCE: Rexroth, Kenneth. "Jazz Poetry." *The Nation* 186 (29 March 1958): 282-3.

In the following essay, Rexroth praises the originators of the literary jazz scene in New York City and San Francisco, and laments the possibility that the popularity of jazz poetry may degrade its quality or betray its roots.

A little short of two years ago, jazz poetry was a possibility, a hope and the memory of a few experiments. Today it runs the danger of becoming a fad. The life of fads is most often intense, empty and short. I feel, on the contrary, jazz poetry has a permanent value or I would not have undertaken it.

When it is successful there is nothing freakish or faddish about it nor, as a matter of fact, is there anything especially new. At the roots of jazz and Negro folk son, especially in the Southwest, is the "talking blues."It is not much heard today, but if you flatten out the melodic line, already very simple, in Big Bill Broonzy or Leadbelly, you have an approximation of it, and some of their records are really more talked than sung. This is poetry recited to a simple blue guitar accompaniment. Long before this, in the mid-nineteenth century, the French poet Charles Cros was reciting, not singing, his poems to the music of a *bal musette* band. Some of his things are still in the repertory of living *café chantant* performers, especially the extremely funny *Le Hareng Saur*. Even today some Rock 'n Roll "novelties"are recited, not sung, and they are some of the most engaging, with music that often verges into the more complex world of true jazz. It has become a common custom in store front churches and Negro revival meetings for a member of the congregation to recite a poem to an instrumental or wordless vocal accompaniment. I believe Langston Hughes recited poems to jazz many years ago. I tried it myself in the twenties in Chicago. In the late forties Kenneth Patchen recited poems to records. Jack Spicer, a San Francisco poet, tried it with a trio led by Ron Crotty on bass. The result, more like the Russian tone color music of the first years of the century, was impressive, if not precisely jazz. Lawrence Lipton has been working with some of the best musicians in Los Angeles for almost two years. William Walton's "Facade, " Stravinsky's "Persephone,"compositions of Auric, Honegger, Milhaud, are well-known examples of speaking rather than singing, to orchestra in contemporary classical music. Charles Mingus and Fred Katz, two of the most serious musicians in jazz—to narrow that invidi-

Charles Mingus plays bass during a live performance at the Five Spot Cafe in Greenwich Village, New York. Copyright © by Fred W. McDarrah.

ous distinction between jazz and serious music—have been experimenting with the medium for some time. The music has been impressive, but in my opinion, speaking as a professional poet, the texts could be improved.

What is jazz poetry? It isn't anything very complicated to understand. it is the reciting of suitable poetry with the music of a jazz band, usually small and comparatively quiet. Most emphatically, it is not recitation with "background"music. The voice is integrally wedded to the music and, although it does not sing notes, is treated as another instrument, with its own solos and ensemble passages, and with solo and ensemble work by the band alone. It comes and goes, following the logic of the presentation, just like a saxophone or piano. Poetry with background music is very far from jazz. It is not uncommon, and it is, in my opinion, usually pretty corny.

Why is jazz poetry? Jazz vocalists, especially white vocalists and especially in the idiom of the most advanced jazz, are not very common. Most Negro singers stay pretty close to the blues, and

there is more to modern jazz than blues. Frank Sinatra, Ella Fitzgerald, there are not many singers whom all schools of jazz find congenial. Curiously, enough, the poet reciting, if he knows what he is doing, seems to "swing" to the satisfaction of many musicians in a way that too few singers do. I think it is wrong to put down all popular ballad lyrics as trivial; some of them are considerable poetry in their own right, but certainly most are intellectually far beneath the musical world of modern jazz, and far less honest, the best jazz is characterized by its absolute emotional honesty. This leaves us with the words of the best blues and Negro folk song, often very great poetry indeed, but still a limited aspect of experience, and by no means everything, translated into words, that modern jazz has to say. In other words, poetry gives jazz a richer verbal content, reinforces and expands its musical meaning and, at the same time, provides material of the greatest flexibility.

How is it done, in actual practice? Kenneth Patchen has been working with Allyn Ferguson and the Chamber Jazz Sextet. The music is composed; it is actually written out, with of course, room for solo improvisation, but with the voice carefully scored in. There is nothing wrong with this. Far more of the greatest jazz is written music than the lay public realizes. Some of even the famous King Oliver and Louis Armstrong records of long ago were scored by Lil Hardin, a very sophisticated musician. Duke Ellington and his arranger, Billy Strayhorn, are among America's greatest composers. for the past year, i have been working with my own band, led by Dick Mills, trumpet, and including brew Moore, tenor, Frank Esposito, trombone, Ron Crotty, bass, Clair Wiley, piano, and Gus Gustafson, drums. Recently in Los Angeles, I played a two-week engagement with a fine band led by Shorty Rogers. In each case we worked from carefully rehearsed "head arrangements."The musicians had each in front of them the text of the poetry, and the sheets were used as cue sheets, scribbled with "inners and outers," chord progressions, melodic lines and various cues.

I feel that this method insures the maximum amount of flexibility and spontaneity and yet provides a steadily deepening and thickening (in the musical sense) basis, differing emotionally more than actually from a written score. The whole thing is elaborately rehearsed—more than usual for even the most complicated "band number."I would like to mention that jazz, contrary to lay opinion, is not just spontaneously "blown"out of the musicians heads. Behind even the freest improvisations lies a fund of accepted patterns, chord changes, riffs, melodic figures, variations of tempo and dynamics, all understood by the musicians. In fact, they are there, given, as a fund of material almost instinctively come by. Even in a jam session, when the soloist gets as far out as possible, everybody has a pretty clear idea of how he is going to get back and of how everybody is going to go off together again. Then the major forms of common jazz are almost as strict as the sonata—the thirty-two bar ballad, the twelve bar blues—bridges, choruses, fillers, all usually in multiples of the basic four bar unit, in four-four time. Needless to say, the poetry is not "improvised"either. This has been tried with disastarously ridiculous results, and not by me. On the other hand, several poets have read over their things with sensitive musicians once and then put on a thoroughly satisfactory show. I have done this with Marty Paitch on piano or Ralph Pena on bass—both musicians with extraordinary feeling for the rhythms and meanings of poetry. It all depends on the musician.

I hope the faddist elements of this new medium will die away. The ignorant and the pretentious, the sockless hipsters out for a fast buck or a few drinks from a Village bistro, will soon exhaust their welcome with the public, and the field will be left clear for serious musicians and poets who mean business. I think that it is a development of considerable potential significance for both jazz and poetry. It reaches an audience many times as large as that commonly reached by poetry, and an audience free of some of the serious vices of the typical poetry lover. It returns poetry to music and to public entertainment as it was in the days of Homer or the troubadours. It forces poetry to deal with aspects of life which it has tended to avoid in the recent past. It demands of poetry something of a public surface—meanings which can be grasped by ordinary people—just as the plays of Shakespeare had something for both the pit and the intellectuals in Elizabethan times, and still have today. And, as I have said, it gives jazz a flexible verbal content, an adjunct which matches the seriousness and artistic integrity of the music.

Certainly audiences seem to agree. Wherever it has been performed properly, the college auditorium, the night clubs, the concert halls have been packed, and everybody—musicians, poets and audiences—has been enthusiastic.

In the past two years it has spread from the Cellar, a small bar in San Francisco, to college campuses, to nightclubs in Los Angeles, St. Louis, New York, Dallas, and I believe, Chicago; to the Jazz Concert Hall in Los Angeles, where Lawrence Lipton put on a program with Shorty Rogers, Fred Katz, two bands, myself, Stuart Perkoff and lipton himself, heard by about six thousand people in two weeks. Kenneth Patchen and Allyn ferguson followed us, and played there for the better part of two months. Dick Mills and his band have performed with me at several colleges and at the San Francisco Art festival, and we are now planning to take the whole show on the road.

If we can keep the standards up, and keep it away from those who don't know what they are doing, who have no conception of the rather severe demands the form makes on the integrity and competence of both musicians and poets, I feel that we shall have given, for a long time to come, new meanings to both jazz and poetry.

BOB DYLAN (SONG DATE 1962)

SOURCE: Dylan, Bob. "Blowin' in the Wind" on *The Free-Wheeling Bob Dylan*. Columbia, 1962.

The following song, one of Dylan's best-known works, is representative of the writer's facility with imagery and symbolism.

"BLOWIN' IN THE WIND"

How many roads must a man walk down
Before you call him a man?
Yes,'n' how many seas must a white dove sail
Before she sleeps in the sand?
Yes,'n' how many times must the cannon balls
    fly
Before they're forever banned?
The answer, my friend, is blowin' in the wind,
The answer is blowin' in the wind.

How many times must a man look up
Before he can see the sky?
Yes,'n' how many ears must one man have
Before he can hear people cry?
Yes,'n' how many deaths will it take 'till he
    knows
That too many people have died?
The answer, my friend, is blowin' in the wind,
The answer is blowin' in the wind.

How many years can a mountain exist
Before it's washed to the sea?
Yes,'n' how many years can some people exist
Before they're allowed to be free?
Yes,'n' how many times can a man turn his head
Pretending he just doesn't see?
The answer, my friend, is blowin' in the wind,
The answer is blowin' in the wind.

BOB DYLAN (SONG DATE 1963)

SOURCE: Dylan, Bob. "The Times They are A-Changing" on *The Times They are A-Changing*. Columbia, 1963.

The following song is a prime example of Dylan's socially conscious lyrics.

"THE TIMES THEY ARE A-CHANGIN'"

Come gather 'round people
Wherever you roam
And admit that the waters
Around you have grown
And accept it that soon
You'll be drenched to the bone.
If your time to you
Is worth savin'
Then you better start swimmin'
Or you'll sink like a stone
For the times they are a-changin'.

Come writers and critics
Who prophesize with your pen
And keep your eyes wide
The chance won't come again
And don't speak too soon
For the wheel's still in spin

And there's no tellin' who
That it's namin'.
For the loser now
Will be later to win
For the times they are a-changin'.

Come senators, congressmen
Please heed the call
Don't stand in the doorway
Don't block up the hall
For he that gets hurt
Will be he who has stalled
There's a battle outside
And it is ragin'.
It'll soon shake your windows
And rattle your walls
For the times they are a-changin'.

Come mothers and fathers
Throughout the land
And don't criticize
What you can't understand
Your sons and your daughters
Are beyond your command
Your old road is
Rapidly agin'.
Please get out of the new one
If you can't lend your hand
For the times they are a-changin'.

The line it is drawn
The curse it is cast
The slow one now
Will later be fast
As the present now
Will later be past
The order is
Rapidly fadin'.
And the first one now
Will later be last
For the times they are a-changin'.

CAROLYN CASSADY (LETTER DATE SUMMER 1986)

SOURCE: Cassady, Carolyn. Letter to *Moody Street Irregulars* (summer 1986).

Cassady wrote the following letter to an editor of Moody Street Irregulars, *a Kerouac fanzine, regarding the music that was used in* Heart Beat, *a film loosely based on her memoirs. Cassady wrote the letter to clarify the types of music that she, Neal Cassady, and Kerouac enjoyed.*

Dear Joel Scherzer,

I cheered your comments on the Jack Nitzsche score for the deplorable film, *Heart Beat*. Some of the fault must lie with John Byrum, I suspect, who mesmerized everyone into his interpretation of "my" story, except me and Mr. and Mrs. Jack Fisk.

When I first received the script and had recovered enough from the shock and dismay (to put it very mildly), I was compelled to send them scenes I set down from the true events which had dramatic effects—Alan Griesman having stated in print that "*No*body's real life is dramatic enough from cinema." Included with these scenes were suggestions for some of the musical numbers that not only had been an integral part of the events but would also enhance the sense of period and deepen the dramatic mood.

Some of them that come to mind are:

1. Anything by the younger Lester Young, for he was the cause of my meeting Neal in the first place.

2. Benny Goodman's "Sing, Sing, Sing" was played enthusiastically for me by Neal in a record booth on the day we met; neither of us ever forgot *that*.

3. "Peg O' My Heart," an accidental part of his wooing, not only of me but of my interest in auto racing.

4. Soon after meeting Jack in Denver, the record on the juke box we danced to, believe it or not, was "Too Close for Comfort."

5. Billie Holiday's "No Good Man" and the flip side, "Good Morning, Heartache," routinely played respectively night and morning when Neal was off on the first road.

6. Helen Hume's "He May Be Your Man But He Comes To See Me Sometimes." We didn't own the record, but, whenever we'd hear it together we were both amused by the irony. I could be even that objective occasionally! One line in particular was all too apt: ". . . 'cause if he flags my train, I'm shore gonna let him ride."

7. Jack's crooning of "A Foggy Day in London Town" and "Funny Valentine" are among those that recall intimate moments between us.

8. When Jack and Neal would talk together in an excited way with rapid-fire glee, I equate the sound with Dizzy Gillespie's "Salt Peanuts."

Well-documented is Jack's taste in jazz which Neal shared, although I think Neal was more taken by the Bop style than was Jack. Both of them enjoyed a wide range of all kinds of music, but our radio was set at either Pat Henry on KJAZ or Jumpin' George on a station whose call letters I've

---

ON THE SUBJECT OF...

DAN PROPPER

Poet Dan Propper's career was shaped by the intersection of two epochal movements: the New York jazz scene of the 1950s and the Beat literary stylistic revolt. The former, jazz, played an integral role in his early life. He pursued little in the way of higher education, though from the early 1950s clubs such as Birdland and the Five Spot and musicians like Thelonious Monk, John Coltrane, and Dizzie Gillespie provided Propper with the cultural education upon which he would draw as a poet. An amateur musician, Propper began working with Decca Records as an assistant sales promoter in 1957. This job, which transformed his passion into a livelihood, was crucial to his entrée into the jazz world. Literature did not figure in his worldview until 1957 when he read the *Evergreen Review* issue on the San Francisco scene. In 1957, Propper's first awareness of the San Francisco literary renaissance combined with jazz to produce the bebop rhythms—evocative of Alan Ginsberg's works—of Propper's most famous poem, "The Fable of the Final Hour" (1958). In 1958 Propper left New York and spent two years in New Orleans and Houston. From 1960 to 1963 he was in San Francisco, and he did not return to New York until the end of 1963. The peak events in Propper's life during those years were his three major jazz readings: one in 1958 at the Five Spot with Thelonious Monk, another that same year in Houston with Dizzie Gillespie, and a third in 1960 with the Jazz Quartet on a half-hour nationwide CBS broadcast from St. Louis. Although Propper acknowledged the importance of Ginsberg's work in his literary development, it was the influence of jazz music that defined his creative output.

---

forgotten. Rarely mentioned has been Stan Kenton, a great favorite, and by whose strains of "Artistry in Rhythm" and the others in that series I was taught the fine points of pot-smoking by Neal. Vocalists who warble consistently through my memory include, of course, Sinatra, Mel

Torme, Ella, both Dinahs, Julie Christie, Al Hibler, Joe Williams, Pearl Bailey, Anita O'Day, and even Helen O'Connell's "Green Eyes," among the hosts of others less well-known. Soon after we got our first TV in 1954, I found it hard to credit Neal's insistence on tuning in Patti Page every evening, although I'm not convinced it was her singing alone that kept him on the edge of his seat.

Both Jack and Neal loved mambos, and we even managed to raise the price of a ticket and engineer a night out to go to a concert by our favorite, Prez Prado, the little jumping bean even more fun to watch.

Our children can better testify to Neal's favorites in the Chubby Checkers, Buddy Holly eras and beyond, and, as often noted, Neal's tastes in later years were perhaps more varied than Jack's. If Neal had favorites or priorities, who knows; he said "yes" to almost everything.

Other musicians and performers and tunes lap at the shores of memory, and I'm sure I'll capture important ones as soon as I mail this, but from this vast pool what a wonderfully complementary score could have been selected for a film. Still, one thing to be said for Byrum's—it was consistent.

BEATS AND FILM

DAVID CRONENBERG AND KAREN JAEHNE (INTERVIEW DATE SPRING 1992)

SOURCE: Cronenberg, David, and Karen Jaehne. "David Cronenberg on William Burroughs: Dead Ringers Do *Naked Lunch.*" *Film Quarterly* 45, no. 3 (spring 1992): 2-6.

In the following interview, Jaehne focuses on Cronenberg's film as a semiautobiography of Burroughs, discussing with the director Burroughs's struggles with misogyny and the accidental killing of his wife, his homosexuality, and his drug addiction. Cronenberg distances his film from Burroughs himself and the novel Naked Lunch, *asserting that the film more closely reflects his own thoughts about Burroughs and about the creative process.*

It is hard to imagine two people more allied by phantasmagoric visions than David Cronenberg and William Burroughs. Both men are attracted to the shiny metallic but mercurial intellectual vein in their subject matter, even though at first blush their imagery is often grotesque, visceral, and unnerving. Plot is always secondary. In *Naked Lunch,* Cronenberg uses Burroughs' life and art as a reason to explore the writer as addict. The film is a nightmare set in Interzone (the International Zone of Tangier, a sort of Berlin of North Africa), where typewriters talk when they're not turning into giant insects, and life, like writing, is boring or repulsive.

Interview

[*Jaehne*]: *Let's start with the critical crux: Is this a David Cronenberg film, the subject of which happens to be William Burroughs, or is this the film about Burroughs and his novel* Naked Lunch *that was inevitable and only happened to be made by Cronenberg?*

[Cronenberg:] It probably has more of me in it than of William Burroughs, because he had very little to do with the process. I never set out to make an historical or quasi-historical account, or to be faithful to the source. I think of it as the product of a dream I would have about Burroughs and his book, a dream to which I bring all my particular obsessions and idiosyncrasies.

What impact did William Burroughs have on the film-making?

Bill had nothing to do with the writing or the directing or the film. He told me that he had once tried to write a script—the memoirs of Dutch Schultz, I believe—and he said this is an entirely different art form, you can save it for the professionals.

And perhaps because the film is about writing and, very specifically, about Burroughs as a writer and an intellect, he had the good grace to stay out of the process. He was very liberal, very intelligent about it and basically told me to go make my movie. As it happens, he likes the result, which pleases me, but that was not my aim either. I wanted to be as honest and interesting as I could about the intellectual makeup of "Bill Lee," the alter ego of William Burroughs during the time he wrote *Naked Lunch.*

Were you ever worried about going too far out on a limb about his experiences or experiments?

Would they come to me if they wanted the kind of discretion you're suggesting? Many of the issues raised by *Naked Lunch*—homosexuality, misogyny, drug use, obscenity and censorship—are still controversial in America today. You have no choice but to face them head on, as bluntly and as crudely as you find in his writing, if you want this film to have any credibility whatsoever. And I'm not sure an American director could approach it in the same way. American culture is not introspective. It's at a white heat and boiling, and I like it, but as a Canadian I'm also in exile from American culture. I can't help but consume it, but I have choices that Americans might not have.

I think in some way it took a Canadian director and an English producer to deal with Burroughs and his world. Not because we are superior, but only because we share an arm's length perspective on the really controversial elements that needs to be preserved. The misogyny alone . . .

What about Burroughs', or Bill Lee's, relationship with the representational woman in this picture—who is played by Judy Davis first as Joan, Burroughs' wife whom he murdered in Mexico, then as Jane Bowles, whom he knew when he was living in Tangier?

Murder is not an appropriate term here. I don't think it was a murder, legally speaking, although he did kill her and felt pain and guilt about it. There were undoubtedly a lot of things at work—jealousy, which I try to allude to in the scene in which he walks in on her with another man. . . .

But that is a famous incident usually portrayed as a paradigm of "Beat" hipness—the lack of jealousy, the idea of tolerance of people acting out their desires despite bourgeois norms.

Maybe, but jealousy is a very important emotion, even when it is repressed. Burroughs loved Joan, admired her, and thought of her as an equal. There is nothing misogynistic about Burroughs' work, and I realize that it's a twisted element of his psychological makeup, but you have to get beyond the surface. His work represents the essence of struggling with misogyny without fear of the dark side. The incident represented in the film as the occasion of Joan's death is the central experience of his life, you see.

"Let's do our William Tell routine." They were out of their minds, and he says he doesn't know why he did it. He also worries about something in her that was self-destructive. . . .

He has said he suspected her brain pulled the bullet to it.

Which is another way of expressing his awareness of her self-destructive state. You see, Burroughs believes in things like possession in a medieval sense and in things that I don't endorse.

Yes, he thought at one time that women were from another planet.

No, he thought they were a different species—a very different thing from being alien. This is not scientific thinking; this is mythological or a kind of primitive poetry. That women and men are "other" is a commonplace, but Bill extended that to an extreme I may find interesting but cannot take literally.

How are we to take Bill's killing Joan in the film— twice?

It was the central event of his life, and everything began from that point, again and again. There was no way to erase it or forget it or pay for it. He has to relive that trauma repeatedly, and it's meant to be about his suffering, not about him getting rid of the woman in his life so he could be creative. It was only after he came to terms with her loss that he began to write seriously again.

Burroughs was very much obsessed with Allen Ginsberg during the time he was in Tangier—long, passionate letters and confessions of depending upon him as a writer are part of the record. You don't seem to want to make much of their relationship, and in your film Kerouac and Ginsberg seem to be more like Tweedledum and Tweedledee than like the two comrades with whom Burroughs had launched the Beat era.

Admittedly, I didn't want to get into the history of Ginsberg or Kerouac, and I didn't want to have to take them on as well, because this is only secondarily a film about the Beats. For me, they worked well in that way, because that's how Bill Lee saw them. You see, Burroughs had been their mentor. He was older and they looked up to him, but he was also this guru who required care, and in looking after him they fulfilled their bond. They saw it as their duty to pull together what spewed out of Bill's creative genius.

Why do you shy away from Burroughs' homosexuality—a Hollywood taboo or just too kinky?

His friend Kiki is portrayed as his lover, but it was something that I just didn't feel that I could delve into. I was sort of damned if I did and damned if I didn't. I myself am not homosexual and do not feel prepared to create a character as extreme in his homosexuality as in *Naked Lunch*. Believe me, I struggled with it aesthetically and morally, because it seemed a kind of transgression, but I finally decided to let go of it.

I approached Bill about it to inform him of my decision because it felt like the fair thing to do. He just said, don't worry, it's your movie, do whatever you want. He likes to invoke the famous line of Raymond Chandler, when people asked him if he liked what Hollywood had done to all his books: "They haven't done a thing to my books. They're all right up there on the shelf."

What does Burroughs think of the film?

He's told countless people it's a great film. He's also said that he doesn't recognize any of the people up there. And why should he? There is this *act* that occurs between the life of the person creating and the work of art that transforms and separates the two of them. That's what this movie is about.

Did Ginsberg have anything to say?

Through a friend, he let me know that he liked it very much and found it funny and true to the spirit of Burroughs—because, I believe, the film is an inquiry into the particular kind of intelligence they had which does not depend upon homosexuality.

A lot of the gay press would disagree.

Well, I did have this contretemps with *The Advocate*, because they refused to believe or to print my statement that Burroughs had actually renounced his homosexuality at one stage. . . .

Yes, it seems that after finishing Naked Lunch, *Burroughs claimed that writing it had exorcized some of his devils and that it had provided a resolution to the sexual conflicts he suffered.[1] Of course, he also regularly gave up drugs!*

I did so much research for this that I cannot remember all the sources, and when somebody challenges you in that way, you think, why bother? My film is about creativity—its anxieties, its lifestyle, its dangers.

What do you mean by that?

It's interesting that Jane Bowles once spoke to Burroughs about her fear of the danger of writing—of exposing yourself and your ideas to things entirely beyond your control.

Is that the point of the Mugwump ordering Bill to the Interzone to file reports on enemy agents—or of typewriters turning into threatening bugs and heads? They're not so much threatening as funny.

I haven't thought about it in exactly that way, but we did want that surreal aspect of the film to carry an absurd humor. Think about it! The talking asshole is a very literal image of the serious social taboo against expressing anything with, through, or about human orifices. That was one of Burroughs' more infamous contributions to literature, which somehow strikes a chord, you know? It breaks through the organization of our bodies and our lives into proper, acceptable forms of presentation.

Likewise, the bugs have escaped from the conscious mind, through the architecture of ideas, through the cracks that release creative ideas. To have mechanical devices transformed into bugs is a way of showing how they are really subservient to the organic flow of the imagination.

The second typewriter he borrows turns into a head; he has to stick his hands in its mouth to type.

That's surreal, isn't it? I don't have an explanation for choosing a head in that case, but I do believe it must go back to the dangerous aspect of writing. To stick your hands into the maw of the beast is dangerous, and it's also like trying to perform brain surgery through the mouth.

What about the hand that also thrusts into a surprisingly vaginal orifice?

The fear's the same: the implications of a vagina dentata have been built up through previous imagery. I want to emphasize my reasons for such sexual imagery, because it is so commonly misunderstood. It is not sexist. It's the visual life of this particular story, and it's not a pronouncement on women. This is the story of one Bill Lee, who is not even William Burroughs, but rather a man who must write himself out of a nightmare.

Is that the nightmare of drug addiction? I recall that Burroughs was supposedly not addicted during the time he was writing Naked Lunch.

Well, the trouble is Burroughs *was* an addict, and he wrote out of addiction. There's no getting around it, even if he was not an addict during the act of creating his novel. There is something about the addictive personality that is more compelling than the fact that he satisfies it with narcotics. For example, Burroughs' wife Joan had a really vile habit and took drugs throughout the time she carried their child; people saw her wasting away right in front of them. She couldn't survive her own addiction, but Bill could. I'm not sure why, but his addiction rose out of exploration rather than escape. He figured out a way to go back and forth from the straight world to the world of the addict. Literati view him as a translator from that world.

Theories Burroughs has proposed or notions threaded through his work make him sound like a crackpot, but in his public appearances he always seems coherent and very controlled. He has a kind of glacial monumentality.

He does, but personally he is a very sweet and surprisingly gentle person. When I first met him—the day before his 70th birthday and arranged by our producer, Jeremy Thomas—what struck me was his shyness and gentle nature. We established a kind of trust, and I felt almost protective of him, which provided even stronger incentives to develop the character away from the man Burroughs and make of him a fictional hero caught between Tangier and the completion of *Naked Lunch*.

Were you ever tempted to put Burroughs in the film, even in a cameo?

Never. It would have been a total betrayal of what the film is about. I might put him in another film, because I like his presence and self-possession in something like *Drugstore Cowboy*. Here, it would point in a self-conscious way to the source. The use of a writer in that way can become exploitative and confuse an audience as to your purpose.

The acting styles of Weller as Bill Lee and the guys riffing on the personalities of other characters drawn from the days in Tangier as well as from Burroughs' book form a very rich jumble. Dr. Benway is from sci-fi, Bill Lee from Pilgrim's Progress . . .

What you're getting at is interesting, because the characters have the quality of apparitions and a symbolic force which rises from an extreme presentation by that particular actor that is, in addition, appropriate to the character's position in the overall odyssey. It's a gallery, not a society.

You spent some time in North Africa yourself in pre-production before the Gulf War broke out . . .

God, yes. We had done our homework and toured Tangier "in the footsteps of the master" with Jeremy and Bill, trying to trace the atmosphere, influences. The landscape has such a strong pull that it's hard to resist attempting to put it on screen. It's remarkably stark and has a magical or maybe mystical sensibility that is completely at one with Burroughs' sensibility.

But then the war broke out and there was no way we could insure the film or actors, and we had no choice but to pack up and go back to Toronto and rewrite it as an interior tale of a man's mind rather than of his environment being peopled by monsters. I think it was a blessing in disguise and forced the film into a claustrophobic feeling that is perfectly appropriate.

How much control did you have over the music for Naked Lunch?

Actually, that was very exciting. Howard Shore came up with the idea of using jazz, and of course everybody agreed that it was the right idea, the right tone, the right mood. But then that simply opens up a wide choice. Then someone came up with Ornette Coleman and he liked the idea. You see, he'd known Burroughs in Tangier back in 1973, when Coleman went to a village called Joujouka to take part in certain rituals and play with the musicians who had been studying ancient techniques. Burroughs had been there to see Coleman participate in the annual ritual, so the reunion of Coleman doing a sound track for the experiences that Burroughs had formulated out of Tangier was . . . kismet. Coleman worked out a score that is so sensitive, it provides a kind of pulse for Bill Lee's emotions. It's a perfect sound track—subtle, a little spooky, full of mystical implications—like the film.

Note

1. See Ted Morgan, *Literary Outlaw* (New York: Henry Holt, 1988).

DAVID STERRITT (ESSAY DATE 1998)

SOURCE: Sterritt, David. "Introduction." In *Mad to Be Saved: The Beats, the '50s, and Film*, pp. 1-15. Carbondale: Southern Illinois University Press, 1998.

In the following essay, Sterritt delineates the history and development of the Beat Generation, relating the myriad artistic and cultural influences to the visual sensibilities portrayed in works by Beat and Beat-inspired filmmakers.

The Beat Generation was a generation of beatitude, and pleasure in life, and tenderness. But they called it in the papers Beat mutiny, Beat insurrection—words I never used. Being a Catholic, I believe in order, tenderness, and piety.
> —Jack Kerouac to William F. Buckley Jr., *Firing Line*, 1968

Recent history is the record of a vast conspiracy to impose one level of mechanical consciousness on mankind. . . . The suppression of contemplative individuality is nearly complete. The only immediate historical data that we can know and act on are those fed to our senses through systems of mass communication. . . . America is having a nervous breakdown.
> —Allen Ginsberg, "Poetry, Violence, and the Trembling Lambs," 1959

Writers are potentially very powerful indeed. They write the script for the reality film.
> —William S. Burroughs, "A Historic Memoir of America's Greatest Existentialist," 1977

The Beats

The so-called Beat Generation flourished in the United States between the mid-'40s, when World War II drew to a close amid widespread uncertainty as to what the American future might hold, and the mid-'60s, when the so-called Hippie movement took over as the nation's most influential countercultural phenomenon. The term "Beat Generation" has been used in different ways by different historians, sociologists, critics, and commentators. For some it connotes the entire youth culture of the first postwar decades. For others it refers to a particular handful of authors, poets, dreamers, and dropouts whose activities reflected a conscious determination to rebel against what they perceived as a highly oppressive sociocultural atmosphere. While the label is regrettably imprecise, it suggestively evokes a youth-centered ethos that felt the weight of conventional social norms as a burden at once punishing and exhausting—inflicting on individuals a sense of being both "beaten," or assailed and tormented, and "beat," or worn down and defeated.

The early Beats have been likened to the Existentialists who emerged in Western Europe at approximately the same time. Both groups were driven by a commingling of alienation, anxiety, idealism, and intellectual energy, and both rejected the social given in favor of an aggressive insistence that humans must define themselves and their reality through their choices, decisions, and actions.[1] The actions of the Beats took the form of a negative dialectic that sought to oppose conventionality, materialism, repressiveness, regimentation, and corruption with the opposites of those qualities; this activity led the group to what critic Gregory Stephenson describes as a libertarian-egalitarian-populist-anarchist orientation that proposed not political rebellion but rather "a revolt of the soul, a revolution of the spirit" (6) that would gather strength as its adherents flung accepted notions of logic, sense, and sanity to the winds and, in Beat chronicler John Tytell's evocative phrase, "danced to the music of the absurdity they saw around them" (9). The importance of absurdity is a key notion for Beats and Existentialists alike, and has played a provocative role in postwar art (e.g., the Theater of the Absurd) and philosophy.

The negativity that prompted the Beat sensibility to its early stirrings never vanished from its social, spiritual, and aesthetic expressions, as later events in Beat history—from William S. Burroughs's radical rejection of linear prose to Jack Kerouac's ultimate embrace of a withdrawn and alcoholic life—have demonstrated in ways both metaphoric and literal. Yet the Beats during their ascendancy were by no means a recessive group. Indeed, they were strikingly productive, counterat-

tacking the '50s idea of rationalized consensus with literary acts reflecting a Romantic insistence on the moral, ethical, and spiritual potency of creative selfhood. Their sense of energy and community were drawn partly from the fascination with language that such core Beats as Kerouac, Burroughs, and Allen Ginsberg displayed in the prose and poetry that made them famous. In addition, they were invigorated by the great outpouring of artistic experimentation that began in the '40s, including the bebop jazz of Miles Davis and Charlie Parker, the proscenium-free theater of Julian Beck and Judith Malina, and the abstract-expressionist painting of Jackson Pollock and the New York School.

To their enthusiasm for various artistic forms the Beats added a sophisticated awareness of the bohemian tradition—with roots a century old on both sides of the Atlantic when the Beats began making their contributions to it—and a passion for street-level city life. This passion was sparked by the hustlers they met during their nighttime wanderings and above all by the hipsters who preceded the Beats as a paradigmatic American counterculture: quintessentially urban rebels who prowled "through our cities like [members] of some mysterious, nonviolent Underground" (1988b, 73), as Beat fellow traveler John Clellon Holmes phrased it. Hipsters took the risks of what Norman Mailer called, in a widely influential Beat-sympathetic essay of 1957,

> the decision . . . to encourage the psychopath in oneself, to explore that domain of experience where security is boredom and therefore sickness, and one exists in the present, in that enormous present which is without past or future, memory or planned intention, the life where a man must go until he is beat, where he must gamble with his energies through all those small or large crises of courage and unforeseen situations which beset his day, where he must be with it or doomed not to swing.
>
> (588)

Other influences on the Beats included the transcendentalism of Walt Whitman and the romanticism of William Blake; major figures in Dadaism and Surrealism, with whom the Beats shared a group identity, a preference for subversiveness that was sociocultural rather than directly political, and a leaning toward extremism in thought and expression; and the more radical of the post-World War I writers known as the Lost Generation, from Hart Crane to Henry Miller and Ezra Pound, all of whom anticipated the Beats in their determination to replace the most widely disseminated views and values of their age with new, more viable ideas. In the spirit of all these predecessors and progenitors, the Beats combined outrage at a status quo perceived as senseless (at best) and psychotic (at worst) with a determination to create what the early Beat figure Lucien Carr called a "New Vision" of art (Charters xviii);[2] this vision would be dynamized by "world-and-mind weariness, the continual moulting of consciousness, and the spirit's arduous venture toward its own reconciliations" (1988b, 89), which Holmes saw as the underrecognized and undervalued foundation of the Beat sensibility. The forerunners who inspired them were less the official intellectuals of canonical wisdom than a heterodox collection of real and apocryphal friends, family members, and half-imagined heroes whom Kerouac called, in one of the most frequently cited passages of Beat literature,

> the mad ones, the ones who are mad to live, mad to talk, mad to be saved, desirous of everything at the same time, the ones who never yawn or say a commonplace thing, but burn, burn, burn like fabulous yellow roman candles exploding like spiders across the stars and in the middle you see the blue centerlight pop and everybody goes "Awww!"
>
> (1991, 8)

Given the energy, inventiveness, and ethos-challenging carnivalism that surge through so much Beat writing, turning even "world-and-mind weariness" into a productive arena for exploration and adventure, the phrase "positive negation" might be more appropriate than "negative dialectic" to describe the group's thought and activity. The latter term suggests somber opposition to a deadening society perceived in the near-apocalyptic terms of, say, the Frankfort School's critique of the modern sociopolitical era. By contrast, positive negation suggests a stance—in keeping with the ideas of Mikhail Bakhtin, the innovative Russian theorist of carnivalism and dialogism—that is not merely antithetical, even toward a scorned status quo. Rather, in the words of Bakhtin exegete Michael Gardiner, it incorporates "the positive pole of popular-festive energy" (57), tapping into sensory and experiential knowledge so as to entail not nihilism or despair but affirmation, renewal, and the inversion of that which is rejected.[3]

Such a conception cannot be applied to the Beats in overly generalized terms, since important aspects of their collective *oeuvre* do have despairing and even nihilistic tendencies. One thinks of the electrifying hallucinations and corrosive metaphors that coexist with the manic humor and explosive satire of Burroughs's dyspeptic world,

and of the profound sadness that courses through a good deal of Ginsberg's outwardly gregarious work.

Perhaps most poignantly, one thinks of how the exuberance and exhilaration of Kerouac's early *On the Road* (1957) and *The Dharma Bums* (1958) were shadowed by the insinuating self-doubt and self-pity of *The Subterraneans* (1958), which themselves gave way to the ineluctable discontents of *Tristessa* (1960) and ultimately to the nightmares that erupt in *Book of Dreams* (1961), *Big Sur* (1962), and *Desolation Angels* (1965). Even in his early works, the presence of happiness is often accompanied by a tentative and worried undertone. "In fact I realized I had no guts. . . . But I have joy" (90), says the Kerouac surrogate in *The Dharma Bums* at a hard moment during a mountain-climbing expedition. This self-analytic statement sounds affirmative enough at first, but glossing it, critic Warren French notes that Kerouac's idea of joy was accompanied by the necessity for Lenten regret, reflecting his acceptance (ever since his Roman Catholic childhood) of the notion that unfettered happiness "is a release valve from the tensions of life that must be paid for with long periods of repentance [and] demands too much energy to sustain itself in the human condition" (126).[4] Kerouac seems instinctively to have viewed carnivalistic pleasure as affording only a temporary catharsis and a quickly dissipated sense of liberation. In this attitude, he reminds one of the medieval subjects described by Bakhtin as "too weak before the forces of nature and society" to resist the "seriousness of fear and suffering in their religious, social, political, and ideological forms. . . . Freedom granted by laughter often enough was mere festive luxury." The bright side of this situation is that when "distrust of the serious tone and confidence in the truth of laughter" did occur, they brought with them "a spontaneous, elemental character" (1984b, 94-95). Spontaneity and an elemental distrust of all seriousness—including his own—were among Kerouac's most appealing traits. Although he saw carnivalistic joy as ultimately a temporary and unsustainable phenomenon, it never entirely departs from his work, even at junctures where what he calls a "Beethoven gloominess"[5] threatens most boldly to take over; and his insistence on utterly intuitive writing with audaciously self-inventing structures ("spontaneous bop prosody") bears out his continual resistance to a closed-off or "official" vision of the world. In this openness and open-endedness, his *oeuvre* bears out Bakhtin's claim that "the carnival sense of the world . . . knows

Jay Landesman, 1919-.

no period, and is, in fact, hostile to any sort of *conclusive conclusion:* all endings are merely new beginnings; carnival images are reborn again and again" (1984a, 165).

In sum, the Beats as a group generated a carnivalistic aura in many of the works that have lived most vividly in the popular imagination, such as Kerouac's peripatetic *On the Road,* Burroughs's uproarious *Naked Lunch* (1962), and Ginsberg's visionary "Wichita Vortex Sutra" (1966), which proclaims: "No more fear of tenderness, much delight in weeping, ecstasy / in singing, laughter rises that confounds / staring Idiot mayors / and stony politicians . . ." (1984, 395). As urgent as their denial of the sociocultural status quo consistently was, and as deeply felt as their own sorrows persistently were, their rebellion was finally a positive phenomenon, producing art that aspired to be celebratory, transcendent, and transformative. This carnival sensibility had special importance in the '50s, a rigorously normative age when restrictive dogmas, doctrines, creeds, and screeds of official thought were striving mightily to exercise unchallenged hegemony over all within their reach. When the young Ginsberg equilibrated his "Howl" (1955-56) by juxtaposing anguished cries of "Moloch! Moloch! Nightmare of Moloch! Moloch the loveless! Mental Moloch! Moloch the heavy judger of men!" with ecstatic

yowls of "The word is holy! The soul is holy! The skin is holy! The nose is holy! The tongue and cock and hand and asshole holy!" (1984, 131, 134), he was practicing a richly Bakhtinian aesthetic in which high and low are scrambled, the lower body is celebrated and sacramentalized, and the staring Idiot mayors of the established system find themselves turned on their richly deserving heads.

Unfortunately, similar things cannot be said of much other cultural production in the postwar era, including the Hollywood cinema, which generally tried to function as a guardian of traditional values and the sociopolitical status quo. Even in the largely monologic domain of American film, however, currents of carnivalistic subversion managed to make themselves felt with surprising frequency. These currents emerged in the work of studio renegades who turned the industrial apparatus to their own sly purposes, in "personal" works or excursions into comparatively flexible territory such as *film noir* melodrama, and also in the efforts of avantgarde experimentalists who functioned as artisans outside the industrial setting. Like the Beat writers, these filmmakers were a minority—often a beleaguered one—within their field. But the best of them believed deeply in the necessity of confronting the social given with new and daring ideas, and their activities helped enrich and expand the Beat challenge to an increasingly ossified society.

BEATNESS

> How frail, beat, final, is Tristessa as we load her into the quiet hostile bar. . . .
> —Jack Kerouac, *Tristessa*

A sense of the derivation and evolution of Beat attitudes can be gleaned from the history of "beat" as a descriptive term. The first to employ this adjective in something like its Beat Generation meaning appear to have been jazz musicians and street hustlers[6] for whom it meant "down and out" or "poor and exhausted" (Charters xvii). Burroughs learned it in 1944 from Herbert Huncke, a friend whose interest in drugs and street survivalism became an inspiration for all the Beat writers. Other core Beats picked up the word in turn, charging it with their own nuances and connotations. Ginsberg found its "original street usage" to suggest "exhausted, at the bottom of the world, looking up or out, sleepless, wideeyed, perceptive, rejected by society, on your own, streetwise" (Charters xviii). Kerouac interpreted the term through the grain of Huncke's voice, recalling how his friend "appeared to us and said 'I'm beat' with radiant light shining out of his despairing eyes." Bringing his own associations to it, Kerouac noted possible echoes of "some midwest carnival or junk cafeteria" (1959b, 42) and connected it with a "melancholy sneer" worn by "characters of a special spirituality who didn't gang up but were solitary Bartlebies [sic] staring out the dead wall window of our civilization" (Charters xviii). These associations accorded with Kerouac's opinion that his generation shared

> a kind of furtiveness. . . . Like we were a generation of furtives . . . with an inner knowledge there's no use flaunting on . . . the level of the "public," a kind of beatness—I mean, being right down to it, to ourselves, because we all *really* know where we are—and a weariness with all the forms, all the conventions of the world. . . . So I guess you might say we're a *beat* generation.[7]

In his first and most conventional novel, *The Town and the City* (1950), Kerouac wrote of someone "wandering 'beat' around the city" on a search for money or support, and in his later novel *Desolation Angels,* he said the term "beat" originally implied "mind-your-own-business," as in "beat it" (Foster 7). Kerouac further reported, in his 1958 essay "The Philosophy of the Beat Generation," that the Beat Generation concept was first embodied by a handful of friends (including Burroughs, Ginsberg, Huncke, Holmes, and himself) who had long since moved from New York and gone their separate ways; yet the concept had sprung back to life after the Korean War when "postwar youth emerged cool and beat . . . bop visions became common property of the commercial, popular cultural world. . . . The ingestion of drugs became official . . . even the clothes style of the beat hipsters carried over to the new rock'n' roll youth . . . and the Beat Generation, though dead, was resurrected and justified" (Charters xxi). The following year, in "The Origins of the Beat Generation," he wrote that "Beat" meant "poor, down and out, deadbeat, on the bum, sad, sleeping in subways" (1959b). In an appearance on Steve Allen's television show he observed, rather cryptically, that "Beat" meant "sympathetic."

Perhaps the most resonant of Kerouac's contributions to the word's developing usage is his punning association of "Beat" with the notion of beatification. In Kerouac's early novel *On the Road,* narrator Sal Paradise, a Kerouac surrogate, says of protagonist Dean Moriarty (a surrogate for Neil Cassady, who strongly influenced Kerouac's early evolution as a thinker and writer) that he "was

ON THE SUBJECT OF...

JAY AND FRAN LANDESMAN
Husband and wife Jay and Fran Landesman have distinguished individual credits: he was the editor of the ground-breaking magazine *Neurotica* in the late 1940s and early 1950s; and Fran wrote lyrics for jazz-influenced popular songs such as "Season in the Sun" and "The Ballad of the Sad Young Men" recorded by such singers as Tony Bennett and Ella Fitzgerald. The Landesman's significance to the Beat movement came from their collaboration on what is considered the first (and, by many accounts, the only) Beat musical, *The Nervous Set* (1959). The couple's other stage works display a take on contemporary life reflective of the New York Beat writers who were their friends. The Landesmans functioned in their different ways as artists; and they were always on the frontiers of the representative experiences of the Beat era: drug–experimentation; sexual progressiveness; a radical social view that eschewed politics; an irreverence that would later be labeled black humor; and a highly personal lifestyle.

BEAT—the root, the soul of Beatific" (161).[8] This marks another connection between Kerouac's writing and his longtime susceptibility to the Roman Catholic beliefs that he learned in childhood, particularly the notion of a "dark night of the soul" leading to a state of grace. Yet this usage did not wrench "Beat" away from its roots in down-and-outness, as Holmes—an author associated with the Beats, although not a member of the core Beat group—indicated when he wrote of it in 1952:

> More than mere weariness, it implies the feeling of having been used, of being raw. It involves a sort of nakedness of mind, and, ultimately, of soul; a feeling of being reduced to the bedrock of consciousness. In short, it means being undramatically pushed up against the wall of oneself. A man is beat whenever he goes for broke and wagers the sum of his resources on a single number; and the young generation has done that continually from early youth.
>
> (1952, 10)

Fran Landesman, 1927-.

The Beats and Visual Thinking

What Lee is looking for is contact or recognition,
like a photon emerging from the haze of
insubstantiality to leave an indelible recording. . . . Failing to find an adequate
observer, he is threatened by painful
dispersal, like an unobserved photon.
—William S. Burroughs, *Queer*

A pungent visuality often pervades Beat writing and thinking. Beats and their commentators
have cited concepts drawn from contemporary
music (especially jazz improvisation) more often
than visual art when identifying key influences
on Beat works; yet practices in fine-art production
(especially action painting) and cinema also
played an important role in shaping and crystal-
lizing Beat notions of creativity. For instance, in
the second half of an *Evergreen Review* piece called
"Belief & Technique for Modern Prose"—a 1959
article that is really a fragmented "list of essentials" for generating spontaneous writing—
Kerouac returns with striking regularity to visual
metaphors that suggest his strong investment in
pictorial, cinematic, and mind's-eye imagery:

16. The jewel center of interest is the eye
within the eye

18. Work from pithy middle eye out, swimming in language sea

21. Struggle to sketch the flow that already exists intact in mind

22. Dont think of words when you stop but to
see picture better

25. Write for the world to read and see yr exact
pictures of it

26. Bookmovie is the movie in words, the
visual American form

30. Writer-Director of Earthly movies Sponsored & Angeled in Heaven (57)

Kerouac's interest in verbal "sketching" has
been traced to a friend's suggestion, early in his
career, that he "just sketch in the streets like a
painter but with words" (Tytell 143). Major
consequences ensued when he followed this
advice, and *On the Road* changed from what had
promised to be a conventional story (in the
Thomas Wolfe-like vein of *The Town and the City,*
perhaps) to a complex and superenergized verbal
tapestry modeled partly on the jazzlike flow of
breath patterns but also on the ideal of transcribing streams of mental imagery with all their
experiential ebbs, flows, and upheavals.[9]

Additionally, Kerouac had been fascinated by
movies in his early years. He had a special fondness for French films; coming from a French-
Canadian family,[10] he spoke English haltingly as
late as age eighteen. He was particularly taken
with the Walt Disney production *Fantasia,* which
he saw fifteen times at Manhattan's well-known
Thalia revival theater (Nicosia 32, 112). With the
boldly colored forms and freewheeling movements of its most imaginative sequences, this film
may have influenced the color symbolism and
shifting visual perspectives found in his most
adventurous books. He was not immune to dreams
of success as a Hollywood screenwriter, moreover,
or to avant-garde visions of producing a reflexive
film about himself and his friends, capturing them
in their real-life personae and perhaps filming
both the performers and the crew unawares "so
that the movie would also reveal the process by
which it was made" (Nicosia 274, 470). The film
Pull My Daisy (1959), in which Kerouac played an
important off-screen part, is rather different in
nature but has a hint of this ambience about it.

Kerouac was not alone among the Beats in
cultivating an important visual component within
his work. Ginsberg conceived his first enthusiasm
for Zen Buddhism as a result of exploring what he
described to Cassady as the "sublimity and sophistication . . . learning and experience" of Asian
painting. In poetry he wished to use tensions

between words much as Paul Cézanne used space between colors, and he found in Cézanne a use of juxtaposed planes and synaesthetic "*petite sensation*" that induced "eyeball kicks" similar to those Ginsberg had experienced in mystical visions of his own (Schumacher 153, 95, 197). He was interested in cinema as well, and harbored occasional ideas about film production. During a period of comparative financial security in the mid-'50s, for instance, he fantasized about making (among other projects) a kind of Buddhist science-fiction movie with "Burroughs on Earth" as its title (Nicosia 469-70).

As for Burroughs, the greater part of his work is grounded in a vast mythology of conflict between humanity and a parasitic enemy (known as the Nova Mob or the Board in most of its appearances) that has seized control of human consciousness through manipulation of images and words, turning the biosphere into a psychic battleground infested with "virus sheets constantly presented and represented before your mind screen to produce more virus word and image around and around . . . the invisible hail of bring down word and image" (1980, 68). Burroughs's major works constitute not only an account of this mythological struggle but also a line of defense against the Nova Mob's infiltration and control, insofar as the radical discontinuities of his montage-based prose (generated through deliberately disruptive cut-up and fold-in procedures) serve as antidotes to the enemy's lethal machinations, which are themselves as profoundly cinematic as they are ruthlessly monologic. "Remember i was the movies," says Mr. Bradly Mr. Martin, the arch villain of Burroughs's mythos, as one of his adventures reaches its final fadeout (1987b, 201).[11]

While it cannot be said that cinema played a specifically privileged role in the lives and works of most of the Beats, their inclinations toward nonliterary modes of expression (such as visuality and musicality) helped motivate an interest in film that asserted itself in many small ways and a few large ways (such as Burroughs's deployment of a recurrent "reality film" metaphor) at sundry points in their various careers. This interest represented, among other things, a creative response by the Beats to the relatively interesting state of American cinema during the period (the late '40s to the early '60s) that witnessed the major phase of their own activities as a "generation" with shared personal and aesthetic ideas. As already suggested, Hollywood studios during the

long reign of the classical filmmaking style (which was largely unchallenged from the '20s to the early '60s) tended to think of themselves as sustainers of mainstream values and sociocultural consensus. Yet gaps and contradictions were always present in this enterprise—some were manifested in the flourishing of *film noir,* for instance, as cited above—and the '50s saw an increase in their number. On one hand, declining revenues and the new challenge of television led studios to relax their formula-bound production habits and loosen the constraints of self-censorship that had been enforced in one form or another throughout their history; these changes allowed a somewhat more fluid and at times even experimental atmosphere (in works by such innovative filmmakers as Samuel Fuller and Nicholas Ray, for example) to creep into commercial cinema. At the same time, a number of veteran filmmakers who had mastered Hollywood's most popular and productive idioms—and who in some cases had given those idioms distinctive inflections of their own, earning recognition as individualistic visual artists from a budding generation of *auteur*-oriented critics—were still actively at work within the studio system, taking advantage of its newfound (if still very limited) creative flexibility to shape some of their most personal and idiosyncratic work.

This is not to say that experienced directors like Alfred Hitchcock and John Ford or inventive newcomers like Fuller and Ray were giving postwar Hollywood as radical a jolt as the action painters were giving to postwar art, the beboppers to postwar music, or the Beats to postwar literature. As will be argued below, mainstream cinema remained a deeply monologic phenomenon in most respects. Nor can it be claimed that the Beats, either as moviegoers or as artists subject to influences from the cultural *Zeitgeist,* zeroed in on the most stimulating cinema that *was* being made. Kerouac, for example, was capable of recognizing a good movie when he saw one; in his novel *Vanity of Duluoz: An Adventurous Education, 1935-46,* he recalls "walking out of the Royal Theater all elated because I had just seen Orson Welles' *Citizen Kane* and by God, what a picture! I wanted to be a genius of poetry in film like Welles. I was rushing home to figure out a movie play" (104). Yet he repeatedly gave his affection to all sorts of films, ranging from critically respected works to movies designed for the most uncritical audiences. In the same novel, he describes the irresistible urge he felt as a Columbia University student to ride on down to Times Square and go see a French movie, go see Jean Gabin press his lips together sayin "*Ca me navre,*" or Louis Jouvet's baggy behind going up the stairs, or that bitter lemon smile of Michele Morgan in the seaside bedroom, or Harry Bauer kneel as Handel praying for his work, or Raimu screaming at the mayor's afternoon picnic, and then after that, an American doublefeature, maybe Joel McRae in *Union Pacific,* or see tearful clinging sweet Barbara Stanwyck grab him, or maybe go see Sherlock Holmes puffing on his pipe with long Cornish profile as Dr. Watson puffs at a medical tome by the fireplace and Missus Cavendish or whatever her name was comes upstairs with cold roast beef and ale so that Sherlock can solve the latest manifestation of the malefaction of himself Dr. Moriarty. . . .

(76)

While this is an eclectic list, it smacks more of eager entertainment-hunting than of refined cinematic taste; that Georg Friedrich Händel biopic appears to have impressed Kerouac not with any musical or historical excellence it had to offer, for instance, but with a walloping dose of sentimental religiosity that made Kerouac literally cry (Nicosia 77).[12] Still, although such movies struck him for reasons having more to do with his personal moods and ephemeral emotions than with his fundamental aesthetic sensitivities, they were not merely a private quirk for him, like cheeseburgers or Twinkies for a renowned chef who respects simple pleasures and likes an occasional respite from elevated cuisine. They had a perceptible effect on his vision and on the writing that emerged from his highly heterogeneous inner life. It is hard not to think of a Walt Disney nature movie or cartoon from the '40s or '50s, for example, when reading a passage like this one in *Big Sur,* paradoxically one of Kerouac's most despairing works:

> I rose that following morning with more joy and health and purpose than ever, and there was me old Big Sur Valley all mine again, here came [the mule] good old Alf and I gave him food and patted his big rough neck with its various cocotte's manes, there was the mountain of Mien Mo in the distance just a dismal old hill with funny bushes around the sides and a peaceful farm on top. . . . And there's the bluejay idiot with one foot on the bar of soap on the porch rail, pecking at the soap and eating it, leaving the cereal unattended, and when I laugh and yell at him he looks up cute with an expression that seems to say "What's the matter? wotti do wrong?"—"Wo wo, got the wrong place," said another bluejay landing nearby and suddenly leaving again—And everything of my life seems beautiful again. . . .

(117-18)

Here such celebrated Kerouac personae as the peripatetic hipster, the transcendental mystic, and the jazz-inspired poet seem less in evidence than the fifteen-time viewer of *Fantasia* and the wide-eyed fan of Louis Jouvet's baggy behind. He shares his "bad taste" with other art-mavericks such as the Surrealists, of course, but they often seem more knowing and ironic in indulging their Kitschy proclivities.

Ginsberg appears to have developed somewhat more sophisticated tastes, yet without demonstrating a notably deep appreciation for cinematic excellence. Like his friend Kerouac, he loved movies from an early age, writing in his diary with precocious world-weariness at the age of eleven, "Movies afford me great pleasure and are about the only relief from boredom which seems to hang around me like a shadow." He received a jarring "nightmare vision of my own future" upon seeing Frederic March in Rouben Mamoulian's *Dr. Jekyll and Mr. Hyde* (1932) and wept sincerely at both the dying protagonist of James Whale's *The Invisible Man* (1933) and a lonely dog chasing after its prison-bound master in the finale of some lachrymose drama (Miles 1989, 26). In much later years, when he became a familiar face in avant-garde movies by a variety of filmmakers, he showed wide-ranging tastes in nonnarrative cinema, praising Andy Warhol's work and Barbara Rubin's audacious *Christmas on Earth* (1963), which he described as "a lot of porn, beauty, in which she made an art object out of her vagina. I thought that was in the right spirit" (Miles 1989, 334). This accolade may have been motivated in part by Ginsberg's personal affection for the filmmaker, however, since he was very close to her at the time of his exposure to her work.

Burroughs also showed an interest in film during much of his life, and cited screenplay writing as a major influence on his other literary work. "As soon as a writer starts writing a film script—that is, writing in terms of what appears on screen—he is no longer omniscient," he has said. The reason is that "information must be shown on the screen, unless the writer falls back on the dubious expedient of the off-stage voice. . . . You cannot get away with an indescribable monster. The audience wants to *see* the monster. . . . The ability to think in concrete visual terms is almost essential to a writer" (1993, 35-36). Yet for all his cogitation on visual thinking, his radicalism as an author, and his profound suspicion of mass media as manipulators of the mind and spirit, Burroughs's mature preferences in cinema appear to have followed mass taste—albeit the more adventurous aspects of mass taste—fairly closely. Discussing the motion pictures of 1969, he called

Dennis Hopper's *Easy Rider* a "pretty good" film, praising the "great wide vistas that are really America. Kerouac would have loved that movie. . . . Or maybe he wouldn't have liked what it said the way he was talking those last years you could never be sure." (As will be shown later in this study, Kerouac's dislike for violence in films grew to almost paranoiac dimensions by the late '50s.) Haskell Wexler's ambitious *Medium Cool* was "[n]ot bad, a step in the right direction . . . with the *cinema verite* stuff, but not an exceptional movie . . . like [Sam Peckinpah's] *The Wild Bunch.*" The film that really excited Burroughs was *The Damned,* which he called "a movie by a real master," a production that could only have been made by "a real European with roots that go way back" and who "knows how the European family works—and that is really what that movie is all about" (B. Cook 183-84). Luchino Visconti's melodrama about the Nazi era is indeed a worthwhile film, but Burroughs hardly seems to have hit upon particularly clever or original arguments for its merit.

Notwithstanding the inconsistencies in cinematic taste shown by the Beat writers, and the presence of much formula-bound cinema to bring out their worst instincts, it remains true that the Beats and the movies both experienced a very interesting phase in the postwar years—the former working to sustain vigorous literary careers, the latter finding new expressive possibilities as Hollywood nurtured (or tolerated) a minority of innovative filmmakers and television navigated its "golden age" of live production and media-specific experimentation. In addition, a new wave of avant-garde cinema emerged in the postwar era, conceived partly as a reaction to commercial film practice and partly as an outgrowth of aesthetic tendencies (poetic, nonlinear, expressionistic) that held little mainstream appeal but had wellestablished records in other art forms. This exercised a clear attraction for artists who wanted to adapt and extend Beat attitudes, ideas, methodologies, and practices in the field of cinema.

The interest of the Beats in visual expression, in high-energy communication, in multidimensional narrativity, in art sparked by spontaneous insight rather than canonical wisdom, in the possibility of a hip *Gesamtkunstwerk* joining the pictorial, the musical, the verbal, and the physical into an orgasmic concatenation of aesthetic joy—all of this lured them at various times to the cinematic world, whether through direct participation, plans or hopes for such participation, an urge to write on cinematic subjects, or simply the desire to reflect a cinematically influenced *Weltanschauung* in works dealing with ostensibly different themes.

BEATS AND CINEMA

The traces left in film history by interaction between Beat/avantgarde and mainstream/commercial discourses are often ephemeral. The reason is partly that the Beat writers deeply distrusted (at least when they gave the matter some deliberate thought) the sort of massproduced culture that Hollywood represented, rightly or wrongly, for them and for most "establishment" intellectuals of the period. Hollywood took a complementary position of opposing Beat values (sexual license, anticonsumerism, utopianism, etc.) through strategies of mockery, cooptation, and containment. Under these conditions, it is not surprising to find the different camps occupying different portions of the sociocultural terrain.

Still, the crosswind of social questioning and cultural criticism that ran through Hollywood cinema during the '50s era—in the continuing output of *film noir,* the increasingly complex moral tapestries of a Douglas Sirk or a Vincente Minnelli, the escalating experimentalism of an Alfred Hitchcock, and so on—prevented Hollywood from congealing into the monolithic establishmentarianism to which its moguls generally aspired. This crosswind also provided Beat and Beat-influenced thinkers with provocative filmrelated material that they could readily identify and approve. Much the same happened with television, where the fluidity of still-emerging production modes offset commercial pressures enough to allow for occasional irruptions of Beatreflective and even Beat-sympathetic expression. Also present on both sides of the Beat-Hollywood divide was a grudging fascination with the "other" that led Hollywood to occasional flirtations with the Beat spirit, and the Beats to occasional dreams of joining, purifying, and reforming the movie industry that held such decadent allure.

For these and other reasons there were numerous intersections between Beat and Hollywood activity; and even when they traveled down pathways that did not come close to converging, the very differences between their respective projects (in all the diversified forms that those projects took) can be read as symptomatic of the social, cultural, political, and economic environment that was shared by these two highly visible loci of artistic production. Like the Hollywood studios, the Beat writers wanted to communicate with a broad and diversified audience and were in fact widely known by the very stratum of American society—the middle class, the bourgeoisie, the squares—that was their most frequent and most avidly attacked target. They aspired to dissemination, respect, and influence just as actively as their studio-bred counterparts did, if with divergent motives and strategies. Their novels, poems, stories, and other works reflect actual, perceived, and fantasized realities of '50s culture as vividly as the period's movies and television programs do, if in different ways and with different goals; and their preoccupations and obsessions were received with interest by a wide range of Americans not limited to particular classes, communities, or degrees of aesthetic sophistication.

Movies and Beats, then, were equally integral aspects of the '50s scene. Fascination with the frontier and the rootless life gave impetus to Hollywood westerns as well as Kerouac's novels on the wilderness and the open road; interest in somatic expressivity spurred avant-garde ciné-poems as well as Ginsberg's breath-measured oral verses; and immersion in atomic-age terror and cold-war aggressivity spawned low-budget monster movies and experimental psychodramas as well as the zany deliriums of Burroughs's cut-up nightmares. The '50s provided fertile ground for all these artistic manifestations, which are as closely linked as they are dauntingly diverse. Much can be gained by considering each through the lens of the others.

Notes

1. John Tytell is one commentator who makes this comparison, designating "the social given" as the common enemy of both groups (9).

2. Carr appears as Claude de Maubris, the "falling star Lucifer angel boy demon genius" of a youthful clique, in *Vanity of Duluoz: An Adventurous Education, 1935-46*, one of Kerouac's most important novels. The narrator reports, "Claude kept yelling stuff about a 'New Vision' which he'd gleaned out of Rimbaud, Nietzsche, Yeats, Rilke, Alyosha Karamazov, anything" (Kerouac 1968, 211).

3. Bakhtin's analysis of Rabelais provides useful insights when applied to Beat writing. For instance, just as Rabelais used folk laughter as a source of "ideological weaponry to rescue human consciousness from [a] stultifying conceptual framework," in Gardiner's words, it can be said that the Beats used various forms of spontaneously generated language "to help prevent what [Walter] Benjamin once called the 'paralysis of the imagination.'" Like the language of Rabelais's novel, moreover, that of Beat works often "drew on popular oral sources and reinvested tired clichés and platitudes with new meanings by placing them in unexpected and often disturbing contexts," involving words in "a 'carnival game of negation' which was enlisted to 'serve utopian tendencies.'" Rabelais was certainly an influence on all of the core Beat writers;

Ginsberg, for instance, invoked Rabelais's tradition of "social satire" in a petition aimed at exonerating comedian Lenny Bruce from obscenity charges (see Schumacher 410-11).

4. Cf. Terry Eagleton's statement that carnivalesque activity tends to be "a licensed affair in every sense, a permissible rupture of hegemony, a contained popular blow-off" (quoted in Gardiner 231).

5. Kerouac makes a half-serious association between Beethoven and "gloom" in more than one book, including *On the Road*.

6. Charters observes that jazz musician Mezz Mezzrow used "beat" in compound words and phrases in his 1946 book *Really the Blues*, as when he writes, "I was dead beat" and "a beat-up old tuxedo with holes in the pants." It is interesting to note that Kerouac used Mezz as the nickname of Pat Mezz McGillicuddy, the musician character in *Pull My Daisy*.

7. Kerouac, in a 1948 conversation with John Clellon Holmes, is responding to Holmes's suggestion that he succinctly characterize his generation's new attitude (quoted in Charters xix).

8. As glossed by Stephenson, the suggestion is that for Kerouac "the condition of weariness, emptiness, exhaustion, defeat, and surrender is antecedent to and causative of a state of blessedness. In being Beat the ego is diminished and in abeyance" (23).

9. Tytell concisely recounts the evolution of *On the Road* (143). The friend of Kerouac was Ed White, an artist.

10. In a description of Jack Duluoz, his alter ego, Kerouac reports that he "couldn't speak anything but French till [he] was six" (1994, 28).

11. With regard to one more Beat figure and the notion of visual thinking, Lawrence Ferlinghetti was not one of the core Beats but had a longtime association with them; in his prose and poetry, Stephenson finds a complex "Spiritual Optics" that constitutes "a way of being and seeing, a mode of identity and vision" involving a psychic struggle toward "integration of the fragmented, fallen consciousness into a unity" and "reconciliation of subject and object, of ego and nonego, in the communion of creative perception" (140). Note the echoes here of Jacques Lacan's psychoanalytic theory of psychic fragmentation and longing for a lost prelapsarian state.

12. Kerouac's tears flowed "as [the composer] knelt to pray for inspiration."

CHUCK WORKMAN AND MARY ELIZABETH WILLIAMS (INTERVIEW DATE 1 JUNE 1999)

SOURCE: Workman, Chuck, and Mary Elizabeth Williams. "The Beats Go on: Filmmaker Chuck Workman on *The Source*, His Fawning Tribute to the Beat Generation." *Salon* (online magazine) <http://archive.salon.com/ent/movies/int/1999/06/02/beat/> (1 June 1999).

In the following interview, Williams queries Workman, director of the documentary The Source, *about the place of the Beats in modern popular culture. Workman suggests that his interests as a filmmaker mirror those of the Beats, in seeking the connection between non-elite consumers of popular culture and serious art.*

By now, Jack Kerouac is almost as famous for his Gap ad as he is for his books. And William Burroughs and Allen Ginsberg are, to some, just those quirky writer guys whose closely timed deaths a couple of years ago sparked a flurry of reflective eulogies about alternative lifestyles in every newspaper across the country. Today all three are icons: Their names and faces are famous and their books are still selling well (even if they're not always as well-read as they are well-bought). Everybody knows who the Beats were, and Beat culture survives and thrives in modern manifestations of poetry readings and jazz jams. But the roots of the movement and the intoxicating words that ignited a generation of writers are less familiar, especially to audiences who've struggled helplessly through *Naked Lunch* or missed their "angry person with a copy of *Howl*" phase.

Director Chuck Workman (*Superstar: The Life and Times of Andy Warhol*) wants to change that. Starting with the meeting of Kerouac, Ginsberg and Burroughs in 1944 and going up to the present, Workman's documentary *The Source* traces the rise and continuing legacy of the Beats in an affectionate, appropriately dreamy and collagelike fashion. Using the original holy trinity as his anchor, he threads in vintage clips of other Beat writers, jazz and pop music, and contemporary interviews with Burroughs, Ginsberg, Ken Kesey, Phillip Glass and a host of other writers and thinkers.

And, just to remind you of what all the fuss was originally about, he offers Johnny Depp reading from *On the Road*, John Turturro doing *Howl* and a hair-raising interpretation of *Naked Lunch* from Dennis Hopper. The result is a work that's both exuberant and elegiac, a high-speed journey through 50 years of driving and drugging, writing and fighting, that's also a tender testament to enduring friendships.

The Source is showing this Thursday at "docfest," the second annual New York International Documentary Festival, and from there, will open in major cities across the country in late August. Workman, meanwhile, is starting work on his next film, a dramatic feature called *A House on a Hill*. The Beats, however, are still very much on his mind.

Workman spoke to Salon Arts & Entertainment over the phone from Los Angeles, where he is working on his next film.

Tell us a little about the genesis of The Source, *and why you chose to do a film on the Beat generation.*

I'm very interested in pop culture—serious pop culture—poetry and theater and art, especially as it interfaces with everyday people. I'm into the sorts of things where there's serious pretense but there's connection with what's happening sociologically and historically. I feel there is a major connection between the nonintellectual consumer and fine art, and it's never given enough credit. There's a big world out there, especially in movies. So I was interested in Warhol, in the Beats, in poetry and jazz. Someone who'd seen *Superstar* called me about doing a movie about Ginsberg [executive producer Hiro Yamagata], and I said I was more into the counterculture that began in the '40s with Allen and how it changed the world, and how that was the source of so much of what we have today.

There's so much music and so many clips in the film—how long did it take to make the movie and gain clearance for all that material?

Four years. One of the jokes about being a director is that the most important trick is to never take no for an answer. I'd just say, "I can get the Bob Dylan song; I can get the Rolling Stones song." We did have a good budget for the film, but we still couldn't spend more than a few thousand dollars for each song and each clip. But people understood and wanted to participate. They knew it was being done in a serious manner, and I tried to do that.

The music was really important. I felt an obligation to get all the right moments in there so you'd watch and think, "There's Monk, there's Gillespie." I got the Dead and Billie Holiday and "Hey, Jack Kerouac." At the end I knew I had to get them all in somehow if I wanted to show this world.

One of the things that's different about The Source *is how much time you spend on actually presenting the words of the authors, and doing it in a way that's unique—like using the actors to perform them.*

If you're making a film about writers, how do you do that? You have to sample the writers. And in this case, the writing is fairly dense. I said, I'm going to subjugate the audience to really listen and pay attention. These actors were all my first choice for these guys. I had to wait a long time for their schedules to open up, but I was happy with the result.

There's also a lot of text in the film. You see the words and there's a lot of typing, all these metaphors for writing that go through the movie. There are people who feel the scenes are too long, who don't really get it, and I say, 'I'm sorry, that's what the movie's about.' It's like saying you don't like the art in a Jackson Pollack movie.

ON THE SUBJECT OF...

The construction of the film is very mosaic. How influenced by the Beat style were you in assembling the images and sounds of the film?

I didn't consciously do that; it's basically my style. I force you to watch hard and to catch connections. I guess it is like jazz. There is that loose lyrical quality that comes out and that may be from the subject and the music. I know what I want in every reel, and what goes first and what goes second, but I want to allow for something that will keep people in their seats and give it a theatricality. I'm always trying to bring a dramatic structure even to a non-dramatic story.

In this case, the material does that: It's great and outrageous and it forces you to cut that way. And when I shot my own stuff, I tried to be kind of loose. I wanted a non-structured, edgy, anything-can-happen feel.

During the making of the film, some of the participants passed away [in addition to Burroughs and Ginsberg, the film also features Jerry Garcia and Timothy Leary]. Do you think the fact its subjects are now gone will change how people view this movie?

People are saying now it's the only thing left. There are other Beat films, there are other Beat projects, but the resources we had were great. We wanted to lay a document down that nailed these guys in a certain way.

Since the Beats are so widely written about and talked about, how did you find ways to say things that hadn't been said before?

I don't think anyone has ever looked at 50 years of counterculture in this way, and shown in a linear way how one thing built on another. That was my take on it.

As you started researching the film and talking to people, were there things that surprised you?

There are certain things you take for granted. The positive was that the literature was so great. Some of that work is very important literature. And I met people whose lifestyle was so far away from mine, even though I was close to their ages. The quality of the literature and the quality of the people were amazing. They were such classy and such cool people. They were very fun-loving; they loved to get stoned, they loved to run around and get naked, they loved sex and rock 'n' roll, and I had to constantly remember that about them. I wasn't in that world but I'm fascinated by it. On the downside, these were such smart men, but I knew what male chauvinist pigs they were.

What do you think the allure of the Beats is today? Do you think that people today think of Kerouac as a writer or an image in a khakis ad?

I think this is greater than just an idea of something that comes and goes. There was definitely something in the air after World War II that changed us, and whether the Beats' own work is still relevant, I don't know. I think it is. *On the Road* is certainly one of the most popular books in college bookstores. When we were filming and went out with Burroughs or Kesey, they were mobbed. People look at their lifestyles and say, there's so much venality and hypocrisy now, and these guys stuck to their guns. People at the turn of this century can respect that. They didn't bullshit; they did their own thing. And maybe that is their legacy.

NICHOLAS ZURBRUGG (ESSAY DATE 1999)

SOURCE: Zurbrugg, Nicholas. "Will Hollywood never Learn? David Cronenberg's *Naked Lunch*." In *Adaptations: From Text to Screen, Screen to Text*, edited by Deborah Cartmell and Imelda Whelehan, pp. 98-112. London: Routledge, 1999.

In the following essay, Zurbrugg critiques Cronenberg's film version of Naked Lunch *as an example of cinematic license gone awry, arguing that in attempting to make the film as much about Burroughs's own life and writing as an adaptation of his novel, Cronenberg strays far from Burroughs's original style. Zurbrugg laments that Burroughs opted to participate minimally in the making of* Naked Lunch, *comparing the movie to earlier films—* Towers Open Fire, Burroughs: The Movie, Drugstore Cowboy, *and others—in which Burroughs participated more fully.*

My nephew . . . was not an author. . . . Very few of those employed in writing motion-picture dialogue are. The executives of the studios just haul in anyone they meet and make them sign contracts. Most of the mysterious disappearances you read about are due to this cause. Only the other day they found a plumber who had been missing for years. All the time he had been writing dialogue for the Mishkin Brothers. Once having reached Los Angeles, nobody is safe.

(Wodehouse [1935] 1954: 236-7)

If you go to Hollywood. . . . And if you really believe in the art of the film . . . you ought to forget about any other kind of writing. A preoccupation with words for their own sake is fatal to good film making. It's not what films are for. . . . The best scenes I ever wrote were practically monosyllabic. And the best short scene I ever wrote . . . was one in which the girl said 'uh huh' three times with three different intonations, and that's all there was to it.

(Chandler, in Gardiner and Walker 1984: 138)

For God's sake Bill, play ball with this conspiracy.

(*Naked Lunch,* 1993)

Like P. G. Wodehouse and Raymond Chandler, William Burroughs has long anticipated the worst from mainstream cinematic adaptations. Writing to the painter Brion Gysin in a letter of 24 May 1977, for example, he memorably complains: 'What can happen to your script is not to be believed. It's like you came back from Istanbul and there was a Dali bent watch right in the middle of your picture. You write a part for James Coburn and you wind up with Liberace' (Morgan 1988: 541).

One way or another, Burroughs suggests, Hollywood invariably imposes the kind of pseudo-surreal effects that the French cultural theorist Paul Virilio equates with 'the poverty of the trivial dream, which is so curiously lacking in variety and imagination that the representation of our desires becomes a load of drivel, with endless repetitions of a few limited themes'. For Virilio, the same can be said for both 'digital imagery' in particular, 'which merely imitates the special effects and tricks of old 3D cinema' (Virilio [1993] 1995: 71), and for the accelerated pace of media culture in general, which in his terms ruins 'the pause of luminous contemplation' and exhausts 'the fragile sphere of our dreams' (Virilio [1993] 1995: 70-1).

As his notes on the American multimedia performance artist Robert Wilson's 'visionary' capacity to present 'beautiful life-saving dream images' indicate, Burroughs regards dreams as both a poetic necessity, circumventing 'the crippling conventions of dramatic presentation' and 'soap opera plots', and quite literally as 'a *biological necessity*' (Burroughs 1991: 17). In this respect, Burroughs—like Virilio and Wilson—is best understood as an ecologist of the dream, striving to remedy what Walter Benjamin calls 'the shock effect of the film' by identifying multimediated forms of 'heightened presence of mind' and re-establishing 'time for contemplation and evaluation' (Benjamin [1936] 1970: 240).

Likewise, as the subtitle of *Nova Express—* demanding 'WILL HOLLYWOOD NEVER LEARN?' (Burroughs 1966: 70)—suggests, Burroughs seems to have little sympathy for the mass-cultural banality of what he thinks of as the American 'non-dream'. So far as Burroughs is concerned:

America is not so much a nightmare as a *non-dream.* The American non-dream is precisely a move to wipe the dream out of existence. The dream is a spontaneous happening and therefore dangerous to a control system set up by the non-dreamers.

(Burroughs [1969] 1974: 102)

Paradoxically perhaps, some quarter century after the French edition of *The Job* first published this warning, the independent Canadian film-maker David Cronenberg met Burroughs for the first time in New York and initiated a project to film Burroughs' supposedly 'unfilmable' anti-novel, *The Naked Lunch* (1959), for mass-market distribution, and against all odds, to endorse Burroughs' prodigal career with the seal of Hollywood approval.

Cronenberg carefully defines his plans for *Naked Lunch* (1993) as the attempt to create 'a combination of Burroughsian material but put into a structure that's not very Burroughsian'. Such an adaptation, Cronenberg contends, 'still deserves to be called *Naked Lunch*' by virtue of "accurately reflecting some of the tone of Burroughs, what his life stands for, and what his work has been"' (Emery and Silverberg in Silverberg 1992: 65). For his part, Burroughs affirmed that Cronenberg's script offered 'a good example of the cinematic license the film-maker takes . . . to realize his vision on film' (Burroughs 1992b: 14-5).

Significantly though, far from considering Cronenberg's film to have anything of the interactive quality of his early 1960s cut-up experiments in the Beat Hotel with Brion Gysin, Harold Norse and Ian Somerville, when they 'held constant meetings and conferences with exchange of ideas and comparison of cut-up writing, painting and tape-recorder experiments' (Burroughs 1983: Introduction), Burroughs clearly regarded Cronenberg's film as 'a profoundly personal interpretation' rather than any kind of collaboration, stipulating that he 'had no writing input into the script whatsoever, and only courtesy rights to request any changes, which I didn't' (Burroughs 1992b: 15).

Cronenberg, by contrast, relates how he felt 'forced to . . . fuse my own sensibility with Burroughs and create a third thing that neither he nor I would have done on his own' (Cronenberg 1997: 162); at once confirming Burroughs' dictum that: 'No two minds ever come together without, thereby, creating . . . a third mind' (Burroughs 1979: 25), and partially fulfilling Burroughs' dream of 'taking over a young body' in 'an experiment of transference which would be of benefit to both of us, perhaps of incalculable benefit, but in all fairness not without danger' (Burroughs 1974: 28-9).

What are the advantages and disadvantages of a cinematic adaptation that foregrounds 'the tone' of a writer, what their life 'stands for' and what their 'work has been'? And what are the most obvious benefits or dangers of placing literary 'material' within a structure that's 'not very' typical of its author? In Burroughs' case, such questions are best considered in terms of the significant differences in 'tone' between Cronenberg's highly personal but in many ways predominantly mainstream cinematic adaptation of *Naked Lunch,* the more dynamic collaborative register of earlier adaptations of Burroughs' writings such as Antony Balch's underground classics *Towers Open Fire* (1963) and *The Cut-Ups* (1967), and such subsequent increasingly 'overground' ventures as Howard Brookner's *Burroughs: The Movie* (1983), Gus Van Sant's *Drugstore Cowboy* (1989), and Robert Wilson, Tom Waits and Burroughs' collaborative opera, *The Black Rider* (1990).

But what does it mean to 'adapt' a novel for the screen? And what, after all, is a novel? Such questions seem best approached by comparing Burroughs' and Cronenberg's writings and observations about text/screen adaptation. Burroughs dismisses soap opera as being 'not—sort of—even *below* lowbrow' (Burroughs 1990: 47), and speculates that 'if you have a film that has, oh say, ten good minutes in it' that's 'a pretty good film', '[a] *very* good film, actually. You can't expect much

more' (Burroughs 1990: 45). He generally concedes, however, that most novels lend themselves to certain 'old, old' formulas.

> Take any novel that you like, and think about making a film out of that novel. Or say in one sentence what this book is about. What is *Lord Jim* about?' . . . Two sentences, 'Honour lost. Honour regained.'
>
> (Burroughs 1990: 43)

But as he equally readily emphasizes, 'some novels won't break down like that', and even if they do, 'just because you can get a novel into one sentence doesn't mean you can make a film out of it'.

> You can get *The Great Gatsby* into a couple of sentences, but you can't make a film out of it. What is this about? 'Poor boy loses girl. Poor boy tries to get girl back, which results in tragedy.' 'Poor boy loses girl to rich man, and tries to get her back. Does get her back for a brief interlude, and then there is a tragic dénouement, because he's trying something that isn't going to work— he's trying to put back the clock.' But this isn't film material.
>
> (Burroughs 1990: 43)

And why isn't this 'film material'? Because— for Burroughs at least—the impact of *The Great Gatsby* arises not so much from its plot as from what Barthes defines as the 'grain' of the text, or what Chandler equates with a 'particular preoccupation with words for their own sake' (in Gardiner and Walker 1984: 138). 'It's all in the prose, in Fitzgerald's prose. That's where Gatsby exists', Burroughs concludes, and nothing but nothing, can translate this into film:

> Well, you remember the end of *The Great Gatsby,* that's one of the famous scenes in English prose, like the end of 'The Dead' by James Joyce, the famous 'snow falling faintly—like the descent of their last end, upon all the living and the dead'. There's no way that you can put that effectively into film. I mean, you can show snow, but what does that mean? It doesn't mean anything. And the same way with the end of *The Great Gatsby.* And all they could do was a voice-over.
>
> (Burroughs 1990: 43)

While Burroughs insists that film cannot do language's job more effectively, he acknowledges that words are equally powerless to emulate such cinematic effects as the *trompe-l'oeil* montages in Antony Balch's film *Bill and Tony* (1972). Here—in a 'little experiment' in 'face-projection', 'intended to be projected onto the faces of its cast'—Balch and Burroughs 'are seen first independently, then side-by-side, introducing themselves (as each other) and then speaking short texts', before dubbing each other's voices in the otherwise identical 'second half' (Balch 1972: 12). Even a summary of *Bill and Tony* becomes daunting, and as Burroughs concludes: 'there's no way you could put that on the printed page' (Burroughs 1990: 43).

Contending that '[w]hen someone says, "Well, the film didn't do justice to the book", or vice versa, they're talking about things which aren't the same medium', generally observing that whenever 'Hollywood gets hold of something that's a classic . . . the results are usually terrible' and speculating that 'films made from quite mediocre books' usually 'make the best films', Burroughs concludes that '[t]he film must stand up as a separate piece of work, quite apart from the book' (Burroughs 1990: 43-5), resting his case upon the precedent of *Chandler* v. *Hollywood*.

> Raymond Chandler was once asked, 'How do you feel about what Hollywood has done to your novels?' He reportedly answered, 'My novels? Why, Hollywood hasn't done anything to them. They're still right there, on the shelf.'
> (Burroughs 1992a: xv)

But as Chandler indicates, Hollywood certainly does do things to novels, not least by contorting verbal complexity into what Beckett dismisses as the 'sweet reasonableness of plane psychology à la Balzac' (Beckett 1934: 976). Or as Homer Mandrill puts it in Burroughs' *Exterminator!*, Hollywood poetics (like redneck politics) compulsively turns the clock back 'to 1899 when a silver dollar bought a steak dinner and good piece of ass' (Burroughs 1974: 106), and—one might add—when a silver dollar also bought a good, no-nonsense read, rather than what P. G. Wodehouse memorably calls 'those psychological modern novels where the hero's soul gets all tied up in knots as early as page 21 and never straightens itself out again' (Wodehouse [1935] 1954: 246).

As the author of convoluted anti-narrative which 'actually caused at least one unprepared square to vomit on the carpet' (Nuttall [1968] 1970: 108), Burroughs very reasonably warns that '[i]t is probably an understatement to say that the novel does not obviously lend itself to adaptation for the screen' (Burroughs 1992a: xiii). In turn, as the ill-fated adapter of a 'mother of epics' into which he felt he could at best 'dip', rather than read 'from start to finish', Cronenberg determined 'to be absolutely ruthless when it came to using Burroughs' material' (Silverberg 1992: 161-2):

> I started to think about what I didn't want to do with *Naked Lunch*. I didn't want it to be a movie about drugs . . . I wanted it to be about writing . . . I wanted the movie to have characters . . . I wanted a woman to have an important character . . . I wanted it to have narrative cohesiveness.
> (Cronenberg, in Silverberg 1992: 164-5)

At the same time, Cronenberg's 'wants' list admits a number of symbolic exceptions. Following his early sense 'that drugs were for jazz musicians' (Silverberg 1992: 164), Cronenberg sets the scene for *Naked Lunch* with 'meandering alto sax notes from Ornette Coleman, gracing the highly stylized graphic design of the opening credits' (Conomos 1992: 16). Thereafter Cronenberg evokes addiction increasingly indirectly in terms of alien invasion imagery, as 'a metaphor for control'. 'I understood the metaphorical side. That's what I responded to' (Silverberg 1992: 164).

But Burroughs' vision is as much about low-life as hi-sci-fi life, and one neglects Burroughs' more or less direct evocations of the 'junk-sick dawn' at one's peril. As the virtuosity of *Naked Lunch*'s early pages suggests, Burroughs is at once the Balzac, the Baudelaire and the Ballard of New York's underworld, confidently charting its sordid, spectral or stomach-turning detail in narrative hovering between dispassionate restraint and paranoid anxiety, and generally anticipating the alacrity with which his later 'routines' evince 'simultaneous insight and hallucination', as 'three-dimensional fact merges into dream, and dreams erupt into the real world' (Burroughs 1993: 243, 300).

While Cronenberg's evocation of addiction in terms of the mechanized, fluid-emitting Mugwump offering 'the teat on its head to addicts eager to partake of its irresistible substance' (Duncan, in Silverberg 1992: 94-6) certainly suggests the presence of alien creatures in the real world, the prospect of his plastic monsters in a vaulted, Hammer-style 'Mugwump dispensary' (Duncan, in Silverberg 1992: 96) smacks of the world of Dr Who rather than of Dr Benway. Cronenberg accurately observes that there is 'a lot of hi-sci-fi and horror imagery in Burroughs', particularly the 'Mugwumps, and all kinds of creatures' (Cronenberg, in Silverberg 1992: 166). But as a glance at *Naked Lunch* indicates, most of Burroughs' creatures are not so much exotic 'hi-sci-fi' mutants as vagrant 'terrestial dogs' (Burroughs 1966: 18). Alienated both at home and abroad, these are quintessentially flesh-and-blood aliens, whether clinically described in terms of the kind of 'real scene' in which 'you pinch up some leg flesh and make a quick stab hole with a pin', before fitting the dropper 'over, not in the hole and feed the solution slow and careful so it doesn't squirt out the sides', or whether self-consciously caricatured in such 'pin and dropper' routines as:

> She seized a safety-pin caked with blood and rust, gouged a great hole in her leg which seemed to hang open like an obscene, festering mouth waiting for unspeakable congress with the dropper which she now plunged out of sight into the gaping wound.
>
> (Burroughs [1959] 1982: 20)

Occasionally, to be sure, Burroughs' world rocks to the 'Monster Mash', as mutants like Bradley the Buyer spread terror 'throughout the industry':

> Junkies and agents disappear. Like a vampire bat he gives off a narcotic effluvium, a dank green mist that anesthetizes his victims and renders them helpless in his enveloping presence. . . . Finally he is caught in the act of digesting the Narcotics Commissioner and destroyed with a flame thrower—the court of inquiry ruling that such means were justified in that the Buyer had lost his citizenship and was, in consequence, a creature without species and a menace to the narcotics industry on all levels.
>
> (Burroughs [1959] 1982: 27)

But usually Burroughs depicts business as usual. Blandly concluding: 'Isn't life peculiar?' (Burroughs [1959] 1982: 15), he catalogues an underworld populated by such everyday grotesques as Willy the Disk, 'blind from shooting in the eyeball' (Burroughs [1959] 1982: 17); by the unwashed, such as 'Old Bart . . . dunking pound cake with his dirty fingers, shiny over the dirt'; by the frailty of 'spectral janitors, grey as ashes, phantom porters sweeping out dusty old halls with a slow old man's hand, coughing and spitting in the junk-sick dawn'; or by shameless 'old junkies'—'Really disgust you to see it' (Burroughs [1959] 1982: 15).

Ironically, while Cronenberg spares his viewers graphic representation of the 'unspeakable congress' between 'dropper' and 'wound' (Cronenberg, in Silverberg 1992: 20), his most powerful symbols of addiction evince an almost Burroughsian propulsion towards 'only the most extreme material' (Burroughs 1993: 262). Indeed, as Emery and Silverberg report, initial responses to the film's evocations of 'unspeakable congress' between the latex organs of 'fifty Mugwumps suspended horizontally and attended to by a hundred "slaves"' (Silverberg 1992: 71), occasionally proved equally disturbing to both Cronenberg and cast:

> Of the hundred extras . . . three defected. One of the defectors, a lawyer, said, 'I just can't have my clients see me sucking on a Mugwump teat,' and

fled. One visitor who thoroughly enjoyed his encounter with a Mugwump, however, was Burroughs. 'I was impressed with the Mugwump,' he says. 'He's very engaging, rather simpatico.' . . . This rather worried Cronenberg, who had designed the Mugwumps . . . to resemble old, elongated junkies that represent the evil spirit pervading the film.

> (Silverberg 1992: 71-2)

Both enjoying the Mugwump's immediate 'simpatico' presence, and condoning the 'masterstoke' of Cronenberg's 'substitution of . . . Mugwump jissom—for the rather more mundane heroin and marijuana depicted in the novel', Burroughs generously concludes: 'One of the novel's central ideas is that addiction can be metaphorical, and what could underscore this better than the film's avoidance of actual narcotics?' (Burroughs 1992a: xiv).

Naked Lunch is self-evidently anything but a purely metaphorical novel without reference to the 'actual'. As Burroughs himself emphasizes, it abounds in 'endless parenthesis' (Burroughs 1989: 128), multiplying realistic and metaphoric perspectives across his 'banquet of thirty, forty components' (Mailer 1965: 42), and hinges upon a sense of obligation towards all facts at all levels, whether metaphoric or literal, indirect or direct. Writing to Jack Kerouac on 18 September 1950, for example, Burroughs insists that '[f]acts exist on infinite levels' and that 'one level does not preclude another' (Burroughs 1993: 71), and in a letter to Kerouac of 12 February 1955 he still more explicitly determines to refine an 'absolute, direct transmission of *fact* on all levels' (Burroughs 1993: 265).

In turn, *Naked Lunch* unequivocally asserts that there is 'only one thing a writer can write about: *what is in front of his senses at the moment of writing*', and that its title 'means exactly what the words say . . . a frozen moment when everyone sees what is on the end of every fork' (Burroughs [1959] 1982: 218, 1). If Allen Ginsberg's sensitivity to the literal quality of Burroughs' 'actual visions' leads his poem 'On Burroughs' Work' (1954) to caricature them as being free from 'symbolic dressing' (Burroughs 1993: 40), Cronenberg's admiration for the general—rather than the local—satirical register of *Naked Lunch* leads him to overemphasize its symbolic content by treating much of the novel's most disturbing verbal content 'in a metaphorical way' (Cronenberg, in Silverberg 1992: 64).

At the same time, Cronenberg frequently modifies the particularity of the novel's detail in terms of his general insights into what Burroughs' life as a whole 'stands for' and 'what his work has been' (Cronenberg, in Silverberg 1992: 65). Acknowledging, for example, that his treatment of *Naked Lunch* is 'not as aggressive and predatory in its homosexuality' as Burroughs' novel, Cronenberg hints that his film may be closer to reality than the novel itself, insofar as it reflects Burroughs' more tentative evocations of his sexuality in 'letters, prefaces and other things': 'I was trying to see beyond, to the reality of the situation, which is much more ambivalent and ambiguous in terms of sexuality' (Silverberg 1992: 163). At such points Cronenberg's film becomes 'as much an adaptation of Ted Morgan's biography of Burroughs, *Literary Outlaw* . . . as it was *Naked Lunch*' (Rodley, in Silverberg 1992: 171).

But, as Burroughs remarks in *Interzone,* he is far more interested in Paul Klee's notion of art with 'a life of its own', placing the artist in 'real danger' (Burroughs 1989: 128), than in literary self-portraiture. While Cronenberg certainly evokes this kind of danger thematically, his general approach is often that of a biographical *roman-à-clef,* rather than that of a more dangerously corrosive *roman-à-Klee.* Gaining much of its iconic force from the deadpan detachment of Peter Weller, who as 'Lee' seems a dead-ringer both for a younger Burroughs and a younger Joseph Beuys, Cronenberg's *Naked Lunch* invites the viewer to play 'Spot the Bowles', to 'Spot the Ginsbergian "Martin"' and to 'Spot the Kerouacian "Hank"'. Declining to play, Burroughs bluntly observes: 'I don't recognize anyone I ever knew in those characters' (Burroughs 1992b: 15).

Far from arising from the concrete details of veiled autobiography, *Naked Lunch*'s impact surely derives primarily from its evocations of what Burroughs calls the 'poltergeist knockings and mutterings of America's putrefying unconscious' and the 'incredibly obscene, thinly disguised references and situations that slip by in Grade B Movies' (Burroughs 1993: 259). Reluctant to offer a literal translation of Burroughs' cathartic 'shitting out my educated Middlewest background' (Burroughs, in Morgan 1988: 264) for fear of being 'banned in every country in the world', Cronenberg takes *Naked Lunch* to Disneyland, mechanizing and masking its menace with all the inventions of 'a heavy-duty effects movie' (Cronenberg, in Silverberg 1992: 161, 166).

Dispensing with Burroughs' most offensive characters and delegating their dialogue to 'effects that also talk a lot', *Naked Lunch* enlivens its decimated cast with the 'Bugwriter'—a robotic 'talking sphincter' (Duncan, in Silverberg 1992:

99, 101) with all the charm of what Burroughs calls 'a Dali bent watch' (Morgan 1988: 541). As Lyden Barber observes (1992: 34), the more one sees of this pulsating incarnation of Dr Benway's routine about 'the man who taught his asshole to talk' (Burroughs [1959] 1982: 133-5), the more tiresome it becomes, and the more grateful one feels for Burroughs' inspired role as Benway in the brief adaptation of the operating scene from *Naked Lunch* (Burroughs [1959] 1982: 66-7) in Howard Brookner's *Burroughs: The Movie* (1983).

Put another way, Burroughs' most forceful accounts of his literary crises derive not so much from the iconic quality of obscene descriptive detail, as from the ironic discursive energy with which Burroughs introduces such detail. Nowhere is this more apparent than in a letter to Kerouac (7 December 1954) outlining the difficulties of writing in 'a popular vein' (Burroughs 1993: 242), recording the involuntary genesis of *Naked Lunch*'s 'interzone' section, and generally generating the vitriolic humour so frequently missing from Cronenberg's adaptation of his novel.

> I sat down seriously to write a best-seller Book of the Month Club job on Tangier. So here is what comes out first sentence: 'The only native in Interzone who is neither queer nor available is Andrew Keif's chauffeur . . . Aracknid is the worst driver in the Zone. On one occasion he ran down a pregnant woman in from the mountains with a load of charcoal on her back, and she miscarried a bloody, dead baby on the street, and Keif got out and sat on the curb stirring the blood with a stick while the police questioned Aracknid and finally arrested the woman.' I can just see that serialized in . . . *Good Housekeeping.*
> (Burroughs 1993: 241-2)

Amusingly confirming that nothing about 'Burroughs in Tangier' was ever *Good Housekeeping* material, Paul Bowles' reminiscences suggest the ways in which Burroughs' distinctive performative energies subsequently offered remarkably good film-making materials to such early collaborative adaptations of his work as Balch's *Towers Open Fire* (1963). Doubtless the same cinematic energy might also have invigorated Cronenberg's adaptation of *Naked Lunch* had the disparity between fact and fiction not led to his exclusion from the film for fear that his presence 'might jar the viewer out of the story' (Burroughs 1992b: 15).

> The litter on his desk and under it, on the floor, was chaotic, but it consisted only of pages of *Naked Lunch,* at which he was constantly working. When he read aloud from it, at random (any sheet of paper he happened to grab would do) he laughed a good deal, as well he might, since it is very funny, but from reading he would suddenly (paper

still in hand) go into bitter conversational attack upon whatever aspect of life had prompted the passage he had just read.

(Bowles 1959: 43)

Following Bowles' lead, and remarking how 'Burroughs' humour is peculiarly American, at once broad and sly', Mary McCarthy persuasively argues that while there are 'many points of comparison between Burroughs and Swift', what saves *Naked Lunch* 'is not a literary ancestor but humor'. More specifically, McCarthy explains:

It is the humor of a comedian, a vaudeville performer playing in 'one,' in front of the asbestos curtain of some Keith Circuit or Pantages house long converted to movies. . . . Some of the jokes are verbal ('Stop me if you've heard this atomic secret' or Dr Benway's 'A simopath . . . is a citizen convinced he is an ape or other simian. It is a disorder peculiar to the army and discharge cures it'). Some are 'black' parody (Dr Benway, in his last appearance, dreamily, his voice fading out: 'Cancer, my first love'). . . . The effect of pandemonium, all hell breaking loose, is one of Burroughs' favorites and an equivalent of the old vaudeville finale, with the acrobats, the jugglers, the magician, the hoofers . . . all pushing into the act.

(McCarthy [1963] 1991: 4-5)

Sadly, Cronenberg virtually pushes such humour out of 'the act' in order to save his film from degenerating into what he calls 'a very nasty kind of soft, satirical social satire of the *Britannia Hospital* variety, with no emotional content and without the beauty, grace and potency of Burroughs' literary style' (Silverberg 1992: 161). But Burroughs' style is quintessentially a 'nasty' mixture of beauty, grace and the worst extremes of *Britannia Hospital* and *Carry On* humour, and any attempt to rarify it falls on its face. Lee's deadpan rendition of 'Bobo's death', for example—a funereal soliloquy stifling the bedpan hilarity of Benway's account of the quite literally 'sticky end' of Professor Fingerbottom, whose 'falling piles blew out the Duc de Ventre's Hispano Suiza and wrapped around the rear wheel'—prompts alarm rather than amusement, and the suggestion, 'You sound as if you could use a drink' (Burroughs [1959] 1982: 165). While Burroughs resists simplistic categorization as 'a stand-up comedian' (Bockris 1981: 27), his writing is certainly that of a 'sit-down' comedian, and Cronenberg's forkwaving and lunch-contemplating 'Lee' pales before Harry Dean Stanton's far more convincing Burroughsian presence as the sardonic Bud in Michael Nesmith's quirkily urban magic-realist *Repo Man* (1984).

In this respect, Cronenberg's greatest successes are surely his humourless evocations of the long-gone scenes that Burroughs distils from 'many sources: conversations heard and overheard, movies and radio broadcasts' (Burroughs 1986: 19). From the opening shot of Lee's silhouetted fedora, we enter what Burroughs persuasively calls a 'masterful thriller' (Silverberg 1992: 14) made up of third-hand images borrowed by Cronenberg from Burroughs, and borrowed by Burroughs from 'Grade B movies' (Burroughs 1993: 259). Yet as John Conomos observes (1992: 16), against all odds such refined cinematic simulation is 'extraordinarily atmospheric'. Typifying Cronenberg's tendency to borrow images and phrases from both *Naked Lunch* and other Burroughsian novels, Lee's visit to the 'bug drug' building builds on the opening section of *Exterminator!*; an episode written in surprisingly cinematic prose, rich in anecdotal bit-parts and still richer in such evocative sound-bites as Lee's catch-phrase—'Exterminator! You need the service?'—and the 'older' Cohen brother's rant—'You vant I should spit right in your face!? You vant!? You vant? You vant!?' (Burroughs 1974: 4, 3). Clearly sharing Burroughs' acute 'ear for dialogue' (Burroughs 1986: 185), even if unwilling or unable to find a way of integrating Burroughsian utterance into his film, Cronenberg beefs things up with a bonus one-liner from the Chinese druggist whose abrupt four worder brings *Naked Lunch*'s last six lines (quoted here in full) to their fragmentary conclusion.

"They are rebuilding the City."

Lee nodded absently. . . . "Yes . . . Always . . ."

Either way is a bad move to The East Wing. . . .

If I knew I'd be glad to tell you. . . .

"No good . . . no bueno . . . hustling himself. . . ."

"No glot . . . C'lom Fliday"

(Burroughs [1959] 1982: 232)

Is this appropriate mainstream movie dialogue? One thinks not. And yet as Paul Bowles remarks, Burroughs' improvisations offered a remarkably theatrical spectacle: 'Surely . . . worth hearing, and worth watching', as he 'stumbled from one side of the room to the other, shouting in his cowboy voice' (Bowles 1959: 43). In turn, subsequent expatriate celebration of Burroughs' voice on the Paris-based English Bookshop's LP, *Call Me Burroughs* (1965), prompted the American poet Emmett Williams to write:

The first time I heard Burroughs' voice . . . I thought: Mark Twain must have talked like this . . . and I'm sure he likes apple pie. Later when I first heard these excerpts from *The Naked Lunch* . . . Twain . . . and apple pie were still in evidence, plus a large dose of Texas Charley the medicine-show man selling tonic to a lot of rubes. . . . His voice is terrifyingly convincing.

(Williams 1965: n.p.)

It is precisely this terrifyingly convincing voice that the British film-maker Antony Balch uses to capture the viewer's attention in the opening scene of Burroughs' first major cinematic adaptation and collaboration, *Towers Open Fire*. Described as 'an 11-minute collage of all the themes and situations in the book, accompanied by a Burroughs soundtrack narration' (Balch 1972: 10), *Towers Open Fire* rushes in where Cronenberg fears to tread (and where Cronenberg can no longer tread), documenting Burroughs shooting up, partially documenting Balch masturbating to Burroughs' incantation 'silver arrow through the night', and offering little other characterization or narrative continuity than fleeting images of Burroughs and Gysin inside or outside the Paris Beat Hotel.

Towers Open Fire opens with a static close-up of Burroughs staring blankly at the camera for fifty seconds or so, before finally blinking and almost smiling, as a burst of trance music signals a cut to the next scene in which he acts as chairman of 'The Board'. Nothing happens, one might say. Or at least, nothing happens but Burroughs' impassive reading and audition of the horrendous 'old white schmaltz' droned out by 'the District Supervisor' in *The Soft Machine*. Here, for a highly unnerving minute, the viewer quite literally has 'no place to go' other than this forced encounter with disquieting dramatization of what the next sentence in *The Soft Machine* calls: 'Most distasteful thing I ever stood still for'.

Now kid what are you doing over there with the niggers and the apes? Why don't you straighten out and act like a white man? After all they're only human cattle—You know that yourself—Hate to see a bright young man fuck up and get off on the wrong track—Sure it happens to all of us one time or another—Why the man who went on to invent Shitola was sitting right where you're sitting now twenty-five years ago and I was saying the same things to him—Well he straightened out the way you're going to straighten out. . . . You can't deny your blood kid—You're white white white— And you can't walk out on Trak—There's just no place to go.

(Burroughs [1961] 1968: 140-1)

As becomes evident, Burroughs in the 1960s was altogether different to the Burroughs of the 1990s who claimed to be 'relieved' that Cronenberg did not ask him to 'write or co-write' the screenplay for *Naked Lunch*, who expressed surprise that writers still 'think they can *write* a film script, not realizing that film scripts are not meant to be read, but acted and photographed' (Burroughs, in Silverberg 1992: 14); and who generally argued that 'the rule of film is that movies move, with minimal talk' (Silverberg 1992: 13). Here, in black and white, Burroughs demonstrates the considerable impact of maximal 'talk' set against almost wholly motionless imagery, writing for—and reading and acting in—a cinematic adaptation built both around and upon the auratic energy of his cinematic presence.

Four years later, Balch's film *The Cut-Ups* (1967) explored still more radical text-screen collaboration and adaptation. On the one hand, as Gysin explains, Balch randomly spliced documentary footage of his collaborators:

Antony was applying . . . the 'cut-up' technique where he simply took all the footage he had and handed it over to an editor, just telling her to set up four reels, and put so many feet on each one in order—one, two, three, four, and start again, the same number.

(Gysin 1997: 177)

On the other hand, Gysin and Burroughs produced an independent made-to-measure soundtrack, patiently intoning such mind-numbing greetings as 'Yes—hello', before juggling with the question, 'Does this image seem to be persisting?' and other phrases 'taken directly from the Scientology classes that [Burroughs] was going to at the time' (Gysin 1997: 180). As Gysin relates, predictably neither *Towers Open Fire* nor *The Cut-Ups* enjoyed commercial success when first screened at the Academy Cinema, Oxford Street, which 'finally asked if we could please take them off the screen because they'd had such a high incidence of people forgetting very strange things in the theatre'. Surprisingly, though, even greater hostility awaited them in New York, where even the artistic underground recoiled from Burroughs' 'very heavy aura' as a writer who 'had shot his wife' and 'published the most shocking book of its time' (Gysin 1997: 182).

Neither literary adaptation nor literary adoption seemed on Burroughs' cards in the late 1960s and early 1970s, and only in 1974 did his 'aura' grow lighter, following the success of his first New York readings. Recalling that 'Burroughs had gotten very paranoid in London', Andreas Brown describes how '[y]ou could see his face change as he realized that people wanted to hear him' (Bockris 1981: 77-8). In New York, as in Tangier and Paris, Burroughs once again wowed his contemporaries with his prowess as a performer and raconteur of semi-autobiographical texts, and in his film *Burroughs: The Movie* (1983), Howard Brookner gave Burroughs *carte blanche* to adapt or perform his writings and generally reminisce about the past. Here we see a besuited Burroughs reading on stage at a desk; a begarbed Burroughs in operating theatre greens, acting out one of the Dr Benway routines from *Naked Lunch;* and an avuncular Burroughs, nostalgically guiding Grauerholz around his old St Louis haunts. Without doubt, Burroughs was back in town.

In May 1983, Burroughs' induction into the American Academy and Institute of Arts and Letters marked his formal literary rehabilitation, and in October 1983, the first major public screening of *Burroughs: The Movie* at the New York Film Festival offered him the approval of independent cinema culture. Five years later, Hollywood itself confirmed that Burroughs was no longer *persona non grata,* as fact, fiction and Burroughs' conflicting personae as literary outlaw and grand old man of American letters coalesced in his role as Tom the Priest—based on The Priest in *Exterminator!* (Burroughs 1974: 156)—in Gus Van Sant's film *Drugstore Cowboy* (1989). Here, as in *Burroughs: The Movie,* Burroughs exemplifies the streetwise old-timer, this time guiding Bob (played by Matt Dillon) around town. And here, once again, Burroughs worked on his script, suggesting to Van Sant that his character—the 'middle-aged' junkie Bob Murphy—should become 'an old junkie', and describing 'how he would have behaved in Murphy's circumstances'. When Van Sant's 'rewrite didn't really capture it', Grauerholz 'rewrote four scenes for William . . . and then William put his own unique polish on it, his own imprimatur' (Grauerholz, in Miles 1992: 14).

The following year, Burroughs entered his final collaboration with the postmodern multimedia avant-garde, writing the libretto for Robert Wilson's opera *The Black Rider* (1990). Hailing Burroughs as a fellow visionary willing 'to destroy the codes in order to make a new language', Wilson welcomed the opportunity to set Burroughs' 'dreamy, cloud-like texts' against his own anti-naturalistic practice of telling stories 'visually, in scenery and in gestures' (Wilson 1992: 50-1). Wilson set Burroughs' words within multimedia narratives evincing 'an ongoing thing . . . a continuum . . . something that never, never finishes', unlike commercially viable cinematic 'one-liners' in which 'you get information in three seconds, and then that's it' (Wilson 1992: 52). This time, collaborative multimedia adaptation and

integration of Burroughs' writings struck gold, and (as Burroughs reports) when *The Black Rider* opened at Hamburg's Thalia Theatre in March 1990, 'There were fifteen curtain calls, which is almost unheard of' (Burroughs 1994: 70).

Revered as a living legend on almost all fronts, Burroughs now presented the ideal subject-matter for Hollywood legend. And so it came to pass, in Cronenberg's strangely puritanical homage to the undeniable 'beauty, grace and potency' of much of 'Burroughs' literary style' (Cronenberg, in Silverberg 1992: 161): a film made too late to integrate the dynamic authorial performances in *Towers Open Fire* and *The Cut-Ups,* made too cautiously to countenance the burlesque Burroughsian 'routines' authorial hammed to perfection in *Burroughs: The Movie,* made too conventionally to opt for the 'dreamy, cloud-like' logic welcomed by Wilson in *The Black Rider,* and made too wisely to replicate the authorial self-caricature in *Drugstore Cowboy.*

Cronenberg's adaptation of *Naked Lunch* surely works best when its camerawork lugubriously glides through beautifully observed sets with exemplary deceleration, partially compensating for its sins of omission with remarkable atmospheric intensity and spectacular 'adult' special effects, generating what Burroughs calls a 'miasma of paranoia' (Burroughs 1992b: 15) entirely commensurate with the 'dead-end despair' (Burroughs 1993:255) permeating the bleaker sections of his 'very funny book' (Burroughs 1990: 38).

As Cronenberg indicates, writing as demanding as Burroughs' fiction almost inevitably places the cinematic adapter in a no-win situation, in which they can at best 'dip' into their subject, 'a little bit here, a little bit there' (Cronenberg, in Silverberg 1992: 161). Given such circumstances, Balch, Brookner, Van Sant and Wilson suggest, the most winning way to work with living experimental authors may well be the 'double-dipping' strategy of integrating the interactive 'special effects' offered by *collaborative* intertextual adaptation.

Bibliography

Balch, A. (1972) Interview, *Cinema Rising,* 1: 10-4.

Barber, L. (1992) 'A little hard to swallow', *The Sydney Morning Herald,* 7 May: 34.

Beckett, S. (1934) 'Proust in pieces', *Spectator,* 22 June: 975-6.

Benjamin, W. (1936) 'The work of art in the age of mechanical reproduction', repr. in H. Zohn (trans.), *Illuminations,* Glasgow: Fontana/Collins, 1970.

Bockris, V. (1981) *With William Burroughs: A report from the bunker,* New York: Seaver.

Bowles, P. (1959) 'Burroughs in Tangier', *Big Table,* 2: 42-3.

Burroughs, W. S. (1959) *The Naked Lunch,* London: John Calder; repr. 1982.

—— (1966) *Nova Express,* London: Jonathan Cape.

—— (1969) *The Job: Interviews with Daniel Odier,* New York: Grove; repr. 1974.

—— (1974) *Exterminator!,* London: Calder and Boyars.

—— (with Gysin, B.) (1979) *The Third Mind,* London: John Calder.

—— (1983) Foreword to H. Norse, *Beat Hotel,* San Diego: Atticus.

—— (1990) 'The Devil's Bargain', interview with N. Zurbrugg, *Art and Text* (Sydney) 35: 38-55.

—— (1991) 'Robert Wilson', in T. Fairbrother (ed.), *Robert Wilson's Vision,* Boston: Museum of Fine Arts (in association with New York: Harry N. Abrams).

—— (1992a) Introduction to I. Silverberg (ed.), *Everything is Permitted: The making of Naked Lunch,* New York: Grove Weidenfeld.

—— (1992b) '. . . 15 questions you never asked. William S. Burroughs', interview, *The Age* (Melbourne), 1 May: 15.

—— (1993) *The Letters of William S. Burroughs: 1945-1959,* ed. O. Harris. New York: Viking.

Conomos, J. (1992) 'A fascinating and phantasmagoric universe', *Filmnews* (Sydney) 22 (4): 16.

Cronenberg, D. (1997) *Cronenberg on Cronenberg,* ed. C. Rodley, London: Faber and Faber.

Gardiner, D. and Walker, K. S. (eds) (1984) *Raymond Chandler Speaking,* London: Allison and Busby.

Gysin, B. (1997) 'Interview with Arthur and Corinne Cantrill', in J. Sargeant, *The Naked Lens: An illustrated history of beat cinema,* London: Creation, pp. 177-83.

Mailer, N. (1965) 'The Boston trial of *Naked Lunch*', *Evergreen Review,* 36: 40-49, 87-8.

McCarthy, M. (1963) 'Burroughs' *Naked Lunch*'; repr. in *New York Review of Books,* 1991, 1 (1): 4-5.

Miles, B. (1992) *William Burroughs: El hombre invisible,* London: Virgin.

Morgan, T. (1988) *Literary Outlaw: The life and times of William S. Burroughs,* New York: Henry Holt.

Nuttall, J. (1968) *Bomb Culture,* London: Paladin; repr. 1970.

Silverberg, I. (ed.) (1992) *Everything is Permitted: The making of 'Naked Lunch',* New York: Grove Weidenfeld.

Virilio, P. (1993) *The Art of the Motor,* trans. J. Rose, Minneapolis: University of Minnesota Press, 1995.

Williams, E. (1965) Untitled sleeve notes for the LP *Call Me Burroughs,* Paris: The English Bookshop.

Wodehouse, P. G. (1935) *Blandings Castle and Elsewhere,* London: Penguin; repr. 1954.

BEATS AND MUSIC

MICHAEL MCCLURE (ESSAY DATE 1974)

SOURCE: McClure, Michael. "Bob Dylan: The Poet's Poet." In *Lighting the Corners: On Art, Nature, and the Visionary, Essays and Interviews,* pp. 26-35. Albuquerque: University of New Mexico College of Arts and Sciences, 1993.

In the following essay, originally published in Rolling Stone *magazine in 1974, McClure remembers his first experiences with Dylan and reflects on Dylan as a poet. McClure suggests that Dylan and the Beat poets, especially Ginsberg, shared sympathies if not many direct connections, though he concludes that the Beats still writing in the 1970s (Ginsberg, Gary Snyder, Robert Duncan, and a few others) were developing a direction in poetry in similar to that of Dylan's music.*

Memory is a beautiful thing—as I get older I learn to cherish it. It seems so beautiful or ugly that it is often more than real. Sometimes the vision is lit up with imagination; sometimes the imaginings have the shapes of real acts and gestures we call experience.

Experience is physical matter—and there is no sense in hanging onto it. It is a pleasure to let memory pour through the consciousness like nuggets of gold and moss agates and crystals of quartz clicking through the fingers at the rock shop. One never plans to keep those stones but the pleasure of feeling them is lovely.

The autoharp Bob Dylan gave me early in 1966 sat on the mantelpiece for six weeks before I picked it up and strummed it. A black and magical autoharp. Afraid of playing music, I had always felt totally unmusical—except in my appreciation. Bob had asked me what instrument I'd like to play (I was writing song lyrics). I said autoharp out of the clear blue though I had no picture of what an autoharp looked like. There must have been people playing them on farms in my Kansas childhood.

San Francisco poets were poor in 1965 and it was an impressive present and it committed me to music. There was the interest in writing lyrics and perhaps a new way to use rhyme.

Rock had mutual attraction for all; a common tribal dancing ground whether we were poets, or printers, or sculptors, it was a form we all shared. I spent a year and a half learning how to play the autoharp in an eccentric way and wrote songs like "The Blue Lyon Laughs," "The Allen Ginsberg For President Waltz" and "Come on God, and Buy Me a Mercedes Benz."

I bought an amplifier and stood for hours whanging on the autoharp. Obsessed with John

ON THE SUBJECT OF...

BOB DYLAN

By most accounts, Dylan's influence on popular music (as well as popular culture) is vast and powerful. He invented for himself myriad personas of pop songcraft, from the confessional singer/songwriter to the stream-of-conscious narrator to the world-weary rock balladeer. Dylan defied the widely held belief that pop singers had to have conventionally "good" singing skills, thereby opening the pop idiom to countless gravel-voiced vocalists. From a musical standpoint, he drew from a broad palette of American and British styles, infusing his work with obvious elements of folk, country, blues, and spirituals. Dylan's force was never more evident than during the 1960s when he influenced numerous popular artists as diverse as the Beatles, whose shift toward introspective songwriting is credited to Dylan, and Jimi Hendrix, who took Dylan's social consciousness to electrified levels. Subsequent decades have proven Dylan's staying power and continued influence. Many of his songs are now considereds popular standards, and critics generally agree that albums such as *The Freewheeling Bob Dylan* (1963), *Highway 61 Revisted* (1965), and *Blonde on Blonde* (1966) are landmark acheivements in the annals of rock music.

There are a number of important relationships between Dylan and writers of the Beat Generation. Throughout his career Dylan has shared with the Beats the aesthetic assumption that true artistic expression is the result of a spontaneous outpouring of the soul and that revision often leads to overrefinement and falsification. In addition he is indebted to the Beats for having combined poetry with music, thus creating an audience that was ready to respond to unconventional lyrics sung to rock accompaniment, a combination folk-music purists were unwilling to accept. During the mid-1960s Dylan also shared the Beats's attitudes toward social authority, politics, and drugs, emphasizing the primacy of the self and rejecting institutionally prescribed norms. Finally, and most important, from the beginning of his rock period, the style of Dylan's most characteristic lyrics unmistakably reveals that Beat poetry was a strong influence on him as he developed into the most provocative and imaginative lyricist of his generation.

Keats's question: What weapon has the lion but himself, I tried to make it a song and sang it so many times so loudly that I wonder what the neighbors thought in those old days when acid rock was a baby.

In December, 1965, when we had been bombing Vietnam for eight months, Dylan read "Poisoned Wheat," a long anti-war poem of mine. One day as we were eating chicken, I handed him another copy. He left huge greasy fingerprints and he did it with great aplomb. It seemed very non-materialistic and natural not to notice the blotches. It seemed right to treat works of art as part of the transformations of life. Later I gave the copy to a woman who wanted Bob's fingerprints.

The first person to play a Dylan album for me was poet David Meltzer. It was Dylan's first album, and I heard it shortly after it came out in March or April of 1962. I could not understand what David heard in the album. In high school I knew slightly older people at the University of Chicago and in New York City who were singing like that—just some hillbilly-intellectual music that I'd gotten bored with earlier. In retrospect, Dylan must have shown a direct creative thrust without the "Art" self-consciousness of other singers.

Early in 1965 a friend of my wife Joanna came to visit and brought the Dylan album with "She Belongs to Me." The album had changed her life-image from a tragic loser to a proud artist. My wife heard and understood Dylan at once and completely, I think.

In 1965 everyone had been after me to listen to Dylan carefully—to sit down and listen to the words *and* the music. I absolutely did *not* want to hear Dylan. We had a banged-up record player in the hallway at the top of the stairs. Late at night, in the pale-grey hallway-light, Joanna sat me down in front of the speaker and told me to listen to the words. I began to hear what the words were saying, not just the jangling of the guitar and the harmonica and the whining nasal voice. The next thing I knew I was crying. It was "Gates of Eden": "At dawn my lover comes to me / And tells me of her dreams / With no attempts to shovel the glimpse / Into the ditch of what each one means. . . ."

I had the idea that I was hallucinating, that it was William Blake's voice coming out of the walls and I stood up and put my hands on the walls and they were vibrating.

Then I went back to those people who had tried to get me to listen and I told them that I thought the revolution had begun. "Gates Of

Eden" and those other songs seemed to open up the post-Freudian and post-Existentialist era. No longer did everyone have to use the old explanations and the mildewed rationalities. By the time I met Bob, his poetry was important to me in the way that Kerouac's writing was. It was not something to imitate or be influenced by; it was the expression of a unique individual and his feelings and perceptions.

There is no way to second-guess poetry or to predict poetry or to convince a poet that the best songs in the world are poetry if they are not. Bob Dylan is a poet; whether he has cherubs in his hair and fairy wings, or feet of clay, he is a poet. Those other people called "rock poets," "song poets," "folk poets," or whatever the rock critic is calling them this week, will be better off if they are appreciated as songwriters.

At a party after his concert in Berkeley in 1965, Dylan told me that he had not read Blake and did not know the poetry. That seemed hard to believe so I recited a few stanzas. One was the motto to "the Songs of Innocence and Experience" which begins: "The Good are attracted by Men's perceptions / And think not for themselves."

In 1965 that first Dylan concert in the Bay Area was at San Francisco's Masonic Auditorium. In those days the Masonic seemed huge and rather plush. It was the first time I had heard Bob Dylan in person. The records were beautiful but this was better—an immaculate performance with inflections or nuances different from the albums. Dylan was purest poet. Like an elf being, so perfect he was and so ferocious in his persistence for perfection. There was a verge of anger in him waiting for any obstacle to the event.

After the Masonic Auditorium concert we went to the Villa Romano Motel, where Bob and his group the Hawks were staying, and met with agent Al Grossman. He, Joan Baez, Allen Ginsberg, and I spoke for a while. Joan said that Allen and I should be Bob's conscience. It seemed a beautiful thing to say, though not clear at the time. Later Joan wrote that we should hold Bob in our consciousness.

A night or two later, after another concert, there was a party for Bob in San Francisco. Ken Kesey bounced through the door with a few of his Merry Pranksters. Ruddy with the vigor of good health, Los Gatos sunshine, and acid, Kesey immediately hit Dylan with something like, "Hey man, you should try playing while you're high on acid." Without a pause Dylan said, "I did and it threw off my timing." There was no way to one-up

Bob Dylan, 1941–.

Bob or to get ahead of him at any level or any time. You knew that pop stars like Dylan or Lennon drove around in black cars and they were careful and they were very fast and they were staying where they were and they were not kidding.

. . . . .

Nine years later, on the plane going to meet Dylan's tour in Philadelphia, I reread Robert Duncan's small book, *Seventeenth Century Suite*. Duncan had vowed not to publish any of his new poetry publicly for fifteen years, so that no pressure would direct him to write anything other than what he wishes most deeply. By canceling formal publication he was essentially vowing to please only himself. Robert made an edition of two hundred copies of the *Seventeenth Century Suite* poems and gave them to friends as Christmas gifts.

How incredibly far it is from Duncan's private edition of *Seventeenth Century Suite* to Dylan's millions of albums. Both are fine poetry and though they seem poles apart, they almost touch in their subtle images and music. One can imagine the radiance and spectrum of the poetry between.

It is a mistake to wonder which poetry will matter thirty years from now. We should wonder what is wrong if Dylan's songs do not mean something to us today. We are all moved by spiritual experiences. For some of us the spiritual experiences can be the grossest hit songs or the most kitsch style of painting. It really is a matter of whether we are ogres or elves—or something in between drawn one way or the other at one moment and another.

. . . . .

The Philadelphia concert made the Masonic Auditorium of San Francisco 1965 seem like a jam session in a small nightclub. The crowd was not in their late twenties and early thirties as friends had predicted—this was an audience of nice-looking, scruffy young people in their early twenties. All in all, except for the number of bodies (making one think of the pictures of a Japanese beach), one did not mind being there. There were some of the best people around, a part of the backbone of the future—the people with hope and some enthusiasm in a country run over for eight years by the War Machine.

The lights went down accompanied by a burst of enthusiasm from the 19,000 living souls.

To open the first set, houselights came down into darkness very fast. Colored spotlights flashed to the stage and banks of colored lights shone. The Band and Bob Dylan almost ran onstage and began playing without a pause while the audience was still cheering their enthusiasm.

There were two thoughts that someone had imparted to me. One was that Bob was redoing his old songs as rock for the new generation who did not know him well. The second was that Dylan was in danger of disappearing into his own creation; that as one of the founders of the giant rock scene he had spawned so many followers, so many imitators, and Dylan-influenced groups and movements that he stood in danger of blending in among his own offspring and hybrids—ending up in the public eye as another surviving folk-rocker.

Dylan a grown man . . . a young man still, but a man. The elfish lightness of foot is gone and the perfection of timing is replaced by sureness; the nasal boy's voice replaced by a man's voice.

Another poet's singing came to mind: Allen Ginsberg at the 1966 Human Be-In singing his strange "Peace in America—Peace in Vietnam," and I was there too, using the black autoharp and singing, "The god I worship is a lion."

Now Dylan is official culture—like Brecht and Weill. He played "Mr. Jones"—in 1965 a glove thrown in the public face, a statement of revolt; now it is Art.

I could not take my eyes off the lights, hypnotized by the spots of amber, lavender, blue, red that kept playing on Dylan. The banks of lights up above the bandstand stage to the right and left kept bleeding and blinking off and on in time with the drama and melody of the songs. Bright lights kept popping in the blackness—intensely bright and silvery white in their flash. Flashbulbs! It seemed crazy that anyone sitting three blocks from the bandstand in the darkness would be setting off flashbulbs. It seemed demented.

"My God, it is a long way since the Avalon Ballroom," I thought. A long way since the artist's light shows and the smallness of the dance floors and the tribal dancers of 1966. We felt so crowded together, transpersonal and magical in those days. In Philadelphia what I saw was gigantic! The incredible subtlety of the earlier light shows was surpassed by a blending of colors, the motility of the spotlights and the sheer candlepower. The devastating volume of the music made it unpleasant trying to pick Dylan's words out of the roar.

One became aware that the enormous volume of the amplified music mimicked, as it bounced off the walls, the roar of the crowd. The music became a response to itself. The effect would trigger in the audience a response to the music. Loud cheering. When it happened I wondered if that was entertainment or ethological manipulation—or if entertainment could be ethological manipulation.

I loved what I could hear of Dylan's new love songs—they seemed inspired. The melodies, lost in the amplified blare, were not impressive but I was able to hear: "May you always stay courageous / Be forever young. . . ."

In the darkness at the end of the concert, the audience lit matches and cigarette lighters, making a Milky Way of wavering lights and cheers—a universe of tiny flaming stars.

If a scholar goes seriously into an analysis of the poetry convergent with the rock movement, there will be interesting contrasts between Lennon, Kerouac, Dylan, and Morrison. The whole thing started with the poets of the fifties. It was an alchemical-biological movement, not a literary one. Bob Dylan's "Dylan" is from Dylan Thomas, the Welsh poet so popular in the fifties. Allen Ginsberg asked if I'd heard that Dylan was titling his album *Planet Waves*. I asked Allen what he thought of that. Allen said, "Charming! Delightful! Great!" I think so too. Allen's last book was *Planet News*. There's plenty of room for feedback back and forth.

At the Toronto concert, media philosopher Marshall McLuhan and his wife were in the audience. McLuhan told me that he had played Dylan albums to a poetry class that morning. McLuhan believes that rock 'n' roll comes out of the English language—using its rhythms and inflections as a basis for melody. (Exactly what I believe—and also that it comes out of the Beat mutation or it has the same root.) The future of rock, he felt, would be the same as that of the language; that it would have its ups and downs as the language does.

As a mode, the ballad and story-song seemed mined-out, I said. Anyone can write a story-song in almost any manner and it becomes uninteresting to listen to. McLuhan felt it is the background, not the mode, that gives out. The background is violence, and Dylan was singing violently. McLuhan feels that "violence is the result of a loss of identity—the more loss the greater the violence."

Sitting among 19,000 people McLuhan said, "Gravity is like acoustic space—the center is everywhere."

I told Marshall that I wanted to go out into the hallway in the last set of the concert when Dylan and the Band played "Like a Rolling Stone." The night before I had been carried away and wept so hard that I did not want to have the experience again. This was my third concert and the incredible volume of the speakers was beginning to undermine my nerves.

I first heard "Like a Rolling Stone" when my wife and I were driving in an open MG across the Arizona-California desert with our daughter curled up asleep behind us next to our wolfhound and our pet black-and-white rat sleeping in his cage on the floor of the sports car. The moon was on the horizon. A song never hit me so hard except as a child when my mother sang to me. Much of our poetic sensibility may have its origin with cradle songs—I remember my mother singing songs from Disney cartoons and movies and reciting Mother Goose and Kipling.

After the concert there was a moment to introduce McLuhan and his wife to producers Bill Graham and Barry Imhoff and Dylan before Bob and the Band went back onstage for their encore.

Pouring sweat, his face puffy, his eyes partially blanked by the concert he'd just delivered, Bob smiled as much as he could. In the auditorium almost 20,000 people were screaming and yelling for him to come back so he could reconnect them briefly with the godhead.

When Dylan and the Band ran back onstage, McLuhan said that this was his first rock concert. Bill Graham replied: "I wish I could say the same thing!" Bill had been concerned because everything on this tour was going too well. There is a theater superstition that if small things don't go wrong then something major will.

. . . . .

Dylan has slipped into people's dream baskets. He has been incorporated into their myths and fantasies. They worry about him: whether he is understood, what his next album will be like, if he is appreciated by the press, whether he might get a cold and how he performs his pieces.

My particular fantasy is that he is underpaid. I would not stand in front of 20,000 people and those lights and amplifiers and do what he is doing for all the dollars in the world or for a stack of gold records ten miles high.

Bob is a prisoner of his fame and fortune. When he says, "I'm anyone who lives in a vault . . . ," he means himself. He is a real poet who lives the poems that he sings. A lot of people who hold Dylan in their dream baskets think the songs are a confection—that they are cute and sweet the way Rod McKuen is. But everything I've seen convinces me that Bob is the real thing, that he is no joke, that he has no answers, that he is a poet, that he is trapped most of the time.

The several new songs that I heard in the concerts were domestic (about wife and home) and inspirational. I hope this is the direction that Dylan is going. It would be good to see lots of young Americans put back on their feet—not through renewed faith in the old values that have been shot down, but through greater awareness of themselves on an earth that was once beautiful—and that still has pockets of beauty. I'd like everyone to begin to get some sense of what, and who, they are—and a further sense that something can be done to elevate the vicious mindlessness of politics and bio-environmental destruction and the extinction of the species of living plants and animals. A lot of poets are moving in that direction—Ginsberg, Snyder, Duncan, Creeley, Waldman.

Thinking of Dylan's poetics I had brought along some books as background material: *Seventeenth Century Suite* by Robert Duncan, poems by Gary Snyder and Allen Ginsberg, *Black Music* by Imamu Amiri Baraka (LeRoi Jones), and Kafka's "Josephine The Singer."

ON THE SUBJECT OF...

NAPHTALI KUPFERBERG

Naphtali "Tuli" Kupferberg is a political satirist, poet, cartoonist, and songwriter. He is best known as a member of the Fugs, the "literary folk-rock group" that he cofounded with poet Ed Sanders. Kupferberg wrote many of the band's outrageous and popular songs as well devising the theatrical skits that accompanied their live performances. Kupferberg sang and played the maracas and the erectorine, an instrument of his own invention comprised of a vertical tambourine mounted on a sawed-off hockey stick. The Fugs (the name is a euphemism for a more offensive expletive) gained recognition for their outrageous brand of music about sex, drugs, and political protest; performances were often heavily improvised and the band became notorious for its unpredictable, irreverent humor. Some of the band's printable song titles include "Kill for Peace," "Group Grope," and "What Are You Doing After the Orgy?" While the Fugs are not known for their musical expertise, they are considered important for their expression of the values and attitudes of the youth of the far Left from the mid-1960s to the end of the Vietnam War. Though commercial success eluded the band in their heyday, they boast an enthusiastic cult following and have influenced the subject matter and language of such later bands as Frank Zappa and the Mothers of Invention, Iggy Pop and the Stooges, Alice Cooper, and numerous punk groups.

In *Black Music,* published in 1968, Baraka says that the content of white-rock, anti-war and anti-authoritarian songs generalizes "passionate luxurious ego demonstrations"; that the artists want to prove that they are good human beings though, in fact, Baraka contends, they are really sensitive antennae of the brutalized and brutalizing white social mass. Baraka insists that is a cop-out and the music is still wealthy white kids playing around. We should remember Baraka's viewpoint:

it may be narrow but light sometimes passes through a thin slit. The Beatles didn't write anti-war songs. When asked about that they replied that all their songs are against war. There may be some beams of light in that crack too.

In Toronto I read Kafka's "Josephine The Singer," from *The Penal Colony.* A mouse-narrator relates an account of a woman-mouse named Josephine who is a singer. She proclaims herself a great artist and the other mice congregate around to hear her at the risk of their lives. But nothing will satisfy her ambition. She has a coterie of worshipful followers. Many of the mice people, however, are not at all sure that what she does, as fascinating and important as it is, is singing. They think that it may be only "piping" and perhaps it is her childishness (as she reflects simple attitudes of her people back to them) that is attractive: "Here is someone making a ceremonial performance out of the usual thing." Josephine demands freedom from the labor quota of the mouse people. But no matter how much they love her or worship her, they will not free her from the work law. Josephine disappears—perhaps she has gone into hiding—to force people to accept her demands. Anyone interested in Dylan and/or poetry should look at the story.

. . . . .

I thought of the creation of a demigod and prophet that took place in the multicolored spotlights and amplification and banks of stage-lights—better known to the modern world than Plato or Confucius or Buddha; watched by thousands with millions wishing to see him in other cities. One can become a statue of one's self, mimicking what one is in eternity. Immortality (or its substitute) can be turned off and on and directed by voice over wires and captured on disks of black plastic. There is the possibility that the background has swallowed up the object and that we are in the process of whiting-out. If so, I think we stand in need of it.

> Poetry, in a general sense, may be defined to be the expression of the imagination; and poetry is connate with the origin of man. Man is an instrument over which a series of external and internal impressions are driven, like the alterations of an ever-changing wind over an Aeolian lyre, which move it by their motion to ever-changing melody. But there is a principle within the human being, and perhaps within all sentient beings, which acts otherwise than in the lyre, and produces not melody alone, but harmony, by an internal adjustment of the sounds or motions thus excited to the impressions which excite them. . . .

So said Shelley in 1821 in *A Defence of Poetry.*

TULI KUPFERBERG AND THERESA STERN (INTERVIEW DATE 1997)

SOURCE: Kupferberg, Tuli, and Theresa Stern. "Interview." *Furious* (online magazine) <www.furious.com/perfect/tuli.html> (1997).

In the following interview, Kupferberg discusses The Fugs, a folk-rock band known for their protest songs and political activism, of which Kupferberg, along with Ed Sanders, was a founding member.

[Stern]: *What were you working on before the Fugs?*

[Kupferberg]: Well, I was the world's greatest poet before I became the world's oldest rock n'roll star. I wasn't with the Fugs until I was 42 but before that my life was trivial. I went to graduate school for sociology in Brooklyn. I dropped out and became a bohemian, living in Greenwich Village. The rest is mystery and history. It's all one blur now.

I was a free-formist. I never took to the traditional forms. I never bothered to learn them. It's OK to learn the old forms though and study what you've inherited in any art. I valued spontaneity a lot and being young, you're always afraid that you're going to be overwhelmed by the masters so you try to avoid it.

What kind of things were influencing you then?

The usual things. Ego, sex, money, in that order I think. Money wasn't actually up there though. You could actually live on much less than you can today. I was sort of influenced by anybody I read.

How did you get interested in politics?

I was very political at an early age. When I was in my pre-teens they had those 'Hoover-villes' during the Depression. My father had a retail store that failed three times. We were just on the brink of going on welfare. You'd be amazed at how that can make you politically and economically conscious. My generation really experienced adversity so a dime is still big money to me! You had to be REALLY STUPID not to be political then. Even when things got better, you didn't see it was better for you personally. It could always happen again and it always does. Besides the economy, you also had wars. When there's a crisis in society, sometimes you see things more clearly. Otherwise, it just kind of waves right over you, especially when you're young.

What did think of the Beat movement when it first started happening?

I remember being shocked by it. I guess I was still in some sort of traditional mode. Shocked,

jealousy and then adaptation. It was liberating. I was shocked by Ed Sander's freedom of sexual expression. I'm sure people were shocked by mine when I started. Ginsberg is your best example of a liberating force. It's not just the language or the freedom of the language because that just reflects character structure. A person who drops dead or wants to kill someone would use all those words you're not supposed to use. It's more than language. It's attitude towards sexuality and human relations along with domination and love. It's not that people who shout about sexual freedom understand everything that's involved. In order to have good sex, you have to have good human relationships and vice versa. When I grew up, in my community, you weren't going to have sex until you got married- this was a middle-class Jewish community. Maybe you went to a prostitute . . . But that gradually broke down. That was all for the good and not just for me but also for most of America.

So you got to be part of the Beats yourself then?

Everyone was. But I felt that they had a heritage with the bohemians. The term comes from 12th century University of Paris. The craziest students came from Bohemia and they gave them this name. There's this old tradition of living outside of the mores of society. Until the bourgeois revolution, most artists lived on the patronage of the ruling class. LA VIE DE BOHEME, the libretto for that opera, tells you what was happening then in the 18th century. So that's a 150 year old tradition that's still going on. It used to be linked to geography with places like New York, San Francisco, Munich, Paris. But now, with the Internet, you could be crazy, wild, free and self-destructive anywhere you want. But hopefully, there's still communities of people out there. Utopian colonies who are just friends.

Before the Fugs, did you have any interest in music?

I'm not a musician—I can't read music. The only thing I know how to play is the radio. I sing and write and compose songs. I have a memory of thousands of songs. There was always some music in the house. I seem to remember melodies better than some musicians I know. I had a silver of that particular kind of intelligence. I listened to a lot of pop music on the radio but there were no musicians around me. Poetry and music used to be the same thing so if I had an interest in poetry, it was part of a musical interest as well.

Speech is music. It's bad music. Some languages are very musical. When you hear certain people read, it's almost music. Some people who do music, it's almost speech. It's a continuance.

A lot of your music comes from chants and sing-a-longs.

I like to involve the audience like a number of writers, directors and political people do. I like to break down the barriers. The artist wants to move people and see the results. That's why performing is more pleasurable than just writing, to me at least.

How did you start out with Ed and the Fugs?

We were both poets on the lowest East Side. We met at a place called the Metro. They sold furniture and since they had the tables and chairs there already, so they decided to open a coffee shop. Once the coffee house was established, it became the center of poetry readings. This was in the early '60s. After the poetry, we would go to a place called the Dom on St. Marks. We would go there and try to dance, listening to the Beatles and the Stones. The early Beatles were not great poets but they did become great poets later. We decided that we could do something like that. So we decided to enter the field and we were sort of an instant hit. We had a wide range—Ed was a wild, crazy, mid-Western young man and I was a New York radical Jew. So together he had everything or, as some people would say, nothing.

Peter Stampfel said that he was impressed with all the songs that you and [Ed] had written before the Holy Modal Rounders joined you.

He was a great help to us. He sort of gave us the illusion that we were musicians and a band. We were sort of a punk band. Our idea was that anybody could do this. Peter and Steve Weber gave us a lot of encouragement. We didn't give a fuck actually. We weren't out to do high art. For our first performances, our friends joined us on stage and carried on. We had a few people who would write songs like Ted Berrigan. The most archetypical Fug line was 'I ain't ever gonna go to Vietnam, I prefer to stay here and screw your mom' which was from Ted. That's from 'Doing Alright.' That was enough to get us beaten up if we did it in the right place.

With the War going on then, it was a desperate time. There were thousands of dead and all the young men were facing that attempt to murder them. The nation was still supporting 'our boys.' We were really the ones being patriotic because we were trying to save lives. Other people were just trying to kill other people that they had

never seen. That's what war is—you go somewhere and kill people you've never met.

What happened with the Fugs after Peter and Steve left?

We got other musicians. I was sort of opposed with the idea of perfecting our music. I felt that it would interfere with our message: love, sex, dope. The only thing I think is safe or worth doing is marijuana. Also, as Ed put it 'all kinds of freedoms given to us that the First Amendment hadn't taken care of.' We were poets. Poets can say whatever they want about anything. So we felt that we did that with music. Pop music from the '20s to the '60s was mostly courtship music. In pop music, the Beatles sang about everything in life and so did everyone else, including us.

Do you think a lot of people who were getting serious about politics at that time were phonies or were they genuine?

There's the problem that if you keep faking something long enough, you start to believe your own lies. But I think mostly they were genuine. The '60s were a time of great crisis in America. The war was the focal point. There was also minorities who demanded equal rights and the women's' movement and various kinds of socialism, communism and anarchism. Then you saw that these things were connected. For instance, a woman couldn't have equal pay unless you had some sort of control over the economy unless you fixed it in the law (though I really don't believe in the law). It's still inter-related but people aren't conscious of this. You have to be very clever, quick and lucky to escape such an oppressive system.

You think that you did that?

Well, we were never arrested, which is amazing. We were threatened many times. Ed has these FBI advisories. Someone in the FBI probably realized what a farce it would be and what asses they would make of themselves if they put Ed on the stand. 'What exactly do you mean by 'Coca-Cola Douche' Mr. Sanders?' 'You know, Coke! No Pepsi!' There were suggestions that we'd be prosecuted but nothing ever happened. People in the government aren't THAT stupid. After 'Howl' was being prosecuted, it became the most famous poem in the country and thousands of people wanted to read it. So if we HAD been arrested, we would have probably sold a few hundred thousand more albums.

Since you were talking about it before, what kind of interactive things were you doing with the Fugs?

Pete Seeger used to do it but going way back. There were whole societies that had huge choral groups. Mass singing was done with the Welsh and the Russians. You could do it in two ways. You could print up the lyrics and force the audience to sing with you. You could also repeat a line or do the song once and then give the audience the line. Depending on what mood they're in, you get audience response. It depends on the song too. The best audience was the third audience at midnight on a Saturday at a club we used to play at on MacDougal Street. They were all drunk so you could come out on stage and wave your hands and they'd scream and yell for you. In our first performances in the East Village, the audience would come on stage and do all sorts of things.

In the sixties, we were really the USO of the Left. We did a lot of benefits. We were one of the most conscious bands but we weren't the only ones. It was really the attitude and style, which later became co-opted. In all due modesty, I don't think there other bands that were as radical then. Zappa was kind of a cultural radical but he was a libertarian and a political idiot as far as I'm concerned. He started out in advertising and he stayed there to some extent. Ginsberg started out in advertising but he never looked back. The Who, The Stones and Beatles were saying very radical things. A lot of folk music is culturally and politically radical. There is a tradition in folk music for that though a lot of the songs are bad. It goes back to the Wobblies in the 19th Century. Woody Guthrie also. Dylan started very political. Phil Ochs too. Folk purists used to argue about playing rock n' roll but good music is good music where ever it comes from. Music by itself can move people, sometimes very destructively like with a military march.

A lot of your songs involved writing new lyrics for songs.

It's a very old tradition. I used it a lot when I didn't have a band. The earliest singers I remember that did this was (Martin) Luther who took popular songs of the period and made church hymns out them. He said 'why should the devil have the best of tunes.' Then Joe Hill in the early part of the 1900's used church hymns and changed them into radical pop songs.

> Long-haired preachers come out every night
> Try and tell you what's wrong and what's right
> But when asked about something to eat
> They are sure, they are sure to repeat
> 'You'll get pie . . .

> You'll get pie in the sky when you die (that's a
>   lie)
> Work and pray
> Live on hay
> You'll get pie in the sky when you die (it's a lie)'

So it's an old tradition. I call them para-songs.

Did the Fugs have any particular goals?

Our goal was to make the revolution. That would have been a complete revolution, not just an economic or political one. We had utopian ideals and those are the best ideals. What happened was that this movement that flourished then had a lot of problems. A lot of promises weren't as deeply rooted or as well grounded as we thought. The technological revolution and the movement of world capital created problems that no one had ever thought possible. The sixties never connected. It was basically a youth movement and basically a middle-class, male movement. That's not enough. There were students but the war fed itself on that part of the movement and the previous radical history. There were a lot of 'grown-ups' and academic people and ordinary people but its roots were not deep enough and its analysis (Marxist and anarchist) wasn't enough to take over. We didn't know how to get from our good ideas to the society we wanted.

Then it slowly collapsed once the draft ended and once the war ended. Obviously the forces of the old society (religion and tradition) were much stronger than we thought. So things continued the way they are. We still don't have the ideology to get out of this. We never connected to the working class and now they seem to be disappearing into microchips—you have a lot of 'surplus' people. We need some sort of understanding of what's going on because everything is out of control, especially out of our control. We have very little influence, we radicals today.

The sixties were a complete surprise because in the fifties, American society was just recovering from World War II and young man just wanted to go back to school and start a family. There was no politics. Then the sixties happened. You can never predict when it's going to happen because it's rooted in human nature that you can only take so much oppression before you do something. But sometimes you do the wrong thing. We don't have the answers but if they only gave us a chance . . . It was not a complete failure because a lot of the things we believed in have gone a long way to being realized. We were not the idealists. We manifested them and learned from other people.

With the Fugs, what was happening with the band after '65?

I think that our songs developed and become more sophisticated and complicated. We spread into different areas and the music got better. I don't think we should have disbanded. It was due to personal conflicts which I really don't completely understand. We would have been really needed in the '70s because that was a slow decline where everything that that generation thought was going to happen, just disappeared slowly.

What were you doing after the Fugs broke up?

I formed a group called the Revolting Theater, which sort of carried on in the tradition of the Fugs. Basically we acted out artifacts that we had found in society—advertisements or crazy songs or poetry. That had a mild reason for being. We played mostly at colleges. Then I formed a group called the Fuxxons and that was me and anybody that was around—we did some Fugs songs and other stuff.

Then in '84, the Fugs were reformed. I would have been always ready to reform but I think Ed decided that it should happen at that particular time. We did a reunion concert with new musicians at the Bottom Line. A lot of people came and it was fun. We've been playing on and off since then. I don't think that we had the impact that we did in the sixties for a number of reasons. We did the Real Woodstock Festival in '94 where Ed lives. That same year, we played in Italy.

Before you said the Fugs were about dope and fucking. What about now?

No, I said that the Fugs were about dope and fucking and any kind of mind liberation that didn't kill you or damage your internal organs. I was always careful about that because I'd been a medical librarian and I knew all about that. My phrase was 'better to be a live ogre than a dead saint.' I knew a lot of dead saints. It was about politics and it was about life and relations between people and 'freedom,' meaning the ability to explore and express yourself and other peoples' feelings. We were all about creating a utopia and we had our ideas about what it was. We tried to work for it and to live it because we weren't going to wait—'we want the world and we want it now.' We were impatient, especially in the sixties where young people faced death and they weren't going to wait to enjoy anything after they were dead.

It's a mistake to put it (freedom) in terms of physiology. Nothing wrong with that. The basic unit of human society is the human body. You have to know how to use it and enjoy it. That's only part of it though because if you have a human body and you put it in the dark and leave them there, you get something that isn't quite human. It needs nourishment and human society. It doesn't have to be the patriarchal family. In the age of AIDS, I recommend group marriages with four couples. More than eight people would be too much.

Basically, the Fugs are the same except we're more refined and more clever and more worked out and more beautifully put and less listened to.

You were saying that things are different for the Fugs now.

What's different isn't the Fugs—it's the society around which we function. There was more of a community for the arts before. If you lived in the Village, you knew the film makers and the painters. Due to mass media, there's no much of a community because there are many, many small communities and groups. If you go into Tower Records, you can find 2500 bands—that's good because it means a lot of people are doing things. But audiences have also become more broken down. There's no large community. The question is whether the times create the great artist or whether the great artist helps to create the times. It works together. If you're incredibly great, you can surpass the times. If you're just a little good, then times will push you onward and make you better. If the times are terrible, you've got to work against all of it. It's really complicated but we're always ready for more good music and more good times.

RONALD D. COHEN (ESSAY DATE 1999)

SOURCE: Cohen, Ronald D. "Singing Subversion: Folk Music and the Counterculture in the 1950s." In *Beat Culture: The 1950s and beyond*, edited by Cornelis A. van Minnen, Jaap van der Bent, and Mel van Elteren, pp. 117-27. Amsterdam: VU University Press, 1999.

In the following essay, Cohen provides an overview of the folk music and musicians associated with the Beat Generation, providing details of the cultural and social context within which this association began and developed.

Memories and current scholarship essentially agree that U.S. society and culture in the 1950s generally experienced smooth sailing, despite a few rough spots, perhaps even a squall or two. Domestic prosperity, coming on the heals of the twin disasters of the Depression and World War II, fueling the brisk move to suburbia, lulled the masses into welcomed complacency. Still, there were disturbing elements: the Cold War abroad and Red Scare at home, heightened fears of youth's corruptibility, even delinquency, straight-jacketed corporate jobs and suburban angst, racial unrest, unsettling music and movies. Resulting from this queasy intermingling of serenity and trepidation, various countercultural movements— literary, musical, political, lifestyle—emerged from society's interstices, questioning and challenging, although hardly threatening, the status quo.[1]

Beat counterculture appeared by mid-decade as one such challenge. As a literary movement and lifestyle image, if not always reality, the Beat movement connected with modern jazz to shape an anti-suburban, anti-corporate, anti-Tin Pan Alley sensibility. Simultaneously, folk music emerged as an anti-establishment musical form and style through the decade, contrasting with, but also somewhat overlapping, the Beat social and cultural matrix. Folk and Beat bohemian communities existed cheek by jowl, in New York's Greenwich Village, San Francisco's North Beach, and selected neighborhoods of Chicago, Denver, and other urban meccas. Folk music possessed a renegade image, partly from its connection with communism, real or manufactured, partly from its challenge to accepted musical standards. When exploring the decade's countercultural movements, proper attention must be paid to folk music's maverick, flickering role, an expressive force paving the way for the turbulent sixties.

"10,000 Beatniks Riot in Greenwich Village," the *Daily Mirror*'s headline screamed in early April 1961, describing a confrontation between folk music enthusiasts and the police over a ban on performing in Washington Square Park. "At 2 P.M., a group of fifty, many in beatnik clothes and beards, advanced from the square's southwest corner," the more staid *New York Times* commented, in cementing the now obvious connection between folk music and the popular stereotype of Beat culture. How did this happen?[2]

The fifties dawned on a mixed note of promise and dread. The powerful success of the Weavers— Pete Seeger, Fred Hellerman, Lee Hays, Ronnie Gilbert, all veterans of radical causes—the prototype folk group, combined with distressing domestic and foreign corruptions, portents of a troubled future. Following six months at the Village Vanguard in New York City, garnering increasing accolades, their recording of "Tzena, Tzena" for Decca Records shot up the pop music charts in mid-summer 1950, peaking at number two.

ON THE SUBJECT OF...

DAVID MELTZER

Meltzer has described himself as a "second generation Beat," a writer who drew his early inspiration from the work of seminal poets such as Michael McClure, Lew Welch, and Robert Duncan. Meltzer arrived in San Francisco in 1957, a time in the city's cultural history often described as a literary renaissance. His identification with Beat literature has continued in the subsequent decades that he has lived in the Bay Area. Since his first poetry collection, *Clowns,* was published in 1959, Meltzer has published more than thirty books. Meltzer has particularly explored the link between poetry and jazz music, authoring two collections on the subject: *Reading Jazz* in 1993 and *Writing Jazz* in 1999. He recorded several albums combining these two forms, including 1968's *Poet Song.*

"Goodnight, Irene" quickly reached number one, and for the next year or so the group's astounding popularity sailed along. Mounting attacks from the right, fanned by the FBI's clandestine maneuverings, led to escalating problems into 1952, however, when Harvey Matusow labeled the group as communists before the House Un-American Activities Committee (HUAC). They disbanded following their annual Town Hall concert in December 1952, but would reemerge three years later, helping to front folk music's mounting resurgence.[3]

Simultaneously, the Red Scare ground on into mid-decade, with Senator Joe McCarthy as the visible cheerleader, but he had plenty of company. Through an odd combination of political repression, general prosperity, technological marvels— led by the spread of television—and the burgeoning baby boom, popular culture entertained while it generally lulled the masses. Around 1955, however, a combination of forces, including the mounting popularity of folk music along with the rise of Beat culture, seemingly broke through the shell of conformity. Stirrings of rebellion, on many fronts, shook and frightened the status quo, which responded in appropriate ways. The blacklist continued in force, however, with many writers,

Village Vanguard nightclub in Greenwich Village, January, 1967.

performers, and countless others unable to regain their former employment and lives.

Part of the rebellion seemed to come from below, in the form of a youthful protest, perhaps more of a media construct than full-blown movement, but nonetheless with solemn overtones. Rock 'n' roll served as one such challenge, marked by Elvis Presley's vibrating torso and black-inflected country songs. The establishment reacted in predictable ways, through economic pressures and heightened rhetoric. Fear brought repression, in various forms—the Comics Code of 1954, censoring sex and violence, even titles that included *horror* or *terror,* from the colorful kids magazines; concern about the spate of delinquency films pouring out of Hollywood; the backlash against rock 'n' roll, fueled by fears of race mixing, which led to the payola scandal of 1959 and onslaught on popular dj Alan Freed. Such cultural issues seemed mild compared to the perceived rise of juvenile delinquency, centered in black and Hispanic minority neighborhoods.

Seemingly placid suburbia had nervous jitters. The enemy could be lurking anywhere, even in the kids' bedrooms.[4]

Reaction to political, cultural, social conformity took various forms and guises, including the rise of Beat culture. Sprouting up in various urban pockets, the Beats rejected the straight-jacketed lives of middle America rushing from office buildings to train stations to suburban dwellings to Little League games to market shopping to country club living, and back again. What about creativity, independence, freedom? Beats dropped out physically and spiritually, aided by alcohol and a variety of drugs, and dropped in artistically and tangibly, with their minds and bodies. They also preferred modern jazz with its pulsating Beat and Black overtones to other musical styles.

Folk performers and their audiences overlapped with Beat culture and society, but also parted company in various ways. Unlike Beat culture (except for Allen Ginsberg and those few with Red backgrounds), folk music had a definite left wing political taint, although many would reject the label and commitment. *Sing Out!* magazine, emerging in 1950 from the rubble of People's Songs and carrying the banner of the Old Left, edited by Irwin Silber, represented the overt link between folk music and activist politics, in promoting civil rights, world peace, labor unions, and economic justice. Many were called to testify before the HUAC. Pete Seeger appeared before the committee in 1955, was soon cited for contempt of Congress, and had a prison sentence hanging over him until 1962. Besides its lingering Red taint, folk's anti-establishment aura derived also from its backward glance at a perceived rustic past. Drawing heavily on Anglo-Saxon ballads, black blues, work songs, the tunes of Woody Guthrie and Leadbelly, and so much else from the world's musical reservoir, folk appealed to those needing a respite from Tin Pan Alley's moon-spoon-june formulas. Indeed, needing a respite from life's seemingly mindless daily rituals.

Folk music represented an alternative milieu, even if essentially aural, and began to attract those searching for something different, particularly in Greenwich Village, New York's bohemian heart. Here the folk and Beat worlds overlapped, while not necessarily connecting, rubbing shoulders on the streets, in the White Horse Tavern, and in the clubs. Joyce Johnson found herself hanging around Washington Square, a few years before plunging into the Beat scene. A young teen in 1949, she approached Washington Square by bus with awe and trepidation: "Here is the arch, as described by the Trotskyite girls, and there is the fountain, the circle in the square, where, according to them, people gather every Sunday to sing folk songs. I'd imagined hordes of people, a whole guitar- and banjo-strumming population, their music ringing through the park." Spotting only six proved somewhat disappointing, although the chilling rain seemed the cause. "I've fallen in love with them all," she later averred. "It's as though a longing I've carried inside myself has suddenly crystallized. To be lonely within a camaraderie of loneliness." Of recent vintage, Sunday folk gatherings would soon become the mecca for budding performers and audiences. "My whole being during the humdrum week is focused on these Sundays," Johnson recalled. As she matured, involved with Jack Kerouac for two years in mid-decade, there is no further mention of folk music. But the connection had been made, spatially and spiritually.[5]

Greenwich Village attracted all sorts of mavericks, increasingly because of its magnetic bohemian image. "Going to the Village for the first time in 1952 was like walking into a dream" for Dan Wakefield. "The special quiet of the Village suggested creation rather than commerce and conveyed a tone of mystery." He also recalls long nights at the White Horse Tavern: "There the talk continued over pints of ale or beer, or the favored combination of arf 'n' arf, and soon everyone broke into songs of Irish rebellion, or love, or protest, folk songs joined and swelled by the Clancy Brothers or long-haired, blond Mary Travers, who also hung out in the back room of the Horse." Johnson records the flood of offbeat talent into the area five years later: "The new cultural wave that had crested in San Francisco was rolling full force into Manhattan—poets, painters, photographers, jazz musicians, dancers— genuine artists and hordes of would-be's. . . . Young and broke, they converged upon the easternmost edges of the Village, peeling off into the nondescript district of warehouses and factory lofts." The Village's cultural vitality surged through the remaining years of the decade. Harry Smith, a true eccentric, arrived in 1950, by way of Seattle and Berkeley, with a load of seventy-eight blues, hillbilly, and gospel records from the 1920s and 1930s. Two years later he had compiled an extravagant, fascinating six-record set for Folkways Records, *Anthology of American Folk Music*, that took on a life of its own. An artistic maverick, Smith spanned the gap between the folk and Beat worlds, yet remained apart from each, even as Allen Ginsberg supported him in later life and he became known for his ingenious films. The *Anthology* served to introduce budding folk music addicts to a wide-ranging body of earlier recordings; many of the performers soon turned up and became energizing folk icons in the 1960s.[6]

The *Anthology of American Folk Music* proved fertile ground for a number of budding northern folk enthusiasts, including John Cohen. While attending Yale in the early 1950s, Cohen had met banjo player Tom Paley, and by decade's end they joined with Mike Seeger, half brother of Pete, to form the New Lost City Ramblers, a seminal group sparking the revival of southern string band music. Cohen was also a documentary film maker and photographer, intrigued by all sorts of cultural incarnations, including the Beats. The photographer Robert Frank, his neighbor in Greenwich Village, asked Cohen to take still shots during the filming of the third act of Jack Kerouac's play *The Beat Generation*, soon transformed into the Beat classic *Pull My Daisy*. Cohen captured the wrap party, with Ginsberg, Gregory Corso, Larry Rivers, and David Amram, and subsequently sold the photos to *Life*, although they were never published. Frank's photos, in turn, appeared on the Ramblers' Folkways Records' covers. Hillbilly music and Beat sensibilities might seem strange bedfellows, polar opposites, yet oddly co-existed in the Village, disparate facets of a bohemian culture struggling for meaning and recognition against the straitjacket of bourgeois values and pretensions.[7]

In April 1957, Israel G. "Izzy" Young, nearing thirty and selling folklore books from his parents' home in Brooklyn, opened the Folklore Center on MacDougal Street in the heart of the Village. Stocking records, books, magazines, and folk instruments, Izzy quickly transformed the store into a drop-in center for folkies of all stripes, one of the Village's cultural nerve centers. He also began staging concerts in his cramped, narrow space. While Izzy became known for his promotion of folk music, he also had an abiding love for poetry and jazz; for example, he co-published the flashy, short-lived *The Jazz Review*, edited by Nat Hentoff and Martin Williams. Full of articles and reviews, the slick monthly, which lasted for twenty issues, included the cream of jazz experts, performers, and producers; Young, however, departed after five issues, forced out by his partners. A few years later, in his illustrated guide to the Village, Fred McDarrah believed Izzy "has been a most influential factor in the development of contemporary folk music. . . . Although the Folklore Center services all seem charitable, Israel

Young does sell books, records, song sheets, and instruments." With no radical roots, he yet quickly drifted into the left milieu, a natural iconoclast bridging the Beat and folk worlds.[8]

Bohemian neighborhoods proved fertile, overlapping ground for both Beat culture and folk music enthusiasts. San Francisco's North Beach, for example, served as the west coast terminus of Beat travels, site of the Six Gallery's ground breaking poetry reading in October 1955, when Ginsberg unveiled "Howl." The scene was rife with Beat poets, hanging out at the Cellar, the Iron Pot, the Place, Vesuvio's bar, Fugazi Hall, and the hungry i. Enrico Banducci had opened the latter (the i standing for id, not intellectual) in 1949 as a hangout for actors and other artists at 149 Columbus, with only informal shows on Sundays. Starting with folk singer Stan Wilson in 1952, however, the eighty-two-seat venue began nightly entertainment. Banducci also co-owned The Purple Onion, with Keith Rockwell, across the street, which initially attracted the hungry i's overflow crowd after opening in 1953. The next year Banducci moved into larger quarters around the corner at 599 Jackson, and the hungry i, now seating over four hundred and sporting a regular liquor license, became the city's favorite night spot for folk music and topical comics. Writer Alvah Bessie, one of the Hollywood Ten—writers and directors who had refused to cooperate with the HUAC and served prison time—and long blacklisted, served as Banducci's light man. The hungry i starred a variety of performers, including Lenny Bruce and Maya Angelou as a folk singer before she switched to literature and poetry, and produced J.F. Goodwin's Beat opera The Pizza Pusher.[9]

Stan Wilson spearheaded the folk revival in San Francisco, which quickly attracted a range of styles and talents. While performing in "Finian's Rainbow" (with Sonny Terry), Odetta Felious first traveled with the stage production to San Francisco and connected with Jo Mapes. Jo and Odetta had met on the first day of junior high school in Los Angeles a few years earlier and formed a strong interracial bond. Jo moved to the North Beach area in 1951, quickly becoming part of the bohemian scene, and married merchant seaman Paul Mapes. They mostly hung around Vesuvio's and began playing folk music with Nan Fowler and Stan Wilson. Jo and Paul had already separated when Odetta returned to Los Angeles, where she improved her guitar playing, then moved north again for a longer stay. While listening to Nan Fowler at the hungry i, Jo talked Banducci into letting Odetta perform. She temporarily filled in on Stan Wilson's night off, but soon moved to the Tin Angel. An immediate hit at the crowded club, she quickly signed for two weeks at the glamorous Blue Angel nightclub in New York, then returned to the Tin Angel for another year, through 1953 and into 1954. Simultaneously, the Gateway Singers, a local Weavers clone, developed an infectious style that landed them a nightly slot at the hungry i in 1955, sharing the bill with a jazz trio and comedian, perhaps Mort Sahl or the zany Professor Irwin Corey.

Chicago had no exact match for Greenwich Village or North Beach, but somewhat the scattered equivalent on the North Side. Myron Reed "Slim" Brundage, symbolically born in the Blackfoot, Idaho, lunatic asylum, where his parents worked, was the noted founder and janitor of the College of Complexes, a bar opened in 1951 that served as the heart of bohemian culture. Mixing poetry, jazz, blues, plays, old movies, ethnic dance—just about everything hard to find anywhere else—the College became a magnet for the politically and artistically disillusioned. "Music was another regular feature," Brundage recalled. "Big Bill Broonzy . . . used to sing at the College on Wednesday nights. Several times a month we had folk songs, jazz concerts, jam sessions," including Bob Gibson, Fleming Brown, and Bernie Asbell. "From mid-1958 through the closing of the College in May 1961, Beat activities and polemics dominated The Curriculum," the College's newsletter, Franklin Rosemont explains. "Beatnik Poetry Nights, Beatnik Party Nights, Beat plays (notably Jack Gelber's 'The Connection'), harangues by Beats and anti-Beats and supporters of Beats were daily affairs. For those who were new to the scene, the College provided its own free Hipsicon defining seventy-five Beatnik terms." Brundage staged a "Miss Beatnik" contest in 1959, and organized a national Beatnik Party the following year, with a nominating convention for its presidential anti-candidate at the College's newly opened New York branch on West 10th Street. (His aborted attempt at opening a North Beach branch ran into local antibeatnik hysteria.) Having reached its peak, the College ran into the buzz saw of the Internal Revenue Service, which seized Brundage's assets for claimed back taxes. For ten brief years the College had mixed folk and jazz, poetry and politics, creating a haven for rebels of all stripes.[10]

Another odd connection between Beat poetry and folk music happened at the Gate of Horn, the city's premier folk club. Opened in 1956 by Les Brown, a reporter for Down Beat, and Albert Grossman, the Gate soon featured Broonzy, Gibson, Odetta, Theo Bikel, and comic Shelly Berman. In 1959, Allen Ginsberg, Peter Orlovsky, and Gregory Corso traveled to Chicago to raise money for *Big Table,* a fledgling literary magazine that was about to publish fragments from William Burroughs' *Naked Lunch.* "We got to Chicago and what was really amazing was that it was like front page news that THE BEATNIKS WERE COMING; and it was like amazing," Ginsberg remembered. "Yeah, those fags are coming, the beatniks are arriving in Chicago! Beatniks are invading Chicago." After a reading at the posh Sherman Hotel of "Howl" and "Kaddish," "I went on Irving Kupcinet's program at some point or other, we all did, and then there was a folk club there called the Gate of Horn, run by Albert Grossman, later Dylan's manager, so he invited us down to read poetry at the Gate of Horn," Ginsberg continued. "[I]t was poetry in a nightclub, and nobody ever had poetry in a nightclub." Perhaps an exaggeration, yet Ginsberg realized the seeming incongruity of the situation, although Beat culture was by nature incongruous, and a fitting companion to folk music. A few years later, after Grossman had sold the Gate of Horn, Lenny Bruce was busted after a performance for obscenity.[11]

Jazz and poetry, vital aspects of Beat culture, and folk had numerous connections in terms of record companies, George Wein with the Newport jazz and folk festivals, various clubs, and so much more. Moe Asch, starting with Asch Records during World War II, followed by Disc Records, and finally Folkways Records in 1949, issued folk as well as jazz records, the latter including Mary Lou Williams, along with the first few volumes of Norman Granz's Jazz at the Philharmonic (JATP) albums, with Dizzy Gillespie, Lester Young, Charlie Parker—the cream of the boppers. Granz branched out in 1947 with his own Clef label, with impressive results. Through the later 1950s Riverside and Prestige, essentially jazz labels, issued a steady stream of creative folk albums. Jac Holzman at Elektra Records, on the other hand, a folk label, produced six jazz records, with Art Blakey and the Jazz Messengers, Herbie Mann, and "Hairy Jazz" with Shel Silverstein. Even Vanguard Records, known for high quality classical and folk recordings, hired John Hammond to oversee its jazz series—Mel Powell, Buck Clayton, Sir Charles Thompson.

"If all art aspires to the condition of music, then in the postwar coteries that would sometimes be called Beat, that music was jazz, and its salient qualities were spontaneity, improvisation, collaboration, subversion, low and outlaw status, hipness/coolness, and an indigenous, hybrid, vernacular Americanism distinct from the Europhilia that had overwhelmed their predecessors," Rebecca Solnit argues.[12] Folk music hardly fit all of these criteria, yet essentially connected with a nativist cultural strain, while also appearing highly incendiary, smacking of subversion. The latter partly derived from the Old Left's adoption of native folk music in the 1930s, in attempting to create a singing labor movement. By the early 1950s the Red Scare had targeted many folk singers and their supporters, in addition to the Weavers. Burl Ives, Josh White, Richard Dyer-Bennet, Oscar Brand, Tom Glazer—all had political troubles. Still, they survived, and others, including a budding group of younger performers, demonstrated that folk maintained an audience and appeal, although the pop charts were dominated by the likes of Perry Como, Patti Page, Eddie Fischer, Doris Day, Jo Stafford, and Rosemary Clooney.[13]

In mid-decade folk music began to emerge from the rubble of the Cold War, battered but intact, with a lingering red taint. Korean War veteran Sonny, the protagonist in Dan Wakefield's novel *Going All the Way,* set in Indianapolis in the mid-1950s, accompanied his friend Gunner to a party. He heard "a record of a guy singing and playing the guitar, but it wasn't hillbilly music exactly. It sounded to Sonny more like old English folk songs but it was about America. Something about This land is your land, and it's my land. . . . The words seemed a little communistic." Highly influenced by the lingering Red Scare, and noticing scattered about the apartment "those little egghead weeklies that were printed on rough paper and didn't have any pictures on the covers just names of articles," he feared, "Maybe the whole place was a secret communist cell; with the magazines and the folk music and everything."[14]

About the same time, in Marge Piercy's novel *Braided Lives,* college student Jill was relieved to hear folk music at a party, the "only music actually sung and played in our peer group. Pop music is crooners soggily serenading our parents. White rock music belongs to the high-school crowd none of us were in with. Black music I knew only because I lived in a partly Black neighborhood. We think folk music is real, gritty, authentic. We like songs about old labor struggles." Whether feared or welcomed, for many folk music held the promise of solace and intrigue, romance and adventure, history and maturity, anything but establishment politics, suburban life, and teenage hijinks, indeed vaguely subversive without sectarian overtones.[15]

Despite its suspect political overtones, folk music's popularity was on the rise. RCA Victor released Harry Belafonte's first album in 1954, *"Mark Twain" And Other Folk Favorites,* closely followed by the best selling *Calypso,* then the popular single "Day-O" in early 1957. A few weeks before, however, the integrated Tarriers's version, under the name "The Banana Boat Song," climbed to number six on the pop charts; Sarah Vaughan, the Fontaine Sisters, and Steve Lawrence had somewhat successful cover versions. Other calypso-style songs captured the public's fancy, including Terry Gilkyson's "Marianne" and Rosemary Clooney's "Mangos." In late 1955, Tennessee Ernie Ford's rendition of Merle Travis's coal mining song "Sixteen Tons" had topped the charts for over two months, another sign that Tin Pan Alley songs had some gritty competition.

The year 1958 witnessed folk music's surging popularity, first with Jimmie Rodgers's pop version of "Kisses Sweeter Than Wine," a hit for the Weavers seven years earlier, which remained on the charts for five weeks. But the big surprise came a bit later, when the Kingston Trio's "Tom Dooley" captured the public's imagination and pocketbook, soon after it appeared on their first album, released in June; it reached number one before Christmas. Dave Guard and Bob Shane, who grew up in Hawaii, and Nick Reynolds, a product of southern California, presented a glossy, novel image of folk singers. Fresh faced and fair haired, they changed folk's look and sound, a combination that particularly appealed to the surging youth market. Following hard on the heels of their monster hit, the group followed with a string of popular singles—"Tijuana Jail," "M.T.A.," "A Worried Man,"—as well as best-selling albums for the next four years. Invited to the Roy Rogers-Dale Evans television show, they shared the stage with country stars Johnny Cash, Jimmy Dean, the Everly Brothers, and Roy Acuff.

Heavily indebted for their style and repertoire to their immediate predecessors—the Weavers, the Tarriers, the Gateway Singers—the trio's publicity yet centered as much on their physical image and domestic lifestyle as on their folksy yet upbeat musical appeal. After all, the Weavers, recently rejuvenated, continued to labor under the cloud of communism, while the Tarriers and Gateway Singers, both racially integrated, always faced prejudice. "It is hard to recall an instance when as wholesome a group of entertainers as the King-ston Trio has won as swift and widespread a popularity as they have," *Redbook Magazine* began its puff piece in mid-1959. Raking over the soon-familiar story of their college backgrounds and sudden rise to stardom, the article stressed, they "score sensationally without catering to any of the current 'sure-fire' vogues," and predicted they "are bringing about a far broader appreciation of folk songs than we have ever had before, and one that is likely to prove lasting."[16]

Life featured a cover photo and two page spread, certifying their pop status. "The brightest new sounds heard through all the racket of rock 'n' roll come from the voices and the instruments of three college grad cutups," the article intoned, quickly establishing its tenor. Indeed, it focused as much on "their three bright and pretty wives," who now traveled with the group, joining "in the fraternity house chorales the boys learned when they were carefree California under grads." Accompanied by a photo captioned "dutiful wives tend[ing] to their tired husbands in club dressing room between song sessions," the article explained, "with success, domesticity came to the softsell folk singers." Shane married an heiress from Atlanta, Guard the daughter of the treasurer of a chain of department stores, and Reynolds a comedienne also due to inherit a fortune. As Reynolds noted, "We may look like tennis bums, but man, underneath we've got stability."[17]

They had the perfect combination of charm, wealth, security, and modesty. "Rockless, roll-less and rich," *Time* proclaimed the next year. Only recently, before success, Guard had been a "preb-eatnik who was heading nowhere," Reynolds a tennis bum, and Shane a Waikiki Beach surfer and drinker. But with their triumph at the Purple Onion "they acquired purpose," then dutiful wives, which "stabilized them further." Despite their instant success, crowned with the honor of appearing at both the Newport Jazz and Folk Festivals in 1959, they "still divide up the household chores as they did in the days when they used to sleep three in a bed in fleabag hotels." *Down Beat* stressed they were "something more than another bunch of campus whiz kids"; they had high "regard for quality and integrity," and would not tolerate any "sacrifice of intelligence or taste." The opening essay in *The Kingston Trio,* a publicity booklet, echoed such sentiments: "Though thoroughly professional in every sense, they are still basically the three young guys first heard at the Cracked Pot, three talented collegians who get a genuine kick out of singing together." What saints! Professionals yet with youthful zest.

A far cry from the scruffy, unwashed, lewd rock 'n' roll singers, or even the slightly subversive folk singers, at least in much of the public mind.[18]

The Kingston Trio emerged at an optimal time for the nation's cultural, moral gatekeepers. Rock 'n' roll's upsurge during the mid-1950s had shaken society's aesthetic and moral foundations, leading to escalating recriminations and additional soul searching in the midst of the Cold War. Could middle class culture survive? Were young people out of control? How to reestablish safe values? The baby boom generation, beginning in 1946, had not yet reached much into their teens, but still the youth market began growing by mid-decade. More importantly, teenage consumer spending, fueled by the general prosperity, continued to climb; their average weekly income of $8.50 in 1957 allowed for the purchase not only of records, but also radios, concert tickets, cars, food, and clothes. Producers and advertisers closely followed these developments, flooding the marketplace with increasing consumer goods geared to the country's youth, but not without friction and controversy.

Heightened consumerism and sophisticated marketing stratagems produced increasingly segmented musical markets, with pop capturing the adults, rock 'n' roll the teen market, and folk appealing more to the college crowd. Indeed, following on the heels of the Kingston Trio's amazing success, folk became increasingly acceptable for the next few years, reaching its peak of commercial popularity in 1964. Countless freshly scrubbed trios, quartets, and larger ensembles crowded the concert stages, airwaves, and record racks for the next few years, somewhat transporting folk music into a marketable commodity comfortable in suburban America. Folk music lost much of its radical taint, yet still managed to cling to its political, counterculture, slightly shady roots, personified by Pete Seeger, whose political problems remained—oddly, while he recorded for Columbia Records, he was blacklisted from CBS television, as well as ABC, which programed the mainstream Hootenanny show in 1963. Folk also connected to the emerging, dynamic civil rights and anti-war movements.

Through the 1950s popular (urban) folk music had experienced sundry incarnations, beginning with the Weavers' immense popularity, through the bleak years of the Red Scare, rejuvenation in mid-decade, only to emerge in 1960 with the clean-cut image of the Kingston Trio. During these years it had been associated with various countercultural forces, in tandem with the Beat culture just emerging, often sharing the stage and audience with jazz and poetry, part and parcel of a bohemian lifestyle. While it might appear in the early 1960s that folk had entered a new phase, somewhat free from previous handicaps and associations, it was shortly captured by the enigmatic, creative, charming Bob Dylan—the cultural offspring not only of Woody Guthrie, Pete Seeger, and Jimmie Rodgers, but also Allen Ginsberg and the Beat poets. In understanding folk's political roots this should not have come as a surprise. Dylan brought it all together.

"Bob Dylan is the incarnation of Beatness in our time," Glenn O'Brien comments, in *Beat Culture and the New America*. "Our greatest poet and not a bad guitar player." Ann Charters includes three Dylan songs and an excerpt from *Tarantula* in *The Portable Beat Reader*, in noting: "Over the next decade Dylan continued to be influenced by the Beats—through his reading, through his association with such Beat writers as Allen Ginsberg and Michael McClure, and by his vision of himself as a solitary creative artist in the rebellious and liberating atmosphere of the 1960s, which the Beats partly inspired and helped sustain." It is no accident that Ginsberg appears in the opening scene of *Don't Look Back,* Don Pennebaker's film of Dylan's English tour in 1965. Allen and Dylan generally shared a cordial relationship; Ginsberg joined Bob's nationally touring "Rolling Thunder Review" a decade later.[19]

In any accounting of countercultural trends and tendencies of the 1950s, folk music's adherents and settings can hardly be ignored. The music appealed to those Northerners bucking the status quo, overtly or covertly, knowingly or not, those seeking alternative musics and inspirations during a dangerous time. "America's rebellious culture of anxiety presented an image of America in conflict with Eisenhower's America," Margot Henriksen has recently written. "No one and no place was safe from madness. Alienation, loneliness, and nervous disillusion seemed the norm in anxious America. . . . And the dissenters who inhabited this postwar culture offered some of the most sane and critical commentary on the diminishment of life in an anxious and schizoid atomic age." Beat cultural offered one alternative comprehension and lifestyle, folk music's search for a sensible past and radical understanding of the present, yet another.[20]

Notes

1. Stephen Whitfield, *The Culture of the Cold War* (Baltimore: Johns Hopkins University Press, 1991).

2. Paul Hofmann, "Folk Singers Riot in Washington Square," *New York Times,* 10 April 1961.

3. For a good overview of the dark side of 1950: Greg Mitchell, *Tricky Dick and the Pink Lady: Richard Nixon vs. Helen Gahagan Douglas—Sexual Politics and the Red Scare, 1950* (New York: Random House, 1998).

4. Ronald D. Cohen, "*The Delinquents*: Censorship and Youth Culture in Recent U.S. History," *History of Education Quarterly* 37.3 (Fall 1997): 251-270.

5. Joyce Johnson, *Minor Characters: A Young Woman's Coming of Age in the Beat Generation* (New York: Washington Square Press, 1990), 28, 32.

6. Dan Wakefield, *New York in the Fifties* (Boston: Houghton Mifflin, 1992), 81, 116; Johnson, *Minor Characters,* 167; Harry Smith, ed., *Anthology of American Folk Music* (reissue, Washington, DC: Smithsonian Folkways Recordings, 1997), with accompanying booklet; Greil Marcus, *Invisible Republic: Bob Dylan's Basement Tapes* (New York: Henry Holt, 1997), chapter 4; Robert Cantwell, *When We Were Good: The Folk Revival* (Cambridge, MA: Harvard University Press, 1996), chapter 6. In the "Sociogram of the Beats, 1950-1965," constructed by Steven Watson and appearing in Lisa Phillips, *Beat Culture and the New America: 1950-1965* (New York: Whitney Museum of American Art, 1995), Harry Smith appears as a "performer or filmmaker" in the upper left corner of the West Coast networks diagram, 260.

7. Peter Goldsmith, *Making People's Music: Moe Asch and Folkways Records* (Washington, DC: Smithsonian Institution Press, 1998), 264-265.

8. Fred McDarrah, *Greenwich Village* (New York: Corinth Books, 1963), 62.

9. Steven Watson, *The Birth of the Beat Generation: Visionaries, Rebels, and Hipsters, 1944-1960* (New York: Pantheon Books, 1995), 189-191.

10. Franklin Rosemond, ed., *From Bughouse Square to the Beat Generation: Selected Ravings of Slim Brundage* (Chicago: Charles Kerr, 1997), 32, 114.

11. Edward de Grazia, *Girls Lean Back Everywhere: The Law of Obscenity and the Assault on Genius* (New York: Random House, 1992), 359, 361.

12. Rebecca Solnit, "Heretical Constellations: Notes on California, 1946-61," in Phillips, *Beat Culture and the New America,* 69.

13. Ibid.

14. Dan Wakefield, *Going All the Way* (New York: Dell Pub. Co., 1970), 199, 201 (ellipses in the original).

15. Marge Piercy, *Braided Lives* (New York: Fawcett Crest, 1982), 114.

16. "Three Daring Young Men," *Redbook Magazine* (May 1959): 12.

17. "A Trio in Tune Makes the Top," *Life* (3 August 1959): 61, 64.

18. "Tin Pan Alley: Like from Halls of Ivy," *Time* (11 July 1960): 56-57; Richard Hadlock, "Tom Dooley—Tom Dooley!," *DownBeat* (11 June 1959): 19-20; *The Kingston Trio* (New York: Random House, 1960), 9.

19. Glenn O'Brien, "The Beat Goes On," in Phillips, *Beat Culture and the New America,* 184; Ann Charters, ed., *The Portable Beat Reader* (New York: Penguin Books, 1992), 370; Barry Miles, *Ginsberg: A Biography* (New York: Harper Collins Pub., 1989), chapter 14 and passim; Robert Shelton, *No Direction Home: The Life and Music of Bob Dylan* (New York: William Morrow, 1986), passim.

20. Margot A. Henriksen, *Dr. Strangelove's America: Society and Culture in the Atomic Age* (Berkeley: University of California Press, 1997), 111 and passim. As usual, while Henriksen includes some discussion of rock 'n' roll and Beat literature, there is no mention of folk music.

DAVID AMRAM (ESSAY DATE 1999)

SOURCE: Amram, David. "This Song's for You, Jack: Collaborating with Kerouac." In *Beat Culture: The 1950s and beyond,* edited by Cornelis A. van Minnen, Jaap van der Bent, and Mel van Elteren, pp. 131-48. Amsterdam: VU University Press, 1999.

In the following essay, Amram provides a detailed personal recollection of his musical collaborations with Kerouac, as well as a first-hand description of key people and places of the jazz music scene in 1950s Greenwich Village.

Collaborating with Kerouac was as natural as breathing. That is because the breath and breadth of Jack's rhythms were so natural that even the most stodgy musician or listener or reader could feel those rhythms and cadences, those breathless flowing phrases, the subtle use of dynamics that are fundamental to the oral (i.e., spoken) and aural (i.e., to be listened to) tradition of all musics and poetic forms of expression.

Whoa, you might say. Why such a long sentence? Because Jack himself spoke, wrote, improvised and sang in long flowing phrases, like the music of Franz Schubert, George Gershwin, Hector Berlioz, Haydn, Charlie Parker, Lester Young, Billie Holiday, like the poetry of Walt Whitman, Dylan Thomas, Baudelaire, Langston Hughes, and other lyric artists whose work we both loved and admired.

The 1950s were the pinnacle years for great conversationalists and great rappers, the last generation to grow up reading voraciously, traveling by extension of the thumb, and trusting the Great Creator to get you to your destination. Part of your requirement of being a successful hitchhiker was to engage your patron saint of the moment, the person who picked you up, in conversations about anything and everything. Storytelling was still practiced as a people-to-people activity. TV and the internet were not part of the picture. Entertainment and communication came from the interaction of people to one another. Many of the greatest poets, authors and jazz artists, whether reading or playing in public, could carry on for hours for an audience of one other person. Our expectations and goals were to achieve excellence, with the hope that once we did, someone out there would dig it.

I participated in incredible concerts, jam sessions, poetry-music readings, classical music concerts, and dance events where the performers usually out-numbered the audience. That was more or less expected. On the rare occasions when there was a large audience, that sense of intimacy was still retained by the performers and considered to be the most important goal to strive for. Our universal motto was "Be for Real." "Just find one person and play for that person all night long, Dave," Charlie Mingus told me in the fall of 1955, when I had just arrived in New York and was fortunate enough to be chosen by him to be in his quintet. "All you need is one person in your whole life to really be listening."

Jack was one of those people who listened and observed as well as he wrote and performed. When Jack and I first began performing together in 1956, we would run across one another at Bring Your Own Bottle (also known as BYOB) parties, often held at painters' lofts. The guests would bring wine, beer, Dr. Brown's Black Cherry Soda, sometimes just paper cups, or potato chips, graham crackers, or a musical instrument, a new poem, a monologue from Shakespeare, or Lord Buckley's latest comedic-philosophical rap, a song or simply their unadorned selves, looking for romance, fun, excitement, and a chance to celebrate Friday and Saturday night, where you could stay up till dawn, because you did not have to go to your day job! The great American weekend frenzy was upon us, but unlike most of our brother and sister pilgrims to the mad canyons of New York's vast and terrifying cement jungle, we could find a harmonious home in our own temporary oasis for weekend adventures, wherever we ended up. Enduring friendships were often formed in the most modest of milieus.

This was the part of New York where Jack and I each felt most at home, in an environment that was inclusive, informal, almost rural, temporarily created for a few hours in the midst of the vast sky-scrapered metropolis, where we miraculously found temporary cocoons of warmth and camaraderie. These party environments were like back porch Lukenbach, Texas picking parties in the summer, or Lowell, Massachusetts, get-togethers over beer with Acadian accordions and singing of old songs, or the pubs of Dublin, Ireland, where unheralded natural poets celebrated the rising of the moon, or great jam sessions in the South, like the ones with Charlie Parker and Dizzy Gillespie

in my basement apartment in 1951-1952 in Washington, D.C., before I met Jack. These informal, spontaneous gatherings were like magic. Jack talked about these one-time-only New York all-night weekend bashes that we shared years later, but when Jack and I first spent time at these great sessions performing together during the course of the evening, we hardly said a word to each other. Just as I related to Thelonious Monk, Miles Davis, Bud Powell, and scores of other great musicians I was blessed to play with who never said much and let their music do the talking, Jack and I had that same musician's extrasensory perception. It was an unspoken communication that came to us naturally. I could play while he read or improvised words, and I knew exactly what to do. When I would make up a throw-away topical rhymed rap at 3 A.M., and he would bang on the piano accompanying me, we related in the same way. We both knew how to *listen,* to lay back, to breathe together, to curb aggression and search for harmony, to tune into one another and surrender ourselves to the particular rhythm and pulse of the evening. That rhythm and pulse was always connected to the Native American drum we both felt so strongly, the African drum that permeated all the great music of our time, even when it was portrayed in movies by white people only, the drum of the Middle East, and the soulful song-stories, prayers and chants of the Catholic Church Jack had in his bones and the Jewish liturgical wailing of ancient songs that reverberated in my unconscious. As soon as we were done performing, we would both give each other a wink, a nod, or a smile, and become part of the party, flirting with young women and searching for food, drink, and adventure.

Several months after we had crossed paths at many of these one-time-only occasions, my weekend excursions to these parties temporarily came to a halt. I began an eleven-week-long stint with my quartet at the Five Spot, a funky bar in the Bowery that became the hangout for painters like Franz Kline, Willem de Kooning, Joan Mitchell, Alfred Leslie (who later directed the film *Pull My Daisy* that Jack and I collaborated on), and Larry Rivers (who appeared in *Pull My Daisy* as a saxophone-playing railroad train conductor, performing duets with me when I portrayed a deranged French hornist).

The Five Spot was crowded with painters, sculptors, actors, composers, authors, poets, moving men, postal workers, winos, office workers, off-duty firemen—just about anyone and everyone was welcome at the Five Spot, where you could get a huge pitcher of beer for 75 cents. My quartet was sometimes joined by as many as eighteen musicians (on the night when the whole Woody Herman Band sat in with us). Late at night, poets and actors would sometimes join us, reciting poetry or improvising verse with music. This was never planned. It just happened, partly because as the leader of the quartet, I was open and enthusiastic to have this happen. Our era was always *in*clusive, not *ex*clusive. Jazz was about sharing and spontaneity.

Jack was often there, and all of us in the quartet could always feel his presence the minute he arrived. We could telepathically feel his power as a listener, just as we could feel his ability to observe, reflected in his dark, brooding eyes as he always became a part of every place he visited. I remembered our great encounters at the weekend loft parties where we played together. *On the Road* was not published, and the terrible pressures of celebrity had not yet arrived in his life. Even though he often sat alone, like a wayward meditative Canadian lumberjack in his plaid redcheckered work shirt, he always exuded a special energy. He was that one special person Mingus alluded to, the one person we always knew we could play for. We began to know one another as two fellow transplanted hicks, trying to relate to Golgothian New York City. Jack was from Lowell, Massachusetts, and I was brought up on a farm in Feasterville, Pennsylvania. Even though we had both seen a lot of the world, we still had the bond of being outsiders in sophisticated New York City, searching for something we knew was there. Jack told me how being a football player had opened the doors for him to leave Lowell, go to an eastern prep school and be accepted at Columbia University, and how playing football had resulted in breaking his leg, but not his spirit. I told Jack about my childhood, always dreaming of becoming a musician. I described the trauma of moving to Washington, D.C. at the age of twelve, and deciding to become a musician and composer, the joy of my job as a part-time gym teacher at a French school then being drafted in the army and beginning my travels around the world.

We found we shared a mutual interest in sports and speaking fractured French, which often annoyed the 4 A.M. stoned-out customers at Bickford's greasy spoon, where we would congregate after the Five Spot closed, to eat hamburgers with fried onions and mayonnaise on English muffins, while we drank coffee and planned our conquest of New York.

A few months later, after my eleven-week engagement at the Five Spot was over, poet and drummer Howard Hart and San Francisco poet Philip Lamantia climbed up the six flights of stairs to my tiny apartment on Christopher Street, which was always open to guests, and told me of their idea to give a jazz-poetry reading in New York City.

"It will be the first one," said Howard Hart, in his hyper-breathless style. "Jack said he'll do it with us. He'll be the MC, and you and he can do all that spontaneous stuff where you both make up rhymed scat-verses and accompany each other, and Philip and I will read from poems we've written out. We'll give you carbon copies of our poems to look at. We can even rehearse, but I know you and Jack don't need to. You guys already can do it naturally better than anyone else."

I read some typed copies of Howard's and Philip's poems, that Howard had brought with him, and understood why Jack wanted to do a planned reading with them. Their poems were lyrical, original, honest, touching, with brilliant flights of fancy, combined with contemporary sounds of everyday urban life. Howard Hart and Philip Lamantia were trying to say something to touch the heart.

"Where are we going to do it, and when?" I asked. "I don't know if I'll have much time to rehearse. I'm writing music for Joe Papp's Free Shakespeare in Central Park, and working part-time in the Post Office, playing with my band and composing music too. I've always played with Jack spontaneously without ever planning anything."

"Don't worry," said Howard. "It will happen when and where it is supposed to happen, and we'll all be there together."

The next day we all met with Jack at my sixth floor walkup. I could hear Jack bellowing as he climbed the stairs.

"Merde alors!" said Jack. "I've ascended the cherubic heights to join the lonely bell ringer up in the tower of St. Amram's Synagogue. Get an elevator, Davey. These six flights will be responsible for your premature demise. *A la santé and lechayim.*" Jack pulled a bottle of Thunderbird wine from his red-checked lumberjacket, removed it from its soiled brown paper bag, and took an enormous gulp.

"We'll make history, Davey. The mad poets and sainted musicians will make New York City become the new international shrine for Buddha-like meditation. All the jaded big city Philistines will smile at one another as we lay our scatological tomes on their weary souls. Let's play something for Philip and Howard to show these boys how Baudelaire and Erik Satie are reborn in Greenwich Village."

I began playing the twelve-bar blues, and Jack and I made up verses, played and scat-sang four-bar breaks, while Howard took a pair of wire brushes from his jacket and played drum parts on a phone book. Philip Lamantia watched us in amazement.

"My God, Jack. I wish everyone in San Francisco could see this. I didn't know you could sing."

"I can't," said Jack. "That's the voice of the Holy Spirit coming through me. Like Stravinsky said about composing 'Sacre du Printemps': 'I'm merely the vessel through which this new creation was given to the World.'"

"I see New York's helping you to overcome your shyness and modesty, Jack," said Philip, laughing.

"Naw, I'm *serious,* man," said Jack. "When Davey and I start *cooking.* I feel like I'm flying. Like Charlie Parker. A bird in flight. He didn't *talk* about it. He *did* it."

"*We'll* do it," said Howard. "We'll be the Jazz Poetry Trio."

"I'll drink to that," said Jack. "Let's get some more wine and go out to the Café Figaro at McDougal and Bleecker Street and meet some beautiful gals. And we'll discuss our plans to invade New York's literary jungle, and overwhelm the masses with our spontaneous madness."

We ambled down the six flights of stairs and headed towards the Café Figaro. We walked in silence for a few blocks. Jack turned to me as we crossed Sheridan Square.

"Did you ever feel you knew someone all your life when you met them?"

"Yes, Jack. I felt that with you, the first time we played together at one of those loft parties, but never would have said it."

"You didn't need to say it," said Jack.

We walked to the Figaro and sat in the back room. I took out my horn, and we gave an impromptu improvised performance. Brooklyn Bernie, an old Village moving man, applauded and came over to our table.

"I'll tell ya what, Dave. I'll buy all you guys free coffee, sandwiches, and pastry if you'll let me recite 'The Rhyme of the Ancient Mariner' with

you, all right? Listen Dave, you play the horn, like the sea sounds making the boat rock, and you other guys hum when I signal you. I always wanted to do this at the Figaro. This is my *chance!*"

Then he whispered confidentially, "There's a bunch of bee-*yoo*-tiful young ladies from Barnard College and Mt. Holyoke College for Women sitting up in the front two tables by the window. They're here to meet some real Bohemian artists. What you guys are doin', no offense, but it's too *weird,* it's too far out, but when they hear *me* do 'The Rhyme of the Ancient Mariner' . . . they'll *flip out*! And I'll buy you all whatever you want."

"I accept your kind offer," said Philip Lamantia. "I'll have the apple turnover, a double expresso and salmon platter."

"I'll have the same," said Howard.

"I'm not hungry. I'm thirsty," said Jack. "I'll take a sip of whatever holy spirits are in that bottle I see in the side pocket of your coat."

"I'm starving, Bernie," I said. "I'll have the vegetarian special plate, a tuna roll, a cappuccino, and toasted bagel with lox, onions and cream cheese, with a side order of cole slaw and French fries."

Brooklyn Bernie, the moving man, ordered us our feast. After we chowed down, Jack and I did a few impromptu numbers, punctuated by Jack taking loud slurps of Wild Turkey whiskey from Brooklyn Bernie's brown-bagged bottle, before launching into his next improvised story-song-poem. Jack sat down and attacked my remaining coleslaw and French fries, Brooklyn Bernie took a huge belt from his near-empty bottle of Wild Turkey, cleared his throat and climbed on top of his chair, waving his arms to let the patrons of the Café Figaro know it was show time.

The denizens of the Café Figaro were used to unannounced performances by anyone who felt like giving impromptu readings of their latest poems, monologues from Shakespeare or Chekov, ranting and raving about world politics, or home-made public service announcements requesting a place to stay for the night.

Brooklyn Bernie clapped his hands, gestured like a crazed symphony conductor from his chair-podium for quiet, and launched into a raspy-voiced version of "The Rhyme of the Ancient Mariner." No one paid any attention. He gave Howard, Jack, Philip and myself signals to accompany him with sound effects suggesting, the sea, but his ship was sinking rapidly. He was receiving the fabled New York freeze. The customers began talking to each other, gradually drowning him out. Many of them turned their chairs so that gradually Bernie could see a room filled with people whose backs were turned towards him.

"He's like Ralph Ellison's 'Invisible Man,'" whispered Howard. "No one knows he's here."

Brooklyn Bernie concluded and was rewarded by withering silence and cold stares of contempt. We could feel his despair. Jack leaped up and started singing "Pennies from Heaven," interspersing "Bernie from Brooklyn" into the lyrics, while I accompanied him.

Jack made up a whole song about Brooklyn Bernie coming through the rain to make Manhattan his new home, and what a *moving man* this moving man was. At the end, the whole Figaro burst into applause and laughter, and one of the women from the table full of intellectual lovelies invited us to join them, and we were asked to go with them to a friend's loft, where we partied till dawn. Brooklyn Bernie was in heaven and was having an elated conversation with a gorgeous philosophy major which was prematurely terminated when he passed out in the armchair he was emoting from.

There was an old upright piano in their loft, and Jack played his particular style of crashing Beethoven-esque chords when I was scat-singing, and I backed him up when he sang, spoke or scatted, and we traded rhymed verses together, with Jack playing the bongos. His natural musicality and style of poetic speaking was extraordinary, and the young women were transfixed to see someone who looked more like Paul Bunyon than the tortured introspective poet, carrying on and emoting streams of dialogue, stories, songs, and poetry that all made sense.

We both knew that night that together we could do anything anywhere, for anybody, and that people who were there with us would no longer be the traditional passive audience. All of us would feel part of one another, sharing in the moment, knowing it would never happen in the same way again.

Howard Hart and Philip Lamantia got up and read their poems. Accompanied by Brooklyn Bernie's snores, my French horn, and the old upright piano I played, their performing style, like their poetry, was powerful, lyrical, intense, severe, sincere, and disciplined. Their formality fit perfectly with the totally spontaneous moments that Jack and I had created earlier in the evening. That night in the spring of 1957, Philip, Howard, Jack

and I did what later became the basis for the first jazz-poetry reading in New York City.

Finally the sun came up, and the gorgeous philosophy major, Helen, put an afghan blanket over Brooklyn Bemie's slumbering hulk, and punctuated by his loud snores, we ate an omelet of hot dogs, mushrooms, Swiss cheese, canned peas, olives, and strawberry yogurt that I whipped up as a culinary thank-you bouquet to our hostesses for allowing us to have what became our only rehearsal for our future public performance, although, of course, we did not know it at the time.

I staggered home, slowly climbed the six flights of stairs and collapsed into an early-morning 8 A.M. slumber. At noon, there was a loud pounding on my door. Howard Hart, knowing it was never locked, burst into the room. "My God, man. What a night! I've got a terrible hangover, but we've got to be at the Museum of Modern Art in an hour. I called Frank O'Hara, and he made an appointment to see the events coordinator at 1:30. He's going to try to get us a jazz-poetry reading at the Museum this fall. We're ready to storm the Bastille of uptown uptightness in the Big Apple. Jack's still sleeping, so we'll meet Frank O'Hara and Philip in 85 minutes. Get dressed. Hurry up! Wear anything."

I threw on my old gray sweater, no socks, mismatching sneakers, and paint-stained jeans.

"I hope I look okay," I said.

"You're fine," said Howard. "Frank O'Hara will take care of everything. We're going to make history. Roll over Picasso, Frank O'Hara's going to let us play the Museum of Modern Art Jazz-Poetry Blues!"

Frank O'Hara was highly respected in the uptown world and was established as an important figure in New York's cultural life. Aside from his gifts as a poet, he was much beloved by all of us and acknowledged as a link to the burgeoning community of artists, poets, painters, musicians, and friends who later became known (or some of us did, through no effort on our part) as the founding members of the Beat Generation, a term we never heard or thought of at the time.

We got to the museum two minutes early, gave Frank O'Hara and Philip Lamantia a hug, and were escorted into the event coordinator's plush office. The man in charge of performance events at the museum listened patiently as Frank extolled the virtues of Howard Hart, Philip Lamantia, Jack Kerouac and myself. I noticed the events coordinator was wearing an elegant crushed velvet jacket and smoked French Gitanes cigarettes from a long ivory cigarette holder. He was wearing patent leather shoes. He eyed my sockless mismatched sneakers and grimaced. After a glowing report of nearly a half an hour, I thought Frank O'Hara's recommendation of our list of achievements would make us candidates for the Nobel Peace Prize.

"Frank, let's be brutally honest," said the events coordinator. "These two poets and Amram are just about totally un*known,* outside of the Bohemian circles of *Down*town. The Museum of Modern Art is not a talent show for hopeful emerging artists. We have an international reputation to uphold. And that Jack *Kerouac.* I've met him at the Cedar Tavern. He acts like a *TRUCK DRIVER!* He's a *TOTAL* unknown and so *GAUCHE!* We would *never* have someone so crude appear at one of our events. I didn't even know he was a writer. I can't believe Viking is going to publish a novel of his this Fall. Do you think he wrote it himself?"

Philip Lamantia looked dismayed. Howard Hart looked at me despairingly. "Let's split," he murmured. We walked towards the exit of the museum.

"What will we tell Jack?" said Philip, in a glum tone.

"He'll roar with laughter," said Frank O'Hara. "Especially the part about him looking like a truck driver and not being able to write a book. Jack's already written *ELEVEN* books. *The Town and the City* was marvelous, even though my colleagues here at the museum *refused* to read it because it never made the best seller list. Don't despair. When my colleague loses his job as the events coordinator at the Museum and is selling lingerie somewhere, all of *you* will be scaling the heights and opening doors to new vistas. Do it *down*town, where you're already loved. It was a mistake for me to try to break down the walls of pretension here at the museum. When you get better known, they'll *fawn* and *grovel* all over you . . . at least until you fall out of fashion. Do it *down*town. Let's try the Brata Art Gallery on East 10th Street. You've already played for their art openings, David. They know your scores for the Free Shakespeare in the Park you started composing, and they've heard you with Mingus and with your quartet at the Five Spot. They trust my judgment of the value of your poetry, Howard and Philip. And they love Jack, and sense he is a genius, as we all do. Let's do it *down*town."

We went downtown, and I called up Jack and told him the whole story. He roared with laughter.

"*Je m'en fou,* Davey. Let's go hang out in the Village and *épater la bourgeoisie.* This may be the holy night that you find the dream-wife life-companion you've searched for on your musicological field trips through the lonely streets of Aulde Manhattenoes (which was Jack's affectionate nickname for downtown New York). You need to find a soulmate. You can write symphonies and cook omelets for her. I don't need to look anymore. I'm cool, Dave. I have the finest woman on Earth. We should both get married tonight at City Hall and celebrate with a champagne dinner in your Mt. Everest walk-up Himalayan-high cabin in the sky on Christopher Street. We can serenade our new young wives with our Rimbaud-Baudelaire-Lester Young-Thelonious Monk-Bartòk-Kerouacian inspired soulful ditties."

I grabbed my French horn, Jack packed up his notebooks, and we strolled through Greenwich Village. I sat in with Art Blakey's band at a nearby jazz club for a set, and then we wandered over to the Café Figaro. Brooklyn Bernie, the moving man, wearing the same clothes he had on when we had left him snoring, at earlier the same day, greeted us in his loud raspy voice.

"Jack, Dave, let's do 'The Rhyme of the Ancient Mariner.'" The manager of the Figaro, came over immediately.

"Listen, Bernie, no offense, but you almost emptied the house last night. I'll buy you all supper if you'll promise to keep quiet. Face it, Bernie. 'The Rhyme of the Ancient Mariner' doesn't go over with the weekend crowd. Let Jack and Dave do their spontaneous stuff. New York's a tough town. Stick to moving furniture."

Bernie looked crestfallen.

"Let Bernie play the bongo drums, and accompany us with his highly evolved moving man rhythms," said Jack graciously.

The manager handed Bernie the house set of bongos, and Jack made up a new version of "Brooklyn Bernie, the moving man, a *Moving Man.*"

Everyone in the Figaro was snapping their fingers and singing alone, in a rhymed choral refrain I made up from Jack's words.

"Thank you, Jack," said Bernie, after the twenty-five minute improvised tribute celebrating Bernie, his native Brooklyn, the Brooklyn Dodgers, and Hart Crane on the Brooklyn Bridge. As everyone applauded, Jack lifted Bernie's hand up as if he were the new heavy weight champion of the world.

Bernie was beaming. "Jack," he said, "You're a generous soul, you're what we call in Yiddish a real *mensche*. You gotta lotta *neshuma*. That means *soul*, man."

"*Merci*," said Jack. "I come from Soul People. The Kerouacs have been on a long journey since the twelfth century, in France, Canada, and the US and I feel that in my blood everywhere I go. Jesus and St. Francis and Buddha guide me on my journey, and *you*, Bernie, are the reincarnation of the Ancient Mariner, a landlubber, trapped in a port-of-call. You're in dry-dock on a pier crowded with Philistines. But despair not, Bernie, I have the sacred wine to anoint your tortured soul."

Jack pulled out a fresh bottle of Thunderbird wine and we surreptitiously poured it into coffee cups and drank it all. Bernie staggered off to take the subway back to Brooklyn, and Jack and I went up to my apartment and played music and talked till dawn.

He told me stories about his travels, and how we could someday create a band of musicians from all over the world and combine them with a symphony orchestra. How we could write a huge piece like Berlioz's "Requiem" for chorus, band and orchestra, and tour the world, inviting local poets, jazz and folk players to join in at each concert. We could give our guest artists a special moment when we would all improvise, and give the symphony orchestra players ten minutes' rest during the concert as the poets and jazz musicians improvised, so that they could someday learn to do the same thing, as they watched us on stage from behind their music stands.

"We can open up the doors, the minds and hearts of everybody," said Jack. "Music and words are all part of the same cloth. Like Yin and Yang, they give the perfect balance to existence. The perfect duality."

A few months later, Howard Hart, Philip Lamantia, Jack Kerouac and I gave the first-ever jazz poetry reading in New York City at the Brata Art Gallery on East 10th Street in November of 1957. There were no posters and no advertising. Just a mimeographed type-written handbill that we handed out at the Cedar Bar, the Five Spot, and the Café Figaro, Kettle of Fish, White Horse Tavern and San Remo.

The Brata was packed. We did what we had already done before. Even so, we felt a tremendous spirit, as if we were doing something for the very first time. We did not know it at the time, but the seeds were sown. Shortly after, we performed at the Circle-in-the-Square Theater. I still have a copy of the original poster for that reading. Over the last forty years, copies of that poster have circulated around the world.

The Circle-in-the-Square lighting designer improvised with us throughout the night. He must have utilized everything in his lifetime of experience in the theater, flashing all the different-colored lights, dimming and brightening every lamp at different angles and tempos, blinking and pulsating, contrasting different hues, creating instant blackouts and even beaming lights in the audience's faces from time to time, all synchronized to the rhythms of the poetry and music. This was ten years before so-called psychedelic lighting came into existence. Jack and I told him to watch, listen, and do what he felt the poetry and music told him to do. He did it and the audience loved it.

When Jack, Howard, and Philip disappeared after intermission to celebrate and drink Thunderbird wine with their fans at the tiny Sheridan Park across the street from the Circle-in-the-Square Theater, I had to play the piano and make up rhymed scat-songs, based on suggestions from the audience to fill up time till Jack and the poets returned from their winetasting expedition. That is how I started doing this in public. Sometimes, desperation is the mother of invention. During our concerts, when Jack was reading, singing or scatting, I never knew *what* was written down beforehand, who wrote it, or what was made up on the spot. It was all spellbinding and fun.

It was three years later in 1960 on a flight from Los Angeles to New York City that I finally read *On the Road,* for the first time. I recognized passages we had performed together for years. We gave several more readings in 1958 and spent time hanging out whenever he was in New York. In 1959, we collaborated together on the film *Pull My Daisy.* In addition to appearing in the film as Mezz McGillicuddy, the deranged French horn player in the moth eaten sweater, I composed the entire score for the film and wrote the music for the title song "Pull My Daisy" with lyrics by Jack, Neal Cassady, and Allen Ginsberg.

The idea of making a film based on Jack's work was easier to talk about than to actually accomplish. Many people felt that the experience of reading *On the Road* was like watching a film, projected on the screen of your mind, as you devoured the pages of his classic adventure story-poem-novel. All of his writing, like his spontaneous raps, conjured up kaleidescopic imagery that made you feel that you were a member of the cast in a great documentary film about the quintessential America we all longed to be part of. He described everyday occurrences in life as the framework of endless descriptions of places and people we could all relate to. Like most of the high-energy musicians, poets, painters and assorted dreamers we hung out with, Jack relished every precious moment of each day and night. He often told me his books were sight and sound journeys, told in the style of a great jazz solo, to be shared by the readers, joining him on his endless odyssey.

A short time after Anita Ellis had recorded the title song, the film was mixed and we had a screening of *Pull My Daisy*. Afterwards, we were all invited to a cast party, with a lot of other friends to celebrate the film's completion. After a few hours of merriment, Franz Kline stood up and raised his hands for silence. Everyone of us in the room that night, even the most incorrigible egomaniacs and hyperactive nut-cases all paid attention. Franz was one of the people we all respected and admired.

"I want to say a few words to all of you. I congratulate all of you for making a film that brings us all together, and documents some precious moments of everyday life. It shows us as we really are as artists. Hanging on and hanging in and hanging tough. But I don't want to talk about the film. I want to talk about our lives. I'm older than almost all of you. Most of my life I barely got by. Recently, the art scene exploded and I've become a rich man. But my life is not built around fame and money. I was just as good an artist when I painted portraits for a dollar in the Village. Now those portraits are worth thousands. But they're no better or worse than when I drew them to be able to buy myself a meal. They're part of the body of my life's work, a document of my survival.

My older landscapes of Pennsylvania are worth so much now that I have to hide them so I don't get put in an even higher tax bracket. For years, nobody would pay a dime for them. They're still the same paintings. They didn't get any better. I treasure them as much as the recent black and white abstracts that made me famous overnight. What I'm doing now made me a rich man, but all that is beyond my control, and has nothing to do with my work or my commitment. My dealer is furious. I've shown him my latest work.

I'm returning to color. He tells me to ride it out and change when the fashions change. I told him *no!*"

We interrupted Franz with a spontaneous series of cheers.

"Yeah, Franz." "All right." "Right on."

"Sock it to that greedy sucker," shouted Gregory Corso.

"I told my art dealer, 'I paint each picture from my heart.' I've followed my heart all my life. I can't change *that*! And none of you should, either. Don't confuse fame and money with art. Rejoice in your fame if you get any. Spend your money if you get any. But don't *ever* forget what our job is. Don't forget we're in this for *life*! Now as for your film about the Beat Generation, whatever that is, Jack, without you, none of this would have happened. We all know there is no Beat Generation or Beatniks. The *poseurs,* merchandisers and mediocrities that adopt a label to sell what is worthless have a right to live. But let's not confuse fashion with fact. The fact is that *On the Road* is a great book that spoke to people where they live—in their hearts.

Jack, I remember you and Amram performing at the Five Spot and painters' lofts before *On the Road* came out. I remember you, Alfred [Leslie] and Robert [Frank] and Larry [Rivers] from years ago. I know almost all of you in this room.

Let's all thank Jack. He has the cross to bear. He is recognized more for a false image created by a merchandising myth than he is for his true gifts—as an artist. I'm in the same position. I'm no spokesman for Abstract Expressionism, or any other ism. I'm Franz, from a small town in Pennsylvania. Anything people want to know about me they can see in my paintings or read in a library. So, Jack, thank you for making it possible for all of us to be together and make a little film about our lives. I like it. It's simple, fun and unpretentious. And it's in black and white!

Now in order for my wonderful philosophy and sociologic insights to be imprinted forever in your memories. I need a god-damn drink so I can toast you all." Robert poured Franz a tumbler full of Scotch whiskey.

"Here's to *Pull My Daisy*," said Franz, raising his glass. "Here's to Jack Kerouac. Here's to all of you here tonight. And here's to Jackson Pollock and Charlie Parker and Louis Armstrong, King Oliver, Bunk Johnson, Bessie Smith, Bela Bartòk and all those now on the other side in that spirit world. You're in our hearts. You are part of us.

Remember us poor bastards down here and know that we remember you. We're still all sinners, so put in a word for us so we can join you upstairs when our time comes. Here's to life!" Franz gulped down the entire tumbler, and walked over to Jack. He put his arm over Jack's shoulders.

"Jack," he said, "let's show these big-city sophisticates how to party."

As bedlam broke loose, with drinking, smoking, dancing, poetry being read, insults and jokes shouted, bongos, congas, pots and pans being banged and the whole loft shaking with all of us carousing till dawn, I felt the end of an era. I had no idea why, but I think all of us sensed that our underground network of friends, bound together by the desperation of our situation, bonds of mutual compassion and respect that were fragile at best, were now being demolished by changing times.

The fifties were over. The company store had bought up our ideas and repackaged them into an image so horrific that we realized that we were no longer welcome unless we wanted to join the charade. I think Robert and Alfred knew better than Jack and I why *Pull My Daisy* should be made. As Robert said, with *Pull My Daisy* we captured a moment in time.

In 1960, a year after *Pull My Daisy* came out and Jack had heard the finished score, he reminded me of our idea in 1957 of writing a symphonic piece for chorus, soloists and orchestra, along, with a band and guest artists.

"I love the counterpoint and voicings in *Pull My Daisy,* with the alto sax, English horn, viola and bassoon," said Jack. "Imagine if we had a whole symphony and chorus."

"Someday we will," I said.

In 1964 I finally had the chance to write a piece I knew would get performed for chorus, soloists and orchestra, where I could honor Jack's words in a formal written-down, thoroughly composed orchestral work. We talked about it one night, when he stayed at my tiny triangular shaped apartment on Sixth Avenue. Since he loved the classical European tradition in music as much as I did, he liked the idea of a cantata for chorus and orchestra that was inspired by Vivaldi's "The Four Seasons." I told him my cantata, "A Year in Our Land," would celebrate the four seasons in America, and each of the four seasons would be set in a different part of the country. Jack suggested about fifty books to read, and wrote the names of them all down. After long days and nights of reading, I found my texts for the cantata "A Year in Our Land." I thanked Jack for his suggestions of books to read and told him what I had selected.

The "Prologue" was by James Baldwin, sung by the chorus and accompanied by the orchestra. "Spring in the East" was set for soprano soloist and orchestra, featuring the strings of the orchestra, with texts by John Dos Passos. "Summer in the West" would be set for a tenor soloist, featuring the woodwinds of the orchestra, from excerpts of *The Lonesome Traveler* by Jack. "Fall in the North" would be set for an alto soloist featuring the brass of the orchestra, with selections from John Steinbeck's *Travels with Charlie.* "Winter in the South" would be set for a bassbaritone soloist featuring the percussion with excerpts from portions of Thomas Wolfe's *The Web and the Rock.* The cantata would conclude with an "Epilogue" using part of Walt Whitman's poem, "Take my Leaves, America," with all four soloists accompanied by their respective choirs of the orchestra all joining with the chorus for a triumphant conclusion. The chorus would participate throughout the cantata, sometimes accompanying the soloists and with solo passages of their own.

"Do it!" said Jack. "Stick to your guns!"

I thought of Jack as I composed the cantata. All the conversations about our respective travels, all the adventures, dreams, flavors, smells, sounds, and people he met and wrote about, and all the places I had been and people I had played with and for inspired me. I thought about the great times we had together as I composed and orchestrated the cantata. Sometimes, when Jack would visit, I would sit at the piano, pounding away and croaking out as best I could the passages for the chorus and soloists and try to sing some of the virtuosic interludes composed for the orchestra alone. Occasionally, after a few drinks, he would join in. He had such a remarkable ear he could remember portions that I had sung to him over the phone or played on a previous visit, and sing them with me, even though I could only play a rough outline of what these portions of the cantata would sound like. His phenomenal memory of conversations extended to his encyclopedic knowledge of music. Anything he heard once could be instantly recalled.

We always had a great time together and always had fun. Jack remained a purist and an idealist all of his life. Even though we always ended up laughing, I could see and feel the pain he was experiencing. This was 1964. The new pop culture had become a colossus that seemed intent on simultaneously rewriting history while making a fortune for a handful of entrepreneurs. According to the New Order, no one over thirty was to be trusted. We were informed that jazz was dead, and that novels, symphonies, operas, and acoustic folk music of the world were now all irrelevant. Ironically, Jack was accused of being responsible for all of this, while being called a red-necked reactionary conservative because he refused to go along with it. At the same time, he was reviled by the literary establishment as some kind of a Cro-Magnon Philistine, whose only talent was his ability as a speed demon at the typewriter. As the deposed King of the Beat Generation (a title he abhorred), he was held responsible for the self-indulgent excesses of the 1960s.

"I love America, Davey," he used to say. "Our country created jazz. It gives a place to come to for the wretched of the earth to seek a haven. All of our families came here to join the Indian people in their great circle. Our lost continent, from Canada to Mexico, is precious. I know what's wrong with America. But how can they blame this self-hatred and the exploitation of innocent kids by greedy merchants on Jack Kerouac? Didn't anyone ever *read my books*?"

He felt betrayed by some of his old friends who, because of his refusal to join the tune-in, turn-on, drop-out, LSD Brigade, or because of their jealousy of his past success or their own craziness, were no longer able to support his needs: to be appreciated, respected and loved for the generosity of his spirit, and the enduring value of his work. He felt they were no longer concerned with his vulnerability and the hurt he felt by critical rejection for the most important thing in his life, his writing. I loved his work. All musicians I knew felt the same way. He was the towering figure of our so-called Beat Generation. All of us knew that. And he did not need a Beat Generation to justify his work. He was an eloquent and original voice in American letters, like Mark Twain, Walt Whitman, Carson McCullers, Hemingway, Faulkner or F. Scott Fitzgerald.

We had long since stopped reading and jamming together in public. It was too stressful for Jack. We would go to Lucien Carr's home and play music till dawn, or sneak to the back of the Figaro in the darkest part of the café and do a little impromptu improvisation for college kids who thought we were two over-the-hill Greenwich Village nut-cases, or play at my place.

I could always cheer him up, but I knew his road was a long one, and it would be years before America would appreciate what a treasure he was to the world. I feared he would not live long enough to see his greatness appreciated. Even though I was eight years younger, I was not sure in my heart of hearts that I would be around to see Jack get his due. But I knew then, as I knew when we first worked together, as I knew when I first played with Dizzy Gillespie, Charlie Parker, Thelonious Monk, Charlie Mingus, and when I worked with symphony conductors Dimitri Mitropolous and Leonard Bernstein, or when I collaborated with W.H. Auden and Langston Hughes and Arthur Miller, that I was with someone whose work would *endure forever*. It had nothing to do with fame. Jack was unknown in 1956 when we first got together. It was not about celebrity or fashion. It had to do with being in the presence of greatness that was as pure and simple and brilliant as a bright, cloudless summer day at the beach, when you look at the perfect azure blue of the ocean and the sun's glitter on a wave in the distance almost knocks you over with the power of its reflection.

You can feel this kind of greatness without a word ever being spoken. And the greatness of Jack's writing and purity of his intent all illuminate the pages of his thirty-one published books.

I tried to honor some of that yea-saying positive spirit in my cantata, "A Year in Our Land." The world premiere in 1965 had a rousing reception in New York City's Town Hall, and was later televised in 1968 in a concert where I conducted the Houston Symphony, sponsored by a chain of book stores in Houston to celebrate the publication of my autobiography *Vibrations*, for which Jack had graciously written a quote for the dust jacket. Jack had written me a letter about the cantata, "A Year in Our Land" from Florida in 1965 after I had sent him a tape of the first performance at Town Hall. I told him we would do more together. He saw the 1968 telecast of the piece, and we talked on the phone for nearly two hours. Towards the end of the conversation, I played the horn and piano into the receiver of the telephone which I had tucked between my ear and shoulder so that we could do some long distance improvising together.

"We're still wailing, Jack," I said.

"Ah, Davey, we have to do more," he said. "I'm tired, man. Fame is such a drag."

Thelonious Monk in performance.

I could hear the sadness in his voice, and even though I could still get him to chuckle, I sensed the overwhelming pain that seemed to engulf him. He talked about his new book *Vanity of Duluoz.* He said it was dedicated to his wife Stella Sampas. He told me how she was saving his life and his mother's life.

"Some day, we'll all get together, if you ever settle down and get married, and we can all go off in the mountains, grow our own food, and write an opera and play music with the Indians, while our wives look after our adoring children. Ah-h-h, man. *C'est triste.* No one comes to see me, or calls. Neal's dead. But I'm writing. You'll have to read my new book, Davey. I can still write."

"I know that, Jack. *Bien sûr,*" I said.

"Read it soon, Davey," he said.

He knew I was always years late in reading his books. That was because being with him was exactly like reading his books. Often Jack would read me favorite passages of whatever he had written or was writing over the phone, as he used to do over the years when were together in New York City.

"Some day, Davey, when we're old men, we'll sit in hammocks and rock back and forth, picking our teeth and discussing our life's works. You can read all my published books, and I'll study all your published symphony scores, and we'll show our grandchildren *Pull My Daisy* so that they can see how crazy we were and then we'll play the recordings of our symphonic collaborations and leap from our hammocks to give an impromptu *soiree* seminar on the secret joys of music and poetry, filling the air with Mozartean delights. Ah-h-h *mon Dieu, cher* Davey . . . I feel tired man. Don't lose your energy. Ruskin said, 'An artist burns with a hard and gem-like flame.' Don't let the fire go out! Keep the flame alive."

When Jack finally left us, I could not go to Lowell for the funeral. I knew some people would use it as a media event, leaping in front of the TV cameras, disrespecting his family, his childhood friends and his roots in the place he loved so much, that was so much a part of his essence.

I sat down at the piano and played. I prayed for his soul and said a Kaddish and kissed an old mass card he had given me in 1957. I could hear his voice fill the room. He always retained the music of his Massachusetts accent, the special sounds of Lowell's Little Canada, a sound that still speaks to my heart every day.

In the fall of 1994, twenty-five years after his death, I went to Lowell for the first time. I had been invited to a place I had always wanted to go to. I performed with my quartet and Sioux poet-painter-narrator-architect Geoffrey Carpentier in a concert I dedicated to the memory of Jack presented by Lowell Celebrates Kerouac.

I finally got to meet some of the people he told me about so often through the years. People he grew up with who were his true life-time soulmates.

And I finally met all of Stella Sampas' family, who knew Jack since childhood and always stuck by him, even in the final years when he felt most of the world had abandoned him. Still I felt a warmth and joy I had not felt since Jack had passed away. I finally was in a place where Jack was truly loved and understood.

After I had completed a marathon series of workshops, lectures, and rap sessions in Lowell, as well as schools and universities in the greater Boston area, my quartet came to join me in the celebratory concert dedicated to Jack. They told me after the concert that they could feel Jack's spirit fill the room that night.

Today, my life is filled with joy to see him being honored at last around the world. I try to make young people aware every place I go in my constant concert tours of what Jack was and is still about. And I stay in touch with Carolyn Cassady, Lawrence Ferlinghetti, Alfred Leslie, Dody Müller, Lucien Carr, Gregory Corso, Joyce Johnson, Barney Rossett, Howard Hart, Diane DiPrima, George Plimpton, Sterling Lord and scores of musicians who knew and loved Jack throughout his life and who were always there for him. None of us consider ourselves to be official representatives of the Beat Generation. We all had and have our own lives, but maintain the enduring friendships formed long ago.

I recently included Jack's texts, narrated by master actor E.G. Marshall in a concert at the Kennedy Center, where I conducted members of Washington's National Symphony Orchestra. The Library of Congress had commissioned me to compose a new work for orchestra and narrator, "A Little Rebellion: Thomas Jefferson," using the words of Thomas Jefferson. In addition to the world premiere of this piece, I conducted music of Copland, William Grant Still, Mexico's Carlos

Chavez, and Canada's Sir Ernest McMillan. I suggested since we were celebrating the continental music of the Americas, we should include Jack Kerouac. We should have E.G. Marshall narrating Jefferson's words with music in the first half of the program, and have him narrate Kerouac in the second half, also accompanied by the National Symphony, with music I had composed. There was one section where I played piano and flutes, alone, as I did with Jack.

I had done readings in Central Park in the 1960s with E.G. Marshall. He made it easy with his effortless style. He is the quintessential American actor and an avid scholar of American letters. E.G. said he wanted to bring a spontaneous feeling to the Kennedy Center performance.

"I like the idea, David. Having you conduct the orchestra accompanying Kerouac's words in some of the selections from *On the Road* and then having you jump off the podium and play some jazz or whatever you feel at the moment behind my narration. We'll give 'em hell at the Kennedy Center and still make them feel like they're in heaven. Jefferson and Kerouac. Makes perfect sense to me. And the spontaneous aspect will give the audience what they need—a certain intimacy we had in the 1930s when I was a young actor. When the theater was a personal experience, and every member of the audience felt they were an integral part of an experience they knew was happening just for them at that moment, an experience they shared that would never happen again. Let's do it!"

E.G. Marshall read the parts of *On the Road* with the same fervor and dignity that he had imbued Jefferson's texts with, and the audience loved it. At the postconcert reception in the Green Room, a distinguished-looking woman with immaculately coifed white hair, wearing a lovely green evening gown, approached me.

"Maestro Amram, may I trouble you for a moment to tell you I never knew Mr. Kerouac (I do hope I'm pronouncing his name correctly) wrote in such a lovely descriptive style. His portrayal of the Rocky Mountains reminded me of how lovely it is to be in the West in the summer. I do thank you for a most enjoyable and unusual evening. I'm a member of friends of the Kennedy Center. We need to have more programs like this that honor our native-born artists. This was certainly different from the all-Beethoven program I heard recently."

As I shook her hand and thanked her, and began talking about Jack, she eyeballed my necklace of beads I wear at every concert and public performance around the world. My white tie and tails were immaculate, and my hair was short, but she still was trying to adjust to the necklace of amulets, all gifts from people around the world I had strung together around to bring good luck to everybody, everywhere I go. I continued telling her of how E.G. and I thought Thomas Jefferson and Jack Kerouac belonged together.

"I always associated Mr. Kerouac with a more, how should I say, *primitive* style of writing. To my surprise, I found his work quite touching. Your music was marvelous and the new composition commissioned by the Library of Congress was *smashing*. Bravo! I also enjoyed the little moment of jazz when you accompanied Mr. Marshall during the recitation of Mr. Kerouac's description of George Shearing performing. It was so evocative. It reminded me of music I heard played by the natives when my husband was the American Consul-General in Tobago. Those native boys have such *rhythm!* Do you play weddings?"

"Only for old friends," I said. "I don't know all the new songs young couples want to hear nowadays. But I do appreciate your asking."

"Very diplomatic maneuvering," E.G. Marshall whispered to me when the woman left the Green Room.

I am still collaborating with Jack, in a series of projects produced by his nephew Jim Sampas. We used Jack's words and my music for part of a CD-rom of Jack's life's work. We also did an audio book for Viking-Penguin. Graham Parker narrated *Visions of Cody.* I created the musical accompaniment, using all my instruments, to give different colors to the different passages. Graham read three hundred pages of text, all accompanied by music I made up on the spot. We did the entire recording in a day-and-a-half. Graham Parker would show me what he was going to read, I would make an instant decision of what instrument to play and go for it. Forty years later, the same fire was there. Jack's words and spirit told me what to do.

"Jim, it would take me a year of uninterrupted composing to write this much music," I said.

"How do you do it?" said Jim.

"I don't know," I said. "I just listen to Kerouac's words and go for it. That's the way we did it in the fifties. Sink or swim. After all these years, desperation is still the mother of invention."

I reminded Jim Sampas of how much Jack wanted to have *Visions of Cody* published. As hard

as he tried, he could never act to see this monumental work issued in print during his lifetime.

"It's with us now," I said to Jim. "And it won't go out of print." "I know," said Jim. "It's being read all over the world, and being translated in several languages."

I am currently composing a new work, commissioned by flutist James Galway, entitled "Giants of the Night." The three movements are dedicated to bassist Oscar Pettiford, author Jack Kerouac, and Dizzy Gillespie. I worked with all three of these giants, and Jack was with me on occasions when I played with Oscar and Dizzy. They knew him, cared for him, and read his books. I am also setting Jack's words to music in a new choral composition, and writing a new work for narrator and orchestra, using Jack's texts. His words still tell me what to do.

Jim Sampas is also completing a new CD of Jack's work, using old tapes, never heard before, of Jack himself reading. I am providing the musical accompaniment in the same way I always did for Jack—spontaneously.

Sometimes when I am composing, I spend a whole day writing and re-writing one measure of music, to get it just right. My orchestral scores are impeccable. I spend most of my commission money having the scores and parts copied and recopied, with every tiny nuance, tempo change, metronome marking, dynamic and phrase clearly indicated. But the *music,* the breathing, living, human, mystical, mysterious part comes *naturally.* That naturalness is what Jack and I strived for when we performed together. When we wrote alone we created formal works (his books and my symphonies) inspired by the natural energy of these real-life experiences. When we performed together, we were celebrating the moment, dealing with the informal, and daring to improvise like tight-rope walkers. We wanted to create formal works, built to last, that retained this same energy. That is what we were all about. That was the basis of our friendship and our work together.

When I go to high schools, colleges or any place where there are young people today, they all know who Jack Kerouac is. None of them have ever told me they thought he was the King of the Beatniks. A great many of them tell me that *they read his books.*

That is Jack's ultimate triumph. His work speaks for itself. I hope, as I know Jack always did, that young people who dream must know that each of them and each of their dreams are precious, and like enduring friendships must never have their flame extinguished.

Until the very end, through all the pain and rejection, Jack continued to write. When I talked to him on the phone in those last sad months, in late-night earlymorning phone calls, he still spoke of work he had to do, and dreams he wished to fulfill.

I feel blessed and lucky to still be here. I try every day to share the joy of seeing my own dreams in music finally coming true as I approach seventy. I also try every day, in some small way, to share that gift of Jack's spirit, energy and human kindness with everyone I meet. As a giant of twentieth century letters, Jack's work can enable future generations to look back on the second half of the twentieth century and see the beauty part.

When Jack and I used to talk about his desire to find his lost Canadian-Indian heritage, I reminded him of the Navajo Prayer of the Twelfth Night. How the men and women prayed to walk on the trail of beauty. I sang him some of the old songs I had learned from Native American musicians. Jack and I both prayed in different languages, but the trail of beauty remained the same. Many of us walked and still walk that trail today. It is accessible to anyone and it is endless, and if you stand tall as Jack did throughout his life, and walk that trail of beauty, you will surely meet him there some day.

DAVID MELTZER (ESSAY DATE 2001)

SOURCE: Meltzer, David. "Poetry and Jazz." In *Beat Down to Your Soul: What Was the Beat Generation,* edited by Ann Charters, pp. 397-406. New York: Penguin, 2001.

In the following essay, Meltzer combines memories of listening to music in the Beat era and criticism of the assimilation of Beat style and jazz style into the mainstream. Meltzer writes in a quasi-Beat style and consciously avoids ascribing too much meaning or clarity to the phenomenon of the Beats' jazz-poetry fusion.

Text

1.

Okay what was poetry & jazz all about? how was it done? who did it? did it really make it? Nobody knows its origins while many claim to be its progenitor: Rexroth says he did it in Chicago with Jelly Roll Morton in the late 20s early 30s; ruth weiss claims to have started it all in 1946 in New Orleans; Vachel Lindsay in the 20s with his "fat black bucks . . . boomalay boomalay" and

"Daniel Jazz" (with marginalia cueing the jazz band); Langston Hughes did it in Harlem during the 20s Renaissance. Maybe it's all moot or, as they used to say in the 50s, "a matter of semantics." Poets have been singing their stuff probably starting in the caves moving into Babylonia Mesopotamia *shir hasharim* Bible plains chanting Kali and Kwan-Yin mantrum and plectrum Sapphic lyre into qawalli singing Sufis rapidfire fanning gutstrings duende cante troubadour courts of tzaddikim ecstatic upholding the universe *nigunim* into Brit balladeers across winter drifts to Schoenberg's *sprechstimme* and Louis Armstrong's amnesia inspired *Heebie Jeebies* 1926 glossolalia; Edith Sitwell ratatatat to *Facade* Walton's teadance jazz band hotcha; the Weimar cabaret and pop operas like Ernst Krenek's *Jonny spielt auf* in 1926, Kurt Weill and Bert Brecht's 1928 *Die Dreigroschenoper,* it's rumored Jean Cocteau played a mean drum kit in Paris Jazz Age joints. How about Gilbert & Sullivan, especially the "patter songs"? The Zurich Dada art demolition derby Cabaret Voltaire cats like Tzara? The "talking blues" form made popular in the Popular Front days of the 40s by Woody Guthrie? From Africa West to Delta South to Kansas City to Broadway, through blues griots, post-pogrom Jews Hart, Gershwin, Berlin, Dorothy Fields, Harburg, African-American poet James Weldon Johnson, Andy Razaf; Duke's recitatives; swing shift into bop mad mouths: Babs Gonsalves Leo Watson Slim Gaillard "putty putty"; acoustic blues poets like Robert Johnson, Blind Willie McTell; urban electric bluesmen like Little Walter, Howling Wolf; the constant stream of rural poetry from poet-singers called hillbilly, cowboy, country—like Jimmie Rodgers and Hank Williams; you get the drift? Post WW2 glossolaliacal Letterists led by Isidore Isou (which rooted into the late 60's Situationist International)? Any way you look at it (or hear it), we're dealing with kinds of song and we all know poetry started as song before being silenced, stamped into paper into a shut book, and another long history of enchantment, *encantare*. So, again, what is this thing called poetry and jazz? "What is this thing called love?"

2.

Okay, what was poetry and jazz in the halcyon daze of the Beat 50s in 'Frisco? Essentially it was poets holding onto the paper of their poems as cripts and cribs to recite to the accompaniment of a small jazz group. Flip the coin and clear the table. It's confession time. In the late 50s, as a lad, I too read my poems to jazz at The Jazz Cellar in North Beach; the same place Ferlinghetti and Rexroth strutted their stuff at. (Also Rod McKuen.

He'd sometime do Sunday afternoon performances which I regret I never attended.) I was a kid, a bebop true believer barely drinking age, while the poets on stage were, jeez, fuckin' middle-aged. The Beats were over-the-hill guys; they didn't, like, swing. Rexroth, Ferlinghetti, and Kenneth Patchen read alerting and often alarming words while the musicians played in the background. Listen to the "live" Fantasy recordings of Rexroth and Ferlinghetti. Both are formidable poets, public charmers and disarmers, but neither seemed connected to the jazz comped behind their words. The words came first, music second. As a greenhorn poet, my jazz poets were singers. Whatever poetry was it wasn't jazz. Jazz was dialogic not logocentric.

The impact of jazz and jazz culture on European and American poets, writers, artists, musicians, was permanently profound; the idiom signified new freedoms and permission to pilfer and transform, create and recreate a fantasy of slavery redeemed by white folk into masks of modernism. The new gets old as soon as it's announced as the new. Haute yearns to get down as long as they can take a cab back home. Both blacks and whites in the States took jazz and blues as an outcast (and cast away) art more profound than the uptown thunder of concert halls.

Barry Wallenstein writes, "The performance of jazz is not unlike the performing language of poetry, one could note how improvised solos break away from the original harmonic and melodic structure. Similarly, in much of modern poetry, especially free verse, the range of improvisatory gesture is immense."[1] The writing process is solitary confinement, silent, on the page, the inward jumps and skips serve the page. When the poet performs words on the page it's like a musician reading sheet music. But it's not the same; it's a different creative act. Poet and musician are interpreting marks on paper, but they're not improvising, i.e., inventing on the spot alternate ways of expressing words and music, creating new moments in time that are ineffable and beyond captivity.

Back to North Beach

During the quick burnout of the Beat moment in the late 50s, greenbacks galore were made off a dissident anti-materialist movement, just as now nouveaux techno riche resell the Beat thing. Then entreprenurial zeal flourished in hit-&-run boutiques, galleries, cafes, opened up and down Grant Avenue (like today's Valencia Street yuppie glut of high-end 50s redux shoppes, pubic goatees, exotic dogs, multicultural themepark eateries, shades, capris, beanbag chairs, &c., all further oversold by umbilical computer throb lines). Daily Gray Line Bus tours to North "Beat" Beach, and on weekends, suburban beatnik wannabes donned black tights, berets, shades, goatees, bongos, and in nervous fibrillating groups ventured into the go-man-go vortex, often predated on by hipster slicksters and tricksters. Hey, baby, it's the looks (style, surface), not the books.

By the way, nostalgia.com tripsters, the 50s expressed and repressed the death of Western Civ revealed in Hiroshima, Nagasaki, and the Holocaust. Business was good; a startlingly abundant postwar economy after the Great Depression and its antidote World War 2. Affordable incredible stuff shaped out of new cheap malleable materials; insaturation of a creditcard economy, a buy-now-pay-later trance triggered by motivationally researched ads (concocted by Leftist European exiles from Fascism), the rise of advertising as a major cultural power. And, uh, the fabulous Cold War, the Military Industrial Complex, Reds versus Feds, decades of top-down crunching of any or all dissent. Ah, the "cool" Fifties.

3.

In the late 50s Jonathan Williams, publisher of trailblazing Jargon Press (early publishers of Olson's *Maximus,* Creeley, Mina Loy, Lorine Neidecker, Stuart Z. Perkoff, &c.), drove a van through the States peddling his books to likely bookstores, art galleries, eccentrics, and rank strangers. He parked his van on La Cienega before the Ferus Gallery where Ed Keinholz, Bob Alexander and Walter Hopps struggled to curate the premiere avant-garde gallery in Los Angeles, site of Andy Warhol's first West Coast show and Wallace Berman's first public one-man show. I used to hang out there, a scussy 19-year-old poet from Brooklyn in exile. Went with Jonathan and a crew of others on a field trip to Venice, California to visit Lawrence Lipton, P. T. Barnum of the "Venice West" sideshow. Lipton, from Lodsz, had been a newspaperman with a street-smart desire for the uptown heights of Literature. Cigar clenched between choppers, Lipton proclaimed the coming revolution of the word, a world of voice spooled out of reel-to-reel tapes and the relatively recent LP. His book of toney *National Enquirer* wireservice Walter Winchell dit dit dot dot on the Venice enterprise, *The Holy Barbarians,* celebrated dissident stirrings with a rapt prose adhering to Euro-Romantic fixation with the heroic Self. The proviso was that he, Maestro Lipton, was the Toscanini or DeMille of the project. All would ultimately follow his lead as capo of the spoken word, jazz & poetry crusade. Man, books were dead, obsolete; the poet had better get with it and jam the jive and riff the raff. He proceded to perform his poetry which was, alas, cornball. The *poete maudit* hipster subcult of Venice was more realized by Stuart Z. Perkoff and his posse of Frank Rios and Tony Scibella. But these, again, were younger guys, hipsters, and deep into the subculture which, in those days, meant drugs as much as jazz as much as art. The profound and influential artist of that time and geography was Wallace Berman whose mantra was, loud and proud, "Art Is Love Is God." As I recall, the Southland was a great place for image; movie folks and artists did well. Not young bebop baptized poets.

4.

Exiled from Brooklyn to L.A. in '54, left for S.F. in '57. With a crew of hungry poets and artists, we spent all night hanging the annual art show at L.A.'s Barnsdell Park, were paid cash under the table and fed breakfast at the house of some hip Board member, and cut loose. Berman and I were driven to Burbank Airport to hop a cheapo Pacific Air flight to 'Frisco. He was going for a long weekend, I was going to stay. Had a job waiting at Paper Editions as a warehouse worker through Norman Rose, managing the operation, whose "pad" he graciously let me stay in. (It was a former radio repair shop on Larkin Street near California. I slept in the window counter, the window covered with ricepaper slapped into place with a mixture of Wilhold and water. We had a toilet and a sink and $25 monthly rent. Not much else.) In those days you could go to the plane toilet and turn on and zone out gazing through a round glass porthole. (People smoked cigarettes everywhere. It was the rule of cool and the law of the land. There was even a cigarette called "Kools.") A full moon night. When herb's bell rang, Luna was cushioned by dark cloudbanks lacked with radiant edges, shining like a radium watchface.

5.

The Jazz Cellar was a basement club on Green Street off Grant Avenue. The long staircase leading down to it took up more space than the club itself which was a narrow room with a bar on one side, a row of tables and chairs on the other side, and a small stage where the band played. When I started there on an off-night in 1958, the house band consisted of Bill Weisjahn, piano, Max Hartstein, drums, and club-owner Sonny Wayne,

drums, with regular appearances by valve trombonist Frank Phipps and multi-reed player Leo Wright.

What happened when it happened? I'd make a "head arrangement" of my poems, i.e., a spine of elements, incomplete clues and prompts (like filecards or a fakebook) in order to improvise beyond the finished entity set deep on the page. (If poetry is the page, ideally poetry and jazz should be beyond the page. A potential form, open ended, dependent on the interactions of musical elements in musician and poet. We'll get back to that.)

I'd indicate the tempo and general ozone of sound like blues, samba, or generic bebop ballad, and tell the bass to walk the first chorus, followed by the drum in dialogue with the bass, then the piano's chorus in a trio format before jumping in for my chorus. We'd improvise, stretching out choruses until each of us said our say and could bring the work to a close. Sometimes it would be voice and drum or bass and voice, pushing each other into deeper dialogue. That was always the key to the process. Whatever would happen was unknown yet entered into with faith to knowing. Irregardless. No different than any kind of ordinary profound. Equilibrium, the dream. Receiving and transmitting all at once; shaping and being shaped.

Ah the good old bad old days. Maybe I got $20 a night at The Cellar, a once a week gig, which went for the usual fuel: cigarettes, rent, biscotti, Chinatown feasts on the cheap (another story). As a poet in those days I was too young to know much except the pulse of music and the often inscrutable paradox of words on paper and their shape-shifting flux of meaning. My workingclass immigrant Brooklyn popularfront coming of age propelled both by Old World and New World energies: *shtetl* orthodox Judaism and CP/USA storefront; Euro classical music and High Culture backup systems back to back (or toe to toe) with Boogie Woogie, Duke Ellington, Bebop, hipster culture, comicbooks, radio, movies, and sanctuary in Public Libraries, pushed me out into a new world that ultimately couldn't renew itself, fixed as it was in irreconcilable oppositions made more acute in 1945 in the faces of the Holocaust, Hiroshima and Nagasaki.

6.

As the beboppers turned pop music and blues inside-out to create an avant-garde, the "Beats" turned the Euro-American modernist avant-garde into a populist movement. One of the Beats' more radical gestures was returning poetry to people, not academicians and New Critic Calvinists. The beboppers, in turn, took jazz away from the body, the dance floor, into the mind of a seated person in a club digging the music as if in Carnegie Hall deep into a Bartók string quartet. The very body and spontaneity white Beat poets celebrated and fetishized in African-American expressivity, black Bebop innovators were relocating into a new formalism. The Beats claimed both a disaffiliated and populist stance even though most of the movement's assigned progenitors were as traditionally literary as the Enemy, as well as privileged. The difference was seeking acceptance by rejecting the accepted. A familiar strategy. Yesterday's anti-boogy warriors become today's high culture heroes for the class they violated and desecrated. Masochism, schism, or flux? Bebop led the way to Free Jazz and the Black Arts movements which was a slave rebellion in the '60s out of the familiar unresolved politics of race and art. From these movements emerged a new jazz and poetry more connected to a renewed populist energy multicultural gumbo of inner-city creativity and defiance which turned on and nourished not only mall malaise but became a global phenomena thanks to increasingly affordable technologies. Like Reggae, hip-hop is insurgent pleasure; agit-prop where the rapper, the MC, the word wizard, holds forth against the beats and mixes of the DJ. It's what jazz and poetry fussed with and pretended but never owned. Baraka, Jayne Cortez, Gil Scott-Heron, The Last Poets, KRS-1, NWA, Michael Frante, Sistah Souljah, are just some of the different generations of performers, stylists doing it. Much of the groundwork for hip-hop was mulched by The Black Arts movement in the 60s, one that also worked to unite factions and redefine cultural perimeters in the same way the Beat moment worked. But the Black Arts movement was never accorded the ever increasing cultural value that the Beats have accumulated.

7.

Am flown down to Hollywood by Jim Dickson, owner and producer of Vaya Records, Lord Buckley's first label. I'm 22 and it's 1959. Miles Davis and Coltrane are on Columbia. Bird's been dead four years. My first book of poetry has been printed (a two-fer shared with Donald Schenker's first book), hand-set by Don and Alice Schenker on the late Weldon Kees's press in a Potrero Hill basement. I knew Jim in L.A. earlier when he was married to the actress Diane Varsi, who I knew through Dean Stockwell. I remember Dean, Diane

and yours truly going to a Hollywood Boulevard movie house to see a restored print of *Citizen Kane,* the same theater I earlier saw the first run of *Salt of the Earth* before it was sucked into McCarthy era anticommunist limbo.

Jim had caught me at The Cellar and set me up to perform a one-nighter at the Club Renaissance on Sunset Boulevard and do an after-hours recording session. Flew down with a handful of books to sell in the club's store and did a two-set gig.

You've got to visualize the Renaissance. It was sunk beneath the lip of a hill on Sunset and its rear was a glass Cinemascope panorama scoping out nighttime L.A. From The Cellar to the Renaissance. Top of the world, ma.

In the band was Allan Eager, a tenor sax hero of mine, and Bob Dorough was the pianist, but I draw a blank on the bass player and drummer. To be trading fours with these guys was astounding. Lots of glitter in the house. Show biz hipsters, actors, artists; it was (ugh) an "in" place. This was the moment of James Dean and Brando where the "movie star" was now an Artist, no longer a plank of glitter meat for an eroding Studio system evaporating into TV's reign of error.

An opulently huge space, lit seductively to create intimacy in between sets. A massive bar and barfood I couldn't imagine. (Earlier, when I lived in L.A. I'd go with other scroungy writer types to Rand's Round Up, "All You Can Eat" for something like $1.98, for our daily meal. We worked out a wolfish strategy: go for the high protein meats, fowl and fish, and hedge on easy landfill of potato salad, macaroni, rolls, fries, onion rings, &c. We figured the meat cost more than the rest of it and in our own way we were beating the system and denting the profit of Rand's Round Up.)

Each set was an awakening; we'd assign each poem to blues and standards whose changes had gotten innate for me, or freeform. Count tempo down and, bam! move into it. Permutations of vocal and instrumental solos, duos, ensemble riffing. When the club closed we recorded a group of poems for an LP to be issued by Vaya Records.

In dawn's early blight Jim and I went to his place to drink and smoke weed. He was a WW2 vet who came back to a United States that was sleepwalking into an immensely reductive paradigm shift of stupefying abundance and regulation. Even rebellion became market managed. He was a founding member of the Hell's Angels, composed mostly of vets who had nothing left to gain, deracinated by the moral contradictions of War and amped up in the face of a sleepy postwar world and its fatuous denial of complicity in the collapse of Western Civ.

Little sleep that night and then off to Burbank to catch my PSA flight back to the Bay Area.

Net result: a few books sold at the club and a toecurling acetate sent to us weeks later. It wasn't the music or spirit of the voice but my dorky poetry.

8.

What came first: the beatnik or the image of the beatnik? Not a trick question. The word was coined, as our forebears remind us, by S.F. *Chronicle* columnist Herb Caen c. 1958, whose daily local chitchat column was the Bay Area version of Walter Winchell's Manhattan daily must-read. The moniker was a play on coldwar panic around the arms and space race, directly referring to the Soviet Union's 1957 satellite "sputnik" which means "fellow traveler of Earth." It was a panic play on rebellion and nonconformity, diminishment via mockery, like "yuppie." It also intended to dis suburban effluvia seeking kicks in North Beach, i.e., "slumming." Paradoxically, it minted a new identity one could grow into and out of at a moment's notice. A new and renewable archetype, a mask, a comicbook safe house called "beatnik."

9.

In media's magic-act of erasing difficulty, the beatnik became a hipster Mickey Mouse whose four white minstrel gloved fingers on each hand emanated immense cuddly safety, not danger. Maynard G. Krebs, highschool beatnik jazzhead whose mantra yelp "Work?" made clear his shiftlessness and de facto that of the beatnik or artist. Then the generic anonymous jazz-poet dressed in black turtleneck, beret, shades, pants, riffing to a beat bongo player's laidback paradiddles at Mother's waterfront dive in *Peter Gunn* or in *Mad Comics* or *The New Yorker*. The instantly camp flicks: as a young hipster & disdainful beatnik, movies like *The Man with the Golden Arm* and *The Subterraneans* were sublimely unauthentic, especially the M.G.M.ing of Kerouac's novella which premiered in San Francisco. Local poets, artists, beatniks, & other marginals & harmless colorful folk were given free passes to attend the opening. We sauntered into the red plush carpet of the Warfield Theater & laughed ourselves to near puke at the idiocy on the screen: a bent remix of Judy

Garland/Mickey Rooney movies with Leslie Caron as Judy, Mickey played by George Peppard wearing the same dazed preppy Wildroot glaze as in *Breakfast at Tiffany's* (another fiction deprogrammed by Metro) pretending to be Jack Kerouac. The City Lights Bookstore set came off the same backlot street Gene Kelly danced & sang in the rain upon. Literal bends set in when Gerry Mulligan pretended to be a paper doll pastiche of Pierre Delattre, Grant Avenue's Bread & Wine Mission minister. The obligatory jazz club scene in mandatory smoke smogged haze as beat poet Roddy McDowall, a giggly graft of Corso and Ginsberg, incants irate yet inexplicable Them/Us (Squares v. Hip) verse. Everpresent cool dude bangs bacchantic on a pair o' bongos; another remote cat bends over his tenor sax, another burrows into the piano, forehead almost touching the keyboard. The poet and jazz trope also trooped into comicbooks, pop music, op-ed cartoons, in the same way hip-hop does today. But what was it and—was it? It was, it wasn't, just like the "Beat Generation" was and wasn't. As always the past is more "now" than it was then. . . .

On the other hand, poetry & jazz (whatever it is) hasn't gone away and is always more or less than it's imagined to be. If the 50s poets were vanguardists, all that's followed in its wake is worthy of regard: freeform radio, adverts, hip hop, spoken word, the mainstreaming of cowboy poetry, poetry slams, presidential townhall debates, wherever words with insinuating beats and musical MSG are agents of seduction and transformation. The edge of the word, its utopic anger and optimism, coexists with its evil twin in a cacophony of power and powerlessness, smeared and glossed by a massive unmeaning making industry; where the word wounded, it is now affirms, reassures; where history had the potential for insight it now is cataracted by hindsight and certainty. When it gets down to essentials, whatever was Beat—the gesture of reading poetry to jazz as an act of inconclusive solidarity—resonates in different currents and will continue to mutate despite the fact that nobody was or will be sure about what it was when it was and what it is when it is and what is left.

Note

1. "Poetry and Jazz: A Twentieth Century Wedding," by Barry Wallenstein in *Black American Literature Forum*. Volume 25, Number 3, 1991; p. 595. One of the more astute takes on the genre.

FURTHER READING

Biographies

Buhle, Paul, and Dave Wagner. *A Very Dangerous Citizen: Abraham Lincoln Polonsky and the Hollywood Left.* Berkeley: University of California Press, 2001, 275 p.

Biography of Polonsky, including discussion of blacklisting of Hollywood authors and directors for their political beliefs. Includes bibliographical references and index.

Eisenschitz, Bernard. *Nicholas Ray: An American Journey,* translated by Tom Milne. London and Boston: Faber and Faber, 1993, 599 p.

Biography of Ray, including criticism and analysis of his ouevre. Includes bibliographical references and filmography.

Goldman, Albert. *Ladies and Gentlemen: Lenny Bruce!* New York: Random House, 1971, 565 p.

Biography of Lenny Bruce, a controversial comedian associated with the Beat Generation.

Heylin, Clinton. *Bob Dylan: Behind the Shades.* New York: William Morrow, 2001, 780 p.

A critically acclaimed, expanded revision of Heylin's 1991 book of the same title that provides a detailed, comprehensive overview and analysis of Dylan's life and career from the 1940s to 2001.

Priestley, Brian. *Mingus: A Critical Biography.* London: Quartet Books, 1982, 308 p.

Full-length biography of Mingus, including a compilation of critical response to his music.

Reisner, Rob George. *Bird: The Legend of Charlie Parker.* New York: Citadel Press, 1962, 256 p.

Full-length biography. Depicts Parker's life and career and includes first-hand information from friends, family, and peers.

Shelton, Robert. *No Direction Home: The Life and Music of Bob Dylan.* Cambridge: DaCapo Press, 1997, 573 p.

Full-length biography of Bob Dylan.

Van der Bliek, Rob, editor. *The Thelonious Monk Reader.* Oxford University Press, 2001, 320 p.

Full-length, comprehensive biography of Monk's life and career.

Criticism

Beard, William. *The Artist as Monster: The Cinema of David Cronenberg.* Toronto: University of Toronto Press, 2001, 469 p.

An academic examination of many of Cronenberg's films through 1996.

————. "Insect Poetics: Cronenberg's *Naked Lunch.*" *Canadian Review of Comparative Literature* 23, no. 3 (September 1996): 823-52.

Examines the common themes in the work of director David Cronenberg and author William S. Burroughs. Beard focuses on Naked Lunch, *but also looks at other works by the two men, noting Cronenberg's artistic debt to Burroughs as well as the points at which the director diverges from Burroughs's vision.*

Ellison, James, editor, and Bob Dylan. *Younger than that Now: The Collected Interviews with Bob Dylan.* New York: Thunder's Mouth Press, 2003, 400 p.

Collection of interviews with Dylan ranging from the 1960s to 2001. Ellison aims to provide an overview of Dylan's personal and artistic development.

Gill, Andy. "Bob Dylan." In *Don't Think Twice, It's All Right: Bob Dylan, The Early Years,* pp. 9-16. New York: Thunder's Mouth Press, 1998.

Relates Dylan's introduction to the music business, including his meetings with record company executive John Hammond and folk icon Woody Guthrie. As Gill notes, Dylan's career began as folk music was assuming greater popularity and credibility in bohemian and Beat culture.

Grant, Michael, editor. *The Modern Fantastic: The Films of David Cronenberg.* Westport, Conn.: Praeger, 2000, 217 p.

Collection of seven critical essays that examines Cronenberg's complete career. Includes an interview with Cronenberg, a full filmography, and a bibliography.

Klinger, Barbara. *Melodrama and Meaning: History, Culture, and the Films of Douglas Sirk.* Bloomington: Indiana University Press, 1994, 200 p.

A full-length analysis of Sirk's career, including the historical and cultural influences on works, focusing particularly on his use of melodrama. Includes a filmography and bibliographic references.

Kofsky, Frank. *Lenny Bruce: The Comedian as Social Critic and Secular Moralist.* New York: Monad Press, 1974, 128 p.

Investigates the impact of Lenny Bruce on American culture.

Malcolm, Douglas. "'Jazz America': Jazz and African American Culture in Jack Kerouac's *On the Road.*" *Contemporary Literature* 40, no. 1 (spring 1999): 85-110.

Considers the influence of jazz improvisation on the experimental narrative style of On the Road.

Mullins, Patrick. "Hollywood and the Beats: MGM Does Kerouac's *The Subterraneans.*" *Journal of Popular Film and Television* 29, no. 1 (spring 1992): 32-41.

Surveys the mainstream representation of Beats in film and television, focusing on the Hollywood production of Kerouac's novel The Subterraneans.

Rodriguez, Elena. *Dennis Hopper: A Method to His Madness,* pp. 55-66. New York: St. Martin's Press, 1988.

Chronicles the filming and impact of Dennis Hopper's film Easy Rider; *Hopper is a noted associate of San Francisco "Beat" artist Bruce Conner.*

Sterritt, David. "Social Criticism." In *Mad to Be Saved: The Beats, the '50s, and Film,* pp. 83-123. Carbondale: Southern Illinois University Press, 1998.

Surveys the relationship between film and Beat literature with a focus on photographers and filmmakers who highlighted the darker side of American life.

Thomas, Lorenzo. "'Communicating by Horns': Jazz and Redemption in the Poetry of the Beats and the Black Arts Movement." *African American Review* 26, no. 2 (summer 1992): 291-8.

Maintains that both Beat poets and writers of the later Black Arts movement viewed jazz as a potential medium for liberation. Thomas is mildly critical of the Beats for their sometimes-unthinking imitation of Black stereotypes and argues for the importance of the Black poet Bob Kaufman in influencing the style of white Beat writers.

Thomas, Tony. *The Films of Marlon Brando.* Secaucus, N.J.: Citadel Press, 1973, 243 p.

Collection of critical essays on Brando's cinematic oeuvre.

Tynan, Kenneth. Foreword to *How to Talk Dirty and Influence People: An Autobiography,* by Lenny Bruce, pp. vi-xi. New York: AMS Press, 1972.

Calls the comedian Lenny Bruce "a night-club Cassandra bringing news of impending chaos, a tightrope walker between morality and nihilism, a pearl miscast before swine."

Woideck, Carl, editor. *The Charlie Parker Companion: Six Decades of Commentary.* New York: Schirmer Books, 1998, 294 p.

Collected critical analyses of Parker's musical achievements. Includes bibliographical references, index, and discography.

VISUAL ARTS AND THE BEAT GENERATION

The relationship between Beat literature and the visual arts mirrors the relationship the Beats had with other areas of society. While such famous Beat authors as Jack Kerouac, Allen Ginsberg, and William S. Burroughs demanded attention for their work, they were not necessarily the first advocates or practitioners of the artistic philosophy that came to be associated with Beat writers. However, the notoriety they gained as well as the media attention their actions and work generated allowed other artists, who had hitherto been working outside the mainstream, opportunities to merge into a larger alternative movement that revolutionized art and literature. Although many artists and painters clearly affiliated themselves with the Beats, others had philosophical common ground with them—for example, they, too, wanted to use their art in new and nontraditional ways, rebelling against established standards, and working to bring "high" art to ordinary people by addressing subjects relevant to society in their own works. Others came to reject the association and the label of "Beat," dubbing themselves "Ratbastards" in protest: "Ratbastard" was also the title of one of artist Bruce Connor's first assemblages. One of the most important predecessors to the so-called Beat artists was Jackson Pollack, whose artistic modus operandi was similar to that of the Beats: experimental, driven by experience and sensation, and anti-

academic. Pollack's drip-and-splatter paintings of the early 1950s opened the door for artists to follow with further experiments in medium and technique.

One of the most important impetuses to the art movement in the mid-1940s came shortly after the end of World War II. In California, under the leadership of Douglas MacAgy, the California School of Fine Arts began recruiting new faculty that included such artists as Edward Corbett, making the school a center for the development of abstract-expressionist art in the western United States. In New York City, the abstract art movement was initiated by exiled artists, many of whom had escaped from the war in Europe to come live in the United States. Both in California and in New York, the art world and the world of poetry merged, exploring similar concerns in different mediums. For example, in San Francisco, the Six Gallery—founded by Wally Hedrick and several of his friends in 1954—became one of the most significant art galleries in the United States at this time, exhibiting the works of local artists as well as providing a forum for poetry readings including Allen Ginsberg's *Howl*. Although the gallery did not keep records of its exhibitions and poetry readings, nor did it preserve many of the works displayed there, during its three-year existence it served as a hub for experimental art and poetic activity in California. Some of the most well-known artists of the era exhibited their work there, including Jay DeFeo (Hedrick's wife) and David Simpson, a close friend of Hedrick's.

Another central figure in the San Francisco arts scene during the Beat era was Michael McClure. Not only a poet and dramatist, McClure was a visual artist who was an influential member of an art movement that sprung up in the wake of Beat notoriety. Artists such as DeFeo, Wallace Berman, Bruce Connor, and others were part of what McClure later called the California Assemblage movement. Assemblagists created collages out of photographs and anything else at hand, purposefully mixing the high and the low. Assemblages were sometimes transitory by intention, as an aspect of their rejection of traditional notions of art. An example is Berman's *Semina* (1955-64), a collage-magazine consisting of poems and images glued together scrapbook-style and then mailed in unusual envelopes to a circle of friends. Other assemblage artists, such as Connor, DeFeo, Hedrick, and Jess (who dropped his last name), created what was later termed ephemeral art. The philosophy behind this type of art emphasized the notion that the value of art lay in the creative process itself, and not the final creation. Therefore, the materials used to create art were of no significance. In fact, the cheaper, more non-traditional, and temporary the materials were, the better.

The flourishing of Beat writers in San Francisco spurred on the development of the San Francisco art scene. In time, the two movements crossed paths, often inspiring works based on each other's art. For example, a set of five buttons that Berman gave to McClure inspired the latter to write *Semina Three,* an epic poem about that experience. Similarly, a poem by Philip Lamantia served as the muse that inspired DeFeo's drawing *The Eyes* (1958). Additionally, poets and artists often worked together creating illustrations and introductions for each other's work, many of which were published by small publishing houses such as White Rabbit and Auerhahn. By the late 1950s, artists living in the San Francisco area began to garner attention outside of their niche, and in 1959, DeFeo and Hedrick were invited to show their work at *Sixteen Americans,* a show sponsored by the Museum of Modern Art in New York City. Included in this exhibition were *The Veronica* (c.1958) by DeFeo and nine works by Hedrick. However, two of the most significant works by DeFeo, *The Rose* (1958) and *The Jewel* (1958), were not in that exhibit, and these, along with the *Vietnam Series* of paintings began by Hedrick in 1957 are cited as examples that protest the notion

of art as production—instead, they exemplify art and creation as a form of intense personal expression. Assemblage art received media attention again when William Seitz organized an exhibition of over 250 works by artists from the United States and abroad. At its opening in 1961, the show attracted attention as well as controversy. In addition, it established that art was no longer confined to painting and sculpture.

REPRESENTATIVE WORKS

Wallace Berman
Semina (collage, magazine) 1955-64

Joan Brown
Fur Rat (sculpture) 1962

Noel on Halloween (painting) 1964

Gordon, Joan & Rufus in Front of S.F. Opera House (painting) 1969

The Bride (painting) 1970

Bruce Conner
Ratbastard (assemblage) 1958

Spider Lady (assemblage) 1959

The Bride (assemblage) 1960

Snore (assemblage) 1960

Jay DeFeo
Tree (assemblage) c. 1954

Blossom (assemblage) 1956

The Eyes (painting) 1958

The Jewel (painting) 1958

The Rose (painting) 1958-66

The Veronica (painting) c.1958

Robert Frank
The Americans (photographs) 1969

Wally Hedrick
The Ace of Spades Meets the Queen of Hearts (painting) 1953

Anger (painting) 1953

Wally's Pallette (painting) 1957

Vietnam Series (paintings) 1957-73

George Herms
The Librarian (assemblage) 1960

ALLAN KAPROW (ESSAY DATE 1958)

SOURCE: Kaprow, Allan. "The Legacy of Jackson Pollock." In *Jackson Pollock: Interviews, Articles, and Reviews*, edited by Pepe Karmel, pp. 84-9. New York: Museum of Modern Art, 1999.

In the following essay, originally written shortly after Pollock's death in 1956 and published later in Art News, *Kaprow assesses Pollock's contributions to the development of modern painting. Kaprow's portrayal of Pollock suggests the artist's connection to Beat aesthetics—such as the rejection of an orderly and arranged process of creation, the use of art to create sensation or experience, and the embrace of the ordinary or ugly.*

1956-1958

1956 should have been a banner year for Pollock. The Museum of Modern Art had chosen him to initiate a series of exhibitions featuring contemporary artists. But Pollock died in a car crash on August 11, and what was intended as a mid-career retrospective became instead a memorial exhibition. The following essay, by the artist Allan Kaprow, was written shortly after Pollock's death, but Art News *chose not to publish it until 1958. In the years that followed, assemblages, environments, and happenings by Kaprow and other artists sought to extend Pollock's methods beyond the borders of painting.*

The tragic news of Pollock's death two summers ago was profoundly depressing to many of us. We felt not only a sadness over the death of a great figure, but in some deeper way that something of ourselves had died too. We were a piece of him: he was, perhaps, the embodiment of our ambition for absolute liberation and a secretly cherished wish to overturn old tables of crockery and flat champagne. We saw in his example the possibility of an astounding freshness, a sort of ecstatic blindness.

But, in addition, there was a morbid side to his meaningfulness. To "die at the top" for being his kind of modern artist was, to many, I think, implicit in the work before he died. It was this bizarre consequence that was so moving. We remembered Van Gogh and Rimbaud. But here it was in our time, in a man some of us knew. This ultimate, sacrificial aspect of being an artist, while not a new idea, seemed, the way Pollock did it, terribly modern, and in him the statement and the ritual were so grand, so authoritative and all-encompassing in its scale and daring, that whatever our private convictions, we could not fail to be affected by its spirit.

It was probably this latter side of Pollock that lay at the root of our depression. Pollock's tragedy was more subtle than his death: for he did not die at the top. One could not avoid the fact that during the last five years of his life his strength had weakened and during the last three, he hardly worked at all. Though everyone knew, in the light of reason, that the man was very ill (and his death was perhaps a respite from almost certain future suffering), and that, in point of fact, he did not die as Stravinsky's fertility maidens did, in the very moment of creation/annihilation—we still could not escape the disturbing itch (metaphysical in nature) that this death was in some direct way connected with art. And the connection, rather than being climactic, was, in a way, inglorious. If the end had to come, it came at the wrong time.

Was it not perfectly clear that modern art in general was slipping? Either it had become dull and repetitious qua the "advanced" style, or large numbers of formerly committed contemporary painters were defecting to earlier forms. America was celebrating a "sanity in art" movement and the flags were out. Thus, we reasoned, Pollock was the center in a great failure: the New Art. His heroic stand had been futile. Rather than releasing a freedom, which it at first promised, it caused him not only a loss of power and possible disillusionment, but a widespread admission that the jig was up. And those of us still resistant to this truth would end the same way, hardly at the top. Such were our thoughts in August, 1956.

But over two years have passed. What we felt then was genuine enough, but it was a limited tribute, if it was that at all. It was surely a manifestly human reaction on the part of those of us who were devoted to the most advanced of artists around us and who felt the shock of being thrown out on our own. But it did not actually seem that Pollock had indeed accomplished something, both by his attitude and by his very real gifts, which went beyond even those values recognized and acknowledged by sensitive artists and critics. The "Act of Painting," the new space, the personal mark that builds its own form and meaning, the endless tangle, the great scale, the new materials, etc. are by now clichés of college art departments. The innovations are accepted. They are becoming part of text books.

But some of the implications inherent in these new values are not at all as futile as we all began to believe; this kind of painting need not be called the "tragic" style. Not all the roads of this modern art lead to ideas of finality. I hazard the guess that Pollock may have vaguely sensed this, but was unable, because of illness or otherwise, to do anything about it.

He created some magnificent paintings. But he also *destroyed painting*. If we examine a few of the innovations mentioned above, it may be possible to see why this is so.

For instance, the "Act of Painting." In the last seventy-five years the random play of the hand upon the canvas or paper has become increasingly important. Strokes, smears, lines, dots, etc. became less and less attached to represented objects and existed more and more on their own, self-sufficiently. But from Impressionism up to, say, Gorky, the idea of an "order" to these markings was explicit enough. Even Dada, which purported to be free of such considerations as "composition," obeyed the Cubist esthetic. One colored shape balanced (or modified, or stimulated) others and these in turn were played off against (or with) the whole canvas, taking into account its size and shape—for the most part, quite consciously. In short, part-to-whole or part-to-part relationships, no matter how strained, were at least a good fifty percent of the making of a picture. (Most of the time it was a lot more, maybe ninety percent). With Pollock, however, the so-called "dance" of dripping, slashing, squeezing, daubing and whatever else went into a work, placed an almost absolute value upon a kind of diaristic gesture. He was encouraged in this by the Surrealist painters and poets, but next to him their work is consistently "artful," "arranged" and full of finesse—aspects of outer control and training. With a choice of enormous scales, the canvas being placed upon the floor, thus making it difficult for the artist to see the whole or any extended section of "parts," Pollock could truthfully say that he was "in" his work. Here the direct application of an automatic approach to the act makes it clear that not only is this not the old craft of painting, but it is perhaps bordering on ritual itself, which *happens* to use paint as one of its materials. (The European Surrealists may have *used* automatism as an ingredient but hardly can we say they really practiced it wholeheartedly. In fact, it is only in a few instances that the writers, rather than the painters, enjoyed any success in this way. In retrospect, most of the Surrealist painters appear to be derived from a psychology book or from each other: the empty vistas, the basic naturalism, the sexual fantasies, the bleak surfaces so characteristic of this period have always impressed most American artists as a collection of unconvincing clichés. Hardly automatic, at that. And such real talents as Picasso, Klee and Miró belong more to the stricter discipline of Cubism than did the others, and perhaps this is why their work appears to

us, paradoxically, more *free*. Surrealism attracted Pollock as an attitude rather than as a collection of artistic examples.)

But I used the words "almost absolute" when I spoke of the diaristic gesture as distinct from the process of judging each move upon the canvas. Pollock, interrupting his work, would judge his "acts" very shrewdly and with care for long periods of time before going into another "act." He knew the difference between a good gesture and a bad one. This was his conscious artistry at work and it makes him a part of the traditional community of painters. Yet the distance between the relatively self-contained works of the Europeans and the seemingly chaotic, sprawling works of the American indicate at best a tenuous connection to "paintings." (In fact, Jackson Pollock never really had a *"malerisch"* sensibility. The painterly aspects of his contemporaries, such as Motherwell, Hofmann, de Kooning, Rothko, even Still, point up, if at one moment a deficiency in him, at another moment, a liberating feature—and this one I choose to consider the important one.)

I am convinced that to grasp a Pollock's impact properly, one must be something of an acrobat, constantly vacillating between an identification with the hands and body that flung the paint and stood "in" the canvas, and allowing the markings to entangle and assault one into submitting to their permanent and objective character. This is indeed far from the idea of a "complete" painting. The artist, the spectator and the outer world are much too interchangeably involved here. (And if one objects to the difficulty of complete comprehension, I insist that he either asks too little of art or refuses to look at reality.)

Then Form. In order to follow it, it is necessary to get rid of the usual idea of "Form," i.e. a beginning, middle and end, or any variant of this principle—such as fragmentation. You do not enter a painting of Pollock's in any one place (or hundred places). Anywhere is everywhere and you can dip in and out when and where you can. This has led to remarks that his art gives one the impression of going on forever—a true insight. It indicates that the confines of the rectangular field were ignored in lieu of an experience of a continuum going in all directions simultaneously, *beyond* the literal dimensions of any work. (Though there is evidence pointing to a probably unknowing slackening of the attack as Pollock came to the edges of his canvas, he compensated for this by tacking much of the painted surface around the back of his stretchers.) The four sides of the painting are thus an abrupt leaving-off of the activity which our imaginations continue outward indefinitely, as though refusing to accept the artificiality of an "ending." In an older work, the edge was a far more precise caesura: here ended the world of the artist; beyond began the world of the spectator and "reality."

We accept this innovation as valid because the artist understood with perfect naturalness "how to do it." Employing an iterative principle of a few highly charged elements constantly undergoing variation (improvising, like much Oriental music) Pollock gives us an all-over unity and at the same time a means continuously to respond to a freshness of personal choice. But this type of form allows us just as well an equally strong pleasure in participating in a delirium, a deadening of the reasoning faculties, a loss of "self" in the Western sense of the term. It is this strange combination of extreme individuality and selflessness which makes the work not only remarkably potent, but also indicative of a probably larger frame of psychological reference. And it is for this reason that any allusions to Pollock's being the maker of giant textures are completely incorrect. The point is missed and misunderstanding is bound to follow.

But, given the proper approach, a medium-sized exhibition space with the walls totally covered by Pollocks, offers the most complete and meaningful sense of his art possible.

Then scale. Pollock's choice of enormous sizes served many purposes, chief of which for our discussion is the fact that by making mural-scale paintings, they ceased to become paintings and became *environments*. Before a painting, one's size as a spectator, in relation to that of the picture, profoundly influences how much we are willing to give up consciousness of our temporal existence while experiencing it. Pollock's choice of great sizes resulted in our being confronted, assaulted, sucked in. Yet we must not confuse these with the hundreds of large paintings done in the Renaissance. They glorified an everyday world quite familiar to the observer, often, in fact, by means of trompe l'oeil, continuing the actual room into the painting. Pollock offers us no such familiarity and our everyday world of convention and habit is replaced by that one created by the artist. Reversing the above procedure, the painting is continued on out into the room.

And this leads us to our final point: Space. The space of these creations is not *clearly* palpable as such. One can become entangled in the web to some extent, and by moving in and out of the skein of lines and splashings, *can* experience a kind of spatial extension. But even so, this space is an *al*lusion far more vague than even the few inches of space-reading a Cubist work affords. It may be that we are too aware of our need to identify with the process, the making of the whole affair, and this prevents a concentration on the specifics of before and behind, so important in a more traditional art. But what I believe *is* clearly discernible is that the *entire* painting comes out at the participant (I shall call him that, rather than observer) right into the room. It is possible to see in this connection how Pollock is the terminal result of a gradual trend that moved from the deep space of the fifteenth and sixteenth centuries, to the building out from the canvas of the Cubist collages. In the present case the "picture" has moved so far out that the canvas is no longer a reference point. Hence, although up on the wall, these marks surround us as they did the painter at work, so strict a correspondence has there been achieved between his impulse and the resultant art.

What we have then, is a type of art which tends to lose itself out of bounds, tends to fill our world with itself, an art which, in meaning, looks, impulse, seems to break fairly sharply with the traditions of painters back to at least the Greeks. Pollock's near destruction of this tradition may well be a return to the point where art was more actively involved in ritual, magic and life than we have known it in our recent past. If so, it is an exceedingly important step, and in its superior way, offers a solution to the complaints of those who would have us put a bit of life into art. But what do we do now?

There are two alternatives. One is to continue in this vein. Probably many good "near-paintings" can be done varying this esthetic of Pollock's without departing from it or going further. The other is to give up the making of paintings entirely, I mean the single, flat rectangle or oval as we know it. It has been seen how Pollock came pretty close to doing so himself. In the process, he came upon some newer values which are exceedingly difficult to discuss, yet they bear upon our present alternative. To say that he discovered things like marks, gestures, paint, colors, hardness, softness, flowing, stopping, space, the world, life, death—is to sound either naïve or stupid. Every artist worth his salt has "discovered" these things. But Pollock's discovery seems to have a peculiarly fascinating simplicity and directness about it. He was, for me, amazingly childlike, capable of becoming involved in the stuff of his art as a group of *concrete facts* seen for the first time. There is, as I said earlier, a certain blindness, a mute belief in everything he does, even up to the end. I urge that this be not seen as a simple issue. Few individuals can be lucky enough to possess the intensity of this kind of knowing, and I hope that in the near future a careful study of this (perhaps) Zen quality of Pollock's personality will be undertaken. At any rate, for now, we may consider that, except for rare instances, Western art tends to need many more indirections in achieving itself, placing more or less equal emphasis upon "things" and the *relations* between them. The crudeness of Jackson Pollock is not, therefore, uncouth or designed as such; it is manifestly frank and uncultivated, unsullied by training, trade secrets, finesse—a directness which the European artists he liked hoped for and partially succeeded in, but which he never had to strive after because he had it by nature. This by itself would be enough to teach us something.

It does. Pollock, as I see him, left us at the point where we must become preoccupied with and even dazzled by the space and objects of our everyday life, either our bodies, clothes, rooms, or, if need be, the vastness of Forty-Second Street. Not satisfied with the *suggestion* through paint of our other senses, we shall utilize the specific substances of sight, sound, movements, people, odors, touch. Objects of every sort are materials for the new art: paint, chairs, food, electric and neon lights, smoke, water, old socks, a dog, movies, a thousand other things which will be discovered by the present generation of artists. Not only will these bold creators show us, as if for the first time, the world we have always had about us, but ignored, but they will disclose entirely unheard of happenings and events, found in garbage cans, police files, hotel lobbies, seen in store windows and on the streets, and sensed in dreams and horrible accidents. An odor of crushed strawberries, a letter from a friend or a billboard selling Draino; three taps on the front door, a scratch, a sigh or a voice lecturing endlessly, a blinding staccato flash, a bowler hat—all will become materials for this new concrete art.

The young artist of today need no longer say "I am a painter" or "a dancer." He is simply an "artist." All of life will be open to him. He will discover out of ordinary things the meaning of ordinariness. He will not try to make them extraordinary. Only their real meaning will be stated. But out of nothing he will devise the extraordinary and then maybe nothingness as well. People will

be delighted or horrified, critics will be confused or amused, but these, I am sure, will be the alchemies of the 1960s.

CRITICAL COMMENTARY

SIDRA STICH AND BRIGID DOHERTY (ESSAY DATE 1989)

SOURCE: Stich, Sidra, and Brigid Doherty. "A Biographical History." In *Jay DeFeo: Works on Paper,* edited by Sidra Stich, pp. 11-25. Berkeley: University of California Art Museum, 1989.

In the following essay, Stich and Doherty provide a biography of DeFeo detailing the influence of the San Francisco art scene on her work, including her connection with Beat poets such as Jack Kerouac and Allen Ginsberg. Stich and Doherty also assert that DeFeo was among those Californians who, like Michael McClure, tried to distinguish themselves from the narrow classification of the Beat movement.

Though her given name is Mary Joan, DeFeo's family called her Joan (pronounced Jo-ann). She was born on March 31, 1929, in Hanover, New Hampshire, where her father was completing the initial phase of his medical education at Dartmouth College. Three years later DeFeo and her parents moved to California. They lived in San Francisco with her paternal grandparents until her father finished medical school and an internship at Stanford University. During these years, DeFeo was quite ill, and a series of childhood diseases led to her hospitalization in the Stanford Convalescent Home (1934-35).

In 1936 the family moved to rural Northern California, where her father worked as a traveling physician with the Civil Service. DeFeo spent summers with her maternal grandparents in Carbondale, Colorado. At age nine, after her parents divorced, she lived for a full year in Colorado with her mother. She and her mother then returned to California, taking up residence in San Jose, where DeFeo attended junior high school. Although her parents encouraged her interest in art, a neighbor who was a commercial artist provided her first memorable learning experience: a "how-to-draw" book that introduced her to the principles of design. She found herself fascinated by the "perfect circles" demonstrated in the book and attempted to reproduce the shape in her own drawings, focusing on the fundamental forms to which she would frequently return throughout her career. The fascination with geometrical shapes such as the circle, triangle, and cruciform, as well as the insistent copying and reworking process

DeFeo adopted, has persisted throughout her career as an artist, clearly informing major works from the "Florence" series through *The Rose* to the more recent "One O'Clock Jump" and *Reflections of Africa* series.

It was during high school in San Jose that De-Feo came to be called Jay. Her interest in art continued to develop under the influence of her high school art teacher, Mrs. Lena Emery, who introduced her to reproductions of Matisse, Picasso, and the Impressionists. DeFeo's mentor also took her to museums in San Francisco. The summer following her graduation from high school, DeFeo took her first art history course at San Jose State.

In 1946 DeFeo enrolled at the University of California at Berkeley, where she would receive a B.A. in 1950, and an M.A. in 1951. At that time the university population consisted largely of veterans of World War II studying under the G.I. Bill. DeFeo recalls the influence their seriousness had on her as she began her university studies at age sixteen. The climate inspired her to work diligently and competitively in an academic world overwhelmingly dominated by men.

The curriculum at Berkeley followed an academic model in which instruction in painting and drawing was organized progressively, maintaining a separation between media and proceeding from drawing through watercolor to oil painting. Work in sculpture consisted strictly of plasticene modeling—a restriction that prompted DeFeo to begin experimenting with plaster, a medium to which she would later return. Although she responded well to the demands of the program, DeFeo resisted what she describes as the "hierarchy of media." She began to mix media and use unorthodox materials, challenging the conventions of application and appearance that controlled the academic study of art.

While working with instructors John Haley, Margaret Peterson O'Hagan, and Erle Loran, De-Feo encountered the legacy of Hans Hofmann, the tremendously influential German expatriate painter who had taught at Berkeley during the summers of 1930 and 1931. Through the Hans Hofmann School of Fine Arts in New York (1931-58) and its summer complement, an art school in Provincetown, Massachusetts (1935-58), Hofmann came to profoundly affect the teaching and practice of painting on both coasts throughout the thirties, forties, and fifties. His philosophy of painting set the agenda for the strict devotion to a rigorous, reductive notion of modern painting that dominated the teaching at Berkeley during the forties and fifties.[1] Haley, O'Hagan, and Loran as well as the formalist critic Clement Greenberg and the painters Lee Krasner, Larry Rivers, and Helen Frankenthaler studied with Hofmann and attended Hofmann's lectures on modern art.

Both Erle Loran and Margaret Peterson O'Hagan incorporated into their teaching their interest in so-called primitive art. Loran collected African art, and O'Hagan often used Northwest Coast Indian art as a source for her work. O'Hagan's methodological commitment to both academic training and the exploration of art's relation to the unconscious encouraged in DeFeo a concern for the interaction of reductive form and mystical imagism. In particular, O'Hagan's visual and psychological interest in Northwest Coast Native American Art aroused in DeFeo a persistent fascination with using art and objects from outside the history of Western art as sources for her own work. The only female faculty member in the department, O'Hagan also served as a professional role model for DeFeo.

Particularly influential as well was John Haley's course on Picasso's *Guernica,* which set out to trace the making of the "masterpiece" through an examination of Picasso's working method. Picasso's process of producing variations on a theme, his reworking of a focal image in a multitude of sketches and studies, had a tremendous impact on DeFeo. She would subsequently adopt a similar method, producing series throughout her career, and reworking the theme of her monumental painting *The Rose* for seven years. At Berkeley, De-Feo also began to formulate a working method that combined formalist rigor and mixed-media experimentation, drawing from a variety of sources and adapting a number of methodologies.

Courses in English literature and the history of art complemented DeFeo's studio work. In particular, DeFeo recalls the influence of courses in medieval, Renaissance, and Asian art taught by Walter Horn and Otto Maenchen-Helfen. The emphasis on architecture in these courses enhanced her fascination with geometric form and inspired a propensity toward architectonic design that DeFeo has so often invoked in her art.

While DeFeo was studying at Berkeley, the California School of Fine Arts (now the San Francisco Art Institute) became the undisputed center of contemporary art activity in the Bay Area. The CSFA's director, Douglas MacAgy, invited Clyfford Still and Mark Rothko out from New York to teach in 1946. Still remained on the faculty until 1950, and, perhaps more because of his overpowering personality and teaching style than because of his painting style, has been considered the dominant influence on Abstract Expressionist painting in the Bay Area. David Park, Elmer Bischoff, Hassell Smith, and Richard Diebenkorn also taught at the CSFA during the late forties and early fifties. The school attracted a highly motivated group of G.I. Bill students and inspired a lively social scene that engaged both students and faculty. MacAgy allowed the CSFA studios to remain open all night, and often Park and Bischoff's informal Studio 13 Jazz Band—occasionally supplemented by MacAgy himself on the drums—played there.[2]

During the forties the San Francisco Museum of Art (now the San Francisco Museum of Modern Art), under the direction of Grace McCann Morley, acquired a number of paintings by Jackson Pollock, Arshile Gorky, and Mark Rothko. At the same time, Jermayne MacAgy, Douglas MacAgy's wife, organized a number of important exhibitions of contemporary art at the California Palace of the Legion of Honor. Among these were the 1945 exhibition *Contemporary American Painting,* which included works by Gorky, Rothko, and Robert Motherwell; and the one-person shows of Rothko (1946) and Still (1947). In 1948 the San Francisco Museum of Art held an exhibition of new work by Park, Bischoff, and Smith. Park's large, thickly painted, non-objective canvases caused a stir, documented by Erle Loran in his column for *Art News.*[3] Instead of continuing to pursue pure abstraction, Park returned to figuration during 1949-50. The public became aware of this new direction in his art in the spring of 1951 when his *Kids on Bikes* was awarded a prize in the San Francisco Museum of Art's annual exhibition. During the early fifties, a rift developed between Abstract Expressionists such as Hassell Smith and Frank Lobdell and painters such as Bischoff and Diebenkorn who followed Park in recuperating landscape, still life, and the human figure in their paintings. However, the new movement was not defined as such until the 1957 Oakland Museum exhibition *Contemporary Bay Area Figurative Painting,* organized by Paul Mills. Even then the artists involved resisted both definition and association.

DeFeo's Berkeley classmates Sam Francis and Fred Martin involved themselves in the emerging San Francisco art world while still students, carrying news and enthusiasm back to Berkeley. Although DeFeo remained apart from the San Francisco scene, she was aware of the activity across the Bay. In particular, issues of representation and abstraction, which came to the fore in San Francisco in the early fifties, have consistently informed DeFeo's work, and she has always courted the tension between recognizable image and formal abstraction.

There was minimal interest, however, at Berkeley in the New York Abstract Expressionists, DeFeo recalls. Yet she remembers looking with enthusiasm at reproductions of Jackson Pollock's paintings in art magazines. Indeed, Erle Loran's frequent commentaries in *Art News* testify to the existence of a coast-to-coast dialogue. DeFeo would, then, have at least been aware of developments in the East, if knowing of emerging trends only through description and poor-quality magazine illustrations.

After receiving her master's degree, and with strong support from the art faculty, DeFeo was awarded Berkeley's competitive Sigmund Martin Heller Traveling Fellowship. Years later she learned that in her nomination the faculty members had deliberately elided *Jay*'s gender. The fellowship administrators, who were inclined to support male students, therefore did not realize they had awarded the prestigious prize to a woman until one of DeFeo's reports on her travels incidentally revealed her to be female. Although DeFeo never deliberately cultivated a persona based on the gender ambiguity of her name, she remained conscious of it, often exhibiting under the name J. DeFeo. Like Lee Krasner, who also used the neuter signature L. K., DeFeo sensed that her name could allow her to sometimes escape being pigeonholed as a maker of "women's art."[4] While she did not initiate or request her nicknaming (her classmates began to call her "Jay" in high school) or ask the art faculty to suppress her gender in the fellowship competition, she retains a sense of both the irony and importance of her masked gender.

The Heller fellowship allowed DeFeo to travel and live in Europe for eighteen months. She went abroad with another Berkeley art graduate, and they linked up with a third student overseas. Their first stop was Paris, where they spent three months. DeFeo produced a number of works on paper during this period, including various calligraphic and expressionistic compositions. She recalls enjoying the city itself and spending long hours in the Louvre and the Musée de l'Homme. Her contact with contemporary art was limited to visits with Sam Francis, who was living in Paris at the time.

DeFeo subsequently traveled to England, where she devoted most of her time to studying images of African and prehistoric art in London's libraries. She meticulously traced images from books as a means of examining their visual form. Indeed, she had little interest in the meaning or identity of the works she copied; rather, copying served as a means of visualizing objects and patterns by manipulating reproduced images. The process involved both close scrutiny and deliberate distancing, two modes of observation that DeFeo has used throughout her career to refresh her vision of both her sources and her own work. During the seventies, for example, DeFeo turned to two other kinds of methodical copying, photography and photocopying, as sketching tools and aids in evaluating works in progress.

After three months in London, DeFeo and her friends rented a car and drove through France, Spain, North Africa, and Italy. DeFeo particularly remembers the open landscape of Spain, the dramatic, ritualized violence of the bullfight, and the saturated colors of the North African earth and sky. When DeFeo arrived in Florence, she decided to stop traveling in order to devote herself again to making art. Living in virtual isolation in a family *pensione,* she spent six months working intensely. And instead of viewing the masterpieces in Florentine galleries and museums, she undertook an extensive examination of the city and its architecture. This rekindled the interest in architecture that she had developed at Berkeley, and reaffirmed an architectonic basis in her art. She was extremely prolific during this period (a letter to her mother notes a production of two hundred drawings in three months), and considers this work to be the first containing "her own" imagery. These compositions evince DeFeo's interest in spatial and geometric form, as well as her characteristic use of broad, black brushstrokes, divergent directional forces, and contrasting tonalities.

On returning from Europe, DeFeo moved into a large studio near College Avenue in Berkeley and resumed the experiments with plaster she had begun as a student. She made large sculptures, all now either lost or destroyed. Although she did not continue in this direction, her plasters inspired Manuel Neri to take up the medium, which he then developed in a distinctive figurative mode. She also began to produce small wire and metal sculptures. She continued to refine her craft and her conceptions of spatial form in these small pieces, further developing the vocabulary of images that consistently informs her work.

Unable to afford the rent for the large studio, DeFeo moved into a small apartment in North Berkeley. The move meant that she no longer could create large sculptures, and her economic situation led her to transform the small sculptures into jewelry. She achieved a high degree of technical expertise in her jewelry-making, learning the craft of gem-setting using sophisticated jeweler's tools. DeFeo supported herself for a number of years by selling her jewelry, which she sold through the most prestigious contemporary jewelry dealer in San Francisco from 1954 to 1957. In addition to the jewelry, DeFeo produced numerous works on paper during this period, including the collage *Tree.*

Soon after moving to her North Berkeley apartment, DeFeo met the painter Wally Hedrick, then a student at the California College of Arts and Crafts in Oakland and the CSFA, and he soon moved in with her. Hedrick's art differed greatly from DeFeo's both conceptually and aesthetically. His work, which would later be called Funk Art, was characterized by an explicit sociopolitical engagement manifest in the inclusion of words and the cultivation of aggressively "marginal" imagery, often in mixed media.

DeFeo and Hedrick married in 1954 and moved to an apartment on Bay Street in San Francisco, around the corner from the CSFA. Just prior to the move, DeFeo paid her first visit to the CSFA.

In 1954 DeFeo was given her first one-person exhibition, at The Place gallery, a tavern and Beat poets' hangout operated by the artist and critic Knute Stiles in San Francisco's North Beach. DeFeo exhibited works from Florence and Paris. That same year, she entered a sculpture in the juried San Francisco Museum of Modern Art Annual. The piece, an oversized white cruciform structure made of paper stretched over a wooden frame and decorated with gaudy splashes of paint and a large jewel in the center, became a cause célèbre in the San Francisco art community.[5]

In 1954 Hedrick, Deborah Remington, Hayward King, David Simpson, John Allen Ryan, and Jack Spicer founded the Six Gallery at 3119 Fillmore Street in San Francisco, the former location of the King Ubu Gallery, which had been run by the artist Jess and the poet Robert Duncan. Joan Brown, Manuel Neri, and Bruce Conner would later become associates of the Six Gallery. Not yet ready to show her art in the gallery, DeFeo was not officially one of the directing members. However, she often worked in the gallery as an attendant and participated in all the events sponsored by the Six—including Allen Ginsberg's legendary first reading of *Howl* in October 1955.

ON THE SUBJECT OF...

WALLACE BERMAN

Many Beat authors such as Ginsberg and Ferlinghetti pursued art alongside their literary works. One of the artists they most admired was Wallace Berman, whose work is frequently described as "Beat Art." Berman embraced interdisciplinary techniques and influences that characterized the Beat Generation. He is best known for his verifax assemblages, sepia-toned works created using a primitive copy machine. The collages juxtapose readily identifiable images such as football players, a lock and key, and a transistor radio with mystical elements like Hebrew letters, a rabbit's foot, and other cryptic symbols. In addition to his art, Berman wrote poetry and composed rhythm and blues music.

During the two years she lived at Bay Street, DeFeo mainly continued to make jewelry. The opportunity to return to larger works came in 1956, when DeFeo and Hedrick each took a large studio in a tenement building at 2322 Fillmore Street. Over the next twelve years they shared the large house variously with the artists Sonia Gechtoff, James Kelly, Craig Kauffman, Joan and William Brown, Bruce and Jean Conner; the poet Michael McClure and his wife Joanne; the musician Dave Getz; and Jim Newman, later founder of the Syndell Studio in Los Angeles and the Dilexi Gallery in San Francisco.

The house at 2322 Fillmore became a meeting place for a disparate group of young Bay Area artists, poets, and musicians. There was a great deal of communal activity, mostly on a social level, and the building became known as the site of notoriously large and raucous parties throughout the late fifties and early sixties. Jazz was an important part of the Fillmore Street environment; records were often played in the building, and Hedrick played jazz himself, as did Dave Getz and James Kelly. The poets, painters, and musicians at 2322 Fillmore saw, heard, and commented upon each other's work, but DeFeo and the other painters who lived in the building adamantly note the absence of highly critical or theoretical discussions about art and ideas. Among the artists, there were technical discussions as well as the monthly ritual of reviewing together the illustrations in *Art News*—the only source of information about contemporary art in New York. But these interchanges were practical and social, not philosophical.

Many of the Beat poets, including Jack Kerouac and Allen Ginsberg, read at the Six Gallery and passed through the Fillmore Street house. DeFeo sympathized with the Beat spirit, although she never incorporated its characteristic sociopolitical engagement and iconoclasm into her own work. Her inventive use of non-art materials and what was seen as her idiosyncratic mysticism made DeFeo's paintings particularly attractive to the Beat poets.

The artist Wallace Berman, based alternately in Los Angeles and Marin County, was a frequent visitor to 2322 Fillmore, and DeFeo carried on a photocollage correspondence with him and posed for a number of his early experimental photographs. In 1958 McClure and Bruce Conner founded the Rat Bastard Protective Society (RBPS) and initiated DeFeo, Hedrick, Joan Brown, and Manuel Neri as charter members of their ironic negation of the various "associations" or self-proclaimed "movements" of modern artists. The RBPS, a prototypical Beat-generation, Funk Art concept, thus simultaneously invoked and burlesqued even the conventions of the avant-garde by criticizing the exclusivity and implicit hostility of groupings or "movements" intended to insulate artists from the "philistinism" of the "establishment." This sort of theatrical gesture epitomized the self-conscious irony of the "movement": the Beat critique of the "establishment" amounted, for McClure and Conner, to a kind of solipsistic parody. Although a friend of the Beats and the Funk artists, DeFeo remained deliberately on the periphery of any groups. She was included in their "associations," but ultimately preferred the cultivation of what she has called her "private" art—an art deliberately distanced, if not disengaged, from social issues.[6]

The move to Fillmore Street initiated a tremendously productive period for DeFeo. She began to experiment with mixed media and photocollage, as in *Blossom* (1956); and she created drawings based on identifiable objects or borrowed images, as in *Apparition* (1956), which DeFeo adapted from a nature study by Leonardo da Vinci. Having a large studio also allowed her to return to large-scale works. In 1958 she completed, among others, the drawings *Death Wish, Doctor Jazz,* and

The Eyes, and began work on a pair of paintings, *Jewel* and *The Rose,* each of which consisted of a radially symmetrical mandala-like form fanning out in thickly impastoed rays. *The Rose* was painted in DeFeo's characteristic gray-white-black monochrome, while *Jewel* explodes in shades of red and orange. DeFeo soon became obsessed with *The Rose* and ceased producing other work. Not until 1964 did she begin another painting, the huge drawing *Estocada,* which now survives only in the fragments that make up DeFeo's 1973 work *Tuxedo Junction.*

In 1958 DeFeo exhibited *Death Wish, Young Bird of Paradise, Annunciation, Ascension, The Eyes, Doctor Jazz, Daphne, Persephone, Applaud the Black Fact, Blossom, Figure in Landscape, Song of Innocence, The Wise Virgin, The Foolish Virgin,* and an *Untitled* drawing in a one-person show at Jim Newman's Dilexi Gallery on Broadway in North Beach. During the late fifties and throughout the sixties, the Dilexi Gallery was a center of contemporary art activity in San Francisco, showing artists such as Jess, Craig Kauffmann, Roy De Forest, Robert Morris, Hassell Smith, and Manuel Neri. At the same time, the Ferus Gallery, which opened in 1956 under the direction of Newman's friend and former co-director of the Syndell Studio in Los Angeles, Walter Hopps, and the artist Edward Kienholz, served as a similar center of activity in Los Angeles. Exhibitions often moved from one space to the other, and a vital North-South dialogue developed between the two galleries and the artists who showed at them during these years. DeFeo exhibited in a one-person show at the Ferus Gallery in 1960, and both Kienholz and Hopps became close friends and strong supporters of De-Feo.

Patrick Lannan, the adventurous Floridian collector of contemporary art, saw DeFeo's 1958 Dilexi show and purchased *Death Wish, Young Bird of Paradise,* and *Ascension.* Dorothy C. Miller, curator at the Museum of Modern Art, New York, also saw the Dilexi show and visited the artist in her studio. She responded immediately to DeFeo's work and decided to include her in the *Sixteen Americans* exhibition planned for 1959. Wally Hedrick, James Jarvaise, Jasper Johns, Ellsworth Kelly, Alfred Leslie, Landes Lewitin, Richard Lytle, Robert Mallary, Louise Nevelson, Robert Rauschenberg, Julius Schmidt, Richard Stankiewicz, Frank Stella, Albert Urban, and Jack Youngerman were the other artists selected for this important showing of emerging artists. Miller represented DeFeo with *Death Wish, Daphne, Persephone, The Veronica,* and *Origin.* Miller wanted to include *The Rose* as

well, but DeFeo was unwilling to stop work on it in order to ship it to New York. DeFeo did not attend the opening of *Sixteen Americans,* nor did she pursue offers from New York art dealers who showed interest in exhibiting her work. She also refused offers from Patrick Lannan and other collectors to buy *The Rose.*

During its seven-year development *The Rose,* which was at times called *The Deathrose* (a title Ed Kienholz recalls mishearing as *Death Throws*)[7] and the *White Rose,* underwent a number of near-total transformations as DeFeo built up and carved away the picture's high-relief surface. *The Rose* sustained several radical compositional changes, which at one point necessitated expansion onto a larger framed canvas and several times required the addition of wooden surface supports that were quickly covered over with fresh layers of paint. The finished painting would weigh 2,300 pounds and have a surface depth varying from two to eight inches.

The picture became an emphatically expansive and inclusive work which eradicated conventional boundaries between media and persistently challenged the spatial and conceptual boundaries between the work and the world of DeFeo's studio. DeFeo drew directly onto the studio wall in order to determine the necessary dimensions of a second frame for the picture; she began to attach beads, wire, pearls, and other remnants of her jewelry-making into the painting; and as the paint on the canvas grew thicker and thicker, she began to sculpt it as she worked, carving and modeling the paint, and no longer speaking of *The Rose* as a painting, but as a liminal work capable of functioning both pictorially and sculpturally. In a 1961 statement in an *Art in America* feature "New Talent, U.S.A.," DeFeo explained:

> Although a painter by definition, my work as it has emerged in the past two years could more accurately be described as a combination of painting and sculpture. I consider the aspects of each to be inseparable and interdependent. . . . It is not my intention to be first a sculptor and subsequently a painter, adorning the three-dimensional form in a painterly manner. To realize satisfaction in this effort I must cope with the problems of both sculpture and painting as we have understood them in the past, and attempt to solve the new problems that emerge out of the dependency of one upon the other in my work.[8]

The Rose proved to be an extraordinarily demanding work both personally and materially. By the time she stopped working on it in a cramped, fume-filled gallery at the Pasadena

Museum, DeFeo was drained of her energy and health, and had spent more than $5,000 on the paint alone.

Precipitating the completion of *The Rose* was the eviction notice served on DeFeo, Hedrick, and their housemates to vacate 2322 Fillmore Street in December 1964. Moving out of the building required complex arrangements for the removal of *The Rose* and the destruction of all but a few fragments of *Estocada,* the gigantic wall-mounted drawing that was DeFeo's only other work during the previous six years.

Walter Hopps, then director of the Pasadena Museum, arranged to have *The Rose* shipped to the museum. The packing and moving of *The Rose* by a crew of Bekins' movers supervised by Mr. Bekins, Jr. entailed the dismantling of part of the facade of 2322 Fillmore. Bruce Conner recorded the event and set it to the tune of Miles Davis's *Sketches in Spain* in his film *White Rose* (1964). The eviction, which coincided with DeFeo's separation from Hedrick, left her homeless for a time. Hopps arranged for her to move to Los Angeles to finish *The Rose,* and DeFeo spent three months there, living in an apartment in Hopps's house and working daily on *The Rose* at the Pasadena Museum. *The Rose* was exhibited at the Pasadena Museum, February 4-March 2, 1969.

DeFeo had begun teaching at the San Francisco Art Institute in 1962, and during her stay in Los Angeles the Pasadena Museum funded her weekly commute by airplane to San Francisco. Although DeFeo taught night classes and therefore had little contact with other faculty members, she sympathized with the sensibilities of Frank Lobdell and Elmer Bischoff, whom she had known from having worked as a model for their drawing classes at the CSFA during the late fifties and early sixties. She saw a relationship between her own work and the rough, thickly painted surfaces of their paintings.

While living in Los Angeles DeFeo at first actively participated in the art scene, visiting galleries and studios with Walter Hopps and attending a myriad of parties and informal gatherings. All this ended abruptly, however, when she caught the Asian flu and could do little more than fulfill her teaching responsibilities and work on *The Rose.* She did attend Frank Lobdell's 1965 exhibition at the Pasadena Museum and describes Lobdell as "the superhero as far as Abstract Expressionism was concerned."

After finishing *The Rose* DeFeo returned to Northern California and took up residence in a small cottage in Ross, an exclusive suburb north of San Francisco in Marin County. Exhausted from the saga of painting and moving *The Rose,* DeFeo stopped painting for six years and totally isolated herself from the art world except for her contacts with students at the CSFA, where she continued to teach until 1970. While living in Ross, DeFeo met John Bogdanoff, who remained her companion until 1980.

After its showing in Pasadena, *The Rose* was exhibited at the San Francisco Museum of Modern Art, April 1-May 25, 1969, and drew highly favorable responses. Alexander Fried, the *San Francisco Examiner*'s art critic, called *The Rose* a "vividly powerful, expressive work, a dominant masterwork in the profuse San Francisco tradition of abstract expressionism."[9] The *San Francisco Chronicle*'s critic, Thomas Albright, who would become an enthusiastic promoter of DeFeo's work until his death in 1984, hailed *The Rose* as "a product of that heroic, swan-song period in the early sixties when Abstract Expressionism was moving in the direction of more specific imagery, when painting and sculpture were moving closer together and when conflict and drama in black and white were moving toward a more colorful lyrical expression. It is a masterpiece of that transitional age."[10]

Following the SFMMA exhibition, *The Rose* was moved to a conference room at the SFAI. Over the years it suffered great damage from coffee stains, fingerprints, and cigarette smoke. Finally, in 1972, Bruce Conner spearheaded a fundraising campaign within the San Francisco art community to initiate the restoration of the painting. In November 1972 conservator Tony Rockwell began work on *The Rose.* This first stage of conservation, completed in August 1974, encased the painting in a plaster mold, raising its weight to 4,500 pounds. This initial treatment stabilized the picture's surface, but the additional weight and mass so raised the cost of transporting the painting to the Northern California Regional Conservation Laboratory for further restoration that the remaining conservation was never undertaken. Since 1972 this fabled and important painting has remained inaccessible, stored behind a wall at the SFAI.[11]

After three years in Ross, DeFeo and Bogdanoff moved to a small house in Larkspur. She converted the cottage's small back porch into a studio and slowly resumed making art, although she remained largely isolated from the San Francisco art community. From 1970 until 1977 she taught

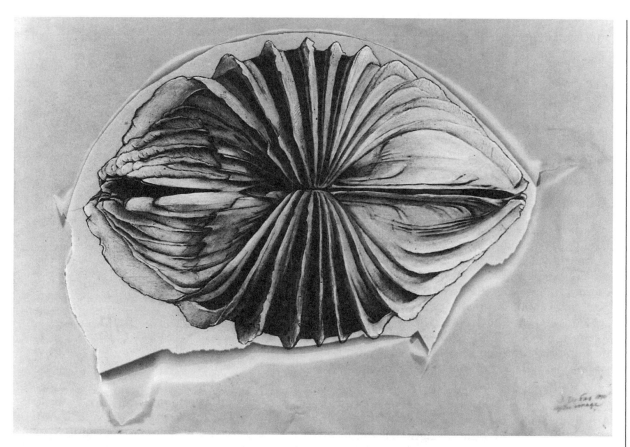

Jay DeFeo's *The After Image* (1970). The Menil Collection, Houston. © 2003 Estate of Jay DeFeo/Artists Rights Society (ARS), New York.

drawing and painting to children and adults at the San Francisco Museum of Modern Art.

In 1970 DeFeo completed *After Image*. The title of the small gray-toned drawing alludes to its role as her first work since *The Rose*. Following *After Image*, DeFeo continued to produce paintings and drawings, creating series whose visual sources were quotidian objects such as lightbulbs, tape dispensers, water goggles, tripods, shoe trees, and jewelry. In these series, which she often rendered in mixed media on paper, DeFeo deliberately distorted and mystified the look of the object by balancing "expressionistic" distortion and a sort of "photo-realistic" depiction: painterly, gestural passages were juxtaposed with areas of linear, hard-edged representation.

During the summer of 1971 DeFeo was included in the show *New Work: Seven Bay Area Artists* at the Oakland Museum.[12] In his review Thomas Albright took note of DeFeo's tendency to use structurally intricate objects as the source of her imagery, describing the "haunting, visionary intensity" of works such as *After Image,* in which

"the images are most sharply defined, most recognizably 'real,' yet filled with mysterious undertones and analogies."[13]

In 1972 DeFeo began using photography and photocopying extensively in her work. She had become quite interested in photography when teaching at CSFA, where her students taught her how to print photographs in the school's darkroom. Now these techniques of reproduction became a means of mediating and examining the relationship of image to object while documenting the process and progress of her work. As her interest in photography grew, DeFeo bought a Hasselblad and Bogdanoff built a darkroom for her at the Larkspur house. Between 1972 and 1974 DeFeo devoted herself to taking photographs, and she exhibited her photographs of objects and still lifes and some photocollages at the California College of Arts and Crafts in 1975.

DeFeo used both photography and photocopying as sketching tools that allowed her to distance herself from the represented object and to exploit the possibilities for exaggerated tonal and compositional relationships that the camera and the photocopier offered. The camera also became important to DeFeo as a focusing and framing mechanism: the aperture, as both device and image, would continue to play a part in paintings and drawings of the "Tripod," "One O'Clock Jump," and "Architecture" series of the seventies and eighties. As in her handmade drawings, she was particularly sensitive to dark-light contrasts and gradations. She became acutely aware of the tonal idiosyncracies of photocopying, knowledgeable, even, about the variations produced by different machines.

In 1973 DeFeo created a series of photocollages that were a kind of game-dialogue with Bruce Conner. During this period, she regularly spoke on the telephone with Conner, who was then campaigning to raise funds to conserve *The Rose.* The contact with Conner inspired her turn to collages imbued with witty, absurd images, somewhat in the spirit of Conner's own art. Her collages, however, were made mainly out of cut-up photographs that she had taken of things that happened to be in her house.

DeFeo received a National Endowment for the Arts Individual Artist Fellowship for 1973-74, and in 1974 she showed at the Wenger Gallery in San Francisco, her first one-person gallery exhibition since the 1960 Ferus show. The exhibition featured paintings and works on paper, including *Tuxedo Junction,* and *Unknown Image.* DeFeo and Bogdanoff hung the show themselves at the understaffed gallery. Though nothing sold, the critical response to the show was favorable. In a review of the exhibition for the *San Francisco Chronicle,* Thomas Albright located the dominant tendency of DeFeo's works of the seventies:

> DeFeo's most masterful efforts . . . are those paintings that steer a middle course between realism and abstraction [and] seem to float in a space that begins on the surface of the canvas and ends somewhere in the psyche of the beholder.[14]

Despite the positive response in the local press, the lack of interest from collectors was disheartening. DeFeo continued to feel estranged from the art world, and was beset by anxiety and regret about having neglected crucial career opportunities during the late fifties and early sixties.

The critical success and commercial failure of the Wenger show intensified DeFeo's determination to reenter the San Francisco art community. Thomas Albright supported her efforts and suggested appropriate dealers and curators to contact. An important breakthrough came with the summer 1978 exhibition in the MATRIX Gallery at the University Art Museum, Berkeley. This exhibition, organized by the then Director of the San Francisco Museum of Modern Art, Henry Hopkins, included fourteen of DeFeo's recent drawings from the "Tripod," "Water Goggles," "Shoe Tree," and "Jewelry" series. In a conversation with Hopkins, recorded in the MATRIX brochure, DeFeo described her recent work and its relation to her previous work:

> Over the years I have worked either from the subjective world of my imagination, finding the image through my response to, and manipulation of the materials I work with or working from the objective world of reality (as in the case of these drawings) discovering the image among the relationships of forms in the common objects that I am using for models. The process becomes a play between my control over the materials and an open or permissive attitude toward technique, allowing it to mold the image as it will. Hopefully even the most literal drawings among the recent work transcend the definition of the objects from which they are derived. I enjoy the paradox of developing something quite organic while using inorganic materials.[15]

Local critical response was once again favorable. Writing in *Artweek,* Judith L. Dunham praised DeFeo's ability to "extract spiritual, metaphysical meaning from her scrutiny of common objects" and the "discipline and sensitivity" of her mixed-media monochromatic (black, white, and gray) works on paper.[16]

In 1979, Ed Kienholz organized an exhibition of DeFeo's work at his Faith and Charity in Hope Gallery, in Hope, Idaho. Included were *September Blackberries, Crescent Bridge I, Crescent Bridge II, Lotus Eater I, Lotus Eater II, Trap,* and *Preliminary Drawing for Eyes.* At the time of the exhibition DeFeo and Kienholz removed the damaged, dirt-encrusted painting *Jewel* from beneath the porch of DeFeo's Larkspur cottage, and Kienholz and his assistants restored it. The restoration revealed anew the painting's intense red and oranges—colors DeFeo so rarely used in her work.

In 1978 DeFeo enthusiastically joined Gallery Paule Anglim in San Francisco and enjoyed a successful one-person exhibition there in 1980. The exhibition included, among other works, two large paintings from the "Loop" series of the early seventies, and the 1980 mixed-media painting *Temple (For WB).* Also included were a number of drawings from the "One O'Clock Jump" series.

Concurrently, DeFeo's teaching career was gathering new momentum. In 1976 she began teaching at Sonoma State University in Rohnert

Park, where she continued as instructor of drawing and painting until 1980. She taught at the California College of Arts and Crafts (CCAC) in Oakland from 1978 until 1981, and during 1980-81 she was a visiting artist at Berkeley. In the autumn of 1981 DeFeo began teaching at Mills College in Oakland and moved to her present studio in West Oakland. The position at Mills became DeFeo's first full-time teaching job, leading to a tenured full professorship.

In 1982 DeFeo received an honorary doctorate from the San Francisco Art Institute, and the following year she received the SFAI's Adaline Kent Award. The Adaline Kent Award exhibition, *Jay DeFeo: Selected Works, Past and Present,* held at the SFAI during the spring of 1984, displayed forty-four paintings and drawings. A number of works from the fifties, including *Blossom, Doctor Jazz, Jewel,* and *The Eyes,* as well as paintings and drawings from the numerous series of the seventies were grouped thematically with compositions from the "Summer Image," "Architecture," and "Eternal Triangle" series, which reveal DeFeo's reintroduction of color into her work of the early eighties.

DeFeo had a second one-person exhibition at the Gallery Paule Anglim in 1983, and in 1983 and 1986 the gallery showed DeFeo's work along with that of Wally Hedrick, Bruce Conner, and George Herms in a pair of group exhibitions entitled "Sight/Vision: The Urban Milieu" (I and II). Part I included works from the fifties along with recent paintings, while Part II focused on new works, including DeFeo's 1983 *Homage to Thomas Albright, #1.*

In 1984 DeFeo traveled to Japan. The trip vivified and expanded her interest in Japanese art and architecture, which dated back to her years as a student at Berkeley. The renewed Japanese sensibility is notable in various large paintings she made upon returning and in the "Samurai" series of drawings.

DeFeo received a second National Endowment for the Arts Individual Artist Fellowship in 1985-86. A 1985 one-person exhibition of seventeen of her recent paintings at the Janus Gallery in Los Angeles renewed the Southern California art community's interest in her work. Writing in the *Los Angeles Times,* critic William Wilson recalled DeFeo's involvement in the Ferus Gallery and its achievement of having "put California art on the map" in the early sixties. Wilson went on to praise the "formal force" of her recent work.[17]

During the summer of 1986 DeFeo traveled to Africa. In anticipation of the trip, she made an extensive series of largely black-and-white, mixed-media works on paper called "Impressions of Africa." The imagery of her *Reflections of Africa* drawings (1987) however, emerged from her examination of a group of black-and-white patterned cardboard tissue boxes, rather than African artifacts.

During the summer of 1987 DeFeo returned to Europe for the first time since her extended stay in 1951-52. She visited Berlin, Paris, and Florence. The trip was partly a nostalgic pilgrimage, though DeFeo made a point of seeing all the museums and attractions she had missed on her student sojourn.

DeFeo's 1988 one-person exhibitions at the Gallery Paule Anglim and the Jan Turner Gallery in Los Angeles showed recent paintings along with works from the *Reflections* and "Impressions of Africa" series, as well as drawings from the 1987 "Samurai" series.

In April 1988 DeFeo learned that she had cancer. While therapeutic treatments have diminished her creative output, she has entered a new phase of work with renewed energy.

In 1989 several of DeFeo's collages were included in the exhibition *Forty Years of California Assemblage* at the Wight Art Gallery in Los Angeles. To celebrate the exhibition, Michael McClure wrote "100 Things of Interest About the Assemblage Movement," which included the following homage to DeFeo:

58. The earliest work of DeFeo's that I saw was in the North Beach, Grant Avenue, bar The Place, where we Beat poets hung out.

59. DeFeo's work was a sudden esthetic illumination: small pieces of posterboard with daubed single splotches of gray and white tempera and maybe a few stringy lines comprising part of a brush stroke or swipey semi-daub of dirty red. But none of it was careless—it was perfect. It was perfectly worn and slightly uncared for pieces of posterboard.

60. When I looked at those pieces I had the sudden feeling that, for visual art, I was happy to be in Frisco and not Paris. That was 1954 or 1955.

61. DeFeo rode abstract expressionism a direction it had never been before—it was the placement of her incredible shabby daubs or exquisitely worn splotches and loose, sprawling, offbeat bars that was the message. She was dealing with the

paint as the assemblagists would deal with worn materials. She was part of a new vision—a new say of seeing. She was Beat, she was elegant, she was worn and glimmery. DeFeo is the visionary of the Assemblagists.

62. DeFeo was as calligraphic and as minimalistic as Motherwell was seen to be, at a slightly later time, in his brush paintings but Motherwell was a very pure painter, an intellectual looking to Paris or perhaps Tokyo. DeFeo was a gambler and an alchemist. She was translating her VISION into painting and gambling her spirit on the *coup* of her dusky materials.

63. I have seen three great crosses: one is by Cimabue or another post-Byzantine master and is in the Accademia in Florence. The second great cross is in my possession and is by George Herms. Herms carried the cross on his back up Downey Street to my home in San Francisco, followed by a group of small children. At the time Herms had very long hair and a beard. The Herms cross is composed of scrap wood and shelving and a tree branch. The crossbar supports a small museum of assemblages ranging from a photo of a man with elephantiasis of the scrotum to a handmade Robbie the Robot to a plastic box containing human teeth. The third cross was entered by DeFeo in the San Francisco Art Annual in the midfifties—and it created a scandal. It was butcher paper stretched over a lumber frame in the shape of a cross, around twelve to fifteen feet high. It was outrageous in scale and beauty—it had an enormous delicacy. The white cross' sole decoration was a large splash or splot of tempera. The piece was graffitied by vandals while hanging in the museum. The obscenities that were added worked to make the piece even more profound and consequently more beautiful.

64. At one point in the late fifties I found that Jay, who then lived in the studio below, had destroyed by cutting in half, nearly all of her tempera on posterboard works. The destroyed stack of work was a foot and a half or two feet high.

I wish she had not done it and I have thought about her act for thirty years.

65. My guess is that DeFeo destroyed the work so that she might go beyond it. It may have taken twenty years to go beyond that work. It was the most advanced work in its spiritual substance that I had seen till that time.

66. Bruce Connor is working with *sensory* and *intellectual fire*—and then *spirit*, in that order. Jay is working with *spirit, contemplation* and *gesture*. She proves that the minute gesture in a perfect daub is as fine as a great slooping drip in Pollock's work or a "field" in Rothko's.[18]

Notes

1. In 1963 Hofmann signed an agreement to give forty-five of his paintings to the University of California at Berkeley. This gift was the impetus for building the University Art Museum.

2. DeFeo's husband, Wally Hedrick, later joined the Studio 13 Jazz Band.

3. E. Loran, "San Francisco," *Art News,* 48, September 1949, 45.

4. Anne M. Wagner, in her essay "Lee Krasner as L. K." posits that Krasner's use of Lee—rather than Lenore, her given name—and the initials L. K. were part of her effort to resist such pigeonholing (*Representations,* 25, Winter 89, 42-57).

5. Michael McClure recalls the impact of DeFeo's cross in his prose-poem "One Hundred Things of Interest About the Assemblage Movement," quoted at length at the end of this essay.

6. *The Dilexi Years,* Oakland Museum, 1984, 38.

7. E. Kienholz, *J. DeFeo* (Faith and Charity in Hope Gallery, catalogue), Hope, Idaho, August 1979.

8. D. C. Miller, J. T. H. Baur, and D. G. Seckler, "New Talent, U.S.A. Painting," *Art in America,* 49, Spring 1961, 30.

9. A. Fried, "After 6 Years and 2300 Pounds of Paint," *San Francisco Examiner,* April 11, 1969.

10. T. Albright, "Just One Single Rose—A Glorious Anachronism," *San Francisco Chronicle,* April 11, 1968.

11. Recently there has been a revival of efforts to raise funds to complete the necessary conservation work so that *The Rose* can again be exhibited.

12. The other artists in the exhibition were Duane Faralla, Nancy Genn, Sidney Gordin, Robert Johnson, Fritz Raugh, and Fred Reichman.

13. T. Albright, "Their Own Artistic Paths," *San Francisco Chronicle,* July 15, 1971.

14. T. Albright, "Paintings Reach Far Beneath the Surface," *San Francisco Chronicle,* September 7, 1974.

15. Conversation with Henry Hopkins, June 23, 1978, in *MATRIX 11: Jay DeFeo* (University Art Museum, Berkeley, brochure), July 1978.

16. J. L. Dunham, "Memorable Visions in Drawing and Sculpture," *Artweek,* July 28, 1978.

17. W. Wilson, "The Art Galleries: La Cienega Area," *Los Angeles Times,* May 24, 1985.

18. McClure read this prose-poem on April 11, 1989, at the Dickson Art Center, University of California at Los Angeles.

REBECCA SOLNIT (ESSAY DATE 1990)

SOURCE: Solnit, Rebecca. "Culture and Counterculture: San Francisco's Fifties." In *Secret Exhibition: Six California Artists of the Cold War Era*, pp. 26-56. San Francisco: City Lights Books, 1990.

In the following essay, Solnit offers an overview of the precursors to and early days of the era of Beat Generation art in California during the 1950s.

The City

"San Francisco was not just a wide-open town," said poet and critic Kenneth Rexroth, who moved there in 1927.[1] "It is the only city in the United States which was not settled overland by the westward-spreading puritanism or by the Walter-Scott fake-cavalier tradition of the South. It had been settled mostly, in spite of all the romances of the overland migration, by gamblers, prostitutes, rascals, and fortune seekers who came across the Isthmus and around the Horn. They had their faults, but they were not influenced by Cotton Mather." San Francisco had become the cultural capital of the West Coast not long after the Gold Rush turned it from a sleepy outpost to a bustling city. Los Angeles has outstripped San Francisco in recent decades, but during the fifties, San Francisco could still regard its museums and symphonies and opera with complacent pride (the San Francisco Museum of Art, which opened in 1935, was the second museum in the United States devoted to modern art). It was less a city of great artists than of self-conscious bohemianism and cosmopolitan appreciation, of art as part of its way of life.

There was genial tolerance for political and social radicalism, and the anarchist tradition begun by Italian workers was continued by artists and writers between the wars and afterward. San Francisco was a favorite spot for conscientious objectors on leave from their wartime camps on the coast, and as a port city, it had sailors-passing through, old-fashioned Madam-run houses of prostitution, and a slightly more visible, less intimidated gay community than most other American cities. It was a diverse and colorful city, with Chinatown and Italian North Beach, the Irish Mission, the Russians out in the foggy Richmond, the black Fillmore district with its jazz clubs.

Michael McClure, who moved here in 1954, recalls, "San Francisco was a hotbed of liberalism and Pacific Coastal rim ideas and environmental consciousness at its early stages and a place where one could live in a lovely apartment with a view and low rent that an artist might be able to af-ford." The small San Francisco-Berkeley cultural enclaves grew rapidly in the years after the war. Robert Duncan, Jack Spicer and Robin Blaser formed a circle of poets in Berkeley; the surrealist Philip Lamantia, the Catholic William Everson (who was, in his monkish incarnation, Brother Antoninus) and Rexroth were their equivalent across the Bay. Madeline Gleason and poet-filmmaker James Broughton formed another locus in San Francisco, and more poets poured in during the early fifties. Gary Snyder came from the north; and Jack Kerouac, Allen Ginsberg, and other Easterners began to flock to the Bay Area. Pacifists and poets were largely responsible for founding KPFA, the radical listener-supported FM station whose broadcasts included Pauline Kael on film, Alan Watts on spirituality and Far Eastern religion, Rexroth on literature, and, on folk music, an extremely irreverent Jack Spicer, who concocted obscene new verses for traditional ballads until he was thrown off the air.[2]

"For years everything was for the War," said Broughton a few years later.[3] "That's why there was this wonderful explosion in 1945 and 1946. Suddenly we knew what we wanted to do. That's when the Bay Area came into flower. Something began to explode for everyone. Wonderful painters. Experimental film began. Wonderful audiences. Everyone was hungry." Artists, as well as poets, gathered in the area, many of them veterans in school on the GI Bill—at conservative University of California, Berkeley, at the materials-oriented California College of Arts and Crafts in Oakland, or at the California School of Fine Arts (now the San Francisco Art Institute), on the fringes of North Beach. The GI Bill enabled thousands of young men to raise their expectations and widen their horizons, and the California School of Fine Arts, with its idealistic agendas, bloomed during the postwar years.

Its transformation had begun when Douglas MacAgy took over as director. He had come to San Francisco via London and Philadelphia to be the assistant director of the San Francisco Museum of Art, then left for the greater challenge of rebuilding the school (which had dwindled to a handful of night classes during the war years). A vigorous organizer with an international perspective on art, MacAgy deserves much credit for making San Francisco more aware of the outside world and raising its artistic standards. In 1949 he organized the Western Round Table on Modern Art, a several-days-long symposium with Marcel Duchamp and Frank Lloyd Wright among the participants. The new faculty he hired included many who acquired fine local reputations, such as Hassel Smith and Edward Corbett, as well as those who later achieved national acclaim: Elmer Bischoff, David Park, Ansel Adams and Clyfford Still, Mark Rothko, and Ad Reinhardt. The painting department was the heart of the school, and early on it became the western outpost of abstract-expressionism.

Abstract-expressionism has been described by one of its leading proponents, Harold Rosenberg, as a religion; one of its most vociferous detractors, Serge Guillbaut, calls it a plot.[4] Many of this movement's ideas came from the abstract surrealists who had spent the war years in exile in the United States, and their interest in psychoanalysis and mythology and their use of automatic drawing as a means of gaining access to the unconscious were central to the new painting. It was the country's first claim to a major modern art movement, and it made New York City the capital of modern art while Europe was still recovering from the war. The interval between inception and institutionalization was unprecedentedly brief for ab-ex, perhaps because America was hungry for a new cultural identity to go with its new role as superpower. Attempts to establish a distinctly American art via social realism and regionalism had collapsed in the war years, partly because these schools were associated with discredited political ideas. "Modern painting is the bulwark of the individual creative expression, aloof from the political left and its blood brother, the right," declared a spokesman at a MOMA forum in 1948.[5] Abstract-expressionism with its emphasis on gesture and spontaneity was upheld as a symbol of freedom, though bereft of overt political content. In Clyfford Still's words: "a single stroke of paint, backed by work and a mind that understood its potency and implications, could restore to man the freedom lost in twenty centuries of apology and devices for subjugation."[6]

Abstract-expressionism was also self-consciously avant-garde, immersed in a realm of eternal verities far from the specifics of contemporary American life. The postwar years saw an increasing fear of vulgarization; the amusing and commercial were widely held to be inimical to high art. Clement Greenberg had paved the way with his "Avant-Garde and Kitsch" essay of the late thirties which, despite its vaguely socialist conclusions, placed faith in "the cultivated of mankind," saw popular culture as both threat and seduction, and celebrated artists who "derive their chief inspiration from the medium they work in." By the beginning of the sixties, Dore Ashton,

another spokesperson for New York's abstract painters could write, "Mass democracy leads to popularization, and popularization is the enemy of the independent artist. . . ."[7] Pop art confronted head-on many of the assumptions of those years, but until that reinvention of kitsch as the avant-garde, a nervously elitist art prevailed.

For all that has been written about abstract expressionism at the California School of Fine Arts, it didn't exactly spread like wildfire. Perhaps its ideals of individualism and self-expression were taken too literally by students such as Jeremy Anderson and Jess, who both forged personal artistic languages full of humor and irreverence. Perhaps the Bay Area has never been fertile ground for "high seriousness"; anarchist sentiments run too deep. Jay DeFeo, perhaps the region's most important abstract painter during the later fifties, came out of Berkeley; Richard Diebenkorn and Frank Lobdell were the only two major abstractionists to emerge from the school's golden age, and even Diebenkorn dipped into figurative painting. Painting instructors Elmer Bischoff and David Park committed apostasy by beginning what would be called the Bay Area Figurative School in the early fifties; in 1950 Park destroyed his abstract work, saying it was "insufficiently troublesome." Ab-ex's legacy in the area was less a continuing painterly tradition than a set of ideals that would serve well even those who reacted against its limitations as a style.

MacAgy's Golden Age was shortlived. Once the influx of GI Bill students slowed, MacAgy's program became financially unfeasible, and the trustees replaced him with solid, reliable, Bauhaus-influenced Ernst Mundt in 1950. MacAgy had resigned (with encouragement, and according to legend, because the trustees wouldn't let him hire Marcel Duchamp), and much of his faculty followed suit or was not rehired in the ensuing years. The school has never been quite the same, though it has had other high points and other distinguished faculty and graduates. The Studio 13 Jass Band seems to typify the spirit of MacAgy's period when, as Bischoff remarked, "there were not really instructors and students so much as there were older artists and younger artists."[8] This traditional jazz group took its name from its practice room at the heart of the school, and its members included both teachers and students—Bischoff on trumpet, Park on piano, students Conrad Janis on trombone and Charlie Clark on trumpet. Wally Hedrick, who joined the band a few years later, remembers walking into the school on his first visit north, in the late 1940s. "The first day I walked in, they were out playing on the patio and they had a complete band. I don't know how many people know it, but MacAgy was a passable drummer."

Painter Among Poets

Jess was a favorite of Clyfford Still's at the California School of Fine Arts, though if that champion of the somber and austere could have foreseen what his pupil would go on to do, his feelings might have been different. Jess had come to the school from Hanford Nuclear Weapons Facility in Washington State, where he was a laboratory chemist involved in plutonium manufacture. Born Burgess Franklin Collins in Long Beach, just south of Los Angeles, in 1923, his journey to the California School of Fine Arts was long and full of detours. His family was "super-Republican" (he dropped his last name in the early fifties to repudiate his connections to them). His vocation asserted itself early and was thwarted early. "I always wanted to be a painter," he said in 1988. "I knew when I was seven years old—the age when you first begin to question your parents. I told my father that's what I wanted to be. He always wanted me to be some sort of scientist. Then he said that maybe there's money in art, and I could become a rich artist: 'I guess Norman Rockwell does all right.' I looked at a Norman Rockwell cover and said to myself, 'If that is art, I don't want it.'"

The playful illustrations in the Oz books were his artistic ideal then, and he never lost his affection for them. He recalls two other things from his childhood that later became influences on his work. His father, a civil engineer, took an avaricious interest in the old mines in California's southeast deserts and brought Jess there as a child. The prospector Old Sourdough was still alive then, and his ramshackle cabins were scattered around the mining territory. "A little palace assembled from scrap wood, pieces of aluminum, junk, tins, almost any type of found object you can imagine," was Jess's description of one of these structures, and its interior was a collage of calendars, posters and advertisements. He credits, too, a great-aunt who made him marvelous scrapbooks of pictures she'd cut out herself.[9]

"I lost touch with the joy they gave me," says Jess, and he lost the scrapbooks as he grew older. His father won out and Jess went to California Institute of Technology to study chemistry. The wartime draft interrupted his studies, and he spent the last two years of World War II at Oakridge, Tennessee, working on the Manhattan Project. In the introduction to Jess's 1971 book *Translations,*

Robert Duncan wrote, "In his former life, the painter Jess was chemist, drafted in 1943 out of Cal Tech to serve his Babylonian Captivity in the Chemical Warfare Division of the US Army and in the Engineers Corps at Oakridge, working in plutonium production, returning after the war to graduate from Cal Tech in chemistry with honor and serving again in the Plutonic legions of the G.E. atomic energy project at Hanford, Washington. The nightmare gravity that colors Jess's canvases and unites his vision with that of the early De Chirico and Max Ernst's hallucinatory collages and paintings has not only its roots in the nightmare reality that we all know in our childhood visions of the world but also has its bitter root in the actuality of the grown-up nightmares which the workers in chemistry and physics have brooded in our time. Xibalba, the land of violent death, whose lords cause bleeding in the road, vomiting of blood, running of pus from open sores, the terrors of revolution and of war, has been known by the artist not only in dreams but in actuality."

On August 6, 1945, Jess's twenty-second birthday, the United States dropped an atomic bomb on Hiroshima and, three days later, another at Nagasaki. A week afterwards, the atomic workers at Oakridge in Tennessee were treated to a screening of a secret government film of the hell they had helped to bring about. The film documented the two shattered cities and included graphic footage of the dead and the grotesquely disfigured survivors. "People were passing out," Jess recalls, "and so was I." Still, the impact of what he was doing didn't arrive until three years later, when he was a chemist at Hanford. "I had a dream—what Jungians call the Big Dream—in which the whole world is being incinerated. It was stated very clearly that the world had only twenty-five years." Deciding that if time was so limited, he ought to begin doing what he really valued, Jess moved to San Francisco, which he had heard his coworkers praise, to become an artist. (He had been, in his words, a Sunday painter before.) On the West Coast, there was almost no chance of becoming financially successful as an artist, so those who chose art were clearly striking out for personal fulfillment and, most often, poverty. For Jess, choosing art meant giving up a secure career. It was a considered decision, and in making it he freed himself to do exactly what he wanted.

He enrolled at the University of California, Berkeley, on the GI Bill, first signing up for graduate chemistry classes as a blind for his true purposes, then switching to art his first week there. The school subjected him to a battery of psychological tests—the chief psychologist concluded he was better suited to art than science anyway—and the head of the art department, after looking at a portfolio of paintings Jess describes as pathetic, told him, "I think you would find it much more valuable to go to the California School of Fine Arts." So in 1949, he found himself enrolled at that West Coast outpost of painterly romanticism. Clyfford Still and the younger painters Edward Corbett, Elmer Bischoff, and Hassel Smith were his most important teachers, and all were then ardent abstract-expressionists.

Still, particularly, was immersed in the mystique of pure painting and played up his role as the Heathcliff of high art. His vast canvases had a melancholy drama about them: huge shards and rifts of color in brushy fields suggesting entropic forces and sublime disasters. He taught art as a sacred vocation, giving his students, in fellow teacher Bischoff's words, "a tremendous feeling of purpose, a tremendous feeling of rectitude."[10] Jess remembers him as an excellent, patient teacher whose lectures were untainted by the dogma that might be expected of an artistic extremist and whose private persona was considerably milder than his public one. Jess's fellow student and friend Harry Jacobus compares Still to a Sufi teacher who teaches by not teaching, by making it clear that learning comes only through doing. As a result, the class that had begun with twenty or so students dwindled to about seven, Jacobus recalls, and of those seven, Jess was the only one Still paid attention to. He liked to talk about metaphysics with the former scientist. (Jess doesn't recall receiving quite so much attention.)

A more easygoing teacher was Clay Spohn, whose 1949 *Museum of Little-Known Objects* is sometimes considered the first assemblage exhibition in the Bay Area. This show at the California School of Fine Arts included constructions such as a conglomerate of bent forks titled *A Forking Situation,* a jar of moldy grayish rice titled *Mouse Seeds,* and a nonfunctional assemblage-chastity belt. Spohn himself took his painting more seriously, and his "museum" was meant as a lighthearted gesture for a school festival. Assemblage and collage were not new when Jess and his peers reinvestigated the medium in the fifties; what was new was their realization that these could be serious, significant media, the central work of an artist's life. At the time, however, the *Museum of Little-Known Objects*' unusual media and prankish tone didn't make an impression on Jess. He was trying

to be an abstract painter, though the approach didn't come naturally to him. He did, however, begin to make representational paintings based on a technique of envisioning the abstract-expressionist paintings Still and others produced as mines for imagery. Michael Auping writes of them, "Jess became intrigued with the idea of transforming Still's craggy fields of color into romantic fictions. This was not simply a matter of seeing picturesque landscape elements (canyons, cliffs, open prairie, waterfalls, etc.) in Still's paintings, but rather of interpreting them as extended fantasies or mythological stories."[11] Abstract-expressionism's ideas of working intuitively sank in, although painting itself wouldn't become a major medium for Jess for many years; instead, as a latecomer to artmaking, he found collage an appealing shortcut to the creation of imagery. Jess's aesthetic was largely formed in his childhood; later events would reawaken it.

In 1950 he met Robert Duncan at a poetry reading. They soon after began a life together that lasted until Duncan's death in 1988, an extraordinary collaboration and partnership. Although only three years older than Jess, Duncan had already ended his early career as a dissolute, roving poet. He knew many important poets and artists and steeped himself in occult lore, art, poetry, history, and politics. In 1944 he caused a stir among East Coast intellectuals by writing "The Homosexual in Society" for Dwight MacDonald's magazine *Politics.*[12] By openly discussing homosexuality and disclosing his own, Duncan offended many straight people; by condemning the voluntary isolationism and elitism of gay subcultures, he closed off what could have been a refuge. *Partisan Review* hastily cancelled publication of his long "African Elegy," and Duncan returned to his native California to study medieval and Renaissance history at the University of California in Berkeley and began yearning to settle down. He was a poet with some solid work behind him and enormous promise, and though his erudite poetry never had much to do with Beat literature, he was one of the major poets to emerge in the 1950s. Some rank his work among the most important American poetry of this century.

When they met, Jess was living in the Ghost House, a decrepit, cavernous Gothic-Victorian on Franklin at Sutter Streets whose three floors of rooms were rented out as studios and illegally inhabited by young writers and artists. Philip Lamantia and Wally Hedrick both spent time in the Ghost House, and Hedrick recalls it as a hangout conveniently located between North Beach and the Fillmore, a place where Thelonius Monk or Miles Davis might drop in, where drugs and parties were common. Duncan joined Jess there briefly, and they took over the ballroom of the place, but they were looking for a more tranquil environment. The Ghost House was Jess's only immersion in the frenetic pace and chaos of bohemian life, and he didn't care for it. He had always shunned boisterous gatherings, and over the years he acquired a reputation as a recluse. When their friend James Broughton went to Europe, they took over his quiet flat at 1724 Baker Street.

The filmmaker Larry Jordan, who became a friend and protégé of Jess and Duncan in the later fifties, recalls their home with great affection as a quiet oasis in an often-chaotic subculture. "Jess was deciding that he would like to build a home and maintain a home and have the magic of, the protection of, a home. And he taught me a great deal of my lifestyle out of that—what the meaning of a home is. It's a whole lot more than bourgeois values, it's a magical kingdom and it needs to be protected from all the wayward vibrations that come and go. So there were rules about who could come and it was very civilized; it was not the usual open American flop pad at all. They abhorred pads, sleeping on the floor on mattresses. And that taught me a great deal about being civilized, which is hard to find in this American culture."

Their household became a salon akin to the Bermans' in southern California, and they themselves became mentors for many younger poets and artists. Jess and Duncan began to build up a vast library—children's picture books were Jess's contribution—and to collect art-nouveau objects and other stuff considered kitsch at the time, to fill their home with the art of their friends and with Jess's art. Assemblage and collage were, among other things, affordable media for artists without money to work in, and the aesthetic of many artists' households owed its origin to economic constraints. Fin-de-siécle and art-nouveau goods were cheap, and their availability as well as their visionary possibilities made them appealing to Duncan and Jess.

They also acquired a lodger. In 1952, the nineteen-year-old Stan Brakhage moved into their basement for a few years while he was exploring both poetry and film (eventually, of course, he became one of most prolific and influential experimental filmmakers in the United States). The basement was full of Broughton's books and films, which the younger artist studied carefully. Bra-

khage described the house with "orange painted walls with giant cats drawn upon them; everything about the place was exotic. I just didn't know what to think. Robert and Jess, his lover, invited me in, and they were civilized and exciting. They were wonderful people and nobody can top them with their deep and active interest in every interstice of life. They were people living out the peculiarities of their lives as a triumph, rather than an abyss."[13] Another time Brakhage recalled, "Duncan's house was my school and he was my teacher. Every evening there was a discussion about films, plays, poems, music, and paintings." This kind of conjunction of artists—a poet, a painter, a filmmaker—was central to the richness of the West Coast subculture, and the common grounds stretch across media. In these three artists' work can be found an emphasis on the subjective, the dream, and the fragment; they all understood collage as a technique applicable to any medium.

In 1955, Brakhage finished a film whose sole character was played by Jess, *In Between,* a ten-minute color narrative about a man withdrawing from the world and traveling into the imagination in search of beauty. Full of flowers, cats, candles, and statues, it was shot in an early version of Brakhage's distinctive handheld camerawork, with a soundtrack of John Cage's music. (Later, Jess and Duncan parted ways with Brakhage, their attitudes about being an artist incompatible with his). McClure says, "there was a mystically independent, deeply intelligent, capricious joy and love of sensibility in all that Jess and Robert did."[14]

Jess was a gentle, quiet rebel in his art, but an absolute rebel. He refused to stay within the confines of the serious, the respectable, and the modern. He took the surrealists as his jumping-off point and became the first major California artist to work with subject matter that would later be called pop. He explored nostalgic imagery and experimented with the appropriation of found images and language in his collage and assemblage. He cites Max Ernst, Jean Cocteau, Antoni Gaudí, and San Francisco's rococo Playland-at-the-Beach (particularly the funhouse) as important influences. A transition between the styles he was schooled in and the styles he developed is visible in the 1953 painting and collage *Seventy XXTH— Success Story.* Its muddy colors and abstracted, brushy forms at first suggest a somber restraint, but on closer inspection the forms resemble jaunty targets, flowers, and clouds; and preposterous phrases cut out from magazines are sprinkled over its surface. The impurity of media and the levity were an outrage in 1953 in a way that is hard to imagine in the laissez-faire art world of the present. Surrealism was supposed to have been superceded by ab-ex. Nineteen fifty-three was the year essayist-pundit Dwight MacDonald had tidily divided the arts into high-brow, middle-brow, and low-brow, so putting lines like "Elsie! What's the Big Id" and "Has God Been Insulted Here?" into a high-culture artifact like a painting was an act of veritable miscegenation.[15]

Actually, if the work of Jess, Berman, Conner, and Kienholz is considered as part of the canon of American art, it becomes clear that surrealism, with its insurrectionary wit and adoration of the absurd, wasn't eclipsed or absorbed by abstract-expressionism (and Hassel Smith has noted that San Francisco ab-ex came out of surrealism without taking the detour through Picasso that shaped East Coast ab-ex). Instead, surrealism became a potent way to address the incongruous realm of American experience. "Originally had a secret notation built to the outside through the evidence. Ay! He used it whenever he wanted dragged back rolled-up partly-worked turned words telling the truth," says a frozen figure in *Case V* of Jess's *Tricky Cad,* one of the many collages he titles pasteups. He was profoundly influenced by Max Ernst's 1934 collage-novel *Une Semaine de Bonte,* which he and Duncan came across in 1952. Ernst's pictorial narratives, which took old engraved scenes and added disruptive incongruities, were very much part of the surrealist assault on bourgeois complacency.

Jess's collage technique is very different. Rather than subvert conventional scenes, he constructs fantastic ones out of smaller bits of imagery, sometimes into fields of colors and textures, like abstract painting. Some of his early pieces are pure clutter, in which cut-out images, typographical elements, and typewritten jokes and puns all swim in an inky sea. There is little or no relationship between the elements, and the work conveys the artist's relish of each Victorian engraving and outré pun. By 1954 the words and images become compositional elements, and a multiplicity of meanings arise from the verbal and visual puns. *Goddess Because* is an exemplary work from this period, both an homage to and parody of the Modess sanitary products ads, which featured a glamorous woman engaged in high-toned activity and the euphemistic slogan "Modess because. . . ." The marble head of an antique goddess dominates Jess's collage, and a genuine power of strangeness manifests itself in the primitive

creatures, the aquatic scenery, and the giant foot. The peculiar color scheme and hilarious phrases, however, anchor the piece firmly in the territory of the absurd.

Its title, *Goddess Because,* is a commentary on American consumerism and the media's elevation of product consumption to the level of meaningful experience. Jess simply goes one step further; elevating the sanitary napkin to the divinely absurd. The *Tricky Cad* series he began the same year uses the same approach, although all its text and material are drawn from one source, just as its changing titles are all anagrams of *Dick Tracy.* This series consists of *Dick Tracy* comic strips made absurd through a process of condensation of imagery and language. Jess's version extends the already surreal qualities of this comic—the cinematic framing of scenes, the grotesque villains, violent action and bizarre details, and the slangy dialogue—though it subverts most of the narrative (the prose narrative, it could be said, has become poetic language, connotation rather than denotation). Jess had been "hooked as a child into the dialectic" of *Dick Tracy,* when it was a crusading strip critical of corrupt police in the early thirties; then in the fifties he found it had become authoritarian and repressive, and so again the collage work combines homage and critique of its original subject. In 1969 Jess wrote of the *Tricky Cad* series, "One surprisingly curmudgeonly Fraternity Sunday in 1953 *Tricky Cad* scrambled out of Chester Gould's *Dick Tracy,* afterwards to concentrate (undertaking 8 cases) in demonstration of the hermetic critique lockt up in Art, here popular.[16] Also here was bad case of sincerest-form-of-flattery; not amusing to the originator. . . . Art is somehow getting-to-the-heart-of-it-all."

In these early works are all the elements of Jess's art. They are adaptations of existing things rather than pure inventions; language is intrinsic to them; they uphold the absurd and mysterious (as two faces of the same thing, the unknown) as exhilarating rather than terrifying. Jess, after all, had taken up art as an "antidote to the scientific method," saying "the real truth—if there is such a thing—that you can learn from science is how little we know about reality. Art seemed to address this more openly." Where the dadaists (John Heartfield and George Grosz, among others) had used collage as a technique for exposing the senselessness of bourgeois society and the state, Jess made nonsense an escape from the stultifying sensibleness of America and the cold rationalism of science. A sense of liberation and joy permeates these pasteups.

"I have gathered a posie of other men's flowers, and nothing but the thread that binds them is mine own," wrote Montaigne, and Jess borrowed the sentence to use as the epigraph to his collage book O! (published in 1960). Nearly all Jess's work is made up of existing images and objects (a series of paintings called *Salvages* was made by painting over his own works and a few canvases found in thrift stores.) "I am ambitious only to emulate, imitate, reconstrue, approximate, duplicate," Duncan asserted in 1953, and Jess's aspirations were similar.[17] His pasteups, of course, recontextualize found images and words, so that the resultant artwork becomes a critique of its components' origins. As in the *Tricky Cad* series, the process is one of turning the prosaic into the poetic, of making scientific diagrams and news photographs into fantastic landscapes and peculiar phenomena. Jess's pasteups often grew into vast, dizzying complex pictures, in which scale and perspective warped and metamorphosed. In *The Mouse's Tale* (1951-54), small black and white bodies cut from magazines form a monumental, pensive figure, rather as the sixteenth-century painter Archimboldo formed faces from fruit, flowers, or animals.

Toward the end of the 1950s, Jess found another way of adapting found images in the "Translations," paintings that transform black-and-white printed and photographic images into impasto paintings in rich, strange colors. The Translations and pasteups are both methods of scavenging and transmuting; the "assemblies" (Jess's term for assemblage) did the same for objects. These small constructions—"votive objects" says the artist—are less central to his work than the two-dimensional art is, and they have only been exhibited a few times, first and most extensively at King Ubu Gallery in 1953—which is another story.

In the Spirit of Ubu

Harry Jacobus, Jess, and Robert Duncan opened the King Ubu Gallery in December of 1952 for the usual reasons—the artists they knew and admired (including Jess and Jacobus) weren't being given exhibitions by the existing Bay Area galleries. It was Jacobus who had the initial idea and who found the place for the gallery at 3119 Fillmore Street. A big airy room with exposed rafters and concrete floors, it had been a carriage house, a garage, and home base for a theater group. The three salvaged an old pair of ten-foot-tall glass and gilt doors from the posh Mark Hopkins Hotel to front the gallery, they put a sign out, but otherwise kept a low profile. King Ubu was located in the quiet neighborhood of Cow Hollow, about a mile due west of North Beach. It was Duncan who named the place, first proposing Aurora Rose (which Jacobus dismissed as "too nelly"), then King Ubu after the hero of Alfred Jarry's absurdist play.

The first exhibition of large-scale drawings by local artists included David Park, Elmer Bischoff, James Weeks, Hassel Smith, Jess, and Jacobus, with sculptures by Miriam Hoffman. It was followed by solo exhibitions of work by artists who, like Hoffman, have disappeared from the public eye, and then, in the summer, by a three-person show of work by Jess, Jacobus, and a painter friend of theirs named Lynn Brockaway Brown. *San Francisco Chronicle* art critic Alfred Frankenstein gave the show a Sunday review that was fairly favorable: "Jess Collins, one of the three artists now showing at the King Ubu Gallery, exemplifies something which is quite rare in the art of the Bay Region— that mixture of bitterness and blarney which goes under the official name of Dada. His constructions of old light bulbs, feather dusters, discarded toasters and similar junk delightfully recall the 1920s and so do his scrambled collages of photographs and headlines. Collins calls his whole display 'Necrofacts, or dead art,' but only the things employed are dead; the ends to which they are put are rather magnificently wild."[18] Jess found the review (in his word) "inane" enough that he made a large painting-collage responding to and quoting extracts of Frankenstein's piece, *Closet Hanging for a Critic*. Frankenstein was flattered. He was an unflappable, broadminded critic who responded more positively to new and unusual work than was common for newspaper critics at the time. An expert on nineteenth-century American trompe l'oeil paintings—still-lifes of such quotidian objects as cards, money, letters, and stamps—Frankenstein saw collage and assemblage as extensions of that genre.

Wallace and Shirley Berman visited Ubu and met Jess and Duncan in early 1954, and the visit had an impact on Berman's sense of artistic possibilities, for Jess was making greater use of surrealism and popular culture than almost any other artist on the coast. Roy DeForest, Sonia Gechtoff, and Deborah Remington had some of their first exhibits at Ubu, when two back-to-back shows of Hassel Smith's students were held. Later in King Ubu's thirteen-month existence, the gallery was open less and less frequently, as its founders tired of sitting in the chilly room, waiting for the occasional visitor—Frankenstein showed up to review exhibitions several times and found the gallery closed. "We did have openings with quantities of wine until we realized what a bore that was too," says Jacobus. "I think that period cured Jess forever of wanting to go to any openings." Stan Brakhage's films, he recalls, had their first public screening there and got a lukewarm response. There were poetry readings at Ubu, which its founders recall with more fondness. Duncan read, of course, as did cohorts from his Berkeley days, Jack Spicer and Robin Blaser, and Jess himself, who wrote galloping madcap alliterative verses, part James Joyce, part Edward Lear. For example:

"A NYEW EAR'S POME BY JESS"

Old Mother Farquahar
kept a wicker cookie jar,
JOLLY MAJOLICA MARMALADE JAM.
for gingercake lads
hunting hotcross bunnytads,
GINGERY JAMBOREE LEMONDROP LAMB.

Down halls of her household
an ogre his yohos howled
NAVAHO BUNGALOW BEE,
no cooking by cuckooclock
with her ogre who struck oclock,
OMAHA TONOPA THREE

All during the fifties, poetry and art were intertwined in San Francisco. Kenneth Rexroth wrote art criticism, and Lawrence Ferlinghetti painted. Duncan drew and even exhibited his work. Allen Ginsberg arrived in town and first set eyes on his future lover Peter Orlovsky in a painting by Robert La Vigne; Michael McClure came to San Francisco in the hope of studying with Rothko and Still and stayed to develop a kind of action poetry. (One of McClure's early poems begins "THE GESTURE THE GESTURE THE GESTURE THE GESTURE THE GESTURE THE / GESTURE THE GESTURE to make fists of it.")[19]

A poetic rebellion was taking place. Ezra Pound and T. S. Eliot had established a modernist tradition of erudite, impersonal poetry—"for thirty years an orthodoxy ruled American poetry," wrote one of the young insurrectionists.[20] "It derived from the authority of T. S. Eliot and the new critics . . . It asked for a poetry of symmetry, intellect, irony and wit." There was no single reaction against that orthodoxy, but there were some widespread tendencies—the assertion of the personal, a grounding in the details of everyday life, and a desire to return to a genuine, American

speech. "My poems contain no wilde beestes, no lady of the lake, music of the spheres, or organ chants," wrote John Wieners, "Only the score of a man's struggle to stay with what is his own. . . ."[21] Walt Whitman's freewheeling rhapsodies and William Carlos Williams' taut, lucid verse became the foundation for a new tradition, in which Allen Ginsberg could write about supermarkets and homosexual encounters, in which Jack Spicer could compare God to a giant white baseball ("who makes the pitcher, catcher and batter look pretty silly"), in which humor and imperfection, confusion and confession were possible.[22]

The territory of their poetic quest was unmistakably American. Kerouac hunted down the Dharma on freight trains and on Skid Road; while Ginsberg wrote of "the drunken taxicabs of Absolute Reality," of "Mohammedan angels staggering on tenement roofs," even of "Zen New Jersey." The search for a point where the lofty and the seedy meet, where sublime encounters ridiculous, where the eternal verities mingle with last week's garbage was also central to the assemblage and collage work coming out of California. Assemblage found the spiritual in the material, the transcendent in the abandoned, just as it rejected traditional orders of beauty and meaning and the ideological barriers between art and life.

In New York, the situation was similar, though by no means the same. For New York artists plaster casts of body parts or pages from *Life* magazine were essentially devices for extending painting, rather than legitimate media in themselves. Robert Rauschenberg's images and objects were pulled into the work with an aesthetic of randomness. John Cage's ideas about chance sounds and noise as music had been a profound influence, and Cage drew from Zen. Berman, Jess, and their associates were involved in more mythologized spiritual traditions and used their materials with greater concern for symbolic meanings. Much of the East Coast work is a reaction against abstract-expressionism, a moving *beyond* it toward pop—the art of the here and now, of the prosaic consumer reality—though not a move beyond painterliness. The contemporaneous West Coast work is, in some respects, a bridge between abstract-expressionism and pop, an art that could reconcile the existence of sanitary napkin ads with the existence of goddesses—though it largely jettisoned formal painterly concerns.

There were again similarities between the New York and San Francisco poetry scenes, though the differences were also significant. New York poet James Schuyler wrote in 1959, "In New York the art world is a painters' world; writers and musicians are in the boat, but they don't steer."[23] In the fifties in San Francisco, the artists and the poets were on a fairly equal footing; in New York the most important new poets—including John Ashbery, Kenneth Koch, Frank O'Hara—seemed to be in orbit around the painter giants, and though there were some collaborations, they never assumed the same importance as they did in the Bay Area. The scenes themselves differed too: San Francisco's bohemia was a self-enclosed world containing almost all its audience, and the outside world wasn't giving it much attention. McClure, who spent time in both places, says. "The art scene here, the painters' scene was more democratic, more underground, more outlaw, more high-strung and independent—and they didn't have any money. In New York, the painters were already kind of becoming an aristocracy. There was money involved, and important galleries." Before the war, comparing New York to San Francisco would have been preposterous. But in Duncan's words, "What's significant here is that San Francisco became a center. You didn't go to New York because you wanted to write poetry. You didn't go to Europe—no, you came to San Francisco in this period."[24] The young poets placed a new emphasis on readings, on poetry as oral, public performance, with the result that poetry audiences grew and poetry became a lively, exciting, front-line art form, not something to dissect in the classroom. "Poetry has become an actual social force," Rexroth declared.

A few months after King Ubu closed in January of 1954, it reopened as the Six Gallery. The Six was not only the most important art gallery in the region during its four-year life-span, but the place where Duncan read *Faust Foutu* and Allen Ginsberg read *Howl*. But the story of Six Gallery begins with Wally Hedrick and a carload of cohorts escaping from Pasadena early in the fifties.

From Pasadena to Fillmore Street

After Wally Hedrick has said something he considers pretentious, he likes to conclude, "But what do I know, I'm just a kid from Pasadena." It was in Pasadena, however, that Hedrick initiated the peculiar style and vision he has adhered to for the last forty years. Neither the figurative nor the abstract-expressionist painters of San Francisco influenced his work, which addressed a trinity of sex, politics, and religion in a style part Paul Klee and part hot-rod-kustomized-kamp, with a sensibility mingling outrage and jubilance. It is now possible to say Hedrick was ahead of his time—

the first American artist to protest the Vietnam War, the artist who painted flags before Jasper Johns painted flags, who made kinetic junk sculpture before Tinguely did. Hedrick was a forerunner of pop art, bad painting neoexpressionism, and image appropriation. It might be more useful to view Hedrick as an artist who was of his time in a unique way, a maverick whose responses to the world showed it in a different light.

Hedrick was born on July 21, 1928, the son of a used car dealer, and he grew up in sunny, tranquil Pasadena in the hills northeast of Los Angeles. He and his friend David Simpson (now a well-known abstract painter) discovered that carrying out art projects for their junior high school art teacher was a good way to avoid P.E. classes, but he didn't yet plan to be an artist. "I didn't even know what a painter was. I was a typical southern California hot rodder and I wasn't even thinking about college or art school or any of that. I was thinking about going to the beach and playing bridge." The picture he paints of himself may be too simple, for Hedrick had an embryonic social conscience and an interest in the world beyond Pasadena. He and David Simpson had the good fortune to find like-minded cohorts—John Allen Ryan, Hayward King, Deborah Remington, Paula Webb—and with them formed a group that called itself the Progressive Art Workers. They all had leftist leanings and avant-garde aspirations. They listened to John Cage and read Moholy-Nagy's book on vision and motion. They opposed the draft, supported the 1948 Progressive Party presidential candidate Henry Wallace, and sang workers' folk songs. The Progressive Art Workers went to Pasadena City College and found a mentor in the teacher Leonard Edmonsen, who had studied with someone who had studied with Paul Klee. The art program was good in its way, set up to prepare students for the Pasadena Art Center's superb training for industrial and graphic designers. They learned lettering, Bauhaus theory, design principles, and such painting basics as stretching canvas and mixing paints.

It was Edmonsen who told them about the California School of Fine Arts in San Francisco. Hedrick recalls, "I came to him naively and said, 'Where do you go to learn how to become an artist?,' and that, if anything, affected that whole group of people, because he said, 'Well, the first thing to do is to get out of Pasadena.'" In 1946, Hedrick and his friends piled into his Model A Ford and drove to San Francisco to see the fabled art school, arriving at two in the morning in dense fog. The following day, they returned to find the

Studio 13 Jass Band rehearsing in Studio 13 next to the courtyard, and MacAgy got up from his drums to show them around. He mistook them for a group of high school students scheduled to come by that day. "It seemed like heaven, full of these crazy artists," Hedrick recalls. They all came back in David Simpson's panel truck to enroll, but Hedrick couldn't afford the tuition. Instead, he found a job—sitting in the window of North Beach's Vesuvio Bar with his full beard, playing bohemian artist for the tourists. This was hardly the fulfillment of his ambitions, so he went back to Pasadena to join the National Guard in order to avoid the draft, and to learn the banjo because when he returned—and he was determined to return—he wanted to be in the Studio 13 Jass Band.

The military left its mark on nearly every man who was born in the twenties and thirties, and it affected the lives of most of the artists under scrutiny here. After spending years in the National Guard to avoid the army proper, Hedrick learned that his unit was going to be the first one called up for Harry Truman's war in Korea. Hedrick spent a year in Japan, where he was disgusted by American racism and delighted with the Japanese respect for artists. For a year he was in the infantry in Korea, in combat—the only subject he doesn't gladly discuss. He won several medals, but says "now anything that has to do with the army I hate, period." The military gave its veterans two things: the GI Bill and a clarified sense of purpose (having had one's personal life taken away strengthened one's determination to enjoy it).

Finally, six years after first conceiving a desire to go to the California School of Fine Arts, Hedrick found it a very different place than he remembered.[25] MacAgy and his faculty were gone, and Ernst Mundt's Bauhausian program was in place; moreover, since the school lacked accreditation, the GI Bill wouldn't cover his tuition. After a semester there, Hedrick enrolled in California College of Arts and Crafts, the low-key, skills-oriented school across the bay in Oakland, and when the California School of Fine Arts instituted a degree program, he transferred back to it. The most significant result of his time at Arts and Crafts was his meeting with Jay DeFeo, a painter a year younger than he but whose work was more mature in terms of formal study and training. DeFeo's mystical, monochromatic abstractions had next to nothing in common with Hedrick's boisterous, colorful explorations of emblems and clichés, but the two wound up marrying each other and stayed that way for a decade. (She claims their relationship began when impoverished Wally started coming around to devour the contents of her refrigerator; Hedrick claims Jay's refrigerator was a repository of years of dirty laundry and that upon seeing it "the scales fell from my eyes like St. Paul and all of a sudden I recognized funk.")

They became the prototypical beat couple, poor, flamboyant, and present at a great many parties. Hedrick's banjo studies had paid off; he was (and still is) a member of the Studio 13 Jass Band, which played oldtime jazz, from the Moose Lodge in Walnut Creek and the Officers' Club at the Presidio to their own parties. The band brought Hedrick into close contact with talented older artists such as David Park and Elmer Bischoff, who became his real teachers. (He no longer remembers his official art instructors.) Saxophonist Paul Beattie brought Hedrick and DeFeo to his own low-rent apartment building at 2322 Fillmore Street, where the young couple lived for nearly a decade and where many other artists took up residence. Hedrick was also still in touch with the former Progressive Art Workers, and several of them took poet Jack Spicer's English class at the California School of Fine Arts.

Spicer was an archetypal poet maudit—foulmouthed, difficult, alcoholic—who was always trying to extend poetry's possibilities, to make "a poem somebody could hide in with a sheriff's posse after him."[26] He conducted a very unorthodox English class. He taught his students to read the tarot and he taught Shakespeare by putting on experimental performances (in which Hedrick was allowed to improvise, since he couldn't memorize). Spicer had them make paintings in response to poems and instigated scandalous happenings with theatrical lighting, nudity, and jazz. The class was outrageous even by the tolerant standards of the California School of Fine Arts and so Spicer and five students decided to leave the academic context. The Ubu Gallery had recently closed, so six of them—Hedrick, Spicer, Ryan, David Simpson, Deborah Remington and Hayward King—rented the space at 3119 Fillmore. They called it the Six Gallery. It was September, 1954 when the Six opened, and the time was ripe for it.

In the larger world, the French were withdrawing from Vietnam, Senator Joseph McCarthy's reign of paranoia was waning, and the Supreme Court was outlawing segregation in public schools. In New York Jasper Johns was painting flags and abstract expressionism was triumphing. In Los Angeles Aldous Huxley was writing about hallucinogenic drugs and Simon Rodia was putting the finishing touches on Watts Towers. In San Francisco more and more young poets were gathering—Allen Ginsberg, Jack Kerouac, and Gary Snyder were on hand, and North Beach was in full swing. Bay Area figurative painting was flourishing, abstract-expressionism still seemed viable to the regions' remaining abstract-expressionists, and mavericks like the sculptor Jeremy Anderson and the painter Roy DeForest were finding their own voices. The Six Gallery continued Ubu's practice of showing lesser-known local artists and holding cultural events. Openings at the Six were riotous, and the Studio 13 Jass Band often played. When Robert Duncan staged *Faust Foutu,* the cavernous gallery was packed with listeners. Later in 1955, Jess and Duncan headed for Europe, and so they weren't around for an event they indirectly instigated, the most important one to take place at the Six.

Michael McClure recalls, "I saw Wally Hedrick on the street one day and he said, 'Hey wow, that was real nice, that thing we had with Robert Duncan. You wanna have a poetry reading? Can you arrange a poetry reading here?' I said, 'Yeah, sure,' and then I met Allen [Ginsberg] at the Auden reception and I told him about it and I said 'I don't have time to do it.' He said, 'Can I do it?' and I said 'Absolutely.' So in the meantime Allen met Gary [Snyder] and Philip [Lamantia] at Rexroth's. But I would say it came about because of *Faust Foutu,* because of Wally Hedrick asking me and my turning it over to Allen. There was a network, as we say today." Rexroth was the master of ceremonies, McClure, Ginsberg, Lamantia, Whalen, and Snyder read. Ferlinghetti and Jack Kerouac were there, and the evening became the best-known set piece in Kerouac's novel *The Dharma Bums.*

One of John Allen Ryan's friends wrote him an account of the reading: "Cultural event at the 6 Gallery last night. Seven poets, of whom six appeared and five read . . . Hemmed in by a lot of insulting black blotches painted on butcher paper that kept getting torn off the walls, there was a fine big crowd, wine punch . . . and a kind of Greek chorus by the name of Carrowac (sp?), of whom more anon. . . . This Carrowac person sat on the floor downstage right, slugging a gallon of Burgundy and repeating lines after Ginsberg, and singing snatches of scat in between the lines; he kept a kind of chanted, revival-meeting rhythm going.[27] Ginsberg's main number was a long descriptive roster of our group, pessimistic dionysian young bohemians and their peculiar and horrible feats, leading up to a thrilling jeremiad at the

end, that seemed to pick up the ponderous main body of the poem and float it along stately overhead as if it were a kite. There was a lot of sex, sailors and language of the cocksuckingmotherfucker variety in it; the people gasped and laughed and swayed, they were psychologically had, it was an orgiastic occasion."

A landmark in postwar literature and harbinger of the liberation movements of the sixties, *Howl* became the subject of a highly publicized censorship trial. Its vindication allowed American publishers to bring out politically radical and sexually explicit writing. The poem began:

"I saw the best minds of my generation destroyed by madness, starving hysterical naked, / dragging themselves through the negro streets at dawn looking for an angry fix angleheaded hipsters burning for the ancient heavenly connection to the starry dynamo in the machinery of night, / who poverty and tatters and hollow-eyed and high sat up smoking in the supernatural darkness of cold-water flats floating across the tops of cities contemplating jazz, / who bared their brains to Heaven under the El and saw Mohammedan angels staggering on tenement roofs illuminated . . . "

McClure's account of that night, written in the eighties, reflected: "At some point Jack Kerouac began shouting 'GO' in cadence as Allen read it.[28] In all of our memories no one had been so outspoken in poetry before—we had gone beyond a point of no return—and we were ready for it, for a point of no return. None of us wanted to go back to the gray, chill, militaristic silence, to the intellective void—to the land without poetry—to the spiritual drabness. We wanted to make it new and we wanted to invent it and the process of it as we went into it. We wanted voice and we wanted vision."

Paint's Faithfuls

The many accounts of *Howl*'s first reading seldom mention that displayed on stage at the Six Gallery were sculptures by Fred Martin. McClure described them as "pieces of orange crates that had been swathed in muslin and dipped in plaster of Paris to make splintered, sweeping shapes like pieces of surrealist furniture."[29] Martin had gone to school at the University of California, Berkeley, with DeFeo and Sam Francis, and it is interesting that all three of them have worked in a peculiarly romantic-mystic vein—and fruitless to look for sources in the cubistic teachings of their alma mater. Martin wasn't much interested in nightlife, having started a family and taken a serious job early on (later he became the administrative mainstay at the California School of Fine Arts/San Francisco Art Institute), and his work at the Six grew out of his home restoration. His sculptures were made of building materials, and the dozens of tiny paintings he exhibited had come out of his feeling that making large-scale paintings was too much like painting walls. The tiny pieces sold for fifty cents each.

What else was shown during the Six Gallery's thirty-nine-month existence is something of a mystery.[30] No one kept records, and many of the works have disappeared. There was no sense of posterity, of future fame. No one was thinking of future art historians yearning for documents and collectors for early work. It was a liberating condition and responsible for a good many experimental works (as well as for a good many that fell apart because their materials were not permanent). Hedrick and DeFeo are the greatest exemplars of this art-for-art-and-the-moment's sake approach, and the term career hardly describes the artistic adventures, singleminded pursuits, unprofitable decisions, and naive rejections of art-world overtures that constitute their artistic history.

"We were pretty loyal to paint," DeFeo once said. Born on March 31, 1929, she was raised by her divorced mother in the Bay Area, discovered her vocation early on and never swerved, going straight from high school in San Jose to the University of California in Berkeley for five years. In 1951 she became the first woman to win the school's Sigmund Martin Heller Traveling Fellowship; on it she went to Europe, where she visited Sam Francis in Paris, spent six months in Florence, and on her return stopped off in New York to see the new work being made by Philip Guston and other ab-ex giants. (The quality of art-magazine reproduction was so poor in those days that artists couldn't discern what was going on elsewhere as easily as they can now. Many people tell stories about how assumptions they had based on small black and white reproductions were dispelled by the works themselves.) DeFeo brought back stacks of her paintings from Florence, "and people were very excited by them. They were actually kind of a new thing. . . . Or at least this was my own style of abstract-expressionism." She describes her work as a dialectic between discipline and freedom, and her paintings are the result of intensive labor leavened by spontaneous inspirations, of carefully achieved textures and lines broken by bold gestures. Much abstract-expressionism relates to a landscapelike field of color or gesture, but De-

Feo's pieces most often concentrate on the depiction of a central form, sometimes a full-fledged object, sometimes only angles and depths resolving out of the paint. Most of her works then and since have been low-key or monochromatic, focusing on the texture and direction of the paint—vast, austere paintings with a strong, somber presence. A very private person, her work was almost never autobiographically referential in the way that many of her peers's was. Born Joan DeFeo, she had changed her name to Jay—sometimes even J.—as a blind for her gender; although she never recalled much overt sexism in the circles she moved in, such ambiguity could hardly hurt.

DeFeo's work elicited a strong response. Walter Hopps was much struck by it and included her in *Action I* and *Action II,* the exhibitions he put together in 1955, and made sure her work was in the inaugural show at Ferus Gallery in 1957 and in several more exhibitions in the following years. Toward the late fifties her work became increasingly obsessive, and she began to make paintings so thick they resembled relief maps or wall sculptures. The heroic, liberating gesture of ab-ex became for DeFeo a longterm ritual of confrontation and decision at the canvas (culminating in the seven-year, one-ton *The Rose*). She also made large representational drawings during this period, such as *Apparition,* whose inspiration seems to be a specimen of plant life, and whose vortex of lines gives it the sense of the concentrating energy that is so much a part of her abstract paintings. During the middle fifties, she made small metal sculptures she sometimes called jewelry, which brought her focus on axes of angles and curves into three dimensions. She also made a series of huge plaster sculptures in her studio, "done with just a lot of wood and wrapping around with rags and slapping on of plaster." The pieces weren't portable enough to be shown and in any case might not have been recognized as sculpture at that point; they did, however, influence Manuel Neri, who made plaster the major medium in his sculpture from the fifties onward. Her photo collages impressed Bruce Conner and Wallace Berman, though DeFeo herself was offhand about them. She was at heart an abstract painter.

"I mean," says Hedrick, "I admire the gesture of it [ab-ex] and it's very heroic and it made it possible to justify whatever kind of craziness I decided to do, but I was never an abstract expressionist. You might say, 'Well then what were you?' and I'd say 'well I had this vision that it was very important (God, it really sounds corny to say) to be me.'" Hedrick's work of the fifties is astonishing the way Jess's is: it simply has nothing to do with what anyone else was doing. It is possible to see Paul Klee as an important influence, but Hedrick has thoroughly transformed what he borrowed. Klee's grids and patterns, his technique of turning doodles into images, his flattening and distorting of space, his conjunctions of words, patterns, symbols, signs, images, even his warm palette of roses and browns and ochres are all present. Hedrick, however, has left Klee's jewel-like scale behind.

One of Hedrick's earliest documented paintings is *Peace Flag* (1953). "Jasper Johns was just out of his mind because I painted that flag before he did,"[31] Hedrick said in 1985, but Hedrick's flag paintings had little in common with Johns's. The latter's were formal exercises in re-creating an existing flat image. Hedrick's *Peace Flag* was rippled, painted in a deliberately sloppy style that would later be called funky, and five plump, squiggly letters spelled out PEACE across it. Johns's American flags were about the picture plane and eschewing illusionism; Hedrick's was about politics. In 1953, after the American death toll in Korea reached 54,000, Eisenhower finally abandoned the war. Hedrick, only a year out of the army and away from the front lines, took the slaughter personally. Curator Sidra Stich writes of this work, "Hedrick's intention . . . was not to celebrate the truce, but to condemn the war and American military involvements, for which the flag served as a call to arms. The work was also a refusal to pledge allegiance to the reigning Abstract Expressionist credo that pictorial images should be abstract and mystical, that art and politics should not be mixed." His interest in the flag image itself grew out of a lecture Hassel Smith had given about the symbolism of flags; Hedrick painted several realistic flag images, of foreign flags—South Korea, Vietnam—and another United States flag. Many were painted black when Hedrick began to paint out his images in protest of the Vietnam war; *Peace Flag* survived until 1963, when (according to Hedrick) the art critic John Coplans borrowed it from a ten-year survey of Hedrick's work and never returned it. He had asked to bring it to a woman interested in buying it, and the work has never been seen since.

It is difficult to discuss Hedrick's work in general terms, because he strives to make each painting genuinely new and different and often destroys work that seems repetitive. In the middle fifties he made metal sculpture and assemblage

and painted in a variety of styles, from the mystical-kitsch of pieces such as *Fred's TV* to symbolist portraiture in *J., Me et Cat*. The latter is typical of Hedrick's approach to style as a vehicle for meaning: each subject is depicted in a way that conveys something about its worldview—DeFeo is an imposing oval with drips, Hedrick a jaunty, geometric figure, and the cat is relatively realistic. In 1956 he explained this painting, "On the right is myself, or rather how I see the form of my world—on the left is my wife, or how she sees the form of our life—in the center is the Cat in all its absurd but real domination of our personal human world. It's a logical portrait containing the paradox of the ridiculousness of the situation together with the frightening revelation that self-delusion haunts all the days of our lives."[32] *Fred's TV*, a more than ten-foot-tall canvas, commemorates a television set that Fred Martin gave Hedrick and DeFeo. In the painting, the television set has become as tall and imposing as an obelisk, and its screen is full of Klee-like hieroglyphic figures. A scarlet Mae West mouth opens at its base, sexual and disconcerting. It took an unusual imagination to represent a television set as a mystical icon in 1956.

Other Hedrick paintings from this period are pure frivolity, such as *Shopping Hour* and *Bottom Jelly*, whose titles and inscriptions are puns on Schopenhauer and Botticelli. Another work made in a spirit of fun deserves more serious consideration, the infamous *Xmas Tree*. Making crystal radio sets and tinkering with electronics had been Hedrick's hobby back in Pasadena, and he had accumulated piles of old electronic devices and machine parts. While still in southern California he had discovered dada and seen Calder's metal mobiles, which prompted him to put his own junk together into kinetic constructions (which he declines to call art, but then the doesn't call his paintings art either). Much of the junk came to San Francisco with him, and some of it found its way into assemblage-sculptures, such as *Sunflower*, whose form suggests an organic-mechanical hybrid. On the principle of using whatever was plentiful, Hedrick made a number of sculptures out of welded beer cans. A few documented pieces such as *His Master's Voice* suggest Hedrick's talent as a found-metal sculptor, along the lines of Richard Stankiewicz, was considerable.

Xmas Tree came about when he was cleaning up and decided to put all the junk on hand into a single construction. The frame consisted of two butterfly-chair wrought-iron frames with three bed rails welded to them, forming a steep pyramid. To this exoskeleton Hedrick added two record players, radios, including one which continuously wandered up and down the frequencies, a siren, an 'ooga' horn, lights, a fan and various other contraptions, all wired to two washing-machine programmers that controlled their activities. The devices established two independent cycles of activity, so the tree's behavior was unpredictable. One record player played Bing Crosby's "White Christmas," the other played a blues song about a poor man who pawned his belongings to buy gifts every year. It hadn't started out as critique of conspicuous consumption and the hollowness of holidays, though Hedrick was happy to consider it one once the work began to resemble a Christmas tree.

The lack of theoretical underpinnings for *Xmas Tree* is typical for West Coast work of that time. Many works paralleled those made by East Coast artists, but without the buttressing of theory and criticism so crucial to establishing the importance and maintaining the caliber of New York art. In California the rise of assemblage sculpture, of a proto-pop art and of multi-media events akin to Kaprow's happenings all took place without the contextualizing and publicizing of criticism. Hedrick's kinetic and metal sculptures have a European counterpart in Jean Tinguely's mechanical constructions, which were at first timorously kinetic and culminated in his epic self-destructing *Homage to New York,* presented at the Museum of Modern Art in 1961. *Xmas Tree* suffered a similar fate that year, when it was exhibited in a group show at the San Francisco Museum of Art. Hedrick wired it to an electrical outlet, set the timers to start the various machines during the trustees' private opening, and left town after warning the museum about the piece. Its effects started up suddenly during the crowded opening. A wealthy trustee jumped in alarm and tangled her furs in its fan, screamed, and became further entangled as lights flashed and sirens blared. Pandemonium ensued until a museum employee severed the electrical cord with a fire axe. The piece never ran again and passed from hand to hand until it was finally abandoned in the early seventies.

However far out on the fringe Hedrick's work seemed in the fifties, he and DeFeo were in the center of the San Francisco art world. Hedrick was managing the Six Gallery, playing with the Studio 13 Jass Band, and socializing at the California School of Fine Arts. After the couple moved into 2322 Fillmore, all these activities consolidated in their flat. The four-unit building on Fillmore Street, was just up the street from the Six and not far from the school. Los Angeles painter Craig Kauffman lived there early on, and painters Sonia Gechtoff and James Kelly moved in before leaving for New York in 1958. Paul Beattie, a friend of George Herms, had brought DeFeo and Hedrick to the building, where they replaced painters Lynn and James Weeks. Gallery owner and collector James Newman took over one of the units, Michael and Joanna McClure settled into another, and Bill and Joan Brown lived there toward the end of the decade.

Fred Martin recalls, "In those days I used to be the director of CSFA exhibitions and one of my jobs was to take visiting curators, critics, directors around, and I would always take them to Jay and Wally's place—for lunch preferably, because the setting would just make their eyes pop. The way the rooms were, the height of these rooms, the way Jay's big *Rose* painting was at the end of these rooms, the way there were Jay's and Wally's things everywhere, the way Jay would do her lunch with a hundred little bits of things; it was like a Chinese lunch. It was by far the most arty. . . . I guess it was fifties bohemia." The flats were big enough to work in, and all the artists used them as studios. DeFeo was famous for never throwing out her Christmas trees, and by the sixties spindly bare pines filled a corner of the room she painted in. Parties were frequent, and in reminiscences, the place assumes the stature of a latter-day Bateau Lavoir.

Many important friendships came out of the 2322 Fillmore households. DeFeo worked closely with Gechtoff, and their work grew to resemble each others; later Joan Brown became a good friend of Hedrick and DeFeo, and her husband Bill joined the Studio 13 Jass Band. Michael McClure moved in several circles, and was active in introducing artists and poets to one another. He had, for example, known Bruce Conner when they were teenagers in Wichita. Jay DeFeo recalled McClure paving the way for Conner's arrival in the fall of 1957: "For a long time there was this talk that 'Bruce is coming, Bruce is coming.' I used to have dreams about all these crates of Bruce Conner's paintings coming. Honest-to-God dreams. And by God, one day, all these trunks came full of Bruce Conner's paintings, preceding his own arrival . . . I marveled at the skill of such a young artist."[33]

Notes

1. "San Francisco was not just . . ." in Cook, *The Beat Generation*

2. an extremely irreverent Jack Spicer: See Robin Blaser's essays in Spicer, *The Collected Books of Jack Spicer*

3. "For years everything was for the war . . ." in Ira Kamin, "Kissed by the Angel of Death," *San Francisco Sunday Examiner and Chronicle* [on James Broughton], Sept. 20, 1981

4. Harold Rosenberg in his *Tradition of the New*, New York: Grove Press, 1962; Serge Guilbaut in *How New York Stole the Idea of Modern Art*

5. "Modern painting is the bulwark . . ." in Guillbaut, *How New York Stole the Idea of Modern Art*

6. "A single stroke of paint . . ." Clyfford Still, in "An Open Letter to An Art Critic," *Artforum*, Dec. 1963

7. Dore Ashton, *The Unknown Shore: A View of Contemporary Art*. Boston: Little, Brown, 1962

8. "there were not really" in Bischoff oral history, AAA [Archives of American Art]

9. "A little palace . . ." in Auping, *Jess: Paste-ups (and Assemblies)*

10. "a tremendous feeling . . ." in Bischoff oral history, AAA

11. "Jess became intrigued . . ." in Auping, "Songs of Innocence," *Art in America*

12. "The Homosexual in Society" and other aspects of Duncan's early years in Faas, *Young Robert Duncan*

13. "Orange painted walls . . ." and "Duncan's house was my school . . ." in Brakhage monograph typescript, Pacific Film Archive, Berkeley

14. "Both Robert and Jess are . . ." McClure in Bertholf, *Robert Duncan: Scales of the Marvelous*

15. Dwight MacDonald in his *Against the American Grain*, New York: Random House, 1962.

16. "One surprisingly curmudgeonly . . ." in John Russell and Suzi Gablik, *Pop Art Redefined*, New York: Praeger, 1969

17. "I am ambitious only to emulate . . ." in Bertholf, *Robert Duncan: Scales of the Marvelous*

18. "Jess Collins, one of the three . . ." in Frankenstein, "Art Exhibits—Large and Small," *This World, San Francisco Chronicle*, June 7, 1953

19. "THE GESTURE THE GESTURE . . ." from McClure's *Hymns to Saint Geryon and Dark Brown*: San Francisco: Grey Fox Press, 1980. See also his "Ode to Jackson Pollock"

20. "For thirty years . . ." introduction to Hall, *Contemporary American Poetry*

21. "My poems contain no . . ." in Wieners's "A Poem for Painters" in Allen, *The New American Poetry*

22. God to a giant white baseball in "Magazine Verse" in Spicer, *The Collected Books of Jack Spicer*

23. "In New York the art world . . ." in Allen, *The New American Poetry,*

24. "What's significant here is . . ." in Duncan oral history, Bancroft Library

25. In 1946, Hedrick . . . In his catalogue essay for the Natsoulas/Novelozo Gallery, Davis, *Lyrical Vision: The Six Gallery 1954-1957*, John Allen Ryan gives 1947 as the year Hedrick first came north, which may be more accurate.

26. "a poem somebody could hide . . ." in "Billy the Kid" in Spicer, *The Collected Books of Jack Spicer*

27. "Cultural event at the 6 . . ." in letter from Jack Goodman, courtesy of John Allen Ryan (though a founder of the Six, Ryan was in Mexico at the time)

28. "At some point Jack . . ." in McClure, *Scratching the Beat Surface*

29. "pieces of orange crate . . ." in McClure, *Scratching the Beat Surface*

30. Since this was written, Natsoulas/Novelozo Gallery in Davis has come out with an extensive catalogue for the exhibition *Lyrical Vision: The Six Gallery 1954-1957*, which gives a fragmentary chronology (of who was shown; what was shown remains relatively obscure). Leo Valledor, Richard Diebenkorn, Joel Barletta, James Budd Dixon, James Weeks, Roy DeForest, Joan Brown (her first solo show, in 1957), Art Grant, William Morehouse, Hassel Smith, Manuel Neri, and, toward the end of the gallery's existence, Bruce Conner showed there. Wallace Berman's postcards may have been shown there as well, in August of 1957.

31. "Jasper Johns was . . ." in *Expo-See* interview with Mark Van Proyen, Summer 1985. Hassel Smith not only lectured about flags, but painted them himself: in the late eighties Natsoulas/Novelozo Gallery, Davis, had a 1949 painting by Smith replete with flags; cars and other pop art motifs rendered in rough, bright color.

32. "On the right is myself . . ." in exhibition brochure for *Wally Hedrick*, Nov. 16-Dec. 7, 1956, SFAI Gallery, California School of Fine Arts

33. "For a long time there was this talk . . ." in Jay DeFeo oral history, AAA

Bibliography

I. BOOKS

Allen, Donald M., ed. *The New American Poetry*. New York: Grove Press, 1960.

Bertholf, Robert J. and Ian W. Reid, eds. *Robert Duncan: Scales of the Marvelous*. New York: New Directions, 1979.

Cook, Bruce. *The Beat Generation*. New York: Charles Scribners and Sons, 1971.

Faas, Ekbert. *Young Robert Duncan: A Portrait of the Poet as Homosexual in Society*. Santa Barbara: Black Sparrow Press, 1983.

Guilbaut, Serge. *How New York Stole the Idea of Modern Art: Abstract Expressionism, Freedom, and the Cold War*. Translated by Arthur Goldhammer. Chicago and London: University of Chicago Press, 1983.

Hall, Donald, ed. *Contemporary American Poetry*. Harmondsworth, England: Penguin Books, 1962.

McClure, Michael. *Scratching the Beat Surface.* San Francisco: North Point Press, 1982.

Spicer, Jack. *The Collected Books of Jack Spicer.* Edited by Robin Blaser. Santa Barbara: Black Sparrow Press, 1975.

II. EXHIBITION CATALOGUE

Auping, Michael. *Jess: Paste-ups (and Assemblies), 1951-1983.* Sarasota, Florida: John and Mable Ringling Museum of Art, 1984.

III. ARTICLES

Auping, Michael. "Songs of Innocence," [on Jess] *Art in America,* vol. 75, no. 1, (January 1987).

"An Interview with Wally Hedrick," Interview by Mark Van Proyen, *Expo-See* (Summer 1985).

IV. ARCHIVES

Archives of American Art, West Coast Regional Center, DeYoung Museum, San Francisco. Oral history interviews: Bruce Conner, Jay DeFeo, Wally Hedrick, Joan Brown, Elmer Bischoff, William Copley, Billy Al Bengston, James Newman, Fred Martin, Hassel Smith. Papers of Jay DeFeo and Wally Hedrick.

Bancroft Library, University of California, Berkeley. Oral history and papers of Robert Duncan. Auerhahn Press archive. Collections of California literary presses.

Pacific Film Archive, Berkeley, California. Filmmakers files: Kenneth Anger, Stan Brakhage, James Broughton, Bruce Conner, Dennis Hopper, Larry Jordan. Films by Joseph Cornell, Stan Brakhage, and Bruce Conner.

REBECCA SOLNIT (ESSAY DATE 1990)

SOURCE: Solnit, Rebecca. "Heyday." In *Secret Exhibition: Six California Artists of the Cold War Era,* pp. 66-98. San Francisco: City Lights, 1990.

In the following essay, Solnit offers an overview of the pinnacle of the Beat Generation art scene in California during the latter half of the 1950s.

In the Swing of Things

Nineteen fifty-seven is often remembered as a year of miracles. Joan Brown, who was nineteen when she moved to 2322 Fillmore, says, "It was a very charged period. And I believe most of us who were working were at a high peak in terms of energy and feeling. That is, not just the artists but North Beach in general. You felt this with the poets too. Of course lots of times we didn't like the poets. And I say *we* because that's how it was. We were a 'we.' And the poets were a 'we' . . . I wouldn't have been anywhere else if I'd had a million dollars and was offered to spend three years in Italy."[1] Although most of the nightlife was in North Beach, and bars there such as The Place provided exhibition space, the upper Fillmore with its galleries was equally important.

In late 1957, the Conners lived just around the corner from 2322, on Jackson Street, and not long after they settled in, the Bermans found an apartment a few doors away. They were part of a Los Angeles diaspora; many of their friends had moved north between 1956 and 1958. David Meltzer settled in the Bay Area for good and Herms moved up in 1957 so his wife Polly could attend the University of California in Berkeley. Berman's close friends Bob Alexander, Artie Richer, and John Reed also came to the Bay Area. For many of them, there was a pragmatic reason: the Los Angeles bookseller Norman Rose had become manager of Paper Editions, a book distribution warehouse in San Francisco, and he offered jobs to his friends at a time when jobs for unconventional people were hard to come by. Meltzer, Herms, Reed, Alexander, and James Newman were among Rose's assistants. Of course there were other reasons to live in San Francisco, which was becoming the crossroads of the new counterculture.

The city began to attract national attention in 1957, partly because of the *Howl* trial. The "San Francisco Scene" issue of the *Evergreen Review* also helped make the city's writers better known. "There has been so much publicity recently about the San Francisco Renaissance and the New Generation of Revolt," wrote Rexroth in the introductory article, "that I for one am getting a little sick of writing about it. . . ." Poetry by Rexroth, Ginsberg, Robert Duncan, James Broughton, Lawrence Ferlinghetti, Jack Spicer, Gary Snyder, and Michael McClure made up the bulk of the issue, with some Kerouac prose and an article by Henry Miller. New York art critic Dore Ashton had been dispatched to write on "The San Francisco School," and she produced a meandering piece about Clyfford Still's "personal use of 'unbound' space," about Sam Francis, Richard Diebenkorn, and a few other painters. "With the absence of Still, who now works in strict seclusion in New York," concluded Ashton, "and the return, four years ago, to figurative painting by David Park, Elmer Bischoff, and several others, activity in San Francisco appears to be less inspired, less significant. Nevertheless, it is still, after New York, the major source of avant-garde painting of quality." The New York art world was still under the sway of abstract-expressionism, and its young turks were second-generation abstractionists like Alfred Leslie and Joan Mitchell. Ashton seems to have been looking for their equivalents out West (certainly she seems to have thought of art as synonymous with painting and disapproved of the figurative painters), and her strongest points were about the romantic idealism of the region. The following year, Johns and Rauschenberg began to be recognized, and after that the East would start to notice other kinds of artistic activity in California.

So, in 1957, Conner, Herms, Berman, Jess, DeFeo, and Hedrick were all working in the Bay Area without attracting much outside attention. Their art was a dialogue with friends, and since no one else was listening almost anything could be said. One result was a lot of ephemeral art. The assemblage and ceramic artist Harold Paris, who came to San Francisco in 1961, addressed this when writing about the art of the sixties that came to be labeled funk: "Almost imperceptibly, funk art has grown away from the funky art of the fifties. Funky art said that material was worthless, that only ideas were important (funky artists showed their art and then often threw it away) and that the value of art was in its making. The meaning of the art was not in any way related to the intrinsic worth of the materials. Funky artists were essentially assemblage people."[2]

Joan Brown, who made sculptures out of cheap, nontraditional materials, recalls, "'Eat, drink and be merry for tomorrow we die' is the attitude which was prevalent at the time. I guess there was a rebellion basically against the slicker materials. There was a delight taken in using ratty materials. The rattier the better." Conner recalls, "I was doing painting, a lot of painting and becoming more and more disgusted with what painting was and with what the situation was as far as exhibiting any work here in San Francisco, because there wasn't anything. If you showed anything it was because somebody had a gallery and they would have a party and everybody would drink a lot of wine and usually you couldn't even get back into the gallery again, because nobody wanted to sit in the gallery. There wasn't any point in having a show—you might as well have parties. And there wasn't much point in making anything that would have any function in the art world itself, because there was no place for it to go, so we had a lot of parties."

Many of Conner's artworks have metamorphosed over the years so that they no longer approximate their original colors and condition. Some even addressed the subject of disintegration: *Bomb* was inspired by the slow annihilation of the Victorian houses of the Western Addition's black community. Another assemblage, *Superhuman Devotion,* was destroyed in shipping to New York, so Conner threw the box off the Staten Island Ferry, in front of the Statue of Liberty. Stories about self-destructing artworks are legion. Neri's plaster and cardboard sculptures, according to one source, crumbled so rapidly while on exhibit at the San Francisco Museum of Art that they left daily droppings, like a pet. Hedrick, whose own paint often cracked and flaked, tells a similar story about a painting by DeFeo that hung in City Lights Bookstore: "I remember Lawrence Ferlinghetti telling me about one of her paintings once . . . it was hung in City Lights Bookstore, and it immediately started falling apart all over the floor. And every day they had to send in a guy to sweep up under it." Work that didn't fall apart disappeared; most of the pieces in Berman's Ferus show eventually vanished, and when Herms was sent to prison for six months in 1957 for possession of marijuana his wife threw away all his work, because there was no place to store it. Later, these disappearances and deteriorations would be regarded as tragic, but at the time nobody was concerned.

Berman actually did very little artwork during the four years he was in the Bay Area, although he was always taking photographs. He showered his friends in Los Angeles with collages-by-mail (and sometimes sent mail to his next-door neighbors), and he produced *Seminas Three, Four, Five, Six,* and *Seven.* And as always, he influenced those around him. Early in 1958, he gave McClure five peyote buttons and McClure wrote an epic about the experience that became the centerpiece of *Semina Three.* (Midway through the poem, McClure writes "I am visited by a man who is the god of foxes / there is dirt under the nails of his paw / fresh from his den / we smile at each other in recognition." Berman had sent Herms by to visit and McClure had taken him for a deity.) Another cross-pollination took place when Berman published Philip Lamantia's poem that includes the lines:

> Tell him that I have eyes only for Heaven
> as I look to you
> > Queen mirror
> of the heavenly court

This poem inspired DeFeo's magnificent *The Eyes,* a four-foot-by-eight-foot pencil drawing. A prodigious accomplishment for its painstaking labor alone, its visionary sensibility seems to forecast the mood of the years to come. Berman photographed DeFeo in front of the drawing as part of a series of portraits of her with her work; in this image she stands shirtless and in black tights between the two eyes, gazing forward. Fine crosshatching flattens the image and gives it an aura of antiquity. The nine portraits in this series seem to try to approach the source of the reverence DeFeo inspired in her friends, and her passionate personal engagement with her artwork. Berman held a private exhibit of the photographs, in his new house on Scott Street. *Semina Four*, with a photograph of Shirley on the cover, was as illustrious an anthology as the *Evergreen Review*, with contributions from McClure, Lamantia, William S. Burroughs, Allen Ginsberg, John Wieners, and Bob Kaufman. Perhaps it was Berman's period of homages to women, for his own pseudonymous poem went:

> Morphine mother
> Heroin mother
> Yage mother
> Benzedrine mother
> Peyote mother
> Marijuana mother
> Cocaine mother
> Hashish mother
> Mushroom mother
> Opium mother
> Mescalin mother
>
> Gave my lover a cherry mother
> Cornbread meat and molasses mother
> Chain gang mother
> Alabamy bound mother
> Bill Bailey mother
> Midnight special mother
> Stockolee mother
> Rock Island mother
> John Henry mother
> Strange fruit mother
> Long John mother

Larry Jordan, who had come out to San Francisco in the early fifties because his friend Stan Brakhage was there, became a link between the wave of filmmakers that departed in the first half of the decade and those who arrived in the second. For a few years he and Conner ran an avant-garde film society called Camera Obscura, the only showcase of its kind in the Bay Area. Like other experimental filmmakers with limited resources, Jordan used his friends as actors: John Reed, Herms, Berman, and McClure all put in appearances. One experimental film, *Visions of a City*, was screened while McClure and Lamantia gave a live reading; another was inspired by a Lamantia poem. Jordan's whole body of work was influenced by the poetry and art in this milieu, sometimes explicitly, in the form of homages, collaborations, and documentations, and sometimes implicitly, in the qualities of image and sequence. In 1960, he collaborated with Jess on *The Forty and One Nights or Jess's Didactic Nickelodeon*, a film of Jess's collages. In 1961, inspired by the collage-novels of Max Ernst, Jordan began making collage films by using stop-motion camerawork to animate old engravings. Conner used a more conceptual collage technique in his first film, the 1958 *A Movie*, which was made up of footage from other movies masterfully edited into new sequences and non-sequiters.[3]

Conner's contribution to the social scene was the Rat Bastard Protective Association, a society whose name derived from the garbage collectors' Scavengers Protective Association and whose first three initials—RBP—alluded to the Pre-Raphaelite Brotherhood. Conner sent out letters to a dozen friends, telling them they were members and that dues were three dollars a year, which entitled members to put the RBP initials on their artworks as a kind of seal of approval. Only the president, Conner, seems to have used the RBP stamp, but the group did have monthly meetings for a while, usually at members' studios (although they met on the Golden Gate Bridge one memorably clammy evening). DeFeo, Brown, McClure, Neri, Martin, Hedrick, Art Grant, Alvin Light, Carlos Villa, and Auerhahn Press publisher Dave Hazelwood were all members, and the Rat Bastard Protective Association staged at least one event. "One time the Rat Bastards and Dave Hazelwood and the poets decided to organize a parade through North Beach with banners and standards," Conner recalls. "It was totally unannounced, and all of a sudden there were about two hundred people walking down Grant Avenue and across Broadway. There was a poetry duel between Philip Lamantia and some bullshit poet who had moved in from New York for about two months to take advantage of the publicity there was about North Beach. Philip Lamantia came in and it was like a ritualistic proclamation. His opposing poet was sitting in a coffee shop and there was a two-foot stack of all the stuff he was going to read. Philip came in with one piece of paper and read his poem and then announced he had written it when he was fourteen years old. Then he turned and walked out. That was the end of the duel."[4]

The ties between artists and poets were many. In addition to projects such as Jordan's films and Berman's *Seminas*, there were many small presses—White Rabbit and Auerhahn among the more prominent, Jess and Duncan provided illustrations and introductions for each other's projects. Jess also illustrated many White Rabbit publications. Conner made images for books of McClure's poetry, and for Lamantia's *Destroyed Works*. Auerhahn had a "Mad Monster Mammoth Poets' Reading" benefit in August of 1959 that featured twelve poets, including Lawrence Ferlinghetti, Bob Kaufman, John Wieners, Philip Whalen, Lamantia, McClure, and Meltzer, as well as "a spectacle of Objects" by Conner and painter Robert LaVigne. "Go, poetry, go!," concluded the announcement.

In the beginning of the fifties, San Francisco had given its artists a sense of sanctuary. By the end of the decade they were feeling not merely safe but exhilarated, and rowdy public events became common. The Six Gallery died with a bang in November of 1957. Pianist and sculptor Ed Taylor organized what might have been called a Happening if it had happened back East, though he called it "Collective Expressionism." A participant cut off Taylor's tie to launch the event, then six poets read their work simultaneously while someone shouted "the horses are off and running." Everyone then demolished the gallery's decrepit piano with axes, blow torches, and sledgehammers. Poet Bob Kaufman had spiked the wine with benzedrine, perhaps making the action more frenetic than planned.[5] Kaufman sponsored an event of his own the following August, a Tour of the Bourgeois Wastelands.[6] The expedition, complete with rented bus, took mock revenge on the tourists and straights who came gawking to North Beach, and it culminated with Kaufman reading poetry on the steps of the luxurious downtown St. Francis Hotel. Jack Spicer's contribution was Blabbermouth Night at the North Beach bar The Place, a kind of running spontaneous poetry fest in which, as one of his fellow poets put it, "you stood up and talked until they sat you down."[7]

Galleries were multiplying too, though the Six closed. "The gallery has been a very valuable impetus to many individuals and groups concerned not only with painting, but with music, dance, experimental photography and sound, and poetry. It has afforded all of us the space and freedom to experiment," said the letter to members announcing the Six's demise. Across the street from the Six site, Sonia Gechtoff's mother ran the East-West Gallery for a few years, until her death in 1958, and she showed work by her daughter's friends, as well as by Hassel Smith and Roy DeForest. Around the corner from the East-West, at 2192 Filbert, in a two-car garage that also served as his home, Dimitri Grachis opened the tiny Spatsa Gallery in 1958. One show included Bruce and Jean Conner, Wally Hedrick, and four other artists; another featured McClure's gestural paintings.[8]

Dilexi, the most important new gallery, opened in 1958. It began as a partnership between Berman's old friend Robert Alexander and James

Newman, a friend of Walter Hopps. Son of a wealthy family, Newman had been involved in some of Hopps's exhibition ventures, and Dilexi was intended as a sort of Ferus Gallery north. Alexander found its name in a Latin dictionary: *dilexi,* to select, to value highly, to love. Knute Stiles, critic, painter and owner of The Place, wrote years later, "The first building to house the Dilexi was upstairs from the Jazz Workshop on Broadway, and the gallery stayed open in the evening, reflecting the neighborhood's habits. Also, Jim Newman's early partner, Bob Alexander, was a more hip type of person, and may very well have been the influence that located the Dilexi in North Beach. . . . I think the Dilexi's presence was an active factor in developing the community of galleries that has made the Bay Area a more important part of the modern art community."[9] Jess, DeFeo, Craig Kauffman, Roy DeForest, Jeremy Anderson, and Robert Morris all showed there in the gallery's first few years. Like Ferus, Dilexi was a link between the underground and the mainstream for many artists, and it was crucial in establishing a thriving art community.

Another child of wealth, William Jahrmarkt, established the wildest of the San Francisco alternative galleries, and Bruce Conner helped get it off the ground. Its name, Batman Gallery, was McClure's suggestion, after the popular comic-book hero; and the black-haired, black-clad Jahrmarkt, who was obsessed with the macabre and gothic, liked the name (eventually he became known as Billy Batman). The gallery, which Conner designed, was at 2222 Fillmore Street, and had black walls. It was probably best suited to showcase Conner's work and it did in its inaugural show. "Batman Gallery will open on November 3, 1960," said the press release. "Bruce Conner, artist who did the infamous CHILD a sculpture of wax, silk stockings and wood, exhibited at the De Young Museum and reproduced in local and national newspapers, will have the inaugural show at the Batman Gallery. His new black-wax and collage sculptures, collages, and paintings show intense grappling with the harmony of pure beauty and the breakthrough to a fiery consciousness of human injustice and a deep anarchic humor. The show is monumental and extremely shocking. A new lyricism in art." The announcement reproduced Conner's *Black Dahlia*.

The initial response was enthusiastic: "The Batman makes its bow with a show of things by Bruce Conner, who has a fabulous eye for junk in the tradition of the 19th-century still life," wrote Alfred Frankenstein. "The effect of the whole is of some magic grotto, full of things that have been put under enchantment and left for years to the bats and spiders, but still alive and waiting to be revivified."[10] Another critic reported, "Dilexi will have to move over, because Batman Gallery has jumped into first place in the avant-garde. It has a crushing opener starring Bruce Conner, that daredevil of the black wax, wood and silk stocking set."[11] (Again, Conner's humor was overlooked, or perhaps overwhelmed by the more somber work. It's worth noting that another exhibition of his that year included the works *Title Removed by Order of Police, Secret Title, Title Lost in Transit, Ma Jolie, Welsh Rabbit, Homage to Minnie Mouse, Lady Brain* and *Scale Model: Birth of the Universe.*[12]) "It opened up very spectacularly," Conner says of Batman Gallery. "But then it didn't function very well, because Billy was a junkie." Conner's show was followed by *GANGBANG*, a show that nowadays would do a museum credit: it included Brown, Conner, DeFeo, Hedrick, Herms, McClure, Neri, James Weeks, and two young newcomers, Carlos Villa and William T. Wiley. Michael McClure's play *!The Feast!* was presented at Batman, and Robert Hudson and George Herms both had their first significant solo shows there. Herms's opened in May of 1961 and Berman did the poster for it, with a bearded and tough-looking Herms in motorcycle regalia next to a huge assemblage. Berman had convinced the shy twenty-six-year-old that if he was going to be an artist, he was going to have to have shows. The new galleries began to change the odds for artists; work now had a chance of being shown, seen, and even sold. Between 1959 and 1961 the artists began to move into the international arena, and for a while it looked as if they'd found an audience.

White Rose Black Flag

The cold-war culture of the fifties began to thaw toward the end of the decade and a spirit of exuberant experimentation arose. John Cage found an audience and disciples, the Beats forged a new poetry, and a whole generation of artists began pushing at the boundaries that had circumscribed visual art. Between 1958 and 1960, Allan Kaprow, George Segal, Roy Lichtenstein, George Brecht, Lucas Samaras, Red Grooms, Claes Oldenburg, Richard Stankeiwicz, and Jim Dine all began to be recognized in New York, most of them for work that went beyond traditional definitions of painting and sculpture. It is impossible to reconstruct anything so amorphous as the mindset of the New York art world of the late fifties, but there was at long last a sense that something had to

succeed abstract expressionism. The Museum of Modern Art actually sent the curatorial equivalent of talent scouts out to California, and two important shows including West Coast artists' work resulted. The first was *Sixteen Americans* in 1959, which included Jay DeFeo and Wally Hedrick; the second was *The Art of Assemblage* in 1961, which included George Herms, Bruce Conner, Jess, and Edward Kienholz.

Sixteen Americans was put together by Dorothy Miller, curator of collections at the museum, as a survey of what was exciting in American art, and did not attempt to postulate a movement or major direction. The museum did such exhibitions regularly, and they functioned as modest precursors of the biennials that now test the zeitgeist. From California, Miller chose Hedrick and DeFeo for her exhibition, which also introduced Robert Rauschenberg, Jasper Johns, Ellsworth Kelly, Frank Stella, Alfred Leslie, and scrap-metal assemblagist Richard Stankiewicz. (It also showcased Louise Nevelson's new painted-wood assemblages.)

Hedrick's big square painting *For Service Rendered* was reproduced in the *New York Times,* and DeFeo's *Veronica* was mentioned favorably in the *New Yorker.* "It never occurred to me until recently that there might be a correlation between the Beat Generation of writers and their fellows in the plastic arts," Robert Coates's piece began. "But I came away from the new showing of paintings and sculptures at the Museum of Modern Art thinking that there is a strong likelihood that one exists. . . . What struck me at the Museum's show was the suggestion that traces of the Beat philosophy—which in one manifestation, is, briefly: Get lowdown; make the best of the least—seems to be invading the plastic artists' point of view too."[13] Coates seems to have been talking mostly about the assemblage and mixed-media works at the museum, though his comments might have been more relevant to DeFeo and Hedrick if their work had been more accurately represented there.

DeFeo's two paintings and three big drawings abstracted, although they were not altogether nonobjective. *The Veronica,* her largest work there, is an eleven-foot-tall panel covered with a spray of impasto hatch-marks that suggest foliage but convey a sense of motion. Hedrick's nine paintings mostly related to the religious aspect of his sex-politics-religion thematic trio. Some depicted a jeweled ornament—an orb, a cross-shaped medal—or a mandala. Some, such as *For Service Rendered,* seemed to refer to Hedrick's experience in the infantry, though it may have been the medal's shape that appealed to him; others had titles like *Spirit* and *Spirit Plus Idea*. Hedrick's *Spirit, 3* suggests an artistic influence from DeFeo; a vertical line down the center of the canvas radiates curving horizontal lines. A fascination with mandalas and patterns of radiating energy is apparent in both artists' work from this period.

Sixteen Americans was the big break young artists are supposed to pray for, but DeFeo and Hedrick weren't looking for it and hardly recognized it when it came. "Wally and I didn't realize the prestige of being included in such a show," DeFeo recalls. "It really surprises many people that we were the only people included in that show who didn't make an effort to go to the opening. The whole show was a kind of coming-out party, I discovered later. I was approached by the Stable Gallery through correspondence, which I turned down, because at this stage of the game I had launched into the painting of *The Rose*."

She began *The Rose* six months before her 1959 Dilexi Gallery show of eleven-foot mandalic drawings that prefigured her masterwork. DeFeo had become obsessed with an image of a radiating form, and she began two large paintings of this motif. One was *The Jewel*, a tall, slender piece in which the paint builds up toward the center of the canvas, forming a convex surface; and the other was the concave *The Rose*. "I started *The Jewel* along with *The Rose* and worked on it for about six months and set it aside thinking it was incomplete, but later realizing that it was complete. *The Jewel* was complete in its unfinished stage and *The Rose* went on and on and on. But I really did know it had a final version. It went through a whole cycle of art history: the primitive, the archaic, the classic, and then on to Baroque. I realized how flamboyant the whole thing had got and I pulled it back to a more classical stage. I knew I had just what I wanted. All those stages were interesting and complete in themselves, but just not what the final version was or what I intended. I don't know if it would have all gone on one canvas if I'd had the kind of studio to spread out in, but I just had one big painting wall. It was truly a subjective, almost visionary piece. It was one of the very few pieces that seemed to make its own demands. I didn't have to think, 'What shall I do now?' That was the easiest part of it, but it was very physically demanding. That period was one where I really pushed myself beyond endurance."

Dorothy Miller had wanted *The Rose* for the MOMA show in 1959, and DeFeo's principal patron, J. Patrick Lannan, wanted to buy it, but she wasn't ready to let it go. "I took a very pre-

ON THE SUBJECT OF...

JAY DEFEO

DeFeo was a part of the avant-garde art and poetry community in San Francisco during the 1950s; as her peer group included several Beat notables, she was often categorized as a Beat artist. Despite her considerable status in this environment, her work was virtually unknown beyond the West coast. In the 1950s, DeFeo's work was often large canvas, semi-abstract oil paintings characterized by religious and mythological themes. Throughout the 1960s, her energy was directed almost solely on what would become her best-known work: a gigantic painting entitled *The Rose* that measures eleven by eight feet and weighs over a ton.

cious, Ivory Towerish attitude about it," she said in 1988, "and said I wanted to retain it until I was finished. I simply refused. It took me six years to realize—that's a long time, that's how long it took me to finish *The Rose,* and when I finished, nobody had ever heard of me." In some respects, it was the ultimate abstract-expressionist work, a statement of commitment and unworldliness; in others, it was the antithesis of spontaneity and the liberating gesture. Built up with a palette knife and carved away at like a block of marble, its gray, radial bulk eventually looked as much like a relief sculpture as a painting. For a while it was called *The Death Rose.*

Fred Martin suggests that the fact that she literally couldn't get rid of the painting—once it was remounted on a larger backing, it wouldn't fit through her studio doors or windows—had something to do with her extended involvement with it. The canvas fit into the bay window at the end of her studio, and light streamed across it from the bay's side windows, picking out the Rose's petals in bold relief. "The whole place had it as the fixed focus," says Martin, "which is why it was so dramatic when you went there. It was like a little cathedral. You came into this room, with very high ceilings, long and narrow, with this sublime number at the end, where the window would have been." The floor and the stool DeFeo had sat on all those years were covered with encrusted paint.

"I saw her studio at that time," says Kienholz, "and the piles of paint scrapings under the easel looked like chicken droppings under a roost that had never been cleaned."[14]

The Rose itself grew into a 2300-pound, eight-inch-thick relief painting. In its final stage, the petals had disappeared, and straight lines radiated out from the center, becoming more expressionistic toward the edges. It had come to resemble a sunburst in a halo of clouds, order dispersing into turbulence. Like a mandala, or a rose window, or a rose itself, the strong centric form conveyed spiritual energy.

It might be considered a site-specific piece today, so rooted was it in the place it was painted. In 1964, when Hedrick and DeFeo had to move because the rent had gone from $65 to $300, *The Rose* was merely unmovable. The eviction was ultimately a handy *deus ex machina* that made DeFeo finish it, or at least regard it as finished. By this time, she had a waiting list of institutions interested in purchasing it, and Dorothy Miller asked that it be promised to the permanent collection of the Museum of Modern Art. Feeling she had an obligation to the West Coast institutions that had been supportive, DeFeo declined to sell the work immediately. Instead, Walter Hopps came to get it to show at the Pasadena Museum of Art, whose director he had become.

Bruce Conner documented its move in the seven-minute movie *The White Rose,* which he later subtitled "Jay DeFeo's painting removed by Angelic Hosts." The black and white movie is an homage and a collaboration, an artwork about another artwork, as well as a lyrical documentary. It opens with establishing shots of the Bekins moving men milling around on the sidewalk outside 2322, looking like doctors or monks in their white coveralls. Interior shots show the dark grove of spindly dead Christmas trees DeFeo had accumulated, then *The Rose* itself, lit from either side like a shrine. It is slowly tipped forward, and a man, then a handful of men, came forward to bear its weight. As it shifts, it blocks out more and more light, until the men became silhouettes and only a halo of light surrounds it, like the sun in eclipse. It descends like Christ from the cross. Shadowy figures converge and disperse. Finally it is lowered by crane through the gouged-out window and trundled away. DeFeo brings a dead Christmas tree to the gaping hole and sits in it, disconsolately dangling her legs over the edge. Miles Davis's *Sketches of Spain* is the soundtrack.

So *The Rose* was not represented in the Museum of Modern Art's *Sixteen Americans*. Hedrick's work had been pruned back to suggest a more respectable, coherent artistic direction. His most famous painting from the late fifties, *Anger,* was not included (to be fair, it may not have been finished when Miller came by), nor were his sculptures, his still-extant *Flag* paintings, or his just-begun *Vietnam Series*. *Anger* is a square painting made from four small stretched canvases stuck together. To the left of a explosive central image, an orb burns like a dark sun, and the inscription reads, "MADAM NHU BLOWS CHIANG ANGER," a reference to the war in Vietnam.

The *Vietnam Series* extended from 1957 until 1973, and it consisted entirely of monochromatic, dark paintings in varying sizes and textures. "The black paintings," recounts Hedrick, "started in about—see, there I'll get in trouble again. If I say 1957, and I'm sure that's when it was, I get static because people start saying, 'Why are you getting upset about Vietnam in 1957?' I was upset about Vietnam in 1954, when the French were in there. I painted out this painting, and this was when I said to myself that since there's no way for me to affect any political decisions (every time I'd vote for somebody they'd lose), what I'll do is I'll deny Western Culture my contribution. (Now, you can see how ridiculous that was.) So I started taking old paintings, including the flags, and painting them out. At the beginning I used old paintings because I was obsessed with the idea that I was going to deny humanity these world-shaking images. It's just like holding my breath and 'you'll be sorry.' And it was as simple as that. I believed it and I did it. That was fine, except I ran out of canvas, and so I was faced with a crisis: do I really believe this enough that I'll go to the trouble of stretching up canvases and then painting them black?" During the Vietnam war, he painted images as well as fields of blackness, but many of his older works disappeared under the darkness of his protest.

From 1957 on Hedrick retreated from any possibility of success. In 1963, he celebrated his first decade in San Francisco with a retrospective at the New Mission Gallery in the Mission District (the exhibition included *Peace Flag*, which was seen publicly for the last time there). John Coplans wrote about the exhibition in the second issue of *Artforum*: "There is something in his particular kind of unpleasantness that seems to break an unwritten agreement, that seems to actually offend where other artists often only pretend to offend. His conduct of himself as an artist—his management, or nonmanagement, of his career also appears as a total rejection of the game. . . . At a time when it is virtually a basic requirement for acceptance at a serious level, let alone the common practice, to create an identity by an easily identifiable and personal image, he resolutely refuses to nurture a style. Uncompromisingly uncommercial, he rejects every channel leading to acceptance. Every aspect of his art is stamped with eccentricity. He loves art, but is full of the most genuine anti-art attitudes—his imagery is a completely crazy mixture of pop, common, popular and even obscene art tendencies."[15]

It may have been in response to this review that Hedrick painted a nearly eleven-foot-tall panel dominated by a huge phallus and called it *Here's Art for'em* (1963). At the time, he was moving away from a period of painting religious and alchemical images, such as *Hermetic Image,* which somewhat mockingly diagrams spiritual forces in a scientific manner. Organizational systems intrigued Hedrick, and several of his paintings use esoteric diagramming systems to chart his personal life (in later years, he used the format of the circuit board to diagram psychological phenomena). One of Hedrick's peculiarities' is that he is both an iconoclast and an icon-lover: he loves symbols and emblems from which he makes powerful symmetrical compositions, although he violates good taste and artistic canons. He responded to Barry Goldwater's 1964 presidential bid with *Bury Berry,* an op-art-style jumbled grid of letters that declares "Bury Berry Now" and ". . . uck the F.B.I." He commemorated a later election with *Big Dick for President,* which shows a monolithic phallus erupting like a fire hydrant into a dark sky.

His most buoyantly iconoclastic gesture took place the same year as *Here's art for'em.* "There was a period when I was very poor, so poor that I stole canvases," he told a Bay Area critic, Mark Van Proyen, in 1985. "Sometimes they weren't the right size, so, literally, I nailed them together. This is a terrible thing to say, but I would go over to the art school and steal paintings. Students' or whoever's. This used to be a secret, but it isn't a secret anymore. I'm probably the only person in the United States who has painted over a Clyfford Still. The reason I'm mentioning it is because I want to find out if they are going to see if they can take my painting off to get to the Still."[16] The Still, he later recalled, had come to him in an assortment of canvases James Weeks gave him when Weeks moved out of town. "I went ahead and used all of these canvases and then one day I looked down and inside of the support bar, there's a little label. It said, 'Clyfford Still, 1947.' I wished I could say I did it on purpose—but I really didn't. I might have, given a chance." It's typical of Hedrick that he committed what might have been a great conceptual act—like Rauschenberg's *Erased de Kooning*—but did it accidentally.

In this period he was engaged in the more serious *Vietnam Series.* Some of the black paintings are smooth, some richly impastoed textures and patterns, some square, some round, but all are dark or black because black was "the absence of light." Hedrick was also marching in parades and otherwise protesting the war; his 1966 Christmas message to friends was a collection of revised Christmas carols, such as:

Hark the local press gang brings Conscripts to the war machine Towns aflame, the dead in piles Body count and scalded child At Johnson City, feast today Lady Bird and L.B.J. While reluctant conscripts bring Death to every living thing.

"I was very strongly and violently against the war. The paintings got bigger as the war got bigger. And in '68 when I made *The Room,* which is a twelvefoot square room, that's when our involvement was at its height." The blackness becomes all-encompassing in this environmental painting, which can be entered through the doorway in one of its four canvas walls. The final *Vietnam* painting is an eleven-by-eighteen-foot expanse of blackness. By 1970, Hedrick had alienated himself out of a job at the San Francisco Art Institute by insisting the school take a stand on the war and encouraging his students to participate in demonstrations.

Hedrick's black paintings parallel *The Rose* as gestures of idealism and obsession. Both back away from art as production, asserting it instead as personal ritual and spiritual commitment.

The Art of Assemblage

Not long after DeFeo and Hedrick had let their chance at fame and fortune slip away, another MOMA curator came out to the West Coast. He was William Seitz from the department of painting and sculpture, and he wasn't looking for sculpture or painting, but for assemblage. He was putting together a vast survey of the medium, and he succeeded in gathering 252 pieces by artists from the United States and Europe. He already knew about Bruce Conner, because his fellow curator Peter Selz had recently given Conner first prize in a national competition. Seitz looked up Conner, and Conner took him around the Bay Area.

The point of Conner's tour was that assemblage was not a new high-art form, but one that had a centuries-long tradition ("Assemblage is a new medium," Seitz wrote anyway). Conner took him to see an old black man whose junk store on McAllister Street was full of arrangements he'd found impressive, and to a Chinese laundry in North Beach with interestingly arranged accretions in its windows. He also took Seitz to see Berman, but Seitz (according to Conner) didn't consider Berman's photographs or *Seminas* to be assemblage. Berman, however, took Seitz next door to meet George Herms. As a result, Herms appeared in *The Art of Assemblage* with a work called *Poet,* a pile of decaying paper and a little sounding-trumpet on a pedestal. It suggests a speaker or broadcast system, and Herms considered it his ambassador to the world. (Like *Fred's TV* by Hedrick, and Berman's later radio pieces, it made vision and visual art stand in for speech.) Two pieces by Conner were included in the exhibition: *The Last Supper,* a small, blackened table bearing dark wax forms that seemed in a state of advanced decay, and *Temptation of Saint Barney Google,* a tall nylon-stocking construction. Jess was represented by a collage of magazine clippings on a window blind.

A few driftwood assemblagists and other northern Californians also made it into the show, and when Seitz headed south, he discovered Kienholz making new work—figurative assemblages that made strong social statements. Like Hedrick, Kienholz broke from the idea that art should be subtle and ambiguous, and his assemblages make overt political statements. Kienholz began his work in assemblage by attaching objects to canvases—antlers and slabs of wood—and then developed large-scale three dimensional works. His approach to assemblage was entirely his own; he used found objects to make figures—a jar or boar's skull for a head, a wheeled shopping basket or table for a body—or he used them just as they were—a couch, a car, a television set. Later works place metaphorical figures in real settings, where the play between representation and actuality enriches the work. Early pieces such as the intentionally crass relief *George Warshington in Drag* (1957) and *Oe'r the Ramparts We Watched Fascinated* (1959) are assaults on unquestioning patriotism. *(It Takes Two to Integrate) Cha, Cha, Cha* (1961), with black and white dolls imprinted with tire tracks, and *The Illegal Operation* (about abortion, 1964) take on specific social issues. *The Art of Assemblage* show included *John and Jane Doe,* two limbless, bloodstained average Americans.

The exhibition opened in October of 1961, attracting considerable attention and even controversy. It made clear that art could no longer be confined to painting and sculpture—at a time when more and more artists were exploring other media, the idea nevertheless seems to have been provocative. Seitz's definition of assemblage was partly drawn from an earlier MOMA show of collages—"collage cannot be defined adequately as merely a technique of cutting and pasting, for its significance lies not in its technical eccentricity but in its relevance to two basic questions which have been raised by twentieth-century art: the nature of reality and the nature of painting itself. Collage has been the means through which the artist incorporates reality into the picture without imitating it." A more functional definition for assemblage followed:

"1) They are predominantly assembled rather than painted, drawn, modeled, or carved.

2) Entirely or in part, their constituent elements are preformed natural or manufactured materials, objects, or fragments not intended as art materials."

The catalogue presented what may be the first extended essay on assemblage, tracing its roots to the linguistic experiments of early modern French poets and tracking its genesis to the visual forays of Picasso and his cubist and dadaist contemporaries. Their incorporation of collage elements in paintings is generally said to have dissolved the distinctions between things and the representation of things and, by extension, between art and life. The idea of metaphor—"the joining of two things which are different"—is central to Seitz's essay. He demonstrates how the poet's metaphorical use of words—a process of dislocating something and making it suggest something else—relates to the artist's use of objects. Assemblage, he says, "is metaphysical and poetic as well as physical and realistic. When paper is soiled or lacerated, when cloth is worn, stained, or torn, when wood is split, weathered, or patterned with peeling coats of paint, when metal is bent or rusted, they gain connotations which unmarked materials lack. . . . Even taken in isolation, the possible meanings of objects and fragments are infinitely rich, where . . . professional art materials such as paint, plastic, stone, bronze, etc., are formless and, in the Platonic sense, are pure essences of redness, hardness or ductility. Found materials are already works in progress: prepared for the artist by the outside world, previously formed, textured, colored, and even sometimes entirely prefabricated into accidental 'works of art.'"

Man Ray wrote of the assemblages he had made in Los Angeles in the forties: "they were made to amuse, bewilder or inspire reflection, but were not to be confused with the aesthetic pretentions or plastic virtuosity usually expected of works of art."[17] Joseph Cornell was almost alone among American artists in regarding assemblage as a serious medium at that time. The artists of the fifties, however, were to bring the richness and scope of painting and sculpture to assemblage. Once the work of young artists such as Rauschenberg, Niki de St. Phalle, and Conner established assemblage—and the MOMA show certified it—as a major medium, the whole definition of art was ready to explode in all directions. It did so in the sixties, when found objects, conceptual art, replicas of consumer goods, performances, installations, texts, and commercial and popular culture appropriations all became legitimized as art.

Seitz asserted, "Assemblage has become, temporarily at least, the language for impatient, hypercritical, and anarchistic young artists." Along with all the older artists affiliated with surrealism or working in isolation, there were three important groups of young artists represented in *The Art of Assemblage,* each with its own aesthetic and relationship to art history: the Nouveaux Realistes of Paris, the California assemblagists, and the New Yorkers. The latter were carrying forward abstract expressionism and at the same time rebelling against it. One of the most dynamic members of this group. Allan Kaprow, wrote, "Pollock, as I see him, left us at the point where we must become preoccupied with and even dazzled by the space and objects of our everyday life, either our bodies, clothes, rooms, or, if need be, the vastness of Forty-Second Street. Not satisfied with the suggestion through paint of our other senses, we shall utilize the specific substances of sight, sound, movements, people, odors, touch. Objects of every sort are materials for the new art: paint, chairs, food, electric and neon lights, smoke, water, old socks, a dog, movies, a thousand other things which will be discovered by the present generation of artists."

New York's new work tended to be conceptually bold and relatively abstruse—concerned with the ideas inherent in a given object. In many respects it was a continuation of modernist sensibility. John Chamberlain's crushed car parts, for example, address issues of polychromy in sculpture, of randomness and mechanical processes;

they are not so much concerned with the meaning of the automobile in contemporary culture as with its formal possibilities. Although it is impossible to describe a Rauschenberg assemblage as austere, the New York work was generally more severe, more concerned with concepts, with engaging art history in a dialogue, than West Coast art. Environment too played a significant role, and New York City produced different garbage and different aesthetics than San Francisco, Los Angeles, or Paris. Whitney Museum curator Barbara Haskell writers, "Much of the work by the younger assemblagists [in New York] aggressively highlighted a crudeness and ugliness in the city landscape."[18] San Francisco, in contrast, presented a sensual, romantic urban landscape. Whatever its particulars, however, the urban environment was both raw material and inspiration for this art. No matter where it was made, assemblage in this period, unlike much contemporary work, did not make use of unaltered organic matter.

Mimmo Rotella and François Dufrène turned the many layers of torn posters on the walls of Rome and Paris into an art form that resembled abstract-expressionist paintings and referred to the turmoil of urban culture—*affiches lacères,* they were called, and many are remarkably beautiful. Daniel Spoerri preserved the jumble left at the ends of meals as a kind of unconsciouslymade art, Arman first made portrait-assemblages by simply putting the contents of his subject's wastebasket into a glass case. The New Yorkers extended an abstract but essentially manual tradition of art-making to include found objects; the Parisians took a more intellectual approach, recontextualizing existing objects without extensively transforming them, as did Duchamp with his readymades. Niki de St. Phalle's work from the early sixties is an exception; it includes triptychs displaying bats and guns and crucifixes, which make an assault on organized religion in a spirit akin to Conner's.

The Californians, in comparison to the eastern artists, seem a hermetic tribe of icon-makers. The damaged car parts that Chamberlain used for sculpture were already sculpture by Cesar's more conceptual standards, whereas George Herms would use crumpled, rusted auto-body metal as a framing element in a literary and nostalgic work such as *Lady Macbeth* (and later he made a series of assemblages out of a dead car as an exercise in recycling). The Nouveaux Realistes did, however, have a kind of wit and irreverence toward the art world that is reminiscent of the Californians, and their work too tended to consist of unmarketable urban debris, rather than saleable representations of it. In a 1987 show of American art of the fifties and sixties, *Made in USA*, the Californians were noticeably dingier than the New Yorkers; the East Coast seems to have tended toward bright, primary colors and big, awkward shapes; the Californians toward browns and blacks and delicate patterns, stains, gradations. In some respects, this California art isn't modern art at all, insofar as modern means a tradition of formal inquiry into the properties of media and perception. Nor were artists elsewhere so concerned with religious and drug-induced experience.

Berman and Herms made art that reflected the state of transcendence central to such experience, a state that blurs traditional distinctions between beautiful and ugly, sacred and profane, precious and worthless. In one way or another, this state of transcendence seems to have been an important goal in the arts of the time. Rauschenberg tried to work "impersonally," without regard for established tastes; the non-sense of Zen influenced artists from John Cage to J. D. Salinger (who wrote, "Seymour once said to me—in a crosstown bus, of all places—that all legitimate religious study *must* lead to unlearning the differences, the illusory differences, between boys and girls, animals and stones, day and night, heat and cold."); Susan Sontag would soon rail against interpretation. The surrealists' goal had been similar; as André Breton put it in the *Second Surrealist Manifesto*: "There is a certain point for the mind in which life and death, the real and the imaginary, the past and future, the communicable and the incommunicable, the high and the low cease being perceived as contradictions."

The virtue of transcendence is central to practices ranging from Zen to psychoanalysis, but the art that preceded mid-fifties work seems opposed to this. Certainly the critics, if not the abstract-expressionists themselves, thought of that earlier art as a bulwark against the avalanche of commercial and popular culture. For example, Herms's arrangement of old buckets and chunks of wood from the dump, with meat-market labels appended aren't really about taste, although ultimately they help redefine what could be worthy of contemplation and capable of carrying meaning. Pop art would pursue the undoing of distinctions more aggressively; such works as Andy Warhol's Coca-Cola bottle paintings and Roy Lichtenstein's comic-strip-derived imagery were less interested in transcending categories than in subverting them.

Assemblage paved the way for pop, and pop superceded it in the hearts of New York dealers and curators. Casting about for a suitable successor to abstract painting in the late fifties, they flirted with art from all over the world—the Californians, the Nouveaux Realistes—then settled on pop, which emerged just about the time of the *Art of Assemblage* exhibition. Pop was a New York phenomenon, with precursors in England, France, and the West Coast, and it seems New York was happy to have the anointed avant-garde in its own back yard again. After 1961, few MOMA curators came to California looking for new talent, and Hedrick, DeFeo, Herms, Kienholz, Jess were left alone again.

The Spinning Wheel

In the late fifties, a measure of fame was coming to the Californian artists, and San Francisco itself was becoming even more famous. The media discovered the Beats, the word beatnik was coined, and a cliché was born: black clothes, promiscuous sex, hip talk, and existentialist alienation. Some of this was pure invention, much seems to have been an attempt to defang something that was genuinely threatening. Scores believed the myth and came to San Francisco to live it out, as they would again in the sixties when hippies were taken up by the media. "The media bring in the creeps," Harry Jacobus said, "That is what has happened to San Francisco all the way through."

For the artists the pace went from lively to frantic. "After a point it really got too damn hard to handle it. It was out of control," said Joan Brown, "There were too damn many parties. And everybody was so damn keyed up, and involving themselves in excessive behavior. Whether it was drinking yourself stupid every night, or getting three hours of sleep, or in some of the musicians' or poets' cases, of drugging yourself to death. To death literally for some of them." Drugs, which had been an adventure and sacrament, became a serious problem when peyote and marijuana were supplemented by hard drugs.

The artist John Reed was one victim, as David Meltzer recalls. "He came to San Francisco, unfortunately, at the time that methamphetamine was introduced into the scene and spent about a year getting eviscerated on speed and burned a lot of bridges. For all the people who got involved in that, especially for creative people, it seemed great. Then there's that transition when you're not in control, it is. And you really can't work, you can't do anything, because you're really paranoid. It's a form of possession. It is directing your life, and speaking out of you, and deforming your perception of reality. The burn-out rate was incredible."

Heroin claimed at least two young poets, and alcohol destroyed many others. "It was a race between affirming life and destroying it," says Meltzer. "And the art was an affirmation."

In the fifties many people were pulled into an exciting vortex of activity; in the early sixties they began to extricate themselves from it. In Brown's words, "You can't keep up. So either you get wiped out or you go away." Larry Jordan observed, "Something that intense can't remain that intense forever. It was like a spinning wheel. People shot off in different directions of their own, in different parts of California or back to the East Coast or down to L.A., to codify their own work." The American political and social climate was changing, and so were the California artists.

* * *

Jess and Duncan had begun withdrawing from the social whirl before anyone else, and left for points east in early 1955. They were stranded in Stan Brakhage's grungy New York apartment for many weeks before finally sailing for Europe. Much of their time was spent in Mallorca, where Jess illustrated Duncan's *Caesar's Gate* and created a series of collages out of a small pile of Spanish-edition *Life* magazines. In 1956, they returned to the United States, to Black Mountain College in North Carolina, where Duncan taught during the spring semester, then back to San Francisco. On their return they felt out of step, and went less often to openings, parties, and readings. They did renew their acquaintance with the Bermans and began a long friendship with Herms. Jess's social life, however, became more and more a matter of having guests come to call. After accompanying Harry Jacobus on a househunting trip in Marin, they moved further away from the center of the subculture. Enchanted by the landscape of the semirural county across the Golden Gate, they took a house in the little coastal hamlet of Stinson Beach and stayed until 1961, when the complications of being carless (neither drove) prompted them to resettle in the city.

Without regard for the desires and disasters of the outside world, Jess continued to build a wonderland of pasteups, assemblies, salvages, and Translations. His career exemplifies the mountain coming to Mohammed. Although he and Duncan moved back to San Francisco, the post office continued to be Jess's main means of contact with the art world. He declined to join the Batman Gallery when he was invited to do so, though he did have one exhibition of pasteups at the Dilexi Gallery in 1960 and another the following year at an eclectic gallery called Borregaard's Museum (run by the poet Ebbe Borregaard). Over the next ten years, however, the art world began to embrace Jess's eccentric work, an acceptance he had never expected. "One thing that helps is to have a scene that you are disaffected with so you can contradict it," he has said. He never set out to please anyone but himself. "I felt, from going to museums, that there was an impetusto to produce things that were for museums. They set a form. There couldn't be intimacy; there couldn't be humor. So I said I'm turning my back on this realm of art—it's art enforcement. That wasn't the way I wanted to do it—I wanted enchantment, I guess. . . ."

The Bermans, sick of media attention and wary of the police, moved to Marin in 1960, settling on the east side, by the bay. The August 1958 issue of *Look* had run an article called "The Bored, The Bearded and the Beat" accompanied by a full-page photograph of the Bermans at home, captioned "Wally Berman and his wife, Shirley, put together an avantgarde magazine. Shirley works while Wally attends to cultural matters and the rearing of their boy, Tosh." In letters to friends Berman complained about this kind of patronizing publicity, which had appeared in a number of other publications, too, even in *Readers' Digest*.

They had been living at 707 Scott Street on Alamo Square, in what Joan Brown called "a big beautiful falling-down mansion," a house that had become a shooting gallery and crash pad for poets. John Wieners, whose *Hotel Wentley Poems* about the Polk Street hotel of that name had just appeared, was the principal problem. He had become a heroin addict and had taken to selling matchboxes of it on nearby streetcorners (while wearing blue eyeshadow, Meltzer recalls). "Rose lit circles . . . poet Johnson / Wieners Grand Duchess of the five / Dollar matchbox" Berman wrote later, in *Semina Seven*. Wiener's activities were the last straw, and when the landlord evicted them, the Bermans were happy to go.

On a visit to the Larkspur home of Billy and Joan Jarhmarkt, the Bermans fell in love with Marin's rustic charm and found a home on the Larkspur marsh. Fed by the creek that flows from Mount Tamalpais into the bay, the marsh had long boardwalks jutting into it with houseboats strung along them. At the time, it was fairly secluded, though Highway 101 ran nearby and San Quentin Federal Penitentiary was visible to the north. Berman liked to refer to their home there as an ark, though a shanty afloat might be more accurate. The Hermses joined them on the waterfront, and Larry and Patricia Jordan moved to nearby Madrone Canyon, a narrow valley at the base of the mountain, shaded by redwoods. Although they always wanted to be near an urban center, the Bermans preferred to live at some distance from the concrete and bustle of the city. Shirley remembers, "It was around the time of Larkspur that we decided we didn't want too many people in our home. It was a retreat in both senses of the word."

Semina Six and *Seven* were produced during the Larkspur stay. *Semina Six* consisted of Meltzer's long poem *The Clown* and a frontispiece drawing by Berman. *Semina Seven,* the only issue dedicated entirely to Berman's work, is a milestone in his career. In his early pencil drawings of jazz figures, a spiritual vision illuminated a specific cultural milieu. All through the fifties, he seemed to be at a loss to bring these realms back together, and the work in the 1957 Ferus show was not rooted in present-day realities the way the drawings had been. *Semina Seven,* however, anticipates his major opus, the Verifax collages, in the way it contextualizes and celebrates his own experience. Most of the copies contain ten to twelve cards bearing images and five discrete texts (as well as inscriptions on the images). On the folder sleeve is written. "ALEPH / a gesture involving photographs drawings & text by Wallace Berman 200 copies Larkspur Calif 1961 for Shirley & Tosh I love you."

Inscribed with curved alephs that dominate and partially obscure them, the images include photographs of a female figure in an electric chair (on the cover), Tosh in a fringed Davy Crocket jacket, and lush marijuana plants. A collage combines Hebrew calligraphy with a picture of Charlie Parker and the handwritten inscription "BIRD 1920-1955." Some of the alephs are black, some are white. The sacred, they seem to suggest, is everywhere; the many are one. Sacred, however, is not synonymous with serene. The poems in *Semina Seven* address such subjects as rape, fear and death. In "Fairytale for Tosh" the line "the wolf is dead" is repeated ten times over; the text of "Rapist & Voicethrower" consists of a series of numbers suggesting police or military communication codes. Berman loved to baffle; the Hebrew letters would grow into a semblance of writing, that spelled out nothing and are simply visual emblems invoking the kabala. *Semina Seven* is a complicated statement, an affirmation of the good and evil and the mystery of life. One card, taller and thinner than the rest, reiterates: "ART IS LOVE IS GOD."

Semina's disseminations took an altogether different form in Larkspur: a roofless shack on the marsh was christened Semina Art Gallery, and George Herms, Artie Richer, and Charles Brittin all had one-day shows there. Like Berman's home shows, they were low-profile, more ceremonial presentations than public displays. With weathered planks and windows framing country scenes, the gallery was as much an object of interest as the work displayed. Photographs that document it make it seem as much a part of Berman's art of context as many of his publications and collages.

During what is called his San Francisco period, George Herms spent time in Berkeley, Tuolumne (in the Motherlode country near Yosemite), Larkspur, and in Santa Rita Prison. He was arrested for marijuana possession (an undercover set-up) and served a six-month sentence; after these hard times, he and Polly Herms separated. On New Year's Eve of 1960, he met Louise Tacklind; they married and moved to Larkspur. Berman pointed out an abandoned boathouse on the marsh near his own ark where they might be able to live. They settled in, hooked up a hose for running water, counting on the tide for plumbing, and brought in a wood stove and oil lamps. "Everybody had boardwalks, but you had to go down the marshes to get to my place," Herms recalls. "That was great. If someone went to see you, they went to *see* you because they couldn't leave until the tides went out again." Acquaintances who visited the Herms's primitive house had the first inklings of what would later be called the hippie lifestyle. Louise gave birth to a daughter, Nalota, at home on Thanksgiving of 1960, and George delivered her.

Herms thrived on the marsh, and most of his earliest extant works date from this productive period. There was a dump nearby, and materials for such works as *Lady MacBeth, All I Wanna Do Is Swing 'N' Nail,* and *Meat Market* were harvested there. *Lady Macbeth* is a wall piece whose crumpled, rusted white-painted metal form framed and partially veiled a small photograph of a stern Victorian, with an effect both joyous and mysterious. *Meat Market,* typical of Herms's work in the Larkspur period, was inspired by a butcher's meat case, which displayed its wares much as museum cases do. From left to right it includes a pair of dressmaker's dummies, a basket, a bureau, a large wooden spool, and a pillar. There's audacity in its proposing such prosaic objects as art—or perhaps humility in the acknowledgment that the piece's power is in the objects and that the artist need merely present them. Not that the arrangement isn't crucial, only that it is at least superficially casual.

A weathered gray picture frame around the dummies confines and defines them as art—like a Giorgio De Chirico painting come to life. The dummies seem locked in an armless embrace, their heads linked by a red from. The basket contains a cow's skull, which is in keeping with the butcher-counter tags that pop up in various places. "Bottom Round Steak" says the tag on the records under the bureau; "Skirt Steak—69¢ lb." says the tag next to the soiled plastic doll on top of the bureau; and the price tags evoke Herms's insistent questions about value. Hanging down from the bureau, at the center of *Meat Market,* is a stained board inscribed "LOVE" with a small drawing of a pair of lips surmounted by a cross. Around this period Herms began stamping LOVE on all his works (a practice he continues today) as a signature and statement of intent. He says he borrowed the idea from Berman's "Art is Love is God" epigram, condensing it down to the one word love—"the keystone of the arch."

It is possible to interpret *Meat Market* as a summary piece about spiritual and carnal love, nourishment and cannibalism, but Herms's work doesn't yield easily to interpretation. He invites the viewer to contemplate the objects as themselves, rather than as symbolic components of a figurative sculpture or social tableau. They're still lifes, and still life is the most inscrutable genre, the one whose subjects are most about themselves as themselves. Like a seventeenth-century Dutch fruit-and-flowers painting, Herms's assemblages both celebrate the beauties of the here and now and remark on their mortality. The patina of time is crucial to his aesthetic, and he has often left things outdoors to "ripen." If Conner's textiles and wax suggest a virulent corruption, Herms's metal and wood describe a natural process of decay and death as part of the cycle of life.

* * *

The death penalty became an important subject in the work of Kienholz, Berman, and Conner. Caryl Chessman, an intelligent and articulate man who'd been fighting for more than a decade to overturn his death sentence, became an international cause célèbre in the year or so before his May 1960 execution at San Quentin Prison in Marin County. The evidence was shaky for the sex crimes he was charged with, and many saw him as an existentialist hero confronting a corrupt society. In his *The Psycho-Vendetta Case,*

Kienholz suggested that death was an inappropriate punishment for sexual misconduct and proposed a kind of eye-for-an-eye retribution (the title alluded to the Sacco-Vanzetti case of the 1920s). *Psycho-Vendetta* was a wooden box containing a kind of rude torso midsection with prominent sphincter, along with a pair of handcuffs and United States and California flags. Kienholz was becoming increasingly blunt about social issues, presenting them in damning tableaux of exploitation and squalor. The dripping resin, dirty materials, and damaged objects in his work represented a dark and repulsive vision of the world.

For the Bermans, the Chessman case was literally close to home; when a *San Francisco Examiner* reporter came out to visit, Berman was pointing out San Quentin to Tosh and saying, "That's where the State burned Chessman." The cover of *Semina Seven* used an image of a woman strapped into an electric chair, from the poster for the movie *I Want to Live.* Conner found the Chessman case, with its nexus of sexuality and state-sanctioned murder, fascinating. In 1961 he made *Homage to Chessman,* a wax-and-assemblage painting in dark, foul colors. It incorporated a telephone line—an allusion to the stay of execution the Supreme Court granted moments too late to save Chessman.[19]

A year earlier, Conner had made a piece with even greater impact—*Child.* Sonia Gechtoff's cast-off high chair provided an impetus for the piece, and Chessman's impending death, the subject. Conner sculpted a contorted blackwax child with its mouth open as if screaming, and bound it with tattered nylons. Conner said in 1988, "After a while it stopped being Caryl Chessman and became a child that had been tied up, gagged, and mutilated. I felt it had some universal message of pain and anguish, and of how natural impulses are thwarted and distorted. It was shown at the annual of the San Francisco Art Association, and it created a scandal; all the papers had big articles about it, saying 'It's not murder, it's art,' and comments like 'He must hate children.'" Viewers found *Child* disturbing, and Conner himself admitted he had to keep it in the closet when it was at home. Later the architect Philip Johnson bought it and donated it to the New York Museum of Modern Art, where it wasn't exhibited for many years and its semblance of deterioration became real.

* * *

Chessman was gassed at San Quentin in May, 1960. Thousands of students from around the Bay

Area went to San Quentin to protest, and many were radicalized by the feelings of outrage and camaraderie the event generated. Less than two weeks later, when the House Un-American Activities Committee began its San Francisco hearings on Communist subversion, several hundred students converged on City Hall in the first big demonstration of the coming decade of activism. "The purpose of this picket line is to protest the invasion by the HUAC of privacy of individual belief and its free expression, and to gain support from the public for the abolition of this Committee," said the statement issued by the newly formed Students for Civil Liberties. "We strive to achieve respect for the dignity of man." As the students attempted to descend the broad marble staircase inside the building, the police clubbed them and turned a fire hose on them. A photograph of the havoc dominated the front page of the *San Francisco Chronicle,* and this event, more than any other, signaled the beginning of the student revolution of the sixties. All during the fifties, demonstrations of dissent had been rare. Some had been cowed into silence, others felt their numbers were too few to take a public stand. For many, their private lives embodied a dissident point of view; making public declarations of principle—as Berman did at the Ferus Gallery, Ginsberg did in *Howl,* Hedrick with *Anger,* or Conner did with *Child*—was perilous.

As the Vietnam War escalated and the Free Speech Movement began, dissent spread across the country, and a wider spectrum of voices was heard. The close-knit underground enclaves that had been essential to artists and poets in the fifties began to dissolve. The vanguard artists and rebels split off in separate directions and began finding hundreds of kindred spirits where there had been at best dozens. Experiences that had been isolated and private became more communal. Bruce Conner remembers wandering through Golden Gate Park high on peyote, wondering if anyone else, anywhere, could also be on peyote. Half a decade later, Golden Gate Park would be full of people experimenting with hallucinogens. In the early sixties, as the artists were dispersing, a younger generation was beginning to gather for the next phase of the counterculture.

Of those who left San Francisco, Conner tried to go the farthest. He had always been obsessed with mortality and death and in 1960, at the Spatsa Gallery, produced a show by "the late Bruce Conner." "I went to Mexico for many reasons," he said in 1984. "One of them was that I was sure the bomb was going to drop and we'd be an-

nihilated. So I'd go to Mexico and figure out how to live in the mountains after the bomb dropped. I got rid of all my worldly goods and decided to change my life forever, and my wife and I got into the car and drove off for Mexico. What I found, though, in retrospect, was that I was basically running away from death. Mexico is a wonderful place to go if you're running away from death, because they celebrate it with bells and parades and everything else."

In 1961, the Herms family and the Bermans also left the Bay Area. The lack of plumbing at the Herms's boathouse finally attracted official attention, and they were evicted as public nuisances. Herms had a fire-sale exhibition called *New Sense on the Marsh* at which he disposed of much of his work and gave away puppies and kittens. They moved back to Topanga Canyon, and the Bermans returned to the little house on Crater Lane. At 2322 Fillmore, only Hedrick and DeFeo remained; the McClures had moved to the Haight-Ashbury, and Brown had gone her own way too. DeFeo was so absorbed in *The Rose* during the early sixties that she too was effactually absent from the scene.

A new generation of artists was emerging in the Bay Area: William T. Wiley, Robert Arneson, Robert Hudson, Stephen DeStaebler, William Geis, Harold Paris. They too explored mixed and unusual media; their art evinced humor, their interest in spirituality and non-European traditions; it was about personal experience and public issues. Herms and Berman returned to Los Angeles to find that the Ferus Gallery stable of former abstract expressionists had turned into (under Irving Blum's insidious influence, by some accounts) the L.A. Look—smooth, plastic, colorful objects. "The patented 'look' was elegance and simplicity, and the mythical material was plastic," says Peter Plagens. "It has, in short, the aroma of Los Angeles in the sixties—newness, postcard sunset color, and intimations of aerospace profundity."[20] Ed Ruscha, Billy Al Bengston, Robert Irwin, Craig Kauffman, Ed Moses were all rejecting the handicraft-and-high-seriousness of fifties art for a kind of cool, manufactured art. Kienholz was rising to prominence with works like *Roxy's,* the symbolic re-creation of a brothel, and a new generation of assemblage-oriented artists was emerging in the southland too: Llyn Foulkes, Betye Saar, Ben Talbert, Fred Mason, Shirley and Richard Pettibone, Tony Berlant, Ed Bereal, Vija Celmins.

The California art world had achieved critical mass. There were enough artists and collectors and galleries and museums and critics that the shadowy California underworld finally emerged into the full light of day. By 1962 California had its own art magazine, *Artforum*, headquartered in San Francisco until the middle of the decade, when it left for the richer pastures of Los Angeles (and then for the richest pasturage, New York). Many of the qualities that would define California art had been established in the fifties and continued in the work of younger artists. The artists of the fifties had broadened the possibilities of art, had let junk, humor, politics, religion, and popular culture into the precincts of art in a new way, and nothing would ever be quite the same.

Notes

1. "It was a very charged period . . ." and subsequent quotes in Joan Brown oral history, AAA

2. "Almost imperceptibly, funk . . ." in Harold Paris, "Sweet Land of Funk," *Art in America*, Mar.-Apr. 1967

3. *A Movie* was yet more avant-garde in its intentions: it was meant to be a film loop projected as part of a cinematic environment, but the necessary projection equipment proved unaffordable, and so Conner finished it as a discrete film.

4. "One time the Rat Bastards . . ." in unpublished interview with Dan Tooker, 1972, cited in Plagens, *Sunshine Muse*

5. See letter from Mark Green to Eugenie Candau, librarian of the San Francisco Museum of Modern Art, in Six Gallery files

6. Tour of the Bourgeois Wastelands in Tim Holt, "North Beach," *San Francisco Magazine*, Dec. 1972

7. "You stood up and talked . . ." in Spicer, *The Collected Books of Jack Spicer*; Knute Stiles's The Place is also memorable for having given shows early on to Jess, DeFeo, Remington, Gechtoff, Joel Barletta, for holding dada shows in 1954 and 1955 and otherwise supporting emerging artists.

8. Much of this gallery information comes from the SFMMA library's gallery files

9. "The first building . . ." and other material on Dilexi: See Oakland Museum's *The Dilexi Years*

10. "The Batman Gallery makes its bow . . ." in Frankenstein, "The Batman Makes Its Bow with Modern 'Junk,'" *This World, San Francisco Chronicle*, Nov. 13, 1960

11. "Dilexi will have to move . . ." A. J. Bloomfield, *San Francisco News-Call Bulletin*, Nov. 1960. Also (undated clipping in Batman file, SFMMA)

12. Another exhibition of his . . . the Alan Gallery in New York

13. "It never occurred . . ." in Coates, *The New Yorker*, Jan. 21, 1960

14. "I saw her studio . . ." Kienholz introduction to brochure for exhibition of her work at his Faith and Charity in Hope Gallery, August 1979, Hope, Idaho

15. "There is something . . ." in Coplans, *Artforum*, May 1963

16. "There was a period . . ." in Van Proyen/Hedrick, *Expo-See*, Summer 1985

17. "they were made to amuse . . ." in Man Ray, *Self-Portrait*

18. "Much of the work . . ." in Barbara Haskell, *Blam! The Explosion of Pop, Minimalism, and Performance, 1958-1964*, New York: Whitney Museum of American Art, 1984

19. *Homage to Chessman* is now in the collection of the Museum of Modern Art, New York

20. Plagens, *Sunshine Muse*

Bibliography

I. BOOKS

Man Ray. *Self-Portrait*. Boston: Little, Brown, 1963.

Plagens, Peter. *Sunshine Muse: Contemporary Art on the West Coast*. New York: Praeger Publishers, 1974.

Spicer, Jack. *The Collected Books of Jack Spicer*. Edited by Robin Blaser. Santa Barbara: Black Sparrow Press, 1975.

II. ARTICLES

Coplans, John. "Wally Hedrick: Offense Intended," *Artforum*, vol. 1, no. 2 (May 1963).

"An Interview with Wally Hedrick." Interview by Mark Van Proyen, *Expo-See* (Summer 1985).

III. ARCHIVES

Archives of American Art, West Coast Regional Center, DeYoung Museum, San Francisco. Oral history interviews: Bruce Conner, Jay DeFeo, Wally Hedrick, Joan Brown, Elmer Bischoff, William Copley, Billy Al Bengston, James Newman, Fred Martin, Hassel Smith. Papers of Jay DeFeo and Wally Hedrick.

Archives of California Art, The Oakland Museum, Oakland, California.

Louise Sloss Ackerman Fine Arts Library. San Francisco Museum of Modern Art. Artist and gallery files.

MICHAEL MCCLURE (ESSAY DATE 1992)

SOURCE: McClure, Michael. "Sixty-six Things About the California Assemblage Movement." In *Lighting the Corners: On Art, Nature, and the Visionary, Essays and Interviews*, pp. 181-90. Albuquerque: University of New Mexico College of Arts and Sciences, 1993.

In the following essay, originally published in Artweek *in 1992, McClure lists principles, trivia, and personal critiques of the assemblage movement, with specific focus on artists Bruce Conner, George Herms, Wallace Berman, and Jay DeFeo. McClure's notes illuminate both his own connection as a Beat poet and author with contemporary artists and the philosophy and motives behind the assemblages.*

1. "Assemblage" in California in its early stages represented a view of how consciousness works. It was a new viewpoint, a new eye, turned on the American cities just as they began to become old. It was keen to the mysterious and almost alchemical meanings of the space between objects and of the emptiness in storefront windows that perhaps contained an old shoe, a tin can standing on a box, and three toothbrushes tied together with a piece of brown twine.

In this sense it was Romantic: esthetic considerations had been heightened to considerations of perception.

2. Only after matters of sensory perception had preeminence was the assemblage movement involved in esthetics.

3. Each mainline assemblage artist has his or her own esthetics.

4. The art was made of ordinary materials but the intent of examining sensory perceptions always verges on the mystical. Perceptions made an even greater thrill with dusty or worn materials. The ordinary became strange, romantic, almost scientific.

5. Decay was involved in perception but not decay of mud and bacteria. Instead, this was the decay of aging, of wear, even sometimes of entropy.

6. Part of the assemblage creed was to reverse entropy—much as living beings reverse entropy and create negentropy. The pieces became thrilling because the unspoken agenda was dynamic: to create objects that had bypassed entropy and become beautiful and alive, even in the aging "urb."

7. With perception as the basic agreement of the field, each artist became an evolved temperament on the background of the field.

8. Bruce Conner was the Leonardo of the assemblagists. He was the renaissance man, equally capable in his energetic subtlety of drawing, his uncanny skill with assembled film, his craft as a sculptor in wax. (Even his skill as a musician and still photographer.)

9. Bruce Conner's youthful skills as an oil painter are not yet acknowledged.

10. Conner's collage *Ratbastard Number One* is a turning point in assemblage. The "ratbastards" are objects of vivid beauty and sexuality and fetishism. They separate the thrust of Conner's intent from Merz, from Dada, and from Cubism, which are European, and though intellectually vivid, fall short in emotional range.

11. The ratbastard is as American as Pollock's "Jungian" work and his drip work. It is the next step.

12. Conner uses the collage to torment, with beauty and sexuality, the consciousness of the onlooker. They are the esthetic tease, so beautiful you want them. The perceptions of space are intense and go beyond perceptions of space and color into texture—into popular consciousness of Ray Charles, big-titted magazines, broken mirrors, and lovely spider goddesses with skulls between their legs.

13. Bruce Conner's work is the work of a little boy who still loves what is bright in sexuality and texture before invention is stifled.

14. In 1957 artist Wallace Berman became my peyote father by giving me five buttons of peyote.

15. Probably no one has pointed out the significance of psychedelic and psychotropic substances on the artists of the assemblage movement. It is of intimate significance in the work of George Herms, Wallace Berman, Dennis Hopper, and Bruce Conner.

16. Wallace Berman sent assemblage artist George Herms to meet me while I was high on the five peyote buttons. I saw that George was the God of Foxes with dirt under the nails of his paws, fresh from his den. (As I put it in my *Peyote Poem*.) A few weeks later, I introduced Bruce Conner and George Herms. They had never seen each others' work.

17. Not long after that, Wallace Berman published *Peyote Poem* with his own cover photo of a peyote button, as an issue of his assemblage magazine *Semina*.

18. George Herms is the most religious of the assemblagists. He believes that art and energy are holy.

19. Herms's work is the most delicately and intentionally negentropic—that is, it goes against entropy—and it is the most involved with creating pristine—even if dusty and cobwebbed—new aggregates of life for the old materials of wood and photo and rubber bands and rusty bike wheels.

20. Each piece of Herms's is a challenge to decay. For a moment, or a month, or a week, or ten years, or a thousand years (but always temporary) the assembled objects defy crumbling and become art. The religious intent is clear if one realizes that this work which defies mortality is eminently and especially mortal.

21. Conner fights the mortality of pieces, hoping to keep them alive. Herms may repair his assemblages but he is sure they will pass on.

22. Herms is interested in the poetic purity of what he is doing—that it shows for a moment, or for a few years, the depth of his love. He has purified things in bringing them together, and they shine even if dusty. Conner is obsessed with the sensory or intellective perceptions that he can bind upon the assemblage awareness of space. He wants to show you blue-black feathers and rhinestones.

23. Herms wants to give you a poem written in faded brown ink on an old photograph stapled to a chairseat lying in a broken aquarium tank.

24. Conner dazzles you so that your mind tells you that you are looking at a poem.

25. Herms is going for the deep strata of profound feeling of silence, or silent music and purity of feelings with perhaps a wry and wistful twist of humor.

26. Sometimes Conner's work is clown-like and sometimes Conner is a social realist in the media of castaway junk or brown-black wax.

27. Oftentimes, seeing Herms's works, one thinks that they are by someone who is near-saintly in his care for the objects that are put together.

28. Bruce Conner lived in the communal group with Timothy Leary in Newton Center, 1963.

29. George Herms was arrested and did time in the late fifties for possession of marijuana.

30. There is a complex relationship between poetry and assemblage.

31. Herms began as a poet and became a visual and tactile artist.

32. Editor Wallace Berman published his own poems in an issue of *Semina* under the *nom de plume* Pantale Xantos. One poem was a list of drugs followed by the word *mother*. It went something like: Heroin mother, Peyote mother, Opium mother . . . and so forth.

33. Among writers most often mentioned by Berman were Cocteau and Hermann Hesse. Hesse appealed because of his bead game mysticism which bears some resemblance in its apparatus and stochasty to assemblage.

34. Conner saw a distinct relationship between the Ratbastard Protective Association, which he formed, and the Pre-Raphaelite Brother-

hood. Membership in the RBPA included Conner, Herms, Jay DeFeo, Joan Brown, Manuel Neri, Wallace Berman, and other artists and poets.

35. Conner set out to illustrate Dante's *Divine Comedy*. The important result of this project were his images of Geryon—the monster Fraud. I appropriated Geryon from Conner and Dante for the title of my first book, *Hymns to Saint Geryon*.

36. In the late fifties, Conner ran the Ezra Pound for President campaign—publishing "Ez for Prez" literature for the election, and he had some correspondence with Pound, who was then incarcerated in Saint Elizabeth's Hospital in Washington, D.C.

37. Conner was an appreciative reader of Michael McClure, Allen Ginsberg, Gregory Corso. Conner created a film portrait of Michael McClure (subsequently lost) and a sculpted portrait bust of Allen Ginsberg in assemblage style. His assemblage sculpture *Bomb* had its source in part in Corso's *Bomb*.

38. Conner was a friend of writer Richard Brautigan. Conner was an admirer of the poetry of Philip Lamantia. One can see a relationship between the styles of the poet and the artist regarding tactile and visual and sensory intensity.

39. It could have not been lost on Conner that Pound's *Cantos* are a collage or assemblage of Pound's mind and history as well as of History itself.

40. The Ubu Gallery was the gallery of art that preceded the Six Gallery in the same location in San Francisco. The Ubu gallery had been supported intellectually and artistically by poet Robert Duncan and his companion, the painter and collagist Jess.

41. When the Ubu Gallery gave way to the Six Gallery, it became cooperative and its members included Wally Hedrick and Jay DeFeo and poet Jack Spicer.

42. In 1955, Wally Hedrick asked Michael McClure to put together a poetry reading for the Six Gallery.

43. Poets Kenneth Rexroth and Robert Duncan did much to furnish the intellectual fundament of the California Bay Area for the tiny but intensely engaged artistic community. Both men were self-taught scholars—both were anarchists. Kenneth Rexroth spoke of the artistic proximity of San Francisco to Asia and the Pacific Rim, and he asserted the importance of Paris and London over New York. Both poets were strong in ego and

self-measured in their success as literary artists—both were anti-academic. Both were anti-materialistic. Both were believers in domesticity and supporters of nature. Both were intensely involved in the arts and especially the plastic arts.

44. Any major show of California assemblage should contain works by Robert LaVigne from the mid and late fifties. Some of these pieces were parts of sets created for the Actors Workshop in San Francisco. Robert LaVigne was the nearest thing to an official Beat artist. However, in the broadest sense, Wallace Berman, George Herms, Jay DeFeo, Joan Brown, and Manuel Neri were all Beats, or were for a time. An assemblage show should also contain collages by Russ Tamblyn (one of the stars of *West Side Story* and seen more recently in *Twin Peaks*). Russ Tamblyn gave up acting for many years, after discovering Wallace Berman and the new art. A major show should also contain collages by Dean Stockwell, who turned his attention to collage and 16mm films after becoming friends with Berman.

45. In the late sixties, actor/director and assemblagist Dennis Hopper was able to recite large passages of the gnostic Gospel of Thomas by rote memory.

46. To my knowledge, no one has ever collected and published poetry by George Herms, though Herms has published books of poems by Michael McClure and Diane di Prima, among others.

47. George Herms has printed small assemblage books and eccentric books with herculean zeal—these books and prints that he made with the printing press deserve to be seen on their own in a special show.

48. Poet David Meltzer is a close friend of George Herms and was good friends with Wallace and Shirley Berman. More than one poet learned his or her sense of style in personal life from the Bermans and from the Jess and Robert Duncan ménage.

49. Herms has used books extensively in his assemblage work. He also has made collage books as single works of art—for instance, he might take an old album for 78 rpm records and glue and staple it with other images and write upon it.

50. Jess is one of the most literate of modern artists. He has written nonsense poetry on a par with Lewis Carroll or Edward Lear, and he has done translations of the German nonsense poetry of Christian Morgenstern.

51. Jess has done many abstract poems as visual works of art. In the early fifties, he took words from periodicals and books and pasted them up in patterns that made haunting and evocative poems as well as esthetic objects. (This literary strand is perhaps even more stunning in the texts of his "Tricky Cad" pieces, which are collaged *Dick Tracy* strips.)

52. Jess has collaborated on books and broadsides with poet Robert Duncan and many other poets, and has illustrated a children's story by Michael McClure.

53. On receiving a copy of McClure's book of poems *September Blackberries*, Jay DeFeo sent the author a collage titled *September Blackberries*.

54. One gets the idea that after the Abstract Expressionists, who were mainly anti-intellectual and macho (with such noteworthy exceptions as Art Reinhardt, Barrett Newman, and Clyfford Still), the mainline assemblage artists were brightly literate.

55. One gets the impression that the drug of choice among Abstract Expressionists was alcohol, and it was either pot or psychedelics among those assemblagists who used drugs.

56. One can almost imagine the assemblagists as the bad, brilliant children of the Abstract Expressionists.

57. The earliest art work of Jay DeFeo's that I saw was in North Beach, in the Grant Avenue bar The Place, where the Beat poets went to drink and socialize in 1954.

58. DeFeo's work was a sudden esthetic illumination: pieces of posterboard with daubed single splotches of grey and white tempera and maybe a few stringy lines or part of a brush stroke or sweep of dirty red. But none of it was careless—it was perfect. And it was on perfectly worn and slightly uncared-for backgrounds.

59. When I looked at her early pieces, I had a sudden feeling that, regarding visual art, I was happy to be in San Francisco and not Paris. That was 1954.

60. DeFeo rode Abstract Expressionism in a direction that it had never been before—it was the placement of her incredible shabby daubs or exquisitely worn splotches and loose sprawling offbeat bars that was the message. She was dealing with paint as the assemblagists would deal with worn materials. She was part of a vision, of a new way of seeing. She was beat, she was elegant, she

was worn, and she was glimmery. DeFeo is the visionary of the assemblagists.

61. Jay DeFeo was as calligraphic and as minimalistic as Robert Motherwell was, in a later decade, in his brush paintings. Robert Motherwell was a pure painter looking to Paris or perhaps Tokyo. DeFeo was a gambler and an alchemist. She was translating her vision into painting and gambling her spirit on the *coup* of her dusky materials.

62. I have seen three great crosses. One is by Cimabue or another post-Byzantine master, and is in the Accademia in Florence. The second is an assemblage by George Herms. Long-haired at the time, Herms carried the cross on his back up Downey Street in San Francisco, followed by a group of children. The Herms cross is composed of scrap wood and shelving and a tree branch. The crossbar supports a small "museum" of assemblage that ranges from a photo of a man with elephantiasis of the scrotum to a statue of Robbie the Robot to a plastic box containing human teeth. The third memorable cross was entered by Jay DeFeo into a San Francisco Art Annual of the mid-fifties. It was of butcher paper stretched over a lumber frame, and around twelve feet high. It was outrageous in scale and beauty—it had an enormous delicacy. The cross's sole decoration was a splash or splot of tempera. At the Museum, the piece was scribbled upon by vandals. The added obscenities made the piece seem more profound and consequently more beautiful.

63. At one point in the late fifties, I found that DeFeo had destroyed, by cutting in half, nearly all of her tempera on posterboard works. The destroyed stack of work was eighteen inches to two feet high.

I wish she had not done it, and I have thought about her act for thirty years.

64. My guess is that DeFeo destroyed the work so that she might go beyond it. It may have taken twenty years for her to go beyond that work. In its spiritual substance, it was the most advanced work that I had seen until that time.

65. Bruce Conner is working with sensory and intellective fire—and then spirit—in that order.

66. Jay DeFeo is working with spirit, contemplation, and gesture. She proves that the minute gesture in a perfect daub is as fine as a great slooping drip in Pollock's work or a color field by Rothko.

MICHAEL MCCLURE AND EDUARDO LIPSCHUTZ-VILLA (INTERVIEW DATE 1992)

SOURCE: McClure, Michael, and Eduardo Lipschutz-Villa. "Wallace Berman and *Semina*." In *Lighting the Corners: On Art, Nature, and the Visionary, Essays and Interviews*, pp. 191-6. Albuquerque: University of New Mexico College of Arts and Sciences, 1993.

In the following interview, originally published in Support the Revolution in 1992, Lipschutz-Villa asks McClure to recall the initial impact of Wallace Berman's assemblage magazine, Semina. *McClure reflects on the number and range of artists and poets who were influenced by Berman's self-produced compilations, and remarks that* Semina *ran parallel, in feeling and philosophy, to other arts of Beat culture.*

[*Lipschutz-Villa*]: *What effect did the assemblage magazine* Semina *have in the creative community?*

[McClure:] First, I want to talk about *Semina* as an act in itself. *Semina*s are a form of love structure that Wallace Berman made, drawing friends together. Friends are drawn together into the assemblage of the magazine, but then the magazine is also sent to acquaintances who are drawn into the circle of friends, so it expands and becomes a larger event. Friends become respondents, that is, to Berman, and some of them become correspondents to the magazine and in that way they are included in the magazine. *Semina* has some aspects of the religion of art and friends. There's an initiation to *Semina*, i.e., if Berman chose you. One is chosen. One cannot purchase or command having a *Semina* but it comes to one. The magazine is out of the line of commodity and merchandising and purchase. There's nothing to consume. And so it's completely different, and precious. In fact, the way one loses *Semina*s is that one lends them to a friend and they keep them because they also find them to be a wonder.

Like George Herms's work, *Semina* is made of the materials of mortality, such as poster papers, cardboard, twine, slick industrial papers. The senses are being appealed to and the magazine *is* an esthetic in itself. The unpurchasable bundle of beautiful art has a color range even more specific than Cubism, when you stop to look at it: the textured range of papers and twines. Also, the actual act of the hand-folding and gluing is there, the artist putting the pieces in the pockets—it's there, still present to the eye, like the smell of the glue in a new *Semina*. *Semina* contrasts the glossiness of hand-produced photographs with the almost Japanese-ness of the background of industrial materials that are used. There is also the luridness of nudity and sexuality contrasted with the various spiritualities of Hesse, or Cocteau, or Artaud, or of David Meltzer, or of John Wieners, or of Allen Ginsberg.

Another thing about *Semina* is that it's un-American. In the fifties, when the magazine first began, it was against what we called "The American Way." *Semina* was a long way from the American Way. The American Way was the Korean War, the starched shirts and ties, the military preparedness to battle against the Iron Curtain or the Bamboo Curtain.

Semina is also about rules. There are so many rules in the putting together of a *Semina* and it is so precise a game of art that new freedom is created for the imagination, as in information theory: the more rules there are, the more specific something must be—then more powerful channels are created for freedom. *Semina* poises like the work of George Herms or Bruce Conner on the crack of crisis, on the lip of entropy—it's about to fall apart. Like love, a *Semina* has to be tended and displayed to exist.

I want to give you an example of what I mean by being poised on the lip of entropy. When Wallace bought a TV set on time from Sears-Roebuck when he first moved to San Francisco, he collaged it. He put drawings and photographs all over it, and it became unrepossessable. It had become poised on the lip of entropy. Another time when Wallace bought a motorcycle, a new motorcycle (and he bought it on time, also), he took olive-drab spray paint and sprayed it. It was then on the lip of entropy. It was no longer useful to the American Way. It was unrepossessable. It had become Wallace, in the same way that the *Seminas* were Wallace, and poised out of the consumer loop. Pushed to the edge, *Semina* became unsellable. What Wallace made was his, and he kept it, and he also gave it to his friends.

I see *Semina* on the cusp exactly between love and generosity and selfish appetite: Wallace's appetite for art, and for friendship, and for spirituality. This is where the most meaningful art exists, and where the most meaningful art comes from, that crack of crisis. A poet said a poem is like an ice cube on the stove, floating on itself. *Semina* melts into itself; it's the ultimately precious object; it's valueless. It gives a gift to the imagination through its net of laws and rules. It gives a glamour of appreciation through the physical textures of twine, board, and papers, and it has the smell of photo chemicals and Wallace's pot-smoke on it. To the eye, it is a fastidious range of

both handmade and glossy (speaking of the photographs) to cheesily machine-made and already about-to-crumble-papers.

One of the things I remember in regard to *Semina* is that when I advised Jim Morrison to publish his poems for the first time, he was concerned that people would not appreciate his poems, that they would only look at them because he was a rock star. I suggested self-publishing to him as being what I had done, and what Shelley had done, and then giving, as Berman had done, the poems to friends to see their reactions. Apparently I'd shown Wallace's *Semina* to Jim because the first secret editions of his poetry, *The Lords* and *The New Creatures,* are brought out in such a way that they look like Wallace might have done them. So Jim also had been influenced by the *Semina* aesthetic. It hit a wide range of poets in surprising ways.

Regarding *Semina,* it was always old by the time you got it because you were interested in it and waiting for it. Since this was a love structure, an assemblage of meaningful materials, that you waited for—an esthetic, a spiritual occasion, an act of soul-building—it was also a slow-moving process. It would take Wallace six months or a year to get an issue of *Semina* out. You'd say, "Well, what are you doing now, Wallace?" and you'd get involved in the process. He wouldn't ever quite tell you what he was doing. So by the time it came out it was old, you'd waited for it for a long time, and then it was in your hands and it was brand-new. But there it was on that edge—it was about to fall apart again. Papers would fall apart, a photograph by Walter Hopps could peel off the page it was glued on; it was poised in a special place where nothing else existed. Even if friends were doing "mail art" or things like that, that was an entirely different thing. *Semina* is not a secular magazine; it's a magazine of the spirit. In the same way that we misunderstand today what the Dadaists were doing, or the early Russians—we misunderstood what Kandinsky was doing, or what Malevich was doing—we don't realize that the roots of those things are in deep, old spiritual beliefs from Hwa Yen Buddhism to Swedenborg to Meister Eckhart. Wallace's work had those old deep roots of spirituality, whereas mail art was secular and immediate. It had to do with the person's spiritual growth, but did not have the roots that Wallace intuitively tapped into with the production of *Semina.*

Like cool jazz or bop, *Semina* didn't ask for any approval. It didn't expect any approval, except from the circle of friends it went to. One couldn't subscribe or purchase it, so it didn't cater to anyone. The only catering it did was to the love of one's friends and their love for you, and the love for art that was part of the instinctive process. It was an outlaw publication. Being outlaw, it reveled in the contradictions of love and pain, and of drugs and of deep thought. We knew these were not contradictions but they were seen as contradictions by mainstream culture. This was something we hadn't really seen before, even in our own Beat milieu. It matched what we poets were doing and it matched what the painters were feeling.

Semina was unwholesome. In the age where the eight-cylinder car and military uniform represented wholesomeness, *Semina* was the ultimately unwholesome object, and we gloried in it. It was a magazine, or an assemblage, that would fling together Jean Cocteau and Orson Welles and David Meltzer and Charles Bukowski with no thought of the inherent contradictions of doing so. Part of the game rules was to do away with rules, with the rules of separation and distinction that were taken for granted. How could you print Bukowski side by side with Artaud and Hesse, or with Cameron? *Semina* is a poseur with the slyness and charm of a swami, but one who does, in fact, quietly and secretly know deep things. *Semina* is like the smoke and mirrors used by the Wizard of Oz in the movie, but behind the smoke and mirrors are views of the reality of the structure of nothingness. That's basically an Eastern, un-American view, regarding seeing through, and moving through, the veil of Maya. *Semina* says, "Everything is as flimsy as this magazine is. Here's a dose of reality for you. It's not like the four-door sedan, it's like this. Everything is all some kind of religious experience. You can look at it all as being love, or God."

Another thing about *Semina* is that it doesn't have any credentials. *Semina* has no credentials, no authority, no badge from the 4-H or the American Insurance Institute. *Semina*'s a real outlaw act, as complex as outlaws in the Old West, as sexy and cool and hip and pop—and at the same time religious. Furthermore, it's sabotage. It's a decor for soul-building. And those of us who were interested in building our souls used it not only as our decor but as a pointer to new directions for us, and as an outlet that we might follow with the portholes it created for our imagination.

I'm looking at this cover of Semina 7, and I see in the corner "Art is Love is God."

Well, "Art is Love is God" may be in that same issue where Wallace prints a part of Juan de la Cruz, St. John of the Cross. You can hear the echo of Gertrude Stein, at the same time feeling the feet of St. John of the Cross on the moist soil of Spain.

I read somewhere that William Burroughs called Berman a poet-maker.

I think that's a wonderful thing for William to say. I would call Wallace a spirit-maker, a soul-maker—because I don't see *Semina* as a poetry magazine. I see *Semina* as an assemblage, and the visual art in it is as interesting as the poetry. The act of creating it is an act that coincides with the poetry. I tend to look at the production of it. In other words, in the era of the slickest production values, here's probably the least slick magazine or the least slick assemblage that anybody had ever seen.

I'd like you to go through Semina 1 and just talk about what comes to you.

All right. I'll pretend I'm twenty-three years old and seeing *Semina* for the first time. Here's *Semina* 1! Hmm—strange-looking woman on the cover, with eyes of such mixed emotion that I think of the paintings of Francesco Clemente. This cover is very beautiful—and it's got a WB under it. What is WB, and what is *Semina*? The face is like a hieroglyph, it's so vivid. I'm not sure of the emotions, or what that face means. I have a lot of ancillary thoughts about it, but . . . And here it all is, this publication in this envelope used by insurance companies or brokers of some unknown substance, or maybe left over from a ship chandler's office. I open it up, I say, "My god, here's a poem by David Meltzer!" I know David Meltzer—we're both renegade Beat poets in San Francisco. I like that! Then I find a poem by E. I. Alexander. I say, "Oh, I've heard of Bob Alexander. He's a legendary figure in Los Angeles. I'll have to read that one later." In the meantime, here's a wild-looking photo. It seems to be a triple exposure, no, a quadruple exposure. It's by Walter Hopps, *that's* why Walter gave me this! So I could see his photo, and see this magazine. That's great! Now I see what Walter's doing. And then here's another strange and beautiful piece by Walter also which could be part of a liquid projection. I heard about liquid projection shows and there's a man named Lee Romero doing them in Venice, California. Maybe this is a photograph that Chico took of a liquid projection—Whoa! And here's a slinky drawing by a woman with a snake's tongue meeting a Mr. Back Door Man, who looks like he escaped from Pavel Tchelichev. I like that, that's interesting. Here's a poem by Cocteau! It's hard in whatever year this is—1965 or 1957—to find anything by Cocteau. Cocteau's seldom printed in English. I've got to look at that in a minute. Then here's something that just says "Marianne Grogan." I don't know who that is. Oh, and then here's an assemblage sculpture! I know about that. My friend Bruce Conner does that. This is called "Homer," and the photo is by Charles Britten. He's one of the Venice or Los Angeles artists. And then here, wait, there's one more thing in here—"To a Toccata by Bach"? It's a poem by Herman Hesse. I didn't even know Herman Hesse wrote poems!

Thank you, Michael. That was great! A surge of remembrance.

RICHARD CÁNDIDA SMITH (ESSAY DATE 1995)

SOURCE: Smith, Richard Cándida. "Woman's Path to Maturation: Joan Brown, Jay DeFeo, and the Rat Bastards." In *Utopia and Dissent: Art, Poetry, and Politics in California*, pp. 172-211. Berkeley: University of California Press, 1995.

In the following essay, Smith traces the development of the works of women artists Joan Brown and Jay DeFeo during the 1950s and 1960s.

From 1957 to 1964 Joan Brown was one of San Francisco's best-known painters. At midcareer she reflected upon the ambitions that nourished her artistic practice, claiming that

[painting]'s the only thing that I have been involved in, or could think of being involved in, where there's no responsibility to anybody else. And this gets into maybe some of my feelings about galleries and the public. Whatever you do is strictly for yourself. And I want the freedom. Anytime I feel the pressure from anybody, from anything outside, I'll retreat from that and push it away and push it aside. Because it's the only thing I've ever done where there's absolute freedom. . . . At any given moment I can make a total ass of myself and I'm responsible. You know, there's just me involved in it and nobody gets hurt, nobody. . . . You can't do that when you're teaching, you can't do that with your family, you can't do that with your child or wife or boyfriend/girlfriend.[1]

We might note immediately that for men art was a way of finding a masculine self, but for Brown art was a way of stepping back from gendered relations. At the time of this statement in 1975, Brown was one of many obscure but talented painters who earned their livings by teach-ing. Yet at the start of her career she seemed, even more than Neri, on the verge of stardom. She began her artistic career in 1955, at the age of seventeen, with an impulsive decision to register at the California School of Fine Arts rather than go to a liberal arts college. She had shown no previous artistic inclinations. Two years later, she had her first commercial exhibition in New York. In 1958 *Holiday* magazine, playing on the national interest in San Francisco's bohemia that developed after the publication of Kerouac's novel *On the Road,* featured her in a series on "North Beach Poet-Makers." *Look* magazine ran a profile on her in an article highlighting the most prominent women artists in the United States. In 1959 Staempfli Gallery in New York began paying her a monthly stipend of $300 for exclusive right to represent her work and presented annual one-artist shows of her work. In 1960 she became the youngest person to exhibit at the Whitney Museum of American Art. *Cosmopolitan* and *Glamour* prepared feature articles on her as a young woman making it in a mostly male profession. In 1962 *Mademoiselle* honored her with its annual Outstanding Single Achievement in Art Award.[2]

"Everybody's Darling," art critic Philip Leider called her. Brown's work, Leider noted, heralded the national success of the aesthetic and pedagogic approach developed at the California School of Fine Arts. Paintings such as *Lolita* epitomized the San Francisco school of painting, with its philosophical preference for ugliness, a coarse four-to-five-inch-thick surface, and cheap materials. Since she came into the art world at a very young age, immature and intellectually undeveloped, Leider argued that Brown focused the ideas of her teachers and peers, without her own ambitions—other than seeking praise—intervening to dilute their expression. Leider sexualized her achievement by describing her as a passive, if talented and energetic, receptacle of "attitudes." Her work "embodied" the "germinating" ideas of Clyfford Still as assimilated by Brown's teachers Elmer Bischoff and Frank Lobdell. Like Bischoff, Brown reduced her figures to the barest amount of information to identify their gender and relative age, while her use of sludgey impasto to create textured three-dimensional shapes echoed Lobdell, although she preferred bright colors to his grimly limited palette.[3]

She recalled the early acclaim she received as "bothersome and difficult." Success limited her sense of freedom. "Some of the pressure was coming from the outside, but some was internal too;

Wallace Berman's *Semina*. Wallace Berman Estate, Courtesy of LA Louver Gallery.

'Is this one as good as the last?' The concerns were going outward where they had been inward. Not 'Do I think this is better than the one I just did?' but worrying about what outside reaction would be. I found that very stifling."[4] This conflict between ambition and inner ideals came to a head in 1964, when she and her dealer, George W. Staempfli, clashed over new directions in her work. After her marriage to Manuel Neri in 1961 and the birth of their son Noel the following year, Brown started painting domestic scenes drawn from her son's baby book. The subject of her painting had moved from creative expression itself to the daily experiences of her life: Noel eating his first ice cream cone or taking a pony ride at the zoo. Her stylistic devices adopted to her new concerns. She recalled:

> I was feeling restless and felt there was more than what I knew about. So in January of 1965 I decided to take a new step forward. I put away all my palette knives and trowels, and decided to do some small still lifes in subtle color. I wanted more conscious control of my work at this point. Staempfli couldn't understand why I would want to change since my paintings were selling well, I

was showing steadily in New York and L.A., and people were taking notice of my work. I tried to explain that I didn't want to show for a while, that I wanted to pursue this new direction. He didn't agree, so then I realized that we must part ways. I never regretted it, either.[5]

Brown's break with Staempfli and her decision to suspend public exhibition of her work coincided with her divorce from Neri. She confronted a crisis hitting all facets of her life by deciding to spend a year remastering her craft. She asked herself what she would need to learn to become a painter if she had never gone to art school. She began, as if a novice, systematically to work through charcoal, crayon, and water color exercises. Discipline and self-control replaced expression and impulse as the key concepts of her working methods. She purposely limited her palette, restricting herself in order to force discovery of what she did not know. She worked with small formats because everybody in San Francisco painted very large canvases. If she was to regain a sense of initiative, her art was no longer to speak of presumed painterly absolutes, but only for herself.[6]

The process broke the patterns she had developed while a student at the California School of Fine Arts. When she returned to public exhibition, her work was radically, and for most critics, shockingly different. The precision of her new style was accentuated by a shift from oil on canvas to enamel on masonite board, which made the surfaces flatter and more brittle. Drafting became vitally important, as she created bright representational images, mostly drawn from dream imagery. She forced the viewer's attention away from the language of painting onto the literal content of the images, the details of which were influenced by her studies of hermetic and gnostic philosophy. The cat in ancient Egyptian religion, for example, was one of the four primal emanations of Ptah, the fundamental life force. The image, painted on the occasion of Brown's third marriage to painter Gordon Cook, merged autobiography with mythology.

This work was consciously out of fashion. She knew that her quotations of Rousseau, van Gogh, and Japanese Ukiyo-e prints appeared naive and quaint in a period dominated by postpainterly abstraction. She assumed, contrary to the prevailing wisdom, that the images could be more important than the form of presentation. Representation meant that she was not afraid of what she felt, even at the risk of sentimentality. She would take a stand in the world by making interpretations. She had progressed from being a brilliant exponent of what was virtually a brand-name style to a more masterful but individual approach that did not at the time relate to the formal preoccupations of any other group of painters. This insistence on the primacy of her own vision over any concept of art orthodoxy problematized her relation to the professional art world and contributed to her decline into the secondary rung of artists.[7]

She had no one-artist shows until a 1971 exhibition at the San Francisco Museum of Modern Art. For ten years she went without a show in New York, and she never again had a commercial gallery as an exclusive representative, although several houses in San Francisco, Los Angeles, and New York exhibited her work. No longer a bright young star or even likely to become famous, she still considered her career to be successful, carefully underscoring that she did not, indeed dare not, use monetary criteria. For her, success meant the ability to create a body of work faithful to her interior vision. She did not conceal her contempt for the purely commercial aspects of the art business. She told *Artweek* magazine in 1971 that she painted only for her-self, but she felt a need "every once in a while" to exhibit her work to see how other people reacted to it.[8]

The objectively foolish, but subjectively necessary decision to drop Staempfli left Brown in a difficult financial situation that would endure for a decade. Since 1960 she had taught at the night school program at the California School of Fine Arts, but the work was sporadic and part-time. Her salary was insufficient to support herself and her son. She received money from Neri and her parents, but she needed to feel that she could rely on her own efforts to provide the basis for her standard of living. She supplemented her income by teaching in hospitals, private schools, and by leading art therapy classes for the physically and mentally disabled. "It was tough at that time," she observed later, but felt that the experience of working with so many different types of people outside the art world gave her a better sense of what art could mean in everyday life. Raising a child convinced her that "being an artist is a by-product of being a human being. . . . I'm not any one thing; I'm not just a teacher, I'm not just a mother, I'm not just a painter. I'm all these things plus, and the more areas I can tap the richer each one of the others will be."[9]

Only in 1974 did she gain financial stability when she joined the faculty of the art department at the University of California, Berkeley. The goal of personal, creative freedom was so necessary for her self-esteem that she willingly accepted ten years of personal hardship without ever publicly regretting the choice she had made. The decision had been hers, she insisted. She refused to blame Staempfli in any way for her difficulties in producing satisfactory product for him. He operated as he did because developing saleable artists was essential to the survival of his business. Brown could not become autonomous working with Staempfli because he himself had no autonomy whatsoever, but led his professional life entirely in reaction to the mechanisms of the market.[10]

Brown's decision was neither unprofessional nor antiprofessional, since her career turned toward an alternative professional model for being an artist, one grounded in the nonprofit, academic aspects of the art world. Her most important shows appeared at museums and university galleries. Her approach to art, shared with many in her generation, included a component irreducibly noncommercial because the institutional framework most important to her advancement took place in the publicly funded sector. She had experienced rebirth in school, and leaving the academy to join the wider world proved difficult and painful. After a plunge into entrepreneurial activity, she discovered that Douglas MacAgy's conception of art as a form of scholarship provided a more secure and independence-giving basis for building a career. She did not reject the value of sales, but she would not make them critical markers of success in her own self-evaluations. The sacralization of creativity in fact helped to support the art market system, because it enhanced the general idea of art as a special autonomous realm. Yet if the public and private sectors were not inherently in conflict, they were not identical, and a potential for conflict underlay the distinction between these two ways of being an artist in America.

The turn from worldly ambition was motivated by a desire to protect personal autonomy and to prevent herself from being reduced to a stereotype. She had discovered that a life based on creativity and work allowed her to live simply and in direct contact with her interior reality. "I trust the unconscious very, very strongly. And I don't trust my conscious, my mind is a mess. It just looks like this painting table. It's just fitted with nonsense, sidetracking, garbage, and crap." Her conscious mind came from the exterior world, from the repetitive dictates of social pressures. Her unconscious tapped into a deeper level of reality, one independent of society. Her dreams were orderly, clean, clear, very bright in color: "They look just like my paintings as a matter of fact."[11]

Three factors in Brown's account of her life help explain the particular contours of her life-course decisions: her parents' status anxiety; an experience of psychological rebirth that the art student peer group gave her; the linkage of sexual stereotypes to commerce. The first factor was her parents' obsessive anxiety over class status. Brown was born in San Francisco in a lower-middle-class Catholic family, the only child of an alcoholic father who worked as a bank clerk and a devoutly religious mother who suffered from epilepsy. Brown began her life story by stressing the disjunction between her parents' psychological disorders and their desire to maintain the façade of a respectable and affluent *professional* family.

Her father's income was modest compared to the image he wished to project. The family lived in an upper-middle-class section of the city, but in a tiny, uncomfortable three-room apartment. Brown was forced to sleep in the dining room with her grandmother, instead of having a room of her own, as she was certain she could have had if they had lived in a neighborhood more appropriate to the family's income level. Brown particularly recalled that she herself was a public emblem of her parents' aspirations. The family often ate poorly, but she wore expensive clothes and attended the most exclusive Catholic schools. The bank clerk concerned about how his peers viewed him arranged his life to conform to the most clichéd images of respectable life, even to using his daughter, without thought to her needs, to allay status anxiety.[12]

She hated the environment her parents provided for her. Life was insular and deprived, rotating between church, school, and the uncomfortable apartment where each member of the family retreated into a personal shell. "It was dark," she recalled. "I mean dark in the psychological way, and it was crazy." She could never bring friends over because the family's private life did not live up to its public façade. The street became the only place where she could escape her parents' obsessive fantasies. "As a child, I never spent one moment alone in that apartment. If my parents weren't home when I came home I would wait in the lobby downstairs. I'd wait out in the street. . . . It was black, dark, scary, like a Dracula house to me."[13]

When she graduated high school in 1955, her parents enrolled her in Lone Mountain College, the city's Catholic women's school, but Brown, only seventeen, impulsively switched to the California School of Fine Arts after seeing an advertisement a few days before classes were to start. As soon as she walked into the school's courtyard, she recalled that the school "was a whole new world for me, and I was just ready for it." The students were "sophisticated" and "worldly" veterans—this time from the Korean War. No one seemed afraid to formulate an opinion about art and society. She felt she learned that the world was hers to interpret, that there were experiences "outside of the damn Catholic San Francisco environment" of her childhood. The continuing appeal of the values and perspectives of World War II veterans-turned-bohemians and the processes by which their interests spread to a younger generation of artists are a striking feature of painter Joan Brown's recollections of her career. She repeated almost verbatim motifs we discussed in chapter 3 [in Smith, Richard Càndida. *Utopia and Dissent*], but her female perspective is a reminder that the male veteran was as much a shared imagination of youthful independence as a sociological reality.

The second critical factor in Brown's transition was the liberating effect of generational confraternity. Instead of competition and infighting, "We'd all meet and be just one big bunch of energies all coming together. . . . We gave each other a great deal at that time. Everybody was excited. It was kind of like a big burst of energy, a rebirth in a sense."[14] Wally Hedrick, a close friend and fellow student, also stressed the importance of a generation developing new lives together: "In this little community we didn't have to have art teachers. It sounds egotistical, but we were our own teachers and we taught each other. We were so close to one another it was as if I could have called them my surrogate parents."[15] Psychological realignment with one's peers helped one separate from unwanted traditions and values, but it was also a way of emphasizing personal accomplishment. Professional identifications provided sociability, but also the group in which one competed to demonstrate personal excellence. By choosing to be orphans, for whom peers were more important than parents or teachers, postwar artists imagined that each person started on an equal footing and achieved what he or she could, according to the strength of talent and vision.

Languages of independence and ambition were closely linked, and thus we must be careful not to assume that youth rebellion was necessarily or inevitably a revolt against patriarchal authority. Fraternity placed the generation in an ambivalent position vis-à-vis fathers and teachers, as we saw in chapter 1 [in Smith, Richard Càndida. *Utopia and Dissent*] when younger artists negated the history of which they were heirs in order to magnify their own accomplishments. The myth of inheriting a cultural desert was a formula for asserting on a social level the powerful feelings of rebirth that students such as Joan Brown felt upon entering the art world. The promise of novelty stimulated ambitions and the possibility of rapid advancement within the chosen profession. Confraternity appeared in the guise of rebellion, but it did not overthrow the patriarchy except in the imagination. Indeed, as careers differentiated and competition intensified for prestige and place, the confraternity dissolved into a memory, idealized and romanticized because it represented hope in a timeless state. As long, however, as ambition conflicted with portions of subjective ideals, the individual remained suspended between accommodation to a mature position within a rejuvenated cultural institution and a position of rebellion defending more egalitarian aims.[16]

Evidence of the psychological realignment Brown underwent in school remains in the formulas in her account that shift her career choice into a purely mythic level. She presented the critical decision of her life as an element of chance, as if the hand of fate had directed her to the new environment for which she, as yet uninitiated into the mysteries of creativity, was totally unprepared.

> I can't really say it was an accident that I ended in art school. I don't believe in accidents, but it certainly wasn't planned. . . . When I went to art school, I had never heard of Picasso. I had heard the name Rembrandt, but never had seen any of the paintings. I had never been to any museums outside San Francisco. All I had looked at was a sarcophagus and a mummy at the de Young Museum.[17]

So foreign was the life she had chosen that she was deeply embarrassed to discover she had to draw life studies from nude models. The first Richard Diebenkorn picture she saw infuriated her because it seemed so pointless. Within a year she wanted to duplicate for others the shock she first felt at seeing an abstract painting.[18]

This motif of chance guiding her continued to appear in her account as she described falling virtually by accident into a teaching career and getting her first shows. The certainty of success that the motif of chance suggested was countered by a second mythic element that introduced factors of suspense *and* personal merit. She loved art school, but she recalled that when she began taking courses, she showed no talent whatsoever and teachers advised her to drop out. To stay in school she had to work extraordinarily hard, fighting lack of aptitude and technique.

> I thought, "I don't have any talent, I have no business here," and I was going to go to work when [William H. Brown] talked me into taking one more class . . . "Landscape Painting." Elmer Bischoff taught the course . . . [and told her] "You don't have to do things right, just paint from your insides, let it go, I'll help you as we go along." He really started teaching me how to see, rather than to be technically proficient.[19]

Brown blossomed under the influence of the "Bischoff attitude": don't worry about the rules, do what feels right, protect your privacy, never forget that it will always be hard work to do something good, and be your own strongest critic, never satisfied until you have achieved something new. She acknowledged that having no "natural" talent, she never mastered the basics of drawing, but her technical inadequacies forced her to explore "internal process" and develop a visual language for her philosophical meditations rather than reproduce surface phenomena.[20]

After her breakthrough in Bischoff's class, she never again considered pursuing a career other than painting, because all alternatives meant returning to her parents' world. Thus her life journey took a path of rebellion only so she might discover the otherwise hidden traditional values of community, apprenticeship, and hard work. She continued as a student until 1961, when she completed a master's of fine arts degree. She escaped forever her parents' "damn Catholic San Francisco environment" that she believed was based on appearances only. She had rebelled, but fundamentally she was not a rebel. "You can't keep working if you're just rebelling," she argued. The media, she thought, imposed an image of the rebel and outcast upon artists and poets, but generalizing from her own experiences to those of her friends, she described the motivations of her generation as positive, as the pursuit of interior truth and moral renewal.[21]

The linked languages of ambition and autonomy are represented by two highly distinctive voices alternating in her accounts. One voice used humorous hyperbole to accentuate the surreality of her parents' life or, on occasion, her own foibles and those of her peers. This inflection drew a veil across the more painful elements of her life by rendering them into sharp, quick images designed to shock and get a laugh. The other voice used a more expansive language of wonder and excitement to express the adventure of a young woman on a journey of initiation that would allow her to overcome her fears and enter into enriching relations with others. Part of this journey included following a very traditional pattern for women: marriage at the age of nineteen to a fellow student, William H. Brown, another "refugee" from a Catholic family, with whom she formed a union based on mutual intellectual interest. For two years he was her teacher and guide: "Bill gave me a bunch of books on painting, on the impressionists, Rembrandt, Goya, and Velásquez. . . . I went through all this stuff, and I was just knocked out. I'd never seen any of this stuff, and I felt this tremendous surge of energy."[22] Her marriage conformed to generational patterns, but it also ensured her independence from her parents. In the context of her progression, an apparently traditional act involved consolidating the rebellion begun when she enrolled in art school. The leading trend was toward assuming personal control over one's life, and thus the 1950s was also a period when one in three marriages ended in divorce. Brown's four marriages follow this trend, but also suggest her determination not to make the mistakes of her parents and continue a relationship that no longer provided growth.

This brings us to the third factor in Brown's subjective progress: the linking of commerce with sexual stereotypes. Entering the realm of aesthetics allowed her to escape the contradictions of her parents' aspirations, in which surface devoured substance. Yet the world she entered linked success and gender so closely that she could not achieve success without betraying the ideal personal freedom that she had discovered in art. She found herself repeating the role that her parents had assigned her, but for a larger audience and with greater rewards. Nell Sinton recalled that the young Brown was a "sparkplug." Sinton meant this as a personal rather than sexual attribute, though in the mid-twentieth century the sexual and personal were seldom distant.[23] Brown's magnetic personality attracted both men and women to her; excitement, verve, and energy could assume distinctly sexual overtones in a male-defined environment, as they often did in reviews of her work.

Brown's response to the sexualization of her art both embraced and rejected the importance of femininity.[24] She did not want to deny her personal charms, yet neither did she want to acknowledge that sexuality, rather than the quality of her ideas, might have been a factor in her success. She confronted contradictions in the art world through a double form of self-representation parallel to the double voice discussed above. She used sexualized imagery to portray her interaction with the absurd world of career building. The language and narrative devices that allow this gendered self to speak were closely connected to those used to discuss her relationship with her parents. Early in her life account, she portrayed herself as a liar who learned to use dress and appearance to protect herself; at the same time, she satisfied her parents' desires for middle-class status by impersonating the role of society princess. This mendacious, opportunistic character reappears in her account as the person who participates to excess in parties, drinks too much, and lets herself be carried to unspecified extremes by the energy levels of "a whole bunch of people . . . constantly butting up against each other on an almost twenty-four-hour-a-day basis."[25]

This figure became an element in her work as well, where it appeared most spectacularly in *Fur Rat* as a decaying animal wrapped in mangy fur. Underneath the fur, Brown had inserted the sharp ends of carpet tacks. The needle points were completely invisible, but if one stroked the work—

Joan Brown's *Fur Rat* (1962). Berkeley Art Museum, University of California.

and only the most privileged patrons of the art world were able actually to touch a work—one's fingers could be lacerated. This object derived from a dream she had in 1961, just as her national career achieved momentum. In later years she recalled that she recognized in the dream her troubled response to the pressures of making a career. The fur rat appeared ironically in *The Bride,* collared and leashed, tamed as a sometimes necessary attribute of dealing with the practical world.[26]

Ironic use of seductive imagery in her art and in her narrative reflected her ambiguous position as a woman in the arts. Like it or not, a woman made her way in the absurd world of practical ambition with "all the dimensions that happen with the absurd—happiness, humor, gentleness, violence."[27] And yet a passion for distinction transformed into ambition for worldly success had led her into a trap. Success under those conditions meant accepting a constricted self-identity, one that gloried in appearances and the ability to use "feminine wiles" to advance herself. To be a successful woman artist was possible, but that life seemed only a reconstruction of her parents' world on another plane.

Opposed to a gendered, sexualized conception of self, another voice called, evoking a vision of an initiate who survived spiritually through recurrent journeys into the freedom of painting. This degendered voice gave her the strength to stand her ground and sever profitable ties with George Staempfli. It also required her to reject the nascent feminist art movement when, in the early 1970s, several feminist critics pointed to Brown's concern with recording personal experience as an example of a specifically female perspective in art.[28] Brown vocally opposed this conclusion and refused to participate in feminist-oriented exhibitions. She accepted feminism when applied to general economic and political questions, but she thought explicitly feminist art was "rotten and contrived" because it elevated one aspect of human experience to universal importance and, perhaps as important, restricted meaning to a priori conclusions. The central act in recovering subjective will was asserting the freedom to establish the meaning of one's experiences. Feminist ideology, when applied to art, struck her as being as narrow and arbitrary as the commercial art world. Powerful images came from a level of thinking, she believed, that preexisted society and all its distinctions. If she were to use her paintings to reflect her experience, she could accept no political ideology as a filter.[29]

A degendered definition of art allowed her to construct a mature identity, but the price was negation of public value and transfer of personal vision onto an ideal, aesthetic level. This surrender did not mean passivity. Retreat was the only way she could continue to function within society as an active, contributing member without being consumed by the contradictions of her position. By embracing those aspects of her experience that were emancipatory but ignoring those that were confining, she could pursue a career as image maker without actively pursuing a commercial career and exposing herself to the demands of the "fur rat" lurking within her. Instead, she reached for a universal subject that could function simultaneously as artist, teacher, mother, wife. The spiritualized reimagination of mature female self appeared in her work as a "mysterious figure" whose spirit is totally distinct from the dreamlike environment in which it finds itself. Speaking of the series of paintings that included *The Bride,* Brown observed that her figures are "involved in a rather placid kind of setting and then something else is going on. . . . You don't know whether the figure is actually thinking about these things or that's just going on and she's thinking about something else or what. I don't know! I don't have the answers. If I did I wouldn't do it."[30] The separation from the environment she invoked suggests the tenuous character of individual empowerment, constantly impinged upon by practical ties. Brown hoped her art connected her to eternity, while daily life was a constant iteration of need. In art, she said, "people are absolutely timeless." In art, one moved from the trivial world of appearances into a "otherworldly" realm where she could function without betraying her own needs.[31]

Brown's course provides a model of life-turnings that appears with variations and nuances in the choices that many of her associates, male and female, made. The institutional shift away from the school and museum toward the primacy of the commercial gallery generated a subjective shift that dismayed her, because it privileged negative aspects present in her personality from her upbringing. She reacted to assert a form of idealized self, hence of institutional position and ultimately of aesthetic form, distinct from the developing market system of "fine art."

This maneuver had a very worldly foundation: the expansion of higher education provided alternative ways of being in the art world, but this factor was not causative. Brown did not achieve a tenured teaching position until 1974, ten years after she made her break with Staempfli. Withdrawal was a procedure for contributing to the world, being within it, without being overwhelmed by the tremendous pressures one could feel to conform to behavior dictated by the necessities of career building. Refusal to submit to the dictates of a commercial career was her way of affirming her personal freedom to make meaning of the world she lived in, a freedom essential to twentieth-century definitions of successful art. Thus withdrawal was closely tied to ambition, to that pursuit of personal excellence propounded so strongly at the time. In part her decision was a reaction to inability to reconcile hopes and realities, but retreat also allowed her to maintain self-control as an artist and thus to preserve the integrity of her own ambition rather than submit to the demands of those who controlled aesthetic institutions. Withdrawal was a way of remaining active and effective *within* a specific imaginary and then seeking out an institutional environment where that imaginary was most comfortable. By constructing a sense of self separated from social reality, she preserved a sense of subjective independence.

This operation did not negate the possibility of worldly success. Withdrawal set limits as to how far a person would go to cooperate, but within those boundaries freed the creative person to acknowledge the empowering aspects of ambition. Because withdrawal was connected to a transcendent view of self, it shaded into forms of hubris, an intent to create a body of work that would overwhelm the social forces with which one normally had to negotiate. To influence without being influenced in return was a heady ambition that projected art and poetry, and therefore the aesthetic creators themselves, as completely "free" elements *within* society, the only elements (many of them believed) capable of disrupting it because they could imagine themselves uncompromised.

Maturation as Differentiation

Because college and university training expanded rapidly in the United States in the 1950s and 1960s, Brown had the option of pursuing an academic career in opposition to working within a commercial structure. Her friend and onetime housemate Jay DeFeo lacked the possibility of that kind of security because in 1954 DeFeo was convicted of shoplifting two cans of paint from a hardware store. This misdemeanor on her record barred her for most of her professional life from working in state-run schools, and most private schools also had policies against hiring individuals with criminal records.

Like Brown, DeFeo came from a troubled family, discovered in art an environment that provided a new productive identity, and achieved early recognition of her talent. A pervasive feature in DeFeo's recollections is the use of antinomies to present herself and her parents. Almost at the very beginning of one interview, she joked about being a schizophrenic. Then to prove the point she recounted the story of her father's life. A doctor committed to ideals of social justice, he worked during the depression in rural northern California treating the poor. DeFeo spent the first eight years of her life moving from community to community, until her father suddenly announced he was in love with another woman and abandoned his family. "He was living two kinds of existence simultaneously," she concluded, and "it all ended in a complete split." Thus as a child there was the "country Jay," the young child who had lived in the woods and the "city Jay," the adolescent who lived in San Jose, where her mother supported herself and her daughter entirely on her own by working nights as a nurse.[32]

She discovered in art a way to reconcile the splits within her by projecting them onto a more abstract plane. Lena Emery, her high school art teacher, recognized DeFeo's considerable talents and encouraged her to consider painting as a profession. Emery was "bohemian," DeFeo recalled, like her father, but her teacher demonstrated that personal freedom required rigorous self-discipline. Emery became a life-long friend, who provided an alternative to the chaos and loneliness of DeFeo's broken family through a vision of modern art as a way of realizing one's potential. For DeFeo, art became a means of physically bringing formal harmony out of chaos, but even here what appealed to her was the possibility of combining the two poles of the artistic tradition coming down to her.

> I think also later I was influenced by two kinds of painting which I'm interested in, or which I consciously or unconsciously tried to resolve in my own work. . . . A kind of classic style, if you wish, for lack of a better word. I don't want to think of it as a sophisticated style necessarily. But something that's classic in nature, influenced by the Renaissance. . . . But at the same time some-

thing that is essentially either funky or primitive. Putting it another way, a very close relationship to the use of materials and my relationship to the process of painting.[33]

DeFeo continued to define her artistic goal as sifting through the capricious elements of chance to locate a salvific underlying structure. She hoped to show through visual form the ways in which the chaos of individual existence was neither arbitrary nor empty. The rational and the irrational would present themselves no longer as contradictions, but as two faces of the same phenomenon.[34]

With financial assistance from Emery, DeFeo entered the art department at Berkeley in 1946. Her teachers there also were impressed by her talent, and DeFeo's first public exhibitions occurred before graduating in 1951. That year she was the first woman to receive the prestigious Sigmund Heller Traveling Fellowship, which allowed her to spend eighteen months in Europe. While living and studying in Paris and Florence, she fell in love with Renaissance and classical art. She did not want to reproduce Renaissance vision, but her personal encounter with the European art heritage helped her preserve an independence from contemporary developments in American art. She remained unawed by the succession of successful artists that appeared every few years. Similarly, Joan Brown remembered her first trip to Europe in 1961 as the beginning of her psychological independence from the art business. She saw firsthand the centuries of work that she had known only from books. The power of it awakened within her suspicions that the achievements of American art since the end of World War II, however significant they were, would not be the last word. This understanding, she thought, gave her courage to change her style and to ignore her dealer's complaints. By placing themselves back in history, both Brown and DeFeo used tradition to distance themselves from the present and achieve a small measure of personal autonomy.[35]

DeFeo returned home and began working in the children's art department of the California College of Arts and Crafts. The certainty of a good academic career was shattered after her arrest. She turned to jewelry making to survive, while she continued to paint. By 1958 she had had several well-received exhibitions in California, had won jury prizes for her work, had seen her paintings published in commercial magazines, and had been selected for the Museum of Modern Art's 1959 *Sixteen Americans* exhibition. Gallery owner Irving Blum recalled that she had developed a reputation of "mythic proportions," not only in California, but in New York. On the basis of three years' work, he and others considered her likely to become one of the very greatest artists of her generation. Edward Kienholz remembered DeFeo as the "seminal force in San Francisco"; her influence extended to Los Angeles, where there was a keen interest in her work among collectors and young artists. Kienholz was impressed by her purist approach. She was one of only two artists he knew who bought pigments and ground her own paints so that she could achieve the exact shades she envisioned.[36]

She had a special affinity for poets, and much of her work derives from poems written by friends of hers. Her monumental pencil drawing *The Eyes,* eight feet wide and four feet tall, was a meditation on a few lines by Philip Lamantia, later published in Wallace Berman's underground journal *Semina:*

> Tell him that I have eyes only for Heaven
> as I look to you
>   Queen mirror
> of the heavenly court[37]

On the verge of establishing a national reputation, DeFeo withdrew from public view as she dedicated herself like a monk to completing one painting, *The Rose* (fig. 16). This work was a continuation of her interest with *The Eyes* to capture the mystic underpinnings to human relationships. She had already painted a series of works, including *The Jewel* and *The Cross,* the visual structures of which emanated from a partially submerged central point, but she was not satisfied that she had demonstrated the necessity of working from a center.

Her obsession with *The Rose* stretched across six years.[38] She felt that in resolving the formal problems posed in this painting she would uncover and systematize the merger of classicist rigor with improvisation. DeFeo's struggle took on titanic proportions. All other activity stopped until she mastered the solution.

Unlike Brown, DeFeo's problem came not from a sense of opposition between "fine art" and commerce, though the critical reputation she developed may have stimulated a pride that matched her natural reticence and modesty. The theme of her art was the compatibility of merely human intentions. Does the interaction of myriad personal ambitions lead to a structured order or to a jumble? Because of the contradictions she felt within her background, she could see plumbing her own depths as a test case. The work was to be a redemption of ambiguity, through a romantic

eclecticism that defined the self through the combination of what appeared to be opposites. "I wanted to create a work that was so precariously balanced between going this way or that way that it maintained itself," she said of the painting.[39]

The gamble was to strip away the fearful, dangerous aspects of rapid, personal change by uncovering a hidden underpinning of a timeless, cosmic reality. Growth and personal choice did not need to be the same thing as irresponsibility, and yet the nature of the problem as posed evaded the tragic dimension of human relationships. One might forgive the father of irresponsibility, but his abandonment still caused pain. Personal differentiation, which we might call growth, could easily mean that the needs of people who have been linked changed at different rates and often in opposing directions. Part of this she experienced in her own marriage to Wally Hedrick. DeFeo was professionally reclusive, while her husband was one of the most active, vocal figures in the local arts community. He was director of the Six Gallery from its opening in 1954 until 1957; he was administrator of the night school program at the California School of Fine Arts after 1957; and he became the leader of the Studio 13 Jazz Band, while continuing to paint and promote his ideas of art as social criticism. In 1959 he mounted what may very well be the first art show protesting American involvement in Vietnam.[40] Antiwar activity would increasingly occupy his time as the pace of American intervention increased. Knute Stiles, commenting on the differences between DeFeo and Hedrick, compared DeFeo working on *The Rose* to Penelope, weaving and unweaving while she waited for her Ulysses to return, struggling through her efforts to keep the ideal of the hearth alive—an ideal that referred both to her marriage and the spiritual necessity of community.[41]

The form of *The Rose* originated in DeFeo's love of hiking in the mountains, where she felt the awesome power of God was most strongly expressed in terms that humans could endure. As she explored the serrated visual structure of valleys, peaks, and canyons, she believed she explored her own spiritual relationship to the earth. Working through the painting's various versions, she found she did not know how to represent female subjectivity. The first version, published in the catalog for *Sixteen Americans,* was called *The Death Rose,* but she decided that this approach was too melodramatic. It overemphasized the existentialist viewpoint that each person must live with her death if she is to find freedom. Because of childbirth, which constantly replenished humanity, she thought women existed at the crossroads of life and death, weaving the two together into an inseparable pattern. She then changed the title to *The White Rose* and recrafted the work to make it more crystalline and airy. This version was significantly larger as she built a new canvas stretching across the bay window of her apartment and glued the old canvas onto the new framework. DeFeo added an armature of wooden beams to *The White Rose,* which gave rigidity to the rays.

Still unsatisfied, she felt that the painting had become too architectural. Her image needed a more organic and biological feeling. She added wire, beads, and pearls, materials she used in her jewelry business, onto the surface; these she used to superimpose a layer of organic shapes on top of the geometric patterns. The overlaying of effects made the painting flamboyant and "super-baroque." Instead of removing the objects she had added to the painting, she painted over them until they disappeared from sight.[42] Their presence, however, was felt in the textures they gave to the surfaces above them. The rational structure that she believed underlay all creation had disappeared under an accretion of emotional reactions. She had to pull back the painting to make it more classic in character. She felt an "absolute necessity to maintain the spirit and freshness of the abstract expressionist ideal—the spontaneity, let's say, and the growth of the image from one layer to the rest. But also I demand from myself and the images, too, a sense of refinement and exactitude."[43] To accomplish this, the painting she remembered "actually had to be carved and hacked." It had become a work of sculpture as well as painting. "It was done with a combination of building up and tearing back during every stage of the game." When she completed the painting, finally feeling that she had embodied a "unity of the opposite ideals," *The Rose* was nearly eleven feet high, nine feet wide, eight inches thick at points, and weighed an incredible 2,300 pounds.[44]

During the nearly seven years she worked and reworked this one image. DeFeo retreated from all exhibition. She turned down inquiries from a New York gallery following her exhibition at the Museum of Modern Art. When her former classmate at Berkeley, Fred Martin, then chair of the exhibitions committee for the San Francisco Art Association, invited her to mount a one-person show, she declined as well, apologizing profusely and hoping he would not misunderstand, but she avowed, "I personally can't do it until I have completed a certain cycle of work. . . . I feel I must be able to understand my work . . . before I hang it up and hope the other people may see it as I do. In this sense, I perhaps place too much importance on the show. . . . As for the actual 'prestige-value' of the show goes—I can very easily give this up as it means little to me. So nothing is lost." Concerned that Martin might be offended by her refusal, she wrote him another letter that confessed that the idea of the show put her "in some kind of fear of being judged by certain prevalent standards that have nothing to do with my paintings . . . our paintings have not been as much visual experiences as perhaps they are 'ideas' on canvas. . . . Somehow abandoning the show also abandoned my ego fears. I was not ashamed of being egocentric but being in a confused state, I wondered if I was losing respect for the 'me' element—which appeared a tremendous threat to my whole motive to paint. . . . I have constant doubts that I will ever be able to satisfy myself in both aspects—that of the personal and the visual . . . at least I can blunder along—as now, at last, no one cares again."

The intersection of private vision and public value was a torturous contradiction for DeFeo. In a third letter to Martin, she observed that "I used to think that *first of all* art was personal and *secondly* it possibly could extend to greatness if the individual were great, which I'm sure I'm not." Then half-retracting her modesty, she added, "I used to think so, oddly enough." Commenting on the ambitions of her friends, DeFeo expressed amazement at how strongly convinced they were that their paintings were important. "They really feel they are struggling to add to the art history of this century and the personal glory plays a part— but it isn't so shallow as *that,* I don't think, I can't dream that it could be that small, I'm sure it isn't." Success seemed to freeze ideas as artists repeated formulas that had achieved a positive response; therefore success barred the path to transcendence. The artist should remained secluded until she had created the best she hoped she could do. DeFeo returned to her concern for "the personal thing," which, although unique to her, she still felt "potentially extends beyond my personal ego."[45]

DeFeo's isolation was sustained by a select group of friends convinced that she was indeed creating something extraordinary. Dorothy Miller, curator at the Museum of Modern Art, followed the progress of the work and promised to purchase it for the museum's permanent collection as soon as DeFeo completed it. Wally Hedrick encouraged her to stop making jewelry and live off his salary. Her former high school art teacher, Lena Emery, and a collector, J. Patrick Lennan, provided her money for supplies. Fred Martin helped her out financially—and he hoped psychologically—by arranging for her to teach an occasional class at the California School of Fine Arts. Walter Hopps from the Ferus Gallery in Los Angeles sold her earlier work and sparked magazine interest in writing about her. The work in progress was published in *Holiday* magazine in 1961, and in 1962 President Kennedy (or his staff), in an article for *Look* magazine, "The Artist in America," selected DeFeo and *The Rose* to illustrate what was best in contemporary American art.[46] In 1964, after becoming curator of the Pasadena Art Museum, Hopps began planning two major shows: the first retrospective of the career of data pioneer Marcel Duchamp and a one-artist exhibit for DeFeo to feature her finally completed *The Rose*.

When the painting was moved in 1965 for exhibition at the Pasadena Art Museum, the movers had to cut out a section of the front wall to her apartment and bring in a crane to lift and lower the work into the moving van. DeFeo laughingly referred to *The Rose* as the "ultimate abstract expressionist auto-da-fé."[47] Bruce Conner, who made a wistful, sweetly sad film on the moving of the painting (*The White Rose*, 1965), described DeFeo's quest as the most heroic of their generation; she had completely subsumed her personality into a single creative act so that the painting reproduced but harmonized the contradictions that moved within her. By this he hastened to add that DeFeo had achieved something few artists had: the painting was physically alive; it was like confronting a living, breathing being.

Except for a thin crust on the surface, the paint had not hardened. This was a common feature to San Francisco painting, but the monumental size of *The Rose* carried a wet surface to another level. The work quivered as people approached it. Viewers could read in the changes on the image's surface a reaction to their own physical, and by extension emotional, effects upon the world. *The Rose* was a physical being, responding to the world around it. The painting recapitulated the action painting aesthetic of projecting the painter's self onto the canvas, but in a baroque elaboration which made the visual image secondary to the visceral reaction evoked within the viewer. DeFeo had manufactured a being that confronted the world, demanding a response, but it was as unstable as a real life.[48]

The painting grew as an effort to bridge a series of interlinked conflicts within DeFeo's life: the tensions of her family background, with pleasure and duty pitted as opposites, and DeFeo's own inability to choose between the models her parents left her, seeing in both father and mother appealing elements. She entered the art profession partly because her teachers presented the aesthetic process as a way of harmonizing the conflicts she felt through a combination of individual freedom and craft discipline. Her aesthetic then was to present the interlocking of chaos and order, so that one need not choose. DeFeo recognized she existed in a competitive social environment, but she refused to participate on that level. The confraternity had started as a utopian community. In her heart, she still lived in the undifferentiated paths of youth. Her heroic effort rallied her friends around her and allowed a sense of community to cohere. The inner center that her work tried symbolically to materialize preserved a community that had to disintegrate as its members aged. While DeFeo's struggle was not against commerce, her attempt to create a material basis to the utopian dream allows us to understand more clearly the nature of Brown's reaction to Staempfli: commerce was the face of antiutopia, introducing through the assignment of rewards and distinctions differentiation and hierarchy among the brethren. Commerce meant the acceptance of external authority, a center that came from without and therefore could only be experienced as arbitrary and dictatorial.

The Rose was predicated on the idea that everything proceeded from a single, interior point from which emanated an undeniable, because subjective, mystic sense of order and value. Just as the painting was fragile, DeFeo was unable to find the center that resolved contradiction into perpetual harmony. Her ideal could not be achieved in the mystic form she sought. The watching eyes remained only one's own, with all one's inner crises still operative.

DeFeo stopped painting for six years after completing *The Rose*. She was deeply depressed and disillusioned, her marriage broke up, and she suffered severe lead poisoning from the quantities of lead white paint she had used. Her teeth fell out, and DeFeo was subject to frequent infections and extreme exhaustion well into the 1970s. Yet she also recalled this period away from painting as a second adolescence that gave her a greater sense of humor in facing the disappointments of her life. By 1968 the canvas and wooden frame support for *The Rose* showed signs of buckling under its ton of weight, and she thought her effort might disintegrate. Bruce Conner organized a campaign in 1972 to save the painting, which conservators decided to sheathe in liquid plastic, linen, and paper and then encase in a plaster truss. The painting with its protective covering weighed two and a half tons and lost the shimmering responsiveness that had made it seem alive. The San Francisco Art Institute provided a home for *The Rose* and stored it in the wall of the school's conference room.

Immature enthusiasm bred ambition for worldly success, but the steps taken to achieve that success generated a crisis of conscience. In Brown's case, the immediate cause was external, the attempt of her dealer to dictate the nature of her work. In DeFeo's case, the cause was internal, a questioning whether her work could possibly live up to the expectations that she and her friends had set. She was proud of the work she had done as a painter. She could speak with confidence as a visual thinker, but her work had failed to hold together the imaginary community brought into being by the arts. The cases of both DeFeo and Brown manifest subjective fissure. Brown and DeFeo experienced ambition and ideals as contradictory, instead of resolving into a structured mature, professional life. This led to withdrawal from the "art world," which did not necessarily mean cessation of production. Withdrawal allowed for the construction of a sense of self that could function within self-determined goals. A return to the art world thus followed the crisis, as the artist created work that reflected more closely the ideals and ambitions that had brought her into the art world in the first place. The artist turned from forms that established the initial reputation and constructed mental categories valuing myth over society, the timeless over the "time-full," freedom over constraint. This resolution was achieved by transferring hopes from worldly to otherworldly success, which allowed the individual to proceed with energy and force since ambition had not been negated but sublated.

I have used two women painters to illustrate a pattern, yet I could as easily have taken male artists and poets as examples, so widespread is this life course in mid-century California. "I want to be anonymous," Bob Kaufman told scholars seeking him out for information on the beat movement. This African-American poet who came to San Francisco in 1957 after discharge from the army was the first person to use the word *beatnik* in print, in his *Abomunist Manifesto,* published by Lawrence Ferlinghetti in 1958. Sales of his first three chapbooks surpassed even Ginsberg's *Howl and Other Poems,* and Kaufman was for a short five years San Francisco's best-known beat poet, a popular figure who held court with his wife, poet Eileen Kaufman, and their toddler at the Coexistence Bagel Shop. He was invited to teach at Harvard in 1963 and New Directions offered him a contract for two collections of his poetry. Then President Kennedy died. Three days later, Kaufman took a ten-year vow of silence, a self-mortification in which he assumed personal responsibility for the tragedy he saw falling on the nation. For a decade he neither spoke in public nor wrote, maintaining his vow until February 1973, when at a gathering commemorating the withdrawal of the last American soldiers from Vietnam he improvised several poems as part of the celebration.[49]

Jay DeFeo's husband Wally Hedrick refused to exhibit his paintings in museums and commercial galleries during the course of the war. He withdrew from full-time teaching and opened a fix-it shop in the suburban community of San Geronimo, while designing costumes and sets for the politically radical San Francisco Mime Troupe. Hedrick continued to paint, but turned down most requests for exhibits even after the war ended. Museum shows, he thought, focused attention on work that was in his past. Curators did not know how to set up a confrontation between artist and audience that would help the artist discover how to solve his current problems. All a show could do, he declared, "was get me in the magazines, and maybe I'd make more money. Then I would just have too much to drink. . . . I know what happens when I get a little money. So I don't need that stuff."[50]

Assemblagist and filmmaker Bruce Conner came to feel imprisoned by the art he produced:

> The object gets my name on them. And it gets to a point where it exists as a personality. If it becomes historical it exists as a weapon to me as a person, as an artist. It can be used against me. It can be used to destroy me as an artist, a living artist.[51]

Conner rebelled against the fetishized art commodity by bringing his dealer in New York, Charles Alan, boxes of found objects simply thrown together without any particular order:

> I remember I went into the Alan Gallery in 1963. I had a cardboard box which had eight or nine objects in it. I said, "This is a new work." He said, "What do you do with it?" I said, "That's it. It's

that box." "You mean you exhibit the box?" I said, "You can if you want to. Or you can take them all out and put them all over the room, or put them in your pocket and walk home, or go to a movie, or put them on a shelf. But you have to remember that they all go together." Charles Alan couldn't deal with that.[52]

Conner's box of objects was as much personal insult against Charles Alan as philosophical reflection on the nature of what made some objects "art." We might recall Joan Brown responding to her success by crafting *Fur Rat* with its hidden nails ready to lacerate the owner's fingers. Wally Hedrick created a sensation in 1958 when one of his mechanical assemblages "attacked" a woman at the San Francisco Museum of Art's annual Christmas party. Three years before, Hedrick had started making sculptures from broken radio and television sets, refrigerators, and washing machines he found in junkyards. He painted over the surfaces with thick layers of impasto and gesso which incorporated the work into the aesthetic of action painting. He was particularly pleased when he could fix an abandoned appliance sufficiently that at least some piece of it would work and he could turn his assemblages into moving sculptures. His *Xmas Tree,* built out of "two radios, two phonographs, flashing lights, electric fans, saw motor—all controlled by timers, hooked so [they] would cycle all these things," was featured at the 1958 San Francisco Museum of Art annual holiday show. One of the record players played "I Hate to See Christmas Come Around." At the opening, which Hedrick refused to attend, he set a timer so that the piece "suddenly began flashing its lights, honking its horns, and playing its records." One woman who was standing next to the piece when it suddenly turned on found her fur coat tangled into it and then received an electrical shock.

> It caused quite a sensation not because of its artistic merit, but because it attacked this lady, which I thought was very nice. . . . I wasn't making it as an art thing. I was more interested in making a "thing," and if it attacked people—well, I guess I knew it was going to attack. . . . I knew it would probably attack because I laid the trap. So it entertained me; I thought the evening was a success.[53]

Critics concluded that the group of young artists were neodada, and some like Hedrick, for whom Marcel Duchamp was a hero, enjoyed the idea that they were continuing in an accepted and honored art tradition of rebellion. But were the insults that Brown, Conner, and Hedrick crafted assaulting art as a system of meaning, or where they directed against the personalities with which

artists had to engage if they wanted to exhibit and sell? Their actions were declarations of personal independence, statements saying that their participation in the professional art world was no longer giving satisfaction, that they would leave to pursue other activities, equally creative, but outside the professional boundaries encasing the "visual arts" in the 1960s. Their insults did not intend to explode those boundaries, and indeed accepted them as facts of life that an individual working within the system was unable to change. Action was aimed at personal empowerment, creating a distance between the artist and an environment that was only partially escapable, while protesting the loss of community, the family of the young, swallowed up in its march into maturity.

In 1965 Conner "dropped out" of the art world. For several years he developed the light show concept at the Avalon Ballroom, utilizing film clips, slides, and reflectors to create a visual accompaniment to the rock music. It was a performance art that could be repeated but never reproduced, and therefore unlike gallery art or the music he was accompanying, immune to the basilisk eye of commerce. He then worked with Dennis Hopper developing motion pictures. He influenced the decor and editing style of Hopper's 1969 film *Easy Rider.*[54] In 1974 Conner felt that he did not have an aggressive enough personality for Hollywood and returned to exhibition in galleries. His reputation remained strong among those who remembered his work from the early 1960s, but withdrawal had reduced him to a figure of historical interest. He preferred to be a marginalized figure, "operating with concerns outside those of most other artists of his day."[55] When asked for photographs of himself for catalogs or magazine articles, he sent in pictures of other people. He enjoyed submitting multiple biographies to reference works:

> I used to have two totally different biographies—one in *Who's Who in American Art* and one in *Who's Who.* In *Who's Who in American Art,* I was born in India and went to exotic schools. Then I got tired of getting letters in the mail that asked me to update my biography. So I sent them back saying "deceased." *Who's Who in American Art* absolutely believed that and never put me back again. And then they sent me a form for information for *Who Was Who.* I updated all the information way beyond the time I died and sent it to *Who Was Who* and they listed me. Then about ten years ago I got another letter that they wanted to include me in *Who's Who*—I'd been recommended. Now I am in *Who Was Who* as a dead artist and *Who's Who* as a living film maker.[56]

Folly and Utopia

Insults are just as easily a sign of immature frustration at the inability to resolve the contradictions of social relations. Similarly the neurotic attachment to one painting. The argument that withdrawal was a path to maturity seems to hold only for Brown, who successfully negotiated a transition from commerce to the university. Yet the challenge each of these artists faced was how to remain productive, and their responses were directed to that goal. Each continued producing, creating new and more unusual work after their crises. DeFeo had the most profound physical and emotional breakdown, but in 1970 she resumed painting. Under doctor's orders, she could no longer work in oil paint, so she began using acrylics on paper. *The Rose* had only replicated, not resolved, the conflict between order and chaos. Her post-1970 paintings, each one readable and precise, powerfully succeeded in fusing her interests in classicism and spontaneity (fig. 17).

In 1971 David Meltzer complained to a longtime friend about the trivialization of avant-garde ideas that seemed to accompany success:

> [Life] zips by so fast, if you fart, it's gone. It was and is and will be always beyond words, which is why we write and excite them into being, which is why we throw our eyes all over canvas and paper and piss rainbows into anywhere knowing it is all perfect. . . . The ones who worship at art's poor used car lots are lost in a world they never made; they sniff at it and think by owning art they are free of its meanings and responsibilities and joys. We were always right to keep those messages around us at all times because those images and works are our amulets, our deepest magics, coming from all kinds of souls in all kinds of knowing and illumination as well as pain and black-hole-in-space density. . . . Our houses are temples, shuls of the most divine reiteration; we can not auction our lives, our magics, our truth.[57]

Long after their activities had generated attention and a market, many in the generation of the 1950s looked back upon its formation and saw a total separation from the arts as commercial ventures. In MacAgy and Still, we saw opposition to art serving an instrumental function subsidiary to other aspects of society. Meltzer's anger hardened into what appeared to be an absolute contradiction between creativity and the market. In another letter, Meltzer returned to the theme as he blamed his colleagues for having surrendered to ambition for worldly success by turning themselves into stereotypes:

> I am so fed up, I mean I am fat to vomiting, with precious sacred cowardness & myth-making. I am sick of men that are poets but pee crookedly. . . .

> I am sick of shamans, hacks & art pushers. . . . Who loves the static man, the man stopped, years ago, copping a safe hole & rotting there?[58]

Meltzer lamented that somehow the original project that artists and poets had embarked upon in the 1950s had gone awry. They had ceased to sing "true songs," coming from the heart in one-on-one communication with reader and viewer so that their work would begin a process of conversion, saying to themselves, "Oh, I never thought of it that way. I never saw it quite like that. Yes, now I see." This art was to create a revolution, to replace the babble of destructive, contentious voices with harmony and productivity.[59] Their generation had the chance to do this, he thought, because creative people had separated from commerce and formed a community. Their ideal of artistic communication was dialogue, the exchange of viewpoints with the goal of achieving some form of higher truth. Jack Hirschman's lines, written to Dean Stockwell in 1971 to thank the actor for hospitality while the San Francisco-based poet was in Los Angeles for a reading, evoked the transcendent goals that creative people shared:

> like the chorus we've always
> made of each other's dialogues,
> multiplying through the long
> distant intimacy of this town
> on the hill of a high,
>   the intonations on a phone,
> the steady help toward
> some quiet dignity quite close
> to the way nature itself works[60]

By the 1970s competition for shows, jobs, and publishers had taken them in many directions. Choices were made, and those who lived through them might view the sundering as a reduction. They could look back upon the ambition and ideals of their youth and see the hope that young artists and poets could create an audience by offering truthful statements about living in America and a way of resolving the contradictions of modern, urban life. "It was a 'we,'" Joan Brown emphasized. The members of the artistic community in the 1950s saw themselves collectively. "It's been an 'I' ever since. But anybody who's really being straight or honest about it *from that time* really should say 'we'" (my emphasis).[61]

As we have seen, this group of artists' memories of their careers revealed crisis and inner conflict. Participants clung to images of youthful rebellion in preference to those of integration and assumption of power.[62] Reactions against the type of maturity that seemed available short-circuited their rise to authority. Their confusions, however, generated an alternative model for maturation, one based on autonomy and transfer of ambitions to "otherworldly" concerns. They redefined personal excellence to give priority to moral ends, which inevitably in a world of permanent war seemed like a dream state. In his 1965 poem "Kral Majales," written after he had been expelled from Czechoslovakia, Allen Ginsberg defined the poet's ambition in terms that portrayed the poet as the "wise youth" whose pursuit of personal excellence was a socially essential task:

> And I am the King of May, which is the power of sexual youth,
> and I am the King of May, which is industry in eloquence and action in amour,
> and I am the King of May, which is long hair of Adam and the Beard of my own body
> and I am the King of May, which is Kral Majales in the Czechoslovakian tongue,
> and I am the King of May, which is old Human poesy, and 100,000 people chose my name
> . . . . .
> And I am the King of May, that I may be expelled from my Kingdom with Honor, as of old,
> To shew the difference between Caesar's Kingdom and the Kingdom of the May of Man—
> and I am the King of May, the paranoid, for the Kingdom of May is too beautiful to last for more than a month[63]

Dare to be as much as you can, Ginsberg told his readers, and the enthusiasm of his language drew upon him the wrath of censors on both sides of the iron curtain. As always, he sang of his own small group of friends, but his ode affirmed the morality of student sit-ins to end segregation and racial discrimination. It affirmed resistance to the Vietnam War and three years later to the Soviet tanks occupying Prague. In the struggle against "conformity," poets helped reinscribe sharp we-they boundaries in a society that many, according to David Riesman in *The Lonely Crowd*, had come to see as a seamless, though articulated, organism in which orders had to be obeyed because they seemed to come from everywhere.[64]

The new inscription evaded social forms of organization to project symbolic imagery of death and rebirth as contending social realities. The sense of anticipation experienced in the community of youth peers combined with a feeling of liberation from the compromised lives of one's parents to give rebirth an active, psychophysical immediacy, the tangibility of which could not be denied by those who experienced it. Art, however, compromised by the expanding webs of commerce, could not sustain the dream. The ideals lived on in the ambitions of political and social resurrection that had accompanied personal choice as an ancillary justification. Youth, considered as an image of lost community, became identified with living in a particularly moral state. This maneuver denied the morality of other forces in society, ultimately making it impossible to confront them politically, since they were associated with the absurdity of parents. Opposing forces stood for death, an imagery that was confirmed by the reliance of the national government upon military solutions.[65]

Poets and artists also redefined the boundaries between public and private spheres by insisting upon public expression of experiences that had before been entirely personal. Their efforts brought resistance from the more conservative sectors of American society. In 1957 the United States Customs Office impounded a British printing of Ginsberg's "Howl" when it arrived at the harbor. Lawrence Ferlinghetti then used an American press to publish his edition. The San Francisco police department arrested him and his manager, Shigeyoshi Murao, for violating antiobscenity laws. The judge directed acquittal, but the case confirmed for those, like Manuel Neri, who did not venture to the scatological or erotic extremes of expression, a sense of danger and risk to the artistic project.

It is in this context of a broad-based, apolitical movement to mobilize the agonal spirit and the beginnings of resistance by cultural conservatives that public fascination with the beats arose in 1958. Artists and poets had symbolic importance in the developing contention because they so easily represented both the positive and the dangerous sides of individualism. It was this contention that imposed stereotypes upon discussion of the avant-garde, even in their own self-presentations.

The contradiction of private freedom and public expression generated a variety of career crises that resulted often in even more powerful art, but also, inevitably, in a sharp curtailment of who saw the work. If we give these artists their due as people who chose their destinies, the impact that many California artists might have made upon the national understanding of contemporary art was limited by their concept of art as spiritual journey that called into being a self independent of the mundane world. The ability to work was the only utopia they could realize. Productivity suspended momentarily the conflict between ambition and autonomy that permeated their relationships with the world. A sense of community decayed as the postwar generation matured and differentiated. Even success could be a mixed blessing because it established conditions within which the work proceeded. As Conner's games with biographical dictionaries allegorized, the happy few were dead to the world and alive to their own creativity.

What was left then was to operate as a dream substratum within American society, influencing without being recognized, exploring the possibility of otherness, occupying the spaces disdained by those who sought overt power and influence. The utopian and the foolish intermingle so closely that it was, and remains, easy to dismiss their activities as irrelevant. But the foolish, an aspect of rejecting the practicality confronting a person, might be the basis for winning out to an alternative standard of practicality. *Might.* Nothing is certain in the never-attained struggle to achieve the utopian. The rejection of the world as it exists flings one into an otherworldly limbo between heaven and hell. By choosing retreat, the avant-garde transformed themselves into a reservoir of pure tendentiousness that would become increasingly attractive and relevant as the mechanisms for extracting consensus in American society collapsed. Like *The Rose,* the avant-garde of the beat era was less a definable image than a response waiting to be activated.

Notes

1. Joan Brown, "Tape-Recorded Interview with Joan Brown, Session #3," interviewed 1975 by Paul Karlstrom, AAA, 25.

2. "North Beach Poet-Makers," *Holiday* (June 1958): 55-62; Charlotte Willard, "Women of American Art," *Look* 24 (27 September 1960): 70 (the article placed Brown next to Georgia O'Keeffe, Louise Nevelson, and Claire Falkenstein); "Joan Brown," *Cosmopolitan* (November 1961); "Joan Brown," *Glamour* 30 (March 1962); "*Mademoiselle*'s Annual Merit Awards," *Mademoiselle* 55 (January 1963): 30-35. Dorothy Walker in the *San Francisco News* predicted a stunning career for Joan Brown in 1957, observing that besides having abundant talent, Brown had flair for self-publicity. See Dorothy Walker, "Painters Shy? These Youngsters Invited Critics To Joint Exhibit," San Francisco News, 26 January 1957, in Joan Brown artist file, SFAA.

3. Philip Leider, "Joan Brown: Her Work Illustrates the Progress of a San Francisco Mood," *Artforum* I (June 1963): 28-31. In a dissenting view on Brown, but one based on similar assumptions, John Coplans argued Brown's paintings were parodies of Clyfford Still and Mark Rothko. See "Westcoast Art: Three Images," Artforum I (June 1963): 25.

4. "Joan Brown: Interview by Lynn Gumpert," in Lynda Benglis, Joan Brown, Luis Jimenez, Gary Stephan, Lawrence Weiner: Early Work (New York: The New Museum, 1982), 17.

5. Quoted in Brenda Richardson, Joan Brown (Berkeley: University Art Museum, 1975), 24. Noel Neri's baby

books, as well as the family photos and sketches that Brown used for her paintings of him, are preserved in the Joan Brown papers, AAA.

6. Brown, "Interview with Lynn Gumpert," 20.

7. For discussions of the status of representational art in the late 1960s and early 1970s, see Lawrence Alloway, "Notes on Realism," Arts Magazine 44 (April 1970): 26-27; Linda Nochlin, "The Realist Criminal and the Abstract Law," Art in America 61 (September-October 1973): 54-61, and 61 (November-December 1973): 97-103; Leo Steinberg, "Other Criteria," in Other Criteria (New York: Oxford University Press, 1972), 55-91; Sidney Tillim, "The Reception of Figurative Art: Notes on a General Misunderstanding," *Artforum* 7 (February 1969), 30-33. Positive critiques of Brown's later work appeared in 1978, when Marcia Tucker described her as a precursor of the New Image school then developing in New York in opposition to the hegemony of formalist thinking (see Introduction, *"Bad" Painting* [New York: New Museum, 1978]; see also Ronny H. Cohen, "Reviews: New York—Joan Brown," *Artforum* 20 [February 1982]: 89). Brown, however, suffered from being too closely identified with a regionalist school. In an article written after her death, Brooks Adams observed that Brown's Bay Area roots had made her seem peripheral and obscured the "international implications of her art" (Brook Adams, "Alternative Lives," *Art in America* 80 [January 1992]: 88).

8. CNM, "Joan Brown's Neo-Naives," *Artweek* 2 (10 July 1971): 3.

9. Andrée Marechal-Workman, "An Interview with Joan Brown," *Expo-See* (March-April 1985); Brown, "Interview with Lynn Gumpert," 19.

10. Ibid., 17.

11. Brown, "Tape-Recorded Interview with Joan Brown, Session #3," AAA, 21-23.

12. Brown's account squared neatly with David Riesman's depiction of the new "other-directed" service-providing middle class in *The Lonely Crowd: A Study of the Changing American Character* (New Haven: Yale University Press, 1950), especially 19-25, 45-49.

13. Joan Brown, "Tape-Recorded Interview with Joan Brown," interviewed 1975 by Paul Karlstrom, AAA, 8, 16. Brown also felt that the antipathy that she felt for the apartment was based on a premonition of her mother's suicide there in 1965. Interviews with artists and poets of Brown's generation tend to portray their childhoods in dark colors and troubled relationships with their parents. Yet the self-images as orphans are belied in occasional details that indicate ongoing relationships with the parents. The question of the nature of the relationships requires biographical investigation to determine what the case was in individual circumstances. The presence of a subjective motif in accounts by a relatively broad spectrum of individuals suggests that they augmented biography with a narrative theme that helped emphasize the idea of a generation embarked on a fundamental break with the past. Despite the rather negative picture Brown presented of her parents, they must have been somewhat open-minded, for they readily agreed to pay her tuition to the art school on what must have been very short notice. She transferred to the California School of Fine Arts days before she was to register

for her classes at Lone Mountain College. Her mementos of Noel's childhood preserved in the AAA show that her son was christened, attended Sunday school, and was confirmed in the Catholic church.

14. Joan Brown, "Tape-Recorded Interview with Joan Brown, Session #2," interview 1975, by Paul Karlstrom, AAA, 17.

15. Hedrick, "Wally Hedrick Interview #1," AAA, 22-23. The structure of Kerouacs's novel *On the Road* links loosely around Dean Moriarty's search for his missing father. That search is unsuccessful, but in the process Moriarty forges a brotherhood with the novel's narrator, Sal Valentine. See Erik Erikson, *Identity, Youth, and Crisis,* 135-136, 167-169, where Erikson argued that maturation required separation from parental authority. Generational confraternity offered a reasonable transition from dependency to autonomy. This contemporary view, presented as a general observation on the process of psychological maturation, suggests that relations between generations was a particular problem in the postwar period. Erikson, however, warned that the attempt to idealize school ties blocked further development to individual integrity and "generativity," that is, the ability to reproduce society through work that others value.

16. See Erikson, *Identity, Youth, and Crisis,* 155-159, for discussion of the age-group identifications and the development of competition. The central importance of peers in forming "other-directed" personality was also a critical element in David Riesman's description of American middle-class structure. See Riesman, *The Lonely Crowd,* 69-77.

17. Brown, "Interview by Lynn Gumpert," 16, 19.

18. Brown, "Tape-Recorded Interview with Joan Brown," AAA, 37. See also Joan Brown, "In Conversation with Jan Butterfield," *Visual Dialog* I (December 1975, January-February 1976): 15; untranscribed audiotape of "Funk Art Symposium," 22 September 1967, University Art Museum, Berkeley, tape at AAA.

19. Brown, "Interview by Lynn Gumpert," 16 19.

20. Brown, "Tape-Recorded Interview with Joan Brown," AAA 19-21, 34-40, 42, 48-49, 65-66.

21. Brown, "Tape-Recorded Interview with Joan Brown, Session #2" AAA, 35.

22. Brown, "Tape-Recorded Interview with Joan Brown," AAA, 40.

23. "Tape-Recorded Interview with Neil Sinton," 15 August 1974, AAA, untranscribed.

24. For a viewpoint that unequivocally embraced the idea of an "essentially feminine attitude" toward art, see Anaïs Nin, "Cornelia Runyon," *Artforum* 2 (August 1963): 54. Runyon, Nin argued, "began with a respect for what the sea or earth had already begun to form in the stone [Runyon used for her sculpture]. She contemplated and meditated over them, permitting them to reveal the inherent patterns they suggested. She never imposed her own will over the image tentatively begun by nature. She discovered and completed that image so that it became visible and clear. She assisted the birth of chaotic masses into recognizable forms . . . In this way, her way, what came through was not some abstraction torn from its basic roots, its textures, its organic growth, but something her tender maternal

intuitive hands allowed to grow organically without losing its connection with the earth or sea . . . Her work, I believe, is the opposite of an act of will,"

25. Brown, "Tape-Recorded Interview with Joan Brown, Session #2" AAA, 22. At the same time, Brown angrily defended herself against accusation that promiscuity advanced her career. She was certain other women artists, jealous of her success, were the source of these rumors.

26. Quotes in Brenda Richardson, *Joan Brown,* 28. *Fur Rat* also reflects Brown's association with the Rat Bastard Protective Association, so one can read the piece as a portrait of the bohemian artist in opposition to the media stereotype of the beats.

27. Brown, "Tape-Recorded Interview with Joan Brown," AAA, 33-34.

28. See Nancy Azara, "Artists in Their Own Image," *Ms.* I (January 1973): 56-60; Lucy Lippard, "Household Images in Art," *Ms.* I (March 1973): 22-25.

29. Brown, "Tape-Recorded Interview with Joan Brown, Session #2," AAA, 49, 51-52, 54-56. She also complained that the feminist movement denied the achievements of women who made careers for themselves prior to 1970. She noted that Marian Schapiro and Judy Chicago claimed that the art movements of the 1950s entirely male and that the Ferus, Six, and Dilexi galleries had never shown women artists. Brown then recalled offhand a dozen women, including herself, Jay DeFeo, Nell Sinton, Deborah Remington, and Cameron, who had had several successful shows at each of these galleries. Brown ignored those aspects of feminist arguments that focused on the marginalization of feminine experience and arts developed by women, such as quilts (see Miriam Schapiro, *Art: A Woman's Sensibility* [Valencia: California Institute of the Arts, 1975]). Brown's position on feminism is a critical marker of the timing of her entrance into the art profession. She began her career at a time when its features were still undifferentiated on the West Coast and a woman could construct a degendered imaginary of art as spiritual journey to find personal autonomy. Women entering art after 1965 encountered a more structured profession, and consideration of their experiences as women offered a more open, autonomous path for the creation of meaning outside of established sets of discourse. See interviews with Miriam Schapiro, Rachel Rosenthal, and Josine Ianco-Starrels, AAA, for examples of how women entering the profession in the 1960s gravitated to feminism as a system explaining heir position *within* the art world, rather than looking to an ideology of aesthetics as a liberation from their position in the world at large.

30. Brown, "Tape-Recorded Interview with Joan Brown, Session #3," AAA, II.

31. Ibid., 24, 25.

32. Jay DeFeo, "Tape-Recorded Interview with Jay DeFeo (I) at the Artist's Home, Larkspur, California," interviewed 1975 by Paul J. Karlstrom, AAA, 2-6. She extended the interior division she used to characterize herself to her mixed ethnic background. Her father was Italian, her mother Austrian, she felt her moods oscillated between the Germanic and the Latin. DeFeo also recalled spending much of her time alone as a child and adolescent.

33. Ibid., 3.

34. Jay DeFeo, "Tape-Recorded Interview with Jay DeFeo (2) at the Artists's Home," interviewed 1975 by Paul J. Karlstrom, AAA, 5.

35. Brown, "Tape-Recorded Interview with Joan Brown," AAA, 60, 65.

36. Irving Blum, "At the Ferus Gallery," interviewed 1976 by Joann Phillips, 1978 and 1979 by Lawrence Weschler, OHP/UCLA, 118-119.

37. Philip Lamantia, untitled, *Semina* 4 (1959).

38. Kienholz said that for years he thought that the painting's title was "Death Throes." He identified trouble with the work as the convulsions of a dying ideal to which she clung to desperately (Kienholz, "Los Angeles Art Community," OHP/UCLA, 119).

39. DeFeo, "Tape-Recorded Interview with Jay DeFeo (1)," AAA, 19.

40. See Six Gallery files, Ackerman Library, San Francisco Museum of Modern Art, for exhibition announcements.

41. "A Discussion Between Sir Avid Penultimate and Knute Stiles about Wally Hedrick," in *Rolling Rock Renaissance: San Francisco Underground Art, 1945-1968* (San Francisco: Intersection/Glide Urban Center, 1968). Reflecting on her marriage to Hedrick, DeFeo complained that they had lived entirely within the insular community of artists and poets. "Wally never took me anywhere in the whole time we were married where there wasn't some kind of a thing where he could perform. Not even once out to dinner in ten years, and that's pretty tough" (DeFeo, "Tape-Recorded Interview with Jay DeFeo (2)," AAA, 24). Stiles's image of Penelope creating the stories of her family community by weaving echoes one of the major themes of Joanne Kyger's first book of poetry, *The Tapestry and the Web* (San Francisco: Four Seasons, 1965).

42. At the time, William Waldren's paintings created by pouring buckets of paint over chicken wire-reinforced canvases were much praised on the West Coast. See *Artforum* I (June 1962): 8-9, for a typical review.

43. Jay DeFeo, "Tape-Recorded Interview with Jay DeFeo (3) at the Artist's Home, Larkspur, California," interviewed 1976 by Paul J. Karlstrom, AAA, 25.

44. Ibid., 6-13. See also "Notes on *The Rose*," prepared by J. Kelemen for Merrill Greene, *Art as a Muscular Principle: 10 Artists and San Francisco* (South Hadley, Massachusetts: Mount Holyoke College, 1975).

45. Jay DeFeo to Fred Martin, five undated letters, ca. 1959, in Fred Martin papers, AAA.

46. "Jay DeFeo, *The White Rose*," *Holiday* (May 1961):34-35; John F. Kennedy, "The Artist in America," *Look* 26 (18 December 1962): 120. See also "New Talent U.S.A.: Painting," *Art in America* 49 (Spring 1961):30-31.

47. DeFeo, "Tape-Recorded Interview with Jay DeFeo (3)," AAA, 26.

48. Conner, "Interview of Bruce Conner," AAA, 18. See also Douglas M. Davis, "Miss DeFeo's Awesome Painting Is Like Living Things Under Decay," *National Observer* 8 (14 July 1969): 12. As of 1993, new conservation efforts seek to restore *The Rose* to its original condition.

49. Raymond Foye, Editor's Note to Bob Kaufman, *The Ancient Rain: Poems 1956-1978* (New York: New Directions, 1981), ix; obituary notice for Bob Kaufman, *San Francisco Chronicle*, 14 January 1986. Eileen Kaufman oversaw the production of the first of the planned New Directions books, *Solitudes Crowded with Loneliness* (1965), as well as another chapbook of previously unpublished material for City Lights Press, *The Golden Sardine* (1967). Bob Kaufman refused to help promote either book or to provide new material for any publisher.

50. Hedrick, "Wally Hedrick Interview #1," AAA, 44-45.

51. Conner, "Tape-Recorded Interview with Bruce Conner," 8-9.

52. Ibid., 14.

53. Wally Hedrick, "Wally Hedrick Interview #2," interviewed 1974 by Paul Karlstrom, AAA, 7-10. See also *San Francisco Chronicle*, 12 December 1958, clipping in Hedrick papers, AAA.

54. Hopper recently reiterated her debts to Conner in his introduction to *Bruce Conner: Assemblages, Paintings, Drawings, Engraving Collages, 1960-1990* (Santa Monica: Michael Kohn Gallery, 1990). See also Stefania Pertoldi, *Il Mito del viaggio in Easy Rider e Zabriskie Point* (Udine: Campanotto Editore, 1987), 145-154.

55. See Frank Gettings, *Different Drummers* (Washington: Smithsonian Institution Press, 1988), 13.

56. "A Conversation with Bruce Conner and Robert Dean," in *Bruce Conner: Assemblages, Paintings, Drawings, Engraving Collages, 1960-1990*.

57. David Meltzer to Bob Alexander, undated, ca. early 1970s, Bob Alexander papers AAA.

58. Meltzer to Alexander, undated, ca. 1977, Bob Alexander papers, AAA.

59. David Meltzer, "Golden Gate: Introduction," in *The San Francisco Poets*, 3-4.

60. Jack Hirschman, "The Crickets," holograph in Bob Alexander papers, AAA.

61. Brown, "Tape-Recorded Interview with Joan Brown, Session #2," AAA, 17. Compare Lawrence Lipton in *The Holy Barbarians* (New York: Julian Messner, 1959). "*We* is what this generation is all about, whether you call it beat or disaffiliated or anything else. *We* is what its books are about, the name of all those characters in those books and what those characters do and say. Everything that happens to them happens to *us*" (p. 48).

62. Generations that claim to initiate fresh starts, Lawrence Lipton thought, put supreme value upon the appearance of youthful behavior (*The Holy Barbarians*, 91).

63. Allen Ginsberg, "Kral Majales," in *The Postmoderns*, 190.

64. Riesman, *The Lonely Crowd*, 236-241.

65. See Kenneth Rexroth, "The Students Take Over," in WOW, for a discussion of the relationship of the new student movement to politics and an existential quest to live in a moral state. However, the importance existentialist writers placed on the finitude of life circumscribed their impact upon a generation intent on extending the condition of youth indefinitely.

FURTHER READING

Criticism

Albright, Thomas. *Art in the San Francisco Bay Area, 1945-1980: An Illustrated History.* Berkeley and Los Angeles: University of California Press, 1985, 349 p.

History of art in the San Francisco Bay area, including art and artists associated with the Beat Generation, written by a noted Bay area art critic.

Assemblage in California, Works from the Late 50's and Early 60's. Alhambra, Calif.: Cunningham Press, 1968, 58 p.

An exhibition catalog from a 1968 exhibition at the University of California Irvine. Includes bibliographical references.

DuPont, Diana C., et al. *San Francisco Museum of Modern Art: The Painting and Sculpture Collection.* Introduction by Katherine Church Holland; foreword by Henry T. Hopkins. New York: Hudson Hills Press, in conjunction with the San Francisco Museum of Modern Art, 1985, 402 p.

Catalog of 1985 exhibition at the San Francisco Museum of Modern Art.

Forty years of California assemblage: UCLA Art Council annual exhibition. Los Angeles: Wight Art Gallery, University of California, Angeles, c. 1989, 241 p.

Catalog of an exhibition held at the Wight Art Gallery and other museums in 1989. Includes bibliographical information.

Galleries of the Beat Generation and Beyond. Davis, Calif.: Natsoulas Press, 1996, 240 p.

Surveys the San Francisco's Beat Generation art galleries of the 1950s and early 1960s, including biographical and photographic documentation of the major figures and works of art. Includes essays by Michael McClure, Rebecca Solnit, Bruce Nixon, Seymour Howard and John Natsoulas.

Hall, James B. and Barry Ulanov, editors. *Modern Culture and the Arts.* New York: McGraw-Hill, 1967, 560 p.

A survey of art and artists within the context of popular American culture.

Lost and Found in California: Four Decades of Assemblage Art, July 16 to September 7, 1988: An Exhibition. Santa Monica, Calif.: James Corcoran Gallery, 1988, 119 p.

Exhibition catalog from exhibition organized by the James Corcoran Gallery in cooperation with the Shoshana Wayne Gallery and Pence Gallery, curated by Sandra Leonard Starr.

Lyrical Vision: The Six Gallery 1954-1957. Davis, Calif: Natsoulas Press, 1990, 96 p.

Catalog of a retrospective of the history of the Six Gallery that includes photos of artists Wally Hedrick, Bruce Conner, James Weeks, David Park and their works. Includes essays by Michael McClure, Rebecca Solnit, and Bruce Nixon.

Phillips, Lisa. "Beat Culture: America Revisioned." In *Beat Culture and the New America: 1950-1965,* pp. 23-40. Paris: Flammarion, 1995.

Provides a historical and artistic context for the artists who were affiliated with the Beat writers. Phillips suggests common artistic values among the musicians, painters, authors, and other artists, and discusses the redemption of the mundane or vulgar, a populist approach to disseminating or publicizing art, and an emphasis on lived experience over mere intellectualization.

Plagens, Peter. *Sunshine Muse: Contemporary Art on the West Coast.* New York: Praeger Publishers, 1974, 200 p.

Delineates the work of West Coast artists from 1945 to the 1970s, providing background information on the art schools and movements of the first half of the 20th century.

Smith, Richard Cándida. "Utopia and the Private Realm: Wallace Berman on Career, Family, and Community." In *Utopia and Dissent: Art, Poetry, and Politics in California,* pp. 212-68. Berkeley: University of California Press, 1995.

Provides detailed history of Berman's life and career, including his experiences as a Beat generation artist.

The Spatsa Gallery, 1958-1961. Davis, Calif.: Natsoulas Press, 1991, 48 p.

Exhibition catalog of 1991 retrospective history of the Spatsa Gallery that includes photographs and biographies of such artists as Michael McClure, Bruce Conner, Art Grant, and Joan Brown, as well as their works.

Tsujimoto, Karen, and Jacquelynn Bass. *The Art of Joan Brown.* Foreword by Brenda Richardson. Berkeley: University of California Press, 1998, 320 p.

The first, full-length, comprehensive overview of Brown's life and artistic career.

Wallace Berman Retrospective, October 24 to November 26, 1978: An Exhibition. Initiated and sponsored by Fellows of Contemporary Art in cooperation with the Otis Art Institute Gallery. Los Angeles: The Fellows, 1978, 118 p.

Exhibition catalog from 1978 exhibit at Otis Art Institute Gallery in Los Angeles.

INDEXES

The main reference

Kerouac, Jack 1922-1969 **1:** 2, 14-18, 20, 21-25, 34,
37-41, 43, 49-52, 106-9, 118-21, 133-34, 141-42,
157-59, 161, 163, 164, 169-71, 179-80, 196, 213-14,
240-46, 305-6, 357-58, 363-68, 398-411; **2:** 113, 123-24,
127-30, 141-50, 318, 379-80, 490; **3:** 4-7, 9-11, 63,
63-142, 207-8, 272, 471

*lists the featured author's entry in either volume 2
or 3 of* The Beat Generation; *it also lists commentary on the featured author in other author
entries and in volume 1, which includes topics associated with the Beat Generation. Page references
to substantial discussions of the author appear in
boldface.*

The cross-references

See also AAYA 25; AITN 1; AMWS 3; BPFB 2; CA 5-8R;
CANR 26, 54, 95; CDALB 1941-1968; CLC 1, 2, 3, 5,
14, 29, 61; CPW; DA; DAB; DAC; DAM MST, NOV,
POET, POP; DLB 2, 16, 237; DLBD 3; DLBY 1995; GLL
1; MTCW 1, 2; NFS 8; RGAL 4; TCLC 117; WLC; WP

*list entries on the author in the following Gale
biographical and literary sources:*

AAL: Asian American Literature

AAYA: Authors & Artists for Young Adults

AFAW: African American Writers

AFW: African Writers

AITN: Authors in the News

AMW: American Writers

AMWR: American Writers Retrospective Supplement

AMWS: American Writers Supplement

ANW: American Nature Writers

AW: Ancient Writers

BEST: Bestsellers (quarterly, citations appear as
Year: Issue number)

BLC: Black Literature Criticism

BLCS: Black Literature Criticism Supplement

BPFB: Beacham's Encyclopedia of Popular Fiction:
Biography and Resources

BRW: British Writers

BRWS: British Writers Supplement

BW: Black Writers

BYA: Beacham's Guide to Literature for Young
Adults

CA: Contemporary Authors

CAAS: Contemporary Authors Autobiography
Series

CABS: Contemporary Authors Bibliographical
Series

CAD: Contemporary American Dramatists

CANR: Contemporary Authors New Revision
Series

CAP: Contemporary Authors Permanent Series

CBD: Contemporary British Dramatists

CCA: Contemporary Canadian Authors

CD: Contemporary Dramatists

CDALB: Concise Dictionary of American Literary
Biography

CDALBS: Concise Dictionary of American Literary
Biography Supplement

CDBLB: Concise Dictionary of British Literary
Biography

CLC: Contemporary Literary Criticism

CLR: Children's Literature Review

CMLC: Classical and Medieval Literature Criticism

CMW: St. James Guide to Crime & Mystery Writers

CN: Contemporary Novelists

CP: Contemporary Poets

CPW: Contemporary Popular Writers

CSW: Contemporary Southern Writers

CWD: Contemporary Women Dramatists

CWP: Contemporary Women Poets

CWRI: St. James Guide to Children's Writers

CWW: Contemporary World Writers

DA: DISCovering Authors

DA3: DISCovering Authors 3.0

DAB: DISCovering Authors: British Edition

DAC: DISCovering Authors: Canadian Edition

DAM: DISCovering Authors: Modules

  DRAM: Dramatists Module; *MST:* Most-
  Studied Authors Module;

  MULT: Multicultural Authors Module; *NOV:*
  Novelists Module;

  POET: Poets Module; *POP:* Popular Fiction and
  Genre Authors Module

DC: Drama Criticism

DFS: Drama for Students

DLB: Dictionary of Literary Biography

DLBD: Dictionary of Literary Biography Documentary Series

DLBY: Dictionary of Literary Biography Yearbook

DNFS: Literature of Developing Nations for Students

EFS: Epics for Students

EXPN: Exploring Novels

EXPP: Exploring Poetry

EXPS: Exploring Short Stories

EW: European Writers

FANT: St. James Guide to Fantasy Writers

FW: Feminist Writers

GFL: Guide to French Literature, Beginnings to 1789, 1798 to the Present

GLL: Gay and Lesbian Literature

HGG: St. James Guide to Horror, Ghost & Gothic Writers

HLC: Hispanic Literature Criticism

HLCS: Hispanic Literature Criticism Supplement

HW: Hispanic Writers

IDFW: International Dictionary of Films and Filmmakers: Writers and Production Artists

IDTP: International Dictionary of Theatre: Playwrights

LAIT: Literature and Its Times

LAW: Latin American Writers

JRDA: Junior DISCovering Authors

LC: Literature Criticism from 1400 to 1800

MAICYA: Major Authors and Illustrators for Children and Young Adults

MAICYA: Major Authors and Illustrators for Children and Young Adults Supplement

MAWW: Modern American Women Writers

MJW: Modern Japanese Writers

MTCW: Major 20th-Century Writers

NCFS: Nonfiction Classics for Students

NCLC: Nineteenth-Century Literature Criticism

NFS: Novels for Students

NNAL: Native North American Literature

PAB: Poets: American and British

PC: Poetry Criticism

PFS: Poetry for Students

RGAL: Reference Guide to American Literature

RGEL: Reference Guide to English Literature

RGSF: Reference Guide to Short Fiction

RGWL: Reference Guide to World Literature

RHW: Twentieth-Century Romance and Historical Writers

SAAS: Something about the Author Autobiography Series

SATA: Something about the Author

SFW: St. James Guide to Science Fiction Writers

SSC: Short Story Criticism

SSFS: Short Stories for Students

TCLC: Twentieth-Century Literary Criticism

TCWW: Twentieth-Century Western Writers

WCH: Writers for Children

WLC: World Literature Criticism, 1500 to the Present

WLCS: World Literature Criticism Supplement

WLIT: World Literature and Its Times

WP: World Poets

YABC: Yesterday's Authors of Books for Children

YAW: St. James Guide to Young Adult Writers

The Author Index lists all of the authors featured in The Beat Generation *set. It includes references to the main author entries in volumes 2 and 3; it also lists commentary on the featured author in other author entries and in volume 1, which includes topics associated with the* Beat Generation. *Page references to author entries appear in boldface. The Author Index also includes birth and death dates, cross references between pseudonyms or name variants and actual names, and cross references to other Gale series in which the authors have appeared. A complete list of these sources is found facing the first page of the Author Index.*

A

Antoninus, Brother
   See Everson, William (Oliver)

B

Blackburn, Paul 1926-1971 **1:** 266;
  2: 1, **1-24, 3:** 326
   See also CA 81-84; CANR 34;
    CLC 9, 43; DLB 16; DLBY
    1981

Brossard, Chandler 1922-1993 **2:**
  25-49
   See also CA 61-64, 142; CAAS 2;
    CANR 8, 56; DLB 16
Brossard, Iris-Marie
   See Brossard, Chandler
Burroughs, William S(eward)
  1914-1997 **1:** 20, 34-35, 38-40,
  45, 51-52, 59-60, 90-91, 125-26,
  162, 211-12, 216, 358-61, 367-69,
  373-80; **2:** 51, **51-121**
   See also AITN 2; AMWS 3; BPFB
    1; CA 9-12R; CANR 20, 52,
    104; CLC 1, 2, 5, 15, 22, 42,
    75, 109; CN 7; CPW; DA; DAB;
    DAC; DAM MST, NOV, POP;
    DLB 2, 8, 16, 152, 237; DLBY
    1981, 1997; HGG; MTCW 1,
    2; RGAL 4; SFW 4; TCLC 121;
    WLC

C

Cassady, Neal 1926-1968 **1:** 34-35,
  41, 119-20, 157-58, 161-62,
  357-58; **2:** 123, **123-52,** 343, 400,
  499-501, 506-10; **3:** 77-81
   See also CA 141; DLB 16, 237
Corso, (Nunzio) Gregory
  1930-2001 **1:** 38, 162, 214-15; **2:**
  153, **153-213, 3:** 91
   See also AMWS 12; CA 5-8R;
    CANR 41, 76; CLC 1, 11; CP 7;
    DLB 5, 16, 237; MTCW 1, 2;
    PC 33; WP

D

di Prima, Diane 1934- **1:** 187; **2:**
  215-41
   See also CA 17-20R; CANR 13;
    CP 7; CWP; DLB 5, 16; WP
Duncan, Edward Howard
   See Duncan, Robert
Duncan, Robert 1919-1988 **1:** 267,
  270, 275, 277, 437, 438-39, 439,
  441-43, 461; **2:** 235, 243, **243-66,**
  3: 57, 182-83, 205-6, 381
   See also CA 9-12R; CANR 28, 62;
    CLC 1, 2, 4, 7, 15, 41, 55;
    DAM POET; DLB 5, 16, 193;
    MTCW 1, 2; PC 2; PFS 13;
    RGAL 4; WP

E

Everson, William (Oliver)
  1912-1994 **2:** 267, **267-304, 3:**
  275-76
   See also CA 9-12R; CANR 20;
    CLC 1, 5, 14; DLB 5, 16, 212;
    MTCW 1

F

Ferlinghetti, Lawrence 1919- **1:** 31,
  53, 269-73, 304-6, 311-21, 323,
  334, 343-44, 346-47; **2:** 160-61,
  305, **305-62**
   See also CA 5-8R; CANR 3, 41,
    73; CDALB 1941-1968; CLC 2,

The Subject Index includes the authors and titles that appear in the Author Index and the Title Index as well as the names of other authors and figures that are discussed in the Beat Generation set. The Subject Index also lists titles and authors of the critical essays that appear in the set, as well as literary terms and topics covered in the criticism. The index provides page numbers or page ranges where subjects are discussed and is fully cross referenced. Page references to significant discussions of authors, titles, or subjects appear in bold-face; page references to illustrations appear in italic.

A

SUBJECT INDEX

W